STEVENS' HANDBOOK OF EXPERIMENTAL PSYCHOLOGY

THIRD EDITION

Volume 1:   Sensation and Perception

STEVENS' HANDBOOK OF EXPERIMENTAL PSYCHOLOGY

THIRD EDITION

Volume 1:   Sensation and Perception

Editor-in-Chief

HAL PASHLER

Volume Editor

STEVEN YANTIS

John Wiley & Sons, Inc.

Library of Congress Cataloging-in-Publication Data

Stevens' handbook of experimental psychology / Hal Pashler, editor-in-chief
— 3rd ed.
        p. cm.
    Includes bibliographical references and index.
    Contents: v. 1. Sensation and perception — v. 2. Memory and cognitive processes — v. 3. Learning, motivation, and emotion — v. 4. Methodology in experimental psychology.

    ISBN 0-471-44333-6 (set) — ISBN 0–471–37777–5 (v. 1 : cloth : alk. paper) — ISBN 0–471–38030–X (v. 2 : cloth : alk. paper) — ISBN 0–471–38047–4 (v. 3 : cloth : alk. paper) — ISBN 0–471–37888–7 (v. 4 : cloth : alk. paper) — ISBN 0–471–44333–6 (set)
    1. Psychology, Experimental. I. Pashler, Harold E.

BF181.H336 2001
150—dc21   2001046809

Contributors

Jamshed J. Bharucha, PhD
Dartmouth College

Randolph Blake, PhD
Vanderbilt University

Jean Bullier, PhD
CNRS/Université Paul Sabatier
Toulouse, France

Laurel H. Carney, PhD
Syracuse University

Pamela Dalton, PhD
Monell Chemical Senses Center

Carolyn Drake, PhD
CNRS/Université René Descartes
Paris, France

Michael J. Farrell, PhD
National Institutes of Health

Richard H. Gracely, PhD
National Institutes of Health

Masilo A. B. Grant, BA
National Institutes of Health

Bruce P. Halpern, PhD
Cornell University

Mark Hollins, PhD
University of North Carolina—
Chapel Hill

Ian Howard, PhD
York University, Toronto, Canada

Kenneth Johnson, PhD
Johns Hopkins University

Peter W. Jusczyk, PhD
Johns Hopkins University

Timothy C. Justus, PhD
University of California, Berkeley

Kenneth Knoblauch, PhD
INSERM U371, Cerveau et Vision
Bron, France

Paul A. Luce, PhD
University at Buffalo, State University
of New York

Steven J. Luck, PhD
University of Iowa

Stephen McAdams, PhD
CNRS/Institut de Recherche et Coordination
Acoustique/Musique, Paris, France

Stephen E. Palmer, PhD
University of California, Berkeley

David A. Rosenbaum, PhD
Pennsylvania State University

Robert Sekuler, PhD
Brandeis University

Michael J. Tarr, PhD
Brown University

Shaun P. Vecera, PhD
University of Iowa

Quoc C. Vuong, BSc
Brown University

Scott N. J. Watamaniuk, PhD
Wright State University

Contents

Preface

The precise origins of experimental psychology can be debated, but by any count the field is more than a hundred years old. The past 10 years have been marked by tremendous progress: a honing of experimental strategies and clearer theoretical conceptualizations in many areas combined with a more vigorous cross-fertilization across neighboring fields.

Despite the undeniable progress, vigorous debate continues on many of the most fundamental questions. From the nature of learning to the psychophysical functions relating sensory stimuli to sensory experiences and from the underpinnings of emotion to the nature of attention, a good many of the questions posed in the late 19th century remain alive and in some cases highly controversial.

Although some have viewed this fact as discouraging, it should scarcely be surprising. As in the biological sciences generally, early hopes that a few simple laws and principles would explain everything that needed to be explained have gradually given way to a recognition of the vast complexity of human (and nonhuman) organisms in general, and of their mental faculties in particular. There is no contradiction between recognizing the magnitude of the progress that has been made and appreciating the gap between current understanding and the fuller understanding that we hope to achieve in the future.

Stanley Smith ("Smitty") Stevens' *Handbook of Experimental Psychology,* of which this is the third edition, has made notable contributions to the progress of the field. At the same time, from one edition to the next, the *Handbook* has changed in ways that reflect growing recognition of the complexity of its subject matter. The first edition was published in 1951 under the editorship of the great psychophysical pioneer himself. This single volume (described by some reviewers as the last successful single-volume handbook of psychology) contained a number of very influential contributions in the theory of learning, as well as important contributions to psychophysics for which Stevens was justly famous. The volume had a remarkably wide influence in the heyday of a period in which many researchers believed that principles of learning theory would provide the basic theoretical underpinning for psychology as a whole.

Published in 1988, the second edition was edited by a team comprised of Richard Atkinson, Richard J. Herrnstein, Gardner Lindzey, and Duncan Luce. The editors of the second edition adopted a narrower definition of the field, paring down material that overlapped with physics or physiology and reducing the role of applied psychology. The result was a set of two volumes, each of which was substantially smaller than the single volume in the first edition.

Discussions of a third edition of the *Stevens' Handbook* began in 1998. My fellow editors and I agreed that experimental psychology had broadened and deepened to such a point that two volumes could no longer reasonably encompass the major accomplishments that have occurred in the field since 1988. We also felt that a greatly enlarged treatment of methodology would make the *Handbook* particularly valuable to those seeking to undertake research in new areas, whether graduate students in training or researchers venturing into subfields that are new to them.

The past 10 years have seen a marked increase in efforts to link psychological phenomena to neurophysiological foundations. Rather than eschewing this approach, we have embraced it without whittling down the core content of traditional experimental psychology, which has been the primary focus of the *Handbook* since its inception.

The most notable change from the previous edition to this one is the addition of a new volume on methodology. This volume provides rigorous but comprehensible tutorials on the key methodological concepts of experimental psychology, and it should serve as a useful adjunct to graduate education in psychology.

I am most grateful to Wiley for its strong support of the project from the beginning. The development of the new *Handbook* was initially guided by Kelly Franklin, now Vice President and Director of Business Development at Wiley. Jennifer Simon, Associate Publisher, took over the project for Wiley in 1999. Jennifer combined a great measure of good sense, good humor, and the firmness essential for bringing the project to a timely completion. Although the project took somewhat longer than we initially envisioned, progress has been much faster than it was in the second edition, making for an up-to-date presentation of fast-moving fields. Both Isabel Pratt at Wiley and Noriko Coburn at University of California at San Diego made essential contributions to the smooth operation of the project. Finally, I am very grateful to the four distinguished volume editors, Randy Gallistel, Doug Medin, John Wixted, and Steve Yantis, for their enormous contributions to this project.

Hal Pashler

CHAPTER 1

Neural Basis of Vision

JEAN BULLIER

This chapter presents an overview of the functional organization of the visual system, with a particular emphasis on the data relevant to psychophysics and cognitive psychology. Most of the reviewed material concerns the visual systems of the most-studied animal species (monkey and cat), and information is also given on the organization of the human cortical areas, as these are the subject of many recent studies using techniques for revealing metabolic activity (such as functional magnetic resonance imaging, or fMRI).

The anatomical organization of the visual system is now well known (see the section titled "Functional Architecture of the Visual System" for details). Visual information is first processed in the retina by different classes of neurons (receptors, horizontal cells, bipolar cells, amacrine cells, and retinal ganglion cells). In the present chapter, the discussion focuses on the retinal ganglion cells that constitute the output stage of the retina. The retinal ganglion cells project to a number of subcortical structures, and the largest projection is sent to a nucleus of the thalamus, the dorsal lateral geniculate nucleus (usually called lateral geniculate nucleus, or LGN). The major projection of the LGN is to area V1 (also called area 17 in some species), which is the largest cortical area of the visual system and contains a complete and detailed representation of the contralateral visual hemifield. Area V1 is reciprocally connected to a few functional areas (areas V2 and V3d as well as area MT, which is also called V5 in humans) that are themselves reciprocally connected to a very dense network of a few dozen cortical areas.

It is generally accepted that each of the cortical areas of the visual system is specialized in the processing of one parameter of visual objects such as color, depth, or direction of movement. Another standard view of the functional organization of the visual system is that simple aspects are coded in area V1 and that areas further away code for more complex aspects of the visual scene. Finally, it is thought that areas of the inferotemporal cortex are devoted to object recognition whereas areas of the parietal cortex process location and movement of objects. We will see that these ideas provide only a limited aspect of the reality of processing in the visual system.

The chapter opens on considerations of two major concepts in vision: the receptive field and the functional maps (the first two sections). The third section presents the anatomical and functional organization of the primate visual system. The fourth section is devoted to the question of the relationship between neuronal activity and perceptual experience, and

The author wishes to thank Frédéric Sarrato for his expert work on the figures.

1

the final section discusses a number of open questions in the biology of vision.

THE RECEPTIVE FIELD CONCEPT

The starting point for our survey of the neural basis of vision is to examine the conditions under which a single neuron is effectively driven by visual stimulation. In practically all cases, a neuron can be activated by photic stimulation when it is confined to a small region of the visual field that is called the receptive field. The set of stimulus properties, including size, color, shape, movement, and so on, together specify the receptive field selectivity of that cell.

Historical Aspects

The notion of receptive field in vision goes back to the early work of Hartline (1940) in the horseshoe crab and Kuffler (1953) in the cat retina. In those days visual physiologists were working on a preparation called the open eyecup, which consisted of an isolated hemi-sectioned eye with the retina left in place. By shining small spots of light directly on the retina and recording from ganglion cells, Kuffler identified the region on the retina that, when stimulated by light, produced a change in the firing rate of the recorded retinal ganglion cell; he called this region the receptive field of the neuron. Subsequently, researchers such as Hubel and Wiesel (1962), recording from neurons in other visual structures of the brain, flashed small spots of light on a screen placed perpendicular to the direction of gaze and defined as the receptive field the screen region in which light stimuli produced a response of the neuron. This method has been carried over to modern techniques of recording in awake behaving monkeys for which the receptive field is defined as the region on a computer monitor for

which contrast changes elicit responses in a neuron.

The receptive field is the central notion of all single-cell investigations in the visual system: Processing in a given structure is studied by comparing the receptive fields of input and output neurons; effects of attention or perceptual learning are studied on the extent and tuning curves of the receptive field of visual neurons. It should be kept in mind that in most experimental studies the receptive field is defined as a small surface region in a given plane of fixation, whereas it is likely that it is a three-dimensional structure, as suggested by results showing that the responses of cortical neurons are strongly modulated by depth in the visual field (Trotter, Celebrini, Stricanne, Thorpe, & Imbert, 1996).

In his pioneering study, Kuffler (1953) made an important observation: retinal neurons code not only for light but for dark as well. He defined two types of retinal ganglion cells: the ON-center cell that responds to luminance increase in its receptive field by increasing its firing rate and to luminance decrease by decreasing its firing rate, and the OFF-center cell that increases its firing rate when luminance is decreased in its receptive field and decreases it when luminance is increased (Figure 1.1). Thus, both ON- and OFF-center cells respond in a push-pull fashion to increases and decreases of light.[1]

One of the major limitations of the receptive field concept is that it requires the eyes to be fixated on a given point on the tangent screen. To study a receptive field, an experimenter flashes or moves spots or bars of light because a standing contrast in luminance

---

[1] This is possible because the spontaneous firing rate of most retinal ganglion cells is high (several tens of spikes per second on average). This is not the case in cortical neurons that are usually silent or produce only a few spikes per second. Thus, cortical neurons, contrary to retinal ganglion cells, transmit information only by increases in firing rates.

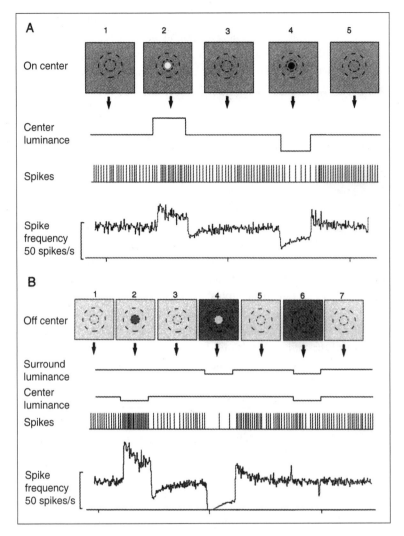

Figure 1.1   ON- and OFF-center receptive fields of retinal ganglion cells.
NOTE: A: Response of an ON-center retinal ganglion cell to a small light or dark spot in its receptive field center. The small circles in dotted lines represent the center and surround outer borders. B: Response of an OFF-center retinal ganglion cell to a small dark spot in its receptive field center, to a luminance decrease in its receptive field surround, and to an extended dark stimulus covering both center and surround. Note that because of the antagonistic effect of the center and surround mechanisms, the neuron does not respond to the extended stimulus.

or chrominance generates little activity in most cortical neurons.[2] Thus, most of what we know from visual neurons results from

an artificial way of studying them: Whereas in a natural visual system—particularly in primates—the eyes are constantly moving and the receptive field of a neuron is probing the world, in an experimental situation the eyes are fixed and the neuron is stimulated by moving or flashed patterns. Only recently

---

[2]This presumably explains the well-known observation that perception fades within a few seconds when images are stabilized on the retina.

have researchers begun to study the responses of visual neurons when the animal is exploring the visual world (see the section titled "How Does the Visual System Deal with Saccades and Microsaccades?").

Center-Surround Organization of Receptive Fields in the Retina

In his study of the vertebrate retina, Kuffler (1953) also identified two regions in the receptive field: the center and the surround. The center corresponds to the region in which luminance increase or decrease of a small spot generates an increase in firing rate. The surround is composed of a wider region that overlaps the center and acts in an antagonistic way. This means that for an OFF-center neuron, stimulating the center alone elicits a response at offset of the light, whereas stimulating the center and the surround together produces little response because of the antagonistic action of the surround (Figure 1.1B).

Center and surround have been modeled as two antagonistic mechanisms with Gaussian-shaped sensitivity domains, the center sensitivity profile being narrow and high and the surround being broad and more extended in space (Figures 1.2A and 1.2B). Center and surround mechanisms are supposed to interact in a linear fashion, and their combination produces the famous Mexican-hat profile of the retinal ganglion cell receptive field (Figures 1.2A, 1.2B, and 1.2C). Because of the sensitivity balance between the center and surround mechanisms, a retinal ganglion cell produces no response to the onset or offset of a light stimulus covering both center and surround mechanisms (Figure 1.1B) but responds optimally to the appearance of a contrast element appropriate in size and contrast for the center mechanism (positive contrast for ON-center cells, negative for OFF-center cells). Moreover, Rodieck (1965) showed that in the case of moving stimuli, the ganglion cell

responds very strongly to small movements of a contrast edge across the steepest part of the center sensitivity curve (Figure 1.2C). The eyes are never perfectly steady but move erratically across a few tenths of a degree when the subject fixates a point (Figure 1.2D), so during fixation the main message sent by the retinal ganglion cells corresponds to the detection of small movements of a contrast border across the transition between center and surround mechanisms.

The Mexican-hat model of retinal ganglion is widely accepted and is appropriate for (at least) one of the main ganglion cell types in the primate, the parasol neuron. In the other major type, the midget ganglion cell (see the section titled "Different Types of Retinal Ganglion Cells"), center and surround components are driven by different combinations of cones and therefore are involved in wavelength discrimination as well as spatial localization.

Discharge Center and Modulatory Surround of Cortical Neurons

A similar type of center-surround organization is found also at the next stage of processing, when the filtering properties of the LGN have been measured by comparing receptive fields of LGN cells with their ganglion cell inputs. The situation changes with the cortical neurons for which the receptive field is generally not circular symmetric. In particular, many neurons in area V1 and in other cortical areas have receptive fields that are selective for a given range of orientations of a contrast element. As in a retinal ganglion cell, the receptive field of a cortical neuron is generally composed of a single discharge region, also called the receptive field center. When this region is stimulated by a contrast border, the neuron responds by increasing its firing rate. In the region surrounding the center, there is a surround mechanism that, as in the retinal

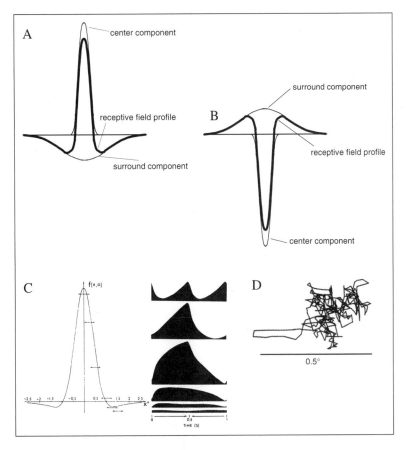

Figure 1.2 Retinal receptive fields and eye movements.

NOTE: A: Center and surround mechanisms in the receptive field of an ON-center retinal ganglion cell. Positive values correspond to increases in firing rate for a light stimulus; negative values correspond to decreases. A light spot limited to the center generates a strong increase in firing rate. An annulus restricted to the surround produces a decrease in response; the addition of the center and surround components produce the Mexican-hat sensitivity profile of the receptive field. B: Center and surround mechanisms and resulting receptive field sensitivity profile for an OFF-center retinal ganglion cell. Here, negative value corresponds to an increase in firing rate for a dark stimulus or a decrease for a light stimulus. C: Responses to movement of a small stimulus oscillating over 0.5 deg across the steepest part of the sensitivity profile. The responses are aligned with the position of the stimulus across the receptive field profile. Note the strong activation at the steepest part of the profile. D: Eye movements of a human observer during fixation. Most of the variation is contained within 0.25 degrees.

SOURCE: C: Reproduced from Rodieck (1965) with permission from Elsevier Science. D: Modified from Rodieck (1998).

ganglion cell, has an antagonistic action to the center mechanism. However, contrary to the retinal neuron, the sensitivity profile is not a Gaussian-shaped domain overlapping the receptive field center. Instead, it is composed of generally one or two main inhibitory hot spots (Figure 1.3A; Walker, Ohzawa, & Freeman, 1999). Another difference with the retinal ganglion cell is that the surround of a cortical neuron does not produce a response when

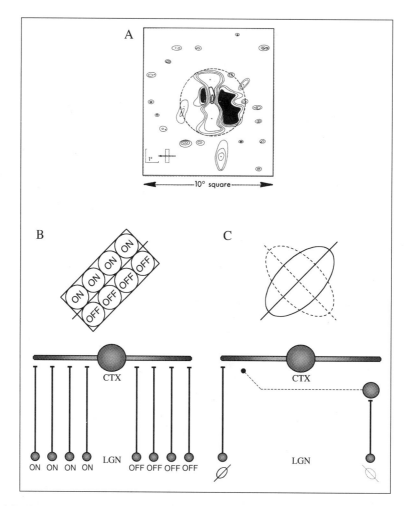

Figure 1.3 Receptive fields of neurons in area 17.

NOTE: A: Center and surround mechanisms of the receptive field of a neuron in cat area 17 (courtesy of J. I. Nelson). Excitatory regions are in white with +s; major inhibitory regions (surround) are in black. Note the patchy distribution of excitatory and inhibitory regions, in contrast to the retinal ganglion cell receptive field (Figure 1.2). B: The Hubel and Wiesel (1962) model of orientation selectivity in cortical neurons. The rectangle with ON and OFF labels represents the elongated receptive field of a neuron in area 17; the ON and OFF regions represent the receptive fields of the afferent excitatory LGN inputs. The wiring diagram is shown below: The cortical neuron (CTX) is driven by two sets of LGN inputs (ON- and OFF-center). Because of the complementary responses of ON- and OFF-center receptive fields, the best response is obtained when a stimulus is aligned with the long axis of the rectangle. C: The Sillito/Bishop model: Some orientation bias is provided by the elongated receptive field of an excitatory LGN input (on the left). Orientation selectivity is provided by the inhibitory input corresponding to another LGN input relayed through a cortical inhibitory neuron. Connections with a small bar correspond to excitatory inputs; those with a black dot correspond to inhibitory input.

SOURCE: Modified from Ferster & Koch (1987).

directly stimulated by light.[3] For this reason, the surrounds of cortical receptive fields are usually called modulatory or silent surrounds.

We saw that the sensitivity to local contrast and the lack of response to luminance changes over the whole receptive field of most retinal ganglion cells could be explained by the antagonistic actions of the center and surround. A similar idea has been proposed to account for the selectivity of cortical neurons to parameters such as orientation, direction of movement, color, and so on. This has not been fully confirmed, and it is possible to demonstrate selectivity of the center mechanism without stimulating the surround.

The role of the surround in shaping the selectivity of cortical neurons is still a controversial issue. Some have argued that neuronal selectivity simply results from a proper arrangement of the excitatory inputs to the center mechanism. Others insist that the antagonism between excitatory and inhibitory parts of the receptive field plays a major role in shaping the selectivity of a cortical neuron. The best example of this controversy is offered by the mechanism of orientation selectivity in neurons of area 17 (Figures 1.3B and 1.3C). Originally, Hubel and Wiesel (1962) proposed that the orientation selectivity of a cortical neuron was due to the properly oriented organization of the receptive field centers of the LGN cells driving the cortical neuron (Figure 1.3B). In the 1970s Peter Bishop and his colleagues (Bishop, Coombs & Henry, 1973) and Adam Sillito (Sillito, 1975) proposed an alternative mechanism: that the orientation selectivity results mainly from the local organization of excitatory (center) and inhibitory (modulatory surround) regions of the receptive field and that much of this organization was due to local corticocortical connections (Figure 1.3C). The debate between the proponents of both models is still very active 40 years after the initial proposition of Hubel and Wiesel. Several lines of evidence suggest that both convergence of thalamic excitatory inputs and inhibitory interactions between cortical neurons play a role in setting up orientation selectivity in neurons of area 17 (Borg-Graham, Monier, & Fregnac, 1998; Chapman, Zahs, & Stryker, 1991). Blocking inhibitory neurons in cortex reduces but does not abolish orientation selectivity of cortical neurons (Ferster & Koch, 1987), thus showing that excitatory/inhibitory interactions between center and surround cannot be the sole mechanism. On the other hand, the width of the orientation selectivity tuning curve of area 17 neurons can be profoundly modified by inactivating neighboring cortical neurons (Crook, Kisvarday, & Eysel, 1997). This finding is impossible to reconcile with the original model of Hubel and Wiesel, and apart from a few extremist teams, most research groups now agree that both a proper selection of LGN inputs and excitatory/inhibitory interactions within cortex are necessary to explain the orientation selectivity of neurons in area 17.

Receptive Field Selectivity of Cortical Neurons: Tuning Curves

The majority of retinal ganglion cells that project to the LGN in primates is only selective to luminance and chrominance contrast between the center and the surround of their receptive fields. In contrast, neurons in the different cortical areas give responses that are selective to a variety of other parameters of the visual scene. Most visual cortical neurons show selectivity to the orientation of a contrast border (Figures 1.4A and 1.4B). Cortical neurons are also selective to the direction of

---

[3]This contrasts with the situation in the retinal ganglion cell: In an ON-center ganglion cell, a large stimulus activating only the surround will produce an antagonistic response (response at offset, instead of onset, in the center). Thus, ON-center ganglion cells are sometimes called ON-center, OFF-surround (vice-versa for OFF-center cells).

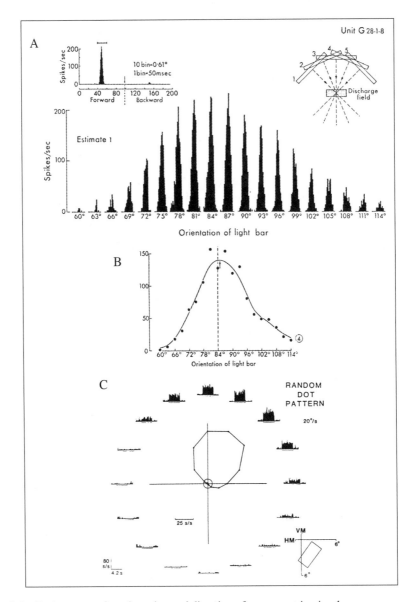

Figure 1.4   Tuning curves for orientation and direction of movement in visual space.

NOTE: A: Tuning for orientation of a neuron in cat area 17. The upper small set of histograms shows the responses to a bar moving at the optimal orientation and in the optimal direction (left histogram) and in the opposite direction (small histogram on the right of the vertical dotted line). This neuron is direction-selective. The large set of histograms below illustrates the neuron responses for different orientations of a bar moving across the receptive field, as indicated on the schematic diagram in the upper right. B: Orientation tuning curve of the neuron illustrated in A. The mean response is plotted as a function of the stimulus orientation. C: Polar plot of the direction selectivity of a neuron in area MT to the movement of a pattern of random dots. The small circle represents the spontaneous activity of the neuron. The receptive field position in the visual field is represented on the lower right (HM: horizontal meridian; VM: vertical meridian).

SOURCE: B: Reproduced from Henry, Bishop, Tupper, & Dreher (1973) with permission from Elsevier Science. C: Reproduced from Albright (1984).

movement of a stimulus on the tangent screen (Figures 1.4A and 1.4C). In both cases, the selectivity is expressed by the tuning curve with an optimal orientation or direction and a tuning curve width (Figure 1.4B).

Because the afferents from the two eyes converge on cortical neurons (see the section titled "Functional Architecture of the Visual System"), one can define three receptive fields for a cortical neuron, one for each eye and one for binocular stimulation. In area V1 a large number of neurons possess only one receptive field in the ipsilateral or contralateral eye. Called monocular neurons, these tend to be concentrated in the layers that receive the LGN afferents. In the other layers and in other cortical areas, most neurons can be driven through stimulation of either eye. These are called binocular neurons. In general, the receptive fields in each eye have similar properties, and most of them are located in corresponding positions in the visual field (i.e., they are tuned to zero binocular disparity). In this case, when the eyes are fixating on a given point, both receptive fields overlap, and the response is larger for a stimulus located on the horopter than for a stimulus located in front or beyond (Figure 1.5A). Other cortical neurons show various amounts of receptive field disparity tuning (i.e., the receptive fields occupy noncorresponding positions on the tangent screen). This arrangement of the monocular receptive fields produces optimal responses for stimuli positioned in front of or beyond the plane of fixation (Figure 1.5B). See Chapter 3 in this volume for a detailed discussion of binocular disparity.

Are Cortical Receptive Fields Tuned for One or for Several Parameters?

Many aspects of the primate visual system exhibit functional specialization. That is, a given neuron is specialized for representing a particular property. One important example is the specialization for wavelength encoding in the retinal cones: Each of three types of cone photoreceptors exhibits a distinct spectral sensitivity to a range of wavelengths in the visible spectrum, and together the three cone classes provide a representation of wavelength that subserves color vision (see Chap. 2, this volume, for details).

The principle of functional specialization has sometimes been extended to many, if not most, visual parameters (e.g., color, movement, orientation, stereoscopic disparity). Textbook treatments hold that distinct populations of neurons or cortical regions are specialized for a single visual property. Although there is evidence for a certain degree of specialization in different cortical areas, most cortical neurons code for several parameters. For example, Figure 1.4A shows a neuron that is tuned to the orientation of a moving stimulus but is also selective for its direction of movement. Color-selective neurons in areas V1 and V2 are often also orientation selective. Direction-selective neurons in area MT are usually tuned for stereoscopic disparity (DeAngelis, Cumming, & Newsome, 1998).

Thus, the idea that color stimuli, for example, activate one population of neurons and moving stimuli activate another distinct population does not accurately characterize neural coding in the visual system. Neural coding is based on the responses of hundreds of thousands of neurons that each provide an intrinsically ambiguous and often multiplexed message (see the section titled "Relation between Neuronal Activity and Perceptual Experience" for a discussion of the relation between neuronal responses and perceptual experience). Even in cortical areas of the inferotemporal (IT) and parietal cortex where very specific receptive fields are found, neurons respond to multiple cues, and each neuron sends an ambiguous message.

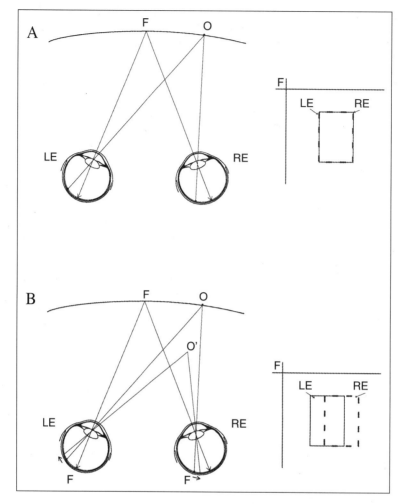

Figure 1.5 Binocular cortical receptive fields and stereoscopic vision.
NOTE: A: Corresponding receptive fields and optimal response for a stimulus O in the fixation plane (diagram on the right illustrates the contralateral visual hemifield around the fixation point F; LE: left eye; RE: right eye). B: Receptive fields with crossed disparity; optimal response for a stimulus O′ in front of the fixation plane.

Complex Receptive Fields

To a rough approximation, when progressing from the lowest to the highest levels of the hierarchy of visual cortical areas (see the section titled "Functional Architecture of the Visual System"), the trigger features of receptive fields become more and more complex: In V1 an oriented bar may activate a given cell, whereas in IT cortex only a quite specific complex object may be required to a activate a given cell. This has been mocked as leading to the logical extreme of the grandmother cell—the one neuron that responds uniquely to the sight of one's grandmother. Although the grandmother cell is unlikely to be found in the brain, there are numerous examples of neurons with receptive fields that are selective to complex features of a stimulus. In the

1970s neurons selective to human and monkey faces and to complex shapes were identified in the IT cortex of monkeys (Gross, Rocha-Miranda, & Bender, 1972; Tanaka, 1996). More recently, researchers have found neurons in the frontal cortex that appear to be specific to classes of objects based on visual features (Freedman, Riesenhuber, Poggio, & Miller, 2001).

The demonstration of highly selective receptive fields in IT and parietal cortex has led to the idea that neurons in these areas have receptive fields that respond to a given stimulus property regardless of the sensory dimension in which that property is rendered. Such cue-invariant responses have been demonstrated by Orban and his collaborators, who showed that some IT neurons respond selectively to a given orientation of a grating stimulus, whether the stimulus is a luminance-defined, motion-defined, or texture-defined grating (Sary, Vogels, Kovacs, & Orban, 1995). These findings suggest that IT neurons abstract away from the sensory input by receiving convergent inputs from neurons at lower stages of cortical processing and that the cue-invariant selectivity is built through this ordered convergence.

However, highly sophisticated selectivity is not observed only in the IT, parietal, and frontal cortex. Recent use of realistic stimuli to study neurons in early visual areas has revealed interesting properties. In an attempt to discover the neuronal basis of the barber-pole illusion,[4] Albright and his collaborators manipulated the depth of the occluding borders to switch the percept induced by a square wave grating (diagonal stripes) moving within a square window (Duncan, Albright, & Stoner,

2001). Changing the relative depths of the four regions bordering the window radically switches the perceived direction of a grating partially occluded by the borders. Albright and his colleagues found a significant proportion of neurons in area MT that responded in a manner consistent with the perceived direction of motion. In other words, such neurons appear to be tuned to what could be called the mental image of the object.

What is particularly interesting is that such specificity to inferred objects is not limited to high-level areas of the inferotemporal or parietal cortex. If one uses latency as an index of the order of activation of cortical areas, area MT is at the same level as area V2 (Bullier, 2001a; Nowak & Bullier, 1997)— just one level above V1—and should therefore be considered as a low-order area (see the section titled "Functional Architecture of the Visual System" for further discussion on this point). Thus, specific responses to inferred properties can be found in an early area such as MT. Similarly, responses to inferred objects have been demonstrated in areas V1 and V2. For example, Sugita (1999) showed that some neurons in V1 strongly respond to a bar moving behind an occluding patch, even though the stimulus does not stimulate the receptive field center. Similar results have been found by Gilbert and his collaborators, who found such selectivity to be more frequent in area V2 than in V1 (Bakin, Nakayama, & Gilbert, 2000). These recent findings extend the well-known results of Peterhans and von der Heydt that showed selective responses of area V2 neurons to illusory contours of the Kanisza type (Peterhans & von der Heydt, 1989; von der Heydt & Peterhans, 1989).

Thus, the classical idea that receptive fields in areas V1 and V2 signal simple features such as edges and terminations and that more complicated three-dimensional shapes are represented only by neurons in higher-order areas is no longer tenable. The main difference

---

[4]In the barber-pole illusion, the stripes of the pole appear to move unambiguously upward, in a direction parallel to the axis of elongation of the pole, although the local motion signal is ambiguous and equally consistent with lateral or diagonal motion.

between receptive fields of neurons in areas V1, V2, and MT and receptive fields of neurons in the IT and parietal cortex is their size, not their complexity. Because neurons in areas V1 and V2 have relatively small receptive fields, they are likely to signal changes in a small area of the visual field, whereas neurons in IT and parietal cortex are selective to larger stimuli.

Receptive Fields That Move in Time

In the 1970s it became evident that the receptive fields of some cortical neurons change in location and configuration as a function of time. The most characteristic case is that of the space-time-inseparable receptive fields of some V1 neurons for which the receptive field center moves together with the stimulus that activates it (DeAngelis, Ohzawa, & Freeman, 1993a, 1993b). This provides the neuron with a direction and speed selectivity through mechanisms of convergent excitatory inputs (Humphrey & Saul, 2001). Other examples of modifications in time of receptive fields have been found in the parietal cortex and in area V4, in which the receptive fields move in the direction of the intended eye movement (Duhamel, Colby, & Goldberg, 1992; Tolias et al., 2001).

FUNCTIONAL MAPS

The spatial layout of neurons in many visual areas is not random. A great deal has been learned about the relation between the spatial layout of neurons in cortex and the spatial and nonspatial properties of the neurons. These spatial layouts are usually referred to as cortical maps.

Retinotopic Mapping in Subcortical Structures and Visual Cortex

Retinotopic mapping constitutes another central notion and an essential tool of visual neu-

roscience. A retinotopic map is an ordered representation of the visual field by neurons distributed across a neural surface. Retinotopic maps are found in subcortical structures as well as in cortical areas. Because no neural structure is a one-neuron wide sheet, the possibility of mapping visual space on a nucleus or a cortical surface requires that when one is moving in a direction perpendicular to that of the neural surface, receptive fields overlap, whereas they move in a predictable fashion when one is moving across the surface. This is illustrated in Figures 1.6A and 1.6B.

Cortical maps of the visual field are enormously distorted: for example, in the map of the contralateral visual hemifield in area V1 of the owl monkey (Figure 1.6C), more than one third of the surface is occupied by the central 10 deg of visual field that correspond to less than 2% of the animal's field of view.[5] This enormous expansion of the central visual field representation is partly a consequence of the higher density of retinal ganglion cells in the central retina (Wassle & Boycott, 1991). One way to quantify the grain of the representation is to calculate the magnification factor, which gives the extent of cortical surface (in linear or surface measure) representing one degree of visual angle. The magnification factor peaks at a value close to 20 mm/deg in the central part of the visual field in macaque monkeys and humans and rapidly declines to 2 mm/deg at an eccentricity of 10 deg. Because of the high values at zero eccentricity and the extremely steep shape of the curve, it is convenient to plot the inverse of the magnification factor (Figure 1.7A) or the relationship between retinal eccentricity and cortical distance (Figure 1.7B). The inverse magnification factor is given by the slope of the curve relating retinal eccentricity and cortical distance (Figure 1.7B).

---

[5] In macaque monkeys and humans, half the surface of V1 is devoted to the central 10 deg of visual field.

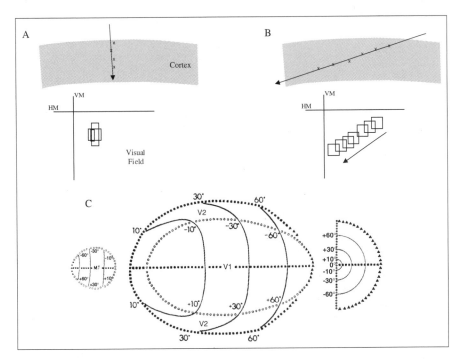

Figure 1.6   Retinotopic maps in the visual cortex.
NOTE: A: Neurons (illustrated by crosses in the cortex) recorded in a penetration perpendicular to the cortical surface have overlapping receptive fields (rectangles in the visual field; HM: horizontal meridian; VM: vertical meridian). B: When successive neurons (crosses) are recorded across the cortical surface in an oblique penetration, the receptive fields move across the visual field. C: Map of the contralateral visual hemifield across the surface of areas V1, V2, and MT in owl monkeys (the hemicircle on the right represents the contralateral visual hemifield). Note that the border between areas V1 and V2 corresponds to neurons coding the vertical meridian (as is the outer border of area MT) and that the neurons at the outer border of area V2 have receptive fields located on the horizontal meridian. This map is a flattened version of that observed on the surface of the owl monkey cortex. Distortion due to flattening is limited because of the smooth nature of the cortex in this animal. Distortions are much more important in macaque monkey and human visual cortex.
SOURCE: C: Redrawn from Allman & Kaas (1974).

Distortions of the visual field differ from one structure to the next in the visual system: Most subcortical nuclei and cortical areas have an expanded representation of the central visual field, but some areas, such as area PO (or area M in New World monkeys), show a proportionally much more important representation of the peripheral visual field than do the other areas (Rosa, 1997). The representation of lower and upper visual fields is comparable in extent in most cortical areas and subcortical structures with some exceptions such as the MIN, a subcortical nucleus in

the cat visual system that contains a vastly expanded representation of the lower visual field (Lee, Malpeli, Schwark, & Weyand, 1984).

Mapping a single visual structure such as the LGN is relatively easy because it contains a single representation of the contralateral visual hemifield. The situation is much more difficult in some subcortical structures, such as the pulvinar, and in the cortex. Each of these structures contains several representations of the contralateral visual hemifield. Because this is the cause of much controversy in the definition of cortical areas in the

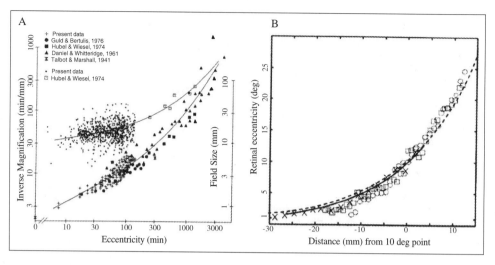

Figure 1.7   Magnification factor as a function of eccentricity.

NOTE: A: Inverse of the magnification factor as a function of eccentricity (lower curve and left scale) and receptive field size (upper curve and right scale) in the macaque monkey area V1. B: Retinal eccentricity as a function of distance on the cortical surface of V1 in human. The origin is taken as the point representing an eccentricity of 10 deg of visual angle along the horizontal meridian. The inverse of the magnification factor is given by the slope of the curve.

SOURCE: A: Redrawn from Dow, Snyder, Vautin, & Bauer (1981). B: Reproduced from Engel, Glover, & Wandell (1997).

animal and human brain, it is important to review it using a hypothetical example (Figure 1.8A). When successive penetrations are made along a line across the visual cortex of an animal with a smooth brain, the locations of receptive fields of neurons recorded in these different penetrations move in a linear fashion in the visual field, reflecting a systematic correspondence between the locations of the cells in the brain and the locations of their receptive fields. This continuous progression is sometimes broken by sudden changes in direction (between 3 and 4 and 13 and 14 in Figure 1.8A). These changes in direction of the progression of the receptive fields usually correspond to the border between one cortical area and another. In some cases, the reversals are observed at the representation of the vertical meridian (e.g., the border between areas V1 and V2 in Figure 1.8A); in other cases, it is at the representation of the horizontal merid-

ian (e.g., the outer border of area V2 in Figure 1.6C). These reversals are sometimes accompanied by changes in receptive field sizes or changes in receptive field properties that help to identify the borders (Rosa, 1997). Confirmation of the location of borders between areas are also provided by histological techniques: The size and density of cell bodies as well as the density of myelin often change abruptly at the border between two functional areas. Areas V1, V2, and MT are relatively easy to identify with histological techniques.

Mapping studies in human visual cortex using fMRI (for details, see Chap. 5, Vol. 4 of this series) follow the same principle as illustrated in Figure 1.8A. Instead of plotting the trajectory of receptive fields of neurons recorded across in an oblique electrode penetration or at successive neighboring points, the movement of the active zone on the cortical surface is recorded for a moving stimulus.

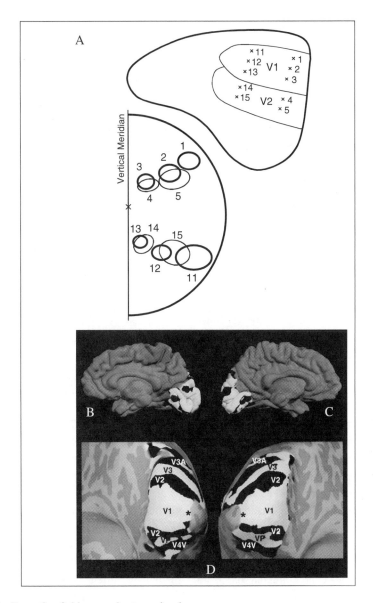

Figure 1.8   Receptive field reversals at area borders.

NOTE: A: Mapping the visual field across cortical borders between areas V1 and V2 in a hypothetical mammal with a smooth brain. Each cross corresponds to a penetration in cortex made perpendicular to the surface. Numbered ellipses correspond to the receptive fields of neurons recorded in these penetrations. Note that the progression of the receptive fields is continuous in the series 1 to 3 and 11 to 13 but that the direction of progression changes abruptly between 3 and 4 and 13 and 14. This corresponds to crossing the border between areas V1 and V2. B and C: Medial views of the human visual cortex. D: Resulting maps on an inflated surface of human cortex. The gray zones correspond to the cortical surface buried in the sulci. V1, V2, V3, VP, V4v, and V3A are identified by the sign of the progression of activity across the cortical surface when a rotating stimulus is used.

SOURCE: Reproduced from Tootell et al. (1998).

Typically, a stimulus consisting of a contrast reversal sector revolves around the center of gaze. This stimulus activates neurons in cortex in a sequence that depends on the type of representation in the area. For example, in the cortical surface shown in Figure 1.8A, as the rotating stimulus moves away from the vertical meridian, it generates two complementary waves of activity in areas V1 and V2, moving in opposite directions away from the border between areas V1 and V2. By measuring the phase of the variation of signal generated by repetitive rotating stimuli, it is possible to identify the borders between functional areas in the visual cortex (Engel, Zhang, & Wandell, 1997; Tootell et al., 1998).

This method has been used for parceling the cortical surface in a number of functional areas, as shown in Figure 1.9. The main species that are used to study vision are the human (Figures 1.9A–C) and the macaque monkey (Figure 1.9D). Although mapping is more precise in the macaque monkey than in the human, there are still controversies concerning the subdivision in cortical areas in the macaque cortex (Kaas, 1997; Rosa, 1997). Homologies between macaque and human brains are valid for areas such as V1, V2, and V5 (called MT in the macaque; Kaas, 1997). There are already differences between monkey and human brains for areas V3 and V3A (Tootell et al., 1997), and the situation is even more complex concerning the role of V4 in color vision in these two species (Tootell & Hadjikhani, 2001). Also, there appear to be areas in the human visual cortex, such as the object-related area LO (Figure 1.9C), for which no homologous area has yet been identified in the monkey (Malach et al., 1995). This constitutes a difficulty in the interpretation of results from imaging studies in human brains because the homologous areas in the monkey have not always been identified, and it is therefore difficult to understand the metabolic responses observed by imaging

methods in terms of responses of single cortical neurons.

Another limitation of the method of retinotopic mapping for identifying the functional areas of the visual cortex is that the retinotopic organization becomes very fuzzy in some regions. This is particularly the case in the IT cortex, where neurons have large receptive fields that are usually centered on the point of fixation and are not restricted to one visual hemifield. Neighboring neurons have receptive fields that overlap extensively, and this makes it nearly impossible to delineate borders between areas on the basis of retinotopic mapping. For this reason, the subdivisions of the IT cortex are usually based on topographic landmarks (e.g., the locations of gyri and sulci). In the monkey these subdivisions are usually confirmed by neuroanatomical studies that characterize regions by their connections with other cortical areas. In the human brain, no such connectivity maps have yet been obtained, and only topographic landmarks can be used. The situation is to some extent similar in the human parietal cortex.

Maps of Nonspatial Properties

Cortical maps are not limited to spatial parameters. A number of nonspatial parameters are also organized in maps across the cortical surface. The most famous example is the map of preferred or optimal orientation on the surface of area V1 (Figure 1.10A). This complicated pattern has been finally identified with the technique of optical imaging that enables the simultaneous recording of activities of large populations of neurons. Such a map has been demonstrated in area V1 for a number of species, and it is highly likely that it also exists in the human (although a satisfactory demonstration will require improvement in the spatial resolution of cortical imaging techniques). The pattern of optimal orientation on the surface of monkey V1

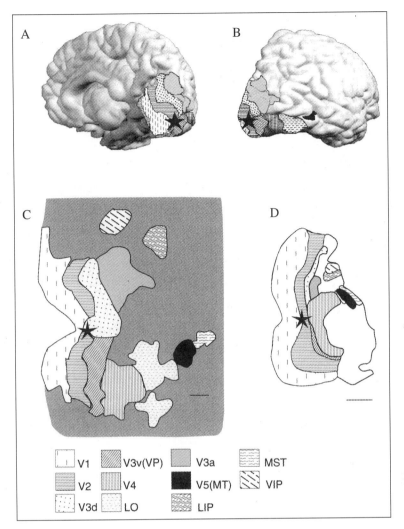

Figure 1.9 Visual cortical areas in the human brain.
NOTE: A and B: Functional cortical areas of the human brain viewed on medial and lateral views of the posterior cortex. The black star marks the representation of the center of gaze. C: Flattened version of the human visual cortical areas. D: Flattened map of the visual cortical areas in the macaque monkey. Note that the sizes of the early visual areas are comparable in human and monkey brains.
SOURCE: Modified from Tootell, Dale, Sereno, & Malach (1996).

(Figure 1.10A) remains practically unchanged for regions measuring several hundreds of microns across. Thus, a stimulus with a given orientation in a given region of the visual field will activate neurons that are grouped on the cortical surface in V1. Because it is known that the source of corticocortical connections are organized in patches of neighboring neurons

(discussed later), it is likely that such an organization of nonspatial parameters is linked to the necessity of connecting together populations of neurons in the source and target cortical area according to their optimal orientations. Regions of constant optimal orientation are separated by smooth or abrupt transitions, and there are special regions called

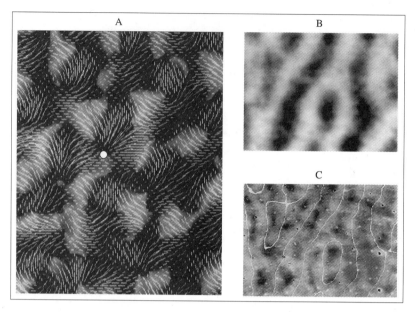

Figure 1.10   Map of optimal orientation on the surface of area V1 in the macaque monkey.
NOTE: A: Regions of iso-orientation are grouped by colors, and the optimal orientation is given by the orientations of the white bars. The bar length indicates the selectivity (long bar: sharp tuning; short bars: region of poor orientation selectivity). The white dot marks a pinwheel. B: Ocular dominance bands on the cortical surface of area V1 in macaque monkey. Dark and white bands correspond to cortical regions dominated by one or the other eye. C: Relationship between cytochrome-oxidase blobs and ocular dominance bands. The borders between ocular dominance bands are represented by the white line. Note how the cytochrome oxidase blobs are aligned in the centers of the ocular dominance bands. Distance between two ocular dominance bands corresponding to the same eye is approximately 1 mm.
SOURCE: Modified from Blasdel (1992). Copyright ©1992 by the Society for Neuroscience. Reprinted by permission.

pinwheels (an example is marked by the white dot in Figure 1.10A) that constitute anchoring points around which the optimal orientation rotates. The relationship between the positions of these pinwheels and the centers of the cytochrome oxidase blobs (discussed later) is a matter of debate.

Although it is best documented for orientation, mapping of nonspatial parameters is not limited to this property. Researchers have noted maps of optimal directions in area 17 of the ferret (Weliky, Bosking, & Fitzpatrick, 1996) and in area MT of the monkey (Albright, Desimone, & Gross, 1984), and the ocular dominance is also systematically mapped on the surface of area V1 (Figure 1.10B). One of the reasons for the large

size of area V1 in all mammalian species may thus be due to the fine grain of the representation (small sizes of the receptive fields) and the multiple mapping of different parameters on the surface of this area. Areas such as MT or V3d, which are more specialized, are smaller, have larger receptive fields, and are organized according to a smaller number of parameters (space, direction of motion, and stereoscopic depth in the case of area MT).

Mapping various parameters across the cortical surface is obviously related to the concept of the cortical column that was in much use in the 1970s. This term is less frequently used nowadays because of the difficulty of defining a column. For example, in the case of orientation one might think that a region of homogeneous optimal orientation constitutes a column. However, the optimal orientation is not uniform for all of the neurons that constitute the column: There are smooth variations within the column as well as random jitters of the optimal orientation from one neuron to the next. The one parameter that is correctly attached to the term *column* is the ocular dominance: Area V1 contains regions that clearly group neurons that respond preferentially to stimulation of one eye. Here, contrary to orientation or direction of movement of a stimulus, the parameter is discrete (right eye, left eye) instead of continuous, as in optimal orientation. However, one might even hesitate to speak strictly of a column of ocular dominance because the domains of ocular dominance are actually organized in bands across area V1 (Figure 1.10B).

The grouping of neurons according to their functional properties is perhaps the most important principle of cortical organization. Sometimes, specific groups also correspond to domains that can be revealed by histological techniques. This is the case of cytochrome oxidase[6] blobs in V1 (Figure 1.10C) and cytochrome oxidase bands in V2. These territories group neurons that share similar response properties (Hubel & Livingstone, 1987). One interesting question is how the spatial and nonspatial maps are superimposed. This has been studied in area V2, and it was found that as one passes from one cytochrome oxidase band to the next, there is a remapping of visual space (Roe & Ts'o, 1995). In other words, a given cortical area does not necessarily correspond to a single smooth retinotopic map, as is often assumed. Instead, a single cortical area can contain a large number of very small

representations of the visual field comprising neurons that share one property (e.g., the same optimal orientation or optimal wavelength). As mentioned earlier, it is probably closely linked to the necessity of organizing connections between areas as groups of neighboring neurons (connection patches).

For a long period after their discovery, it was thought that retinotopic maps in subcortical and cortical structures were invariant features of the visual system. However, it was first demonstrated in the somatosensory cortex that maps are plastic and reorganize after being deafferented by removal of the peripheral sensory inputs (Kaas, Merzenich, & Killackey, 1983). A similar observation was made in the visual system after retinal lesions (Kaas et al., 1990). A few hours after the lesion, some neurons with receptive fields near the lesioned region exhibited shifted receptive fields. After several weeks, the cortical region containing neurons with receptive fields in the lesioned region regained its responsiveness. The receptive fields of these neurons now occupied regions of the visual field that were close to the lesioned area. It appears that both synaptic reorganization and axon regrowth are involved in this phenomenon (Darian-Smith & Gilbert, 1994).

Another form of plasticity was demonstrated in the auditory and somatosensory systems: After repeated use of a cortical region representing a certain tone or position on the body, the extent of cortex responding to these stimuli expand at the same time that the receptive fields become narrower. Similar modifications have been observed in humans by imaging studies. Such modifications after training appear to be much more limited in the visual system, at least in area V1, which has been tested (Crist, Li, & Gilbert, 2001). It is possible that the retinotopic organization in area V1 is more stable than the tonotopic or somatotopic organization in primary areas of the auditory and somatosensory systems. It remains

---

[6]Cytochrome oxidase is an enzyme that is found in cell bodies of neurons with high metabolic activity. Regions of strong cytochrome oxidase activity can be viewed easily with a light microscope after histological treatment (Figure 1.10C). This technique provides useful information about the anatomical structure of cortex.

to be seen whether training can induce changes in retinotopic organization of cortical areas beyond V1 in the visual system.

FUNCTIONAL ARCHITECTURE OF THE VISUAL SYSTEM

Neurons of the visual system present a large diversity in morphology, functional properties, and connectivity. As discussed earlier, a fundamental principle of organization in the nervous system is that neurons with similar properties and connections tend to be grouped together. This also constitutes the basis of the functional architecture of the visual system.

Different Types of Retinal Ganglion Cells

Among the several dozens of retinal ganglion cell types (Rodieck, 1998), it is usual to distinguish three main classes: two relatively homogeneous groups (the midget and the parasol cells) and a heterogeneous group called the W or Koniocellular cells. Midget cells (also called beta cells) are characterized by a small cell body and dendritic arbor and are thought to carry information about fine spatial and chromatic discrimination in the middle and long wavelengths (fed by the M and L cones). It appears to be the most numerous ganglion cell type in the primate retina (about 70%). Parasol cells (also called alpha cells) are much less frequent than the midget (around 10%) and carry information about luminance contrast. The receptive field organization of parasol cells is similar to that demonstrated for the cat retinal ganglion cells (see Figure 1.2). The third group of retinal ganglion cells, the W type, is much more heterogeneous in morphology and receptive field properties: Some neurons are direction-selective, whereas others signal absolute luminance. Recent results (Calkins & Sterling, 1999) suggest that a group of W cells, the bistratified ganglion

cell, carries chromatic opponent signals in the short wavelengths (S/L+M).

All three types of ganglion cells project to the LGN, the thalamic relay of the visual system that receives approximately 90% of the information that leaves the retina. Other destinations of retinal ganglion cell axons are the superior collicullus, the suprachiasmatic nucleus, the nucleus of the optic tract, the pretectum, and the nuclei of the accessory optic tract. Both parasol and W cells project to the superior colliculus. The projections to the nucleus of the optic tract, the pretectum, and the nuclei of the accessory optic tract appear to belong for the most part to the W system and constitute specialized circuits for the stabilization of the eyes when following a moving pattern or during the pupillary reflex or the stabilization of the circadian rhythm (Rodieck, 1998).

In the optic chiasm, the fibers coming from the retinal ganglion cells located in the nasal retina cross to the other hemisphere, whereas the axons coming from the temporal half of the retina are directed to the ipsilateral thalamus (Figure 1.11). This hemidecussation and the rearrangement of fibers at the arrival in the LGN provide the basis for an ordered representation of the contralateral visual hemifield in the LGN and in the visual cortex.

The Lateral Geniculate Nucleus

The LGN is a multilayered nucleus of cells located in the posterior and lateral part of the thalamus. Approximately 80% of the LGN neurons are relay cells that receive inputs from retinal ganglion cells and send an axon to V1. The remaining neurons are local inhibitory interneurons. The LGN also receives inhibitory input from the thalamic reticular nucleus (TRN; called perigeniculate nucleus in the visual system of some species). The TRN contains GABA-ergic neurons that project to the LGN and receive inputs from the cortex and from axon collaterals of the

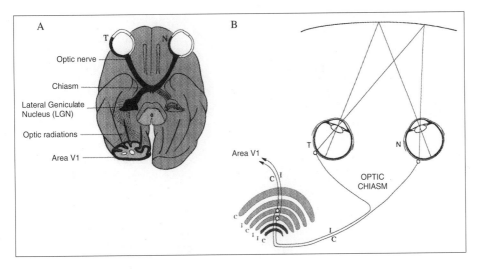

Figure 1.11   Connections between the retina and the cortex.
NOTE: A: Diagram of the connections between the eyes, the LGN and area V1 on a ventral view of the human brain. B: Connectivity between a neuron located in the temporal (T) half of the retina on the ipsilateral (I) side and the LGN and between a neuron located in the nasal (N) half of the contralateral (c) retina and the LGN. Axons from the nasal half of the retina cross at the optic chiasm. Axons from different layers of the LGN transmit information corresponding to ipsi- or contralateral eye. Note that successive layers of the LGN receive alternatively from ipsi- or contralateral retina and that the connectivity is such that a column of cells in the LGN corresponds to a given direction in visual space. The two ventral layers in dark gray are the magnocellular layers.

geniculocortical axons (Sherman & Guillery, 2001).

Three subdivisions are usually distinguished in the LGN: (a) the two ventral layers containing cells with large cell bodies, called the magnocellular layers; (b) the four dorsal layers, which contain smaller neurons and are called parvocellular layers; and (c) the koniocellular layers, which correspond to the regions between these layers and below the magnocellular layers. The magnocellular and parvocellular layers are innervated alternatively by axons from the ipsilateral (I) or the contralateral (c) eye (Figure 1.11B).

This subdivision in magno-, parvo-, and koniocellular layers is extremely important because it corresponds to a functional division due to the specific projections of the different types of retinal ganglion cells to the different sets of layers of the LGN. The magnocellular (M) layers receive inputs from the parasol ganglion cells of the retina; the parvocellular layers (P) are innervated by the midget type of retinal ganglions cells; and the koniocellular layers (K) receive their inputs from the W ganglion cells and the superior colliculus. These three groups of neurons also project to different layers in V1.

Because of these connectivity differences, neurons of the P layers are selective for the wavelength of the stimuli: They have small receptive fields and respond to fine detail (high spatial frequencies). On the other hand, P cells respond poorly to high temporal frequencies (e.g., fast-moving stimuli or flickering lights), and they do not respond to contrasts below 8%. Neurons of the M layers exhibit nearly complementary properties: They are not sensitive to chromatic differences ("color blindness"), have larger receptive fields, and respond poorly to high spatial frequencies (fine detail) but well to rapidly moving targets and to contrasts below 8% (Merigan & Maunsell, 1991). The properties of the K layers are less well known because of the difficulty of recording from small cells. Some neurons selective to wavelength differences in the short-wavelength range have been reported in the K layers, suggesting that the color-opponent signals corresponding to short wavelengths may, at least partly, be transferred through the K layers of the LGN (White, Wilder, Goodchild, Sefton, & Martin, 1998).

Another difference between the layers in the LGN concerns the timing of the responses (Nowak & Bullier, 1997): Neurons in the M layers respond in a transient fashion to changes of contrast in their receptive fields (onset or offset), and they respond more rapidly (by about 10–20 ms) than do the neurons of the P layers. In contrast, P neurons produce a more sustained response to sudden changes in luminance or wavelength contrast. Finally, the response of neurons in the K layers appears to be delayed by another 10 ms with respect to P-layer neurons.

Comparison of the receptive field properties of retinal ganglion cells and LGN neurons leads to the conclusion that no new selectivity is achieved at the LGN level by the arrangement of retinal connections. Thus, the LGN appears to act mostly as a relay structure whose transfer characteristics are governed by nonretinal sources of input: the cortex, the thalamic reticular nucleus, and several brain stem nuclei associated with various vigilance states (Sherman & Guillery, 2001).

The role of the cortical feedback remains unclear. Cortical inputs to LGN relay cells are concentrated on the distal dendrites, and most corticogeniculate axons are slowly conducting. This suggests that the cortex has mainly a slow modulatory action on the transmission of messages through the LGN. It has been recently suggested (Sherman & Guillery, 2001) that LGN neurons occupy one of two states: one in which they transmit mostly bursts of action potentials and another in which they transmit relatively closely the firing rate of their retinal afferents. Switches between these two states may correspond to different vigilance states but could also be used to transmit different types of information to the visual cortex during active vision (Sherman, 2001).

The Superior Colliculus and the Pulvinar

Located in the upper part of the brain stem, the superior colliculus (called the optic tectum in some species) receives a direct input from the retina in its upper layers and cortical input from many visual cortical areas in its deep layers. Although in many species it is the major subcortical visual nucleus, in primates it is a small structure whose role appears to be limited to the control of voluntary eye movements. Projections extend from the superior colliculus to the pulvinar and to the K layers of the LGN. Although the relay from the superior colliculus to the visual cortex concerns only a small region of the pulvinar (Stepniewska, Qi, & Kaas, 1999), these connections are assumed to constitute the nongeniculate route to cortex that could subserve the residual visual capacities of primates with lesions in area V1 (Bullier, Girard, & Salin, 1994; Weiskrantz, 1986).

The pulvinar is divided into multiple nuclei; of these, only the inferior and lateral pulvinar are specifically related to vision. Several retinotopic maps are found in the lateral and inferior pulvinar, and it is assumed that they correspond to different functional entities. Despite its large size in primates, the role of the pulvinar in vision remains largely mysterious. A role in attention has been repeatedly mentioned (Robinson & Petersen, 1992) and included in a number of models of the visual system, but it has not been demonstrated experimentally. Researchers (Rockland, 1998; Sherman & Guillery, 1998) have recently argued that some of the connections from the visual cortex to the pulvinar may be of the "driver" type (similar to the retinal input into the LGN). This has led Sherman and Guillery to suggest that the pulvinar could play a role in processing and relaying information between different visual cortical areas.

Areas V1 and V2

The major cortical projection from the LGN is to area V1. Only a very small contingent of projections from the K layers terminates in areas outside of V1. Area V1 is the largest of all visual cortical areas, and V2 is only slightly smaller. As mentioned earlier, the central 10 deg of visual field are represented by approximately half the cortical surfaces in areas V1 and V2 in macaque monkeys and humans. The border between areas V1 and V2 corresponds to the representation of the vertical meridian, and the anterior border of V2 corresponds to the representation of the horizontal meridian. Because of this organization, stimuli placed on either side of the horizontal meridian activate neighboring neuronal populations in V1, whereas in V2 the upper stimulus activates a region in the ventral part of the area and the lower stimulus activates a region in the dorsal part of V2 (Figure 1.6C). This is important to remember in the interpretation of imaging studies: One stimulus localized in visual space can activate two separate regions in one cortical area.

Cortical neurons are arranged in layers that contain various densities and sizes of neurons (Figure 1.12). These layers constitute the input-output modules of the cortex. In V1 the LGN axons terminate mainly in layer 4C, with additional small inputs in layers 4A and 6 and in the cytochrome oxidase blobs in layers 2 and 3. Layer-4 neurons send connections to layers 2-3 and 5-6 which are also reciprocally

connected (Lund, 1988). Layers 2 and 3 contain the main source of cortical outputs to area V2 and receive inputs from several cortical areas. Layer 4B contain neurons that project to areas V3d and MT and receives return projections from these areas. Layer 5 contains neurons projecting to the superior colliculus and the pulvinar. Layer 6 contains neurons projecting back to the LGN and sending connections to the claustrum. Cortical inputs into area V1 terminate in layers 2-3 and 5-6 (Salin & Bullier, 1995).

The separation between magno-, parvo- and koniocellular neurons in the LGN is maintained at the first processing stages in V1: Magnocellular axons terminate in layer 4C alpha; parvocellular axons project to layer 4C beta and 4A; and koniocellular axons terminate in the cytochrome oxidase blobs in layers 2 and 3 (Figure 1.12). Beyond this stage, however, there is extensive mixing of different types of thalamic inputs in cortical neurons (Callaway, 1998).

Area V2 receives by far the largest projections from V1. These axons terminate in layer 4 and lower layer 3. A strong return projection from V2 to V1 arises from layers 2-3 and 5-6 and terminates outside layer 4 in V1. The very dense network of connections between areas V1 and V2 is organized in separate streams that are identified by the cytochrome oxidase blobs in V1 and the cytochrome oxidase bands in V2. Three types of bands in V2 are identified by their width and density: the thin, thick, and pale bands. The blobs in V1 are reciprocally connected with the thin bands in V2; the zones between the blobs in V1 (the interblobs) are connected to the pale bands. Finally, the thick bands are connected to layer 4B in V1. The cytochrome oxidase bands are also differently connected to the cortical areas beyond V2: The thin and pale bands are reciprocally connected to area V4, and the thick bands are connected to area MT (Salin & Bullier, 1995).

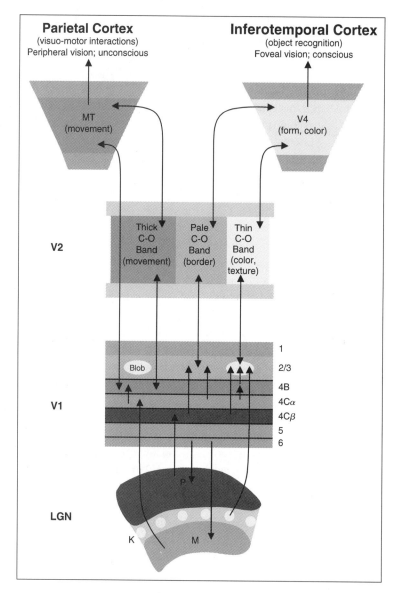

Figure 1.12 Connections between the P, M, and K layers of the LGN and V1 and connections between V1, V2, V4, and MT in the primate visual system.
NOTE: C-O: cytochrome oxidase.

The parallel transfer of information in the different cytochrome-oxidase subdivisions in areas V1 and V2 is maintained beyond V2, as there is evidence that the thin and pale bands of V2 innervate different subdivisions in V4 (Felleman, Xiao, & McClendon, 1997). Hubel and Livingstone (1987; Livingstone & Hubel, 1984) interpreted the connections be-tween the cytochrome-oxidase compartments in V1 and V2 as evidence for parallel processing of color information (in the blobs, thin bands and V4), form (in the interblobs, pale bands and V4), and motion information (in layer 4B and the thick bands in V2). The original finding that color-selective neurons are preferentially found in the thin bands in V2 has not been replicated by more recent quantitative studies, and the functional significance of the parallel channels in V1 and V2 remains to be fully understood (Bullier, 2001a). One likely possibility is that the blobs and thin bands represent territories where surface information is processed (e.g., surface reflectance and texture), whereas the interblobs and pale bands contain neurons that signal borders between different surface elements.

Except for the first-order neurons in layer 4C beta and a small proportion of neurons in layers 2-3 and 5-6, the neurons in V1 are selective for the orientation of contrast edges in the stimulus. As illustrated earlier (Figure 1.10A), the optimal orientation of neurons is distributed in a regular fashion across the surface of V1. Orientation selectivity is a general property of cortical neurons, and it is observed in most visual cortical areas (see the first section for discussion of the mechanisms of orientation selectivity).

Besides orientation selectivity, another important transformation that occurs at the cortical level is the convergence of inputs from both eyes. Neurons in the retina and the LGN have a single receptive field corresponding to the afferent eye. In cortex most neurons beyond layers 4C alpha and beta are driven by both eyes and thus possess two receptive fields. When the two receptive fields are in exact overlap (e.g., when the eye fixates a point), the optimal stimulus is located in the same frontal plane as the fixation point (Figure 1.5A). This neuron is called *tuned excitatory* (Poggio & Fischer, 1977). In cases when the two receptive fields are crossed (Figure 1.5B), the neuron responds optimally to a stimulus that is nearer to the animal than the fixation point, and it is called a *near* neuron. When the two receptive fields are noncrossed, the optimal response is obtained for neurons located further away than the fixation point. Thus, neurons in V1 respond to stereoscopic disparity with respect to the plane of fixation

(Cumming & Parker, 2000), whereas neurons in V2 are sensitive to the relative disparity of neighboring surfaces, thus providing the basis for the identification of borders between separate objects positioned at different distances from the eyes.

Although it is usually assumed that area V1 constitutes a retinotopic map that is invariant with the position of the eyes, this is no longer considered to be true. Several reports have shown that the direction of gaze and the angle of vergence modulate very strongly the gain of the response of a V1 neuron to a visual stimulus. In other words, a stimulus located 2 deg from the fixation point will give a full response when the animal is fixating 10 deg to the right of straight ahead but give no response when the animal is looking to the left (Trotter & Celebrini, 1999). This suggests that area V1 (and all the other visual cortical areas) is coding the visual world not in terms of retinotopic coordinates but in a craniocentric or egocentric system of coordinates (see also the first section).

The role of areas V1 and V2 in vision is usually considered to be limited to constructing a fine-grained representation of the visual world with many simple parameters (orientation, stereo depth, direction of motion, wavelength) and sending information to the several more specialized areas located beyond (discussed later). More elaborate receptive fields are usually found in larger numbers in area V2 than in V1; sizes of receptive fields are larger in V2 than in V1; and it appears likely that area V2 contains neurons that respond specifically to borders in depth as well as borders between regions of different textures or colors (Olson, 2001). This information is used in other areas such as V4 to identify objects or local features in three dimensions. However, the presence of many neurons in areas V1 and V2 responding with long latencies to visual stimulation and the very dense network of feedback connections to these two areas suggest that they may play a more complex role than that of a simple relay and filter, which is the role that is usually attributed to them.

Cortical Areas beyond V1 and V2 and Their Connections

Beyond areas V1 and V2 are a large number of visual cortical areas. Although it is often stated that there are several dozen visual cortical areas (Felleman & Van Essen, 1991), specific information about neuronal responses has been gathered in only about 10 of these areas. The receptive fields are larger in these areas than in areas V1 and V2; indeed, there is a progressive increase in receptive field sizes as one moves from V1 to V2, V4, TEO, and TE. This suggests that neurons in areas such as TEO or TE gain more specific selectivities by the proper convergence of neurons in lower-order areas.

The functional specialization of the different cortical areas beyond V1 and V2 has been the subject of much debate. The original idea that each area analyzes one parameter of the visual scene (e.g., movement in MT and color in V4) was based on the observation that these areas contain neurons with relatively homogeneous properties, such as selectivity to direction of motion in MT or selectivity to shape and color in V4 (Zeki, 1993). Lesion studies in monkeys, however, have not provided confirmation of such a neophrenological view of the brain. In area MT, for example, the concentration of neurons that give responses selective to the direction of motion of a stimulus in three-dimensional space has led to the suggestion that this is the area in which the direction of movement of a stimulus is analyzed (Zeki, 1978). However, removal of area MT by lesion produces only a transient deficit in the animal's ability to process information concerning the direction of movement. It is only when several areas surrounding MT are lesioned together with MT that the animal demonstrates a serious deficit in motion pro-

cessing (Newsome & Pare, 1988). This suggests that several areas in the vicinity of area MT are specialized in processing motion information and that MT is only an important node in that processing network.

Another observation that has been made repeatedly is that clear perceptual deficits can be observed following lesions of visual areas only when focal attention is needed to identify the stimulus that is used to probe the effects of the lesion. This can be the case when the stimulus shape is masked or transformed (Schiller, 1995) or when distracting stimuli are present in the visual field (De Weerd, Peralta, Desimone, & Ungerleider, 1999). This suggests that individual cortical areas may be necessary more to match memory representations to the incoming flow of retinal information based on a given parameter than simply to process one specific parameter of a stimulus for transmission to higher-order recognition areas.

It is widely believed that two groups of cortical areas can be distinguished, the so-called dorsal and ventral streams (Ungerleider & Mishkin, 1982). This subdivision is based on lesion experiments done in the 1970s that showed that lesions of the parietal cortex of the monkey led to deficits in localizing an object with respect to a landmark but produced little deficit in the identification of individual objects. By contrast, lesions of the IT cortex produced strong deficits in object identification but little effect on the animal's capacity to process the respective location of two objects (Pohl, 1973). This led to the classic distinction between the parietal cortex representing "where" an object is and the IT cortex processing "what" the object is (Ungerleider & Mishkin, 1982). This distinction consisted of a replication in the monkey of the well-known double dissociation of deficits observed between patients with lesions in the parietal and temporal cortex, respectively, but it provided a way to classify the different cortical areas in the dorsal occipito-parietal stream and those areas that belong to the ventral occipito-temporal stream. Thus, areas V3d, MT, MST, and FST, as well as the areas of the parietal cortex, belong to the dorsal stream, whereas areas V4, TEO, and TE belong to the ventral stream. Studies in humans have since led to a reappraisal of the original distinction between the dorsal and ventral pathways. More emphasis is placed nowadays on the role played by the dorsal stream in visuomotor interactions (Jeannerod, Arbib, Rizzolatti, & Sakata, 1995; Milner & Goodale, 1995), and it has been proposed that the dorsal stream processes the "how" as well as the "where."

Cortical areas are linked by a very dense network of corticocortical connections. Two main types of connections are identified by their anatomical characteristics: the feedforward connections that arise mostly from layers 2-3 and send axons to layer 4 in the target area and the feedback connections that arise predominantly from layers 5-6 and terminate outside layer 4. It has been demonstrated that feedforward connections carry the major drive to neurons in the target area (Bullier et al., 1994), and only recently have several groups studied the role of feedback connections. Feedback connections appear to act in a nonlinear fashion by boosting the gain of the center and surround mechanisms (Bullier, Hupé, James, & Girard, 2001). Feedback connections have been shown to be important in cases of stimuli that are difficult to identify from the surrounding background (Hupé et al., 1998). This may explain the important deficits in the identification of objects partially masked or placed in a cluttered environment that are observed after lesions of areas V4 or MT (discussed earlier). When these areas are lesioned, they no longer provide the feedback connections to the neurons in areas V1 and V2 that analyze the image with a fine-grained representation, and a proper representation cannot be built in these areas for adequate identification.

The identification of feedforward and feedback connections has led Van Essen and his colleagues (Felleman & Van Essen, 1991; Van Essen & Maunsell, 1983) to classify the cortical areas of the monkey brain in the hierarchy of cortical areas (Figure 1.13A) using a simple rule: One area is placed at a higher level than another if it receives feedforward connections from it and sends feedback connections to it. Areas can be placed at the same level if they exchange connections of another type, called lateral. This classification of cortical areas, which was originally an anatomical model, has been considered by many to be a functional model. According to this model, lower-order areas provide feedforward connections to areas of the higher level, and the processing of visual information is simply a succession of filters that leads eventually to the specific response of a small population of neurons in the highest stages of the hierarchy.

There are several problems with this simplistic view of the visual system. First, it gives no role to the feedback connections that are at least as numerous as the feedforward connections. Second, consideration of the timing of the different cortical areas does not confirm this sequential model. As can be seen in Figure 1.13B, areas such as FEF or MST that are at the highest stages of the original version of the hierarchy (Figure 1.13A) are activated at the same time as are areas V1 and V2! Neurons in areas V1 and V2, which clearly represent two sequential stages in the hierarchy of cortical areas, have latencies that largely overlap and differ by only 10 ms in their means (Nowak, Munk, Girard, & Bullier, 1995). These observations suggest that the cortical areas are not organized as a series of filters, as suggested by the hierarchical organization. Instead, it appears that some cortical areas beyond V1 and V2 are activated extremely rapidly by a visual stimulus. This

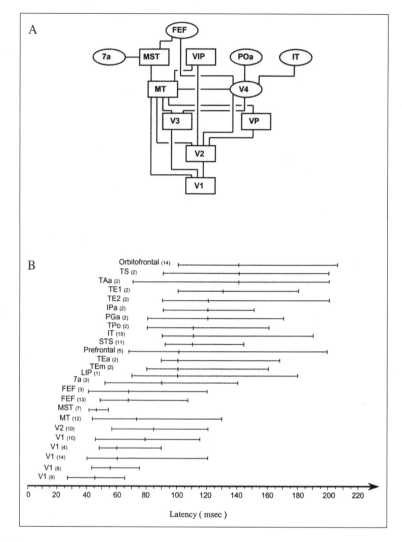

Figure 1.13 Hierarchy of cortical areas and response timing.
NOTE: A: Original version of the hierarchy of cortical areas; for more recent versions see Felleman & Van Essen (1991). B: Latencies of neurons to visual stimulation in different cortical areas. The central bar corresponds to the median, and the extremities of the horizontal bar correspond to the 10th and 90th percentiles. Numbers refer to bibliographic references given in Bullier (2001a). Note the very early responses in areas of the dorsal stream (areas MT and MST) and in area FEF, which were located at the top of the hierarchy in the original version of the hierarchy of cortical areas (A).
SOURCE: A: Modified from Van Essen & Maunsell (1983).

is particularly the case of parietal and frontal areas (Nowak & Bullier, 1997). It is likely that processing in these areas is retroinjected in lower-order areas by feedback connections that are well suited to boost some channels and block others, thus processing information according to analysis done in higher-order areas of the hierarchy (Bullier, 2001b).

Thus, a given object in the visual field generates more or less simultaneous responses in groups of neurons that are distributed in the different visual cortical areas. How are the different properties of an object (its motion, color, shape, etc.), which are apparently represented in a distributed fashion over multiple visual areas, combined into a single coherent percept? This is particularly important in the case of a cluttered natural scene in which several objects may overlap and partly occlude one another so that the activity they elicit cannot be separated on the basis of retinotopic organization. This has been called the binding problem, and it has been proposed (Singer, 1993) that neurons that respond to the presentation of the same object synchronize their responses by locking the time of spike emission to rhythmic bursts in the gamma range (above 20 Hz).

After some initial debate concerning the presence of gamma oscillations in the responses of neurons in visual cortical areas, it is now agreed that such rhythmic bursts do exist. The question that remains is the functional role of these oscillatory responses. Although Singer and his collaborators have provided some evidence in favor of the hypothesis that neurons that code for the same object synchronize their activities, a consensus has not yet been achieved. Recent evidence suggests that when neurons participate in a difficult discrimination task, their responses tend to desynchronize instead of synchronizing, as expected from the synchronization hypothesis (de Oliveira, Thiele, & Hoffmann, 1997). Recordings in humans and monkeys of gamma oscillatory activity indicate that these bursts are most frequently observed when mental images are manipulated, such as when holding a visual pattern in memory (Tallon-Baudry, Bertrand, Peronnet, & Pernier, 1998). It has also been recently reported that attention given to an object increases the level of gamma oscillatory bursts in area-V4 neurons (Fries, Reynolds, Rorie, & Desimone, 2001).

Despite some 20 years of debate concerning the functional role of gamma oscillations in sensory cortex, it must be admitted that no clear role for these forms of neural activity has been definitively established. It is likely that such oscillations are used to synchronize populations of neurons that participate in a common task. Synchronizing the activities of afferents in a given neuron increases enormously the chances of transferring information, and thus the presence of bursts of gamma activity may be related to some mechanisms of multiplexing activity across multiple groups of neurons. It is possible that the role of gamma synchronization in binding reflects primarily mechanisms that may be used also in other aspects of processing of visual information.

RELATION BETWEEN NEURONAL ACTIVITY AND PERCEPTUAL EXPERIENCE

One of the oldest methods for testing the relationship between neuronal activity and behavior consists of studying the consequences of lesions in a localized part of the brain. In the visual system this technique has been used very effectively because of the retinotopic organization of most cortical areas and the possibilities of working with animals that fixate their gazes on a point in the visual field. This has opened the way for making lesions restricted to a single visual area and testing the visual behavior of the animal in the region of visual field that corresponds to the lesion. This method has been used to investigate the role of areas MT and V4 in vision and has confirmed the role of neurons in these areas in processing motion and shape information (Newsome & Pare, 1988; Schiller, 1993).

However, two factors complicate the interpretation of such experiments. The first is that a cortical area processes and transmits information, and it is difficult to decide whether the effects of a lesion are due to the loss of the specialized neurons that process a specific type of information (e.g., motion in the case of MT) or to the fact that other areas no longer receive this type of information because the lesioned area is an important connection node. To give an example, no one would attribute the total blindness due to the loss of area V1 to the fact that all visual information is processed in area V1. It may be that some of the deficits observed after lesions of V4 or MT are due to this function of information transfer to the rest of the visual system.

Another complicating factor is that there is a substantial recovery of function after a lesion. This phenomenon, which is well known to the clinician, suggests that neurons in other areas modify their selectivities to take over the role played by the neurons that are destroyed by the lesion. Results of experiments using reversible methods of inactivation suggest that indeed there is a substantial amount of postlesion recovery (Payne, Lomber, Villa, & Bullier, 1996), and the deficits revealed by the lesion are probably less important than those caused by the inactivation of neurons in a given area.

Studies in which the firing rates of single neurons are recorded while the animal makes perceptual decisions about a sensory stimulus have made it possible to compare behavioral thresholds and single unit responses. The idea is that if neurons in a given cortical area are used to encode the stimulus, there should be neurons that signal the behavioral threshold (i.e., the smallest change in the strength of the sensory stimulus that can be detected by the observer). Contrary to what has been found for neurons in the peripheral part of the somatosensory system, where the psychophysical threshold matches the threshold of the most sensitive neurons (Parker & Newsome, 1998), in area MT the psychophysical thresh-

old matches the *average* sensitivity of individual neurons (Britten, Shadlen, Newsome, & Movshon, 1992). In other words, some neurons in MT detect smaller differences than the psychophysical threshold. This very interesting result has been interpreted as evidence for a pooling model, which states that decisions are based on the activity of a small number of neurons (on the order of a few hundred). The efficiency of this pool of neurons is limited by the internal noise of the neuronal firing and the weak correlation between neighboring neurons (Parker & Newsome, 1998). One important caveat in these studies is that the comparison between neural and behavioral thresholds assumes that the neural activity throughout an arbitrary interval (e.g., 2 s) is used as the basis for the decision. There is no independent evidence for this assumption. Despite this limitation, these studies remain the best evidence to date that the average firing rate of neurons in the visual system carries information that is relevant to the animal's behavior.

A very interesting twist has been added to these studies by Newsome and colleagues: Is it possible to bias the animal's choice by weakly activating some MT neurons by electrical stimulation? When very small current impulses are injected in the vicinity of neurons that optimally respond to a given direction of movement, the decisions made by the animals are biased toward this direction (Salzman, Murasugi, Britten, & Newsome, 1992). These effects are sensitive to small changes in location or current strength of the stimulation and therefore appear to represent a causal relationship between neural activity and behavioral decisions. The only limitation in the interpretation is that electrical stimulation does not activate only the neurons located near the stimulating electrode; it also activates efferent and afferent axons that are located in the vicinity. These remarkable experiments therefore show that the activity of a small network of neurons distributed across a small number of cortical areas can elicit perceptual decisions.

Another group of experiments designed to examine the relationship between single unit activity and visual perception exploited the perceptual phenomenon of binocular rivalry. In these experiments two different images were shown, one to each eye of the animal. In this situation, perception alternates between one and the other of the two monocular stimuli. The animal is trained to press one button when it sees one of the images and another button when it sees the other, thus reporting the contents of its perceptual experience. Logothetis and his colleagues (Logothetis & Schall, 1989; Sheinberg & Logothetis, 1997) have recorded from a variety of cortical areas using this method. The most spectacular result has been obtained in the IT cortex: Almost all the neurons switched their responses when the animal's reported perceptual experience changed from one to the other percept (Sheinberg & Logothetis, 1997). Such changes were not limited to neurons in IT but were observed in smaller numbers also in areas V1, V2, and V4. This suggests that the perception of a given object or face does not result simply from the activity of a small population of neurons in IT (as a simple feedforward conception might suggest), but that it is based instead on the activity of a network of neurons distributed across many areas of the visual system.

The explosion of research on visual attention in humans using experimental psychology and imaging techniques has been paralleled by an increase in the number of studies on the effect of attention on the responses of neurons in the visual system. These are reviewed elsewhere (see Chap. 6, this volume).

As mentioned earlier, in the mid-1980s researchers found that the maps of the visual field are not static but can be profoundly reorganized following lesions of the afferent inputs from the retina. Such a plasticity of cortical neurons has led to the idea that learning could modify the mapping of visual space in the cortical areas as well as the responses of individual neurons. Changes in the responses of individual neurons after training have been difficult to demonstrate in low-order areas (Crist et al., 2001; Schoups, Vogels, Qian, & Orban, 2001). The effect of experience has been demonstrated in the IT cortex by training the animal to achieve difficult discriminations on a stimulus that is new but important because it leads to food rewards. The number of neurons responding optimally to this type of neuron was shown to increase significantly after training, thus suggesting that a number of neurons have modified their tuning to include responses to this behaviorally important stimulus (Logothetis & Pauls, 1995; Logothetis, Pauls, & Poggio, 1995).

UNANSWERED QUESTIONS

Neuronal Basis of Three-Dimensional Vision

The world around us is three-dimensional, and it is surprising that most electrophysiological research deals exclusively with two-dimensional stimuli presented on computer monitors. Of course, one reason for this limitation is the technical difficulty of producing stereoscopic stimuli. Another reason is that it has been traditionally thought that all the early stages of processing in the visual system are organized as two-dimensional maps of the visual field. The early models of the visual system were strongly influenced by the David Marr's (1982) computational model, which stated that three-dimensional vision was a later processing stage and that much of early- and mid-level vision was devoted to producing a two-dimensional representation of the visual field. This perspective is now changing because of evidence that the eye position changes the gain of neural responses in all cortical areas including V1 (Trotter & Celebrini, 1999). However, there is no satisfactory model that explains the perception of three-dimensional structures from the responses of single units in different cortical areas. Results obtained in the parietal cortex demonstrate that neurons are selective to the orientation in space of objects (Murata, Gallese, Luppino, Kaseda, & Sakata, 2000; Taira, Tsutsui, Jiang, Yara, & Sakata, 2000), and there have been a few studies of neurons in IT cortex with three-dimensional stimuli (Janssen, Vogels, & Orban, 2000). The basic mechanisms of segmentation in space of object borders have only recently been investigated with stereoscopic cues (von der Heydt, Zhou, & Friedman, 2000). However, we know very little concerning the use of other depth cues, such as shadows, perspective, and motion parallax (see Chap. 3, this volume), even though these cues are the main determinants of our perception of depth.

Neuronal Bases of Conscious and Unconscious Vision

This extremely popular theme has been fueled by recent results in experimental psychology showing that our conscious perception of details is limited to the central 10 deg of visual field surrounding the point of eye fixation (Mack & Rock, 1998). A number of theories have been advanced, such as the idea that gamma-range oscillations would sustain neuronal processing that corresponds to conscious vision (Crick, 1994) or that only activity in the areas linked to the frontal cortex can lead to conscious perception of visual stimuli (Crick & Koch, 1995). More recently, Lamme and Roelfsema (2000) have proposed that the initial transfer of information that is sustained by feedforward connections is largely unconscious and that conscious perception needs that information to be sent back to early visual

areas by feedback connections. This hypothesis is close to the proposal that I made that visual processing involves a first-pass analysis by the magnocellular channel (Bullier, 2001b). This first analysis most likely does not reach consciousness, and information is then transferred back to lower stages, such as V1 and V2, that act as active blackboards that send information to higher stages of the IT cortex in which neural activity appears to be linked to conscious vision, as mentioned earlier.

Another popular idea is that processing is largely unconscious in the parietal cortex, whereas it is conscious in the IT cortex. The neural evidence rests mainly on the observation that lesions or inactivation of area V1 silences most areas of the ventral stream, whereas most cortical areas of the parietal cortex are still active (Bullier et al., 1994). This difference of the effects on parietal and temporal cortex, as well as the fact that there is largely unconscious residual vision in patients with occipital lesions (Perenin, 1991; Weiskrantz, 1986), is consistent with the idea that parietal cortex participates in unconscious vision. Further support for this idea comes from observations of patients with parietal lesions that are unable to correct the trajectory of their hand while being completely unconscious of it (Pisella et al., 2000). Not all processing in parietal cortex can be unconscious, however, as research has shown that neurons in LIP respond almost exclusively to stimuli that are the target of a future eye movement and that lead to a reward (Gottlieb, Kusunoki, & Goldberg, 1998). Such a relationship between neuronal firing and eye movements programming has been shown also for the FEF area in the frontal cortex (Schall, 2001).

In general, there is a trend toward considering that the earliest stages of processing (at all levels) are unconscious and that conscious perception requires activation of neurons that respond in the late phases of brain activity. For example, the decision to make an eye movement toward a target has been shown to correspond to a late increase in neuronal activity in the parietal (Newsome, 1997) and frontal cortex (Schall, 2001).

Neuronal Basis of Mental Representations

By mental representation I mean an internally generated percept, such as a percept generated from memory or an amodal representation. This is another area in which only a few attempts have been made at understanding its neural basis at the single neuron level, despite a lot of activity in imaging studies. One demonstration has been made in neurons of the parietal cortex of activity related to the presence of an unseen stimulus that passed behind a mask (Assad & Maunsell, 1995). A number of reports from groups recording from neurons in IT cortex have shown that neural responses increase during intervals when the animal holds an image in memory for further processing (Chelazzi, Duncan, Miller, & Desimone, 1998; Miyashita, 1993). Similar results have been reported for the frontal cortex (Miller, Erickson, & Desimone, 1996).

It is difficult to manipulate mental images in animals from which single unit recording can be done. It is much easier to create illusory percepts by manipulating stimuli. This has been a very active field of research since the initial discovery that single units respond to illusory contours (von der Heydt, Peterhans, & Baumgartner, 1984). The general finding is that responses to these stimuli are found at the earliest levels of the hierarchy of cortical areas: in areas V1, V2, and MT. As mentioned in the first section, recent experiments by Albright and colleagues (Duncan, Albright, & Stoner, 2001) show that neurons in area MT respond in a similar fashion to stimuli that move in a given direction and to inferred stimuli that are partially masked by occlusion.

Neurons signaling partially occluded moving or static stimuli have also been reported in areas V1 and V2 (Bakin et al., 2000; Sugita, 1999).

Because mental images and illusory percepts have been largely used in imaging studies, it is important to remember that the blood oxygenated level dependent (BOLD) signal given by fMRI reflects mainly the synaptic activity and only weakly the single unit responses of neurons in one area (Logothetis, Pauls, Augath, Trinath, & Oeltermann, 2001). This explains, for example, why a strong BOLD signal is produced by the waterfall illusion[7] in human area V5 (Tootell et al., 1995), whereas very little neural activity is produced by this stimulus in area V5/MT in monkeys (Marlin, Hasan, & Cynader, 1988; Petersen, Baker, & Allman, 1985). Similarly, a recent demonstration of activity in V1 elicited by moving illusory contours using fMRI (Seghier et al., 2000) does not mean that many neurons in V1 are strongly responding to such a stimulus.

Role of Feedback Connections

Despite their very high densities, feedback connections have been largely absent in models of the visual system until recently (Hupé et al., 1998), and we are far from understanding how these connections may mediate attention, memory, or conscious perception (Bullier, 2001c). Among the technical difficulties of this work is recording the responses of single units in animals actively engaged in behavioral tasks while reversibly inactivating neurons in one or several connected cortical areas that might be providing feedback. It is possible that new techniques may be developed with genetic manipulation when we

---

[7]Following adaptation to motion (e.g., a waterfall) one experiences illusory motion of a static surface in the opposite direction.

know more about the specificities of different types of receptors involved in these connections.

How Does the Visual System Deal with Saccades and Microsaccades?

Practically all the present research in vision uses the classical preparation of a monkey fixating a target while stimuli are flashed in the receptive field of the neuron under study. However, this is not the way we use our visual system. We are constantly making saccadic eye movements from one point to the next in the visual field, and our eyes remain steady during fixations for periods of a few hundreds of milliseconds. Some studies have been devoted to the responses of neurons while the animal engages in free viewing of a natural scene (Burman & Segraves, 1994; Sheinberg & Logothetis, 2001). Sheinberg and Logothetis recently showed that during active search in cluttered environments, IT neurons respond just before the eyes finally land on a target object that has been found and not when it passes over it before it has been noticed.

When we fixate, despite our intention to keep our eyes on one spot, our eyes are constantly making micromovements (Figure 1.2D). As mentioned earlier, such micromovements produce extremely strong activation of neurons whose receptive fields cross and recross a luminance or color border (Rodieck, 1965; see Figure 1.2C). Despite this early demonstration, very little work has been devoted to the study of the responses of cortical neurons. Recent work by Hubel and colleagues suggests that neurons in V1 indeed respond only when the receptive fields are palpating the border of a standing figure (Martinez-Conde, Macknik, & Hubel, 2000). It is not clear how this information is transferred across the different levels of the cortical hierarchy or how it leads to the conscious perception of an object. We may learn more about this process by appreciating how the somatosensory system builds a mental image from active manual exploration of an object (see Chap. 13, this volume) than by continuing to present flashed stimuli in the middle of the receptive field of a neuron.

REFERENCES

Albright, T. D. (1984). Direction and orientation selectivity of neurons in visual area MT of the macaque. *Journal of Neurophysiology, 52,* 1106–1130.

Albright, T. D., Desimone, R., & Gross, C. G. (1984). Columnar organization of directionally selective cells in visual area MT of the macaque. *Journal of Neurophysiology, 51,* 16–31.

Allman, J. M., & Kaas, J. H. (1974). The organization of the second visual area (VII) in the owl monkey: A second order transformation of the visual hemifield. *Brain Research, 76,* 247–265.

Assad, J. A., & Maunsell, J. H. R. (1995). Neuronal correlates of inferred motion in primate posterior parietal carter. *Nature, 373,* 518–521.

Bakin, J. S., Nakayama, K., & Gilbert, C. D. (2000). Visual responses in monkey areas V1 and V2 to three-dimensional surface configurations. *Journal of Neuroscience, 20,* 8188–8198.

Bishop, P. O., Coombs, J. S., & Henry, G. H. (1973). Receptive fields of simple cells in the cat striate cortex. *The Journal of Physiology* (London), *231,* 31–60.

Blasdel, G. G. (1992). Differential imaging of ocular dominance and orientation selectivity in monkey striate cortex. *Journal of Neuroscience, 12,* 3115–3138.

Borg-Graham, L. J., Monier, C., & Fregnac, Y. (1998). Visual input evokes transient and strong shunting inhibition in visual cortical neurons. *Nature, 393,* 369–373.

Britten, K. H., Shadlen, M. N., Newsome, W. T., & Movshon, J. A. (1992). The analysis of visual motion: A comparison of neuronal and psychophysical performance. *Journal of Neuroscience, 12,* 4745–4765.

Bullier, J. (2001a). Cortical connections and functional interactions between visual cortical areas. In M. Fahle (Ed.), *Neuropsychology of vision* (in press). Oxford: Oxford University Press.

Bullier, J. (2001b). An integrated model of the visual system. *Brain Research Reviews, 36,* 96–107.

Bullier, J. (2001c). What is fed back? In T. Sejnowski & L. Van Hemmen (Eds.), *Twenty-three questions for the 21st century*. Oxford: Oxford University Press (in press).

Bullier, J., Girard, P., & Salin, P. A. (1994). The role of area 17 in the transfer of information to extrastriate visual cortex. In A. Peters & K. S. Rockland (Eds.), *Primary visual cortex in primates* (Vol. 10, pp. 301–330). New York: Plenum Press.

Bullier, J., Hupé, J.-M., James, A., & Girard, P. (2001). The role of feedback connections in shaping the responses of visual cortical neurons. *Progress in Brain Research, 134,* 193–204.

Burman, D. D., & Segraves, M. A. (1994). Primate frontal eye field activity during natural scanning eye movements. *Journal of Neurophysiology, 71*(3), 1266–1271.

Calkins, D. J., & Sterling, P. (1999). Evidence that circuits for spatial and color vision segregate at the first retinal synapse. *Neuron, 24*(2), 313–321.

Callaway, E. M. (1998). Local circuits in primary visual cortex of the macaque monkey. *Annual Review of Neuroscience, 21,* 47–74.

Chapman, B., Zahs, K. T., & Stryker, M. P. (1991). Relation of cortical cell orientation selectivity to alignment of receptive fields of the geniculocortical afferents that arborize within a single orientation column in ferret visual cortex. *Journal of Neuroscience, 11,* 1347–1358.

Chelazzi, L., Duncan, J., Miller, E. K., & Desimone, R. (1998). Responses of neurons in inferior temporal cortex during memory-guided visual search. *Journal of Neurophysiology, 80*(6), 2918–2940.

Crick, F. (1994). *The astonishing hypothesis*. New York: Scribner's.

Crick, F., & Koch, C. (1995). Are we aware of neural activity in primary visual cortex? *Nature, 375,* 121–123.

Crist, R. E., Li, W., & Gilbert, C. D. (2001). Learning to see: Experience and attention in primary visual cortex. *Nature Neuroscience, 4*(5), 519–525.

Crook, J. M., Kisvarday, Z. F., & Eysel, U. T. (1997). GABA-induced inactivation of functionally characterized sites in cat striate cortex: Effects on orientation tuning and direction selectivity. *Visual Neuroscience, 14*(1), 141–158.

Cumming, B. G., & Parker, A. J. (2000). Local disparity not perceived depth is signaled by binocular neurons in cortical area V1 of the macaque. *Journal of Neuroscience, 20*(12), 4758–4767.

Darian-Smith, C., & Gilbert., C. D. (1994). Axonal sprouting accompanies functional reorganization in adult cat striate cortex. *Nature, 368,* 737–740.

DeAngelis, G. C., Cumming, B. G., & Newsome, W. T. (1998). Cortical area MT and the perception of stereoscopic depth. *Nature, 394,* 677–680.

DeAngelis, G. C., Ohzawa, I., & Freeman, R. D. (1993a). Spatiotemporal organization of simple-cell receptive fields in the cat's striate cortex: I. General characteristics and postnatal development. *Journal of Neurophysiology, 69,* 1091–1117.

DeAngelis, G. C., Ohzawa, I., & Freeman, R. D. (1993b). Spatiotemporal organization of simple-cell receptive fields in the cat's striate cortex: II. Linearity of temporal and spatial summation. *Journal of Neurophysiology, 69,* 1118–1135.

de Oliveira, S. C., Thiele, A., & Hoffmann, K. P. (1997). Synchronization of neuronal activity during stimulus expectation in a direction discrimination task. *Journal of Neuroscience, 17*(23), 9248–9260.

De Weerd, P., Peralta, M. R., III, Desimone, R., & Ungerleider, L. G. (1999). Loss of attentional stimulus selection after extrastriate cortical lesions in macaques. *Nature Neuroscience, 2*(8), 753–758.

Dow, B. M., Snyder, A. Z., Vautin, R. G., & Bauer, R. (1981). Magnification factor and receptive field size in foveal striate cortex of the monkey. *Experimental Brain Research, 44,* 213–228.

Duhamel, J.-R., Colby, C. L., & Goldberg, M. E. (1992). The updating of the representation of visual space in parietal cortex by intended eye movements. *Science, 255,* 90–92.

Duncan, R. O., Albright, T. D., & Stoner, G. R. (2001). Occlusion and the interpretation of visual motion: Perceptual and neuronal effects of context. *Journal of Neuroscience, 20,* 5885–5897.

Engel, S. A., Glover, G. H., & Wandell, B. A. (1997). Retinotopic organization in human visual cortex and the spatial precision of functional MRI. *Cerebral Cortex, 7,* 181–192.

Engel, S. A., Zhang, X., & Wandell, B. (1997). Colour tuning in human visual cortex measured with functional magnetic resonance imaging. *Nature, 388,* 68–71.

Felleman, D. J., & Van Essen, D. C. (1991). Distributed hierarchical processing in the primate cerebral cortex. *Cerebral Cortex, 1,* 1–47.

Felleman, D. J., Xiao, Y., & McClendon, E. (1997). Modular organization of occipito-temporal pathways: Cortical connections between visual area 4 and visual area 2 and posterior inferotemporal ventral area in macaque monkeys. *Journal of Neuroscience, 17,* 3185–3200.

Ferster, D., & Koch, C. (1987). Neuronal connections underlying orientation selectivity in cat visual cortex. *Trends in Neurosciences, 10,* 487–492.

Freedman, D. J., Riesenhuber, M., Poggio, T., & Miller, E. K. (2001). Categorical representations of visual stimuli in the primate prefrontal cortex. *Science, 291,* 312–316.

Fries, P., Reynolds, J. H., Rorie, A. E., & Desimone, R. (2001). Modulation of oscillatory neuronal synchronization by selective visual attention. *Science, 291,* 1560–1564.

Gottlieb, J. P., Kusunoki, M., & Goldberg, M. E. (1998). The representation of visual salience in monkey parietal cortex. *Nature, 391,* 481–484.

Gross, C. G., Rocha-Miranda, C. E., & Bender, D. B. (1972). Visual properties of neurons in inferotemporal cortex. *Journal of Neurophysiology, 35,* 96–111.

Hartline, H. K. (1940). The receptive field of optic nerve fibers. *American Journal of Physiology, 130,* 690–699.

Henry, G. H., Bishop, P. O., Tupper, R. M., & Dreher, B. (1973). Orientation specificity and response variability of cells in the striate cortex. *Vision Research, 13,* 1771–1779.

Hubel, D. H., & Livingstone, M. S. (1987). Segregation of form, color, and stereopsis in primate area 18. *Journal of Neuroscience, 7,* 3378–3415.

Hubel, D. H., & Wiesel, T. N. (1962). Receptive fields, binocular interaction and functional architecture in the cat visual cortex. *The Journal of Physiology* (London), *160,* 106–154.

Humphrey, A. L., & Saul, A. B. (2001). The emergence of direction selectivity in cat primary visual cortex. In B. Payne and A. Peters (Ed.), *Cerebral cortex: Cat primary visual cortex* (in press). New York: Plenum Press.

Hupé, J. M., James, A. C., Payne, B. R., Lomber, S. G., Girard, P., & Bullier, J. (1998). Cortical feedback improves discrimination between figure and background by V1, V2 and V3 neurons. *Nature, 394,* 784–787.

Janssen, P., Vogels, R., & Orban, G. A. (2000). Three-dimensional shape coding in inferior temporal cortex. *Neuron, 27*(2), 385–397.

Jeannerod, M., Arbib, M. A., Rizzolatti, G., & Sakata, H. (1995). Grasping objects: The cortical mechanisms of visuomotor transformation. *Trends in Neurosciences, 18,* 314–320.

Kaas, J. H. (1997). Theories of visual cortex organization in primates. In K. S. Rockland, J. H. Kaas, & A. Peters (Eds.), *Cerebral cortex: Vol. 12. Extrastriate cortex in primates* (pp. 91–126). New York: Plenum Press.

Kaas, J. H., Krubitzer, L. H., Chino, Y., Langston, A. L., Polley, E. H., & Blair, N. (1990). Reorganization of retinotopic cortical maps in adult mammals after lesions of the retina. *Science, 248,* 229–231.

Kaas, J. H., Merzenich, M. M., & Killackey, H. P. (1983). The reorganization of somatosensory cortex following peripheral nerve damage in adult and developing mammals. *Annual Review of Neuroscience, 6,* 325–356.

Kuffler, S. W. (1953). Discharge patterns and functional organization of mammalian retina. *Journal of Neurophysiology, 16,* 37–68.

Lamme, V. A. F., & Roelfsema, P. R. (2000). The distinct modes of vision offered by feedforward and recurrent processing. *Trends in Neurosciences, 23,* 571–579.

Lee, C., Malpeli, J. G., Schwark, D. H., & Weyand, T. G. (1984). Cat medial interlaminar nucelus: Retinotopy, relation to tapetum and implications for scotopic vision. *Journal of Neurophysiology, 52,* 848–869.

Livingstone, M. S., & Hubel, D. H. (1984). Anatomy and physiology of a color system in the primate visual cortex. *Journal of Neuroscience, 4,* 309–356.

Logothetis, N. K., & Pauls, J. (1995). Psychophysical and physiological evidence for viewer-centered object representations in the primate. *Cerebral Cortex, 5*(3), 270–288.

Logothetis, N. K., Pauls, J., Augath, M., Trinath, T., & Oeltermann, A. (2001). Neurophysiological investigation of the basis of the fMRI signal. *Nature, 412,* 150–157.

Logothetis, N. K., Pauls, J., & Poggio, T. (1995). Shape representation in the inferior temporal cortex of monkeys. *Current Biology, 5*(5), 552–563.

Logothetis, N. K., & Schall, J. D. (1989). Neuronal correlates of subjective visual perception. *Science, 245,* 761–763.

Lund, J. S. (1988). Anatomical organization of macaque monkey striate cortex. *Annual Review of Neuroscience, 11,* 253–288.

Mack, A., & Rock, I. (1998). *Inattentional blindness.* Cambridge: MIT Press.

Malach, R., Reppas, J. B., Benson, R. R., Kwong, K. K., Jiang, H., Kennedy, W. A., Ledden, P. J., Brady, T. J., Rosen, B. R., & Tootell, R. B. (1995). Object-related activity revealed by functional magnetic resonance imaging in human occipital cortex. *Proceedings of the National Academy of Sciences of the United States of America, 92,* 8135–8139.

Marlin, S. G., Hasan, S. J., & Cynader, M. S. (1988). Direction-selective adaptation in simple and complex cells in cat striate cortex. *Journal of Neurophysiology, 59*(4), 1314–1330.

Marr, D. (1982). *Vision.* San Francisco: Freeman.

Martinez-Conde, S., Macknik, S. L., & Hubel, D. H. (2000). Microsaccadic eye movements and firing of single cells in the striate cortex of macaque monkeys. *Nature Neuroscience, 3*(3), 251–258.

Merigan, W. H., & Maunsell, J. H. R. (1991). How parallel are the primate visual pathways? *Annual Review of Neuroscience, 16,* 369–402.

Miller, E. K., Erickson, C. A., & Desimone, R. (1996). Neural mechanisms of visual working memory in prefrontal cortex of the macaque. *Journal of Neuroscience, 16*(16), 5154–5167.

Milner, A. D., & Goodale, M. A. (1995). *The visual brain in action.* Oxford: Oxford University Press.

Miyashita, Y. (1993). Inferior temporal cortex: Where visual perception meets memory. *Annual Review of Neuroscience, 16,* 245–263.

Murata, A., Gallese, V., Luppino, G., Kaseda, M., & Sakata, H. (2000). Selectivity for the shape, size, and orientation of objects for grasping in neurons of monkey parietal area AIP. *Journal of Neurophysiology, 83*(5), 2580–2601.

Newsome, W. T. (1997). The King Solomon lectures in neuroethology: Deciding about motion: Linking perception to action. *Journal of Comparative Physiology A, 181,* 5–12.

Newsome, W. T., & Pare, E. B. (1988). A selective impairment of motion processing following lesions of the middle temporal visual area (MT). *Journal of Neuroscience, 8,* 2201–2211.

Nowak, L. G., & Bullier, J. (1997). The timing of information transfer in the visual system. In K. S. Rockland, J. H. Kaas, & A. Peters (Eds.), *Extrastriate visual cortex in primates* (Vol. 12, pp. 205–241). New York: Plenum Press.

Nowak, L. G., Munk, M. H. J., Girard, P., & Bullier, J. (1995). Visual Latencies in areas V1 and V2 of the macaque monkey. *Visual Neuroscience, 12*(2), 371–384.

Olson, C. R. (2001). Object-based vision and attention in primates. *Current Opinion in Neurobiology, 11,* 171–179.

Parker, A. J., & Newsome, W. T. (1998). Sense and the single neuron: Probing the physiology of perception. *Annual Review of Neuroscience, 21,* 227–277.

Payne, B. R., Lomber, S. G., Villa, A., & Bullier, J. (1996). Reversible deactivation of cerebral network components. *Trends in Neurosciences, 19,* 535–542.

Perenin, M. T. (1991). Discrimination of motion direction in perimetrically blind fields. *Neuroreport, 2,* 397–400.

Peterhans, E., & von der Heydt, R. (1989). Mechanisms of contour perception in monkey visual cortex: II. Contours bridging gaps. *Journal of Neuroscience, 9,* 1749–1763.

Petersen, S. E., Baker, J. F., & Allman, J. M. (1985). Direction-specific adaptation in area MT of the owl monkey. *Brain Research, 346*(1), 146–150.

Pisella, L., Grea, H., Tilikete, C., Vighetto, A., Desmurget, M., Rode, G., Boisson, D., & Rossetti, Y. (2000). An "automatic pilot" for the hand in human posterior parietal cortex: Toward reinterpreting optic ataxia. *Nature Neuroscience, 3*(7), 729–736.

Poggio, G. F., & Fischer, B. (1977). Binocular interaction and depth sensitivity in striate and prestriate cortex of behaving rhesus monkey. *Journal of Neurophysiology, 40*(6), 1392–1405.

Pohl, W. (1973). Dissociation of spatial discrimination deficits following frontal and parietal lesions in monkeys. *Journal of Comparative and Physiological Psychology, 82,* 227–239.

Robinson, D. L., & Petersen, S. E. (1992). The pulvinar and visual salience. *Trends in Neurosciences, 15*(4), 127–132.

Rockland, K. S. (1998). Convergence and branching patterns of round, type 2 corticopulvinar axons. *The Journal of Comparative Neurology, 390*(4), 515–536.

Rodieck, R. W. (1965). Quantitative analysis of cat ganglion cell response to visual stimuli. *Vision Research, 5,* 583–561.

Rodieck, R. W. (1998). *The first steps in seeing.* Sunderland, MA: Sinauer.

Roe, A. W., & Ts'o, D. Y. (1995). Visual topography in primate V2: Multiple representations across functional stripes. *Journal of Neuroscience, 15,* 3689–3715.

Rosa, M. (1997). Visuotopic organization of primate extrastriate cortex. In K. S. Rockland, J. H. Kaas, & A. Peters (Eds.), *Cerebral cortex: Vol. 12. Extrastriate cortex in primates* (pp. 127–203). New York: Plenum Press.

Salin, P.-A., & Bullier, J. (1995). Corticocortical connections in the visual system: Structure and function. *Physiological Reviews, 75,* 107–154.

Salzman, C. D., Murasugi, C. M., Britten, K. H., & Newsome, W. T. (1992). Microstimulation in visual area MT: Effects on direction discrimination performance. *Journal of Neuroscience, 12,* 2331–2355.

Sary, G., Vogels, R., Kovacs, G., & Orban, G. A. (1995). Responses of monkey inferior temporal neurons to luminance-defined, motion-defined, and texture-defined gratings. *Journal of Neurophysiology, 73*(4), 1341–1354.

Schall, J. D. (2001). Neural basis of deciding, choosing and acting. *Nature Reviews Neuroscience, 2,* 33–42.

Schiller, P. H. (1993). The effects of V4 and middle temporal (MT) area lesions on visual performance in the rhesus monkey. *Visual Neuroscience, 10,* 717–746.

Schiller, P. H. (1995). Effect of lesions in visual cortical area V4 on the recognition of transformed objects. *Nature, 376,* 342–344.

Schoups, A., Vogels, R., Qian, N., & Orban, G. (2001). Practising orientation identification improves orientation coding in V1 neurons. *Nature, 412,* 549–553.

Seghier, M., Dojat, M., Delon-Martin, C., Rubin, C., Warnking, J., Segebarth, C., & Bullier, J. (2000). Moving illusory contours activate primary visual cortex: An FRMI study. *Cerebral Cortex, 10,* 663–670.

Sheinberg, D. L., & Logothetis, N. K. (1997). The role of temporal cortical areas in perceptual organization. *Proceedings of the National Academy of Sciences of the United States of America, 94,* 3408–3413.

Sheinberg, D. L., & Logothetis, N. K. (2001). Noticing familiar objects in real world scenes: The role of temporal cortical neurons in natural vision. *Journal of Neuroscience, 21*(4), 1340–1350.

Sherman, S. M. (2001). Tonic and burst firing: Dual modes of thalamocortical relay. *Trends in Neuroscience, 24*(2), 122–126.

Sherman, S. M., & Guillery, R. W. (1998). On the actions that one nerve cell can have on another: Distinguishing "drivers" from "modulators." *Proceedings of the National Academy of Sciences of the United States of America, 95*(12), 7121–7126.

Sherman, S. M., & Guillery, R. W. (2001). *Exploring the thalamus.* San Diego: Academic Press.

Sillito, A. M. (1975). The contribution of inhibitory mechanisms to the receptive field properties of neurones in the striate cortex of the cat. *The Journal of Physiology* (London), *250*(2), 305–329.

Singer, W. (1993). Synchronization of cortical activity and its putative role in information processing and learning. *Annual Review of Physiology, 55,* 349–374.

Stepniewska, I., Qi, H. X., & Kaas, J. H. (1999). Do superior colliculus projection zones in the inferior pulvinar project to MT in primates? *European Journal of Neuroscience, 11*(2), 469–480.

Sugita, Y. (1999). Grouping of image fragments in primary visual cortex. *Nature, 401,* 269–273.

Taira, M., Tsutsui, K. I., Jiang, M., Yara, K., & Sakata, H. (2000). Parietal neurons represent surface orientation from the gradient of binocular disparity. *Journal of Neurophysiology, 83*(5), 3140–3146.

Tallon-Baudry, C., Bertrand, O., Peronnet, F., & Pernier, J. (1998). Induced gamma-band activity during the delay of a visual short-term memory task in humans. *Journal of Neuroscience, 18,* 4244–4254.

Tanaka, K. (1996). Inferotemporal cortex and object vision. *Annual Review of Neuroscience, 19,* 109–139.

Tolias, A. S., Moore, T., Smirnakis, S. M., Tehovnik, E. J., Siapas, A. G., & Schiller, P. H. (2001). Eye movements modulate visual receptive fields of V4 neurons. *Neuron, 29*(3), 757–767.

Tootell, R. B. H., Dale, A. M., Sereno, M. I., & Malach, R. (1996). New images from human visual cortex. *Trends in Neurosciences, 19,* 481–489.

Tootell, R. B. H., & Hadjikhani, N. (2001). Where is "Dorsal V4" in human visual cortex? Retinotopic, topographic and functional evidence. *Cerebral Cortex, 11,* 298–311.

Tootell, R. B. H., Hadjikhani, N. K., Vanduffel, W., Liu, A. K., Mendola, J. D., Sereno, M. I., & Dale, A. M. (1998). Functional analysis of primary visual cortex (V1) in humans. *Proceedings of the National Academy of Sciences of the United States of America, 95,* 811–817.

Tootell, R. B. H., Mendola, J. D., Hadjikhani, N. K., Ledden, P. J., Liu, A. K., Reppas, J. B., Sereno, M. I., & Dale, A. M. (1997). Functional analysis of V3A and related areas in human visual cortex. *Journal of Neuroscience, 17*(18), 7060–7078.

Tootell, R. B. H., Reppas, J. B., Dale, A. M., Look, R. B., Sereno, M. I., Malach, R., Brady, T. J., & Rosen, B. R. (1995). Visual-motion aftereffect in human cortical area MT revealed by functional magnetic resonance imaging. *Nature, 375,* 139–141.

Trotter, Y., & Celebrini, S. (1999). Gaze direction controls response gain in primary visual-cortex neurons. *Nature, 398,* 239–242.

Trotter, Y., Celebrini, S., Stricanne, B., Thorpe, S., & Imbert, M. (1996). Neural processing of stereopsis as a function of viewing distance in primate visual cortical area V1. *Journal of Neurophysiology, 76,* 2872–2885.

Ungerleider, L. G., & Mishkin, M. (1982). Two cortical visual systems. In D. J. Ingle, M. A. Goodale, & R. J. W. Mansfield (Eds.), *Analysis of visual behavior* (pp. 549–586). Cambridge: MIT Press.

Van Essen, D. C., & Maunsell, J. H. R. (1983). Hierarchical organization and functional streams in the visual cortex. *Trends in Neurosciences, 6,* 370–375.

von der Heydt, R., & Peterhans, E. (1989). Mechanisms of contour perception in monkey visual cortex: I. Lines of pattern discontinuity. *Journal of Neuroscience, 9,* 1731–1748.

von der Heydt, R., Peterhans, E., & Baumgartner, G. (1984). Illusory contours and cortical neuron responses. *Science, 224,* 1260–1262.

von der Heydt, R., Zhou, H., & Friedman, H. S. (2000). Representation of stereoscopic edges in monkey visual cortex. *Vision Research, 40*(15), 1955–1967.

Walker, G. A., Ohzawa, I., & Freeman, R. D. (1999). Asymmetric suppression outside the classical receptive field of the visual cortex. *Journal of Neuroscience, 19*(23), 10536–10553.

Wassle, H., & Boycott, B. B. (1991). Functional architecture of the mammalian retina. *Physiological Reviews, 71,* 447–480.

Weiskrantz, L. (1986). *Blindsight: A case study and implications* (Vol. 12). Oxford University Press, Oxford.

Weliky, M., Bosking, W. H., & Fitzpatrick, D. (1996). A systematic map of direction preference in primary visual cortex. *Nature, 379,* 725–728.

White, A. J., Wilder, H. D., Goodchild, A. K., Sefton, A. J., & Martin, P. R. (1998). Segregation of receptive field properties in the lateral geniculate nucleus of a New-World monkey, the marmoset Callithrix jacchus. *Journal of Neurophysiology, 80*(4), 2063–2076.

Zeki, S. (1993). *A vision of the brain.* London: Blackwell.

Zeki, S. M. (1978). Functional specialisation in the visual cortex of the rhesus monkey. *Nature, 274,* 423–428.

CHAPTER 2

Color Vision

KENNETH KNOBLAUCH

INTRODUCTION: GENERAL OBSERVATIONS

Color vision is a vast subject that requires consideration of issues ranging from physics and physiology to psychology and anthropology. Within a chapter, it is impossible to review thoroughly all aspects of a subject to which entire books are devoted. Nevertheless, I will provide an introduction to the fundamental issues in color vision, especially with respect to the early coding of spectral characteristics of the stimulus and its relation to color appearance. I will point the reader to recent data that have clarified particular issues and to questions that remain unanswered.

What Does It Mean to Have Color Vision?

This basic question can be posed and answered in more than one way. Color is a private experience and is not open to examination by anyone but the observer experiencing it.

Seeing Color

Despite its status as a subjective phenomenon, we typically experience color as a characteristic of things in the world, an intrinsic property of surfaces and lights. Thus, a first approach might be to investigate what parameters of lights and surfaces evoke particular color experiences in an observer. This task is complex, however, because the relation between lights and color experience is not one to one, but many to many. The same light reaching our eyes can have many different appearances as a function of its context. Similarly, very different lights reaching our eyes can appear to be the same color.

Nevertheless, colors can be organized along a small number of simple dimensions. It can be supposed that this perceptual organization is constrained by the coding of color in the brain. Thus, the mental representation of color should be an indicator of the neural representation of color, and we would hope that at some level neural activity would be isomorphic with (i.e., follow the same rules of organization as) our experience.

Discriminating between Spectra

The difficulty of accessing the subjective aspects of color has motivated operational definitions of color vision, the use of behavioral (observable) indexes correlated with the presence of color. So to return to our first approach, by varying the characteristics of lights, we can determine what parameter values an observer can distinguish and what parameter values an observer cannot. A typical manipulation consists of varying the spectral composition of the light, thus motivating a minimal definition of color vision in common use: the capacity to distinguish lights on the basis of spectral differences independent of intensity differences. It might be supposed that discriminating spectral differences means that the observer sees color differences, but the logic of this assertion does not necessarily follow.

The benefit of such an approach is that it is objective. It does not depend on language and can be applied to nonlinguistic organisms (e.g., infants and animals; Blough & Yager, 1972; Teller, 1979). Such an approach is the basis of the conventional classification of normal and abnormal human color vision (Pokorny, Smith, Verriest, & Pinckers, 1979).

A significant disadvantage of this approach, however, is that there is nothing in the discrimination task per se that guarantees that the behavior is color-related. Discrimination tasks provide information on the sets of stimuli among which subjects cannot differentiate. Such information is intimately linked with the number and filtering properties of visual mechanisms that encode stimulus differences. It remains, however, to show in what manner such visual mechanisms relate to the experience of color.

Identifying Surfaces/Reflectances

A third approach to defining color vision considers evolutionary factors. One can ask what purpose color vision serves for survival. Color perception is part of an apparatus for observing and accurately deducing characteristics of the world in which organisms must survive. They must correctly infer the properties of objects independent of the variations of the stimulation that they present to our visual systems. Thus, color vision can be viewed as an adaptation over generations to the environment. The capacities for discriminating and seeing color, then, are not independent of the natural properties of surfaces and lights in the environment of the organism. The structure of those parts of the environment critical for the survival and reproduction of the species will be reflected in constraints on processing that are intrinsic to the visual system. This definition resolves the paradox that although color is an experience of the mind, it is invariably perceived as a property of the world.

With this approach, we focus on the characteristics of the natural world. For example, are the lights and surfaces to which we are exposed arbitrary, or are they constrained in some manner? In studying the visual system, we may ask, "Are the limits in what we can discriminate likely to lead to confusions in the natural (constrained) world?" In terms of behavior, "Are there color-dependent behaviors that are critical to survival and reproduction?" and "Given the environmental and physiological constraints, how optimal is the organism's performance?" These are not easy questions because humans live in widely varied and artificially constructed environments. However, the results from primate (and other) species that have visual systems similar to ours and live in the wild are enlightening (Regan et al., 1998).

Nomenclature

It is absolutely essential to avoid terminology that confuses the levels of events. Color names such as red, yellow, and so on will be reserved for the description of appearance and will never be applied to lights (except when describing their appearance), genes, cells, or neural responses. There is a long history of (mis-)applying color names to neural cells either in order to refer to the color of the part of the visual spectrum to which the cell responds best or to refer to the perceptual events to which the cell's response is hypothesized to mediate (or both!). Because color is an experience and not a property of the spectrum, the first usage is misleading. Because we do not know what cell activity is linked directly with the experience of color, the second usage presupposes the truth of an unproven hypothesis. Although the use of careful and clear language can occasionally lead to circuitous phrases, it avoids confusion.

Local and Global Factors

In the last 200 years color vision research has been dominated by questions relating to the coding of the spectral characteristics of light. The mechanisms proposed have typically been local in nature, inasmuch as they are based on processing at individual points in the retinal image; it had been assumed that the coding in a given region is little influenced by the coding in other regions that are sufficiently distant.

In the last 30 years, however, the study of color appearance has repeatedly demonstrated that the colors that we perceive depend intimately on context—other colors in the scene, the objects in the scene, and the observer's interpretation of the nature of these objects. Thus, the appearance of colors depends on factors that are both local and global to a scene. Therefore, understanding how coding of light in the retinal image becomes a representation of the color of objects must ultimately address how local information in the retinal image is integrated to render a global perceptual quality.

LIGHT AND MATTER

Although it is possible to evoke visual sensations by unusual means, such as electrical or magnetic stimulation of the visual cortex (Brindley & Lewin, 1968) or electrical or mechanical stimulation of the eye (Brindley, 1955, 1966), these methods are obviously atypical of how visual sensations arise naturally. It is also possible to evoke visual experiences (albeit weak ones) through visual imagery, a kind of self-induced activity of the brain (D'Esposito et al., 1997; Kosslyn,

1994). Normally, however, what we see is caused by the stimulation of the retina by light. In fact, the retinal image, as the stimulus for vision, can be completely described in terms of its radiance as a function of position, time, and wavelength. Other characteristics of light such as polarization or phase might be included, although the human visual system seems to be insensitive to these variables.

The retinal image is created by light coming from two types of emitters: sources and surfaces. Sources are those emitters of light that we perceive as producing light (e.g., the sun, fire, lamps etc.). Surfaces reflect light when they are illuminated by a source. In physical terms, the distinction between sources and surfaces is not so exact. For example, surfaces with a specular component (e.g., a mirror) produce an image of the source that can illuminate other surfaces. More generally, for a complete description of a scene, the inter-reflections among surfaces require that they be treated as secondary sources (Bloj, Kersten, & Hurlbert, 1999). Although this section introduces some basic physical properties of sources and surfaces, it is important to emphasize that whether a particular patch of light is perceived to be a surface or a source can profoundly influence its color appearance.

Sources

Light is an electromagnetic phenomenon that displays properties associated with both waves and particles. Young's (1802) double-slit experiment demonstrated that coherent beams of light can interfere with each other as do waves. However, in its interaction with matter, light acts as if it were a particle. For example, light is absorbed and emitted in integral amounts. The minimum amount, one part, is referred to as a quantum of light.

As a wave phenomenon, a wavelength, λ, or frequency, ν, is associated with light. The two are related by

$$\lambda = c\nu^{-1}, \qquad (1)$$

where $c = 2.997 \times 10^8 \, \text{m·s}^{-1}$ is the speed of light in a vacuum. The frequency is held to be an invariant characteristic of light. Because the speed of light in a medium depends on the index of refraction of the medium, the wavelength varies as well. The index of refraction of air, being negligibly different from that of a vacuum (defined as $n = 1$), can be ignored for most purposes.

It is convenient to take the visible spectrum as comprising the wavelength range from 400 nm to 700 nm. For practical purposes, it is sometimes necessary to consider a wider range, and accordingly many reference books include visually related data from 380 nm to 780 nm. It should be noted that visual functions are rarely measured outside the former range, however.

Most sources of light emit a range of wavelengths. To describe the light that is emitted from a source, it is necessary to express the radiance of the source at each wavelength, yielding the spectral radiance distribution or, more succinctly, the spectrum of the source (for example, Figure 2.1). Radiance is expressed in energy, for example, W/m^2 or W/deg^2.[1] The energy, E, in a single quantum of light depends on its frequency, ν, or on its wavelength, λ, by,

$$E = h\nu = h/\lambda, \qquad (2)$$

where $h = 6.626 \times 10^{-34}$ J·s is Planck's con-

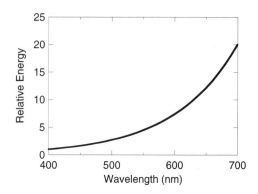

Figure 2.1   Every light is characterized by its spectrum, the distribution of its energy as a function of wavelength.

stant. Thus, there will be more energy per quantum at short than at long wavelengths.[2]

Additive Light Mixture

Light spectra are functions of wavelength. When two light sources with spectra, $f(\lambda)$ and $g(\lambda)$, are combined in a common beam or superposed in a common field, the resulting spectrum, $h(\lambda)$, is the wavelength by wavelength sum of the two:

$$f(\lambda) + g(\lambda) = h(\lambda), \qquad (3)$$

as shown in Figure 2.2.

A light source can also be amplified or attenuated by a constant factor (self-addition) that corresponds to multiplying the spectrum by a real, positive constant. With these two operations, the set of visible sources constitutes an infinite dimensional vector space

---

[1] It can be argued that light expressed in number of quanta is a more fundamental visual quantity. Most radiometers provide results in energy, which partly explains its frequent usage. However, certain comparisons require that light be expressed in quantal units. For example, discrepancies between the dark-adapted, peripheral spectral sensitivity of humans and the extinction spectrum of human rhodopsin were only resolved when it was realized that the latter were on a quantum basis and the two needed to be compared on a common basis (Dartnall, 1953).

[2] Given that frequency is invariant, it has been argued that it is a more fundamental parameter for expressing visual data. This view gained some support by the observation that visual photopigments have a more similar shape when plotted on a scale proportional to frequency (Dartnall, 1953). A related quantity, wavenumber, which is simply the reciprocal of wavelength (expressed in centimeters), is sometimes employed. The visible spectrum, 400–700 nm, in wavenumber varies from 25,000–14,286 cm^{-1}. Nevertheless, most studies continue to express data on a wavelength basis.

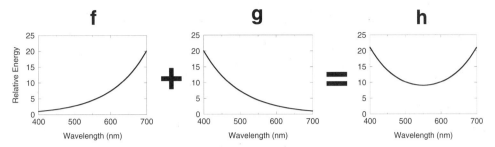

Figure 2.2 The spectrum resulting from the additive mixture of two lights, f and g, is given by the sum of their spectra at each wavelength, yielding the light with spectrum h.

defined on the wavelength interval of 400 nm to 700 nm.

In practice, a source is measured at a finite number of wavelengths and is represented by a list, (λ, E), of pairs of wavelength and energy that represent a sampled version of the spectrum. If the spectrum is sampled every 10 nm (1 nm), then in the visible range the list of energies has 31 (301) elements. Two lists of energy, representing two sampled spectra, can be added element by element and multiplied by real, positive constants in the same way as with the functions described earlier for the superposition of two lights. Thus, the lists can be treated as vectors, and the lights can be represented in a finite dimensional vector space in which the operations correspond to physical manipulations of the spectra of the lights. Note that the dimension of this space depends on the fineness with which one samples the continuous spectrum.

Combining lights in a fashion such that the resulting spectrum can be described within the framework of a linear vector space is referred to as an additive color mixture.

Surfaces

Surfaces interact in a number of complex ways with light depending on the characteristics of the light and of the surface. Light incident on a surface can be absorbed, reflected, or transmitted by it. It is the light returned to our eyes from a surface that is critical for vision. If a light beam is reflected back at the angle of incidence, then it produces a specular reflection or an image of the source. At the other extreme, if the light reflected is scattered uniformly in all directions, then the surface appears matte. Most surfaces are intermediate between these two extremes and have both specular and matte components in the light reflected.

Most surfaces absorb and reflect wavelengths differentially. This characteristic is the one that is most closely related to its color appearance. The reflectance of a surface, $R(\lambda)$, is defined as the ratio of the reflected energy, E_r, and incident energy, E_i, as a function of wavelength

$$R(\lambda) = \frac{E_r(\lambda)}{E_i(\lambda)}. \tag{4}$$

For a surface that is perfectly matte (i.e., Lambertian) with reflectance $R(\lambda)$, and an incident source with spectrum $E_i(\lambda)$, the spectrum reaching the eye is the product, $E_i(\lambda)R(\lambda)$.

This simple model of the interaction of lights and surfaces is widely used and easily applied to the numerous experiments in which the stimuli used are matte surfaces. In reality, many more complex situations arise. For example, the light that is absorbed by a surface can be re-emitted at a different wavelength, producing the phenomenon of fluorescence, or the roughness of a surface can produce internal reflections that cause inhomogeneities in its spectral characteristics, thereby influencing the appearance through contrast phenomena.

Subtractive Mixture

The interaction between the spectra of lights and (matte) surfaces is not additive, but multiplicative. One finds a similar relationship for the transmission spectra that result from the superposition of homogeneous (nonfluorescent and nondiffusing) filters and for the mixture of (nonfluorescent) pigments or paints. This type of interaction is referred to as subtractive mixture because light is lost from the resulting spectra. For example, a paint that absorbs long wavelengths and reflects middle and short wavelengths will appear bluish (Figure 2.3, solid curve). One that absorbs short wavelengths and reflects middle and long wavelengths will appear yellowish (Figure 2.3, long-dashed curve). The mixture of these two paints will absorb in the short and long wavelengths, only reflecting in the overlapping middle-wavelength region (Figure 2.3, short-dashed curve). The resulting paint will probably appear dark greenish.

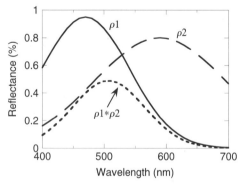

Figure 2.3   In substractive color mixtures, the reflectance spectrum (dotted curve) given by the mixture of two paints with reflectances ρ_1 and ρ_2 (solid and dashed curves) is given by the product of the individual reflectances at each wavelength.

Natural Sources and Surfaces

The task of classifying the invariant properties of surfaces is rendered more complex by the fact that the characteristics of sources vary enormously. It is useful to keep in mind, however, that under natural circumstances this variation is not arbitrary.

The most important natural source of illumination is the sun. Its spectrum is not invariant but changes with the time of day, the seasons, the weather, and the local environment, among other variables. For example, if one lives in a forest, natural sunlight will be partially filtered by the surrounding foliage. Under all conditions, the spectrum of the sun covers the entire visible spectrum. The variations can be described principally as a change in the overall intensity and a smooth family of variations that modify the relative weight of energy coming from the short- and long-wavelength regions of the spectrum. A detailed analysis of the variations of the solar spectrum have shown it to be well described by three parameters or principle components (Judd, MacAdam, & Wyszecki, 1964). Thus, vision evolved under a natural illumination that is not arbitrary in its characteristics.

We also live under a number of artificial illuminants, some of which have characteristics that deviate considerably from the family of solar curves (e.g., fluorescent and narrowband sources). It should not be surprising that our capacity to distinguish surfaces might be impaired under such unnatural conditions. An extreme case is given by the narrowband, yellowish sodium lights used in some parking lots that make it difficult to recognize your car by its color. In this case, all cars reflect the same narrowband spectrum. A more common example is given by some fluorescent lamps that contain a few narrowband peaks of energy. These alter the relations between spectra arriving at the eye from different surfaces in a way different from natural lights, and the color appearances of the surfaces seem to vary markedly with respect to a natural light source.

Although it is more difficult to specify what constitutes the set of natural surfaces, several surveys of the reflectances of natural objects have been performed. Analysis of these sets indicates that surface characteristics are not arbitrary either. The number of parameters necessary to characterize the variation among reflectance functions of these sets is estimated to be in the range of six to nine (Maloney, 1986). Thus, given the limited dimensionality of the sets of natural illuminants and surfaces, the variations in spectra from natural surfaces that are available to our visual systems are, also, significantly constrained. If one considers that for a particular organism in a particular ecological niche, the set of surfaces that play a role in survival and reproduction (i.e., whose correct discrimination and identification play such a role) could well be more limited, then it seems reasonable to suppose that the dimensionality of the space of natural surface reflectances should be viewed as an upper bound.

METAMERIC MATCHES

The experiments of Isaac Newton (1730/1952) serve as a useful departure point in the modern history of color vision. Most people are familiar with his demonstration that sunlight, which appears to be of uniform color, can be decomposed by a prism into a continuous gradient or spectrum of colored lights resembling a rainbow. By introducing a lens in the optical path, Newton showed that the lights in the spectrum could be recombined to produce a field of uniform color, identical to the original sunlight. But which is more fundamental, the sunlight of uniform color or the component lights of the spectrum?

To answer this question, Newton used a slit to select only one part of the spectrum produced by the first prism, say the portion that appears orange. When passed through a second prism, this light was not further decomposed into a finer gradient; it remained orange. From these experiments he argued that sunlight, which appears as a very desaturated color, is heterogeneous, or composed of the sum of homogeneous components, each appearing as a different, highly saturated color. In passing through the prism, these component lights are differentially refracted or bent in their path and are thus spread out differentially over space.

He also employed an argument based on the appearance of surfaces illuminated by narrow bands of his spectrum. He reasoned that reflection at a surface could not change the nature of a homogeneous light. Illuminated by a given narrow band of the spectrum, he found that different surfaces appeared to be the same color as the band, varying only in brightness. Thus, if sunlight were a homogeneous light, all objects illuminated by it would appear one and the same color.

These initial experiments demonstrate the physical characteristics of light. The physical components of the spectrum that are differentially refracted correspond to different wavelengths of the light.

Newton discovered, however, that the colors he saw were not intrinsic to the light. By using multiple slits that permitted the mixing of several narrow bands of the spectrum, he found that different light mixtures could yield lights of identical appearance. In fact, two carefully chosen, narrow bands were sufficient to generate a light mixture that was identical in color to that obtained by recombining the entire spectrum. The fact that the mixture of many different pairs of bands sufficed to produce a light identical in color to that of sunlight demonstrated that the color of sunlight was not a property specific to its

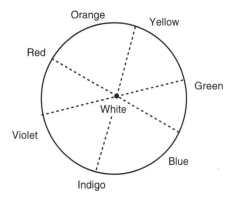

Figure 2.4 Newton represented the spectrum on a circle.

NOTE: Newton used color names to identify the different bands that he isolated. The additive mixtures of two lights are always represented on the line connecting the points representing them in the circle. Different bands of the spectrum could be mixed to match arbitrary lights composed of a distribution of wavelengths. Thus, the light labeled "white" in the center could be matched by many different pairs of lights around the rim of the circle.

spectral distribution, but one shared by many different spectral distributions. Thus, these experiments show that the human visual system is limited with respect to its capacity to encode lights of different spectral composition. Lights that appear identical but have different spectra are called *metamers*.

To organize his observations on light mixtures, Newton proposed a diagram in the form of a circle (Figure 2.4). The homogeneous (or narrowband) lights were distributed on the rim of the circle in the order found in the spectrum. All other lights were distributed within the interior. Lights that matched the mixture of two homogeneous lights from the rim were found on the line segment connecting the points representing them. A center of gravity rule was used to assign the position on this line segment. For example, if a light was a mixture of equal parts of two monochromatic lights, then the point representing the mixture was at the midpoint of the segment connecting the two points representing the monochromatic lights. Sunlight, which is a mixture of all

wavelengths, would be found near the center of the diagram. Note that an infinity of pairs of lights would match sunlight in appearance, because an infinity of line segments passes through an interior point of a circle, each of which has two distinct endpoints on the rim. The basic properties of Newton's color circle are retained in modern chromaticity diagrams.

Although these observations of Newton are repeated in nearly every introductory text on color vision, the fact that they are so fundamental to the topic and that they anticipate the development of modern colorimetry makes them still valuable to consider. Newton used the color of monochromatic lights as an indicator of physical phenomena. Nevertheless, he appreciated that the appearance of a light is a *psychological* characteristic:

> And if at any time I speak of Light and Rays as coloured or endued with Colours, I would be understood to speak not philosophically and properly, but grossly, and accordingly to such Conceptions as vulgar People in seeing all these Experiments would be apt to frame. For the Rays to speak properly are not coloured. In them there is nothing else than a certain Power and Disposition to stir up a Sensation of this or that Colour. (Newton, 1730/1952, pp. 124–125).

What Is the Dimension of Color Discrimination?

Newton's observations demonstrate that the human capacity for discriminating between lights on the basis of their spectral differences is limited. It is not infinitely dimensional, as is the space of lights. The fact that we can discriminate between some lights on the basis of their spectral differences indicates that our vision is at least two-dimensional. Newton's color circle, if accepted as an accurate model of human color matching behavior, suggests that our vision is at least three-dimensional. To see why, consider how many parameters an observer must vary in order to match an arbitrary light using the rules proposed by Newton

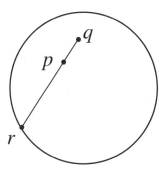

Figure 2.5 Newton's color circle implies that three degrees of freedom are necessary to match an arbitrary light, p.
NOTE: 1) One chooses the light q. 2) Then the light r must be chosen on a line collinear with p and q. 3) Finally, q and r must be mixed in the appropriate proportions to match the light p.

for the color circle. The arbitrary light corresponds to a point, p, in or on the circle in Figure 2.5. Another light, q, cannot be adjusted to match p by varying its amount (one parameter) unless the two points already coincide. One can choose a second light, r, to mix with q. The choice of this light (its position in the color circle) adds a second parameter. Finally, the amount of r to mix with q in order to attain the point p, using the center of gravity rule, provides a third parameter.

Newton did not discuss the issue of the dimensionality of color discrimination. The problem was not addressed explicitly until Palmer (1777) and then Young (1802) suggested that three parameters were sufficient to specify colors. Experimentally, Helmholtz (1911/1962) and Maxwell (1856) showed through rigorous color matching experiments that observers could match an arbitrary light by manipulating three variables. Human vision is defined as *trichromatic* because the control of three parameters is sufficient to match an arbitrary light and because more than three parameters is never necessary. Trichromacy means that with respect to human vision, all lights can be represented in a three-dimensional space. The coordinates of each light are the values of the three parame-

ters that the observer adjusts in order to obtain a perfect match. Lights that are metamers are represented by the same coordinates. Thus, the color-matching experiment establishes an equivalence relation on lights, wherein lights that have identical appearances are deemed equivalent by mapping them to the same point in the parameter or color-matching space.

The parameters could be wavelength and intensity, as indicated earlier. Most frequently, however, three lights called primaries with fixed spectral composition, $P_1(\lambda)$, $P_2(\lambda)$, and $P_3(\lambda)$, are chosen, and the observer manipulates the radiances of each one to obtain a match with a comparison light, $P_0(\lambda)$. The only constraint on the choice of primaries is that not one of them can be matched by a combination of the other two. It is possible that in order to obtain a match, one of the primary lights must be mixed with the comparison match. This will be shown later to be equivalent to subtracting that light from the matching mixture. This situation is not inconsistent with trichromacy because the observer is still required to manipulate just three quantities to obtain a match with a fourth light. The two matching situations can be represented formally by

$$P_0 \sim a * P_1 \oplus b * P_2 \oplus c * P_3 \quad (5)$$

or

$$P_0 \oplus a * P_1 \sim b * P_2 \oplus c * P_3, \quad (6)$$

where $\sim$ means is a metameric match to, $*$ is multiplication by a real constant (a, b, c), $\oplus$ indicates the wavelength-by-wavelength addition of spectra, and the wavelength dependence of the lights is suppressed for conciseness. For each light, P_0, an observer can perform the task of adjusting the quantities of the three primaries so that the light mixtures corresponding to the two sides of the equations are identical in appearance. We say then that the light P_0 has coordinates a, b, c or coordinate vector, (a, b, c), with respect to the primary lights P_1, P_2, and P_3.

Grassmann's Laws

The formal properties of color matching implied by Newton's center of gravity rule were first made explicit by Grassmann (1853). Grassmann proposed that matches should obey four properties: (a) trichromacy, (b) continuity, (c) additivity, and (d) additivity of brightness. These became known as Grassmann's laws of color matching.

Krantz (1975a) reformulated these laws in modern mathematical terms in order to simplify them and to underscore the relationship between color matching and its linear-algebraic representation. He proposed three laws: (a) scalar invariance, (b) additivity, and (c) trichromacy. Formally, these are:

Scalar Invariance: Given lights P_1 and P_2 and real number a, if

$$P_1 \sim P_2$$

then

$$a * P_1 \sim a * P_2$$

Additivity: Given lights P_1, P_2, and P_3, if

$$P_1 \sim P_2$$

then

$$P_1 \oplus P_3 \sim P_2 \oplus P_3$$

Trichromacy:

1. Given lights P_1, P_2, and P_3 such that no mixture of a pair of these lights matches the third and real numbers a_i, b_i $i = 1, 3$, then in the color-matching equation

$$\sum_{i=1}^{3} a_i * P_i \sim \sum_{i=1}^{3} b_i * P_i$$

if and only if $a_i = b_i$.

2. Given lights P_i and real numbers a_i, b_i $i = 1, 4$, then in the color-matching equation if

$$\sum_{i=1}^{4} a_i * P_i \sim \sum_{i=1}^{4} b_i * P_i$$

then for at least one i, $a_i \neq b_i$.

This unusual statement of the principle of trichromacy requires some explanation. Trichromacy 1 states that when adjusting three lights distributed across two fields, the only match possible is one of physical identity (i.e., an isomeric match). Note that the case of complementary lights is excluded by the requirement of independence—that no mixture of two of the lights matches the third. Trichromacy 2 indicates, however, that in the case of four lights, there are matches between the two fields that are not physically identical (i.e., metamers). The unusual form of Trichromacy 2 is designed so that a single formalism covers the situations in which three primaries are mixed in the same field as well as when one primary is mixed with the reference light.

Grassmann's laws can be tested empirically. Under conditions in which they hold, they guarantee that the results of a color-matching experiment may be represented in a linear vector space with the physical operations of superposition and scaling of lights corresponding to vector addition and multiplication by a constant of the coordinate vectors of lights, respectively. Importantly, the results from new mixtures of lights not performed by an observer can also be predicted.

Grassmann's laws are usually considered to be valid at photopic levels[3] that do not produce significant photopigment bleaching and for fields restricted to the central two degrees of vision. Photopigment bleaching causes

---

[3]The term *photopic* refers to luminance levels at which rod photoreceptor signals are saturated. Thus, visual function is due solely to cone photoreceptors. Luminance levels below cone absolute thresholds, and thus at which vision is mediated solely by rods, are referred to as *scotopic*. Photopic vision usually refers to luminance levels above 3 cd/m^2, though the exact value will depend on the wavelength (Pokorny et al., 1979). Scotopic vision occurs below 0.001 cd/m^2, with the same caveat concerning wavelength. Intermediate levels at which vision is mediated by both rods and cones is referred to as *mesopic*.

small changes in the photoreceptor spectra that produce violations of scalar invariance (Brindley, 1953). Fields that are larger than two degrees or that are not photopic can introduce the participation of the rods that will yield violations of additivity (Trezona, 1974, 1987). Inhomogeneities in the visual field related to the distribution of macular pigment and the shortening of cone outer segments may also render extrafoveal matches different from foveal matches.

Color Spaces: A First Look

Grassmann's laws permit the construction of a vector space representation of metameric matching within which the coordinates of any light, given only its spectrum, can be specified with respect to three primary lights. To perform this construction, one needs to know the coordinates of the set of monochromatic lights with respect to the primaries. Because every light is a superposition of monochromatic components of different energies (i.e., its spectrum), then by additivity the coordinates of a light will be the sum of the coordinates of its components weighted by their respective energies in the spectrum. Next, I consider this in detail.

The color-matching coordinates of the set of monochromatic lights of unit energy are called the color-matching or distribution functions. These are determined by having observers perform color matches for a set of monochromatic (or narrowband) lights across the visible spectrum (e.g., 400–700 nm) in 10-nm steps. With these monochromatic lights substituted for the light P_0 in Equations (5) and (6), the values of the coordinates become functions of wavelength $\bar{a}(\lambda)$, $\bar{b}(\lambda)$, and $\bar{c}(\lambda)$, where the bar is traditionally used to indicate that the coordinates or color-matching functions (CMfs) have been normalized for a unit energy at each wavelength. By scalar invariance such a normalization is permitted, even if the matches are performed at different energy levels at different wavelengths. When one primary is added to the test light, P_0, then by additivity its coordinate is given a negative value.

Given an arbitrary light with spectrum, $F(\lambda)$, its three coordinates are computed by weighting its spectrum by each of the three CMF functions and summing over wavelength. In the discrete case, this gives

$$A = \sum_{\lambda=400}^{700} F_\lambda \bar{a}_\lambda = F \cdot \bar{a}$$

$$B = \sum_{\lambda=400}^{700} F_\lambda \bar{b}_\lambda = F \cdot \bar{b} \qquad (7)$$

$$C = \sum_{\lambda=400}^{700} F_\lambda \bar{c}_\lambda = F \cdot \bar{c},$$

where the coordinates A, B, and C of the light F are called *tristimulus values*. The right-hand side of the equation has been added to emphasize that the weighted summation over wavelength can be regarded equally well as a scaler or dot product between the two vectors, representing the light spectrum and the CMF distribution, respectively. Thus, in the present case, the CMFs can be treated as a 3×31 matrix that maps a 31-dimensional vector from the space of light spectra into a three-dimensional tristimulus vector.

In practice, an additional simplification is introduced. Because it is difficult to visualize and plot points in three dimensions (or, at least, it was so in the 19th and early 20th century, when these formalisms were first developed) and because scalar invariance implies that the ratios between the tristimulus values for a light are invariant as the light's radiance is scaled, the tristimulus values are typically projected into a plane, yielding two *chromaticity coordinates*. For example, if the tristimulus values are projected into a plane in which the sum of the three equals 1, we have

$$a = \frac{A}{A + B + C}$$

$$b = \frac{B}{A + B + C} \qquad (8)$$

$$c = \frac{C}{A + B + C} = 1 - a - b,$$

where the value of c is determined given a and b. Given the chromaticity coordinates, (a, b), a third value, typically the luminance, is then required to reconstruct the original tristimulus values.

Several problems arise at this point. First, if different experimenters use different sets of primaries, they will obtain different CMFs and different coordinates for each light. Is there a simple way to relate coordinates with respect to one set of primaries to those with respect to another set? Second, any primaries based on real lights will generate CMFs that are negative (a primary light must be mixed with the test light) over some range of wavelengths. This was generally seen as a disadvantage that increased the probability of making errors in the calculations of the tristimulus values. The solution to the first problem provides the method for generating an all-positive set of CMFs.

Given the linear representation of metameric matching operations, it should be evident that the relation between coordinates (or tristimulus values) obtained with different sets of primary lights corresponds to the relation between coordinates of a vector with respect to different bases. In the latter case, if we can determine a nonsingular matrix that relates one set of basis elements to another set, then we can use this matrix to obtain the map from the coordinates for one basis to those in the new one.

Consider two sets of primaries, $\{P_i\}$ and $\{Q_i\}$, with CMFs, $\{\bar{a}_i(\lambda)\}$ and $\{\bar{b}_i(\lambda)\}$, respec-

tively.[4] The coordinates of the three lights $\{P_i\}$ with respect to the primaries $\{Q_i\}$ are determined by 9 numbers, m_{ij}, that give the quantities of the primaries necessary to obtain the three metameric matches:

$$P_1 \sim m_{11} * Q_1 \oplus m_{12} * Q_2 \oplus m_{13} * Q_3$$
$$P_2 \sim m_{21} * Q_1 \oplus m_{22} * Q_2 \oplus m_{23} * Q_3 \quad (9)$$
$$P_3 \sim m_{31} * Q_1 \oplus m_{32} * Q_2 \oplus m_{33} * Q_3.$$

By Grassmann's laws, the right side of each of these equations can be substituted for the respective $\{P_i\}$ in Equation (5). Collecting the coefficients of each $\{Q_i\}$ demonstrates that the vector of P-primary coordinates, (a, b, c) multiplied by the transpose of the matrix of m_{ij} gives the new Q-primary coordinates, (d, e, f), of the light P_0, or

$$\begin{pmatrix} d \\ e \\ f \end{pmatrix} = \begin{pmatrix} m_{11} & m_{21} & m_{31} \\ m_{12} & m_{22} & m_{32} \\ m_{13} & m_{23} & m_{33} \end{pmatrix} \begin{pmatrix} a \\ b \\ c \end{pmatrix}. \quad (10)$$

Although the nine entries in the matrix M can be determined by performing three trichromatic matches, an alternative method can be employed. If the spectral energy distributions, $Q_i(\lambda)$, of the Q-primaries are known, the entries of the matrix M can be computed directly using the P-primary CMFs and Equation (7).

Given the matrix M, the CMFs of the Q-primaries are related to the CMFs of the P-primaries by the same relation given in Equation (10):

$$\begin{pmatrix} \bar{b}_{1,\lambda_0} & \bar{b}_{1,\lambda_1} & \cdots \\ \bar{b}_{2,\lambda_0} & \bar{b}_{2,\lambda_1} & \cdots \\ \bar{b}_{3,\lambda_0} & \bar{b}_{3,\lambda_1} & \cdots \end{pmatrix}$$
$$= \begin{pmatrix} m_{11} & m_{21} & m_{31} \\ m_{12} & m_{22} & m_{32} \\ m_{13} & m_{23} & m_{33} \end{pmatrix} \begin{pmatrix} \bar{a}_{1,\lambda_0} & \bar{a}_{1,\lambda_1} & \cdots \\ \bar{a}_{2,\lambda_0} & \bar{a}_{2,\lambda_1} & \cdots \\ \bar{a}_{3,\lambda_0} & \bar{a}_{3,\lambda_1} & \cdots \end{pmatrix}.$$
$$(11)$$

---

[4]Note that to avoid a proliferation of letters, the notation has been changed and formalized here. Thus the CMFs labeled above in Equation (7) as $\bar{a}, \bar{b}, \bar{c}$ have here been renamed to $\bar{a}_1, \bar{a}_2, \bar{a}_3$.

The energy in the spectrum for a physical light is nonnegative at all wavelengths. Given the previous formalisms, however, there is nothing that prevents one from choosing a set of spectra that are not physical (i.e., spectra that take on negative values for some wavelengths). Such spectra are not realizable. Nevertheless, one can calculate the coordinates of lights for such unrealizable primaries. Furthermore, the system will be completely consistent with the color-matching behavior of a human observer in the sense that lights that are metameric for such an observer will still map into the same point in the new space. The value of such an exercise is that only with nonphysical primaries can one generate CMFs that are nonnegative.

One nonnegative set of CMFs in widespread industrial use is the Commission Internationale de l'Éclairage's (CIE) two-degree standard observer. The CMFs are based on the average data collected in the 1920s by Guild (1931) and Wright (1928–29), in separate experiments and with different sets of primaries. When the data from each lab were re-expressed in terms of three fixed

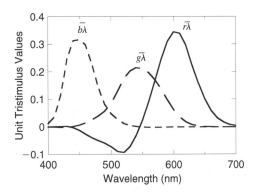

Figure 2.6 The CIE 1931 RGB color-matching functions based on monochromatic primary lights at 700.0 nm, 546.1 nm, and 435.8 nm.

monochromatic stimuli at 700 nm, 546.1 nm, and 435.8 nm, called the *RGB* system (shown in Figure 2.6), they were found to be sufficiently similar to be combined and to serve as an average normal observer. The CIE two-degree observer is a linear transformation of the RGB CMFs called the *XYZ* system. The new nonnegative CMFs, $(\bar{x}(\lambda), \bar{y}(\lambda), \bar{z}(\lambda))$, are shown in Figure 2.7a. These are employed exactly as outlined earlier. The tristimulus values, (X, Y, Z), of a light are calculated from

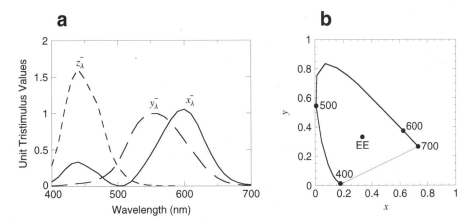

Figure 2.7

NOTE: a) The color-matching functions, $\bar{x}$, $\bar{y}$, and $\bar{z}$ of the CIE 1931 2-degree observer are the tristimulus values for a unit of energy at ech wavelength. b) The CIE xy chromaticity diagram is the modern incarnation of Newton's color circle. It is obtained from the color-matching functions by normalizing their sum to unity and retaining only the first two normalized coordinates (x, y). EE indicates the coordinates of an equal energy spectrum (0.33, 0.33).

its spectral energy distribution as in Equation (7). The chromaticity coordinates, (x, y), are obtained by projecting the tristimulus values in a plane where the sum is equal to one, as in Equation (8). The xy chromaticity diagram is shown in Figure 2.7b.

One particular feature of the XYZ system is that the $\bar{y}(\lambda)$ function was chosen to be equal to the photopic luminosity curve, V_λ, defined by the CIE in 1924. This choice leads to the Y tristimulus value being proportional to luminance. It is common practice to specify a light in terms of its chromaticity coordinates and luminance, (x, y, Y), from which the three tristimulus values are easily recalculated. The 1924 V_λ function, however, was based on data obtained from a variety of techniques, some of which have since been shown to yield a nonadditive sensitivity curve (Wagner & Boynton, 1972). In addition, the CMFs obtained by Wright (1928–29) and Guild (1931) were not measured directly in energy units. Instead, the luminances of the primaries were determined psychophysically, and the data were readjusted to an energy spectrum on the base of the V_λ function. For these reasons, Judd (1951) proposed a modified luminosity curve and recalculated the distribution coefficients. It is generally recognized that the Judd-modified luminosity and CMFs represent a better approximation of an average human observer's color-matching performance and are more widely used in vision research. An even better estimate is given by CMFs measured directly in energy (Stiles & Burch, 1955).

The Receptor Theory of Trichromacy

Trichromacy, the fact that the perceptual equivalence of lights can be encoded in three dimensions, implies that neural information that codes spectral differences is transmitted along three independent paths in the visual system. Interestingly, the first expressions of this idea were not meant to explain trichromacy (Palmer, 1777; Young, 1802), but instead were attempts to account for the variety of color appearances that we can experience. For example, Young suggested that lights of different wavelengths were encoded in three types of receptors, each with spectrally overlapping sensitivities, because it seemed to him unlikely that one could squeeze a large number of receptors—each tuned to a very narrow band of the spectrum—at each spatial position on the retina. He conceived of each receptor as signaling a fundamental hue sensation. The myriad of colors that we perceive corresponds to mixtures of these sensations. Thus, his theory of encoding is also a theory of perception. Later experimentalists who rigorously verified trichromacy (Maxwell, 1856; Helmholtz, 1911/1962) retained this notion of mixtures of sensations, even though there is nothing in the theory of metameric matching that requires it.

With the later discovery of two types of photoreceptors in the eye, rods and cones, and the duplicity theory, which linked the rods with night vision and the cones with day vision, it was hypothesized that three types of cones mediate color matches (Hecht, 1929). It must be emphasized that this is not a sufficient condition for trichromacy. There must also be three independent channels at subsequent stages of neural processing to convey the spectral information encoded in the ensemble response of the cones.

It is supposed that each class of cones obeys the principle of *univariance*. According to this principle, the signals of cone photoreceptors depend on the number of photons absorbed by the photopigment but not on the spectral energy distribution of the incident light. In other words, luminance and spectral differences are confounded in the response of a single class of cones. What differentiates one cone class from another is its spectral sensitivity or efficiency at absorbing photons as a function of wavelength. Let the spectral sensitivity of a cone class be represented as a function of wavelength, $S(\lambda)$. Then, it is supposed that the cone signal is a function of the integrated product of the spectral sensitivity and the spectral energy distribution of the incident light. In the discrete representation that we have been using, the integration becomes a dot product:

$$\rho = f(S_\lambda \cdot E_\lambda), \qquad (12)$$

where E is a spectral distribution, ρ is the cone response, and f is a function that relates quantum catch by the photoreceptor to the signal that it transmits to the next set of cells in the visual pathway.

The spectral differences between two lights are encoded in the differences in the ensemble of activity in the three cone classes. Given three spectral sensitivities, $L(\lambda)$, $M(\lambda)$, and $S(\lambda)$,[5] the matching relation in Equation (5) can be rewritten as three equations relating the quantum catch of each cone class on each side of the bipartite field and in which the quantities of the three primaries, (a, b, c), that are necessary to satisfy the equations play the role of unknowns.

$$
\begin{pmatrix} P_0 \cdot L_\lambda \\ P_0 \cdot M_\lambda \\ P_0 \cdot S_\lambda \end{pmatrix}
$$
$$
= \begin{pmatrix} P_1 \cdot L_\lambda & P_2 \cdot L_\lambda & P_3 \cdot L_\lambda \\ P_1 \cdot M_\lambda & P_2 \cdot M_\lambda & P_3 \cdot M_\lambda \\ P_1 \cdot S_\lambda & P_2 \cdot S_\lambda & P_3 \cdot S_\lambda \end{pmatrix} \begin{pmatrix} a \\ b \\ c \end{pmatrix}.
$$
$$(13)$$

Provided that the matrix on the right of this equation is nonsingular (i.e., the rows are linearly independent), there is a unique solution to the equation corresponding to the required mixture of the three primaries to obtain a metameric match.

---

[5]Notations used to represent the cone spectral sensitivities are arbitrary. However, the use of the letters L, M, and S, signifying long-, middle-, and short-wavelength sensitive cone classes, respectively, has come to be the most widely used in recent years.

The model of color matching can be generalized to any number of photopigments. An eye with n photopigments will require n primaries to obtain equality of the quantum catches in the n photopigments with respect to an arbitrary comparison light. The visual system should not be called n-chromatic, however, unless it can be demonstrated that the minimum dimension of the color space required to account for discriminating spectral differences is also n, in which case it can be supposed that n independent signals are propagated through the visual system. Thus, there exists the theoretical possibility that n photopigments send their signals into m neural pathways. If $n \leq m$, then the system will be n-chromatic. If $n > m$, then a quantum match in the n photopigments will certainly be a metameric match, as the signals from the two fields will be identical at the cone outputs and thus will be identical at every successive stage of processing. The match will not necessarily be unique, however. Additional mixtures of the primaries will render the two fields metameric. In this case, the lights have been equated in the m neural channels and not necessarily for the quantum catch in the n photopigments. If the n signals combine linearly in the m channels, then the system can be modeled as m equations in n unknowns.

This discussion raises the possibility that trichromacy might be explained by alternatives to the receptor hypothesis. Although the receptor hypothesis has historically been the dominant theory of metameric matches, other hypotheses were considered before the rigorous demonstration in the latter 20th century of three classes of cones in the human eye. For example, before the development of microspectrophotometry, it was not known whether the cones might contain mixtures of the photopigments. Three independent mixtures of the photopigments would also yield a trichromacy obeying Grassmann's laws. It is worthwhile, then, to consider some of the evidence supporting the receptor hypothesis as well as some that casts it in doubt.

Persistence of Color Matches

The appearance of a test light will change, in general, if it is placed on a background to which it is not metameric. This implies that the background light differentially adapted some sites controlling the appearance of lights. A pair of metameric lights placed on an adapting field of moderate luminance (insufficient to bleach a significant proportion of the cone photopigments) continues to be metameric even though the appearance of the lights may change. This phenomenon is referred to as the *persistence of color matches* (Wyszecki & Stiles, 1982). It implies that the three mechanisms that are equated in a metameric match have relative spectral sensitivities that are invariant with moderate adaptation. Alternatively, it can be interpreted as implying that the adaptation due to the background occurs at a site in the visual pathways at or beyond the site at which the match is determined. (Additionally, one might infer that the match is determined prior to the site at which the adaptation of appearance occurs.) If the signals from the cone photoreceptors can be differentially light-adapted, then it implies that three classes of photoreceptor mediate trichromacy.

Consider an alternative in which more than three classes of photoreceptors funnel their signals through three channels. If the photoreceptors differentially adapt, then the spectral sensitivities in the three channels will change with the adaptation conditions. If the spectral sensitivities of the sites mediating a metameric match change, $(L_\lambda, M_\lambda, S_\lambda)$ in Equation (13), then the match will change also.

Direct Measurements of Photoreceptors

Although the extraction of the rod photopigment rhodopsin was accomplished with relative ease from the eyes of most animals, similar procedures yielded disappointing results for cone photopigments, probably because there is so little cone pigment present. Only by analysing a large number of cone-dominant chicken retinas could Wald, Brown, and Smith (1955), for example, isolate a cone photopigment, which they named iodopsin.

Rushton (1956) developed the technique of reflection densitometry to demonstrate the presence in vivo of bleachable photopigments in the human eye. The technique works by measuring the change in reflectance of the fundus of the eye before and after a strong bleaching light. With the proper choice of the wavelength and luminance of the bleaching light, one can selectively bleach a particular photopigment with respect to the others. The change in reflectance of the fundus, then, will be related to the spectral characteristics of the bleached pigment. With this technique, Rushton (Baker & Rushton, 1965) was able to demonstrate the presence of two foveal photopigments with different spectral bleaching efficiencies in the long-wavelength portion of the spectrum. Based on their action spectra, these appear to be the photopigments of the M- and L-cones. He was not able to find evidence of the S-cones with this technique, presumably because they comprise only a small percentage of the cones in the eye.

In the 1960s several teams succeeded in measuring the absorption spectra of individual photoreceptors in extracted retinas (Brown & Wald, 1964; Marks, Dobelle, & MacNichol, 1964). The technique, dubbed microspectrophotometry, eventually demonstrated three classes of bleachable cone photopigments in primate and human retinas. The task of measuring the optical characteristics of individual photoreceptors is extremely difficult because of the small size of the photoreceptors with respect to the wavelength range of visible light. Although the wavelength scans of absorption of individual photoreceptors show peaks in different parts of the spectrum, the raw data are extremely noisy and only characterize the absorption curves within less than a factor of 10 with respect to their peaks. Three classes of cone photoreceptors with bleachable pigments peaking in the short-, middle-, and long-wavelength regions of the spectrum have been observed (Bowmaker & Dartnall, 1980).

An accurate characterization of the absorption spectra of individual photoreceptors over an extended wavelength range was finally obtained using suction micropipettes (Baylor, Nunn, & Schnapf, 1984). With this technique, the outer segments of individual photoreceptors are aspirated into the opening of a glass micropipette. The micropipette is filled with a fluid, allowing the measurement of the current flow between the inner and outer segments of the photoreceptor. The experimenter obtains an action spectrum by adjusting the energy of the incident beam to obtain a constant change in the photocurrent. This technique obviates any nonlinear contribution of the receptor response and allows responses to be measured without substantially bleaching away the photopigment. After correcting for the in vivo optical density of the photopigments and preretinal absorption factors caused by the lens and the macular pigment, Schnapf, Kraft, and Baylor (1987) were able to obtain a remarkably good fit between a linear combination of the action spectra obtained using suction micropipettes and human CMFs.

Undoubtedly, one of the key achievements in the last 20 years in the study of human color vision has been the identification and characterization of the genes for the opsins of the human photopigments (Nathans, Piantanida, & Eddy, 1986; Nathans, Thomas, & Hogness, 1986). This advance has permitted enormous progress in our understanding of normal and abnormal individual variations in color vision, of receptoral pathologies, and of the evolution of color vision across species. The rod photopigment opsin gene was localized on chromosome 8, and the S-cone opsin gene was localized on chromosome 7. The L- and M-cone opsin genes were found in tandem array on the X chromosome. Surprisingly, most observers were found to have multiple copies of the M-cone opsin gene, averaging between three and four.

The L- and M-cone opsins are highly similar in their amino acid sequences (differing by only 4%), reflecting their recent evolutionary separation. Their adjacency and similarity have been hypothesized to result occasionally in false pairings during cell division that can yield extra copies, hybrid genes, or loss of one of the genes. The role of the extra copies of the M-opsin gene in normal vision, whether they influence in any manner spectral discrimination or color perception, remains a controversial issue. The possibility of studying the structure of the genotype directly and relating it to phenotypic color discrimination is providing us with a deeper understanding of individual variations in color vision.

Using molecular genetic techniques, Merbs and Nathans (1992a) were able to insert and express individual cone opsin genes in cell culture, thus permitting them to harvest sufficient amounts of cone photopigment to perform the sort of spectral studies that had been performed on isolated rhodopsin. These studies have permitted the isolation of the three classes of photopigment in the human eye, but they also permit the study of the individual differences in absorption characteristics caused by genetic variations due to amino acid substitution or gene hybridization (Merbs & Nathans, 1992b).

Equally spectacular success has been achieved in the application of adaptive optics to imaging of the retina. This technique employs a deformable mirror in the imaging process that introduces distortions that are inverse to those produced by the natural aberrations of the eye. This corrective process allows images of unprecedented quality to be obtained of the retina with a resolution permitting the visualization of individual photoreceptors in vivo (Roorda & Williams, 1999). By obtaining images of an area of the retina before and after exposure of a light of wavelength that selectively bleached the photopigments, Roorda and Williams were able to classify the probable identity of the photopigment in individual photoreceptors. The images demonstrate that the S-cones comprise less than 10% of the cones, that the three cone classes are randomly distributed on the retina, but that the proportion of L- to M-cones is highly variable between individuals, ranging from 4:1 to 1:1.

The randomness of the L- and M-cone arrays might be explained by the fact that the evolutionary event that duplicated the L- and M-opsins on the X-chromosome did not duplicate a region far upstream on the genome that controls their expression, the locus control region (LCR). Thus, there is a single control mechanism for the expression of both L- and M-cone opsins in the photoreceptors. In order for an opsin to be expressed, the LCR must come into contact with the section of the genome that codes for the opsin. The adjacency and similarity between the L- and M-opsin genes may cause the LCR to come into contact with one or the other randomly, resulting in a random expression of the L- and M-opsins from cell to cell.

An interesting consequence of the random arrangement of the cone mosaic is the tendancy, simply on a statistical basis, to find photoreceptors of the same class in small clumps. Consider, for example, the simulated photoreceptor mosaics of Figure 2.8 with cone ratios corresponding to the two extreme cases reported by Roorda and Williams. The presence of such aggregates with identical spectral sensitivity (especially in individuals with unequal numbers of L- and M-cones) poses a number of interesting questions for

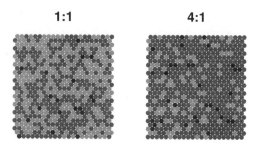

Figure 2.8 Simulated random photoreceptor mosaics resembling those obtained by Roorda & Williams (1999) in vivo in human eyes.
NOTE: The three cone types, L, M, and S, are indicated by colors red, green, and blue, respectively. The proportion of S-cones is 5%. The ratio of L- to M-cones is equal on the left and 4 to 1 on the right. Note that with random placement of cone classes, it is highly probable to find regions populated by single classes of cones. Such regions become larger as the ratio of L- to M-cones deviates from one.

retinal wiring, color discrimination, and color appearance.

Dichromacy

Further evidence for the receptor theory of trichromacy comes from the study of observers with an altered or a reduced capacity for spectral discrimination (i.e., color defective observers). There are many varieties of abnormal color vision, both congenital and acquired secondary to pathology. What interests us here is that there are observers for whom vision is dichromatic; that is, they can match all lights by varying only two primaries. Maxwell (1855) measured the CMFs of some dichromatic observers, verifying that they needed only two primaries to make metameric matches. He believed that they were missing one of the fundamental mechanisms of trichromacy. If trichromacy is mediated by three pathways, then it would seem reasonable to suppose that dichromacy is mediated by two. Consistent with this line of reasoning, there are three well-confirmed varieties of dichromacy, each corresponding to the absence of one class of photoreceptor: protanopia, deuteranopia, and tritanopia, corresponding to the absence of L-, M-, and S-cones, respectively.

Early systematic observations of his own defective color vision led Dalton (1798) to propose that his ocular media abnormally attenuated short-wavelength lights, but postmortem examination of his eyes did not support this hypothesis. Young's three receptor hypothesis (1802) would propose a different explanation in terms of the loss of one of the fundamental sensitivities underlying trichromacy. A recent molecular-genetic analyis of Dalton's ocular remains found no evidence for the presence of M-cone opsin, suggesting that he was indeed a deuteranope (Hunt, Kanwaljit, Bowmaker, & Mollon, 1995). A detailed analysis of the color confusions that he described supported this hypothesis as well.

Under the receptor theory of trichromacy, lights match when they are equated for the three classes of photoreceptors. If one class is missing, then the lights should still be equated for the other two. A test of the idea that dichromats have lost one of the normal pathways conveying spectral information, then, is that their color-matching behavior should be a subset of that of normal trichromats. It is clear, however, that there are significant individual variations in normal and dichromatic color-matching behavior (Alpern, 1979; MacLeod & Webster, 1983; Viénot, 1983), reflecting individual differences in photoreceptor spectral sensitivities, some of which can already be accounted for on the basis of genotypic variations (Neitz & Jacobs, 1986; Sanocki, Shevell, & Winderickx, 1994; Sharpe, Stockman, Jägle, & Nathans, 1999; Winderickx, Lindsey, Sanocki, Teller, & Motulsky, 1992). Thus, the test of confronting an individual dichromatic observer with an individual trichromatic observer's metameric match is probably too stringent. The most that

we can hope for is that average dichromatic CMFs are linearly related to the averages from normal trichromats.

Such a hypothesis is the basis for the psychophysical derivation of the cone spectral sensitivities of normal trichromats based on the color matches of dichromats. In effect, suppose that a dichromat has two cone classes in common with a normal trichromat and is missing the third. Consider a pair of lights that are metameric for the dichromat but not for the normal trichromat. According to the receptor hypothesis, these lights are metameric for the dichromat because they are equated for the quantum catches across his or her two classes of cones. However, these cone classes are the same as two of the classes in the normal trichromat's retina. Thus, the quantum catches are equated for the corresponding cone classes in the trichromat's eye. The basis for the trichromat's discrimination of these two lights, then, is their differential excitation of the third class of cones that is present only in the trichromat's retina. The alternation of these lights, which is silent for the dichromat, is detected by the trichromat because they modulate the quantum catch in one class of cones and not in the other two. These lights are *cone-isolating*. For each class of dichromat, then, we can define, based on the metameric matches, pairs of lights whose alternation modulates the excitation of one of the normal trichromat cone classes in isolation. The vector in a color-matching space connecting the pair of cone-isolating lights defines a cone-isolating direction.

Given cone-isolating directions for each of the three cone classes of a normal trichromat (i.e., based on the metameric matches of each type of dichromat), the spectral sensitivities of the three classes of cones in the normal trichromatic eye can be derived. This is done by calculating the spectral sensitivity directions for each cone class. Given a light,

$E(\lambda)$, with coordinates (e_1, e_2, e_3) in a color matching space and a spectral sensitivity, $S(\lambda)$, then the spectral sensitivity direction, σ, is a direction for which

$$E(\lambda) \cdot S(\lambda) = \sum_i e_i \sigma_i, \qquad (14)$$

where σ_i are the components of σ. In other words, the dot product of the coordinates of a light and the spectral sensitivity direction give the same result as does the dot product of the spectral distribution of the light and the spectral sensitivity as a function of wavelength. The existence of such a direction is guaranteed by a basic theorem of linear algebra (Lang, 1996). The relationship between the cone-isolating directions, c_i, and the spectral sensitivity directions is given by

$$c_i \cdot \sigma_j = \begin{cases} 1 & \text{if } i = j \\ 0 & \text{if } i \neq j. \end{cases} \qquad (15)$$

Recall that the cone-isolating directions cause no modulation of the excitation in two cone classes. Equation (15) defines the spectral sensitivity directions as the duals of the cone-isolating directions. If we let the cone-isolating directions be the columns of a matrix, C, then Equation (15) indicates that the spectral sensitivity directions will be the rows of its inverse, C^{-1}. Given a spectral sensitivity direction, the spectral sensitivity at a given wavelength, λ, is calculated by taking the dot product of the color-matching coordinates for a unit energy at λ with the spectral sensitivity direction. The cone spectral sensitivities derived in this fashion are referred to as König fundamentals, after one of the first investigators to apply this technique (König & Dieterici, 1893).[6]

Refined estimates of dichromatic CMFs and their sources of variation have led to

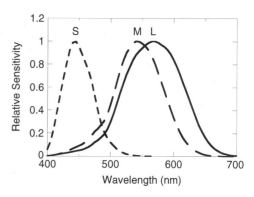

Figure 2.9   The relative spectral sensitivities of the three cone classes, estimated in human eyes (Stockman, MacLeod, & Johnson, 1993).

refined estimates of psychophysically defined cone fundamentals in recent years (Estévez, 1979; Smith & Pokorny, 1975; Stockman, MacLeod, & Johnson, 1993; Vos & Walraven, 1971). But our growing knowledge of the degree of variation of the genetic substrate of the photopigments across individuals indicates the limits of precision on this type of derivation. Cone fundamentals representative of average human behavior remain, however, a valuable datum in theoretical and applied color work.

The most recent König fundamentals (shown in Figure 2.9) are in good agreement with suction electrode recordings from primate retinas, as the previous comparison of Schnapf et al. (1987) would have led one to expect.

Cone Excitation Space

Given the spectral sensitivities of the three classes of cones, $(L(\lambda), M(\lambda), S(\lambda))$, a color space can be defined as in Equation (7) in terms of their excitations, using the cone fundamentals in place of the CMFs $(\bar{a}(\lambda), \bar{b}(\lambda), \bar{c}(\lambda))$. Under the receptor hypothesis of trichromacy, such a space is linearly related to color spaces based on color matching. One of

---

[6]Note that the relation between isolation and spectral sensitivity directions given in Equation (15) is equally valid if applied to linear, postreceptoral mechanisms (Knoblauch, 1995).

its values, however, is that it permits the representation of a light in terms of physiologically significant activity the cone quantum catches. For a light with spectrum, $F(\lambda)$, the cone excitation tristimulus values, (L, M, S), are

$$L = \sum_{\lambda=400}^{700} F_\lambda L_\lambda$$

$$M = \sum_{\lambda=400}^{700} F_\lambda M_\lambda \qquad (16)$$

$$S = \sum_{\lambda=400}^{700} F_\lambda S_\lambda.$$

MacLeod and Boynton (1979) suggested adjusting the heights of the L- and M-cone sensitivities so that they sum to the $V(\lambda)$ curve. With this normalization, the sum of the L and M tristimulus values is proportional to the luminance of the stimulus. They then projected the tristimulus values in a unit luminance plane, giving chromaticity coordinates, (l, m, s), related to cone excitation:

$$l = \frac{L}{L + M}$$

$$m = \frac{M}{L + M} = 1 - l \qquad (17)$$

$$s = \frac{S}{L + M}.$$

The associated chromaticity diagram that has gained widespread acceptance is in the (l, s) plane and is shown in Figure 2.10. Along the axis of abscissae, increases in L-cone excitation are accompanied by decreases in M-cone excitation (and vice versa), whereas S-cone excitation is fixed. Along the axis of ordinates, L and M are fixed, and only S-cone excitation varies.

If the luminance, $L + M$, is added as a third axis, the space is sometimes referred to as *cardinal directions space* and provides an approximate representation of the coding of spectral differences in cells from the retinal

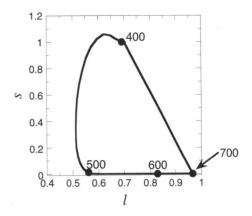

Figure 2.10 The MacLeod-Boynton cone excitation diagram is a chromaticity diagram with axes based on the distribution of activity of the three classes of cone photoreceptors.

output to the cortical input. Supposing the l axis to be orthogonal to the luminance axis, its spectral sensitivity can be shown to be related to the difference of L- and M-cone signals. Just as luminance is constant in the (l, s)-plane, the s-axis spectral sensitivity can be attributed to a mechanism with spectral sensitivity related to the difference of S-cone and luminance signals. These three spectral sensitivities, $(L + M, L - M, S - (L + M))$, bear a striking resemblance to the average spectral sensitivities of the M, P, and K streams, respectively, identified in the retino-geniculate pathway (Derrington, Krauskopf, & Lennie, 1984).

Is Trichromacy a Receptoral Limit?

If the data, just outlined, from numerous approaches overwhelmingly support the presence of three classes of cone photoreceptors in the normal human retina, several arguments question whether the trichromatic limit on human spectral discrimination is imposed at the photoreceptor level. In the three examples that follow, the argument turns around situations in which more than three spectral sensitivities mediate discrimination (or are thought to) and spectral discrimination remains trichromatic.

Variations in Spectral Sensitivity across the Retina

The CMFs vary as a function of retinal eccentricity (Moreland, 1972), reflecting changes in spectral sensitivity of the cones with retinal position as measured at the cornea. These changes can be attributed to at least two factors. First, the macular pigment is inhomogeneously distributed across the retina: It is densest in the fovea and falls to negligible density by 4 deg to 5 deg. This pigment absorbs light differentially in the wavelength band between 400 nm and 540 nm. Thus, the spectra of lights imaged on the visual periphery will differ from those in the fovea.

The differential transmission of light by the macular pigment can be visualized by flickering a large (about 10 deg) field between two wavelengths that are differentially absorbed by the macular pigment (e.g., 460 nm at its peak and 580 nm on one of its tails). Typically, the observer sees a darker region in the center of the field, which moves with the observer's fixation (thus indicating the retinal origin of the phenomenon). This entoptic phenomenon is called Maxwell's spot.

Under most circumstances, however, this inhomogeneity in the proximal stimulus is not visible. If the flicker is stopped, the darker region in the center quickly fades, and the field appears of uniform color again. The differences in the spectral distribution over the retina due to macular pigment filtering could be exploited by the visual system to improve its wavelength discrimination. However, an adaptive process appears to attenuate these differences rapidly, when the observer perceives the stimulus as a single object (e.g., a single field).

A second source of the differences in spectral sensitivity between the fovea and the periphery is due to *self-screening* by the photopigments. Light absorption in photoreceptors is assumed to obey approximately the Beer-Lambert law that relates the fraction of photons absorbed in a medium, $A(\lambda)$, to the concentration of absorbing molecules and to the path length through the medium traversed by the beam of light:

$$A_\lambda = 1 - e^{-\alpha_\lambda c l}, \tag{18}$$

where α is the extinction coefficient that has units of area (cm^2), c is the concentration (molecules/cm^3), and l is the path length (in cm) traversed by the light beam. The argument of the exponential, $\alpha_\lambda c l$, is the napirian optical density and is dimensionless. The more usual decadic form is obtained by dividing the argument by $\ln(10) \approx 2.3$.

Of interest is that the photopigment bearing outer segments of the cones become progressively shorter from the fovea to the periphery. By Equation (18), the reduced path length through the outer segment lowers the optical density of the photopigment. If the photopigment is present in sufficiently high optical density in the fovea (where the cone outer segments are longest), then the exponential form of the relation between the proportion photons absorbed and optical density means that as the optical density decreases, $A(\lambda)$ diminishes less rapidly for wavelengths near the peak of the spectral sensitivity than for those at the tails. The consequence is that the spectral sensitivity of cones in the visual periphery is expected to be narrower than those in the fovea. Changes in color-matching behavior between the fovea and the periphery under conditions in which macular pigment absorption can be ignored (e.g., for wavelengths greater than 540 nm) are consistent with this model (Pokorny, Smith, & Starr, 1976; Viénot, 1983).

Thus, although there are three families of cones, the spectral sensitivity of each changes systematically as a function of eccentricity.

In principle, these variations could aid and increase the dimensionality of color discrimination. That they do not—at least, there is no evidence that they do—suggests that either the variations are not sufficiently large compared with the variability of color-matching behavior or that the potential increased dimensionality due to the eccentricity differences is lost because there are only three subsequent channels for processing the information.

Mesopic Vision

There exists a fourth photopigment in the eye, the rhodopsin of rods. Rods and cones, however, are specialized to operate under different conditions: cones during the day, rods at night. Nevertheless, they function together over the extended range of mesopic vision. Rod influences on cone function and color perception are well documented (Buck, 2001; Stabell & Stabell, 1973). It is significant, however, that color matching remains trichromatic under mesopic conditions (Trezona, 1974, 1987). Observers can obtain metameric matches by adjusting only three primaries under mesopic conditions. These matches are not necessarily equated for the quantum catch in the photoreceptors. The observer adjusts three lights to obtain criterion signals from four classes of photoreceptors. In general, the matches are not additive and do not obey the persistence property; that is, they are upset by the presence of a weak adaptation field. These results support the hypothesis that mesopic color matches with three primaries are constrained by equating three neural signals subsequent to the photoreceptor outputs. Quantum matches that obey additivity and persistence can be obtained only by allowing the observer to perform four primary matches (Trezona, 1974, 1987).

Heterozygous Color Vision

As noted earlier, the genes for the L- and M-cone opsins are adjacent on the X chro-

mosome. Their similarity and proximity are thought to be responsible for the significant variability from individual to individual in the number of these genes and in the composition of their nucleotide base sequences. It seems reasonable to believe that this heterogeneity will eventually explain in detail the significant individual variability in spectral discrimination linked with the L- and M-cone photopigments. The fact that these genes are on the X chromosome explains why the color defects associated with the L- and M-cones are much more prevalent among males. Males have only a single X chromosome, so if they inherit a color vision defect associated with the L/M gene array, it is expressed. On the other hand, females inherit two X chromosomes, one from each parent. The probability of inheriting a color-defective gene array from both parents is approximately the square of the probability of inheriting from one. Thus, the presence of a normal L/M gene array on at least one X chromosome appears to be sufficient to guarantee normal color vision.

Females carriers of an L/M color-defective gene array, or heterozygotes, can sometimes be detected via psychophysical tests. For example, protanopes classically show a loss of luminosity in the long wavelengths owing to the absence of the L-cones. Female carriers of protan defects often display a luminosity curve of sensitivity that is intermediate between the normal and protanopic at long wavelengths. This condition is referred to as Schmidt's sign (Schmidt, 1955).

The presence of Schmidt's sign suggests that the defective gene array is expressed, at least to some extent. The leading hypothesis is that of Lyon (1972), according to which one of the X chromosomes in females is expressed and the other is inactivated in each cell. The inactivation occurs randomly from cell to cell at some time during embryogenesis. The consequence of random inactivation for females who are heterozygous for

X-chromosome-linked traits is that these traits are expressed differentially from cell to cell. Thus, according to this hypothesis, a female carrier of a color-defective L/M gene array can express normal L- and M-opsin genes as well as hybrid ones. Thus, such individuals could have more than three cone photopigments expressed in their retinas.

The color matches of some heterozygous carriers of X-chromosome-linked color deficiencies vary under mild chromatic adaptation (i.e., a failure of persistence; Nagy, MacLeod, Heyemann, & Eisner, 1981). This result is consistent with the idea that these observers code the spectral information in a greater number of adaptable channels than the number of channels that transmit the information centrally. On the other hand, Jordan and Mollon (1993) performed an extensive evaluation of the spectral discrimination of heterozygous females. In a sample of 31 observers, only one made matches consistent with having four photopigments and four channels along which to transmit the outputs of the photoreceptors.

The cases just described suggest that even when more than three classes of spectral sensitivity are present in the retina, only three channels of information are supported in central transmission. Although the receptor hypothesis remains the dominant model to explain trichromacy, the previous discussion suggests several ways in which it may represent only an approximation and indicate some directions currently under investigation to better understand its nuances.

COLOR APPEARANCE

One of the great misunderstandings in the study of color is the belief that the color- (or metameric-) matching experiment provides a measure of a light's color. As stated in the previous section, color matching provides a ba-

sis for specifying what lights look alike, not, however, what they look like.

Consider, for example, a pair of metameric lights surrounded by a field that appears to be of a different color, say red. The pair of lights will still be metameric; they will be represented by the same coordinates in a color-matching space. Indeed, they have not changed physically in the presence of a large surrounding field. Nevertheless, the presence of a surrounding field of a different color is likely to change their appearance via the phenomenon of simultaneous contrast. A similar argument can be advanced using a mild adaptation stimulus instead of a surround field. Adaptation to a colored light that does not significantly bleach the photopigments (to avoid changing the spectral sensitivity by reducing the photopigment concentration; see Equation [18]) will cause a colored afterimage. A pair of metameric lights presented on the adapted region will still be metameric (the persistence of color matches), but their appearance is unlikely to be the same as when the same lights are presented to the unadapted retina, the phenomenon of successive contrast. Thus, the tristimulus values of a light cannot be taken to represent the appearance of the light. What is the relation, then, of the ensemble of cone responses and the perceived color of a light?

Young's Trichromatic Theory

The earliest theory, and the one that dominated for nearly 150 years, was that proposed by Young (1802). He hypothesized that light excited three types of processes in the retina, each with a different but broadband relative sensitivity. This hypothesis is sufficient to account for trichromacy, but he went on. To explain the variety of hues seen across the spectrum, he supposed that excitation of each of these processes generated a fundamental sensation: red, green, and blue (although he modified the latter to violet in 1807). Because the sensitivities of the three processes overlapped, no light could activate one of these processes in isolation. The appearance of a light was determined by the mixing of these fundamental sensations. Thus, a light appears bluish-green because it activates principally the green and blue sensations associated with the excitation of two of the processes. This idea was later adopted by Helmholtz and Maxwell, and the three processes were eventually associated with the three classes of cone photoreceptors (Hecht, 1929).

In the simplest version of this theory, color is determined at each point in the retina by the distribution of activity across the three cones. Thus, in this theory color is coded locally. Afterimage phenomena were treated by considering relative sensitivity changes in the three classes of cones. Simultaneous contrast phenomena required spatial interaction between neighboring retinal regions, but these could still be handled by sensitivity changes within cone classes.

On close examination, however, this theory fails to explain many important details of hue perception. First, given that the fundamental sensations generated by the cones are red, green, and blue, there is no way to account for the appearance of yellow in the spectrum. Thus, the theory does not explain the basic data for which it was proposed. Second, supposing that one class of cones is absent in dichromacy, one would expect that one fundamental sensation would be lost as well. Protanopes and deuteranopes were thought to have lost the red and green sensations, respectively. One would then predict that protanopes would describe hues in terms of blue and green and deuteranopes in terms of blue and red. However, both classes of dichromats describe the hues of the spectrum in terms of blue and yellow (Dalton, 1798; Hurvich, 1972; Knoblauch, Sirovich, & Wooten, 1985; Pole, 1893). Tritanopes, who under this hypothesis would have lost the blue sensation, describe the spectrum as blue and red (Alpern, Kitahara, & Krantz, 1983).

Hering's Opponent-Colors Theory

Whereas Young's theory attempted to explain color perception in terms of the activity of coding mechanisms, Hering (1920/1964) sought to explain the neural mechanisms mediating color perception by analyzing the perceptual organization of color.

Initially, he noted that six hues appear to be psychologically fundamental, in the sense that they cannot be decomposed perceptually into finer components. These are white, black, yellow, blue, red, and green. Orange, for example, is not fundamental because it can be decomposed perceptually into reddish and yellowish components. Violet and purple can be decomposed into reddish and bluish components. What was novel in Hering's approach was the recognition that for several classes of phenomena, these six hues could be regrouped as three pairs (red-green, yellow-blue, white-black), where each member of a pair was in an antagonistic relationship with the other member of the pair. For example, whereas there are colors that are reddish-yellow, reddish-blue, greenish-yellow, and greenish-blue, there are no colors that are reddish-green or yellowish-blue. It would appear that the presence of one component in a hue excludes the other.

The components of these pairs are linked as well in several perceptual phenomena. In simultaneous contrast, a reddish (yellowish or whitish) surround induces a greenish (bluish or blackish) hue in the center and vice versa. In successive contrast, after adapting to a field that is the color of one member of one of the three pairs, upon staring at a white field, one sees an afterimage that is the color of the other member. With respect to normal vision, the hues described in the spectrum by protanopes and deuteranopes are consistent with the loss of the perception of red and green (but refer to the case of the tritanope, discussed earlier, for a problem with this argument).

These observations and others contribute to the idea that color perception is organized around three bipolar dimensions: red-green, yellow-blue, and white-black. The signal along one of these dimensions can take on a sign that corresponds to one of the pairs but not both at the same time, as in positiveness and negativeness. Thus, a color can be reddish (yellowish) or greenish (bluish), but not both. The color of any light can be described with respect to its activation of the three dimensions. Notice that because it postulates three dimensions, the theory is consistent with human color discrimination.

In Hering's conception, opponency was not just between colors but also between events separated in space and over time. Such interactions were postulated to be the basis for simultaneous and successive contrast phenomena. The global nature of the interactions in the determination of color in this theory is in contrast to the local coding in Young's theory.

The subjective nature of the opponent colors theory and the lack of a quantitative database, like the CMFs, probably initially hindered its widespread acceptance, even if it provided a more accurate description of the perception of color than did Young's theory. Additionally, when first proposed, the phenomenon of inhibition in the nervous system was unknown. Thus, there was no physiological basis to support the antagonistic interactions hypothesized by Hering (Hurvich, 1969).

Hue Cancellation

Suppose that a field of monochromatic light is presented on a dark background. As the wavelength is changed (e.g., from long to short-wavelengths), the hue will change in a systematic fashion. At the long-wavelength end of the spectrum, the hue is typically described by normal trichromats as predominately red and slightly yellowish. As the wavelength is decreased, the yellowish component progressively increases its relative contribution to the hue of the field. At a certain wavelength, there is a transition at which the hue switches from appearing reddish-yellow to greenish-yellow. Normal trichromats typically observe this transition somewhere between 570 nm and 590 nm. The wavelength at this point of transition appears as a yellow that is neither reddish nor greenish, or a unique yellow. The residual hue of this wavelength, however, is of less importance than the fact that it represents a criterion point, in effect a zero-crossing or equilibrium point, of the red-green system. As with other criterion points of psychophysical functions, one can study the stimulus conditions that lead to this perceptual criterion to probe the characteristics of the underlying response function.

There is a second red-green spectral equilibrium point around 470 nm that appears unique blue. In a similar fashion, there is a yellow-blue spectral equilibrium point typically found between 495 nm and 520 nm that is a green that is neither yellowish nor bluish, or unique green. The yellow-blue equilibrium that appears red is not spectral but requires the mixture of short-wavelength lights that appear bluish-red with long-wavelength lights that appear yellowish-red. Considering mixtures of lights in general, a set of lights that are in equilibrium for the red-green system (unique yellow, blue, and white) and similarly for the yellow-blue system (unique red, green, and white) can be determined. The possibility of evaluating the properties of each of these sets of equilibrium lights for testing the response functions underlying red-green and yellow-blue perception, respectively, was appreciated early on (Purdy, 1931; Schrödinger, 1920/1994).

The first systematic and extensive attempt at exploiting equilibrium hue judgments for putting the opponent-colors theory on a quantitative basis can be found in a series of papers by Hurvich and Jameson (1955, 1957; Jameson & Hurvich, 1955, 1956), who used the hue cancellation technique. The idea of hue cancellation is to measure the strength of one hue component of a light in terms of the energy required of a second light to bring the mixture of the two to a state of hue equilibrium (either red-green or yellow-blue). For example, for lights of wavelength longer than that appearing unique yellow, the energy is determined of a greenish light necessary to just cancel the redness. This same greenish standard can be used to evaluate the redness at short wavelengths. A reddish standard light is used to cancel the greenness of wavelengths between spectral unique blue and yellow. Similarly, bluish and yellowish standard lights are used to cancel the yellow and blue components, respectively, at wavelengths longer and shorter, respectively, than that appearing unique green. To take an example, if a light has a large component of red, then it will require a greater energy of the greenish standard for the mixture to appear neither red nor green. Varying the wavelength, spectral curves for each hue component can be determined. In order to equate the red (yellow) and green (blue) curves, the curves are typically adjusted by a factor determined by the relative amounts of the two canceling standards in a mixture with each other to obtain an equilibrium hue for the appropriate system. One observer's data are shown in Figure 2.11.

The hue cancellation functions indicate the variation of the four chromatic hues across the spectrum. Hurvich and Jameson (1957) showed how these data could be used to account for a wide range of basic color vision data, including wavelength discrimination, colorimetric purity discrimination, hue perception, saturation perception, color defi-

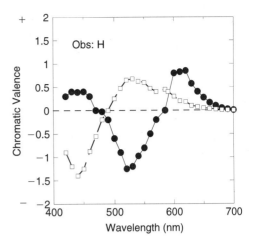

Figure 2.11 Red-green (filled circles) and yellow-blue (unfilled squares) hue cancellation data obtained from one observer by Jameson & Hurvich (1955) for an approximately 1-deg field in a 37-deg adapting surround, adjusted in preliminary experiments to be chromatically neutral.

NOTE: The ordinate indicates the magnitude of a monochromatic light necessary to cancel the hue of one chromatic component at each wavelength. For example, positive red-green values indicate the amount of a greenish light necessary to cancel the reddish component of the stimulus. The magnitude of the negative values indicates the amount of a reddish light necessary to cancel the greenish component of the stimulus. The data were adjusted as if each light were presented at equal energy and as if the cancellation judgments obeyed scalar invariance.

SOURCE: Data are replotted from Jameson & Hurvich (1955).

ciency, spatial and temporal interactions, and so on. For example, they proposed the calculation of hue and saturation coefficients, hc and sc, respectively, based on the hue cancellation functions, to provide an index of the color appearance of a light:

$$hc = \frac{|(r-g)_\lambda|}{|(r-g)_\lambda| + |(y-b)_\lambda|}$$

$$sc = \frac{|(r-g)_\lambda| + |(y-b)_\lambda|}{|(r-g)_\lambda| + |(y-b)_\lambda| + |(w-bk)_\lambda|},$$

(19)

where $(r - g)$ and $(y - b)$ are obtained from the hue cancellation functions and $w - bk$ is an index of activity of the white-black system based on brightness judgments. If the hue of a light can be described in terms of responses in red-green and yellow-blue systems, then the hue coefficient indicates the proportion of redness (greenness) with respect to the total hue. The proportion of yellowness (blueness) is one minus this value. Similarly, the saturation coefficient measures the proportion of chromatic hue with respect to chromatic and achromatic aspects of the appearance. If the hue cancellation functions and a white-black function were taken as a set of CMFs, then the *hc* and *sc* would serve as chromaticity coordinates with a *psychological* significance. In fact, these indexes provide a reasonable description of human perceptual judgments of hue and saturation of spectral lights (Hurvich & Jameson, 1957; Werner & Wooten, 1979).

Zone Models

Opponent-colors theory is perfectly consistent with trichromacy in that three channels carry spectral characteristics of the stimulus. To integrate the ideas of spectral in-teraction implied by this theory with the notion of broadly overlapping sensors proposed by Young (1802), several investigators proposed multiple-stage models in which a first stage was mediated by the absorption of light in photoreceptors and subsequent stages included excitatory and inhibitory interactions among the photoreceptor outputs (Guth, Massof, & Benzschawel, 1980; Hurvich & Jameson, 1955; Ingling, 1977; Vos & Walraven, 1972). These models are sometimes referred to as zone models to indicate that processing occurs in successive zones, an initial spectral coding independently within each cone class followed by a comparison of the cone outputs.

The zone models show how cone signals might interact locally to produce the outputs of opponent mechanisms. The global interactions postulated in opponent-colors theory are not necessarily a part of such models (unless specifically included). As such, a specific relation is implicit between local cone excitation and the hue perceived. For example, in the model in Figure 2.12, *L*-cone signals contribute to the red side of the red-green system and to the yellow side of the yellow-blue system. Thus, it would be predicted that

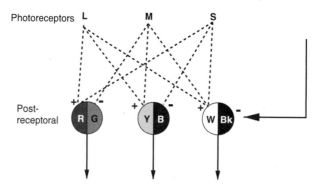

Figure 2.12 A zone model of the mapping of cone photoreceptor outputs, L, M, and S, onto postre-ceptoral opponent-colors channels, r-g, y-b, and w-bk.
NOTE: Each cone class distributes its singals among the three opponent-colors channels. The net activity at the opponent level determines the resulting hue of the stimulus. In this scheme, based on a model of Hurvich & Jameson (1957), L-cones contribute to redness, yellowness, and whiteness. Note that the w-bk system is not spectrally opponent. Its opponency arises from spatial and temporal interactions, indicated by the black arrow to the right.

increasing excitation of *L*-cones would increase the redness and the yellowness of the stimulus. Instead of *L*-cones signaling redness as Young's theory hypothesized, they signal redness and yellowness. Similary, *M*-cones signal greenness and yellowness, and *S*-cones signal reddness and blueness. As long as each cone class contributes to only one side of each opponent mechanism, there will be a fundamental sensation associated with its activity, if stimulated in isolation.

Tests for Linearity

Can the hue cancellation functions be used to calculate cancellation values for lights of arbitrary spectral composition, just as the CMFs can predict matches for arbitrary lights? The value of such calculations, in the case of hue cancellation, would be that the coordinates would specify not only the sets of lights that are of equivalent appearance but also (via the hue and saturation coefficients) their appearance. A minimum requirement for a formalism equivalent to that used for metameric matching is that the hue cancellation functions be a linear combination of the CMFs. Such a relation would imply a model in which the cone signals combined linearly within each opponent-colors channel. Early analyses of equilibrium hues, in fact, assumed linearity (Judd, 1949; Hurvich & Jameson, 1951, 1955; Schrödinger, 1920/1994). If linearity was valid, one could employ the cancellation functions as distribution functions (as in Equation [7]) and calculate red-green and yellow-blue tristimulus values. The white-black values might be based on luminance or brightness judgments. The hue and saturation coefficients of Equation (19) would then yield suitable chromaticity coordinates for representing lights in a color diagram.

Krantz (1975b) proposed a generalization of Grassmann's laws to test the linearity of hue cancellation. These amount to tests of closure within each set of equilibrium lights. For example, two lights in red-green equilib-rium mixed together must give a light that is also in red-green equilibrium. If, for example, adding a unique yellow to a unique blue light produces a greenish or reddish light, then the set of lights in red-green equilibrium is not closed. Formally, the closure of a set of equilibrium lights can be expressed in terms of two axioms:

Suppose a set of lights $\{e\}$ in equilibrium for one color-opponent system.

1) *Scalar Invariance:* Given light P_1 and real number a, if

$$P_1 \in \{e\}$$

then

$$a * P_1 \in \{e\}$$

2) *Additivity:* Given lights P_1, P_2, if

$$P_1 \quad \text{and} \quad P_2 \in \{e\}$$

then

$$P_1 \oplus P_2 \in \{e\}.$$

Scalar invariance implies that the spectral unique hues will be at the same wavelengths independent of the radiance of the field. Most early results concern this axiom. For example, several studies found invariance of the spectral unique hues with intensity (Hurvich & Jameson, 1951; Purdy, 1931). Either the scalar invariance of unique red in early studies was not examined (Hurvich & Jameson, 1951), or the results indicated noninvariance when evaluated (Purdy, 1931). The additivity axiom implies that the locus of equilibrium hues will lie on a straight line in a chromaticity space. An early study suggested that the unique green and unique red sections of the yellow-blue equilibrium locus may not be collinear (Valberg, 1971). More generally, the ensemble of equilibrium lights for an opponent-colors system will fall on a surface in a three-dimensional color space. If the laws of linearity are upheld, this surface will be a plane.

Following Krantz's (1975b) explicit formulation of the laws of linearity for hue cancellation, several studies converged in finding that red-green hue equilibria obeyed linearity but that yellow-blue ones did not (Ayama & Ikeda, 1989; Elzinga & De Weert, 1984; Larimer, Krantz, & Cicerone, 1974, 1975; Nagy, 1979; Werner & Wooten, 1979). Closer examination, however, revealed nonlinearities in red-green judgments as well (Ayama, Ikeda, & Nakatsue, 1985; Burns, Elsner, Pokorny, & Smith, 1984). Of course, the nonlinearity in the hue cancellation judgments invalidates the application of the formalism of Equation (7) for predicting an arbitrary light's cancellation values and implies a nonlinear relation between cone signals and hue cancellation. Complicating the situation, most investigators have remarked significant individual differences in the degree of yellow-blue nonlinearity (Larimer et al., 1975; Werner & Wooten, 1979).

Why Not an Orange-Blue Opponent Mechanism?

There has been frequent confusion between the notions of hue cancellation and complementarity of lights (Saunders & van Brakel, 1997). Complementary lights arise in the context of metameric matching. As Newton observed for sunlight, but more generally for broadband lights, there exist pairs of monochromatic lights whose mixture yields a metameric match. The fact that broadband lights are usually desaturated in appearance and that the monochromatic lights are highly saturated has led some to think of this as akin to hue cancellation. Recall, however, that in the case of metameric matches, the color appearance of the fields enters the judgment only in as much as the two fields are identical or not. On the other hand, in hue cancellation there is no comparison field. The reference for judgment is subjective: a light that appears

neither red (yellow) nor green (blue) for the observer. The judgment itself entails that the observer employ a perceptual criterion related to hue and not identity or nonidentity. Recall, as well, that the endpoints of a hue cancellation judgment are not identical. For example, for red-green equilibrium judgments the residual hue of the lights will be either blue, yellow, or white.

Thus, a second question evoked is why red-green and yellow-blue? Why not orange-blue? This question is more difficult to answer in a fashion that might satisfy psychophysical purists who would require an objective way to verify that a light really is neither reddish nor greenish when the observer states that it is. The fundamental opponent colors were chosen because they seem to be psychologically elementary, which cannot be said to be so for orange, a yellowish-red. Observers find the task of adjusting lights to a state of hue equilibrium relatively easy; the endpoint is well defined. Additionally, the distribution of such lights in color space falls along a surface as one would predict for a visual mechanism (Chichilnisky & Wandell, 1999).

What would be the endpoint for a judgment of neither orangish nor bluish? Orangish and bluish lights are complementary for a light that is perceptually white under some circumstances and, thus, would give an equilibrium locus that corresponds to a point in color space. The lights that are yellowish and greenish are neither orangish nor bluish, but these would fill a *region* of color space. It is not at all clear how one would model a visual mechanism with these characteristics.

Philosophical debates over the validity of the hue cancellation will probably continue. Nevertheless, it can be said that although hue cancellation is based on an intrinsically psychological criterion and many questions concerning its physiological substrate remain unanswered, it is one of the few tasks that directly taps perceptual aspects of color.

CONCLUSION

As indicated in the opening, it is impossible to do justice to all aspects of a vast topic such as color vision in the space allotted in a chapter. Several important areas that are currently the focus of intense research activity have been barely touched upon: chromatic adaptation and discrimination, models of discrimination and perception based on subcortical and cortical physiology, the interaction of local and global factors in color perception, color constancy, and scaling and linguistic constraints on color. I have done my best to provide the reader with a basis for entry into this field and to the ideas, approaches, and data that are a prerequisite to intelligent discussion and further progress.

REFERENCES

Alpern, M. (1979). Variation in the visual pigments of human dichromats and normal human trichromats. In N. R. C. Committee on Vision (Ed.), *Frontiers of visual science: Proceedings of the 1985 symposium* (pp. 169–193). Washington, DC: National Academy Press.

Alpern, M., Kitahara, K., & Krantz, D. H. (1983). Perception of colour in unilateral tritanopia. *Journal of Physiology, 335,* 683–697.

Ayama, M., & Ikeda, M. (1989). Additivity of yellow chromatic valence. *Vision Research, 26,* 763–769.

Ayama, M., Ikeda, M., & Nakatsue, T. (1985). Additivity of red chromatic valence. *Vision Research, 25,* 1885–1891.

Baker, H. D. & Rushton, W. A. H. (1965). The red-sensitive pigment in normal cones. *Journal of Physiology, 176,* 56–72.

Baylor, D. A., Nunn, B. J., & Schnapf, J. L. (1984). The photocurrent, noise and spectral sensitivity of rods of the monkey, *Macaca fascicularis. Journal of Physiology, 357,* 557–607.

Bloj, M. G., Kersten, D., & Hurlbert, A. C. (1999). Perception of three-dimensional shape influences colour perception through mutual illumination. *Nature, 402,* 877–879.

Blough, D. S., & Yager, D. (1972). Visual psychophysics in animals. In D. Jameson & L. M. Hurvich (Eds.), *Handbook of sensory physiology: Vol. 7. Visual psychophysics* (pp. 732–763). Berlin: Springer.

Bowmaker, J. K., & Dartnall, H. J. A. (1980). Visual pigments of rods and cones in a human retina. *Journal of Physiology, 298,* 501–511.

Brindley, G. S. (1953). The effects on colour vision of adaptation to very bright lights. *Journal of Physiology, 122,* 332.

Brindley, G. S. (1955). The site of electrical excitation of the human eye. *Journal of Physiology, 127,* 189–200.

Brindley, G. S. (1966). The deformation phosphene and the tunnelling of light into rods and cones. *Journal of Physiology, 188,* 24P–25P.

Brindley, G. S., & Lewin, W. D. (1968). The sensations produced by electrical stimulation of the visual cortex. *Journal of Physiology, 196,* 479–493.

Brown, P. K., & Wald, G. (1964). Visual pigments in single rods and cones of the human retina. *Science, 144,* 45–51.

Buck, S. L. (2001). What is the hue of rod vision? *Color Research and Application, Supplement volume, 26,* 57–59.

Burns, S. A., Elsner, A. E., Pokorny, J., & Smith, V. C. (1984). The Abney effect: Chromaticity coordinates of unique and other constant hues. *Vision Research, 24,* 475–490.

Chichilnisky, E. J., & Wandell, B. A. (1999). Trichromatic opponent color classification. *Vision Research, 39,* 3444–3458.

Dalton, J. (1798). Extraordinary facts relating to the vision of colours. *Memoires of the Literary and Philosophical Society of Manchester, 5,* 28–45.

Dartnall, H. J. A. (1953). The interpretation of spectral sensitivity curves. *British Medical Bulletin, 9,* 24–30.

Derrington, A. M., Krauskopf, J., & Lennie, P. (1984). Chromatic mechanisms in lateral geniculate nucleus of macaque. *Journal of Physiology, 357,* 241–265.

D'Esposito, M., Detre, J. A., Aguire, G. K., Alsop, D. C., Tippett, L. J., & Farah, M. J. (1997). A functional MRI study of mental image generation. *Neuropsychologia, 35,* 725–730.

Elzinga, C. H., & de Weert, C. M. M. (1984). Nonlinear codes for the yellow/blue mechanism. *Vision Research, 24,* 911–922.

Estévez, O. (1979). *On the fundamental database of normal and dichromatic color vision.* Unpublished doctoral dissertation, Amsterdam University.

Grassmann, H. (1853). Zur Theorie der Farbenmischung. *Poggendorf's Annalen der Phyzik, Leipzig, 89,* 69–84.

Guild, J. (1931). The colorimetric properties of the spectrum. *Philosophical Transactions of the Optical Society (London), A, 230,* 149–187.

Guth, S. L., Massof, R. W., & Benzschawel, T. (1980). Vector model for normal and dichromatic vision. *Journal of the Optical Society of America, 70,* 197–212.

Hecht, S. (1929) Vision: II. The nature of the photoreceptor process. In C. Murchison (Ed.), *The foundations of experimental psychology* (pp. 216–272). Worcester, England: Clark University Press.

Helmholtz, H. v. (1962). *Handbuch der Physiologischen Optik* (Vol. 2; J. P. C. Southall, Ed.) New York: Dover. (Original work published 1911)

Hering, E. (1964). *Outlines of a theory of the light sense* (L. M. Hurvich & D. Jameson, Trans.). Cambridge: Harvard University Press. (Original work published 1920)

Hunt, D. M., Kanwaljit, S. D., Bowmaker, J. K., & Mollon, J. D. (1995). The chemistry of John Dalton's color blindness. *Science, 267,* 984–988.

Hurvich, L. M. (1969). Hering and the scientific establishment. *American Psychologist, 24,* 497–514.

Hurvich, L. M. (1972). Color vision deficiencies. In D. Jameson & L. M. Hurvich (Eds.), *Handbook of sensory physiology: Vol. 7. Visual psychophysics* (pp. 582–624). Berlin: Springer.

Hurvich, L. M., & Jameson, D. (1951). The binocular fusion of yellow in relation to color theories. *Science, 114,* 199–202.

Hurvich, L. M., & Jameson, D. (1955). Some quantitative aspects of an opponent-colors theory. II: Brightness, saturation and hue in normal and dichromatic vision. *Journal of the Optical Society of America, 45,* 602–616.

Hurvich, L. M., & Jameson, D. (1957). An opponent-process theory of color vision. *Psychological Review, 64,* 384–404.

Ingling, C. R. (1977). The spectral sensitivity of the opponent-color channels. *Vision Research, 17,* 1083–1089.

Jameson, D., & Hurvich, L. M. (1955). Some quantitative aspects of an opponent-colors theory: I. Chromatic responses and spectral saturation. *Journal of the Optical Society of America, 45,* 546–552.

Jameson, D., & Hurvich, L. M. (1956). Theoretical analysis of anomalous trichromatic vision. *Journal of the Optical Society of America, 46,* 1075–1089.

Jordan, G., & Mollon, J. D. (1993). A study of women heterozygous for colour deficiencies. *Vision Research, 33,* 1495–1508.

Judd, D. B. (1949). Response functions for types of color vision according to the Müller theory. *Journal of Research of the National Bureau of Standards, 42,* 1–16.

Judd, D. B. (1951). Report of U.S. Secretariat, Committee on Colorimetry and Artificial Daylight. *Proceedings of the CIE 1,* part 7, p. 11 (Stockholm). Paris: Bureau Central CIE.

Judd, D. B., MacAdam, D. L., & Wyszecki, G. W. (1964). Spectral distribution of typical daylight as a function of correlated color temperature. *Journal of the Optical Society of America, 54,* 1031–1040.

Knoblauch, K. (1995). Dual bases in dichromatic color space. In B. Drum (Ed.), *Colour vision deficiencies* (Vol. 12, 165–177). Dordrecht, Netherlands: Kluwer.

Knoblauch, K., Sirovich, L., & Wooten, B. R. (1985). Linearity of hue cancellation in sex-linked dichromacy. *Journal of the Optical Society of America A, 2,* 136–146.

König, A., & Dieterici, C. (1893). Die Grundempfindungen in normalen und anomalen

Farbensystemen und ihre Intensitatsverteilung in spectrum. *Zeitschrift fur Psychologie und Physiologie der Sinnesorgorgane, 4,* 241–347.

Kosslyn, S. M. (1994). In search of occipital acitivation during visual mental imagery. *Trends in Neuroscience, 17,* 294–297.

Krantz, D. H. (1975a). Color measurement and color theory: I. Representation theory for Grassmann structures. *Journal of Mathematical Psychology, 12,* 283–303.

Krantz, D. H. (1975b). Color measurement and color theory: II. Opponent-colors theory. *Journal of Mathematical Psychology, 12,* 304–327.

Lang, S. (1996). *Linear algebra.* New York: Springer.

Larimer, J., Krantz, D. H., & Cicerone, C. (1974). Opponent process additivity: I. Red/green equilibria. *Vision Research, 14,* 1127–1140.

Larimer, J., Krantz, D. H., & Cicerone, C. (1975). Opponent process additivity: II. Yellow/blue equilibria and nonlinear models. *Vision Research, 15,* 723–731.

Lyon, M. (1972). X-chromosome inactivation and developmental patterns in mammals. *Biological Review of the Cambridge Philosophical Society, 47,* 1–35.

MacLeod, D. I. A., & Boynton, R. M. (1979). Chromaticity diagram showing cone excitation by stimuli of equal luminance. *Journal of the Optical Society of America, 69,* 1183–1186.

MacLeod, D. I. A., & Webster, M. A. (1983). Factors influencing the color matches of normal observers. In J. D. Mollon & L. T. Sharpe (Eds.), *Colour vision: Physiology and psychophysics* (pp. 81–92). London: Academic Press.

Maloney, L. T. (1986). Evaluation of linear models of surface spectral reflectance with small numbers of parameters. *Journal of the Optical Society of America A, 3,* 1673–1683.

Marks, W. B., Dobelle, W. H., & MacNichol, E. F. (1964). Visual pigments of single primate cones. *Science, 143,* 1181–1183.

Maxwell, J. C. (1855). Experiments on colour as perceived by the eye, with remarks on colour blindness. *Transactions of the Royal Society of Edinburgh, 21,* 275–298.

Maxwell, J. C. (1856). Theory of the perception of colors. *Transactions of the Royal Society of Arts, 4,* 394–400.

Merbs, S. L., & Nathans, J. (1992a). Absorption spectra of human cone photopigments. *Nature, 356,* 433–435.

Merbs, S. L., & Nathans, J. (1992b). Aborption spectra of the hybrid pigments responsable for anomalous color vision. *Science, 258,* 464–466.

Moreland, J. (1972). Peripheral color vision. In D. Jameson & L. M. Hurvich (Eds.), *Handbook of sensory physiology* (Vol. 7/4: Visual psychophysics, pp. 517–536). Berlin: Springer-Verlag.

Nagy, A. (1979). Unique hues are not invariant with brief stimulus durations. *Vision Research, 19,* 1427–1432.

Nagy, A. L., MacLeod, D. I. A., Heyemann, N. E., & Eisner, A. (1981). Four cone pigments in women heterozygous for color deficiency. *Journal of the Optical Society of America, 71,* 719–722.

Nathans, J., Piantanida, T. P., & Eddy, R. L. (1986). Molecular genetics of inherited variation in human color vision. *Science, 232,* 203–210.

Nathans, J., Thomas, D., & Hogness, D. S. (1986). Molecular genetics of human color vision: The genes encoding blue, green and red pigments. *Science, 232,* 193–202.

Neitz, J., & Jacobs, G. (1986). Polymorphism of the long-wavelength cone in normal human colour vision. *Nature, 323,* 623–625.

Newton, I. (1952). *Opticks.* New York: Dover. Original work published 1730.

Palmer, G. (1777). *Theory of colours and vision.* London: S. Leacroft.

Pokorny, J., Smith, V. C., & Starr, S. J. (1976). Variability of color mixture data: Part II. The effect of viewing field size on the unit coordinates. *Vision Research, 16,* 1095–1098.

Pokorny, J., Smith, V. C., Verriest, G., & Pinckers, A. J. L. G. (1979). *Congenital and acquired color vision defects.* New York: Grune & Stratton.

Pole, W. (1893). On the present state of knowledge and opinion in regard to colour-blindness.

Transactions of the Royal Socieyt of Edinburgh, 37, 441–480.

Purdy, D. M. (1931). Spectral hue as a function of intensity. *The American Journal of Psychology, 43,* 541–559.

Regan, B. C., Julliot, C., Simmon, B., Viénot, F., Charles-Dominique, P., & Mollon, J. D. (1998). Frugivory and colour vision in *Alouatta seniculus,* a trichromatic platyrrhine monkey. *Vision Research, 38,* 3321–3327.

Roorda, A., & Williams, D. R. (1999). The arrangement of the three cone classes in the living human eye. *Nature, 397,* 520–522.

Rushton, W. A. H. (1956). The difference spectrum and photo sensitivity of rhodopsin in the living human eye. *Journal of Physiology, 134,* 11–29.

Sanocki, E., Shevell, S. K., & Winderickx, J. (1994). Serine/alanine amino acid polymorphism of the L-cone photopigment assessed by dual Rayleigh-type colour matches. *Vision Research, 34,* 377–382.

Saunders, B. A. C., & van Brakel, J. (1997). Are there nontrivial constraints on colour categorization? *Behavioral and Brain Sciences, 20,* 167–228.

Schmidt, I. (1955). A sign of manifest heterozygosity in carriers of color deficiency. *American Journal of Optometry, 32,* 404–408.

Schnapf, J. L., Kraft, T. W., & Baylor, D. A. (1987). Spectral sensitivity of human cone photoreceptors. *Nature, 325,* 439–441.

Schrödinger, E. (1994). On the relationship of four-color theory to three-color theory. Translation in *Color Research and Application, 19,* 37–47.

Sharpe, L. T., Stockman, A., Jägle, H., & Nathans, J. (1999). Opsin genes, cone photopigments, color vision, and color blindness. In K. R. Gegenfurtner & L. T. Sharpe (Eds.), *Color vision: From genes to perception* (pp. 3–51). Cambridge: Cambridge University Press.

Smith, V. C., & Pokorny, J. (1975). Spectral sensitivity of the foveal cone photopigments between 400 and 500 nm. *Vision Research, 15,* 161–171.

Stabell, B., & Stabell, U. (1973). Chromatic rod vision-IX: A theoretical survey. *Vision Research, 13,* 449–455.

Stiles, W. S., & Burch, J. M. (1955). Interim report to the Commission Internationale de l'Eclairage, Zurich, 1955, on the National Physical Laboratory's investigation of colour matching. *Optica Acta, 2,* 168–181.

Stockman, A., MacLeod, D. I. A., & Johnson, N. E. (1993). Spectral sensitivities of the human cones. *Journal of the Optical Society of America A, 10,* 2491–2521.

Teller, D. Y. (1979). The forced-choice preferential looking procedure: A psychophysical technique for use with human infants. *Infant Behavior and Development, 2,* 135–153.

Trezona, P. W. (1974). Additivity in the tetrachromatic colour matching system. *Vision Research, 14,* 1291–1303.

Trezona, P. W. (1987). Is the retina trichromatic or tetrachromatic? *Die Farbe, 34,* 211–219.

Valberg, A. (1971). A method for the precise determination of achromatic colours including white. *Vision Research, 11,* 157–160.

Viénot, F. (1983). Can variation in macular pigment account for the variation of colour matches with retinal position? In J. D. Mollon & L. T. Sharpe (Eds.), *Colour vision: Physiology and psychophysics* (pp. 107–116). London: Academic Press.

Vos, J. J., & Walraven, P. L. (1971). On the derivation of the foveal receptor primaries. *Vision Research, 11,* 799–818.

Vos, J. J., & Walraven, P. L. (1972). An analytical description of the line element in the zone fluctuation model of colour vision: I. Basic concepts. *Vision Research, 12,* 1327–1344.

Wagner, G., & Boynton, R. M. (1972). Comparison of four methods of heterochromatic photometry. *Journal of the Optical Society of America, 62,* 1508–1515.

Wald, G., Brown, P. K., & Smith, P. H. (1955). Iodopsin. *Journal of General Physiology, 38,* 623–681.

Werner, J. S., & Wooten, B. R. (1979). Opponent chromatic mechanisms: Relation to photopigments and hue naming. *Journal of the Optical Society of America, 69,* 422–434.

Winderickx, J., Lindsey, D. T., Sanocki, E., Teller, D. Y., & Motulsky, A. G. (1992). Polymorphism in red photopigment underlies variation in colour matching behavior. *Nature, 356,* 431–433.

Wright, W. D. (1928–29). A re-determination of the trichromatic coefficients of the spectral colours. *Transactions of the Optical Society, 30,* 141–164.

Wyszecki, G., & Stiles, W. S. (1982). *Color science: Concepts and methods, quantitative data and formulae* (2nd ed.). New York: Wiley.

Young, T. (1802). On the theory of light and colours. *Philosophical Transactions of the Royal Society of London, 92,* 20–71.

Young, T. (1807). *A course of lectures on natural philosophy and the mechanical arts.* London: J. Johnson.

CHAPTER 3

Depth Perception

IAN P. HOWARD

INTRODUCTION

The problem of how we perceive a three-dimensional world engaged the interest of the Greeks as early as the 5th century B.C. Empedocles proposed the *extromission theory,* which holds that light rays leave the eye and sense the distance of an object by the length of the ray, in the same way that the distance of a touched object is sensed by the extension of the arm. Aristotle (384–322 B.C.) adopted the *intromission theory,* in which images travel to the eye as a disturbance of the transparent medium of the air. In Alexandria around 300 B.C., Euclid wrote his book of *Optics,* in which he laid the foundations of the geometrical analysis of visual space. He described the fundamental facts of perspective and noted that the images in the two eyes differ. Claudius Ptolemy (A.D. 100–175), also in Alexandria, wrote his book of *Optics,* which extended Euclid's geometrical analysis and contained the first geometrical analysis of binocular vision (Howard & Wade, 1996). The next major advance was the *Book of Optics* by Alhazen (A.D. 965–1040), an Arabic scholar working in Cairo. He elaborated Ptolemy's analysis of binocular vision and discovered many visual phenomena that were not rediscovered until the 19th century (Howard, 1996). During the 14th and 15th centuries, the artists of the Italian Renaissance discovered

the precise principles of perspective. By the 17th century, artists such as Rembrandt had a full working knowledge of all monocular cues to depth, such as shading and transparency. Kepler set out the geometrical principles of image formation in his book *Dioptrice* (1611). A full appreciation of the role of binocular disparity in depth perception had to wait until Wheatstone invented the stereoscope in 1836. Developments since that time are described in the following pages.

It is often stated that it is difficult to understand how people perceive a three-dimensional world when retinal images are two-dimensional. The perception of any property of the world, be it color, motion, shape, or depth, depends on the existence of a pattern of activity in a sense organ that is uniquely related to that property. All sensory features are coded in the nervous system in terms of the relative rates of firing of specific nerve cells. Just as the perception of color does not depend on the coloration of nerve impulses, the perception of depth does not require that the dimension be represented by depth in the nervous system. The direction of a visual object is coded locally in terms of which retinal receptor is stimulated. Depth is not coded locally in an eye but rather in terms of patterns of neural activity produced by perspective, relative motion, and shading. Depth is also coded in terms of differences in the positions of images on the two retinas. Thus, several sources of information contribute to the perception of depth. Depth judgments can be based on any of these so-called cues to depth.

To investigate the perception of any feature of the world we must first analyze the available sensory cues. Psychophysicists not only measure the precision and accuracy with which each cue is used in isolation but also study how cues interact. Physiologists study the patterns of nervous activity generated by defined changes in sensory stimulation. Mathematicians and computer scientists construct theoretical models of how sensory information is processed. The study of sensory and perceptual performance in animals and infants reveals the extent to which perceptual mechanisms are innate or learned.

A sensory mechanism can be innate when there is no ambiguity in the stimulus that evokes a given response. For example, a motion of the whole retinal image is an unambiguous stimulus for a pursuit motion of the eyes. This response is present at birth, and adults cannot inhibit it. We cannot rely on innate mechanisms when we must decide to which of several stimuli to respond. For example, when we decide which of several objects to pick up, we direct our attention and gaze to the selected object and ignore other objects and other ways of responding. Also, we cannot rely on innate mechanisms when stimuli are ambiguous. For example, relative motion in the visual field can arise from the motion of objects or from motion parallax generated by motion of the self. In cases like this, we rely on experience to infer the most likely objects and events in the world that could generate the pattern of stimuli that we experience. Infants build up an incredibly rich knowledge of the world, and inferential processes become so well practiced that they are performed without conscious awareness. With novel stimuli or when we learn to respond to old stimuli in novel ways, we must apply conscious effort.

This three-tiered structure of perception, from innate sensory processes to unconscious inference to conscious thought, was first described by Alhazen in the 10th century and was championed by Helmholtz in the 19th century.

I first discuss the cues to depth and then show how they work together to produce that most wonderful phenomenon, the perception of a three-dimensional world.

Several figures require the reader to binocularly fuse two displays. Fusion of the images can be most easily achieved if a piece of paper about 6 inches long is held between the bridge of the nose and a point midway between the two displays. Convergence or divergence of the eyes by the right amount brings the two images onto corresponding locations in the two eyes.

ACCOMMODATION AS A CUE TO DISTANCE

When we look at an object at a certain distance, the ciliary muscles adjust the shape of an eye's lens to bring the image into focus on the retina. This is known as accommodation. The accommodative state of the eyes can serve as a weak cue to distance for near distances in the absence of other cues to depth. Thus, the apparent distance of a high-contrast stimulus at a fixed distance decreases when lenses cause the eyes to accommodate as to a near distance, but there are large individual differences (Fisher & Ciuffreda, 1988; Mon-Williams & Tresilian, 1999). The act of changing accommodation from one object to another may be an effective cue to relative depth, but there do not seem to be any studies on this question.

VERGENCE AS A CUE TO DISTANCE

When we look at an object at a given distance, the eyes converge to bring the images of the object onto corresponding positions in the two eyes—the nearer the object the greater the angle of convergence. When all other cues to depth are removed, the apparent distance of an object increases as vergence angle decreases, but only up to a distance of 1 or 2 m (Leibowitz, Shina, & Hennessy, 1972; Wallach & Floor, 1971). Beyond 2 m the vergence angle changes very little. Looking through base-out prisms increases the convergence required to fixate an object at a fixed distance. This causes the object to appear small and near—an effect known as *micropsia* (Enright, 1989). Base-in prisms have the opposite effect. The dependence of perceived size and distance on vergence is also illustrated by the *wallpaper effect* shown in Figure 3.1. At near distances, judgments of distance based on vergence are no worse than are judgments of direction based on version, when both are expressed in angular terms (Brenner & Smeets, 2000).

When all cues to distance other than vergence are removed, people tend to reach too far for near distances and too near for far distances (Mon-Williams & Dijkerman, 1999). Gogel and Tietz (1973) called this regression to the mean distance the *specific distance ten-*

dency. A similar contraction of judgments toward the mean occurs in any task in which there is uncertainty (Mon-Williams, Tresilian, & Roberts, 2000).

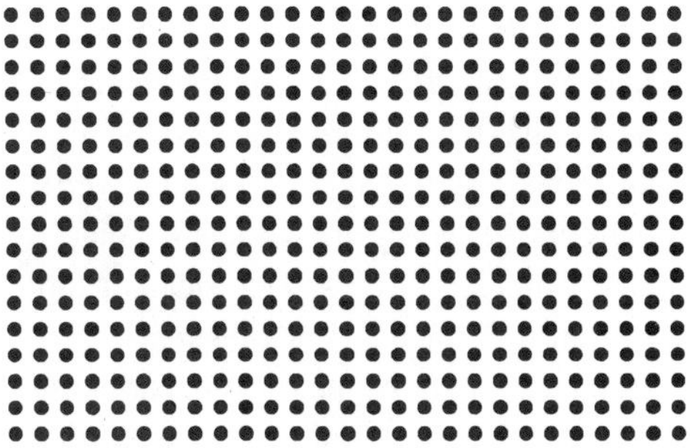

Effects of Altered Vergence

Viewing the world for a few minutes through base-out prisms leads to an overestimation of distance when the prisms are removed (Wallach, Moore, & Davidson, 1963). Wallach and Halperin (1977) produced evidence that prism aftereffects are caused by cue conflict. However, Fisher and Ebenholtz (1986) obtained aftereffects when there was no cue conflict and concluded that they are caused by a change in the tonic state of the extraocular muscles (Fisher & Ciuffreda, 1990). The way muscle tonus affects judgments of depth depends on the presence of other depth cues (Heuer & Lüschow, 1983).

Accommodation and vergence are oculomotor cues to distance because they depend on registration of states of muscular contraction derived from motor commands or from sensory receptors in muscles. The depth cues that I discuss next are all derived from visual stimuli.

Figure 3.1 The wallpaper illusion.
NOTE: When the repeating pattern is viewed with the eyes overconverged (crossed), the angle of vergence corresponds to a distance nearer than the true distance. As a result, the pattern appears nearer and smaller than it is. When the eyes underconverge, the pattern appears farther and larger than it is.

IMAGE BLUR

Blur of the retinal image arising from out-of-focus objects can serve as a cue to relative depth. Thus, artists create an impression of relative depth by blurring the images of certain objects. Photographers reduce the depth of focus of the camera so that only the object of interest is in focus, leaving the surroundings with various degrees of blur. Texture blur in combination with blur of the edge of a textured region can induce unambiguous impressions of relative depth, as illustrated in Figure 3.2 (Marshall, Burbeck, Ariely, Rolland, & Martin, 1996).

(a) Inner square appears near-er than the surround because texture and edges are sharp, as in a near in-focus square.

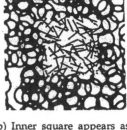

(b) Inner square appears as a distant surface because texture and edges are blurred, as in a surface beyond an aperture.

(c) Inner square can appear as an out-of-focus surface be-yond the surround or as a dif-fuse textured square in front.

(d) Inner square appears near and out-of-focus because texture and edges are blurred.

Figure 3.2   Effects of texture and edge blur on apparent depth.
SOURCE: Adapted from Marshall, Burbeck, Ariely, Rolland, & Martin (1996). *Journal of the Optical Society of America, 13*(4). Used with permission.

INTERPOSITION

Occlusion of One Object by Another

Interposition occurs when one object occludes part of another object. Interposition of station-ary objects provides information about depth order but not about depth magnitude.

Overlapping objects usually produce im-ages that contain edges meeting in T-junctions, as in Figure 3.3. The edge that terminates at a T-junction is the *stem edge.* The two collinear stem edges in Figure 3.3a are seen as be-longing to the more distant of the two shapes (Ratoosh, 1949). This interpretation allows the far object to be seen as having a con-tinuous edge that extends behind the nearer object. This is known as *amodal completion* (Grossberg, 1997; Huffman, 1971). When the

corner of an object is occluded, amodal com-pletion is achieved by visually extending the occluded edges until they meet to form a cor-ner. Other effects illustrated in Figure 3.3 demonstrate that information provided by T-junctions may be supplemented or overrid-den by the tendency to see shapes that are smaller, simpler, more symmetrical, or more meaningful (Chapanis & McCleary, 1953).

A far object can be made to appear in front of a near object by aligning a cut-out portion of the far object with the contour of the near object (Ames, 1955).

Dynamic Accretion and Deletion

When a textured surface moves over another textured surface, images of texture elements

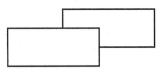

(a) The rectangle appears in front because of T-junctions but also because that allows both figures to appear as simple rectangles.

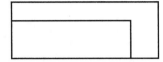

(b) The T-junctions are uninformative, and the figure tends to be seen in one plane. There is some tendency to see the small rectangle in front because the figures appear as simple rectangles.

(c) Even though the T-junctions are uninformative, the small square tends to be seen in front because it is the smaller figure and because both figures form complete squares.

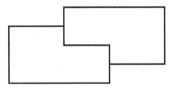

(d) The two T-junctions produce conflicting information about depth order.

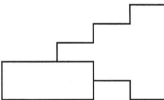

(e) T-junctions indicate rectangle in front, but it is easy to see the pyramid in front because it is then seen as symmetrical.

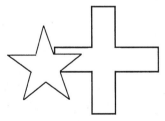

(f) Even though there are no T-junctions, the star tends to be seen in front because both figures are then seen as symmetrical.

Figure 3.3   The perception of depth order from occlusion.
SOURCE: Figures (e) and (f) adapted from Chapanis & McCleary (1953).

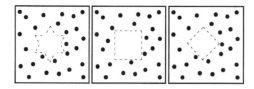

Figure 3.4 Detection of shape by accretion/deletion.
NOTE: People can identify the shapes of the blank areas (indicated here by dashed lines) by the pattern of accretion and deletion of dots as the background moved laterally with respect to the stationary blank areas.
SOURCE: Redrawn from Andersen & Cortese (1989).

are deleted along the leading edge and reappear along the lagging edge. The surface with unchanging texture is seen in front (Gibson, Kaplan, Reynolds, & Wheeler, 1969). The

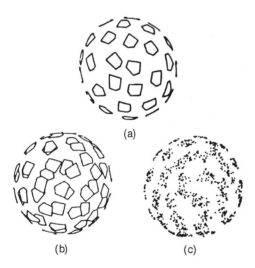

Figure 3.5 Occlusion and resolution of depth ambiguity.
NOTE: (a) The parallel projection of a rotating opaque sphere covered with dots can be seen as concave of convex. Large texture elements resolve the depth ambiguity because of the way they disappear along one edge and reappear along the opposite edge. (b) In the image of a rotating transparent sphere, occlusion of far by near texture elements resolves depth ambiguity. (c) Occlusion of far by near dot clusters does not resolve depth ambiguity because the dot clusters lose their separate identity.
SOURCE: Andersen & Braunstein (1983).

pattern of accretion/deletion produced by motion of a random-dot display with respect to blank regions, as shown in Figure 3.4, reveals the shape of the blank region (Andersen & Cortese, 1989). Dynamic occlusion can resolve the ambiguity of depth order inherent in the projected images of three-dimensional objects, such as the object shown in Figure 3.5 (Braunstein, Anderson, & Riefer, 1982).

SHADING, SHADOWS, AND AERIAL PERSPECTIVE

Shading

A matte, or *Lambertian,* surface, reflects light equally in all directions. A shiny, or **specular,** surface reflects light more in one direction than in other directions. A perfect mirror reflects each incident beam in only one direction. Reflections of small sources of light from a shiny surface produce *highlights.* A beam of light becomes spread over a larger area of a surface as the surface becomes inclined to the beam, as shown in Figure 3.6. Shading is the variation in irradiance caused by changes in surface orientation or by specularity. A smoothly curved matte surface produces gradual shading. A sharply curved surface creates shading with a sharp edge. Shading provides information about the three-dimensional shape of a single object.

Artists gained a practical understanding of shading and shadows long before scientists developed theories. Designers of computer-generated displays are adept at calculating shadows and patterns of shading produced by specified scenes (Foley, van Dam, Feiner, & Hughes, 1990). The mathematics is relatively simple because a given scene always produces the same image. A perceiver must work in reverse to decide which scene produced a given image. This is more difficult because a given image can be produced by a large

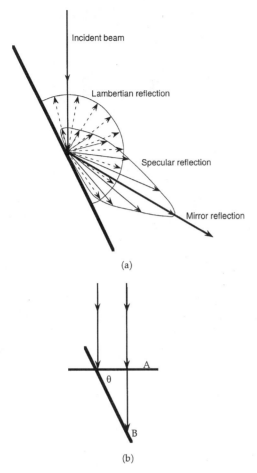

(a)

(b)

Figure 3.6   Properties of reflecting surfaces.
NOTE: (a) Lambertian reflection (dotted lines), specular reflection (solid lines), and mirror reflection (bold line). (b) Collimated light falling on unit area of a normal surface A spreads over an area of $1/\cos\theta$ on surface B inclined at an angle of θ to the direction of the light. For a Lambertian surface, the irradiance of each point on the surface decreases in proportion to $\cos\theta$ as the surface is inclined.

addition of a shadow, shading, and a light source can reduce or eliminate the ambiguity if the rules governing the formation of shadows are known. This illustrates an important principle: To take advantage of increased information provided by more complex scenes, one must consider relationships between features—that is, one must operate globally, not locally (Hayakawa, Nishida, Wada, & Kawato, 1994).

Figure 3.7 demonstrates that shading is an ambiguous depth cue. It is often stated that people resolve the ambiguity by assuming that illumination comes from above as defined by gravity. Observing Figure 3.7 with an inverted head, however, demonstrates that the crucial factor is the orientation of the stimulus with respect to the head (Howard, Bergström, & Ohmi, 1990).

The ambiguity of shading may be resolved by cast shadows, binocular viewing, texture gradients, and highlights on shiny surfaces (Todd & Mingolla, 1983; van den Enden &

number of scenes (Pentland, 1982). The mathematics is simplified by considering only certain features of visual scenes. However, this increases ambiguity because ambiguity in one feature can only be resolved by another feature. For example, the image of an isolated trapezoid can arise from an infinite number of shapes in different orientations. The

Figure 3.7   Convexity-concavity from shading.
NOTE: Convexities and concavities perceptually reverse when the figure is inverted, in conformity with the assumption that light comes from above. Viewing the display with inverted head reveals that the important factor is the direction of light with respect to the head rather than with respect to gravity. The odd disc pops out, showing that shape from shading is a preattentive feature.

Spekreijse, 1989). If the surface is viewed obliquely, occlusion of one surface feature by another may also help (Howard, 1983).

Shading can be a rich source of information about the structure of three-dimensional surfaces, as artists have known for a long time. Todd and Mingolla (1983) found that subjects underestimated the depth of computer-generated cylinders when the shading was Lambertian (matte) but less so when specularities were added. Bulthoff and Mallot (1990) found that the perceived curvature of ellipsoids defined by shading, texture, or both was underestimated relative to that defined by binocular disparity. However, with improved test procedures, Johnston and Passmore (1994) found that depth discrimination based on shading was as good as was that based on disparity.

The perception of the shape of a surface from shading cannot be considered in isolation because it can be influenced by neighboring surfaces (Curran & Johnston, 1996).

Shadows

A shadow is a variation in irradiance from a surface caused by obstruction by an opaque or semiopaque object. Light from one small source forms sharp shadows that may be indistinguishable from surface marks. Light from a diffuse source, scattered light, or light reflected from other objects casts smoothly graded shadows.

A shadow provides information about the shape of an object only if the direction of illumination and the orientation of the surface upon which the shadow is cast are known. If the shape of the object casting the shadow is known, a shadow can provide information about the structure of the surface upon which it is cast.

A shadow cast by an object onto itself or onto another object is known as a detached shadow. A detached shadow can have a large

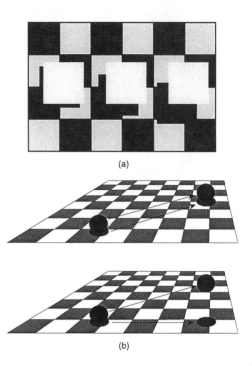

(a)

(b)

Figure 3.8 Relative depth and cast shadows.
NOTE: (a) The light gray squares appear to increase in depth above the background because of the positions of the shadows. (b) When the black disk and its shadow move together diagonally from left to right, the disc appears to move in depth along the surface and grow in size (top diagram). When the disc moves diagonally but the shadow moves horizontally, the disc appears to move in a frontal plane, rise above the surface, and remain the same size (lower diagram).
SOURCE: Adapted from Kersten, Mamassian, & Knill (1997).

effect on the perceived depth between an object and a surface, as illustrated in Figure 3.8 (Kersten, Mamassian, & Knill, 1997).

Aerial Perspective

Aerial perspective is the loss in visibility of distant objects caused by optic haze that is produced by currents of warm air and by the loss of contrast that is produced by dust and mist. The loss in contrast can be measured with a photoelectric telephotometer (Coleman

& Rosenberger, 1950). A disc of light appears to increase in size and advance when the contrast between it and a surrounding annulus is increased, and it appears to shrink and recede when the contrast is reduced (Ames, 1946). Holway and Boring (1940b) found that a tenfold dimming of a 1° disc of light in dark surroundings induced a 10% reduction in apparent size relative to a standard disc.

Table 3.1   Types of perspective.

Type	Effect of greater object distance
Linear perspective	Images of parallel lines converge
Size perspective	Images of objects shrink
Height in field	Images move toward fovea
Texture size	Images of texture elements shrink
Texture density	Image density increases
Aspect-ratio	Relative dimensions of images change

GEOMETRICAL PERSPECTIVE

Geometrical perspective in all its forms arises from the fact that as an object recedes into the distance, its image decreases in size. The various types of perspective are represented in Figure 3.9 and are listed in Table 3.1.

Linear Perspective

Each visual line can be considered to pass through a point near the center of the eye (the nodal point) and intersect the retina in a distinct image point. The central visual line, or visual axis, intersects the retina in the fovea. The images of any set of receding parallel lines converge on a vanishing point. Lines parallel to the visual axis produce images that converge on the fovea, which is the *principal vanishing point* of the eye. The images of receding horizontal planes converge on the *horizon line.* A given image can arise from any of an infinite number of objects that fill the cone of light rays that define the image, as illustrated in Figure 3.10. These are *perspectively equivalent objects.*

One of the main tasks of perception is to register those properties of objects that remain the same (invariant) when we view objects from different positions or orientations, or under different lighting conditions. Because all objects are projected onto a two-dimensional

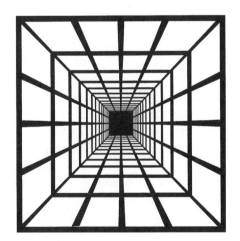

Figure 3.9   General perspective.
NOTE: All types of perspective are represented: simple size perspective, linear perspective, height in the field, texture size gradient, texture density gradient, and aspect-ratio perspective.

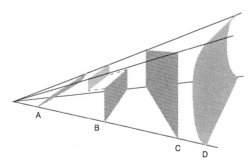

Figure 3.10   Projective equivalence of shapes.
NOTE: All shapes that fill out the same visual pyramid form the same image in the eye. Thus, the dissected square at *B* forms the same image as do an inclined trapezoid at *A*, a slanted trapezoid at *C*, and a curved shape at *D*.

retina, it is important for the visual system to take account of the following invariants in this transformation from three to two dimensions.

1. The image of a straight line is a straight line unless it lies along a line of sight.
2. Neighboring object points produce neighboring image points, although neighboring image points do not necessarily arise from neighboring object points.
3. The order of points is preserved, although parts of one object may be occluded by another object.
4. A polygon remains a polygon and a conic section remains a conic section.
5. The angle subtended at the eye by the vanishing points of any two lines equals the angle in three-dimensional space between those lines.

Parallels, lengths, and angles are not preserved in perspective (Lasenby & Bayro-Corrochano, 1999).

Perspective invariants convey a lot of information about the world, especially for moving objects (Gibson, 1979). When points on a surface appear collinear from one vantage point but not from another vantage point, the surface must be curved. When continuity of neighboring points is not preserved as one views an object from different vantage points, the object has a hole in it or is not a single object. When incidence of lines or surfaces is not preserved, one object is sliding over another. The image of an object receding along a line of sight preserves its shape, and the image of an object moving along a surface concentric with the nodal point of the eye preserves both its shape and size. The image of any two-dimensional figure rotating in depth at a constant velocity compresses at a rate proportional to the cosine of the angle of tilt to a line of sight. The true shape is therefore indicated when the rate of change of the image is at a minimum.

Projective Transformations

Any change of an image produced by the motion of a rigid object is a *projective transformation of the image.* Images on a flat surface, such as the film in a camera, change shape when the camera rotates. Images on a spherical surface, such as the retina, do not change when the eye rotates. Figure 3.11 shows the transformations of the image of a square projected onto a flat image plane as the square is translated within each of three orthogonal planes. The transformations are not always the same for the spherical image plane of the retina.

Perspective in a stationary image is ambiguous. However, the correct appreciation of projective transformations that occur when we view an object from different vantage points allows us to make inferences about object properties. For example, when the image of a nearby object remains constant when we translate, we can infer that the object is moving with us. If the image of an approaching object remains constant, we see the object shrinking as it approaches. If the image grows in inverse proportion to distance, we see an approaching object of constant size. Similarly, an appreciation of the shear transformation of a three-dimensional object as we move the head from side to side allows us to distinguish between motion parallax caused by self motion and plastic deformations of the object. When a rigid object moves, the projective transformation of the image narrows the choice of possible objects. Four noncoplanar points seen from two defined vantage points provide sufficient information to recover the complete three-dimensional structure of the points (Mayhew & Longuet-Higgins, 1982).

Depth from Linear Perspective

Linear perspective by itself can create an impression of inclination. For example, an

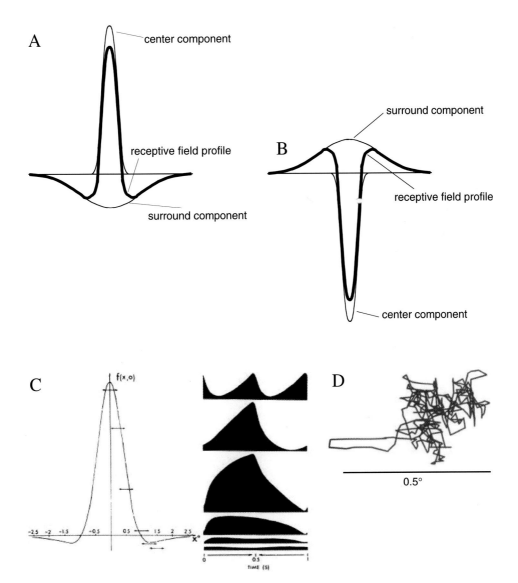

Figure 1.2 Retinal receptive fields and eye movements.
SOURCE: C: Reproduced from Rodieck (1965) with permission from Elsevier Science. D: Modified from Rodieck (1998).

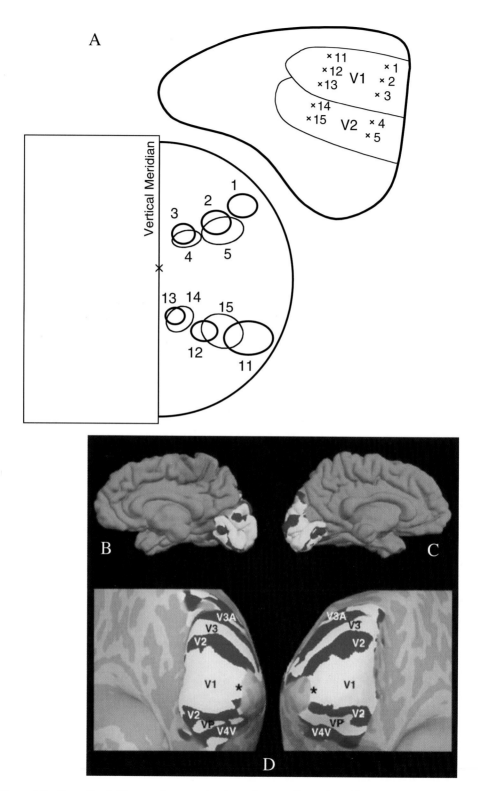

Figure 1.8 Receptive field reversals at area borders. SOURCE: Reproduced from Tootell et al. (1998).

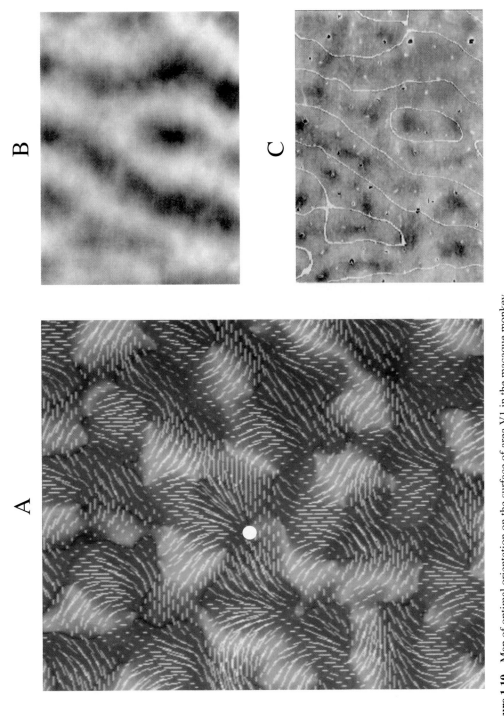

Figure 1.10 Map of optimal orientation on the surface of area V1 in the macaque monkey.
SOURCE: Modified from Blasdel (1992). Copyright © 1992 by the Society for Neuroscience. Reprinted by permission.

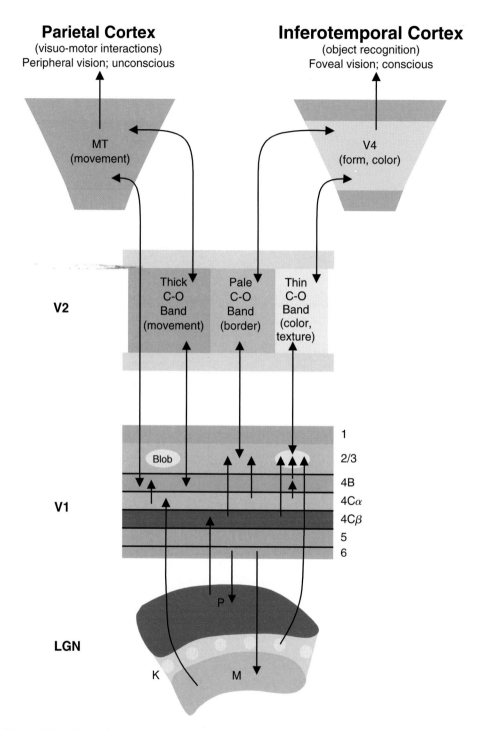

Figure 1.12 Connections between the P, M, and K layers of the LGN and V1 and connections between V1, V2, V4, and MT in the primate visual system.

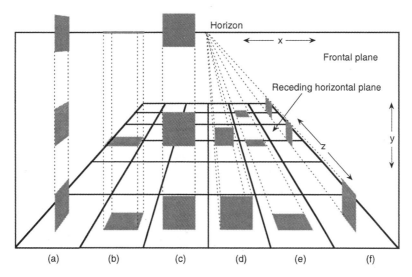

Figure 3.11 Transformations of the image of a two-dimensional object on a frontal image plane.
NOTE: The image of an object moving in a frontal plane from the horizon to eccentricity ε (a) shears through angle ε, (b) grows in dimension y in proportion to cos ε, or (c) remains constant. The image of an object receding along a horizontal plane (d) shrinks overall in proportion to increasing distance, (e) shrinks in dimension x in proportion to distance and in dimension y in proportion to z^2 because of the combined effects of increasing distance and movement toward eye level (or toward the median plane in the case of a vertical plane), or (f) shrinks in dimension y in proportion to distance and in dimension x in proportion to z^2.

illuminated trapezoid in the frontal plane in dark surroundings appears inclined, but not to the extent corresponding to the convergence of the sides of the trapezoid (Clark, Smith, & Rabe, 1955). Outline perspective is a more effective cue to inclination than is a texture gradient, especially when supplemented with binocular disparity (Smith, 1964). The impression of inclination produced by a frontal trapezoid depends on the assumption that the object is rectangular and that image taper is caused by depth. Assumptions about shape are not required when the object rotates in depth because the frontal shape of the object is available when the image is widest and when the rate of change of image shape is at a minimum. The object must be correctly perceived as being rigid. Neither shape nor rigidity assumptions are required when the object is viewed with both eyes (Reinhardt-Rutland, 1990).

The *Ames distorted room* is constructed on the principle of projective equivalence (Ittelson, 1952). The far wall, floor, and ceiling are tapered and slanted so that when viewed through a peephole they create the same image as a rectangular room would. Because of size-distance scaling, a person standing in the more distant corner of the room appears smaller than one standing in the near corner of the room. Distorted rooms were built in Holland in the 17th century.

The *Ames window* is also constructed on the principle of projective equivalence (Ames, 1951). A trapezoidal window rotating about its mid-vertical axis projects the same image as a rectangular window does when at the correct angle to the line of sight, which causes the window to change its apparent shape and direction of rotation in every complete rotation. A rod placed through the window is not subject to the illusory change in direction of rotation and consequently appears to pass through the window or bend round it.

Vogel and Teghtsoonian (1972) asked subjects to estimate the distance and size of a disc presented in a box that was 9-ft long. When the walls of the box converged into the distance, the apparent distance of the disc grew as the 1.4 power of its distance. When the walls diverged, apparent distance grew as the 0.95 power of its distance. Apparent size was not a simple function of apparent distance probably because of size contrasts between the disc and the end of the box.

Size Perspective

The size of an image varies inversely with distance of the object along a line of sight. This is the simple *size-distance law*. A sphere at a fixed distance in otherwise dark surroundings appears to approach when it is inflated and recede when it is deflated (Ittelson, 1952). The same effect is produced by looming textured displays. Thus, people interpret looming as due to the approach motion of an object of fixed size rather than to changing size.

When two stationary discs are presented at the same distance in dark surroundings, the disc subtending the larger visual angle appears more distant (J. E. Hochberg & McAlister, 1955; Ittelson, 1951; Over, 1960). Thus, people assume that the images arise from objects of the same size (Gogel, 1969).

Gogel (1976) argued that under reduced conditions people tend to perceive objects at a default distance, a tendency he called the *specific distance tendency*. This default distance is related to the resting state of vergence (Gogel & Tietz, 1977).

Familiar Size as a Cue to Distance

Ittelson (1951) asked subjects to judge the distance of playing cards of normal size, double size, and half size presented one at a time at the same distance in dark surroundings. He concluded that the perceived distance of a familiar object is, "that distance at which an object of physical size equal to the assumed-size would have to be placed in order to produce the given retinal image (page 66)." C. B. Hochberg and Hochberg (1952) argued that Ittelson had not controlled for relative size. Three blank cards may produce the same result, as in Figure 3.12. However, Ono (1969) found that when photographs of a golf ball and baseball were presented at the same angular size, the baseball appeared more distant.

The apparent sizes and distances of familiar objects are influenced by whether subjects are trying to judge object size or angular size (image size) (Predebon, 1992). Merely informing subjects that an unfamiliar object has a certain size or a certain distance can influ-

Figure 3.12   The influence of size on perceived distance.
NOTE: The effect is most evident when the figure is viewed through a hole or tube.

ence distance estimates under reduced viewing conditions (Tyer, Allen, & Pasnak, 1983). Even if familiar size is not an effective cue for absolute distance, it is a cue for relative distance between objects (Epstein & Baratz, 1964; Gogel & Mertens, 1968).

Perceived Distance and Height in the Field

The image of an object moving in depth below eye level rises in the visual field, and the image of an object moving above eye level falls. The lower of two equal circles on a card below eye level appears nearer and smaller than the upper circle does (Roelofs & Zeeman, 1957). This is a pure *height-in-the-field* effect.

A monocularly viewed object suspended above a horizontal textured surface appears as if it is sitting on a point on the surface that is optically adjacent to the base of the object. The nearer the object is to the horizon, the more distant is the *point of optical adjacency* and the more distant the object appears, as illustrated in Figure 3.13 (Rock,

1975, p. 47). However, an object may appear larger, and therefore more distant, when it lies on the high-density end of the texture gradient than when it lies on the low-density end. This would be a *size-contrast* effect, rather than a height-in-the-field effect or a point-of-optical-adjacency effect.

Texture Perspective

A textured surface produces three types of texture perspective, all of which are illustrated in Figure 3.9.

In *texture size scaling* images of texture elements shrink with increasing distance.

In *texture density scaling* images of texture elements become more densely spaced with increasing distance.

In *aspect-ratio perspective* the depth dimension of the image of a shape is compressed in proportion to the cosine of the angle of inclination to the gaze normal.

The slope and direction of a local texture gradient indicates the slope and direction of the surface relative to the visual axis. An observer must make allowance for any real texture gradients in the actual surface.

The aspect ratio of a single texture element indicates inclination only if the true shape of the texture element is known. For example, one must assume that the bricks in Figure 3.14 are rectangular to use changes in their aspect ratio as a cue to inclination. An aspect-ratio

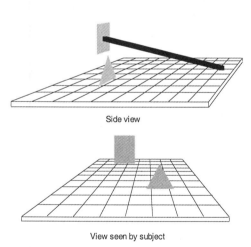

Side view

View seen by subject

Figure 3.13 The depth cue of height in the field. NOTE: The square is supported by a rod above and in front of the triangle but appears on the same level and beyond it when viewed from the front. This occurs because the square is perceived to touch the plane where its base is optically adjacent to the plane.

Figure 3.14 Texture gradients and perception of inclination.
SOURCE: From Gibson (1950b).

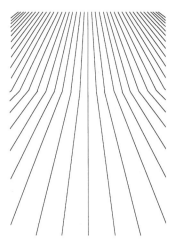

(a) A change in texture gradient produces a change in slope.

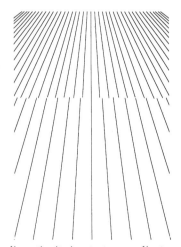

(b) A gap discontinuity in a texture gradient produces a step.

Figure 3.15   Discontinuities in texture gradients.
SOURCE: Redrawn from Gibson (1950a). From *American Journal of Psychology.* Copyright 1950 by the
Board of Trustees of the University of Illinois. Used with permission of the University of Illinois Press.

gradient indicates the direction and magnitude of the three-dimensional curvature of a surface if it is correctly assumed that the aspect ratio of the actual elements is constant over the surface (Rosenholtz & Malik, 1997).

Changes in a texture gradient indicate the changing inclination of a rigid surface rocking in depth even when nothing is known about the distribution or shape of the texture elements on the surface. A change in the slope of a texture gradient indicates a change in the slope of the surface. A gap in an otherwise constant gradient indicates the presence of a step, as shown in Figure 3.15 (Gibson, 1950a).

Using the texture gradients shown in Figure 3.14, Gibson (1950b) found that perceived inclination increased with increasing texture gradient but that judgments were more frontal than was predicted from the gradient.

Phillips (1970) used displays with a texture gradient defined by (a) only the size and aspect ratio of texture elements, (b) only texture density, and (c) the two gradients in agreement or in opposition. Only element size and aspect ratio contributed significantly to perceived inclination. Cumming, Johnston, and Parker (1993) used textured half-cylinders and independently varied element size, texture density, and aspect ratio. Aspect ratio was the only component that contributed significantly to perceived depth, confirming Cutting and Millard (1984).

However, the importance of aspect-ratio perspective depends on the type of display. For example, the cue of aspect ratio is not available for an inclined surface containing vertical objects such as rocks or blades of grass. For such displays, subjects must use texture scaling and texture density.

DEPTH CONSTANCIES

The ability to detect a constant property of an object despite changes in other features is known as *perceptual constancy* (Walsh & Kulikowski, 1998). In depth perception we have the following constancies:

Size constancy is the ability to judge the size of an object at different distances.

Shape constancy is the ability to judge a shape as it rotates in depth.

Constancy of relative depth is the ability to judge relative depth of two objects at different absolute distances.

Orientation constancy is the ability to judge object orientation at different eccentricities (Ebenholtz & Paap, 1973).

Speed constancy is the ability to judge the speed of an object at different distances.

Size Constancy

There are three *size-distance laws* that are true of any optical projection system:

1. For an object of constant size, image size varies inversely with distance.
2. For an image of constant size, object size is proportional to distance.
3. For an object at a fixed distance, image size is proportional to object size.

From these laws of optics we can construct three perceptual hypotheses:

P1. For an object of given perceived size, perceived image size varies inversely with perceived distance.

P2. For an image of a given perceived size, perceived object size is proportional to perceived distance. This is known as the *size-distance invariance hypothesis.*

P3. For an object at a given perceived distance, perceived image size is proportional to perceived object size.

In the classic study by Holway and Boring (1941), a disc of light was varied in size until it appeared the same linear size as a test disc presented in various sizes at various distances, but always subtending 1° of visual angle. With monocular viewing, the size of the test disc was increasingly underestimated as distance increased. When stimuli were viewed through an artificial pupil that eliminated effects of accommodation and through a tube that eliminated the surroundings, judgments came very close to visual subtense matches (image size matches). With binocular viewing, the judged size of the test disc conformed closely to its actual size, although judged size increased slightly with increasing distance, a tendency known as *over-constancy.*

Other investigators have reported over-constancy also at far distances. For example, with good depth cues in an outdoor setting, objects of constant size appear to get larger with increasing distance (Gilinsky, 1955), especially small objects (Joynson, Newson, & May, 1965) and unfamiliar objects (Leibowitz & Harvey, 1969). The topic of over-constancy has been critically reviewed by Carlson and Tassone (1971) and Teghtsoonian (1974).

When vergence is the only cue to distance, size constancy falls off as the distance of the stimulus increases beyond 2 m because vergence ceases to be an effective cue around that distance (Harvey & Leibowitz, 1967). Size constancy for a circle seen in dark surroundings improves with binocular viewing and when subjects are provided with tactile information that they are moving toward or away from the stimulus (Gregory & Ross, 1964).

Figure 3.16 illustrates the size-distance hypothesis qualitatively. The usual explanation is that objects in a picture appear more distant and therefore larger as they approach the vanishing point. However, the lower object may appear smaller because it extends across fewer converging lines than the higher objects do.

Attempts to provide quantitative support for the size-distance invariance hypothesis

Figure 3.16 A distance-size illusion.
NOTE: The three figures are the same physical size but appear to increase in size with increasing apparent distance.

have produced conflicting results and sometimes paradoxical results in which perceived size decreases with increased distance. There are several possible causes of these conflicting results.

First, results depend on whether subjects judge linear size or angular size (image size) and on how well instructions are understood (Leibowitz & Harvey, 1967). Under full cue reduction conditions, size estimates are proportional to distance estimates when subjects judge linear size, in conformity with hypothesis P2. Size estimates vary inversely with perceived distance when subjects judge angular size, in conformity with hypothesis P1 (Baird, 1963). This would be paradoxical from the point of view of judging linear size, but it is not paradoxical in the context of what the subject is trying to judge (Joynson, 1949; McCready, 1985).

Second, when cues to distance are impoverished, size-distance invariance may fail because subjects tend to perceive a larger disc or rectangle as nearer than a smaller one (Over, 1963).

Third, a stimulus factor that makes an object appear more distant will, by the *size-distance hypothesis,* cause it to appear larger. However, the increase in apparent size may feed into an *image-looming mechanism,* which makes an object that grows in size appear to be coming closer. The net result is that the initial increase in apparent distance results in the object's appearing nearer (Rump, 1961).

When familiar objects are used, people can make size judgments without taking account of distance information. Under reduced viewing conditions, an abnormally large familiar object appears in its natural size at a reduced distance (Franklin & Erickson, 1969; Ittelson, 1952). Under natural viewing conditions in an open field, Slack (1956) found that subjects perceived abnormally small or large chairs as closer to the size of a normal chair. Predebon, Wenderoth, and Curthoys (1974) obtained similar results at a distance of 28 yards but not at 14 yards. At the nearer distance, depth cues would be more effective and would allow subjects to make accurate size judgments.

For detailed reviews see Ono (1970), Foley (1980), Sedgwick (1986), and Ross and Plug (1998).

Judgments of Visual Angle

When subjects try to match the angles that two objects subtend at the eye, they perform well when depth cues are reduced (McKee & Welch, 1992). When cues to distance are present, people overestimate the angular subtense of a distant object relative to that of the same object at a nearer distance, as illustrated in Figure 3.16. The habit of comparing the linear sizes of objects intrudes into the task of comparing image sizes (Epstein, 1963). Artists must learn to see objects in terms of their angular extents because that is what determines the relative sizes of objects in a picture.

Judgments of visual subtense are disturbed in size contrast illusions, such as the Ebbinghaus illusion shown in Figure 3.17 (Rock & Ebenholtz, 1959). Inspection of a grating for some minutes causes a coarser grating to appear coarser and a finer grating to appear finer than they normally appear (Blakemore & Sutton, 1969).

Emmert's Law

An afterimage appears to grow in size in proportion to the distance of the surface upon which it is projected. This is known as Emmert's law. The effect can be seen if one fixates a light bulb for about 10 s and then views the afterimage projected on surfaces at different distances. If one views an afterimage in complete darkness and imagines it projected on a card held in the hand, it appears

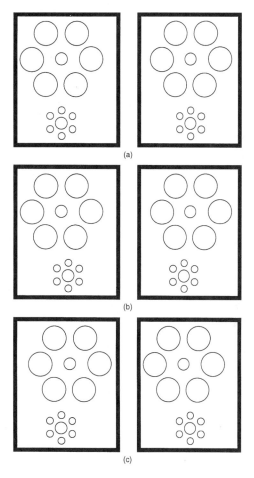

Figure 3.17 The Ebbinghaus illusion.
NOTE: The circle surrounded by large circles appears smaller than does the circle surrounded by small circles. When the images are cross-fused, the illusion is still evident in (a) even though all the circles appear coplanar. In (b) the illusion is enhanced because it is supplemented by a size-distance effect. In (c) the illusion is decreased or eliminated by a counteracting size-distance effect.

to grow and shrink when the unseen hand and card are moved backward and forward (Carey & Allan, 1996; Taylor, 1941). However, experiments to determine whether Emmert's law holds quantitatively have produced different results depending on instructions, methods of measurement, and the nature of the surface upon which the afterimage is projected

(Hastorf & Kennedy, 1957; Teghtsoonian, 1971).

The Moon Illusion

The horizon moon typically appears about 1.5 times larger than the zenith moon, even though the sizes of the retinal images are the same in both cases. Ptolemy mentioned the moon illusion in the 2nd century A.D. (Plug & Ross, 1994). Bishop Berkeley suggested that the illusion occurs because the moon is dimmer and hazier when on the horizon. This may be a factor, but the illusion is still evident when the moon is equally bright in the two positions (Goldstein, 1962).

Holway and Boring (1940a) suggested that the moon illusion is caused by changes in the posture of the head. However, the moon still appears larger when on the horizon even when the scene is viewed through 90° prisms that require subjects to look upward (Kaufman & Rock, 1962). From other experiments, Rock and Kaufman (1962) concluded that the moon illusion arises, at least in part, because the night sky is perceived as a flattened dome so that the moon appears closer in the zenith than in the horizon position.

According to another theory, the moon illusion occurs because the horizon moon is adjacent to familiar objects of known size, such as buildings and trees, whereas the zenith moon is seen among objects of unspecified size, such as clouds and stars. Rock and Kaufman obtained a larger moon illusion when the terrain effect was present, but the illusion persisted when both horizon and zenith moons were seen against a clear sky.

Shape Constancy

The in-depth dimension of the image of a flat object shrinks in proportion to the cosine of the angle of inclination. This is referred to as *foreshortening*. A person is said to exhibit *shape constancy* if the perceived shape of an object remains the same when the object is inclined in depth. For example, a book continues to appear rectangular when it is tilted back despite the fact that its image becomes trapezoidal.

Thouless (1930) asked subjects to select a shape in the frontal plane to match the projected shape (retinal image) of an adjacent inclined shape. When subjects selected a frontal ellipse to match the projected shape of an inclined circle, for example, they selected an ellipse intermediate between a circle and the projected shape of the inclined circle. Their performance was not a measure of shape constancy but rather a measure of failure to judge the projected shapes of inclined stimuli. Thouless referred to the intrusion of the tendency to judge real shape as "regression to the real object."

Measurements of shape constancy are confounded by the problem of instructions. With vague instructions, some subjects match the linear shape of the inclined stimulus and achieve high shape constancy, whereas others attempt to match the projected shapes (images) of the stimulus and achieve compromise judgments (Joynson, 1958; Joynson & Newson, 1962). Furthermore, subjects may interpret instructions correctly but fail to perceive the stimuli according to their intentions (Epstein, 1963; Kaneko & Uchikawa, 1997). As the angle of inclination increases, subjects have an increasing tendency to judge shape in terms of the projected image (Lichte, 1952).

According to the shape/slant invariance hypothesis formulated by Koffka (1935), a given retinal image of a flat rigid object determines a unique inverse relationship between errors of perceived shape and errors of perceived inclination of the object. The shape/slant hypothesis is supported by the following facts.

Under good viewing conditions and with the correct instructions, subjects make nearly perfect shape constancy judgments (Lichte & Borresen, 1967). Beck and Gibson (1955) induced errors in the perceived slant of a triangular target by inclining it with reference to a textured background. The perceived shape of the triangle corresponded to its perceived slant. However, the relationship between perceived shape and perceived slant is inexact under some viewing conditions (Epstein, Bontrager, & Park, 1962). Conflicting results can arise from the use of inadequate psychophysical methods and ambiguous instructions (Epstein & Park, 1963; Kraft & Winnick, 1967).

Perceived shape conforms more closely to projected shape as depth cues are reduced by increasing viewing distance or by viewing the stimuli in dark surroundings (Meneghini & Leibowitz, 1967; Nelson & Bartley, 1956). Thus, it seems that people assume that an object lies in a frontal plane when there is no information to indicate otherwise.

In surroundings devoid of static depth cues, rotation of a shape in depth can restore shape constancy (Langdon, 1955). The projected image of a three-dimensional shape, such as a bent piece of wire, appears flat. But when the object is rotated, the projected image appears three-dimensional, and the shape of the object is accurately perceived. This is the *kinetic depth effect* (Wallach & O'Connell, 1953). Thus, patterns of optic flow can serve as an effective depth cue for shape constancy.

People are accustomed to seeing pictures from an oblique vantage point. As long as they have information that the picture plane is slanted in depth, the picture does not appear unduly distorted (Halloran, 1989). When an oblique picture is made to appear in a frontal plane by removing the perspective taper of its frame, the picture appears grossly distorted.

The literature on shape constancy has been reviewed by Epstein and Park (1963) and Sedgwick (1986).

Constancy of Relative Depth

Different depth cues are affected in different ways by a change in absolute distance. Therefore, constancy of relative depth should depend on which depth cues are available. Image blur from out-of-focus objects is an effective relative depth cue only for near distances and under conditions of narrow depth of focus. Vergence ceases to be an effective cue to distance at distances of more than about 2 m.

When an object moves along a line of sight, constancy of three-dimensional shape indicated by perspective does not require an estimate of distance because all dimensions of the image scale in the same way with distance. However, when an object recedes along a plane below eye level, different dimensions of an object scale with distance in different ways, as shown in Figure 3.11.

MOTION PARALLAX

Motion parallax refers to the relative motion of the images of objects at different distances that is caused by motion of the observer with respect to the objects. For two objects separated by a fixed depth, parallax produced by a given motion of the observer is inversely proportional to the square of the viewing distance. These geometrical relationships are analogous to those for binocular disparity (Rogers, 1993).

Perception of the distance of a single point from motion parallax requires information about the motion of the retinal image, the eye in the head, and the head on the body. Not surprisingly, parallax is not an effective source of information about the distance of a single point (Gogel & Tietz, 1973). However, the complete three-dimensional structure of a scene can be recovered from just three views of four noncoplanar points

(Ullman, 1979) or from just two views of eight points (Longuet-Higgins, 1981). Thus, with multiple views only visual information is required.

Motion parallax works best with rigid objects (Johansson, 1977; Ullman, 1979). The assumption that the world is rigid is known as the *rigidity constraint*. Even though the world contains plastic objects, we can often assume *local rigidity*. For example, the background features of the world and local objects are usually rigid (Koenderink, 1986; Todd, 1982).

Sensitivity to Depth Generated by Motion Parallax

Rogers and Graham (1979) used a monocularly viewed random-dot pattern that appeared flat when the head was stationary. As subjects moved the head from side to side, the dots were sheared to mimic the motion parallax produced by a corrugated surface (Figure 3.18). Observers could match the perceived depth to that defined by disparity with reasonable accuracy. The results were similar when the observer remained stationary and parallactic motion in the display was coupled to sideways movements of the display, thereby simulating motion parallax created by a translating corrugated surface.

Illusory Motion Parallax

If, during sideways motion of the head, the distance of an accurately tracked stationary target is underestimated, the eyes move more slowly than they should for that perceived distance. The stationary target therefore appears to move in the same direction as the head. When the distance of the target is overestimated, the eyes move faster than they should for that perceived distance, and the target appears to move in the opposite direction to the head (Hay & Sawyer, 1969; Wallach, Yablick, & Smith, 1972).

Illusory motion parallax is illustrated by the fact that a face on a poster seems to follow one as one walks past it (Tyler, 1974). In a picture, the expected motion parallax is not present. For a real object, this happens only if the object moves with the viewer.

THE PERCEPTION OF MOTION IN DEPTH

Judging Time to Contact

We judge *time to contact* of an approaching object when we run or drive, dodge an object moving toward us, or play ball games (Cavallo & Laurent, 1988; Lee, Lishman, &

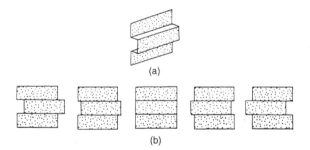

(a)

(b)

Figure 3.18   Motion parallax transformations.
NOTE: When the square-wave surface depicted in (a) is viewed by a moving observer, relative motion is created between surface features at different distances. Figure (b) shows how the random-dot pattern on a screen was transformed with side-to-side head movements to simulate motion parallax. In the experiment, the transformation was continuous and the edges of the pattern were not visible.
SOURCE: Redrawn from Rogers & Graham (1979).

Thompson, 1982; Warren, Young, & Lee, 1986).

When an object moves toward an eye at constant speed, the time to contact is equal to the angular size of its image, θ, at a given time divided by the rate of change of image size at that time. Lee (1976) called this ratio *tau*. Thus, if the image of an approaching object has doubled in size in 1 s, it must have traveled half the distance from its starting point in 1 s and will therefore hit the observer in another second. Judgments about time to impact do not require information about the absolute size or distance of the object.

Knowles and Carel (1958) found that subjects made reasonably accurate estimates of time to impact of a looming grid pattern when time to impact was less than 4 s but that they made progressively larger underestimations of longer times. Subjects are more accurate when they use a natural action such as striking a ball with a bat, than when they press a key (Bootsma, 1989). A catching motion in response to an approaching ball is delayed when the ball deflates as it approaches, because the rate of expansion of the image is less than that of a ball of fixed size (Savelsbergh, Whiting, & Bootsma, 1991).

Todd (1981) asked subjects to judge which of two looming squares on an oscilloscope screen would reach them first. Responses were 90% accurate for a time-to-contact difference of 150 ms and did not reach chance level until the time difference was reduced to 10 ms.

If starting size is held constant, the ratio of angular image size to the rate of image expansion is confounded with the simple rate of angular expansion. Regan and Hamstra (1993) measured the separate contributions of these two factors and concluded that the visual system contains a mechanism specifically sensitive to time to contact that is independent of changes in either the angular size or the rate of change of angular size of the image.

People are more accurate in judging time to contact with binocular vision than with monocular vision (Heuer, 1993; Von Hofsten, Rosengren, Pick, & Needy, 1992). Gray and Regan (1998) asked subjects to estimate time to contact of a $0.7°$ or $0.03°$ disc seen against a fixed array of random dots with reference to a click sound. Like Heuer, they found greater accuracy when both looming and changing disparity cues were provided compared with when only one cue was provided. With only changing disparity available, time to contact was overestimated up to 10% for the large target and up to 3% for the small target. With only looming available, time to contact of the large target was underestimated by between 2% and 12%. Monocular looming is not an effective cue for small objects.

Judging Heading Direction

When an observer approaches a large textured surface, with the gaze fixed on the focus of expansion of the optic array, the focus of expansion of the retinal image indicates the *heading direction*. James Gibson stressed the importance of looming for a pilot landing an aircraft (Gibson, Olum, & Rosenblatt, 1955). When the eyes pursue a part of the expanding image, a translatory component caused by eye tracking is added to the looming due the forward self-motion, and the focus of expansion of the retinal image no longer indicates the heading direction (Regan & Beverley, 1982). A person could recover heading direction if the motion of the eyes were taken into account (van den Berg, 1992; Warren, Morris, & Kalish, 1988).

When an observer moves through an array of objects at different depths, heading direction is specified by the locus of those objects that do not show parallax and remain in alignment. This so-called *locus of zero parallax* is not affected by eye movements and, under the best conditions, reduces to a vernier acuity

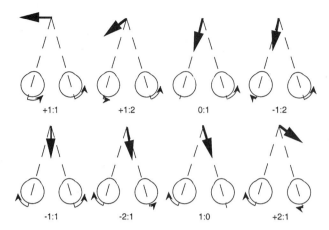

Figure 3.19 Impact direction and relative image velocity.
NOTE: Relative speeds and directions of image motion in the two eyes are related to the impact direction of an object approaching in the plane of regard. The ratio of image velocities in left and right eyes is given below each figure. Positive signs indicate movement in the same direction in the two eyes. Negative signs indicate that there is movement in opposite directions and that the object will hit between the eyes. SOURCE: Adapted from Beverley & Regan (1975).

task, like that involved in aiming a gun (Cutting, 1986; Regan & Beverley, 1984).

A spherical object approaching an eye along any visual line produces an image that expands symmetrically. This signifies that the object will ultimately hit the observer. If the object approaches along any other path, its image expands asymmetrically. If the asymmetry is large enough, the object is destined to miss the head (Regan & Kaushal, 1993).

From a long series of experiments, Regan (1986) concluded that there are visual channels specifically tuned to looming images that are built up from detectors for opposite motion along a particular motion axis. There is evidence that responses to looming involve visual pathways to the superior colliculus that bypass the visual cortex (Dean, Redgrave, & Westby, 1989). Destriate humans can be startled by an approaching object (Weiskrantz, 1986). At the cortical level, looming detectors have been found in the visual cortex of cats (Regan & Cynader, 1979) and in the middle temporal area (MT) and parietal lobe of monkeys and humans (Page & Duffy, 1999).

Binocular Cues to Motion in Depth

When the gaze is fixed on a stationary object while a second object moves toward the head, the relative motion of the images of the moving object in the two eyes varies with the impact direction of the object, as illustrated in Figure 3.19 (Beverley & Regan 1975). Thus, the *relative motion of binocular images* provides information about an object's impact direction.

Aftereffects of Rotation in Depth

Aftereffects may be produced when observers inspect objects rotating in depth. Aftereffects are produced by adaptation to the monocular cues of looming or perspective (Regan & Beverley, 1978; Petersik, Shepard, & Malsch, 1984). Aftereffects also occur after adaptation to rotation in depth produced only by disparity (Nawrot & Blake, 1991; Regan & Beverley, 1973). These latter aftereffects could depend on disparity-specific motion detectors or on changing-disparity detectors

(Anstis & Harris, 1974; Verstraten, Verlinde, Fredericksen, & van de Grind, 1994).

There is physiological evidence for disparity-specific motion detectors in several visual areas of the cerebral cortex. For instance, some cells in areas the primary visual areas (V1 and V2) and medial temporal visual area (MT) of the monkey respond selectively to binocular stimuli moving in a particular direction in a particular depth plane (Maunsell & Van Essen, 1983; Poggio & Talbot, 1981).

Cumming (1994) has reviewed the topic of motion in depth.

STEREOSCOPIC VISION

Visual Fields and Pathways

The *binocular visual field* is the portion of the total field within which an object must lie to be visible to both eyes for a given position of the eyes. It subtends about 80° laterally and 120° vertically and is flanked by left-eye and right-eye monocular sectors, each extending about 37° laterally. The axons of over one million ganglion cells leave the eye to form the *optic nerve*. After leaving the retina at the optic disc, the optic nerve travels to the *optic chiasma*. In most vertebrates, most axons from each eye cross over, or *decussate,* to the contralateral side in the chiasma. In primates (including humans) and some other mammals, axons from the nasal hemiretinas decussate, but those from the temporal hemiretinas remain on the same side. This is known as *hemidecussation.*

The nerves that emerge from the chiasma form the *optic tracts.* Each tract terminates on its own side in a part of the thalamus known as the *lateral geniculate nucleus* (LGN). Within each LGN, inputs from the two eyes remain in distinct layers, or laminae, where they synapse with *relay cells.* Axons of the relay cells fan out to form the *optic radiations,* each of which

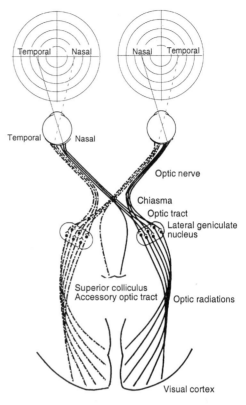

Figure 3.20   The visual pathways.
NOTE: Axons from the right half of each eye (left visual hemifield) project to the right occipital lobe, and those from the left half of each eye (right visual hemifield) project to the left occipital lobe.
SOURCE: From Howard (1982).

terminates in the ipsilateral occipital lobe of the cerebral cortex, as shown in Figure 3.20 (Howard, 1982). Thus, the left half of the visual space is represented in the right cerebral hemisphere, and the right half is represented in the left hemisphere.

Hemidecussation brings inputs from corresponding locations in two eyes to the same location in the brain. This provides the basis for binocular stereoscopic vision in mammals with frontal eyes, such as cats and primates. In these animals, visual inputs from corresponding regions in the two eyes converge on binocular cells in the visual cortex, which are tuned to binocular disparity. See Howard and

Rogers (1995) for a review of the physiology of stereoscopic vision.

Geometry of Binocular Correspondence

The eyes are about 6.5 cm apart and therefore see things from different vantage points. For each point in the binocular portion of the retina of one eye, there is a corresponding point in the retina of the other eye. Images that fall on noncorresponding points exhibit binocular disparity. If the disparity is small enough, the images fuse and are seen as one image. The range of disparities within which images fuse is *Panum's fusional area* (Panum, 1858). Images falling outside this range are seen as double, which is referred to as *diplopia*. The reader is invited to hold a pencil vertically in one hand at arm's length and hold a second pencil in the other hand midway between the first pencil and the face. When the gaze is fixated on the far pencil the near pencil appears double. This is diplopia. When the near pencil is moved slowly toward the far pencil, with fixation held on the far pencil, the position at which it appears single defines the boundary of Panum's fusional area.

The angular subtense of Panum's fusional area depends on retinal eccentricity and on characteristics of the stimulus and the surrounding stimuli. Dissimilar images falling in Panum's fusional area do not fuse but exhibit *binocular rivalry,* in which we see the two images in alternation (Fox, 1991; Howard & Rogers, 1995).

The relative position of two stimulus objects or of their retinal images is indicated by the angle that they subtend at the nodal point at the center of the eye. Side-to-side differences in the positions of similar images in the two eyes are *horizontal disparities*. Figure 3.21 illustrates the geometry of horizontal disparity. The visual axes converge on point *F*, and a second point *P* is placed some distance beyond *F*. The *binocular disparity* of

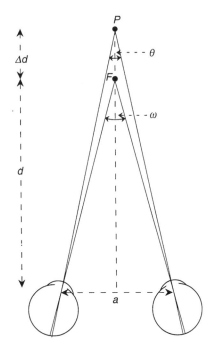

Figure 3.21   Binocular disparity.
NOTE: The distance between fixation point *F* at distance *d* and point *P* is Δd. The interocular distance is a; θ is the binocular subtense of *P*; and ω is the binocular subtense of *F*. The angular disparity, η, of *P* with repect to *F* is $\omega - \theta$. To a first approximation, $\eta = a\Delta d/d^2$.

the images of *F* is zero because each image falls on a fovea. If ω is the binocular subtense of point *F* and θ is the binocular subtense of point *P*, the horizontal disparity of the images of point *P* expressed in angular terms is equal to $\omega - \theta$.

The images of an object nearer to an observer than the point of convergence have *convergent disparity,* or crossed disparity, because the eyes must converge to fuse them. The images of an object beyond the point of convergence have *divergent disparity,* or uncrossed disparity.

Binocular images arising from the same object are *corresponding images.* Corresponding images are usually similar, but need not be identical because they may contain disparities. Noncorresponding images are usually dissimilar but may arise from distinct but identical objects. Images of any type that engage the disparity-detection system are *binocularly linked images.* We see objects in their proper depth relationships only if the visual system links corresponding images. The problem of how the visual system links only corresponding images in natural scenes is known as the *binocular correspondence problem.*

Consider a horizontal row of small dots lying on the horopter, as in Figure 3.22. Corresponding visual lines from each eye intersect in each dot. Each line to one eye intersects all lines to the other eye. Thus, for N dots there are N^2 intersections of visual lines. These intersections form the *Keplerian projection,* which defines the set of possible correspondences plus the set of possible disparities between the images of a set of objects.

For an array of objects in the neighborhood of the horopter, three rules usually guarantee that corresponding images are properly linked. The *nearest-neighbour rule* states that images that are closest to each other are linked. The *unique-linkage rule* states that each image links to only one image. The *similarity rule* states that only similar images are linked.

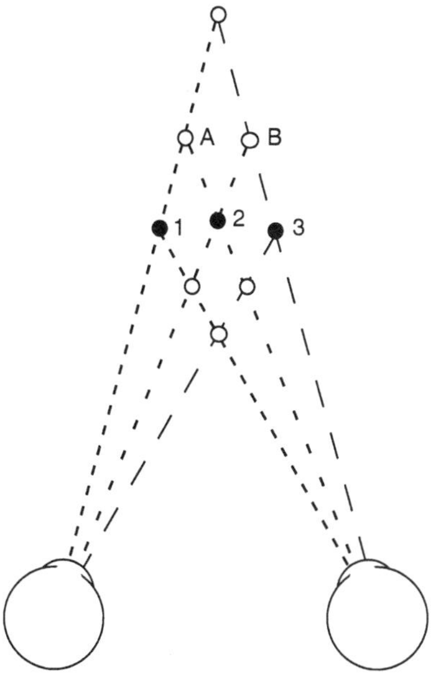

Figure 3.22 The Keplerian projection.
NOTE: Solid dots are three objects lying in the horopter. Dashed lines are pairs of corresponding visual lines. The circles represent objects that produce images with the same disparities. For instance, object B produces images with an uncrossed disparity equal to the angular separation between the images of objects 2 and 3 on either retina. Objects A and B produce a fused pair of images equivalent to those produced by object 2, in adition to unpaired images in each eye in the direction of objects 1 and 3.

The Horopter

The *horopter* is the locus of points in space that projects images onto corresponding points in the two retinas for a given point of binocular convergence. The horopter has two parts: the *horizontal horopter,* or longitudinal horopter, which usually lies in the horizontal plane of regard, and the *vertical horopter,* which lies in the median plane of the head.

Figure 3.23 illustrates the basic geometry of the *theoretical horizontal horopter,* or *Vieth-Müller circle,* which is a circle through the point of convergence and the nodal points of the two eyes. All points on a vertical line in the median plane through the Vieth-Müller circle also have zero disparity. This line is called the *theoretical vertical horopter.* The horizontal and vertical horopters constitute the *space horopter* (Tyler, 1991).

Any point that is not in the space horopter has a horizontal disparity, a vertical disparity, or both. For example, consider a point B in an oblique position with respect to a central fixation point A. The angular separation of B and A is larger to one eye than to the other because B is nearer to one eye than to the other. Because point A is on the horopter, point B can-

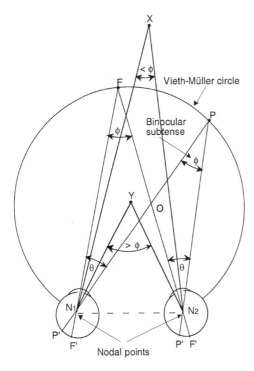

Figure 3.23 Basic geometry of the horizontal horopter.

NOTE: When the eyes are converged on point F, the foveal images, F', have zero disparity. Let Φ be the binocular subtense of point F and place a circle through F and the nodal points of the eyes (Vieth-Müller circle). Any point, P, on the circle has a binocular subtense of Φ, because all points project from chord N1-N2. Because opposite angles at O are equal, angles θ must also be equal. Therefore, the images of P stimulate corresponding points. The Vieth-Müller circle therefore defines the locus points having zero horizontal disparity. Point X beyond the circle subtends an angle smaller than Φ and produces uncrossed images. Point Y nearer than the circle projects an angle larger than Φ and produces crossed images.

not fall on corresponding points, and therefore the horopter cannot include point B.

The horopter determined by a psychophysical procedure is the *empirical horopter*. In one procedure, the subject fixates a central point and moves a test object along a cyclopean line radiating out from a point between the eyes until it appears fused. The procedure is then repeated for other cyclopean lines. In dichoptic procedures, the eyes converge on a central point while a line seen by one eye is moved until it appears aligned with a second line presented to the other eye in a stereoscope. These so-called *nonius lines* are placed one above the other. The procedure is repeated for various positions of the nonius lines. The precision of alignment of nonius lines is about 0.7 arcmin in the central retina (McKee & Levi, 1987), but the method becomes unreliable beyond an eccentricity of about 12° (Ogle, 1964, p. 48).

The empirical horopter deviates from the theoretical ideal when corresponding points in the two retinas are not congruent. The horopter resulting from a gradient of compression of points in one retina and an opposite gradient of compression in the other retina is shown in Figure 3.24. Its shape varies with viewing distance, an effect known as the *Hering-Hillebrand deviation*.

For most people, corresponding vertical meridians are rotated top in by about 2°, which causes the vertical horopter to be inclined top away, as shown in Figure 3.25 (Siderov, Harwerth, & Bedell, 1999). The shear of corresponding vertical meridians relative to corresponding horizontal meridians is probably a consequence of the fact that ground surfaces are inclined top away. The pattern of correspondence may be shaped in early development by alignment of the vertical horopter with the ground (Krekling & Blika, 1983).

Because the eyes are separated horizontally, one might suppose that only horizontal disparities are involved in coding distance. In fact, vertical disparities affect the perception of depth in several ways. Readers interested in this topic are referred to Howard and Rogers (1995).

Visual Features Used for Stereopsis

Stereoscopic vision can work only when corresponding points in the images in the two eyes are correctly matched.

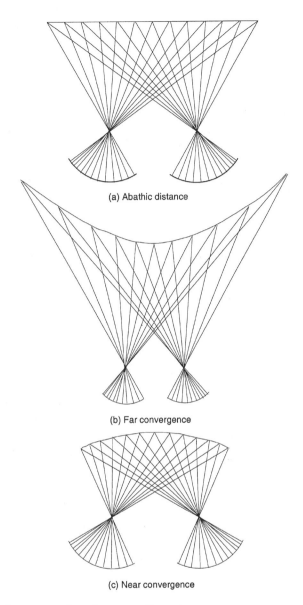

(a) Abathic distance

(b) Far convergence

(c) Near convergence

Figure 3.24   Relative compression of corresponding points.
NOTE: (a) Corresponding visual lines plotted from equally spaced points on a frontal plane define retinal points relatively compressed in the temporal hemiretinas. (b) Horopter constructed with the same spacing of corresponding points but with the visual axes (bold lines) converged on a more distant point. (c) Horopter constructed with the same points but with the visual axes converged on a nearer point.
SOURCE: Adapted from Howard & Rogers (1995).

Stereopsis can occur when the shapes that appear in depth are not visible in either image. Such shapes are called cyclopean shapes. In a *random-dot stereogram* (Julesz, 1960) a cyclopean shape defined by disparity be-tween groups of random dots emerges only after the images have been correctly fused. Figure 3.26 illustrates the construction of a random-dot stereogram. A random-dot stereogram contains no monocular cues to depth.

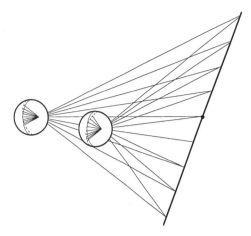

Figure 3.25   The empirical vertical horopter.
NOTE: The empirical vertical horopter for near convergence is a straight line inclined top away within the median plane of the head. The dotted lines of the retinas indicate the corresponding vertical meridians. The solid lines indicate the true vertical meridians.
SOURCE: Adapted from Howard & Rogers (1995).

Some people have difficulty fusing random-dot stereograms.

We can use any of the following visual features for matching binocular images.

Matching Luminance-Defined Edges

An edge defined by luminance contrast is the most prevalent token for detecting disparity. Stereopsis tolerates some difference in contrast between the images in the two eyes. However, the contrast polarity and orientation of the images must be the same (see Howard & Rogers, 1995).

Marr and Poggio (1979) proposed that linkage occurs between regions known as *zero crossings*. These are edge regions where luminance changes most rapidly. In the Marr and Poggio model, linking of zero crossings is done separately on each output of four spatial filters, ranging from fine to coarse. This helps to minimize ambiguities in the linking process. Once achieved, linked images are stored in a buffer memory, referred to

as the $2^1/_2$-D sketch. The output of the low spatial-frequency filter is used also to control vergence. This account cannot be complete, however, because perception of depth can be evoked by disparity between edges that are not defined by zero crossings (Boothroyd & Blake, 1984; Mayhew & Frisby, 1981) or by disparity between smoothly graded changes that lack well-defined zero crossings (Mallot, Arndt, & Bülthoff, 1996).

Matching by Texture

The texture of a homogeneously patterned surface may be defined in terms of the shapes, orientations, sizes, or spacing of the texture elements. Disparity between boundaries of differently textured regions can create a step in depth when the texture for each region is the same in the two eyes (Mayhew & Frisby, 1976).

Matching by Color

The visual system has chromatic detectors of color differences in the absence of luminance gradients and achromatic detectors of differences in luminance independently of color. There is only weak stereopsis with random-dot stereograms at equiluminance with the dots in one color and the background in another color (Lu & Fender, 1972; Osuobeni & O'Leary, 1986). Also, brain potentials in human subjects evoked by depth reversal of a red-green dynamic random-dot stereogram are greatly reduced at equiluminance (Livingstone, 1996).

However, an edge defined by color produces a weaker retinal signal than one defined by luminance. When this factor is allowed for, depth discrimination at equiluminance is as good as the equivalent contrast of the display allows (Simmons & Kingdom, 1995). The chromatic channel is relatively insensitive to transient stimuli and is therefore most sensitive to slow oscillations in depth, whereas the luminance channel is sensitive to

Left-eye image   Right-eye image

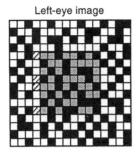 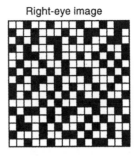

(a) Black dots are arranged at random in about half the squares of a grid, and the pattern is duplicated. A subset of dots is cut out of one of the patterns, with cuts along the sides of the squares so that dots are not dissected.

(b) The cut region is shifted an integral number of small squares. Overlapping dots on one side of the shifted region are transferred to the empty space on the other side.

(c) The grid is removed. When viewed in a stereoscope, the shifted region appears in front of or behind the background, depending on the way the shifted region was moved.

Figure 3.26   The random-dot stereogram.

transient stimuli and therefore is most sensitive to fast oscillations in depth (Tyler & Cavanagh, 1991).

Matching by Motion

Halpern (1991) presented a display of random dots in which a central square moved from side to side with respect to the surrounding dots. The squares in the two eyes moved out of phase to produce changing disparity of the motion-defined edges. When the accretion and deletion cue was removed by flickering the dots, both crossed and uncrossed disparities produced good impressions of depth.

Thus, kinetic boundaries can be used by the stereoscopic system.

Monocular Occlusion

Next to the vertical edge of an opaque object is a region of a far surface that is visible to only one eye. This can easily be verified by holding the hand in front of a page of print and alternately closing one eye. This is *monocular occlusion.*

Fusion of the two images in Figure 3.27 creates the impression of one black square in front of another. This stereogram lacks disparity. Therefore, depth arises from monocular occlusion only (Gillam, Blackburn, & Nakayama, 1999).

Stereoacuity

Stereoacuity (η) is the angular threshold for discrimination of depth based on binocular disparity. Let the eyes be converged on point F in the median plane of the head at distance d (Figure 3.23). Point P is another point in the median plane, distance Δd beyond point F. Let Δd be the least discriminable depth between F and P. Stereoacuity, η, is the threshold difference between the binocular angular subtenses of point F and point P and, to a first approximation, is given by:

$$\eta = \frac{a \Delta d}{d^2} \quad \text{in radians}$$

where a is the interocular distance. Thus, stereoacuity is proportional to the stereo base (distance between the eyes) and is inversely proportional to the square of the viewing distance.

For selected subjects under the best conditions, stereoacuity is in the range 2 to 6 arcsec and is at least as good as vernier acuity. A stereoacuity of 2 arcsec is equivalent to detecting a depth interval of 4 mm at 5 m. For a discussion of the many factors that influence stereoscopic acuity, see Howard and Rogers (1995).

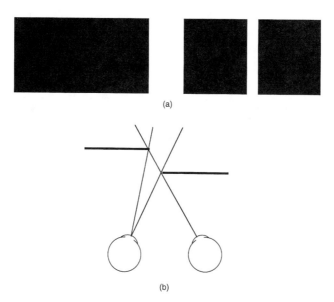

(a)

(b)

Figure 3.27 Monocular occlusion as a cue to depth.
NOTE: (a) Fusion of the two images creates the impression of one square in front of another, even though there are no binocular disparities in the fused image. (b) Two squares at different distances create the images shown in (a) when the squares are arranged so that one eye sees the gap between them but the other eye does not see the gap because the edges of the squares fall on the same line of sight.
SOURCE: (a) Adapted from Gillam, Blackburn, & Nakayama (1999).

The Pulfrich Effect

When a neutral density filter is held in front of one eye, a bob at the end of a pendulum swinging in a frontal plane appears to move in depth in an elliptical path. The motion is clockwise (from above) when the filter covers the left eye and counterclockwise when it covers the right eye (Figure 3.28). The effect was first reported by Carl Pulfrich (1922) and is known as the *Pulfrich effect.*

The generally accepted explanation of the effect is that the dimmer stimulus in the filtered eye is registered with a longer latency than is the unfiltered image in the other eye. Thus, signals about the object's position are relayed to the visual cortex with a temporal offset, and the filtered eye sees the object in a slightly earlier spatial position than does the unfiltered eye. This binocular disparity between the two images creates a sensation of depth. The latency hypothesis correctly predicts that the depth of the Pulfrich effect increases with an increase in filter density, speed of the pendulum bob, viewing distance, luminance, and contrast between bob and background (Lit & Hyman, 1951; Rogers & Anstis, 1972). For a detailed review of this topic, see Howard and Rogers (1995).

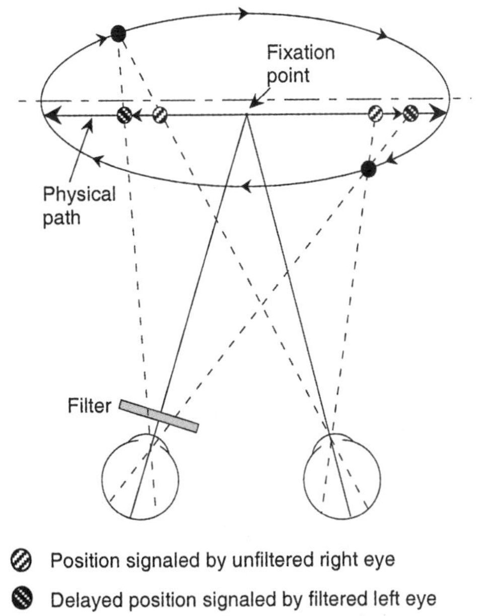

Stereopsis and Figural Organization

Stereopsis can affect the appearance of surface continuity, as shown in Figure 3.29 (Nakayama, Shimojo, & Silverman, 1989).

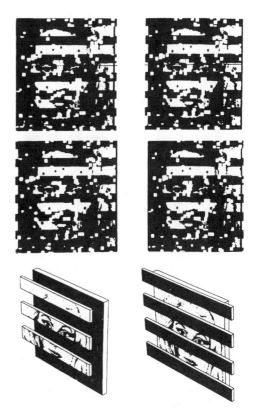

Figure 3.29 Effects of stereopsis on figural continuity.
NOTE: One stereogram creates a face seen through horizontal bars. The other creates strips of a face in front of a black surface.
SOURCE: From Nakayama, Shimojo, & Silverman (1989). *Psych Perception, 18.* Used with permission.

⊘ Position signaled by unfiltered right eye

⦿ Delayed position signaled by filtered left eye

Figure 3.28 The Pulfrich pendulum illusion.
NOTE: With a filter over the left eye, a pendulum bob appears to rotate in a clockwise elliptical path in depth, as seen from above. The bob's physical path (solid line) does not coincide with the major axis (dashed line) of the perceived elliptical path.
SOURCE: Adapted from Howard & Rogers (1995).

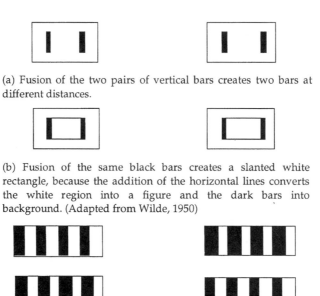

(a) Fusion of the two pairs of vertical bars creates two bars at different distances.

(b) Fusion of the same black bars creates a slanted white rectangle, because the addition of the horizontal lines converts the white region into a figure and the dark bars into background. (Adapted from Wilde, 1950)

(c) When the dark bars are seen as figures on a white ground, they appear as slanted planes, as in (d). When the white bars are seen as figures, they appear as slanted planes, as in (e). The crossed and uncrossed versions alternate independently. These effects may take time to develop. (Adapted from Metzger, 1975)

(d)   (e)

Figure 3.30   Figure-ground reversals and stereopsis.

An imposed change in figure-ground organization can prime or inhibit stereoscopic depth, as illustrated in Figure 3.30b (Wilde, 1950). Depth induced by disparity between parts of a pattern seen as figure has precedence over depth induced by disparity between parts seen as background. A spontaneous change in figure-ground organization can also affect how images are matched stereoscopically, as illustrated in Figure 3.30c (Metzger, 1975).

In Figure 3.31, a subjective triangle appears to overlap three black discs. If the eyes are converged or diverged by the right amount, the reader will see two fused images flanked by two monocular images. In one fused image, the subjective triangle comes forward. In the other fused image, the disparity places the triangle beyond the black discs, and only the corners of the triangle are seen. The stereogram in Figure 3.32 produces three overlapping rectangles above or below the plane of the corner elements.

Figure 3.31   Kanizsa triangle in stereo depth.
NOTE: Crossed or uncrossed fusion creates an illusory triangle in front of the Pac-Men and a triangle beyond the Pac-Men with only its corners visible through three holes.

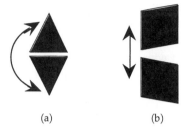

(a)   (b)

Figure 3.33 Three-dimensional apparent motion.
NOTE: (a) Apparent motion occurs in depth when the pyramids are alternated in rapid succession, because their configurational properties prompt a 3-D interpretation. (b) Trapezoids produce deforming motion in a plane.

Figure 3.32 Subjective rectangles in multiple planes.
NOTE: The stereograms create three overlapping rectangles in front of or beyond the black discs.
SOURCE: Redrawn from Ramachandran (1987).

Neurones in the region of the visual cortex known as V2 of the alert monkey respond when a subjective contour falls across the receptive field (Bakin, Nakayama, & Gilbert, 2000). The cells do not respond when the disparity of relationships between the inducing elements and the subjective shape place the shape beyond the inducing elements, as in one of the fused images of Figure 3.31. Anderson and Julesz (1995) have reviewed the subject of illusory contour formation in stereopsis.

Stereopsis and Visual Motion

Apparent motion is seen preferentially between stimuli that appear to lie in the same plane, even though the plane is inclined in depth (He & Nakayama, 1994). However, when configurational cues forbid a good pattern match within the same plane, apparent motion occurs out of the plane containing the moving shape (Wertheimer, 1912). For example, rapid alternation of the two triangles in Figure 3.33a produces a triangle rotat-

ing out of the plane, whereas an alternation of the trapezoids in Figure 3.33b produces a deforming trapezoid moving in a frontal plane.

See Julesz (1971) and Howard and Rogers (1995) for reviews of stereopsis.

**INTERACTIONS BETWEEN
DEPTH CUES**

Multiple depth cues may be combined in any of the following ways.

Cue Summation.   Two or more cues may combine to improve depth sensitivity. For example, the more depth cues that are present, the better able we are to discriminate small differences in depth.

Cue Averaging.   For example, depth produced by binocular disparity may be canceled by an opposite depth produced by motion parallax (Graham & Rogers, 1982). Cue averaging occurs only for cues that have a continuous range of values, that converge early on a common neural process, and that are not widely discordant. Otherwise, depth cues interact in one or other of the following ways.

Cue Confirmation and Perceptual Stability. Some cues confirm or supplement one another rather than average. This is most evident with bistable percepts. For example, the stability of a particular depth interpretation of a three-dimensional cube depends on the additive contributions of disparity and on the relative contrasts of far and near sides (Sperling & Dosher, 1995).

Cue Complementation. Two cues may complement each other. One cue may extend the stimulus range of a second, substitute for it when it is obscured, disambiguate it, or provide it with an error signal. For example, the cue of perspective operates over a larger range of distance than does that of binocular disparity.

Cue Dominance. When two cues conflict, one cue may be suppressed. For example, sound seems to emerge from the moving mouth of a ventriloquist's doll, even though auditory information indicates that it comes from the mouth of the ventriloquist.

Cue Dissociation. Each cue is interpreted as arising from a distinct object. For instance, when a seen bell and the sound it makes are well separated, two bells are perceived.

Cue Reinterpretation. A cue conflict may be resolved by a reinterpretation of the stimulus situation. For example, a looming image usually indicates motion in depth. If looming conflicts with another depth cue, it may be reinterpreted as a change in the size of the object.

Cue Recalibration. Prolonged exposure to conflicting depth cues may lead to a recalibration of one or the other cue (Epstein, 1975).

Interactions between Disparity and Motion Parallax

Binocular disparity and motion parallax interact in various ways. Our ability to discriminate a small difference in depth is improved when both binocular disparity and motion parallax are present (Pong, Kenner, & Otis, 1990). Prior inspection of a surface with corrugations specified by one of the two cues biases the direction of perceived depth of corrugations specified by the other cue (Graham & Rogers, 1982). Also, adaptation to a rotating sphere with unambiguous disparity biases the perceived direction of rotation of a monocularly viewed rotating sphere (Nawrot & Blake, 1991).

Interactions between Disparity and Perspective

Interaction between perspective and disparity depends on the type of perspective, on whether the stimulus is static or moving in depth, and on viewing distance.

Gillam (1968) found that the strong monocular cue of linear perspective at a value of zero slant reduced perceived slant of a surface produced by disparity, but that the weak monocular cue of foreshortening set at zero had no effect on disparity-induced slant.

Harwerth, Moeller, and Wensveen (1998) found that depth perception was dominated by disparity when disparity was varied and that it was dominated by size when size was varied. Thus, dynamic cues dominate static cues. When changing disparity is in conflict with changing perspective, perceived motion in depth is determined by changing disparity at low speeds and by changing perspective at higher speeds (Pong et al., 1990; Allison & Howard, 2000).

Johnston, Cumming, and Parker (1993) used textured stereograms of half cylinders, ridges, and spheres and found that disparity is more effective at near than at far distances than texture gradient is. Adding the correct texture gradient had a stronger effect for vertical cylinders than for horizontal cylinders. This suggests that relative compression disparity produced on surfaces slanted about a vertical axis is a weaker cue to depth than is shear disparity produced on surfaces inclined about a horizontal axis. A similar anisotropy was noted by Gillam, Chambers, and Russo (1988).

Interactions between Disparity and Interposition

An example of a conflict between disparity and interposition is provided by the stereogram in Figure 3.34a (Schriever, 1924). This

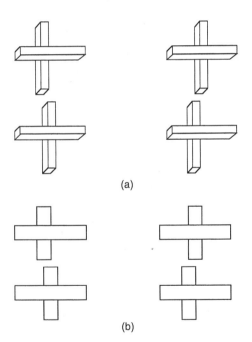

(a)

(b)

is an example of cue dominance. In Figure 3.34b, the ends of the horizontal bar sometimes appear to bend away from the viewer when disparity and overlap cues conflict. In this case, overlap dominates at the intersection, and disparity dominates at the ends of the horizontal bar (Zanforlin, 1982).

There are thus four ways to resolve incompatibility between disparity and overlap:

1. Dominance of overlap over disparity. This is cue dominance.

2. Phenomenal bending, in which both cues are preserved but in different locations. This is cue dissociation.

3. Figure segmentation, in which occlusion is reinterpreted as figural discontinuity.

4. Transparency, in which occlusion is reinterpreted as one surface seen through another.

Interactions between Disparity and Transparency

Figure 3.35 illustrates how disparity can force one to reinterpret occlusion as transparency. Proper convergence creates two stereoscopic, fused images flanked by monocular images. In one fused image the gray square should appear nearer than the black square. At first,

Figure 3.34 Interactions between disparity and overlap.
NOTE: (a) In one fused image the vertical stick appears beyond the horizontal stick. In the other fused image, the figural cue that the horizontal stick is nearer overrides the conflicting disparity information. (Adapted from Schriever, 1924) (b) In one fused image, the ends of the horizontal rectangle sometimes appear curved away from the viewer.

Figure 3.35 Effects of transparency on stereopsis.
NOTE: Fusion of the images produces two displays in depth. Depth is seen readily in the display in which the black square appears in front of the gray square. In the display in which disparity indicates that the grey square is in front, the gray square appears transparent after a time. Then depth in the two cases appears equal.

depth is not seen in the other fused image even though disparity signifies that the black square is in front of the gray square. This is because occlusion information indicates that the gray square is nearer than the black square. After a while, the black square pops out in front, and its physically missing corner is subjectively filled to form a complete transparent black square.

Cognition and Depth-Cue Interactions

A hollow mask of the human face appears as a normal convex face. This has been taken as evidence that familiarity overrides conflicting information from binocular disparity (Gregory, 1970). An upside-down face mask reverses in apparent depth less readily than an upright face does, presumably because an inverted face is more difficult to recognize than an upright face is. An unfamiliar object reverses less frequently still (Klopfer, 1991).

CONCLUSION

This has been a brief review of the types of sensory information that we use for the perception of a three-dimensional world. Even if some of the basic neural mechanisms are innate, they depend on early experience for their refinement. More complex mechanisms that involve interactions between different depth cues are probably learned during the first few months of life, but they continue to be refined and are subject to adaptive modification even in the adult. The coding of visual space is the single most complex process carried out by the cerebral cortex, and it occupies most areas of that organ. Our incomplete understanding of how the system works is reflected in the fact that computer robots operate at only a very rudimentary level.

REFERENCES

Allison, R. S., & Howard, I. P. (2000). Temporal dependencies in resolving monocular and binocular cue conflict in slant perception. *Vision Research, 40,* 1869–1886.

Ames, A. (1946). *Some demonstrations concerned with the origin and nature of our sensations: A laboratory manual.* Dartmouth, NH: Dartmouth Eye Institute.

Ames, A. (1951). Visual perception and the rotating trapezoidal window. *Psychological Monographs, 65*(Whole No. 324), 1–31.

Ames, A. (1955). *The nature of our perceptions, prehensions and behavior.* Princeton, NJ: Princeton University Press.

Andersen, G. J., & Braunstein, M. L. (1983). Dynamic occlusion in the perception of rotation in depth. *Perception and Psychophysics, 34,* 356–362.

Andersen, G. J., & Cortese, J. M. (1989). 2-D contour perception resulting from kinetic occlusion. *Perception and Psychophysics, 46,* 49–55.

Anderson, B. L., & Julesz, B. (1995). A theoretical analysis of illusory contour formation in stereopsis. *Psychological Review, 102,* 705–743.

Anstis, S. M., & Harris, J. P. (1974). Movement aftereffects contingent on binocular disparity. *Perception, 3,* 153–168.

Baird, J. C. (1963). Retinal and assumed size cues as determinants of size and distance perception. *Journal of Experimental Psychology, 66,* 155–162.

Bakin, J. S., Nakayama, K., & Gilbert, C. D. (2000). Visual responses in monkey areas V1 and V2 to three-dimensional surface configurations. *Journal of Neuroscience, 20,* 8188–8198.

Beck, J., & Gibson, J. J. (1955). The relation of apparent shape to apparent slant in the perception of objects. *Journal of Experimental Psychology, 50,* 125–133.

Beverley, K. I., & Regan, D. (1975). The relation between discrimination and sensitivity in the perception of motion in depth. *Journal of Physiology, 249,* 387–398.

Blakemore, C., & Sutton, P. (1969). Size adaptation: A new aftereffect. *Science, 166,* 245–247.

Boothroyd, K., & Blake, R. (1984). Stereopsis from disparity of complex grating patterns. *Vision Research, 24,* 1205–1222.

Bootsma, R. J. (1989). Accuracy of perceptual processing subserving different perception-action systems. *Quarterly Journal of Experimental Psychology, 41A,* 489–500.

Braunstein, M. L., Anderson, G. J., & Riefer, D. M. (1982). The use of occlusion to resolve ambiguity in parallel projections. *Perception and Psychophysics, 31,* 261–267.

Brenner, E., & Smeets, J. B. J. (2000). Comparing extra-retinal information about distance and direction. *Vision Research, 40,* 1649–1651.

Bulthoff, H. H., & Mallot, H. A. (1990). Integration of stereo, shading and texture. In A. Blake & T. Troscianko (Eds.), *AI and the eye* (pp. 119–146). Chichester: Wiley.

Carey, D. P., & Allan, K. (1996). A motor signal and "visual" size perception. *Experimental Brain Research, 110,* 482–486.

Carlson, V. R., & Tassone, E. P. (1971). Familiar versus unfamiliar size: A theoretical derivation and test. *Journal of Experimental Psychology, 71,* 109–115.

Cavallo, V., & Laurent, M. (1988). Visual information and skill level in time-to-collision estimation. *Perception, 17,* 623–632.

Chapanis, A., & McCleary, R. A. (1953). Interposition as a cue for the perception of relative distance. *Journal of General Psychology, 48,* 113–132.

Clark, W. C., Smith, A. H., & Rabe, A. (1955). Retinal gradient of outline as a stimulus for slant. *Canadian Journal of Psychology, 9,* 247–253.

Coleman, H. S., & Rosenberger, H. E. (1950). The attenuation of brightness contrast caused by atmospheric optical haze. *Journal of the Optical Society of America, 39,* 507–521.

Cumming, B. G. (1994). Motion-in-depth. In A. T. Smith & R. J. Snowden (Eds.), *Visual detection of motion* (pp. 333–366). London: Academic Press.

Cumming, B. G., Johnston, E. B., & Parker, A. J. (1993). Effects of different texture cues on curved surfaces viewed stereoscopically. *Vision Research, 33,* 827–838.

Curran, W., & Johnston, A. (1996). Three-dimensional curvature contrast-geometric or brightness illusion. *Vision Research, 36,* 3641–3653.

Cutting, J. E. (1986). *Perception with an eye to motion.* Cambridge: MIT Press.

Cutting, J. E., & Millard, R. T. (1984). Three gradients and the perception of flat and curved surfaces. *Journal of Experimental Psychology: General, 113,* 198–216.

Dean, P., Redgrave, P., & Westby, G. W. M. (1989). Event or emergency? Two response systems in the mammalian superior colliculus. *Trends in Neurosciences, 12,* 137–147.

Ebenholtz, S. M., & Paap, K. R. (1973). The constancy of object orientation: Compensation for ocular rotation. *Perception and Psychophysics, 14,* 458–470.

Enright, J. T. (1989). Manipulating stereopsis and vergence in an outdoor setting: Moon, sky and horizon. *Vision Research, 29,* 1815–1824.

Epstein, W. (1963). Attitudes of judgment and the size-distance hypothesis. *Journal of Experimental Psychology, 66,* 78–83.

Epstein, W. (1975). Recalibration by pairing: A process of perceptual learning. *Perception, 4,* 59–72.

Epstein, W., & Baratz, S. S. (1964). Relative size in isolation as a stimulus for relative perceived distance. *Journal of Experimental Psychology, 67,* 507–513.

Epstein, W., Bontrager, H., & Park, J. (1962). The induction of nonveridical slant and the perception of shape. *Journal of Experimental Psychology, 63,* 472–479.

Epstein, W., & Park, J. N. (1963). Shape constancy: Functional relationships and theoretical formulations. *Psychological Bulletin, 60,* 265–288.

Fisher, S. K., & Ciuffreda, K. J. (1988). Accommodation and apparent distance. *Perception, 17,* 609–621.

Fisher, S. K., & Ciuffreda, K. J. (1990). Adaptation to optically-increased interocular separation under naturalistic viewing conditions. *Perception, 19,* 171–180.

Fisher, S. K., & Ebenholtz, S. M. (1986). Does perceptual adaptation to telestereoscopically enhanced depth depend on the recalibration of binocular disparity? *Perception and Psychophysics, 40,* 101–109.

Foley, J. D., van Dam, A., Feiner, S. K., & Hughes, J. F. (1990). *Computer graphics.* New York: Addison-Wesley.

Foley, J. M. (1980). Binocular distance perception. *Psychological Review, 87,* 411–434.

Fox, R. (1991). Binocular rivalry. In D. Regan (Ed.), *Vision and visual dysfunction: Vol. 9. Binocular vision* (pp. 93–110). London: Macmillan.

Franklin, S. S., & Erickson, N. L. (1969). Perceived size of off-size familiar objects under formal and degraded viewing conditions. *Psychonomic Science, 15,* 312–313.

Gibson, J. J. (1950a). *The perception of the visual world.* Boston: Houghton-Mifflin.

Gibson, J. J. (1950b). The perception of visual surfaces. *American Journal of Psychology, 63,* 367–384.

Gibson, J. J. (1979). *The ecological approach to visual perception.* Boston: Houghton-Mifflin.

Gibson, J. J., Kaplan, G., Reynolds, H., & Wheeler, K. (1969). The change from visible to invisible: A study of optical transitions. *Perception and Psychophysics, 5,* 113–116.

Gibson, J. J., Olum, P., & Rosenblatt, F. (1955). Parallax and perspective during aircraft landings. *American Journal of Psychology, 68,* 372–385.

Gilinsky, A. S. (1955). The effect of attitude upon the perception of size. *American Journal of Psychology, 68,* 173–192.

Gillam, B. (1968). Perception of slant when perspective and stereopsis conflict: Experiments with aniseikonic lenses. *Journal of Experimental Psychology, 78,* 299–305.

Gillam, B., Blackburn, S., & Nakayama, K. (1999). Stereopsis based on monocular gaps: Metrical encoding of depth and slant without matching contours. *Vision Research, 39,* 493–502.

Gillam, B., Chambers, D., & Russo, T. (1988). Postfusional latency in slant perception and the primitives of stereopsis. *Journal of Experimental Psychology: Human Perception and Performance, 14,* 163–175.

Gogel, W. C. (1969). The sensing of retinal size. *Vision Research, 9,* 1079–1094.

Gogel, W. C. (1976). An indirect method of measuring perceived distance from familiar size. *Perception and Psychophysics, 20,* 419–429.

Gogel, W. C., & Mertens, H. W. (1968). Perceived depth between familiar objects. *Journal of Experimental Psychology, 77,* 206–211.

Gogel, W. C., & Tietz, J. D. (1973). Absolute motion parallax and the specific distance tendency. *Perception and Psychophysics, 13,* 284–292.

Gogel, W. C., & Tietz, J. D. (1977). Eye fixation and attention as modifiers of perceived distance. *Perceptual and Motor Skills, 45,* 343–362.

Goldstein, G. (1962). Moon illusion: An observation. *Science, 138,* 1340–1341.

Graham, M. E., & Rogers, B. J. (1982). Simultaneous and successive contrast effects in the perception of depth from motion-parallax and stereoscopic information. *Perception, 11,* 247–262.

Gray, R., & Regan, D. (1998). Accuracy of estimating time to collision using binocular and monocular information. *Vision Research, 38,* 499–512.

Gregory, R. L. (1970). *The intelligent eye.* New York: McGraw-Hill.

Gregory, R. L., & Ross, H. E. (1964). Visual constancy during movement: 2. Size constancy using one or both eyes or proprioceptive information. *Perceptual and Motor Skills, 18,* 23–26.

Grossberg, S. (1997). Cortical dynamics of three-dimensional figure-ground perception of two-dimensional pictures. *Psychological Review, 104,* 618–658.

Halloran, T. O. (1989). Picture perception is array-specific: Viewing angle versus apparent orientation. *Perception and Psychophysics, 45,* 467–482.

Halpern, D. L. (1991). Stereopsis from motion-defined contours. *Vision Research, 31,* 1611–1617.

Harvey, L. O., & Leibowitz, H. W. (1967). Effects of exposure duration, cue reduction, and temporary monocularity on size matching at short distances. *Journal of the Optical Society of America, 57,* 249–253.

Harwerth, R. S., Moeller, M. C., & Wensveen, J. M. (1998). Effects of cue context on the perception of depth from combined disparity and perspective cues. *Optometry and Vision Science, 75,* 433–444.

Hastorf, A. H., & Kennedy, J. L. (1957). Emmert's law and size constancy. *American Journal of Psychology, 70,* 114–116.

Hay, J. C., & Sawyer, S. (1969). Position constancy and binocular convergence. *Perception and Psychophysics, 5,* 310–312.

Hayakawa, H., Nishida, S., Wada, Y., & Kawato, M. (1994). A computational model for shape estimation by integration of shading and edge information. *Neural Networks, 7,* 1193–1209.

He, Z. J., & Nakayama, K. (1994). Perceived surface shape not features determines correspondence strength in apparent motion. *Vision Research, 34,* 2125–2135.

Heuer, H. (1993). Estimates of time to contact based on changing size and changing target vergence. *Perception, 22,* 549–563.

Heuer, H., & Lüschow, U. (1983). Aftereffects of sustained convergence: Some implications of the eye muscle potentiation hypothesis. *Perception, 12,* 337–346.

Hochberg, C. B., & Hochberg, J. E. (1952). Familiar size and the perception of depth. *Journal of Psychology, 34,* 107–114.

Hochberg, J. E., & McAlister, E. (1955). Relative size vs. familiar size in the perception of represented depth. *American Journal of Psychology, 68,* 294–296.

Holway, A. H., & Boring, E. G. (1940a). The moon illusion and the angle of regard. *American Journal of Psychology, 53,* 109–116.

Holway, A. H., & Boring, E. G. (1940b). The dependence of apparent visual size upon illu-mination. *American Journal of Psychology, 53,* 587–589.

Holway, A. H., & Boring, E. G. (1941). Determinants of apparent visual size with distance variant. *American Journal of Psychology, 54,* 21–37.

Howard, I. P. (1982). *Human visual orientation.* Chichester: Wiley.

Howard, I. P. (1983). Occluding edges in apparent reversal of convexity and concavity. *Perception, 12,* 85–86.

Howard, I. P. (1996). Alhazen's neglected discoveries of visual phenomena. *Perception, 25,* 1203–1218.

Howard, I. P., Bergström, S. S., & Ohmi, M. (1990). Shape from shading in different frames of reference. *Perception, 19,* 523–530.

Howard, I. P., & Rogers, B. J. (1995). *Binocular vision and stereopsis.* New York: Oxford University Press.

Howard, I. P., & Wade, N. (1996). Ptolemy on binocular vision. *Perception, 25,* 1189–1203.

Huffman, D. A. (1971). Impossible objects as nonsense sentences. In B. Meltzer & D. Michie (Eds.), *Machine intelligence* (Vol. 6, pp. 295–324). Edinburgh: Edinburgh University Press.

Ittelson, W. H. (1951). Size as a cue to distance: Static localization. *American Journal of Psychology, 64,* 54–67.

Ittelson, W. H. (1952). *The Ames demonstrations in perception.* Princeton, NJ: Princeton University Press.

Johansson, G. (1977). Studies on visual perception of locomotion. *Perception, 6,* 365–376.

Johnston, A., & Passmore, P. J. (1994). Shape from shading. I: Surface curvature and orientation. *Perception, 23,* 169–189.

Johnston, E. B., Cumming, B. G., & Parker, A. J. (1993). Integration of depth modules: Stereopsis and texture. *Vision Research, 33,* 813–826.

Joynson, R. B. (1949). The problem of size and distance. *Quarterly Journal of Experimental Psychology, 1,* 119–135.

Joynson, R. B. (1958). An experimental synthesis of the associationist and Gestalt accounts of the perception of size: II. *Quarterly Journal of Experimental Psychology, 10,* 142–154.

Joynson, R. B., & Newson, L. J. (1962). The perception of shape as a function of inclination. *British Journal of Psychology, 53,* 1–15.

Joynson, R. B., Newson, L. J., & May, D. S. (1965). The limits of over-constancy. *Quarterly Journal of Experimental Psychology, 17,* 209–215.

Julesz, B. (1960). Binocular depth perception of computer generated patterns. *Bell System Technical Journal, 39,* 1125–1162.

Julesz, B. (1971). *Foundations of cyclopean perception.* Chicago: University of Chicago Press.

Kaneko, H., & Uchikawa, K. (1997). Perceived angular and linear size: The role of binocular disparity and visual surround. *Perception, 26,* 17–27.

Kaufman, L., & Rock, I. (1962). The moon illusion: I. Explanation of this phenomenon through the use of artificial moons seen on the sky. *Science, 136,* 953–961.

Kersten, D., Mamassian, P., & Knill, D. C. (1997). Moving cast shadows induce apparent motion in depth. *Perception, 26,* 171–192.

Klopfer, D. S. (1991). Apparent reversals of a rotating mask. A new demonstration of cognition in perception. *Perception and Psychophysics, 49,* 522–530.

Knowles, W. B., & Carel, W. L. (1958). Estimating time-to-collision. *American Psychologist, 13,* 405–406.

Koenderink, J. J. (1986). Optic flow. *Vision Research, 26,* 161–180.

Koffka, K. (1935). *Principles of Gestalt psychology.* New York: Harcourt Brace.

Kraft, A. L., & Winnick, W. A. (1967). The effect of pattern and texture gradient on slant and shape judgments. *Perception and Psychophysics, 2,* 141–147.

Krekling, S., & Blika, S. (1983). Development of the tilted vertical horopter. *Perception and Psychophysics, 34,* 491–493.

Langdon, J. (1955). The role of spatial stimuli in the perception of changing shape: I. *Quarterly Journal of Experimental Psychology, 7,* 19–27.

Lasenby, J., & Bayro-Corrochano, E. (1999). Analysis and computation of projective invariants from multiple views in the geometric algebra framework. *International Journal of Pattern Recognition and Artificial Intelligence, 13,* 1105–1121.

Lee, D. N. (1976). A theory of visual control of braking based on information about time-to-collision. *Perception, 5,* 437–459.

Lee, D. N., Lishman, J. R., & Thompson, J. A. (1982). Regulation of gait in long jumping. *Journal of Experimental Psychology: Human Perception and Performance, 8,* 448–459.

Leibowitz, H. W., & Harvey, L. O. (1967). Size matching as a function of instructions in a naturalistic environment. *Journal of Experimental Psychology, 74,* 378–382.

Leibowitz, H. W., & Harvey, L. O. (1969). The effect of instructions, environment, and type of test object on matched size. *Journal of Experimental Psychology, 81,* 36–43.

Leibowitz, H., Shina, K., & Hennessy, R. T. (1972). Oculomotor adjustments and size constancy. *Perception and Psychophysics, 12,* 497–500.

Lichte, W. H. (1952). Shape constancy: Dependence upon angle of rotation, individual differences. *Journal of Experimental Psychology, 43,* 49–57.

Lichte, W. H., & Borresen, C. R. (1967). Influence of instructions on degree of shape constancy. *Journal of Experimental Psychology, 74,* 538–542.

Lit, A., & Hyman, A. (1951). The magnitude of the Pulfrich stereophenomenon as a function of distance of observation. *American Journal of Optometry and Archives of American Academy of Optometry, 28,* 564–580.

Livingstone, M. S. (1996). Differences between stereopsis, interocular correlation and binocularity. *Vision Research, 36,* 1127–1140.

Longuet-Higgins, H. C. (1981). A computer algorithm for reconstructing a scene from two projections. *Nature, 293,* 133–135.

Lu, C., & Fender, D. H. (1972). The interaction of color and luminance in stereoscopic vision. *Investigative Ophthalmology, 11,* 482–490.

Mallot, H. A., Arndt, P. A., & Bülthoff, H. H. (1996). A psychophysical and computational analysis of intensity-based stereo. *Biological Cybernetics, 75,* 187–198.

Marr, D., & Poggio, T. (1979). A computational theory of human stereo vision. *Proceedings of the Royal Society of London B, 204,* 301–328.

Marshall, J. A., Burbeck, C. A., Ariely, D., Rolland, J. P., & Martin, K. E. (1996). Occlusion edge blur: A cue to relative visual depth. *Journal of the Optical Society of America, 13,* 681–688.

Maunsell, J. H. R., & Van Essen, D. C. (1983). Functional properties of neurons in middle temporal visual area of the macaque monkey: II. Binocular interactions and sensitivity to binocular disparity. *Journal of Neurophysiology, 49,* 1148–1167.

Mayhew, J. E. W., & Frisby, J. P. (1976). Rivalrous texture stereograms. *Nature, 264,* 53–56.

Mayhew, J. E. W., & Frisby, J. P. (1981). Psychophysical and computational studies towards a theory of human stereopsis. *Artificial Intelligence, 17,* 349–385.

Mayhew, J. E. W., & Longuet-Higgins, H. C. (1982). A computational model of binocular depth perception. *Nature, 297,* 376–378.

McCready, D. (1985). On size, distance, and visual angle perception. *Perception and Psychophysics, 37,* 323–334.

McKee, S. P., & Levi, D. M. (1987). Dichoptic hyperacuity: The precision of nonius alignment. *Journal of the Optical Society of America A, 4,* 1104–1108.

McKee, S. P., & Welch, L. (1992). The precision of size constancy. *Vision Research, 32,* 1447–1460.

Meneghini, K. A., & Leibowitz, H. W. (1967). Effect of stimulus distance and age on shape constancy. *Journal of Experimental Psychology, 74,* 241–248.

Metzger, W. (1975). *Gesetze des Sehens.* Frankfurt: Kramer.

Mon-Williams, M., & Dijkerman, H. C. (1999). The use of vergence information in the programming of prehension. *Experimental Brain Research, 128,* 578–582.

Mon-Williams, M., & Tresilian, J. R. (1999). Some recent studies on the extraretinal contribution to distance perception. *Perception, 28,* 167–181.

Mon-Williams, M., Tresilian, J. R., & Roberts, A. (2000). Vergence provides veridical depth perception from horizontal retinal image disparities. *Experimental Brain Research, 133,* 407–413.

Nakayama, K., Shimojo, S., & Silverman, G. H. (1989). Stereoscopic depth: Its relation to image segmentation, grouping, and the recognition of occluded objects. *Perception, 18,* 55–58.

Nawrot, M., & Blake, R. (1991). The interplay between stereopsis and structure from motion. *Perception and Psychophysics, 49,* 230–244.

Nelson, T. M., & Bartley, S. H. (1956). The perception of form in an unstructured field. *Journal of General Psychology, 54,* 57–63.

Ogle, K. N. (1964). *Researches in binocular vision.* New York: Hafner.

Ono, H. (1969). Apparent distance as a function of familiar size. *Journal of Experimental Psychology, 79,* 109–115.

Ono, H. (1970). Some thoughts on different perceptual tasks related to size and distance. *Psychological Monograph Supplements, 3*(Whole No. 45), 143–151.

Osuobeni, E. P., & O'Leary, D. J. (1986). Chromatic and luminance difference contribution to stereopsis. *American Journal of Optometry and Physiological Optics, 63,* 970–977.

Over, R. (1960). Size and distance judgements under reduction conditions. *Australian Journal of Psychology, 12,* 162–168.

Over, R. (1963). Size- and distance-estimates of a single stimulus under different viewing conditions. *American Journal of Psychology, 76,* 452–457.

Page, W. K., & Duffy, C. J. (1999). MST neuronal responses to heading direction during pursuit eye movements. *Journal of Neurophysiology, 81,* 596–610.

Panum, P. L. (1858). *Physiologische Untersuchungen über das Sehen mit zwei Augen.* Keil: Schwers.

Pentland, A. P. (1982). Finding the direction of illumination. *Journal of the Optical Society of America, 72,* 448–455.

Petersik, J. T., Shepard, A., & Malsch, R. (1984). A three-dimensional motion aftereffect produced by prolonged adaptation to a rotation simulation. *Perception, 13,* 489–497.

Phillips, R. J. (1970). Stationary visual texture and the estimation of slant angle. *Quarterly Journal of Experimental Psychology, 22,* 389–397.

Plug, C., & Ross, H. E. (1994). The natural moon illusion: A multifactor angular account. *Perception, 23,* 321–33.

Poggio, G. F., & Talbot, W. H. (1981). Mechanisms of static and dynamic stereopsis in foveal cortex of the rhesus monkey. *Journal of Physiology, 315,* 469–492.

Pong, T. C., Kenner, M. A., & Otis, J. (1990). Stereo and motion cues in preattentive vision processing: Some experiments with random-dot stereographic image sequences. *Perception, 19,* 161–170.

Predebon, G. M., Wenderoth, P. M., & Curthoys, I. S. (1974). The effects of instructions and distance on judgments of off-size familiar objects under natural viewing condition. *American Journal of Psychology, 87,* 425–439.

Predebon, J. (1992). The role of instructions and familiar size in absolute judgments of size and distance. *Perception and Psychophysics, 51,* 344–354.

Pulfrich, C. (1922). Die stereoskopie im Dienste der isochromen und heterochromen Photometrie. *Naturwissenschaften, 10,* 553–564.

Ramachandran, V. S. (1987). Visual perception of surfaces: A biological approach. In S. Petry and G. E. Meyer (Eds.), *The perception of illusory contours* (pp. 93–108). New York: Springer.

Ratoosh, P. (1949). On interposition as a cue for the perception of distance. *Proceedings of the National Academy of Sciences, 35,* 257–259.

Regan, D. (1986). Visual processing of four kinds of relative motion. *Vision Research, 26,* 127–145.

Regan, D., & Beverley, K. I. (1973). Some dynamic features of depth perception. *Vision Research, 13,* 2369–2379.

Regan, D., & Beverley, K. I. (1978). Looming detectors in the human visual pathway. *Vision Research, 18,* 415–421.

Regan, D., & Beverley, K. I. (1982). How do we avoid confounding the direction we are looking and the direction we are moving? *Science, 215,* 194–196.

Regan, D., & Beverley, K. I. (1984). Psychophysics of visual flow patterns and motion in depth. In L. Spillmann & B. R. Wooten (Eds.), *Sensory experience, adaptation and perception* (pp. 215–40). Hillsdale, NJ: Erlbaum.

Regan, D., & Cynader, M. (1979). Neurons in area 18 of cat visual cortex selectively sensitive to changing size: Nonlinear interactions between responses to two edges. *Vision Research, 19,* 699–711.

Regan, D., & Hamstra, S. J. (1993). Dissociation of discrimination thresholds for time to contact and for rate of angular expansion. *Vision Research, 33,* 447–462.

Regan, D., & Kaushal, S. (1993). Monocular discrimination of the direction of motion in depth. *Vision Research, 34,* 163–178.

Reinhardt-Rutland, A. H. (1990). Detecting orientation of a surface: The rectangularity postulate and primary depth cues. *Journal of General Psychology, 117,* 391–401.

Rock, I. (1975). *An introduction to perception.* New York: Macmillan.

Rock, I., & Ebenholtz, S. (1959). The relational determination of perceived size. *Psychological Review, 66,* 387–401.

Rock, I., & Kaufman, L. (1962). The moon illusion: II. The moon's apparent size is a function of the presence or absence of terrain. *Science, 136,* 1023–1030.

Roelofs, C. O., & Zeeman, W. P. C. (1957). Apparent size and distance in binocular and monocular distance. *Ophthalmologica, 133,* 183–204.

Rogers, B. J. (1993). Motion parallax and other dynamic cues for depth in humans. In F. A. Miles & J. Wallman (Eds.), *Visual motion and its role in the stabilization of gaze* (pp. 119–137). Amsterdam: Elsevier.

Rogers, B. J., & Antis, S. M. (1972). Intensity versus adaptation and the Pulfrich stereophenomenon. *Vision Research, 12,* 909–928.

Rogers, B. J., & Graham, M. E. (1979). Motion parallax as an independent cue for depth perception. *Perception, 8,* 125–134.

Rosenholtz, R., & Malik, J. (1997). Surface orientation from texture: Isotropy or homogeneity (or both)? *Vision Research, 37,* 2283–2293.

Ross, H. E., & Plug, C. (1998). The history of size constancy and size illusions. In V. Walsh & J. Kulikowski (Eds.), *Perceptual constancy* (pp. 499–528). Cambridge: Cambridge University Press.

Rump, E. E. (1961). The relationship between perceived size and perceived distance. *British Journal of Psychology, 52,* 111–124.

Savelsbergh, G. J. P., Whiting, H. T. A., & Bootsma, R. J. (1991). Grasping tau. *Journal of Experimental Psychology: Human Perception and Performance, 17,* 315–322.

Schriever, W. (1924). Experimentelle Studien über stereoskopisches Sehen. *Zeitschrift fur Psychologie, 96,* 113–170.

Sedgwick, H. A. (1986). Space perception. In K. R. Boff, L. Kaufman, & J. P. Thomas (Eds.), *Handbook of human perception and performance.* New York: Wiley (pp. 21-1 to 21-57).

Siderov, J., Harwerth, R. S., & Bedell, H. E. (1999). Stereopsis, cyclovergence and the backward tilt of the vertical horopter. *Vision Research, 39,* 1347–1357.

Simmons, D. R., & Kingdom, F. A. A. (1995). Differences between stereopsis with isoluminant and isochromatic stimuli. *Journal of the Optical Society of America A, 12,* 2094–2104.

Slack, C. W. (1956). Familiar size as a cue to size in the presence of conflicting cues. *Journal of Experimental Psychology, 52,* 194–198.

Smith, A. H. (1964). Judgment of slant with constant outline convergence and variable surface texture gradient. *Perceptual and Motor Skills, 18,* 869–875.

Sperling, G., & Dosher, B. A. (1995). Depth from motion. In T. V. Papathomas (Ed.), *Early vision and beyond* (pp. 133–43). Cambridge: MIT Press.

Taylor, F. V. (1941). Changes in the size of the after-image induced in total darkness. *Journal of Experimental Psychology, 29,* 75–80.

Teghtsoonian, M. (1971). A comment on "The apparent size of 'projected' afterimages under conditions where size-constancy holds." *Perception and Psychophysics, 10,* 98.

Teghtsoonian, M. (1974). The doubtful phenomenon of over-constancy. In H. R. Moskowitz, B. Scharf, & J. C. Stevens (Eds.), *Sensation and measurement.* Dordrecht, Netherlands: Reidel.

Thouless, R. H. (1930). Phenomenal regression to the real object: I. *British Journal of Psychology, 21,* 339–359.

Todd, J. T. (1981). Visual information about moving objects. *Journal of Experimental Psychology: Human Perception and Performance, 7,* 795–810.

Todd, J. T. (1982). Visual information about rigid and nonrigid motion: A geometric analysis. *Journal of Experimental Psychology: Human Perception and Performance, 8,* 238–252.

Todd, J. T., & Mingolla, E. (1983). Perception of surface curvature and direction of illumination from patterns of shading. *Journal of Experimental Psychology: Human Perception and Performance, 9,* 583–595.

Tyer, Z. E., Allen, J. A., & Pasnak, R. (1983). Instruction effects on size and distance judgments. *Perception and Psychophysics, 34,* 135–139.

Tyler, C. W. (1974). Induced stereomovement. *Vision Research, 14,* 609–613.

Tyler, C. W. (1991). The horopter and binocular fusion. In D. Regan (Ed.), *Vision and visual dysfunction: Vol. 9. Binocular Vision* (pp. 19–37). London: Macmillan.

Tyler, C. W., & Cavanagh, P. (1991). Purely chromatic perception of motion in depth: Two eyes as sensitive as one. *Perception and Psychophysics, 49,* 53–61.

Ullman, S. (1979). *The interpretation of visual motion.* Cambridge: MIT Press.

van den Berg, A. V. (1992). Robustness of perception of heading from optic flow. *Vision Research, 32,* 1285–1296.

van den Enden, A., & Spekreijse, H. (1989). Binocular reversals despite familiarity cues. *Science, 244,* 959–961.

Verstraten, F. A. J., Verlinde, R., Fredericksen, R. E., & van de Grind, W. A. (1994). A transparent motion aftereffect contingent on binocular disparity. *Perception, 23,* 1181–1188.

Vogel, J. M., & Teghtsoonian, M. (1972). The effects of perspective alterations on apparent size and distance scales. *Perception and Psychophysics, 11,* 294–298.

Von Hofsten, C., Rosengren, K., Pick, H. L., & Needy, G. (1992). The role of binocular information in ball catching. *Journal of Motor Behavior, 24,* 329–338.

Wallach, H., & Floor, L. (1971). The use of size matching to demonstrate the effectiveness of accommodation and convergence as cues for distance. *Perception and Psychophysics, 10,* 423–428.

Wallach, H., & Halperin, P. (1977). Eye muscle potentiation does not account for adaptation in distance perception based on oculomotor cues. *Perception and Psychophysics, 22,* 427–430.

Wallach, H., Moore, M. E., & Davidson, L. (1963). Modification of stereoscopic depth perception. *American Journal of Psychology, 76,* 191–204.

Wallach, H., & O'Connell, D. N. (1953). The kinetic depth effect. *Journal of Experimental Psychology, 45,* 205–217.

Wallach, H., Yablick, G. S., & Smith, A. (1972). Target distance and adaptation in distance perception in the constancy of visual direction. *Perception and Psychophysics, 12,* 139–145.

Walsh, V., & J. Kulikowski, J. (Eds.). (1998). *Perceptual constancy.* Cambridge: Cambridge University Press.

Warren, W. H., Morris, M. W., & Kalish, M. (1988). Perception of translational heading from optical flow. *Journal of Experimental Psychology: Human Perception and Performance, 14,* 646–660.

Warren, W. H., Young, D. S., & Lee, D. N. (1986). Visual control of step length during running over irregular terrain. *Journal of Experimental Psychology: Human Perception and Performance, 12,* 259–266.

Weiskrantz, L. (1986). *Blindsight: A case study and implications.* London: Oxford University Press.

Wertheimer, M. (1912). Experimentelle Studien über das Sehen von Bewegung. *Zeitschrift für Psychologie und Physiologie des Sinnesorgane, 61,* 161–265.

Wilde, K. (1950). Der Punktreiheneffekt und die Rolle der binocularen Querdisparation beim Tiefensehen. *Psychologische Forschung, 23,* 223–262.

Zanforlin, M. (1982). Figural organization and binocular interaction. In J. Beck (Ed.), *Organization and representation in perception* (pp. 251–67). Hillsdale, NJ: Erlbaum.

CHAPTER 4

Motion Perception

ROBERT SEKULER, SCOTT N. J. WATAMANIUK, AND RANDOLPH BLAKE

INTRODUCTION AND OVERVIEW

Gordon Lynn Walls, a comparative anatomist, observed, "If asked what aspect of vision means the most to them, a watchmaker may answer 'acuity,' a night flier 'sensitivity,' and an artist 'color.' But to the animals which invented the vertebrate eye, and hold the patents on most of the features of the human model, the visual registration of *movement* was of the greatest importance" (Walls, 1942) p. 342.

The rich and rapidly expanding scientific literature on visual motion perception suggests that Walls was right: To organisms all up and down the phylogenetic scale, visual motion perception is of unmatched importance. Visual motion serves a wide variety of crucial roles: wayfinding (optic flow), perception of shape from motion, depth segregation, judgments of coincidence (time to collision, time to filling a tea cup), judgments of motion direction and speed, and perception of animate, biological activity. Sometimes, the presence of motion can compensate for deficiencies in other forms of visual information, as Figure 4.1 shows. The three images in the figure are frames from a video showing a person performing a common action. Clearly, no single frame conveys sufficient spatial structure to permit recognition that a person is present, let alone recognition of what the person might be doing. However, the complex patterns of

visual motion generated when these frames are displayed as part of a video convey immediately that a person is present and that the person is in the process of sitting down (Bobick & Davis, 2001).[1]

Recent decades have produced major advances in understanding of visual motion perception.[2] Many such advances have come from complementary approaches to analyzing motion: psychophysical, computational, and neurophysiological. It is now known that the detection and analysis of motion are achieved by a cascade of neural operations, starting with the registration of local motion signals within restricted regions of the visual field and continuing with the integration of those local motion signals into more global descriptions of the direction and speed of object motion. Physiological studies of animals—most notably cats and monkeys—have revealed some of the neural hardware comprising this hierarchical processing scheme. Recently, exciting

---

[1] To download the video from the Internet, go to http://www.cis.ohio-state.edu/~jwdavis/Archive/blurmotion.mpg or http://www.cis.ohio-state.edu/~jwdavis/Archive/blurmotion.mov.

[2] Previous editions of this handbook paid scant notice to the topic of our chapter. In the first edition, Graham (1951) spent just six pages on motion perception, emphasizing research on apparent motion. In the second edition, more than three decades later, the coverage was increased by only ten pages distributed over two chapters (Hochberg, 1988; Westheimer, 1988).

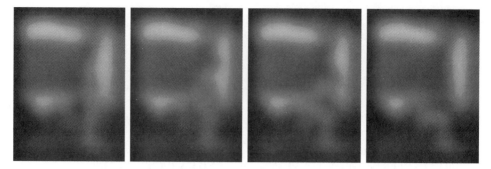

Figure 4.1   Four still frames cut from a video by Bobick and Davis (2001). Used with permission. NOTE: The video shows a person engaged in a common, everyday activity. The low-pass spatial filtering of video makes it difficult, from any individual frame, to discern the person, let alone what the person is doing. However, when the video is played at normal rate, the pattern of motions makes both the person and the person's action immediately apparent.

new techniques including brain imaging and transcranial magnetic stimulation have been deployed in concert with psychophysics to identify neural concomitants of motion perception in the human visual system.

Our goal in this chapter is to highlight some of these exciting developments. However, limitations on space—together with the exponential growth of the literature on motion perception—forced on us hard choices about what to include and what to omit. Thus, this chapter emphasizes motion in the front-parallel plane, unavoidably deemphasizing work on motion in depth and "cyclopean" motion perception (Patterson, 1999). In addition, the chapter focuses on motions of objects defined by luminance contrast, with little discussion of important work on the role of chromatic information in motion processing (Dobkins, 2000; Gegenfurtner & Hawken, 1996). The chapter slights numerous interesting and potentially informative illusions of motion (e.g., Hikosaka, Miyauchi, & Shimojo, 1993; Krekelberg & Lappe, 2001; Viviani & Stucchi, 1989). Moreover, our coverage primarily focuses on motion perception in primates, particularly Homo sapiens. Consequently, interesting work on motion perception in birds (e.g., Bischof, Reid, Wylie,

& Spetch, 1999; Wylie, Bischof, & Frost, 1998), fish (e.g., Albensi & Powell, 1998; Orger, Smear, Antis, & Baier, 2000) and insects (e.g., Dror, O'Carroll, & Laughlin, 2001; Gabbiani, Mo, & Laurent, 2001) has been left out. Our chapter does include research on "atypical observers," particularly individuals with diminished motion sensitivity consequent to brain damage.

Stimuli

In introducing the first edition of this handbook, Stanley Smith Stevens (1951, pp. 31–32) observed that "In a sense there is only one problem of psychophysics, the definition of the stimulus. . . . [T]he complete definition of the stimulus to a given response involves the specification of all the transformations of the environment, both internal and external, that leave the response invariant. This specification of the conditions of invariance would entail, of course, a complete understanding of the factors that produce and that alter responses." We agree. As this chapter underscores, contemporary research on visual motion perception has advanced in large measure because researchers are able to generate and deploy suitable stimuli, including innovative computer-generated animations, that simulate complex, real-life events.

Commenting on one aspect of this challenge, Graham (1965, pp. 579–580) cautioned that "we must take care that parameters are not confounded, a danger that arises only too readily from the fact that velocity itself involves the variables of distance and time. In any given experiment the variables of time, distance, interval between stimuli, and cycle of repetition of stimuli must be clearly analyzed before we can be confident that unequivocal conclusions may be drawn."

Researchers have developed many clever ways around the confounds that Stevens warned against. Consider just two examples. Under normal circumstances, a visual target's movement always involves a change of that object's shape, position, or both. This confounding of motion and position change has made it difficult to connect psychophysical responses to motion alone. To break the confound, Nakayama and Tyler (1981) generated matrices in which black and white cells alternated at random. All cells in a row were shifted back and forth, left and right; with appropriate rates of shift, observers saw oscillatory motion. The cells were small (<3 minarc) and spatially quite dense. Moreover, because all cells of the same color were indistinguishable from one another, the positions of individual elements could not be tracked. Despite the absence of position information, observers could detect the oscillatory motion generated by shifts of pattern elements.

Consider a second example of a stimulus designed to test a hypothesis about motion perception. To explore how the visual system combines or segregates spatially intermingled motions in different directions, Qian, Andersen, and Adelson (1994) created displays whose every local region contained balanced, opposite directions of motion. The locally opposed directions tended to cancel one another, which caused observers to see no overall motion. This chapter offers numerous other examples of complex stimuli specifically designed to probe particular aspects of motion perception.

Overview of Motion Processing Stages

Where appropriate, this chapter relates psychophysical results on motion perception to underlying neural mechanisms. An interest in establishing such connections drives much contemporary research into visual motion. For this reason, it will be helpful to provide a broad overview of the anatomy and physiology of those portions of the primate visual system explicitly involved in the analysis of motion information (see Figure 4.2); for a more detailed account, see Croner and Albright (1999).

Among the neurons in the visual systems of primates, cells selectively responsive to the direction of motion are first encountered in area V1, the primary visual cortex, which is located in the occipital lobe. Such neurons are often described as "tuned" for direction.[3] Beginning with the landmark work of Hubel and Wiesel (1968), it has been known that a significant fraction of V1 neurons respond best when a contour moves through their receptive fields in a particular direction; responses are significantly diminished when movement is in the opposite direction. Different neurons have different preferred directions of motion, with all directions around the clock represented within the ensemble of neurons. This inaugural stage of processing comprises a local analysis of motion energy. In this analysis, direction-selective neurons act as filters that register the presence of component features of moving objects within

---

[3] As Parker and Newsome put it (1998, p. 229), "A neuron is considered to be 'tuned' if the response is strongest to a particular value (or narrow range of values) of the stimulus and declines monotonically as stimulus values depart from this 'preferred' value."

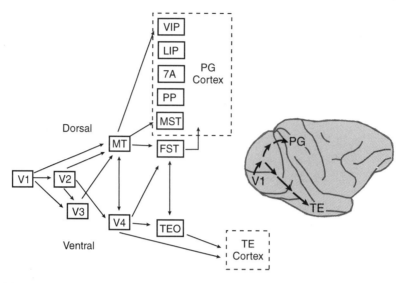

Figure 4.2 Diagram illustrating proposed functional and anatomical streams in the primate cerebral cortex.

NOTE: Partially separate streams carry information from area V1 either dorsally, toward the inferior parietal cortex (PG), or ventrally, toward the inferior temporal cortex (TE). Arrows indicate the main feedforward projections between areas. Abbreviations used in the diagram: V1, primary or striate cortex; MT, middle temporal area (also known as V5); VIP, ventral intraparietal; LIP, lateral intraparietal; PP, posterior parietal, MST, medial superior temporal; FST, fundus superior temporal; PG, inferior parietal cortex; TE, inferior temporal cortex.

SOURCE: After Ungerleider and Haxby (1994).

the local regions of their receptive fields (Emerson, Bergen, & Adelson, 1992).

The outputs of these local filters in area V1, in turn, activate second-stage analyzers that integrate motion signals over more extended regions of visual space. This second-stage analysis begins with neurons in the middle temporal visual area, or area MT, as it is typically called. Area MT receives some of its input directly from area V1 and the rest indirectly from area V1 via areas V2 and V3. Nearly all neurons in area MT are selective for the direction and speed of stimulus motion, again with the range of preferred directions among neurons spanning 360 degrees. MT neurons have larger receptive fields than do V1 neurons, which means that they can integrate motion signals over larger regions of visual space. Moreover, a given MT neuron will respond to motion in its preferred

direction regardless of whether those motion signals are carried by luminance, color, or texture. MT neurons, in other words, exhibit form invariance (Croner & Albright, 1999), implying that those neurons register motion information per se. MT neurons, in turn, project to higher visual areas that encode more complex forms of motion, including expansion and rotation (Tanaka & Saito, 1989) and motion-defined boundaries (Van Oostende, Sunaert, Van Hecke, Marchal, & Orban, 1997). Outputs from area MT also make their way to visual areas in the frontal lobe that are concerned with the control of eye movements (Bichot, Thompson, Chenchal Rao, & Schall, 2001; Schall, 2000).

A great many studies implicate area MT in the perception of motion. Though neurons in area MT certainly contribute to the perception of motion, it is clear that this is not the sole site where neurons extract significant motion information. Actually, various aspects of motion perception depend on the neural computations carried out in different areas of the cortex. Normally, motion perception depends on activity distributed over many areas of the brain, each extracting somewhat different information from the retinal image. Complicating matters, in macaque monkeys, which have visual systems that are highly similar to those of Homo sapiens, back-projections from area MT to area V1 have been demonstrated (Beckers & Homberg, 1992). Initial evidence suggests that in humans this back-projection may be important for conscious awareness of visual motion. To explore this idea, Pascual-Leone and Walsh (2001) applied brief pulses of magnetic energy[4] to spatially restricted regions of the scalps of human observers. This technique is known as transcranial magnetic stimulation (TMS). When the localized pulses are adjusted in duration, frequency, and amplitude and are delivered to particular regions of the scalp, TMS creates sensations of flashes of light. Called *phosphenes,* these flashes appear to move when the pulses are delivered to the scalp overlaying visual area MT, but they are stationary when TMS is delivered to the scalp that overlays area V1. By applying separate TMS pulses asynchronously to area V1 and area MT, Pascual-Leone and Walsh obliterated observers' conscious experience of the moving phosphenes that were ordinarily evoked by MT stimulation. This result

required the investigators to deliver TMS to area V1 some tens of milliseconds after area MT was stimulated. Presumably, the obliteration of motion perception is caused by a disruption of a re-entrant: back-projections from area MT to area V1. A similar result was reported by Beckers and Homberg (1992).

The preceding description of the motion pathway was based mainly on physiological and anatomical studies of nonhuman primates. During the past decade, understanding of motion perception's neuronal substrates in humans has been advanced significantly by the use of brain imaging techniques, primarily functional magnetic resonance imaging (fMRI). This growing literature has identified at least a dozen distinct regions in which neurons respond to visual motion. These regions in the human brain stretch from the occipital lobe to the frontal lobe (Culham, He, Dukelow, & Verstraten, 2001; Sunaert, Van Hecke, Marchal, & Orban, 1999). Among the regions responsive to motion are area V1 (which responds to almost any moving pattern, as well as to stimulus flicker) and the MT/medial superior temporal (MST) complex, located on the brain's lateral surface near the junction of the occipital, parietal, and temporal lobes. This region, which we shall refer to as MT+, responds weakly to flicker but strongly to coherent motion, including optic flow patterns (discussed later). Other important motion areas include area KO (for kinetic occipital), which responds preferentially to motion-defined boundaries, and area STS (for superior temporal sulcus), which is especially responsive to patterns of motion that portray biological motion. As appropriate, brain imaging results are introduced throughout this chapter to clarify the neural computations that make motion perception possible.

With this overview in place, we can now explore several aspects of motion perception that make it so crucially important for guidance of people's everyday activities.

---

[4]TMS offers a powerful tool for investigating cognitive or perceptual neural circuitry (Pascual-Leone, Walsh, & Rothwell, 2000), including circuitry that supports various aspects of motion perception (e.g., Hotson & Anand, 1999; Walsh, Ellison, Battelli, & Cowey, 1998). When the TMS coil is positioned against an observer's skull, a powerful, focused magnetic field hits and penetrates the skull. The field penetrates superficial layers of the cerebral cortex, and can temporarily terminate or modify currently ongoing neural activity or alter neural activity that is about to begin.

THE LIMITS OF MOTION PERCEPTION

Motion Detection

Visual motion can be construed as an event that unfolds over space and time. Distilled to the simplest case, motion involves a continuous change in the spatial position of a single object over time; this can be depicted in the form of a space-time plot in which spatial position along one dimension is plotted as the function of time in Figure 4.3. Intuitively, one might expect that the ease with which this kind of simple event can be seen would depend on the magnitude of the displacement over time and on the rate at which that

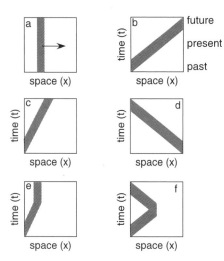

Figure 4.3   Illustrative space-time (x-t) diagrams that are used to represent motion.
NOTE: Panel A: Vertical bar moves rightward at constant speed. Panel B: The space-time representation of the movement in Panel A. Panel C: Space-time representation for bar moving rightward at higher speed than in Panel A. Panel D: Space-time representation for bar moving leftward at same speed as in Panel A. Panel E: Space-time representation for bar that moves rightward, stops suddenly, and remains stationary. Panel F: Space-time representation for bar that moves rightward and then abruptly reverses direction.

displacement occurred. There is truth to this intuition. Consider, for example, the movement of a clock's minute hand. People cannot see the clock hand's gradual progression, but intuitively we know that it has moved because its position has changed over time. Motion perception, however, need not involve any kind of intuitive process; motion is a direct experience, uniquely specified by the visual system (Exner, 1888; Nakayama, 1981; Thorson, Lange, & Biederman-Thorson, 1969). But how sensitive is the system that generates this experience? What is the lower limit for detection of motion? Measurements with a single moving object show that an object must traverse at least 1 minarc for a sensation of motion to be experienced. (This distance is approximately the edge-to-edge lateral separation between adjacent alphanumeric characters on this page when viewed at arm's length.) This value varies, however, with the object's duration, velocity, and luminance, as well as with the region of the retina stimulated. An up-to-date summary of this literature is given by Tayama (2000).

Very seldom, however, are people called upon to detect the motion of a single object appearing in isolation. Instead, most everyday detection of motion involves the detection of an object's (or a group of objects') motion *relative* to another object (or another set of objects). And at this challenge—detecting relative motion—humans excel. We are vastly better at detecting relative motion than we are at detecting absolute motion (e.g., Leibowitz, 1955). This is strikingly demonstrated in a study by Lappin, Donnelly, and Kojima (2001) in which observers viewed an array of three horizontally aligned "blobs" (circular, Gaussian luminance patches). In one condition, all three blobs moved laterally back and forth in unison (in-phase motion), and in another condition the center blob's direction of motion was opposite to that of the flanking blobs (antiphase, or relative, motion).

Motion acuity—the smallest detectable motion displacement—was actually better for the antiphase condition compared with the in-phase condition. In other words, tiny motion displacements visible in the antiphase condition were impossible to see when there was no relative motion. This finding dovetails nicely with earlier results showing that humans are keenly sensitive to shearing motion (Nakayama, 1981; Snowden, 1992), which also entails relative motion instead of overall rigid displacement. This direction contrast amplifies differences in motion vectors in neighboring regions of the visual field. One must keep in mind that in the research described later, motion performance is measured for moving targets that appear within some background framework.

Intuition suggests that motion might render an object less detectable. (Consider, for example, the difficulty that a person experiences when trying to read a newspaper in a moving subway.) Under most circumstances, however, exactly the opposite is true. Especially for objects with significant energy at low spatial frequencies, motion can render an otherwise invisible object visually conspicuous (Robson, 1966). To experience this for yourself, hold an object between the uniform surface of a wall and a light source in order to create a large, very faint shadow on the wall. When the nonmoving dim shadow fades to invisibility, move the occluding object and notice how the shadow abruptly springs into existence. The familiar textbook example of seeing the retinal blood vessels in your own eye by jiggling (i.e., moving) a light source on your sclera is another instance of motion's ability to reveal what otherwise would have been undetectable.

To characterize more precisely the optimal stimulus for the motion system, researchers have exploited the lower envelope principle. Barlow first called attention to the principle 40 years ago and most recently framed it this way: "Sensory thresholds are set by the class of sensory unit that has the lowest threshold for the particular stimulus used and are little influenced by the presence or absence of responses in the enormous number of other neurons that are less sensitive to that stimulus" (Barlow, 1995, p. 418). Discussing various applications of the principle to sensory systems, Parker and Newsome (1998, p. 242) noted that "in its pure form, the lower envelope principle means literally that a single neuron governs the behavioral threshold. The development of the lower envelope principle has been very much a reaction by neurophysiologists to the formerly prevalent notion that single neurons are inherently unreliable devices."

In an attempt to apply the lower envelope principle to motion, Watson and Turano (1995) measured the minimum contrast at which observers could discriminate direction of movement. Their test stimuli were drawn from a family of patterns known as Gabor functions. Each Gabor function comprises a sinusoidal grating that has been multiplied, point by point, by the values of a two-dimensional Gaussian function. This multiplication modulates the sinusoid's contrast, producing a pattern whose contrast falls off smoothly in all directions from a maximum at the pattern's center.[5] In search of the most easily seen moving stimulus, Watson and Turano independently varied the spatiotemporal characteristics of both the sinusoidal grating and its modulating Gaussian function. The stimulus yielding the lowest contrast threshold was a sinusoidal grating with spatial frequency of 3 cycles/degree and drift rate of 5 Hz, with a width and height of 0.44 degrees

---

[5]These functions bear the name of Dennis Gabor, a Hungarian engineer and applied physicist. Gabor won the 1971 Nobel Prize in Physics for his work on wavefront reconstruction in optical holography. In vision research, Gabor functions are used as stimuli; also, they are good approximations to the spatiotemporal receptive fields of many visual neurons.

visual angle and a duration of 0.13 s. Applying the lower envelope principle, these parameters describe the most sensitive of the neural filters in the direction-extracting system.

Stimuli like those used by Watson and Turano (1995) and others have the advantage of limiting stimulus energy to particular bands of spatial and temporal frequencies. Although such grating patterns are often used to explore motion perception, they bring some disadvantages. For example, they confound motion with orientation and can appear to move only in the directions perpendicular to their orientation. To get around these limitations, researchers devised an entirely different class of motion stimuli, arrays of irregularly spaced moving elements such as blobs or dots. These computer-generated stimuli are commonly known as random dot cinematograms (RDCs), and there are several different algorithms for generating them. Distilled down to their essence, most RDCs consist of "signal" dots that move in a given direction (or within a given range of directions) and are intermingled randomly with "noise" dots that move in random directions.[6] When the proportion of signal dots is high, dots in the RDC appear to move coherently in the general direction of those signal dots; when signal dots comprise only a small fraction of the RDC, the sense of motion coherence is weak or, in the limit, absent entirely. Motion threshold is defined as the minimum percentage of signal dots necessary for detection of coherent motion. It should be stressed that the information supporting detection performance in these stochastic stimuli must be extracted globally: Observers cannot perform well simply by attending to a single dot or to a restricted region of the display.

Humans exhibit remarkable sensitivity to coherent motion in RDCs. Under optimal conditions, observers can detect signal percentages as small as 5% (Scase et al., 1996), and this holds for signal dots portraying translational motion, rotational motion, and expansion and contraction (but see Ahlström & Börjesson, 1996; Blake & Aiba, 1998). Absolute threshold values vary with display size (Burr, Morrone, & Vaina, 1998), dot density (Watamaniuk, 1993), and exposure duration (Watamaniuk, Sekuler, & Williams, 1989), but not with direction of motion (Gros, Blake, & Hiris, 1998). Visual cues that allow segmentation of signal dots from noise dots—such as color or contrast polarity—can substantially enhance detection of motion (Croner & Albright, 1997). Prior exposure, or adaptation, to strongly coherent motion in a given direction temporarily elevates coherence thresholds for directions of motion within roughly 40 degrees of the adapting direction, with the elevation in threshold being largest at the adapting direction. Thresholds are also affected by higher-order variables such as visual attention to a particular direction of motion (Raymond, 2000; Raymond, O'Donnell, & Tipper, 1998), a point discussed later in this chapter.

In an influential series of experiments, Newsome and colleagues used RDCs to test motion detection in monkeys. They recorded neural responses from single cells in areas MT and MST of the monkey's brain while the monkey tried to detect motion (see a review of this work by Parker and Newsome, 1998). In general, the monkey's behavioral threshold for detecting motion was very close to the neural threshold derived for some individual directionally selective neurons. The

---

[6]The terms *signal* and *noise,* commonplace in psychophysics, derive from engineering and communication sciences. There, the task facing a biological or machine detector is portrayed as the extraction of a message (signal) from a stream of input, some portion of which (noise) is irrelevant or even antithetical to the extraction of the message. These definitions enable investigators to characterize a detector's sensitivity in terms of the ratio of signal to noise that just allows signal extraction.

correspondence between neural thresholds and behavioral thresholds points to a tight linkage between neural activity in areas MT and MST and the monkey's performance, with "neural" thresholds corresponding closely to behavioral thresholds (Celebrini & Newsome, 1994; Newsome, Britten, & Movshon, 1989).

This linkage was further strengthened by the finding that electrical stimulation of neurons in area MT (Salzman, Murasugi, Britten, & Newsome, 1992) or in area MST (Celebrini & Newsome, 1994) can bias a monkey's perceptual report of motion direction in RDCs. Thus, direct stimulation of MT neurons tuned to leftward motion increased the probability that the RDC would appear to move in that direction. Direct electrical stimulation of particular clusters of MT neurons, then, was perceptually equivalent to the effect normally produced by an RDC moving in the neurons' preferred direction with a particular coherence level. Lesion studies lend additional support to the idea that area MT participates in motion perception. Lesions encompassing area MT, area MST, or both areas produce permanent impairments in the ability to extract coherent motion from RDCs (Newsome & Paré, 1988; Rudolph & Pasternak, 1999). Comparable deficits in motion sensitivity to RDCs are found in human patients with damage to an area of the brain homologous to area MT in primates (Schenk & Zihl, 1997).

Trajectory Detection

Algorithms that generate RDC stimuli ordinarily prevent any signal dot from moving in a constant direction throughout the entire animation sequence. This is done to prevent observers from basing judgments on any single dot's trajectory, instead forcing judgments to arise from the integration of many motion vectors. In the natural environment, however, there are many instances in which it is important to detect one object's movement in the presence of other, distracting moving objects, and, for that matter, despite temporary occlusions in the target object's path. To take an unpleasant example, a lion in hunting mode can visually track the path of one particular zebra in a herd, even when all other members of the herd are moving about in random directions, and even though the target zebra is temporarily obscured by vegetation or other opaque objects. To learn how vision manages such feats, Watamaniuk, McKee, and Grzywacz (1995) measured observers' abilities to detect the presence of a single dot moving on a fixed straight path in a field of noise dots whose directions changed randomly over time. The signal dot was identical to the noise dots in luminance, size, and speed. For a stimulus duration of 500 ms, motion was detected 90% of the time, even when there were as many as 250 noise dots. Under such conditions, the proportion of signal dots was minute: only 0.4%.

Watamaniuk and McKee (1995) also found that a single moving dot's trajectory is easily seen even when that trajectory is interrupted by a series of opaque occluders (Figure 4.4). Detection of the dot's motion across three path segments, each separated by an occluder

Figure 4.4 Diagram of display used by Watamaniuk and McKee (1995) to examine effects of occlusion on trajectory detection. NOTE: See text for further details.

1 degree wide, was essentially as good as detection of the same motion over a single uninterrupted path of equivalent length. Therefore, the motion signal generated by the moving object was essentially unaffected by temporary interruptions of that signal when the object was occluded. However, when the dot's trajectory was momentarily interrupted by a different kind of occluder, detection of the moving dot fell dramatically. Here, occluding regions were filled with random-direction motions (noise) similar to the random motions in the display's other regions. The dot disappeared when it entered a noisy occluding region and reappeared when it left that region. Within each noisy occluder the virtual path of the signal dot was probably masked or distorted by similarly directed motion vectors in the noise. These noise directions led the directional signal astray, reducing the precision of matches from one segment of the dot's trajectory to the next. (This is an instance of the so-called motion correspondence problem, which is discussed in a subsequent section.) Because the reduction in detectability persisted even when noise-filled occluders lay in a depth plane different from the regions containing the trajectory, it seems that trajectory detection operates prior to the assignment of depth to image components.

Grzywacz, Watamaniuk, and McKee (1995) proposed a model that can account for many observations on trajectory detection. In their model, local connections among motion mechanisms enhance responses that result when mechanisms are stimulated in sequence and roughly in the direction of their directional tuning. These connections are spatiotemporal analogues to the spatial association fields that have been implicated in contour integration (Field, Hayes, & Hess, 1993; Geisler, Perry, Super, & Gallogly, 2001; Sigman, Cecchi, Gilbert, & Magnasco, 2001). From a perceptual perspective, the connections postulated by Grzywacz et al. promote what Gestalt psychology dubbed "good continuation": Perception will favor trajectories that are smooth over trajectories that have large and abrupt changes in direction. Such spatiotemporal preferences were demonstrated in Metzger's (1934) observations with objects moving on independent but intersecting paths.

Because of the spatiotemporally tuned local connections in Grzywacz et al.'s (1995) model, each successively stimulated motion mechanism will produce a response that is larger than that produced by the previously stimulated mechanism. Eventually, the response grows large enough to be accurately detected, even though other motion detectors are responding to the background motion noise. Because local connections involve mechanisms with a range of similar directional tuning (spanning about ± 30 degrees), the model can account also for the detection of curved trajectories as well as straight ones (Grzywacz et al., 1995; Verghese, Watamaniuk, McKee, & Grzywacz, 1999).

Grzywacz et al.'s (1995) trajectory network model postulates facilitation of signals in sequentially stimulated motion mechanisms, a result observed by Verghese et al. (1999), who compared the detectability of two kinds of trajectories. In one, the moving elements followed a single continuous trajectory of length L; in the other, the same elements traced out n separate trajectories, with a gap between successive segments. Because each segment was L/n long, their summed lengths were the same as the length of the single uninterrupted trajectory. Verghese et al. wanted to know how the motion system would sum the motion signals contained in these segments. For a computational benchmark, they drew upon the notion of probability summation. In its simplest form, probability summation predicts that detection of a signal should be equal to the sum of the square of the number of independent stimulus elements (Graham, 1989; Watson,

1979). In Verghese et al.'s experiments, the number of independent stimulus elements is n. This computational rule gave a good account of detection when trajectory segments were so short that each segment was likely to be detected by only a single mechanism. With longer trajectories, however, probability summation failed badly. For example, a single 200-ms trajectory was approximately three times more detectable than were two spatially isolated 100-ms trajectories presented one after another, which kept L constant. Thus, the detection of an extended trajectory cannot be explained by activation of a series of independent motion detectors whose outputs are summed linearly. Instead, the result points to significant spatiotemporally tuned interactions among local motion units, of the kind postulated in Grzywacz et al.'s trajectory network model.

Motion Discrimination: Direction, Speed, and Coherence

Having highlighted key determinants of motion detection, we turn now to motion discrimination. In tasks used to measure discrimination, observers must not only detect the motion (i.e., see that motion is present) but also judge one or more of the motion's essential characteristics, such as direction, speed, or coherence.

In experiments on motion perception, sinusoidal grating stimuli were used to investigate *discrimination* of direction of motion at or near the contrast *detection* threshold for that moving stimulus. In general, the contrast at which observers could just detect the presence of a moving stimulus was also sufficient to identify its direction of motion (Derrington & Henning, 1993; Levinson & Sekuler, 1975; Watson, Thompson, Murphy, & Nachmias, 1980). Such results suggested that visual mechanisms that extract motion signals are labeled for direction. In this context, a neural mechanism is said to be labeled for some elementary sensation, Φ, if activity in the mechanism is sufficient to generate the experience of Φ (Watson & Robson, 1981). Although much has been learned about motion from experiments using grating stimuli, an exclusive reliance on such stimuli encounters substantial limitations. If an observer cannot see the ends of the grating (the usual case in motion experiments), unambiguous motions can be produced only in the two directions orthogonal to the grating's orientation, an ambiguity known as the aperture problem (discussed later). Thus, creating other directions of motion requires a change in the orientation of the grating, thus confounding direction and orientation. Partly to avoid this potential confound, Westheimer and Wehrhahn (1994) measured direction discrimination for a single moving spot. They found that at high speeds (30 deg/s) direction discrimination was equal to that for orientation discrimination of a static line of the same length as the distance traveled by the moving spot and presented for the same duration. This suggests that at high speeds the moving spot created an oriented smear (a virtual line) on which observers could have based their judgments (work by Geisler, 1999, makes a similar point). This potential problem is avoided, however, by using RDCs in which the directions of individual dots change frequently or in which each dot has a limited lifetime.

Williams and Sekuler (1984) created RDCs in which individual elements were assigned new directions of motion in each frame. When directions were drawn from a distribution of directions spanning 180 degrees or less, observers saw the entire fields of dots move in the direction of the distribution's mean, even though the random movements of individual dots were also visible. This meant that the motion mechanisms responsible for this global motion integrated direction information over much of the motion display, if not over the entire display. Using a RDC in which each dot chose a new direction of motion each frame from a distribution of directions spanning 30 degrees, Ball, Sekuler, and Machamer (1983) determined that the direction tuning of these motion mechanisms is broad: Two directions of motion had to be separated by 120 degrees before they no longer stimulated the same mechanism.

With such broadly tuned motion mechanisms to draw upon, how well can observers discriminate small differences in direction? To answer this question, Watamaniuk et al. (1989) measured direction discrimination for fields of random dots. When all dots moved in the same direction, observers reliably discriminated directions that differed by only 1 degree. Moreover, this threshold was relatively resistant to the inclusion of random motions that potentially interfere with signal extraction. When similar measures were made with RDCs whose elements moved in a range of directions, once the range of directions in the RDC exceeded 30 degrees, direction discrimination thresholds increased with direction range. In addition, direction discrimination improved as exposure duration lengthened, up to at least 300 ms to 400 ms, and as size of the stimulus increased, up to at least a 10-degree diameter (Watamaniuk & Sekuler, 1992; Watamaniuk et al., 1989). Thus, the motion system is robust in the presence of random motions, and it can produce precise discriminations using mechanisms that are broadly tuned.

RDCs can generate motion percepts simultaneously on two different spatial scales. In particular, the perception of global flow can coexist with the perception of the small random motions of individual dots. Watamaniuk and McKee (1998) showed that direction information was encoded independently on the two spatial scales, global and local. In their RDCs, a single central dot moved in a constant direction while the remaining 100 to 150 dots were assigned a new direction of motion in each frame from a distribution spanning 160 degrees. The direction of global flow and the direction of the constant-direction dot were always similar, but both varied from trial to trial. After a brief presentation of the RDC, a tone told the observer which motion, global or local, was to be judged. Under these conditions, observers judged either direction just as well as if they had been told in advance which direction to judge. This suggests that visual information on different spatial scales is processed simultaneously with little interference.

As indicated earlier, motion detection is isotropic. For direction discrimination, however, performance is anisotropic, varying strongly with the test direction. Discrimination thresholds are lowest (i.e., performance is best) for directions at and near the "cardinal" directions of up, down, left, and right (Gros, Blake, & Hiris, 1998). This oblique effect could reflect a disproportion in the number of neurons tuned to cardinal directions; alternatively, it could arise from narrower directional tuning for neurons tuned to cardinal directions. The absence of an oblique effect for the *detection* of motion suggests that the second interpretation is correct, but the question remains open.

Direction Change

In the natural world, objects often change direction, and responses to such changes can be quite important. For example, direction changes by inanimate objects may result from a collision; direction changes by living creatures may convey biologically significant information, such as the information produced by a series of hand gestures. Direction-tuned neurons in area MT of primate cortex have been shown to be efficient encoders of such changes (Buracas, Zador, DeWeese, & Albright, 1998). Synchronized changes in direction of motion among an array of small objects promote perceptual grouping of those objects into a coherent shape (Lee & Blake, 1999).

Dzhafarov, Sekuler, and Allik (1993) proposed a formal computational model for responses to changes in speed and direction of motion. The model, which has been extended by Mateeff, Genova, and Hohnsbein (1999), incorporated a process that normalized all stimulus velocity signals registered prior to any change.[7] Velocity normalization is an instance of visual adaptation processes that reduce redundancy in neural responses by minimizing the total neural activity elicited by any stimulus input (Barlow, 1990). For Dzhafarov et al.'s implementation, assume that some stimulus has an initial velocity V_0, which changes abruptly to a different velocity, V_1. As a result of normalization, this change from V_0 to V_1 is detected as though the change were the onset of an initial motion with velocity $|V_1 - V_0|$. In other words, the actual value of V_0 is irrelevant; all that matters is the absolute difference between V_1 and V_0. This basic computation successfully predicted observers' speeds of response to change with a considerable variety of values for V_0 and V_1. A. B. Sekuler and R. Sekuler (1993) examined this normalization process further. In an attempt to disrupt the extraction of information about V_0, they injected transients such as temporary occlusion or disappearance into the trajectory prior to the change to V_1. By injecting a transient at various times during and after V_0, they were able to interrupt or freeze normalization. Even a relatively brief disappearance of the moving target reset normalization entirely, erasing all the velocity information that had been extracted up to that point.

Speed Discrimination

During their daily routines, humans frequently make judgments about the speeds of moving objects. Consider, for example, the simple acts of judging the speeds of nearby cars when changing lanes on the highway or running across the lawn to intercept a small child who is crawling toward a street. How do humans judge speed in these kinds of situations? Because objects moving at different speeds cover different distances in any given temporal interval, observers could use distance traveled as a cue to speed. Alternatively, the time needed to travel some criterion distance might also be used as a cue to speed. So how can one measure speed discrimination without confounding influences of time and distance? The usual experimental approach is to randomize presentation time over a range so large that duration and therefore distance cues become unreliable (McKee & Watamaniuk, 1994).

Speed discrimination thresholds are typically presented as Weber fractions ($\Delta V/V$) that specify the proportional difference in speed needed to produce reliable discrimination. The smallest increment in speed that can be reliably detected (ΔV) is divided by the mean or base speed (V). Most studies have reported Weber fractions in the range 0.04 to 0.08 with various types of stimuli, including moving lines, dot fields, and sinusoidal gratings (Bravo & Watamaniuk, 1995; Brown, 1961; De Bruyn & Orban, 1988; McKee, 1981;

---

[7]Normalization refers to various linear operations that transform some data set, $\mathbf{D}$, into a new set, $\mathbf{D'}$, while preserving particular types of numerical relationships among the set's members. Of two common forms of normalization, subtractive normalization of $\mathbf{D}$ can be described as $\mathbf{D'} = \mathbf{D} - k$; divisive normalization is represented by $\mathbf{D'} = \mathbf{D}/k$. Subtractive normalization, which is the form used in Dzhafarov et al.'s model, preserves the relative magnitudes of members of $\mathbf{D}$; divisive normalization preserves the proportional relationships among members of $\mathbf{D}$. Heeger (1994; Heeger, Simoncelli, & Movshon, 1996) describes another type of normalization, which operates in the visual cortex to suppress partially the responses of individual neurons.

Nakayama, 1981; Orban, de Wolf, & Maes, 1984; Pasternak, 1987; Turano & Pantle, 1989; Watamaniuk & Duchon, 1992). The Weber fraction's constancy means that the smallest detectable increment in speed increases with the base or starting speed.

Although the Weber fraction for speed discrimination is fairly constant over a variety of test conditions, perceived speed can be altered by any number of stimulus parameters. For example, Katz, Gizzi, Cohen, & Malach (1990) reported that drifting stimuli that are only briefly presented appear to move faster than do stimuli that are presented for longer durations. A grating's drift or movement rate takes degree/second as its units, where "degree" signifies degrees of visual angle. It is important to distinguish drift rate from a related variable, temporal frequency, which takes units of Hz or, equivalently, cycles/s. The relationship between a grating's drift rate and the temporal frequency produced by that drift takes account of the grating's spatial structure:

$$\text{Temporal frequency (Hz)} = \text{Drift rate(deg/s)} \times \text{Spatial frequency (cycles/deg)}$$

Perceived speed of movement (perceived drift rate) varies with a grating's spatial frequency, which takes units of cycles/degree. Sinusoidal gratings presented at lower temporal frequencies (and hence lower spatial frequencies) appear to be slower than gratings moving at the same speed but with higher temporal frequency (Diener, Wist, Dichgans, & Brandt, 1976; McKee, Silverman, & Nakayama, 1986; Smith & Edgar, 1991). Turning to other variables that affect perceived speed, when gratings of different contrast move at the same physical speed, a lower-contrast grating appears to move more slowly (Stone & Thompson, 1992; Thompson, 1982). Furthermore, objects seen in the periphery appear to move more slowly than do foveal objects of

the same speed (Johnston & Wright, 1986; Tynan & Sekuler, 1982). Finally, the perception of an object's speed is adversely affected at low luminance levels, which correspond to rod-mediated, scotopic vision. Gegenfurtner, Mayser, and Sharpe (2000) showed that a moving object's perceived speed is considerably slowed in rod-mediated vision, compared to its perceived speed in cone-mediated vision. To understand the likely basis for this result, note that differences in constants of rod time and cone time indicate that rods average information over longer periods than do cones. Gegenfurtner et al. speculated that the rods' extended temporal averaging attenuates motion signals that would be generated in detectors that are tuned to high velocities. The reduction in such signals causes the reduction in perceived speed under rod-dominated conditions. Grossman and Blake (1999) found that the perception of biological motion and structure from motion were also impaired under scotopic viewing conditions. Such findings have clear implications for driving safety at night on poorly illuminated roads.

IDEAL OBSERVERS AND MOTION ANALYSIS

Early studies established that the visual system was an extraordinarily efficient detector of light (Hecht, Shlaer, & Pirenne, 1942; Rose, 1948). To assess the efficiency of vision when it performs other tasks, researchers often turn to ideal-observer models. In its most common form, an ideal observer comprises a mathematical model of a theoretical observer who has complete and perfect knowledge of all relevant stimulus and task statistics; in addition, this theoretical ideal makes statistically optimal decisions when transforming sensory information into psychophysical responses. Ideal-observer models afford interesting benchmarks for the fallibility of human observers, in comparison with the theoretical limit represented by an ideal observer. Ideal observer models have been used to compare human and ideal performance for tasks such as detecting changes in spatial patterns (e.g., Barlow, 1978; Barlow, 1980; Barlow & Reeves, 1979; Burgess & Barlow, 1983; Burgess, Wagner, Jennings, & Barlow, 1981; van Meeteren & Barlow, 1981).

Random and unpredictable variability in the stimulus limits an ideal observer's performance because it subverts the observer's otherwise perfect knowledge of the stimulus to be detected. Such random variability is known as noise.[8] Ideal-observer models try to predict how humans and ideal observers might perform when each must extract information from a noisy stimulus. Increasing stimulus noise leads any observer—human as well as ideal—to make more errors, such as failures to detect the stimulus, misclassifications of a stimulus, or declarations that a stimulus is present when it actually is not. How closely a human observer approximates the theoretical ideal defines the human observer's efficiency. This statistic is given by the square of the ratio of human performance to ideal performance, where both performance measures are expressed as d' values (Chap. 2, Vol. 4 of this series). Thus, if a human observer's performance is ideal, efficiency is 1.0. Detailed

comparisons of human and ideal observers create valuable diagnostic opportunities for identifying and quantifying components that limit human performance (Geisler, 1989).

In the first application of ideal-observer analysis to visual motion perception, Watamaniuk (1993) devised an ideal-observer model that discriminated the direction of global flow generated in RDCs. In specially constructed RDCs, the directions in which each dot moved over successive frames were chosen randomly, with replacement, from a Gaussian distribution of directions. The unusual algorithm for generating the movements or elements made the stimulus noisy: The algorithm introduced a random discrepancy between the actual directional content of the stimulus and the nominal, or average, directional content represented by the sampled distribution. To vary the magnitude of this discrepancy, in different conditions directions were drawn from one of five Gaussian distributions with different standard deviations. The larger the standard deviation, the greater the mean absolute discrepancy between actual and nominal-direction information in the stimulus. This introduced random sampling noise into the stimuli. Because the ideal observer had to rely on its knowledge only of the *nominal* stimulus, introduction of variability (noise) into the *actual* stimulus reduced the observer's performance.

Direction discrimination was measured for each direction distribution for a range of stimulus durations, stimulus areas, and spatial densities of dots. As expected, human performance was always poorer than the ideal observer's performance. Efficiency generally decreased with increased stimulus area or density and remained constant as duration increased from 100 ms to 500 ms. However, the data clearly showed that efficiency increased as stimulus noise increased, reaching averaged values of 0.35. This suggests that the human visual system was influenced

---

[8] In virtually any psychophysical experiment, valuable information can be gained from measurements made with stimuli to which various amounts of noise have been added (Pelli & Farell, 1999). Noise can assume different forms, depending on the observer's task. For example, when the task involves detection of a static form, the noise usually comprises independent, random luminance values added to each element in the stimulus display (Bennett, Sekuler, & Ozin, 1999; Gold, Bennett, & Sekuler, 1999); when the task involves detection of symmetry in a pattern, noise may be introduced by randomly altering the position of each of the pattern's elements (Barlow & Reeves, 1979); or, when the task requires identification of global motion direction in an RDC, noise can be generated by randomizing the directions comprising the RDC (Watamaniuk, 1993).

by the random noise less than the ideal observer was. Note that high efficiency does not mean high level of performance. Because efficiency is a ratio of human performance to ideal performance, high efficiency can be obtained at any level of performance. In fact, Watamaniuk (1993) found highest efficiency for direction discrimination when average performance was at a d' of about 0.75, which translates to a percent correct discrimination of about 70%. Finally, Watamaniuk identified several factors that undermine human performance, including the limited spatial and temporal summation of human vision.

Watamaniuk's (1993) ideal observer was designed to *discriminate* one motion from another, but a comparable ideal observer could be designed for another task: to *detect* motion. Because the visual system exploits a different source of neural information both for direction discrimination and for motion detection (Hol & Treue, 2001), specifying an ideal-observer analysis for a new task can be far from a trivial matter. Barlow and Triparthy (1997) applied an ideal-observer analysis to the detection of coherent motion embedded in random motion noise. Human as well as ideal observers received two-alternative forced choice tests. They had to identify which of two intervals contained coherent motion rather than completely random directional noise. Noise was introduced into the stimulus by making the frame-by-frame positioning of the coherently moving dots less precise. As precision declined, efficiency increased, reaching values of approximately 0.3. This result points to the relatively coarse spatial resolution of human vision and shows that adding spatial position noise affects the ideal observer more than it affects the human. This coarse spatial resolution represents a low-pass spatial filtering operation, which, as Barlow and Triparthy speculated, enhances sensitivity to naturally occurring motion.

Extending this analysis of motion detection, Baddeley and Triparthy (1998) examined some limitations that might possibly undermine the performances of human observers. Using a novel statistical procedure that examined the frame-by-frame movements of each dot, Baddeley and Triparthy determined that whereas an ideal observer bases decisions on the motions of all dots in the display, human observers seem to use only a proportion of the dots in the display. The same frame-by-frame analysis allowed them to rule out other possible limiting factors, including the idea that human observers differentially weighted directional information generated at various locations in the visual field.

OPTIC FLOW AND STRUCTURE FROM MOTION

Motion affords potentially powerful information about the three-dimensional shapes of moving objects as well as about an observer's own movements within the environment populated by those objects. In particular, the movements of objects within an environment create spatiotemporal changes in the light distribution on the retina of a stationary observer. Likewise, an observer's movements through a stationary environment change his or her own retinal images. Such spatiotemporal changes, whatever their origin, are termed *optic flow,* and they constitute significant sources of visual information. For example, optic flow provides information about the speed, direction, and path of an observer's movements; it can also provide information about the three-dimensional structure of the environment (Koenderink, 1986). In the natural environment, an otherwise camouflaged object—such as an edible insect—stands out conspicuously when it moves relative to its background. Any creature that possesses the neural machinery to extract and register the presence and shape of this target can secure a meal courtesy of visual motion.

Historically, research on optic flow has tended to bifurcate into distinct branches. One branch has focused on the use of optic flow in steering an observer's movement and heading; the other branch has focused on the use of optic flow in revealing the shape and structure of moving objects. In discussing the uses of optic-flow information, we will respect this bifurcation, but it is worth remembering that both uses of optic flow arise ultimately from the same source.

Optic Flow Supports Perception of Heading

Conventionally, the patterns of retinal image flow produced by self-motion are represented by an instantaneous velocity field, as illustrated for simple translatory movement in the top panel of Figure 4.5. Each vector signifies the velocity (direction and speed) in the retinal image of an environmental element. For the case illustrated, the observer's gaze is assumed to coincide with the direction in which the observer is moving. This creates a radial pattern of optic flow in which the focus of the flow corresponds to the observer's heading. Note that the representation contains no information about the physical attributes of the elements, such as their color, shape, and size. Instead, they are treated as uniform entities, known as *tokens*. The lower panel of Figure 4.5 represents the velocity field resulting from an observer's circular movement parallel to the ground plane. This velocity field would be generated, for example, on the retina of a driver whose automobile made a smooth turn.

Although snapshot representations like those in Figure 4.5 omit information such as acceleration-produced changes or temporary occlusions (Warren, Blackwell, Kurtz, Hatsopoulos, & Kalish, 1991), they are still

Figure 4.5 Optic-flow patterns.
NOTE: Panel A: Optic-flow pattern produced when an observer translates along a straight path; diagram assumes that observer is directed toward destination point. Panel B: Optic-flow pattern produced when an observer translates along a curved path.
SOURCE: From Warren, Blackwell, and Morris (1988). Used with permission.

useful in understanding optic flow's possible role in steering and wayfinding. Koenderink (1986) provided a thorough and accessible mathematical account of the optic-flow dynamics that result from various basic types of observer movement. Transformations generated by such movement, no matter how complex, can be decomposed into four basic components: translation, isotropic expansion, rigid rotation, and shear. Summing these basic components in varying amounts can reproduce the original complex optic-flow field. As a result, visual mechanisms specialized for extracting these basic components could generate signals that, in aggregate, would represent the complex flow field and, therefore, an observer's movements. The receptive field properties of neurons in area MST make those neurons well suited to extracting optic-flow information related to an observer's heading. The participation of such neurons in navigation has been confirmed empirically. Direct electrical stimulation of local clusters of neurons in area MST of monkeys altered the monkeys' judgments of heading direction (Britten & van Wezel, 1998). With human observers and human brains, functional neuroimaging reveals large areas of MT+ that respond to particular components of optic flow—such as either circular or radial motion—but not to simple translation motions in a front-parallel plane (Morrone, Tosetti, Montanaro, Fiorentini, Cioni, & Burr, 2000).

Research into optic flow's role in wayfinding has addressed two key issues. First, psychophysical experiments had to determine whether observers could extract heading information from displays containing only optic-flow information. Second, knowing that such extraction was indeed feasible, researchers have tried to identify any conditions under which such optic-flow information is actually used. We consider these two lines of investigation in turn.

Accuracy of Heading Judgments Based on Optic Flow

For modes of human locomotion such as walking, running, skiing, and driving, Cutting (1986, pp. 277–279) estimated the accuracy with which people needed to assess their own heading in order to avoid obstacles. For example, suppose a person who is 1.75 m tall and weighs 65 kg runs steadily at 5 m/s (approximately 11 mph). Assuming that the runner has normal reaction time, in order to swerve to avoid an obstacle such as a tree, the runner would have to judge his or her own heading to an accuracy of at least 1.6 deg visual angle. If the same person walked rather than ran, far less precise heading judgments would still afford a margin of safety. For downhill skiing, in which velocities may be nearly three times

that of running, the margin of safety narrows to 0.78 deg visual angle, which heightens skiing's potential risk.

How do such theoretical estimates square with what human observers can actually do? Empirical measurements of such judgments showed that with paths generated by pure translation across a ground plane, human observers achieve the performance level that Cutting stipulated (Warren, Blackwell, & Morris, 1988). Warren et al. created two-dimensional displays in which movements of display elements simulated an optic-flow field produced by an observer's movement. When viewing random dot displays that represent various directions of self-movement through the environment, observers can judge direction to an accuracy of about 1 deg visual angle (Warren et al., 1988). This level of visual precision is maintained whether the observer's gaze remains fixed or shifts with eye movements of the sort that observers might make while walking through a real environment. Furthermore, direction judgments are relatively robust in the face of visual noise added to the otherwise consistent motions of simulated flow fields (van den Berg, 1992).

Most experiments on the accuracy of heading judgments have used displays that simulate retinal consequences of simple, straight paths through the environment. In an important departure from this approach, Warren, Mestre, Blackwell, and Morris (1991) simulated self-motion on a curved path. After viewing random dot fields that simulated some curved path through the environment, observers were shown a distant target and had to judge whether the path they had seen would have taken them to the left or to the right of the target. Warren et al. measured heading thresholds for paths with varying radii of curvature and densities of dots in the flow field. Paths with typical curvature supported thresholds of 1.5 deg; performance was unchanged by even dramatic reductions in the number of random elements in the display. This finding carries theoretical weight. Neural network-based explorations predicted that a pair of elements seen in two successive views would provide visual information sufficient to support perception of an observer's curved path (Warren, Blackwell et al., 1991). As a public service for drivers and downhill skiers, we note that accuracy of path judgments is severely degraded at small radii of curvatures (sharper turns).

Under many conditions, then, observers can judge their own paths quite accurately based on optic flow. However, examination of this ability has been limited to movement over single, simple paths. Does optic flow play a role when people attempt to navigate complex, multilegged paths? To answer this question, Kirschen, Kahana, Sekuler, and Burack (2000) asked people to navigate computer-generated synthetic environments with and without salient optic flow. Using the arrow keys on a computer keyboard to control their own simulated self-movement, Kirschen's participants made repeated trips over what had originally been a novel path. Trips grew faster as participants learned the environment's layout. Because these test environments were series of identically textured virtual corridors and intersections, participants needed to construct some mental representation of the environment in order to perform the task. By varying the rates at which the display was updated, the researchers created optic flow that was either smooth or choppy. The choppy condition created the impression of a series of separate still views of the environment. The availability of smooth optic flow promoted faster learning of complex paths, mainly by preventing disorientation and backtracking. In a second experiment, participants navigated within a virtual city-block environment, experiencing two different kinds of optic flow as they went. Smooth optic flow enhanced observers' ability to navigate accurately to

the remembered position of target objects. Kirschen et al. concluded that when other cues (e.g., distinctive landmarks) are not available, optic flow can be a significant aid to navigation.

Mere availability of reliable optic-flow information does not guarantee that all observers will be equally able to exploit such information. Here we consider two classes of observers for whom the quality of heading judgments is diminished.

Ball and Sekuler (1986) showed that healthy older people in their 70s and 80s had elevated direction discrimination thresholds. Although these measurements involved random dot motion in a front-parallel plane rather than heading-related judgments, the older observers' elevated thresholds might be a sign of some general age-related decline in motion perception, particularly perception of multi-element displays and tasks requiring heading judgments. Warren et al. (1988) measured heading thresholds for two groups of people, young (mean age about 20 years) and old (mean age of late 60s). Observers saw optical velocity fields that would be produced by observer translation or by observer movement along a curved path. After each display, which lasted about 4 s, a vertical line was presented, and observers had to judge whether the heading direction that they had seen would have taken them to the left or right of the line. With straight paths, young observers' heading thresholds averaged 1.1 deg visual angle, whereas older observers' heading thresholds were significantly higher, 1.9 deg visual angle. With curved paths, the corresponding threshold values averaged 1.4 and 2.9 deg visual angle. After ruling out ocular and other peripheral causes, Warren et al. suggested that these substantial age-related declines in heading acuity resulted from changes in high-level visual processing.

Patients with Alzheimer's disease, a progressive, degenerative disease of the brain, often have difficulty finding their way around their surroundings, even when those surroundings are familiar. Two groups of researchers have connected this difficulty to subnormal processing of information contained in optic flow. If optic-flow information actually guides navigation, at least under some circumstances, then failure to process that information fully could produce spatial confusion and loss of one's bearings. Rizzo and Nawrot (1998) showed that patients with mild to moderate Alzheimer's disease have particular trouble extracting form or shape information from stimuli in which the form is defined by movement (shape from motion). Moreover, Tetewsky and Duffy (1999) showed that some patients with Alzheimer's disease are impaired in extracting directional information from optic-flow stimuli. Many of these same patients showed correspondingly poor performance on a test of spatial navigation (wayfinding) ability.

Is Optic Flow Normally Used to Guide Locomotion?

Observers' abilities to exploit the information in optic flow in order to judge heading does not guarantee that such ability is actually used to control locomotion. To see whether the information was used, Warren, Kay, Zosh, Duchon, & Sahuc (2001) allowed individuals to walk freely in a very large room while wearing a head-mounted display that afforded wide-field stereoscopic vision of computer-generated imagery. At the same time, head position was tracked, and head-position signals were used to update the computer imagery at 60 Hz. While viewing several different sorts of display images, observers attempted to walk as quickly as possible to a visible target such as vertical line or a doorway. Under normal viewing conditions outside the laboratory, walkers could base their locomotion on information other than the optic flow generated by their own movements. There-

fore, a walker could register the position of a seen target in egocentric coordinates and then walk toward that target's position, trying to remain centered on the target. Ordinarily, the optic flow generated by this egocentering strategy would be identical to the flow generated if an observer used the flow itself to control locomotion. Warren et al. broke this normal correlation by feeding participants optic-flow information that deviated systematically from what their movements alone would have generated. In a control condition, when no optic-flow information was provided, observers' paths indicated that they had walked in the egocentric direction of the target. Thus, they homed in on the target by keeping it centered with respect to their bodies. In other conditions, optic flow was introduced, with the unusual arrangement that the focus of expansion was offset from the walking direction (by 10 deg visual angle). As additional optic flow was introduced into the displays—by adding texture to floors and ceilings—observers' navigation behavior changed dramatically. Now, instead of walking toward the target as observers had been instructed to, they tended to follow the optic flow, which was intentionally misleading. It appears, then, that under normal conditions the visual system depends on both optic flow and egocentric localization, using the two sources of information in a complementary fashion. Warren et al. noted that when flow is reduced (e.g., on a grass lawn or at night), reliance on flow is also reduced, but that in environments that afford considerable optic flow (e.g., forested areas), locomotor behavior is likely to be dominated by flow.

Optic Flow Supports Collision Avoidance

When an observer is on a collision course with an object, the object generates a characteristic spatiotemporal expansion on the observer's retina. This fact holds equally well, of course, for a moving observer and a stationary object, or vice versa. If the rate of movement is constant, the retinal angle subtended by the object grows nonlinearly in a nearly exponential fashion.

Animals as dissimilar as fiddler crabs, chicks, monkeys, and human infants all try to avoid looming patterns created artificially on television screens (Schiff, 1965). This is true even for newborn infants who have never before encountered a looming stimulus. Apparently, learning plays little role in this behavior.

The rate of retinal image expansion specifies the time to collision, that is, the moment at which a moving observer would reach the object. If at time t an observer D meters away from the object starts moving steadily toward the object, time to collision is given by travel distance divided by travel rate, D/R. Recognizing that solving for time to collision would require information about both D and R, Lee (1980) suggested that vision exploited another dynamic source of information about time to arrival, which would make it unnecessary to know either D or R.

Tau, the variable that Lee (1980) introduced, is the ratio between the current retinal image size and the rate of change in that image size. If the visual system computed a value approximating tau, time to collision would be given by tau's reciprocal. Note that this calculation's result is independent of object size.

The connection between imminent collision and the rate of expansion of retinal image size holds for any moving creature that has its eyes open—including birds that fly along and then dive at great speeds in order to catch a fish in the water below. Among the best studied of these diving birds is the gannet, a large web-footed seabird with a sharply pointed beak. Gannets fly along with their wings spread wide until just before their diving bodies would hit the water's surface, at which point

they tuck their wings tight to their sides. Timing is everything. If a gannet performs this maneuver too late, the impact with the water could be quite damaging; if a gannet folds it wings prematurely, its body will be buffeted by cross-winds that will alter the point of entry into the water. Although we have no wings that need folding, the human visual system carries out similarly complex computations. For example, information about the rate of expansion can be used to control the braking of an automobile (Lee, 1976), the split-second changes in gait needed when running across rough terrain (Warren, Young, & Lee, 1986), or the various movements and adjustments of the hand that are required for catching a ball (Savelsbergh, Whiting, & Bootsma, 1991). This coupling between optical expansion and action is not performed consciously. People succeed in these tasks despite being unaware—or being unable to articulate—what they are doing (Savelsbergh et al., 1991).

Although tau may be helpful in many circumstances in which people must recognize collision time, it cannot be the only effective cue to collision. In fact, tau would fail under a number of conditions (Tresilian, 1999). For example, if the approach rate is not constant, tau evaluated at any single moment fails to give the correct collision time. Gravity-induced acceleration also undermines tau's usefulness as a predictor of when a falling body will strike some surface. Additionally, with a very slow approach to an object, the rate of image expansion could become so small as to drop below threshold.

Tresilian (1999) discusses tau's limitations, and catalogs other cues that observers could and, in fact, do use. Human observers seem to be quite flexible in making use of available information to solve the collision problem. Thus, Schrater, Knill, and Simoncelli (2001) showed that observers can estimate expansion rates in the absence of optic-flow information by using only gradual changes in the scale of random texture elements. In a simulated ball-hitting task, Smith, Flach, Dittman, and Stanard (2001) demonstrated that observers optimize performance by adjusting the relative weights given to cues such as the approaching object's angular subtense and rate of expansion.

It is both plausible and theoretically attractive to postulate that observers adjust cue weights to match task demands and to reflect the reliability and availability of various cues. This theoretical proposition, however, raises a series of theoretical questions about the control architecture that might be used to integrate task-specific processes (Hildreth, personal communication, May 2001). For example, do observers always generate the values of all potential information sources and then use an optimization strategy to select the most reliable? Or do observers actually generate only one or two preselected weights, based on the characteristics of the situation and task? Such questions must be asked and answered in order to clarify the real value of postulating observers's flexibility in choice of strategy.

Optic Flow Supports Perception of Object Structure

Kinetic Shape

In the laboratory, motion is a potent specifier of shape. This potency was demonstrated in studies by Regan (1989), who created displays in which alphanumeric characters were defined by clusters of dots moving in different directions. To illustrate, imagine a dense array of tiny dots, each of which moves. Now suppose that dots in a subset of those dots, which fall within the boundaries of a virtual shape, all move in the same direction, while dots outside the shape's boundaries move in a different direction. (It is important to realize that the region of the virtual shape itself is not necessarily moving; only the dots defining that area move.) People readily see a figure defined by those common motion vectors, and they can judge with excellent accuracy the shape of that figure. Called "kinetic form perception," this ability is conserved in the face of substantial amounts of random motion noise.

The perception of biological motion provides another compelling example of vision's ability to recover object information from motion. When an animal's body moves, the body deforms; that is, various parts of the body move relative to one another. These characteristic relative movements are signatures of normal biological motion. In fact, when a human moves with stiff or locked body joints, reducing the normal movement of body parts relative to one another, the body's movement looks unnatural, artificial. Because normal biological motion involves deformation of the body, biological motion is classified as nonrigid motion. Although there are many nonbiological sources of nonrigid motion (e.g., the movement of a flag waving in the breeze), perception of human body movement has drawn the most interest and research.

In studies of biological motion, the activity and identity of an animate creature are extracted quickly and compellingly from merely a dozen or so "light points" placed strategically on the creature's body (Johansson, 1973). In animation sequences that represent the points' movements over time, no single point conveys information about the object or event being depicted. Individual points merely undergo translational or elliptical motions, or both. The lights promote perception best when they are placed on joints, the parts of the body whose movements are most diagnostic. Perception of a biological organism that is engaged in an activity requires global integration of motion signals over space and time. As a result, the perception of such animation sequences is literally the *creation* of motion information (in the same sense that perception of an object in a random-point stereogram is the creation of binocular disparity information). Even a brief view of a point-light display allows an observer to identify the gender of the person in the display (e.g., Kozlowski & Cutting, 1977; Mather & Murdoch, 1994), the activity in which the person is engaged (Johansson, 1973), or the person's emotional state (e.g., Brownlow, Dixon, Egbert, & Radcliffe, 1997). Human infants as young as 3 months of age can perceive biological motion (e.g., Fox & McDaniel, 1982), as can adult cats (Blake, 1993). Perception of biological motion is remarkably robust in that observers can readily discriminate biological from nonbiological motion even when the points' contrast changes randomly over time or when the points are defined entirely by texture and not by luminance (V. Ahlström, Blake, & Ahlström, 1997).

The perception of biological motion may be mediated, at least in part, by unique motion mechanisms. First, information specifying biological motion can be summed over much longer temporal intervals than can information for simple translational motion (Neri, Morrone, & Burr, 1998). Second, damage to specific regions of the brain can impair perception of biological motion while leaving intact other forms of motion perception (Cowey & Vaina, 2000). Conversely, damage to other regions of the brain impairs perception of translational motion but has no influence on perception of biological motion (Vaina, Lemay, Bienfang, Choi, & Nakayama, 1990). Finally, functional neuroimaging (Grossman, Donnelly, Price, Morgan, Pickens, Neighbor, & Blake, 2000) has identified regions of the brain, located on the posterior STS, that are active during the viewing of biological motion, but not during the viewing of the same local motion vectors scrambled in space. These specialized regions are located anterior and superior to area MT+.

Kinetic Depth

In addition to object shape, motion information can also convey the three-dimensional spatial structure of surfaces. A single view of a stationary two-dimensional projection of a three-dimensional object affords little unambiguous depth information. When the object is set into motion, however, its projection can produce a clear impression of the object's depth and spatial structure. Wallach and O'Connell (1953) provided an early report of this phenomenon, which they dubbed the "kinetic depth effect." Today, the preferred term for the general class of phenomena is "structure-from-motion," which encompasses not only the emergence of depth from motion but also the generation of surfaces and other object-related properties. Specially constructed motion displays have been crucial to understanding the computational and neural bases of structure from motion. Figure 4.6 illustrates the construction of one such stimulus display. A computer is programmed to create a flat, two-dimensional projection

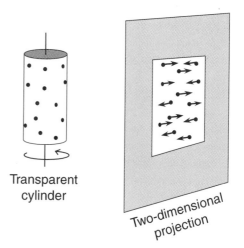

Transparent cylinder

Two-dimensional projection

Figure 4.6 Two-dimensional projection (right) of transparent rotating cylinder (left).
NOTE: The dots on the cylinder's surface create intermingled left- and right-moving dots in the two-dimensional projection.

of a revolving, speckled, transparent, vertical cylinder. Viewing this two-dimensional projection, an observer sees intermingled rightward-moving and leftward-moving dots (arising from front and rear surfaces of the cylinder). Additionally, the speeds of individual dots will vary systematically across the display, and the fastest-moving elements will be projections of dots that lie closest to the left and right edges of the cylinder's projection. This two-dimensional projection typically produces a strong percept of structure from motion, giving rise to a bistable percept: a cylinder whose direction of rotates alternates between front leftward and front rightward (Andersen & Bradley, 1998).

In humans, the ability to exploit motion as the source of three-dimensional shape information seems to develop very early. Using a habituation technique, Arterberry and Yonas (2000) showed that infants as young as 8 weeks can perceive three-dimensional object shapes defined only by optic flow. This early access to structure from motion is fortunate because mechanisms that extract static-form information are relatively immature in early infancy.

Having seen the potential importance of shape from motion, one can ask how that information is actually extracted from the optic array. Originally, it was thought that three-dimensional structure in displays such as the one in Figure 4.6 resulted from a series of matches, over successive samples, of the spatial locations at which elements are located (Ullman, 1984). Such an algorithm, in which spatial positions were matched, ignored contributions from local motions, whose central role in structure from motion has been proven conclusively (Andersen & Bradley, 1998).

To explain the neural basis for structure from motion, Nawrot and Blake (1991b) devised a neural network incorporating interactions between stereopsis and direction-selective neurons (1991a). Because some neurons in area MT are tuned not only for motion but also for stereo depth, Nawrot and Blake's model incorporated units tuned to combinations of disparity (e.g., near vs. far) and of direction of motion (e.g., left vs. right). The display shown in Figure 4.6 would activate two different types of units in a network of neurons: units sensitive to the conjunction of near disparity and rightward motion and units sensitive to far disparity and leftward motion. Mutual inhibition among units tuned to a given depth plane put them into an opponent relationship, and activation of one type of unit (e.g., near-depth leftward) tended to reduce responses in units signaling the opposite direction of motion (in this case, near-depth rightward). These within-plane interactions ensured that activity at a given depth plane was associated with only one direction of motion. In addition, units tuned to the same direction of motion in near- and far-depth planes also exerted mutual inhibition on one another. These between-plane interactions promoted segregation of different directions of motion into different depth planes. Together, these opponent arrangements keep the network from generating contradictory percepts within any local area, just as in the physical world any single, local region on the cylinder's surface cannot simultaneously move leftward and rightward.

Nawrot and Blake (1991b) assigned their units nonlinear stimulus-response activation functions. This nonlinearity, together with excitatory connections among similarly tuned units, allows structure from motion to build up over time, which is consistent with human observers' experiences with many such displays. For example, under many conditions the full structure of a display such as the cylinder in Figure 4.6 can take as long as a second or more to emerge fully. Similar cooperative interactions among like-tuned neural units have been implicated in other aspects of motion perception (Nawrot & Sekuler, 1990;

Williams, Phillips, & Sekuler, 1986). Finally, the model's combination of noise (moment-to-moment variability in response) and opponent organization caused it to reproduce another notable feature of human perception of structure from motion: a perceptual bistability produced by ambiguous displays such as the cylinder. Confirming this general idea, analogous bistability can be seen in the behavior of MT neurons in the brains of monkeys who view ambiguous two-dimensional displays such as the projection of the cylinder (Andersen & Bradley, 1998).

Nawrot and Blake's (1993) model makes some interesting predictions. First, because kinetic depth and stereoscopic depth are computed within the same neural network, the model predicts that it should be possible to create stimulus conditions in which the two forms of depth—kinetic and stereoscopic—will produce equivalent perceptual experiences. That prediction was confirmed in a series of experiments. In one experiment, observers viewed two successive animations depicting a rotating sphere. In one display, the impression of a three-dimensional sphere was created solely by kinetic depth; in the other display, retinal disparity was used to portray the sphere. For some disparities, these two displays were indistinguishable under forced-choice testing. A related experiment revealed that a weak sense of depth from retinal disparity could be reinforced or, alternatively, canceled by a strong kinetic-depth stimulus that itself contained no explicit disparity information. This finding, too, points to a common neural substrate for kinetic depth and dynamic stereopsis. A kinetic-depth stimulus's capacity to bias stereoscopic depth is comparable to the effect of direct, localized electrical stimulation of direction-selective MT neurons. In monkeys, stimulation of area MT has been shown to bias perceptual judgments of depth (DeAngelis, Cumming, & Newsome, 1998).

MOTION TRANSPARENCY

When an observer views a display in which two or more velocities are spatially intermingled, the percept can be one of transparency (two or more separate patterns moving through one another) or coherence (patterns cohering and moving in a single direction). Gibson, Gibson, Smith, and Flock (1959) reported that observers could detect two overlapping planes in a display in which the planes moved at different speeds. Subsequently, Andersen (1989) demonstrated that observers could accurately identify the presence of up to three planes in similar displays with a duration of 2 s. When duration is reduced to only 250 ms, observers can distinguish between a display comprising as many as five transparent sheets of dots moving in different directions from a display of dynamic random noise (Mulligan, 1992). Furthermore, with translatory movements the process of segregating a display into different planes is fast: With just a 60-ms exposure, observers can correctly identify a two-plane stimulus. However, if more complex motion patterns such as expansion/contraction and rotations are superimposed and presented for brief durations (85 ms followed by a random noise mask), observers cannot accurately identify the component motions (De Bruyn & Orban, 1993).

In transparent displays, the dots defining each separate plane usually move in phase, as an intact pattern in a given direction and speed. However, transparency can also be observed if individual dots in the display alternate between two different speeds (Bravo & Watamaniuk, 1995). In these cases, transparency is perceived, as evidenced by observers' abilities to judge accurately the speeds of individual component motions.

Although two spatially superimposed sets of dots moving in different directions can generate perceptual transparency, the two sets of motion signals do not operate without mutual interactions. Specifically, the perceived directions of the two sets of dots appear to be further apart than they actually are, a phenomenon referred to as motion repulsion (e.g., Hiris & Blake, 1996; Marshak & Sekuler, 1979). If the directions of the superimposed sets of dots differ by less than approximately 90 deg, the perceived direction of each motion will be pushed away from the direction of the other motion. The magnitude of this repulsion effect depends on the speeds of the component motions and on the density of the moving elements (Dakin & Mareschal, 2000; see also Lindsey, 2001). In addition, Snowden (1990) and Verstraten, Fredericksen, van Wezel, Lankheet, and van de Grind (1996) showed that sensitivity to the direction of each motion plane decreases as the speeds of the two motion planes become more similar. Thus, although the percept of transparency shows that vision segregates component motions from one another, when the two motion signals are sufficiently similar, each can influence the perception of the other.

The percept of transparency requires a single local region to contain more than a single direction of motion. But what is the size of such transparency-producing regions? Qian, Andersen, and Adelson (1994) addressed this issue by generating direction-balanced displays in which dots moving in opposite directions (left and right) were either paired, so that a dot from each set was in close spatial proximity to the other, or unpaired. The observer's task was to judge the degree of transparency in the display. When the paths of the briefly presented dot pairs crossed or when they were separated vertically by 0.2 deg or less, the percept of transparency was abolished. In both cases in which transparency is abolished, the oppositely moving dots were close to one another. A similar lack of transparency is perceived if

two oppositely moving sine-wave gratings are superimposed.

Transparency can be restored to dot and grating displays if the components are sufficiently separated in depth, or if component gratings differ in spatial frequency by about two octaves.[9] Curran and Braddick (2000) refined this work, showing that if paired dots moved in directions separated by just 60 deg to 120 deg, rather than in opposite directions, then the percept was that of coherent global flow in the direction of the dots' vector average. Presumably, paired directions differing by only 60 deg to 120 deg does not trigger the inhibition that would be generated had the directions opposed one another, that is, had they differed by 180 degrees. Similarly, Lindsey and Todd (1998) found that motion signals embedded in random noise were more easily detected when the component motions moved at right angles to one another, rather than in opposite directions. These data are consistent with the existence of a suppressive stage of motion processing in which oppositely tuned motion detectors inhibit each other locally. When the directions of spatially proximate motions are opposite one another, directional signals are perfectly balanced, and mutual, direction-selective inhibition results in no net perceived motion (Qian, Andersen, & Adelson, 1994). When spatially proximate signals differ by just 90 deg, the absence of directional inhibition enables observers to see the motion easily, as Lindsey and Todd found.

Neurophysiology provides further support for this hypothesis. Qian and Andersen (1994) recorded responses from V1 and MT neurons during presentation of paired or unpaired motion stimuli and found that V1 cells

---

[9]A difference of two octaves means that the spatial frequencies differ by a factor of four. With a difference this large, the two gratings will be initially registered by different spatial frequency tuned visual mechanisms (Graham, 1989).

responded equally well to both types of stimuli, but that MT cells responded better to stimuli in which local motions were unpaired. Snowden, Treue, Erickson, and Andersen (1991) reported data that were consistent with these results. But what about the brains of humans? Does the human motion complex (area MT+) behave as its nonhuman primate homologues do? Does area MT+ exhibit motion opponency? To answer this, Heeger, Boynton, Demb, Seidemann, and Newsome (1999) compared multiunit recordings from neurons in monkey cortex to the fMRI activation patterns generated in the human brain. A multiunit recording collects responses from local aggregates of neurons, rather than from individual neurons in isolation. This approach was meant to enhance comparability with fMRI measurements, which represent aggregated neural activity. Heeger et al. used equivalent stimuli for both measures of neural activity, and with both species. In humans as well as in monkeys, area V1 showed no evidence of motion opponency: Responses to paired and unpaired stimuli (dot patterns or gratings) were essentially the same. However, area MT in the monkey and its homologue in humans showed considerable motion opponency. In particular, the fMRI activation in area MT+ was far stronger with nonpaired dot stimuli than with dot patterns in which local, opposite motions were pitted against one another. Thus, area MT+ is a site at which direction opponency could initiate the assessment of transparency.

HOW THE VISUAL SYSTEM MEASURES MOTION: THREE PROBLEMS TO SOLVE

This section provides an overview of three major problems that vision must solve in order to provide observers with useful accounts of motion in the visual field.

Direction Selectivity/Reichardt Detectors

The first computational account of motion perception arose five decades ago, from the collaboration of Bernhard Hassenstein, a biologist, and Werner Reichardt, a physicist (Borst, 2000). Their product was a simple multiplicative correlation detector made up of two oppositely tuned subunits. To understand the detector's operation, imagine that a spotlight moves across the retina, successively stimulating different groups of adjacent photoreceptors one after another. To simplify, assume that the direction of the moving spot caused the spot to fall first on photoreceptor A and then, after some delay Δt, on photoreceptor B. As a result, the luminance signal elicited from A precedes the signal generated from B by Δt. This delay depends on two variables, the spatial separation between A and B, and the speed with which the spot moves. Now to the detector's circuitry: For one of the detector's subunits the luminance signal generated in photoreceptor A is multiplied by a delayed luminance signal from a second neighboring photoreceptor set, B. This basic operation is replicated in the detector's other subunit, but in mirror-symmetrical fashion: The two photoreceptors are switched, and the delay is now applied to the signal from the previously nondelayed photoreceptor. Because of the delays, a spot that reaches first A and then B generates a response that is larger in the second subunit than in the first; the same spot traveling at the same speed but in the opposite direction generates a response that is larger in the first subunit than in the second. In other words, the numerical difference between the two subunits' responses is directionally selective: Motion in one direction generates a positive difference, whereas motion in the opposite direction generates a negative difference.

The model's simple circuit guarantees that motion sensitivity will reflect a stimulus's temporal and spatial parameters, which is certainly true of vision. In its first tests, the model was applied to insect vision to exploit as a behavioral index of motion perception the optomotor reflex of the beetle *Chlorophanus*. The model's success inspired a good deal of research, including work on higher animals. It also promoted the creation of other models that performed a similar computation using different circuitry (Sperling & Lu, 1998).

Although the Hassenstein-Reichardt motion circuit has many virtues, it also has one property that could be considered a flaw: It fails to distinguish between two classes of stimuli that are physically quite different from one another. In particular, the circuit would give equivalent responses to (a) a spot that moved smoothly with the proper velocity from the receptive fields of one subunit's receptors to the receptive fields of the other subunit's receptors and (b) a spot that was presented to one set of receptive fields, then extinguished, and, after a delay, presented to the other receptive fields. With proper delays between presentations of the spot, this latter sampled or stroboscopic motion stimulus would be indistinguishable from its smooth counterpart. Scaled up to an entire human visual system, this perceptual "error" becomes quite important because it allows the sampled images that comprise film and video sequences to mimic smooth motion. The result of such a sampling process is known as "apparent motion," a designation meant to contrast with smooth or "real" motion. The quality of apparent motion (i.e., how smooth the motion appears) varies with a number of parameters, particularly the rate at which the stimulus is sampled in both space and time domains. As the interval lengthens between successive frames of display, the sampling rate is said to decrease. Intuitively, as sampling rate increases—and successive frames come closer together in time—the appearance of the sampled stimulus approaches that of a smoothly-moving stimulus.

Watson, Ahumada, and Farrell (1986) developed a simple model that predicts whether any spatial and temporal sampling rate would produce the appearance of smooth motion. Their model defines a spatiotemporal range of each observer's window of visibility. The boundaries of this window, a region in joint spatial- and temporal-frequency space, define the spatial- and temporal-frequency limits of the observer's sensitivity to energy in the stimulus. When the stimulus is sampled in time, as for video or film or computer displays, the sampling process generates energy at temporal frequencies in addition to the fundamental frequency. A low sampling rate produces energy over a range of low temporal frequencies; a high sampling rate produces energy over a range of high temporal frequencies. As a result, the higher the sampling rate, the more likely it is that the resulting energy will fall outside the window of visibility, which renders them invisible and perceptually inconsequential. Therefore, two stimuli—one smoothly moving and the other representing sampled motion—will appear identical if their spectra within the window of visibility are identical; portions of their spectra that lie outside the window are irrelevant. Using two different strategies for sampling stimuli, Watson et al. confirmed the essential validity of their elegantly simple model.

Following Hassenstein and Reichardt, most studies of motion perception have examined responses to drifting modulations of luminance (or chromatic contrast). These stimuli, termed first-order stimuli or Fourier stimuli, would evoke responses in visual mechanisms that are responsive to spatiotemporal variations in luminance or chromatic contrast. Such stimuli correspond to a dominant species of spatiotemporal modulation that are encountered every day, but such stimuli do not exhaust the possibilities. Some stimuli, termed second-order or non-Fourier stimuli, would elude detection by such mechanisms (Chubb & Sperling, 1988; Pantle, 1973). Nevertheless, perceptually, such stimuli elicit strong motion responses. It is worth emphasizing that second-order motion is not merely a creation of the laboratory. A well-camouflaged creature moving against a background with the same texture markings as the creature's own will generate second-order motion only. The same is true for the waving of tree branches when wind blows through a forest, or wheat stalks waving in a wheat field.

Many psychophysical studies comparing first- and second-order motion have demonstrated clear distinctions between the two. The distinction between the two classes of motion stimuli has gained increasing theoretical significance from reports that localized lesions of the brain can selectively impair either first- or second-order motion perception, while sparing the nonaffected form (Vaina, Cowey, & Kennedy, 1999; Vaina, Grzywacz, LeMay, Bienfang, & Wolpow, 1998).

The Correspondence Problem

Some of the computational prerequisites of motion perception reflect computational obstacles to perception more generally. To appreciate this point, consider the problem of motion correspondence. It has long been recognized that the proximal stimulus underspecifies the distal stimulus. In describing this fact, Helmholtz (1866) noted that at any instant the distribution of light on the retina (the proximal stimulus) is consistent with an indefinitely large combination of stimulus objects and patterns of object illumination (distal stimuli). To resolve, or at least reduce, the proximal stimulus's massive underspecification of the distal stimulus, the visual system exploits various sources of supplementary information, including constraints and regularities embodied in the physics of the natural world.

Although motion perception must overcome the underspecification that is common to all perception, as a spatiotemporal process, motion faces some additional, unique sources of underspecification. An early stage of motion extraction requires correspondence matching. Some local pattern—for example, a luminance perturbation centered on retinal coordinates x_0, y_0—is detected at time t_0 and matched at later time, t_1, to the pattern located at new coordinates, x_1, y_1. As this description implies, motion depends on a match or correspondence in space and time. As Attneave (1974) pointed out, when a stimulus comprises more than one element that moves, identification of correspondences over time becomes a challenge.

Measurements of element positions in successive samples insufficiently determine the motion correspondences of the samples.[10] Simple demonstrations of this point are shown in Figure 4.7. If there are **n** elements in each of two samples, then there are at least **n!** sets of correspondences consistent with the samples. (This calculation assumes that one and only one element in the second sample is matched to each element in the first sample.) Dawson (1991) argued that to resolve this motion correspondence, the visual system exploits a trio of global spatiotemporal constraints that mimic the properties of motion in the natural world. ("Global" implies that the constraints are applied simultaneously to the entire field of dots, or to large portions of the field.) These constraints are known as the nearest neighbor principle (minimize the mean displacements between points matched

---

[10]To illustrate the correspondence problem, we have used examples in which stimuli are time-sampled at a relatively low rate. For historical reasons, when such stimuli generate the experience of motion, that motion is often designated as *apparent motion*. It is important to note that despite our limited choice of illustrative examples, the correspondence problem confronts any biological motion system.

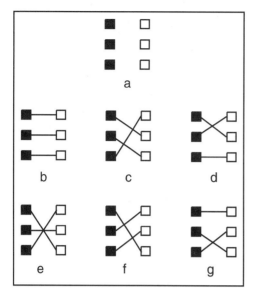

Figure 4.7 Illustration of motion's correspondence problem.

NOTE: In each panel, the three black squares represent items presented in the first frame of a cinematogram, and the three white squares represent items in the second frame. Panels illustrate various ways that items from the two frames could be matched.

SOURCE: After Dawson (1991).

between successive samples), the smoothness principle (because natural surfaces tend to vary smoothly, motion arising from the displacement of elements on such surfaces should be as smooth as possible, minimizing

abrupt changes in velocity among neighboring elements), and the element integrity principle (because surfaces do not tend to pop in and out of existence, elements on such surfaces should persist over time; i.e., one element should not split into two, and two elements should not fuse into one).

By emphasizing global motion matching, Dawson's (1991) model assumes that properties such as chromatic or shape similarities exert only a minor influence on motion correspondence. Although some empirical results have been taken as justifying that assumption, we believe that the preponderance of evidence leaves little doubt that motion correspondence is powerfully influenced by the similarity between stimuli. For example, A. B. Sekuler and Bennett (1996) examined motion correspondence generated by stimuli of differing calibrated discriminability. Manipulating relative phase—a crucial determinant of form perception—they assessed strength of correspondence produced by quartets of stimuli. Each quartet comprised four stimuli that were evenly spaced on a virtual circle. To emphasize the figural relationships among members of the quartet, we can designate the four stimuli as A, B, A, B.

Figure 4.8 illustrates the entire quartet rotated rigidly over 45 deg between successive display frames. Consider the four successive frames represented in that figure. If there

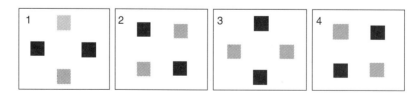

Figure 4.8 Four frames of a quartet display.

NOTE: In each frame, two tokens are black, and two are gray; the quartet of tokens rotates rigidly by 45 deg between successive frames. In the absence of color-based correspondence matching, the display's motion would be ambiguous, as likely to move clockwise as counterclockwise. However, color-based matching generates consistent motion in a clockwise direction, and the probability of seeing motion in the direction dictated by color matches increases with the perceptual difference between the two pairs of tokens.

were no color-based correspondence matching, the motion produced by the display would be ambiguous (i.e., as likely to move clockwise as counterclockwise). However, color-based matching would generate consistent motion in a clockwise direction. The elements in A. B. Sekuler and Bennett's (1996) quartets were compound sinusoidal gratings, each comprising a fundamental component and one harmonic component, at twice the frequency of the fundamental. A. B. Sekuler and Bennett manipulated the contrast and relative phase of the harmonic component in order to generate pairs of stimuli that varied in discriminability. When such stimuli were placed in quartet configuration (as in Figure 4.8), the probability of seeing motion in the direction dictated by figural matches varied with the perceptual difference between the two pairs of compound gratings. Tse, Cavanagh, and Nakayama (1998) described a novel class of displays in which figural parsing and matching are requisites for perception of motion. ("Parsing" refers to the segmentation, spatial isolation, and identification of separate stimulus elements.)

Before leaving the topic of motion correspondence, we should take special note of bistable motion sequences (i.e., stimuli in which the correspondence problem has two equally likely outcomes). An example of this unusual situation is illustrated in Figure 4.9, which shows two successive frames of animation sequence in which a pair of discs moves back and forth between two positions. Note that the upper disc in frame 1 could correspond either to the left-hand disc or to the right-hand disc in frame 2 (and likewise for the lower disc in frame 1). Because the two alternative motion paths are exactly equal in length, the motion system has no basis for deciding which pattern of motions is correct: Motion correspondence is entirely ambiguous. When stimuli like this are viewed for an extended period, people perceive both possible paths (Anstis & Ramachandran, 1987; Kramer &

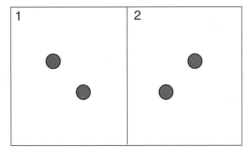

Figure 4.9   Two successive frames of a display that illustrates feature matching in the solution of a correspondence problem.
NOTE: The upper disc in frame 1 could correspond either to frame 2's left-hand disc or to its right-hand disc (and likewise for the lower disc in frame 1). Because the two alternative motion paths are equal in length, the motion system has no basis for deciding which pattern of motions is correct: motion correspondence is entirely ambiguous. When such stimuli are viewed for an extended period, both possible paths are seen in alternation.

Yantis, 1997; Pantle & Picciano, 1976; Ramachandran & Anstis, 1985), with each pattern of motion dominating for a few seconds and then giving way to the alternative pattern. Such ambiguous motion displays are useful tools for studying the stimulus factors that influence solutions to the correspondence problem (Francis & Kim, 1999; Yu, 2000). Multimodal stimuli, such as auditory signals, can influence the perception of bistable motion displays (Lewkowicz, in press; R. Sekuler, Sekuler, & Lau, 1997; Watanabe & Shimojo, 2001).

The Aperture Problem

As described earlier, local motion is extracted from the retinal image by neurons in area V1. The receptive fields of such neurons can be construed as apertures, spatially delimited windows within which neurons register the presence of motion in a given direction. If an extended moving edge or bar is seen within such an aperture, then regardless of the direction in which the edge or bar actually moves, the neuron will respond as though the edge or bar were moving perpendicular to the orientation in the neuron's receptive field (Bradley, 2001). To take a specific instance, imagine that a smooth, featureless, vertically oriented bar moves obliquely (up and to the left) at a constant velocity. Any small receptive field positioned along the contour's length signals only the motion component that is perpendicular to the contour's orientation, in this case the leftward motion component. Because the contour extends beyond the boundaries of the small receptive field, the contour's upward motion component produces no information that changes with time (Pack & Born, 2001).

Because each directionally selective (DS) unit sees only what is happening within its own receptive field, the resulting signals from DS units are necessarily ambiguous. This ambiguity, now known as the aperture problem, was pointed out more than 60 years ago by Hans Wallach (Wuerger, Shapley, & Rubin, 1996). Figure 4.10 illustrates what Wallach had in mind. The circular area in the figure represents the receptive field of a DS neuron. Its preferred direction of movement is rightward. As the vertical edge of a large black line moves rightward at an appropriate speed through the receptive field, the neuron responds strongly (Panel A). However, this is not the only direction of movement that could evoke such a response. As long as the black line is large compared to the aperture (the receptive field), the same local spatiotemporal event—movement at the same velocity (meaning the same speed and direction)—could be generated by any number of other combinations of direction and speed, some of which are suggested in Panels B and C. This equivalence means that the neuron's response is inherently ambiguous. Because the neuron's view of the world is limited to the confines of its receptive field, the neuron responds exactly the same way to each of

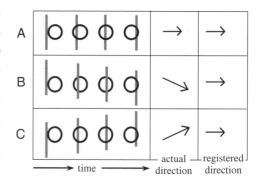

Figure 4.10   Illustration of the aperture problem: The ambiguity of directional information within a receptive field aperture.

NOTE: The circular area represents the receptive field of a directionally selective neuron tuned to rightward motion. As the vertical bar moves rightward through the receptive field, the neuron signals rightward motion (Panel A). However, movement of the same bar downward and to the right (Panel B), or movement upward to the right (Panel C) also generates rightward movement within the receptive field. The equivalence of these and other directions of actual movement renders the neuron's response ambiguous.

SOURCE: Modified from R. Sekuler and Blake (2001).

these different velocities of movement. As a prelude to explaining the visual system's strategy for resolving this ambiguity, consider one side effect of this ambiguity:

Movement seen within any single receptive field could have arisen from a variety of distinctly different visual events. This ambiguity opens the door to numerous illusions of perceived motion. With some of these, observers watch as a line or bar moves through an aperture whose shape strongly influences the perceived direction of movement. For example, suppose that an L-shaped aperture is cut in a piece of paper. Suppose also that a long oblique line (at 45 deg) behind the aperture moves steadily straight downward (Figure 4.11A). Initially, an observer sees an oblique line that moves downward. Then, once the line reaches the base of the

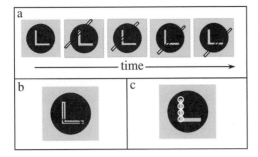

Figure 4.11   Wallach's demonstration of the influence of aperture shape on perceived motion.
NOTE: Panel A: Motion of an obliquely oriented line into, through, and then out of an L-shaped aperture. Panel B: The line initially appears to move vertically downward; then, when the line enters the aperture's horizontally oriented portion, its apparent direction abruptly changes to horizontal. Panel C: See text for an explanation.
SOURCE: Modified from R. Sekuler and Blake (2001).

L-shaped aperture, the movement abruptly changes (Figure 4.11B). Now the observer sees a rightward-moving oblique line. Wallach investigated this and several dozen related aperture illusions (Wuerger et al., 1996). To appreciate the basic elements of his approach, return to the L-shaped aperture.

One can approximate the L-shaped aperture's upright portion by a set of colinear circular receptive fields (Figure 4.11C). An oblique, downward-moving line would traverse each of these fields, one after another. However, this pattern of stimulation underspecifies the distal stimulus; in fact, the pattern of stimulation could have arisen from any number of distal stimuli. For example, it could have been produced by several different but similarly oriented lines, each of which traverses just one receptive field and then disappears, just as the next line appears at the top of the next receptive field and begins its own descent. Or, the same pattern of stimulation across all the receptive fields could have resulted, as it did in Wallach's

demonstration, from a single line that moved from top to bottom, entering and then exiting one receptive field after another. Given the limited information available to it, how does the visual system select the scenario that most likely was responsible for that information? In the spirit of Gestalt psychology, Wallach proposed that the single perceptual choice made in such multiple-choice situations tends to be the simplest global motion. In this case, an observer sees a single steadily moving line rather than a series of different lines in succession. An alternative view might portray the single perceptual outcome as the product of a Bayesian perceptual inference (Knill, Kersten, & Yuille, 1996). Choosing between these alternative accounts requires additional, carefully designed empirical measurements.

Perceived motion, then, is not determined solely by local responses to stimulus velocity that are generated within separate restricted regions of the field. Instead, local measurements of velocity are integrated at some place in the visual system at which the local velocity-related signals from area V1 are collected and combined. Such a combination of signals is the nervous system's standard operating procedure for resolving neural ambiguity in the signals of individual neurons. When the response of one neuron is ambiguous, the nervous system can diminish the ambiguity by aggregating outputs from a number of differently tuned neurons. For visual motion, the nervous system reduces ambiguity about individual, local, spatiotemporal events by channeling outputs from the first stage of direction processing to its second stage of neural processing in area MT.

Some neurons in area MT receive input from V1 neurons with different preferred directions of motion. As a result, the directional selectivity of these MT neurons differs qualitatively from that of their predecessors in area V1. Furthermore, these differences enhance the importance of area MT's contribution to the perception of motion. To see this, return to Wallach's demonstration with two overlaid, moving gratings. When analogous two-component grating displays are imaged within the receptive fields of V1 neurons, the neurons tend to respond to the separate components. Some of Wallach's psychophysical observations foreshadowed these physiological results. He showed observers patterns composed of two different line gratings such as those shown Figures 4.12A and 4.12B. When the two are overlaid, as in Figure 4.12B, they generate a series of diamond-shaped structures. When the bars of the two gratings move downward at the same rate, the display's appearance fluctuates between (a) a field of diamonds that moves downward (Figure 4.12C) and (b) two line gratings that move at different

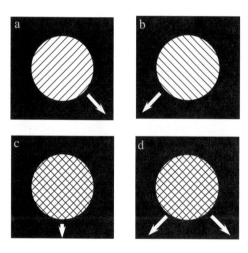

Figure 4.12 Superimposition of two diagonal, moving gratings (A and B) produces a diamond pattern whose motion is bistable.

NOTE: When either moving grating is presented alone, it appears to move in a consistent direction, which is indicated by the arrows in A and B. When the gratings are superimposed, they cohere to form a single downward-moving pattern (Panel C), or they appear to slide over one another, in two different superimposed directions.

SOURCE: Demonstration devised by Wallach. Diagram modified from R. Sekuler and Blake (2001).

velocities, sliding over each other in the process (Figure 4.12D). As Wallach found, the relative potency of the two alternative perceptual outcomes varies with a number of factors, including the angle between the two line gratings. This bistability is reminiscent of Rubin's vase/face illusion and of various phenomena of binocular rivalry (see R. Sekuler & Blake, 2001).

This perceptual bistability points to something quite important about motion perception. In order to parse the display into two gratings that move in different directions, the nervous system requires mechanisms that separate the different directions within each local region. However, to produce the alternative outcome—the moving diamond—the nervous system needs a second mechanism that collects dissimilar directional signals from regions across the display and binds those signals into coherent perceptual wholes rather than independent, isolated elements. This may sound challenging, but it is utterly necessary. In the example shown in Figure 4.12, these directions would be obliquely downward to the left and to the right. When the same displays are presented in the receptive fields of MT neurons, however, many of those cells respond to the motion not of the components, but of the overall moving pattern (Movshon, Adelson, Gizzi, & Newsome, 1986). In the case illustrated in Figure 4.12, this would be coherent motion directly downward. It is thought, then, that important aspects of motion perception arise from two stages of processing: one stage in which local motion vectors are extracted, and a second stage in which those vectors are sorted into object-related combinations. As Braddick put it, "[W]e do not live in a world of independent fragments, but of objects and surfaces that move coherently" (1993, p. 263). Vision needs some way to combine velocity signals that belong to the same moving object. It also needs to separate velocity signals that do not belong together, that is, signals that arise from different objects (Snowden & Verstraten, 1999). Obviously, the characteristics of the world mandate precisely the sort of complex behavior that Wallach demonstrated.

Several computational strategies could be exploited in order to resolve the ambiguity represented by the aperture problem. Fennema and Thompson (1979) were the first to observe that the ambiguity could be overcome by combining two or more ambiguous measurements of local motion. Movshon et al. (1986) demonstrated that some neurons in area MT seem to perform precisely such a disambiguating computation, a computation that produces what is known as an intersection of constraints (Adelson & Movshon, 1982).

Pack and Born (2001) demonstrated a dynamic form of disambiguation in macaque MT neurons. As expected from the influence of the aperture problem, MT neurons initially responded primarily to the component of motion perpendicular to the orientation of a moving contour. Then, over approximately 60 ms, the neurons' responses shifted steadily. At the end of this dynamic process, neurons' responses began to signal the actual direction of the stimulus, no matter what the stimulus's orientation. This shift in neural activity had a striking correlate in the monkeys' oculomotor behavior, in smooth pursuit eye movements. The initial velocity of pursuit eye movements deviates in a direction perpendicular to local contour orientation, suggesting that the earliest neural responses influence the oculomotor behavior. These results suggest that the primate visual system derives an initial estimate of motion direction by integrating ambiguous and unambiguous local-motion signals over a fairly large spatial region and then refines this estimate over time. Lorenceau, Shiffrar, Wells, and Castet (1993) demonstrated an analogous result with human observers: The perceived direction of a field of moving bars is initially perpendicular to the bars' orientation but shifts slowly toward the actual direction of movement.

Geisler (1999) called attention to yet another avenue to the disambiguation of motion signals. With a stimulus that moves relatively rapidly, the visual system's temporal integration produces an oriented *virtual* contour, which Geisler labeled a visual streak. (It is important to appreciate the virtual character of such streaks; they should not be confused with the actual streaks, or trails, sometimes generated as a wake when a bright target moves rapidly across the display of a cathode ray tube.) The orientation selectivity of neurons in area V1 means that motion streaks, which accurately reflect the direction of contour motion, could generate reliable orientation signals that can help disambiguate direction of motion (see also Jancke, 2000). Geisler buttressed his ingenious hypothesis with measurements of motion thresholds with simultaneous orientation masking and after orientation adaptation.

MOTION AFTEREFFECTS

When one stares at motion in one direction for some period of time and then gazes at a stationary scene, the static scene appears to move in the direction opposite to the previously viewed motion. Although prolonged exposure to motion has other consequences—such as direction-selective threshold changes and alterations in perceived velocity—illusory postexposure motion defines what is known as the motion aftereffect (MAE).[11] Reports of this visual phenomenon can be traced back to Aristotle (about 330 B.C.) and Titus Lucretius Carus in about 56 B.C. (Wade &

---

[11]Even very brief exposures to motion can generate substantial consequences, such as twofold, directionally selective decreases in sensitivity or clear alterations in perceived direction (Pantle, Gallogly, & Piehler, 2000).

Verstraten, 1998). The best-known early description of the phenomenon was given by Addams (1834), whose observation of the effect at Scotland's Falls of Foyer gave the phenomenon its common name, the waterfall illusion. Wade and Verstraten (1998) provided an excellent historical treatment of MAE, which is a widely used tool for studying motion processing more generally. In fact, the explosive growth in the literature on MAE, as documented by Mather, Verstraten, and Anstis (1998, p. viii) parallels the growth in published works on many aspects of visual motion.

The conditions under which MAE occurs were extensively studied by Wohlgemuth (1911). The strength of MAE can be assessed by any of a number of measures, including apparent speed, apparent direction, and duration (Pantle, 1998). Using MAE duration as an index of strength, Wolgemuth found that maintaining fixation during the adaptation period increased the effect and that adapting one eye would produce an aftereffect in the other, an example of interocular transfer. This surprising finding was initially reported by Dvorak (1870) and has been replicated recently by others (e.g., Raymond, 1993; Steiner, Blake, & Rose, 1994; Symons, Pearson, & Timney, 1996; Wade, Swanston, & De Weert, 1993). The interocular effects are usually only half as strong as the monocular effects.

Many motion studies generated adaptation with drifting sinusoidal grating, whose effect was measured with a stationary test grating. Not unexpectedly, the MAE was tuned to spatial frequency: The strongest effect occurred when adapting both the grating and the stationary test grating had the same spatial frequency (Bex, Verstraten, & Mareschal, 1996; Cameron, Baker, & Boulton, 1992; Thompson, 1998). The effect also showed temporal frequency tuning; the strongest effect was reported at a temporal frequency of

5 Hz, regardless of spatial frequency (Pantle, 1974).

Although the aftereffect is evoked usually with a stationary test stimulus, more recent experiments have used dynamic RDCs as test stimuli (e.g., Blake & Hiris, 1993; Ledgeway, 1994). Using such test stimuli, aftereffect strength can be measured by having a proportion of dots in the RDC move in the adapted direction to null the illusory motion. Moreover, adapting to non-Fourier motion does not produce an aftereffect with static tests (McCarthy, 1993; Nishida, Ashida, & Sato, 1994; von Grünau, 1986), but an aftereffect is observed when the test stimulus is dynamic, such as a pattern of flickering elements (Ledgeway, 1994; McCarthy, 1993; Nishida & Sato, 1995). Some investigators feel that dynamic, rather than static, test patterns provide the most accurate reflection of the properties of motion mechanisms (Hiris & Blake, 1992).

The MAE ordinarily lasts for a relatively brief time following adaptation, typically decaying after about 1 s to 15 s. Although the passage of time strongly influences the decay of the aftereffect, other factors also play a role. In fact, certain conditions of test viewing can freeze the aftereffect's normal decay, causing the aftereffect to be stored (Spigel, 1960, 1962a, 1962b, 1964). Immediately after adaptation, if one closes one's eyes for a period that exceeds the MAE's expected duration, then the MAE will still be seen when the eyes are reopened. In other words, closing the eyes slows the MAE's normal decay. This phenomenon is often described as an example of *aftereffect storage.* Such storage has some interesting characteristics that have changed researchers' views of the MAE. For example, suppose that after adaptation the MAE is tested with a dynamic field (randomly moving dots). If the MAE is allowed to run its course with this dynamic test field and if a static test field is then presented, a MAE will be seen on that field. Most surprising, the duration of the MAE on the static field will be little affected by the intervening dynamic MAE. Reversing the order of the two test fields (i.e., the static MAE followed by the dynamic MAE), the duration of the dynamic MAE is affected by the intervening static MAE (Verstraten et al., 1996). This relative independence of the static and dynamic MAEs, and other divergences between these two types of test fields, has encouraged the idea that adaptation can occur in at least two distinct regions of the brain. Specifically, Nishida et al. (1994) suggested that the static MAE is caused by adaptation in the primary motion detectors, whereas the dynamic MAE reflects adaptation in a higher cortical area, such as area MT.

Early modern accounts of the MAE assigned a central role to the fatiguing of cells during adaptation. These accounts exploited two key ideas: first, that neurons in the motion system fire spontaneously in the absence of motion, and second, that perceived direction of motion reflects the relative firing rates of neurons tuned to opposite directions. Suppose that the spontaneous activity of fatigued cells is significantly reduced for a brief time after adaptation. Therefore, the presentation of a stationary stimulus generates an imbalance in the spontaneous firing of the motion cells, and the nonadapted cells have a proportionately higher rate. According to this hypothesis, the brain takes this imbalance as signaling the presence of actual motion in a direction opposite to the earlier adapting direction (Barlow & Hill, 1963; R. Sekuler & Ganz, 1963; Sutherland, 1961). Such illusory motion is, of course, what people perceive. This model was labeled the ratio model because it held that perceived direction was controlled by the ratio of responses among motion cells that are tuned to different directions of motion. A somewhat modified version of this theory, dubbed the distribution shift model (Mather, 1980), recognized that adaptation would

affect a range of directionally tuned mechanisms, not just the one mechanism that was most sensitive to the adapting direction. The result would be a more widespread change in postadaptation spontaneous activity.

By incorporating various forms of inhibition, recent theories of the mechanisms of the MAE depart from earlier emphases on fatigue. This new emphasis reflects in part a recognition of the central role that inhibition plays in the cortex and, therefore, in visual computations. For example, Barlow (1990) proposed that the MAE results from a buildup of mutual inhibition among populations of motion-sensitive neurons during adaptation.[12] This mutual inhibition remains for some time after the adapting stimulus is removed. As a result, the pattern of responses among the motion cells is modified such that a neutral (stationary) stimulus is perceived as moving in the opposite direction. Because this inhibitory buildup could occur at any site where motion-sensitive cells are found, adaptation can occur at one or more sites in the motion system. Nishida and Sato's (1995) MAE results, mentioned earlier, are consistent with this idea.

Motion aftereffects can also be produced by stimuli comprising two superimposed directions of motion. Here, the resulting aftereffect is opposite the vector sum of the two adapting directions (Riggs & Day, 1980; Verstraten, Fredericksen, & van de Grind, 1994). Thus, for example, simultaneous adaptation to leftward motion and to upward motion subsequently causes a stationary test figure to appear to drift down and to the right (the vector sum of the downward component and the rightward component). When the two adapting components are unequal in strength

---

[12]For Barlow (1990), the MAE exemplified a general principle of neural operation. In his view, the mutual inhibition, to which he ascribes MAE, reduces redundancy in the firing of different sets of neurons, thereby minimizing the total activity at any site in the visual system.

(e.g., one component is of higher contrast than is the other), the aftereffect direction shifts toward the stronger component, and the size of the shift tracks the inequality between stimulus components.

MEMORY AND LEARNING FOR MOTION

Vision's essential purpose is to guide behavior, and that purpose is served best when vision's current products can be compared to stored representations of vision' earlier products. Such comparisons, or recognitions, enable animals to prepare situation-appropriate behaviors before they are necessary. Although much of the research on human memory has focused on memory for symbolic or verbal material, long before words came on the evolutionary stage, animals had a crucial need to remember and recognize scenes, objects, and events that they had encountered earlier. Although motion is certainly among the visual attributes that are worth remembering, relatively little research has been done on memory for motion.

Magnussen and Greenlee (1992) examined observers' short-term memory for stimulus velocity. Using drifting luminance grating, they measured the difference threshold for velocity, ΔV. They explored the retention of velocity information in memory by varying the interstimulus intervals (ISI) separating the first (reference) stimulus and the second (test) stimulus. Weber fractions ($\Delta V/V$) proved to be independent of ISIs ranging from 1 s to 30 s. This invariance showed that memory for velocity is quite robust over delays of up to 30 s.

Blake, Cepeda, and Hiris (1997) explored memory for direction of movement by using RDCs with 100% coherence. After a 1-s presentation of an RDC, an observer used a computer mouse to indicate the direction in which motion had been seen. The mean absolute value of observers' errors was about 5 deg (Blake, Cepeda, & Hiris, 1997). This level of performance is remarkably robust when pre-response delays force the perceived direction to be stored and then retrieved from memory. For example, performance is unchanged when the subject's response is delayed by 8 s. The memory on which responses were based is unlikely to be of an iconic nature; performance was unimpaired by random visual noise interposed between the RDC and the report of the remembered direction. Nor did memory depend on stored information from eye movement, such as observers might make while viewing the RDC: Performance was unaffected when observers executed random tracking-eye movements before making their judgments. Although memory for RDC direction was preserved over short intervals, such memory was dramatically undermined when Blake et al.'s observers saw not just one direction but a succession of different directions on each trial. Performance fell off substantially as the number of seen directions grew. For example, average error climbed from 5 deg with just one presentation to 25 deg to 30 deg when observers saw and tried to remember seven different directions of motion.

Pasternak and colleagues have studied the role of area MT in remembering the direction of visual motion (Bisley & Pasternak, 2000; Bisley et al., 2001). They trained monkeys to compare the directions of motion portrayed in two successively presented animation sequences, the "sample" and the "test." Task difficulty was manipulated by varying the coherence of these random-dot motion displays and the delay interval between sample and test. During the delay period—while the monkey was trying to remember the sample direction that it had seen—small, brief electrical pulses were delivered directly to clusters of neurons in area MT. This electrical stimulation, which artificially activated the recipient neurons, influenced the monkey's subsequent judgment about the test direction (Bisley, Zaksas, & Pasternak, 2001). This result supports the notion that area MT is involved in the short-term retention and retrieval of information about the direction of visual motion. This conclusion receives further support from the same researchers' studies of the effects of unilateral lesions to motion centers of the monkey cortex (Bisley & Pasternak, 2000).

As mentioned in the introduction to this section, visual memory is an important guide for behavior. Memory of what people have seen allows us to prepare situation-appropriate behaviors and to execute them in a timely fashion. For visual movement, preparation of appropriate behavior requires recognition that some motion that is being experienced at a given time has in fact been seen before. Chun and Jiang (1999) showed that with repeated exposure to particular complex movement sequences, subsequent recognition of those sequences remains at the implicit level. In their experiment, observers searched for a single rotated-T target embedded in a field of L-shaped distractors. An animation sequence made all the search items—target as well as distractors—move randomly over the display screen; each item's random trajectory was independent of the trajectory of the other items. Because all the search items started the sequence as crosses, and only slowly morphed into their final form—a rotated-T or L distractors—observers had to monitor the entire set of randomly moving items. Unbeknownst to observers, some of the random sequences were repeated during the 72 experimental trials. Search time improved for all sequences, repeated as well as nonrepeated, but the improvement was dramatically stronger with repeated sequences. Because explicit recognition accuracy was no better than chance, Chun and Jiang applied the label "implicit" to the perceptual learning that they observed. This result supports the notions that

subjects can pick up and encode dynamic regularities or invariances and that they can do so without explicitly recognizing those repeating features.

KNOWLEDGE, ATTENTION, AND MOTION PERCEPTION

Attention takes many forms, all of which promote preferential processing of stimuli or stimulus attributes that are relevant to a particular task and inhibit processing of task-irrelevant stimuli or stimulus attributes (Chap. 6, this volume; Raymond, 2000). The selectivity that is represented by attention modulates the behavioral impact of any moving stimulus—up or down—in accord with an observer's task and goals. Performance on any task, whether in the laboratory or as part of everyday activity, implicitly reflects this modulation, which ordinarily operates unnoticed in the background. In this section, we consider a sample of experiments designed especially to highlight selectivity.

Tracking Multiple Objects

William James distinguished among forms of attention, noting that whereas people can attend to sensory stimuli (e.g., particular locations or objects), they can attend also to "ideal or represented objects" (1890, p. 393). In other words, James recognized that people could attend either to a thing that was physically present or to an object that existed only in the mind, which today might be called a virtual object. Attention's ability to influence virtual moving objects is demonstrated by results from a procedure devised by Pylyshyn and Storm (1988). The procedure measures the ability to keep track, over time, of multiple, spatially dispersed, independently moving targets. The task can be likened to watching some crows feeding in a field, and then,

Phase of Trial

1. Target Designation
(potential target
discs blink)

2. Movement
(discs move
randomly, 5 s)

3. Probe
(the target disc brightens)

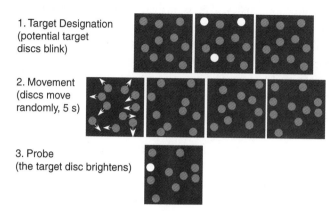

Figure 4.13   Typical trial structure for multiple-target tracking experiment.
NOTE: During trial's initial phase (target designation) several discs are singled out by a momentary brightening. During the second phase (movement) all discs undergo a series of random movements. In phase 3 (probe) a single disc is brightened, and the observer must judge whether that disc was among the ones that had been identified as potential targets during the trials's initial phase.
SOURCE: Modified from R. Sekuler and Blake (2001).

when the crows fly off in different directions, keeping track of each and every crow.

In a typical experiment on multiple-object tracking, a trial consists of three phases, called *target designation, movement,* and *probe.* Figure 4.13 illustrates each of the three phases. Target designation begins with the presentation of 10 targets, such as discs, scattered about on a computer display. Then three, four, or five of the 10 discs, chosen randomly, blink several times. This informs the observer of the discs that will be targets for that trial. In the movement phase, all 10 discs move about smoothly on the screen in various directions, each changing course unpredictably. After several seconds of movement, the trial's probe phase begins. One of the 10 discs is highlighted, and the observer must report whether that one probe item had or had not been one of the targets designated during the designation phase, several seconds before. Performance, summarized as the proportion of correct responses, is most accurate when people have to keep track of fewer targets (e.g., 3 instead of 4 or 5). This is consistent with earlier find-

ings that attention loses potency for any one item when additional items must also be attended to.

Yantis (1992) examined the influence of perceptual grouping on multiple-object tracking. In one experiment, for example, targets either were chosen at random or were chosen to lie at the vertices of virtual simple geometric figures, such as diamonds. At the outset of the experiment, performance was much superior when the target to be recognized had started out as part of a nice geometric perceptual group (during the target designation phase of a trial). However observers quickly learned to impose virtual groupings on elements that had not been part of ready-made, regular geometrical groupings. This erased the early advantage found with ready-made groupings.

Unless grouping is maintained during the movement phase, grouping at the start of a trial is no help at trial's end (the probe phase). By varying the targets' movements during the movement phase of a trial, Yantis controlled the likelihood that any existing grouping would be maintained. In one condition, targets moved about randomly, which allowed one or more targets occasionally to cross over an opposite edge of the virtual polygon. This crisscrossing destroyed the original grouping, undermining the coherence of the virtual polygon and causing elements to lose identity as designated targets in that virtual polygon. In another condition, movements of targets were constrained, ensuring that none ever crossed over an opposite edge of the virtual polygon. Here, movements of individual targets produced moment-to-moment fluctuations in the shape of a virtual figure that would be created by connecting those targets. However, not one of these fluctuations was drastic enough to destroy the convexity of the virtual polygon. Performance was distinctly better when the virtual polygon was preserved. This suggests that observers' attention creates (in the target designation phase) and maintains (in the movement phase) an updatable virtual object that is used (in the probe phase) to determine whether the probed target was in the object.

To track multiple *moving* objects, the brain exploits neural circuits that are ordinarily dedicated to a different purpose, namely, shifting attention from one location in space to another. Culham et al. (1998) used fMRI to identify the brain circuits that participated in multiple-object tracking. Their results provide a clear picture of how the brain manages this difficult task. Attentive tracking of multiple, independently moving objects is mediated by a network of areas that includes parietal and frontal regions—known to be responsible for shifts of attention between locations and for eye movements—as well as area MT and related regions, which, as noted earlier, are central regions for processing motion information.

Uncertainty and Motion Detection

When it comes to detecting weak motion signals that are embedded in noise, it helps greatly to know in advance in which direction the signal dots are moving: uncertainty about direction of motion impairs detection performance. In one study, Ball and Sekuler (1981) determined the ease with which people detected very dim dots moving across a computer display. From trial to trial, the direction of the dots' motion changed unpredictably. In addition, during half the trials, no dots at all were presented; the viewer saw only a blank screen. The dots were made dim enough that a viewer had great difficulty telling whether or not any dots were present. Ball and Sekuler measured the intensity threshold for detecting the dots under various conditions. Thresholds were initially determined simply by randomizing from trial to trial the direction in which the dots moved. Thresholds were then measured with an explicit cue that reduced the viewer's uncertainty about direction of motion. This directional cue was a short line flashed very briefly at different times relative to the presentation of the dots. The orientation of the line indicated the direction in which the dots, if present at all, might move (recall that no dots were presented on half of the trials).

Ball and Sekuler (1981) made several noteworthy discoveries. First, when the cue specified the direction of the dots' motion precisely, the dots were easier to see; that is, the intensity threshold was low. Second, the cue was not helpful unless it preceded the dots by about 500 ms, indicating that selective attention required some time to operate. Third, if the cue's orientation did not match the dots' direction precisely, but only approximated it, the cue could still lower the detection threshold, but not as much as when it was precisely accurate. Generally, the greater the discrepancy between the cue's orientation and the direction of the dots' motion, the more difficult it was to see the moving dots. In the extreme, a cue that misdirected the observer's expectation by 180 deg was worse than no cue at all: Detection fell below a no-cue baseline.

How do directional cues or certainty about direction exert the effect that they do? Cues or prior knowledge are not part of the stimulus, but they certainly do affect the response evoked by the stimulus. Obviously, some information extracted from the cue must be recoded into a format capable of influencing subsequent processing of the test stimulus. After this recoding process, the nonmoving cue then seems able to boost selectively responses in particular sets of directionally selective neurons.

Shulman et al. (1999) extended Ball and Sekuler's (1981) study by measuring brain activity while people performed the cued-motion detection task. As before, the stationary cue, presented prior to the moving target, specified the direction of motion that people would see. As revealed by fMRI signals, the nonmoving cue activated brain areas that included area MT, as well as adjacent regions that normally respond to motion. Also, some areas of parietal lobe that are not normally responsive to motion were activated. Together, these motion-sensitive and motion-insensitive areas constitute a neural circuit that encodes and maintains the cue during the interval between the cue and the onset of motion.

Presumably, prior information about the direction of motion temporarily boosts the signals of MT neurons that are particularly responsive to that direction of motion (Treue & Maunsell, 1999; Treue & Trujillo, 1999). This internally generated boost response is equivalent to what happens when the responses of particular directionally selective neurons are strengthened, either by the presentation of a strong visual stimulus or by direct electrical stimulation, as in the study by Salzman et al. (1992).

A. B. Sekuler, Sekuler, and Sekuler (1990) used direction uncertainty to explore detection of changes in direction of movement. *Direction uncertainty* refers to an observer's prior knowledge of stimulus direction; as described earlier, uncertainty diminishes the detectability of motion, as indexed by elevated thresholds or lengthened reaction times. In this study, observers had to respond as quickly as possible to a constant relative change in stimulus direction: 30 deg clockwise. The prechange direction either was fixed within a block of trials (certainty condition) or was completely random (maximum uncertainty). Generally, responses to change in the certainty condition were considerably faster than in conditions of uncertainty. However, if the prechange motion lasted 500 ms or longer, observers' reaction times to change were no longer affected by uncertainty about initial direction. However, for shorter initial durations, reaction time increased with increased uncertainty (i.e., increased in the range of possible initial directions). A. B. Sekuler et al. proposed that the visual system requires approximately 500 ms to normalize the initial direction of motion in order to be able to detect the direction *change* by essentially converting the nominal task to one of detecting motion *onset*.

Alais and Blake (1999) used the MAE to probe the influence of attention on motion perception. As mentioned earlier, when the adapting stimulus comprises two directional components, the direction of the MAE is usually the vector sum of the two components; but when the components are unequal in strength, the resulting MAE tracks that inequality. By varying the relative contrasts of the two component adapting motions, Alais and Blake were able to manipulate how much attention an observer had to pay to one of the components. In their experiments, observers viewed a computer display consisting of two superimposed fields of moving dots. In one group, all dots moved coherently in a single direction, shown as "upward" in Figure 4.14. Dots in the other group moved in random directions most of the time, producing no net directional drift. Occasionally, a subset of the random dots joined forces to move in the same

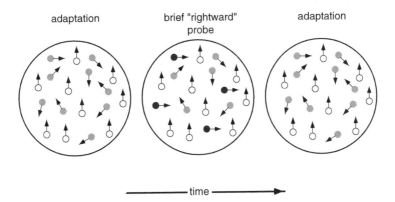

adaptation   brief "rightward"   adaptation
                              probe

—————————— time ——————————▶

Figure 4.14 Schematic of stimulus conditions used by Alais and Blake (1995) to test attention's influence on motion adaptation.

NOTE: During most of the adaptation period, a subset of adaptation dots moved coherently upward (open circles in left panel), and the remaining noise dots moved randomly in all directions (gray circles in left panel). Unpredictably, a subset of the noise dots moved briefly rightward (black dots in center panel) and then quickly resumed their normal motions (right panel). Observers had to detect this brief motion, which required considerable attention. Note that throughout the experiment all dots were actually the same color; differences of shading are used here for illustrative purposes only.

SOURCE: Modified from R. Sekuler and Blake (2001).

direction, shown as "rightward" in Figure 4.14. The proportion of dots moving rightward was only about 25%, making it necessary for observers to look carefully to detect their presence. On some trials observers were required to indicate when this weak coherent motion was present; on the remaining trials observers simply saw the same stimuli but did not have to perform the detection task and, therefore, did not have to attend selectively to the rightward motion. Alais and Blake reasoned that the first of these conditions would demand more attention than would the second, passive viewing condition. In the passive control condition, the brief insertions of weak rightward motion had little effect on MAE's direction; however, when observers had to attend to it, the inserted motion dramatically altered the aftereffects' direction, shifting it by about 20 deg. This same shift, which was mediated solely by observers' attention to a weak signal, was equivalent to the shift that would have been produced by a very powerful signal (motion with dots 70% correlated). Therefore,

attention to motion in one direction boosted the response to that motion by almost three times, rendering a 25% correlated stimulus as effective as one that was 70% correlated. Extrapolating from neural responses within area MT to changes in degree of stimulus correlation, Alais and Blake deduced that the attentional effects seen in human observers were equivalent, on average, to what would be expected from doubling the stimulus correlation in a nonattended stimulus. There is no doubt that attention can exert a very powerful influence on perceived motion.

Parsing Everyday Activities

Although considerable progress has been made toward an understanding of motion perception, a number of important questions remain unresolved. Among them is the question of how human observers recognize and categorize everyday actions. To clarify the problem, Bobick (1997) has distinguished between what he calls movements, such as the lifting of arm, and what he calls actions, which include interactions with the environment and other actors, as well as inferred causal relationships among image components. To take just a few examples, actions include a soccer player's heading the ball, a cook's making a cheese sandwich, and your making a bed or ironing a shirt. In all these cases, the actor (the soccer player, the cook, and you) generates a more-or-less continuous stream of movements. An observer's understanding of the visual information could begin with a parsing of the action into distinct perceptual events (Tong, 2001). One perceptual component event could be distinguished from a succeeding component by changes in velocity or in the movement of one body part relative to another. Therefore, motion perception is essential for our ability to parse complex actions. Combining behavioral observations and a novel fMRI paradigm, Zacks et al. (2001) examined motion's possible contribution to action parsing. Participants first watched movies of everyday activities. The movies, 2 min to 5 min long, showed someone making a bed, fertilizing a houseplant, ironing a shirt, or washing dishes. Movies were viewed three times each, in random order. During the first viewing of any movie, observers merely watched the action passively. During this viewing, fMRI measurements were taken. During subsequent viewings of a movie, participants used a button to signal when they thought that one natural and meaningful unit of action had ended and another had begun. During the original, passive viewing of everyday activities, fMRI signals reflected transient changes occurring in several related regions of the brain, including area MT+, which participates in motion perception. The onset of transient changes in neural activity did not occur randomly during the action but were in temporal register with moments that observers deemed to be boundaries between components of the overall action. Thus, it may be that motion information

plays a key role in the segmentation and understanding of everyday actions.

It is worth noting when these transient changes in MT+ activation occurred. On average, they began a few seconds *before* the perceived boundary between action components. As a result, it could be that these anticipatory transient changes in brain activation signify top-down influences, that is, influences of observers' familiarity with the actions and therefore observers' expectancies about upcoming changes in motion. Support for this hypothesis comes from fMRI research with motion that is imagined but not actually seen (Grossman & Blake, 2001; Kourtzi & Kanwisher, 2000).

SUMMING UP AND LOOKING FORWARD

Without question, our understanding of motion perception has been pushed to a level scarcely imaginable just two decades ago. New psychophysical, physiological, and computational research tools have made possible huge strides toward unraveling the mysteries of the visual registration of motion, which Walls (1942) and we consider to be most important among the talents that comprise vision. The application of functional neuroimaging has begun to identify rough but intriguing relationships between particular sites in the visual brain and performance of particular tasks. Obviously, this development has only just started, and many difficult challenges lie just ahead.

Our present knowledge of links between brain sites and aspects of visual motion perception throws only the dimmest of lights onto the complex neural transformations and computations that support performance on various tasks. Motion perception emerges from a shifting partnership between exogenous influences, represented by stimulus attributes,   and   endogenous   influences, including expectation, attention, memory, and learning. We have relatively little understanding of the parameters and limiting conditions of this partnership. Also, we have no understanding whatever of the control architecture that sets and adjusts the relative weights for the two partners, exogenous and endogenous influences. Furthermore, it is not clear to us whether traditional behavioral paradigms will contribute much to the development of such understanding.

Vernon Mountcastle (quoted in Shadlen & Newsome, 1996) sketched out an ambitious and broad agenda not only for the study of visual motion but also for the entire field of sensory science. He urged researchers to study the complete chain of events that "lead from the initial central representation of sensory stimuli, through the many sequential and parallel transformations of those neural images, to the detection and discrimination processes themselves, and to the formation of general commands for behavioral responses and detailed instructions for their motor execution (p. 628)." This last part of Mountcastle's unfulfilled agenda would connect decisions about sensory signals to the preparation and execution of motor acts that are appropriate to those decisions, an exciting area in which work has only just begun (see, e.g., Gold & Shadlen, 2001).

REFERENCES

Addams, R. (1834). An account of a peculiar optical phenomenon seen after having looked at a moving body. *London and Edinburgh Philosophical Magazine and Journal of Science, 5,* 373–374.

Adelson, E. H., & Movshon, J. A. (1982). Phenomenal coherence of moving visual patterns. *Nature, 300,* 523–525.

Ahlström, U., & Börjesson, E. (1996). Segregation of motion structure from random noise. *Perception, 25,* 279–291.

Ahlström, V., Blake, R., & Ahlström, U. (1997). Perception of biological motion. *Perception, 26,* 1539–1548.

Alais, D., & Blake, R. (1999). Neural strength of visual attention gauged by motion adaptation. *Nature Neuroscience, 2,* 1015–1018.

Albensi, B. C., & Powell, J. H. (1998). The differential optomotor response of the four-eyed fish Anableps anableps. *Perception, 27,* 1475–1483.

Andersen, G. J. (1989). Perception of three-dimensional structure from optic flow without locally smooth velocity. *Journal of Experimental Psychology: Human Perception & Performance, 15,* 363–371.

Andersen, R. A., & Bradley, D. C. (1998). Perception of three-dimensional structure from motion. *Trends in Cognitive Science, 2,* 222–228.

Anstis, S., & Ramachandran, V. S. (1987). Visual inertia in apparent motion. *Vision Research, 27,* 755–764.

Arterberry, M. E., & Yonas, A. (2000). Perception of three-dimensional shape specified by optic flow by 8-week-old infants. *Perception & Psychophysics, 62,* 550–556.

Attneave, F. (1974). Apparent movement and the what-where connection. *Psychologia, 17,* 108–120.

Baddeley, R., & Tripathy, S. P. (1998). Insights into motion perception by observer modeling. *Journal of the Optical Society of America A, 15,* 289–296.

Ball, K., & Sekuler, R. (1981). Cues reduce direction uncertainty and enhance motion detection. *Perception & Psychophysics, 30,* 119–128.

Ball, K., & Sekuler, R. (1986). Improving visual perception in older observers. *Journal of Gerontology, 41,* 176–182.

Ball, K., Sekuler, R., & Machamer, J. (1983). Detection and identification of moving targets. *Vision Research, 23,* 229–238.

Barlow, H. B. (1978). The efficiency of detecting changes of density in random dot patterns. *Vision Research, 18,* 637–650.

Barlow, H. B. (1980). The absolute efficiency of perceptual decisions. *Philosophical Transactions of the Royal Society of London (Series B), 290,* pp. 71–82.

Barlow, H. B. (1990). A theory about the functional role and synaptic mechanism of visual after effects. In C. Blakemore (Ed.), *Coding and Efficiency* (pp. 363–375). Cambridge: Cambridge University Press.

Barlow, H. B. (1995). The neuron doctrine in perception. In M. S. Gazzaniga (Ed.), *The cognitive neurosciences* (pp. 415–435). Cambridge: MIT Press.

Barlow, H. B., & Hill, R. M. (1963). Evidence for a physiological explanation for the waterfall phenomenon and figural aftereffects. *Nature, 200,* 1345–1347.

Barlow, H. B., & Reeves, B. C. (1979). The versatility and absolute efficiency of detecting mirror symmetry in random dot displays. *Vision Research, 19,* 783–793.

Barlow, H. B., & Tripathy, S. P. (1997). Correspondence noise and signal pooling in the detection of coherent visual motion. *Journal of Neuroscience, 17,* 7954–7966.

Beckers, G., & Homberg, V. (1992). Cerebral visual motion blindness: Transitory akinetopsia induced by transcranial magnetic stimulation of human area V5. *Proceedings of the Royal Society of London, Series B, 249,* 173–178.

Bennett, P. J., Sekuler, A. B., & Ozin, L. (1999). Effects of aging on calculation efficiency and equivalent noise. *Journal of the Optical Society of America A, 16,* 654–668.

Bex, P. J., Verstraten, F. A. J., & Mareschal, I. (1996). Temporal and spatial frequency tuning of the flicker motion aftereffect. *Vision Research, 36,* 2721–2727.

Bichot, N. P., Thompson, K. G., Chenchal Rao, S., & Schall, J. D. (2001). Reliability of macaque frontal eye field neurons signaling saccade targets during visual search. *Journal of Neuroscience, 21,* 713–725.

Bischof, W. F., Reid, S. L., Wylie, D. R., & Spetch, M. L. (1999). Perception of coherent motion in random dot displays by pigeons and humans. *Perception & Psychophysics, 61,* 1089–1101.

Bisley, J. W., & Pasternak, T. (2000). The mutiple roles of visual cortical areas MT/MST in remembering the direction of visual motion. *Cerebral Cortex, 10,* 1053–1065.

Bisley, J. W., Zaksas, D., & Pasternak, T. (2001). Microstimulation of cortical area MT affects performance on a visual working memory task. *Journal of Neurophysiology, 85,* 187–196.

Blake, R. (1993). Cats perceive biological motion. *Psychological Science, 4,* 54–57.

Blake, R., & Aiba, T. S. (1998). Detection and discrimination of optic flow components. *Japanese Psychological Research, 40,* 19–30.

Blake, R., Cepeda, N. J., & Hiris, E. (1997). Memory for visual motion. *Journal of Experimental Psychology: Human Perception & Performance, 23,* 353–369.

Blake, R., & Hiris, E. (1993). Another means for measuring the motion aftereffect. *Vision Research, 33,* 1589–1592.

Bobick, A. F. (1997). Movement, activity and action: The role of knowledge in the perception of motion. *Philosophical Transactions of the Royal Society of London (Series B), 352,* 1257–1265.

Bobick, A. F., & Davis, J. (2001). The recognition of human movement using temporal templates. *IEEE Transactions on Pattern Analysis and Machine Intelligence, 23,* 257–268.

Borst, A. (2000). Models of motion detection. *Nature Neuroscience, 3*(Suppl.), 1168.

Braddick, O. (1993). Segmentation versus integration in visual motion processing. *Trends in Neuroscience, 16,* 263–268.

Bradley, D. (2001). MT signals: Better with time. *Nature Neuroscience, 4,* 346–348.

Bravo, M. J., & Watamaniuk, S. N. J. (1995). Evidence for two speed signals: A coarse local signal for segregation and a precise global signal for discrimination. *Vision Research, 35,* 1691–1697.

Britten, K. H., & van Wezel, R. J. (1998). Electrical microstimulation of cortical area MST biases heading perception in monkeys. *Nature Neuroscience, 1,* 59–63.

Brown, R. H. (1961). Visual sensitivity to differences in velocity. *Psychological Bulletin, 58,* 89–103.

Brownlow, S., Dixon, A. R., Egbert, C. A., & Radcliffe, R. D. (1997). Perception of movement and dancer characteristics from point-light displays of dance. *Psychological Record, 47,* 411–421.

Buracas, G. T., Zador, A. M., DeWeese, M. R., & Albright, T. D. (1998). Efficient discrimination of temporal patterns by motion-sensitive neurons in primate visual cortex. *Neuron, 20,* 959–969.

Burgess, A. E., & Barlow, H. B. (1983). The efficiency of numerosity discrimination in random dot images. *Vision Research, 23,* 811–829.

Burgess, A. E., Wagner, R. F., Jennings, R. J., & Barlow, H. B. (1981). Efficiency of human visual signal discrimination. *Science, 214,* 93–94.

Burr, D. C., Morrone, M. C., & Vaina, L. M. (1998). Large receptive fields for optic flow detection in humans. *Vision Research, 38,* 1731–1743.

Cameron, E. L., Baker, C. L., & Boulton, J. C. (1992). Spatial frequency selective mechanisms underlying the motion aftereffect. *Vision Research, 32,* 561–568.

Celebrini, S., & Newsome, W. T. (1994). Neuronal and psychophysical sensitivity to motion signals in extrastriate area MST of the macaque monkey. *Journal of Neuroscience, 14.*

Chubb, C., & Sperling, G. (1988). Drift-balanced random stimuli: A general basis for studying non-Fourier motion perception. *Journal of the Optical Society of America A, 5,* 1986–2006.

Chun, M. M., & Jiang, Y. (1999). Top-down attentional guidance based on implicit learning of visual covariation. *Psychological Science, 10,* 360–365.

Cowey, A., & Vaina, L. M. (2000). Blindness to form from motion despite intact static form perception and motion detection. *Neuropsychologia, 38,* 566–578.

Croner, L. J., & Albright, T. D. (1997). Image segmentation enhances discrimination of motion in visual noise. *Vision Research, 37,* 1415–1427.

Croner, L. J., & Albright, T. D. (1999). Seeing the big picture: Integration of image cues in the primate visual system. *Neuron, 24,* 777–789.

Culham, J. C., Brandt, S. A., Cavanagh, P., Kanwisher, N. G., Dale, A. M., & Tootell, R. B. (1998). Cortical fMRI activation produced by attentive tracking of moving targets. *Journal of Neurophysiology, 80,* 2657–2670.

Culham, J. C., He, S., Dukelow, S., & Verstraten, F. A. J. (2001). Visual motion and the human brain: What has neuroimaging told us? *Acta Psychologica, 107,* 69–94.

Curran, W., & Braddick, O. J. (2000). Speed and direction of locally-paired dot patterns. *Vision Research, 40,* 2115–2124.

Cutting, J. E. (1986). *Perception with an eye for motion.* Cambridge: MIT Press.

Dakin, S. C., & Mareschal, I. (2000). The role of relative motion computation in "direction repulsion." *Vision Research, 40,* 833–841.

Dawson, M. R. W. (1991). The how and why of what went where in apparent motion: Modeling solutions to the motion correspondence problem. *Psychological Review, 98,* 569–603.

DeAngelis, G., Cumming, B. G., & Newsome, W. T. (1998). Cortical area MT and the perception of stereoscopic depth. *Nature, 394,* 677–680.

De Bruyn, B., & Orban, G. A. (1988). Human velocity and direction discrimination measured with random dot patterns. *Vision Research, 28,* 1323–1335.

De Bruyn, B., & Orban, G. A. (1993). Segregation of spatially superimposed optic flow components. *Journal of Experimental Psychology: Human Perception and Performance, 19,* 1014–1027.

Derrington, A. M., & Henning, G. B. (1993). Detecting and discriminating the direction of motion of luminance and colour gratings. *Vision Research, 33,* 799–811.

Diener, H. C., Wist, E. R., Dichgans, J., & Brandt, T. H. (1976). The spatial frequency effect on perceived velocity. *Vision Research, 16,* 169–176.

Dobkins, K. R. (2000). Moving colors in the lime light. *Neuron, 25,* 15–18.

Dror, R. O., O'Carroll, D. C., & Laughlin, S. B. (2001). Accuracy of velocity estimation by Reichardt correlators. *Journal of the Optical Society of America A, 182,* 241–252.

Dvorak, V. (1870). Versuche über Nachbilder von Reizveränderungen. *Sitzungsberichte der*

Weiner Akademie der Wissenschaften, 61, 257–262.

Dzhafarov, E. N., Sekuler, R., & Allik, J. (1993). Detection of changes in speed and direction of motion: Reaction time analysis. *Perception & Psychophysics, 54,* 733–750.

Emerson, R. C., Bergen, J. R., & Adelson, E. H. (1992). Directionally selective complex cells and the computation of motion energy in cat visual cortex. *Vision Research, 32,* 203–218.

Exner, S. (1888). Über optische Bewegungsempfindungen. *Biologisches Centralblatt, 8,* 437–448.

Fennema, C. I., & Thompson, W. B. (1979). Velocity determination via scenes containing several moving images. *Computer Graphics and Image Processing, 9,* 301–315.

Field, D. J., Hayes, A., & Hess, R. F. (1993). Contour integration by the human visual system: Evidence for a local "association field." *Vision Research, 33,* 173–193.

Fox, R., & McDaniel, C. (1982). The perception of biological motion by human infants. *Science, 218,* 486–487.

Francis, G., & Kim, H. (1999). Motion parallel to line orientation: Disambiguation of motion percepts. *Perception, 28,* 1243–1255.

Gabbiani, F., Mo, C., & Laurent, G. (2001). Invariance of angular threshold computation in a wide-field looming-sensitive neuron. *Journal of Neuroscience, 21,* 314–329.

Gegenfurtner, K. R., & Hawken, M. J. (1996). Interaction of motion and color in the visual pathways. *Trends in Neuroscience, 19,* 394–401.

Gegenfurtner, K. R., Mayser, H. M., & Sharpe, L. T. (2000). Motion perception at scotopic light levels. *Journal of the Optical Society of America A, 17,* 1505–1515.

Geisler, W. S. (1989). Sequential ideal-observer analysis of visual discriminations. *Psychological Review, 96,* 267–314.

Geisler, W. S. (1999). Motion streaks provide a spatial code for motion direction. *Nature, 400,* 65–69.

Geisler, W. S., Perry, J. S., Super, B. J., & Gallogly, D. P. (2001). Edge co-occurrence in natural images predicts contour grouping performance. *Vision Research, 41,* 711–724.

Gibson, E. J., Gibson, J. J., Smith, O. W., & Flock, H. (1959). Motion parallax as a determinant of perceived depth. *Journal of Experimental Psychology, 58,* 40–51.

Gold, J., Bennett, P. J., & Sekuler, A. B. (1999). Identification of band-pass filtered letters and faces by human and ideal observers. *Vision Research, 39,* 3537–3560.

Gold, J. I., & Shadlen, M. N. (2001). Neural computations that underlie decisions about sensory stimuli. *Trends in Cognitive Science, 5,* 10–16.

Graham, C. H. (1951). Visual perception. In S. S. Stevens (Ed.), *The handbook of experimental psychology* (pp. 868–920). New York: Wiley.

Graham, C. H. (1965). Perception of motion. In C. H. Graham (Ed.), *Vision and visual perception* (pp. 575–588). New York: Wiley.

Graham, N. V. S. G. (1989). *Visual pattern analyzers.* New York: Oxford University Press.

Gros, B. L., Blake, R., & Hiris, E. (1998). Anisotropies in visual motion perception: A fresh look. *Journal of the Optical Society of America A, 15,* 2003–2011.

Grossman, E. D., & Blake, R. (1999). Perception of coherent motion, biological motion and form-from-motion under dim-light conditions. *Vision Research, 39,* 3721–3727.

Grossman, E. D., & Blake, R. (2001). Brain activity evoked by inverted and imagined biological motion. *Vision Research, 41,* 1475–1482.

Grossman, E. D., Donnelly, M., Price, P., Morgan, V., Pickens, D., Neighbor, G., & Blake, R. (2000). Brain areas involved in perception of biological motion. *Journal of Cognitive Neuroscience, 12,* 711–720.

Grzywacz, N. M., Watamaniuk, S. N. J., & McKee, S. P. (1995). Temporal coherence theory for the detection and measurement of visual motion. *Vision Research, 35,* 3183–3203.

Hecht, S., Shlaer, S., & Pirenne, M. H. (1942). Energy, quanta, and vision. *Journal of General Physiology, 25,* 819–840.

Heeger, D. J. (1994). The representation of visual stimuli in primary visual cortex. *Current Directions in Psychological Science, 3,* 159–163.

Heeger, D. J., Boynton, G. M., Demb, J. B., Seidemann, E., & Newsome, W. T. (1999). Motion opponency in visual cortex. *Journal of Neuroscience, 19,* 7162–7174.

Heeger, D. J., Simoncelli, E. P., & Movshon, J. A. (1996). Computational models of cortical visual processing. *Proceeding of the National Academy of Science USA, 93,* 623–627.

Heidenreich, S. M., & Zimmerman, G. L. (1995). Evidence that luminant and equiluminant motion signals are integrated by directionally selective mechanisms. *Perception, 24,* 879–890.

Hikosaka, O., Miyauchi, S., & Shimojo, S. (1993). Visual attention revealed by an illusion of motion. *Neuroscience Research, 18,* 11–18.

Hiris, E., & Blake, R. (1992). Another perspective on the visual motion aftereffect. *Proceeding of the National Academy of Science USA, 89,* 9025–9028.

Hiris, E., & Blake, R. (1996). Direction repulsion in motion transparency. *Visual Neuroscience, 13,* 187–197.

Hochberg, J. (1988). Visual perception. In R. C. Atkinson, R. J. Herrnstein, G. Lindzey, R. D. Luce (Eds.), *Stevens' handbook of experimental psychology:* Vol. 1, Perception and Motivation (2nd ed., pp. 195–276). New York: Wiley.

Hol, K., & Treue, S. (2001). Different populations of neurons contribute to the detection and discrimination of visual motion. *Vision Research, 41,* 685–689.

Hotson, J. R., & Anand, S. (1999). The selectivity and timing of motion processing in human temporo-parieto-occipital and occipital cortex: A transcranial magnetic stimulation study. *Neuropsychologia, 37,* 169–179.

Hubel, D. H., & Wiesel, T. N. (1968). Receptive fields and functional architecture of monkey striate cortex. *Journal of Physiology, 195,* 215–243.

James, W. (1890). *Principles of psychology.* New York: Holt.

Jancke, D. (2000). Orientation formed by a spot's trajectory: A two-dimensional population approach in primary visual cortex. *Journal of Neuroscience, 20,* RC86(1–6).

Johansson, G. (1973). Visual perception of biological motion and a model for its analysis. *Perception & Psychophysics, 14,* 201–211.

Johnston, A., & Wright, M. J. (1986). Matching velocity in central and peripheral vision. *Vision Research, 26,* 1099–1109.

Katz, E., Gizzi, M. S., Cohen, B., & Malach, R. (1990). The perceived speed of an object is affected by the distance it travels. *Perception, 19,* 387.

Kirschen, M. P., Kahana, M. J., Sekuler, R., & Burack, B. (2000). Optic flow helps humans learn to navigate through synthetic environments. *Perception, 29,* 801–818.

Knill, D. C., Kersten, D., & Yuille, A. (1996). A Bayesian formulation of visual perception. In D. C. Knill & W. Richards (Eds.), *Perception as Bayesian inference.* Cambridge: Cambridge University Press, pp. 1–21.

Koenderink, J. J. (1986). Optic flow. *Vision Research, 26,* 161–180.

Kourtzi, Z., & Kanwisher, N. G. (2000). Activation in human MT/MST by static images with implied motion. *Journal of Cognitive Neuroscience, 12,* 48–55.

Kozlowski, L. T., & Cutting, J. E. (1977). Recognizing the gender of walkers from dynamic point-light displays. *Perception & Psychophysics, 21,* 575–580.

Kramer, P., & Yantis, S. (1997). Perceptual grouping in space and time: Evidence from the Ternus display. *Perception & Psychophysics, 59,* 87–99.

Krekelberg, B., & Lappe, M. (2001). Neuronal latencies and the position of moving objects. *Trends in Neuroscience, 24,* 335–339.

Lappin, J. S., Donnelly, M. P., & Kojima, H. (2001). Coherence of early motion signals. *Vision Research, 41,* 1631–1644.

Ledgeway, T. (1994). Adaptation to second-order motion results in a motion aftereffect for directionally-ambiguous test stimuli. *Vision Research, 34,* 2879–2889.

Lee, D. N. (1976). A theory of visual control of braking based on information about time-to-collision. *Perception, 5,* 437–459.

Lee, D. N. (1980). The optic flow field: The foundation of vision. *Philosophical Transactions of the Royal Society of London (Series B), 290,* 169–179.

Lee, S. H., & Blake, R. (1999). Detection of temporal structure depends on spatial structure. *Vision Research, 39,* 3033–3048.

Leibowitz, H. (1955). Effect of reference lines on the discrimination of movement. *Journal of the Optical Society of America, 45,* 829–830.

Levinson, E., & Sekuler, R. (1975). The independence of channels in human vision selective for direction of movement. *Journal of Physiology, 250,* 347–366.

Lewkowicz, D. J. (in press). Heterogeneity and heterochrony in the development of intersensory perception. *Cognitive Brain Research.*

Lindsey, D., & Todd, J. T. (1998). Opponent motion interactions in the perception of transparent motion. *Perception & Psychophysics, 60,* 558–574.

Lindsey, D. T. (2001). Direction repulsion in unfiltered and ring-filtered Julesz textures. *Perception & Psychophysics, 63,* 226–240.

Lorenceau, J., Shiffrar, M., Wells, N., & Castet, E. (1993). Different motion sensitive units are involved in recovering the direction of moving lines. *Vision Research, 33,* 1207–1217.

Magnussen, S., & Greenlee, M. W. (1992). Retention and disruption of motion information in visual short-term memory. *Journal of Experimental Psychology: Learning, Memory & Cognition, 18,* 151–156.

Marshak, W., & Sekuler, R. (1979). Mutual repulsion between moving visual targets. *Science, 205,* 1399–1401.

Mateeff, S., Genova, B., & Hohnsbein, J. (1999). The simple reaction time to changes in direction of visual motion. *Experimental Brain Research, 124,* 391–394.

Mather, G. (1980). The movement aftereffect and a distribution-shift model for coding direction of visual movement. *Perception, 9,* 379–392.

Mather, G., & Murdoch, L. (1994). Gender discrimination in biological motion displays based on dynamic cues. *Proceedings of the Royal Society of London, Series B, 258,* 273–279.

Mather, G., Verstraten, F. A. J., & Anstis, S. (1998). Preface. In G. Mather, F. Verstraten, & S. Anstis (Eds.), *The motion aftereffect: A modern perspective* (pp. vii–xii). Cambridge: MIT Press.

McCarthy, J. E. (1993). Directional adaptation effect with contrast modulated stimuli. *Vision Research, 33,* 2653–2662.

McKee, S. P. (1981). A local mechanism for differential velocity detection. *Vision Research, 21,* 491–500.

McKee, S. P., Silverman, G. H., & Nakayama, K. (1986). Precise velocity discrimination despite random variations in temporal frequency and contrast. *Vision Research, 26,* 609–619.

McKee, S. P., & Watamaniuk, S. N. J. (1994). The psychophysics of motion perception. In A. T. Smith, & R. J. Snowden, Eds., *Visual detection of motion* (pp. 85–114). New York City: Academic Press.

Metzger, W. (1934). Beobachtungen über phänomenale Identität [Observations on phenomenal identity]. *Psychologische Forschung, 19,* 1–60.

Morrone, M. C., Tosetti, M., Montanaro, D., Fiorentini, A., Cioni, G., & Burr, D. C. (2000). A cortical area that responds specifically to optic flow, revealed by fMRI. *Nature Neuroscience, 3,* 1322–1328.

Movshon, J. A., Adelson, E. H., Gizzi, M. S., & Newsome, W. T. (1986). The analysis of moving visual patterns. In C. Chagas, R. Gattas, & C. G. Gross (Eds.), *Pattern recognition mechanisms* (pp. 177–151). New York: Springer.

Mulligan, J. B. (1992). Motion transparency is restricted to two planes. *Investigative Ophthalmology and Visual Science, 33,* 1049.

Nakayama, K. (1981). Differential motion hyperacuity under conditions of common image motion. *Vision Research, 21,* 1475–1482.

Nakayama, K., & Tyler, C. W. (1981). Psychophysical isolation of movement sensitivity by removal of familiar position cues. *Vision Research, 21,* 427–433.

Nawrot, M., & Blake, R. (1991a). The interplay between stereopsis and structure from motion. *Perception & Psychophysics, 49,* 230–244.

Nawrot, M., & Blake, R. (1991b). A neural-network model of kinetic depth. *Visual Neuroscience, 6,* 219–227.

Nawrot, M., & Blake, R. (1993). On the perceptual identity of dynamic stereopsis and kinetic depth. *Vision Research, 33,* 1561–1571.

Nawrot, M., & Sekuler, R. (1990). Assimilation and contrast in motion perception: Explorations in cooperativity. *Vision Research, 30,* 1439–1451.

Neri, P., Morrone, M. C., & Burr, D. C. (1998). Seeing biological motion. *Nature, 359,* 894–896.

Newsome, W. T., Britten, K. H., & Movshon, J. A. (1989). Neuronal correlates of a perceptual decision. *Nature, 341,* 52–54.

Newsome, W. T., & Paré, E. B. (1988). A selective impairment of motion perception following lesions of the middle temporal visual area (MT). *Journal of Neuroscience, 8,* 2201–2211.

Nishida, S., Ashida, H., & Sato, T. (1994). Complete interocular transfer of motion aftereffect with flickering test. *Vision Research, 34,* 2707–2716.

Nishida, S., & Sato, T. (1995). Motion aftereffect with flickering test patterns reveals higher stages of motion processing. *Vision Research, 35,* 477–490.

Orban, G. A., de Wolf, J., & Maes, H. (1984). Factors influencing velocity coding in the human visual system. *Vision Research, 24,* 33–39.

Orger, M. B., Smear, M. C., Anstis, S. M., & Baier, H. (2000). Perception of Fourier and non-Fourier motion by larval zebrafish. *Nature Neuroscience, 3,* 128–1133.

Pack, C. C., & Born, R. T. (2001). Temporal dynamics of a neural solution to the aperture problem in visual area MT of macaque brain. *Nature, 409,* 1040–1042.

Pantle, A. (1973). Stroboscopic movement based upon global information in successively presented visual patterns. *Journal of the Optical Society of America, 63,* 1280.

Pantle, A. (1974). Motion aftereffect magnitude as a measure of spatio-temporal response properties of direction-selective analyzers. *Vision Research, 14,* 1229–1236.

Pantle, A. (1998). How do measures of the motion aftereffect measure up? In G. Mather, F. Verstraten, & S. Anstis (Eds.), *The motion aftereffect: A modern perspective* (pp. 25–39). Cambridge: MIT Press.

Pantle, A., Gallogly, D. P., & Piehler, O. C. (2000). Direction biasing by brief apparent motion stimuli. *Vision Research, 40,* 1979–1991.

Pantle, A., & Picciano, L. (1976). A multistable movement display: Evidence for two separate motion systems in human vision. *Science, 193,* 500–502.

Parker, A. J., & Newsome, W. T. (1998). Sense and the single neuron: Probing the physiology of perception. *Annual Review of Neuroscience, 21,* 227–277.

Pascual-Leone, A., & Walsh, V. (2001). Fast backprojections from the motion to the primary visual area necessary for visual awareness. *Science, 292,* 510–512.

Pascual-Leone, A., Walsh, V., & Rothwell, J. (2000). Transcranial magnetic stimulation in cognitive neuroscience: Virtual lesion, chronometry, and functional connectivity. *Current Opinion in Neurobiology, 10,* 232–237.

Pasternak, T. (1987). Discrimination of differences in speed and flicker rate depends on directionally-selective mechanisms. *Vision Research, 27,* 1881–1890.

Patterson, R. (1999). Stereoscopic (cyclopean) motion sensing. *Vision Research, 39,* 3329–3345.

Pelli, D., & Farell, B. J. (1999). Why use noise? *Journal of the Optical Society of America A, 16,* 647–653.

Pylyshyn, Z. W., & Storm, R. W. (1988). Tracking multiple independent targets: Evidence for a parallel tracking mechanism. *Spatial Vision, 3,* 179–197.

Qian, N., & Andersen, R. A. (1994). Transparent motion perception as detection of unbalanced motion signals: II. Physiology. *The Journal of Neuroscience, 14,* 7367–7380.

Qian, N., Andersen, R. A., & Adelson, E. H. (1994). Transparent motion perception as detection of unbalanced motion signals: I. Psychophysics. *The Journal of Neuroscience, 14,* 7357–7366.

Ramachandran, V. S., & Anstis, S. M. (1985). Perceptual organization in multistable apparent motion. *Perception, 14,* 135–143.

Raymond, J. E. (1993). Complete interocular transfer of motion adaptation effects on motion coherence thresholds. *Vision Research, 33,* 1865–1870.

Raymond, J. E. (2000). Attentional modulation of visual motion perception. *Trends in Cognitive Science, 4,* 42–50.

Raymond, J. E., O'Donnell, H. L., & Tipper, S. P. (1998). Priming reveals attentional modulation of human motion sensitivity. *Vision Research, 38,* 2863–2867.

Regan, D. (1989). Orientation discrimination for objects defined by relative motion and objects defined by luminance contrast. *Vision Research, 29,* 1389–1400.

Riggs, L. A., & Day, R. H. (1980). Visual aftereffects derived from inspection of orthogonally moving patterns. *Science, 208,* 416–418.

Rizzo, M., & Nawrot, M. (1998). Perception of movement and shape in Alzheimer's disease. *Brain, 121,* 2259–2270.

Robson, J. G. (1966). Spatial and temporal contrast-sensitivity functions of the visual system. *Journal of the Optical Society of America, 56,* 1141–1142.

Rose, A. (1948). The sensitivity performance of the human eye on an absolute scale. *Journal of the Optical Society of America, 38,* 196–208.

Rudolph, K., & Pasternak, T. (1999). Transient and permanent deficits in motion perception after lesions of cortical areas MT and MST in the macaque monkey. *Cerebral Cortex, 9,* 90–100.

Salzman, C. D., Murasugi, C. M., Britten, K. H., & Newsome, W. T. (1992). Microstimulation in visual area MT: Effects on direction discrimination performance. *Journal of Neuroscience, 12,* 2331–2335.

Savelsbergh, G. J. P., Whiting, H. T. A., & Bootsma, R. J. (1991). Grasping tau. *Journal of Experimental Psychology: Human Perception and Performance, 17,* 315–322.

Scase, M. O., Braddick, O. J., & Raymond, J. E. (1996). What is noise for the motion system? *Vision Research, 36,* 2579–2586.

Schall, J. D. (2000). From sensory evidence to a motor command. *Current Biology, 10,* R404–R406.

Schenk, T., & Zihl, J. (1997). Visual motion perception after brain damage: I. Deficits in global motion perception. *Neuropsychologia, 35,* 1289–1297.

Schiff, W. (1965). Perception of impending collision. *Psychological Monographs, 79,* 1–26.

Schrater, P. R., Knill, D. C., & Simoncelli, E. P. (2001). Perceiving visual expansion without optic flow. *Nature, 410,* 816–819.

Sekuler, A. B., & Bennett, P. J. (1996). Spatial phase differences can drive apparent motion. *Perception & Psychophysics, 58,* 174–190.

Sekuler, A. B., & Sekuler, R. (1993). Representational development of direction in motion perception: A fragile process. *Perception, 22,* 899–915.

Sekuler, A. B., Sekuler, E. B., & Sekuler, R. (1990). How the visual system detects changes in the direction of moving targets. *Perception, 19,* 181–196.

Sekuler, R., & Blake, R. (2001). *Perception.* New York: McGraw-Hill.

Sekuler, R., & Ganz, L. (1963). A new aftereffect of seen movement with a stabilized retinal image. *Science, 139,* 419–420.

Sekuler, R., Sekuler, A. B., & Lau, R. (1997). Sound changes perception of visual motion. *Nature, 384,* 308–309.

Shadlen, M. N., & Newsome, W. T. (1996). Motion perception: Seeing and deciding. *Proceeding of the National Academy of Science USA, 93,* 628–633.

Shulman, G. L., Ollinger, J. M., Akbudak, E., Conturo, T. E., Snyder, A. Z., Petersen, S. E., & Corbetta, M. (1999). Areas involved in encoding and applying directional expectations to moving objects. *Journal of Neuroscience, 19,* 9480–9496.

Sigman, M., Cecchi, G. A., Gilbert, C. D., & Magnasco, M. O. (2001). On a common circle: Natural scenes and Gestalt rules. *Proceeding of the National Academy of Science USA, 98,* 1935–1940.

Smith, A. T., & Edgar, G. K. (1991). The separability of temporal frequency and velocity. *Vision Research, 31,* 321–326.

Smith, M. R. H., Flach, J. M., Dittman, S. M., & Stanard, T. (2001). Monocular optical constraints on collision control. *Journal of Experimental Psychology: Human Perception & Performance, 27,* 395–410.

Snowden, R. J. (1990). Suppressive interactions between moving patterns: Role of velocity. *Perception & Psychophysics, 47,* 74–78.

Snowden, R. J. (1992). Sensitivity to relative and absolute motion. *Perception, 21,* 563–568.

Snowden, R. J., Treue, S., Erickson, R. G., & Andersen, R. A. (1991). The response of area MT and V1 neurons to transparent motion. *The Journal of Neuroscience, 11,* 2768–2785.

Snowden, R. J., & Verstraten, F. A. J. (1999). Motion transparency: Making models of motion perception transparent. *Trends in Cognitive Sciences, 3,* 369–377.

Sperling, G., & Lu, Z.-L. (1998). A systems analysis of visual motion perception. In T. Watanabe (Ed.), *High-level motion processing: Computational, neurobiological and psychophysical perspectives* (pp. 153–186). Cambridge: MIT Press.

Spigel, I. M. (1960). The effects of differential post-exposure illumination on the decay of the movement after-effect. *Journal of Psychology, 50,* 209–210.

Spigel, I. M. (1962a). Contour absence as a critical factor in the inhibition of the decay of a movement aftereffect. *Journal of Psychology, 54,* 221–228.

Spigel, I. M. (1962b). Relation of MAE duration to interpolated darkness intervals. *Life Sciences, 1,* 239–242.

Spigel, I. M. (1964). The use of decay inhibition in an examination of central mediation in movement aftereffects. *Journal of General Psychology, 70,* 241–247.

Steiner, V., Blake, R., & Rose, D. (1994). Interocular transfer of expansion, rotation, and translation motion aftereffects. *Perception, 23,* 1197–1202.

Stevens, S. S. (1951). Mathematics, measurement and psychophysics. In S. S. Stevens (Ed.), *Handbook of experimental psychology* (pp. 1–49). New York: Wiley.

Stone, L. S., & Thompson, P. (1992). Human speed perception is contrast dependent. *Vision Research, 32,* 1535–1549.

Sunaert, S., Van Hecke, P., Marchal, G., & Orban, G. A. (1999). Motion-responsive regions of the human brain. *Experimental Brain Research, 127,* 355–370.

Sutherland, N. S. (1961). Figural aftereffects and apparent size. *Quarterly Journal of Experimental Psychology, 13,* 222–228.

Symons, L. A., Pearson, P. M., & Timney, B. (1996). The aftereffect to relative motion does not show interocular transfer. *Perception, 25,* 651–660.

Tanaka, K., & Saito, H. (1989). Analysis of motion of the visual field by direction, expansion/contraction, and rotation cells clustered in the dorsal part of the medial superior temporal area of the macaque monkey. *Journal of Neurophysiology, 62,* 626–641.

Tayama, T. (2000). The minimum temporal thresholds for motion detection of grating patterns. *Perception, 29,* 761–769.

Tetewsky, S. J., & Duffy, C. J. (1999). Visual loss and getting lost in Alzheimer's disease. *Neurology, 52,* 958–965.

Thompson, P. (1982). Perceived rate of movement depends on contrast. *Vision Research, 22,* 377–380.

Thompson, P. (1998). Tuning of the motion aftereffect. In G. Mather, F. Verstraten, & S. Anstis (Eds.), *The motion aftereffect: A modern perspective* (pp. 41–55). Cambridge: MIT Press.

Thorson, J., Lange, G. D., & Biederman-Thorson, M. (1969). Objective measure of the dynamics of a visual movement illusion. *Science, 164,* 1087–1088.

Tong, F. (2001). Brain at work: Play by play. *Nature Neuroscience, 4,* 560–561.

Tresilian, J. R. (1999). Visually timed action: Timeout for "tau"? *Trends in Cognitive Science, 3,* 301–310.

Treue, S., & Maunsell, J. H. R. (1999). Effects of attention on the processing of motion in macaque middle temporal and medial superior temporal visual cortical areas. *Journal of Neuroscience, 19,* 7591–7602.

Treue, S., & Trujillo, J. C. (1999). Feature-based attention influences motion processing gain in macaque visual cortex. *Nature, 399,* 575–579.

Tse, P., Cavanagh, P., & Nakayama, K. (1998). The role of parsing in high-level motion processing. In T. Watanabe (Ed.), *High-level motion processing: Computational, neurobiological and psychophysical perspectives* (pp. 249–266). Cambridge: MIT Press.

Turano, K., & Pantle, A. (1989). On the mechanism that encodes the movement of contrast variations: Velocity discrimination. *Vision Research, 29,* 207–221.

Tynan, P. D., & Sekuler, R. (1982). Motion processing in peripheral vision: Reaction time and perceived velocity. *Vision Research, 22,* 61–68.

Ullman, S. (1984). Maximizing rigidity: The incremental recovery of a 3-D structure from rigid and non-rigid motion. *Perception, 13,* 255–274.

Ungerleider, L. G., & Haxby, J. V. (1994). "What" and "where" in the human brain. *Current Opinion in Neurobiology, 4,* 157–165.

Vaina, L. M., Cowey, A., & Kennedy, D. (1999). Perception of first- and second-order motion: Separable neurological mechanisms? *Human Brain Mapping, 7,* 67–77.

Vaina, L. M., Grzywacz, N. M., LeMay, M., Bienfang, D., & Wolpow, E. (1998). Perception of motion discontinuities in patients with selective motion deficits. In T. Watanabe (Ed.), *High-level motion processing: Computational, neurobiological and psychophysical perspectives* (pp. 213–247). Cambridge: MIT Press.

Vaina, L. M., Lemay, M., Bienfang, D. C., Choi, A. Y., & Nakayama, K. (1990). Intact "biological motion" and "structure from motion" perception in a patient with impaired motion mechanisms: A case study. *Visual Neuroscience, 5,* 353–369.

van den Berg, A. V. (1992). Robustness of perception of heading from optic flow. *Vision Research, 32,* 1285–1296.

van Meeteren, A., & Barlow, H. B. (1981). The statistical efficiency for detecting sinusoidal modulation of average dot density in random figures. *Vision Research, 21,* 765–777.

Van Oostende, S., Sunaert, S., Van Hecke, P., Marchal, G., & Orban, G. (1997). The kinetic occipital (KO) region in man: An fMRI study. *Cerebral Cortex, 7,* 690–701.

Verghese, P., Watamaniuk, S. N. J., McKee, S. P., & Grzywacz, N. M. (1999). Local motion detectors cannot account for the detectability of an extended trajectory in noise. *Vision Research, 39,* 19–30.

Verstraten, F., Fredericksen, R. E., & van de Grind, W. A. (1994). The movement aftereffect of bivectorial transparent motion. *Vision Research, 34,* 349–358.

Verstraten, F. A., Fredericksen, R. E., van Wezel, R. J. A., Lankheet, M. J. M., & van de Grind, W. A. (1996). Recovery from adaptation for dynamic and static motion aftereffects: Evidence for two mechanisms. *Vision Research, 36,* 421–424.

Verstraten, F. A. J., Fredericksen, R. E., van Wezel, R. J. A., Boulton, J. C., & van de Grind, W. A. (1996). Directional motion sensitivity under transparent motion conditions. *Vision Research, 36,* 2333–2336.

Viviani, P., & Stucchi, N. (1989). The effect of movement velocity on form perception: Geometric illusions in dynamic displays. *Perception & Psychophysics, 46,* 266–274.

von Grünau, M. W. (1986). A motion aftereffect for long-range stroboscopic apparent motion. *Perception and Psychophysics, 40,* 31–38.

Wade, N. J., Swanston, M. T., & De Weert, C. M. M. (1993). On interocular transfer of motion aftereffects. *Perception, 22,* 1365–1380.

Wade, N. J., & Verstraten, F. A. J. (1998). Introduction and historical overview. In G. Mather, F. Verstraten, & S. Anstis (Eds.), *The motion aftereffect: A modern perspective* (pp. 1–23). Cambridge: MIT Press.

Wallach, H., & O'Connell, D. N. (1953). The kinetic depth effect. *Journal of experimental Psychology, 45,* 205–217.

Walls, G. (1942). *The vertebrate retina and its adaptive radiation.* Bloomfield Hills, MI: Cranbrook Press.

Walsh, V., Ellison, A., Battelli, L., & Cowey, A. (1998). Task-specific impairments and enhancements induced by magnetic stimulation of human visual area V5. *Proceeding of the Royal Society of London, Series B, 265,* 537–543.

Warren, W. H., Jr., Blackwell, A. W., Kurtz, K. J., Hatsopoulos, N. G., & Kalish, M. L. (1991). On the sufficiency of the velocity field for perception of heading. *Biological Cybernetics, 65,* 311–320.

Warren, W. H., Jr., Blackwell, A. W., & Morris, M. W. (1988). Age differences in perceiving the direction of self-motion from optical flow. *Journal of Gerontology, 44,* P147–P153.

Warren, W. H., Jr., Kay, B. A., Zosh, W. D., Duchon, A. P., & Sahuc, S. (2001). Optic flow is used to control human walking. *Nature Neuroscience, 4,* 213–216.

Warren, W. H., Jr., Mestre, D. R., Blackwell, A. W., & Morris, M. W. (1991). Perception of circular heading from optical flow. *Journal of Experimental Psychology: Human Perception & Performance, 17,* 28–43.

Warren, W. H., Jr., Young, D. S., & Lee, D. N. (1986). Visual control of step length during running over irregular terrain. *Journal of Experimental Psychology: Human Performance and Perception, 12,* 259–266.

Watamaniuk, S. N. J. (1993). An ideal observer for discrimination of the global direction of dynamic random dot stimuli. *Journal of the Optical Society of America A, 10,* 16–28.

Watamaniuk, S. N. J., & Duchon, A. (1992). The human visual system averages speed information. *Vision Research, 32,* 931–941.

Watamaniuk, S. N. J., & McKee, S. P. (1995). "Seeing" motion behind occluders. *Nature, 377,* 729–730.

Watamaniuk, S. N. J., & McKee, S. P. (1998). Simultaneous encoding of direction at a local and global scale. *Perception & Psychophysics, 60,* 191–200.

Watamaniuk, S. N. J., McKee, S. P., & Grzywacz, N. M. (1995). Detecting a trajectory embedded in random-direction motion noise. *Vision Research, 35,* 65–77.

Watamaniuk, S. N. J., & Sekuler, R. (1992). Temporal and spatial integration in dynamic random dot stimuli. *Vision Research, 32,* 2341–2347.

Watamaniuk, S. N. J., Sekuler, R., & Williams, D. W. (1989). Direction discrimination in complex dynamic displays: The integration of direction information. *Vision Research, 29,* 47–59.

Watanabe, K., & Shimojo, S. (2001). When sound affects vision: Effects of auditory grouping on visual motion perception. *Psychological Science, 12,* 109–116.

Watson, A. B. (1979). Probability summation over time. *Vision Research, 19,* 515–522.

Watson, A. B., Ahumada, A. J., Jr., & Farrell, J. E. (1986). Window of visibility: A psychophysical theory of fidelity in time-sampled visual motion displays. *Journal of the Optical Society of America A, 3,* 300–307.

Watson, A. B., & Robson, J. G. (1981). Discrimination at threshold: Labeled detectors in human vision. *Vision Research, 21,* 1115–1122.

Watson, A. B., Thompson, P. G., Murphy, B. J., & Nachmias, J. (1980). Summation and discrimination of gratings moving in opposite directions. *Vision Research, 20,* 341–347.

Watson, A. B., & Turano, K. (1995). The optimal motion stimulus. *Vision Research, 35,* 325–336.

Westheimer, G. (1988). Vision: Space and movement. In R. C. Atkinson, R. J. Herrnstein, G. Lindzey, & R. D. Luce (Eds.), *Stevens' handbook of experimental psychology:* Vol. 1. Perception and Motivation (2nd ed., pp. 165–193). New York: Wiley.

Westheimer, G., & Wehrhahn, C. (1994). Discrimination of direction of motion in human vision. *Journal of Neurophysiology, 71,* 33–37.

Williams, D., Phillips, G., & Sekuler, R. (1986). Hysteresis in the perception of motion direction as evidence for neural cooperativity. *Nature, 324,* 20–26.

Williams, D. W., & Sekuler, R. (1984). Coherent global motion percepts from stochastic local motions. *Vision Research, 24,* 55–62.

Wohlgemuth, A. (1911). On the after-effect of seen movement. *British Journal of Psychology,* (Suppl. 1), 1–117.

Wuerger, S., Shapley, R., & Rubin, N. (1996). "On the visually perceived direction of motion" by Hans Wallach: 60 years later. *Perception, 25,* 1317–1367.

Wylie, D. R., Bischof, W. F., & Frost, B. J. (1998). Common reference frame for neural coding of translational and rotational optic flow. *Nature, 392,* 278–282.

Yantis, S. (1992). Multielement visual tracking: Attention and perceptual organization. *Cognitive Psychology, 24,* 295–340.

Yu, K. (2000). Can semantic knowledge influence motion correspondence? *Perception, 29,* 693–707.

Zacks, J. M., Braver, T. S., Sheridan, M. A., Donaldson, D. I., Snyder, A. Z., Ollinger, J. M., Buckner, R. L., & Raichle, M. E. (2001). Human brain activity time-locked to perceptual event boundaries. *Nature Neuroscience, 4,* 651–655.

CHAPTER 5

Perceptual Organization in Vision

STEPHEN E. PALMER

Visual perception begins when light entering the eye activates millions of individual photoreceptors in the retina. The initial sensory state of the organism at a given moment in time can therefore be completely described by the neural activity in each of these receptors. Perhaps the most astonishing aspect of this description of the initial retinal state, aside from its sheer complexity, is how enormously it differs from the nature of the visual experience that ultimately arises from it. We perceive the visual world as structured into complex scenes and events, consisting of meaningful objects such as people, houses, trees, and cars in meaningful spatial, temporal, and causal relations to each other. This transformation from activity in independent receptors to highly structured perceptions of meaningful objects, relations, and events is the subject matter of perceptual organization in vision.

THEORETICAL APPROACHES

The term *perceptual organization* refers somewhat ambiguously both to the structure of experiences based on sensory activity and to the underlying processes that produce that perceived structure. The importance and difficulty of achieving useful organization in the visual modality can perhaps be most easily appreciated by considering the output of the retinal mosaic simply as a numerical array in which each number represents the neural response of a single receptor. The main organizational problem faced by the visual nervous system is to determine image *structure:* what parts of this array "go together" in the sense of corresponding to the same objects, parts, or groups of objects in the environment. This way of stating the problem implies that much of perceptual organization can be understood as the process by which a *part-whole hierarchy* is constructed for an image (Palmer, in press-b). There is more to perceptual organization than just part-whole structure, but it is the single most important issue.

The first problem is therefore to understand what part-whole structure people perceive in a given scene and how it might be characterized. Logically, there are limitless possible organizations for any particular image, only one (or a few) of which people actually perceive. A possible part-whole structure for the leopard image in Figure 5.1A is given in Figure 5.1C. It is represented as a hierarchical graph in which each node stands for a perceptual unit or element, and the various labels refer to the image regions distinguished in Figure 5.1B. The top (or root) node represents the entire image. The scene is then divided into the leopard, the branch, and the background sky. The leopard is itself a complex perceptual object consisting of its own

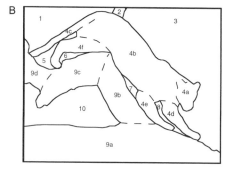

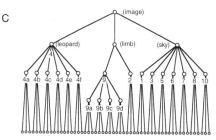

Figure 5.1 Perceptual organization of a natural image.

NOTE: An image of a leopard on a branch against the sky (A) can be segmented into a set of uniform connected regions (B) that eventually lead to the perception of a part-whole hierarchy (C).

hierarchy of parts: head, body, tail, legs, and so forth. The branch also has parts consisting of its various segments. The sky is articulated into different regions in the image, but it is perceived as unitary and uniform because it is completed behind the leopard and branches. The bottom (or terminal) nodes of the graph represent the (literally) millions of individual receptors whose outputs define this particular image.

The second problem is how such a part-whole hierarchy might be determined by the visual system. This problem, in turn, has at least three conceptual parts. One is to understand the nature of the stimulus information that the visual system uses to organize images. This includes not only specifying the crucial stimulus variables but also determining their ecological significance: why they are relevant to perceiving part-whole structure. This first problem corresponds to what Marr (1982) called a computational analysis. The second problem is to specify the processing operations involved in extracting this information: how a particular organization is computed from an image via representations and processes. It corresponds to what Marr called an algorithmic analysis. The third is to determine what physiological mechanisms perform these operations in the visual nervous system. It corresponds to what Marr called an implementational analysis. Not surprisingly, researchers currently know more about the computational level of perceptual organization than about the algorithmic level, and almost nothing yet about the neural implementation.

Before I begin to consider empirical constraints on the answers to these theoretical questions, I briefly consider three historically important approaches to perceptual organization based on structuralist, Gestalt, and ecological principles. Then I describe the kind of computational proposals that characterize modern theorizing about perceptual organization.

Structuralist Theory

The structuralist approach to perceptual theory was an outgrowth of British empiricist philosophy, particularly the writings of Berkeley, Hume, and Locke. Their views were strongly based on an empirical perspective that claimed that visual organization is *learned* through statistical regularities in the stimulus input.

Structuralists viewed perception as arising from a process in which basic sensory atoms (i.e., the color experiences in each tiny region of the visual field, presumably resulting from the activity of individual photoreceptors) evoke other sensory atoms that have been associated in memory through repeated, prior, joint occurrences. These primitive sensations were assumed to combine into perceptions by simple *concatenation,* putting them together much as one could create a picture by overlaying many transparencies, each of which contained a small spot of color at a single location. These local sensations were thought to be concatenated in memory because they were observed to be juxtaposed many times in the same or similar patterns over an organism's lifetime.

As the earlier reference to "atoms" of sensory experience suggests, structuralists relied heavily on a theoretical analogy to chemistry. They proposed that the relation between simple sensations (e.g., the experience of redness in a particular location of the visual field) and complex perceptions (e.g., the perception of an apple at a particular location in three-dimensional space) is analogous to the relation between primitive atoms and more complex molecules in chemistry. Structuralists claimed that the glue that holds sensations together in more complex percepts was learned associations that resulted from their spatial and temporal contiguity in past experience.

Gestalt Theory

The topic of perceptual organization is primarily identified with Gestalt psychology. It was the centerpiece of this approach, which encompassed not only perception but also memory, thinking, and social interaction (see Koffka, 1935; Rock & Palmer, 1990). Gestaltist views about organization arose historically as a rejection of the piecewise structuralist claim that perceptions were simple concatenations of local sensory atoms. The Gestalt rallying cry, "The whole is *different* from the sum of its parts," conveyed their contrary belief that complex perceptions had their own intrinsic structure as wholes that could not be reduced to parts or even to piecewise relations among parts. This doctrine is generally known as *holism.* As evidence for holism, Gestaltists pointed to visual configurations that have *emergent properties* that are not present in any of their local parts. Imagine a line segment made up of series of small, equally spaced circular dots. Each dot, by itself, has only the properties of color, size, and location. When they are arranged in a line, however, the whole configuration has additional emergent properties, such as its length, orientation, and density, none of which are defined for its individual parts.

The central tenet of the Gestalt approach to perceptual organization was the principle of Prägnanz: The percept will be as "good" as the prevailing conditions allow. This means that observers will perceive the simplest, most regular (i.e., "best") interpretation that is consistent with the constraints imposed by the retinal image (i.e., the prevailing conditions). Gestaltists tried to explain such tendencies in terms of the structure of the brain itself and how it interacts with visual stimulation (e.g., Köhler, 1920/1950). They were never very clear about exactly what constituted simplicity or how the brain arrived at the simplest perception, so the principle of Prägnanz remained almost impossible to test in this abstract form.[1]

To specify a concrete mechanism by which perceptual organization might occur, Köhler

---

[1] Several decades later, Dutch psychologist Emanuel Leeuwenberg and his colleagues developed a formal theory—originally called *coding theory* and later renamed *structural information theory*—that provides a well-defined interpretation of the principle of Prägnanz (Leeuwenberg, 1971; Buffart & Leeuwenberg, 1981). See also the section titled "Representational Simplicity."

(1920/1950) proposed that the brain is a physical Gestalt: a holistic physical system that converges toward an equilibrium state of minimum energy. Gestaltists often used the formation of a soap bubble to illustrate the concept. Free-floating soap bubbles have the intriguing property that, whatever their initial shape, they inevitably evolve over time into a perfect sphere, a state of global stability in which the forces on the surface reach minimum physical energy. There are many other physical systems defined by minimum energy, and the Gestaltists believed that the brain was among them. They also believed that the brain achieved maximum simplicity in perception by arriving at some corresponding brain state that was characterized by minimum energy in electromagnetic field structure (Köhler, 1920/1950). Unfortunately, subsequent physiological experiments disconfirmed key predictions of this electromagnetic hypothesis (Lashley, Chow, & Semmes, 1951; Sperry & Milner, 1955), and Gestalt theory fell out of favor.

Ecological Approaches

There is no question that the visual system is sensitive to certain kinds of structure, as the Gestaltists demonstrated, but there is still the question of *why*. Structuralists assumed that it is implicit in statistical regularities of the proximal stimulus. Gestaltists claimed that it was determined by the interaction between the structure of retinal images and the structure of the brain. Ecological[2] theorists take a different approach, claiming that it is a reflection of the structure of the environment (or distal stimulus).

If the basic problem of perceptual organization is to determine part-whole structure in the environment, the most straightforward approach to solving it is to do whatever will maximize achieving the correct answer. This is the rationale behind Helmholtz's well-known likelihood principle: The visual system interprets retinal stimulation as the environmental situation that most likely gave rise to that pattern of stimulation. This makes great evolutionary sense because an organism that can correctly perceive the structure of the environment will have enormous survival advantages over an organism that cannot.

Ecological theories explain organizational phenomena, such as grouping (discussed later), by appealing to the utility of certain visual features for correctly structuring scenes into object and parts. Color similarity, for example, is a good cue for grouping because objects and their significant parts tend to be reasonably homogeneous in surface reflectance and therefore tend to have the same or similar colors in their projected images. Likewise, common fate is a good cue for grouping because environmental objects tend to move rigidly (or piecewise rigidly) in the world, so that their projected motions are similar in direction and speed.

Ecological approaches to perceptual organization are powerful and persuasive, but they are prone to at least two difficulties (Palmer, in press-b). First, there is an epistemological problem: How does the organism gain access to information about the actual state of the external world? If organizational processes are optimized to conform with the structure of the environment, then implicitly or explicitly the visual system must have knowledge about the actual state of the world. It is unclear how this is possible because there appears to be no unimpeachable sensory or perceptual access to the nature of the external world. Second,

---

[2]In the context of theories of perception, the term *ecological* is usually reserved to refer to Gibson's views, as in his theory of ecological optics. It is actually a far more general concept that can be applied to any theory that attempts to explain perception by appealing to the nature of the environment. I therefore consider Helmholtz (1867/1925) to be as much of an ecological theorist as Gibson is.

there is an ontological problem: Is there really an objectively true organizational state of affairs in the environment to which an ecological account can appeal? Current physical theory supposes that the world is just a distribution of probability density clouds of quantum particles over space-time. Where is the objective part-whole hierarchy here? Might different organisms not legitimately perceive different structures in the same physical environment? And if so, are "objects" and "parts" not more properly considered the *result* of organizational processes rather than their *cause*? These are difficult questions for which ecological theory provides no clear answers.[3]

Computational Approaches

Modern theories of vision typically take a computational form: Perception is viewed as the result of achieving a useful representation of the environment from optical stimulation by information processing operations. There are at least two different levels at which computational theories are relevant to the problem of perceptual organization: the macrolevel of overall systemic architecture and the microlevel of detailed mechanisms.

At the macrolevel, the goal is to analyze perceptual organization in terms of the kinds of architectures that are suitable for computing the perceptual structure that people see. The usual procedure is to analyze perception via a flowchart of simpler component processes, consistent with the tenet of recursive decomposition (Palmer & Kimchi, 1986) of

nearly decomposable systems (Simon, 1969). Although this general theoretical orientation has been around for more than 30 years, little systematic work has been done to apply it to the processes of perceptual organization until recently.

Palmer and Rock (1994a, 1994b) proposed one of the more ambitious attempts at a macrolevel, information-processing theory of perceptual organization. The flowchart they proposed is diagramed in Figure 5.2. It shows what they believe to be the key organizational processes and how they are structured in terms of information flow. I do not consider this theory in detail now because none of the components have yet been discussed, but I refer to it at various points later in the chapter.

At the microlevel, particular computational elements that can perform the required computations are analyzed. One computational approach that is particularly relevant for perceptual organization comes from recurrent connectionist networks, that is, networks of neuron-like elements that contain feedback loops (e.g., Grossberg & Mingolla, 1985; Kienker, Sejnowski, Hinton, & Schumacher, 1986). They are of special interest because of their relation to the ideas of Gestalt theorists about physical Gestalts. Although Köhler (1920/1950) was apparently wrong in thinking that electromagnetic fields were the substrate of the brain's operation, recurrent networks of neuron-like elements are a more plausible candidate. Hopfield (1982) clarified the situation by proving that symmetric recurrent networks (i.e., recurrent networks with equal weightings in both directions between any pair of units) necessarily converge to an equilibrium state that satisfies an informational constraint that is formally isomorphic to minimum energy. This means that although the Gestaltists may have been wrong in thinking that the brain was an electromagnetic Gestalt system, they may turn out to have been right at a more abstract level: Recurrent neural

---

[3]It is worth noting that neither the structuralist nor the Gestalt approaches run afoul of either problem. Because both statistical regularities and structural simplicity of the input patterns can be computed over internal representations without access to any external realities, the epistemological problem just mentioned does not arise. Furthermore, because neither of these approaches presumes that there is any true or objective organization in the external world, they do not run into the ontological problem described earlier either.

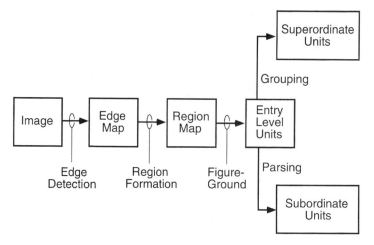

Figure 5.2   A flow diagram theory of visual organization.
SOURCE: From Palmer & Rock (1994a).

networks might be the real physiological implementation of their principle of Prägnanz.

PERCEPTUAL GROUPING

The visual phenomenon most closely associated historically with the concept of perceptual organization is *grouping:* the fact that observers perceive some elements of the visual field as "going together" more strongly than do others. Indeed, perceptual grouping and perceptual organization are sometimes presented as though they were synonymous. They are not. Grouping is just one kind of organizational phenomenon, albeit a very important one.

Principles of Grouping

Max Wertheimer (1923/1950), one of the founding fathers of Gestalt psychology, wrote the groundbreaking paper on perceptual grouping in 1923. First he posed the problem itself, and then he attempted to solve it by asking what stimulus factors influence perceived grouping of discrete elements. He began his demonstrations with a single line of equally spaced dots (Figure 5.3A) that do not group together into any larger perceptual units—except, of course, the whole line of dots. He then noted that when he altered the spacing between adjacent dots so that some dots were closer together and others were farther apart (Figure 5.3B), the closer ones grouped together strongly into pairs. This factor of relative distance, which Wertheimer called *proximity,* was the first of his famous *laws of grouping.* Henceforth, I call them principles or factors of grouping because they are not quantitative scientific laws in the usual sense (see Kubovy & Gepshtein, 2000).

Wertheimer went on to illustrate other principles of grouping, several of which are portrayed in Figure 5.3. Parts C, D, and E demonstrate different versions of the general principle of *similarity:* All else being equal, the most similar elements (in color, size, and orientation for these examples) tend to be grouped together. Another powerful grouping factor is *common fate:* All else being equal, elements that move in the same way tend to be grouped together. Notice that both common fate and proximity can be considered special

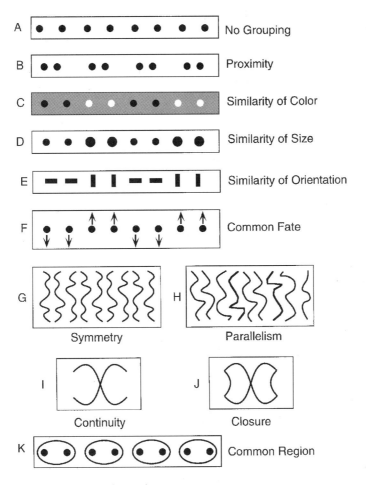

Figure 5.3   Principles of perceptual grouping.
SOURCE: From Palmer (1999).

cases of similarity grouping in which the similar properties are velocity and position, respectively.

Gestalt psychologists also described several further factors that influence perceptual grouping of more complex elements. *Symmetry* (Figure 5.3G), *parallelism* (Figure 5.3H), and *continuity* or *good continuation* (Figure 5.3I), for example, are factors that influence the grouping of lines and curves. Continuity is manifest in Figure 5.3I because observers perceive the figure as two continuous intersecting lines rather than as two angles

whose vertices meet at a point. Figure 5.3J illustrates the further factor of *closure:* All else being equal, elements that form a closed figure tend to be grouped together. Note that this display shows that closure can overcome continuity because the very same elements that were organized as two intersecting lines in part I are organized as two angles meeting at a point in part J.

The demonstrations of continuity and closure illustrate that, as formulated by Gestalt ists, grouping principles are ceteris paribus rules—rules in which a given factor has the stated effect only if all other factors are equal (i.e., eliminated or otherwise neutralized). The difficulty with ceteris paribus rules is that they provide no general scheme for integrating several potentially conflicting factors into an overall outcome (i.e., for predicting the strength of their combined influences). For example, continuity governs grouping when the elements do not form a closed figure (Figure 5.3I), but it can be overpowered when closure opposes its influence (Figure 5.3J). The same problem arises for all of the previously mentioned principles of grouping. If proximity influences grouping toward one outcome and color similarity toward another, then which grouping will be perceived depends heavily on the particular degrees of proximity and color similarity.

There has been surprisingly little modern work on principles of perceptual grouping in vision. Recently, however, two new grouping factors have been suggested: *synchrony* (Palmer & Levitin, in press) and *common region* (Palmer, 1992). Common region refers to the fact that all else being equal, elements that are located within the same closed region of

space tend to be grouped together. Figure 5.3K shows an example analogous to Wertheimer's classic demonstrations (Figures 5.3B–F): A line of otherwise equivalent, equally spaced dots is strongly organized into pairs when they are enclosed within the same surrounding contour. Common region may be at least partly responsible for the fact that the leopard's spots are grouped together (Figure 5.1), because they all lie within the region defined by its outer contour.

The principle of synchrony states that all else being equal, visual events that occur at the same time tend to be perceived as grouped (Palmer & Levitin, in press). Figure 5.4 depicts an example similar to those in Figure 5.3B–F. Each element in an equally spaced row of dots flickers alternately between dark and light. The arrows indicate that half of the circles changes color at one time and that the other half of the circles changes at a different time. When the alternation rate is about 5 to 25 changes per second or less, observers see the dots as strongly grouped into pairs based on the synchrony of these changes. At much faster rates there is no grouping in what

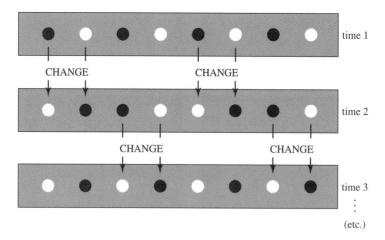

Figure 5.4   Grouping by synchrony.
NOTE: Elements that change at the same time are perceived as grouped together, even if they do not change in the same way.
SOURCE: From Palmer (1999).

appears to be chaotically flickering dots. At much slower rates there is momentary grouping into pairs when the changes occur, but this grouping dissipates during the unchanging interval between them.

Blake and his associates have shown that synchrony grouping also occurs when elements change their brightnesses continuously, becoming brighter at the same time or dimmer at the same time (e.g., Alais, Blake & Lee, 1998; Blake & Yang, 1997). This form of synchrony grouping can be interpreted as an extension of common fate, however, because the changes are in the same direction on the same dimension, so that their "fate" is indeed common. Palmer and Levitin (in press) have shown that synchrony alone is sufficient for grouping by demonstrating not only that the changes can occur in different directions (e.g., some elements get brighter while others get dimmer), but that the changes can even occur along different dimensions (e.g., some elements change in brightness while others change in color, size, or orientation). Synchrony grouping thus appears to be possible for a wide variety of discrete visual changes, provided that they occur simultaneously.

One might think from this discussion of grouping principles that they are mere textbook curiosities, only distantly related to anything that occurs in normal perception. Nothing could be further from the truth. Even the very simple leopard scene in Figure 5.1 requires extensive use of grouping principles to be organized as people experience it. The separate patches of sky, for example, must be grouped together to be seen as part of the same perceptual object, as must the distinct pieces of the branch supporting the leopard. Even the leopard's spots may require grouping by virtue of common region, as well as their similarity in size, shape, and color. Some dramatic examples in which perceptual organization goes wrong can be identified in natural camouflage, as illustrated in Figure 5.5.

Camouflage results when grouping processes that would normally make an object stand out from its environment are foiled. When successfully camouflaged, an object is grouped with its surroundings, primarily due to similarity grouping of various forms. The leopard stands out against the branch and sky in Figure 5.1, for example, but against a mottled background of dried grasses and leaves,

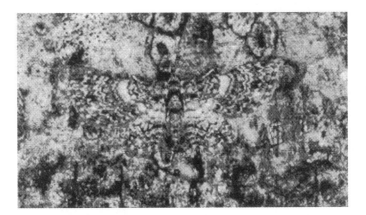

Figure 5.5   An example of natural camouflage.
NOTE: The organism shown here is so similar to its surroundings that it is difficult to discriminate from its environment.
SOURCE: Photograph by David C. Rentz.

it would be all but invisible. Camouflage can be nearly perfect as long as the object remains stationary, but even perfect camouflage is undone by the principle of common fate once the camouflaged object moves. The common motion of its markings and contours against the background causes them to be strongly grouped together, providing a vigilant observer with strong evidence that it is an object separate from the background.

Measuring Grouping Effects Quantitatively

Gestalt demonstrations were the first method used to study grouping phenomena. These demonstrations were adequate for establishing the existence of ceteris paribus rules but not for determining how multiple factors are integrated. To answer this important question, one needs quantitative methods that allow the strength or degree of grouping to be measured. One way to do this is to quantify direct behavioral reports of phenomenal grouping (e.g., Geisler & Super, 2000; Kubovy & Wagemans, 1995). Another is to measure performance on an objectively defined perceptual task that provides an indirect indication of grouping (e.g., Palmer & Beck, in press; Palmer & Nelson, 2000). The best approach to studying grouping—or indeed any organizational phenomenon—is probably to use a combination of all three methods.

Kubovy and Wagemans (1995) examined the relative strengths of different groupings in dot lattices (Figure 5.6A) by measuring the probability with which subjects reported seeing them organized into lines in one of the four orientations indicated in Figure 5.6B. After being shown a given lattice for 300 ms, their subjects indicated which of the four organizations they saw. Over many trials the probability of perceiving each grouping could be accurately estimated. Consistent with the Gestalt principle of proximity, their results showed

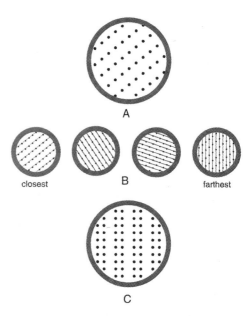

Figure 5.6 Dot-lattice stimuli employed by Kubovy & Wagemans (1995) and by Kubovy, Holcombe, & Wagemans (1998).
NOTE: Dot lattices (A) are ambiguous in their perceived organization, as illustrated in part B, which explicitly shows the four most likely groupings. Part C shows a split dot lattice, which has hierarchical grouping structure.
SOURCE: A and B from Palmer (1999).

that the most likely organization is the one in which the dots are closest together, and other organizations were less likely as the spacing between the dots increased.

More precisely, Kubovy and Wagemans (1995) found that their data fit a mathematical model in which the attraction between dots decreases exponentially as a function of distance:

$$f(v) = e^{-\alpha(v/a - 1)},$$

where $f(v)$ is the attraction between two elements in the lattice as a function of the distance, v, between them, α is a scaling constant, and a is the shortest distance between any pair of elements. Kubovy, Holcombe, and Wagemans (1998) extended this work to show that the same exponential function can account for hierarchical grouping of split dot lattices (Figure 5.6C). Observers appear to organize the dots in split lattices into pairs that become new perceptual units whose relative separations then govern how the pairs group at a higher level. Further experiments using lattices in which the dots differed in color similarity as well as in proximity showed that the rule by which multiple grouping factors combine is multiplicative (see Kubovy & Gepshtein, 2000).

Another quantitative method for studying grouping, called the *repetition discrimination task,* has been devised recently by Palmer and Beck (in press; Beck & Palmer, in press). This paradigm relies on a task in which there is an objectively correct answer for each response. Subjects are presented with displays such as those shown in Figure 5.7. Each consists of a row of squares and circles that alternate except for a single adjacent pair of identical shapes. The subject's task on each trial is to determine, as quickly as possible, whether the adjacent repeated pair is composed of squares or circles. There are three main conditions. On within-group trials, a grouping factor (proximity in Figure 5.7A) biases the target pair to be organized into the same group. On between-group trials, the same factor biases the target pair to be organized as part of two different groups (Figure 5.7B). On neutral trials, the factor does not bias the pair one way or the other (Figure 5.7C).

Responses were much faster on the within-group trials than on the between-group trials for the proximity stimuli (Figure 5.7A vs. 5.7B). Responses on the within-group trials were nearly as fast as those on the neutral trials shown in Figure 5.7C, presumably because the shape similarity of the target pair caused them to be grouped together even in the absence of other grouping factors. Similar results were obtained for detecting adjacent pairs of squares or circles when they were grouped by color similarity, common region, and element connectedness (Palmer & Beck, in press), even though not one of these factors produces any difference in distance between the elements in the target pair.

Is Grouping an Early or Late Process?

If perceptual organization is to be understood as the result of computations, the question of where in the stream of visual processing grouping occurs is important. Is it an early process that works at the level of two-dimensional image structure, or does it work

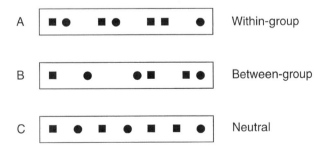

Figure 5.7   Proximity grouping stimuli for the repetition discrimination task (RDT).
NOTE: Subjects must determine whether the repeated pair of adjacent items consists of squares or circles as quickly as possible when the target items are within the same group (A), in two different groups (B), or in a neutral control condition (C).
SOURCE: From Palmer (1999).

later—after depth information has been extracted and perceptual constancy has been achieved?[4]

Wertheimer (1923/1950) discussed grouping as though it occurred at a very low level, presumably corresponding to what is now called image-based processing (see Palmer, 1999). He may even have believed that it was at work in organizing the output signals of individual retinal receptors, although he presented no empirical evidence to support this position. The view that has been generally held since his seminal paper, however, is that organization must occur early in order to provide virtually all higher-level perceptual processes with discrete units as input (e.g., Neisser, 1967). Indeed, this "early" view of grouping has seldom been seriously questioned until recently (see Palmer, in press-a).

Following previous work by Corbin (1942), Rock and Brosgole (1964) sought to determine the level at which proximity grouping occurred. They asked whether the relevant distances are defined in the two-dimensional image plane or in perceived three-dimensional space. They showed observers a two-dimensional rectangular array of luminous beads in a dark room either in the frontal plane (perpendicular to the line of sight) or slanted in depth so that the horizontal dimension was foreshortened to a degree that depended on the angle of slant. The beads were actually closer together vertically, so that when they were viewed in the frontal plane, observers always reported them as grouped vertically into columns rather than horizontally into rows.

The crucial question was what would happen when the same lattice of beads was presented to the observer slanted in depth so that

the beads were closer together horizontally when measured in the retinal image, even though they were still closer together vertically when measured in the three-dimensional world. When observers viewed this slanted display with just one eye, so that binocular depth information was not available, they reported that the beads were organized into rows as predicted by retinal proximity. When observers achieved compelling depth perception by viewing the same display binocularly, however, their reports reversed: They reported seeing the slanted array of beads organized into vertical columns, just as they did in the frontal viewing condition. This finding supports the hypothesis that grouping occurs after stereoscopic depth perception.

Rock, Nijhawan, Palmer, and Tudor (1992) addressed a similar issue in lightness perception: Is similarity grouping by achromatic color based on the retinally measured luminances of elements or on their phenomenally perceived lightnesses after lightness constancy has been achieved? Their first experiment used cast shadows to decouple luminance and lightness. Observers were shown displays similar to the one illustrated in Figure 5.8 and were asked to indicate whether the central column of elements grouped with the elements on the left or on the right.

The critical constancy display, illustrated in Figure 5.8, was carefully constructed so that the central squares were identical in reflectance to the ones on the left (because they were made of the same shade of gray paper), but were seen under a shadow cast by an opaque vertical strip of cardboard hanging nearby. As a result, the luminance of the central squares was identical to the luminance of the squares on the right. The results showed that grouping followed the predictions of the postconstancy grouping hypothesis: Similarity grouping was governed by the perceived lightnesses of the squares rather than by their retinal luminances.

---

[4]Perceptual constancy refers to the ability to perceive the unchanging properties of distal environmental objects despite variation in the proximal retinal images caused by differences in viewing conditions.

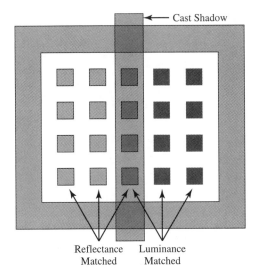

Figure 5.8 A stimulus display to determine whether grouping by color similarity is based on retinal luminance or perceived lightness.
NOTE: Subjects report that the central column of squares (in shadow) groups with the reflectance-matched squares to the left rather than with luminance-matched squares on the right.
SOURCE: From Rock, Nijhawan, Palmer, & Tudor (1992).

Further results using analogous methods have shown that perceptual grouping is also affected by amodal completion (Palmer, Neff, & Beck, 1996) and by illusory contours (Palmer & Nelson, 2000), both of which are phenomena believed to depend on depth per-ception in situations of occlusion (see Rock, 1983). Such results show that grouping cannot be attributed entirely to early, preconstancy visual processing; rather, they are compati-ble also with the possibility that grouping is a temporally extended process that includes components at both early and later levels of processing. A provisional grouping might be determined at an early, preconstancy stage of image processing, but it might be overrid-den if later, object-based information (from depth, lighting conditions, occlusion, etc.) requires it.

This multistage hypothesis would be sup-ported if grouping can be shown both to af-fect constancy operations and to be affected by them. The logic is that if grouping both influences a given type of constancy and is influenced by it, then grouping must both pre-cede and follow the processes that achieve that form of constancy. Figure 5.9 demon-strates that grouping affects depth perception and shape constancy. The central element in part A is ambiguous in that it can be seen as ei-ther as an ellipse in the frontal plane or as a cir-cle tilted in depth. Part B shows that when the central figure is grouped with the surrounding square according to proximity and color sim-ilarity, it tends to be perceived as an ellipse in the frontal plane. Part C shows that when it is grouped with the surrounding trapezoid

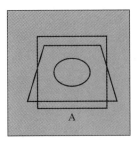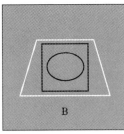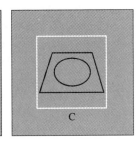

Figure 5.9   Effects of grouping on relative depth and shape constancy.
NOTE: The ellipse in part A can be perceived either as a circle in depth or as an ellipse in the frontal plane. Altering the proximity and color similarity relations between the surrounding contextual elements and the target figure can strongly bias perception toward the elliptical (B) or circular (C) shape interpretation.

by the same factors, it tends to be seen as a circle slanted in depth. The grouping effects illustrated in Figure 5.9 are even more pronounced when the powerful grouping factor of common fate is employed. Even so, this is but one example of a grouping effect on constancy. It would be premature at this point to claim that grouping therefore generally occurs both before and after constancy.

The Role Of Past Experience

Before leaving the topic of grouping, it is worth mentioning that Wertheimer (1923/1950) discussed a further factor in perceptual grouping that is seldom mentioned: past experience. According to modern visual theory, such effects would also support the hypothesis that grouping effects can occur relatively late in perception because they would have to happen after contact between the stimulus display and representations in memory. The idea is that elements that have been previously grouped in certain ways will tend to be seen as grouped in the same way when they are seen again.

Figure 5.10 provides a particularly strong demonstration of the effects of prior experience. People who have never seen this image before usually see it as a seemingly random array of meaningless black spots and blobs on a white background. However, once they have seen it as a dalmatian with its head down, sniffing along a street, the picture becomes dramatically reorganized. Certain of the blobs go together because they are part of the dog, and others go together because they are part of the street or some other object. The most interesting fact relevant to prior experience is that once you have seen the dalmatian in this picture, you will see it that way for the rest of your life! Prior experience can thus have a dramatic effect on grouping and organization, especially if the organization of the image is highly ambiguous.

Figure 5.10   The effects of past experience on perceptual organization.
NOTE: Although this image initially looks like a bunch of random black dots, it actually depicts a dalmatian sniffing along a street.
SOURCE: Photograph by R. C. James.

REGION SEGMENTATION

The vigilant reader may have noticed an important gap in the story of perceptual organization told thus far. We have neglected to explain how the to-be-grouped "elements" (e.g., the dots and lines in Figure 5.3) arise in the first place. Wertheimer (1923/1950) appears simply to have assumed the existence of such elements, but they are not directly given by the stimulus array. Rather, their formation requires an explanation, including an analysis of the factors that govern their existence as perceptual elements and how such elements might be computed from an optical array of luminance values.

This initial organizational operation is usually called *region segmentation:* the process of partitioning an image into an exhaustive set of mutually exclusive two-dimensional areas. In graph-theoretical terms, the problem is to specify how a set of intermediate nodes can be constructed in a part-whole hierarchy between the top, or root, node corresponding to the entire scene and the bottom, or terminal, nodes corresponding to the individual receptor outputs.

Uniform Connectedness

Palmer and Rock (1994a, 1994b) postulated that region segmentation is determined by an organizational principle that they called *uniform connectedness*. They claimed that the first step in constructing the part-whole hierarchy of an image is to partition it into a set of uniformly connected (UC) regions, much like

a stained-glass window. A region is uniformly connected if it constitutes a single connected subset of the image that either is uniform or slowly varies in its image-based visual properties, such as color, texture, motion, and/or binocular disparity. Figure 5.11B shows one observer's division of the penguin scene in Figure 5.11A into a set of UC regions.

Uniform connectedness is an important principle of perceptual organization because of its informational value in designating connected objects or object parts in the

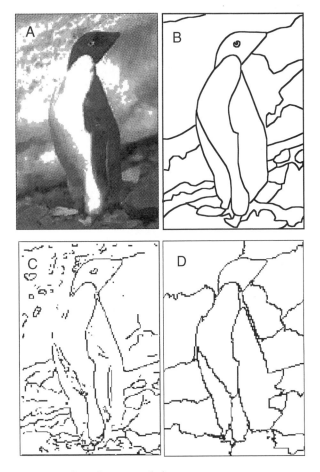

Figure 5.11   Region segmentation of a gray-scale image.
NOTE: Partitions of the penguin image (A) are shown for one human observer (B), for the Canny edge detection algorithm, which requires edge integration to produce regions (C), and for the normalized cuts algorithm (D) of Malik and colleagues.
SOURCE: Parts A and D from Shi & Malik (1997); part C courtesy of Thomas Leung.

environment. As a general rule, if an area of the retinal image constitutes a UC region, it almost certainly comes from a single connected environmental object or part. What we normally perceive as an object usually consists of many UC regions, as does the penguin in Figure 5.11B, but very few UC regions come from more than one object. This is *not* true for successful camouflage (e.g., Figure 5.5), but because such situations are quite rare, uniform connectedness is an excellent heuristic for finding image regions that correspond to parts of single connected objects in the environment.

There are two basic ways of approaching the task of partitioning an image into UC regions. One is to detect *differences* in local visual properties (i.e., boundary-based segmentation), and the other is to assess the *sameness* of adjacent portions of the image (i.e., region-based segmentation). They are different sides of the same coin, so to speak, but they imply different computations.

Boundary-Based Approaches

Whenever luminance edges form a closed contour, they define two regions: the fully bounded interior and the partly bounded exterior. An image can therefore be segmented into a set of connected regions by using an edge-detection algorithm to locate closed contours. This idea forms a theoretical bridge between well-known physiological and computational work on edge detection (e.g., Canny, 1986; Hubel & Wiesel, 1962; Marr & Hildreth, 1980) and work on perceptual organization. This bridge suggests that edge detection may be the first step in perceptual organization. Some edge-detection algorithms naturally produce a partition of the image (e.g., Marr & Hildreth, 1980), whereas others produce sets of disconnected line segments (Figure 5.11C) that require complex, segment-integration processes to link the locally defined edges into connected regions.

Region-Based Approaches

Malik and colleagues (Shi & Malik, 1997; Leung & Malik, 1998) recently designed a global and explicitly region-based procedure for region segmentation. This *normalized cuts algorithm* for region segmentation is a graph theoretic procedure that works by finding the binary partition of a given region—initially, the whole image—into two sets of pixels that maximizes a particular measure of pair-wise pixel similarity within the same subregion, normalized relative to the total pair-wise pixel similarity within the entire region. Similarity of pixel pairs is defined by the weighted integration of a number of Gestalt-like grouping factors, such as proximity, color similarity, texture similarity, and motion similarity. Malik and colleagues also included a grouping factor based on evidence for the presence of a local edge between the given pair of pixels, which reduces the likelihood that they are part of the same subregion.

When this normalized cuts algorithm is applied repeatedly to a given image, dividing and subdividing it into smaller and smaller regions, perceptually plausible partitions emerge. Figure 5.11D shows an example for the penguin image in Figure 5.11A. Notice that Malik's region-based approach produces closed regions by definition. The regional parsing of the normalized cuts algorithm, though not perfect, is certainly plausible as a first approximation because it finds important regions early, with minimal presence of the inconsequential disconnected contours that plague most edge-based algorithms. Although it is not yet clear how such a graph-theoretical approach might be implemented in the brain, this work is an important reminder that a local edge-based approach to region segmentation is not the only way—nor necessarily the best way—to partition an image into UC regions.

Texture Segmentation

A special case of region segmentation that has received considerable attention is texture segmentation (e.g., Beck, 1966, 1972; Julesz, 1981). In displays such as Figure 5.12A, for example, most observers perceive the tilted *T*s in the left region as being different from the upright *T*s in the center region more quickly and easily than they perceive the upright *L*s in the right region as being different from the upright *T*s in the center. The factors that govern texture segmentation are not necessarily the same as those that determine explicit judgments of shape similarity for the very same elements when they are perceived as individual figures. For instance, the texture segmentation evident in Figure 5.12A is the opposite of what would be predicted from simple shape similarity ratings. When subjects judged these same elements for sim-

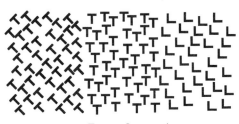

A. Texture Segregation

B. Shape Similarity

Figure 5.12 Texture segregation versus shape similarity.
NOTE: The texture of upright *T*s segregates more strongly from the texture of tilted *T*s than from that of upright *L*s, even though the shape of a single upright *T* looks more similar to a tilted *T* than to an upright *L*.
SOURCE: From Palmer (1999).

ilarity in shape as individual figures (Figure 5.12B), a tilted *T* was judged more similar to an upright *T* than was an upright *L* (Beck, 1966). From the results of many such experiments, Beck (1972, 1982) concluded that texture segmentation resulted from detecting differences in the feature density (i.e., the number of features per unit of area) of certain simple attributes, such as line orientation, overall brightness, color, size, and movement.

Julesz (1981) formulated a similar proposal in which textures were segregated by detecting changes in the density of simple local textural features that he called *textons* (Julesz, 1981). He proposed three different types of textons: (a) elongated blobs defined by their color, length, width, orientation, binocular disparity, and flicker rate; (b) line terminators; and (c) line crossings or intersections. Julesz also claimed that normal, effortless texture segmentation based on differences in texton densities was a preattentive process, that is, one that occurs in parallel over the whole visual field prior to the operation of focused attention. He further suggested that there were early detectors in the visual system that were sensitive to textons, such that texture segmentation took place through the differential activation of the texton detectors. Julesz's textons are similar to the critical features ascribed to simple cells in cortical area V1 (Hubel & Wiesel, 1962) and to some of the primitive elements in Marr's *primal sketch* (Marr, 1982; Marr & Nishihara, 1978). This work on texture segmentation by Julesz and Beck forged theoretical links among three interrelated topics: perceptual findings on texture segmentation, the physiology of visual cortex, and computational theories of vision. From these beginnings, computational theories have emerged that attempt to present a unified account of their interrelation (e.g., Malik and Perona, 1990).

FIGURE-GROUND ORGANIZATION

If the goal of perceptual organization is to construct a scene-based hierarchy consisting of parts, objects, and groups, then region segmentation can be no more than a very early step, because UC regions in images seldom correspond directly to the projection of environmental objects. As illustrated in Figure 5.1, some UC regions need to be grouped into higher-level units (e.g., the patches of sky), and others need to be parsed into lower-level units (e.g., the leopard's various body parts) to flesh out the part-whole hierarchy. Before this grouping and parsing can occur, however, further organizational processing must take place.

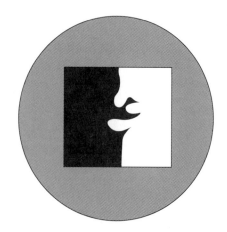

Figure 5.13   Edge assignment and figure-ground organization.
NOTE: This image is ambiguous in terms of whether the central edge is assigned to the black or white region.
SOURCE: From Palmer (1999), after Rock (1983).

Boundary Assignment

Each bounding contour in an image partition has a region on either side. Because most environmental surfaces projected onto the retina are opaque, the region on one side corresponds to a closer, occluding surface, and the region on the other side corresponds to a farther, occluded surface that extends behind the closer one. *Boundary assignment* is the process of determining to which region the contour "belongs," thus determining the shape of the surface corresponding to that region but not to the other.

To demonstrate the profound difference that alternative boundary assignment can make, consider Figure 5.13. Processes of region segmentation will partition the square into two UC regions, one white and the other black. But to which side does the boundary belong? If you perceive the edge as belonging to the white region, you will see a white object with rounded fingers protruding in front of a black background. If you perceive the edge as belonging to the black region, you will see a black object with pointed claws in front of a white background. This particular display is highly ambiguous, so that sometimes you see the white fingers and other times you see the black claws.[5] This further aspect of perceptual organization is known in the classical perceptual literature as *figure-ground organization* (Rubin, 1921). The thing-like region is referred to as the *figure,* and the background-like region is referred to as the *ground.*

Attention and Figure-Ground Organization

The fact that the figure is always perceived as lying in front of the ground region further suggests that figure-ground organization is intimately related to relative depth perception, particularly to pictorial information from occlusion (see Chap. 3, this volume). Relative

---

[5]It is also possible to see a *mosaic* organization in which the boundary belongs to both sides at once, as in the case of jigsaw puzzle pieces that fit snugly together to form a single contour. This interpretation is infrequent probably because it does not arise very often in normal situations, except when two adjacent and parallel contours are clearly visible.

depth based on edge assignment is thus the core of the figure-ground distinction. Figure-ground organization appears to have an additional component, however, that is attentional: Observers usually attend to the figure rather than to the ground. Because the figural region is perceived as closer, it makes sense for an observer to attend to it, all else being equal. The image is also more informative about the figural region along that boundary because it is the one whose shape is given by the visible contour. It therefore seems reasonable that figural regions should strongly influence the allocation of visual attention and therefore be correlated with it.

There is some evidence that attention can influence edge assignment, such that attended regions are more likely to be perceived as figural. Using a short-term visual memory task, Driver and Baylis (1996) found that if observers were asked to attend voluntarily to one region in an ambiguous figure-ground display, that region was more likely to be perceived as figural. If their attention were involuntarily drawn to one region, however, it was not more likely to be perceived as figural, at least by the researchers' experimental criteria. The relation between figure-ground organization and attention is thus complex and interesting. Given such complexities, however, it seems misleading to consider edge assignment and attention as components of a single process of figure-ground organization. The issues would probably be better served by a clean division between processes for edge assignment and those for region-based attention.

Principles of Figure-Ground Organization

Figure 5.13 is highly ambiguous in its figure-ground organization because it is approximately equally easy to see the black and white regions as figures, but this is not always—or even usually—the case. Consider Figure 5.14A. Observers nearly always see a white figure on a gray background. Notice that it is also possible to see this image as a gray rectangle with an irregular hole in the center that reveals a white surface in the background, but that is almost never one's initial perception. The fact that you see the white-blob interpretation first and that it is much harder to achieve the hole interpretation shows that the visual system has distinct preferences for perceiving certain kinds of regions as figural.

Analogous to the Gestalt principles of perceptual grouping, the principles of figure-ground organization are ceteris paribus rules. Among the most important factors are the following:

1. *Surroundedness:* A surrounded region tends to be perceived as a figure (Figure 5.14A).

2. *Size:* The smaller region tends to be perceived as a figure (Figure 5.14B).

3. *Orientation:* Regions that are oriented vertically and horizontally tend to be perceived as figures (Figure 5.14C).

4. *Contrast:* Regions with greater contrast to the surrounding area tend to be perceived as figures (Figure 5.14D).

5. *Symmetry:* Symmetrical regions tend to be perceived as figures (Figure 5.14E).

6. *Convexity:* Convex regions tend to be perceived as figures (Figure 5.14F; Kanizsa & Gerbino, 1976).

7. *Parallelism:* Regions with parallel contours tend to be perceived as figures (Figure 5.14G).

8. *Lower region:* The lower region in a vertically stratified display tends to be perceived as a figure (Figure 5.14H; Vecera, Vogel, & Woodman, in press).

9. *Meaningfulness:* Regions whose shapes are meaningful tend to be perceived as figures (Figure 5.14I; Peterson & Gibson, 1991).

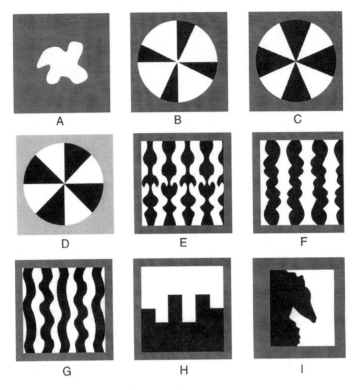

Figure 5.14 Principles of figure-ground organization.
NOTE: Figural regions tend to be surrounded (A), smaller (B), horizontal and/or vertical (C), higher in contrast (D), symmetrical (E), convex (F), parallel (G), lower (H), and meaningful (I).
SOURCE: Parts A–G from Palmer (1999).

10. *Attention:* Voluntarily attended regions tend to be seen as figures (Driver & Baylis, 1996).

11. *Higher spatial frequency:* Regions containing higher spatial frequencies tend to be seen as figures (Klymenko & Weisstein, 1986).

As qualitative ceteris paribus rules, these principles of figure-ground organization have the same weaknesses as have the principles of grouping, including the inability to predict the outcome when several conflicting factors are at work in the same display.

Theoretical Issues

One of the most important theoretical questions about figure-ground processing is whether it precedes object recognition. The standard argument that it does is logical: If object recognition is based on the results of shape perception (which seems virtually certain), and if shape perception is based on the results of figure-ground organization (which seems very likely, given that edge assignment is required to determine shape), then object recognition must be based on the results of figure-ground processing. Furthermore, if visual processing is a sequence of operations, then these considerations imply that figure-ground processing must precede object recognition.

The problem with this claim is that recent results have shown that a meaningfully shaped region tends to be perceived as a figure more often than as a ground (e.g., Peterson

& Gibson, 1991, 1993). To account for such findings, Peterson and her colleagues proposed that an initial "prefigural" recognition took place before edge assignment and therefore could influence figure-ground organization (e.g., Peterson, 1994). Other theorists objected to this proposal, claiming that the results could be explained adequately by an interactive cascade of processes in which results from a later object recognition process could feed back to an earlier but as-yet-incomplete figure-ground process to influence figural perception (Palmer & Rock, 1994b; Vecera & O'Reilly, 1998). More recently, Peterson and her colleagues have advanced a parallel interactive model (PIM) of figural assignment (Peterson, de Gelder, Rapcsak, Gerhardstein, & Bachoud-Levi, 2000) in which two regions that share an edge contour compete with each other for figural status through a neural network architecture that involves cooperation within regions and competition between regions.

PARSING

I have now discussed three fundamental processes of perceptual organization: region segmentation, figure-ground organization, and grouping. Another important process involved in the organization of perception is *parsing* or *part segmentation:* dividing a single element or region into two or more parts. Parsing is therefore essentially the opposite of grouping.

Parsing is an important aspect of perceptual organization because it determines what subregions of a perceptual unit are perceived as "belonging together" most coherently. To illustrate, consider the leopard scene in Figure 5.1. Suppose that the principle of uniform connectedness defines the entire leopard as a single region on the basis of uniform or slowly changing texture. This result conforms well

to our experiences of seeing it as a single object. However, we also experience the leopard as being composed of a number of clear and obvious parts: its head, body, tail, and legs. How do these organizational elements enter the part-whole hierarchy if they are initially subsumed by the undifferentiated UC region of the entire leopard?

Palmer and Rock (1994a) argued that parsing must logically follow region segmentation because parsing presupposes the existence of a unitary region that must be divided. There is no logical constraint, however, on the order in which parsing and grouping must occur relative to each other. They could very well happen simultaneously. This is why the flowchart of Palmer and Rock's theory (Figure 5.2) shows that grouping and parsing take place at the same time after regions have been defined. According to Palmer and Rock's analysis, parsing should occur also after figure-ground organization. Their reason is that parsing, like grouping, is based on properties (such as concavity/convexity, discussed in the following section) that are properly attributed to regions only after a boundary has been assigned to one region or another.

Boundary Rules

There are at least two different ways to divide an object into parts: using *boundary rules* or *shape primitives.* The boundary rules approach defines a set of general rules that specify where the boundaries lie between parts. The best-known theory of this type was developed by Hoffman and Richards (1984). Their key observation was that the two-dimensional silhouettes of multipart objects can usually be divided at *deep concavities* (or local negative minima of curvature): places where an object's contour is maximally curved inward (concave) toward the interior of the region. This rule specifies that the leopard's three legs (regions 4d, 4e, and 4f in

Figure 5.1B) will be parsed at the paired concavities along the leopard's outer contour, as indicated by the dashed lines. An important gap in Hoffman and Richards' original theory was that it merely identified the points at which cuts should be made to divide an object into parts; it did not specify which pairs of points should be the endpoints of which cuts. Their examples were well chosen to avoid problematic cases, but real-world cases such as the leopard with multiple concavities are not nearly as clear. This gap has been filled recently by an analysis of rules for matching concavities according to further sets of rules, one of which is to make cuts between the nearest dividing points (Singh, Seyranian, & Hoffman, 1999).

Shape Primitives

An alternative to parsing by boundary rules is the shape primitive approach. It is based on a set of atomic, indivisible shapes that constitute a complete listing of the most basic parts. Objects that are more complex are then analyzed as configurations of these primitive parts. This approach can be considered analogous to dividing cursive writing into parts by knowing the cursive alphabet and finding the component letters by a parallel visual search process. Such a shape-primitive scheme for parsing works well if there is a relatively small set of primitive components, as there might be in the case of cursive writing (at least for one individual writer), but it is far from obvious what the two-dimensional shape primitives might be in the case of parsing two-dimensional projections of natural scenes.

If the shape primitive approach is going to work, it seems plausible that the shape primitives appropriate for parsing the projected images of three-dimensional objects would be the projections of three-dimensional *volumetric* shape primitives. Such an analysis has

been provided by Binford's (1971) influential proposal that complex three-dimensional shapes can be analyzed into *generalized cylinders:* appropriately sized and shaped volumes that are generalized from standard cylinders in the sense that they have extra parameters that enable then to encompass many more shapes (see also Marr, 1982; Biederman, 1987). The extra parameters specify the shape of the base (rather than always being circular), the curvature of the axis (rather than always being straight), and so on. If one has a set of shape primitives and some way of detecting them in two-dimensional images, they can be used to parse complex three-dimensional objects. If the primitives are sufficiently general, part segmentation will be possible, even for novel objects.

With these four basic organizational processes—region segmentation, figure-ground organization, grouping, and parsing—configured into the flow diagram that Palmer and Rock (1994a) proposed (Figure 5.2), it is possible to see how a part-whole hierarchy such as the one shown in Figure 5.1C could be constructed by a plausible sequence of operations. To illustrate how these operations might relate to each other in arriving at a hierarchy of perceptual organization, consider the leopard scene again (Figure 5.1). An initial set of UC regions is shown as the 10 regions in Figure 5.1B. Some of these are compound regions that need to be parsed into two or more subordinate parts, such as the leopard (region 4) into its bodily parts (subregions 4a–4f) and the lower branch (region 9) into its branch segments (9a–9d). Other regions need to be grouped into larger aggregations or configurations, such as the seven patches of sky (regions 1, 3, 5, 6, 7, 8, and 10) into a single uniform background of sky. Many of these further organizational processes can be performed based on bottom-up stimulus factors without access to stored knowledge about leopards, branches, and sky, but it seems likely that some of this reorganization will be facilitated by accessing stored knowledge about familiar objects, such as the usual structure of branches and the general anatomy of leopards.

VISUAL INTERPOLATION

Even after regions of similar visual properties have been segmented, figures have been discriminated from grounds, and both grouping and parsing have taken place, the visual system is far from finished in organizing the visual field into the objects and surfaces that populate visual experience. One of the main complications is that most surfaces are opaque and therefore routinely hide portions of farther objects from view. As we move around in the three-dimensional world, for example, surfaces continually undergo occlusion and disocclusion by edges of closer surfaces. To cope with this incomplete, piecewise, and

changeable montage of visible surfaces, we need some way to infer the nature of hidden parts from visible ones. Following Kellman and Shipley (1991), I call this phenomenon *visual interpolation.*

Amodal Completion

The phenomenon of *amodal completion* is that the visual system often infers automatically that partly occluded surfaces and objects are whole and complete, including the shape, texture, and color of unseen portions (Michotte, Thinès, & Crabbé, 1964). A simple example is provided in Figure 5.15A. Observers spontaneously perceive a full circle behind a square, as indicated in Figure 5.15B, even though one quarter of its area is not visible. Amodally completed portions of surfaces and objects seem to fall midway between full sensory experience of visible objects and purely

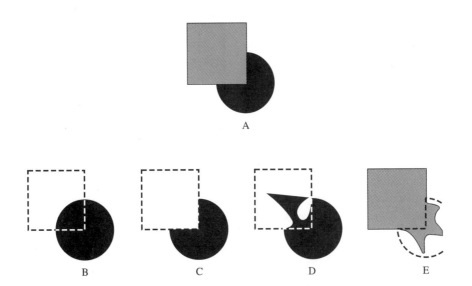

Figure 5.15   Amodal completion.
NOTE: Image A is always perceived as a square occluding an amodally completed circle (B) rather than as a square abutting a Pac-Man (C), as a square occluding some odd-shaped object (D), or as a Pac-Man occluding some odd-shaped object (E).
SOURCE: Parts A–D from Palmer (1999).

cognitive knowledge of the existence of completely unseen objects, for example, in the next room. If the occluded portion of the contour is relatively small, then the experience of its completed shape, though still not visual, can be nearly as certain as if it were viewed in its entirety.

Amodal completion is logically underdetermined. The real state of affairs corresponding to Figure 5.15A might be a square covering a whole circle (B), a "mosaic" of a square abutting a three-quarter circle (or Pac-man) (C), a square in front of a circle with odd protrusions (D), a Pac-Man in front of a square with odd protrusions (E), or an infinite number of other possibilities. The visual system therefore appears to have strong preferences about how to complete partly occluded objects, and these preferences are clearly aimed at achieving veridical perception of whole objects in the world. How might this happen?

Figural Familiarity

One possibility is that we complete the circle behind the square because of prior experience in seeing whole circles. We have also had experiences of seeing three-quarter circles, of course, but most people probably see a good many more full circles. This line of thinking, similar to the structuralist approach described earlier, leads to the familiarity hypothesis: Partly occluded figures are completed according to the most frequently encountered shape that is compatible with the visible information. One problem with this theory is that we easily complete objects that we have never seen before (Gregory, 1972).

This argument does not prove that familiarity has no effect on amodal completion; it merely indicates that something more must be involved. In fact, there are some compelling examples of familiarity effects on completion. In viewing the following, uppercase WO**R**D, most people perceive the partly occluded letter as an *R* even though it could logically be perceived as a *P*, a *B*, or as some other geometrical pattern that does not form a letter at all. That *R*, *P*, and *B* are familiar letters and that *WORD* is a familiar English word—whereas *WOPD* and *WOBD* are not—seems to be an important factor in this example, not to mention the fact that the semantic context leads one to expect the word *WORD*. Familiarity at the level of the completed figure cannot be the whole story, however, so we must look for other kinds of explanations as well.

Figural Simplicity

A second possibility is that partly occluded figures are completed in the way that results in the "simplest" perceived figures. A square occluding a complete circle in Figure 5.15A, for example, is intuitively simpler than any of the alternatives, and the same could be true for completion of quite novel shapes. Explaining phenomena of perceptual organization in terms of maximizing simplicity—or, equivalently, minimizing complexity—was the theoretical approach favored by Gestalt psychologists (discussed earlier). It seems to fit particularly well with many completion phenomena.

The Gestaltists called their hypothesis that the visual system perceives the simplest possibility the principle of Prägnanz, although others later dubbed it the *minimum principle* (Hochberg & McAlister, 1953): The percept will be as good as the prevailing conditions allow. The problem is that for such a hypothesis to generate testable predictions about what will be perceived, one needs a definition of *goodness*. This is a difficulty that the Gestaltists never fully resolved, but other theorists have since offered explicit theories (e.g., Leeuwenberg, 1971; see the section titled "Figural Goodness").

To illustrate this kind of theory, suppose that a figure's goodness could be measured by simply counting the number of axes of bilateral symmetry, where more axes correspond to greater figural goodness. The matter is actually much more complex, as discussed in the section on figural goodness, but this definition will do for purposes of illustration. By this account, the perception of a square occluding a circle is the simplest alternative shown in Figure 5.15 because the circle is bilaterally symmetric about all central axes. In contrast, the mosaic interpretation has only one axis of symmetry (about a left-diagonal line through its center), and the irregularly completed circle has no symmetries at all. Perceiving a square in front of a circle thus turns out to be the simplest possible interpretation, at least given this definition of goodness. A general problem with this type of theory of completion is that it is only as good as the measure of simplicity on which it is based. Failures to account for experimental results can thus be easily dismissed on the grounds that a better measure would bring the predictions into line with the results. This may be true, of course, but it makes the general theory almost impossible to falsify.

Ecological Constraints

Theories in the third class try to explain amodal completion by appealing directly to ecological evidence of occlusion. For example, when a contour of one object is occluded by that of another, they typically form an intersection known as a *T-junction*. The continuous contour (the top of the *T*) is interpreted as the closer edge whose surface occludes the other edge (the stem of the *T*). A further assumption required to account for amodal completion is that the occluded edge (and the surface attached to it) somehow connects with another occluded edge in the scene.

One such ecological theory of completion is Kellman and Shipley's (1991) *relatability theory,* which can be understood as a more complete and well-defined version of the classic grouping principle of good continuation (Wertheimer, 1923/1950). Pairs of occluded edges in *T*-junctions are said to be relatable in this theory if and only if (a) their extensions intersect at an angle of 90° or more and (b) they can be smoothly connected to each other, as illustrated in Figure 5.16. Once they

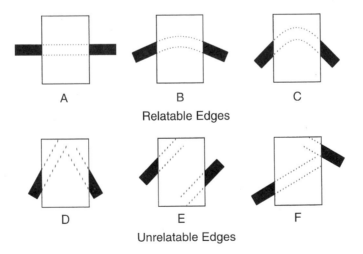

Figure 5.16 Conditions for edge relatability.
NOTE: Because edge pairs in A, B, and C are relatable, the figures of which they are part are completed behind the occluding rectangle. The edges in D, E, and F are not relatable and therefore are not completed.
SOURCE: From Palmer (1999), after Kellman & Shipley (1991).

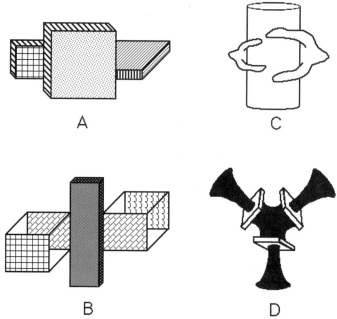

Figure 5.17 Image-, surface-, and volume-based approaches to amodal completion.
NOTE: In part A the outer contours are highly relatable, but fail to support amodal completion. In part B there are no relatable contours, yet people readily perceive amodal completion. In part C there are relatable surfaces on opposite sides of the occluder, yet people perceive two distinct objects. In part D, there are no relatable surfaces, yet amodal completion is perceived.
SOURCE: After Tse (1999).

are related, a new perceptual unit is formed when such a pair of edges forms an enclosed area. Units are then assigned positions in depth based on the depth information available in the T-junctions: The surface to which the stem segment belongs is farther than the surface to which the top segment belongs. It may seem counterintuitive that such a complex process could be required to perceive something as simple as the completed circle in Figure 5.15A. Experiments have shown, however, that the process of completing simple geometrical shapes such as squares and circles can take as long as 400 ms (Sekuler & Palmer, 1992).

Kellman and Shipley's (1991) relatability theory of amodal completion is couched in terms of image-based information: the relatability of edges in the two-dimensional image.

Figures 5.17A and 5.17B provide evidence that this cannot be the whole story, however. Part A shows an example in which the outer contours on the left and right side of the closest object line up perfectly, thus conforming ideally to the requirements of edge relatability. However, they fail to support amodal completion. Figure 5.17B shows the opposite situation, in which there are no relatable contours (because they are themselves occluded), yet people readily perceive amodal completion behind the cylinder. These examples thus suggest that image-relatable contours are neither necessary nor sufficient for perceiving amodal completion.

An alternative possibility is that completion takes place within a surface-based representation by relating two-dimensional surfaces embedded in three-dimensional space (e.g., Nakayama & Shimojo, 1992; Nakayama, Shimojo, & Silverman, 1989). Figure 5.17C shows a case in which there are relatable surfaces on the left and right sides of the occluder, yet people usually perceive two distinct objects instead of one that is completed behind it. Finally, Figure 5.17D shows an example in which there are no relatable surfaces, yet amodal completion is still perceived. These two examples therefore suggest that relatable surfaces are neither necessary nor sufficient for perceiving amodal completion. A third alternative is that amodal completion occurs when three-dimensional volumes are merged (Tse, 1999). The examples in Figure 5.17 suggest that this approach may indeed be preferable, but the details of such a theory have not yet been formulated. It is not entirely clear, for example, how volumes are relatable if their surfaces are not.

Illusory Contours

Another important form of visual interpolation produces a fascinating illusion in which contours are seen that do not actually exist in the stimulus image. This phenomenon of *illusory contours* (also called *subjective contours*) was first described almost a century ago (Schumann, 1904), but modern interest in it was sparked by the striking demonstrations of Kanizsa (1955, 1979). One of the best-known examples is the so-called *Kanizsa triangle* shown in Figure 5.18. The white triangle so readily perceived in this display is defined by illusory contours because the stimulus image consists solely of three Pac-Man shapes. Most observers report actually seeing well defined luminance edges where the contours of an occluding triangle should be, with the interior region of the triangle appearing brighter than the surrounding ground. These edges are not physically present in the image, however.

Figure 5.18   Illusory contours in a Kanizsa triangle.
NOTE: People usually perceive a white triangle occluding three black (amodally completed) circles on a white background, including visible edges between the white triangle and white ground where no luminance edges exist.

The perception of illusory contours is accompanied by amodal completion of the inducing elements. For example, when one perceives the illusory triangle in Figure 5.18, one simultaneously perceives the Pac-Man shapes as partly occluded circles. In fact, if the inducing elements are not perceived as incomplete, no illusory contours or figures are seen, as illustrated in Figure 5.19. In panel A, an illusory rectangle is usually perceived because the inducing elements are seen as incomplete octagons. In panel B, however, no illusory rectangle is seen, even though exactly the same cut-out corners are present as in panel A. The difference appears to be that in Figure 5.19B the cut-out corners are perceived as integral parts of the plus signs, which are visible in their entirety. The inner notches therefore require no perceptual "explanation" in terms of occluding objects. This contrast shows that illusory figures and contours are relatively complex phenomena that depend on more than local conditions of stimulation. This demonstration is a good example of the Gestalt claim that what is perceived depends importantly on the structure of the whole

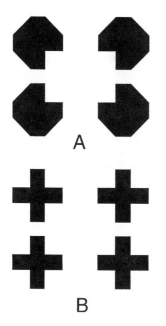

Figure 5.19   Conditions for perceiving illusory figures.
NOTE: A white rectangle occluding four octagons is perceived in A, but no such rectangle is perceived in B despite the presence of the same local contours. Factors such as symmetry and parallel edges in B appear to block the perception of illusory contours.
SOURCE: From Palmer (1999).

configuration and cannot easily be predicted from the structure of local parts.

Subjective contours and illusory figures may be closely related to amodal completion. In fact, Kellman and his colleagues have claimed that both result from the same set of underlying processes of unit formation and that both can be described in terms of relatability theory (Kellman & Loukides, 1987; Kellman & Shipley, 1991). However, if the same processes are at work in both cases, why do examples of the two phenomena *look* so different? According to relatability theory, the answer lies in the perceived depth relations between the figures in question. If the missing contours are part of the closer occluding figure, then illusory contours are perceived. If the missing contours are part of the farther occluded figure, then they are amodally completed behind the closer figure.

Perceived Transparency

Another phenomenon of visual interpolation is *perceived transparency:* the perception of an object as being viewed through a closer, translucent object (e.g., Metelli, 1974). A translucent object is one that transmits some portion of the light reflected from the farther figure instead of blocking it entirely. Under conditions of translucency, the light striking the retina at a given location provides information about (at least) two different external points along the same viewer-centered direction: one on the farther opaque object and the other on the closer translucent object (Figure 5.20A).

Perception of transparency depends on both spatial and color conditions. For example, transparency will be perceived if the translucent surface is positioned so that reflectance edges on the opaque surface behind it can be seen both through the translucent surface and outside it, as illustrated in Figure 5.20A. When this happens, a phenomenon called *color scission* or *color splitting* occurs, and the image colors in the regions of the translucent surface (y and z) are perceived as a combination of one that belongs to the background and one that belongs to the translucent surface. Color scission will not occur, however, if the translucent surface lies completely within a single reflectance region (Figure 5.20B). It can be blocked also by destroying the unity of the translucent region (Figure 5.20C) or by merely weakening it (Figure 5.20D). Color scission in transparency perception is thus a good example of the importance of spatial organization: the effect does not occur unless the organization of the regions is appropriate (Metelli, 1974).

Proper spatial conditions alone are not sufficient, however, because improper color

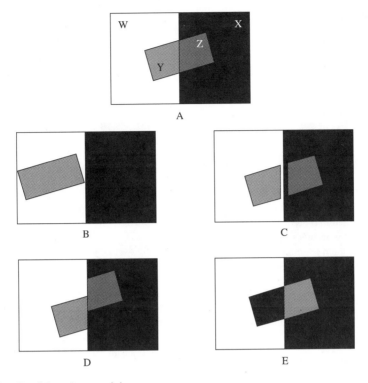

Figure 5.20   Conditions for perceiving transparency.
NOTE: Observers will perceive transparency if the color and spatial relations among four (or more) regions are all compatible with a single translucent surface in front of two (or more) overlapping regions, as illustrated in A. If any of these relations is incompatible (B, C, D, and E), transparency is not perceived.
SOURCE: From Palmer (1999).

relations will block transparency perception in the very same spatial configuration that produces perception of transparency with appropriate color relations (Figure 5.20E versus 5.20A). In simple two-surface displays such as those considered here, the color relations among four spatial regions must be considered (Figure 5.20A). Two of these (w and x) show the two different reflectances of the underlying opaque surfaces. The other two (y and z) show these same underlying reflectances as filtered through the translucent surface. Metelli (1974), Gerbino (1994), and Anderson (1997) have formulated precise quantitative theories of the conditions under which color scission will occur.

Figural Scission

Yet another example of visual interpolation is *figural scission:* the division of a single homogeneous region into two overlapping figures of the same color, one in front of and occluding the other. This phenomenon, illustrated in Figure 5.21, has many interesting features. One is that no local sensory information requires the single region to be split at all: That is, there are no luminance or color edges in the interior of the region where they would be if two figures were actually present. The visual system constructs the missing contours where it expects to find them. Thus, when figural scission occurs, *illusory contours* appear in the interior of the region where the closer figure occludes

Figure 5.21   Figural scission.
NOTE: A single homogeneous region is sometimes perceptually divided into two overlapping objects, one of which partly occludes the other. The depth relation between them is ambiguous, and illusory contours are generally perceived where the closer figure occludes the farther one.
SOURCE: From Palmer (1999).

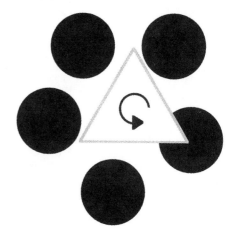

Figure 5.22   Kinetic illusory figures.
NOTE: When white wedges rotate through the five black circles at appropriate times, an illusory white rectangle is perceived as rotating in front of the circles and alternately occluding and disoccluding them. (The light gray edge of the triangle is not actually present in the display.)
SOURCE: From Palmer (1999), after Kellman & Loukides (1987).

the farther one. The visual system also *completes* the portions of the farther figure that are occluded by the closer one. Because the stimulus conditions do not determine which figure is in front and which is behind, however, either possibility can be perceived. Indeed, after you stare at such displays for a while, the depth relations of the two parts become *multistable:* They spontaneously reverse so that you now see the interior edges of what used to be the farther figure, which is now the nearer one (see the section titled "Multistability").

Kinetic Interpolation

Still other examples of visual interpolation involve motion. Kellman and Cohen (1984) have developed demonstrations of dynamic illusory figures that are like classical illusory figures (e.g., the Kanisza triangle; see Figure 5.18) but are defined dynamically as they unfold over time. An example of this *kinetic completion* effect is depicted in Figure 5.22. (The light gray edge of the triangle is not present in the dynamic display.) Notice that any single image in the sequence is insuffi-

cient to produce either illusory contours or an illusory figure, because each consists of just four circles and a single Pac-Man. When they are presented as part of a coherent motion sequence, however, the movement gives rise to the compelling perception of an illusory white triangle rotating in front of black circles on a white ground. It is revealed over time as it rotates so that its vertices occlude different black circles at different times. Similar effects can also be produced when the inducing elements themselves are defined solely by movement (Kellman & Loukides, 1987).

Another phenomenon of kinetic interpolation occurs when all but a small part of an object is occluded behind another object, but the shape of the entire object can be perceived over time due to the motion either of the object or of the occluder. An everyday example is that of perceiving a person walking past a door that is open just a crack. You perceive the entire person passing by the door even

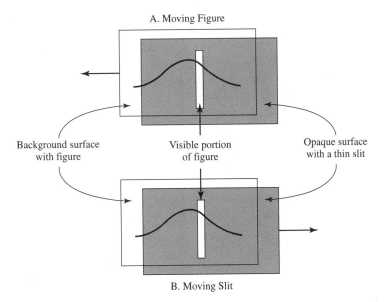

Figure 5.23   Anorthoscopic perception.

NOTE: If an object is seen moving behind a stationary slit such that only a small part is revealed at any time (A), observers perceive it in its entirety. The same is true if the object is stationary and the slit moves across the figure (B).

SOURCE: From Palmer (1999).

though only a thin slice is actually present on your retina at any one time. This phenomenon, usually called *anorthoscopic perception,* was first studied by Zöllner (1862) and Helmholtz (1867/1925) and was later rediscovered by Parks (1965). It occurs under both moving-figure and moving-slit conditions. Moving-figure conditions refer to a figure translating back and forth behind a stationary slit through which only a small portion of the figure is visible at any one time, as illustrated in Figure 5.23A. Moving-slit conditions refer to a stationary figure situated behind a slit that translates back and forth, as illustrated in Figure 5.23B. In both cases, the object is revealed piecemeal through the slit, and the visual system must somehow integrate the results over time into a complete object. Careful research has shown that this completion phenomenon is not achieved by eye movements that "paint" the full image onto the retina over time

(Fendrich & Mack, 1980; Morgan, Findlay, & Watt, 1982). Rather, some more central form of visual memory must perform an integration over space and time.

OF PARTS AND WHOLES

Until now I have presumed that visual perception of a complex image is organized into a part-whole hierarchy. Phenomenal experience strongly suggests that this is the case. People also have the distinct impression that the parts they perceive in objects are stable and nonarbitrary. People further believe that other people perceive them in pretty much the same way that they do. Is there any experimental evidence for the assertion that people perceive objects as composed of parts?

Evidence for Part Perception

Palmer (1977) performed studies using several converging operations to investigate the perception of part structure in novel two-dimensional figures that contained six line segments. In one experiment subjects were asked simply to divide figures like those shown in Figure 5.24 into "natural parts." In a second experiment they were asked to rate the goodness or naturalness of several different subsets of each figure. In a third they were required to decide as quickly as possible whether various three-segment parts—constituting good, medium, or bad parts as defined by the ratings in the second experiment—were contained within a given six-segment figure (Figure 5.24).

The results of all three experiments supported the hypothesis that even these novel figures were spontaneously perceived as having well-defined part structure. In the speeded part verification task, for example, good parts were found much more quickly and accurately than were medium or bad parts within the same figure (see also Reed & Johnsen, 1975). Moreover, using stimuli in which the same three-segment part was embedded in different six-segment figures, Palmer (1977) was able to show that the variation in verification time was not due simply to the properties of the three-segment test probe. The goodness of parts clearly depends on the nature of

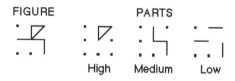

FIGURE   PARTS

High   Medium   Low

Figure 5.24 Stimuli for experiments on part detection.
NOTE: Subjects had to verify the presence of parts within wholes for parts whose goodness within wholes varied from high to low.
SOURCE: After Palmer (1977).

the relation between the part and the whole figure.

Using very different stimuli and procedures—drawings of meaningful three-dimensional objects in an explicit recognition task—Biederman and Cooper (1991) reported evidence that supports the hypothesis that people perceive well-known, meaningful objects in terms of parts. The priming experiments that they conducted showed that recognition times were faster (i.e., there was more priming) when the same parts of the same objects were shown a second time than when different parts of the same objects were shown a second time. A variety of well-chosen control conditions ruled out several alternative hypotheses.

Global versus Local Processing

Assuming that objects are indeed perceived as structured into something like a hierarchy of parts, subparts, and so on, a question that naturally arises is whether parts are perceived before wholes or wholes are perceived before parts. Although Gestaltists never posed the question in precisely this form, their doctrine of holism suggests that wholes may be processed first in some important sense. Nearly all other approaches to perception imply the opposite: that wholes are constructed by integrating smaller parts into increasingly larger aggregations. Which view is correct?

Like many theoretical questions, the answer depends on how it is posed. Within a physiological framework the answer is that local structure is initially processed before global structure is. Retinal receptors respond to exceedingly tiny regions of stimulation, and as one traces the path of neural information processing inward, synapse by synapse, the receptive fields of visual neurons become ever larger and responsive to ever more complex stimulus configurations (Van Essen & DeYoe,

1995). From this physiological perspective, then, there is little doubt that processing proceeds from local stimulation to global structure.

There are problems in accepting this line of argument as settling anything about perceptual experience, however. First, the order in which processing is *initiated* may not be nearly as relevant for determining perceptual experience as the order in which it is *completed,* and it is by no means clear that neural processing is completed in a local-to-global order. Indeed, there is good evidence that the flow of neural information processing is not unidirectional from the retina to higher centers of the brain. Massive backward projections from higher to lower cortical areas suggest that a great deal of feedback occurs, although nobody yet knows precisely what form it takes or even what functions it serves. Feedback raises the possibility that the order in which perceptual experiences arise is not given by the simplistic reading of the physiological facts given in the previous paragraph. I now consider evidence from psychological experiments suggesting that we take seriously the possibility that the perception of global objects precedes that of local parts.

Navon (1976) posed the question about the priority of wholes versus parts by studying discrimination tasks with hierarchically structured stimuli: typically, large letters of many appropriately positioned small letters. On some trials subjects were shown *consistent configurations* in which the global and local letters were the same, such as a large *H* made of small *H*s or a large *S* made of small *S*s. On others, they were shown *inconsistent configurations* in which the global and local letters conflicted, such as a large *H* made of small *S*s or a large *S* made of small *H*s. They were cued on each trial to report the identity of the letter represented at either the global or the local level. Response times and error rates were measured.

The results of Navon's experiment supported the predictions of *global precedence:* the hypothesis that observers perceive the global level of hierarchical stimuli before they perceive the local level. Response times are faster to global than to local letters, and global inconsistency interferes when subjects are attending to the local level. However, local inconsistency does not interfere when they are attending to the global level. The data thus appear to indicate that perceptual processes proceed from global, coarse-grained analysis to local, fine-grained analysis.

Further investigation suggested a more complex story, however. Kinchla and Wolfe (1979) found that the speed of naming local versus global letters depended on the letters' retinal sizes. Other experiments suggested that global and local levels of information are processed simultaneously rather than sequentially (Miller, 1981). Neuropsychological findings by Robertson and her colleagues have also shown that global and local information is processed differently in the two cerebral hemispheres. There is an advantage for global processing in the right temporal-parietal lobe, whereas there is an advantage for local processing in the left temporal-parietal lobe (Robertson, Lamb, & Knight, 1988). All of these results suggest that global/local processing may thus be better understood as the result of parallel processing in channels of different spatial resolution, with coarser channels being processed slightly faster than finer channels, rather than as reflecting a fixed global-to-local order of processing.

Global Superiority Effects

Other psychological evidence that global properties are primary in human vision comes from experiments in which perception of parts is found to be superior when the parts are embedded within meaningful or well-structured wholes than when they are not. The first findings of improved perceptual performance within meaningful wholes were reported by Reicher (1969), who confirmed the existence of a phenomenon that has come to be known as the *word superiority effect:* subjects are better able to perceive single letters when they are presented as part of meaningful words than when they are presented alone or in meaningless strings. Subjects were presented with either a word (such as *WORD*) or a comparable scrambled letter string (such as *ORWD*). This image was presented very briefly (for about 50 ms) and was followed by a masking pattern over the area that had contained the crucial letters. Just above the mask was a pair of letters—*D* and *K*, shown one over the other—that might have been presented in the position indicated. The subject's task on each trial was to indicate which of the two letters in the test had actually been presented in the corresponding position.

Reicher (1969) found that letter discrimination in word contexts had a substantial advantage over that for nonword contexts. The obvious conclusion is that identification of letters is indeed influenced by context: Letters in words are identified more accurately than are letters in random strings. This effect is often called the *word-nonword effect.* He also found that a single target letter was perceived less accurately than when it appeared in a word, a finding often referred to as the *word-letter effect.* Further research showed that letters in pronounceable nonwords are identified more accurately than are letters in unpronounceable nonwords (McClelland & Johnston, 1977), a finding often called the *pseudoword effect.*

Weisstein and Harris (1974) reported a similar contextual effect, known as the *object superiority effect,* with line drawings of objects versus nonobjects. Subjects were required to determine which target among a certain set of line segments was contained within

displays consisting of many line segments. The results showed that subjects were more accurate in the three-dimensional object condition than in either of the other two conditions.

Another example of superior discrimination performance for parts within larger wholes is provided by the *configural superiority effect* (Pomerantz, Sager, & Stoever, 1977). Again, subjects were instructed to discriminate simple elements that were presented either alone (e.g., a left- versus right-diagonal segment) or as part of a larger configuration. To ensure that the extra configural elements themselves could not be used to perform the discrimination task, exactly the same elements were added to both targets in the configural condition (e.g., a right angle that formed a triangle with one diagonal target versus an arrow vertex with the other diagonal target). Response-time measurements showed that subjects were much faster at discriminating the configurations than at discriminating the isolated parts.

The word, object, and configural superiority effects indicate that perceptual performance on these simple discrimination tasks does not occur in a strictly local-to-global order. Exactly how these contextual effects should be interpreted is open to debate, however. One possibility is that neural processing proceeds from local parts to global wholes, but that feedback from the holistic level to the earlier part levels then facilitates processing of local elements if they are part of coherent patterns at the global level. This is the mechanism proposed in the well-known *interactive activation model* of letter and word processing (McClelland & Rumelhart, 1981; Rumelhart & McClelland, 1982) that was developed to account for word superiority effects. Another possibility is that although neural processing proceeds from local parts to global wholes, people may gain conscious access to the results in the opposite order, from global wholes to local parts (Marcel, 1983). Regardless of what mechanism is ultimately found to be responsible, the experiments just described clearly rule out the possibility that the perception of local structure necessarily precedes that of global structure. The truth, as usual, is much more complex and interesting.

FRAMES OF REFERENCE

Another perceptual phenomenon that indicates the priority of large-scale structure in perceptual organization is the existence of what are called *frames of reference* (Palmer, 1989; Rock, 1990). A frame of reference in visual perception is a set of theoretically hypothesized reference standards with respect to which the properties of perceptual objects are presumed to be represented. Visual reference frames are often considered analogous to coordinate systems in analytic geometry. Reference-frame effects are important in perceptual organization because the reference frame for a given visual element is often defined by the next-higher level in the perceptual part-whole hierarchy. In this section I present a brief sample of reference-frame effects in orientation, shape, and motion perception.

Orientation Perception

One of the most compelling demonstrations of reference-frame effects on orientation perception occurs when you enter a tilted room such as those in a fun house or mystery house of an amusement park. Although you may notice the slant of the floor as you first enter, you rapidly come to perceive the room as gravitationally upright. Once this misperception occurs, all sorts of other illusions follow. You perceive the chandelier as hanging askew from the ceiling, for example, and you perceive yourself as leaning precariously to one side, despite the fact that both the chandelier and your body are gravitationally upright. If you then try to correct your posture to align yourself with the orientation of the room, you may lose your balance, or even fall.

Normally, the vertical orientation in the reference frame of the large-scale visual environment coincides with gravitational vertical because the dominant orientations—caused by walls, floors, tree trunks, standing people, and so forth—are either aligned with or perpendicular to gravity. The heuristic assumption that the walls, floor, and ceiling of a room are vertical and horizontal thus generally serves us well in perceiving the orientations of objects accurately. When you walk into a tilted room, however, this assumption is violated, giving rise to illusions of orientation.

One particularly well-known reference-frame effect on orientation perception is the *rod and frame effect* (Asch & Witkin, 1948a, 1948b). Subjects were shown a luminous rod within a large, tilted, luminous rectangle and were asked to set a luminous rod inside it to gravitational vertical. Asch and Witkin found large, systematic errors in which subjects set the rod to an orientation somewhere between true vertical and alignment with the frame's most nearly vertical sides. Further experiments showed that the effect of the frame is greatest when the rectangle is large, and that small ones just surrounding the line have little effect (Ebenholtz, 1977; Wenderoth, 1974). Other studies have shown that when two frames are present, one inside the other, it is the larger surrounding frame that dominates perception (DiLorenzo & Rock, 1982). These facts are consistent with the interpretation that the rectangle in a rod and frame task induces a visual frame of reference that is essentially a world-surrogate for the visual environment (Rock, 1990). By this account, a visual structure will be more likely to induce a frame of reference when it is large, surrounding, and stable over time, like the tilted room in the previous example.

Configural orientation effects also indicate that the perceived orientation of local elements depends on global orientational structure (e.g., Palmer 1980, 1989). The basic phenomenon comes from an observation by Attneave (1968) that equilateral triangles are directionally ambiguous figures: They can be seen as pointing in any of three directions, but in only one of them at once. For example, in Figure 5.25A the triangle can look like it is pointing toward 3, 7, or 11 o'clock. The fact of interest for reference-frame effects on orientation is that when several triangles are aligned in particular ways, the configuration can strongly affect the direction in which the

individual triangles are perceived to point. For example, if the triangles are aligned along an axis of symmetry (Figures 5.25B and 5.25D), observers tend to see them point along the configural line. If they are aligned along one of their sides (Figures 5.25C and 5.25E), observers tend to see them point perpendicular to the configural line. Similar orientation effects can be induced by placing a rectangle surrounding a single triangle at orientations parallel or perpendicular to the direction of pointing (Palmer, 1989), by placing textural stripes within or around a single triangle at these same orientations (Palmer & Bucher, 1981), and by creating motion along the direction of pointing (Bucher & Palmer, 1985).

Shape Perception

Because perceived shape depends on perceived orientation, robust reference-frame effects also occur in shape perception. One of the first, simplest, and most elegant demonstrations of the relation between shape and orientation was Mach's (1914/1959) observation that when a square (Figure 5.26A) is rotated 45° (Figure 5.26B), people generally perceive it as an upright diamond rather than as a tilted square. You can see this figure as a tilted square, if you take the flat side at 45° to be its top; but if the upper vertex is perceived as the top, the shape of the figure is seen as diamond-like and quite different from that of an upright square.

This relation suggests that the perceived shape of a shape-ambiguous object, such as the square/diamond, should be influenced by the orientation of a frame of reference, and this is indeed true. One of the earliest and most compelling demonstrations was given by Kopferman (1930), who showed that a gravitational diamond is perceived as a square when it is enclosed within a 45° tilted rectangle, (Figure 5.26C). Palmer (1985) later

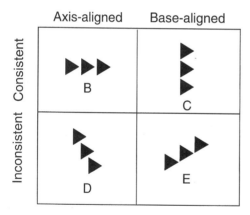

Figure 5.25 Perceived pointing of ambiguous triangles.
NOTE: A single equilateral triangle is ambiguous in that it can be seen to point in any of three directions (A). Alignment of several triangles along their axes of symmetry (B and D) or sides (C and E) strongly affects the direction in which the component triangles are seen to point, either consistent (B and C) or inconsistent (D and E) with a task that requires subjects to see them point directly left (not shown) or directly right (shown here).

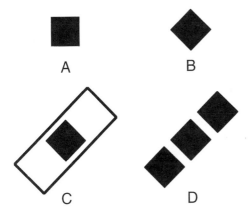

Figure 5.26   Reference-frame effects on the ambiguous square/diamond.
NOTE: The same figure is perceived as a square when its sides are vertical and horizontal (A) but as a diamond when its sides are diagonal (B). The diamond's perceived shape can be changed to that of a tilted square by placing it in a context in which a diagonal reference frame is established, for example, by surrounding it with a diagonal rectangle (C) or by locating it within a diagonal configuration (D).
SOURCE: C after Kopferman (1930); D after Palmer (1985).

generalized this result to other factors that he had previously shown to influence orientation perception, such as the orientation of configural lines (Figure 5.26D), textural stripes, and rigid motion. In all of these cases, when contextual factors induce a perceptual frame of reference that is aligned along a 45° axis of a gravitationally defined diamond, its shape is then perceived relative to that diagonal orientation, leading to the perception of a tilted square.

Rock (1973) has shown that the relation between perceived shape and the orientation of a perceptual reference frame generalizes beyond Mach's (1914/1959) square/diamond. He presented subjects with a sequence of several amorphous, novel shapes in a particular orientation during an initial presentation phase and later tested their recognition memory for the figures in the same orientation versus a different orientation (see Figure 5.27A). The results showed that people were far less likely to recognize the shapes if they were tested in a different orientation than if they were tested in the same orientation. Their poor recognition performance, which approached chance for 90° rotations, indicates that subjects often fail to perceive shape equivalence of the presented and tested figures when they are differently oriented.

In a series of further studies, Rock (1973) showed that the primary factors that determine the reference orientation for these poorly structured figures are not retinal, but environmental, gravitational, or both. For instance, when observers tilted their heads by 90° between presentation and test without changing the figure's orientation in the world, recognition performance was much better than when the orientation of the figures was changed by 90° without tilting the observer's head. Rock took these and related results as evidence that shape is perceived relative to a global, environmental frame of reference in which the sense of gravitational upright defines the reference orientation. If the environmental orientation of the figure changes from the initial presentation to the later testing, the description of the test figure will not match the description stored in memory, and the observer will fail to perceive the equivalence of two figures.

This finding seems to conflict with everyday experience in that people seldom fail to recognize, for example, a chair when they see it lying on its side rather than standing up. The difference appears to be that many objects, chairs included, have enough orientational structure that they effectively carry their own intrinsic, object-centered reference frames along with them. Roughly speaking, an *object-centered reference frame* is a perceptual reference frame that is chosen on the basis of the intrinsic properties of the object that is

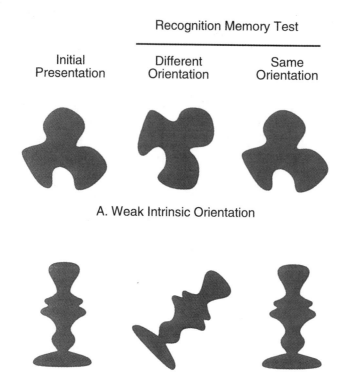

A. Weak Intrinsic Orientation

B. Strong Intrinsic Orientation

Figure 5.27 Effects of orientation on perceived shape.
NOTE: When subjects were shown figures with poor intrinsic axes (A) in one orientation and tested for recognition memory with figures in the same versus different orientations, they were much better at remembering when the figure's orientation was the same. Figures with good intrinsic axes (B) showed no such difference when orientation was changed at testing.
SOURCE: From Palmer (1999).

to be described, one that is somehow "made to order" for that particular object (see Palmer, 1999, pp. 368–371). For example, if the orientations of two otherwise identical objects are different, such as an upright and a tipped-over chair, the orientation of each object-centered reference frame (e.g., the axis of elongation that lies in its plane of symmetry) will be defined such that both objects will have the same shape description relative to their object-centered frames.

Wiser (1981) used Rock's memory paradigm to study shape perception for objects with good intrinsic axes and found that they were recognized as well when they are presented and tested in different orientations as when they were presented and tested in the same orientation (Figure 5.27B). In further experiments, Wiser (1981) showed that when a well-structured figure was presented initially so that its axis was not aligned with gravitational vertical, subsequent recognition was actually fastest when the figure was tested in its vertical orientation. She interpreted this result to mean that the shape was stored in memory as though it were upright, relative to its own object-centered reference frame.

Motion Perception

Reference-frame effects are also present in motion perception. Two of the most important examples are induced motion and configural motion. *Induced motion* is an illusion in which a small stationary object is perceived as moving when it is surrounded by a larger moving object. Known to ancient scientists such as Euclid and Ptolemy, this effect was studied systematically by the Gestalt psychologist Karl Duncker (1929/1937). In a completely dark room, he showed observers a small luminous dot inside a luminous rectangle. When the rectangle was moved slowly back and forth with respect to the stationary dot, they reported seeing the dot move (forth and back) inside a stationary rectangle. The dot's perceived motion was opposite that of the rectangle's actual motion so that the *relative* motion of dot and rectangle was preserved.

It appears that perceived motion relies on a reference frame in which stationarity is one of the reference parameters of perceived spacetime. Induced motion can then be understood as the misperception of true environmental stationarity, much as the rod and frame effect can be understood as the misperception of environmental vertical. The majority of known facts about induced motion fit an account based on two assumptions (Rock, 1983): (a) The visual system is more sensitive to relative motion between two objects than to absolute motion of a single object alone (Wallach, 1959), and (b) when the relative motion between two objects is above threshold and the absolute motion of each object is below threshold, the visual system assumes that the larger or surrounding object is stationary. It therefore assigns the registered relative motion to the smaller, enclosed object.

Allowing the observer to perceive the actual motion of the frame usually destroys the illusion of induced motion because the motion is then correctly attributed to the moving frame (Rock, 1983). If the frame moves fast enough that it is clearly above the threshold for perception of absolute motion, induced motion of the stationary object generally does not occur, although sometimes both the frame and the central object are seen moving at the same time (Rock, Auster, Shiffman, & Wheeler, 1980). The heuristic of attributing motion to the smaller object makes ecological sense because moving objects are generally smaller than their surrounding visual framework. Because the environment is largely stable and unmoving; assuming it to be stationary is often correct and produces veridical perception. In the unusual cases where it is wrong, however, the illusion of induced motion results.

Perceptually assigning stationarity to moving objects can sometimes produce a compelling illusion of induced self-motion. This frequently occurs, for example, when you are sitting in an unmoving train and look out the window. If the train next to yours begins to pull slowly out of the station, you often vividly experience your own train as moving in the opposite direction instead. This is an example of induced motion because your visual system registers the relative motion between your train and the other train but erroneously attributes the motion to your train (and you) rather than to the other one. The other train does not literally enclose or surround your train, of course, but if it is the only thing visible through the window, the visual system responds as though it is part of the stationary exterior world.

Other potent reference-frame effects in motion perception go under the general heading of *configural motion*. Johansson (1950) discovered this phenomenon when he realized that two or more moving dots sometimes caused different motions to be experienced than the ones he explicitly programmed into the displays. A simple example is the "L" configuration shown in Figure 5.28A. The

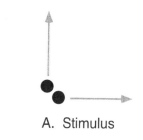

A. Stimulus

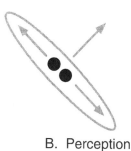

B. Perception

Figure 5.28 Dynamic organization of Johansson's "L" configuration.
NOTE: Two dots moving synchronously vertically and horizontally (A) are perceived as a group moving diagonally while they move apart and together within the group (B).
SOURCE: From Palmer (1999).

display consists of two dots, one moving harmonically up and down and the other moving harmonically right and left. When each dot is viewed in isolation, this is precisely how they are perceived. When they are viewed moving together in synchrony, however, the perception often changes in a surprising way. The two dots are experienced as a group moving in unison along a diagonal path while they simultaneously move toward and away from each other along the opposite diagonal, as depicted in Figure 5.28B. The *common motion component* of the group is represented by the arrow attached to the gray oval enclosing the group, and the *relative motion component* is represented by the arrows attached to the individual dots within the group.

Johansson (1950) proposed a theory of configural motion perception based on a gen-

eralization of the idea of common fate. Specifically, he suggested that object motions can be represented as vectors and that these vectors can be decomposed by the visual system into two components: *Common motion* is a vector component shared by the motion of several different objects. These objects are grouped together by virtue of this common motion component, which is, by definition, the same for all objects in the group. *Relative motions* are vectors that specify how each object is moving relative to the whole group (and relative to each other). It is not clear exactly how this computation is performed. One possibility is that the common motion component might be extracted first, with the relative motion vector as the residual (e.g., Johansson, 1950). Another is that relative motion might be detected first, with the common motion vector as the residual (e.g., Cutting & Proffitt, 1982). A third is that they might be codetermined simultaneously.

However it is performed, Johansson's (1950) vector analysis of motion configurations into common and relative components is a good example of how hierarchical reference frames can organize motion perception. In the cases we have just been discussing, there are three frames of reference: the entire visual environment, the whole group of elements, and the individual elements. The stationary environment is the largest frame of reference, and the common motion of the whole group is perceived relative to it. The common motion of the group is the next-largest frame of reference, and the motion of each individual dot is perceived relative to it.

MULTISTABILITY

In most naturally occurring scenes, a single, rock-solid organization completely dominates perception. However, carefully chosen examples illustrate the possibility of arriving

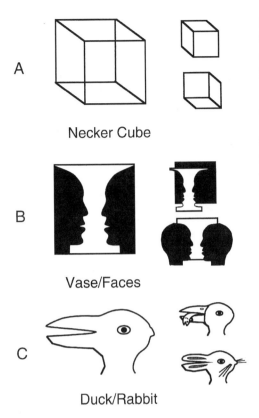

Necker Cube

Vase/Faces

Duck/Rabbit

Figure 5.29 Ambiguous figures and unambiguous version of their interpretations.
NOTE: Figure A can be seen as a cube viewed from above or below. Figure B can be seen either as a white vase against a black background or as a pair of black faces against a white background. Figure C can be seen as a duck (facing left) or a rabbit (facing right).
SOURCE: From Palmer (1999).

at different organizations for the same image, organizations that can profoundly change our perceptual experiences. Figure 5.29 shows three different examples of ambiguous figures. The Necker cube (Figure 5.29A) is ambiguous in depth; the vase/faces display is ambiguous in figure-ground organization (edge assignment; Figure 5.29B); and the duck/rabbit display is ambiguous in its perceptual categorization (Figure 5.29C). Not only do such ambiguous figures allow for more than one interpretation, but they are

multistable as well: They can produce spontaneous alternations among the different perceptual interpretations once the different interpretations have been seen.

The Neural Fatigue Hypothesis

One interesting question about multistability is why it occurs. The most widely accepted theory is the *neural fatigue hypothesis* of Köhler (1940). He claimed that perception of ambiguous figures alternates among different interpretations because different sets of neurons tire of firing after they have done so for a long time. To make the neural fatigue hypothesis more concrete, we will apply it to a particular theory of the perception of a Necker cube, shown in Figure 5.30 (Rumelhart, Smolensky, McClelland, & Hinton, 1986). The network representations of the two interpretations of the cube are two subnetworks embedded within the larger interconnected network. These two subnetworks are shown in the top left and top right regions of Figure 5.30 next to an unambiguous cube illustrating the perceptions to which they correspond. The left subnetwork represents the perception of the cube viewed from above, and the right subnetwork represents it viewed from below. The underlying theoretical assumptions required to explain its multistability appear to be that (a) different interpretations are represented by different patterns of neural activity in the two subnetworks, (b) perception corresponds to whichever pattern is most active in the brain at the time, and (c) neural fatigue causes different patterns of activation to dominate at different times.

The behavior of this network exemplifies bistability: Activation spreads dynamically throughout the network, and it eventually settles into one of two stable states. Sometimes all the nodes in the left network end up active, whereas those in the right network are not, and sometimes the reverse

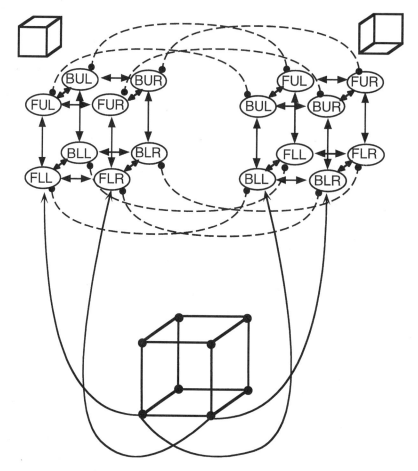

Figure 5.30   A connectionist network model of perceiving a Necker cube.

NOTE: The left and right subnetworks at the top correspond to perceiving the two ambiguous organizations of this reversible, multistable figure. Solid lines represent excitatory connections, and dashed lines represent inhibitory connections. See text for more details.

SOURCE: From Palmer (1999), after Rumelhart, Smolensky, McClelland, & Hinton (1986).

happens. This bistability arises from the network's *architecture:* the pattern of connections among its nodes. In this case, the architecture is such that the mutually excitatory connections (solid lines with arrows at both ends) between pairs of nodes from the same interpretation produce *cooperation,* whereas the mutually inhibitory connections (dashed lines with dots at both ends) between pairs of nodes from different interpretations produce *competition.* Together, the cooperative and competitive connections make each sub-

network function as a cohesive unit that tends to settle into a state in which either all its units or none of them are active. This mutual exclusivity in the behavior of the network thus mimics an important aspect of the perception of Necker cubes: One interpretation or the other is experienced at any given time, not both.

The further assumption of neural fatigue allows this network to alternate between these two interpretations of the same stimulus: First one subnetwork becomes dominant, but its dominance decreases as its units fatigue until the second subnetwork dominates. This cycle of domination, fatigue, and reversed domination can continue indefinitely to the very same input. The same general architecture—which features distinct subnetworks defined by mutual excitation within each subnetwork, by mutual inhibition between the two subnetworks, and by neural fatigue of all individual units—can be used to model multistability in other ambiguous figures. They would require quite different subnetwork representations, of course, but whatever the neural network representations might be, if the subnetworks have the three properties just listed—cooperation within subnetworks, competition between subnetworks, and neural fatigue—they should exhibit multistability.

Data from experiments on the perception of ambiguous figures support several predictions of neural fatigue theories. One is that if subjects view an unambiguous version for an extended period, they should then tend to see the *other* interpretation when they are finally exposed to the ambiguous version (Hochberg, 1950). Such effects have been reported with a variety of different ambiguous stimuli (e.g., Carlson, 1953). Another confirmed prediction of the neural fatigue hypothesis is that the rate of alternation between the two interpretations accelerates over time (Köhler, 1940). This acceleration should occur if the fatigue that has built up during extended perception of one interpretation (A) does not completely dissipate during the perception of the other interpretation (B). Then, when interpretation A is perceived for the second time, its neural representation will already be partially fatigued. As a result, the level of activation in the neural representation of A will decrease more quickly the second time than it did the first time. By the same logic, similar reductions in duration will occur for the third, fourth, and later perceptions of A and B.

The Role of Eye Fixations

Despite its success, the neural fatigue hypothesis has not gone unchallenged. An alternative idea is that reversals are caused by eye movements to different fixation points. You may have noticed, for example, that if you fixate on the upper central Y-vertex of the Necker cube, you tend to perceive the cube-from-above interpretation. Fixating the lower Y-vertex similarly biases the cube-from-below interpretation. In general, the fixated vertex tends to be perceived as nearer, as Necker himself noticed. Further studies have shown that this cannot be the whole story, however, because afterimages (Gregory, 1970) and even stabilized images (Pritchard, 1958) of a Necker cube have been found to reverse. Moreover, there is evidence that the causal relation between eye fixations and reversals may run in the opposite direction: Eye movements may be the *result* of perceptual reversals rather than their cause (Noton & Stark, 1971; Woodworth, 1938).

More recent findings by Peterson and Hochberg (1983) using a modified Necker cube have confirmed that local information around the position at which the eye is fixated does indeed exert a disproportionately strong influence on what is perceived. Depth-biased information around the fixated vertex caused subjects to report the interpretation consistent with that bias for longer durations than they reported the inconsistent interpretation. Their results also showed strong effects of the subject's *intention* to perceive a given interpretation. Subjects reported seeing the instructed interpretation for much longer periods than they reported seeing the uninstructed interpretation.

Instructional Effects

Another challenge to the neural fatigue hypothesis has come from Rock and his colleagues, who have questioned whether this simple mechanism is indeed sufficient to explain multistability of ambiguous figures (Girgus, Rock, & Egatz, 1977; Rock, Gopnik, & Hall, 1994; Rock & Mitchener, 1992). Rock pointed out that in virtually all earlier research on ambiguous figures, the experimenter *informed* subjects about the two alternative perceptions beforehand.

To discover the role of such instructions on spontaneous perception, Rock and Mitchener (1992) showed subjects three ambiguous figures (akin to the duck/rabbit in Figure 5.29C), saying only, "Tell me what you see, and continue to look at the picture, since I am going to ask you some questions about it later." After viewing the three figures sequentially for 30 s each, the subjects were interviewed to determine whether they had perceived any interpretation other than the one they had reported initially. To aid in eliciting reports of perceptual change in the interview phase, the experimenter showed subjects unambiguous versions of each stimulus figure. By their own report, fully one third of the subjects reported *never* seeing any of the three figures reverse. Once they were given the standard instructions, however, all of them reported seeing frequent reversals.

Rock interpreted these results as challenging the idea that neural fatigue alone is sufficient to explain multistability. Recall, however, that in the network theory of the Necker cube described earlier, two additional conditions were required for a network to be multistable: (a) The alternative interpretations had to be represented within different, internally cooperative subnetworks, and (b) these subnetworks had to compete with each other through mutual inhibition. The implications of these conditions in network architecture for eliciting multistability in human observers are that (a) subjects must have perceived the two alternative interpretations previously in order for both alternative subnetworks to be available in the first place, and (b) the subjects

must realize (at a perceptual level) the competitive, mutually exclusive relation between the alternative interpretations. These conditions are just what the standard experimental instructions ensure, of course, and just what are (purposely) missing in Rock's experiments.

In light of the network-based theory of multistability, then, it is perhaps not too surprising that Rock and Mitchener (1992) found many subjects who failed to report spontaneous reversals. Indeed, the surprising thing is that *any* subjects experienced reversals under these conditions—*if* they were truly naive about ambiguous figures. After all, science museums, television programs, and perception textbooks often include material on ambiguous figures, making it difficult to find truly naive adults. Rock, Gopnik, and Hall (1994) therefore reasoned that young children were far more likely to be naive than were adults. They found that without explicit instructions about the alternative interpretations, 3- to 4-year-old children *never* report spontaneous reversals during extended viewing of three ambiguous figures (including the vase/faces and the duck/rabbit shown in Figures 5.29B and 5.29C). These children also showed reversal rates that were slower than those for adults once they were given instructions about the alternative perceptions.

FIGURAL GOODNESS

I have supposed that each perception of a given image or event has a particular organization—or, rarely, two alternating organizations—but I have not yet addressed in detail the important question of why it has the particular organization that it does. There are, after all, innumerable logical possibilities, only one of which is typically realized by the visual system. Gestalt theorists believed that perceptions are organized according to their principle of Prägnanz (as discussed earlier):

Perception will be as good as the prevailing conditions allow. The notion of goodness was thus key to their understanding of basic organizational mechanisms. In this section I examine what this means and how it has been analyzed.

Gestalt psychologists grounded their notion of goodness in an aspect of perceptual experience that they called *gute Gestalt:* literally, "good shape" or "good form." In the modern literature, the more usual term for this concept is *figural goodness,* which refers to the aspect of perceptual experience that is perhaps best described as a composite of (at least) simplicity, order, and regularity. Certain shapes, such as circles, seem highly simple, regular, and orderly. Virtually any change one might make in a circle reduces the experience of goodness in viewing it. In contrast, a chaotic jumble of lines of approximately the

same overall size seems bad in comparison: complex, irregular, and random. Why might this be? What factors determine the perceived goodness of a figure?

One obvious factor that influences figural goodness is the number of component parts an object has. As the number of sides of a figure increases, so does the complexity of its perceived shape. Number of parts is not the whole story, however, because objects can differ in figural goodness even if they have the same number of physical parts. For example, consider the set of five-dot figures shown in the left column of Figure 5.31. Observers generally agree that there is an ordering from simple, regular figures at the top to more complex, irregular figures at the bottom. These differences in figural goodness cannot depend solely on the number of physical parts that the figure contains, because all of them contain

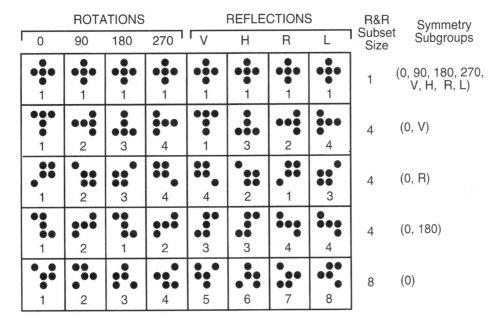

Figure 5.31 Stimuli used to study figural goodness and their analysis according to transformational theories.
NOTE: The figural goodness of each pattern can be predicted from the size of its rotation and reflection (R&R) subset and from the transformations in its symmetry subgroup. See text for more details.
SOURCE: After Palmer (1991).

exactly five dots. Rather, the differences seem to stem from the way in which the dots are arranged or configured.

Garner (1974) showed that human performance on a number of objective tasks with such dot configurations is closely related to people's ratings of their subjective goodness. He found, for example, that people match pairs of good figures more quickly for physical identity than they match pairs of bad ones, that they remember good figures more accurately than they remember bad ones, that they describe good figures in fewer words than they describe bad ones, and that they learn good figures more quickly than they learn bad ones. All these findings fit together nicely if good patterns can somehow be more easily and economically represented and processed within the visual system. How this might occur has been the focus of several theories of figural goodness.

Information Theory

The first significant advance in objective theories of figural goodness came from applying basic concepts from *information theory,* a mathematical theory of communication that measures a commodity (in units called *bits*) that depends on the degree of predictability or certainty associated with a given signal in a particular context (Shannon, 1948; Shannon & Weaver, 1949).[6] Shannon called this commodity "information," but its relation to the everyday, common-sense notion

of information is perhaps less obvious than it might be.

Relations between information theory and the Gestalt concept of figural goodness were formulated independently by Attneave (1954) and Hochberg and McAlister (1953) at about the same time. They realized that if the perceptual system coded figures optimally by eliminating redundancies (e.g., symmetries and repetitions), good figures could be encoded and stored more efficiently than bad ones. In effect, they proposed that good figures could be described in fewer bits than could bad figures. This informational analysis of figural goodness is based on breaking figures down into local components such as angles and lines and analyzing them for structural regularities, such as the sameness of angle sizes or line lengths within the same figure (Hochberg & McAlister, 1953). Both a square and an irregular quadrilateral consist of four lines and four angles, but the square is better than the irregular quadrilateral because all of its sides are the same length and all of its angles are 90°. Such regularities mean that fewer bits of information are required to describe it, although information theorists were never very clear about what the descriptions might be or how many bits of information a given figure contained. Still, these informational analyses were applauded as an advance over Gestalt ideas because they showed that good figures were objectively simpler than bad ones in a well-defined sense.

Transformational Invariance

Although information theorists sought to explain the Gestalt construct of figural goodness in objective terms, their ideas do not fit well into the Gestalt style of explanation, which generally opposed piecewise theories of perception (Wertheimer, 1924/1950). Formulations more in keeping with the holistic approach of Gestalt theory were later provided

---

[6]"Bit" is actually a shortened form of "binary digit," defined as the amount of information required to reduce the number of equally probable alternatives by half. Because the content of the alternatives does not matter, knowing whether a tossed coin lands heads or tails is one bit of information, and so is knowing whether the roll of a die produces an odd- or even-numbered outcome (i.e., 6 equally likely alternatives reduced to 3). More generally, there are $\log_2(N)$ bits of information in N equally likely alternatives.

by Garner (1974) and Palmer (1991) in terms of *transformational invariance.* Garner proposed that figures are good to the extent that they are the same as transformed versions of themselves, a notion he formalized in his theory of *rotation and reflection* (R&R) *subsets.* Palmer refined this idea in terms of *symmetry subgroups.*

When a set of spatial transformations is applied to a figure, the transformations produce a set of transformational variants of that figure. The key observation for Garner's (1974) theory of figural goodness is that better figures produce fewer transformational variants than do worse figures. In the original formulation of this theory, Garner and Clement (1963) applied a set of eight possible transformations to five-dot configurations (see Figure 5.31): four central rotations (through angles of 0°, 90°, 180°, and 270°) and four central reflections (about vertical, horizontal, left-diagonal, and right-diagonal axes). Within this set is a subset of distinguishably different figures, the R&R subset, which is enumerated in Figure 5.31 by the numbers below the transformational variants. Garner and Clement (1963) found that patterns rated as good (e.g., the top one in Figure 5.31) had few transformational variants, whereas those rated as bad (e.g., the bottom one) had many transformational variants. Thus, they proposed that the goodness of a figure was an inverse function of the size of its R&R subset. This analysis is appealing from the Gestalt point of view because it applies to whole figures. There is no sense in which patterns need to be broken into piecewise components in order to apply it.

One problem with Garner's theory is that it lumps together a number of qualitatively different structures. For example, the figures in the three middle rows in Figure 5.31 all have exactly four different figures in their R&R subsets, but most people find the vertically symmetrical figure to be better than the other two, and many experimental findings support

this fact (e.g., Palmer, 1991). Palmer (1991) offered an alternative formulation in terms of the symmetries a figure possesses that differentiates between bilateral symmetry about vertical, horizontal, and diagonal axes. Even the fourth row of Figure 5.31, which has no bilateral symmetry, has rotational symmetry. In modern mathematics, a figure is symmetrical with respect to a given transformation if applying that transformation leaves the figure unchanged (Weyl, 1952). Thus, patterns that remain the same after being rotated 180 degrees about their centers have 180° rotational symmetry (e.g., S, N, and Z), which is precisely the symmetry possessed by the dot pattern shown in the fourth row of Figure 5.31. (Notice that patterns with two symmetries of reflection, such as the top one in Figure 5.31, always have 180° rotational symmetry as well.)

The symmetry subgroup of a given figure can therefore be characterized as the subset of spatial transformations over which it is invariant. The rightmost column of Figure 5.31 shows these symmetry subgroups for Garner's five-dot patterns. Palmer (1991) extended Garner's theory by proposing that the goodness of a figure can be identified with its symmetry subgroup rather than with R&R subset size. Palmer also argued that local symmetries (i.e., symmetries that hold only within a diameter-limited region of space) are important for understanding figural goodness (see also Alexander & Carey, 1968; Blum, 1973), and he reported data supporting this possibility.

Representational Simplicity

Many of the ideas about figural goodness have been brought together and formalized by Leeuwenberg (1971) and his colleagues (e.g., Buffart & Leeuwenberg, 1981; Van der Helm & Leeuwenberg, 1991). Leeuwenberg's theory—initially called *coding theory* and later called *structural information theory*—provides a well-defined method for constructing different symbolic descriptions of the same object and for relating them to perception via a version of the Gestalt principle of Prägnanz. It fits with the information-theoretical approach because different codes have different degrees of compactness and with transformational approaches because the way in which codes are simplified corresponds to explicitly encoding certain kinds of transformational invariances.

A shape description is derived in structural information theory by first generating a symbolic perceptual description called a *code* that is sufficient to generate the figure and then simplifying the code to remove redundancies. Ideas closely akin to Gestalt theory are introduced into coding theory through a measure called *information load*, which is the metric used to identify the best possible code, more or less as advocated in the principle of Prägnanz. Coding theory proposes that the alternative that most observers perceive is the one that has the simplest code as measured by the lowest information load. Not only does the theory account well for judgments of figural goodness, but it has also successfully predicted a number of interesting organizational effects, such as amodal completion, transparency perception, and configural motion (e.g., Buffart & Leeuwenberg, 1981; Leeuwenberg, 1978; Restle, 1979). Of the possible completions of the image in Figure 5.15A, for example, it can be shown that the circular completion has the lowest information load.

The general outline of structural information theory is as follows:

1. Construct a *primitive code* by tracing the contour of the figure and describing it symbolically as a sequence of line segment lengths and the angles between them. (This description is much like generating the figure in the "turtle geometry" computer language LOGO.)

2. Use a set of *semantic operators* (or *rewrite rules*) to simplify the primitive code by removing as many structural redundancies as possible. The resulting simplified codes are called *reduced codes*.

3. Compute the *information load* of each reduced code by counting the number of parameters (numerical values) it contains. This value corresponds inversely to the figural goodness of the perception that contains the structure specified in the reduced code.

4. The reduced code with the lowest information load, called the *minimum code*, is the one that structural information theory predicts will be perceived most often. Others may also be perceived with a probability that depends on their information load relative to the alternatives.

Leeuwenberg and his colleagues have used this simplicity-based theory of perceptual representation to explain many organizational phenomena in terms of the principle of Prägnanz. Partly occluded objects (e.g., Figure 5.15) are amodally completed such that the hidden figure has the simplest minimum code among all the possible completions that are compatible with the image (Buffart & Leeuwenberg, 1981). Similarly, illusory contours (e.g., Figure 5.18) are perceived when the minimum code for a surface occluding the amodally completed inducer elements is simpler than the alternative minimum code of the unoccluded inducer elements. This simplicity-based explanation is thus able to explain why the notched octagons in Figure 5.19A give rise to illusory figures, whereas the locally similar crosses in Figure 5.19B do not: The codes for the amodally completed octagons have a much lower information load than do the uncompleted notched octagons, whereas the codes for amodally completed crosses (i.e., crosses with the occluded corner added in) actually have a higher information load than do the uncompleted crosses (i.e., the true crosses). The same kinds of analyses can be given for perceived transparency, figural scission, various cases of configural motion, and a number of other organizational effects (e.g., Buffart & Leeuwenberg, 1981; Restle, 1979).

ECOLOGICAL APPROACHES REVISITED

Even if a theory based on structural simplicity were able to provide explanations of all known organizational phenomena—and there is as yet no such theory—a puzzle remains about why it should succeed in so many cases. It is not clear what advantage would accrue to an organism that perceived the *simplest* alternative interpretation. Helmholtz's likelihood principle seems to provide a more satisfying rationale for an organism perceiving one organization instead of another: The organism perceives the most likely environmental situation that could have caused the pattern of sensory stimulation. That is clearly a statement of an evolutionarily ideal organizational algorithm, and it is quite compatible with ecological approaches to perception.

Rejection of Coincidence

Many of the phenomena of perceptual organization that we have described thus far can be understood within the ecological framework of maximum likelihood (Pomerantz & Kubovy, 1986). One important contribution to this approach is what has recently come to be called the principle of *nonaccidentalness* or *genericity:* the idea that the visual system avoids interpreting structural regularities in an image as arising from unlikely accidents

of viewing. Underlying these analyses is the notion of *general viewpoint:* viewing conditions in which a small change in viewpoint makes only minor changes in a scene's optical projection. Viewing a pair of vertical lines at different distances from the observer so that they are precisely aligned can thus be understood as a violation of general viewpoint, because any small change in viewpoint to either side will cause the lines to move out of alignment in the retinal image. In the psychological literature this idea was discussed by Rock (1983) as the *rejection-of-coincidence* principle. He pointed out that many phenomena of perceptual organization can be explained by assuming that the visual system rejects interpretations in which the properties of the retinal image arise from coincidences of any sort. Similar ideas were independently proposed within a computational framework by Lowe (1985) and extended by others (e.g., Albert & Hoffman, 1995). Whatever it is called, this general idea can be viewed as a corollary of Helmholtz's ecologically motivated likelihood principle.

Grouping phenomena provide many good examples of rejecting coincidences. It might be true that two image regions moving in the same direction and at the same rate belong to two different, unrelated objects that coincidentally happen to be moving the same way, but it is far more likely that they do so because they are parts of a single object moving as a unitary whole. The visual system prefers the nonaccidental interpretation that they are parts of the same object. The same is true of good continuation. We perceive the segments in the X of Figure 5.32A as consisting of two intersecting straight lines (B) rather than as two angles that just happen to align at their vertices (C) because the latter arrangement is a rather unlikely coincidence compared to the former. One way of assessing which interpretation is less coincidental is to examine the consequences

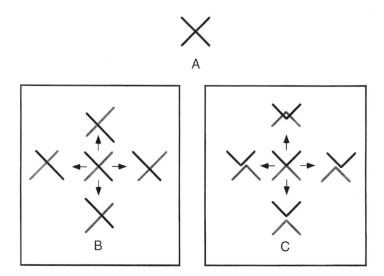

Figure 5.32   Nonaccidentalness in good continuation.
NOTE: Slight changes in the position from which A is viewed (arrow directions) lead to minor quantitative changes in image geometry if it consists of two continuous lines at different depths (B). The same changes in viewing position lead to much more drastic qualitative changes if the scene consists of two angles at different depths that accidentally align at their vertices (C).
SOURCE: From Palmer (1999).

of slight changes in the viewpoint of the observer. Notice in the crossed-lines case that the observer moving slightly in any direction changes only minor details of the resulting figure (B), but in the aligned-angles case moving slightly in any direction (except along the line of sight) produces far more radical changes (C). It is logically possible that the continuity of the segments is actually an accident caused by the precise alignment of two angles, but it is far more likely that they are aligned because they are continuations of the same environmental lines.

Ecological considerations also lead to functional hypotheses about why the visual system exhibits figure-ground organization and why it is affected by the particular factors described earlier. The functional role of figure-ground organization in region interpretation appears to be determining which two-dimensional image regions correspond to objects and which correspond to spaces between objects. Sur-

roundedness may be relevant because it is more likely that there is an object in front of a larger one than that there is a hole in the large object. Orientation may have its effect because objects in the real world tend to be more gravitationally stable in horizontal or vertical orientations than in oblique ones. Real-world objects tend also to be more convex than concave, and the regions of empty space around them tend to be correspondingly more concave than convex. Objects are also much more likely to have symmetrical or parallel sides than are the spaces between the objects, for which such properties would arise only by unlikely accidents. And, perhaps most obviously, regions that have the shape of known object types are much more likely to be the projections of those objects than they are to arise accidentally from the juxtaposition of occluding objects that happen to line up in just the right way. Related analyses of accidental properties can be given for amodal completion, perceived transparency, and illusory figures.

Simplicity and Likelihood

The final question that must be discussed is how the structural-simplicity approach might relate to this ecological approach. Are they fundamentally incompatible, or might both be part of some larger integrated story? Palmer (in press-b) has argued that they are actually complementary in a particularly interesting way. Ecological arguments are useful for understanding the evolutionary utility of perceptual organization, but they have trouble explaining how the requisite knowledge gets into the system to be used in the actual mechanisms. How does the system know the likelihoods of actual environmental situations? (This is the epistemological problem mentioned briefly in the section on ecological approaches). Structural simplicity arguments are useful for understanding how the visual system can select among alternative interpretations based on internally available criteria, but it has trouble explaining why such mechanisms are useful. The most appealing connection between them is that the interpretation that is most likely (and thus evolutionarily most useful) in an ecological sense may be strongly correlated with the simplest interpretation in a structural sense. If structural simplicity is correlated with environmental likelihood, the visual system could use simplicity as a surrogate for likelihood. The conjecture, to put it somewhat crudely, is that evolution may have built simplicity mechanisms into the visual system as a heuristic for likelihood.

This possibility is perhaps most easily understood through an analogy to eating behavior.[7] Evolutionarily speaking, it is advanta-geous for an organism to eat things that are nourishing and to avoid eating things that are poisonous. However, we do not have veridical nourishment detectors or poison detectors in any sensory modality for deciding what to eat and what not to eat. That is, we do not have sensory access to the objective external conditions that will help versus harm us nutritionally. Rather, the actual mechanism of selective consumption—the internal criterion of eating behavior, if you will—is *taste:* We eat things that taste *good* and avoid eating things that taste *bad*. This works because there is a pretty high correlation between what tastes good and what is nourishing and between what tastes bad and what is nonnourishing or even poisonous. It is not perfect, of course, because some nonnourishing things taste good (like saccharine), and some nourishing things taste bad (like liver, at least to this writer). The intriguing possibility is that something similar may be occurring in perception: Perhaps evolution built simplicity into the visual system as a heuristic because it correlates well enough with the relevant ecological realities of the physical world that it regularly provides organisms with useful information about the environment. Adjustments can be made during the lifetime of the organism, of course, to optimize the process based on prior experiences, much as people can learn to avoid eating good-tasting things that have previously made them sick.

SUMMARY

Organization is an important and ubiquitous phenomenon in visual perception. Without it, we would not be able to perceive the visual world as structured into the groups, objects, parts, and subparts that we so readily experience when we view natural scenes. Our ability to perceive this hierarchical part-whole structure depends on the interactions

---

[7]I first heard this analogy from Michael Leyton.

among several basic organizational processes, including region segmentation, boundary assignment (figure-ground organization), grouping, and parsing. Further processes of visual interpolation produce perceptual phenomena, such as amodal completion, illusory contours, translucency, and figural scission, that fill in partly seen portions of the visual world.

Experimental evidence in several different tasks indicates that the global structure of whole configurations is often perceived before the local structure of its constituent parts. Global structure also appears to provide the frame of reference within which more local properties (such as the orientation, shape, and motion of subordinate perceptual elements) are perceived. The question of which of all possible organizations is perceived for a given image has been addressed primarily through the Gestalt idea of maximal simplicity (or minimum complexity). Alternative accounts for a number of organizational phenomena have been proposed in terms of ecological likelihood principles, such as nonaccidentalness. Simplicity and likelihood explanations may be related, however, by natural correlations that evolution has exploited to improve organisms' fitness for survival and reproduction.

REFERENCES

Alais, D., Blake, R., & Lee, S.-H. (1998). Visual features that vary together over time group together over space. *Nature Neuroscience, 1*(2), 160–164.

Albert, M. K., & Hoffman, D. D. (1995). Genericity in spatial vision. In R. D. Luce, M. D'Zmura, D. D. Hoffman, G. J. Iverson, & A. K. Romney (Eds.), *Geometric representations of perceptual phenomena: Papers in honor of Tarow Indow on his 70th birthday* (pp. 95–112). Mahwah, NJ: Erlbaum.

Alexander, C., & Carey, S. (1968). Subsymmetries. *Perception and Psychophysics, 4,* 73–77.

Anderson, B. L. (1997). A theory of illusory lightness and transparency in monocular and binocular images: The role of contour junctions. *Perception, 26,* 419–453.

Asch, S. E., & Witkin, H. A. (1948a). Studies in space orientation: I. Perception of the upright with displaced visual fields. *Journal of Experimental Psychology, 38,* 325–337.

Asch, S. E., & Witkin, H. A. (1948b). Studies in space orientation: II. Perception of the upright with displaced visual fields and with body tilted. *Journal of Experimental Psychology, 38,* 455–477.

Attneave, F. (1954). Some informational aspects of visual perception. *Psychological Review, 61,* 183–193.

Attneave, F. (1968). Triangles as ambiguous figures. *American Journal of Psychology, 81,* 447–453.

Beck, D. M., & Palmer, S. E. (in press). Top-down influences on perceptual grouping.

Beck, J. (1966). Effects of orientation and shape similarity on perceptual grouping. *Perception and Psychophysics, 1,* 300–302.

Beck, J. (1972). Similarity grouping and peripheral discriminability under uncertainty. *American Journal of Psychology, 85*(1), 1–19.

Beck, J. (1982). Textural segmentation. In J. Beck (Ed.), *Organization and representation in perception* (pp. 285–318). Hillsdale, NJ: Erlbaum.

Biederman, I. (1987). Recognition-by-components: A theory of human image understanding. *Psychological Review, 94*(2), 115–117.

Biederman, I., & Cooper, E. E. (1991). Priming contour-deleted images: Evidence for intermediate representations in visual object recognition. *Cognitive Psychology, 23*(3), 393–419.

Binford, T. O. (1971). *Visual perception by computer.* Paper presented at the IEEE Conference on Systems and Control, Miami.

Blake, R., & Yang, Y. (1997). Spatial and temporal coherence in perceptual binding. *Proceedings of the National Academy of Sciences, 94,* 7115–7119.

Blum, H. (1973). Biological shape and visual science, Part 1. *Journal of Theoretical Biology, 38,* 205–287.

Bucher, N. M., & Palmer, S. E. (1985). Effects of motion on perceived pointing of ambiguous triangles. *Perception & Psychophysics, 38,* 227–236.

Buffart, H., & Leeuwenberg, E. L. J. (1981). Structural information theory. In H. G. Geissler, E. L. J. Leeuwenberg, S. Link, & V. Sarris (Eds.), *Modern issues in perception.* Berlin, Germany: Erlbaum.

Canny, J. F. (1986). A computational approach to edge detection. *IEEE Transactions on Pattern Analysis and Machine Intelligence, 8,* 769–798.

Carlson, V. R. (1953). Satiation in a reversible perspective figure. *Journal of Experimental Psychology, 45,* 442–448.

Corbin, H. H. (1942). The perception and grouping of apparent motion in visual depth. *Archives of Psychology, No. 273.*

Cutting, J. E., & Proffitt, D. R. (1982). The minimum principle and the perception of absolute, common, and relative motions. *Cognitive Psychology, 14*(2), 211–246.

DiLorenzo, J. R., & Rock, I. (1982). The rod-and-frame effect as a function of the righting of the frame. *Journal of Experimental Psychology: Human Perception & Performance, 8*(4), 536–546.

Driver, J., & Baylis, G. (1996). Edge-assignment and figure-ground segmentation in short-term visual matching. *Cognitive Psychology, 31*(3), 248–306.

Duncker, K. (1937). Induced motion. In W. D. Ellis (Ed.), *A sourcebook of Gestalt psychology* (pp. 161–172). London: Routledge & Kegan Paul. (Original work published 1929)

Ebenholtz, S. M. (1977). Determinants of the rod-and-frame effect: The role of retinal size. *Perception & Psychophysics, 22*(6), 531–538.

Fendrich, R., & Mack, A. (1980). Anorthoscopic perception occurs with a retinally stabilized image. *Supplement in Investigative Ophthalmology and Vision Science, 19,* 166.

Garner, W. R. (1974). *The processing of information and structure.* Hillsdale, NJ: Erlbaum.

Garner, W. R., & Clement, D. E. (1963). Goodness of pattern and pattern uncertainty. *Journal of Verbal Learning & Verbal Behavior, 2*(5–6), 446–452.

Geisler, W. S., & Super, B. J. (2000). Perceptual organization of two-dimensional patterns. *Psychological Review, 107,* 677–708

Gerbino, W. (1994). Achromatic transparency. In A. L. Gilchrist (Ed.), *Lightness, brightness, and transparency* (pp. 215–255). Hillsdale, NJ: Erlbaum.

Girgus, J. J., Rock, I., & Egatz, R. (1977). The effect of knowledge of reversibility on the reversibility of ambiguous figures. *Perception & Psychophysics, 22*(6), 550–556.

Gregory, R. L. (1970). *The intelligent eye.* New York: McGraw-Hill.

Gregory, R. L. (1972). Cognitive contours. *Nature, 238,* 51–52.

Grossberg, S., & Mingolla, E. (1985). Neural dynamics of form perception: Boundary completion, illusory figures, and neon color spreading. *Psychological Review, 92*(2), 173–211.

Helmholtz, H. v. (1925). *Treatise on physiological optics.* New York: Dover. (Original work published 1867, Translator, J. P. C. Southall).

Hochberg, J. (1950). Figure-ground reversal as a function of visual satiation. *Journal of Experimental Psychology, 40,* 682–686.

Hochberg, J., & McAlister, E. (1953). A quantitative approach to figural "goodness." *Journal of Experimental Psychology, 46,* 361–364.

Hoffman, D. D., & Richards, W. A. (1984). Parts of recognition [Special issue]. *Cognition, 18*(1–3), 65–96.

Hopfield, J. J. (1982). Neural networks and physical systems with emergent collective computational abilities. *Proceedings of the National Academy of Sciences USA, 79*(8), 2554–2558.

Hubel, D. H., & Wiesel, T. N. (1962). Receptive fields, binocular interaction, and functional architecture of the cat's visual cortex. *Journal of Physiology (London), 160,* 106–154.

Johansson, G. (1950). *Configuration in event perception.* Uppsala, Sweden: Almqvist & Wiksell.

Julesz, B. (1981). Textons, the elements of texture perception, and their interactions. *Nature, 290*(5802), 91–97.

Kanizsa, G. (1955). Margini quasi-percettivi in campi con stimolazione omogenea. *Rivista di Psicologia, 49,* 7–30.

Kanizsa, G. (1979). *Organization in vision: Essays on Gestalt perception.* New York: Praeger.

Kanizsa, G., & Gerbino, W. (1976). Convexity and symmetry in figure-ground organization. In M. Henle (Ed.), *Vision and artifact.* New York: Springer. 25–32.

Kellman, P. J., & Cohen, M. H. (1984). Kinetic subjective contours. *Perception & Psychophysics, 35*(3), 237–244.

Kellman, P. J., & Loukides, M. G. (1987). An object perception approach to static and kinetic subjective contours. In S. Petry & G. E. Meyer (Eds.), *The perception of illusory contours* (pp. 151–164). New York: Springer.

Kellman, P. J., & Shipley, T. F. (1991). A theory of visual interpolation in object perception. *Cognitive Psychology, 23*(2), 141–221.

Kienker, P. K., Sejnowski, T. J., Hinton, G. E., & Schumacher, L. E. (1986). Separating figure from ground with a parallel network. *Perception, 15*(2), 197–216.

Kinchla, R. A., & Wolfe, J. M. (1979). The order of visual processing: "Top-down," "bottom-up," or "middle-out." *Perception & Psychophysics, 25*(3), 225–231.

Klymenko, V., & Weisstein, N. (1986). Spatial frequency differences can determine figure-ground organization. *Journal of Experimental Psychology: Human Perception & Performance, 12,* 324–330.

Koffka, K. (1935). *Principles of Gestalt psychology.* New York: Harcourt, Brace.

Köhler, W. (1940). *Dynamics in psychology.* New York: Liveright.

Köhler, W. (1950). Physical Gestalten. In W. D. Ellis (Ed.), *A sourcebook of Gestalt psychology* (pp. 17–54). New York: Humanities Press. (Original work published 1920)

Kopferman, H. (1930). Psychologishe Untersuchungen über die Wirkung zweidimensionaler korperlicher Gebilde. *Psychologische Forschung, 13,* 293–364.

Kubovy, M., & Gepshtein, S. (2000). Gestalt: From phenomena to laws. In K. Boyer & S. Sarker (Eds.), *Perceptual organization for artificial vision systems.* Dordrecht, NL: Kluwer. pp. 41–72.

Kubovy, M., & Holcombe, A. O. (1998). On the lawfulness of grouping by proximity. *Cognitive Psychology, 35*(1), 71–98.

Kubovy, M., & Wagemans, J. (1995). Grouping by proximity and multistability in dot lattices: A quantitative Gestalt theory. *Psychological Science, 6*(4), 225–234.

Lashley, K. S., Chow, K. L., & Semmes, J. (1951). An examination of the electrical field theory of cerebral integration. *Psychological Review, 58,* 123–136.

Leeuwenberg, E. L. J. (1971). A perceptual coding language for visual and auditory patterns. *American Journal of Psychology, 84*(3), 307–349.

Leeuwenberg, E. L. J. (1978). Quantification of certain visual pattern properties: Salience, transparency, and similarity. In E. L. J. Leeuwenberg. & H. F. J. M. Buffart (Eds.), *Formal theories of visual perception.* New York: Wiley (pp. 277–298).

Leung, T., & Malik, J. (1998). *Contour continuity in region-based image segmentation.* Paper presented at the Proceedings of the 5th European Conference on Computer Vision, Freiburg, Germany.

Lowe, D. G. (1985). *Perceptual organization and visual recognition.* Boston: Kluwer Academic.

Mach, E. (1959). *The analysis of sensations.* Chicago: Open Court. (Original work published 1914)

Malik, J., & Perona, P. (1990). Preattentive texture discrimination with early vision mechanisms. *Journal of the Optical Society of America A, 7*(5), 923–932.

Marcel, A. J. (1983). Conscious and unconscious perceptions: An approach to the relations between phenomenal experience and perceptual processes. *Cognitive Psychology, 15,* 238–300.

Marr, D. (1982). *Vision: A computational investigation into the human representation and processing of visual information*. San Francisco: Freeman.

Marr, D., & Hildreth, E. C. (1980). Theory of edge detection. *Proceedings of the Royal Society of London: Series B, 207*, 187–217.

Marr, D., & Nishihara, H. K. (1978). Representation and recognition of the spatial organization of three-dimensional shapes. *Proceedings of the Royal Society London, 200*, 269–294.

McClelland, J. L., & Johnston, J. C. (1977). The role of familiar units in perception of words and nonwords. *Perception and Psychophysics, 22*, 249–261.

McClelland, J. L., & Rumelhart, D. E. (1981). An interactive activation model of context effects in letter perception: I. An account of basic findings. *Psychological Review, 88*(5), 375–407.

Metelli, F. (1974). The perception of transparency. *Scientific American, 230*(4), 90–98.

Michotte, A., Thinès G., & Crabbé, G. (1964). Les compliments amodaux des structures perceptives. Publications U. Louvain, Louvain, Belgium.

Miller, J. (1981). Global precedence in attention and decision. *Journal of Experimental Psychology: Human Perception & Performance, 7*(6), 1161–1174.

Morgan, M. J., Findlay, J. M., & Watt, R. J. (1982). Aperture viewing: A review and a synthesis. *Quarterly Journal of Experimental Psychology: Human Experimental Psychology, 34*(2), 211–233.

Nakayama, K. & Shimojo, S. (1992). Experiencing and perceiving visual surfaces. *Science, 257*(5075), 1357–1363.

Nakayama, K., Shimojo, S., & Silverman, G. H. (1989). Stereoscopic depth: Its relation to image segmentation, grouping, and the recognition of occluded objects. *Perception, 18*, 55–68.

Navon, D. (1976). Irrelevance of figural identity for resolving ambiguities in apparent motion. *Journal of Experimental Psychology: Human Perception and Performance, 2*, 130–138.

Neisser, U. (1967). *Cognitive psychology*. Englewood Cliffs, NJ: Prentice-Hall.

Noton, D., & Stark, L. (1971). Scanpaths in eye movements during pattern perception. *Science, 171*(3968), 308–311.

Palmer, S. E. (1977). Hierarchical structure in perceptual representation. *Cognitive Psychology, 9*(4), 441–474.

Palmer, S. E. (1980). What makes triangles point: Local and global effects in configurations of ambiguous triangles. *Cognitive Psychology, 12*(3), 285–305.

Palmer, S. E. (1985). The role of symmetry in shape perception. *Acta Psychologica, 59*(1), 67–90.

Palmer, S. E. (1989). Reference frames in the perception of shape and orientation. In B. E. Shepp & S. Ballesteros (Eds.), *Object perception: Structure and process* (pp. 121–163). Hillsdale, NJ: Erlbaum.

Palmer, S. E. (1991). Goodness, Gestalt, groups, and Garner: Local symmetry subgroups as a theory of figural goodness. In G. R. Lockhead & J. R. Pomerantz (Eds.), *The perception of structure: Essays in honor of Wendell R. Garner* (pp. 23–39). Washington, DC: American Psychological Association.

Palmer, S. E. (1992). Common region: A new principle of perceptual grouping. *Cognitive Psychology, 24*(3), 436–447.

Palmer, S. E. (1999). *Vision science: Photons to phenomenology*. Cambridge: MIT Press.

Palmer, S. E. (in press-a). Perceptual grouping: It's later than you think. *Current Directions in Psychological Science*.

Palmer, S. E. (in press-b). Understanding perceptual organization and grouping. In R. Kimchi, M. Behrman, & C. Olson (Eds.), *Perceptual organization*. Hillsdale, NJ: Erlbaum.

Palmer, S. E., & Bucher, N. M. (1981). Configural effects in perceived pointing of ambiguous triangles. *Journal of Experimental Psychology: Human Perception & Performance, 7*(1), 88–114.

Palmer, S. E., & Beck, D. M. (in press). The repetition discrimination task: An objective method for studying perceptual grouping.

Palmer, S. E., & Kimchi, R. (1986). The information processing approach to cognition. In T. J. Knapp & L. C. Robertson (Eds.), *Approaches to Cognition: Contrasts and Controversies*. Hillsdale, NJ: Erlbaum.

Palmer, S. E., & Levitin, D. (in press). *Synchrony: A new principle of perceptual organization.* Manuscript in preparation.

Palmer, S. E., Neff, J., & Beck, D. (1996). Late influences on perceptual grouping: Amodal completion. *Psychonomic Bulletin & Review, 3*(1), 75–80.

Palmer, S. E., & Nelson, R. (2000). Late influences on perceptual grouping: Illusory contours. *Perception & Psychophysics, 62*(7), 1321–1331.

Palmer, S. E., & Rock, I. (1994a). On the nature and order of organizational processing: A reply to Peterson. *Psychonomic Bulletin & Review, 1,* 515–519.

Palmer, S. E., & Rock, I. (1994b). Rethinking perceptual organization: The role of uniform connectedness. *Psychonomic Bulletin & Review, 1*(1), 29–55.

Parks, T. E. (1965). Post-retinal visual storage. *American Journal of Psychology, 78,* 145–147.

Peterson, M. A. (1994). The proper treatment of uniform connectedness. *Psychological Bulletin & Review, 1,* 509–514.

Peterson, M. A., De Gelder, B., Rapcsak, S. Z., Gerhardstein, P. C., & Bachoud-Levi, A. C. (2000). Object memory effects on figure assignment: Conscious object perception is not necessary or sufficient. *Vision Science, 40,* 1549–1568.

Peterson, M. A., & Gibson, B. S. (1991). The initial identification of figure-ground relationships: Contributions from shape recognition processes. *Bulletin of the Psychonomic Society, 29*(3), 199–202.

Peterson, M. A., & Gibson, B. S. (1993). Shape recognition inputs to figure-ground organization in three-dimensional grounds. *Cognitive Psychology, 25,* 383–429.

Peterson, M. A., & Hochberg, J. (1983). Opposed-set measurement procedure: A quantitative analysis of the role of local cues and intention in form

perception. *Journal of Experimental Psychology: Human Perception & Performance, 9*(2), 183–193.

Pomerantz, J. R., & Kubovy, M. (1986). Theoretical approaches to perceptual organization: Simplicity and likelihood principles. In K. R. Boff, L. Kaufman, & J. P. Thomas (Eds.), *Handbook of perception and human performance: Vol. 2. Cognitive processes and performance* (pp. 1–46). New York: Wiley.

Pomerantz, J. R., Sager, L. C., & Stoever, R. J. (1977). Perception of wholes and of their component parts: Some configural superiority effects. *Journal of Experimental Psychology: Human Perception & Performance, 3*(3), 422–435.

Pritchard, R. M. (1958). Visual illusions viewed as stabilized retinal images. *Quarterly Journal of Experimental Psychology, 10,* 77–81.

Reed, S. K., & Johnsen, J. A. (1975). Detection of parts in patterns and images. *Memory & Cognition, 3*(5), 569–575.

Reicher, G. M. (1969). Perceptual recognition as a function of meaningfulness of stimulus material. *Journal of Experimental Psychology, 81*(2), 275–280.

Restle, F. (1979). Coding theory of the perception of motion configurations. *Psychological Review, 86,* 1–24.

Robertson, L. C., Lamb, M. R., & Knight, R. T. (1988). Effects of lesions of the temporal-parietal junction on perceptual and attentional processing in humans. *Journal of Neuroscience, 8,* 3757–3769.

Rock, I. (1973). *Orientation and form.* New York: Academic Press.

Rock, I. (1983). *The logic of perception.* Cambridge: MIT Press.

Rock, I. (1990). The frame of reference. In I. Rock (Ed.), *The legacy of Solomon Asch: Essays in cognition and social psychology* (pp. 243–268). Hillsdale: Erlbaum.

Rock, I., Auster, M., Shiffman, M., & Wheeler, D. (1980). Induced movement based on subtraction of motion from the inducing object. *Journal of Experimental Psychology: Human Perception & Performance, 6,* 391–403.

Rock, I., & Brosgole, L. (1964). Grouping based on phenomenal proximity. *Journal of Experimental Psychology, 67,* 531–538.

Rock, I., Gopnik, A., & Hall, S. (1994). Do young children reverse ambiguous figures? *Perception, 23*(6), 635–644.

Rock, I., & Mitchener, K. (1992). Further evidence of failure of reversal of ambiguous figures by uninformed subjects. *Perception, 21*(1), 39–45.

Rock, I., Nijhawan, R., Palmer, S., & Tudor, L. (1992). Grouping based on phenomenal similarity of achromatic color. *Perception, 21*(6), 779–789.

Rock, I., & Palmer, S. E. (1990). The legacy of Gestalt psychology. *Scientific American, 262* (December), 84–90.

Rubin, E. (1921). *Visuell wahrgenommene Figuren* [Visual perception of figures]. Copenhagen: Glydenalske.

Rumelhart, D. E., & McClelland, J. L. (1982). An interactive activation model of context effects in letter perception: II. The contextual enhancement effect and some tests and extensions of the model. *Psychological Review, 89*(1), 60–94.

Rumelhart, D. E., Smolensky, P., McClelland, J. L., & Hinton, G. E. (1986). Schemata and sequential thought processes in PDP models. In J. L. McClelland & D. E. Rumelhart (Eds.), *Parallel distributed processing: Explorations in the microstructure of cognition: Vol. 2. Psychological and biological models* (pp. 7–57). Cambridge: MIT Press.

Schumann, F. (1904). Beitrage zur Analyse der Gesichtswahrnehmungen. *Zeitschrift für Psychologie, 36,* 161–185.

Sekuler, A. B., & Palmer, S. E. (1992). Perception of partly occluded objects: A microgenetic analysis. *Journal of Experimental Psychology: General, 121*(1), 95–111.

Shannon, C. E. (1948). A mathematical theory of communication. *Bell System Technical Journal, 27,* 379–423.

Shannon, C. E., & Weaver, W. (1949). *The mathematical theory of communication.* Urbana: University of Illinois Press.

Shi, J., & Malik, J. (1997). *Normalized cuts and image segmentation.* Paper presented at the Proceedings of the IEEE Conference on Computation: Vision and Pattern Recognition, San Juan, Puerto Rico.

Simon, H. A. (1969). *The sciences of the artificial.* Cambridge: MIT Press.

Singh, M., Seyranian, G. D., & Hoffman, D. D. (1999). Parsing silhouettes: The short-cut rule. *Perception & Psychophysics, 61*(4), 636–660.

Sperry, R., & Miner, N. (1955). Pattern recognition following insertion of mica plates into the visual cortex. *Comparative and Physiological Psychology, 48,* 463–469.

Tse, P. U. (1999). Volume completion. *Cognitive Psychology, 39,* 37–68.

Van der Helm, P. A., & Leeuwenberg, E. L. (1991). Accessibility: A criterion for regularity and hierarchy in visual pattern codes. *Journal of Mathematical Psychology, 35*(2), 151–213.

Van Essen, D. C., & DeYoe, E. A. (1995). Concurrent processing in the primate visual cortex. In M. S. Gazzaniga (Ed.), *The cognitive neurosciences* (pp. 383–400). Cambridge: MIT Press.

Vecera, S. P., & O'Reilly, R. C. (1998). Figure-ground organization and object recognition processes. *Journal of Experimental Psychology: Human Perception and Performance, 24*(2), 441–462.

Vecera, S. P., Vogel, E. K., & Woodman, G. F. (in press). *Lower region: A new cue for figure-ground segregation.* Manuscript in preparation.

Wallach, H. (1959). The perception of motion. *Scientific American, 201,* 56–60.

Weisstein, N., & Harris, C. S. (1974). Visual detection of line segments: An object-superiority effect. *Science, 186*(4165), 752–755.

Wenderoth, P. M. (1974). The distinction between the rod-and-frame illusion and the rod-and-frame test. *Perception, 3*(2), 205–212.

Wertheimer, M. (1950). Untersuchungen zur Lehre von der Gestalt. *Psychology Forschung, 4,* 301–350. (Original work published 1923)

Wertheimer, M. (1950). Gestalt theory. In W. D. Ellis (Ed.), *A sourcebook of Gestalt psychology* (pp. 1–11). New York: Humanities Press. (Original work published 1924)

Weyl, H. (1952). *Symmetry*. Princeton: Princeton University Press.

Wiser, M. (1981). *The role of intrinsic axes in shape recognition*. Paper presented at the Third Annual Conference of the Cognitive Science Society, Berkeley, CA.

Woodworth, R. S. (1938). *Experimental psychology*. New York: Holt.

Zöllner, F. (1862). Über eine neue Art anorthoscopischer Zerrbilder. *Poggendorf's Annalen der Physik und Chemie, 117,* 477–484.

CHAPTER 6

Attention

STEVEN J. LUCK AND SHAUN P. VECERA

WHAT IS ATTENTION?

The term *attention* has been used in the title or abstract of over 40,000 journal articles, books, and book chapters over the past 30 years. This greatly exceeds the 8,300 works that have used the term *emotion,* and it almost equals the 48,000 works that have used the term *memory.* But what is attention? Perhaps the most commonly used definition was given by William James in his landmark monograph, *Principles of Psychology:*

> Everyone knows what attention is. It is the taking possession by the mind, in clear and vivid form, of one out of what seem several simultaneously possible objects or trains of thought. Focalization, concentration, of consciousness are of its essence. It implies withdrawal from some things in order to deal effectively with others. (James, 1890, pp. 381–382)

This is an excellent definition of attention, but it is limited because it defines attention in a unitary manner. In contrast, the term attention has multiple definitions in common usage (see, e.g., any dictionary definition of attention), and it is used in many different ways in the psychological literature (see, e.g., the 40,000+ articles, books, and chapters on attention written in the past 30 years). Moreover, it is natural to assume from a definition like this that there is a unitary psychological process that corresponds to the term

attention, but it seems unlikely that any complex psychological term in a natural language will map onto a single psychological process. Indeed, recent evidence indicates that multiple dissociable cognitive processes may all be related to the term *attention.* In this review, we first consider the different ways that the term attention is used and the different paradigms that have been used to study attention, and we then describe several specific mechanisms of attention that have been isolated over the past few decades.

Task-Defined Attention

People who study attention usually use the term *attention* to refer to a psychological process, but the term can also be used in a more descriptive manner. For example, consider the experiment shown in Figure 6.1A, in which a pigeon is reinforced for pecking a key when a red vertical bar or red horizontal bar is displayed and is not reinforced for pecking when a green vertical bar or a green horizontal bar is displayed. If the pigeon pecks when red is present and does not peck when red is absent, regardless of the orientation of the bar, then the pigeon is said to be attending to color and not to orientation. As a second example, consider a neuroimaging experiment in which subjects view arrays of dots and must indicate whether the dots are red or green in one

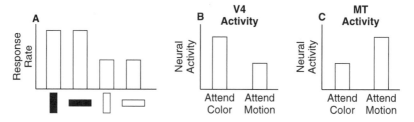

Figure 6.1   Examples of attention manipulations.
NOTE: (A) Pecking rates for a hypothetical experiment in which a pigeon is reinforced for pecking a key when a red bar is presented (indicated here by the filled bars), whether horizontal or vertical, and is not reinforced for pecking when a green bar is presented (indicated here by the open bars). (B) Neural activity levels in area V4 in a hypothetical experiment in which the subject makes color or motion discriminations. (C) Neural activity levels in area MT in a hypothetical experiment in which the subject makes color or motion discriminations.

condition and must indicate whether they are moving upward or downward in a different condition. If the subjects respond on the basis of color in the former condition and on the basis of motion in the latter condition, they are said to be attending to color in the former case and motion in the latter case.

In both of these examples, the concept of attention is intrinsic to the definition of the task. That is, if the subject correctly performs the task, then he or she is said to be attending to some stimuli and not to others, no matter what internal mechanisms are used to achieve correct task performance. We call this *task-defined attention* because the use of attention can be inferred solely on the basis of accurate performance of the task. More precisely, we define task-defined attention as responding on the basis of some stimulus values or dimensions rather than others, under experimental control.

The last phrase of this definition ("under experimental control") is important for two reasons. First, it requires a demonstration that the subject actually could respond on the basis of the ignored stimulus dimension. For example, if pigeons could not perceive orientation, then the first example experiment would not be a demonstration that the pigeons were attending to color and ignoring orientation. A

demonstration of attention therefore requires that subjects can attend to different dimensions in different conditions, as in the example of the neuroimaging experiment. A second important aspect of this definition is that it does not require that attention be under voluntary control, but allows the possibility of automatic control of attention. For example, if a sudden flash occurs in the periphery, this may automatically attract attention to a location, leading subjects to respond to information at that location rather than to information at other locations.

When attention is task-defined, any entity—whether human, animal, or machine—would be said to be using attention as long as it responded on the basis of the appropriate stimulus dimension according to the rules of the task. Thus, this use of the term *attention* is purely descriptive and does not have any implications for the *mechanisms* of attention. In fact, an exceedingly simple mechanism (composed of only a few neurons or a few transistors) would be sufficient to demonstrate this variety of attention.

Task-defined attention is often used in experiments that are focused on issues other than attention per se. In a typical memory experiment, for example, the experimenter might present subjects with a set of words and ask them to make either semantic judgments or letter-case judgments, and the effects of this attentional manipulation on subsequent recall or recognition would be used to draw conclusions about memory processes. Similarly, the neuroimaging example just described would use different attentional conditions to draw conclusions about the brain areas involved in color perception versus motion perception.

Occasionally, however, task-defined attention is confused with a mechanism of attention. For example, neuroimaging investigators sometimes interpret task-defined attention effects as reflecting *processes* of attention when they actually reflect the *consequences* of attention. As illustrated in panels B and C of Figure 6.1, area V4 might be more active when subjects attend to the color of the stimuli than when they attend to the direction of motion, and area MT might be more active when subjects attend to motion than when they attend to color; however, one would not want to conclude from such results that area V4 contains specific mechanisms for attending to color and that area MT contains specific mechanisms for attending to motion. It would be more parsimonious to conclude that area V4 plays a role in discriminating color and area MT plays a role in discriminating motion, and that these discriminative processes can be turned on or off by task instructions. Indeed, the changes in V4 and MT activity might reflect a mechanism that operates to modulate the flow of information at an earlier stage, such as V1. Thus, a task-controlled modulation of activity in a given brain area is not sufficient evidence for the operation of attention in that area. Claiming that area V4 contains specific mechanisms for attending to color implies that this area does more than just discriminate colors, and such a conclusion would not be warranted without further evidence (for a good example of further evidence, see Corbetta, Miezin, Dobmeyer, Shulman, & Petersen, 1990). Put yet another way, if any task-related change in neural activity is taken as evidence of an attention effect, then virtually any experimental effect is an attention effect, making the term attention so broad that it would be virtually meaningless.

Although task-defined attention clearly corresponds to the way the term *attention* is often used by both psychologists and the general public, it does not fit well with William James's classic definition of attention. In the sample neuroimaging experiment, for example, it is entirely possible that subjects in the attend-color condition could clearly see the motion as well as the color of the array, even though they based their responses solely on the color. That is, the subjects in this experiment are not "taking possession . . . in clear and vivid form" the color and not the motion of each array, and there is no "focalization, concentration, of consciousness." Thus, task-defined attention should be viewed as a useful experimental tool, but it should not be confused with the psychological *process* that we call attention.

Maintaining Attention

Although task-defined attention is conceptually simple and does not seem to require a sophisticated mechanism, there are many situations in which individuals fail to maintain this simple type of attention. For example, consider an experiment in which a child performs a *continuous performance task* in which red and green letters are presented sequentially, one every 2 s, and the child is asked to press a button whenever a red letter is presented, regardless of the identity of the letter. If the child indeed presses the button for each red letter and does not press for green letters, the child is said to be attending to red and ignoring green. This is another case of task-defined attention, because any entity that performed the task correctly would be said to be attending. Note, however, that the term *attention* in this experiment refers to a value along a dimension (red) rather than to the entire dimension (color), and we could just as easily say that the subjects in this experiment are attending to color and ignoring letter identity. Thus, task-defined attention can refer to dimensions or to values, and both are possible within a single experiment, which is a potential source of confusion.

Most children can perform the continuous performance task for at least a few seconds, but some children will start making errors or stop responding altogether after only a minute or two, and very few children can perform a task like this for more than 20 to 30 minutes. If a child starts making frequent errors on this task after only one minute, it would be tempting to make a diagnosis of attention-deficit disorder. That is, even though it may be trivial for this child to direct attention to red (or to color) momentarily, it is difficult for the child to maintain attention to the task for a long period of time, and this may indicate the presence of a cognitive deficit that will have important implications for real-world activities. Thus, even when attention is task-defined and a simple mechanism could be used to direct attention, the maintenance of this type of attention may be quite difficult.

It is crucial to make a distinction between the process of directing attention and the process of maintaining attention because these processes may be completely different. For example, stroke patients with parietal lesions may have difficulty directing attention to the contralesional side of space while having relatively little difficulty maintaining attention; in contrast, children with attention-deficit disorder may be able to direct attention normally but may be unable to maintain attention. In addition, deficits in maintaining attention may arise from systems that are not directly related to attention. As an analogy, consider a car that steers poorly: This could reflect a problem with the steering system per se, but it could

also reflect underinflated tires or problems with the electrical system. Similarly, an inability to maintain attention could result from an impairment in working memory that makes it impossible to maintain a representation of the task. Indeed, Cohen and his colleagues have proposed that schizophrenia involves impairments in working memory that lead to deficits in the continuous performance task (Cohen, Barch, Carter, & Servan-Schreiber, 1999). Thus, a failure to maintain attention does not indicate that the attention system itself is impaired.

Process-Oriented Attention

Until this point we have considered attention descriptively, and we now begin considering attention as a psychological process, which was William James's view of attention. In his definition, attention is described as an active process that focuses the mind on one of many possible sensory inputs or trains of thought, thus increasing the quality of the selected input, task, or train of thought. This definition of attention has two essential properties. First, attention is viewed as a process of selection among alternatives. Second, the purpose of selection is to improve the effectiveness of mental processes. In other words, we focus on a subset of the available inputs or tasks to speed processing and to avoid errors that would otherwise occur. Using more modern terminology, we can recast James's definition as "restricting cognitive processes so that they operate on a subset of the available information for the purpose of improving the speed or accuracy of the processes." We call this the *process-oriented* definition of attention.

According to this definition, attention is needed only when mental processes cannot operate at maximal efficiency because too many stimuli or too many tasks are present. For example, in the continuous performance paradigm described earlier, pressing a button when a red letter is presented and not pressing when a green letter is presented does not require significant attentional *processes*. Given that the stimuli are presented at a rate of one letter every two seconds, the processing of one letter should be completed before the onset of the next letter, and there would be no reason to focus sensory, memory, or decision processes on the red letters and exclude the green letters from these processes. Motor processes operate only when a red stimulus is perceived, and this could be construed as attention operating at the level of response systems. Indeed, that is why this paradigm qualifies as a case of task-defined attention.

However, it is not necessary to posit a separate attention process to explain performance of this task. For example, consider what would happen if we changed this *go/no-go* task into a *two-alternative forced-choice* (2AFC) task by requiring subjects to press one button for red letters and a different button for green letters. In the 2AFC version, subjects simply make different responses for different colors, and there is no sense in which they are attending to one color and not the other. The only difference between the 2AFC task and the go/no-go task is that subjects make no response to green letters in the go/no-go task; it is therefore unnecessary to postulate an additional attention mechanism for the go/no-go task. Thus, the go/no-go version is a case of task-defined attention (i.e., subjects were instructed to attend to the dimension of color and to respond when the color was red), but it is not an interesting case of process-oriented attention (i.e., no "focalization" or "concentration" on the red letters need be postulated, to use William James's terms).

Consider, in contrast, the visual search task shown in Figure 6.2. In this task, 20 red and green letters are presented simultaneously, and the subjects are instructed to indicate whether a red O is present. It seems plausi-

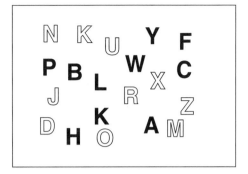

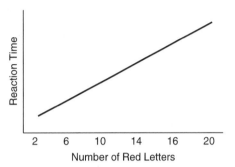

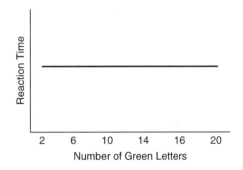

Figure 6.2 Examples of a visual search task in which subjects look for a red O among red letters (shown in black here) and green letters (shown in gray here).

NOTE: As the number of red letters in the stimulus array is increased, reaction times for detecting the target are increased. However, reaction time is independent of the number of green letters, indicating that subjects attend only to the red letters.

ble that the human visual system cannot efficiently process all 20 letters at the same time, and it would therefore be worthwhile for the subjects to focus their processing onto a subset of the letters. Indeed, Egeth, Virzi, and

Garbart (1984) conducted an experiment of this nature and found that subjects could focus attention on the red letters, ignoring the green letters. Consequently, response speed was influenced by the number of red letters in each array but was not affected by the number of green letters. That is, some mental processes were restricted to the red items, leading to more efficient detection of the target. This fits well with the process-oriented definition of attention because the computational role of attention in this task is to increase the speed and accuracy of cognitive processes that would otherwise be negatively influenced by an overload of inputs.

COMMON PARADIGMS IN ATTENTION RESEARCH

Now that we have made a distinction between task-defined attention and process-oriented attention, let us turn to the main paradigms used to study process-oriented attention. Attention paradigms can be categorized in several different ways; here we group them into cuing paradigms, search paradigms, filtering paradigms, and dual-task paradigms.

Cuing Paradigms

In *cuing paradigms* a stimulus or an instruction is used to lead subjects to expect a specific source of inputs, and then the processing of this source of inputs is compared with the processing of other inputs. These paradigms are useful for studying the processes involved in shifting attention to the cued source and for comparing the processing of attended versus unattended stimuli. The most common example of this is the spatial cuing paradigm, a typical example of which is shown in Figure 6.3A (for classic examples, see Averbach & Coriel, 1961; Eriksen & Hoffman, 1972; Posner, 1980). In the example shown in

Figure 6.3A, each trial begins with a cue at one of two locations, which indicates the likely location of a subsequent target stimulus. After a delay of a few hundred milliseconds, a target is presented, and the subject makes a simple detection response. On most trials a single location is cued, and the target appears at the cued location; this is called a *valid* trial because the cue validly indicates the location of the target. On other trials one location is cued, but the target appears at the other location; this is called an *invalid* trial. Many experiments also include *neutral* trials, in which both locations are cued, providing the subject with no information about the likely location of the subsequent target. Subjects are encouraged to respond as quickly as possible, and occasional no-target catch trials are included to prevent subjects from making anticipatory responses. As shown in Figure 6.3B, reaction times are typically fastest on valid trials, slowest on invalid trials, and intermediate on neutral trials, consistent with the idea that attention is focused on the cued location, leading to benefits at the cued location and costs at the uncued location (both relative to neutral trials).

In the spatial cuing paradigm—and in most studies of spatial attention—the goal is to assess covert shifts of attention (i.e., shifts of the "mind's eye") rather than overt shifts in eye position. If subjects actually fixate the cued location, then faster and more accurate processing would be expected simply on the basis of the greater density of photoreceptors in the fovea. Thus, although studies of overt shifts in gaze can be useful for studying the mechanisms that control orienting, they are not generally useful for studying the effects of attention. Most spatial cuing studies therefore either require subjects to maintain central fixation (verified with measurements of eye position) or present the target so quickly after the cue that subjects do not have time to program and execute an eye movement to

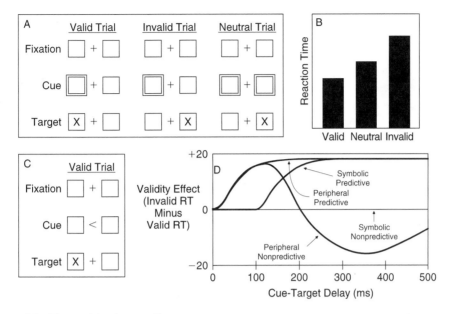

Figure 6.3   The spatial cuing paradigm.
NOTE: (A) Example of the spatial cuing paradigm with peripheral cues. Each trial begins with a fixation point, which is followed by a cue and then a target. (B) Typical pattern of cuing results. (C) Example of a symbolic cue. (D) Size of the validity effect—measured as the difference in reaction time between valid trials and invalid trials—as a function of the delay between cue onset and target onset.

the cued location (which typically requires at least 200 ms).

In most spatial cuing paradigms, valid trials are much more common than are invalid trials, and this motivates subjects to attend to the cued location. However, if the cue is a salient sensory event, such as the appearance of a new object, the cue may automatically attract attention, regardless of the subject's motivations (for a classic study of this, see Jonides, 1981; for more recent debates, see Folk, Remington, & Johnston, 1993; Yantis, 1993). Cues that appear at the to-be-attended location are typically called *peripheral cues,* and if they automatically attract attention they are sometimes called *exogenous cues.* The cues shown in Figure 6.3A are examples of peripheral cues. In contrast, the cue may be an arbitrary symbol indicating that attention should be directed toward some other location, such as an arrow pointing from the

fixation point toward the likely target location; cues of this nature do not automatically cause attention to be allocated toward the cued location and are called *central cues, symbolic cues,* or *endogenous cues.* The cues shown in Figure 6.3C are examples of symbolic cues.

In addition to being endogenous or exogenous, cues can also be *predictive,* meaning that the target appears more often at the cued location than at uncued locations, or *nonpredictive,* meaning that the target appears no more often at the cued location than at any of the uncued locations. In the example shown in Figure 6.3A, for example, the target might appear at the cued location on 80% of trials and at the uncued location on 20% of trials; this would be an example of a predictive cue. If the cue were nonpredictive, however, then the target would appear at either location—cued or uncued—with 50% probability. Predictive cues are used to encourage subjects to attend voluntarily to the cued location; because the target usually appears at the cued location, performance can be improved by focusing attention onto the cued location, which motivates subjects to attend to that location. Nonpredictive cues are typically used to study the automatic capture of attention by the cue. This is based on the assumption that because the cue does not reliably predict the location of the target, subjects will have no reason to attend to the cued location; thus, any allocation of attention to the cued location is presumed to be unintentional. This is a fairly weak inference, however, and additional evidence is necessary to reach a firm conclusion about automaticity (see Jonides, 1981).

Any given spatial cue can be classified as a combination of symbolic or peripheral and predictive or nonpredictive. The typical results obtained with each of these combinations are illustrated in Figure 6.3D, which plots the size of the cuing effect (the difference in reaction time, or RT, between valid and invalid trials) as a function of the delay between the cue and the target. First, *nonpredictive symbolic* cues do not produce an orienting of attention to the cued location; there is simply no motivation for subjects to shift attention to the cued location if that location is not particularly likely to contain a target. Second, *predictive symbolic* cues will elicit a long-lasting orienting of attention, but because it takes time to decode and interpret a symbolic cue, attention does not shift to the cued location until 100 ms to 200 ms after the onset of the cue. Third, *predictive peripheral* cues elicit a rapid and long-lasting orienting of attention; less time is necessary to decode these cues, so attention shifts within 50 ms to 100 ms after cue onset. Fourth, *nonpredictive peripheral* cues automatically produce a rapid and brief shift of attention; the shift is brief because subjects voluntarily stop attending to the cued location after a few hundred milliseconds. In fact,

the initial period of facilitation at the cued location is followed by a period of slowed reaction times for targets at the cued location. This slowing is called *inhibition of return* because it is thought to reflect a process that biases attention against returning to a recently attended location (Posner & Cohen, 1984). Inhibition of return typically begins approximately 200 ms after the onset of the cue, but Tassinari, Aglioti, Chelazzi, Peru, and Berlucchi (1994) showed that it is actually triggered by the offset of the cue. Collie, Maruff, Yucel, Danckert, and Currie (2000) also have argued that the initial facilitation and the subsequent inhibition actually reflect two separate, temporally overlapping processes, differing in their spatial distributions. Indeed, the inhibition may be primarily motor in nature (for an extensive discussion, see Taylor & Klein, 2000).

There are many other examples of cuing paradigms in addition to the spatial cuing paradigm. For example, Graham and her colleagues have investigated the extent to which sine wave gratings of a cued spatial frequency can be more accurately detected than can sine wave gratings of other spatial frequencies (Graham, 1989; Graham, Kramer, & Haber, 1985). Cuing can also be combined with other tasks, such as when subjects are told that a visual search target is more likely to be one color than another (Woodman & Luck, 1999).

Search Paradigms

In *search paradigms* subjects look for one or more target stimuli embedded in a set of nontarget stimuli, presented either simultaneously or sequentially. These tasks reflect the overload of information that is present in many real-word contexts, and they are particularly useful for studying how attention is used to eliminate interference from irrelevant stimuli. These tasks are also useful for studying how attention shifts among different sensory inputs. The most common variety of search task is the visual search task, in which multiple objects are presented in a simultaneous stimulus array and the subject indicates whether a target is present in the array (see, e.g., Figure 6.2). In most visual search experiments, the number of items in each search array (the *set size*) varies, and the experimenter examines the function relating reaction time to set size. In addition, this *search function* is often compared across different conditions in which the nature of the targets and nontargets is varied. As an example, Figure 6.4 shows an experiment that compared two conditions, one in which the target was

a triangle with a line and the nontarget items were simple triangles, and another in which the target was a simple triangle and the nontarget items were triangles with a line (Luck & Hillyard, 1990). Separate search functions were obtained for target-present and target-absent trials in these two conditions.

Each search function is characterized by a slope and an intercept. The slope is generally taken as a measure of the efficiency of the search process, whereas the intercept reflects primarily the duration of the processes that precede and follow the search processes. In some cases, such as the condition shown in Figure 6.4A, the slope is near zero. This

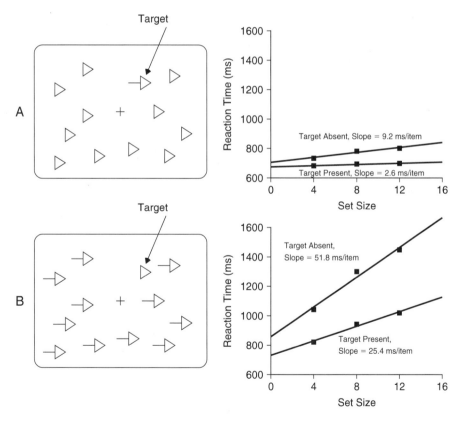

Figure 6.4   Visual search for feature presence and absence.
NOTE: (A) Example of a visual search task in which the target is defined by the presence of a simple feature and reaction times are not strongly influenced by the number of items in the stimulus array. (B) Example of a visual search task in which the target is defined by the absence of a feature and reaction times increase as a function of the number of items in the array.

typically indicates that a target-nontarget decision can be made independently, without inference, for each item in the array (an *unlimited-capacity parallel search*). In other cases, such as the condition shown in Figure 6.4B, RT increases steeply as the set size increases, and the slope is often greater for target-absent trials than for target-present trials. This pattern is typically taken to mean that the target-nontarget decision cannot be made independently for each item and that the discrimination of one item interferes with the discrimination of other items. Some investigators interpret results such as these as evidence for a *serial search* process, in which attention is shifted from item to item until the target is found (e.g., Treisman & Gelade, 1980). The steeper slope for nontarget trials can be explained by positing that subjects must search the entire array to ensure that the target is not present, whereas only half the items need to be searched on average to find the target, which would yield a slope that is twice as steep for target-absent trials than for target-present trials. Alternatively, subjects may simply search until they find the target or give up, which would also lead to greater slopes on target-absent trials (although the target-absent slopes may not be exactly twice as great as are the target-present slopes). Steep slopes may also be explained by a *limited-capacity parallel search* process, in which attention is directed to all of the items simultaneously and each item is processed more slowly at larger set sizes. As is discussed later, however, it may be possible to explain steep search slopes without appealing to attention.

In some search paradigms, the to-be-searched items are presented sequentially rather than simultaneously. For example, in the rapid serial visual presentation (RSVP) paradigm, a stream of objects is presented at fixation, one at a time, at a very rapid rate (e.g., 10/s). RSVP is discussed in greater detail in the section on dual-task paradigms.

Filtering Paradigms

In *filtering paradigms* attention is directed to one source of information, and the processing of other, unattended sources of information is assessed. These paradigms are useful for studying the processes involved in suppressing irrelevant inputs, including the stage or stages of processing at which irrelevant inputs are suppressed. The classic example of this is the *dichotic listening* task, in which subjects listen to two streams of auditory information, one in each ear, and are required to repeat, or shadow, everything they hear in one ear (for a classic example, see Cherry, 1953; see also a recent follow-up by Wood & Cowan, 1995a). For example, a different story might be read into each ear, and the subject would be required to repeat each word of the story in the left ear (in real time), ignoring the story in the right ear. In some experiments, the similarity between the two sources of information is varied, and the accuracy of shadowing performance is assessed to determine how well subjects can pay attention to one message and ignore the other. In other experiments, the goal is to determine how much of the ignored message is actually processed. For example, Moray (1959) found that subjects could report almost nothing from the unattended ear, except for the subject's own name (see also Wood & Cowan, 1995b).

The *Stroop* task (Stroop, 1935) is another classic example of a filtering paradigm. As illustrated in Figure 6.5A, subjects in this paradigm are presented with the names of colors drawn in different colors of ink. In some conditions they must report the word, and in other conditions they must report the color of the ink. When subjects are required to report the ink color, they are slowed if the ink color does not match the word. When they are required to report the word, however, there is little or no effect of whether the ink color matches or mismatches the word. These

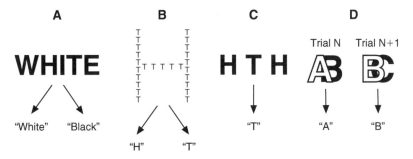

Figure 6.5   Examples of several common paradigms used to study attention.
NOTE: (A) The Stroop task. (B) The global-local task. (C) The Eriksen flankers paradigm. (D) The negative priming paradigm.

results are typically interpreted as evidence for fast and automatic processing of the word and slower or less automatic processing of the ink color. The Stroop task has been used extensively to assess the extent to which various populations, such as psychiatric patients and children, are able to suppress dominant responses (e.g., Cohen et al., 1999; Diamond & Taylor, 1996).

A similar asymmetric pattern of interference was reported by Navon (1977) for hierarchical stimuli in which a large shape is formed by a set of small shapes (this is often called the *global-local* paradigm). As an example, Figure 6.5B shows a global H formed by a set of local Ts. When subjects must report the local letters, reaction times are slowed if the global letter mismatches the local letters. When they report the global letter, however, there is typically little or no effect of whether the local letters match or mismatch the global letter. Navon concluded that this asymmetrical interference pattern reflects a precedence of global processing. That is, the global letter is identified before the local letters, making it possible for the global letter to interfere with the processing of the local letter but not vice versa. More recent experiments indicate that absolute size (or spatial frequency) may play an important role and that intermediate-size objects may be processed faster than either

very large or very small objects are (Lamb & Robertson, 1990). In general, the global-local paradigm has been useful for studying interactions between attentional processes and sensory features such as size and spatial frequency.

In the Stroop and global-local paradigms, different features of a single stimulus lead to interference, and other filtering paradigms examine interference between separate stimuli. For example, in the *flankers* task shown in Figure 6.5C, subjects are asked to report the name of a letter presented at fixation and to ignore flanking letters presented on either side of the target (for a review, see Eriksen, 1995). In this example, subjects would make a left-hand response when the central target is the letter T and a right-hand response when the central target is the letter H. On some trials the target and flankers are associated with the same response (e.g., a central T surrounded by flanker Ts), and on other trials the target and flankers are associated with different responses (e.g., a central T surrounded by flanker Hs). When the flanking letters and the target are associated with different responses, RTs are typically slowed compared to when the target and flankers are associated with the same response. However, if the flankers are sufficiently far from the target, this interference is reduced or eliminated (although this may reflect poorer perceptibility at greater eccentricities; see Egeth, 1977). The interfering effects of the flankers reflect the extent to which subjects fail to focus attention perfectly on the target and, consequently, process the flankers as well. Thus, this paradigm is useful for studying the extent to which attention spreads from the target location to nearby locations (see, e.g., LaBerge, 1983; LaBerge, Brown, Carter, & Bash, 1991; Pan & Eriksen, 1993).

Another common filtering paradigm is the *negative priming* paradigm (for a review, see Fox, 1995). In this paradigm two stimuli are presented on each trial, one of which is attended and requires a response. Figure 6.5D shows an example of this paradigm in which overlapping black and white letters are presented and the subject is required to say the name of each white letter. When an item that was unattended on one trial (e.g., the black B in Figure 6.5D) becomes the attended item on the next trial (e.g., the white B in Figure 6.5D), responses are slowed, indicating that the unattended letter was identified and remembered. This paradigm is often used to assess the extent to which ignoring a stimulus at one point in time can influence the processing of that stimulus at a later time.

Dual-Task Paradigms

In the paradigms just described, attention is distributed among several stimuli within a single task. However, attention also plays an important role in coordinating the performance of multiple tasks, and this is typically studied in *dual-task paradigms*. A dual-task paradigm is defined as one in which subjects perform two distinctly different tasks and the investigators assess the degree to which the two tasks interfere with each other. In the prototypical dual-task design, subjects are asked to perform two tasks simultaneously, and the amount of effort devoted to each

task is varied. For example, subjects might be asked to devote 10% of their attention to Task A and 90% to Task B in one condition, 50% to each task in a second condition, and 90% to Task A and 10% to Task B in a third condition. The results of such an experiment can be plotted in the form of an *performance operating characteristic* function (see Norman & Bobrow, 1976), in which performance on one task is plotted as a function of performance on the other task.

There are three common patterns of results, as illustrated in Figure 6.6. First, if the two tasks involve the same cognitive processes, paying more attention to one task and thereby increasing the level of performance on that task may lead to a reciprocal decrease in performance on the other task. This is illustrated in Figure 6.6A, which shows that increases in the level of Task A performance are perfectly matched by decreases in Task B performance. For example, if Task A requires the subject to retain in working memory a series of letters spoken in the left ear and Task B requires the subject to retain a series of letters spoken in the right ear, a nearly perfect tradeoff will occur between left-ear performance and right-ear performance. The second common pattern occurs when the two tasks are relatively independent, such that both can be performed simultaneously almost as well as either task can be performed alone (see Figure 6.6B). For example, a split-brain patient might be able to remember left-ear and right-ear information independently such that left-ear performance is independent of right-ear performance. The third common pattern, shown in Figure 6.6C, occurs when performance of one task is somewhat affected by performance of the second task but does not show a perfectly reciprocal relationship. For example, an experienced pianist may be able to carry on a conversation quite well while playing a moderately difficult piece of music but would show some impairment when

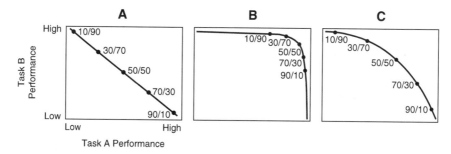

Figure 6.6   Three typical patterns of results in dual-task resource-sharing experiments.
NOTE: In each case, performance on Task B is plotted as a function of performance on Task A. Each data point is labeled to indicate the relative apportionment of attention between the tasks, with the first number indicating the percentage of attention devoted to Task A and the second number indicating the percentage of attention devoted to Task B (e.g., "10/90" means 10% of attention to Task A and 90% to Task B).

playing a difficult piece or engaging in a complex discussion.

Although it is possible to pit real-world tasks against each other in this manner, such tasks are usually so complex that it is difficult to determine exactly why two tasks interfere with each other. In addition, it may be possible to use time-sharing strategies to perform two closely related tasks simultaneously. For example, if both Task A and Task B use cognitive processes X and Y, Task A could engage process X while Task B engages process Y, and then the tasks and pro-

cesses could switch. To avoid these difficulties, many recent experiments have used simple tasks and have explicitly examined subjects' abilities to engage specific cognitive processes simultaneously versus sequentially. The two most common paradigms of this nature in the current literature are the *psychological refractory period* paradigm and the *attentional blink* paradigm, which are illustrated in Figure 6.7.

First used by Telford (1931), the psychological refractory period paradigm consists of two targets (labeled T1 and T2), each of

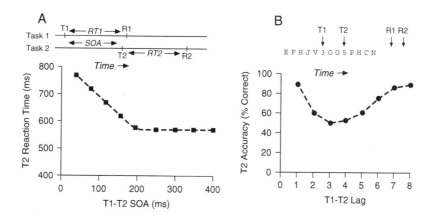

Figure 6.7   Typical experimental designs and results for the psychological refractory period (A) and the attentional blink paradigm (B).

which requires a speeded response (labeled R1 and R2). In addition, the delay between the onset of T1 and the onset of T2 (called the stimulus onset asynchrony, or SOA) is varied. For example, T1 might be a high or low pitch, leading to a response with the index or middle finger of the left hand, respectively, and T2 might be a red or green square, leading to a response with the index or middle finger of the right hand, respectively (see the review by Pashler, 1994). When the SOA between T1 and T2 is long, the processing of T1 is complete before the processing of T2 begins, and the subjects can respond rapidly to both T1 and T2. When the SOA is short, however, the processing of T1 is still occurring when T2 is presented, leading to delayed T2 responses. In most experiments, the subjects are encouraged to give priority to T1, leading to no effect of SOA on R1 and a progressive slowing of R2 as the SOA increases (as illustrated in Figure 6.7A). Remarkably, substantial slowing of R2 is present even when T1 and T2 are very simple, are presented in different sensory modalities, and require very different responses (e.g., a manual response and a vocal response).

The attentional blink paradigm was developed independently by Broadbent and Broadbent (1987) and by Weichselgartner and Sperling (1987), and interest in it increased dramatically after the paradigm was refined and named by Raymond, Shapiro, and Arnell (1992). This paradigm is conceptually similar to the psychological refractory period paradigm, but accuracy rather than RT is the main dependent variable. Most attentional blink experiments use an RSVP procedure. In the experiment shown in Figure 6.7B, for example, each trial consists of a sequence of 20 alphanumeric characters presented at a rate of 10 characters per second at the center of a computer screen. Two of the characters are digits, and the rest are letters, and the sub-

ject's task is to report the two digits at the end of the trial. These two digit targets are again labeled T1 arid T2, and the corresponding responses are labeled R1 and R2. Just as the SOA between T1 and T2 is varied in the psychological refractory period paradigm, the lag between T1 and T2 is varied in the attentional blink period. At long lags, the processing of T1 has been completed before T2 is presented, and accuracy is high for both T1 and T2. At short lags, however, T2 is presented before the processing of T1 is complete, leading to impaired accuracy for T2. This is called the attentional blink because it is similar to the effect of a T1-triggered eyeblink. It should be noted that in many experiments T2 accuracy is quite good when T2 is the first item after T1 (i.e., at lag 1), which appears to reflect a temporal imprecision that leads T1 and T2 to be processed together (Visser, Bischof, & Di Lollo, 1999).

WHY IS ATTENTION USEFUL?

Now that we have described several of the major paradigms currently used to study attention, we turn to the issue of why mechanisms of attention are necessary. In other words, what is the computational role of attention? The usual answer is that the human brain is often faced with a huge array of sensory stimuli that could be perceived and many tasks that could be performed, leading to information overload. It is assumed that we cannot fully process all incoming stimuli and perform all possible tasks, and attention is therefore necessary to focus the mind on a subset of stimuli and tasks. However, the brain is a massively parallel computational system, capable of processing a great deal of information simultaneously, so we still need an explanation of why the brain suffers from information overload and therefore requires attentional mechanisms. Here we consider several specific problems that attention might be used to solve: (a) resource limitations, (b) decision noise, (c) processing bottlenecks, (d) the binding problem, (e) internal noise, and (f) limited working memory capacity.

Resource Limitations

In the 1970s it became popular to use the concept of *resource allocation* to describe the role of attention (Kahneman, 1973). According to the resource-allocation framework, the human mind contains a limited pool of some unspecified cognitive processing resource, and this resource can be allocated flexibly among the various stimuli and tasks facing an individual. In the visual search task shown in Figure 6.2, for example, resources could be allocated to the red letters and not to the green letters, allowing the red letters to be processed faster or more accurately than would be possible if the resources were divided among both the red letters and the green letters. Moreover, as the number of red letters increases, RTs are slowed because the limited pool of resources is being divided among more red letters, slowing the processing of each letter. This framework can be applied also to the allocation of resources among multiple tasks. For example, an individual who is driving a car while speaking on a telephone might allocate more resources to driving if traffic is heavy, leaving fewer resources for speaking; more resources might later be allocated to speaking if the traffic becomes lighter and fewer resources are therefore needed for driving. In addition, this framework posits that the total amount of resources may vary as a function of the level of arousal.

The term *capacity* is used frequently in the context of resource-allocation theories. Just as an electrical generator has a limited output capacity, the pool of cognitive resources is assumed to have a limited capacity. Moreover, just as the capacity of a generator may be exceeded when many electricity users simultaneously demand a large amount of current, the capacity of the attentional system may be exceeded when multiple tasks must be performed at the same time.

The resource-allocation framework provides a convenient terminology for the process-oriented view of attention. For example, the same terminology can be used to describe both the allocation of resources among several stimuli and the allocation of resources among several tasks. This framework can also handle cases in which attention does not seem to be necessary for a given task by assuming that some tasks do not require limited resources, and this can apply to tasks that do not seem to require any attention (e.g., breathing) and to tasks that require progressively less attention over a period of training (e.g., typing). In addition, this framework can readily be extended to include multiple pools of resources (Navon & Gopher, 1979; Wickens, 1980). That is, tasks A and B might require one type of resource, whereas tasks C and D might require a different type of resource, leading to interference when A and B are performed together or when C and D are performed together, but not when A and C are performed together.

Although the resource-allocation framework provides a convenient terminology that is widely used by attention researchers, it has not proven to be a useful theory of the *mechanisms* of attention. There are two main limitations of the resource-allocation framework. First, the nature of the limited resource is usually unspecified, and the research program implied by this framework tends to merely specify the degree to which various pairs of tasks share a common resource without exploring the nature of the resource. Second, the resource-allocation framework tends to be circular and unfalsifiable. That is, if a pair of tasks cannot be performed simultaneously without impaired performance, it is concluded that they require the same limited resource, but if no impairment is observed, it is concluded that they do not require the same limited resource. Moreover, any complex set of results across multiple pairs of tasks can be explained by postulating the existence of addition resource pools. Consequently, there is no pattern of data that cannot be accommodated by this framework (for more details, see Allport, 1989; Navon, 1984).

Nonetheless, the concepts of capacity limitations and resource allocation still play an important descriptive role in attention research. Specifically, any cognitive process that operates less efficiently when the number of inputs is increased can be described as a limited-capacity process, and any attention mechanism that operates by restricting the inputs to such a process can be described as a resource-allocation mechanism. It may seem that all attention mechanisms are resource-allocation mechanisms, and many researchers have assumed that the sole purpose of attention is to guide the allocation of limited resources. That is, many researchers assume that "If the brain had infinite capacity for information processing, there would be little need for attentional mechanisms" (Mesulam, 1985, p. 125). As a result, many studies of attention seek to specify the nature of the limited-capacity processes and the role of attention in controlling these processes. However, the attention literature contains a long thread of studies arguing that attention is not used only for resource allocation and that many results that are attributed to limited resources can be explained without postulating resource limitations (see, e.g., Eckstein, 1998; Eriksen & Hoffman, 1974; Graham et al., 1985; Green, 1961; Lappin & Uttal, 1976; Palmer, Ames, & Lindsey, 1993; Palmer, Verghese, & Pavel, 2000; Shaw, 1984; Shiu & Pashler, 1994;

Sperling & Dosher, 1986). These theories use the concept of *decision noise* to explain the results that are usually attributed to limited resources.[1]

Decision Noise

The basic idea behind decision noise is very simple: In tasks that require multiple decisions, accuracy will necessarily decline as the number of the decisions increases simply because there are more opportunities to make errors. Here we discuss how this idea has been used to explain visual search and cuing results.

Decision Noise and Visual Search

Consider a variant of the search task shown in Figure 6.2 in which response accuracy is measured instead of response speed, and the stimuli are presented very briefly to bring accuracy away from ceiling. If accuracy were found to decrease as the number of red items increased but did not vary as a function of the number of green items, it would be tempting to conclude that some perceptual processing resource was being allocated to the red items and not to the green items. In addition, one might suppose that as the number of red items increases, each red item receives fewer resources and therefore has a lower probability of being correctly identified. However,

---

[1]The general concept of noise is discussed in detail in the chapter on signal detection theory (see Chap. 10, this volume). Briefly, the input to any psychological process can be divided into two components: signal and noise. The signal is the part of the input that provides relevant information to the process, and the noise is any residual input that is not relevant to the process. Consider, for example, a visual search task in which the target is the letter X and the distractors are the letters Y and Z. In this case, the target would be a signal and the distractors would be noise. Noise would also be present in each individual letter (e.g., small random variations in luminance across the letter), making each individual letter more difficult to perceive. Noise may arise also from internal sources, as in the case of random variations in the firing rates of the neurons that provide the input to some process.

Palmer and his colleagues have shown that this pattern of results can be explained by decision noise without invoking capacity limitations (Eckstein, Thomas, Palmer, & Shimozaki, 2000; Palmer, 1994; Palmer, 1998; Palmer et al., 1993; Palmer et al., 2000).

Palmer's logic is as follows: Because sensory representations always contain some noise, there is always a nonzero probability of misperceiving a given nontarget item as a target. Consequently, as the number of nontarget stimuli being discriminated increases, the probability of misperceiving at least one of them as a target increases, leading to decreased accuracy. That is, as the number of decisions increases, accuracy necessarily decreases. Importantly, this is true even for an *ideal observer* with no capacity limitations. Thus, the finding of decreased accuracy for larger set sizes does not necessarily imply the existence of capacity limitations. This conclusion applies to all visual search experiments (and to all experiments in which a single decision is made on the basis of varying numbers of inputs). In the context of our example experiment, we can further assume that decisions are made only for red letters and not for green letters. Consequently, the number of decisions will increase as the number of red letters increases but will not vary as a function of the number of green letters, and this explains why accuracy would decrease as the number of red letters increases but would not vary as a function of the number of green letters. The size of the increased error rate produced by an increased number of decisions will depend on the amount of noise (which influences the probability that any given decision will be incorrect), but Palmer and his colleagues have argued that this model is useful for explaining search results for any amount of noise, large or small (Palmer et al., 2000).

This logic can easily be extended to RT results, such as those shown in Figure 6.2, by invoking the idea of speed-accuracy trade-offs. The basic idea behind speed-accuracy tradeoffs is that subjects accumulate evidence about sensory inputs over time, and when the evidence reaches a certain level (called the *response criterion*), they respond. By spending more time accumulating evidence (i.e., using a higher response criterion), subjects can respond more accurately; by spending less time accumulating evidence (i.e., using a lower response criterion), subjects can make faster responses. Thus, changes in response criterion will influence the speed and accuracy of responses in a reciprocal manner. In the case of visual search with speeded responses, the experimenter insists that subjects maintain a uniformly high level of accuracy at all set sizes. To avoid making more errors at large set sizes, subjects will spend more time accumulating evidence when the set size is large, leading to longer RTs (for more details, see Palmer, 1998). Thus, the mere finding of increases in reaction times or error rates at larger set sizes is not sufficient to warrant a conclusion of capacity limitations.

Decision Noise in Spatial Cuing

The results of many spatial cuing experiments can also be explained without invoking capacity limitations. Before considering the role of decision noise, however, it is first necessary to describe the possible role of speed-accuracy tradeoffs when reaction time is the primary dependent variable. As an example, consider the cuing experiment shown in Figure 6.3A. When one location is cued, the target usually appears at that location, and subjects are therefore motivated to attend to the cued location, leading to faster RTs on valid trials than on invalid trials. The resource-allocation framework explains such results by positing that subjects allocate their perceptual processing resources to the cued location at the expense of the uncued location. However, these results can be explained by the use of different response criteria for the cued and the uncued

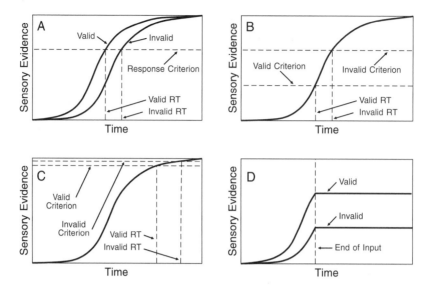

Figure 6.8 Hypothetical patterns of the relationships among cue validity, accumulation of sensory evidence, and reaction time in spatial cuing experiments.

locations (Shaw, 1984; Sperling & Dosher, 1986). This is illustrated in panels A–C of Figure 6.8, which show the accumulation of sensory information over time for valid and invalid trials in three cases. In all cases, information about the target is assumed to accumulate over time, and subjects respond when the amount of information reaches the response criterion.

Figure 6.8A illustrates the case in which perceptual processing resources are preferentially allocated to the cued location. This causes the rate of information accumulation to be greater on valid trials than on invalid trials. This in turn causes the response criterion to be reached earlier on valid trials than on invalid trials, resulting in faster RTs on valid trials than on invalid trials. Figure 6.8B illustrates how this same pattern of RT effects can result from changes in the response criterion. Because the subject knows that a target is more likely to appear at the cued location than at the uncued location, it would be sensible to use a lower response criterion at the cued location. In other words, subjects might

reasonably choose to respond as soon as they have the smallest hint of a target at the cued location on valid trials, but they may wait until they are sure that the target is present at the uncued location before responding on invalid trials. Thus, faster responses might be obtained on valid trials than on invalid trials even if sensory evidence accumulates at the same rate on valid and invalid trials.

If subjects respond on the basis of less sensory evidence on valid trials than on invalid trials, then a higher error rate should be obtained on valid trials (because of the logic of speed-accuracy tradeoffs, as discussed earlier). Many investigators therefore use choice RT tasks rather than the simple RT task shown in Figure 6.3A. For example, the target might be either an X or an O, and subjects would be required to press one button for X and another for O. Subjects are instructed to maintain high accuracy on both valid trials and invalid trials. Consequently, there is typically no significant difference in accuracy, whereas RTs are significantly shorter on valid trials than on invalid trials. This pattern of results is sometimes taken as evidence in favor of the resource-allocation model shown in Figure 6.8A and against the speed-accuracy trade-off model shown in Figure 6.8B. However, this conclusion relies on accepting the null hypothesis of no significant decrease in accuracy on valid trials, and this is especially problematic given that the accumulation of information typically follows a sigmoidal time course. As illustrated in Figure 6.8C, when subjects adopt a very high response criterion so that accuracy is high, a very small shift in the response criterion (corresponding to a small shift in accuracy) can yield a large change in RT. Thus, it is difficult to rule out the possibility of speed-accuracy tradeoffs unless accuracy is well below ceiling, which is rarely the case.

To eliminate speed-accuracy tradeoffs, several investigators have conducted cuing experiments using unspeeded responses, masked targets, and accuracy measures (e.g., Bashinski & Bacharach, 1980; Downing, 1988; Hawkins et al., 1990). As illustrated in Figure 6.8D, the logic of these experiments is as follows: If resources are allocated to the cued location and the rate of information acquisition is therefore greater on valid trials than on invalid trials, then the amount of

information acquired will be greater on valid trials than on invalid trials at the time that the mask terminates the accumulation of new sensory evidence. Consequently, accuracy will be greater on valid trials than on invalid trials.

Shiu and Pashler (1994) reviewed the previous studies of cuing that used this approach and found that many such experiments yielded no effect of cue validity on discrimination accuracy (e.g., Grindley & Townsend, 1968; Nazir, 1992). Some experiments did yield large cue validity effects (e.g., Henderson, 1991; Henderson & Macquistan, 1993), but these effects could be explained in terms of decision processes. Consider, for example, the cuing experiment illustrated in Figure 6.9A. In this experiment, there are four possible target locations, one of which is precued. The target is a 100-ms digit (4, 5, 6, or 7), and subjects are required to report which digit was presented. To bring accuracy away from ceiling, masks are presented at all four possible target locations.

If accuracy is found to be greater for valid trials than for invalid trials, the usual conclusion would be that subjects allocated processing resources to the cued location, increasing the rate of information acquisition at that location (as in Figure 6.8D). However, Shiu and

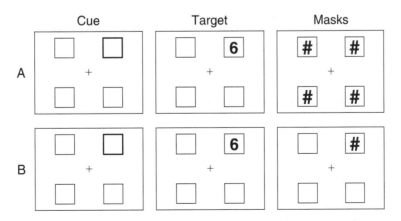

Figure 6.9 Cuing tasks.
NOTE: In (A) there is significant decision noise due to uncertainty about which location contains the target. In (B) there is no uncertainty about target location and therefore minimal decision noise.

Pashler (1994) proposed an alternative explanation. Because masks are presented at all four locations, they argued, the subjects do not know which location contains the target (which is quite plausible given typical timing parameters). Therefore, subjects must base their responses on a weighted combination of noise from the nontarget locations and signal-plus-noise from the target location, and the accuracy of the responses will therefore depend on the relative weight given to the information at the target and nontarget locations. Because subjects know that the target is more likely to occur at the cued location, they will place greater weight on the information at the cued location. On valid trials, this will lead to high accuracy because subjects will be placing greater weight on the target information presented at the cued location than on the noise presented at the uncued locations. On invalid trials, however, accuracy will be low because subjects will be placing greater weight on the noise presented at the cued location than on the target information presented at one of the uncued locations. According to this argument, the role of attention is to modulate the decision process so that sources of information that are likely to contain only noise receive a low weight and sources that are likely to contain the target receive a high weight. Importantly, this role of attention would be useful even in an ideal observer with no capacity limitations.

To provide evidence for this explanation, Shiu and Pashler (1994) conducted an experiment in which they compared a condition like that shown in Figure 6.9A with a condition like that shown in Figure 6.9B. In the former condition masks were presented at all four locations, and the subjects could not easily determine which location contained the target. In the latter condition only the target location was masked. Shiu and Pashler argued that if the cue is used to redirect perceptual processing resources to the cued location, then in both conditions performance should be better on valid trials than on invalid trials. However, if the cue simply provides the subject with information about which location to report, then no effect of cuing should be observed in the single-mask condition, because the location of the target is unambiguous in that condition. Consistent with this latter prediction, a very large effect of cue validity was observed in the multiple-mask condition, but no significant effect was observed in the single-mask condition. From these results, Shiu and Pashler concluded that cuing does not lead to a reallocation of perceptual processing resources, but instead influences decision processes.

Are Resources Dead?

From the studies of Palmer et al. (1993) and Shiu and Pashler (1994), it might be tempting to conclude that there is no evidence that visual search involves the use of limited-capacity processes or that spatial cues lead to a reallocation of limited resources. However, such a conclusion would be premature. First, Palmer (1994) has shown that there are cases of visual search—such as the search for a target defined by a spatial relationship among parts—that cannot be explained solely on the basis of decision noise. In addition, electrophysiological studies have provided evidence that difficult visual search tasks involve shifts of attention (Luck, Girelli, McDermott, & Ford, 1997; Woodman & Luck, 1999). Second, Shiu and Pashler (1994) did not argue against the general possibility of resource allocation, but instead argued against the more specific proposal that resource allocation plays a role when high-contrast alphanumeric stimuli are presented in isolation. Moreover, several recent studies have demonstrated that even when such stimuli are used, the single-mask condition used by Shiu and Pashler (1994) can yield significant cue validity effects under certain conditions (Cheal & Gregory, 1997; Henderson, 1996;

Luck, Hillyard, Mouloua, & Hawkins, 1996; Luck & Thomas, 1999). In addition, electrophysiological studies have shown that early sensory responses are larger for validly cued targets than for invalidly cued targets, consistent with a modulation of limited-capacity perceptual processes (Eimer, 1994; Luck et al., 1994; Mangun & Hillyard, 1991). Thus, there is good evidence that resource allocation plays a role in both visual search and spatial cuing tasks, though only under certain conditions (more will be said about the necessary conditions in later sections). In addition, there is abundant evidence that attention controls the allocation of resources in postperceptual processes, such as working memory. However, the studies of Palmer et al. (1993) and Shiu and Pashler (1994) have made it clear that caution must be exercised when one attempts to draw conclusions about resource allocation.

Information-Processing Bottlenecks

The first modern theory of attention (Broadbent, 1958) invoked the concept of *bottlenecks* to explain the role of attention in information processing. This idea developed in the context of communication systems. Imagine, for example, two cities connected by a single analog telephone line. Each city may have a great deal of information being communicated within its local telephone system, but only a single message can pass between the two cities at any given moment. This is analogous to a liquid flowing from one large container into another large container through a bottleneck, and a low-capacity stage interposed between two high-capacity stages is therefore called a bottleneck. In the psychological domain, one might imagine that the human mind has a very large sensory processing capacity and a very large long-term memory capacity, but that sensory information may have to pass through a system that can process only one sensory input at a time

(e.g., perceptual categorization) before reaching memory. This one-at-a-time system would be a bottleneck, and attentional processes would presumably be used to control which sensory signals were selected for transmission through this bottleneck. Note that the concept of an information-processing bottleneck does not just imply a general restriction on processing, but has come to imply one-at-a-time processing.

The concept of an immutable bottleneck at an early processing stage was abandoned fairly quickly, primarily because of overwhelming evidence that at least some information from unattended sources ultimately reaches higher stages of processing (see, e.g., Deutsch & Deutsch, 1963; Moray, 1959). However, there is substantial evidence for an attention-controlled bottleneck at a central stage of processing (i.e., a stage that follows perception but precedes response execution), although the nature and precise locus of this bottleneck are not yet entirely clear. In addition, this central bottleneck is primarily observed in dual-task paradigms that assess the allocation of attention among tasks instead of in filtering paradigms that assess the allocation of attention among stimuli.

The strongest evidence for a central bottleneck arises from the psychological refractory period paradigm (see Figure 6.7A). Specifically, the delayed responses observed for the second target (T2) at short T1-T2 SOAs does not reflect a slowing of the perception of T2 or the execution of the T2 response (R2), but instead appears to reflect a postponement of some interposed process rather than a concurrent sharing of resources between the tasks (for a review, see Pashler, 1994).

The evidence for postponement comes from experiments that use a *locus-of-cognitive-slack approach,* as shown in Figure 6.10. This approach involves manipulating a factor known to influence a particular stage of processing (e.g., manipulations of

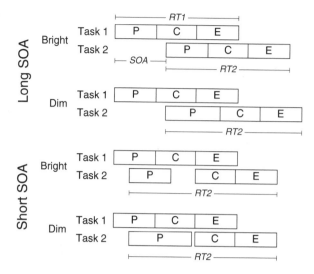

Figure 6.10 Diagram of the locus-of-slack concept in the psychological refractory period paradigm. NOTE: Each box represents a stage of processing, with P for perception, C for central processes, and E for response execution.

brightness or contrast influence the duration of perceptual processing). Figure 6.10 shows the sequence of perceptual (P), central (C), and response execution (E) processes for Task 1 and Task 2 at long and short T1-T2 SOAs and for dim and bright T1 and T2 stimuli. This figure reflects the hypothesis that central processes can operate on only one task at a time, such that central processing of Task 2 is postponed while central processes are occupied by Task 1. In contrast, perceptual processes and response execution processes are hypothesized to operate on both tasks simultaneously.

To understand the logic behind the locus-of-cognitive-slack approach, first consider the bright stimulus conditions. At the long SOA, the central processing of T1 is complete before the central processing of T2 begins, so RT2 is not delayed. At the short SOA, in contrast, the central processing of T1 is still occurring when the perceptual processing of T2 is completed, leading to a period of time during which no T2 processing occurs. Once the central processing of T1 is completed, the central processing of T2 can begin. The period between the end of perceptual processing and

the beginning of central processing for T2 is called a slack period.

Now consider the dim stimulus conditions. When T2 is dimmed and the SOA is long, perceptual processing is prolonged by the dimming, and every millisecond of delayed perceptual processing leads to a millisecond of delay in the onset of each subsequent stage. Thus, RT2 increases by exactly the amount of time that perceptual processing is prolonged. In the short-SOA condition, however, the increased duration of perceptual processing is absorbed into the slack period rather than being wholly propagated to the subsequent stages. Indeed, if the slack period is long enough to accommodate the entire increase in perceptual processing time, central processes and response execution processes will not be delayed at all. As a result, dimming T2 should have a large effect on RT2 at long SOAs, but should have a smaller effect on RT2 at short SOAs. This is exactly the pattern of results that have been obtained in several experiments (see, e.g., McCann & Johnston, 1992; Pashler & Johnston, 1989). In contrast, manipulations of the duration of central processes or response execution processes typically lead to the same delay in RT2 at all SOAs, indicating that these processes follow the slack period (see Pashler, 1994). The overall pattern of results is therefore consistent with a true bottleneck between perceptual processes and central processes (for a contrasting viewpoint, see Meyer & Kieras, 1997; Schumacher et al., 2001).

What, exactly, is the nature of the central process that is postponed in the psychological refractory period paradigm? Pashler and his colleagues have argued that *response selection*—the process of mapping the perceptual representation of T2 onto the appropriate response—is the postponed process (see Pashler, 1994; see also Pashler & Johnston, 1988, for a discussion of other central processes that may be postponed). This conclusion receives support from RT studies based on the locus-of-cognitive-slack approach and also from event-related potential (ERP) studies showing that ERP components that precede response selection are not delayed (Luck, 1998), whereas components that follow response selection are delayed (Osman & Moore, 1993).

However, multiple processes may exhibit bottleneck-like properties. First, there is evidence that response initiation is also postponed at short SOAs (De Jong, 1993; Ivry, Franz, Kingstone, & Johnston, 1998). Second, several studies using a hybrid of the psychological refractory period paradigm and the attentional blink paradigm indicate that making a speeded response to T1 causes a reduction in accuracy for T2, even when the T2 response is unspeeded (e.g., Jolicoeur, 1998, 1999a, 1999b). Because delays in response selection for T2 cannot plausibly underlie a decline in T2 accuracy, some earlier process is implicated by this result. However, it is important not to confuse *stages* with *processes*. That is, some bottleneck process may be used at the stage of response selection as well as at earlier stages. For example, the process of working memory access may be necessary during response selection, and this process has also been implicated as a source of errors in the attentional blink task (discussed later). Thus, when subjects make a speeded response to T1, the processes that underlie response selection for T1 may be unavailable for encoding T2 into working memory, leading to errors in the T2 response (for an extended discussion, see Luck & Vogel, 2001).

The Binding Problem

The brain represents information by means of the pattern of activation over large numbers of neurons. This can be a very efficient strategy but it may lead to problems when multiple items are represented simultaneously. Specifically, when multiple items are simultaneously active, how does the brain know which neurons correspond to each representation? This is called the *binding problem,* and it is pervasive in neural coding. A specific example is given in Figure 6.11, which shows a set

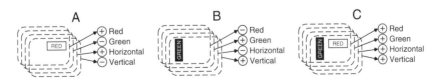

Figure 6.11   Example of the binding problem in area V4 of visual cortex.
NOTE: Each circle represents a neuron, and the regions indicated by the broken lines represent the receptive fields of the neurons. The + symbol indicates that the neuron is active, and the − symbol indicates that the neuron is inactive.

of neurons in area V4, an intermediate visual processing area in the occipital lobe. These four neurons have essentially the same receptive field (i.e., they all respond to stimuli in the same part of space), and each neuron is activated by a different feature. When a red horizontal bar is presented alone in the receptive field (Figure 6.11A), the red-selective and horizontal-selective neurons are active (indicated by the + symbol), and the green-selective and vertical-selective neurons are inactive (indicated by the − symbol). Similarly, a green vertical bar is represented by activity in the green and vertical neurons and no activity in the red and horizontal neurons. (Figure 6.11B). The binding problem arises when both stimuli are presented simultaneously (Figure 6.11C). This leads to activity in all four neurons, but because there is no means to specify which features belong together, the neural activity could indicate a red vertical bar and a green horizontal bar or a red horizontal bar and a green vertical bar (for more details, see Luck, Girelli, et al., 1997; Treisman, 1996). One possible solution to this problem would be neurons that code combinations of features, but this approach quickly leads to a combinatorial explosion in the number of neurons needed to code all possible higher-order combinations (Feldman, 1985).

Several solutions to the binding problem have been proposed (e.g., Luck, Girelli, et al., 1997; Mozer, 1991; Singer & Gray, 1995), but Treisman's feature integration theory (Treisman, 1988; Treisman & Sato, 1990; Treisman & Schmidt, 1982; Treisman & Gelade, 1980) is the best known. This theory proposes that the role of attention in visual perception is to bind features together into objects. The focusing of attention onto an object has several interrelated consequences for the features of the attended object; specifically, those features (a) become the only effective inputs to the receptive fields of the neurons, (b) become bound together, and

(c) can be localized. Without attention, in contrast, features may be miscombined and mislocalized.

Treisman and her colleagues have provided several pieces of evidence in support of this theory. For example, when attention is distracted by a second task, subjects sometimes miscombine features from different objects (i.e., they report *illusory conjunctions*). In addition, subjects can accurately report the identity of a feature even when they cannot accurately report its location, but they cannot accurately report the identity of a multifeature object unless they can also report its location. Moreover, visual search experiments showed that subjects can detect simple features in parallel, leading to near-zero search slopes, but search slopes are steep for targets defined by combinations of features, at least under some conditions (for an extensive review, see Wolfe, 1994).

Evidence supporting feature integration theory has also been obtained from studies of neurological patients with parietal damage and concomitant deficits in attention. For example, subjects with unilateral parietal damage exhibit impaired search in the contralesional field for conjunction targets, but not for feature targets (Eglin, Robertson, & Knight, 1989). These patients also exhibit elevated rates of illusory conjunctions in the impaired field (Cohen & Rafal, 1991). However, the most striking evidence has been obtained from a rare patient with bilateral parietal damage and bilateral attentional deficits (Robertson, Treisman, Friedman-Hill, & Grabowecky, 1997). When presented with multiple objects, this patient is able to accurately report which features are present, but he is at chance when asked which features are parts of the same object. He can therefore perform search tasks relatively normally when the target is defined by a simple feature, but he fails completely when asked to search for conjunctively defined targets. Thus, in the absence of attention the visual system perceives the world as a set of disconnected features, and this supports the hypothesis that one function of attention is to bind object features together.

Electrophysiological studies in humans and monkeys are also consistent with the general proposal that attention solves the binding problem by restricting processing to a subset of the input array. In single-cell recordings from macaque visual cortex during visual search tasks, Chelazzi and his colleagues found that neurons coding nontarget stimuli become suppressed approximately 175 ms after the onset of the search array, such that only the target-selective neurons remain responsive (Chelazzi, Duncan, Miller, & Desimone, 1998; Chelazzi, Miller, Duncan, & Desimone, 1993). This effect was largest under the conditions that would be expected to emphasize the need to localize and bind the features of the target such as (a) when multiple stimuli are present inside the receptive field, (b) when the target is a complex combination of form and color rather than a simple colored square, and (c) when the target must be localized so that an eye movement can be made to it. In humans, there is an ERP component labeled *N2pc* (negative component 2, posterior contralateral) that appears to reflect the same attentional process as is observed in the monkey recordings, and this component is larger (a) when the target is surrounded by nearby distractors, (b) when the target is defined by a conjunction rather than a simple feature, and (c) when the target must be localized so that an eye movement can be made to it (Luck, Girelli, et al., 1997). Moreover, this component is lateralized to the hemisphere contralateral to the attended object, and it has been shown to shift rapidly between the left and right hemispheres as attention shifts between the left and right hemifields, consistent with a serial search process (Woodman & Luck, 1999). When combined with the behavioral results from normal and neuro-logical subjects, these electrophysiological results provide strong evidence that attention plays an important role in solving the binding problem.

Internal Noise

Although some attention effects are present primarily under conditions that would tend to emphasize the binding problem, others are present under conditions that would not seem to involve binding, such as the detection of simple features (Luck et al., 1994; Prinzmetal, Presti, & Posner, 1986). Some of these attention effects appear to take the form of a simple amplification of signals from the attended location (for a review, see Hillyard, Vogel, & Luck, 1998). However, it would seem pointless merely to increase the gain of an input source, because this would presumably increase both the signal and the noise, yielding no net improvement in perceptibility. Hawkins et al. (1990) provided a solution to this conundrum by noting that the brain faces two sources of noise: noise in the input (external noise) and noise in the brain (internal noise). Consequently, increasing the gain of a sensory input source would increase the size of the signal and the associated external noise but would not increase the internal noise, thus yielding an overall increase in the signal-to-noise ratio.

Lu and Dosher (1998) provided a formal model of this role of attention and developed an elegant approach to testing this hypothesis. They reasoned that if attention operates like a sensory amplifier, then attention should greatly improve target detection performance when there is very little noise in the sensory input and performance is limited by internal noise. In contrast, attention should have little or no effect when the sensory input is very noisy and performance is primarily limited by this external noise. As an analogy, imagine that you are listening to a CD-quality recording on a noisy subway; by turning up the volume, you will be much better able to hear the music clearly. In contrast, imagine that you are listening to an old, low-quality tape recording in a quiet room; turning up the volume will not help very much because it will increase the noise as well as the music. Similarly, an attentional volume control should be useful primarily when the sensory input has relatively little noise. Consistent with this reasoning, Lu and Dosher found that attention influenced perceptual quality primarily for low-noise signals. Thus, one role of attention is to improve the overall signal-to-noise ratio of perception by increasing the relative strength of the sensory input relative to internal neural noise.

Limited Working Memory Capacity

Although the resource-allocation approach to attention has been much maligned, there is one specific cognitive resource that is widely regarded as being highly limited in capacity and controlled by attention—namely, working memory. Working memory is an active representation of information that can be manipulated for the purposes of complex cognitive tasks such as following a map or comprehending a sentence. The most influential model of working memory posits several independent storage systems, each with a very limited capacity, and a central executive that controls and manipulates the information in the storage systems (Baddeley, 1986; Baddeley & Hitch, 1974). Each storage system appears to have a capacity of only about three to four items (Cowan, 2001; Vogel, Woodman, & Luck, 2001), and this small capacity places significant constraints on a variety of cognitive tasks (see, e.g., Hummel & Holyoak, 1997; Just & Carpenter, 1992). It is therefore reasonable to suppose that attentional mechanisms would be used to control the transfer of information into working memory, thus making the best use of this highly limited resource.

The first well-known studies that used attention to control the access of perceptual representations to working memory are the classic iconic memory studies of Sperling (1960) and Averbach and Coriel (1961). In the study of Averbach and Coriel, subjects were presented with arrays of 10 letters—exceeding the storage capacity of working memory—and a spatial cue was used to indicate which letter to report. If the cue was presented before the onset of the letter array, subjects were able to report the identity of the letter with near-perfect accuracy. Performance continued to be excellent when the cue was simultaneous with the array and even when it followed the array by 50 ms to 100 ms, consistent with the idea that attentional processes were used to transfer persisting sensory representations into working memory. As the delay increased, performance declined, and the results indicated that the sensory representation faded over the course of several hundred milliseconds.

Duncan and Humphreys (1989) extended this idea to explain the results of visual search experiments. According to their *attentional engagement* theory, all visual inputs are fully identified in parallel and without capacity limitations, and the finding of steep search slopes for some tasks and not for others can be explained by the nature of the process that transfers perceptual representations into visual working memory (they actually used the term *visual short-term memory,* but this appears to be the same concept as visual working memory). Specifically, they proposed that subjects form a representation of the target (called a *search template*) and that the probability that a perceptual representation will be transferred into visual working memory is a function of the similarity between the perceptual representation and the search template. In addition, they proposed that perceptual grouping processes are used to link similar items together and that grouped items can be entered into visual working memory together.

This model predicts that search will be inefficient when the target is similar to the distractors, because both will match the search template fairly closely, and as a result distractors will often be transferred into visual working memory before the target is. This model also predicts that search will be more efficient when the distractors are similar to each other than when they are heterogeneous, because similar distractors can be linked together by gestalt grouping processes and rejected as a group. This model therefore predicts that search will be efficient when the target contains a feature that is absent from a homogeneous set of distractors, which is the prototypical case of feature-based search. This model also predicts that search will be less efficient for conjunctions, because the target is similar to each of the distractors along at least one dimension and because the distractors are heterogeneous. Thus, the attentional engagement theory can explain many of the results that have been taken as evidence for feature integration theory, even though it posits no special role for attention in binding features together.

The relative merits of these two theories have been argued extensively, and different behavioral experiments appear to favor different theories (for a debate, see Duncan & Humphreys, 1992; Treisman, 1991, 1992). As discussed earlier, however, feature integration theory also is supported by significant neuropsychological and electrophysiological research. Moreover, a recent study indicates that visual search does not involve the transfer of perceptual information into visual working memory because the efficiency of visual search is not impaired when visual working memory is filled by a secondary task (Woodman, Vogel, & Luck, 2001).

A MULTIPLICITY OF ATTENTION MECHANISMS

The preceding section considered six problems that attention might be used to solve, and it reviewed evidence that attention is actually used to solve each of these six problems. To summarize, the existing evidence indicates that (a) attended stimuli (and tasks) receive more resources; (b) attended stimuli are given greater weight in noisy decision processes; (c) attended stimuli receive preferential access to bottleneck processes; (d) the features of attended stimuli are bound together, whereas the features of unattended stimuli are free-floating; (e) attended stimuli are processed at a higher gain than are ignored stimuli; and (f) attended stimuli (and tasks) receive preferential access to working memory.

A great many studies in the attention literature are attempts to demonstrate that *one* of these six effects of attention effects is *the* effect of attention (or that a single mechanism can explain all the effects of attention). However, it seems much more likely that the term *attention* applies to many separable processes, each of which operates within a different cognitive subsystem and in a manner that reflects the representational structure and processing demands of that cognitive subsystem. In other words, all six of the possible attention effects described in the previous section are true effects of attention, but they may be effects of separate mechanisms that are all given the same label of *attention.*

Textbook writers seem to have drawn this same conclusion. For example, one cognitive psychology textbook states that "Human attention appears to be accomplished through overlapping but partially independent subsystems that operate on different types and levels of information" (Medin & Ross, 1996, p. 112). However, this point is often lost on attention researchers, who tend to think that various properties that attention might have are mutually exclusive. For example, Treisman has argued that attention is not necessary for the detection of simple features (Treisman, 1988), and this claim was challenged by a study showing that a significant attentional blink can be observed even when T2 is a simple feature target (Joseph, Chun, & Nakayama, 1997). However, it is entirely possible that feature detection can occur without attention at the level of perception (as emphasized in visual search tasks), but that attention is equally necessary to transfer feature and conjunction targets into working memory (which appears to be the key process in attentional blink tasks).

In the remainder of this section, we describe the evidence supporting this multiple-attention-systems viewpoint. In particular, we describe how this viewpoint helps to solve a longstanding debate about whether attention operates at the level of perception or whether attention operates only after perception is complete. It is now clear that attention operates at both perceptual and postperceptual stages of processing, depending on the nature of the stimuli and task. Moreover, recent evidence indicates that the properties of attention are different at perceptual and postperceptual stages, which in turn indicates that these varieties of attention are truly separable.

The Locus-of-Selection Debate

Most theories of attention are either *early-selection* theories, positing that attention operates at an early stage to protect sensory processes from being overloaded, or *late-selection* theories, positing that attention operates after perception is complete to protect higher-level processes, such as working memory, from being overloaded (for classic examples, see Broadbent, 1958; Deutsch & Deutsch, 1963; Norman, 1968; Treisman, 1964). The essential difference between these

classes of theories is whether attention influences the perception of stimuli. Although it might seem that it should be easy to differentiate between two classes of theories that differ in such a significant and well-defined way, almost any effect of attention on behavior that can be explained by one class of theories can also be explained by the other.

For example, the classic evidence for late selection comes from dichotic listening experiments in which subjects are instructed to shadow information presented in one ear and ignore information in the other ear; subjects are typically unable to remember information presented to the unattended ear, but a subject can detect and remember his or her own name (Moray, 1959). Late-selection theorists argue that this result indicates that selection operates after perception is complete because the semantic content of an unattended message can influence whether it is remembered. How would this be possible, they ask, if unattended stimuli were not identified to the point of semantic access? However, early-selection theorists explain this result by noting that people have lower sensory detection thresholds for familiar stimuli such as one's own name. As a result, a partial sensory attenuation of unattended stimuli would lead to poor performance for most sensory inputs but not for one's own name.

Over time, it became clear that attention does sometimes operates at a late, postperceptual stage. For example, the finding that a cue can influence memory performance even when it appears slightly after the offset of a stimulus array (Averbach & Coriel, 1961; Sperling, 1960) seems difficult to reconcile with early selection. That is, it seems unlikely that a cue could improve the perception of a stimulus that is no longer visible. As a result, research began to focus on the question of whether attention might operate at early stages as well as at late stages. This question was difficult to answer primarily because stimuli must pass through both early and late stages to influence behavioral responses, making it difficult to isolate the locus of selection on the basis of behavioral response data.

The Search for Early Selection

A few behavioral studies have implicated an early locus of selection (e.g., Pashler, 1984; Yantis & Johnston, 1990), but the most convincing evidence for early selection has been obtained from electrophysiological recordings in humans and in monkeys. Electrophysiological measures are advantageous for addressing the locus-of-selection issue because they provide a continuous measure of processing between a stimulus and a response, making it possible to determine the precise time at which the processing of attended and ignored stimuli differs.

Consider, for example, the experiment illustrated in Figure 6.12A. While maintaining fixation on the central cross, subjects attend to the left visual field in some trial blocks and to the right visual field in others. Subjects try to detect occasional target stimuli at the at-tended location, embedded in a rapid series of left and right nontarget stimuli. The ERP response is found to be larger for attended-location stimuli than for unattended-location stimuli, and in many studies this effect begins within 100 ms of stimulus onset (see the review by Mangun, 1995). Sensory processing has only reached intermediate stages at this time, so this early effect provides clear support for early selection (for a more detailed analysis of the ERP evidence for early selection, see Hillyard et al., 1998).

Even more precise measurements of attentional modulations of sensory processing have been obtained in single-cell recordings from macaque monkeys in the intermediate visual processing area V4 (Luck, Chelazzi, Hillyard, & Desimone, 1997). As illustrated in Figure 6.12B, attended-location stimuli elicit greater neural firing rates in area V4, and this effect begins at 60 ms poststimulus, which is the onset time of stimulus-evoked activity in this area. Thus, attention modulates the initial feedforward volley of sensory information in extrastriate areas of visual cortex, at least under some conditions.

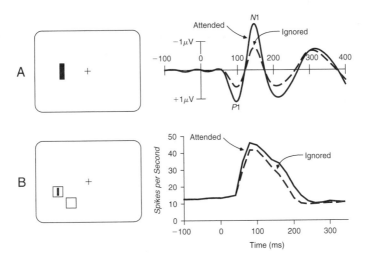

Figure 6.12 Electrophysiological studies of spatial attention.
NOTE: (A) Typical event-related potential paradigm and results for studying the influence of attention on sensory processes. (B) Stimuli and results from a study in which the effects of attention were measured in area V4 (Luck, Chelazzi, et al., 1997).

Although attention can modulate perceptual processes under some conditions, in other conditions attention appears to have no effect on perceptual processes but to have a profound effect on postperceptual processes. For example, ERP recordings in the attentional blink paradigm show no suppression of sensory ERP responses during the period of the attentional blink, although working memory related ERP responses are completely suppressed during the attentional blink period (Vogel, Luck, & Shapiro, 1998).

Perceptual Load and Interference

What are the conditions that cause attention to operate at an early versus a late stage? Lavie argued that the key variable is the amount of *perceptual load* imposed by the stimuli and task (Lavie, 1995, 1997; see also an early discussion of this issue by Treisman, 1969). If perceptual systems are not overloaded, Lavie argued, then all stimuli should be identified, and selection can happen at a later stage. This is sensible because it avoids discarding information that might turn out to be useful. Consider, for example, the Eriksen flankers task shown in Figure 6.5C. This task involves the presentation of only three letters, presented with high contrast and minimal noise, and the subject must make a simple 2AFC response. This is clearly a low-load situation, so Lavie would predict that the irrelevant flanker letters would not be suppressed at an early stage. Indeed, responses are typically found to be slowed when the flankers are incompatible with the central target, consistent with a late selection process. Lavie (1995) showed that interference from the flankers could be eliminated simply by increasing the number of distractors surrounding the target, presumably because this increased the perceptual load. Several other manipulations that were designed to increase the perceptual load also yielded a decrease in interference. Simi-

larly, a functional magnetic resonance imaging (fMRI) study showed that activity in visual cortex elicited by task-irrelevant parafoveal motion was suppressed when subjects performed a demanding foveal task relative to when they performed an easy foveal task (Rees, Frith, & Lavie, 1997).

Luck and Hillyard (1999) expanded on this perceptual-load hypothesis, proposing that attention will operate in a given cognitive subsystem whenever that system faces interference from multiple inputs. That is, the locus of selection is determined by the locus of interference. This proposal has the potential to be as unfalsifiable as the multiple-resource concept, and it will be testable only when independent sources of evidence are used to demonstrate (a) that a cognitive subsystem faces interference for a given combination of task and stimuli but not for others and (b) that attention operates at that stage whenever the combination of task and stimuli yields interference at that stage.

As an example, consider the attentional blink task (see Figure 6.7B). Previous studies have demonstrated that the visual system can identify letters and even complex real-world scenes at rapid rates of presentation (Potter, 1976; Shiffrin & Gardner, 1972). However, there is good evidence indicating that this task should overload the storage capacity of working memory (Luck & Vogel, 1997; Sperling, 1960) and that perceptual representations cannot be transferred into working memory at the high presentation rates used in attentional blink experiments (Potter, 1976). We thus have independent evidence (i.e., not from attentional blink experiments) that the attentional blink paradigm does not overload perceptual systems but does overload working memory. The next step is to provide a means of determining whether the attentional blink reflects an impairment in perceptual processing or an impairment in working memory. As discussed earlier, ERP recordings have been used to show that there is no suppression of perceptual processing during the attentional blink (up to the point of contact with semantic information) but that working memory-related processes are suppressed (Vogel et al., 1998). Thus, it is possible to test independently for interference effects and for attention effects in a given cognitive subsystem.

Different Properties at Different Stages

If attention operates within different cognitive subsystems in different tasks, then it is reasonable to suppose that the properties of attention within a given subsystem will match the representational format and processing role of that subsystem. For example, because occipital-lobe visual areas are spatially organized, attentional mechanisms that operate during visual feature analysis would be expected to show spatial properties such as a relatively broad spatial gradient and the inability to attend to noncontiguous regions of space. That is, spatial properties such as these make sense only in a system in which space plays a key role. In contrast, because there is little spatial organization in the frontal and inferotemporal

areas that underlie visual working memory for objects, attentional mechanisms that operate in object working memory would not be expected to show a spatial gradient and should be capable of being allocated to noncontiguous areas of space (with the exception of attentional mechanisms that operate within the working memory subsystem that is devoted to spatial information).

This proposal was recently tested by Vogel (2000), who compared the properties of attention in two cuing tasks, one designed to overload perceptual processes and one designed to overload working memory. The memory-intensive task is shown in Figure 6.13A. A change-detection paradigm was used in which a *memory array* consisting of 10 colored squares was presented, followed by a 1000-ms delay and then a *test array,* which was either identical to the memory array or differed in the color of one square. Subjects made an unspeeded same-different response for each trial. Each memory array was preceded by a cue that indicated the side of the display in which the color change was most likely to occur. The test array contained items only in the cued region, which is important for

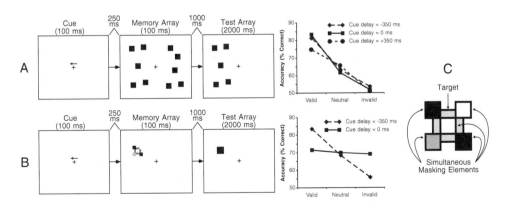

Figure 6.13   *Stimuli and results from the study of Vogel (2000).*
NOTE: (A) The memory-intensive condition. The black squares were actually colored squares, each of which was randomly selected from a set of seven possible colors. (B) The perception-intensive condition. (C) An expanded view of the target stimulus used in the perception-intensive condition. The target was the large central square, which was one of seven possible colors. The colors of the five masking elements (four at the corners and one in the center) were selected at random from the remaining colors.

avoiding the decision-noise interpretation of Shiu and Pashler (1994).

This task overloads working memory by presenting many more items than can be stored in working memory, and previous studies have shown that performance in this task is not limited by perceptual factors (Vogel et al., 2001). Thus, we would expect the cues to influence the transfer of perceptual information into working memory, but we would not expect the cues to influence the perception of the colored squares. Consistent with this reasoning, Vogel (2000) found that cue validity had the same effect on accuracy whether the cue preceded or followed the memory array (see Figure 6.13A). That is, because the cue was effective even when it followed the offset of the memory array by 250 ms, it is unlikely that the validity effects reflect improved sensory processing (i.e., it would be difficult for a cue to improve the sensory processing of a stimulus that terminated 250 ms previously).

To isolate the operation of attention in perception, Vogel (2000) modified this paradigm slightly, as shown in Figure 6.13B. Specifically, he made the perceptual component of the task very difficult by adding simultaneous masking noise (see Figure 6.13C), and he used only a single item so that working memory would not be overloaded. This created a high perceptual load and a low memory load, which would be expected to yield perceptual-level attention effects rather than working memory–level attention effects. Consistent with this reasoning, Vogel found that significant cue-validity effects were found only when the cue preceded the memory array.

To demonstrate that attention has different properties when it operates in different cognitive subsystems, Vogel (2000) examined the extent to which noncontiguous locations can be attended without attending to the region between them. Previous experiments that have found that attention can be split between noncontiguous locations have generally used

paradigms that stress working memory, decision, or response systems (Bichot, Cave, & Pashler, 1999; Egly & Homa, 1984), whereas experiments that have found evidence for a contiguous attended region have generally stressed perceptual systems (Heinze et al., 1994). Thus, Vogel predicted that noncontiguous regions could be attended in the memory-intensive task shown in Figure 6.13A but not in the perception-intensive condition shown in Figure 6.13B. And that is exactly what he found. Specifically, performance in the memory-intensive task was just as accurate when two noncontiguous locations were cued as when two adjacent locations were cued, but performance in the perception-intensive condition was significantly less accurate when two noncontiguous locations were cued than when two adjacent locations were cued.

These results indicate that the properties of attention are different for different cognitive subsystems, reflecting the nature of the specific subsystems. Consequently, many potential properties of attention that have been treated as mutually exclusive may simply describe the operation of attention within different cognitive subsystems or within different tasks. For example, some types of attention may influence both features and conjunctions, whereas other may influence conjunctions but not features. Similarly, some types of attention may be spatial, whereas others are object-oriented. Furthermore, some types of attention may be automatically attracted by peripheral transients, whereas others may not. Thus, whenever a claim is made about the properties of attention, it is important to ask which types of attention have those properties.

WHAT IS ATTENDED?

Now that we have considered why attention is necessary and how it affects the processing of stimuli, we turn to the issue of exactly what is attended. Consistent with our earlier discussion of multiple attentional processes, attention can select a wide range of stimuli that occur both within a single sensory modality and across different modalities.

Automatic Allocation of Attention to Abrupt Onsets

The presentation of a sudden, intense, and unexpected stimulus leads to an automatic orienting response with several components, including a shift of gaze toward the stimulus, a galvanic skin response, and a momentary slowing of the heart rate (see, e.g., Ohman, 1979). This overt orienting of attention is mirrored by a covert orienting of attention that can be automatically triggered by a sudden, but less intense, sensory transient. This automatic covert orienting of attention is often studied by means of nonpredictive peripheral cues, as discussed earlier (see Figure 6.3). Even when a cue is nonpredictive, responses to cued-location targets are typically faster than are responses to uncued-location targets, although this effect lasts for only a few hundred milliseconds.

A classic study by Jonides (1981) provided evidence that the effects of peripheral cues are highly automatic. This study provided three pieces of evidence supporting automaticity for peripheral cues: (a) Peripheral cues attract attention even when the target is actually less likely to appear at the cued location than at an uncued location, whereas symbolic cues are effective only when they reliably predict the target location; (b) peripheral cues are just as effective when central processes are occupied by a secondary memory task, but symbolic cues are less effective under these conditions; and (c) when instructed to ignore the cues, symbolic cues became ineffective, but peripheral cues remained effective. More recent studies have shown that the capture of atten-

tion by abruptly onsetting peripheral stimuli can be overridden when attention is strongly focused onto a different location or onto a different stimulus dimension (Folk, Remington, & Johnston, 1992; Yantis & Jonides, 1990), but it is still clear that abrupt onsets attract attention in a relatively automatic manner.

The usual explanation for the automatic capture of attention by abrupt onsets is that peripheral sensory transients often signal ecologically important events, such as the appearance of a predator. However, the cuing paradigm is somewhat artificial because the sensory transient created by the cue is not itself the target, but is merely presented at the location of a subsequent target. A more ecologically valid paradigm was developed by Yantis and Jonides (1984), who combined elements of cuing with elements of visual search. As illustrated in Figure 6.14A, each trial began with a set of figure-eight placeholders. The search display was created by removing elements of the figure-eight placeholders to reveal letters and by simultaneously presenting a letter at a previously blank location. Subjects were required to search for a particular target letter ("A" in this example), and this target could be either the new letter (called the *onset* letter) or one of the letters formed by removing elements from a figure-eight placeholder (called *offset* letters). The target was no more likely to be the onset letter than any of the offset letters, and subjects therefore had no incentive to attend to this item. Thus, the onset item is analogous to a nonpredictive peripheral cue except that it serves both as the attention-attracting stimulus and the to-be-detected target stimulus.

As shown in Figure 6.14B, reaction times were faster when the target was the onset letter than when it was one of the offset letters, consistent with the automatic capture of attention by the onset letter. In addition, the slope of the function relating RT to set size was very shallow for onset targets, which suggests that

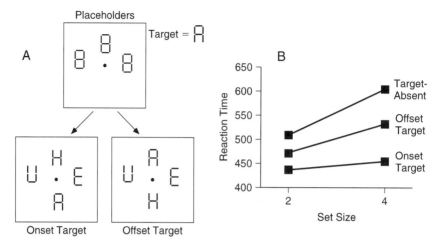

Figure 6.14   Typical stimuli (A) and results (B) from the sudden-onset paradigm (based on the study of Yantis & Jonides, 1984).

subjects did not bother searching the offset letters when the onset letter was the target. Thus, this more ecologically valid paradigm also provides evidence that certain types of stimuli can automatically attract attention.

Subsequent experiments have tried to determine exactly what types of stimuli will automatically attract attention. For example, a red visual search target among green distractors appears to "pop out" from the display, and it seems plausible that this popout effect reflects the automatic capture of attention by feature discontinuities. Jonides and Yantis (1988) tested this hypothesis by determining whether the pattern of results obtained for onset targets (see Figure 6.14B) would also be obtained for targets that differed in color or brightness from the rest of stimulus array. They found that differential color or brightness did *not* automatically attract attention, and they concluded that the popout phenomenon reflects an intentional orienting of attention (see also Yantis & Egeth, 1999).

Yantis and his colleagues have subsequently argued that attention is captured whenever the visual system detects the presence of a new object, regardless of the low-

level visual events that give rise to the perception of a new object (Hillstrom & Yantis, 1994; Yantis & Hillstrom, 1994). However, Miller (1989) found that offsets attract attention just as effectively as do onsets when perceptual salience is controlled. In addition, Folk and his colleagues have argued that the capture of attention depends on high-level *attentional control settings* that bias the visual system toward task-relevant classes of stimuli (Folk & Remington, 1999; Folk et al., 1992; Folk, Remington, & Wright, 1994). In most cuing experiments, for example, the target is defined by a luminance transient, and subjects are therefore biased to attend to luminance transients. Folk et al. (1992) argued that this accounts for the apparently automatic capture of attention by peripheral cues. In contrast, when the target is defined by color, they found that attention was automatically captured by uniquely colored items and not by luminance transients. However, in a cuing experiment that used unspeeded responses and accuracy measures rather than speeded responses and RT measures, Luck and Thomas (1999) found that luminance-defined peripheral cues automatically attracted attention even when the targets were defined by color rather than by luminance. Thus, we do not yet have a complete understanding of the factors that determine whether a particular stimulus will automatically capture attention, and this issue is currently the focus of a great deal of research (see, e.g., Atchley, Kramer, & Hillstrom, 2000; Folk & Remington, 1999; Gellatly, Cole, & Blurton, 1999; Gibson & Kelsey, 1998; Yantis & Egeth, 1999).

Attention to Objects and Surfaces

For many years, most studies of visual attention focused on spatial attention. However, as first noted by Kahneman and Henik (1977), we are usually more concerned with objects than with the locations that they occupy, and attention may therefore be focused on the object regions that are defined by Gestalt grouping processes at an early stage of visual processing. Given that objects are presented at a specific location, it is difficult to distinguish between the allocation of attention to an object or to the object's location. However, several experimental paradigms have been developed to dissociate between object-based and space-based attention mechanisms (e.g., Duncan, 1984; Egly, Driver, & Rafal, 1994), resulting in many demonstrations of object-based attentional processes. The emerging consensus is that there may be multiple forms of perceptual-level attention, including both space-based and object-based attention.

In many experimental paradigms, object-based selection is intimately related to object segmentation (Vecera, 2000). Object segmentation involves determining which visual features combine to form a single shape and which features combine to form other shapes (see Chap. 5, this volume). The ability to distinguish foreground figures from background regions also involves segmentation processes. Object-based attention involves selecting a segregated shape from among several segre-

gated shapes (or, alternatively, focusing attention on one shape versus dividing attention among several shapes). Thus, before object-based attention operates, a candidate shape or region must first be segregated from other shapes or regions.

Because segmentation processes provide candidate objects to the attentional system, most of the object-based attention literature can be characterized as a search for the bottom-up segmentation cues that influence attentional allocation. For example, many studies have used the flankers task (Figure 6.5C) to show that the spatial selection in this task can be overridden by object-grouping cues. In the earliest report, Driver and Baylis (1989) showed that targets and flankers that move together are selected as a single perceptual group (but see Kramer, Tham, & Yeh, 1991, for a failure to replicate). Subsequent research showed that other grouping cues, such as similarity of color, good continuation (Baylis & Driver, 1992), and connectedness (Kramer & Jacobsen, 1991), bias the allocation of attention in the flankers paradigm. In each of these cases, targets that are perceptually grouped with spatially distant flankers are selected as a chunk of visual information.

Stimulus-based influences on object attention have also been observed in spatial cuing tasks, such as the widely used task developed by Egly et al. (1994). In their task, depicted in Figure 6.15, subjects viewed two rectangles, each of which is essentially a perceptual group formed by closure and common region. One end of one rectangle was briefly cued with a predictive peripheral cue, and a target appeared after a short delay. Subjects pressed a button as soon as they detected the target, which could appear in one of three locations: at the cued location (position A; 80% of trials); at the opposite end of the cued rectangle (position B; 10% of trials); or in the uncued rectangle (position C; 10% of trials). The latter two locations were equidistant from

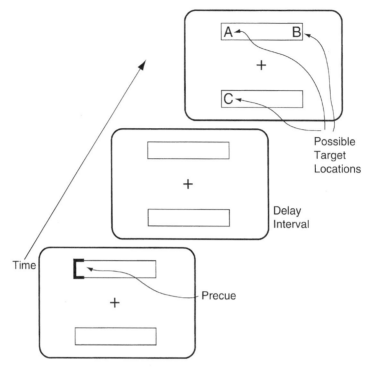

Figure 6.15   Sequence of stimuli in the study of Egly et al. (1994).
NOTE: One end of one rectangle is cued, and then a target appears at the same location (labeled location A), in a different location in the same rectangle (location B), or at an equidistant location in the other rectangle (location C). Note that the rectangles were sometimes horizontal, as illustrated here, and sometimes vertical.

the cued location and equally likely to contain a target, but one was in the same object as the cued location, and the other was in a different object. Egly et al. found both space-based and object-based effects. First, invalid-trial responses were faster when the target appeared at the uncued end of the cued rectangle than when the target appeared in the uncued rectangle; because these two locations were equidistant from the cued location, this effect cannot reflect purely space-based attentional allocation and must be object-based. Second, responses to targets at the uncued end of the cued rectangle were slower than were responses to targets at the cued location. If attention were entirely object-based, responses should have been equally fast at both ends of the cued rectangle, so this is

presumably a space-based effect. Thus, closure and connectedness can bias—but do not completely control—the allocation of attention. When spatial attention is summoned to a location, attention can spread or move within a closed, connected region more easily than between closed, connected regions.

In addition to defining whole objects, some visual segmentation cues allow an object to be decomposed into its parts (e.g., minima of curvature cues; see Hoffman & Richards, 1984). Vecera and colleagues (Vecera, Behrmann, & Filapek, 2001; Vecera, Behrmann, & McGoldrick, 2000) recently demonstrated that attention can be directed selectively to the parts of an object. In attending to multipart objects, subjects are more accurate in reporting features from a single part than from multiple parts. This part-based attentional selection is not reducible to simple spatial (perceptual-level) attention because increasing the spatial separation between the parts of an object influences part selection very little, if at all (Vecera et al., in press).

Most research on object-based attention has aimed simply to demonstrate the existence of object-based attention. However, recent studies have begun to explore more detailed issues, such as the locus-of-selection issue. For example, Valdes-Sosa, Bobes, Rodriguez, and Pinilla (1998) recorded ERPs during an object attention task in which subjects viewed displays containing two superimposed surfaces (two transparent surfaces composed of different colored dots that rotated in opposite directions). Subjects selectively attended to one of the two dot surfaces and monitored this surface for an infrequently occurring target. ERPs were elicited by task-irrelevant stimuli that did not require an overt response. Task-irrelevant stimuli associated with the attended surface produced ERP waveforms with larger P1 and N1 amplitudes than did task-irrelevant targets associated with the unattended surface. These results suggest that surface-based attention begins to operate at an early, perceptual stage. Attending to surfaces is presumably an important component of object-based attention, so these results suggest that object-based selection may operate at an early stage. Moreover, the similarity of these surface-based P1 and N1 effects to the space-based P1 and N1 effects described previously suggests that some object-based effects may be generated by neural processes shared with spatial attention. Specifically, both object-based attention and spatial attention may involve changes in sensory gain.

Other studies have more directly examined the relationship between space-based and object-based mechanisms of selection. Several studies have reported object-based effects in which the spatial location of the objects

also influences selection (e.g., Kramer & Jacobsen, 1991; Vecera, 1994). That is, in some tasks it is easier to divide attention between objects when the objects are spatially near one another, suggesting that object attention is selecting from an early, spatially organized representation that involves perceptual segmentation (a grouped array; see Vecera, 1994; Vecera & Farah, 1994). However, other studies have found little or no influence of the spatial distance between objects (Kramer, Weber, & Watson, 1997; Lee & Chun, 2001; Vecera & Farah, 1994), suggesting that object selection may occur from a later, object-centered representation that contains little spatial information.

It is possible to resolve this discrepancy by proposing two object-based attention mechanisms, an early-selection mechanism that uses perceptual grouping principles to control the allocation of attention within a grouped spatial array, and a late-selection mechanism that operates on a more abstract representation. Moreover, the use of these different mechanisms might depend on the cognitive subsystem required by a particular task (see Vecera & Farah, 1994), just as perceptual-level and working memory-level attentional mechanisms appear to be invoked under different task conditions (Vogel, 2000).

Cross-Modal Links in Attention

Until this point we have focused almost exclusively on the visual modality. However, attention can also operate in other modalities (e.g., auditory attention in dichotic listening tasks). This raises a basic question: Are the attention mechanisms for different modalities linked together? For example, can a spatial cue in one modality influence the allocation of attention in another modality?

Early studies of cross-modal links in attention were equivocal. Many studies either reported null results regarding cross-modal cuing effects or had methodological difficulties that led to ambiguous results. For example, Posner, Nissen, and Ogden (1978) investigated links between visual and tactile attention by cuing subjects either to the likely spatial location of a target (left or right) or to the likely modality of a target (visual or tactile). Subjects were required to distinguish between high- and low-intensity light flashes or between high- and low-intensity tactile vibrations. Subjects were faster to discriminate targets when the modality of the target was validly cued than when it was invalidly cued. However, there was no cuing effect for spatial location in the uncued modality: If the target's modality was unknown, targets on the cued side of space were discriminated about as fast as were targets on the uncued side. The few early studies that did report spatial cuing effects using cues and targets in different modalities (e.g., Rhodes, 1987) tended to use localization responses (e.g., is the target to the left or right?). Results using localization responses may reflect response priming and not necessarily cross-modal attentional selection.

To overcome the methodological difficulties in previous research, Spence and Driver (1996) developed an orthogonal cuing method to study cross-modal attention. In this task subjects are cued to the left or right side of space and perform an orthogonal discrimination by reporting a target's spatial elevation (up or down, determined by whether the target appears above or below the horizontal meridian). This procedure eliminates the possibility of response priming; any cuing effect must be due to attentional links between two modalities. Using this procedure, Spence and Driver found that subjects were faster to discriminate validly cued auditory targets than invalidly cued auditory targets, even with visual cues. These results support a link between visual and auditory endogenous attention. Links also exist between visual and auditory exogenous

attention. When nonpredictive peripheral auditory or visual cues are used in the orthogonal cuing method, auditory cues elicit shifts of both visual and auditory attention to the cued location (Spence & Driver, 1997). Subjects are faster to discriminate both visual and auditory targets following a valid peripheral auditory cue than following an invalid peripheral auditory cue. However, this link between exogenous visual and auditory attention is asymmetrical. Nonpredictive peripheral visual cues do not automatically elicit an orienting of auditory attention, although the same cues do elicit an orienting of visual attention.

Results from neuropsychological studies also support cross-modality links in attention. Patients with unilateral damage to the parietal lobe (usually due to stroke) fail to attend to both visual and auditory stimuli presented in the hemispace opposite the lesioned hemisphere, suggesting that some attentional processes operate on a representation of space that includes both visual and auditory components. Similar results have been reported from multimodal versions of Posner's spatial precuing task (Farah, Wong, Monheit, & Morrow, 1989). In the multimodal version of this task, neglect patients are asked to detect the appearance of a lateralized visual target. The visual target is preceded by a lateralized visual or auditory precue. Neglect patients exhibit difficulty disengaging attention from both visual and auditory precues presented on the good (ipsilesional) side of peripheral space. These results support a supramodal representation for attentional control processes of the parietal lobe. However, it is possible that separate auditory and visual systems are present in the parietal lobes and that both tend to be damaged together.

Finally, electrophysiological studies with neurologically intact observers have investigated the operation of selective attention across different modalities. Hillyard, Simpson, Woods, Van Voorhis, and Münte

(1984) asked subjects to attend to either the left or right side of space, monitoring for auditory targets in one condition and visual targets in another condition. ERPs were elicited by task-irrelevant probe stimuli that were presented in either modality. Consistent with the presence of cross-modality links, the probe-elicited ERPs in the ignored modality were found to be enhanced for stimuli presented in the attended location compared to the unattended location.

Although visual and auditory attention appear to operate in concert, it is difficult to determine if these effects are due to linked but separate unimodal attention systems or to a single supramodal attention system. Consistent with our view that there are multiple attentional processes, there are likely to be both unimodal attentional mechanisms that operate in a manner the reflects the nature of each stimulus modality and supramodal attentional mechanisms that are used for the coordination of attention across sensory modalities.

HOW DO ITEMS BECOME ATTENDED?

In the previous section we discussed what types of stimuli are selected by attention. Attention selects abruptly occurring stimuli, objects, and spatial locations in different sensory modalities. But how do these items become attended? This is the question of attentional control, which involves the parameters and processes that are involved in determining what becomes attended and what does not. The parameters of attentional control influence the items that attention selects. For example, abruptly appearing stimuli not only are attended themselves, but they also control the allocation of attention to subsequent stimuli. Thus, although we separate our discussion of what is attended and how items become attended, these two issues are interrelated.

A Framework for Attentional Control

Attentional control is relatively trivial when a single stimulus appears abruptly in an otherwise empty display: Attention will be captured by the abrupt onset. Attentional control becomes more computationally challenging when multiple objects of roughly equal salience appear in a complex scene. In a multi-item scene the different objects will compete for attention, and some control process is required to resolve this competition to allow some objects to be selected over others.

A general framework for conceptualizing attentional control is Desimone and Duncan's (1995) *biased competition* model (see also Kinsbourne, 1977). In the biased competition model, two classes of parameters influence attentional control: bottom-up (stimulus-based) parameters and top-down (goal-driven) parameters (see Yantis, 2000, for a review). In a visual search task, for example, the visual information presented to a subject contains bottom-up information that can capture attention. Bottom-up parameters include the sudden appearance of a stimulus, as discussed earlier, and local inhomogeneities in an array of stimuli (Sagi & Julesz, 1984). Top-down parameters include the target template—the mental representation of the target being searched for (Desimone & Duncan, 1995; Downing, 2000; Duncan & Humphreys, 1989)—as well as subjects' expectancies about the location and timing of stimuli (Chun & Jiang, 1998).

In the biased competition model, stimuli and tasks compete with each other for control over both neural representations and motor output. For example, when two stimuli are presented simultaneously inside a neuron's receptive field, as in Figure 6.11C, they compete for control over the neuron's responses: Should a red-selective neuron fire at a high rate to indicate that red is present in one object, or should it fire at a low rate to indicate the red is absent in the other object? Similarly, in the Stroop task (Figure 6.5A), the color of the ink and the name of the word compete for control over the vocal apparatus. Incompatible representations are assumed to be mutually inhibitory to avoid a merging of different representations, such as a subject saying "blite" when shown the word "white" written in black ink. In a network of mutually inhibitory representations, representations that are slightly stronger will tend to suppress other representations, leading eventually to a single, winning representation. Consequently, any bottom-up or top-down factors that strengthen a representation will give it a competitive advantage for neural representations and for control of behavior.

According to the biased competition model, the brain generates an *attentional template* that represents task demands and goals. For example, if subjects perform a visual search task with the letter T as the target and are told that the target will usually appear in the left visual field, the attentional template will specify the shape and likely location of the target. Any incoming sensory representations will then be compared with the attentional template, and representations will be strengthened to the extent that they match the template. In addition, bottom-up factors such as contrast will also influence the strengths of representations. In this manner, bottom-up and top-down sources of information together bias the competition between stimuli.

The general principles of biased competition also can be applied to attentional control in tasks other than visual search, such as object-based attention tasks. Several recent reviews have described the roles of bottom-up and top-down parameters in object-based attention (Behrmann & Haimson, 1999; Vecera, in press; Vecera & Behrmann, in press). Bottom-up influences on object attention include the Gestalt principles of perceptual grouping, as discussed earlier (see also

Chap. 5, this volume). Top-down influences on object attention include spatial attention and perceptual set (often defined by an experimenter's instructions). The principles of biased competition also find support in parallel distributed processing models of cognition, which have been successful in describing potential attentional mechanisms (e.g., Mozer & Sitton, 1998).

Neural Systems for the Control of Attention

Now that we have presented a framework for understanding how bottom-up and top-down factors are integrated to control attention, we briefly review the neural systems that are involved in the control of attention. More detailed reviews of the neural mechanisms of attention are also available (Colby, 1991; Desimone & Duncan, 1995; Farah, 2000; Kastner & Ungerleider, 2000; Posner & Petersen, 1990; Rafal, 2000).

Neglect and Extinction

Several cortical and subcortical areas participate in the control of spatial attention. For example, the pulvinar nucleus of the thalamus is involved in filtering or suppressing irrelevant stimuli in a cluttered display (LaBerge, 1995), and the superior colliculus is involved in executing both overt and covert shifts of attention (Rafal, Posner, Friedman, Inhoff, & Bernstein, 1988). However, the cortical region that occupies a central role in the control of spatial attention is the posterior parietal region. Damage to the parietal region (especially in the right hemisphere) results in a profound attentional impairment referred to as *neglect*. Patients with neglect fail to pay attention to stimuli falling on the side of space opposite to the lesion (the contralesional side). For example, a patient with damage to the right parietal lobe may fail to eat food on the left half of the plate, acknowledge people who approach from the left side, or read words on the left half of a page. Neglect occurs soon after damage to the parietal region, but the neglect typically becomes less severe over time. Recovering patients can typically detect a single stimulus presented in the contralesional visual field, but they may still fail to notice a contralesional stimulus if it is presented simultaneously with an ipsilesional stimulus. This is called *extinction* because the contralesional stimulus is extinguished by the ipsilateral stimulus. Both neglect and extinction appear to involve an inability to deploy attention to the contralesional field voluntarily.

Extinction can be observed in the spatial cuing task (see Rafal, 2000, for a review), and the results from extinction patients suggest that the parietal lobe gives the ipsilesional field a competitive advantage over the contralesional field. In cuing experiments, extinction patients can use valid exogenous cues to allocate attention to the contralesional field prior to the appearance of the target. However, when a peripheral cue appears in the good (ipsilesional) field and a target appears in the bad (contralesional) field, responses are very slow. That is, the patients are impaired primarily when the good field is cued and the target then appears in the bad field. A straightforward interpretation of these results is that the contralesional and ipsilesional sides of space compete for the control of attention (e.g., Cohen et al., 1994). A cue can bias the competition in favor of the cued field, and damage to the parietal lobe weakens the contralesional field's ability to compete for attention. When both the cue and the target are in the same field, there is no competition, and the target can be detected quickly. However, when the good field is cued and the target appears in the bad field, the good field wins the competition for attention even though the target is in the bad field, leading to abnormally slow responses.

Which aspect of attentional control— bottom-up or top-down—is disrupted in these patients? Although parietal-damaged patients appear to have intact perceptual processes such as object segmentation (Mattingley, Davis, & Driver, 1997), this disorder of attention appears to involve bottom-up control: Attention is not captured effectively by contralesional inputs. Further, some forms of top-down attentional control appear to be intact in parietal-damaged patients. These patients can make use of top-down expectancies or task-relevant goals. For example, a contralesional stimulus may not be extinguished if the ipsilesional stimulus is irrelevant to a task and the patient is instructed to ignore this ipsilesional stimulus (e.g., Baylis, Driver, & Rafal, 1993). Presumably, some top-down control of attention is intact in these patients and can bias attention to select the task-relevant stimulus in the bad field.

Neuroimaging Studies

The role of the posterior parietal lobe in the control of spatial attention has been corroborated by neuroimaging studies. Because the whole brain can be examined using some of these techniques, multiple brain regions that influence spatial attention can be observed, making it possible to isolate the sources of bottom-up and top-down control.

Positron-emission tomography (PET) studies of spatial cuing have provided evidence for two neuroanatomically distinct control processes. Corbetta, Miezin, Shulman, and Petersen (1993) presented subjects with visual targets that appeared in a predictable sequence that was designed to engage endogenous attentional allocation. The predictable sequences were leftward or rightward "hops" of a target; the target first appeared just to the left or right of fixation and then jumped to increasingly lateral locations. This sequence allowed the subjects to anticipate the next target location and to endogenously allocate attention to that location. Each time a target appeared, the subject pressed a button. Thus, the targets in this task involved both exogenous and endogenous components—the appearance of the target was an exogenous event, and the predictable sequence encouraged endogenous shifts of attention. Two neural regions of interest exhibited increased blood flow during this task: the superior parietal lobe and the superior frontal cortex.

To separate the attentional processes mediated by the superior parietal and superior frontal areas, Corbetta et al. (1993) included a control task. The control task involved the presentation of randomly presented peripheral targets in one visual field; instead of detecting these peripheral targets, however, subjects detected targets presented at fixation. Thus, subtracting the control task from the predictive sequence should isolate blood flow changes associated with endogenous shifts of attention in the periphery and motor responses to lateralized stimuli. When peripheral shifts of attention were isolated in this manner, both superior parietal and superior frontal areas were active. However, unlike the superior parietal area, the superior frontal area was not active unless subjects responded to the peripheral targets. Corbetta et al. concluded that superior parietal regions are involved in both exogenous (bottom-up) and endogenous (top-down) control of spatial attention, whereas superior frontal regions are involved in the endogenous control of spatial attention. These results broadly support a biased competition view of attentional control by demonstrating different neuroanatomical substrates for bottom-up and top-down control. More direct support for the biased competition view comes from recent studies that demonstrate that attention may resolve the competition among stimuli (see Kastner & Ungerleider, 2000, for a discussion). Simultaneously presented stimuli compete with one another and suppress one another, leading to weaker fMRI responses in ventral visual areas. Directing focal attention to one of several simultaneously presented stimuli increases the fMRI response, suggesting that focal attention can resolve the competition that occurs among items that appear at the same time (Kastner, De Weerd, Desimone, & Ungerleider, 1998).

Finally, the parietal-lobe control processes appear to participate in attentional control across very different visual tasks. A recent fMRI study found activation in two parietal lobe areas in three very different tasks: (a) a spatial shifting task, (b) an object matching task in which subjects reported if two attended objects were the same or different, and (c) a nonspatial conjunction task in which subjects searched for a target letter in an RSVP paradigm (Wojciulik & Kanwisher, 1999). Parietal-lobe involvement across widely different tasks may depend on the suppression of visual distractors; neuroimaging studies with visual search tasks that do not require the suppression of distractors have not found parietal lobe involvement across tasks (Corbetta, Miezin, Dobmeyer, Shulman, & Petersen, 1991).

Neurophysiology of Attentional Control

Evidence for parietal lobe involvement in covert shifts to spatial attention has also been obtained from single-unit recordings in the lateral intraparietal (LIP) area in monkeys (Colby & Goldberg, 1999). Neurons in LIP have topographic receptive fields that respond to visual stimulation. When a monkey makes an eye movement to a new location, the receptive field of an LIP neuron also will fall in a new location. Prior to the eye movement, however, an LIP neuron will respond to visual stimuli at a location that is the target of a planned eye movement that has not yet been executed. That is, the receptive fields of LIP neurons are remapped in anticipation of an eye movement. This shift of the LIP representation of space may provide the neural mechanism for covert shifts of attention that precede and anticipate overt shifts involving eye movements.

The LIP neurons' ability to update their representation of space implies that this area receives inputs regarding the intended eye movement. This input likely comes from the frontal eye fields (FEFs), suggesting that the updating of the spatial representation is based on endogenous, top-down factors. In visual search, FEF is involved in selecting the target to which an eye movement will be directed (see Schall & Thompson, 1999). Monkeys viewed displays that contained a target that popped out from a field of distractors (e.g., Figure 6.4A) and were trained to make an eye movement to the popout target. Prior to the saccade, FEF neurons discriminated target items from distractor items: If the target fell within an FEF neuron's receptive field, the neuron responded vigorously; if a distractor fell within the receptive field, the neuron responded weakly (Schall & Thompson, 1999). Additional studies demonstrated that the enhanced firing of these FEF neurons was not caused solely by the capture of attention by the odd item in the display. With training, FEF neurons can become sensitive to target features that do not pop out from a display. For example, if multiple targets are present, FEF neurons show larger firing rates when any of the targets fall in their receptive fields than when a single distractor falls within their receptive field (Schall & Thompson, 1999).

SUMMARY

The concept of attention has played a significant role in many areas of psychology, ranging from animal behavior to cognition to psychopathology. In many cases, the term *attention* is used descriptively, such that correct performance of a task is sufficient to claim that attention has been used. In other cases, attention is treated as a psychological process, the operation of which leads to specific patterns of behavior, above and beyond mere correct task performance. This distinction between task-defined and process-oriented attention helps to bring some order to the thousands of published studies that use the term *attention*.

We have argued that attentional processes are primarily useful when a given cognitive system is faced with too many inputs and could therefore benefit from a reduction in the number of inputs. This sort of information overload often occurs for limited-capacity cognitive processes, which operate less efficiently when the number of inputs is increased and therefore benefit when attention is used to reduce the number of inputs. However, attention can also be beneficial for processes that are not capacity-limited because reducing the number of inputs to a process reduces the number of decisions that must be made, which improves accuracy purely for statistical reasons.

Because different cognitive systems might be faced with excess inputs under different conditions, it is plausible that attention might operate in the different cognitive systems at different times. In this chapter we discussed evidence consistent with this hypothesis. Moreover, not only does attention operate in different cognitive systems under different conditions, but the specific characteristics of attention appear to reflect the characteristics of the cognitive systems in which attention is operating in a given task as well. In addition, we have discussed evidence that attention can be allocated to different types of information, ranging from entire tasks to specific stimulus features and from spatial locations to surface and object representations. This allocation of attention to different types of information (i.e., attentional control) is influenced by both bottom-up and top-down factors. It is our hope that as research on attention progresses, it will be possible to define several distinct attention mechanisms that vary along a variety of dimensions, including (a) the computational role of each mechanism, (b) the cognitive systems that are influenced by each mechanism, (c) the representational format of the information selected by each mechanism, and (d) the neural systems that control and implement the operation of each mechanism.

REFERENCES

Allport, A. (1989). Visual attention. In M. I. Posner (Ed.), *Foundations of cognitive science* (pp. 631–682). Cambridge: MIT Press.

Atchley, P., Kramer, A. F., & Hillstrom, A. P. (2000). Contingent capture for onsets and offsets: Attentional set for perceptual transients. *Journal of Experimental Psychology: Human Perception & Performance, 26,* 594–606.

Averbach, E., & Coriel, A. S. (1961). Short-term memory in vision. *Bell System Technical Journal, 40,* 309–328.

Baddeley, A. D. (1986). *Working memory.* Oxford: Clarendon.

Baddeley, A. D., & Hitch, G. J. (1974). Working memory. In G. H. Bower (Ed.), *The psychology of learning and motivation: Vol. 8* (pp. 47–90). New York: Academic Press.

Bashinski, H. S., & Bacharach, V. R. (1980). Enhancement of perceptual sensitivity as the result of selectively attending to spatial locations. *Perception & Psychophysics, 28,* 241–248.

Baylis, G. C., & Driver, J. (1992). Visual parsing and response competition: The effect of grouping factors. *Perception & Psychophysics, 51,* 145–162.

Baylis, G. C., Driver, J., & Rafal, R. D. (1993). Visual extinction and stimulus repetition. *Journal of Cognitive Neuroscience, 4,* 453–466.

Behrmann, M., & Haimson, C. (1999). The cognitive neuroscience of visual attention. *Current Opinion in Neurobiology, 9,* 158–163.

Bichot, N. P., Cave, K. R., & Pashler, H. (1999). Visual selection mediated by location: Feature-based selection of noncontiguous locations. *Perception & Psychophysics, 61,* 403–423.

Broadbent, D. E. (1958). *Perception and communication.* New York: Pergamon.

Broadbent, D. E., & Broadbent, M. H. P. (1987). From detection to identification: Response to multiple targets in rapid serial visual presentation. *Perception & Psychophysics, 42,* 105–113.

Cheal, M., & Gregory, M. (1997). Evidence of limited capacity and noise reduction with single-element displays in the location-cuing paradigm. *Journal of Experimental Psychology: Human Perception and Performance, 23,* 51–71.

Chelazzi, L., Duncan, J., Miller, E. K., & Desimone, R. (1998). Responses of neurons in inferior temporal cortex during memory-guided visual search. *Journal of Neurophysiology, 80,* 2918–2940.

Chelazzi, L., Miller, E. K., Duncan, J., & Desimone, R. (1993). A neural basis for visual search in inferior temporal cortex. *Nature, 363,* 345–347.

Cherry, E. C. (1953). Some experiments on the recognition of speech with one and with two ears. *Journal of the Acoustic Society of America, 25,* 975–979.

Chun, M. M., & Jiang, Y. (1998). Contextual cueing: Implicit learning and memory of visual context guides spatial attention. *Cognitive Psychology, 36,* 28–71.

Cohen, A., & Rafal, R. D. (1991). Attention and feature integration: Illusory conjunctions in a patient with a parietal lobe lesion. *Psychological Science, 2,* 106–110.

Cohen, J. D., Barch, D. M., Carter, C., & Servan-Schreiber, D. (1999). Context-processing deficits in schizophrenia: Converging evidence from three theoretically motivated cognitive tasks. *Journal of Abnormal Psychology, 108,* 120–133.

Cohen, J. D., Romero, R. D., Servan-Schreiber, D., & Farah, M. J. (1994). Mechanisms of spatial attention: The relation of macrostructure to microstructure in parietal neglect. *Journal of Cognitive Neuroscience, 6,* 377–387.

Colby, C. L. (1991). The neuroanatomy and neurophysiology of attention. *Journal of Child Neurology, 6,* 90–118.

Colby, C. L., & Goldberg, M. E. (1999). Space and attention in parietal cortex. *Annual Review of Neuroscience, 22,* 319–349.

Collie, A., Maruff, P., Yucel, M., Danckert, J., & Currie, J. (2000). Spatiotemporal distribution of facilitation and inhibition of return arising from the reflexive orienting of covert attention. *Journal of Experimental Psychology: Human Perception and Performance, 26,* 1733–1745.

Corbetta, M., Miezin, F. M., Dobmeyer, S., Shulman, G. L., & Petersen, S. E. (1990). Attentional modulation of neural processing of shape, color, and velocity in humans. *Science, 248,* 1556–1559.

Corbetta, M., Miezin, F. M., Dobmeyer, S., Shulman, G. L., & Petersen, S. E. (1991). Selective and divided attention during visual discriminations of shape, color, and speed: Functional anatomy by positron-emission tomography. *Journal of Neuroscience, 11,* 2383–2402.

Corbetta, M., Miezin, F. M., Shulman, G. L., & Petersen, S. E. (1993). A PET study of visuospatial attention. *Journal of Neuroscience, 13,* 1202–1226.

Cowan, N. (2001). The magical number 4 in short-term memory: A reconsideration of mental storage capacity. *Behavioral and Brain Sciences, 24,* 87–185

De Jong, R. (1993). Multiple bottlenecks in overlapping task performance. *Journal of Experimental Psychology: Human Perception and Performance, 19,* 965–980.

Desimone, R., & Duncan, J. (1995). Neural mechanisms of selective visual attention. *Annual Review of Neuroscience, 18,* 193–222.

Deutsch, J. A., & Deutsch, D. (1963). Attention: Some theoretical considerations. *Psychological Review, 70,* 80–90.

Diamond, A., & Taylor, C. (1996). Development of an aspect of executive control: Development of the abilities to remember what I said and to "Do as I say, not as I do." *Developmental Psychobiology, 29,* 315–334.

Downing, C. J. (1988). Expectancy and visual-spatial attention: Effects on perceptual quality. *Journal of Experimental Psychology: Human Perception and Performance, 14,* 188–202.

Downing, P. E. (2000). Interactions between visual working memory and selective attention. *Psychological Science.*

Driver, J., & Baylis, G. C. (1989). Movement and visual attention: The spotlight metaphor breaks down. *Journal of Experimental Psychology: Human Perception and Performance, 15,* 448–456.

Duncan, J. (1984). Selective attention and the organization of visual information. *Journal of Experimental Psychology: General, 113,* 501–517.

Duncan, J., & Humphreys, G. (1989). Visual search and stimulus similarity. *Psychological Review, 96,* 433–458.

Duncan, J., & Humphreys, G. (1992). Beyond the search surface: Visual search and attentional engagement. *Journal of Experimental Psychology: Human Perception and Performance, 18,* 578–588.

Eckstein, M. P. (1998). The lower visual search efficiency for conjunctions is due to noise and not serial attentional processing. *Psychological Science, 9,* 111–118.

Eckstein, M. P., Thomas, J. P., Palmer, J., & Shimozaki, S. S. (2000). A signal detection model predicts the effects of set size on visual search accuracy for feature, conjunction, triple conjunction, and disjunction displays. *Perception & Psychophysics, 62,* 425–451.

Egeth, H. (1977). Attention and preattention. In G. H. Bower (Ed.), *The psychology of learning and motivation: Volume 2* (pp. 277–320). New York: Academic Press.

Egeth, H. E., Virzi, R. A., & Garbart, H. (1984). Searching for conjunctively defined targets. *Journal of Experimental Psychology: Human Perception and Performance, 10,* 32–39.

Eglin, M., Robertson, L. C., & Knight, R. T. (1989). Visual search performance in the neglect syndrome. *Journal of Cognitive Neuroscience, 1,* 372–385.

Egly, R., Driver, J., & Rafal, R. D. (1994). Shifting visual attention between objects and locations: Evidence from normal and parietal lesion subjects. *Journal of Experimental Psychology: General, 123,* 161–177.

Egly, R., & Homa, D. (1984). Sensitization of the visual field. *Journal of Experimental Psychology: Human Perception and Performance, 10,* 778–793.

Eimer, M. (1994). "Sensory gating" as a mechanism for visuospatial orienting: Electrophysiological evidence from trial-by-trial cuing experiments. *Perception & Psychophysics, 55,* 667–675.

Eriksen, C. W. (1995). The flankers task and response competition: A useful tool for investigating a variety of cognitive problems. *Visual Cognition, 2,* 101–118.

Eriksen, C. W., & Hoffman, J. E. (1972). Temporal and spatial characteristics of selective encoding from visual displays. *Perception and Psychophysics, 12,* 201–204.

Eriksen, C. W., & Hoffman, J. E. (1974). Selective attention: Noise suppression or signal enhancement? *Bulletin of the Psychonomic Society, 4,* 587–589.

Farah, M. J. (2000). *The cognitive neuroscience of vision.* Malden, MA: Blackwell.

Farah, M. J., Wong, A. B., Monheit, M. A., & Morrow, L. A. (1989). Parietal lobe mechanisms of spatial attention: Modality-specific or supramodal? *Neuropsychologia, 27,* 461–470.

Feldman, J. (1985). Connectionist models and parallelism in high-level vision. *Computer Vision, Graphics, and Image Processing, 31,* 178–200.

Folk, C. L., & Remington, R. (1999). Can new objects override attentional control settings? *Perception & Psychophysics, 61,* 727–739.

Folk, C. L., Remington, R. W., & Johnston, J. C. (1992). Involuntary covert orienting is contingent on attentional control settings. *Journal of Experimental Psychology: Human Perception and Performance, 18,* 1030–1044.

Folk, C. L., Remington, R. W., & Johnston, J. C. (1993). Contingent attentional capture: A reply to Yantis (1993). *Journal of Experimental Psychology: Human Perception and Performance, 19,* 682–685.

Folk, C. L., Remington, R. W., & Wright, J. H. (1994). The structure of attentional control: Contingent attentional capture by apparent motion, abrupt onset, and color. *Journal of Experimental Psychology: Human Perception and Performance, 20,* 317–329.

Fox, E. (1995). Negative priming from ignored distractors in visual selection: A review. *Psychonomic Bulletin & Review, 2,* 145–173.

Gellatly, A., Cole, G., & Blurton, A. (1999). Do equiluminant object onsets capture visual attention? *Journal of Experimental Psychology: Human Perception and Performance, 25,* 1609–1624.

Gibson, B. S., & Kelsey, E. M. (1998). Stimulus-driven attentional capture is contingent on attentional set for displaywide visual features. *Journal of Experimental Psychology: Human Perception & Performance, 24,* 699–706.

Graham, N. (1989). *Visual pattern analyzers.* New York: Oxford University Press.

Graham, N., Kramer, P., & Haber, N. (1985). Attending to the spatial frequency and spatial position of near-threshold visual patterns. In M. I. Posner & O. S. M. Marin (Eds.), *Attention and performance: Vol. 11* (pp. 269–284). Hillsdale, NJ: Erlbaum.

Green, D. M. (1961). Detection of auditory sinusoids of uncertain frequency. *Journal of the Acoustical Society of America, 33,* 897–903.

Grindley, G. C., & Townsend, V. (1968). Voluntary attention in peripheral vision and its effects on acuity and differential thresholds. *Quarterly Journal of Experimental Psychology, 20,* 11–19.

Hawkins, H. L., Hillyard, S. A., Luck, S. J., Mouloua, M., Downing, C. J., & Woodward, D. P. (1990). Visual attention modulates signal detectability. *Journal of Experimental Psychology: Human Perception and Performance, 16,* 802–811.

Heinze, H. J., Luck, S. J., Münte, T. F., Gös, A., Mangun, G. R., & Hillyard, S. A. (1994). Attention to adjacent and separate positions in space: An electrophysiological analysis. *Perception & Psychophysics, 56,* 42–52.

Henderson, J. M. (1991). Stimulus discrimination following covert attentional orienting to an exogenous cue. *Journal of Experimental Psychology: Human Perception and Performance, 17,* 91–106.

Henderson, J. M. (1996). Spatial precues affect target discrimination in the absence of visual noise. *Journal of Experimental Psychology: Human Perception and Performance, 22,* 780–787.

Henderson, J. M., & Macquistan, A. D. (1993). The spatial distribution of attention following an exogenous cue. *Perception & Psychophysics, 53,* 221–230.

Hillstrom, A. P., & Yantis, S. (1994). Visual motion and attentional capture. *Perception & Psychophysics, 55,* 399–411.

Hillyard, S. A., Simpson, G. V., Woods, D. L., Van Voorhis, S., & Münte, T. (1984). Event-related brain potentials and selective attention to different modalities. In F. Reinoso-Suarez & C. Ajmone-Marsen (Eds.), *Cortical integration* (pp. 395–414). New York: Raven Press.

Hillyard, S. A., Vogel, E. K., & Luck, S. J. (1998). Sensory gain control (amplification) as a mechanism of selective attention: Electrophysiological and neuroimaging evidence. *Philosophical Transactions of the Royal Society: Biological Sciences, 353,* 1257–1270.

Hoffman, D. D., & Richards, W. A. (1984). Parts of recognition. *Cognition, 18,* 65–96.

Hummel, J. E., & Holyoak, K. (1997). Distributed representations of structure: A theory of analogical access and mapping. *Psychological Review, 104,* 427–466.

Ivry, R. B., Franz, E. A., Kingstone, A., & Johnston, J. C. (1998). The psychological refractory period effect following callosotomy: Uncoupling of lateralized response codes. *Journal of Experimental Psychology: Human Perception & Performance, 24,* 463–480.

James, W. (1890). *The principles of psychology.* New York: Holt.

Jolicoeur, P. (1998). Modulation of the attentional blink by on-line response selection: Evidence from speeded and unspeeded Task-sub-1 decisions. *Memory & Cognition, 26,* 1014–1032.

Jolicoeur, P. (1999a). Concurrent response-selection demands modulate the attentional blink. *Journal of Experimental Psychology: Human Perception & Performance, 25,* 1097–1113.

Jolicoeur, P. (1999b). Restricted attentional capacity between sensory modalities. *Psychonomic Bulletin & Review, 6,* 87–92.

Jonides, J. (1981). Voluntary versus automatic control over the mind's eye's movement. In J. B. Long & A. D. Baddeley (Eds.), *Attention and performance: Vol. 9* (pp. 187–203). Hillsdale, NJ: Erlbaum.

Jonides, J., & Yantis, S. (1988). Uniqueness of abrupt visual onset in capturing attention. *Perception & Psychophysics, 43,* 346–354.

Joseph, J. S., Chun, M. M., & Nakayama, K. (1997). Attentional requirements in a "preattentive" feature search task. *Nature, 387,* 805–808.

Just, M. A., & Carpenter, P. A. (1992). A capacity theory of comprehension: Individual differences in working memory. *Psychological Review, 99,* 122–149.

Kahneman, D. (1973). *Attention and effort.* New Jersey: Prentice Hall.

Kahneman, D., & Henik, A. (1977). Effects of visual grouping on immediate recall and selective attention. In S. Dornic (Ed.), *Attention and performance: Vol. 2, Proceeding of the Donders centenary symposium on reaction time* (pp. 307–331). NJ: Erlbaum.

Kastner, S., De Weerd, P., Desimone, R., & Ungerleider, L. G. (1998). Mechanisms of directed attention in the human extrastriate cortex as revealed by functional MRI. *Science, 282,* 108–111.

Kastner, S., & Ungerleider, L. G. (2000). Mechanisms of visual attention in the human cortex. *Annual Review of Neuroscience, 23,* 315–341.

Kinsbourne, M. (1977). Hemi-neglect and hemispheric rivalry. In E. A. Weinstein & R. P. Friedland (Eds.), *Advances in neurology: Vol. 18, Hemi-inattention and hemisphere specialization* (pp. 41–49). New York: Raven Press.

Kramer, A. F., & Jacobsen, A. (1991). Perceptual organization and focused attention: The role of objects and proximity in visual processing. *Perception & Psychophysics, 50,* 267–284.

Kramer, A. F., Tham, M.-P., & Yeh, Y.-Y. (1991). Movement and focused attention: A failure to replicate. *Perception & Psychophysics, 50,* 537–546.

Kramer, A. F., Weber, T. A., & Watson, S. E. (1997). Object-based attentional selection: Grouped arrays or spatially invariant representations? Comment on Vecera and Farah (1994). *Journal of Experimental Psychology: General, 126,* 3–13.

LaBerge, D. (1983). Spatial extent of attention to letters and words. *Journal of Experimental Psychology: Human Perception & Performance, 9,* 371–379.

LaBerge, D. (1995). *Attentional processing.* Cambridge: Harvard University Press.

LaBerge, D., Brown, V., Carter, M., & Bash, D. (1991). Reducing the effects of adjacent distractors by narrowing attention. *Journal of Experimental Psychology: Human Perception & Performance, 17,* 65–76.

Lamb, M. R., & Robertson, L. C. (1990). The effect of visual angle on global and local reaction times depends on the set of visual angles presented. *Perception & Psychophysics, 47,* 489–496.

Lappin, J. S., & Uttal, W. R. (1976). Does prior knowledge facilitate the detection of visual targets in random noise? *Perception & Psychophysics, 20,* 367–374.

Lavie, N. (1995). Perceptual load as a necessary condition for selective attention. *Journal of Experimental Psychology: Human Perception & Performance, 21,* 451–468.

Lavie, N. (1997). Visual feature integration and focused attention: Response competition from multiple distractor features: *Perception & Psychophysics, 59,* 543–556.

Lee, D., & Chun, M. M. (2001). What are the units of visual short-term memory: Objects or spatial locations? *Perception & Psychophysics, 63,* 253–257

Lu, Z., & Dosher, B. A. (1998). External noise distinguishes attention mechanisms. *Vision Research, 38,* 1183–1198.

Luck, S. J. (1998). Sources of dual-task interference: Evidence from human electrophysiology. *Psychological Science, 9,* 223–227.

Luck, S. J., Chelazzi, L., Hillyard, S. A., & Desimone, R. (1997). Neural mechanisms of spatial selective attention in areas V1, V2, and V4 of macaque visual cortex. *Journal of Neurophysiology, 77,* 24–42.

Luck, S. J., Girelli, M., McDermott, M. T., & Ford, M. A. (1997). Bridging the gap between monkey neurophysiology and human perception: An ambiguity resolution theory of visual selective attention. *Cognitive Psychology, 33,* 64–87.

Luck, S. J., & Hillyard, S. A. (1990). Electrophysiological evidence for parallel and serial processing during visual search. *Perception and Psychophysics, 48,* 603–617.

Luck, S. J., & Hillyard, S. A. (1999). The operation of selective attention at multiple stages of processing: Evidence from human and monkey electrophysiology. In M. S. Gazzaniga (Ed.), *The new cognitive neurosciences* (2nd ed., pp. 687–700). Cambridge: MIT Press.

Luck, S. J., Hillyard, S. A., Mouloua, M., & Hawkins, H. L. (1996). Mechanisms of visual-spatial attention: Resource allocation or uncertainty reduction? *Journal of Experimental Psychology: Human Perception & Performance, 22,* 725–737.

Luck, S. J., Hillyard, S. A., Mouloua, M., Woldorff, M. G., Clark, V. P., & Hawkins, H. L. (1994). Effects of spatial cuing on luminance detectability: Psychophysical and electrophysiological evidence for early selection. *Journal of Experimental Psychology: Human Perception & Performance, 20,* 887–904.

Luck, S. J., & Thomas, S. J. (1999). What variety of attention is automatically captured by peripheral cues? *Perception & Psychophysics, 61,* 1424–1435.

Luck, S. J., & Vogel, E. K. (1997). The capacity of visual working memory for features and conjunctions. *Nature, 390,* 279–281.

Luck, S. J., & Vogel, E. K. (2001). Multiple sources of interference in dual-task performance: The cases of the attentional blink and the psychological refractory period. In K. L. Shapiro (Ed.), *The limits of attention* (pp. 124–140). London: Oxford University Press.

Mangun, G. R. (1995). Neural mechanisms of visual selective attention. *Psychophysiology, 32,* 4–18.

Mangun, G. R., & Hillyard, S. A. (1991). Modulations of sensory-evoked brain potentials indicate changes in perceptual processing during visual-spatial priming. *Journal of Experimental Psychology: Human Perception & Performance, 17,* 1057–1074.

Mattingley, J. B., Davis, G., & Driver, J. (1997). Preattentive filling-in of visual surfaces in parietal extinction. *Science, 275,* 671–674.

McCann, R. S., & Johnston, J. C. (1992). Locus of the single-channel bottleneck in dual-task interference. *Journal of Experimental Psychology: Human Perception & Performance, 18,* 471–484.

Medin, D. L., & Ross, B. H. (1996). *Cognitive psychology* (2nd ed.). Fort Worth: Harcourt Brace.

Mesulam, M. M. (1985). Attention, confusional states, and neglect. In M. M. Mesulam (Ed.), *Principles of behavioral neurology.* Philadelphia: Davis.

Meyer, D. E., & Kieras, D. E. (1997). A computational theory of executive cognitive processes and multiple-task performance: Part 1. Basic mechanisms. *Psychological Review, 104,* 3–65.

Miller, J. (1989). The control of attention by abrupt visual onsets and offsets. *Perceptual Psychophysics, 45,* 567–571.

Moray, N. (1959). Attention in dichotic listening: Affective cues and the influence of instructions. *Quarterly Journal of Experimental Psychology, 11,* 56–60.

Mozer, M. C. (1991). *The perception of multiple objects.* Cambridge: MIT Press.

Mozer, M. C., & Sitton, M. (1998). Computational modeling of spatial attention. In H. Pashler (Ed.), *Attention* (pp. 341–393). Hove, England: Psychology Press.

Navon, D. (1977). Forest before trees: The precedence of global features in visual perception. *Cognitive Psychology, 9,* 353–383.

Navon, D. (1984). Resources—a theoretical soup stone? *Psychological Review, 91,* 216–234.

Navon, D., & Gopher, D. (1979). On the economy of the human processing system. *Psychology Review, 86,* 214–255.

Nazir, T. A. (1992). Effects of lateral masking and spatial precueing on gap-resolution in central and peripheral vision. *Vision Research, 32,* 771–777.

Norman, D. A. (1968). Toward a theory of memory and attention. *Psychology Review, 75,* 522–536.

Norman, D. A., & Bobrow, D. G. (1976). On the analysis of performance operating characteristics. *Psychological Review, 83,* 508–510.

Ohman, A. (1979). The orienting response, attention and learning: An information-processing perspective. In H. D. Kimmel, E. H. Van Olst, & J. F. Orlebeke (Eds.), *The orienting reflex in humans* (pp. 443–447). Hillsdale, NJ: Erlbaum.

Osman, A., & Moore, C. M. (1993). The locus of dual-task interference: Psychological refractory effects on movement-related brain potentials. *Journal of Experimental Psychology: Human Perception & Performance, 19,* 1292–1312.

Palmer, J. (1994). Set-size effects in visual search: The effect of attention is independent of the stimulus for simple tasks. *Vision Research, 34,* 1703–1721.

Palmer, J. (1998). Attentional effects in visual search: Relating search accuracy and search time. In R. D. Wright (Ed.), *Vancouver studies in cognitive science: Vol. 8. Visual attention* (pp. 348–388). New York: Oxford University Press.

Palmer, J., Ames, C. T., & Lindsey, D. T. (1993). Measuring the effect of attention on simple visual search. *Journal of Experimental Psychology: Human Perception and Performance, 19,* 108–130.

Palmer, J., Verghese, P., & Pavel, M. (2000). The psychophysics of visual search. *Vision Research, 40,* 1227–1268.

Pan, K., & Eriksen, C. W. (1993). Attentional distribution in the visual field during same-different judgments as assessed by response competition. *Perception & Psychophysics, 53,* 134–144.

Pashler, H. (1984). Evidence against late selection: Stimulus quality effects in previewed displays. *Journal of Experimental Psychology: Human Perception & Performance, 10,* 429–448.

Pashler, H. (1994). Dual-task interference in simple tasks: Data and theory. *Psychological Bulletin, 116,* 220–244.

Pashler, H., & Johnston, J. C. (1988). Attentional limitations in dual-task performance. In

H. Pashler (Ed.), *Attention* (pp. 155–189). East Sussex, England: Psychology Press.

Pashler, H., & Johnston, J. C. (1989). Chronometric evidence for central postponement in temporally overlapping tasks. *Quarterly Journal of Experimental Psychology, 41A,* 19–45.

Posner, M. I. (1980). Orienting of attention. *Quarterly Journal of Experimental Psychology, 32,* 3–25.

Posner, M. I., & Cohen, Y. (1984). Components of visual orienting. In H. Bouma & D. G. Bouwhuis (Eds.), *Attention and performance: Vol. 10, Control of language processes* (pp. 531–556). Hillsdale, NJ: Erlbaum.

Posner, M. I., Nissen, M. J., & Ogden, W. C. (1978). Attended and unattended processing modes: The role of set for spatial location. In H. L. Pick & E. Saltzman (Eds.), *Modes of perceiving and processing information* (pp. 137–157). Hillsdale, NJ: Erlbaum.

Posner, M. I., & Petersen, S. E. (1990). The attention system of the human brain. *Annual Review of Neuroscience, 13,* 25–42.

Potter, M. C. (1976). Short-term conceptual memory for pictures. *Journal of Experimental Psychology: Human Learning and Memory, 2,* 509–522.

Prinzmetal, W., Presti, D. E., & Posner, M. I. (1986). Does attention affect visual feature integration? *Journal of Experimental Psychology: Human Perception and Performance, 12,* 361–369.

Rafal, R. (2000). Neglect II: Cognitive neuropsychological issues. In M. J. Farah & T. E. Feinberg (Eds.), *Patient-based approaches to cognitive neuroscience* (pp. 125–141). Cambridge: MIT Press.

Rafal, R. D., Posner, M. I., Friedman, J. H., Inhoff, A. W., & Bernstein, E. (1988). Orienting of attention in progressive supranuclear palsy. *Brain, 111,* 267–280.

Raymond, J. E., Shapiro, K. L., & Arnell, K. M. (1992). Temporary suppression of visual processing in an RSVP task: An attentional blink? *Journal of Experimental Psychology: Human Perception & Performance, 18,* 849–860.

Rees, G., Frith, C. D., & Lavie, N. (1997). Modulating irrelevant motion perception by varying attentional load in an unrelated task. *Science, 278,* 1616–1619.

Rhodes, G. (1987). Auditory attention and the representation of spatial information. *Perception & Psychophysics, 42,* 1–14.

Robertson, L., Treisman, A., Friedman-Hill, S., & Grabowecky, M. (1997). The interaction of spatial and object pathways: Evidence from Balint's syndrome. *Journal of Cognitive Neuroscience, 9,* 295–317.

Sagi, D., & Julesz, B. (1984). Detection versus discrimination of visual orientation. *Perception, 13,* 619–628.

Schall, J. D., & Thompson, K. G. (1999). Neural selection and control of visually guided eye movements. *Annual Review of Neuroscience, 22,* 241–259.

Schumacher, E. H., Seymour, T. L., Glass, J. M., Fencsik, D. E., Lauber, E. J., Kieras, D. E., & Meyer, D. E. (2001). Virtually perfect time sharing in dual-task performance: Uncorking the central cognitive bottleneck. *Psychological Science, 12,* 101–108.

Shaw, M. L. (1984). Division of attention among spatial locations: A fundamental difference between detection of letters and detection of luminance increments. In H. Bouma & D. G. Bouwhuis (Eds.), *Attention and performance: Vol. 10, Control of language processes* (pp. 109–121). Hillsdale, NJ: Erlbaum.

Shiffrin, R. M., & Gardner, G. T. (1972). Visual processing capacity and attentional control. *Journal of Experimental Psychology, 93,* 72–83.

Shiu, L., & Pashler, H. (1994). Negligible effect of spatial precuing on identification of single digits. *Journal of Experimental Psychology: Human Perception & Performance, 20,* 1037–1054.

Singer, W., & Gray, C. M. (1995). Visual feature integration and the temporal correlation hypothesis. *Annual Review of Neuroscience, 18,* 555–586.

Spence, C., & Driver, J. (1996). Audiovisual links in endogenous covert spatial attention. *Journal of Experimental Psychology: Human Perception & Performance, 22,* 1005–1030.

Spence, C., & Driver, J. (1997). Audiovisual links in exogenous covert spatial orienting. *Perception & Psychophysics, 59,* 1–22.

Sperling, G. (1960). The information available in brief visual presentations. *Psychological Monographs, 74* (Whole No. 498).

Sperling, G., & Dosher, B. A. (1986). Strategy and optimization in human information processing. In K. R. Boff, L. Kaufman, & J. P. Thomas (Eds.), *Handbook of perception and human performance: Vol. 1* (pp. 2–65). New York: Wiley.

Stroop, J. R. (1935). Studies of interference in serial verbal reactions. *Journal of Experimental Psychology, 18,* 643–662.

Tassinari, G., Aglioti, S., Chelazzi, L., Peru, A., & Berlucchi, G. (1994). Do peripheral non-informative cues induce early facilitation of target detection? *Vision Research, 34,* 179–189.

Taylor, T. L., & Klein, R. M. (2000). Visual and motor effects in inhibition of return. *Journal of Experimental Psychology: Human Perception and Performance, 26,* 1639–1656.

Telford, C. W. (1931). The refractory phase of voluntary and associative responses. *Journal of Experimental Psychology, 14,* 1–36.

Treisman, A. (1988). Features and objects: The Fourteenth Bartlett Memorial Lecture. *Quarterly Journal of Experimental Psychology, 40,* 201–237.

Treisman, A. (1991). Search, similarity, and integration of features between and within dimensions. *Journal of Experimental Psychology: Human Perception & Performance, 17,* 652–676.

Treisman, A. (1992). Spreading suppression or feature integration? A reply to Duncan and Humphreys (1992). *Journal of Experimental Psychology: Human Perception & Performance, 18,* 589–593.

Treisman, A. (1996). The binding problem, *Current Opinion in Neurobiology, 6,* 171–178.

Treisman, A., & Sato, S. (1990). Conjunction search revisited. *Journal of Experimental Psychology: Human Perception & Performance, 16,* 459–478.

Treisman, A., & Schmidt, H. (1982). Illusory conjunctions in the perception of objects. *Cognitive Psychology, 14,* 107–141.

Treisman, A. M. (1964). Selective attention in man. *British Medical Bulletin, 20,* 12–16.

Treisman, A. M. (1969). Strategies and models of selective attention. *Psychological Review, 76,* 282–299.

Treisman, A. M., & Gelade, G. (1980). A feature-integration theory of attention. *Cognitive Psychology, 12,* 97–136.

Valdes-Sosa, M., Bobes, M. A., Rodriguez, V., & Pinilla, T. (1998). Switching attention without shifting the spotlight: object-based attentional modulation of brain potentials. *Journal of Cognitive Neuroscience, 10,* 137–151.

Vecera, S. P. (1994). Grouped locations and object-based attention: Comment on Egly, Driver, and Rafal (1994). *Journal of Experimental Psychology: General, 123,* 316–320.

Vecera, S. P. (2000). Toward a biased competition account of object-based segregation and attention. *Brain and Mind, 1,* 353–384.

Vecera, S. P., & Behrmann, M. (in press). Attention and unit formation: A biased competition account of object-based attention. In T. F. Shipley & P. Kellman (Eds.), *From frames to objects: Segmentation and grouping in vision.* New York: Elsevier.

Vecera, S. P., Behrmann, M., & Filapek, J. C. (2001). Attending to the parts of a single object: Part-based selection limitations. *Perception & Psychophysics, 63,* 308–321.

Vecera, S. P., Behrmann, M., & McGoldrick, J. (2000). Selective attention to the parts of an object. *Psychonomic Bulletin & Review, 7,* 301–308.

Vecera, S. P., & Farah, M. J. (1994). Does visual attention select objects or locations? *Journal of Experimental Psychology: General, 123,* 146–160.

Visser, T. A. W., Bischof, W. F., & Di Lollo, V. (1999). Attentional switching in spatial and non-spatial domains: Evidence from the attentional blink. *Psychological Bulletin, 125,* 458–469.

Vogel, E. K. (2000). *Selective storage in visual working memory: Distinguishing between perceptual-level and working memory-level mechanisms of attention.* Iowa city: University of Iowa.

Vogel, E. K., Luck, S. J., & Shapiro, K. L. (1998). Electrophysiological evidence for a postperceptual locus of suppression during the attentional blink. *Journal of Experimental Psychology: Human Perception & Performance, 24,* 1656–1674.

Vogel, E. K., Woodman, G. F., & Luck, S. J. (2001). Storage of features, conjunctions, and objects in visual working memory. *Journal of Experimental Psychology: Human Perception & Performance, 27,* 92–114.

Weichselgartner, E., & Sperling, G. (1987). Dynamics of automatic and controlled visual attention. *Science, 238,* 778–780.

Wickens, C. D. (1980). The structure of attentional resources. In R. S. Nickerson (Ed.), *Attention and performance: Vol. 8* (pp. 239–257). Hillsdale, NJ: Erlbaum.

Wojciulik, E., & Kanwisher, N. (1999). The generality of parietal involvement in visual attention. *Neuron, 23,* 747–764.

Wolfe, J. M. (1994). Guided search 2.0: A revised model of visual search. *Psychonomic Bulletin & Review, 1,* 202–238.

Wood, N., & Cowan, N. (1995a). The cocktail party phenomenon revisited: Attention and memory in the classic selective listening procedure of Cherry (1953). *Journal of Experimental Psychology: General, 124,* 243–262.

Wood, N., & Cowan, N. (1995b). The cocktail party phenomenon revisited: How frequent are attention shifts to one's name in an irrelevant auditory channel? *Journal of Experimental Psychology: Human Perception & Performance, 21,* 255–260.

Woodman, G. F., & Luck, S. J. (1999). Electrophysiological measurement of rapid shifts of attention during visual search. *Nature, 400,* 867–869.

Woodman, G. F., Vogel, E. K., & Luck, S. J. (2001). Visual search remains efficient when visual working memory is full. *Psychological Science, 12,* 219–224.

Yantis, S. (1993). Stimulus-driven attentional capture and attentional control settings. *Journal of Experimental Psychology: Human Perception & Performance, 19,* 676–681.

Yantis, S. (2000). Goal-directed and stimulus-driven determinants of attentional control. In S. Monsell & J. Driver (Eds.), *Attention and performance: Vol. 18, Control of cognitive processes* (pp. 73–103). Cambridge: MIT Press.

Yantis, S., & Egeth, H. E. (1999). On the distinction between visual salience and stimulus-driven attentional capture. *Journal of Experimental Psychology: Human Perception & Performance, 25,* 661–676.

Yantis, S., & Hillstrom, A. P. (1994). Stimulus-driven attentional capture: Evidence from equiluminant visual objects. *Journal of Experimental Psychology: Human Perception & Performance, 20,* 95–107.

Yantis, S., & Johnston, J. C. (1990). On the locus of visual selection: Evidence from focused attention tasks. *Journal of Experimental Psychology: Human Perception & Performance, 16,* 135–149.

Yantis, S., & Jonides, J. (1984). Abrupt visual onsets and selective attention: Evidence from visual search. *Journal of Experimental Psychology: Human Perception & Performance, 10,* 601–621.

Yantis, S., & Jonides, J. (1990). Abrupt visual onsets and selective attention: Voluntary versus automatic allocation. *Journal of Experimental Psychology: Human Perception & Performance, 16,* 121–134.

CHAPTER 7

Visual Object Recognition

MICHAEL J. TARR AND QUOC C. VUONG

OVERVIEW

The Recognition Problem

The study of object recognition concerns itself with a twofold problem. First, what is the form of visual object representation? Second, how do observers match object percepts to visual object representations? Unfortunately, the world is not color coded or conveniently labeled for us. Many objects look similar (think about four-legged mammals, cars, or song birds), and most contain no single feature or mark that uniquely identifies them. Even worse, objects are rarely if ever seen under identical viewing conditions: Objects change their size, position, orientation, and relations between parts; viewers move about; and sources of illumination turn on and off or move. Successful object recognition requires generalizing across such changes. Thus, even if observers have never seen a bear outside the zoo, on a walk in the woods they can tell that the big, brown, furry object with teeth 20 ft in front of them is an unfriendly bear and is probably best avoided, or that the orange-yellow blob hanging from a tree is a tasty papaya.

Consider how walking around an object alters one's view of it. Unless the object is rotationally symmetric (e.g., a cylinder), the visible shape of the object will change with observer movement—some surfaces will come into view, whereas other surfaces will become occluded and the object's geometry will change both quantitatively and qualitatively (Tarr & Kriegman, 2001). Changes in the image as a consequence of object movement are even more dramatic: Not only do the same alterations in shape occur, but the positions of light sources relative to the object change as well. This alters both the pattern of shading on the object's surfaces and the shadows cast by some parts of the object on other parts. Transformations in size, position, and mean illumination also alter the image of an object, although somewhat less severely when compared to viewpoint/orientation changes.

Recognizing Objects across Transformations of the Image. Theories of object recognition must provide an account of how observers compensate for a wide variety of changes in the image. Although theories differ in many respects, most attempt to specify how perceptual representations of objects are derived from visual input, what processes are used to recognize these percepts, and what representational format is used to encode objects in visual memory. Broadly speaking, two different approaches to these issues have been adopted. One class of theories assumes that specific invariant cues to object identity may be recovered under almost all viewing conditions. These theories are said to

287

be *viewpoint-invariant* in that these invariants provide sufficient information to recognize the object regardless of how the image of an object changes (within some limits; Biederman, 1987; Marr & Nishihara, 1978). A second class of theories argues that no such general invariants exist[1] and that object features are represented much as they appeared when originally viewed, thereby preserving *viewpoint-dependent* shape information and surface appearance. The features visible in the input image are compared to features in object representations, either by normalizing the input image to approximately the same viewing position as represented in visual memory (Bülthoff & Edelman, 1992; Tarr, 1995) or by computing a statistical estimate of the quality of match between the input image and candidate representations (Perrett, Oram, & Ashbridge, 1998; Riesenhuber & Poggio, 1999).

Viewpoint-invariant and viewpoint-dependent approaches make very different predictions regarding how invariance is achieved (these labels are somewhat misleading in that the goal of *all* theories of recognition is to achieve invariance, i.e., the successful recognition of objects across varying viewing conditions). Viewpoint-invariant theories propose that recognition is itself invariant across transformations. That is, across changes in viewpoint, illumination, and so on, there is no change in recognition performance; that is, as long as the appropriate invariants are recoverable, the response of the system remains constant. In comparison, viewpoint-dependent theories hypothesize that recognition is dependent on specific viewing parameters. That is, across changes in viewpoint,

illumination, and so on, there may be changes in recognition performance because objects are represented according to how they appeared when originally learned.

Recognizing Objects across Different Instances of a Class.   Generalization across object views is only one of several demands placed on the visual recognition system. A second factor is the ability to generalize across different instances of a visual object class. Because such instances are typically treated as members of the same category and thus should elicit the same response, an observer must be able to use one or more instances of a class to recognize new instances of the same class—the bear we are staring at is unlikely to be the same one we saw on our last trip to Alaska or on "Animal Planet," but it would be fatal not to realize that this, too, is a bear. At the same time, an observer must not confuse somewhat similar objects that should be recognized as different individuals: It is important that one does not confuse poisonous Ugli fruit with edible papayas. Marr and Nishihara (1978) termed these two goals of object recognition *stability* and *sensitivity,* respectively. These two goals seem to trade off against one another: As recognition abilities become more stable (i.e., the more one can generalize across objects), the less an observer may be able to distinguish between objects. Conversely, as recognition abilities become more sensitive (i.e., the better one is at telling objects apart), the worse an observer may be at deciding that two objects are really the same thing. How to deal with these two competing goals is at the heart of most theories of object recognition and is central to the debate that has ensued about the "correct" theory of human recognition abilities.

Recognizing Objects at Different Levels of Specificity.   A third factor that is important to developing such theories is the nature

---

[1]Of course invariants can be found under certain contexts. For example, if there are only three objects to be distinguished and these objects are red, green, and blue, object color becomes an invariant in this context (Tarr & Bülthoff, 1995).

of recognition itself. That is, what exactly is the recognition task? Imagine that one spies a bear in the distance and wants to know a variety of different things: Recognition: Is that a bear? Discrimination: Is that a bear or a person wearing a fur hat? Is that a grizzly or a brown bear? Identification: Is that the friendly Gentle Ben? The key point highlighted by these different recognition tasks is that objects may be visually recognized in different ways and—critically—at different *categorical levels*. In the cognitive categorization literature a distinction is made between the superordinate, basic, subordinate, and individual levels (Rosch, Mervis, Gray, Johnson, & Boyes-Braem, 1976). A bear can be classified as an animal, as a bear, as a grizzly bear, and as Gentle Ben, and each of these labels can correspond respectively to a different categorization of the same object.

Visual recognition can occur roughly at these same levels, although visual categorization is not necessarily isomorphic with the categorization process as studied by many cognitive psychologists. For example, some properties of objects are not strictly visual but may be relevant to categorization: Chairs are used to sit on, but there is no specific visual property that defines "sitability." A second distinction between visual and cognitive categorization is the default level of access. Jolicoeur, Gluck, and Kosslyn (1984) pointed out that many objects are not recognized at their basic level. For example, the basic level for pelicans is "bird," but most people seeing a pelican would label it "pelican" by default. This level, referred to as the entry level, places a much greater emphasis on the similarities and differences of an object's visual features relative to other known objects in the same object class (Murphy & Brownell, 1985). The features of pelicans are fairly distinct from those of typical birds; hence, pelicans are labeled first as "pelicans"; in contrast, the features of sparrows are very typical, and sparrows are much more likely to be labeled as "birds."

Why are these distinctions between levels of access important to object recognition? As reviewed in the next section, several controversies in the field center on issues related to categorical level. Indeed, the stability/sensitivity tradeoff just discussed is essentially a distinction about whether object recognition should veer more toward the subordinate level (emphasizing sensitivity) or toward the entry level (emphasizing stability). This issue forms the core of a debate about the appropriate domain of explanation (Biederman & Gerhardstein, 1995; Tarr & Bülthoff, 1995). That is, what is the default (and most typical) level of recognition? Furthermore, the particular recognition mechanisms applied by default may vary with experience; that is, perceptual experts may recognize objects in their domain of expertise at a more specific level than do novices (Gauthier & Tarr, 1997a). Some theorists—most notably Biederman (1987)—presuppose that recognition *typically* occurs at the entry level and that any theory of recognition should concentrate on accounting for how the visual system accomplishes this particular task. In contrast, other theorists—Bülthoff, Edelman, Tarr, and others (see Hayward & Williams, 2000; Tarr & Bülthoff, 1998)—argue that the hallmark of human recognition abilities is *flexibility* and that any theory of recognition should account for how the visual system can recognize objects at the entry, subordinate, and individual levels (and anything in between). This distinction is almost isomorphic with the viewpoint-invariant/viewpoint-dependent distinction raised earlier. Specifically, viewpoint-invariant theories tend to assume the entry level as the default and concentrate on accounting for how visual recognition at this level may be achieved. In contrast, viewpoint-dependent theories tend to assume that object recognition functions at many different categorical levels, varying with context and task demands.

A second, somewhat related, debate focuses on the scope of posited recognition mechanisms. Some theorists argue that at least two distinct mechanisms are available for recognition, generally breaking down along the lines of whether the recognition discrimination is at the entry or the subordinate level (Farah, 1992; Jolicoeur, 1990). Some researchers have suggested that several "special purpose devices" may be devoted to the task of recognizing specific object classes (e.g., a neural module for face recognition, another for place recognition, and one for common object recognition; Kanwisher, 2000). Alternatively, it has been argued that recognition at many levels and for all object categories can be accomplished by a single, highly plastic system that adapts according to task constraints and experience (Tarr, in press; Tarr & Gauthier, 2000). This and the aforementioned debates have produced an extensive research literature addressing the nature of visual object recognition. In order to understand these controversies better, we next review the particular dimensions typically used both to characterize object representations and to constrain potential mechanisms of recognition.

THE NATURE OF OBJECT REPRESENTATIONS

An overwhelming body of evidence addresses the nature of representation in object recognition and visual cognition. Despite this, there is an alarming absence of a comprehensive account of object recognition. Rather, as outlined earlier, most theorists have more or less tried to develop a framework along a particular subset of issues in order to frame a particular theory (Biederman, 1987; Edelman, 1995; Marr & Nishihara, 1978; Pinker, 1984; Poggio & Edelman, 1990; Tarr, 1995). More-

over, although there have been some attempts to integrate low- and mid-level visual processing into theories of object perception and recognition (Marr, 1982), most researchers have restricted themselves to a narrower problem that isolates recognition mechanisms from the processing that precedes it.

The range of behavioral and neural data indicates that the representations of objects and the mechanisms used to recognize objects are highly flexible (Tarr & Black, 1994). This presents a challenge to any theory of object recognition (including those that argue for flexibility but cannot explain it). Selecting a representational format typically depends on how a particular theory addresses a broad set of interdependent issues, including the factors reviewed earlier. The critical issues include (a) the features of the representation; (b) the degree to which three-dimensional structure, if any, is encoded; (c) the spatial relationships among features within the representation; (d) the frame of reference used to specify the locations of features; and (e) the normalization mechanisms, if any, used to operate on the input image or on the representation. Together, these issues are crucial to understanding the problem of object recognition; they also provide metrics by which the strengths and weaknesses of theories can be identified (Bülthoff & Edelman, 1993; Hummel, 1994).

Object Features

What are features? A loose definition is that features are the elementary units used in the representation of objects (Marr & Nishihara, 1978). This definition, however, leaves open a wide range of possible feature types, from local features that measure metric properties of objects at specific locations to global features that represent only qualitative characteristics of objects. Examples of local features include receptive field responses measuring brightness or color, oriented lines, T-junctions, corners, and so on (K. Tanaka, 1996). Examples of global features include three-dimensional component parts realized as simple volumes that roughly capture the actual shape of an object (Biederman, 1987; Marr & Nishihara, 1978).

Significant differences between these two approaches are immediately apparent. On the one hand, an appealing aspect of local features is that they are readily derivable from retinal input and that they are the natural result of earlier visual processing as discussed in prior chapters in this volume. However, three-dimensional parts must be recovered from two-dimensional images in a manner that is not entirely obvious given what is currently known about visual processing. On the other hand, it is hard to imagine how stability is achieved using only local features; the set of features visible in one viewpoint of an object is likely to be very different from the feature sets that are visible in other viewpoints of the same object or other similar objects. Even slight variations in viewpoint, illumination, or configuration may change the value of local responses and, hence, the object representation. Furthermore, three-dimensional parts yield stability; as long as the same invariants are visible, the same set of three-dimensional parts may be recovered from many different viewpoints and across many different instances of an object class. Thus, variations in viewpoint, illumination, or configuration are likely to have little impact on the qualitative representation of the object.

Dimensionality

The range of features that may form the representation is quite wide, but cutting across all possible formats is their degree of dimensionality, that is, how many spatial dimensions are encoded. The physical world is three-dimensional, yet the optic array sampled by the retinas is two-dimensional. As discussed in earlier chapters in this volume, one goal of vision is to recover properties of the three-dimensional world from this two-dimensional input (Marr, 1982). Indeed, three-dimensional perception seems critical for grasping things, walking around them, playing ping-pong, and so on. However, recovery of three-dimensional shape may not be critical to the process of remembering and recognizing objects. Thus, one can ask whether object representations are faithful to the full three-dimensional structure of objects or to the two-dimensional optic array, or to something in between. As discussed earlier, some theories argue that complete three-dimensional models of objects are recovered (Marr & Nishihara, 1978) or that object representations are three-dimensional, but can vary depending on the features visible from different viewpoints (Biederman, 1987). Others have argued that object representations are strictly two-dimensional (i.e., preserving the appearance of the object in the image with no reference to three-dimensional shape or relations; Edelman, 1993). An intermediate stance is that object representations are not strictly two-dimensional or three-dimensional, but rather that they represent objects in terms of visible surfaces, including local depth and orientation information. Such a representation is sometimes termed $2^{1}/_{2}$-dimensional ($2^{1}/_{2}$-D; Marr, 1982). Critically, both two-dimensional and $2^{1}/_{2}$-D representations only depict surfaces visible in the original image; there is no recovery, reconstruction, or extrapolation about the three-dimensional structure of unseen surfaces or parts. Instead, three-dimensional information arises from more local processes such as shape-from-shading, stereo, and structure-from-motion. In contrast, three-dimensional representations include not only surface features visible in the input (the output of local three-dimensional recovery mechanisms) but also additional globally recovered information about an object's three-dimensional structure (e.g., the three-dimensional shape of an object part). Such three-dimensional representations are appealing because they encode objects with a structure that is isomorphic with their instantiation in the physical world. However, deriving three-dimensional representations is computationally difficult because three-dimensional information must be recovered and integrated (Bülthoff & Edelman, 1993).

Spatial Relationships

Features are the building blocks of object representations. By themselves, however, they are not sufficient to characterize, either quantitatively or qualitatively, the appearance of objects. A face, for example, is not a random arrangement of eyes, ears, nose, and mouth, but rather is a particular set of features in a particular spatial arrangement. Object representations must therefore express the spatial relations between features. One aspect of how this is accomplished is whether the spatial relations between features are represented at a single level, in which all features share the same status, or whether there is a hierarchy of relations. For instance, Marr and Nishihara (1978) hypothesized that a small number of parts at the top of a hierarchy are progressively decomposed into constituent parts and their spatial relationships at finer and finer scales (e.g., an arm can be decomposed into an upper arm, forearm, and hand). The hand, in turn, can be further decomposed at an even finer scale into a palm and fingers. Local image features can similarly be structured: Elaborate features can be decomposed into simpler ones (Riesenhuber & Poggio, 1999). Thus, entry-level categories might be captured by a higher level of the hierarchy (in that the common features that define an entry-level category—e.g., "bear"—are typically more global), and subordinate-level categories might be cap-

tured only by finer levels (e.g., the subtle features that distinguish a grizzly bear from a brown bear). Alternatively, object representations might encode only the coarsest level of structure: two to three parts (and their relations) at most with no hierarchy specifying structure at finer scales (Biederman, 1987; Hummel & Biederman, 1992).

Because visual input is inherently spatial, early and intermediate visual representations necessarily encode the quantitative positions of features; in essence, representations within the visual system are inherently *spatial* early on (Marr, 1982). At issue, however, is the degree to which metric information is preserved in higher-level, long-term object representations. Building on the examples cited in the previous section, there is a dichotomy between a local, quantitative approach and a global, qualitative approach. At one extreme, the metric relations between features present in the image are kept more or less intact in higher-level object representations. The resulting *template* would be highly sensitive to changes in the image, such that any variation in the spatial relations between features—no matter how slight—would require a new representation (although this variation may be compensated for by using a variety of strategies; see the discussion on normalization mechanisms later). Typically, however, even if one were to posit local, quantitative features, the relations between them are assumed to be somewhat more flexible. For example, many local feature theories posit that the relative positions of features are probabilistic (Edelman, 1995; Riesenhuber & Poggio, 1999; Tarr & Bülthoff, 1998). The resulting object representation would still be sensitive to metric variations between a known version of an object and a new image of that object but would not fail to find correspondences between like features in slightly different locations—a *deformable template,* so to speak (Ullman & Basri, 1991). Models that assume local, quantitative measures as the molar features along with relatively precise localization of these features in the image have been dubbed *image-based models* (although this term still encompasses a wide variety of approaches).

Global, qualitative models tend to assume a much coarser coding of the spatial relations between features. Biederman (1987; Hummel & Biederman, 1992) argues that spatial relations are encoded in a qualitative manner that discards metric relations between object features but preserves their critical structural relations. On this view, for example, the representation would code that one part is above another part, but it would not code how far above or how directly above (a "top-of" relation). The resulting concatenation of features (in Biederman's model with three-dimensional parts) and qualitative structural relations is often referred to as a *structural description*.

One other possibility should be noted. *All* spatial relations between features might be discarded so that only the features themselves are represented: Thus a face, for instance, might just be a jumble of features! Such a scheme can be conceptualized as an array of nonlocalized *feature detectors* uniformly distributed across the retinal array (dubbed *Pandemonium* by Selfridge, 1959). The resulting representation might be more stable, but only as long as the same features or a subset of these features are present somewhere in the image and their presence uniquely specifies the appropriate object. Although there are obvious problems with this approach, it may have more merit than it is often given credit for, particularly if one assumes an extremely rich feature vocabulary and a large number of features per object (see Tarr, 1999).

Frames of Reference

As pointed out in the previous section, most theorists agree that intermediate stages of visual processing preserve at least the rough geometry of retinal inputs. Thus, from the perspective of the observer there is an implicit specification of the spatial relations between features for intermediate-level image representations. Ultimately, however, the spatial relations between features are typically assumed to be explicit in high-level object representations. This explicit coding is generally thought to place features in locations specified relative to one or more anchor points or frames of reference (Marr, 1982).

The most common distinction between reference frames is whether they are *viewpoint-independent* or *viewpoint-dependent*. Embedded in these two types of approaches are several different kinds of frames, each relying on different anchor points. For example, viewpoint-independent models encompass both object-centered and viewpoint-invariant representations. Consider what happens if the features of an object are defined relative to the object itself: Although changes in viewpoint alter the appearance of the object, they do not change the position of a given feature relative to other features in the object (as long as the object remains rigid). Thus, the representation of the object does not change with many changes in the image. The best-known instantiation of an object-centered theory was proposed by Marr and Nishihara (1978). They suggested that an object's features are specified relative to its axis of elongation, although other axes, such as the axis of symmetry, are also possible (McMullen & Farah, 1991). As long as an observer can recover the elongation axis for a given object, a canonical description of that object can be constructed for any image of it. Ideally, only a single viewpoint-independent representation of each object would be encoded in visual memory for that object to be recognized from all viewpoints. Although this approach has some advantages, in practice it has proven rather difficult to develop methods

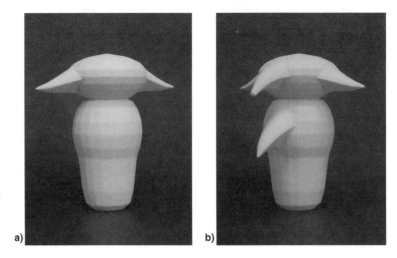

a)

b)

Figure 7.1   Different viewpoints of objects often reveal (or occlude) different features.

for the reliable derivation of canonical axes of elongation for most objects without recourse to at least some aspects of the object's identity. Moreover, it seems unlikely that a single representation of an object could suffice when there exist many viewpoints from which some significant features of the object are completely occluded (Figure 7.1).

Biederman's (1987) theory of recognition attempts to address some of these shortcomings. Like Marr and Nishihara, he assumes a structural description comprised of three-dimensional parts, but his theory posits viewpoint-invariant (not object-centered) object representations. What, precisely, is the distinction? Rather than attempt to encode the position of features in any specific coordinate system, Biederman sidestepped the problem by proposing that particular collections of viewpoint-invariant features (sometimes referred to as nonaccidental properties, i.e., local configurations of edges that are so unlikely to have occurred by accident that they must reflect meaningful three-dimensional structure) map onto a given three-dimensional volume. For example, if several Y-vertices and arrow-vertices appear in an image along with three parallel lines, they might specify

a brick. In Biederman's model, the brick's three-dimensional primitive would entirely replace the image features that specified the part. Because the parts themselves and their relations are represented only at a nonmetric, qualitative level (e.g., brick on top of cylinder), the representation does not use a strictly object-centered frame of reference (although the spatial relations are still object-relative). The trick here is that the particular features specifying the three-dimensional parts are invariants with respect to viewpoint (and possibly illumination). Thus, many changes in viewpoint would not change which particular three-dimensional primitives were recovered. Biederman, however, acknowledges that it is impossible to recover parts that are not visible from a given viewpoint. Thus, he allows for multiple representations for each object: Each depicts different collections of visible parts for the same object under different viewing conditions (Biederman & Gerhardstein, 1993).

In contrast to viewpoint-invariant models, viewpoint-dependent models inherently encompass retinotopic, viewer-centered (egocentric), and environment-centered (spatiotopic or allocentric) frames, anchored to the retinal image, the observer, or the environment, respectively. That is, objects are represented from a particular viewpoint, which entails multiple representations. Put another way, object representations that use a viewer-centered reference frame are tied more or less directly to the object as it appears to the viewer or, in the case of allocentric frames, relative to the environment. As such, they are typically assumed to be less abstract and more visually rich than are viewpoint-independent representations (although this is simply a particular choice of the field; viewpoint-dependence/ independence and the richness of the representation are technically separable issues). It is often thought that viewpoint-dependent representations may be more readily computed from retinal images as compared to viewpoint-independent representations. However, there is an associated cost in that viewpoint-dependent representations are less stable across changes in viewpoint because they necessarily encode distinct viewpoints of the same object as distinct object representations. Thus, theories adopting this approach require a large number of viewpoints for each known object. Although this approach places higher demands on memory capacity, it potentially reduces the degree of computation necessary for deriving high-level object representations for recognition.

Normalization Procedures

Regardless of the molar features of the representation—local features, three-dimensional parts, or something in between—if some degree of viewpoint dependency is assumed, then the representation for a single object or class will consist of a set of distinct feature collections, each depicting the appearance of the object from a different vantage point. This leads to a significant theoretical problem: Different viewpoints of the same object must somehow be linked to form a coherent representation of the three-dimensional object. One solution might be to find a rough correspondence between the features present in different viewpoints. For example, the head of the bear is visible from both the front and the side, so this might be a clue that the two images arose from the same object. Unfortunately, simple geometric correspondence seems unlikely to solve this problem; if such correspondences were available (i.e., if it were possible to map one viewpoint of an object into another viewpoint of that same object), then recognition might proceed without the need to learn the new viewpoint in the first place! Thus it would seem that viewpoints are either distinct or not (Jolicoeur, 1985).

The conundrum of how an observer might recognize a novel viewpoint of a familiar object was addressed by Tarr and Pinker (1989). They built on the finding that human perceivers have available a mental rotation process (Shepard & Metzler, 1971) by which they can transform a mental image of a three-dimensional object from one viewpoint to another. Shepard and others had reasoned that although the mental rotation process was useful for mental problem solving, it was not appropriate for object recognition. The argument was that in order to know the direction and target of a given rotation, an observer must already know the identity of the object in question; therefore, executing a mental rotation would be moot. Put another way, how would the recognition system determine the correct direction and magnitude of the transformation prior to recognition? Ullman (1989) pointed out that an alignment between the input shape and known object representations could be carried out on the basis of partial information. That is, a small portion of the input could be used to compute both the most likely matches for the current input, as well as the transformation necessary to align this input with its putative matches. In practice, this means that a subset of local features in the input image is compared, in parallel, to features encoded in stored object representations. Each comparison returns a goodness-of-fit measure and the transformation necessary to align the image with the particular candidate representation (Ullman, 1989). The transformation actually executed is based on the best match among these. Thus, observers could learn one or more viewpoints of an object and then use these known viewpoints plus normalization procedures to map from unfamiliar to familiar viewpoints during recognition.

Jolicoeur (1985) provided some of the first data suggesting that such a process exists by demonstrating that the time it takes to name a familiar object increases as that object is rotated farther and farther away from its familiar, upright orientation. However, this result was problematic in that upright viewpoints of mono-oriented objects are canonical in that they are the most frequently seen and most preferred views (Palmer, Rosch, & Chase, 1981). Thus, the pattern of naming times obtained by Jolicoeur might speak more to the "goodness" of different object views than to the mechanisms used in recognition.

Tarr and Pinker's (1989) innovation was to use novel two-dimensional objects shown to subjects in multiple viewpoints. Subjects learned the names of four of the objects and then practiced naming these objects plus three distractors (for which the correct response was "none of the above") in several orientations generated by rotations in the picture-plane (Figure 7.2a). Tarr and Pinker's subjects rapidly became equally fast at naming these objects from all trained orientations. Subjects' naming times changed when new picture-plane orientations were then introduced: They remained equally fast at familiar orientations, but naming times were progressively slower as the objects were rotated further and further away from a familiar orientation (Figure 7.2b). Thus, subjects were learning to encode and use those orientations that were

seen most frequently (and were not merely geometrically "good" views). This suggests that observers were able to invoke normalization procedures to map unfamiliar orientations of known objects to familiar orientations of those same objects. Tarr and Pinker hypothesized that these normalization procedures were based on the same mental rotation process discovered by Shepard and Metzler (1971). Tarr (1995) reported corroborating evidence using novel three-dimensional versions of Tarr and Pinker's two-dimensional objects rotated in depth.

Some researchers have pointed out that mental rotation is an ill-defined process. What does it really mean to "rotate" a mental image? Several researchers have offered computational mechanisms for implementing normalization procedures with behavioral signatures similar to that predicted for mental rotation. These include linear combinations of views (Ullman & Basri, 1991), view interpolation (Poggio & Edelman, 1990), and statistical evidence accumulation (Perrett et al., 1998). Some of these normalization mechanisms make further predictions regarding recognition behavior for new viewpoints of known objects. For example, Bülthoff and Edelman (1992) obtained some evidence consistent with the view-interpolation models of normalization, and Perrett et al. found that responses of populations of neurons in monkey visual cortex were consistent with the evidence-accumulation account of normalization.

Note that viewpoint-invariant theories of recognition do not require normalization as a way for recognizing unfamiliar viewpoints of familiar objects. In particular, Marr and Nishihara (1978) assumed that viewpoint-invariant recovery mechanisms are sufficient to recognize an object from any viewpoint, known or unknown. Biederman (1987) assumed that viewpoint-invariant mechanisms are viewpoint-limited but span extremely wide viewpoint regions, effectively making recog-

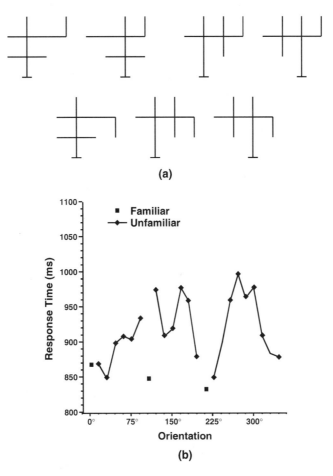

(a)

(b)

Figure 7.2   Recognizing objects over changes in viewpoint.

NOTE: a) The novel two-dimensional objects used as stimuli in Tarr and Pinker (1989). b) Average response times for subjects to name these objects in trained, familiar orientations and in unfamiliar orientations. Naming times increased systematically with distance from the nearest familiar orientation.

SOURCE: Adapted from Tarr and Pinker (1989, Figures 1, p. 243, and 6, p. 255).

nition behavior viewpoint-independent (Biederman & Gerhardstein, 1993; see Tarr & Bülthoff, 1995, for a critique of these claims and Biederman & Gerhardstein, 1995, for their reply).

Although these normalization mechanisms show how disparate viewpoints of objects may be mapped onto one another, they still leave open one of our original questions: When two viewpoints of a single object are so distinct as to require separate representations, how does the recognition system ever map these onto the same object name or category (or are observers destined never to know that it was the same thing coming as going)? One intriguing possibility is that statistical mechanisms similar to those that seem to function in learning distinct viewpoints are used to connect disparate visual information over time. Consider that when people view an object, the single image they are most likely to see next is another viewpoint of that same object (Tarr & Bülthoff, 1998). Thus, a mechanism that associates what one sees at one instant with what one sees at the next instant would produce the necessary relationships. Recent neural (Miyashita, 1988) and computational (Wallis, 1996) evidence indicates that primate visual memory does learn to associate distinct images if they co-occur over time. Thus, whether views are defined by three-dimensional parts or by local features, temporal associations may provide the glue for building coherent mental representations of objects (Tarr & Bülthoff, 1998).

THEORIES OF OBJECT RECOGNITION

Structural-Description Models

We have now set the stage for an enumeration of two primary approaches to visual object recognition: *structural-description* and *image-based* theories. For historical reasons we begin by reviewing the structural-description approach. One consequence of the computing revolution of the late 1960s and early 1970s was the development of sophisticated tools for generating realistic computer graphics (Foley & Van Dam, 1982). To generate images of synthetic three-dimensional objects, graphic programmers employed volumetric primitives (i.e., three-dimensional volumes that depicted the approximate shape of a part of a real three-dimensional object). Thus, a teakettle might be synthesized by a sphere flattened on the top and bottom, a very flat cylinder for the lid, and two bent thin cylinders for the handle and spout. Based on such techniques, some researchers suggested that similar representations might be used by both biological and machine vision systems for object recognition (Binford, 1971). Specifically, objects would be learned by decomposing them into a collection of three-dimensional parts and then remembering that part configuration. Recognition would proceed by recov-

ering three-dimensional parts from an image and then matching this new configuration to those stored in object memory. One appealing element of this approach was the representational power of the primitives, called generalized cones (or generalized cylinders) by Binford. A generalized cone represents three-dimensional shape as three sets of parameters: (a) an arbitrarily shaped cross section that (b) can scale arbitrarily as (c) it is swept across an arbitrarily shaped axis. These three parameter sets are typically defined by algebraic functions that together capture the shape of the object part.

Marr and Nishihara built on this concept in their seminal 1978 theory of recognition. In many ways they proposed the first viable account of human object recognition, presenting a model that seemed to address the factors of invariance, stability, and level of access. As mentioned previously, they placed a significant computational burden on the reconstruction of the three-dimensional scene. In particular, in their model a necessary step in the recognition process consists of recovering three-dimensional parts from the input image. Recognizing the power of generalized cones, Marr and Nishihara suggested that observers use information about an object's bounding contour to locate its major axis of elongation. This axis can then be used as the sweeping axis for the creation of a generalized cone structural description relating individual three-dimensional parts to one another at multiple scales (Figure 7.3). Invariance was accomplished by virtue of the object-centered coordinate system in which these three-dimensional parts were parameterized. Thus, regardless of viewpoint and across most viewing conditions, the same viewpoint-invariant, three-dimensional structural description would be recovered by identifying the appropriate image features, (e.g., the bounding contour and major axes of the object), recovering a canonical set of

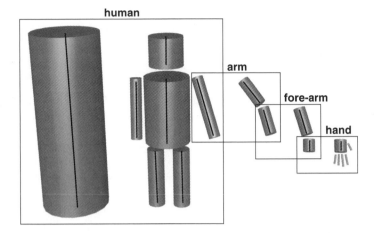

Figure 7.3 Schematic diagram of the multiscale three-dimensional representation of a human figure using object-centered generalized cones.
NOTE: Although cylinders are used for illustrative purposes, Marr and Nishihara's (1978) model allows for the representation of much more complex shapes for each part of an object.
SOURCE: Adapted from Marr and Nishihara (1978, Figure 3, p. 278).

three-dimensional parts, and matching the resultant three-dimensional representation to like representations in visual memory.

Biederman's (1987; Hummel & Biederman, 1992) model—recognition by components (RBC)—is quite similar to Marr and Nishihara's theory. However, two innovations made the RBC model more plausible in the eyes of many researchers. First, RBC assumes a restricted set of volumetric primitives, dubbed *geons* (Figure 7.4). Second, RBC assumes that geons are recovered on the basis of highly stable nonaccidental image properties (i.e., shape configurations that are unlikely to have occurred purely by chance; Lowe, 1987). One example of a nonaccidental property is three edges meeting at a single point (an arrow or Y junction): It is far more likely that this image configuration is the result of an inside or outside corner of a rectangular three-dimensional object than the chance meeting of some random disconnected edges. Biederman considered the set of 36 or so three-dimensional volumes specified by the combinations of nonaccidental properties in the image: the presence of particular

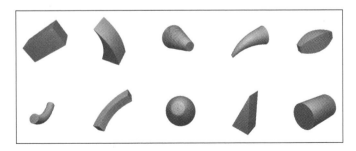

Figure 7.4 Ten of the 30 or so geons that Biederman's (1987) RBC model posits as the building blocks of object representations.

edge junctions or vertices, the shape of the major axes, symmetry of the cross section around these axes, and the scaling of the cross section. For example, a cylinder is specified as a curved cross section (i.e., a circle) with rotational and reflection symmetry, constant size, and a straight axis. An important point is that these attributes are defined qualitatively. For instance, a cross section is either straight or curved; there is no in-between or degree of curvedness. Although the reader might be skeptical about how one might represent the huge range of objects that exist using this limited toolkit, consider Tinkertoy; there are only a few different kinds of building blocks and connectors in the can, yet one can construct models that approximate almost any type of object.

The possible combinations of nonaccidental properties not only enumerate a restricted set of three-dimensional volumes (geons) but also allow a method for recovering these particular volumes. The fact that geons are generated by contrasting qualitative differences in nonaccidental properties is crucial to this process. Consider a brick and cylinder. Most nonaccidental projections of a brick have three parallel edges and three outer arrow vertices (points of cotermination). In contrast, most nonaccidental projections of a cylinder have only two parallel edges and two tangent Y-vertices. These and other contrasts provide the leverage for inferring the presence of specific geons in the image. Hypothetically, an observer needs only to examine the image of a three-dimensional object for the presence of the critical nonaccidental properties and then replace these properties with the appropriate, qualitatively specified geon. The complete configuration is referred to as a geon-structural description. Because the RBC approach restricts the set of possible three-dimensional volumes and, consequently, can rely on a more plausible method of three-dimensional part recovery, RBC is compu-

tationally more tractable than is Marr and Nishihara's theory.

RBC deviates from Marr and Nishihara's model in three related respects: RBC assumes only one level of representation (i.e., 2 or 3 geons per object); RBC attempts to account for object recognition only at the entry level; and, as reviewed earlier, RBC posits qualitative spatial relations between parts.

Evaluating Structural-Description Models

What are the strengths and weaknesses of Marr and Nishihara's approach to object recognition? Perhaps the two most appealing aspects of the model are (a) the invariance across viewpoint and other image transformations obtained by adopting a viewpoint-independent object-centered frame of reference for the description of parts and (b) the balance between stability and sensitivity achieved by representing objects at multiple scales in a hierarchical fashion. However, the model is in some ways almost too powerful. That is, generalized cones are represented by an arbitrary axis and cross section; therefore the mathematical description of these elements may be quite complex. Moreover, even at coarser scales it is not clear whether different instances of an object class will give rise to the same generalized cone descriptions; thus, class generalization may be difficult. Another serious issue is that the method for recovering generalized cones is not well-specified and has never been implemented successfully. Finally, empirical studies of human object recognition have not obtained much evidence in support of the sort of invariances predicted by Marr and Nishihara. All in all, while promising in some respects, these and other shortcomings of Marr and Nishihara's model rendered it a less than plausible account of human object recognition. Indeed, many of the extensions to Marr and Nishihara's model proposed in RBC seem explicitly designed to address these shortcomings.

What are the implications of these additional assumptions in RBC? On the positive side, RBC provides a more specific account of how three-dimensional primitives might be derived from two-dimensional images. Moreover, by severely restricting the vocabulary of three-dimensional primitives to only 36 or so geons, RBC removes the potential computational complexity of describing complicated three-dimensional parts as a series of mathematical functions. Further efficiency is derived from the fact that RBC limits the number of parts in each object description. Finally, the fact that geons and the relations between geons are qualitatively defined provides invariance across a wide range of viewpoints, as well as position, size, and other variations in viewing conditions. Moreover, different instances of an object category often contain similar parts; thus, the use of geons facilitates a many-to-one mapping between individual exemplars and their visual object class.

At the same time, some researchers have argued that much as with Marr and Nishihara's model, RBC specifies a theory that does not account for many aspects of human visual recognition behavior. First, consider the recovery process. RBC relies heavily on particular configurations of edges. However, there is little evidence to suggest that early vision and mid-level vision provide an edge map that looks anything like a clean line drawing (Sanocki, Bowyer, Heath, & Sarkar, 1998). For instance, depending on the direction of the lighting, shadows may produce spurious edges on many of an object's surfaces. Thus, although using edge-based, nonaccidental properties may seem appealing at first blush, the reliability of recovery mechanisms based on such features remains suspect. Moreover, by insisting on a singular approach that is edge-based, RBC relegates surface characteristics, including color, texture, and shading, to a secondary role in recognition (Biederman & Ju, 1988). However, a growing body of data indicates that surface properties are critical to the recognition process and are more or less integrated into object representations (see Price & Humphreys, 1989; J. W. Tanaka, Weiskopf, & Williams, in press; Tarr, Kersten, & Bülthoff, 1998).

Second, consider the nature of the representation. RBC assumes a single level of two to three qualitatively defined geons. This is a major reason why the theory attempts to explain only entry-level recognition. Such an impoverished object representation would be useless for the recognition of objects at the subordinate level or of specific individuals, could easily confuse objects that are actually distinct (but visually similar) at the entry level, or distinguish between objects that are actually members of the same entry-level class (Tarr & Bülthoff, 1995).

Third, as discussed earlier, RBC (as well as Marr & Nishihara's theory) predicts that over a wide range of changes in viewpoint, recognition performance should be viewpoint-invariant. Although there are some limited circumstances in which observers can invariantly recognize known objects that are shown in never-before-seen viewpoints, by and large the common finding has been some cost in both accuracy and response time when objects must be recognized across changes in viewpoint (Hayward & Tarr, 1997; Tarr, Bülthoff, Zabinski, & Blanz, 1997; Tarr, Williams, Hayward, & Gauthier, 1998).

In sum, there are limitations to RBC and a need for alternative mechanisms. Indeed, Hummel and Biederman (1992) and Biederman and Gerhardstein (1995) acknowledge that RBC captures some, but not all, recognition phenomena. The question is whether RBC forms the bulk of the explanation or, as claimed by Tarr and Bülthoff (1995), constitutes a restricted model that is inconsistent with much of the psychophysical and neural data. Thus, although some aspects of the structural-description approach are appealing and have been incorporated into recent models of recognition, it is still unclear whether the overall concept of a single-level, three-dimensional, qualitative, part-based representation can account for human object recognition abilities.

Image-Based Models

The most common alternative to a structural-description account is an image-based representation. Although the term *image-based* (or *view-based;* within the computer-vision community such models are also sometimes called *appearance-based*) has been criticized as too vague, certain assumptions constrain the theories. Perhaps the most critical element of any image-based model is that the features of the representation preserve aspects of an object as it *originally appeared* in the image. Note that this statement does not restrict the representation only to shape features but instead allows for measures of almost any property, including color, texture, shading, local depth, and spatial frequency, as well as shape (e.g., Edelman, 1993). The inclusion of nonshape properties is a significant difference between the image-based and structural-description approaches. A second important difference is how image-based theories encode three-dimensional structure: Instead of a single three-dimensional object model or a set of three-dimensional models, image-based theories represent three-dimensional objects as a collection of *views,* each view depicting the appearance of the object under specific viewing conditions (Tarr, 1995). This multiple-views representation supports the invariant recognition of three-dimensional objects in much the same manner as do structural descriptions.

In light of the framework outlined earlier, the majority of image-based models posit local features that are generally thought of as visual information processed over restricted regions (i.e., the output of the filtering that is implemented in early and mid-level vision). Often this information is characterized as part of the *surface* representation, and, indeed, there are many reasons why surfaces are attractive as the molar unit of high-level visual representations. At the same time, how individual surfaces are spatially related to one another is an issue of some debate. At one extreme, some researchers have argued that the overall representation simply preserves the quantitative two-dimensional spatial relations visible in the image (e.g., a rigid template; Poggio & Edelman, 1990). At another extreme, others have argued for a completely unordered collection of features that preserve nothing about their spatial relationship (Mel, 1997). Both approaches have some merit but break under fairly obvious conditions. Thus, the trend has been to implement hybrid models in which the features are image-based but are related to one another in a hierarchy that captures multiple levels of object structure (Hummel & Stankiewicz, 1996; Lowe, 2000; Riesenhuber & Poggio, 1999; Ullman & Sali, 2000). In some sense, such models are structural descriptions in that they relate the positions of object features to one another in a multi-scale hierarchy, but they are different from either Marr and Nishihara's or Biederman's models in that they assume that the features are viewpoint-dependent, local features rather that viewpoint-independent, three-dimensional parts.

Consider two other aspects that are used to characterize object representations. In terms of dimensionality, image-based models rarely assume a unitary three-dimensional representation. Rather, they posit features either that remain two-dimensional or, through the recovery of local depth, that are $2\frac{1}{2}$-D. At most, then, image-based features represent local depth (i.e., surface slant and orientation from the perspective of the viewer). Critically, this representation of depth does not impart viewpoint invariance (Bülthoff & Edelman, 1992). This brings us to the last characteristic of image-based models: the use of a viewpoint-dependent frame of reference, which is implied by the nature of the features themselves and by the way in which depth information is represented (if at all). Indeed, a major characteristic of image-based theories is that they are viewpoint-dependent; that is, as the input image deviates from the originally learned viewing conditions, there are systematic costs in recognition accuracy and speed. This prediction is central to many studies that have examined the object-recognition process.

Image Normalization

Because an object's representation is tied to specific viewing conditions, even minimal changes in viewing conditions may produce a mismatch between a viewpoint-based representation and a new viewpoint of the same object. Consequently, one must posit either a large number of views to represent a single object—with the potential to exceed the limits of human memory capacity—or a mechanism to *normalize* the processed input image to object viewpoints encoded in visual memory. As discussed earlier, there are several different proposals for how normalization might be accomplished. These can be divided roughly into four classes: mental transformation models (Shepard & Metzler, 1971; Tarr & Pinker, 1989); interpolation models (Bülthoff & Edelman, 1992; Poggio & Edelman, 1990; Ullman & Basri, 1991); alignment models (Ullman, 1989); and evidence accumulation models (Perrett et al., 1998).

What do these different approaches to normalization have in common, and how do they differ from one another? First and foremost, almost all predict that the normalization process is capacity-limited so that the magnitude of the normalization impacts recognition performance. That is, the larger the difference

between the input image and stored representations, the larger the cost in recognition time and accuracy. At the same time, different view-based models make different predictions regarding how these costs will manifest themselves, particularly across changes in viewpoint.

Mental transformation models (Tarr, 1995; Tarr & Pinker, 1989) predict that the costs will vary as a direct function of the angular difference between familiar and unfamiliar viewpoints of an object. Put another way, recognition performance will be straightforwardly determined by how far away a new viewpoint is from a known viewpoint. This prediction is based on the idea that mental transformations are analogs to physical transformations, following a continuous path that traverses the same space that the object would if it were actually being rotated. Thus, larger transformations take more time and incur more errors as compared with smaller transformations, and the magnitudes of both response times and error rates are proportional to the magnitude of the transformation (Shepard & Cooper, 1982).

View-interpolation models (Bülthoff & Edelman, 1992; Poggio & Edelman, 1990; see also Ullman & Basri, 1991) predict that costs will vary depending on how the view space is spanned by familiar viewpoints. That is, a better estimate—and consequently smaller performance costs—of how the image of an object is likely to change with rotation in depth can be made if the rotation is bounded by two or more known viewpoints. On the other hand, if a rotation in depth is not bounded by known viewpoints, approximations of the appearance of an object from a new view will be poorer, and the costs associated with normalization will be larger. Remember interpolating between points on a graph in high-school math: You could do a better job predicting the shape of the curve if you interpolated between two points and if the points were closer together; if there were few points and they were far apart, your ability to predict was diminished. The same applies to view interpolation: Simply think of each known viewpoint as a point on a three-dimensional graph and a new viewpoint as a point between these actually plotted points. Unfamiliar viewpoints between familiar viewpoints are likely to fall on the "line" connecting the two known points and hence are better recognized than are unfamiliar viewpoints that do not fall on this line.

Alignment models (Ullman, 1989) actually do not predict performance costs per se, but they do posit that three-dimensional objects are represented as multiple viewpoint-specific feature sets. The reason is that they assume that once the alignment transformation has been determined between an input image and the correct view in memory, the alignment may be executed in a single step. There are several reasons why, in practice, this single-shot approach is unlikely to work. First, the appropriate alignment transformation is determined by comparing a small subset of the input with object representations in visual memory (the same sort of preprocessing used to determine the rotation in mental transformation models). Although this process might appear to be time-consuming, there are methods for executing the comparison in parallel, thereby simultaneously comparing a given feature subset from the input with all candidate object representations. However, the reliability of this process will decrease as the alignment features increase in their dissimilarity from those in visual memory. Thus, larger viewpoint differences will, in all probability, lead to less reliable recognition performance. Second, the idea that an alignment can be performed by a single-step transformation, regardless of magnitude, works only if object features are represented in a form that allows rigid three-dimensional rotations to be applied to all features simultaneously (e.g., a three-

dimensional matrix of shape coordinates). If the features of the representation are not in this format (e.g., their three-dimensional positions are unknown), then other, most likely incremental, processes must be used to align input images with views in object memory. Indeed, most researchers now consider alignment models to be mathematical approximations of the normalization process, rather than actual models of how normalization is implemented in biological systems (Ullman, 1996).

Finally, evidence accumulation models (Perrett et al., 1998) attempt to account for normalization-like behaviors without actually positing any transformation of the input image. Recall that image-based representations are often characterized by a large number of local viewpoint-specific measures of image properties: color, shape, texture, and so on. What happens to these measures if viewing conditions change? Here intuition may fail us: It might seem that even a small object rotation or shift in lighting direction would change every local feature in a manner that would lead to an entirely different image description. In truth, this is not the case. The appearance of some features will not change at all or only marginally, whereas others will change more dramatically, though generally in a systematic fashion. Furthermore, only a fraction of the visible features will appear entirely different or disappear. Thus, for a large collection of local image features, the overall difference between the original image of an object and a new image of the same object under different viewing conditions will be related to how much the viewing conditions have changed. That is, given a large number of features in an object representation, the cumulative response of these features is related almost monotonically to the degree of rotation or the magnitude of lighting change from the known to unknown image. The implication is that objects may be represented as image-specific views, but that rather than using normalization mechanisms, image similarity across large numbers of features provides a means for generalizing from known to unknown viewpoints.

Why is this approach referred to as an evidence accumulation model? Consider that each measure of an object image can be thought of as a statistical feature detector: For a given location, the better an actual feature matches the preferred feature of the detector, the stronger the response. Thus, each detector accumulates evidence about the presence of particular features, and the overall response of the collection provides an estimate of the likelihood of a particular image of a particular object given the current image. What is perhaps most interesting about such models is that they make predictions that are quite similar to those of mental transformation and interpolation models. That is, as the magnitude of the change increases, so will the magnitude of response times and error rates. Consequently, a recognition system that relies on evidence accumulation to generalize from known to unknown viewpoints will produce a response pattern that *appears* as if the image is being normalized.

Evaluating Image-Based Models

How do the assumptions of image-based models stand up to the data? Consider the most critical characteristic of the approach: that object representations are view-based. The implication is that observers should better remember what objects looked liked under familiar viewing conditions (i.e., when seeing viewpoints that they have seen before). A corollary of this prediction is that recognition performance should decrease as the object image is transformed further and further from a known viewpoint. The precise pattern of how performance will change in relation to changes in the image will depend on the particular version of normalization that one

adopts, but the basic point of diminished performance with larger changes remains constant in most image-based models.

A considerable body of behavioral and neurophysiological results is consistent with this basic prediction of image-based models. As mentioned earlier, several studies observed that it took longer for subjects to name familiar common objects as those objects were rotated in the picture plane away from their upright, canonical orientation (Jolicoeur, 1985) or for subjects to name novel objects in new, unfamiliar viewpoints as those objects were rotated away from trained viewpoints (Tarr, 1995; Tarr & Pinker, 1989). These and other results provide evidence for viewpoint-specific, image-based object representations that are generalized to new viewing conditions using a mental transformation process.

An analogous result was obtained by Bülthoff and Edelman (1992; Edelman & Bülthoff, 1992). They found that recognition performance diminished as novel viewpoints were located farther and farther away from familiar viewpoints, but they also observed differences in the magnitudes of the cost depending on whether new viewpoints were located between or beyond familiar viewpoints (a pattern also obtained in Tarr, 1995). Thus, not only did Bülthoff and Edelman provide further evidence for object representations based on multiple image-based views, but also their data suggest that the normalization mechanism used for the recognition of novel viewpoints is view interpolation, not mental transformation. Over the past decade researchers have added to these results, generating a sizable collection of data that clearly support image-based models (Humphrey & Khan, 1992; Lawson & Humphreys, 1996; Srinivas, 1995; Tarr, Williams, Hayward, & Gauthier, 1998; for a review, see Tarr & Bülthoff, 1998).

Similar conclusions can be made based on results from single-unit recording studies

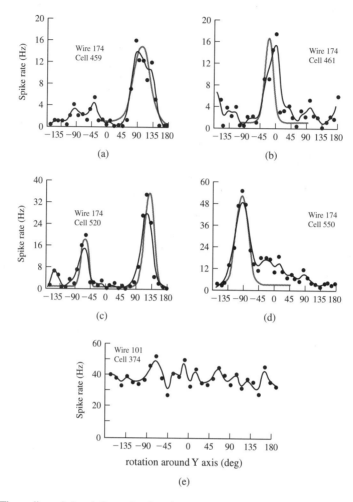

Figure 7.5 The coding of view information in primate visual cortex.
NOTE: a–d) Viewpoint-sensitive responses of four separate neurons in the inferior temporal (IT) cortex of a monkey trained to recognize novel three-dimensional objects in specific viewpoints. These responses are for a single object seen from multiple viewpoints. e) An IT neuron that responds in a viewpoint-independent manner to a trained object.
SOURCE: Adapted from Logothetis, Pauls, & Poggio (1995, Figure 5, p. 557).

in the inferior temporal cortex (IT) of monkeys. For example, Logothetis, Pauls, and Poggio (1995) found that if monkeys were trained to recognize novel three-dimensional objects (the same as those used in Bülthoff and Edelman, 1992) from specific viewpoints, neurons in their IT became "view-tuned." That is, individual neurons were found to be selective for specific objects, but only for view-

points that the monkey had actually seen (Figure 7.5). At the same time, the monkey's recognition performance was invariant across these highly familiar viewpoints—similar to the finding by Tarr and Pinker (1989) that following familiarization with a set of viewpoints, human observers represent three-dimensional objects as multiple image-specific views at those viewpoints. Although it seems unlikely that objects or views of objects are represented by single neurons (Booth & Rolls, 1998), the fact that neurons selective for particular objects—indicating that such neurons at least participate in the object representation—are also selective for familiar viewpoints of those objects provides evidence that the overall object representations are themselves image-based (a similar study by Booth & Rolls, 1998, was interpreted as evidence for viewpoint-invariant coding, but in fact they obtained approximately the same proportion of view-tuned cells as was observed in Logothetis et al., 1995).

Further evidence for this claim comes from several studies that examined the viewpoint sensitivity of single IT neurons selective for images of human and monkey heads. That is, not only do researchers often find neurons that are highly active when presented with particular faces, but their strongest response is viewpoint dependent as well—typically for the frontal or profile viewpoints (Perrett, Mistlin, & Chitty, 1987; Perrett, Rolls, & Caan, 1982). Recently, Perrett et al. (1998) have built on this finding, showing view-tuned single neurons selective for various body parts (head, hands, arms, legs, torso) in their upright orientations. They found that the cumulative response of the neurons' coding for different features of the figure predicted the monkey's recognition performance. That is, as the stimulus figure was rotated in the picture plane, the response of the individual feature detectors diminished. When summed together, their responses decreased in monotonic manner with increasing misorientation, much as would be predicted by a mental transformation or interpolation model. Note, however, that the response of the system was actually determined by a set of summed local responses—exactly what the evidence accumulation model predicts (see also Gauthier & Tarr, 1997b).

Overall, a great deal of behavioral and neurophysiological data may be accommo-

dated in an image-based model. One oft-cited criticism, however, must be addressed. Specifically, it has been argued that although image-based models are quite good at identifying specific instances of objects, they are poor at generalizing across instances (i.e., recognizing objects at the entry level). Given known images of several bears, for example, within an image-based framework how is a new bear recognized as a bear (Biederman & Gerhardstein, 1993)? The answer is surprisingly simple. Most recent image-based models rely on stochastic feature detectors that respond more or less as an input feature deviates from the originally measured feature. It is this sort of response that mediates the overall responses in Perrett et al.'s (1998) evidence accumulation model and in Riesenhuber and Poggio's (1999) HMAX model. Thus, such models can explain decreases in recognition performance, for instance due to changes in viewpoint as a consequence of decreases in image similarity (typically computed over image features, not single pixels or undifferentiated images). The *same* principle may be used to account for generalization across specific instances in an image-based framework. Two instances from the same object class are likely to be similar to one another in image-feature space; therefore, stochastic feature detectors representing a given object will respond more strongly to that object's cohorts (i.e., to other instances of the same object class). Not only does this account provide a plausible mechanism for class generalization in image-based models, but two recent psychophysical studies provide evidence for image-based class generalization as well (Gauthier & Tarr, 1997b; Tarr & Gauthier, 1998). The critical results in both studies are that observers are able to recognize novel objects that are visually similar to previously learned novel objects and that their pattern of responses implicates viewpoint-dependent, image-based mechanisms. At the same time, there is no generalization for visually different objects, suggesting that the observed viewpoint-dependent generalization is used for recognizing new instances of a known object class.

A second criticism of image-based models is that they are memory-intensive. That is, there is a potential "combinatorial explosion" in the number of images or views that may be needed to represent completely each known object. Consider even a relatively simple object such as our bear. Depending on what information is encoded in each familiar view of the bear, even a slight change in its appearance or in one's viewing position would produce a new collection of features in the image of the bear and, hence, lead to the representation of a new, separate view. Thus, even a single bear might come to be represented by thousands of views—a combinatorial explosion that would tax the capacity of our visual memory. One possible response to this concern is that memory in the human brain is plentiful and that thousands of views per an object is not actually implausible. This is not an entirely satisfying response in that the same argument may not hold if the numbers increase by an order of magnitude or more. Perhaps a more plausible answer is that only a small number of views are used to describe each object and that images that deviate from known views are recognized using normalization mechanisms. If a new image is sufficiently different from known views or if it occurs quite frequently, it too will come to be represented. However, this explanation does not provide any hard and fast numbers on exactly how many views per an object are necessary or on exactly what features are used to determine the similarity between views.

In summary, image-based models are able to posit a single mechanism that appears to account for behavior in a wide range of recognition tasks, including both entry-level recognition and the recognition of specific individuals within a class (Tarr, in press). At the same time, important aspects of image-based models are still underspecified in many respects, including the specific features of the representation, the number of views sufficient to represent an object or object class, and the exact normalization mechanisms used to match unfamiliar views to familiar ones.

IS A SINGLE MECHANISM REALLY SUFFICIENT?

In the previous section we raised the possibility that a single recognition mechanism might be capable of supporting a wide array of recognition tasks, ranging from the individual level to the entry level. Although some image-based computational implementations appear able to handle this range of recognition tasks, there looms the larger question of whether any empirical evidence supports such unified approaches. Indeed, a logical argument regarding the nature of object recognition has often been used to argue for dual systems: one system that supports the recognition of objects at the entry level (discriminating between visually *dissimilar* objects such as dogs and chairs) and that relies on separable object parts, and another system that supports the recognition of objects at the subordinate level (discriminating between visually *similar* objects such as different faces) and relies on more holistic object representations (Farah, 1992; Humphreys & Riddoch, 1984; Jolicoeur, 1990). Different versions of this approach are possible, but generally they are all motivated not only by the processing demands of different levels of recognition, but more specifically by the demands of face recognition as compared to normal object recognition (Biederman, 1987; Farah, 1992; Kanwisher, 2000).

The argument is as follows: However normal object recognition is accomplished, face recognition (and possibly other forms of subordinate-level recognition) is different in that it requires subtle discriminations between individuals that are members of a highly homogeneous object class. As such, face recognition recruits more holistic or configural information than is ordinarily called for. According to this view, then, face and object recognition should be seen as separable processes. Supporting this claim is a wide range of behavioral studies that appear to demonstrate face-specific processing (e.g., J. W. Tanaka & Farah, 1993; Yin, 1969). Reinforcing this conclusion, a neuropsychological impairment from brain-injury (prosopagnosia) of object recognition appears to be restricted exclusively to the recognition of individual faces (Farah, 1990). Finally, there are recent findings from neuroimaging (PET and fMRI) that seem to reveal a small region of inferotemporal cortex—the fusiform face area (FFA)—that is selectively more active for faces than for other objects (Kanwisher, McDermott, & Chun, 1997).

Evaluating this evidence, however, requires careful consideration of both the *default* level of categorical access for control object class (faces are recognized at the individual level by default) and the degree of perceptual expertise with the object class (all subjects are perceptual experts at face recognition). When these two factors are taken into account, a far different picture of visual object recognition emerges. Specifically, behavioral studies have found that once subjects are perceptual experts with a class of novel objects (e.g., "Greebles"; one Greeble is shown in Figure 7.1), subjects show the same recognition behaviors that all individuals show with faces. Consider what makes someone an expert: the fact that they recognize objects in the domain of expertise *automatically* at the individual level (J. W. Tanaka & Taylor, 1991). This is true for faces (I recognize my sister first as "Joanna," not as a woman or as

a Caucasian) and for Greebles once a subject has become a Greeble expert (i.e., they apply the individual-level names for Greebles by default). Given such perceptual expertise, the same holistic or configural effects obtains for faces and for Greebles: Within a domain of expertise, moving some parts of an object affects the recognition of other parts (Gauthier & Tarr, 1997a), but the same is not true for objects that are not from a domain of expertise. Similarly, when subjects with prosopagnosia are forced to make individual-level discriminations between Greebles, snowflakes, or even familiar, common objects, their recognition impairment for faces and objects appears equivalent across all object classes. Therefore, these brain-injured subjects do not have the hypothesized face-specific recognition deficit (Gauthier, Behrmann, & Tarr, 1999). Finally, neuroimaging studies that have compared the subordinate-level recognition of familiar, common objects to the recognition of faces have revealed common neural substrates for both recognition tasks (Gauthier, Anderson, Tarr, Skudlarski, & Gore, 1997; Gauthier, Tarr et al., 2000). At the same time, the putative FFA has been found to activate not only for faces, but also for Greebles once subjects become Greeble experts (Gauthier, Tarr, Anderson, Skudlarski, & Gore, 1999). Reinforcing the importance of expertise in putatively face-specific effects, bird and car experts also show activation in their FFAs for birds and cars, but only in their domains of expertise (Gauthier, Skudlarski, Gore, & Anderson, 2000a). Thus, there is little evidence to support the existence of face-specific perceptual processes or neural substrates. Rather, current results point to a single visual recognition system that can be tuned by experience to recognize specific object classes by default at a more subordinate level than is ordinarily the case (Tarr & Gauthier, 2000). The exact nature of this system, however, is still open to debate.

CONCLUSIONS: IS ANY MODEL ADEQUATE?

Despite our earlier statement that image-based models do a better job of accounting for extant data, it is unclear whether any model provides an adequate explanation of human object recognition. Although various groups have argued that one model or another offers a comprehensive theory (Biederman & Gerhardstein, 1995; Tarr & Bülthoff, 1995), the truth is, at present, that no single model can explain the range of behavioral, neurophysiological, and neuropsychological data that has been obtained under various conditions. Indeed, perhaps the most significant challenge to any theory is that human object recognition is so flexible, supporting accurate recognition across a myriad of tasks, levels of specificity, degrees of expertise, and changing viewing parameters.

Consider the case of viewpoint. Many studies have attempted to assess whether object recognition is viewpoint-dependent or viewpoint-invariant (Biederman & Gerhardstein, 1993; Bülthoff & Edelman, 1992; Lawson & Humphreys, 1996; Tarr, 1995; Tarr et al., 1998), but asking the question in a strictly dichotomous manner is futile. The fact is that recognition performance varies almost continuously depending on the similarity of the target object relative to the distractor objects (Hayward & Williams, 2000). There is no canonical "viewpoint-dependent" result, and there are few cases in which recognition is truly viewpoint-invariant (Tarr & Bülthoff, 1995). As an alternative, one might abandon the notion of viewpoint-dependency as a guiding principle in favor of similarity metrics between to-be-recognized objects, rendering viewpoint-dependent effects a byproduct of the way in which similarity is measured (Edelman, 1995; Perrett et al., 1998). The problem is that there is currently no reasonable notion of how to measure similarity. What is the correct feature set? How are features compared to one another? These questions remain unanswered, yet they are central to any theory of object recognition, even if one sidesteps many other potentially difficult issues.

Given that there is no such thing as a definitive experiment and there are data that in some sense can invalidate every theory, what can be said about the current state of models of visual object recognition? To begin with, the debate between proponents of structural-description models and image-based models boils down to an argument about the molar features of object representations. On one side, researchers such as Biederman (1987) and Hummel (Hummel & Stankiewicz, 1996) have posited the use of three-dimensional volumes that approximate the three-dimensional appearance of individual object parts, an approach that has its origins in computer graphics (Foley & Van Dam, 1982) and long-standing popularity in the field of computer vision (Binford, 1971; Brooks, 1983; Marr & Nishihara, 1978). On the other side, theorists such as Tarr (Tarr, 1995; Tarr & Pinker, 1989), Poggio and Edelman (1990), and Bülthoff and Edelman (1992) have posited the use of local two-dimensional and 2½-D image features, an approach that is rooted in what is known about the architecture of the primate visual system (Hubel & Wiesel, 1959).

At the same time, both camps effectively agree about many of the properties that are critical in any plausible model of recognition:

- The decomposition of an image into component features

- The coding of the spatial relations between such features

- Multiple views for single objects to encode different collections of features arising from different viewpoints

- Generalization mechanisms to normalize over viewpoint and other changes in viewing conditions
- Plasticity that can support recognition tasks ranging from the highly specific individual level to the categorical entry level

In the end, things might not be so bleak after all. That there is any agreement at all about such a list suggests that vision scientists have made some progress.

REFERENCES

Biederman, I. (1987). Recognition-by-components: A theory of human image understanding. *Psychological Review, 94,* 115–147.

Biederman, I., & Gerhardstein, P. C. (1993). Recognizing depth-rotated objects: Evidence and conditions for three-dimensional viewpoint invariance. *Journal of Experimental Psychology: Human Perception and Performance, 19*(6), 1162–1182.

Biederman, I., & Gerhardstein, P. C. (1995). Viewpoint-dependent mechanisms in visual object recognition: Reply to Tarr and Bülthoff (1995). *Journal of Experimental Psychology: Human Perception and Performance, 21*(6), 1506–1514.

Biederman, I., & Ju, G. (1988). Surface versus edge-based determinants of visual recognition. *Cognitive Psychology, 20,* 38–64.

Binford, T. O. (1971, December). *Visual perception by computer.* Paper presented at the IEEE Conference on Systems and Control, Miami.

Booth, M. C. A., & Rolls, E. T. (1998). View-invariant representations of familiar objects by neurons in the inferior temporal visual cortex. *Cerebral Cortex, 8*(6), 510–523.

Brooks, R. A. (1983). Model-based three-dimensional interpretations of two-dimensional images. *IEEE Transactions on Pattern Analysis and Machine Intelligence, 5*(2), 140–149.

Bülthoff, H. H., & Edelman, S. (1992). Psychophysical support for a two-dimensional view interpolation theory of object recognition. *Proceedings of the National Academy of Sciences USA, 89,* 60–64.

Bülthoff, H. H., & Edelman, S. (1993). Evaluating object recognition theories by computer graphics psychophysics. In T. A. Poggio & D. A. Glaser (Eds.), *Exploring brain functions: Models in neuroscience* (pp. 139–164). New York: Wiley.

Edelman, S. (1993). Representing three-dimensional objects by sets of activities of receptive fields. *Biological Cybernetics, 70,* 37–45.

Edelman, S. (1995). Representation, similarity, and the chorus of prototypes. *Minds and Machines, 5*(1), 45–68.

Edelman, S., & Bülthoff, H. H. (1992). Orientation dependence in the recognition of familiar and novel views of three-dimensional objects. *Vision Research, 32*(12), 2385–2400.

Farah, M. J. (1990). *Visual agnosia: Disorders of object recognition and what they tell us about normal vision.* Cambridge: The MIT Press.

Farah, M. J. (1992). Is an object an object an object? Cognitive and neuropsychological investigations of domain-specificity in visual object recognition. *Current Directions in Psychological Science, 1*(5), 164–169.

Foley, J. D., & Van Dam, A. (1982). *Fundamentals of interactive computer graphics.* Reading, MA: Addison-Wesley.

Gauthier, I., Anderson, A. W., Tarr, M. J., Skudlarski, P., & Gore, J. C. (1997). Levels of categorization in visual recognition studied with functional Magnetic Resonance Imaging *Current Biology, 7,* 645–651.

Gauthier, I., Behrmann, M., & Tarr, M. J. (1999). Can face recognition really be dissociated from object recognition? *Journal of Cognitive Neuroscience, 11*(4), 349–370.

Gauthier, I., Skudlarski, P., Gore, J. C., & Anderson, A. W. (2000). Expertise for cars and birds recruits brain areas involved in face recognition. *Nature Neuroscience, 3*(2), 191–197.

Gauthier, I., & Tarr, M. J. (1997a). Becoming a "Greeble" expert: Exploring the face recognition mechanism. *Vision Research, 37*(12), 1673–1682.

Gauthier, I., & Tarr, M. J. (1997b). Orientation priming of novel shapes in the context of viewpoint-dependent recognition. *Perception, 26,* 51–73.

Gauthier, I., Tarr, M. J., Anderson, A. W., Skudlarski, P., & Gore, J. C. (1999). Activation of the middle fusiform "face area" increases with expertise in recognizing novel objects. *Nature Neuroscience, 2*(6), 568–573.

Gauthier, I., Tarr, M. J., Moylan, J., Anderson, A. W., Skudlarski, P., & Gore, J. C. (2000). Does visual subordinate-level categorisation engage the functionally defined Fusiform Face Area? *Cognitive Neuropsychology, 17*(1/2/3), 143–163 Special Issue on Face Recognition (N. Karwisher and M. Moscovitch; eds.).

Hayward, W. G., & Tarr, M. J. (1997). Testing conditions for viewpoint invariance in object recognition. *Journal of Experimental Psychology: Human Perception and Performance, 23*(5), 1511–1521.

Hayward, W. G., & Williams, P. (2000). Viewpoint dependence and object discriminability. *Psychological Science, 11*(1), 7–12.

Hubel, D. H., & Wiesel, T. N. (1959). Receptive fields of single neurons in the cat's striate cortex. *Journal of Physiology, 148,* 574–591.

Hummel, J. E. (1994). Reference frames and relations in computational models of object recognition. *Current Directions in Psychological Science, 3*(4), 111–116.

Hummel, J. E., & Biederman, I. (1992). Dynamic binding in a neural network for shape recognition. *Psychological Review, 99*(3), 480–517.

Hummel, J. E., & Stankiewicz, B. J. (1996). An architecture for rapid, hierarchical structural description. In T. Inui & J. McClelland (Eds.), *Attention and performance: Vol. XVI* (pp. 93–121). Cambridge: MIT Press.

Humphrey, G. K., & Khan, S. C. (1992). Recognizing novel views of three-dimensional objects. *Canadian Journal of Psychology, 46,* 170–190.

Humphreys, G. W., & Riddoch, M. J. (1984). Routes to object constancy: Implications from neurological impairments of object constancy. *Quarterly Journal of Experimental Psychology, 36A,* 385–415.

Jolicoeur, P. (1985). The time to name disoriented natural objects. *Memory & Cognition, 13,* 289–303.

Jolicoeur, P. (1990). Identification of disoriented objects: A dual-systems theory. *Mind & Language, 5*(4), 387–410.

Jolicoeur, P., Gluck, M., & Kosslyn, S. M. (1984). Pictures and names: Making the connection. *Cognitive Psychology, 16,* 243–275.

Kanwisher, N. (2000). Domain specificity in face perception. *Nature Neuroscience, 3*(8), 759–763.

Kanwisher, N., McDermott, J., & Chun, M. M. (1997). The fusiform face area: A module in human extrastriate cortex specialized for face perception. *Journal of Neuroscience, 17,* 4302–4311.

Lawson, R., & Humphreys, G. W. (1996). View specificity in object processing: Evidence from picture matching. *Journal of Experimental Psychology: Human Perception and Performance, 22*(2), 395–416.

Logothetis, N. K., Pauls, J., & Poggio, T. (1995). Shape representation in the inferior temporal cortex of monkeys. *Current Biology, 5*(5), 552–563.

Lowe, D. G. (1987). The viewpoint consistency constraint. *International Journal of Computer Vision, 1,* 57–72.

Lowe, D. G. (2000). Towards a computational model for object recognition in IT Cortex. In S.-W. Lee, H. H. Bülthoff, & T. Poggio (Eds.), *Biologically motivated computer vision* (Vol. 1811, pp. 20–31). Berlin: Springer.

Marr, D. (1982). *Vision: A computational investigation into the human representation and processing of visual information.* San Francisco: Freeman.

Marr, D., & Nishihara, H. K. (1978). Representation and recognition of the spatial organization of three-dimensional shapes. *Proc. R. Soc. of Lond. B, 200,* 269–294.

McMullen, P. A., & Farah, M. J. (1991). Viewer-centered and object-centered representations in the recognition of naturalistic line drawings. *Psychological Science, 2,* 275–277.

Mel, B. (1997). SEEMORE: Combining color, shape, and texture histogramming in a neurally inspired approach to visual object recognition. *Neural Computation, 9,* 977–804.

Miyashita, Y. (1988). Neuronal correlate of visual associative long-term memory in the primate temporal cortex. *Nature, 335,* 817–820.

Murphy, G. L., & Brownell, H. H. (1985). Category differentiation in object recognition: Typicality constraints on the basic level advantage. *Journal of Experimental Psychology: Learning, Memory, and Cognition. 11,* 70–84.

Palmer, S., Rosch, E., & Chase, P. (1981). Canonical perspective and the perception of objects. In J. Long & A. Baddeley (Eds.), *Attention and performance: Vol. IX* (pp. 135–151). Hillsdale: Erlbaum.

Perrett, D. I., Mistlin, A. J., & Chitty, A. J. (1987). Visual neurones responsive to faces. *Trends in Neuroscience, 10*(96), 358–364.

Perrett, D. I., Oram, M. W., & Ashbridge, E. (1998). Evidence accumulation in cell populations responsive to faces: An account of generalisation of recognition without mental transformations. *Cognition, 67*(1/2), 111–145.

Perrett, D. I., Rolls, E. T., & Caan, W. (1982). Visual neurones responsive to faces in the monkey temporal cortex. *Experimental Brain Research, 47,* 329–342.

Pinker, S. (1984). Visual Cognition: An Introduction. *Cognition, 18,* 1–63.

Poggio, T., & Edelman, S. (1990). A network that learns to recognize three-dimensional objects. *Nature, 343,* 263–266.

Price, C. J., & Humphreys, G. W. (1989). The effects of surface detail on object categorization and naming. *The Quarterly Journal of Experimental Psychology, 41A,* 797–828.

Riesenhuber, M., & Poggio, T. (1999). Hierarchical models of object recognition in cortex. *Nature Neuroscience, 2*(11), 1019–1025.

Rosch, E., Mervis, C. B., Gray, W. D., Johnson, D. M., & Boyes-Braem, P. (1976). Basic objects in natural categories. *Cognitive Psychology, 8,* 382–439.

Sanocki, T., Bowyer, K. W., Heath, M. D., & Sarkar, S. (1998). Are edges sufficient for object recognition? *Journal of Experimental Psychology: Human Perception and Performance, 24*(1), 340–349.

Selfridge, O. G. (1959). *Pandemonium: A paradigm for learning.* Paper presented at the Symposium on the Mechanisation of Thought Processes, London.

Shepard, R. N., & Cooper, L. A. (1982). *Mental images and their transformations.* Cambridge: MIT Press.

Shepard, R. N., & Metzler, J. (1971). Mental rotation of three-dimensional objects. *Science, 171,* 701–703.

Srinivas, K. (1995). Representation of rotated objects in explicit and implicit memory. *Journal of Experimental Psychology: Learning, Memory, and Cognition, 21*(4), 1019–1036.

Tanaka, J. W., & Farah, M. J. (1993). Parts and wholes in face recognition. *Quarterly Journal of Experimental Psychology, 46A,* 225–245.

Tanaka, J. W., & Taylor, M. (1991). Object categories and expertise: Is the basic level in the eye of the beholder? *Cognitive Psychology, 23,* 457–482.

Tanaka, J. W., Weiskopf, D., & Williams, P. (In press). The role of color in object recognition. *Trends in Cognitive Science.*

Tanaka, K. (1996). Inferotemporal cortex and object vision. *Annual Review of Neuroscience* (Vol. 19, pp. 109–139). Palo Alto, CA: Annual Reviews.

Tarr, M. J. (1995). Rotating objects to recognize them: A case study of the role of viewpoint dependency in the recognition of three-dimensional objects. *Psychonomic Bulletin and Review, 2*(1), 55–82.

Tarr, M. J. (1999). News on views: Pandemonium revisited. *Nature Neuroscience, 2*(11), 932–935.

Tarr, M. J. (in press). Visual object recognition: Can a single mechanism suffice? In M. A. Peterson & G. Rhodes (Eds.), *Analytic and holistic processes in the perception of faces, objects, and scenes.* New York: JAI/Ablex.

Tarr, M. J., & Black, M. J. (1994). A computational and evolutionary perspective on the role of representation in vision. *Computer Vision, Graphics, and Image Processing: Image Understanding, 60*(1), 65–73.

Tarr, M. J., & Bülthoff, H. H. (1995). Is human object recognition better described by geon-structural-descriptions or by multiple-views? *Journal of Experimental Psychology: Human Perception and Performance, 21*(6), 1494–1505.

Tarr, M. J., & Bülthoff, H. H. (1998). *Object recognition in man, monkey, and machine.* Cambridge: MIT Press.

Tarr, M. J., Bülthoff, H. H., Zabinski, M., & Blanz, V. (1997). To what extent do unique parts influence recognition across changes in viewpoint? *Psychological Science, 8*(4), 282–289.

Tarr, M. J., & Gauthier, I. (1998). Do viewpoint-dependent mechanisms generalize across members of a class? *Cognition, 67*(1–2), 71–108.

Tarr, M. J., & Gauthier, I. (2000). FFA: A Flexible Fusiform Area for subordinate-level visual processing automatized by expertise. *Nature Neuroscience, 3*(8), 764–769.

Tarr, M. J., Kersten, D., & Bülthoff, H. H. (1998). Why the visual system might encode the effects of illumination. *Vision Research, 38*(15/16), 2259–2275.

Tarr, M. J., & Kriegman, D. J. (2001). What defines a view? *Vision Research, 41*(15), 1981–2004.

Tarr, M. J., & Pinker, S. (1989). Mental rotation and orientation-dependence in shape recognition. *Cognitive Psychology, 21*(2), 233–282.

Tarr, M. J., Williams, P., Hayward, W. G., & Gauthier, I. (1998). Three-dimensional object recognition is viewpoint-dependent. *Nature Neuroscience, 1*(4), 275–277.

Ullman, S. (1989). Aligning pictorial descriptions: An approach to object recognition. *Cognition, 32,* 193–254.

Ullman, S. (1996). *High-level vision.* Cambridge: MIT Press.

Ullman, S., & Basri, R. (1991). Recognition by linear combinations of models. *IEEE Transactions on Pattern Analysis and Machine Intelligence, 13*(10), 992–1006.

Ullman, S., & Sali, E. (2000). Object classification using a fragment-based representation. In S.-W. Lee, H. H. Bülthoff, & T. Poggio (Eds.), *Biologically motivated computer vision* (Vol. 1811, pp. 73–87). Berlin: Springer.

Wallis, G. (1996). Using spatio-temporal correlations to learn invariant object recognition. *Neural Networks, 9*(9), 1513–1519.

Yin, R. K. (1969). Looking at upside-down faces. *Journal of Experimental Psychology, 81*(1), 141–145.

CHAPTER 8

Motor Control

DAVID A. ROSENBAUM

INTRODUCTION

Most readers of this chapter will probably hope to find answers to one or more of these questions: (a) What is motor control, and what are the main issues investigated in this field? (b) Which of these issues have special connections to experimental psychology, and of these, which have witnessed significant advances, especially since the treatment of this topic in the last edition of the *Stevens' Handbook* (Pew & Rosenbaum, 1988)? (c) Finally, what are the directions that this area of research is likely to take in the future?

Before addressing these questions, it is helpful to introduce some definitions and to establish the limits of the present survey. Motor control is that set of processes that enables creatures (living or artificial) to stabilize or move the body or physical extensions of the body (tools) in desired ways. Typical activities studied by investigators of motor control are walking, reaching, making facial expressions, talking, typing, and writing.

Four main problems are studied in this area of research:

1. *The serial order and timing problem:* How are the elements of movement sequences assigned ordinal, ratio, or interval values in time?

2. *The learning problem:* How does motor activity change as a function of practice?

3. *The degrees of freedom problem:* How do particular forms of motor activity emerge when more than one form allows a task to be completed?

4. *The perceptual-motor integration problem:* How are motor activity and perceptual activity interrelated?

These four issues served as the organizing themes of the last chapter on motor control in the previous *Stevens' Handbook* (Pew & Rosenbaum, 1988), and they remain at the center of experimental psychological research on this topic, although the degree of emphasis placed on them and the methods used to study them have changed somewhat since the earlier chapter was prepared.

Like any chapter of its kind, this one has limitations. First, it has been prepared both to emphasize classic studies and to highlight important new developments. Second, although neuroscience has come to occupy a more prominent role than it did earlier in this and other fields of experimental psychology, the aim of much of that work—to discover what functions are served by which brain areas—will be subordinated here to the primary aim of psychological investigation—namely, to discern from behavior how behavior is functionally organized. Third, much valuable work will not be presented here because of space limitations. More will be said about fine motor control than about gross motor control, about hand and arm movements than other kinds of movements, and about the performance of university students than of babies, children, older adults, patients, or animals. Readers wishing other summaries of motor control research may find them in the following texts: For emphasis on neuroscience, see Gazzaniga, Ivry, and Mangun (1998); Kandel, Schwartz, and Jessell (2000); Latash (1993); and Rothwell (1987); for emphasis on computation, see Gallistel (1999) and Jordan and Rosenbaum (1989); for emphasis on kinesiology, see Schmidt and Lee (1999); and for emphasis on psychology, see Keele (1986), Rosenbaum (1991), and Rosenbaum and Krist (1996).

A note on terminology: I will speak of the control of movement without meaning to downplay the role of holding still. I will also interchange the terms "movements," "movement sequences," "motor acts," and "actions." One term I will not substitute for actions is "responses." Responses are reactions to external events. Voluntary movements are intentional. They are not afterthoughts and should not be treated as such in experimental psychology.

THE SERIAL ORDER AND TIMING PROBLEM

How are motor acts sequenced? Prior to the cognitive revolution of the 1950s and 1960s, it was thought that motor acts are sequenced via stimulus-response (SR) chaining. According to this hypothesis, feedback from one movement—what is now called *reafference*—triggers the next movement. Hardly anyone takes the SR chaining view seriously anymore, so it may seem gratuitous to mention it here. Nonetheless, showing how the SR chaining model has been overturned provides a useful entry into the material to be covered.

Lashley's Arguments

In a famous paper, Karl Lashley (1951) offered three main arguments against the SR chaining view. First, he said that if the hypothesis were correct, one would expect delays between successive movements to be long enough to permit feedback from one movement to trigger the next. Yet, as Lashley noted, the actual delays are often shorter than feedback delays. Adams (1984) protested that the delays are in fact shorter than Lashley believed, and one can allow that feedback from movement n need not trigger movement $n + 1$ but instead can trigger movement $n + 2$ or $n + 3$, and so on (Rosenbaum, 1991). Thus, Lashley's first argument carries less weight than one might think.

Lashley's (1951) second argument was that physical interruption of feedback paths does not interrupt the unfolding of movement sequences, even though it should according to the SR chaining hypothesis. As Lashley noted, severing the dorsal roots of the spinal cord, through which afferent signals pass, does not render the patient or experimental animal motionless. (See Taub & Berman, 1968; Bard, Fleury, Teasdale, Paillard, & Nougier, 1995; Sanes, 1990 for recent evidence).

Lashley's (1951) third argument against SR theory amounted to the assertion that one knows what one will do before one does it. In support of this assertion, Lashley relied on the facility with which people can transform words in language games such as Pig Latin and on the systematic nature of mistakes in spontaneous writing, typing, and speech. If one commits a Spoonerism, for example, saying "He hissed all my mystery lectures," rather than "He missed all my history lectures," it is plausible that information is available to the speaker about the words cued for later production.

Lashley's conclusion that plans mediate language extends to other forms of expression as well. Just as language is generative, so too are nonverbal activities. Furthermore, because errors in nonverbal behavior are similar to those made in speech (Norman, 1981), plans can be said to underlie these other activities much as they do language.

Further Evidence For Motor Plans

Experimental psychologists have provided additional evidence for motor plans. One measure that they have used is reaction time (RT). In an important study that used this measure, Henry and Rogers (1960) had participants respond to the onset of a signal by lifting the hand from a switch, by lifting the hand from the switch and then performing one more action, or by lifting the hand from the switch and then performing two more actions. In all three cases, participants knew in advance what motor task was supposed to be performed, and the signal was the same. Nonetheless, the RT, defined as the time from the onset of the signal to the onset of the movement, increased with the number of actions to be performed. Based on this result, Henry and Rogers suggested that information about the forthcoming movement sequence was held in memory and that the amount of information, which Henry and Rogers assumed would grow with the number of forthcoming acts, affected the rate at which information about the first act could be accessed.

Subsequent investigations confirmed Henry and Rogers's (1960) inference. RTs were found to increase with the length of the sequence to be produced in tasks involving speaking (Sternberg, Wright, Knoll, & Monsell, 1980), typing (Sternberg, Monsell, Knoll, & Wright, 1978), key pressing (Rosenbaum, 1987), and generating saccades (Inhoff, 1986).

RTs have also been found to depend on features of what one does in sequences of fixed length. For example, the RT to make a key press is different if the keypress to be produced will be a Morse code "dit" or a Morse code "dah" (Klapp, 1977). Similarly, the RT to make an utterance is different if the utterance to be produced will begin with a simple or complex initial consonant cluster (Frederiksen & Kroll, 1976; Klapp, 1977). In choice RT tasks, in which subjects must perform one action or another depending on which signal appears, RTs have been found to depend on the relation between the actions (Kornblum, 1965). For example, when the response alternatives are reaching movements, it has been found that the RT for a reach in a given direction and over a given distance depends on the direction and distance of the other possible reach. When the other reach has the same direction but a different distance, the RT is shorter than when the other possible reach has the same distance and a different direction (Megaw, 1972). Further work suggested that direction and distance are specified independently (Rosenbaum, 1980). This view was later supported by studies of distributions of endpoints of aiming movements (J. Gordon, Ghilardi, & Ghez, 1997) and by studies of errors in recalled pointing movements (Chieffi & Allport, 1997).

Another source of evidence for advance planning of movement sequences is the activity of the brain prior to movement. Different parts of the brain become active at different times relative to the onset of movement. The supplementary motor cortex, for example, becomes active a full second before voluntary movement occurs, whereas the primary motor cortex usually becomes active only 50 ms or so before voluntary movement begins. This difference suggests that the supplementary motor cortex is involved in a higher level of motor preparation than is the primary motor cortex. Consistent with this inference, when people perform finger-tapping sequences (e.g., alternately touching the tips of the fingers with the thumb of the same hand) both the primary motor cortex and supplementary motor cortex light up when the brain's activity is recorded using positron-emission tomography scans (Roland, 1993). By contrast, when the finger-tapping sequence is only imagined, the supplementary motor cortex lights up, but the primary motor cortex does not.

One can also examine behavior itself to see how it reflects the behavior that follows. This approach has already been alluded to in connection with language, but similar evidence has been obtained in studies of typewriting, eye movements, and reaching (for a review, see Rosenbaum, 1991). With respect to reaching, it has been found that when the hand leaves a start position to move toward a target as quickly as possible, the initial speed of the movement predicts the distance to be covered (Hollerbach & Atkeson, 1987; Megaw, 1972). Similarly, in studies of prehension (reaching out to grasp an object) it has been observed that as the hand approaches an object to be grasped, the fingers spread apart before coming into contact with the object, with the peak separation of the fingers being closely related to the size of the object (Jeannerod, 1984). The hand's behavior as it approaches the object reveals the actor's considerable knowledge of what still must be done.

Serial Order and Timing of Motor Acts

Having considered the main lines of evidence that support Lashley's view that behavioral sequences are planned, let us now probe more deeply into the nature of those plans and the means by which they are realized. It is fitting that we approach this problem by considering the mechanisms responsible for ensuring that elements of behavioral sequences occur in desired orders (serial order) and with desired interelement delays (timing).

A popular theory of serial order holds that plans for behavioral sequences are structured hierarchically. According to this theory, the highest-level representation of a sequence to be produced corresponds to the sequence's main constituents, lower-level representations correspond to lower-level constituents, and so on. Actual performance consists, on this view, of producing movement elements that correspond to the lowest-level elements (Mackay, 1982).

An appealing feature of the hierarchical theory is that it accords with the fact that skill learning progresses from simple to more complex routines. A piano student must learn to play rudimentary series of notes before attempting chord progressions, just as a telegrapher must learn to recognize individual letters before recognizing entire words (Bryan & Harter, 1897).

Another appealing feature of the hierarchical theory is that it provides a convenient way of combining and altering movement elements. With hierarchical representations, entire constituents can be reordered easily (P. C. Gordon & Meyer, 1987), and features of entire motor sequences (e.g., whether to perform a finger-tapping sequence with the right hand or the left) can be determined in an instant (for a review, see Rosenbaum, 1987).

Consistent with the hierarchical theory, times between movements during the production of memorized sequences can be predicted on the basis of hierarchical decoding (Figure 8.1). Here, constituents are successively unpacked to their lowest levels, and the higher the level of the transition, the longer the transition takes. Data consistent with this claim have been obtained both in rapid keyboard performance (Povel & Collard, 1982; Rosenbaum, 1987) and in speech production (Cooper & Paccia-Cooper, 1980; Reitman & Rueter, 1980). The similarity in outcomes across the domains hints at the fundamental similarity between computations underlying

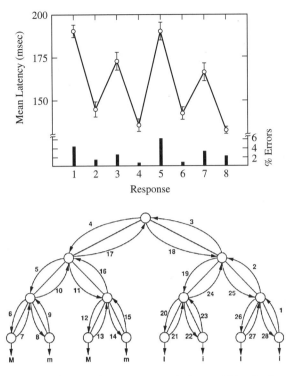

Figure 8.1 Times and errors of successive movements during rapid production of memorized finger sequences (top panel) and an account of the data in terms of hierarchical decoding (bottom panel).

NOTE: *Top panel:* Data from a study (Rosenbaum, Kenny, & Derr, 1983) in which adults tapped on keys with the left middle (m), left index (i), right index (I), and right middle (M) fingers so that successive taps were always made with alternating hands and a given finger was never tapped more than twice in a row. A representative sequence was MmMmIiIi. The sequence was produced as quickly as possible over and over again until a stop tone sounded. The times and errors shown are for each tap after the preceding tap; the very first tap is not included. *Bottom panel:* A hierarchical decoding (tree traversal) model for the results. The number beside each arrow indicates the internal step number for the shift of control from one node to the next. Activation of a terminal node triggers a finger tap.

SOURCE: *Top panel:* Rosenbaum, Kenny, & Derr (1983). Copyright © 1983 by the American Psychological Association. Reprinted with permission. *Bottom Panel:* Adapted from Rosenbaum, Kenny, & Derr (1983). Copyright © 1983 by the American Psychological Association. Adapted with permission.

movement generation on the one hand and recall of verbalizable facts on the other (Rosenbaum, Carlson, & Gilmore, 2001).

However appealing the hierarchical theory is and however strong its support may be, it does not specify the biological mechanism that ensures the ordering and timing of movement elements. One mechanism that may help in this regard is an internal clock. Such a mechanism consists of a source that

generates periodic or quasi-periodic signals, a counter that registers the number of signals, and a trigger that initiates events when a requisite number of signals have occurred. With an internal clock, it is possible to control delays between motor elements.

The most influential clock model in the field of motor control was proposed by Wing and Kristofferson (1973). These authors suggested that in tasks such as regular finger tapping, delays between successive taps may be controlled by allowing p pulses to occur, at which time a command is sent to the musculature to trigger the ith finger tap. Wing and Kristofferson hypothesized that intervals between successive pulses are variable and stochastically independent. From this one can predict that the variance of the p pulses should grow linearly with the size of p. Wing and Kristofferson also proposed that efferent delays are variable and stochastically independent. From this one can predict that adjacent interresponse intervals should be negatively correlated because a long efferent delay for the completion of one interresponse interval will tend to shorten the next interresponse interval, and vice versa. Nonadjacent interresponse intervals, by contrast, should be uncorrelated.

The Wing-Kristofferson (1973) model has enjoyed a great deal of attention and a considerable amount of empirical support. As it predicts, the variability of interresponse intervals grows with the length of the intervals, and adjacent interresponse intervals tend to be negatively correlated, whereas nonadjacent interresponse intervals tend to have correlations closer to zero. The model does not have an unblemished record, however. Some studies have found correlations significantly different from zero for nonadjacent intervals (Chen, Ding, & Kelso, 1997; Gilden, 2001); the standard deviation rather than the variance of interresponse intervals is often seen to increase linearly with the mean of the intervals produced (Ivry & Hazeltine, 1995); and marked feedback effects can occur during production (Wing, 1980), although these are not strictly allowed by the theory, given its exclusive reliance on top-down control. The importance of feedback in timing is especially pronounced in synchronization tasks, in which participants try to synchronize finger taps, for example, with external signals or with taps made with some other part of the body (e.g., the foot).

Typically, the taps lead the external signals by a short amount of time, as if the subjects try to synchronize the central registration of the tap-produced reafference with the central registration of the external signal (Aschersleben & Prinz, 1995). In like manner, when subjects tap with the foot and hand, the foot leads the hand by the time that permits the hand and foot reafference to reach the brain simultaneously (Paillard, 1949).

The Wing-Kristofferson (1973) model relies on a central timekeeper, but other work has led to the proposal that coupled oscillators rather than clocks underlie timing and rhythm control. A finding that has led to this view comes from tasks in which subjects tap with two hands rather than one. When the left- and right-hand taps are supposed to be generated in phase (relative phase equal to 2π radians) or antiphase (relative phase equal to π radians), the tapping has low timing variability, but when the taps are interleaved such that the delay between the left hand and right are unequal (i.e., relative phase not equal to π or 2π radians), the timing variability increases (Yaminishi, Kawato, & Suzuki, 1980). Yaminishi et al. ascribed this result to interactions between nonlinear coupled oscillators. A recent paper suggested that it might be due to central timekeepers (Semjen & Ivry, 2001).

There has been debate between those who think timing is based on clocks, including hierarchically arranged clocks (Vorberg & Hambuch, 1978), and those who think timing emerges from the dynamics of nonlinear coupled oscillators (Schöner & Kelso, 1988). Those who endorse the clock view generally advocate cognitive processing (Gibbon, Church, & Meck, 1984; Rosenbaum, in press; Semjen & Ivry, 2001), whereas those who endorse the coupled-oscillator view eschew appeals to internal computations and representations (Beek, Peper, & Stegeman, 1995; Turvey, 1990).

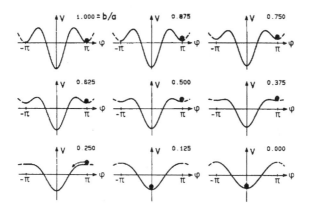

Figure 8.2   Potential landscape that can account for the growing attraction of in-phase finger oscillation as frequency increases.

NOTE: The potential function, V(ϕ), of relative phase, ϕ, obeys the relation $V(\phi) = -a\cos(\phi) - b\cos(2\phi)$, where the ratio b/a is a real number that decreases with frequency. The landscape provides just one basin of attraction for the system's state (depicted by the "marble") when the frequency is so high that $b/a = 0$.

SOURCE: Reprinted from *Human Movement Science, 7,* J. A. S. Kelso & G. Schöner, "Self-organization of coordinative movement patterns," pp. 1–27, Copyright © 1988, with permission from Excerpta Medica Inc.

One set of results in the motor timing literature seems much easier to explain with coupled oscillators than with central timekeepers. These findings come from a phenomenon first discovered by Cohen (1970) and then investigated in considerable detail by Kelso and colleagues (e.g., Haken, Kelso, & Bunz, 1985; Schöner & Kelso, 1988). In the canonical version of this task subjects oscillate the left and right index fingers simultaneously, swinging the fingers in time with a metronome whose frequency may change. The main result is that the fingers are generally attracted to one of two phase lags—either in phase or antiphase—much as in the study of Yaminishi et al. (1980), although the in-phase mode dominates as frequency increases. Using the metaphorical language of dynamical systems analysis, Kelso and colleagues called these phase lags *attractors*. The fact that other phase lags are possible when the driving frequency is low suggests that the potential landscape containing possible attractors (represented by basins in which the state of the system can fall) can change as a function of the driving frequency (Figure 8.2). The landscape can be flatter when the driving frequency is low than when it is high, but as the frequency increases, the basins deepen at the preferred phase lags. This model, whose mathematical formulation is presented in Haken et al. (1985), has managed to account for the full set of results from this paradigm more effectively than any central timekeeper model of which I am aware.

THE LEARNING PROBLEM

In this section I turn to the problem of learning. I made reference to this issue earlier when I mentioned that an appealing feature of hierarchical plans is that their constituents may be learned at different stages. Expressing this idea in another way and relying on a familiar analogy from computer science, plans or programs for skilled action may draw on previously prepared subroutines much as computer programs do (Miller, Galanter, & Pribram, 1960). What is the evidence for this view?

The Power Law

One of the earliest views of skill learning was that the actor (human or animal) learns through trial and error. Thorndike (1911) championed this idea, and it has been revisited often since then. Crossman (1959) suggested that trial and error learning may underlie the functional relation between speed of performance and amount of practice, as found, for example, in Crossman's own recordings of cigar factory workers (Figure 8.3). Crossman found that the time, T, to roll a typical cigar varied with the amount of practice, P, according to a power law, $T = aP^{-b}$, where a and b are nonnegative constants. This formula implies that a task such as cigar rolling gets faster with practice, although the rate of speeding up slows down as practice continues. It has recently been shown that an exponential function may provide a better fit to the data than a power function can (Heathcote, Brown, & Mewhort, 2000), but this does not challenge the basic claim of the power law. Findings consistent with the power law have been obtained in a wide set of circumstances. The time to draw figures viewed only in a mirror changes with practice as predicted by the power law (Snoddy, 1926). So does the time to do computer text editing (Singley & Anderson, 1989), prove mathematical theorems (Neves & Anderson, 1981), and even to write books (Ohlsson, 1992). The generality of these findings suggests that the power law may reflect the formation of ever more inclusive routines (Newell & Rosenbloom, 1981) and that the mechanisms underlying the acquisition of perceptual-motor skills on the one hand and of more "intellectual" skills on the other may be more fundamentally

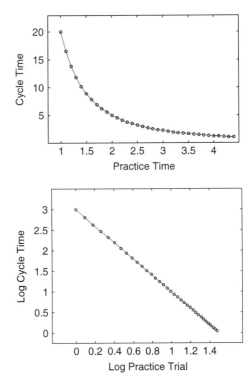

Figure 8.3 Speed-up with practice in cigar rolling.
NOTE: (A) Cycle time as a function of number of cigars produced; (B) Same data plotted on log-log coordinates.

alike than different (Schmidt & Bjork, 1992; Rosenbaum et al., 2001).

Similarities between Motor Learning and Intellectual Learning

A number of other similarities between learning in the perceptual-motor and intellectual domains can also be noted:

First, both in verbal learning (Glenberg, 1997) and in perceptual-motor learning (Shea & Morgan, 1979) one sees better immediate performance following massed practice than following spaced practice and better long-term retention following spaced (or random) practice than following blocked or massed practice. Magill and Hall (1990) offered relevant data for perceptual-motor skills, as did Melton (1970), Landauer and Bjork (1978), and Rea and Modigliani (1985) for intellectual skills.

Second, variations in feedback frequency have similar effects in perceptual-motor learning and in intellectual learning. Good short-term retention but poor long-term retention is seen when subjects receive frequent feedback, whereas poor short-term retention but good long-term retention is seen when subjects receive infrequent feedback. Schmidt and Bjork (1992) and Rosenbaum et al. (2001) reviewed the evidence.

Third, constant training (using the same materials) leads to better performance just after training than after a delay, but variable training (using different materials) leads to worse performance just after training than in later tests. Shapiro and Schmidt (1982) summarized data relevant to this claim for perceptual-motor tasks, and Bransford, Franks, Morris, and Stein (1977) did the same for intellectual tasks.

Fourth, consolidation effects are also observed in both domains. In explicit memory tasks subjects suffer from interruptions of memory consolidation (Weingartner & Parker, 1984). Recent work on perceptual-motor learning shows similar behavioral effects. Learning to compensate for predictable force perturbations in manual aiming (Brashers-Krug, Shadmehr, & Bizzi, 1996) and learning to perform finger-thumb opposition sequences (Karni et al., 1998) benefit from breaks between training and subsequent tests. Brain imaging studies also reveal task-related changes during rests following practice (Karni et al., 1998).

Fifth, rehearsal plays a role in learning, both in acquisition of verbal material and in acquisition of nonverbally expressed skills. The benefits of rehearsal in verbal learning are well known from studies of short-term memory. Rehearsing items increases the likelihood that they will be remembered, and some forms of rehearsal (elaborative rehearsal) are more effective than others (rote rehearsal). Mental rehearsal also turns out to be a useful adjunct to learning perceptual-motor skills, although mental rehearsal is usually not as effective as physical practice (for a review, see Schmidt & Lee, 1999). Mental rehearsal of movements (movement imagery) faithfully reflects the time to complete the movements (Decety & Jeannerod, 1995; Decety, Jeannerod, & Prablanc, 1989; Johnson, 2000; MacKay, 1982; Sirigu et al., 1996).

Sixth, an influential theory of the stages of skill acquisition applies just as well to intellectual skill development as to perceptual-motor skill development (Anderson, 1982). According to this theory (Fitts, 1964), there are three main stages in skill acquisition. First, there is a *declarative* stage in which the performer learns the basic steps of the task, often speaking privately to him- or herself (e.g., "OK, to put the car in first gear I have to push the gear shift forward while also pushing in on the clutch"). During a second, or *associative* stage, the task becomes more fluent, as if the steps become more strongly associated to one another and to the environment than they were before. The need for verbalization also tends to drop out during this second period. In a third stage—the so-called *autonomous* stage—the steps become faster and require less mental effort. Greater automaticity is possible, and the performer can perform the task while also engaging in other tasks—something that was impossible before (Spelke, Hirst, & Neisser, 1976).

Special Features of Motor Learning

From the fact that perceptual-motor learning is similar to intellectual learning, it does not follow that one should ignore the physical aspects of performance that must be learned during perceptual-motor learning. Clearly, what must be learned differs if one is learning to play the piano or learning to play chess. Palmer and Meyer (2000) showed that children learning to play the piano were adversely affected in their piano playing when they had to change the assignment of fingers to keys, although skilled adult pianists were less adversely affected by this change. Rosenbaum and Chaiken (2001) showed that when university students moved a joystick to a visually specified location without on-line visual guidance, they performed the task more accurately if the hand was the same as in earlier training. Accuracy was also better if the hand movements could be performed in the same part of the workspace as in earlier training.

A finding that turned up a surprising feature of memory for perceptual motor tasks was obtained by Marteniuk and Roy (1972). These investigators asked participants to direct the hand to a position in space, after which the experimenter brought the hand to its original starting position or to a different starting position. In both cases, participants could easily bring the hand to the terminal position that they had previously adopted. However, when the instruction was to cover the distance traveled before, subjects did very poorly when the hand was brought to a starting position that was different from its original takeoff point. This and other results suggest that movements are not remembered as well as final positions are (for a review, see Smyth, 1984). Work by Baud-Bovy and Viviani (1998) and Rosenbaum, Meulenbroek, and Vaughan (1999) shows that remembered final positions include remembered postures, not just locations in space.

As one becomes more proficient at a task, one's movement efficiency also improves (Sparrow & Newell, 1998). One way this happens is that actors learn about the dynamics

Figure 8.4   A baby in a Jolly Jumper.
Source: From Thelen (1995).

of the environment in which they perform. A charming demonstration of this learning concerns infants in a "Jolly Jumper" (see Figure 8.4; Goldfield, Kay, & Warren, 1993). With exposure to this device (a seat hung with elastic straps), infants get more and more "bounce for the buck." Their bounce amplitudes increase, and their bounce periods become less variable.

Other work on the learning of dynamics has provided insights into more detailed aspects of motor learning and control. Conditt, Gandolfo, and Mussa-Ivaldi (1997) studied subjects' adaptation to a velocity-dependent force field. Subjects moved a manipulandum from one visual target to another while the robot to which the manipulandum was attached generated forces proportional to the hand's velocity. Conditt et al. found that subjects could adapt in this situation. The subjects' initially highly curved movements, induced by the artificial force field, became increasingly straight (the normal path shape).

If the subjects later drew shapes (e.g., circles) that were not simply composed of the individual target-aiming movements that they had produced during learning, they were able to draw the shapes quite well. This led Conditt et al. to title their paper "The motor system does not learn the dynamics of the arm by rote memorization of past experience." Instead, actors form an internal model of the dynamics of the environment of which they are a part (cf. Atkeson, 1989; Jordan, 1994).

THE DEGREES OF FREEDOM PROBLEM

In reaching for a visually perceived target, people may adopt many postures at the end of the movement and on the way to the final posture. Much work on motor control has been concerned with this overabundance of degrees of freedom in the body relative to the ostensive description of a task to be performed. The question addressed by researchers in the field of motor control is how particular solutions emerge when infinitely many solutions are possible.

Coupling

A proposed solution to the degrees of freedom problem was advanced by the person who first recognized that redundant behavioral options pose a challenge for motor control research (Bernstein, 1967). Bernstein's idea was to rely on interactions between effectors. Abstractly, the basis for this approach is captured by considering two points in a plane (Saltzman, 1979). The points have a total of four degrees of freedom (their horizontal and vertical positions), but if the points are connected with a segment of fixed length, the number of degrees of freedom shrinks to three (the horizontal and vertical position of one point and the angle of the link). Coupling

between effectors may similarly provide a way of reducing the degrees of freedom to be managed.

A great deal of evidence exists for effector coupling. Some of it has already been mentioned in connection with bimanual finger coordination (Cohen, 1970; Haken et al., 1985; Semjen & Ivry, 2001; Yaminishi et al., 1980). These findings were inspired by earlier observations of extremity coupling in humans and in fish (von Holst, 1939/1973).

An interesting finding about the basis of effector coupling comes from the observation that neurologically normal individuals have great difficulty drawing two different shapes with the two hands, whereas patients whose corpus callosum has been severed can draw a shape with one hand with nary an effect of the shape drawn by the other hand (Franz, Eliassen, Ivry, & Gazzaniga, 1996). Such decoupling of the two hands in split-brain patients suggests that communication between the hemispheres normally plays a role in bimanual coupling.

Whether effectors are coupled does not depend only on whether their neural control centers are anatomically linked. Two people watching each other may synchronize their behavior. Thus, if one person swings a leg at some frequency, the other person may swing his or her leg at a similar frequency and phase (see Turvey, 1990). This phenomenon indicates that coupling may be informationally and not just anatomically based.

Coupling can also be turned on or off within an individual depending on the task he or she is performing. During speech production, the vertical positions of the upper and lower lip are negatively correlated when the lips need to meet, as in [apa], but their vertical positions are essentially uncorrelated when the lips do not need to meet, as in [afa] (Abbs, Gracco, & Cole, 1984). Analogous results have been obtained for finger coordination (Cole, Gracco, & Abbs, 1984).

Does coupling solve the degrees of freedom problem? It may when the task calls for coupling (e.g., while swimming the breaststroke), but it is doubtful that coupling is the final answer because, as seen earlier, it can be turned on or off. This leaves open the question of who or what activates the synergy. There is also the problem that many physical decisions do not rely simply on the activation or deactivation of synergies. Deciding to take hold of a stick with an overhand or underhand grip, for example, depends on where it will later be carried, so this is a decision that relies on other decision processes.

Equilibrium Point Control

Another candidate solution of the degrees of freedom problem is reliance on reflexes. If the nervous system has innate reflex patterns, perhaps these can be used to reduce the complexity of planning. This idea is difficult to evaluate because the definition of a reflex is slippery (Latash, 1993). Moreover, the way in which reflexes might be combined is potentially limitless.

One hypothesis about the use of reflexes that has received a great deal of attention is the *equilibrium point* hypothesis of Feldman (1986). According to this hypothesis, thresholds for muscle stretch reflexes are centrally altered, causing the limb to be out of equilibrium until it is brought to the new equilibrium position established by the central nervous system. The beauty of this proposal is that it potentially provides a way of obviating detailed control of movement to new positions.

Space does not permit a review of the extensive debate that has arisen about the equilibrium point hypothesis. Questions have been raised about the necessity of sensory feedback for successful operation of an equilibrium point mechanism (Polit & Bizzi, 1978) and about the modifiability of movement based on

learned force perturbations (Dizio & Lackner, 1995; Gomi & Kawato, 1996). Modifiability of movement trajectories seems at first to contradict the idea of a movement that proceeds without guidance to an equilibrium position. On the other hand, one may also say that if movements *can* be guided, this does not mean they always *must* be.

The debate about the equilibrium point hypothesis will no doubt continue and will, as it has in the past, produce useful findings (e.g., Bizzi, Mussa-Ivaldi, & Giszter, 1991). Regardless of how the debate is resolved, it is unlikely that equilibrium point control can be the sole solution to the degrees of freedom problem, for even if equilibrium points are established and limbs move faithfully to them, the issue remains of how particular equilibrium points are chosen.

Cost Containment

Another approach to the degrees of freedom problem that has gained prominence in recent years is reliance on cost containment. Impetus was given to this notion by Flash and Hogan (1985), who were impressed by the regularity of hand-path kinematics in simple point-to-point positioning tasks. In general, the hand speeds up as it leaves its start position and then slows down as it comes to rest at its final position such that the function relating hand speed to time is symmetric and bell-shaped. Flash and Hogan suggested that such movements are performed as if the mean squared rate of change of acceleration (mean squared jerk) is minimized.

Subsequent research challenged this interpretation on the grounds that the minimum jerk model ignored dynamics. That is, Flash and Hogan's (1985) principle was concerned only with the movement of a massless point (usually corresponding to the hand) in external space. It cannot account for effects of physical loads (Uno, Kawato, & Suzuki,

1989) or for differences in the power of various muscles (Dornay, Uno, Kawato, & Suzuki, 1996). Uno et al. were better able to handle such effects by positing a variant of Flash and Hogan's model. According to Uno et al., movements generally minimize mean squared torque change. Other minimization models have been proposed as well. For example, Soechting, Buneo, Herrmann, and Flanders (1995) suggested that the operative minimization principle concerns peak work.

Later models allowed for minimization of multiple rather than single costs (Kawato, 1996; Rosenbaum, Muelenbroek, Vaughan, & Jansen, in press). The multiple-cost approach provides a way of accounting for performance flexibility as illustrated, for example, in a violonist's deliberate switch from a legato to a staccato style of bowing depending on what the music calls for. A complete model of motor planning must allow for such flexibility. One model that strives for it has modifiable constraint hierarchies (Rosenbaum et al., in press). Here, costs are assigned different priorities depending on the task to be performed. This model departs from earlier ones, including Kawato's (1996), in that it relies on satisficing (Simon, 1955) rather than minimization. It also uses elimination by aspects (Tversky, 1972) rather than weighted averaging (Georgopoulos, Schwartz, & Kettner, 1986; Rosenbaum, Loukopoulos, Muelenbroek, Vaughan, & Engelbrecht, 1995) to weed out competitors. The way in which elimination by aspects works is that competitors that fail to satisfy the most important constraint are weeded out first, those that fail to satisfy the second most important constraint are weeded out second, and so on. This model yields reasonable solutions to a broad range of action problems such as writing with different effectors (Meulenbroek, Rosenbaum, Thomassen, Loukopoulos, & Vaughan, 1996) and reaching around obstacles (Rosenbaum et al., in press), but like its predecessors it

begs the question of how the degrees of freedom problem is ultimately solved. The reason is that it leaves unanswered who or what modifies the constraint hierarchies used to choose movement solutions.

THE PERCEPTUAL-MOTOR INTEGRATION PROBLEM

The final problem addressed here concerns perceptual-motor integration. How are our actions linked to perception? The question can be divided into two parts: (a) How are movements affected by perceptual processing? and (b) how is perceptual processing affected by movement?

Effect of Perception on Movement

A basic way in which movement is affected by perception is through feedback. A movement is made, and perception is used to evaluate the outcome, whereupon a corrective movement may follow (Woodworth, 1899). The time to move to the target depends on this series of events. When a handheld stylus is moved as quickly as possible to a target, the movement time increases with the distance to the target at a rate that depends on the width of the target; the wider the target, the lower the rate of increase (Fitts, 1954). This relation can be accounted for with an *optimized submovement* model (Meyer, Abrams, Kornblum, Wright, & Smith, 1988). According to this model, endpoint variability grows with velocity (distance divided by time), so even though the actor may wish to maximize velocity to reach the target as quickly as possible, doing so would imperil placement of the endpoint in the target. By taking into account how endpoint variability increases with velocity, the actor can select distance-time combinations that minimize movement time while ensuring target attainment after one or more submoves

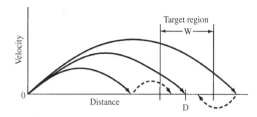

Figure 8.5   Possible sequences of submoves to a target region of width W whose center is distance D from the starting position.
SOURCE: Adapted from Meyer et al. (1988).

(see Figure 8.5). Meyer et al. showed that Fitts's observed relation between movement time, distance from the start position to the target center, and target width can be derived from the variability assumption just mentioned. Substantively, this outcome is interesting because it suggests that anticipation of motor variability plays a key role in aiming. Said another way, the seemingly simple task of bringing a stylus to a spatial target turns out to depend on surprisingly sophisticated computations.

Aiming for a stationary target, as just discussed, is only one kind of aiming. Another kind involves aiming for a continuously moving target (pursuit tracking). It turns out that anticipation plays a role in pursuit tracking as well. When the path of the moving target is simple and predictable, as in a sine wave, pursuit tracking can be virtually perfect (Poulton, 1974). An interesting recent finding is that pursuit tracking errors can be greatly reduced by taking feedback delays into account (Miall, Weir, Wolpert, & Stein, 1993). If one generates pursuit movements whose feedback is delayed, one's tracking can become highly unstable. On the other hand, if the expected reafference is buffered until the actual feedback is expected, performance can improve dramatically. Miall et al. argued that the cerebellum may serve, among other things, as a neural substrate for such a buffer (or, as it is called in control theory, a Smith predictor). Damage to the cerebellum impairs compensation for longer-than-normal feedback delays, in keeping with this hypothesis. Moreover, because successful use of a Smith Predictor entails estimation of delays for feedback, it is fitting that the cerebellum has been considered by others to be a primary site for timing (Ivry & Keele, 1989).

Effect of Movement on Perception

Perception affects movement, as indicated in the preceding section, but movement also affects perception. It does so in ways that are helpful (e.g., letting one perceive things that could not be perceived if movement did not occur) and also in ways that are challenging (e.g., deciding whether the external environment moved or remained stationary when its image shifted or remained fixed on the retina following a saccade).

An ingenious solution to the challenge just mentioned was introduced in the mid-19th century by Helmholtz (see Gregory, 1973). Helmholtz noticed that if he gently pushed on his eye with his finger while trying to maintain fixation on a stationary scene, the scene appeared to move. However, if he let his eye scan the scene, the scene appeared to remain stationary. What differed in the two cases, Helmholtz argued, was that oculomotor commands for saccades were present in one case but not in the other. Associated with the generation of the oculomotor commands was an expectancy about the shift in retinal position of the scene. If the expected retinal shift occurred when such an expectancy was present, the scene could be perceived as stationary, but if the expected retinal shift did not occur when it was expected, the scene was perceived to move. When oculomotor commands were not issued (when the finger nudged the eyeball), the shift of the retinal image was compared to an implicit expectancy for no shift at all, in which case the presence of a retinal shift led to the perception of external motion.

Helmholtz's argument entailed unconscious inference, which meant that Helmholtz, rather than Freud (who came later), actually "discovered" the unconscious. Others have resisted the idea that inference—conscious or unconscious—underlies perception (Michaels & Carello, 1981), but the evidence, at least in my opinion, supports the view that inferences and expectancies play some role in how we perceive.

Two other demonstrations attest to the generality of inferences and expectancies in contexts involving motor control and vision. One used the housefly (see Figure 8.6). Placed in a cylinder with vertical black and white stripes, this insect turns freely about its vertical axis, undisturbed by the shifting projections of the stripes on its compound eyes. But if the fly's head is rotated 180° and is glued in place so that its left eye is on the right and its right eye is on the left, the fly is flummoxed (von Holst & Mittelstaedt, 1950). Attempting to turn left, it immediately turns to the right, and vice versa. Soon the fly hardly moves at all,

though it is not physically paralyzed; when the environment is darkened, it moves freely. Von Holst and Mittelstaedt's account of the fly's strange behavior was basically the same as Helmholtz's. They argued that when the fly turned in one direction, it expected a visual change in the opposite direction. If the expectation was fulfilled, the fly inferred that the external environment was stationary, but if the expectation was not fulfilled—and in particular if there was a visual change in the same direction as the fly's whole-body rotation (as occurred when the fly's eye positions were inverted)—the fly inferred that the world was moving and stood still to regain its balance. Von Holst and Mittelstaedt's experiment, then, demonstrated expectancies and inferences in the housefly.

The other demonstration of the role of expectancies in movement-related visual perception pertains to receptive field properties of neurons in the parietal cortex (see Figure 8.7; Duhamel, Colby, & Goldberg, 1992). Duhamel et al. found neurons whose receptive fields shifted in anticipation of saccades. Before the saccades, the neurons responded to stimulation of one part of the visual scene, but as the time of the saccades approached, the neuron's receptive field shifted to the part of the visual scene that would have the same position relative to the line of gaze *after* the forthcoming saccade as the original receptive field did relative to the line of gaze *before* the saccade. This finding corroborates Helmholtz's claims and provides a portal into its neural circuitry.

Many other demonstrations have been offered for the effects of movement on perception. During and shortly before saccades, visual sensitivity declines, giving rise to saccadic suppression (Volkmann, 1976). The same is true during and shortly before blinks (Volkmann, Riggs, & Moore, 1980). Blink suppression was shown with an ingenious experiment in which an optic fiber was used

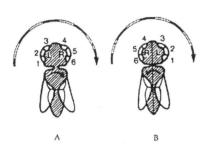

A   B

Figure 8.6 Turning behavior of a fly whose left and right eyes are either (a) in their normal positions or (b) on the right and left, respectively, because the fly's head is rotated 180°. The numbers show eye segments. The arrow on the fly's body shows how the fly is likely to turn when the vertical stripes it faces turn clockwise as viewed from above.
SOURCE: From Gallistel (1999).

Oculomotor events

Visual events

Fixate

Intend eye movement

Refixate

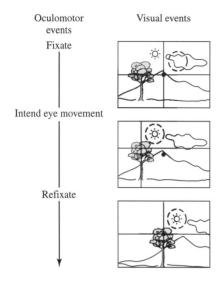

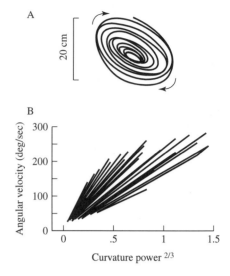

A

20 cm

B

Angular velocity (deg/sec)

300

200

100

0

0 .5 1 1.5

Curvature power $^{2/3}$

Figure 8.7 Change in the receptive field properties of the parietal cortex of a monkey as it looks at one location (top panel), prepares to direct its gaze to another location (middle panel), and then brings its gaze to that new location.
NOTE: The dot shows the current gaze location; the dashed line shows the receptive field of the neural pool whose activity is recorded along with the monkey's eye position; and the crosshairs show the center of the frame of reference of the presumed cortical representation.
SOURCE: Reprinted from Duhamel, Colby, & Goldberg (1992).

Figure 8.8 A drawn spiral (A) and its pen-tip kinematics (B).
NOTE: The angular velocity of the pentip is proportional to curvature raised to the 2/3 power. The constant of proportionality increases with the linear extent of the arc defined by its characteristic curvature.
SOURCE: From Lacquaniti, Terzuolo, & Viviani (1984).

to project light onto the roof of the mouth (Volkmann et al., 1980). With this setup, illumination of the retina was achieved without having to pass through the closed or closing lids.

The way things are visually perceived often depends on what actions they afford, as argued by Gibson (1979). For instance, a chair affords sitting, a ball affords throwing, and so on. Two recent findings lent noteworthy support to this claim. One, by Viviani and Stucchi (1989), was related to the fact that when one draws with a pen, the angular velocity of the pentip depends on the curvature of the stroke being drawn and on the length of the segment with that degree of curvature. If one draws a spiral,

for example, the angular velocity of the pentip increases as the curve gets tighter and as the linear extent of each segment with fixed curvature increases (see Figure 8.8). As shown by Lacquaniti, Terzuolo, and Viviani (1984), the angular velocity is proportional to curvature raised to the 2/3 power. This has been called the two-thirds power law. By definition, curvature for three contiguous points on an arc is the inverse of the radius of the circle on whose circumference the three points lie. The length of the arc for which curvature remains constant establishes the constant of proportionality for the two-thirds power law. Regarding visual perception, Viviani and Stucchi (1989) showed that to make a dot moving on a screen be seen to move with constant speed, its speed must be adjusted so that it obeys the two-thirds power law. If the dot moves at an objectively constant speed, it appears to move at a speed that varies. This finding supports the view that how we perceive depends on how we move.

Another recent finding that supports this conclusion was provided by Proffitt, Bhalla, Gossweiler, and Midgett (1995). These researchers asked subjects to judge hill angles and give their estimates of slant either verbally or by tilting a board with the hand (as well as with another method not critical for present purposes). The hand-tilt method was most accurate, escaping the overestimation of geographical slant found with verbal reports. Proffitt et al. concluded that the perception of hill inclination was more accurate when a direct behavioral measure could be given than when an indirect verbal report was desired. Others have obtained similar results (e.g., Bridgeman, Lewis, Heit, & Nagle, 1979).

The final discovery to be reviewed in this section concerns mirror neurons (Gallese, Fadiga, Fogassi, & Rizzolatti, 1996; Rizzolatti & Arbib, 1998). These neurons fire when the same task is either observed or performed. When a macaque watches someone perform a grasp or performs the same grasp itself, neurons in its premotor cortex fire selectively. Mirror neurons like these seem to exist as well in humans. When a person watches someone perform a grasping movement, transcranial magnetic stimulation of the observer's brain induces an increase in excitability of the muscles that the observer would use for that same movement. The increase in excitability exceeds what is seen in control conditions (Fadiga, Fogassi, Pavesi, & Rizzolatti, 1995). The presumed mechanism for this enhancement is heightened activity in neural pools analogous to the mirror neurons of the macaque. Analogous effects can also be obtained with RT techniques (Craighero, Fadiga, Rizzolatti, & Umiltà, 1998).

Prediction

Findings such as those just summarized suggest that seeing others perform actions has sympathetic effects in the observer's brain. This may provide a basis for the benefits of modeling as a training technique (Bandura, 1965), and it may help explain the ease with which the actions of others can be imitated (Iacobini et al., 1999; Meltzoff & Moore, 1977). The capacity to represent movements without actually performing the movements may also provide a basis for prediction. A growing body of evidence indicates that anticipating the perceptual consequences of one's acts is a part of action planning (Prinz, 1997). The notion that action planning entails perceptual anticipation was advanced in the 19th century (see Prinz, 1997) and was revived and substantially confirmed through later studies by Greenwald (1970) and, more recently, by Prinz (1997) and his colleagues (e.g., Hommel, 1996).

Predicting what will occur when one acts makes sense from a teleological standpoint. Because most or possibly all voluntary actions are carried to effect desired perceptual consequences, it is reasonable that the representations of those expected consequences play a role in action planning. Having representations of anticipated consequences is also likely to help in feedback processing because feedback must be compared to a standard to be used effectively.

The final reason for believing that predictions are made about the consequences of motor acts is that it has come to be understood that such predictions may be needed to issue appropriate motor commands. To adapt to external force fields, for example, predictions or forward models are vital. How else could one alter the way one behaves when the wind kicks up or when the currents in which one is swimming change? As already indicated, Conditt et al. (1997) showed that subjects exposed to velocity-dependent force fields developed models of those force fields, enabling them to generate forces that anticipated rather than merely followed the forces that were externally imposed. Other research has confirmed that actors learn to make accurate force-related predictions (Dizio & Lackner, 1995; Shadmehr & Mussa-Ivaldi, 1994) as well as adaptive anticipatory changes to altered visual feedback, as in prism adaptation (Redding & Wallace, 1997). Recent theoretical work on the detailed processes underlying motor planning has also come to rely on the notion that predicting what will happen given different courses of action is an important means of selecting actions (Mel, 1991; Rosenbaum et al., 2001; Wolpert & Kawato, 1998).

CONCLUSIONS

This chapter opened with a set of questions about motor control, some of which pertained to how movements are controlled or learned and some of which pertained to the relevance of this field for experimental psychology at large. I hope that the questions about the relevance of motor control for experimental psychology have been answered positively. With respect to those questions, one could say that the most striking feature of motor control research from the past few decades is its discovery of the richness of the computational machinery on which action relies. Rather than being a mere matter of reflexes, as is commonly held by the public and even by some experimental psychologists, motor control relies on rich generative capabilities made possible by computations that we are only beginning to understand.

Will motor control hold more interest for experimental psychologists than it has in the past? One reason to think that it will is that many experimental psychologists have

been drawn to the claim that action may be more intimately related to attention than was previously recognized (Rizollati, Riggio, & Sheliga, 1994; Tipper, Howard, & Jackson, 1997). Experimental psychologists have also been intrigued by the proposition that a special visual system may exist for action apart from the one used for identification (Milner & Goodale, 1995). Both suggestions have been controversial, but work on them has helped—and will doubtless continue to help—reveal the rich psychological substrates of action.

Where will the experimental psychological study of motor control go in the future? Two trends are unmistakable. One is the growing importance of neuroscience, a trend that was reflected in the fact that this review made more frequent reference to neurophysiological data than did the chapter on motor control in the previous *Stevens' Handbook* (Pew & Rosenbaum, 1988). The other unmistakable trend is the growth of computational approaches. Experimental psychological research has been complemented by increasingly detailed quantitative models of behavior. Such work has been pursued by behavioral scientists as well as computer scientists, control systems engineers, and the like. More and more effort has been aimed at marrying experimental psychological techniques with techniques from physics, mathematics, and engineering. This is a healthy development that will doubtless help advance our knowledge.

Finally, work in this area is likely to yield practical benefits. Areas such as medicine, human factors, education, and the arts (e.g., computer animation) are likely to witness advances thanks to research on motor control conducted by experimental psychologists and others. The notion that signals from the brain can be used to operate external devices is moving from fantasy to reality. Robots are being endowed with more capabilities than ever, making the prospect of their autonomous operation in places as remote as Mars the stuff of reality rather than of fiction. Teams of robots are also able to do now what no single robot could do before. This may be an especially important new direction for the field. Actions are often carried out in social contexts. It is impossible for one person to move a piano down a flight of stairs and have it survive the descent, for example, but a team of interacting movers can get the job done. Social action is, I think, one area in which significant advances will be made in the future. Just as modern motor-control research has shown that actors rely on internal models to plan movements and evaluate reafference, internal models related to action may include an appreciation of what others can and cannot do. Future research may show how such models work. Conceivably, the internal modeling of what others can and cannot do at the motor level will translate into other forms of modeling that may make us more sympathetic creatures than the course of history has so far shown us to be.

REFERENCES

Abbs, J. H., Gracco, V. L., & Cole, K. J. (1984). Control of multimovement coordination: Sensorimotor mechanisms in speech motor programming. *Journal of Motor Behavior, 16,* 195–231.

Adams, J. A. (1984). Learning of movement sequences. *Psychological Bulletin, 96,* 3–28.

Alexander, R. M. (1984). Walking and running. *American Scientist, 72,* 348–354.

Alexander, R. M. (1992). *Exploring biomechanics.* New York: Freeman.

Anderson, J. R. (1982). Acquisition of cognitive skill. *Psychological Review, 89,* 369–406.

Aschersleben, G., & Prinz, W. (1995). Synchronizing actions with events: The role of sensory information. *Perception & Psychophysics, 57,* 305–317.

Atkeson, C. G. (1989). Learning arm kinematic and dynamics. *Annual Review of Neuroscience, 12,* 157–183.

Bandura, A. (1965). Vicarious processes: A case of no-trial learning. In L. Berkowitz (Ed.), *Advances in experimental social psychology: Vol. 2* (pp. 1–55). New York: Academic Press.

Bard, C., Fleury, M, Teasdale, N., Paillard, J., & Nougier, V. (1995). Contribution of proprioception for calibrating and updating the motor space. *Canadian Journal of Physiology and Pharmacology, 73,* 246–254.

Baud-Bovy, G., & Viviani, P. (1998). Pointing to kinesthetic targets in space. *The Journal of Neuroscience, 18,* 1528–1545.

Beek, P. J., Peper, C. E., & Stegeman, D. F. (1995). Dynamical models of movement coordination. *Human Movement Science, 14,* 573–608.

Bernstein, N. (1967). *The coordination and regulation of movements.* London: Pergamon.

Bizzi, E., Mussa-Ivaldi, F. A., & Giszter, S. (1991). Computations underlying the execution of movement: A biological perspective. *Science, 253,* 287–291.

Bransford, J. D., Franks, J. J., Morris, C. D., & Stein, B. S. (1977). Some general constraints on learning and memory research. In L. S. Cermak & F. I. M. Craik (Eds.), *Levels of processing in human memory* (pp. 331–354). Hillsdale, NJ: Erlbaum.

Brashers-Krug, T., Shadmehr, R., & Bizzi, E. (1996). Consolidation in human motor memory. *Nature, 382,* 252–255.

Bridgeman, B., Lewis, S., Heit, G., & Nagle, M. (1979). Relationship between cognitive and motor systems of visual position perception. *Journal of Experimental Psychology: Human Perception and Performance, 5,* 692–700.

Bryan, W. L., & Harter, N. (1897). Studies in the physiology and psychology of the telegraphic language. *Psychological Review, 4,* 27–53.

Chen, Y., Ding, M., & Kelso, J. A. S. (1997). Long memory processes ($1/f^\square$ type) in human coordination. *Physical Review Letters, 79,* 4501–4504.

Chieffi, S., & Allport, D. A. (1997). Independent coding of target distance and direction in visuo-spatial working memory. *Psychological Research, 60,* 244–250.

Cohen, L. (1970). Interaction between limbs during bimanual voluntary activity. *Brain, 93,* 259–272.

Cole, K. J., Gracco, V. L., & Abbs, J. H. (1984). Autogenic and nonautogenic sensorimotor actions in the control of multiarticulate hand movements. *Experimental Brain Research, 56,* 582–585.

Conditt, M. A., Gandolfo, F., & Mussa-Ivaldi, F. A. (1997). The motor system does not learn the dynamics of the arm by rote memorization of past experience. *Journal of Neurophysiology, 78,* 554–560.

Cooper, W. E., & Paccia-Cooper, J. (1980). *Syntax and speech.* Cambridge: Harvard University Press.

Craighero, L., Fadiga, L., Rizzolatti, G., & Umiltà, C. (1998). Visuomotor priming. *Visual Cognition, 5,* 109–125.

Crossman, E. R. F. W. (1959). A theory of the acquisition of speed skill. *Ergonomics, 2,* 153–166.

Decety, J., & Jeannerod, M. (1995). Mentally simulated movements in virtual reality: Does Fitts's law hold in motor imagery? *Behavioral Brain Research, 72,* 127–134.

Decety, J., Jeannerod, M., & Prablanc, C. (1989). The timing of mentally represented actions. *Behavioral Brain Research, 34,* 35–42.

Dizio, P., & Lackner, J. R. (1995). Motor adaptation to coriolis force perturbations of reaching movements: Endpoint but not trajectory adaptation transfers to the nonexposed arm. *Journal of Neurophysiology, 74,* 1787–1792.

Dornay, M., Uno, Y., Kawato, M., & Suzuki, R. (1996). Minimum muscle-tension change trajectories predicted by using a 17-muscle model of the monkey's arm. *Journal of Motor Behavior, 2,* 83–100.

Duhamel, J.-R., Colby, C. L., & Goldberg, M. E. (1992). The updating of the representation of visual space in parietal cortex by intended eye movements. *Science, 255,* 90–92.

Fadiga, L., Fogassi, L., Pavesi, G., & Rizzolatti, G. (1995). Motor facilitation during action observation: A magnetic stimulation study. *Journal of Neurophysiology, 73,* 2608–2611.

Feldman, A. G. (1986). Once more on the equilibrium-point hypothesis (λ model) for motor control. *Journal of Motor Behavior, 18,* 17–54.

Fitts, P. M. (1954). The information capacity of the human motor system in controlling the amplitude of movement. *Journal of Experimental Psychology, 47,* 381–391.

Fitts, P. M. (1964). Perceptual-motor skill learning. In A. W. Melton (Ed.), *Categories of human learning* (pp. 243–285). New York: Academic Press.

Flash, T., & Hogan, N. (1985). The coordination of arm movements: An experimentally confirmed mathematical model. *The Journal of Neuroscience, 5,* 1688–1703.

Franz, E., Eliassen, J., Ivry, R., & Gazzaniga, M. (1996). Dissociation of spatial and temporal coupling in the bimanual movements of callosotomy patients. *Psychological Science, 7,* 306–310.

Frederiksen, J. R., & Kroll, J. F. (1976). Spelling and sound: Approaches to the internal lexicon. *Journal of Experimental Psychology: Human Perception and Performance, 2,* 361–379.

Gallese, V., Fadiga, L., Fogassi, L., & Rizzolatti, G. (1996). Action recognition in the premotor cortex. *Brain, 119,* 593–609.

Gallistel, C. R. (1999). Coordinate transformations in the genesis of directed action. In B. M. Bly & D. E. Rumelhart (Eds.), *Cognitive science* (pp. 1–42). San Diego: Academic Press.

Gazzaniga, M. S., Ivry, R. B., & Mangun, G. R. (1998). *Cognitive neuroscience: The biology of the mind.* New York: Norton.

Georgopoulos, A. P., Schwartz, A. B., & Kettner, R. E. (1986). Neuronal population coding of movement direction. *Science, 233,* 1416–1419.

Gibbon, J., Church, R. M., & Meck, W. H. (1984). Scalar timing in memory. In J. Gibbon & L. Allan (Eds.), *Timing and time perception. Annals of the New York Academy of Sciences, 423,* 52–77.

Gibson, J. J. (1979). *The ecological approach to visual perception.* Boston: Houghton-Mifflin.

Gilden, D. L. (2001). Cognitive emissions of 1/f noise. *Psychological Review, 108,* 33–56.

Glenberg, A. M. (1997). What memory is for. *Behavioral and Brain Sciences, 20*(1), 1–55.

Goldfield, E. C., Kay, B. A., & Warren, W. H. (1993). Infant bouncing: The assembly and tuning of action systems. *Child Development, 64,* 1128–1142.

Gomi, H., & Kawato, M. (1996). Equilibrium-point control hypothesis examined by measured arm stiffness during multijoint movement. *Science, 272,* 117–120.

Gordon, J., Ghilardi, M. F., Ghez, C. (1997). Accuracy of planar reaching movements: I. Independence of direction and extent variability. *Experimental Brain Research, 99,* 97–111.

Gordon, P. C., & Meyer, D. E. (1987). Control of serial order in rapidly spoken syllable sequences. *Journal of Memory and Language, 26,* 300–321.

Greenwald, A. G. (1970). Sensory feedback mechanisms in performance control: With special reference to the ideo-motor mechanism. *Psychological Review, 77,* 73–99.

Gregory, R. L. (1973). *Eye and brain* (2nd ed.). New York: McGraw-Hill.

Haken, H., Kelso, J. A. S., & Bunz, H. (1985). A theoretical model of phase transitions in human hand movements. *Biological Cybernetics, 51,* 347–356.

Heathcote, A., Brown, S., & Mewhort, D. J. K. (2000). The power law repealed: The case for an exponential law of practice. *Psychonomic Bulletin and Review, 7,* 185–207.

Henry, F. M., & Rogers, D. E. (1960). Increased response latency for complicated movements and a "memory drum" theory of neuromotor reaction. *Research Quarterly, 31,* 448–458.

Hollerbach, J. M., & Atkeson, C. G. (1987). Deducing planning variables from experimental arm trajectories: Pitfalls and possibilities. *Biological Cybernetics, 56,* 279–292.

Hommel, B. (1996). The cognitive representation of action: Automatic integration of perceived action effects. *Psychological Research, 59,* 176–186.

Iacobini, M., Woods, R. P., Brass, M., Bekkering, H., Mazziotta, J. C., & Rizzolatti, G. (1999). Cortical mechanisms of human imitation. *Science, 286,* 2526–2528.

Inhoff, A. W. (1986). Preparing sequences of saccades under choice reaction conditions: Effects of sequence length and context. *Acta Psychologica, 61,* 211–228.

Ivry, R. B., & Hazeltine, R. E. (1995). Perception and production of temporal intervals across a range of durations: Evidence for a common timing mechanism. *Journal of Experimental Psychology: Human Perception and Performance, 21,* 3–18.

Ivry, R. B., & Keele, S. W. (1989). Timing functions of the cerebellum. *Journal of Cognitive Neuroscience, 1,* 136–152.

Jeannerod, M. (1984). The timing of natural prehension movement. *Journal of Motor Behavior, 26*(3), 235–254.

Johnson, S. H. (2000). Thinking ahead: The case for motor imagery in prospective judgments of prehension. *Cognition, 74,* 33–70.

Jordan, M. I. (1994). Computational motor control. In M. S. Gazzaniga (Ed.), *The cognitive neurosciences* (pp. 597–609). Cambridge: MIT Press.

Jordan, M. I., & Rosenbaum, D. A. (1989). Action. In M. I. Posner (Ed.), *Foundations of cognitive science* (pp. 727–767). Cambridge: MIT Press.

Kandel, E. R., Schwartz, J. H., & Jessell, T. M. (Eds.). (2000). *Principles of neural science* (4th ed.). New York: McGraw-Hill.

Karni, A., Meyer, G., Rey-Hipolito, C., Jezzard, P., Adams, M. M., Turner, R., & Ungerleider, L. G. (1998). The acquisition of skilled motor performance: Fast and slow experience-driven changes in primary motor cortex. *Proceedings of the National Academy of Science, 95,* 861–868.

Kawato, M. (1996). Bidirectional theory approach to integration. In T. Inui & J. L. McClelland (Eds.), *Attention and performance: 16. Information integration* (pp. 335–367). Cambridge: MIT Press.

Keele, S. W. (1986). Motor control. In J. K. Boff, L. Kaufman, & J. P. Thomas (Eds.), *Handbook of human perception and performance: Vol. 2* (pp. 30-1–30-60). New York: Wiley.

Kelso, J. A. S., & Schöner, G. (1988). Self-organization of coordinative movement patterns. *Human Movement Science, 7,* 27–46.

Klapp, S. T. (1977). Reaction time analysis of programmed control. *Exercise and Sport Sciences Reviews, 5,* 231–253.

Kornblum, S. (1965). Response competition and/or inhibition in two choice reaction time. *Psychonomic Science, 2,* 55–56.

Lacquaniti, F., Terzuolo, C., & Viviani, P. (1984). Global metric properties and preparatory processes in drawing movements. In S. Kornblum & J. Requin (Eds.), *Preparatory states and processes* (pp. 357–370). Hillsdale, N.J.: Erlbaum.

Landauer, T. K., & Bjork, R. A. (1978). Optimal rehearsal patterns and name learning. In M. M. Gruneberg, P. E. Morris, & R. N. Sykes (Eds.), *Practical aspects of memory* (pp. 625–632). London: Academic Press.

Lashley, K. S. (1951). The problem of serial order in behavior. In L. A. Jeffress (Ed.), *Cerebral mechanisms in behavior* (pp. 112–131). New York: Wiley.

Latash, M. L. (1993). *Control of human movement.* Champaign, IL: Human Kinetics.

MacKay, D. G. (1982). The problem of flexibility, fluency, and speed-accuracy trade-off in skilled behavior. *Psychological Review, 89,* 483–506.

Magill, R. A., & Hall, K. G. (1990). A review of the contextual interference effect in motor skill acquisition. *Human Movement Science, 9,* 241–289.

Marteniuk, R. G., & Roy, E. A. (1972). The codability of kinesthetic location and distance information. *Acta Psychologica, 36,* 471–479.

Megaw, E. D. (1972). Direction and extent uncertainty in step-input tracking. *Journal of Motor Behavior, 4,* 171–186.

Mel, B. W. (1991). A connectionist model may shed light on neural mechanisms for visually guided reaching. *Journal of Cognitive Neuroscience, 3,* 273–292.

Melton, A. W. (1970). The situation with respect to the spacing of repetitions and memory. *Journal of Verbal Learning and Verbal Behavior, 9,* 596–606.

Meltzoff, A. N., & Moore, M. K. (1977). Imitation of facial and manual gestures by human neonates. *Science, 198,* 75–78.

Meulenbroek, R. G. J., Rosenbaum D. A., Thomassen, A. J. W. M., Loukopoulos, L. D., & Vaughan, J. (1996). Adaptation of a reaching model to handwriting: How different effectors can produce the same written output, and other results. *Psychological Research/Psychologische Forschung, 59,* 64–74.

Meyer, D. E., Abrams, R. A., Kornblum, S., Wright, C. E., & Smith, J. E. K. (1988). Optimality in human motor performance: Ideal control of rapid aimed movements. *Psychological Review, 95,* 340–370.

Miall, R. C., Weir, D. J., Wolpert, D. M., & Stein, J. F. (1993). Is the cerebellum a Smith predictor? *Journal of Motor Behavior, 25,* 203–216.

Michaels, C. F., & Carello, C. (1981). *Direct perception.* Englewood Cliffs, NJ: Prentice-Hall.

Miller, G. A., Galanter, E., & Pribram, K. H. (1960). *Plans and the structure of behavior.* New York: Holt, Rinehart, & Winston.

Milner, A. D., & Goodale, M. A. (1995). *The visual brain in action.* New York: Oxford University Press.

Neves, D. M., & Anderson, J. R. (1981). Knowledge compilation: Mechanisms for the automatization of cognitive skills. In J. R. Anderson (Ed.), *Cognitive skills and their acquisition* (pp. 57–84). Hillsdale, NJ: Erlbaum.

Newell, A. M., & Rosenbloom, P. S. (1981). Mechanisms of skill acquisition and the law of practice. In J. R. Anderson (Ed.), *Cognitive skills and their acquisition* (pp. 1–55). Hillsdale, NJ: Erlbaum.

Norman, D. A. (1981). Categorization of action slips. *Psychological Review, 88,* 1–15.

Ohlsson, S. (1992). The learning curve for writing books: Evidence from Professor Asimov. *Psychological Science, 3,* 380–382.

Paillard, J. (1949). Quelques donnés psychophysiologiques relatives au déclenchment de la commade motrice [Some psychophysiological data relating to the triggering of motor commands]. *L'Annee Psychologique, 48,* 28–47.

Palmer, C., & Meyer, R. E. (2000). Conceptual and motor learning in music performance. *Psychological Science, 11,* 63–68.

Pew, R. W., & Rosenbaum, D. A. (1988). Human motor performance: Computation, representation, and implementation. In R. C. Atkinson, R. J. Herrnstein, G. Lindzey, & R. D. Luce (Eds.), *Stevens' handbook of experimental psychology* (2nd ed., pp. 473–509). New York: Wiley.

Polit, A., & Bizzi, E. (1978). Processes controlling arm movements in monkeys. *Science, 201,* 1235–1237.

Poulton, E. C. (1974). *Tracking skill and manual control.* New York: Academic Press.

Povel, D.-J., & Collard, R. (1982). Structural factors in patterned finger tapping. *Acta Psychologica, 52,* 107–124.

Prinz, W. (1997). Perception and action planning. *European Journal of Cognitive Psychology, 9,* 129–154.

Proffitt, D. R., Bhalla, M., Gossweiler, R., & Midgett. K. (1995). Perceiving geographical slant. *Psychonomic Bulletin & Review, 2,* 409–428.

Rea, C. P., & Modigliani, V. (1985). The effect of expanded versus massed practice on the retention of multiplication facts and spelling lists. *Human Learning, 4,* 11–18.

Redding, G. M., & Wallace, B. (1997). *Adaptive spatial alignment.* Mahwah, NJ: Erlbaum.

Reitman, J. S., & Rueter, H. H. (1980). Organization revealed by recall orders and confirmed by pauses. *Cognitive Psychology, 12,* 554–581.

Rizzolatti, G., & Arbib, M. A. (1998). Language within our grasp. *Trends in Neurosciences, 21,* 188–194.

Rizzolatti, G., Riggio, L., & Sheliga, B. M. (1994). Space and selective attention. In C. Umilta & M. Moscovitch (Eds.), *Attention and performance: Vol. 15.* Conscious and nonconscious information processing (pp. 231–265). Cambridge: MIT Press.

Roland, P. E. (1993). *Brain activation.* New York: Wiley.

Rosenbaum, D. A. (1980). Human movement initiation: Specification of arm, direction, and extent. *Journal of Experimental Psychology: General, 109,* 444–474.

Rosenbaum, D. A. (1987). Successive approximations to a model of human motor programming. In G. H. Bower (Ed.), *Psychology of learning and motivation: Vol. 21* (pp. 153–182). Orlando, FL: Academic Press.

Rosenbaum, D. A. (1991). *Human motor control.* San Diego: Academic Press.

Rosenbaum, D. A. (in press). Time, space, and short-term memory. *Brain and Cognition.*

Rosenbaum, D. A., Carlson, R. A., & Gilmore, R. O. (2001). Acquisition of intellectual and perceptual-motor skills. *Annual Review of Psychology, 52,* 453–470.

Rosenbaum, D. A., & Chaiken, S. (2001). Frames of reference in perceptual-motor learning: Evidence from a blind manual positioning task. *Psychological Research, 65,* 119–127.

Rosenbaum, D. A., Kenny, S., & Derr, M. A. (1983). Hierarchical control of rapid movement sequences. *Journal of Experimental Psychology: Human Perception and Performance, 9,* 86–102.

Rosenbaum, D. A., & Krist, H. (1996). Antecedents of action. In H. Heuer & S. W. Keele (Eds.), *Handbook of Perception and Action: Vol. 2* (3–69). London: Academic Press.

Rosenbaum, D. A., Loukopoulos, L. D., Meulenbroek, R. G. M., Vaughan, J., & Engelbrecht, S. E. (1995). Planning reaches by evaluating stored postures. *Psychological Review, 102,* 28–67.

Rosenbaum, D. A., Meulenbroek, R. G., & Vaughan, J. (1999). Remembered positions: Stored locations or stored postures? *Experimental Brain Research, 124,* 503–512.

Rosenbaum, D. A., Meulenbroek, R. G., Vaughan, J., & Jansen, C. (2001). Posture-based motion planning: Applications to grasping. *Psychological Review, 108,* 709–734.

Rothwell, J. C. (1987). *Control of human voluntary movement.* London: Croom-Helm.

Saltzman, E. (1979). Levels of sensorimotor representation. *Journal of Mathematical Psychology, 20,* 91–163.

Sanes, J. (1990). Motor representations in deaf-ferented humans: A mechanism for disordered movement performance. In M. Jeannerod (Ed.), *Attention and performance: Vol. 13. Motor representation and control* (pp. 714–735). Hillsdale, NJ: Erlbaum.

Schmidt, R. A., & Bjork, R. A. (1992). New conceptualizations of practice: Common principles in three paradigms suggest new concepts for training. *Psychological Science, 3,* 207–214.

Schmidt, R. A., & Lee, T. D. (1999). *Motor control and learning: A behavioral emphasis* (3rd ed.). Champaign, IL: Human Kinetics.

Schöner, G., & Kelso, J. A. S. (1988). Dynamic pattern generation in behavioral and neural systems. *Science, 239,* 1513–1520.

Semjen, A., & Ivry, R. B. (2001). The coupled oscillator model of between-hand coordination in alternate-hand tapping: A reappraisal. *Journal of Experimental Psychology: Human Perception and Performance, 27,* 251–265.

Shadmehr, R., & Mussa-Ivaldi, F. A. (1994). Adaptive representation of dynamics during learning of a motor task. *The Journal of Neuroscience, 14,* 3208–3224.

Shapiro, D. C., & Schmidt, R. A. (1982). The schema theory: Recent evidence and developmental implications. In J.A.S. Kelso & J. E. Clark (Eds.), *The development of movement control and coordination* (pp. 113–150). New York: Wiley.

Shea, J. B., & Morgan, R. L. (1979). Contextual interference effects on acquisition, retention, and transfer of a motor skill. *Journal of Experimental Psychology: Human Learning and Memory, 5,* 179–187.

Simon, H. (1955). A behavioral model of rational choice. *Quarterly Journal of Economics, 69,* 99–118.

Singley, K., & Anderson, J. R. (Eds.). (1989). *The transfer of cognitive skill.* Cambridge: Harvard University Press.

Sirigu, A., Duhamel, J.-R., Cohen, L., Pillon, B., Dubois, B., & Agid, Y. (1996). The mental representation of hand movements after parietal cortex damage. *Science, 273,* 1564–1568.

Smyth, M. M. (1984). Memory for movements. In M. M. Smyth & A. M. Wing (Eds.), *The psychology of human movement* (pp. 83–117). London: Academic Press.

Snoddy, G. S. (1926). Learning and stability: A psychophysical analysis of a case of motor learning with clinical applications. *Journal of Applied Psychology, 10,* 1–36.

Soechting, J. F., Buneo, C. A., Herrmann, U., & Flanders, M. (1995). Moving effortlessly in three dimensions: Does Donders' Law apply to arm movement? *Journal of Neuroscience, 15,* 6271–6280.

Sparrow, W. A., & Newell, K. M. (1998). Metabolic energy expenditure and the regulation of movement economy. *Psychonomic Bulletin & Review, 5,* 173–196.

Spelke, E., Hirst, W., & Neisser, U. (1976). Skills of divided attention. *Cognition, 4,* 215–230.

Sternberg, S., Monsell, S., Knoll, R. L., & Wright, C. E. (1978). The latency and duration of rapid movement sequences: Comparisons of speech and typewriting. In G. E. Stelmach (Ed.), *Information processing in motor control and learning* (pp. 117–152). New York: Academic Press.

Sternberg, S., Wright, C. E., Knoll, R. L., & Monsell, S. (1980). Motor programs in rapid speech. In R. Cole (Ed.), *Perception and production of fluent speech* (pp. 507–534). Hillsdale, NJ: Erlbaum.

Taub, E., & Berman, A. J. (1968). Movement and learning in the absence of sensory feedback. In S. J. Freeman (Ed.), *The neuropsychology of spatially oriented behavior* (pp. 173–192). Homewood, IL: Dorsey.

Thelen, E. (1995). Motor development: A new synthesis. *American Psychologist, 50,* 79–95.

Thorndike, E. L. (1911). *Animal intelligence.* New York: Hafner.

Tipper, S. P., Howard, L. A., & Jackson, S. R. (1997). Selective reaching to grasp: Evidence for distractor interference effects. *Visual Cognition, 4,* 1–38.

Turvey, M. T. (1990). Coordination. *American Psychologist, 45*(8), 938–953.

Tversky, A. (1972). Elimination by aspects: A theory of choice. *Psychological Review, 79,* 281–299.

Uno, Y., Kawato, M., & Suzuki, R. (1989). Formation and control of optimal trajectory in human multijoint arm movement: Minimum torque-change model. *Biological Cybernetics, 61,* 89–101.

Viviani, P., & Stucchi, N. (1989). The effect of movement velocity on form perception: Geometric illusions in dynamic displays. *Perception & Psychophysics, 46,* 266–274.

Volkmann, F. C. (1976). Saccadic suppression: A brief review. In R. A. Monty & J. W. Senders (Eds.), *Eye movements and psychological processes* (pp. 73–84). Hillsdale, NJ: Erlbaum.

Volkmann, F. C., Riggs, L. A., & Moore, R. K. (1980). Eyeblinks and visual suppression. *Science, 207,* 900–902.

von Holst, E. (1973). *The behavioural physiology of animal and man: The collected papers of Erich von Holst* (R. Martin, Trans.). London: Methuen. (Original work published 1939)

von Holst, E., & Mittelstaedt, H. (1973). *The behavioural physiology of animal and man: The collected papers of Erich von Holst* (R. Martin, Trans.). London: Methuen. (Original work published 1950)

Vorberg, D., & Hambuch, R. (1978). On the temporal control of rhythmic performance. In J. Requin (Ed.), *Attention and performance: Vol. 7* (pp. 535–555). Hillsdale, NJ: Erlbaum.

Weingartner, H., & Parker, E. (1984). *Memory consolidation: Psychobiology of cognition.* Hillsdale, NJ: Erlbaum.

Wickens, D. (1938). The transference of conditioned excitation and conditioned inhibition from one muscle group to the antagonistic group. *Journal of Experimental Psychology, 22,* 101–123.

Wing, A. M. (1980). The long and short of timing in response sequences. In G. E. Stelmach & J. Requin (Eds.), *Tutorials in motor behavior* (pp. 469–486). Amsterdam: North-Holland.

Wing, A. M., & Kristofferson, A. B. (1973). Response delays and the timing of discrete motor responses. *Perception & Psychophysics, 14,* 5–12.

Wolpert, D. M., & Kawato, M. (1998). Multiple paired forward and inverse models for motor control. *Neural Networks, 11,* 1317–1329.

Woodworth, R. S. (1899). The accuracy of voluntary movement. *Psychological Review Monograph Supplements, 3,* (supp. 13), 1–119.

Yaminishi, J., Kawato, M., & Suzuki, R. (1980). Two coupled oscillators as a model for the coordinated finger tapping by both hands. *Biological Cybernetics, 37,* 219.

CHAPTER 9

Neural Basis of Audition

LAUREL H. CARNEY

INTRODUCTION

The nervous system's ability to detect, analyze, and segregate dynamic acoustic stimuli in complex environments surpasses the signal-processing powers of even the most sophisticated machines and algorithms in existence. The auditory system is as fast as it is complex, a quality necessitated by the fleeting nature of auditory information. The goal of this chapter is to provide an introduction to the physiology of the auditory pathway. The level of detail is intended to be accessible to students and researchers new to the field of audition as well as to those familiar with the psychology of audition but not with its physiology. This review provides a relatively comprehensive overview of the entire auditory pathway, but the emphasis is on topics that have received significant attention and yielded interesting results in recent years, especially since the last publication of this handbook.

The review starts with an introduction to the structure of the auditory pathway followed by a description of the physiology. This review focuses on basic neuroanatomy and on neurophysiology at the extracellular level. Biophys-

ical descriptions of cells in the various auditory nuclei, as well as descriptions of the neurochemical properties of these cells, are beyond the scope of this review. Comprehensive book-length reviews of the anatomy (Webster, Popper, & Fay, 1992) and physiology (Popper & Fay, 1992) provide much more detailed descriptions of the auditory pathway. Other reviews that are specific to certain topics will be referenced later.

A primary function of the auditory system is to encode the frequency spectrum of a sound, that is, the level of energy at each frequency within a stimulus. The physical dimensions of frequency and sound level convey most of the important information in sounds. Studies of frequency and level coding have traditionally focused on pure-tone stimuli, and the responses to these simple stimuli are considered first. Then, the encoding of information in more realistic sounds that are made up of more than one tone, or so-called complex sounds, is presented. The representation of complex sounds in the auditory system is not related in a simple way to the representation of pure tones because the auditory system is not linear. Complex sounds that are discussed include sounds with noise maskers and amplitude-modulated sounds. The other major dimension of sound is its spatial location; this chapter concludes with a discussion of the physiology of spatial hearing.

Preparation of this chapter was supported by NIH-NIDCD DC01641. David Cameron, Susan Early, and Michael Heinz provided helpful comments on drafts of this manuscript.

Because a large body of literature in this field is based on experimental work in different species, some introduction to the general structure of the auditory pathway across species is provided. Although space does not allow a comprehensive overview of the comparative anatomy, interesting specializations in a few species are pointed out, as these often play a role in the interpretation of physiological results. Comprehensive reviews of comparative anatomy and physiology of the auditory system have been provided by Manley (1990) and Popper and Fay (1980). In this review, description is limited to species with an auditory periphery that is characterized by a basilar membrane or papilla, which includes mammals, birds, and reptiles (Manley, 1990).

THE AUDITORY PERIPHERY

External and Middle Ears

In the auditory periphery, sound is transduced from mechanical energy (sound pressure) into a neural signal, resulting in a pattern of neural activity in the fibers of the auditory nerve (Figure 9.1).

Sound reaches the ear as a pressure wave, having traveled through either air or water to reach the tympanic membrane, which serves to couple the pressure wave into motion of the bones of the middle ear, or the ossicles. The ossicles are coupled directly to the inner ear, and their motion is translated into a pressure wave in the fluid-filled inner ear. The efficiency with which energy in the environment is transmitted from one part of the ear to

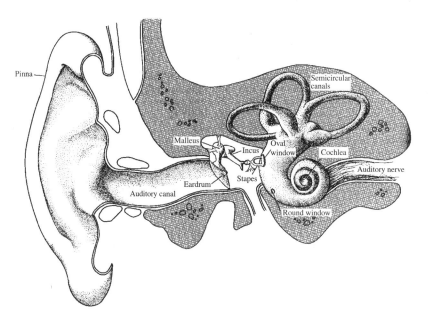

Figure 9.1   Drawing of the peripheral auditory system in human.
NOTE: The external ear consists of the pinna and auditory canal. The middle ear is the air-filled space between the tympanic membrane (eardrum) and the inner ear (cochlea); the motion of the tympanic membrane is coupled to the inner ear by three small bones, the ossicles (malleus, incus, and stapes). The primary afferent fibers of the auditory nerve each innervate a single sensory receptor cell located at a place along the cochlea.
SOURCE: Figure from *Human Information Processing: An Introduction to Psychology,* Second Edition by Peter Lindsay and Donald Norman. Copyright © 1977 by Harcourt College Publishers. Reproduced by permission of the publisher.

the next, before it is finally transduced into a neural signal, depends on the matching of the acoustical impedances at each interface between media and tissues (i.e., the difference in acoustical properties between air and cochlear fluid presents an impedance mismatch). Thus, the middle ear is often described in terms of the degree to which it successfully matches the radiation and input impedances. The lever action of the ossicles and the ratio of the sizes of the tympanic membrane and the oval window contribute to the middle ear's ability to match these impedances. A perfect match would result in optimal transfer of energy. The radiation impedance (the acoustic impedance looking outward from just outside the tympanic membrane) is dominated by the external ear and the atmosphere through which the sound travels. The input impedance (the acoustic impedance looking inward from just outside the tympanic membrane) is dominated by the properties of the middle and inner ears (Hemila, Nummela, & Rueter, 1995; Peake & Rosowski, 1991; Rosowski, 1996).

The sound waves that reach the two ears are influenced by many factors, including the acoustical environment (e.g., nearby surfaces or objects that may reflect, refract, or absorb the sound waves), as well as by the presence of the head and torso. The physical and acoustical properties of the external and middle ears differ dramatically from species to species (mammals: Huang, Rosowski, & Peake, 2000; birds and reptiles: Manley, 1990). For example, the mammalian middle ear is characterized by three ossicles forming a chain between the tympanic membrane and the cochlea, whereas the middle ear of birds and reptiles contains a single ossicle (Manley, 1990). The mechanical and acoustical properties of the auditory periphery influence the sound that reaches the inner ear and play an important role in determining the frequency range and sensitivity of hearing (for a review of external and middle ear function, see Rosowski, 1996).

The Inner Ear

The mechanical properties of the inner ear further shape the detailed properties of the effective stimulus for each neural element in the auditory periphery. The cochlea is often described as performing a mechanical frequency analysis that results in a sharply tuned and very sensitive input to the neural transduction elements, or hair cells. The mechanical resonant frequency of the basilar membrane changes systematically along the length of the cochlea because of a combination of systematic gradients of the stiffness, structural dimensions, and tissue properties along the length of the basilar membrane (Figure 9.2; von Békésy & Rosenblith, 1951;

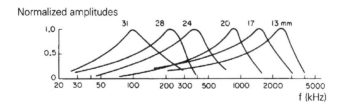

Figure 9.2   Illustration of the response amplitudes of six places along the length of the cochlea (location identified by numbers at top) to tones at different frequencies.
NOTE: Each place along the cochlea is tuned, or most responsive, to a particular frequency. This frequency tuning is a result of systematic changes in the mechanical properties of the cochlea along its length.
SOURCE: From von Békésy & Rosenblith (1951). Copyright ©1951 by John Wiley & Sons, Inc. Reprinted by permission of John Wiley & Sons, Inc.

von Békésy, 1960; Naidu & Mountain, 1998). Von Békésy's influential studies of basilar membrane motion date to 1942, when he first used stroboscopic illumination of the cochlea in the human cadaver in response to extremely high level stimuli (approximately 140 dB SPL). Since then, improved techniques have allowed measurements at lower sound levels, and these have transformed our understanding of the mechanics of the cochlea (e.g., Rhode, 1971; Ruggero, Rich, Recio, Narayan, & Robles, 1997; reviews by Zwislocki, 1986; de Boer, 1991; Ruggero, 1992b).

A pure-tone stimulus causes a maximal mechanical vibration at the place along the cochlear partition that is tuned to the stimulus frequency, as well as a spread of excitation to neighboring areas, depending on the sound level of the tone. In the mammalian cochlea, the pattern of excitation, or vibration, in response to a stimulus propagates along the length of the spiral-shaped cochlea in what is referred to as the traveling wave (von Békésy, 1960; Johnstone et al., 1986; de Boer, 1991). Figure 9.3 illustrates a cross-section of one turn of the spiral-shaped mammalian inner ear. The vibration of the cochlear partition results in excitation of the hair cells, whose stereocilia are deflected by means of the shear forces set up by the relative motion of the basilar membrane and tectorial membrane (reviewed by de Boer, 1991; Ruggero, 1992b).

There are two types of hair cells in the mammalian ear (Figure 9.4). The inner hair cells (IHCs) provide the major afferent input to the brainstem via the type I auditory-nerve (AN) fibers, which make up approximately 95% of the auditory nerve (reviewed by Ryugo, 1992). (See Table 9.1 for list of abbreviations used in the text.) The outer hair cells (OHCs), which are larger and outnumber the inner hair cells by a 3:1 ratio, are contacted by the relatively small number of type II AN fibers (5% of AN fibers; Ryugo, 1992). OHCs

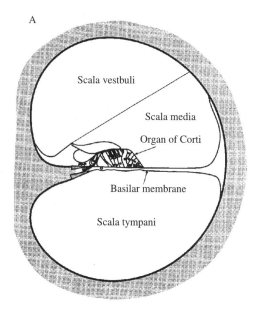

A

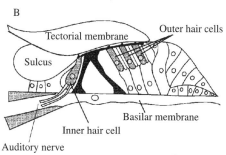

B

Figure 9.3 Schematic diagram of the key structures in the mammalian inner ear.
NOTE: A) Cross section of the cochlea shows the three major fluid-filled chambers, or scalae, and the organ of Corti, which lies on top of the basilar membrane. B) The organ of Corti includes the inner and outer hair cells, a large number of supporting cells and tissues, and the gelatinous tectorial membrane that overlies the stereocilia of the hair cells.
SOURCE: Reprinted from *Trends in Neurosciences, 15*, G. K. Yates, B. M. Johnstone, R. B. Patuzzi, & D. Robertson, "Mechanical preprocessing in the mammalian cochlea," pp. 57–61. Copyright © 1992, with permission from Elsevier Science.

are thought to be involved primarily in modifying the mechanical response of the basilar membrane itself (discussed later). It has become clear in recent years that essentially all major features of the responses of mammalian

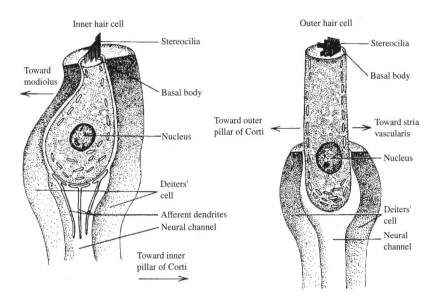

Figure 9.4   Drawing of the major features of mammalian inner and outer hair cells.
SOURCE: From *Hearing: Physiology and Psychophysics* by W. Lawrence Gulick, R. Frisina, & G. Gescheider, copyright © 1971 by Oxford University Press, Inc. Used by permission of Oxford University Press, Inc.

AN fibers (e.g., the sharpness of tuning, sensitivity, and nonlinear response features such as compression and two-tone suppression) can be observed in mechanical responses of the cochlea (e.g., Ruggero, Robles, & Rich, 1992; Cooper, 1996).

In nonmammalian species, frequency analysis in the inner ear takes advantage of different mechanical and electrical mechanisms (reviewed by Fettiplace & Fuchs, 1999). The ultimate result of this analysis, as in the mammalian cochlea, is that individual hair cells and the AN fibers that innervate them are tuned in frequency. However, the mechanisms by which this tuning is achieved vary significantly. For example, in the ear of the alligator lizard, systematic differences in length of the stereocilia result in different passive resonant frequencies along the length of the basilar papilla (Freeman & Weiss, 1990). In the turtle cochlea, electrical resonances set up by different ionic conductances through the hair cells contribute to frequency tuning (Crawford &

Fettiplace, 1981; Art, Crawford, & Fettiplace, 1986).

The sensory hair cells (Figure 9.4) transduce mechanical vibration into an electrical signal, the receptor potential, by means of transduction channels associated with the stereocilia (reviewed by Fettiplace & Fuchs, 1999). The mechanisms by which motion of the basilar membrane, the surrounding fluids and tissues, or both results in the motion of the stereocilia of the hair cells differs from species to species, and in some cases from region to region within the ear (depending upon the presence of accessory structures, such as the tectorial membrane, shown in Figure 9.3, or tectorial sallets, reviewed by Manley, 1990, and Fettiplace & Fuchs, 1999). A common property of hair-cell transduction is a receptor potential consisting of both AC and DC components. At low frequencies (below about 1000 Hz, as discussed later), the AC component dominates and the receptor potential follows the fine temporal details of the

Table 9.1 List of Abbreviations

Anatomical Terms

AN	auditory nerve
IHC	inner hair cell
OHC	outer hair cell
CN	cochlear nuclear complex
AVCN	anteroventral cochlear nucleus
PVCN	posteroventral cochlear nucleus
DCN	dorsal cochlear nucleus
NM	nucleus magnocellularis
NA	nucleus angularis
SOC	superior olivary complex
MSO	medial superior olive
LSO	lateral superior olive
TB	trapezoid body
MNTB	medial nucleus of the trapezoid body
LNTB	lateral nucleus of the trapezoid body
VNTB	ventral nucleus of the trapezoid body
NL	nucleus laminaris
SON	superior olivary nucleus
COCB	crossed olivocochlear bundle
LL	lateral lemniscus
VNLL	ventral nucleus of the lateral lemniscus
DNLL	dorsal nucleus of the lateral lemniscus
INLL	intermediate nucleus of the lateral lemniscus
IC	inferior colliculus
ICC	central nucleus of the inferior calculus
LN or ICx	lateral nucleus, or external nucleus, of the inferior calculus
DN	dorsomedial nucleus of inferior calculus
SC	superior colliculus
MGB	medial geniculate body

Auditory Cortex

AI	primary auditory cortex
AII	secondary auditory cortex
EP	posterior ectosylvian region
ss	suprasylvian fringe
A or AAF	anterior field
P	posterior field
V	ventral field
VP	ventralposterior field

Periolivary regions

VNTB	ventral nucleus of the trapezoid body
AVPO	anteroventral periolivary nucleus
ALPO	anterior lateral periolivary nucleus
DPO	dorsal periolivary nucleus
PPO	posterior periolivary nucleus
DMPO	dorsomedial periolivary nucleus

Stimulus-related Terms

dB SPL	decibels sound pressure level
ITD	interaural time difference
ILD	interaural level difference
HRTF	head-related transfer function
AM	amplitude modulated

Physiological Terms

CF	characteristic frequency
SR	spontaneous rate
PST	peri-stimulus time histogram
EE	cells that are excited by stimuli delivered to either ear
IE	cells that are inhibited by stimuli to the contralateral ear and excited by stimuli to the ipsilateral ear
EI	cells that are inhibited by stimuli to the ipsilateral ear and excited by stimuli to the contralateral ear
MTF	modulation transfer function

stimulus waveform. At higher frequencies, the low-pass filtering introduced by the capacitance and resistance associated with the hair-cell membrane attenuate the AC component, and the DC component dominates, resulting in a response to the envelope of the sound (e.g., Palmer & Russell, 1986).

The sensitivity and frequency tuning in the mammalian ear are not caused simply by passive mechanics of the inner ear but are strongly influenced by what has been called an active process or "cochlear amplifier" (Davis, 1983), which refers to an enhancement of the mechanical response of the inner ear. Responses of the healthy basilar membrane to a low-level sound input are larger in amplitude, because of this enhancement or amplification, than are responses of the ear in the presence of ototoxic drugs (which block transduction by the hair cells) or after death (e.g., Ruggero & Rich, 1991). Although the details of the neural, electrical, and mechanical mechanisms by which this amplification occurs are not completely understood, there is a body of evidence suggesting that in mammals the OHCs are involved, possibly by means of length changes of these cells in response to sound (Figure 9.5; first reported by Brownell, Bader, Bertrand, & de Ribaupierre, 1985; see the review by Yates, Johnstone, Patuzzi, & Robertson, 1992). The length changes of the OHCs are believed to provide forces that enhance (or "amplify") the mechanical vibration on a cycle-by-cycle basis (Dallos & Evans, 1995; Frank, Hemmert, & Gummer, 1999; reviewed by Ashmore & Geleoc, 1999). A protein that is abundant in the membranes of OHCs has recently been proposed to be the motor protein associated with OHC motility (Zheng et al., 2000). An alternative mechanism for OHC motility based on membrane biophysics (flexoelectricity) has also been recently proposed (Raphael, Popel, & Brownell, 2000). Further, an alternative mechanism for the cochlear amplifier based on active movements of the OHC stere-

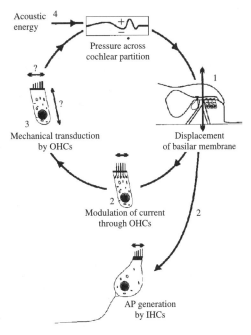

Figure 9.5 How the motile response or active process is thought to operate as a positive feedback loop within the cochlea.

NOTE: (1) Acoustic stimulation produces pressure fluctuations in scala vestibuli, causing the basilar membrane to vibrate. (2) The resulting shearing between the tectorial membrane and the tops of the hair cells modulates the standing current, driven by a K^+ electrochemical gradient. (3) The resulting receptor potential within the outer hair cells triggers the active process, causing some form of mechanical activity in the outer hair cell. (4) This in turn feeds pressure fluctuations back into the scala vestibuli to complete the loop. The receptor potential within the hair cell leads to transmitter release across the afferent synapse.

SOURCE: Figure and caption reprinted from *Trends in Neurosciences, 15,* G. K. Yates, B. M. Johnstone, R. B. Patuzzi, & D. Robertson, "Mechanical preprocessing in the mammalian cochlea," pp. 57–61. Copyright ©1992, with permission from Elsevier Science.

ocilia, rather than on length changes of the cell body, has also been proposed (reviewed by Yates, 1995).

It is worth noting that species that do not have OHCs also exhibit an active process in the inner ear (Manley & Koppl, 1998).

There appear to be a number of different electrical, mechanical, and molecular mechanisms involved in the sensitive responses of the inner ear to sounds that vary across and within species, as well as across frequency (e.g., active motion of stereocilia: Crawford & Fettiplace, 1985; Martin & Hudspeth, 1999; molecular aspects of electrical tuning in the turtle: Ricci, Gray-Keller, & Fettiplace, 2000; reviewed by Fettiplace & Fuchs, 1999).

The active process can be conceptualized as a level-dependent amplifier: It amplifies low-level sounds by up to 50 dB to 60 dB, and its amplification decreases at middle to high sound levels. It has been hypothesized that the amplification is driven by a mechanism that saturates, which would explain the systematic drop in amplification (often referred to as compression) as level increases (Mountain, Hubbard, & McMullen, 1983). Because the properties of the amplifier change with sound level, the overall response of the cochlea (and thus of the IHCs and AN fibers) is quite nonlinear; that is, responses to stimuli at one sound level do not necessarily provide a prediction of responses at other levels, and responses to simple stimuli do not provide predictions for complex sounds. In particular, the nonlinear properties of the inner ear cause complex interactions between components of sounds that are important for understanding physiological responses to complex sounds.

The active process is also associated with the generation of vibrations in the inner ear, which are then conducted back along the basilar partition and through the middle and outer ear, where they can be measured as acoustic signals in the ear canal (Kemp, 1978; reviewed by Lonsbury-Martin, Martin, McCoy, & Whitehead, 1995). These otoacoustic emissions may be spontaneous, or they may be evoked by auditory stimuli in an ear with a healthy auditory periphery. These emissions have been studied extensively as a tool for understanding cochlear function (e.g., Shera & Guinan, 1999), as well as for a noninvasive and objective diagnostic tool for audiologists.

The electrical, mechanical, and molecular basis of the active process, and the differences in mechanisms across species, is the topic of much current work. One goal of this research is to understand how the brains of different species achieve the exquisite sensitivity and discrimination ability that is generally believed to depend on the active process. In addition, the active process is typically described as a fragile process that is present in the healthy ear, and reduced or absent in the impaired ear (e.g., Patuzzi, Yates, & Johnstone, 1989). Thus, a better understanding of how the nonlinear properties of the active process influence the responses of the AN population should provide a better understanding of how the input to the central nervous system is altered in common forms of hearing impairment.

THE STRUCTURE OF THE AUDITORY PATHWAY

Ascending Pathways in the Central Nervous System

The auditory central nervous system is typically described in terms of ascending and descending pathways. Currently, much more is known about the ascending pathways than about the descending pathways. In general, the pathways of most species are characterized by a similar series of monaural, then binaural, nuclei along the ascending auditory pathway (Figure 9.6). Above the first level of binaural processing at the brainstem level, the anatomical and neurochemical pathways set up a general representation of acoustical stimuli arising from the contralateral hemifield on either side of the brain, as is true for the central representations of other sensory modalities.

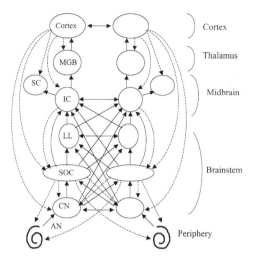

Figure 9.6 Schematic diagram of the mammalian auditory pathway showing the major ascending (solid arrows) and descending (dotted arrows) pathways.

NOTE: The details of the connections of individual nuclei are not shown, but rather the general scheme of connectivity across the two sides of the brain and across levels in the pathway. Abbreviations: auditory nerve (AN), cochlear nucleus (CN), superior olivary complex (SOC), lateral lemniscus (LL), inferior colliculus (IC), superior colliculus (SC), and medial geniculate body (MGB).

(Note that this is not strictly accurate for the auditory system because there are neurons with panoramic receptive fields, especially at the higher levels of the pathway.) The key features of each level along these pathways are briefly reviewed in the next sections.

First Level of Brainstem Processing

The first level of processing in all species is the projection of the auditory nerve to a brainstem region where distinct groups of cells receive excitatory inputs from AN fibers (Figure 9.7). In the mammal, this region is the cochlear nuclear (CN) complex, which consists of three regions: the anteroventral (AVCN), posteroventral (PVCN), and dorsal cochlear nuclei (DCN; reviewed by Cant, 1992). Each AN fiber bifurcates as it enters the CN and sends projections into all three regions of the CN (Figure 9.7). In general, there appear to be parallel representations of stimulus features in the responses of different cell groups in the CN (discussed later), and these cells project to different regions of the brainstem and midbrain (Figure 9.8).

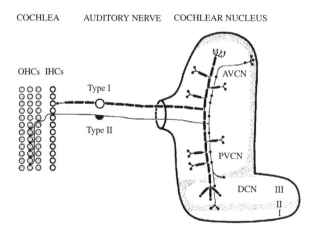

Figure 9.7 Schematic illustration of the projections of auditory nerve fibers in mammal showing their pattern of inputs from the inner and outer hair cells and the bifurcation of the AN fibers as they project into the cochlear nuclear complex.

SOURCE: From Ryugo (1992). Reprinted with permission.

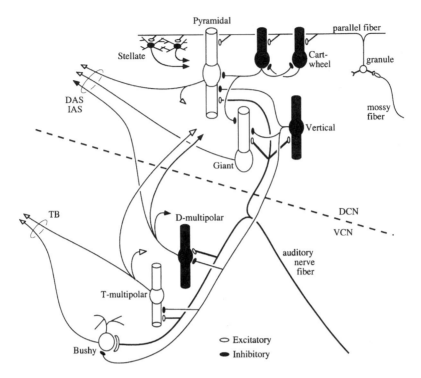

Figure 9.8   Schematic illustration of the major cell types in the cochlear nuclear complex in mammal and their primary projections.

NOTE: The VCN contains two major cell types: bushy cells, which send excitatory projections to the ipsilateral medial and lateral superior olives (MSO and LSO), and multipolar cells, which project to the inferior colliculus (IC) with collaterals to other brainstem and lemniscal nuclei. The DCN contains two major types of projection neurons, the pyramidal and giant cells, which project to the IC, and several types of interneurons, including cartwheel, vertical, stellate, and granule cells. The output pathways from the cochlear nucleus form three bundles, the trapezoid body (TB), which heads toward the superior olivary complex, and the dorsal (DAS) and intermediate (IAS) acoustic striae, which coarse through the lateral lemniscus toward the IC (reviewed by Osen, 1969; Harrison & Feldman, 1970; Osen & Mugnaini, 1981; Cant, 1992).

SOURCE: From Young (1998). From *Synaptic Organization of the Brain, Fourth Edition,* edited by Gordon Shepherd, copyright © 1998 by Oxford University Press, Inc. Used by permission of Oxford University Press, Inc.

The first level of processing in the brainstem is typically described as monaural, and responses are certainly dominated by the stimulus to the ipsilateral ear; however, connections between the two cochlear nuclei have been identified (e.g., Schofield & Cant 1996).

The avian brain, particularly that of the barn owl or chick, has also been a popular model for studies of binaural processing (reviewed by Knudsen, 1987; Takahashi, 1989).

In avian species, the first level of brainstem processing occurs in two regions, the nucleus magnocellularis (NM) and the nucleus angularis (NA; Figure 9.9). NM cells have morphologies, connections, and response properties similar to that of the bushy cells in the mammalian AVCN, and the cells in NA are most similar to the stellate cells in the AVCN (e.g., Carr & Konishi, 1990; Hausler, Sullivan, Soares, & Carr, 1999; Sullivan, 1985; Warchol & Dallos, 1990).

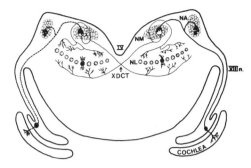

Figure 9.9 Anatomy of the chick brainstem illustrating the projections of the AN to the first level of brainstem processing, the nucleus magnocellularis and nucleus angularis.

NOTE: The nucleus magnocellularis in turn projects to the first major binaural brainstem region, the nucleus laminaris.

SOURCE: From Rubel, Born, Deitch, & Durham (1984).

Binaural Nuclei in the Brainstem

The first major binaural convergence takes place at the second stage of processing in the brainstem (Figure 9.6). There are two major binaural response types in the auditory brainstem: cells that are excited by stimuli delivered to either ear (EE), and those that are inhibited by stimuli to the contralateral ear and excited by stimuli to ipsilateral ear (IE). In the mammal the AVCN provides the major inputs to the first level of binaural processing, which occurs in the superior olivary complex (SOC; Figure 9.10; Cant & Casseday, 1986; Harrison & Feldman, 1970). The medial superior olive (MSO) receives inputs from the spherical bushy cells in both cochlear nuclei and is characterized by EE responses. The morphologies of the excitatory inputs from the contralateral side resemble delay lines (Beckius, Batra, & Oliver, 1999; Smith, Joris, & Yin, 1993), as was hypothesized in models for binaural hearing (Jeffress, 1948; discussed later). The lateral superior olive (LSO) receives excitatory inputs from spherical bushy cells in the ipsilateral cochlear nucleus and inhibitory inputs from the ipsilateral medial nucleus of the trapezoid body (MNTB) and

is characterized by IE responses. The MNTB receives excitatory inputs from the contralateral AVCN. Although they are typically described as EE, cells in the MSO also receive inhibitory inputs from the ipsilateral lateral nucleus of the trapezoid body (LNTB; Cant & Hyson, 1992) and from the contralateral side, via the ipsilateral MNTB (Adams & Mugnaini, 1990). Furthermore, the LSO receives ipsilateral inhibition in addition to its classical IE inputs (Wu & Kelly, 1994). The SOC also contains a number of so-called periolivary regions (Figure 9.10) that are

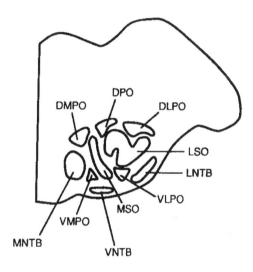

Figure 9.10 Drawing of a cross section of the mammalian brainstem at the level of the superior olivary complex (SOC).

NOTE: The three largest cell groups in this complex are the two major olivary nuclei, the medial superior olive (MSO) and lateral superior olive (LSO), and the medial nucleus of the trapezoid body (MNTB). Two other cell groups located in the trapezoid body (the bundle of fibers that arises in the cochlear nuclei) are the lateral and ventral nuclei of the trapezoid body (LNTB, VNTB). The major periolivary groups are shown: The dorsomedial, dorsal, and dorsolateral periolivary nuclei (DMPO, DPO and DLPO) span the dorsal extent of the SOC, and the ventromedial (VMPO) and ventrolateral (VLPO) periolivary nuclei lie ventral to the major nuclei in the SOC.

SOURCE: From Schwartz (1992). Reprinted with permission.

involved in both the ascending and (especially) in the descending pathways (discussed later; J. K. Moore, 1987; reviewed by Schwartz, 1992).

In the avian brainstem, the first primary site of binaural interaction is the nucleus laminaris (NL), which receives excitatory inputs from both sides of the brainstem. The inputs from the contralateral side have morphologies that resemble delay lines (Carr & Konishi, 1990; Overholt, Rubel, & Hyson, 1992). The NL is often described as a homologue to the mammalian MSO. Like the MSO, the NL receives not only binaural excitation but also inhibitory inputs from other cells in the brainstem (the avian superior olivary nucleus, or SON; Yang, Monsivais, & Rubel, 1999). The inhibitory inputs to the NL have been proposed to play a role in gain control for the binaural circuitry involved in spatial localization (Yang et al., 1999).

Nuclei of the Lateral Lemniscus

The major pathway for auditory nuclei from the brainstem to the midbrain is the lateral lemniscus (LL; Figure 9.11; reviewed by Schwartz, 1992). Two major cell groups lie in the LL: the ventral nucleus of the lateral lemniscus (VNLL) and the dorsal nucleus of the lateral lemniscus (DNLL). (An additional group, the intermediate nucleus of the lateral lemniscus, or INLL, has similar properties to and an indistinct boundary with the VNLL.) The VNLL is predominantly monaural, receiving inputs from spherical and globular bushy cells and octopus cells in the contralateral cochlear nucleus and the ipsilateral MNTB; the VNLL projects to the ipsilateral inferior colliculus and the medial geniculate body (Adams, 1997; Schofield & Cant, 1997). The DNLL is predominantly binaural, receiving bilateral inputs from the CN, LSO, MSO,

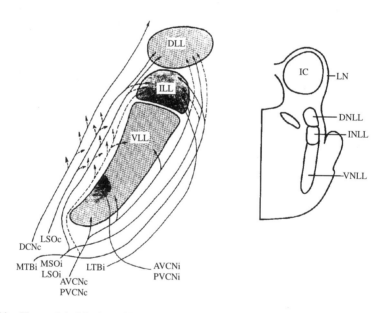

Figure 9.11   The nuclei of the lateral lemniscus, which lie along the major ascending pathway from the auditory brainstem to the auditory midbrain.
Note: The left-hand drawing shows the orientation and major inputs of the three lemniscal nuclei: the ventral, intermediate, and dorsal nuclei of the lateral lemniscus (VNLL, INLL, and DNLL). The right-hand drawing shows their orientation with respect to the inferior colliculus (IC) in the coronal plane.
Source: From Schwartz (1992). Reprinted with permission.

and from the contralateral DNLL. The DNLL projects to both inferior colliculi, as well as to the contralateral DNLL (Kelly, 1997).

The Auditory Midbrain: Inferior Colliculus and Superior Colliculus

The next major level in the ascending pathway is in the midbrain of most species, where there is convergence of inputs from monaural brainstem regions, binaural nuclei, and the lemniscal nuclei. In mammals this midbrain region is the inferior colliculus (IC; Figure 9.12; reviewed by Oliver & Huerta, 1992); the homologous region in birds and reptiles is the torus semicircularis (G. E. Meredith, 1988). The pattern of inputs from the brainstem to the midbrain sets up the contralateral representation of auditory space, which predominates at all levels above the brainstem. A combination of crossed projections (which effectively convert EI responses—i.e., from cells that are excited by stimuli to the contralateral ear and inhibited by stimuli to the

ipsilateral ear—to IE responses) and neurochemical sign changes (i.e., inhibitory projections to ipsilateral targets) is involved in this process, which is referred to as the acoustic chiasm (e.g., Glendenning, Baker, Hutson, & Masterton, 1992).

The main projections in the acoustic chiasm are as follows: The MSO, which is already dominated by stimuli in the contralateral field (Yin & Chan, 1990; discussed later), sends an excitatory projection to the ipsilateral IC. The high-frequency region of the LSO, which is IE, sends an excitatory projection to the contralateral IC; thus, high-frequency cells in the IC have EI responses and are excited by stimuli on the contralateral side. The low-frequency limb of the LSO is monaural and is excited by ipsilateral stimuli; this limb sends an inhibitory projection to the ipsilateral IC (Glendenning et al., 1992).

The IC has several divisions that are distinguished by different cell types and connections (Figure 9.12; Morest & Oliver, 1984;

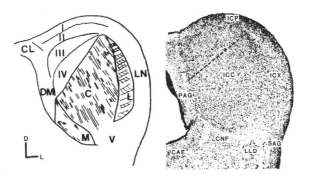

Figure 9.12 Drawings of coronal sections through the inferior colliculus in cat showing the two parceling schemes that have been proposed for the IC.
NOTE: The left-hand drawing shows the divisions of Morest & Oliver (1984). The central nucleus of the ICC is divided into several subdivisions: the pars centralis (C), pars medialis (M), pars lateralis (L), and pars ventralis (V). The dorsal cortex is indicated by the four layers, I–IV. Other labeled regions are the central nucleus of the commissure (CL), dorsomedial nucleus (DM), and lateral nucleus (LN). The right-hand drawing shows the traditional divisions (e.g., Rockel and Jones, 1973a, 1973b). Abbreviations: central nucleus (ICC), pericentral nucleus (ICP), external nucleus (ICX), periaqueductal gray (PAG), nucleus caeruleus (CAE), cuneiform nucleus (CNF), dorsal nucleus of lateral lemniscus (LLD), and sagulum (SAG).
SOURCE: Left-hand drawing from Oliver and Huerta (1992). Reprinted with permission. Right-hand drawing from Irvine (1986). Copyright ©1986 by Springer-Verlag. Reprinted with permission.

Rockel & Jones, 1973a, 1973b; reviewed by Oliver & Huerta, 1992). The largest region of the IC is the central nucleus, or ICC, which receives tonotopic inputs from the contralateral cochlear nucleus and the ipsilateral MSO and VNLL, and bilaterally from the LSO (discussed earlier) and DNLL. The ICC also receives a diffuse, nontonotopic input from the periolivary nuclei (Adams, 1983; Henkel & Spangler, 1983). The dorsal cortex of the IC (layers I–IV, based on cytoarchitecture; Figure 9.12) receives its major input from the auditory cortex (Morest & Oliver, 1984). The lateral nucleus (LN), or the external nucleus (ICx; Rockel & Jones, 1973b), receives inputs from the ICC as well as from a large number of other sources, such as somatosensory regions, the dorsal column nuclei, and possibly the auditory cortex (Oliver & Huerta, 1992). The dorsomedial nucleus (DN) receives inputs from the LL as well as the auditory cortex (Morest & Oliver, 1984).

There are two major ascending targets of the IC: One is the superior colliculus (SC), which integrates sensory and motor information and is involved in the control of reflexive movements of the eyes, pinnae, head, and body (Huerta & Harting, 1984). In birds and reptiles the homologous region is the optic tectum. The SC is a layered structure (Figure 9.13); the superficial layer has both inputs and outputs that are restricted to the visual system (Oliver & Huerta, 1992). The deep SC receives ascending auditory inputs from the IC, the dorsomedial periolivary nucleus, the nuclei of the trapezoid body, and the VNLL (Edwards, Ginsburg, Henkel, & Stein, 1979) and descending inputs from the auditory cortex (M. A. Meredith & Clemo, 1989). The somatosensory system also projects to the deep SC from the spinal cord, the dorsal column nuclei, trigeminal nuclei, and cortex. Topographic maps of the different modalities have been reported to be approximately in register with each other (discussed later; e.g.,

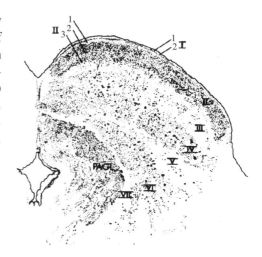

Figure 9.13   Cross section of the superior colliculus (SC) in cat.
NOTE: Layers I, II, and III comprise the superficial SC; layers IV–VII are the deep layers of the SC.
SOURCE: From Kanaseki & Sprague (1974). Reprinted by permission of McGraw-Hill.

Middlebrooks & Knudsen, 1987; Stein, Magalhaes-Castro, & Kruger, 1976; Wise & Irvine, 1985).

Auditory Thalamus

The other major target of the IC is the auditory region of the thalamus. In mammals the auditory thalamus is the medial geniculate body (MGB); birds and reptiles also have auditory regions of thalamus, which are comparable to the MGB in terms of their connectivity to auditory regions in the midbrain and telencephelon. The mammalian MGB has been parceled into two (Rioch, 1929; Rose & Woolsey, 1949) or three (Winer, 1992) regions, based on the anatomical properties of cells and fibers in the MGB, their connectivity to the auditory cortex, physiological properties, neuropharmacology, and development. The three regions in the more recent description are the ventral, dorsal, and medial divisions (Figure 9.14); the earlier parceling scheme grouped the ventral and dorsal divisions into a single division.

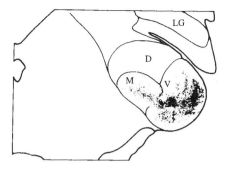

Figure 9.14 Coronal section through the medial geniculate body (MGB) in cat.
NOTE: The MGB is the auditory region of the mammalian thalamus. The three major divisions of the MGB are indicated: ventral (V), dorsal (D), and medial (M). The stippled areas represent regions that were labeled by an injection of tritiated leucine into the central nucleus of the IC. This labeling indicates locations in the MGB that receive inputs from the ICC.
SOURCE: From Kudo & Niimi (1980). Copyright © 1980 John Wiley & Sons, Inc. Reprinted by permission of McGraw-Hill.

The ventral division is a heterogeneous group of cells that receives its primary input from the ipsilateral ICC (R. A. Anderson, Knight, & Merzenich, 1980; Roullier & de Ribaupierre, 1985); this division receives input also from the thalamic reticular nucleus, a property common to the other sensory regions of the thalamus (reviewed by Winer, 1992; Rouiller, 1997). The dorsal division, also heterogeneous in terms of cellular morphologies, receives inputs from a vast number of auditory regions, including ICC, SC, and auditory cortex. The dorsal division receives inputs also from a number of nonauditory regions, including limbic areas, nonauditory areas of cortex, and regions of the basal ganglia, suggesting that this division plays a role in sensory-motor processing (reviewed by Winer, 1992). The medial division of the MGB is a heterogeneous group of cells that receives nontopographic input from diverse, predominantly nonauditory regions of the brainstem and midbrain.

The projections of the three divisions of MGB reflect the nature of their inputs. The ventral division has topographic and highly reciprocal connections with auditory cortex; the dorsal division has more diverse and less regular reciprocal connections with a wider range of cortical regions; and the medial division has a very diverse set of cortical targets, many of which are outside the classical auditory regions (see Winer, 1992, for a detailed review).

Auditory Cortex

The final stage in the ascending pathway is the projection from the thalamus to the cortex. The mammalian auditory cortex is typically described in terms of four major regions, which are distinguished by their physiological response properties and cytoarchitectures. Primary auditory cortex, AI, was the first to be described in terms of its tonotopic arrangement (Woolsey & Walzl, 1942). Rose (1949) described four regions of cortex based on cytoarchitecture: AI, AII, which is located ventral to AI, the posterior ectosylvian region (EP), and the suprasylvian fringe (ss; Figure 9.15). Rose and Woolsey (1949) also described the essential and orderly connectivity between auditory thalamus and area AI, with sustaining projections from the thalamus to the other cortical regions. Woolsey (1961) described complete tonotopic maps in each of these four central areas, plus an additional five peripheral regions.

Woolsey's map has been refined over time by additional mapping studies, but it has generally served as the standard map for subsequent studies (Goldstein & Knight, 1980). Detailed mapping studies have proposed that there are regions in the band around AI that also contain tonotopic maps, receive thalamic input, and have sharply tuned neurons (e.g., Reale & Imig, 1980). Thus, the auditory cortex cannot be thought of as one primary tonotopically mapped region (AI) that

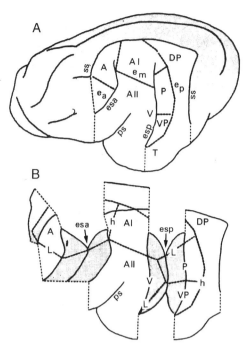

Figure 9.15 Major areas of the auditory cortex. NOTE: A) Drawing of the auditory cortex in cats showing the location of the auditory areas (left temporal cortex is shown). Four regions have clear tonotopic arrangements: anterior, primary, posterior, and ventral posterior areas (A, AI, P, VP). Other abbreviations: suprasylvian fissure (ss); anterior, medial, and posterior ectosylvian gyrus (e_a, e_m, e_p); anterior and posterior ectosylvian (esa, esp); dorsal posterior, temporal, ventral and secondary areas (DP, T, V, AII). B) "Flattened" representation of the cortical regions, showing the areas that lie within the fissures (shown in gray). The tonotopic arrangements of the major areas are indicated by "L" for low-frequency regions, and "h" for high-frequency regions.
SOURCE: From Buser & Imbert (1992), after Reale & Imig (1980). Copyright © 1980 by the MIT Press. Reprinted with permission.

then projects to other regions for higher processing (Goldstein & Knight, 1980).

A detailed review of the cytoarchitecture and neurochemistry associated with each of the cortical layers of the different regions of auditory cortex is provided by Winer (1992). The layered structure of the auditory cortex

is generally similar to that of other sensory cortical regions, despite the fact that the basic pattern of connectivity of the auditory cortex differs significantly from that of other sensory areas, especially in terms of the interconnections between auditory fields and hemispheres (reviewed by Winer, 1992; Rouiller, 1997). Detailed descriptions of the laminar sources of input—as well as targets of projections—for AI are available but are not described here (reviewed by Winer, 1992).

Descending Pathways

The ascending pathways describe only half of the auditory nervous system. Although much less is known about the descending pathways, they have received increasing attention in recent years. The bias toward study of the ascending system stems probably from the fact that responses at higher levels of the auditory pathway, and thus the descending signals, are increasingly sensitive to anesthesia. Work in awake, and in some cases behaving, animals may be necessary to understand the interplay between ascending and descending systems. The descending pathways are implicated in a diverse set of roles, including attention, gating of ascending signals, modulation of intensity and frequency selectivity, spatial localization, and protection of the auditory periphery (see reviews by Huffman & Henson, 1990; Rouiller, 1997; Spangler & Warr, 1991).

Several anatomical studies have mapped out the substrate for the descending system. The classic studies of Rose and Woolsey (1949) mapped out the corticothalamic projections, which largely reflect the thalamocortical pattern of connectivity (discussed earlier; reviewed by Winer, 1992). Nearly all fields in the auditory cortex (except A, P, and VP) have strong projections from layer V (Kelly & Wong, 1981) to more than one area of the inferior colliculus; these cortical inputs do not terminate in the central nucleus of the IC (except possibly from AII; Diamond, Jones, & Powell, 1969) but rather target the paracentral regions, such as LN (also referred to as the external nucleus; discussed earlier; Aitkin, Dickhaus, Schult, & Zimmerman, 1978). Auditory cortical fields also project to several other regions, including superior colliculus (M. A. Meredith & Clemo, 1989), cochlear nucleus (Feliciano, Saldaña, & Mugnaini, 1995; Weedman & Ryugo, 1996), pons, basal ganglia, and limbic regions (reviewed by Harrison & Howe, 1974; Huffman & Henson, 1990; Rouiller, 1997; Winer, 1992). The MGB does not play a significant role in the descending pathway; although it receives a strong ascending projection from the IC (discussed earlier), its projections are primarily to auditory cortex, which then projects directly down to the level of the IC.

The IC has a large number of descending projections to the superior olivary complex, primarily to the periolivary regions, which have descending projections to the cochlear nuclei. The two periolivary regions that receive the strongest collicular inputs are the ventral nucleus of the trapezoid body (VNTB) and anteroventral periolivary nucleus (AVPO); these regions project to all three regions of both contralateral and ipsilateral cochlear nuclei (Schofield & Cant, 1999). The IC also projects directly to the dorsal cochlear nucleus and granule cell area of the CN (Saldaña, 1993).

The periolivary nuclei of the SOC send a large number of projections to the cochlear nuclei. The lateral/dorsal periolivary regions (anterior lateral (ALPO), dorsal (DPO), posterior (PPO), and lateral nucleus of the trapezoid body (LNTB) have a strong projection to the ipsilateral CN, and a relatively weak projection to contralateral CN (Spangler, Cant, Henkel, Farley, and Warr, 1987). The medial regions (dorsomedial periolivary region, or DMPO, and the medial and ventral nuclei of the trapezoid body, or MNTB and VNTB, respectively) project more strongly to the contralateral than to ipsilateral CN (Spangler et al., 1987). The terminals of these projections are widespread throughout the regions of the CN, and they are tonotopic in some cases (Spangler et al., 1987).

The descending pathway extends to the cochlea. Two systems of fibers project from the periolivary regions of the superior olive to the cochlea, where they synapse directly on the OHCs or on the AN fibers underneath the IHCs (reviewed by Warr, Guinan, & White, 1986; Warr, 1992). The two olivocochlear systems are illustrated in Figure 9.16. The lateral olivocochlear neurons arise from lateral periolivary regions and project mainly to the IHC region of the ipsilateral cochlea. The medial olivocochlear system arises from medial periolivary regions and projects mainly to the OHCs of the contralateral cochlea (reviewed by Warr et al., 1986; Warr, 1992).

Comparison of Brainstem Regions across Species

Several interesting species have auditory specializations that are apparent in the anatomy of the auditory periphery, central pathway, or both (Figure 9.17; Glendenning & Masterton, 1998; J. K. Moore & Moore, 1971). Animals that are most sensitive to or communicate with high-frequency sounds have correspondingly enlarged high-frequency brainstem nuclei (e.g., the MNTB and LSO). Animals that are most sensitive to or communicate with low-frequency sounds have larger MSOs. For example, extreme biases in the anatomy are seen for echo-locating bats, which have a magnified region in their tonotopic maps, beginning in the inner ear and persisting at higher levels of the auditory pathway, that is tuned to the frequencies that dominate their vocalizations and thus their echoes (reviewed by Simmons et al., 1996). Also note that the

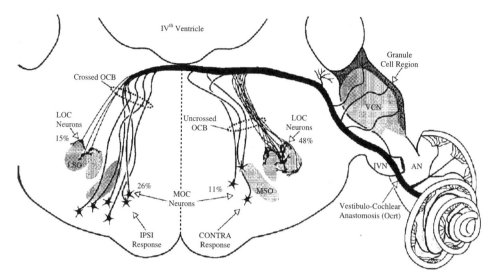

Figure 9.16 Major projections associated with the olivocochlear system, which arises from cells groups in the periolivary regions of the superior olivary complex and projects directly to the cochlea.
NOTE: The olivocochlear bundles (OCB) comprise two subsystems: the medial olivocochlear (MOC) and lateral olivocochlear (LOC) systems.
SOURCE: From Warr (1992). Reprinted by permission of McGraw-Hill.

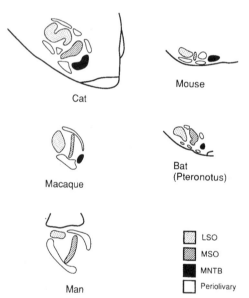

Figure 9.17 Diagram of typical cross sections through the brainstem for several different species, showing the relative sizes of different regions.
SOURCE: From Schwartz (1992). Reprinted with permission. Cat, mouse, monkey, and human data are from J. K. Moore & Moore (1971). Bat drawing based on Zook & Casseday (1982).

human brainstem has no MNTB and a relatively small LSO; although researchers have identified a few cells that have characteristics similar to those of the MNTB, they are not organized into a well-defined nucleus in human (Richter, Norris, Fullerton, Levine, & Kiang, 1983). These variations in the basic structure of the auditory pathways must be kept in mind when generalizing physiological results across species, for example, to relate physiology in nonhuman species to psychoacoustical performance in humans.

ACOUSTIC STIMULI

Before reviewing physiological responses, this section briefly reviews the units of measurement and important parameters of acoustic stimuli. Sounds can be either simple stimuli, which consist of a sinusoid (or tone) at a single frequency, or complex stimuli, which refer to all other sounds. Simple stimuli can be described completely in terms of their frequency, amplitude, and starting phase, as well as duration and onset/offset ramp shapes. Complex sounds can be represented as combinations of multiple sinusoids of different frequencies by using the Fourier transform. Descriptions of complex sounds must contain the amplitudes and phases of all component frequencies (i.e., the spectral magnitudes and phases), in addition to duration and onset/offset ramp shapes.

Sound waves are pressures that propagate through a medium, typically air or water. (Note that sound can also be conducted by bone or other solid materials.) The amplitudes of acoustic stimuli are typically measured as sound pressure in units of Pascals (1 Pa = 1 Newton of force per square meter of area) or as intensity in units of Watts. Logarithmic units are typically used to describe sound amplitudes because the auditory system is sensitive to changes in stimuli over a wide range of amplitudes and because log units seem to provide a representation that makes sense in terms of many physiological and psychophysical response properties. The standard reference pressure that is used for acoustic stimuli is 20 μPa, which is approximately the threshold of hearing at 1000 Hz for human listeners (Sivian & White, 1933). Sounds represented in terms of dB SPL (sound pressure level) are referenced to this standard pressure; that is, the level in dB SPL $= 20 \log(P/P_0)$, where P_0 is 20 μPa. Note that the amplitude of air particle motion associated with sounds at the threshold of hearing is similar to the dimensions of a hydrogen atom.

The description of stimuli in three-dimensional space requires additional parameters, and these parameters are of interest in experiments that explore binaural processing (such as how the information that arrives to the two ears is combined to improve detection of signals in a noisy environment) and sound localization. The physical dimensions of sounds that arrive at the two ears differ because of the different path lengths from a sound source to the ears located on each side of the head and because of the presence of the head between the two ears. There are three major cues for binaural processing: (a) differences in time between the stimuli to the two ears (both at the onset of a stimulus and during ongoing differences in the phases of the two stimuli due to a delay to one side), (b) differences in the sound levels at the two ears due to different distances to the target from the two ears as well as to head-shadowing effects, and (c) spectral cues introduced by the anatomical structure of the external ear that are sensitive to the angle of incidence of the sound.

The importance of each cue for binaural processing varies according to the stimulus frequency. At low frequencies (below about 2000 Hz in humans) the size of the head is small compared to a wavelength of the stimulus, so the presence of the head does not have a large effect on the propagation of sound waves. Therefore, at low frequencies the predominant binaural cue is simply the difference in arrival time of sounds to the two ears, or interaural time difference (ITD), which is caused primarily by the different distances to the two ears from sources located at nonzero azimuths (zero azimuth conventionally refers to the location straight ahead). At high frequencies, the size of the head is large with respect to the wavelength of sound, and head-shadow effects are significant. The head-shadow effect refers to the increase in pressure caused by reflection of sound from the side of the head nearer to the source, in addition to the reduction in pressure at the side of the head that is farthest from the source. Both of these effects contribute to significant interaural level differences (ILDs) for sounds that are located at nonzero azimuths.

These differences in the physical cues that dominate at low and high frequencies are reflected in both physiology and psychophysics.

For example, at low frequencies the phase differences of sounds arriving at the two ears from different locations are well encoded by the temporal response properties of auditory neurons, whereas at high frequencies fine temporal details of pure tone stimuli are not as well encoded (discussed later). Psychophysically, localization of pure tones is relatively good at low frequencies (below approximately 1500 Hz), relatively poor at middle frequencies (approximately 2000 Hz), and relatively good at higher frequencies (e.g., Mills, 1972; reviewed by Blauert, 1997; Durlach & Colburn, 1978). The different cues and mechanisms that dominate at different frequencies have led to what is called the duplex theory of sound localization (Lord Rayleigh, 1907; reviewed by Kuhn, 1987; physiological aspects reviewed by Kuwada & Yin, 1987). Note that complex sounds are typically rich in combinations of dynamic temporal and level cues across all frequencies, so it is not reasonable, for example, to ignore temporal information when considering the encoding of high-frequency complex sounds.

The third type of cue for localization is the so-called spectral cue, which refers to the complex spectral shapes that are associated with sounds arriving from different angles of incidence (Figure 9.18). Spectral cues are often described by head-related transfer functions (HRTFs), which show the effect of the reflections in the pinna and ear canal as a function of frequency (e.g., Batteau, 1967; Blauert, 1969; reviewed by Blauert, 1997; Kuhn, 1987; Shaw, 1982). The reflections in the pinna that result in spectral cues essentially impose these spectral shapes upon the spectrum of the acoustic source. (Note that the strong notches and peaks associated with spectral cues are at high frequencies, so they do not interfere with the low-frequency spectrum of sounds.) Spectral cues are relevant only for complex sounds because the relative amplitudes and phases

across a range of frequencies must be interpreted in order to use this cue. These cues are particularly significant for stimuli that vary in position along the vertical meridian (the plane that bisects the head along the saggital plane) for which there are essentially no ITD or ILD cues because of the head's symmetry.

ENCODING OF PURE TONES ALONG THE AUDITORY PATHWAY

The acoustic stimulus employed in most physiological experiments has been the pure tone. Many basic response properties can be characterized with pure tones, and responses of neurons at different levels along the pathways can be compared. However, because the auditory periphery and subsequent neural processing mechanisms are highly nonlinear, responses to pure tones do not typically provide accurate predictions for responses to more complex stimuli. Therefore, responses to several different complex stimuli are discussed separately.

Responses of auditory neurons can be described in terms of discharge rate or in terms of temporal response patterns. In general, both aspects of the responses are involved in the encoding of both frequency and level. Discharge rate, usually measured as the average rate over the stimulus duration, plays a role in encoding both frequency and level, but only at relatively low levels; at middle to high levels, the discharge rate saturates for the majority (but not all) of auditory neurons. Discharge timing, which reflects the synchronization of discharge times to the temporal fluctuations of the stimulus, can provide information at very low sound levels (below the rate threshold for low frequencies) and also varies with sound level over a wide dynamic range because of the nonlinearity of the inner ear. The following sections describe

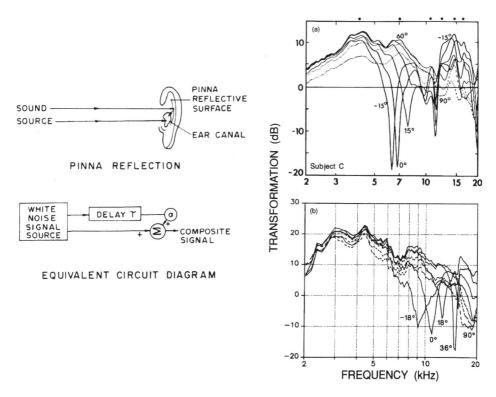

Figure 9.18   Drawing of the pinna schematically showing the interaction between an incident waveform and a slightly delayed version of the waveform that is reflected off the pinna (left).
NOTE: Summing a waveform with a delayed replica results in deep spectral notches, such as those seen in the head-related transfer functions (HRTFs; right). The amount of delay depends on the angle of incidence, due to the asymmetry of the pinna, and thus the spectral notches change systematically with angle of incidence. The HRTFs represent the sound pressure measured using a probe tube placed near the tympanic membrane, referenced to the free-field sound in the absence of the head.
SOURCE: Left: from Wright, Hebrank, & Wilson (1974). Reprinted with permission. Right: from Musicant, Chan, & Hind (1990). Reprinted with permission. Top panel: originally from Shaw (1982). Reprinted with permission.

aspects of both rate and temporal coding, as well as their interactions, for several different stimuli.

Frequency Tuning

One of the most basic properties of the responses of auditory neurons is frequency tuning. At every level of the auditory pathway there are neurons that are sharply tuned in frequency; the frequency to which a neuron is most sensitive will be referred to as its characteristic frequency (CF). The frequency tuning of a neuron can be described by a frequency-threshold tuning curve, which shows the sound level that just elicits a measurable excitatory response, plotted as a function of frequency (Figure 9.19; Kiang, 1984; Kiang & Moxon, 1978). The general nature of tuning curves is similar across species; relatively sharp, V-shaped tuning curves are seen in the periphery and in at least some cells at all levels, including the auditory cortex. More complex tuning, in some cases

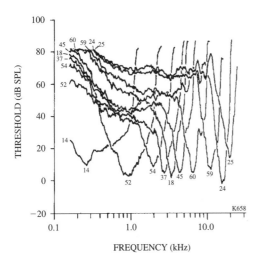

Figure 9.19 Tuning curves for AN fibers in the cat (data redrawn from Kiang, 1984).
SOURCE: From Irvine (1986). Copyright © 1986 by Springer-Verlag. Reprinted with permission.

reflecting interactions between excitatory and inhibitory inputs, is often observed at higher levels in the pathway. The sharpness of tuning and the range of frequencies over which the population of peripheral fibers is tuned varies from species to species (Manley, 1990).

In addition to being tuned in frequency, most auditory nuclei have a tonotopic spatial arrangement. The frequency maps vary in specifics (e.g., orientation and orderliness of maps) from place to place, but they are generally maintained at all levels of the pathway, from the AN to the cortex (Irvine, 1992). An additional complexity of frequency tuning is that the best frequency shifts with sound level; in cats, the best frequency shifts downward with increased level for CFs greater than approximately 1500 Hz, upward for CFs less than approximately 750 Hz, and stays constant for CFs between 750 and 1500 Hz (Carney, McDuffy, & Shekhter, 1999). These shifts in frequency tuning are caused by the interaction between the nonlinear cochlear amplifier (related to the active process in the inner ear; discussed earlier) and frequency glides in the impulse responses of the basi-

lar membrane, hair cells, and AN fibers (e.g., Zhang & Zwislocki, 1996; Carney et al., 1999; de Boer & Nuttall, 1997; Recio, Narayan, & Ruggero, 1997; reviewed in Carney, 1999).

If the response rates of auditory neurons were linearly related to the energy in the neurons' receptive fields (as defined by their tuning curves), the frequency tuning and tonotopy would be sufficient to provide a substrate for encoding the frequency and sound level of pure tones. Also, such a scheme could encode the spectra of complex sounds in the form of average discharge rate versus place or location within the tonotopic map (indeed, only knowledge of the neuron's frequency tuning is required, not strict tonotopy). However, discharge rates are typically related to sound level in a nonlinear manner at all levels of the pathway, and it is necessary to look in more depth at other neural response properties to determine how even simple stimulus attributes, such as sound level and frequency, are encoded. In general, changes in both average discharge rate and temporal response properties, combined across populations of neurons, are required to explain encoding of sounds. Different response features and different neurons convey information, depending on the frequency, level, and complexity of the stimulus.

Response to Tones of Auditory-Nerve Fibers

The discharge rate (average rate over the time course of the stimulus, in spikes/s) of an AN fiber to a tone at its CF is characterized by (a) Poisson-distributed spontaneous activity at very low sound levels; (b) a range of levels at which discharge times become phase-locked, or aligned in time, with temporal features of the stimulus for low stimulus frequencies; (c) a threshold at which the rate is just increased (typically by a criterion of 20 spikes/s, measured over a 50-ms time window; Liberman, 1978); (d) a dynamic range of levels over which the response rate increases as tone level increases; and (e) a maximal, or saturated, rate that remains relatively constant at higher levels. (For detailed reviews of AN response properties, see Javel, 1986; Ruggero, 1992a.)

In mammals, AN fibers vary in their spontaneous rates (SRs), which are correlated to their tone thresholds (Liberman, 1978): The majority (61%) have high-SRs (>18 spikes/s) and low thresholds; medium-SR fibers (23%, 1–18 spikes/s) have higher thresholds; and low-SR fibers (16%, <1 spike/s) have the highest thresholds. The form of rate-level functions varies across these groups (Figure 9.20). High-SR fibers have steep rate-level functions because of their low thresholds,

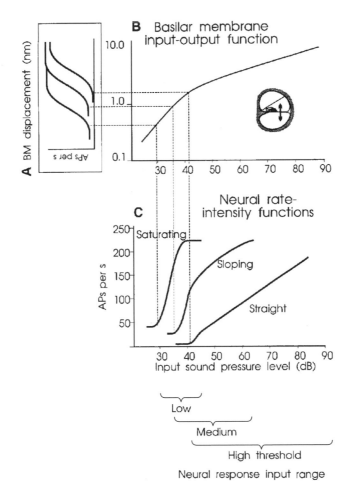

Figure 9.20   Illustration of rate vs. level functions for AN fibers with different spontaneous rates, and the dependence of the rate-level functions on the basilar-membrane (BM) input-output function.

NOTE: The BM output is enhanced at low levels, due to the cochlear amplifier. The gain of the cochlear amplifier is reduced at moderate to high levels by saturation of the active process, reflected in the slope of the BM input-output function (discussed in the text).

SOURCE: Reprinted from *Trends in Neurosciences, 15,* G. K. Yates, B. M. Johnstone, R. B. Patuzzi, & D. Robertson, "Mechanical preprocessing in the mammalian cochlea," pp. 57–61. Copyright © 1992, with permission from Elsevier Science.

which are in the low-SPL range where the cochlear amplifier is at maximal gain (discussed earlier). Medium- and low-SR fibers have higher thresholds, and their rate-level functions are less steep because of the reduction in gain of the cochlear amplifier as sound level increases (Figure 9.20; Sachs & Abbas, 1974; Sokolowski, Sachs, & Goldstein, 1989; Yates et al., 1992). Thus, the range of levels over which discharge rate varies with sound level, or the dynamic range, varies significantly across the three SR groups.

Obviously, the discharge rate's ability to encode sound level is constrained by these dynamic ranges. To explain quantitatively level coding over a wide range of levels requires combinations across frequencies (Siebert, 1968) or across groups of fibers with different SRs (Colburn, 1981; Delgutte, 1987; Viemeister, 1988; Winter & Palmer, 1991; reviewed by Delgutte, 1996). However, it is important to note that the presence of the straight rate-level functions for the low-SR fibers depends on a large amount of cochlear amplification, which is only present at the high-frequency end of the cochlea. Straight rate-level functions are not observed at CFs below 1500 Hz in guinea pig (Winter & Palmer, 1991) and are not observed in cats at any CF (e.g., Sachs & Abbas, 1974; Winslow & Sachs, 1988). Thus, encoding of level by low-CF fibers cannot depend on wide-dynamic range fibers and must be explained either by spread of excitation across the population (which only applies to pure tones) or by temporal response properties (Carney, 1994; Colburn, Carney, & Heinz, 2001; Heinz, Colburn, & Carney, 2001b).

Two different temporal cues are available in the responses of AN fibers: synchrony and phase. Synchrony, or phase locking to the fine structure of the stimulus waveform (Figure 9.21A), is detectable at levels of approximately 20 dB below the rate threshold (for high-SR fibers) and persists up to the highest

levels tested (Johnson, 1980). As shown in Figure 9.21A, synchronized discharges typically do not occur on every cycle of the stimulus; when they do occur, however, they are aligned in time with a particular phase of the stimulus (phase-locked). The strength of synchrony of the response times to the stimulus waveform increases to a maximum over a relatively narrow range of levels, peaks at about 20 dB above rate threshold, and then drops slightly at higher levels (Johnson, 1980). Thus, changes in synchrony with sound level may contribute to encoding of sound level at very low levels, but not at medium to high sound levels (Colburn, 1981; Colburn et al., 2001). In addition, the ability of AN fibers to synchronize to the fine structure of tones is limited to low frequencies (Figures 9.21B–D; Johnson, 1980; Koppl, 1997). This limitation is imposed by the low-pass filtering associated with the membranes of IHCs, as well as by other neural processes (Weiss & Rose, 1988). Although high-CF fibers do not synchronize well to tones at their CF (Figure 9.21C), high-CF fibers do synchronize extremely well to low-frequency tones presented at high levels (Joris, Smith, & Yin, 1994) and to the envelopes of complex high-frequency sounds (discussed later).

The synchronized activity of AN fibers provides the substrate for another temporal cue. The phase of the synchronized discharges also conveys information about tone level. Because the gain of the cochlear amplifier changes with sound level, the bandwidth and phase properties of the tuning in the auditory periphery also change with level (e.g., Cheatham & Dallos, 1998; Geisler & Rhode, 1982; Ruggero et al., 1997). The phase of the responses in the cochlea determines the timing of synchronized responses of AN fibers. Thus, the responses of AN fibers to tones near CF have phases that systematically change as sound level is varied (Figure 9.22; D. J.

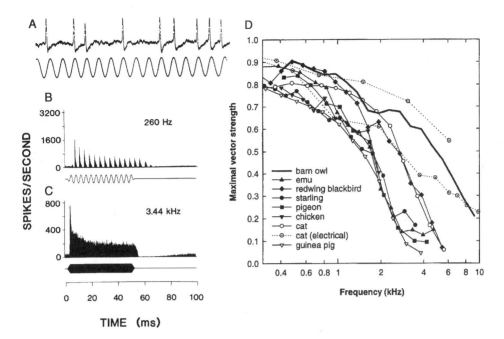

Figure 9.21 Phase-locking of AN responses.

NOTE: A) Example of an auditory nerve fiber's discharges that are phase-locked to the stimulus waveform. The fiber does not discharge on every cycle of the stimulus; when it does discharge, however, it is synchronized, or phase-locked, to a particular phase of the stimulus. B–C) Poststimulus time histograms for two AN fibers responding to tones at CF. Discharge times for 3,000 tone bursts were superimposed to form these histograms. The low-CF fiber responds in synchrony with the temporal features of the sinusoidal stimulus (shown just below the response). The higher-CF fiber's response is not clearly phase-locked to the high-frequency stimulus (shown just below response); at 3.44 kHz, the strength of synchrony is relatively weak (see D). D) Synchronization coefficient of AN responses to tones at CF as a function of frequency for several species. Each measurement was made at the level that yielded the maximum synchronization coefficient for that fiber. Strength of phase locking is typically measured using the synchronization coefficient (equivalent to vector strength), where a value of 0 represents no phase locking and 1 represents perfect phase locking; this measure is the ratio between the energy in the PST histogram at the tone frequency (determined with a Fourier transform) and the overall average rate.

SOURCE: A) Evans (1975). Copyright © 1986 by Springer-Verlag. Reprinted with permission. B–C) From Irvine (1986); redrawn from Kiang (1984). Copyright © 1986 by Springer-Verlag. Reprinted with permission. D) From Koppl (1997). Copyright © 1997 by the Society for Neuroscience. Reprinted with permission.

Anderson, Rose, Hind, & Brugge, 1971), providing a cue for encoding sound level at low frequencies (Carney, 1994; Colburn et al., 2001; Heinz et al., 2001b). This cue can be decoded by a neural coincidence-detection mechanism; no absolute phase reference is required because the relative timing, or degree of coincidence, of discharges on neurons tuned to different CFs systematically varies with sound level (Carney, 1994; Heinz et al., 2001b). It is interesting to note that the non-linear phase cue, which is associated with the OHC-driven active process in the mammalian cochlea (e.g., Ruggero et al., 1997; discussed earlier), is present also in AN responses of the starling (Gleich & Narins, 1988). The active process in birds is hypothesized to involve active movements of stereocilia, as opposed to

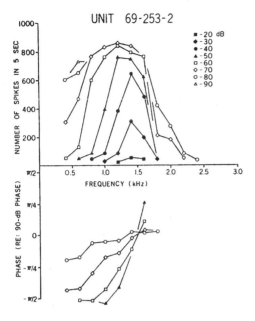

Figure 9.22 The phase of phase-locked responses of low-frequency fibers varies systematically with sound level.

NOTE: Response area for a 1400-Hz CF AN fiber in cats is shown. The upper panel shows average discharge rate as a function of tone frequency at several sound levels. The lower panel shows the phases of the phase-locked responses, referenced to the phase of the response to the 90 dB SPL tone at each frequency.

SOURCE: From Anderson, Rose, Hind, & Brugge (1971). Reprinted by permission of McGraw-Hill.

length changes of the hair cells (see Fettiplace & Fuchs, 1999). Thus, the presence of the level-dependent phase cues may be present across diverse species as a result of different active mechanisms.

Figure 9.22 demonstrates that a combination of rate and temporal encoding strategies can encode level across a wide range of levels, even when processing is restricted to fibers tuned to a limited range of frequencies near the tone (which is important when considering complex stimuli, or masked stimuli; discussed later). For this neuron, discharge rate changes with sound level at frequencies near CF from threshold (about 20 dB SPL) up to

about 60 dB SPL, and then saturates. However, the phase of the phase-locked discharges of fibers tuned just below or above the frequency of the tone continues to change up to at least 90 dB. By combining the information available in rate and temporal response properties, sound level can be encoded over the wide range of levels required to explain psychophysical performance (e.g., Heinz et al., 2001a).

These three cues—level-dependent rate, synchrony, and phase—can be combined to encode information over a wide range of stimulus parameters, with different aspects of the responses providing information in different situations, depending on the frequency and sound level of the stimulus (Heinz et al., 2001a). The previous discussion pertains to encoding of pure tones presented in a quiet background; the effects on these different encoding schemes of background noise or other stimulus components, such as in complex sounds, are a topic for future investigation. Also, other factors may play a role in the contribution of average rate to level coding in certain situations. For example, the dynamic range of the onset response of AN fibers is much wider than that of the sustained response (Smith, 1988). Furthermore, the activity of olivocochlear efferents (stimulated electrically or acoustically) may act to shift dynamically the rate-level and phase-level functions of AN fibers, effectively enlarging their dynamic ranges (discussed later; May & Sachs, 1992; Winslow & Sachs, 1988).

Responses to Tones in the Cochlear Nuclear Complex

Responses of neurons at the first level of processing in the brainstem have received a great deal of study. These neurons are of interest because they represent the first level of processing or decoding the information that is initially encoded in the patterns of discharge of populations of AN fibers. Thus, a better understanding of the response properties of cells in the CN may shed more light on how information is encoded in the AN. In addition, the responses of the various cell types in the brainstem are inherently interesting from a biophysical standpoint; these cells receive essentially the same excitatory inputs—convergent AN fibers—but respond in many different ways. Differences in responses from cell to cell, and from cell type to cell type, presumably depend on the number and synaptic strengths of the inputs, the location of the inputs on the cell, the cell morphology, and the properties of the cell membrane. All of these characteristics vary across the cells of the cochlear nucleus (reviewed by Cant, 1992). Pfeiffer (1966) classified responses in the CN based on the onset responses and the temporal patterning of the sustained responses seen in these peri-stimulus time histograms (PSTs; Figure 9.23). Subsequent classification schemes incorporated information on the inter-spike interval statistics (e.g., Blackburn & Sachs, 1989; Young, Robert, & Shofner, 1988) and on response maps (discharge rate vs. frequency and sound level) that include both excitatory and inhibitory response features (Figure 9.24; Shofner & Young, 1985).

In the mammalian cochlear nucleus, the AVCN contains two major cell types: bushy cells, which are associated with primary-like (i.e., AN-like) PSTs in response to tones at CF (Rhode, Oertel, & Smith, 1983; Rouiller & Ryugo 1984; Smith & Rhode, 1987), and stellate cells, which are associated with chopper (i.e., regularly firing) response PSTs (Figure 9.23; Rhode et al., 1983; Smith & Rhode, 1989). The PVCN contains stellate cells that are associated with onset-chopper responses (Smith & Rhode, 1989) and octopus cells that are associated with onset responses (Rhode et al., 1983). The DCN has several cell types associated with different response properties that are often described in terms of response maps and rate-level functions in response to noise and tones (Figure 9.24), in addition to their PSTs to tones (Figure 9.23).

The mammalian AVCN and PVCN project to the major binaural nuclei in the brainstem and midbrain. The temporal encoding of low-frequency tonal stimuli is apparently enhanced in the AVCN, where bushy cells have synchronization coefficients that are higher than those of AN fibers in response to low-frequency tones (Joris, Carney, Smith, & Yin, 1994). In birds and reptiles, AN fibers project to two brainstem regions, the NM and the NA. Cells in the NM have response properties similar to bushy cells in mammalian AVCN, while those in NA are similar to the stellate cells in mammalian AVCN (Carr & Konishi, 1990; Hausler et al., 1999; Sullivan, 1985; Warchol & Dallos, 1990). Bushy and stellate cells are often described in terms of parallel paths, with the bushy cells conveying temporal information to higher levels and stellate cells conveying information about sound level in terms of average rate (e.g., Shofner & Dye, 1989; Takahashi, Moiseff, & Konishi, 1984). However, most stellate cells have relatively limited dynamic ranges (Carney & Burock, 1997; May & Sachs, 1992), and while they do not phase-lock well to tonal stimuli at CF, stellate cells do phase-lock well to the envelopes of complex sounds (Frisina, Smith, & Chamberlain, 1990; Rhode & Greenberg, 1994). Furthermore, both bushy cells and stellate cells are sensitive to manipulations of the phase spectrum of complex sounds, suggesting that they are sensitive to the relative timing of convergent AN inputs (Carney, 1990). Thus, it is not clear whether the segregation of the pathways is very strict in terms of temporal or average-rate information.

Responses to tones of cells in the DCN, especially the type IV and V neurons, are

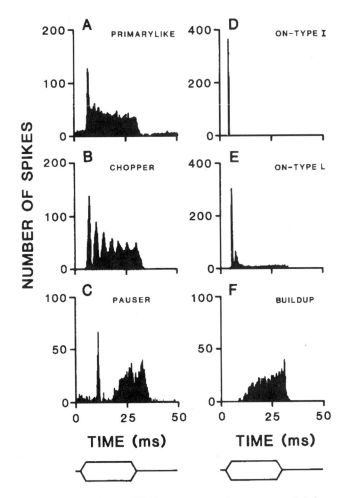

Figure 9.23   Examples of six different PST histogram types in response to brief tone pulses at CF for cells in the cochlear nucleus.

NOTE: The categories proposed by Pfeiffer (1966) are illustrated. Primary-like PSTs are associated with spherical and some globular bushy cells in the AVCN; different varieties of chopper PSTs are associated with the stellate cells in AVCN and multipolar cells in PVCN; Onset-I (pure onset response) PSTs are associated with octopus cells in the PVCN; Onset-L (onset with low-sustained rate) PSTs are associated with globular bushy cells; Pauser and Buildup PSTs are associated with cells in the DCN (reviewed by Young, 1984, 1998; Rhode & Greenberg, 1992).

SOURCE: From Irvine (1986). Copyright © 1986 by Springer-Verlag. Reprinted by permission of McGraw-Hill.

highly nonmonotonic as a function of level and usually are not factored into models for encoding of the level and frequency of single tones. Rather, the DCN's more complex response properties have been proposed to reflect a role in the decoding of spectral notches that are associated with the pinna cues for sound localization of stimuli in the vertical plane (discussed later). The neural circuitry of the DCN has been a topic of several physiological and anatomical studies exploring the interactions of the different cell types (reviewed by Young, 1984, 1998).

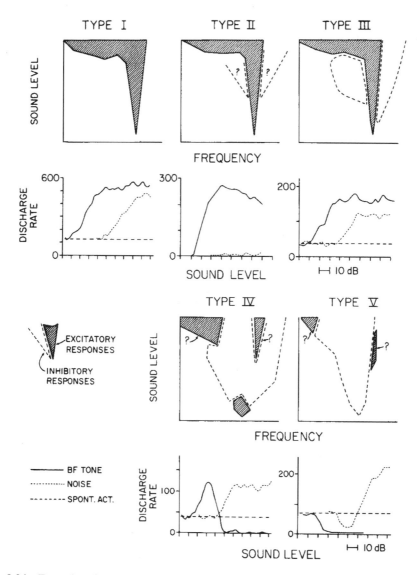

Figure 9.24 Examples of the categories of cells in the cochlear nucleus based on response maps.
Note: These response maps (RMs; Shofner & Young, 1985) show the excitatory and inhibitory responses of a neuron to tones across a wide range of frequencies and sound levels. Below each RM are rate-level functions in response to tones at CF and wideband noise. Cells in the AVCN tend to have type I RMs; type III RMs are found in VCN and DCN; and types II, IV, and V are found primarily in DCN (Young, 1984; Rhode & Greenberg, 1992).
Source: From Young (1984). Reprinted with permission.

Responses to Tones in the Superior Olivary Complex and Lateral Lemniscus

Cells in the binaural region of the brainstem have been studied primarily from the viewpoint of sound localization (discussed below). This section presents the basic response properties of these cells to tonal stimuli.

Of all the auditory brainstem nuclei, the thin sheet of cells that makes up the MSO has been the most difficult to study, partly because the large extracellular fields due to the synchronous activity of these cells makes them difficult to isolate for single-unit recording (Guinan, Norris, & Guinan, 1972; Yin & Chan, 1990). The MSO of the mammal is dominated by cells that are tuned to low frequencies, excited by stimuli to each ear, and often facilitated by stimuli presented to both ears with appropriate binaural parameters. MSO cells have frequency tuning curves in response to stimuli delivered to either ear that are comparable in shape to AN fibers, but with slightly broader tuning, suggesting some convergence across CFs (Yin & Chan, 1990). Rate-level functions for most MSO cells are monotonic and saturating, with dynamic ranges of 20 dB to 30 dB; a few cells have nonmonotonic rate-level functions (Yin & Chan, 1990). The temporal response properties of low-frequency MSO neurons are highly synchronized to tonal stimuli, typically exceeding the highest synchronization coefficients seen in the AN, and comparable to those in bushy cells of the AVCN (Joris et al., 1994; Yin & Chan, 1990). MSO cells are highly sensitive to the relative timing of stimuli to the two ears (Goldberg & Brown, 1969; Yin & Chan, 1990).

Cells in the LSO are typically excited by stimuli to the ipsilateral ear and have frequency tuning that is comparable to that in the AN (Tsuchitani, 1977). The tonotopic map in the LSO is dominated by high-frequency CFs, which do not exhibit significant phase-locking to tones at CF (although, like AN fibers, they phase-lock to the envelopes of complex sounds; discussed later). In response to tones presented to the ipsilateral ear, LSO cells have chopper response patterns that differ in the details of their chopping patterns as well as in their interspike-interval statistics (Tsuchitani & Johnson, 1985). These cells are inhibited by sounds to the contralateral ear, and are thus sensitive to interaural level differences and presumed to play a role in

the localization of high-frequency sounds (reviewed by Irvine, 1986, 1992). The inhibitory inputs to the LSO are provided by the principal cells of the ipsilateral MNTB, which receives its input in the form of the large calyces of Held from the globular bushy cells of the contralateral cochlear nucleus (e.g., Smith, Joris, Carney, & Yin, 1991; Stotler, 1953). Because of the secure synapses associated with the calyceal terminals, responses of MNTB are very similar to those of globular bushy cells in the CN (Smith, Joris, & Yin, 1998).

The nuclei of the lateral lemniscus have been the focus of relatively few studies. As it has become increasingly clear that the responses of the IC are significantly more complex than are those of the MSO and LSO, however, the motivation to understand these nuclei that provide strong inputs to the IC has grown. Most of the neurons in the VNLL and DNLL are sharply tuned; a minority has broad or unusual tuning-curve shapes (Guinan et al., 1972). The DNLL has a clear tonotopic arrangement, whereas that of the VNLL and the neighboring INLL is less consistent (Aitkin, Anderson, & Brugge, 1970). Cells in the DNLL have binaural responses due to the inputs from the SOC (e.g., Brugge, Anderson, & Aitkin, 1970; Markovitz & Pollak, 1994; reviewed by Kelly, 1997). Cells in the VNLL are primarily monaural and excited by the contralateral ear, reflecting the dominant input from the contralateral CN. The function of these nuclei is somewhat unclear because all the inputs to the nuclei of the LL provide inputs also to the IC, which is the major target of the NLL outputs (Irvine, 1986). Additional connections between the two DNLLs, and the projections of these nuclei to both ICs, provide a potential for explaining some of the more complex binaural response properties seen for the cells in the IC as compared to the cells in the SOC. For example, to explain responses to some complex stimuli in the IC (discussed later), one requires convergence of excitatory and inhibitory inputs tuned to different binaural configurations. Binaural processing within the DNLL and its inhibitory projections to both ICs have also been proposed to enhance the laterality of the representation of contralateral space and to enhance the sensitivity of IC neurons to small changes in interaural level and time (Kelly, 1997).

Responses to Tones in the Midbrain: Inferior and Superior Colliculi

In most species the midbrain auditory region is relatively large and is accessible for physiological studies, especially as compared to the lower binaural nuclei in the SOC. For these reasons, it is one of the most studied levels of the auditory pathway. The cells in the IC are typically sensitive to particular combinations of binaural stimuli, reflecting the binaural processing at lower levels of the brainstem, as well as further processing within the IC itself. For example, both EE and EI responses to tones have been described for IC neurons in cats, reflecting the response properties of the MSO and LSO neurons that project to the IC. However, more complex stimulus paradigms (discussed later) make it clear that not all properties of IC neurons can be explained simply by processing at the level of the MSO and LSO.

The shapes of frequency tuning curves of neurons in the ICC are more diverse than at lower levels, probably because of the high degree of convergence at this level. Although there is clearly a tonotopic organization of the nucleus (e.g., Merzenich & Reid, 1974; reviewed by Irvine, 1992), the details of the map are unclear, as are the relationships to other proposed maps, such as those of sharpness of tuning (Schreiner & Langner, 1988), threshold (Stiebler, 1986), or tuning for amplitude-modulated stimuli (Schreiner & Langner, 1988).

Responses of IC neurons to tones also reflect the diversity of inputs to the IC. In contrast to neurons at the levels of the MSO and below, phase-locking to low-frequency stimuli in the ICC is rare and is also seldom observed for frequencies above 600 Hz (Kuwada, Yin, Syka, Buunen, & Wickesberg, 1984). Rate-level functions of ICC neurons vary over a continuum from monotonic to highly nonmonotonic (Figure 9.25; Irvine and Gago, 1990). From these rate-level functions one could hypothesize that level is encoded in terms of the average rates of the monotonic cells, or in terms of a place code based on the nonmonotonic cells (or a combination of both; Irvine, 1992). Neither of these models has been quantitatively tested. In addition to the diversity of rate-level functions, the temporal response patterns in the IC vary significantly; many cells have onset responses followed by long pauses (50-ms pauses are not uncommon) before sustained activity begins, if it is present at all (D. R. Moore & Irvine, 1980; Irvine, 1986). Recent studies of the ICC have also explored the influence of inputs from the contralateral DCN by using response maps to characterize IC responses (e.g., Ramachandran, Davis, & May, 1999). Cells in the ICx are reported to have more complex and typically broader frequency tuning characteristics than ICC has (e.g., Aitkin, Webster, Veale, & Crosby, 1975). A spatial map has been reported in the ICx of the barn owl (e.g., Knudsen & Knudsen, 1983), and most studies of the ICx focus on its role in spatial hearing.

One of the major projections of the central nucleus of the IC is to the deep layers of the superior colliculus (SC). Auditory, visual, and somatosensory inputs converge in this region (e.g., M. A. Meredith & Stein, 1983; Knudsen, 1987), along with inputs from proprioceptive, vestibular, and other systems that are involved in the generation of motor commands. The organization of the deep SC is

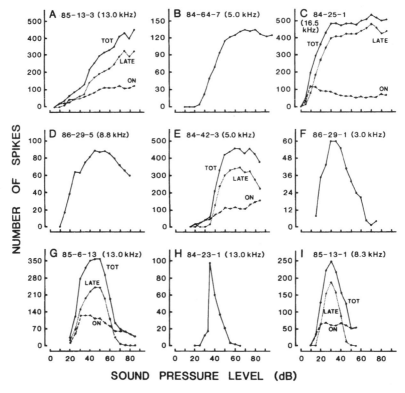

Figure 9.25 Examples showing the diversity of rate-level functions for cells in the ICC in response to tones at CF.

NOTE: The number at the top of each panel (e.g., 85-13-3) is an identifier for each neuron; the number in parentheses refers to the CF of the cell. Responses are averaged over 30 presentations; in some cases, the onset and sustained (late) responses are shown in addition to the total response.

SOURCE: From Irvine & Gago (1990). Reprinted with permission.

described as a motor map; responses of cells depend on the difference between the current and desired locations of the eyes, head, and body (reviewed by Sparks, 1999).

Reponses to tonal stimuli in the SC (which have been recorded primarily in anesthetized animals, in which eye movements were neither elicited nor behaviorally controlled) show a wide diversity of frequency tuning, including very sharp, very broad, and complex multipeaked threshold-tuning curves (Hirsch, Chan, & Yin, 1985; Wise & Irvine, 1983). The SC is dominated by cells tuned to high CFs (Carlile & Pettigrew, 1987; Hirsch et al., 1985; Wise & Irvine, 1983). The SC does not have a simple tonotopic map, but several groups

have reported evidence for spatial maps (King & Palmer, 1983; Middlebrooks & Knudsen, 1987). Carlile & Pettigrew (1987) have argued that the complex tonotopy makes sense if it is interpreted in terms of the spectral cues provided by the pinna, which thus may provide the basis for a spatial map in the SC.

The roles of sensory maps for the different represented modalities in the SC, their interactions, and ultimate transformation into motor commands are a fascinating topic. For example, the fact that the eyes move relative to the head (and thus relative to the ears) and that the head moves relative to the rest of the body (and thus relative to the somatosensory system), necessitates the use of proprioceptive or sensory inputs in order to interpret the dynamic spatial relationships between the different modalities. In the barn owl, which has very limited eye movements, it has been reported that the visual map in the superficial layers of optic tectum and the auditory map of space in deep layers are aligned with each other (Knudsen, 1987). The responses of auditory neurons in the SC are influenced by the position of the eyes (in the monkey, Jay & Sparks, 1984) and the pinnae (in the cat, Middlebrooks & Knudsen, 1987). Recent studies of gaze control (i.e., control of combined eye and head movements) suggest that neural activity in the SC is most consistent with gaze, as opposed to eye, head, or body movements in isolation (Freedman & Sparks, 1997). Furthermore, studies of the SC motor maps conducted on animals with fixed heads have yielded distorted maps (reviewed by Sparks, 1999). The role of the dynamic sensory maps in deep SC and their interaction with a gaze control system are topics for further study.

Responses to Tones in the Thalamus

The other target of cells in the IC is the MGB in the thalamus. The three major regions of the thalamus have basic physiological response properties that mirror the general nature of their anatomical inputs and outputs (reviewed by Clarey, Barone, & Imig, 1992). The ventral division, which receives its input primarily from ICC and projects strongly to auditory cortex, is characterized by an orderly tonotopic map (Aitkin & Webster, 1972; Calford & Webster, 1981; Imig & Morel, 1985b). The dorsal division, which has a more diverse set of inputs and projections, is less strongly tonotopic; most cells in this region have broad and complex (multipeaked) frequency-threshold tuning curves (Calford & Webster, 1981). The medial division, which is most diverse in terms of its cell types, inputs, and projec-

tions, has an irregular tonotopic arrangement (Imig & Morel, 1985a; Roullier, Rodrigues-Dagaeff, Simm, de Ribaupierre, Villa, & de Ribaupierre, 1989).

The rate-level functions of the majority of cells in the MGB are nonmonotonic (Aitkin & Dunlop, 1968; Galambos, Rose, Bromiley, & Hughes, 1952; Rouiller, de Ribaupierre, Morel, & de Ribaupierre, 1983). There seems to be a general organization of responses throughout the MGB along the anterior-posterior axis: The anterior regions have a higher percentage of monotonic cells that are more responsive to broad-band stimuli such as noise and clicks, whereas the posterior regions have a higher percentage of non-monotonic cells that are more responsive to tones and respond poorly to broadband stimuli (Rodrigues-Dagaeff et al., 1989; Rouiller et al., 1983). The anterior and posterior regions also have different projection patterns to the auditory cortex (Morel & Imig, 1987; Rodrigues-Dagaeff et al., 1989).

Responses to Tones in the Auditory Cortex

The tonotopic arrangement of auditory cortex was described earlier because it plays an essential part in the parceling of the different regions of auditory cortex. Responses of cortical neurons to pure tones are sharply tuned in frequency in several of the cortical regions that have orderly tonotopic maps: primary auditory cortex (AI), the anterior field (A or AAF), the posterior field (P), the ventral cortical field (V), and the ventral posterior part of e_p (VP; Figure 9.15; e.g., Reale & Imig, 1980; Winer, 1992). A topographic representation of tone level along iso-frequency strips was reported in AI (Heil, Rajan, & Irvine, 1994). Tone level is also reflected in the synchronization of neural responses in AI and between AI and AAF (Eggermont, 2000). The representation of temporal features of acoustic stimuli in auditory cortex has been recently reviewed

(Schreiner, Mendelson, Raggio, Brosch, & Krueger, 1997).

Regions of auditory cortex other than AI, AAF, V, and VP are notoriously difficult to stimulate with pure tones, and recent studies have turned to the use of more complex stimuli, including vocalizations (e.g., Wang, 1998; discussed later). The difficulty in studying cortex was surmounted most notably by Suga and his colleagues, who have conducted a number of studies of the bat auditory cortex (reviewed in Suga, 1989). Their studies take advantage of the fact that bats echolocate their prey using relatively simple and thoroughly studied vocalizations; thus the processing of cues associated with the task of echolation can be studied using a stimulus that is known to be behaviorally important to the animal.

Physiology of the Descending Pathways

The physiology of the descending pathways that terminate in the central nervous system has only recently become a focus of study. A general framework describing three parallel corticofugal systems was proposed by Huffman and Henson (1990). A series of recent studies have demonstrated a variety of effects of the corticofugal pathways on the response properties of neurons at lower levels in the mustache bat (e.g., Chowdhury & Suga, 2000; Yan & Suga, 1996; Zhang, Suga, & Yan, 1997).

A large number of studies have focused on the olivocochlear system. The influence of the descending auditory pathway has generally been studied by stimulating these neurons and monitoring the effect on AN and basilar membrane responses, rather than by recording from the efferent neurons themselves. In general, stimulation of the crossed olivocochlear bundle (COCB; accessible at the floor of the fourth ventricle) results in a reduction of AN responsiveness. In quiet, stimulation of the COCB elevates thresh-

olds and shifts the RL functions to higher levels (Gifford & Guinan, 1983; Guinan & Gifford, 1988; Wiederhold, 1970; reviewed by Wiederhold, 1986). In the presence of noise, stimulation of the COCB also restores the dynamic range of AN fibers to nearly that observed in quiet and thus may play a role in maintaining information about sound level in the presence of background sounds (Winslow & Sachs, 1987, 1988). Based on the effect of COCB stimulation on basilar-membrane responses to different tones near CF, a likely mechanism for the reduced response is a reduction of the cochlear amplification associated with OHC motility (e.g., Dolan, Guo, & Nuttall, 1997; Murugasu & Russell, 1996). However, more complex features of the effects of COCB stimulation on responses to frequencies away from CF and at high SPLs suggest that additional mechanisms may be necessary to explain the effects (Guinan & Stankovic, 1996; Russell & Murugasu, 1997; Stankovic & Guinan, 1999, 2000).

RESPONSES TO COMPLEX ACOUSTIC STIMULI

Most studies of the auditory system, at all levels of the pathway, have been conducted with pure-tone stimuli. The motivation for this approach is guided by the general strategy of trying to understand the responses of a system to the simplest possible stimulus, after which complex stimuli can be understood. (Using Fourier analysis, complex sounds can be represented as straightforward combinations of simple stimuli). Of course, this strategy works only for linear systems, for which responses to combinations of simple stimuli are just combinations of responses to the simple stimuli. Since the late 1960s and early 1970s, it has become increasingly clear that the auditory system is nonlinear. Indeed, because of the fragile nature of the active process in the inner ear, the healthy auditory system is much more nonlinear than the impaired system is.

To understand how the nonlinear auditory system processes complex sounds, they must be studied (essentially) one at a time, which opens the door to an infinite parameter space. Psychophysical studies provide insight as to which complex stimuli may be interesting to pursue in physiological studies; for example, it is interesting to consider stimuli, such as masking stimuli, that illustrate significant differences between the healthy and the impaired ear. In contrast, tones in quiet produce relatively little deficit, other than raised thresholds, in impaired listeners. Because the healthy ear has an exquisite ability to pull signals out of noisy backgrounds—an ability that is lost after impairment (e.g., B. C. J. Moore, 1995)—masking stimuli are effective in demonstrating differences between healthy and impaired ears.

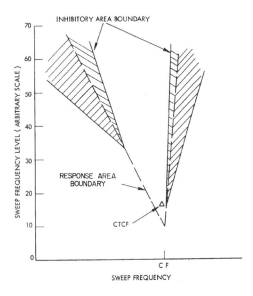

Figure 9.26   Idealized two-tone suppression tuning curve for an AN fiber.
SOURCE: From Sachs & Kiang (1968). Reprinted with permission.

Responses to Combinations of Tones

The simplest and most studied masking stimulus is a second tone; tone-on-tone masking provided one of the earliest and most classic illustrations of auditory nonlinearity: two-tone suppression (Arthur, Pfeiffer, & Suga, 1971; Sachs & Kiang, 1968). The basic illustration of two-tone suppression is the suppression tuning curve (Figure 9.26; note that the term *two-tone suppression* is now used in favor of *two-tone inhibition*). After finding the excitatory threshold tuning curve with a single pure tone, a continuous tone is presented at CF (CTCF) at a fixed level above threshold (indicated by the triangle); then a second tone is varied in frequency and sound level to map the boundary at which it just suppresses the response to the tone at CF. If the frequency and level of the second tone lie within the hatched area (Figure 9.26), this tone is able to suppress the response to the tone at CF. The details of two-tone suppression (e.g., not only

its threshold but also the slope at which suppression grows above threshold) vary depending on the CF as well as on the frequency of the suppressor relative to CF (Delgutte, 1990). Recent studies of mechanical responses of the basilar membrane have demonstrated that the features of two-tone suppression reported for the AN are present in the mechanics of the inner ear (Cooper, 1996; Nuttall & Dolan, 1993; Ruggero et al., 1992). Furthermore, when the active process is experimentally manipulated (e.g., by applying reversible ototoxic drugs), two-tone suppression is eliminated and recovers with the same time course as does the cochlear amplifier (Ruggero & Rich, 1991). Thus, the effect of the suppressor can be thought of as turning down the gain of the cochlear amplifier (just as a moderate- to high-level tone at CF results in a reduction in amplifier gain). The suppression tuning curve provides information concerning the stimulus frequency range that can affect the gain of the amplifier at a given place (CF).

Responses of AN fibers to harmonic complexes also reveal complex nonlinear interactions (Horst, Javel, & Farley, 1985), which are presumably caused by the interactions of the individual tones and their combined effect on the gain of the cochlear amplifier. Changes in the gain result in a change not only in the magnitude of the response (which is often masked by neural saturation) but also in the phase of responses (discussed earlier). The temporal patterns of responses to complex stimuli are influenced by the relative phases of the responses to the different components of the sounds.

Responses of neurons at higher levels of the auditory pathway to two-tone complexes are more challenging to interpret because they are affected by two-tone suppression at the level of the auditory nerve, as well as by inhibitory interactions at higher levels (e.g., see the response maps in Figure 9.24; Rhode and Greenberg, 1992; Young, 1984, 1998). Two-tone stimuli have been used to investigate the nonlinear response properties of cells in the cochlear nucleus (Nelken, Kim, & Young, 1997; Shofner, Sheft, & Guzman, 1996; Spirou, Davis, Nelken, & Young, 1999).

Responses to Noise and Tones Masked by Noise

Responses of AN fibers to wideband and band-limited noise have been pursued as another approach to the study of the nonlinear response properties of the auditory periphery (Ruggero, 1973; Schalk & Sachs, 1980). Rate-level functions of AN fibers in response to noise typically have a shallower slope than do tone responses. This effect can be understood in terms of the reduction in cochlear amplification by the frequency components in the noise stimulus within the two-tone suppression regions (see Figure 9.26).

Noise responses have been used also as a tool for characterizing peripheral tuning using reverse-correlation techniques (e.g., de Boer & de Jongh, 1978). The reverse-correlation technique provides a transfer-function description (at a given sound level) that can be used to predict responses to other stimuli (Carney & Yin, 1988). Noise has been used also as a tool for testing the cross-correlation model for binaural processing at the level of the MSO (Yin & Chan, 1990) and ICC (Yin, Chan, & Carney, 1987).

The encoding of tones in the presence of wideband noise is a classic problem that has been pursued in many psychophysical studies. Physiologically, responses of AN fibers to tones in the presence of noise have rate-level functions that are shifted to higher levels and have compressed dynamic ranges (Costalupes, Young, & Gibson, 1984; Sinex & Geisler, 1980; Winslow & Sachs, 1988; Young & Barta, 1986). These responses can be interpreted in terms of a wideband suppressive effect elicited by the noise (Sinex & Geisler, 1980) that reduces the gain of the cochlear amplifier. Young and Barta (1986) performed a statistical analysis of discharge rates of AN fibers in comparison with behavioral thresholds and found that performance could be explained by the rates of a few fibers. Miller, Barta, and Sachs (1987) reported that the temporal response properties of AN fibers tuned near the tone frequency provided reliable information for detection of a tone in noise. Neurons with rate-level functions that shift to high sound levels in the presence of noise are also observed at higher levels of the pathway (e.g., auditory cortex; Phillips, 1990). Several binaural physiological studies have investigated responses to tones in the presence of noise, which is relevant to psychophysical studies of binaural detection (e.g., Palmer, Jiang, & McAlpine, 1999).

Responses to Amplitude-Modulated Stimuli

Another class of complex stimuli that has received a significant amount of study, in both physiology and psychophysics, is amplitude-modulated (AM) sounds. These stimuli typically consist of a tone or noise as a carrier, which is modulated in amplitude by a low-frequency sinusoid. This stimulus is useful because it can be described with relatively few parameters, which can be systematically manipulated. AM stimuli can provide a useful probe into the neural processes involved in analyzing complex stimuli, including naturally occurring sounds with amplitude fluctuations, such as vocalizations.

Detailed studies of neural responses to AM stimuli have been conducted in the AN (e.g., Cooper, Robertson, & Yates, 1993; Joris & Yin, 1992; Palmer, 1982), cochlear nucleus (Frisina et al., 1990; Rhode & Greenberg, 1994), SOC (Joris, 1996; Joris & Yin, 1995, 1998; Kuwada & Batra, 1999), IC (Batra, Kuwada, & Stanford, 1993; Langner & Schreiner, 1988; Rees & Møller, 1983), and auditory cortex (Eggermont, 1999; Schreiner & Urbas, 1988). These studies report modulation transfer functions (MTFs), which describe the magnitude of the response that is synchronized to the envelope of the stimulus as a function of frequency. At the level of the AN, neurons have low-pass MTFs, suggesting that the neurons follow the dynamics of the stimulus envelope for low frequencies and are limited in their ability to follow faster fluctuations (similar to their limited ability to follow the fine structure in the phase-locked responses to pure tones; Joris & Yin, 1992). At higher levels in the auditory pathway, many neurons have bandpass MTFs, suggesting that they are tuned to a specific range of modulation frequencies (e.g., Frisina et al., 1990; Langner & Schreiner, 1988). One interesting feature of neural responses to AM stimuli is their level-dependence, especially in the periphery; envelopes are well represented in the modulated discharge rates of AN fibers near threshold, but the responses saturate at higher levels (Joris & Yin, 1992). The representa-

tion of AM across a wide range of SPLs at higher levels in the pathway suggests that (a) information is encoded in AN responses at high SPLs, potentially in the details of the temporal response properties (e.g., nonlinear phase cues), and (b) that neural processing extracts this information into the form of the modulated rates seen at higher levels in the pathway.

Responses to Speech Sounds and Other Vocalizations

Communication sounds represent one of the most interesting classes of acoustic stimuli, but one of the most difficult to study (see Chap. 12, this volume). The use of communication sounds in species that have a limited repertoire of calls can provide an advantage; the specificity of the acoustic cues allows the investigator to zero in on important questions and look for specific processing mechanisms (e.g., bat echolocation, birdsong, frog mating calls). The study of human speech presents a challenge because of the huge diversity of stimuli. The complex acoustical properties of speech are made even more difficult to study by the fact that utterances that are perceived as being the same can have very different acoustical properties (the same problem is faced in automatic speech recognition.) The basic response properties of AN fibers to a wide range of speech sounds have been characterized (reviewed by Delgutte, 1982; May, Le Prell, Hienz, & Sachs, 1997; Sachs, 1984). Nonlinear cochlear amplification influences AN responses to speech sounds by enhancing the representations of spectral peaks, or formants, in the average discharge rate (e.g., Sachs, 1984) and in the temporal response properties, due to capture of synchrony (e.g., Wong, Miller, Calhoun, Sachs, & Young, 1998). The representation of simple speech sounds in terms of discharge rate is enhanced for some cell groups in the AVCN (e.g., May et al., 1997).

An ongoing series of studies of responses to vocalizations (Wang, 1998; Wang, Merzenich, Beitel, & Schreiner, 1995) has focused on the auditory cortex of the marmoset, which has a relatively large, but countable, set of communication sounds (Figure 9.27). These studies have quantitatively characterized the acoustic properties of the animal's vocalizations, and have then systematically studied the responses of neurons to actual vocalizations, as well as to prototypes and sounds that contain only certain temporal or spectral properties of the sounds. One of the most promising outcomes of this approach has been the discovery that mammalian cortical cells are much more responsive than was previously thought, as long as a suitably diverse (and appropriate) arsenal of stimuli are employed.

PHYSIOLOGY OF SPATIAL HEARING

Unlike vision and touch, for which spatial locations of stimuli are mapped directly onto the receptor arrays, the auditory system must compute the location of stimuli. The information provided for this task consists of the signals from the two ears, which are mapped onto the receptor array in terms of frequency, which is not (in general) correlated to spatial location. By comparing the sounds to the two ears, or by analyzing the profile of the spectrum at either (or both) ears, spatial location can be deduced for simple stimuli in simple acoustical environments. This section begins with a summary of the current knowledge of binaural physiology related to these simple cues and then briefly mentions some of the challenges that are faced as part of the problem of localization in realistic, reverberant environments.

The three primary stimulus features that provide information for localization are interaural time differences (ITDs), interaural level differences (ILDs), and spectral cues (discussed earlier). ITDs are the predominant cue for source azimuth at low frequencies, and the psychoacoustics and physiology of ITD sensitivity have been the subject of a great deal of study. Human listeners are sensitive to changes in ITD on the order of tens of microseconds (reviewed by Durlach & Colburn, 1978). In 1948, Jeffress proposed a neural model for ITD sensitivity that was based on neural delays and coincidence detection of signals from the two ears (Figure 9.28). This model has provided hypotheses for a large number of physiological, anatomical, and behavioral experiments over the last

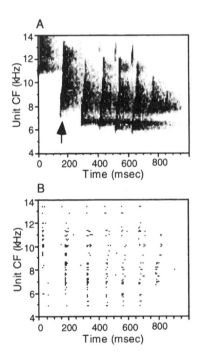

Figure 9.27   Auditory cortex response to a vocalization.
NOTE: A) Spectrogram of a marmoset twitter call. B) Population response from 100 auditory cortex (AI) cells, plotted in 2 ms bins along the time axis. Both temporal and spectral features of the call are represented in the population response.
SOURCE: Reproduced with permission from Wang (1998). Copyright © 1998 by Whurr Publishers Ltd.

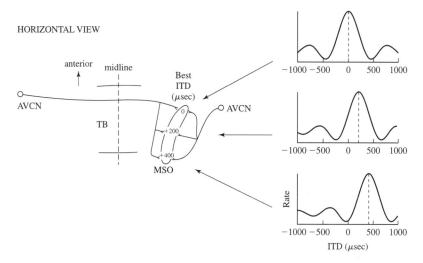

HORIZONTAL VIEW

Figure 9.28 Illustration of the anatomical features and basic physiological responses associated with the Jeffress (1948) model.

NOTE: Monaural channels feed into a binaural processor consisting of a bank of cross-correlators that each tap the signal at a different ITD. The contralateral signals arrive with different neural delays, due to the delay line configuration of the axon. There is no apparent delay line on the ipsilateral side, unlike the configuration in Jeffress's original model (Overholt, Rubel, & Hyson, 1992; Smith et al., 1993; Beckius et al., 1999). Cells respond maximally to stimuli with interaural delays (ITDs) that are exactly offset by the neural delays. ITD is mapped out along the length of the MSO in cats (Yin & Chan, 1990) and chicks (Overholt et al., 1992). In owls the ITDs are reported to be mapped across the width of the MSO (Carr & Konishi, 1990).

SOURCE: Figure provided by P. X. Joris, after Joris et al. (1998). Reprinted with permission.

50 years, most of which provide general support for the mechanism of binaural coincidence detection (or, more generally, cross-correlation) in the MSO (e.g., Beckius et al., 1999; Carr & Konishi, 1990; Goldberg & Brown, 1969; Overholt et al., 1992; Smith et al., 1993; Yin & Chan, 1990; reviewed by Kuwada & Yin, 1997; Joris, Smith, & Yin, 1998).

MSO cells are classically described as EE, receiving excitatory inputs from bushy cells in the AVCN of both sides. Their exquisite sensitivity to interaural times (on the order of tens of μ-s, times much smaller than the duration of the input action potentials) can be explained by the nonlinear membrane properties of these cells (Smith, 1995). A slow, low-threshold K+ channel (similar to that de-

scribed in AVCN bushy cells; Manis & Marx, 1991), which is partially open at rest, is further activated by an excitatory input. In response to a subthreshold input, the activation of the slow, low-threshold K+ channel results in a drop in the membrane resistance, which lasts for a relatively long time due to the long time-constant of the channel. A subsequent input is thus not able to depolarize the cell. The only event that can result in depolarizing the cell to threshold is the coincident arrival of excitatory inputs that act together before the low-threshold K+ channel has a chance to drop the membrane resistance (reviewed by Trussell, 1999).

Recent studies of ITD sensitivity, both in the MSO and at the level of the IC, have begun to explore the role of inhibitory inputs to these cells (Grothe & Park, 1998). Physiologically based models for sound localization based on ITD have also gone beyond the original Jeffress model to incorporate inhibitory inputs at the level of the MSO (Brughera, Stutman, Carney, & Colburn, 1996), as well as higher-order binaural processing involving the DNLL and IC (Cai, Carney, & Colburn, 1998a, 1998b). Finally, although sensitivity to ITDs is primarily associated with low-frequency processing, subjects are also sensitive to ITDs of the envelopes of complex high-frequency sounds (e.g., Henning, 1974). Physiological studies of ITD sensitivity in the high-frequency regions of the LSO demonstrate that these cells are sensitive to ITDs. This sensitivity is related to their sensitivity to dynamic ILDs, which are created by the envelope ITDs (Joris & Yin, 1995).

ILDs are a major cue for localization of high-frequency sounds (discussed earlier). The LSO, which is biased toward high frequencies, has long been associated with establishing the sensitivity to ILDs by comparison of the excitatory input from the ipsilateral AVCN and inhibitory input (via the MNTB) from the contralateral AVCN (reviewed by Irvine 1986, 1992). For this mechanism to apply over a wide range of sound levels, these cells must depend strongly on the rate information that is initially provided by nonsaturating AN fibers (discussed earlier).

Responses of neurons in the IC and MGB to ITDs and ILDs reflect, in general, the first-order binaural process that occurs in the brainstem, with some sharpening of the representation occurring at higher levels (e.g., Ivarsson, de Ribaupierre, & de Ribaupierre, 1988; Stanford, Kuwada, & Batra, 1992). However, there are cases for which it is clear that further binaural processing, in particular convergence across cells tuned to different ITDs, must occur above the level of the SOC (Kuwada, Stanford, & Batra, 1987; McAlpine, Jiang, & Palmer, 1998).

A separate pathway has been indicated for the processing of spectral cues. The response properties of type IV cells in the DCN (see Figure 9.24) led to the hypothesis that the responses of these cells represent the spectral notches associated with monaural spectral cues (e.g., Young, Spirou, Rice, & Voigt, 1992). These cells are inhibited by spectral notches near CF (Imig, Bibikov, Poirier, & Samson, 2000; Joris, 1998; Nelken & Young, 1994; Spirou & Young, 1991). Behavioral studies involving lesions of the dorsal acoustic stria (the output pathway of the DCN) show little deficit in discrimination of sounds on the vertical meridian, for which spectral cues are most important (Sutherland, Glendenning, & Masterton, 1998). However, this lesion does affect an animal's ability to orient toward sounds in this plane (Sutherland, Masterton, & Glendenning, 1998), suggesting that other pathways may be able to analyze the spectral cues but that the DCN is involved in the orientation response.

Physiological studies of spatial hearing at higher levels of the pathway have explored interactions between the different components of these three spatial cues. Although the cues can be independently manipulated using stimuli delivered over headphones, the three cues covary for free-field stimuli. Using recordings of spectral cues in the ear canal of the cat (e.g., Musicant, Chang, & Hind, 1990), and by manipulating the ITDs, ILDs, and spectral profiles, the relative contributions of these cues to the responses of IC neurons have been investigated (e.g., Delgutte, Joris, Litovsky, & Yin, 1999). The spatial tuning of MGB and cortical neurons has also been studied with wideband free-field stimuli that include combinations of localization cues (e.g., Brugge et al., 1994; Imig, Poirier, Irons, & Samson, 1997; Samson, Clarey, Barone, & Imig, 1993). A recent study involving a combination of neuroanatomical and physiological techniques described separate (but interacting) pathways for "what" and "where" processing in the auditory cortex (Romanski et al., 1999); these pathways were compared to similar dual-stream organization of the visual and somatosensory cortical pathways. The temporal response patterns of cortical neurons to free-field sounds may also contribute to encoding of spatial position in terms of discharge rate, particularly in cells with "panoramic" responses to stimuli from all directions (Middlebrooks, Clock, Xu, & Green, 1994).

The spatial cues of ITDs and ILDs and spectral cues provide straightforward information about azimuth and elevation of a sound source in a simple, anechoic (echo-free) environment. However, in a realistic environment that contains multiple sound sources and reverberations, these cues are highly distorted. However, the most realistic percepts of space are achieved by simulating reverberant sound fields. The auditory system must do much more than simply compute time and level differences, or detect spectral peaks and notches, in order to localize stimuli in reverberant environments. Suppression of echoes (which is one aspect of the precedence effect; e.g. Blauert, 1997; Litovsky, Colburn, Yost, & Guzman, 1999) by mechanisms such as long-duration inhibition is believed to play an important role in processing complex acoustical environments (e.g., Fitzpatrick, Kuwada, Kim, Parham, & Batra, 1999; Litovsky & Yin, 1998a, 1998b).

FUTURE CHALLENGES

This review has focused on several areas that either are new or have received increasing attention in the years since the last edition of this handbook was published. It is interesting to consider the areas that might be the focus of a future review of this nature. Three areas come to mind:

First, the relationships between physiological response properties and psychophysics and behavior have been based on a combination of lesion studies and comparison of the physiological responses and psychophysical performance. For the most part, the latter have been limited to simple stimuli and simple psychophysical tasks, partly because of the daunting problem of recording or simulating neural population responses to complex sounds. Furthermore, the most interesting difficulties for the impaired auditory system are with complex stimuli, especially in situations in which noise maskers are present. New computational tools for simulating neural responses and for quantifying information in population responses should allow great progress on this front in the next few years.

A related challenge is in developing a better understanding of the active process in the cochlea and how it is involved in encoding complex stimuli. Improved techniques for measuring and imaging the motion of the basilar membrane should allow tests for different hypotheses concerning the electromechanical mechanisms involved in the cochlear amplifier. These tests will allow a clearer picture of the influence of the active process on responses of AN fibers and thus of its impact on encoding complex sounds. Again, it is for complex sounds that the benefits of the cochlear amplifier seem to be most important, as it is these stimuli that present the greatest difficulties for hard-of-hearing listeners in whom the active process is damaged.

Finally, the role of the descending auditory pathways will be an important area for progress in the next few years. The use of awake and behaving animals provides an experimental approach to probing this system, which appears to be as complex as the ascending pathways. The influence of the descending pathways on information processing at all levels of the auditory pathway and their interaction with the active process in the cochlea are important areas for future study.

REFERENCES

Adams, J. C. (1983). Cytology of periolivary cells and the organization of their projections in the cat. *Journal of Comparative Neurology, 215,* 275–289.

Adams, J. C. (1997). Projections from octopus cells of the posteroventral cochlear nucleus to the ventral nucleus of the lateral lemniscus in cat and human. *Auditory Neuroscience, 3,* 335–350.

Adams, J. C., & Mugnaini, E. (1990). Immunocytochemical evidence for inhibitory and disinhibitory circuits in the superior olive. *Hearing Research, 49,* 281–298.

Aitkin, L. M., Anderson, D. J., & Brugge, J. F. (1970). Tonotopic organization and discharge characteristics of single neurons in nuclei of the lateral lemniscus of the cat. *Journal of Neurophysiology, 33,* 421–440.

Aitkin, L. M., Dickhaus, H., Schult, W., & Zimmerman, M. (1978). External nucleus of the inferior colliculus: Auditory and spinal somatosensory afferents and their interactions. *Journal of Neurophysiology, 41,* 837–847.

Aitkin, L. M., & Dunlop, C. W. (1968). Interplay of excitation and inhibition in the cat medial geniculate body. *Journal of Neurophysiology, 31,* 44–61.

Aitkin, L. M., & Webster, W. R. (1972). Medial geniculate body of the cat: Organization and responses to tonal stimuli of neurons in ventral division. *Journal of Neurophysiology, 35,* 365–380.

Aitkin, L. M., Webster, W. R., Veale, J. L., & Crosby, D. C. (1975). Inferior colliculus: I. Comparison of response properties of neurons in central, pericentral, and external nuclei of adult cat. *Journal of Neurophysiology, 38,* 1196–1207.

Anderson, D. J., Rose, J. E., Hind, J. E., & Brugge, J. F. (1971). Temporal position of discharges in single auditory nerve fibers within the cycle of a sinewave stimulus: Frequency and intensity effects. *Journal of the Acoustical Society of America, 49,* 1131–1139.

Anderson, R. A., Knight, P. L., & Merzenich, M. M. (1980). The thalamocortical and corticothalamic connections of AI, AII, and the anterior auditory field (AAF) in the cat: Evidence for two largely segregated systems of connections. *Journal of Comparative Neurology, 194,* 663–701.

Art, J. J., Crawford, A. C., & Fettiplace, R. (1986). Electrical resonance and membrane currents in turtle cochlear hair cells. *Hearing Research, 22,* 31–36.

Arthur, R. M., Pfeiffer, R. R., & Suga, N. (1971). Properties of "two-tone inhibition" in primary auditory neurones. *Journal of Physiology, 212,* 593–609.

Ashmore, J., & Geleoc, G. S. (1999). Cochlear function: Hearing in the fast lane. *Current Biology, 9,* 572–574.

Batra, R., Kuwada, S., & Stanford, T. R. (1993). Temporal coding of envelopes and their interaural delays in the inferior colliculus of the unanesthetized rabbit. *Journal of Neurophysiology, 61,* 257–268.

Batteau, D. W. (1967). The role of the pinna in human localization. *Proceedings of the Royal Society of London B, 168,* 158–180.

Beckius, G. E., Batra, R., & Oliver, D. L. (1999). Axons from anteroventral cochlear nucleus that terminate in medial superior olive of cat: Observations related to delay lines. *Journal of Neuroscience, 19,* 3146–3161.

Blackburn, C. C., & Sachs, M. B. (1989). Classification of unit types in the anteroventral cochlear nucleus: PST histograms and regulatory analysis. *Journal of Neurophysiology, 62,* 1303–1329.

Blauert, J. (1969). Sound localization in the median plane. *Acustica, 22,* 205–213.

Blauert, J. (1997). *Spatial hearing: The psychophysics of human sound localization* (Rev. ed.). Cambridge: MIT Press.

Brownell, W. E., Bader, C. R., Bertrand, D., & de Ribaupierre, Y. (1985). Evoked mechanical responses of isolated cochlear outer hair cells. *Science, 227,* 194–196.

Brugge, J. F., Anderson, D. J., & Aitkin, L. M. (1970). Responses of neurons in the dorsal nucleus of the lateral lemniscus to binaural tonal stimulation. *Journal of Neurophysiology, 33,* 441–458.

Brugge, J. F., Reale, R. A., Hind, J. E., Chan, J. C., Musicant, A. D., & Poon, P. W. (1994). Simulation of free-field sound sources and its application to studies of cortical mechanisms of sound localization in the cat. *Hearing Research, 73,* 67–84.

Brughera, A., Stutman, E., Carney, L. H., & Colburn, H. S. (1996). A model with excitation and inhibition for cells in the medial superior olive. *Auditory Neuroscience, 2,* 219–233.

Buser, P., & Imbert, M. (1992). *Audition* (R. H. Kay, Trans.). Cambridge: MIT Press.

Cai, H., Carney, L. H., & Colburn, H. S. (1998a). A model for binaural response properties of inferior colliculus neurons: I. A model with ITD-sensitive excitatory and inhibitory inputs. *Journal of the Acoustical Society of America, 103,* 475–493.

Cai, H., Carney, L. H., & Colburn, H. S. (1998b). A model for binaural response properties of inferior colliculus neurons: II. A model with ITD-sensitive excitatory and inhibitory inputs and an adaptation mechanism. *Journal of the Acoustical Society of America, 103,* 494–506.

Calford, M. B., & Webster, W. R. (1981). Auditory representation within principal division of cat medial geniculate body: An electrophysiological study. *Journal of Neurophysiology, 45,* 1013–1028.

Cant, N. B. (1992). The cochlear nucleus: Neuronal types and their synaptic organization. In D. B. Webster, A. N. Popper, & R. R. Fay (Eds.), *The mammalian auditory pathway: Neuroanatomy* (pp. 66–116). New York: Springer.

Cant, N. B., & Casseday, J. H. (1986). Projections from the anteroventral cochlear nucleus to the lateral and medial superior olivary nuclei. *Journal of Comparative Neurology, 247,* 457–476.

Cant, N. B., & Hyson, R. L. (1992). Projections from the lateral nucleus of the trapezoid body to the medial superior olivary nucleus in the gerbil. *Hearing Research, 58,* 26–34.

Carlile, S., & Pettigrew, A. G. (1987). Distribution of frequency sensitivity in the superior colliculus

of the guinea pig. *Hearing Research, 31,* 123–136.

Carney, L. H. (1990). Sensitivities of cells in the anteroventral cochlear nucleus of cat to spatio-temporal discharge patterns across primary afferents. *Journal of Neurophysiology, 64,* 437–456.

Carney, L. H. (1994). Spatiotemporal encoding of sound level: Models for normal encoding and recruitment of loudness. *Hearing Research, 76,* 31–44.

Carney, L. H. (1999). Temporal response properties of neurons in the auditory pathway. *Current Opinions in Neurobiology, 9,* 442–446.

Carney, L. H., & Burock, M. A. (1997). Encoding of sound level by discharge rates of auditory neurons. *Comments on Theoretical Biology, 4,* 315–337.

Carney, L. H., McDuffy, M. J., & Shekhter, I. (1999). Frequency glides in the impulse responses of auditory-nerve fibers. *Journal of the Acoustical Society of America, 105,* 2384–2391.

Carney, L. H., & Yin, T. C. T. (1988). Temporal coding of resonances by low-frequency auditory nerve fibers: Single fiber responses and a population model. *Journal of Neurophysiology, 60,* 1653–1677.

Carr, C. E., & Konishi, M. (1990). A circuit for detection of interaural time differences in the brain stem of the barn owl. *Journal of Neuroscience, 10,* 3227–3246.

Cheatham, M. A., & Dallos, P. (1998). The level dependence of response phase: Observations from cochlear hair cells. *Journal of the Acoustical Society of America, 104,* 356–369.

Chowdhury, S. A., & Suga, N. (2000). Reorganization of the frequency map of the auditory cortex evoked by cortical electrical stimulation in the big brown bat. *Journal of Neurophysiology, 83,* 1856–1863.

Clarey, J. C., Barone, P., & Imig, T. J. (1992). Physiology of thalamus and cortex. In A. N. Popper & R. R. Fay (Eds.), *The mammalian auditory pathway: Neurophysiology* (pp. 232–334). New York: Springer.

Colburn, H. S. (1981). Intensity perception: Relation of intensity discrimination to auditory-nerve firing patterns. Internal Memorandum, Research Laboratory of Electronics, Massachusetts Institute of Technology, Cambridge.

Colburn, H. S., Carney, L. H., & Heinz, M. G. (2001). *Quantifying the information in auditory-nerve responses for level discrimination.* Manuscript submitted for publication.

Cooper, N. P. (1996). Two-tone suppression in cochlear mechanics. *Journal of the Acoustical Society of America, 99,* 3087–3098.

Cooper, N. P., Robertson, D., & Yates, G. K. (1993). Cochlear nerve fiber responses to amplitude-modulated stimuli: Variations with spontaneous rate and other response characteristics. *Journal of Neurophysiology, 70,* 370–386.

Costalupes, J. A., Young, E. D., & Gibson, D. J. (1984). Effects of continuous noise backgrounds on rate response of auditory nerve fibers in cat. *Journal of Neurophysiology, 51,* 1326–1344.

Crawford, A. C., & Fettiplace, R. (1981). An electrical tuning mechanism in turtle cochlear hair cells. *Journal of Physiology (London), 312,* 377–412.

Crawford, A. C., & Fettiplace, R. (1985). The mechanical properties of ciliary bundles of turtle cochlear hair cells. *Journal of Physiology (London), 364,* 359–379.

Dallos, P., & Evans, B. N. (1995). High-frequency motility of outer hair cells and the cochlear amplifier. *Science, 267,* 2006–2009.

Davis, H. (1983). An active process in cochlear mechanics. *Hearing Research, 9,* 79–90.

de Boer, E. (1991). Auditory physics: III. Physical principles in hearing theory. *Physics Reports (Review Section of Physics Letters), 203,* 125–231.

de Boer, E., & de Jongh, H. R. (1978). On cochlear encoding: Potentialities and limitations of the reverse correlation technique. *Journal of the Acoustical Society of America, 63,* 115–135.

de Boer, E., & Nuttall, A. L. (1997). The mechanical waveform of the basilar membrane: I. Frequency modulations ("glides") in impulse responses and cross-correlation functions. *Journal of the Acoustical Society of America, 101,* 3583–3592.

Delgutte, B. (1982). Some correlates of phonetic distinctions at the level of the auditory nerve. In R. Carlson & B. Granstrom (Eds.), *The representation of speech in the peripheral auditory system* (pp. 131–149). Amsterdam: Elsevier.

Delgutte, B. (1987). Peripheral auditory processing of speech information: Implications from a physiological study of intensity discrimination. In M. E. H. Schouten (Ed.), *The psychophysics of speech perception* (pp. 333–353). Dordrecht, Netherlands: Nijhoff.

Delgutte, B. (1990). Two-tone rate suppression in auditory nerve fibers: Dependence on suppression frequency and level. *Hearing Research, 49,* 225–246.

Delgutte, B. (1996). Physiological models for basic auditory percepts. In H. L. Hawkins, T. A. McMullen, A. N. Popper, & R. R. Fay (Eds.), *Auditory computation* (pp. 157–220). New York: Springer.

Delgutte, B., Joris, P. X., Litovsky, R. Y., & Yin, T. C. T. (1999). Receptive fields and binaural interactions for virtual-space stimuli in the cat inferior colliculus. *Journal of Neurophysiology, 81,* 2833–2851.

Diamond, I. T., Jones, E. G., & Powell, T. P. S. (1969). The projection of the auditory cortex upon the diencephalon and brain stem of the cat. *Brain Research, 15,* 305–340.

Dolan, D. F., Guo, M. H., & Nuttall, A. L. (1997). Frequency-dependent enhancement of basilar membrane velocity during olivocochlear bundle stimulation. *Journal of the Acoustical Society of America, 102,* 3587–3596.

Durlach, N. I., & Colburn, H. S. (1978). Binaural phenomena. In E. C. Carterette & M. P. Friedman (Eds.), *Handbook of perception: Vol. 4. Hearing* (pp. 365–466). New York: Academic Press.

Edwards, S. B., Ginsburg, C. L., Henkel, C. K., & Stein, B. E. (1979). Sources of subcortical projections to the superior colliculus in the cat. *Journal of Comparative Neurology, 184,* 309–330.

Evans, E. F. (1975). Cochlear nerve and cochlear nucleus. In W. D. Keidel and W. D. Neff (Eds.), *Handbook of sensory physiology,* Vol. 5,

Auditory system, part 2, *Physiology (CNS), behavioral studies, psychoacoustics* (pp. 1–108). Berlin: Springer.

Eggermont, J. J. (1999). The magnitude and phase of temporal modulation transfer functions in cat auditory cortex. *Journal of Neuroscience, 19,* 2780–2788.

Eggermont, J. J. (2000). Sound-induced synchronization of neural activity between and within three auditory cortical areas. *Journal of Neurophysiology, 83,* 2708–2722.

Feliciano, M., Saldaña, E., & Mugnaini, E. (1995). Direct projections from the rat primary auditory neocortex to nucleus sagulum, paralemniscal regions, superior olivary complex and cochlear nuclei. *Auditory Neuroscience, 1,* 287–308.

Fettiplace, R., & Fuchs, P. A. (1999). Mechanisms of hair cell tuning. *Annual Review of Physiology, 61,* 809–834.

Fitzpatrick, D. C., Kuwada, S., Kim, D. O., Parham, K., & Batra, R. (1999). Responses of neurons to click-pairs as simulated echoes: Auditory nerve to auditory cortex. *Journal of the Acoustical Society of America, 106,* 3460–3472.

Frank, G., Hemmert, W., & Gummer, A. W. (1999). Limiting dynamics of high-frequency electromechanical transduction of outer hair cells. *Proceedings of the National Academy of Sciences USA, 96,* 4420–4425.

Freedman, E. G., & Sparks, D. L. (1997). Activity of cells in the deeper layers of the superior colliculus of the rhesus monkey: Evidence for a gaze displacement command. *Journal of Neurophysiology, 78,* 1669–1690.

Freeman, D. M., & Weiss, T. F. (1990). Hydrodynamic analysis of a two-dimensional model for micromechanical resonance of free-standing hair bundles. *Hearing Research, 48,* 37–67.

Frisina, R. D., Smith, R. L., & Chamberlain, S. C. (1990). Encoding of amplitude modulation in the gerbil cochlear nuclei: I. A hierarchy of enhancement. *Hearing Research, 44,* 99–122.

Galambos, R., Rose, J. E., Bromiley, R. B., & Hughes, J. R. (1952). Microelectrode studies on medial geniculate body of cat: II. Responses to clicks. *Journal of Neurophysiology, 15,* 359–380.

Geisler, C. D., & Rhode, W. S. (1982). The phases of basilar-membrane vibrations. *Journal of the Acoustical Society of America, 71,* 1201–1203.

Gifford, M. L., & Guinan, J. J., Jr. (1983). Effects of crossed olivocochlear bundle stimulation on cat auditory-nerve fiber responses to tones. *Journal of the Acoustical Society of America, 74,* 115–123.

Gleich, O., & Narins, P. M. (1988). The phase response of primary auditory afferents in a songbird (*Sturnus vulgaris* L.). *Hearing Research, 32,* 81–92.

Glendenning, K. K., Baker, B. N., Hutson, K. A., & Masterton, R. B. (1992). Acoustic chiasm V: Inhibition and excitation in the ipsilateral and contralateral projections of LSO. *Journal of Comparative Neurology, 319,* 100–122.

Glendenning, K. K., & Masterton, R. B. (1998). Comparative morphometry of mammalian central auditory systems: Variation in nuclei and form of the ascending system. *Brain, Behavior, and Evolution, 51,* 59–89.

Goldberg, J. M., & Brown, P. B. (1969). Response of binaural neurons of dog superior olivary complex to dichotic tonal stimuli: Some physiological mechanisms of sound localization. *Journal of Neurophysiology, 32,* 613–636.

Goldstein, M. H., Jr., & Knight, P. L. (1980). Comparative organization of mammalian auditory cortex. In A. N. Popper & R. R. Fay (Eds.), *Comparative studies of hearing in vertebrates* (pp. 375–398). New York: Springer.

Grothe, B., & Park, T. J. (1998). Sensitivity to interaural time differences in the medial superior olive of a small mammal, the Mexican free-tailed bat. *Journal of Neuroscience, 18,* 6608–6622.

Guinan, J. J., Jr., & Gifford, M. L. (1988). Effects of electrical stimulation of efferent olivocochlear neurons on cat auditory-nerve fibers: III. Tuning curves and thresholds at CF. *Hearing Research, 37,* 29–45.

Guinan, J. J., Jr., Norris, B. E., & Guinan, S. S. (1972). Single auditory units in the superior olivary complex: I. Responses to sounds and classifications based on physiological response properties. *International Journal of Neuroscience, 4,* 101–120.

Guinan, J. J., Jr., & Stankovic, K. M. (1996). Medial efferent inhibition produces the largest equivalent attenuations at moderate to high sound levels in cat auditory-nerve fibers. *Journal of the Acoustical Society of America, 100,* 1680–1690.

Gulick, W. L., Gescheider, G. A., & Frisina, R. D. (1989). *Hearing: Physiological acoustics, neural coding, and psychoacoustics.* New York: Oxford University Press.

Harrison, J. M., & Feldman, M. L. (1970). Anatomical aspects of the cochlear nucleus and the superior olivary complex. In W. D. Neff (Ed.), *Contributions to sensory physiology: Vol. 4* (pp. 95–142). New York: Academic Press.

Harrison, J. M., & Howe, M. E. (1974). Anatomy of the descending auditory system (mammalian). In W. D. Keidel, W. D. Neff (Eds.), *Handbook of sensory physiology: Vol. 5. Auditory system Part I. Anatomy, physiology (ear)* (pp. 364–388). New York: Springer.

Hausler, U. H., Sullivan, W. E., Soares, D., & Carr, C. E. (1999). A morphological study of the cochlear nuclei of the pigeon (Columba livia). *Brain, Behavior and Evolution, 54,* 290–302.

Heil, P., Rajan, R., & Irvine, D. R. F. (1994). Topographic representation of tone intensity along the isofrequency axis of cat primary auditory cortex. *Hearing Research, 76,* 188–202.

Heinz, M. G., Colburn, H. S., & Carney, L. H. (2001a). Rate and timing cues associated with the cochlear amplifier: Level discrimination based on monaural cross-frequency coincidence detection. *Journal of the Acoustical Society of America, 110,* 2065–2084.

Heinz, M. G., Colburn, H. S., & Carney, L. H. (2001b). Evaluating auditory performance limits: I. One-parameter discrimination using a computational model for the auditory nerve. *Neural Computation, 13,* 2273–2316.

Hemila, S., Nummela, S., & Rueter, T. (1995). What middle ear parameters tell about impedance matching and high frequency hearing. *Hearing Research, 85,* 31–44.

Henkel, C. K., & Spangler, K. M. (1983). Organization of the efferent projections of the medial superior olivary nucleus in the cat as revealed by HRP and autoradiographic tracing methods. *Journal of Comparative Neurology, 221,* 416–428.

Henning, G. B. (1974). Detectability of interaural delay in high-frequency complex waveforms. *Journal of the Acoustical Society of America, 55,* 84–90.

Hirsch, J. A., Chan, J. C. K., & Yin, T. C. T. (1985). Responses of neurons in the cat's superior colliculus to acoustic stimuli: I. Monaural and binaural response properties. *Journal of Neurophysiology, 53,* 726–745.

Horst, J. W., Javel, E., & Farley, G. R. (1985). Extraction and enhancement of spectral structure by the cochlea. *Journal of the Acoustical Society of America, 78,* 1898–1901.

Huang, G. T., Rosowski, J. J., & Peake, W. T. (2000). Relating middle-ear acoustic performance to body size in the cat family: Measurements and models. *Journal of Comparative Physiology [A], 186,* 447–465.

Huerta, M. F., & Harting, J. K. (1984). The mammalian superior colliculus: Studies of its morphology and connections. In H. Vanegas (Ed.), *Comparative neurology of the optic tectum* (pp. 687–773). New York: Plenum.

Huffman, R. F., & Henson, O. W., Jr. (1990). The descending auditory pathway and acousticomotor systems: Connections with the inferior colliculus. *Brain Research Reviews, 15,* 295–323.

Imig, T. J., Bibikov, N. G., Poirier, P., & Samson, F. K. (2000). Directionality derived from pinna-cue spectral notches in cat dorsal cochlear nucleus. *Journal of Neurophysiology, 83,* 907–925.

Imig, T. J., & Morel, A. (1985a). Tonotopic organization in ventral nucleus of medial geniculate body in the cat. *Journal of Neurophysiology, 53,* 309–340.

Imig, T. J., & Morel, A. (1985b). Tonotopic organization in lateral part of posterior group of thalamic nuclei in the cat. *Journal of Neurophysiology, 53,* 836–851.

Imig, T. J., Poirier, P., Irons, W. A., & Samson, F. K. (1997). Monaural spectral contrast mechanism for neural sensitivity to sound direction in the medial geniculate body of the cat. *Journal of Neurophysiology, 78,* 2754–2771.

Irvine, D. R. F. (1986). *The auditory brainstem: A review of the structure and function of the auditory brainstem processing mechanisms.* In D. Ottoson (Ed.), *Progress in sensory physiology: Vol. 7* (pp. 1–279). Berlin: Springer.

Irvine, D. R. F. (1992). Physiology of the auditory brainstem. In A. N. Popper & R. R. Fay (Eds.), *The mammalian auditory pathway: Neurophysiology* (pp. 153–231). New York: Springer.

Irvine, D. R. F., & Gago, G. (1990). Binaural interaction in high-frequency neurons in inferior colliculus of the cat: Effects of variation in sound pressure level on sensitivity to interaural intensity differences. *Journal of Neurophysiology, 63,* 570–591.

Ivarsson, C., de Ribaupierre, Y., & de Ribaupierre, F. (1988). Influence of auditory localization cues on neuronal activity in the auditory thalamus of the cat. *Journal of Neurophysiology, 59,* 586–606.

Javel, E. (1986). Basic response properties of auditory nerve fibers. In R. A. Altschuler, D. W. Hoffman, & R. P. Bobbin (Eds.), *Neurobiology of hearing: The cochlea* (pp. 213–245). New York: Raven Press.

Jay, M. F., & Sparks, D. L. (1984). Auditory receptive fields in primate superior colliculus shift with changes in eye position. *Nature (London), 309,* 345–347.

Jeffress, L. A. (1948). A place theory of sound localization. *Journal of Comparative Physiology and Psychology, 41,* 35–39.

Johnson, D. H. (1980). The relationship between spike rate and synchrony in responses of auditory-nerve fibers to single tones. *Journal of the Acoustical Society of America, 68,* 1115–1122.

Johnstone, B. M., Patuzzi, R., & Yates, G. K. (1986). Basilar membrane measurements and the travelling wave. *Hearing Research, 22,* 147–153.

Joris, P. X. (1996). Envelope coding in the lateral superior olive: II. Characteristic delays and comparison with responses in the medial superior olive. *Journal of Neurophysiology, 76,* 2137–2156.

Joris, P. X. (1998). Response classes in the dorsal cochlear nucleus and its output tract in the chloralose-anesthetized cat. *Journal of Neuroscience, 18,* 3955–3966.

Joris, P. X., Carney, L. H., Smith, P. H., & Yin, T. C. T. (1994). Enhancement of neural synchronization in the anteroventral cochlear nucleus: I. Responses to tones at the characteristic frequency. *Journal of Neurophysiology, 71,* 1022–1036.

Joris, P. X., Smith, P. H., & Yin, T. C. T. (1994). Enhancement of neural synchronization in the anteroventral cochlear nucleus: II. Responses in the tuning curve tail. *Journal of Neurophysiology, 71,* 1037–1051.

Joris, P. X., Smith, P. H., & Yin, T. C. T. (1998). Coincidence detection in the auditory system: 50 years after Jeffress. *Neuron, 21,* 1235–1238.

Joris, P. X., & Yin, T. C. T. (1992). Responses to amplitude-modulated tones in the auditory nerve of the cat. *Journal of the Acoustical Society of America, 91,* 215–232.

Joris, P. X., & Yin, T. C. T. (1995). Envelope coding in the lateral superior olive: I. Sensitivity to interaural time differences. *Journal of Neurophysiology, 73,* 1043–1062.

Joris, P. X., & Yin, T. C. T. (1998). Envelope coding in the lateral superior olive: III. Comparison with afferent pathways. *Journal of Neurophysiology, 79,* 253–269.

Kanaseki, T., & Sprague, J. M. (1974). Anatomical organization of pretectal nuclei and tectal laminae in the cat. *Journal of Comparative Neurology, 158,* 319–338.

Kelly, J. B. (1997). Contribution of the dorsal nucleus of the lateral lemniscus to binaural processing in the auditory brainstem. In J. Syka (Ed.), *Acoustical signal processing in the central auditory system* (pp. 329–352). New York: Plenum.

Kelly, J. B., & Wong, D. (1981). Laminar connections of the cat's auditory cortex. *Brain Research, 212,* 1–15.

Kemp, D. T., (1978). Stimulated acoustic emission from within the human auditory system. *Journal of the Acoustical Society of America, 64,* 1386–1391.

Kiang, N. Y. S. (1984). Peripheral neural processing of auditory information. In I. Darian-Smith (Ed.), *Handbook of physiology (Section 1: The Nervous System): Vol. 3. Sensory Processes (Part 2)* (pp. 639–674). Bethesda: American Physiological Society.

Kiang, N. Y. S., & Moxon, E. C. (1978). Tails of tuning curves of auditory-nerve fibers. *Journal of the Acoustical Society of America, 55,* 620–630.

King, A. J., & Palmer, A. R. (1983). Cells responsive to free-field auditory stimuli in guinea-pig superior colliculus: Distribution and response properties. *Journal of Physiology, 342,* 361–381.

Knudsen, E. I. (1987). Neural derivation of sound source location in the barn owl: An example of a computational map. *Annals of the New York Academy of Science, 510,* 33–38.

Knudsen, E. I., & Knudsen, P. F. (1983). Space-mapped auditory projections from the inferior colliculus to the optic tectum in the barn owl (*Tyto alba*). *Journal of Comparative Neurology, 218,* 187–196.

Koppl, C. (1997). Phase locking to high frequencies in the auditory nerve and cochlear nucleus magnocellularis of the barn owl, *Tyto alba. Journal of Neuroscience, 17,* 3312–3321.

Kudo, M., & Niimi, K. (1980). Ascending projections of the inferior colliculus in the cat: An autoradiographic study. *Journal of Comparative Neurology, 191,* 545–556.

Kuhn, G. F. (1987). Physical acoustics and measurements pertaining to directional hearing. In W. A. Yost & G. Gourevitch (Eds.), *Directional hearing* (pp. 3–25). New York: Springer.

Kuwada, S., & Batra, R. (1999) Coding of sound envelopes by inhibitory rebound in neurons of the superior olivary complex in unanesthetized rabbit. *Journal of Neuroscience, 19,* 2273–2287.

Kuwada, S., Stanford, T. R., & Batra, R. (1987). Interaural phase-sensitive units in the inferior colliculus of the uanesthetized rabbit: Effects of changing frequency. *Journal of Neurophysiology, 57,* 1338–1360.

Kuwada, S., & Yin, T. C. T. (1987). Physiological studies of directional hearing. In W. A. Yost & G. Gourevitch (Eds.), *Directional hearing* (pp. 146–176). New York: Springer.

Kuwada, S., Yin, T. C. T., Syka, J., Buunen, T. J. F., & Wickesberg, R. E. (1984) Binaural interaction in low-frequency neurons in inferior colliculus of the cat: IV. Comparison of monaural and binaural response properties. *Journal of Neurophysiology, 51,* 1306–1325.

Langner, G., & Schreiner, C. E. (1988). Periodicity coding in the inferior colliculus of the cat: I. Neuronal mechanisms. *Journal of Neurophysiology, 60,* 1799–1822.

Liberman, M. C. (1978). Auditory-nerve responses from cats raised in a low-noise chamber. *Journal of the Acoustical Society of America, 63,* 442–455.

Lindsay, P. H., & Norman, D. A. (1977). *Human information processing: An introduction to psychology* (2nd ed.). Orlando, FL: Academic Press.

Litovsky, R. Y., Colburn, H. S., Yost, W. A., Guzman, S. J. (1999). The precedence effect. *Journal of the Acoustical Society of America, 106,* 1633–1654.

Litovsky, R. Y., & Yin, T. C. T. (1998a). Physiological studies of the precedence effect in the inferior colliculus of the cat: I. Correlates of psychophysics. *Journal of Neurophysiology, 80,* 1285–1301.

Litovsky, R. Y., & Yin, T. C. T. (1998b). Physiological studies of the precedence effect in the inferior colliculus of the cat: II. Neural mechanisms. *Journal of Neurophysiology, 80,* 1302–1316.

Lonsbury-Martin, B. L., Martin, G. K., McCoy, M. J., & Whitehead, M. L. (1995). New approaches to the evaluation of the auditory system and a current analysis of otoacoustic emissions. *Otolaryngology: Head and Neck Surgery, 112,* 50–63.

Manis, P. B., & Marx, S. O. (1991). Outward currents in isolated ventral cochlear nucleus neurons. *Journal of Neuroscience, 11,* 2865–2880.

Manley, G. A. (1990). *Peripheral hearing mechanisms in reptiles and birds.* Berlin: Springer.

Manley, G. A., & Koppl, C. (1998). Phylogenetic development of the cochlea and its innervation. *Current Opinions in Neurobiology, 8,* 468–474.

Markovitz, N. S., & Pollak, G. D. (1994). Binaural processing in the dorsal nucleus of the lateral lemniscus. *Hearing Research, 73,* 121–140.

Martin, P., & Hudspeth, A. J. (1999). Active hair-bundle movements can amplify a hair cell's response to oscillatory mechanical stimuli. *Proceedings of the National Academy of Science USA, 96,* 14306–14311.

May, B. J., Le Prell, G. S., Hienz, R. D., & Sachs, M. B. (1997). Speech representation in the auditory nerve and ventral cochlear nucleus: Quantitative comparisons. In J. Syka (Ed.), *Acoustical signal processing in the central auditory system* (pp. 413–429). New York: Plenum.

May, B. J., & Sachs, M. B. (1992). Dynamic range of neural rate responses in the ventral cochlear nucleus of awake cats. *Journal of Neurophysiology, 68,* 1589–1602.

McAlpine, D., Jiang, D., & Palmer, A. R. (1998). Convergent input from brainstem coincidence detectors onto delay-sensitive neurones in the inferior colliculus. *Journal of Neuroscience, 18,* 6026–6039.

Meredith, G. E. (1988). Comparative view of the central organization of afferent and efferent circuitry for the inner ear. *Acta Biologica Hungarica, 39,* 229–249.

Meredith, M. A., & Clemo, H. R. (1989). Auditory cortical projection from the anterior ectosylvian sulcus (field AES) to the superior colliculus in the cat: An anatomical and electrophysiological study. *Journal of Comparative Neurology, 289,* 687–707.

Meredith, M. A., & Stein, B. E. (1983). Interactions among converging sensory inputs in the superior colliculus. *Science, 221,* 389–391.

Merzenich, M. M., & Reid, M. D. (1974). Representation of the cochlea within the inferior colliculus of the cat. *Brain Research, 77,* 397–415.

Middlebrooks, J. C., Clock, A. E., Xu, L., & Green, D. M. (1994). A panoramic code for sound location by cortical neurons. *Science, 264,* 842–844.

Middlebrooks, J. C., & Knudsen, E. I. (1987). Changes in external ear position modify the spatial tuning of auditory units in the cat's superior colliculus. *Journal of Neurophysiology, 57,* 672–687.

Miller, M. I., Barta, P. E., & Sachs, M. B. (1987). Strategies for the representation of a tone in

background noise in the temporal aspects of the discharge patterns of auditory-nerve fibers. *Journal of the Acoustical Society of America, 81,* 665–679.

Mills, A. W. (1972). Auditory localization. In J. V. Tobias (Ed.), *Foundations of modern auditory theory: Vol. 2.* (pp. 303–348). New York: Academic Press.

Moore, B. C. J. (1995). *Perceptual consequences of cochlear damage.* New York: Oxford University Press.

Moore, D. R., & Irvine, D. R. F. (1980). Development of binaural input, response patterns, and discharge rate in single units of the cat inferior colliculus. *Experimental Brain Research, 38,* 103–108.

Moore, J. K. (1987). The human auditory brain stem: A comparative view. *Hearing Research, 29,* 1–32.

Moore, J. K., & Moore, R. Y. (1971). A comparative study of the superior olivary complex in the primate brain. *Folia Primatol (Basel), 16,* 35–51.

Morel, A., & Imig, T. J. (1987). Thalamic projections to fields A, AI, P, and VP in the cat auditory cortex. *Journal of Comparative Neurology, 265,* 119–144.

Morest, D. K., & Oliver, D. L. (1984). The neuronal architecture of the inferior colliculus in the cat: Defining the functional anatomy of the auditory midbrain. *Journal of Comparative Neurology, 222,* 209–236.

Mountain, D. C., Hubbard, A. E., & McMullen, T. A. (1983). Electromechanical processes in the cochlea. In E. de Boer & M. A. Viergever (Eds.), *Mechanics of hearing* (pp. 119–126). The Hague, Netherlands: Delft University Press.

Murugasu, E., & Russell, I. J. (1996). The effect of efferent stimulation on basilar membrane displacement in the basal turn of the guinea pig cochlea. *Journal of Neuroscience, 16,* 325–332.

Musicant, A. D., Chan, J. C. K., & Hind, J. E. (1990). Direction-dependent spectral properties of cat external ear: New data and cross-species comparisons. *Journal of the Acoustical Society of America, 87,* 757–781.

Naidu, R. C., & Mountain, D. C. (1998). Measurements of the stiffness map challenge a basic tenet of cochlear theories. *Hearing Research, 124*, 124–131.

Nelken, I., Kim, P. J., & Young, E. D. (1997). Linear and nonlinear spectral integration in Type IV neurons of the dorsal cochlear nucleus: II. Predicting responses with the use of nonlinear models. *Journal of Neurophysiology, 78*, 800–811.

Nelken, I., & Young, E. D. (1994). Two separate inhibitory mechanisms shape the responses of dorsal cochlear nucleus type IV units to narrowband and wideband noise. *Journal of Neurophysiology, 71*, 2446–2462.

Nuttall, A. L., & Dolan, D. F. (1993). Two tone suppression of inner hair cell and basilar membrane responses in the guinea pig. *Journal of the Acoustical Society of America, 93*, 390–400.

Oliver, D. L., & Huerta, M. F. (1992). Inferior and superior colliculi. In D. B. Webster, A. N. Popper, & R. R. Fay (Eds.), *The mammalian auditory pathway: Neuroanatomy* (pp. 168–221). New York: Springer.

Osen, K. K. (1969). Course and termination of the primary afferents in the cochlear nuclei of the cat: An experimental anatomical study. *Archives Italienne de Biologie, 108*, 21–51.

Osen, K. K., & Mugnaini, E. (1981). Neuronal circuits in the dorsal cochlear nucleus. In J. Syka & L. Aitkin (Eds.), *Neuronal mechanisms of hearing* (pp. 119–125). New York: Plenum.

Overholt, E. M., Rubel, E. W., & Hyson, R. L. (1992) A circuit for coding interaural time differences in the chick brainstem. *Journal of Neuroscience, 12*, 1698–1708.

Palmer, A. R. (1982). Encoding of rapid amplitude fluctuations by cochlear-nerve fibers in the guinea-pig. *Archives of Otorhinolaryngology, 236*, 197–202.

Palmer, A. R., Jiang, D., & McAlpine, D. (1999). Desynchronizing responses to correlated noise: A mechanism for binaural masking level differences at the inferior colliculus. *Journal of Neurophysiology, 81*, 722–734.

Palmer, A. R., & Russell, I. J. (1986). Phase-locking in the cochlear nerve of the guinea-pig and its relation to the receptor potential of inner hair-cells. *Hearing Research, 24*, 1–15.

Patuzzi, R. B., Yates, G. K., & Johnstone, B. M. (1989). Outer hair cell receptor currents and sensorineural hearing loss. *Hearing Research, 42*, 47–72.

Peake, W. T., & Rosowski, J. J. (1991). Impedance matching, optimum velocity, and ideal middle ears. *Hearing Research, 53*, 1–6.

Pfeiffer, R. R. (1966). Classification of response patterns of spike discharges for units in the cochlear nucleus: Tone-burst stimulation. *Experimental Brain Research, 1*, 220–235.

Phillips, D. P. (1990). Neural representation of sound amplitude in the auditory cortex: Effects of masking. *Behavioral Brain Research, 37*, 197–214.

Popper, A. N., & Fay, R. R. (Eds.). (1980). *Comparative studies of hearing in vertebrates*. New York: Springer.

Popper, A. N., & Fay, R. R. (Eds.). (1992). *The mammalian auditory pathway: Neurophysiology*. New York: Springer.

Ramachandran, R., Davis, K. A., & May, B. J. (1999). Single-unit responses in the inferior colliculus of decerebrate cats: I. Classification based on frequency response maps. *Journal of Neurophysiology, 82*, 152–163.

Raphael, R. M., Popel, A. S., & Brownell, W. E. (2000). A membrane bending model of outer hair cell electromotility. *Biophysical Journal, 78*, 2844–2862.

Rayleigh, Lord (J. W. Strutt). (1907). On our perception of sound direction. *Philosophical Magazine (6 Ser.) 13*, 214–232.

Reale, R. A., & Imig, T. J. (1980). Tonotopic organization in auditory cortex of the cat. *Journal of Comparative Neurology, 182*, 265–291.

Recio, A., Narayan, S. S., & Ruggero, M. A. (1997). Weiner-kernel analysis of basilar-membrane responses to white noise. In E. R. Lewis, G. R. Long, R. F. Lyon, P. M. Narins, C. R. Steele, & E. Hecht-Poinar (Eds.), *Diversity in auditory mechanics* (pp. 325–331). Singapore: World Scientific.

Rees, A., & Møller, A. R. (1983). Responses of neurons in the inferior colliculus of the rat to AM and FM tones. *Hearing Research, 10*, 301–330.

Rhode, W. S. (1971). Observations of the vibration of the basilar membrane in squirrel monkeys using the Mössbauer technique. *Journal of the Acoustical Society of America, 64,* 158–176.

Rhode, W. S., & Greenberg, S. (1992). Physiology of the cochlear nuclei. In A. N. Popper & R. R. Fay (Eds.), *The mammalian auditory pathway: Neurophysiology* (pp. 94–152). New York: Springer.

Rhode, W. S., & Greenberg, S. (1994). Encoding of amplitude modulation in the cochlear nucleus of the cat. *Journal of Neurophysiology, 71,* 1797–1825.

Rhode, W. S., Oertel, D., & Smith, P. H. (1983). Physiological response properties of cells labelled intracellularly with horeseradish peroxidase in cat ventral cochlear nucleus. *Journal of Comparative Neurology, 213,* 448–463.

Ricci, A. J., Gray-Keller, M., & Fettiplace, R. (2000). Tonotopic variations of calcium signalling in turtle auditory hair cells. *Journal of Physiology (London), 524,* 423–436.

Richter, E. A., Norris, B. E., Fullerton, B. C., Levine, R. A., & Kiang, N. Y. S. (1983). Is there a medial nucleus of the trapezoid body in humans? *The American Journal of Anatomy, 168,* 157–166.

Rioch, D. M. (1929). Studies on the diencephalon of carnivora: I. The nuclear configuration of the thalamus, epithalamus, and hypothalamus of the dog and cat. *Journal of Comparative Neurology, 49,* 1–119.

Rockel, A. J., & Jones, E. G. (1973a). The neuronal organization of the inferior colliculus of the adult cat: I. The central nucleus. *Journal of Comparative Neurology, 147,* 22–60.

Rockel, A. J., & Jones, E. G. (1973b). The neuronal organization of the inferior colliculus of the adult cat: II. The pericentral nucleus. *Journal of Comparative Neurology, 149,* 301–334.

Rodrigues-Dagaeff, C., Simm, G., de Ribaupierre, Y., Villa, A., de Ribaupierre, F., & Rouiller, E. M. (1989). Functional organization of the medial division of the medial geniculate body of the cat: Evidence for a rostral-caudal gradient of response properties and cortical projections. *Hearing Research, 39,* 103–126.

Romanski, L. M., Tian, B., Fritz, J., Mishkin, M., Goldman-Rakic, P. S., & Rauschecker, J. P. (1999). Dual streams of auditory afferents target multiple domains in the primate prefrontal cortex. *Nature Neuroscience, 2,* 1131–1136.

Rose, J. E. (1949). The cellular structure of the auditory region of the cat. *Journal of Comparative Neurology, 91,* 409–440.

Rose, J. E., & Woolsey, C. N. (1949). The relations of the thalamic connections, cellular structure and evokable electrical activity in the auditory region of the cat. *Journal of Comparative Neurology, 91,* 441–466.

Rosowski, J. J. (1996). Models of external- and middle-ear function. In H. L. Hawkins, T. A. McMullen, A. N. Popper, & R. R. Fay (Eds.), *Auditory computation* (pp. 15–61). New York: Springer.

Rouiller, E. M. (1997). Functional organization of the auditory pathways. In G. Ehret & R. Romand (Eds.), *The central auditory system* (pp. 193–258). New York: Oxford University Press.

Rouiller, E. M., & de Ribaupierre, F. (1985). Origins of afferents to physiologically defined regions of the medial geniculate body of the cat: ventral and dorsal divisions. *Hearing Research, 19,* 97–114.

Rouiller, E. M., de Ribaupierre, Y., Morel, A., & de Ribaupierre, F. (1983). Intensity functions of single unit responses to tones in the medial geniculate body of cat. *Hearing Research, 11,* 235–247.

Roullier, E. M., Rodrigues-Dagaeff, C., Simm, G., de Ribaupierre, Y., Villa, A., & de Ribaupierre, F. (1989). Functional organization of the medial division of the medial geniculate body of the cat: Tonotopic orgnization, spatial distribution of response properties and cortical connections. *Hearing Research, 39,* 127–142.

Rouiller, E. M., & Ryugo, D. K. (1984). Intracellular marking of physiologically characterized cells in the ventral cochlear nucleus of the cat. *Journal of Comparative Neurology, 225,* 167–186.

Rubel, E. W., Born, D. E., Deitch, J. S., & Durham, D. (1984). Recent advances toward understanding auditory system development. In

C. Berlin (Ed.), *Hearing science* (pp. 109–157). San Diego: College-Hill Press.

Ruggero, M. A. (1973). Responses to noise of auditory-nerve fibers in the squirrel monkey. *Journal of Neurophysiology, 36,* 569–587.

Ruggero, M. A. (1992a). Physiology and coding of sound in the auditory nerve. In A. N. Popper & R. R. Fay (Eds.), *The mammalian auditory pathway: Neurophysiology* (pp. 34–93). New York: Springer.

Ruggero, M. A. (1992b). Responses to sound of the basilar membrane of the mammalian cochlea. *Current Opinions in Neurobiology, 2,* 449–456.

Ruggero, M. A., & Rich, N. C. (1991). Furosemide alters organ of Corti mechanics: Evidence for feedback of outer hair cells upon the basilar membrane. *Journal of Neuroscience, 11,* 1057–1067.

Ruggero, M. A., Rich, N. C., Recio, A., Narayan, S., & Robles, L. (1997). Basilar-membrane responses to tones at the base of the chinchilla cochlea. *Journal of the Acoustical Society of America, 101,* 2151–2163.

Ruggero, M. A., Robles, L., & Rich, N. C. (1992). Two-tone suppression in the basilar membrane of the cochlea: Mechanical basis of auditory-nerve rate suppression. *Journal of Neurophysiology, 68,* 1087–1099.

Russell, I. J., & Murugasu, E. (1997). Medial efferent inhibition suppresses basilar membrane responses to near characteristic frequency tones of moderate to high intensities. *Journal of the Acoustical Society of America, 102,* 1734–1738.

Ryugo, D. K. (1992). The auditory nerve: Peripheral innervation, cell body morphology, and central projections. In D. B. Webster, A. N. Popper, & R. R. Fay (Eds.), *The mammalian auditory pathway: Neuroanatomy* (pp. 23–65). New York: Springer.

Sachs, M. B. (1984). Speech encoding in the auditory nerve. In C. Berlin (Ed.), *Hearing science* (pp. 263–307). San Diego: College-Hill Press.

Sachs, M. B., & Abbas, P. J. (1974). Rate versus level functions for auditory-nerve fibers in cats: Tone-burst stimuli. *Journal of the Acoustical Society of America, 56,* 1835–1847.

Sachs, M. B., & Kiang, N. Y. S. (1968). Two-tone inhibition in auditory-nerve fibers. *Journal of the Acoustical Society of America, 43,* 1120–1128.

Saldaña, E. (1993). Descending projections from the inferior colliculus to the cochlear nucleus in mammals. In M. A. Merchan, J. Juiz, D. Godfrey, & E. Mugnaini (Eds.), *The mammalian cochlear nuclei: Organization and function* (pp. 153–165). New York: Plenum Press.

Samson, F. K., Clarey, J. C., Barone, P., & Imig, T. J. (1993). Effects of ear plugging on single-unit azimuth sensitivity in cat primary auditory cortex: I. Evidence for monaural directional cues. *Journal of Neurophysiology, 70,* 492–511.

Schalk, T. B., & Sachs, M. B. (1980). Nonlinearities in auditory-nerve fiber responses to bandlimited noise. *Journal of the Acoustical Society of America, 67,* 903–913.

Schofield, B. R., & Cant, N. B. (1996). Origins and targets of commissural connections between the cochlear nuclei in guinea pigs. *The Journal of Comparative Neurology, 375,* 128–146.

Schofield, B. R., & Cant, N. B. (1997). Ventral nucleus of the lateral lemniscus in guinea pigs: Cytoarchitecture and inputs from the cochlear nucleus. *Journal of Comparative Neurology, 379,* 363–385.

Schofield, B. R., & Cant, N. B. (1999). Descending auditory pathways: Projections from the inferior colliculus contact superior olivary cells that project bilaterally to the cochlear nuclei. *The Journal of Comparative Neurology, 409,* 210–223.

Schreiner, C. E., & Langner, G. (1988). Periodicity coding in the inferior colliculus of the cat: II. Topographical organization. *Journal of Neurophysiology, 60,* 1823–1840.

Schreiner, C. E., Mendelson, J., Raggio, M. W., Brosch, M., & Krueger, K. (1997). Temporal processing in cat primary auditory cortex. *Acta Otolaryngologica (Stockholm), Suppl. 532,* 54–60.

Schreiner, C. E., & Urbas, J. V. (1988). Representation of amplitude modulation in the auditory cortex of the cat: II. Comparison between cortical fields. *Hearing Research, 32,* 49–64.

Schwartz, I. R. (1992). The superior olivary complex and lateral lemniscal nuclei. In D. B. Webster, A. N. Popper, & R. R. Fay (Eds.), *The mammalian auditory pathway: Neuroanatomy* (pp. 117–167). New York: Springer.

Shaw, E.A.G. (1982). External ear response and sound localization. In R. Gatehouse (Ed.), *Localization of sound: Theory and applications* (pp. 30–41). Groton, CT: Amphora.

Shera, C. A., & Guinan, J. J., Jr. (1999). Evoked otoacoustic emissions arise by two fundamentally different mechanisms: A taxonomy for mammalian OAEs. *Journal of the Acoustical Society of America, 105,* 782–798.

Shofner, W. P., & Dye, R. H., Jr. (1989). Statistical and receiver operating characteristic analysis of empirical spike-count distributions: Quantifying the ability of cochlear nucleus units to signal intensity changes. *Journal of the Acoustical Society of America, 86,* 2172–2184.

Shofner, W. P., Sheft, S., & Guzman, S. J. (1996). Responses of ventral cochlear nucleus units in the chinchilla to amplitude modulation by low-frequency, two-tone complexes. *Journal of the Acoustical Society of America, 99,* 3592–3605.

Shofner, W. P., & Young, E. D. (1985). Excitatory/inhibitory response types in the cochlear nucleus: Relationships to discharge patterns and responses to electrical stimulation of the auditory nerve. *Journal of Neurophysiology, 54,* 917–939.

Siebert, W. M. (1968). Stimulus transformations in the peripheral auditory system. In P. A. Kollers & M. Eden (Eds.), *Recognizing patterns* (pp. 104–133). Cambridge: MIT Press.

Simmons, J. A., Saillant, P. A., Ferragamo, M. J., Haresign, T., Dear, S. P., Fritz, J., & McMullen, T. A. (1996). Auditory computations for biosonar target imaging in bats. In H. L. Hawkins, T. A. McMullen, A. N. Popper, & R. R. Fay (Eds.), *Auditory computation* (pp. 401–468). New York: Springer.

Sinex, D. G., & Geisler, C. D. (1980). Responses of primary auditory fibers to combined noise and tonal stimuli. *Hearing Research, 3,* 317–334.

Sivian, L. J., & White, S. D. (1933). On minimum sound audible fields. *Journal of Acoustical Society of America, 4,* 288–321.

Smith, P. H. (1995). Structural and functional differences distinguish principal from nonprincipal cells in the guinea pig MSO slice. *Journal of Neurophysiology, 73,* 1653–1667.

Smith, P. H., Joris, P. X., Carney, L. H., & Yin, T. C. T. (1991). Projections of physiologically characterized globular bushy cell axons from the cochlear nucleus of the cat. *Journal of Comparative Neurology, 304,* 387–407.

Smith, P. H., Joris, P. X., & Yin, T. C. T. (1993). Projections of physiologically characterized spherical bushy cell axons from the cochlear nucleus of the cat: evidence for delay lines to the medial superior olive. *Journal of Comparative Neurology, 331,* 245–260.

Smith, P. H., Joris, P. X., & Yin, T. C. T. (1998). Anatomy and physiology of principal cells in the medial nucleus of the trapezoid body (MNTB) of the cat. *Journal of Neurophysiology, 79,* 3127–3142.

Smith, P. H., & Rhode, W. S. (1987). Characterization of HRP-labeled globular bushy cells in the cat anteroventral cochlear nucleus. *Journal of Comparative Neurology, 266,* 360–376.

Smith, P. H., & Rhode, W. S. (1989). Structural and functional properties distinguish two types of multipolar cells in the ventral cochlear nucleus. *Journal of Comparative Neurology, 282,* 595–616.

Smith, R. L. (1988). Encoding of sound intensity by auditory neurons. In G. M. Edelman, W. E. Gall, & W. M. Cowan (Eds.), *Auditory function: Neurobiological bases of hearing* (pp. 243–274). New York: Wiley.

Sokolowski, B. A. H., Sachs, M. B., & Goldstein, J. L. (1989). Auditory nerve rate-level functions for two-tone stimuli: Possible relation to basilar membrane nonlinearity. *Hearing Research, 41,* 15–23.

Spangler, K. M., Cant, N. B., Henkel, C. K., Farley, G. R., & Warr, W. B. (1987). Descending projections from the superior olivary complex to the cochlear nucleus of the cat. *Journal of Comparative Neurology, 259,* 452–465.

Spangler, K. M., & Warr, W. B. (1991). The descending auditory system. In R. Altschuler, D. W. Hoffman, R. P. Bobbin, & B. M. Clopton (Eds.), *The neurobiology of hearing: Vol. 2, The central auditory system.* New York: Raven Press.

Sparks, D. L. (1999). Conceptual issues related to the role of the superior colliculus in the control of gaze. *Current Opinion in Neurobiology, 9,* 698–707.

Spirou, G. A., Davis, K. A., Nelken, I., & Young, E. D. (1999). Spectral integration by Type II interneurons in dorsal cochlear nucleus. *Journal of Neurophysiology, 82,* 648–663.

Spirou, G. A., & Young, E. D. (1991). Organization of dorsal cochlear nucleus type IV unit response maps and their relationship to activation by band-limited noise. *Journal of Neurophysiology, 66,* 1750–1766.

Stanford, T. R., Kuwada, S., & Batra, R. (1992). A comparison of the interaural time sensitivity of neurons in the inferior colliculus and thalamus of the unanaesthetized rabbit. *Journal of Neuroscience, 12,* 3200–3216.

Stankovic, K. M., & Guinan, J. J., Jr. (1999). Medial efferent effects on auditory-nerve responses to tail-frequency tones: I. Rate reduction. *Journal of the Acoustical Society of America, 106,* 857–869.

Stankovic, K. M., & Guinan, J. J., Jr. (2000). Medial efferent effects on auditory-nerve responses to tail-frequency tones: II. Alteration of phase. *Journal of the Acoustical Society of America, 108,* 664–678.

Stein, B. E., Magalhaes-Castro, B., & Kruger, L. (1976). Relationship between visual and tactile representations in cat superior colliculus. *Journal of Neurophysiology, 39,* 401–419.

Stiebler, I. (1986). Tone-threshold mapping in the inferior colliculus of the house mouse. *Neuroscience Letters, 65,* 336–340.

Stotler, W. A. (1953). An experimental study of the cells and connections of the olivary complex of the cat. *Journal of Comparative Neurology, 98,* 401–432.

Suga, N. (1989). Principles of auditory information-processing derived from neuroethology. *Journal of Experimental Brain Research, 146,* 277–286.

Sullivan, W. E. (1985). Classification of response patterns in the cochlear nucleus of barn owl: Correlation with functional response properties. *Journal of Neurophysiology, 53,* 201–216.

Sutherland, D. P., Glendenning, K. K., & Masterton, R. B. (1998). Role of acoustic striae in hearing: Discrimination of sound source elevation. *Hearing Research, 120,* 86–108.

Sutherland, D. P., Masterton, R. B., & Glendenning, K. K. (1998). Role of acoustic striae in hearing: Reflexive responses to elevated sound sources. *Behavioral Brain Research, 97,* 1–12.

Takahashi, T. (1989). The neural coding of auditory space. *Journal of Experimental Biology, 146,* 307–322.

Takahashi, T., Moiseff, A., & Konishi, M. (1984). Time and intensity cues are processed independently in the auditory system of the owl. *Journal of Neuroscience, 4,* 1781–1786.

Trussell, L. O. (1999). Synaptic mechanisms for coding timing in auditory neurons. *Annual Reviews in Physiology, 61,* 477–196.

Tsuchitani, C. (1977). Functional organization of lateral cell groups of cat superior olivary complex. *Journal of Neurophysiology, 40,* 296–318.

Tsuchitani, C., & Johnson, D. H. (1985). The effects of ipsilateral tone-burst stimulus level on the discharge patterns of cat lateral superior olivary units. *Journal of the Acoustical Society of America, 77,* 1484–1496.

Viemeister, N. F. (1988). Psychophysical aspects of intensity discrimination. In G. M. Edelman, W. E. Gall, & W. M. Cowan (Eds.), *Auditory function: Neurobiological bases of hearing* (pp. 213–241). New York: Wiley.

von Békésy, G. (1960). *Experiments in hearing* (E. G. Wever, Trans.). New York: McGraw-Hill.

von Békésy, G., & Rosenblith, W. (1951). The mechanical properties of the ear. In S. Stevens (Ed.), *Handbook of experimental psychology* (pp. 1075–1180). New York: Wiley.

Wang, X. (1998). What is the neural code of species-specific communication sounds in the auditory cortex of primates? In A. R. Palmer, A. Rees, A. Q. Summerfield, & R. Meddis (Eds.), *Psychophysical and physiological advances in hearing* (pp. 521–528). London: Whurr.

Wang, X., Merzenich, M. M., Beitel, R., & Schreiner, C. E. (1995). Representation of a species-specific vocalization in the primary auditory cortex of the common marmoset: Temporal and spectral characteristics. *Journal of Neurophysiology, 74,* 2685–2706.

Warchol, M. E., & Dallos, P. (1990). Neural coding in the chick cochlear nucleus. *Journal of Comparative Physiology [A], 166,* 721–734.

Warr, W. B. (1992). Organization of olivocochlear efferent systems in mammals. In D. B. Webster, A. N. Popper, & R. R. Fay (Eds.), *The mammalian auditory pathway: Neuroanatomy* (pp. 410–448). New York: Springer.

Warr, W. B., Guinan, J. J., Jr., & White, J. S. (1986). Organization of the efferent fibers: The lateral and medial olivocochlear systems. In R. Altschuler, D. W. Hoffman, & R. P. Bobbin (Eds.), *The neurobiology of hearing: The cochlea.* New York: Raven Press.

Webster, D. B., Popper, A. N., & Fay, R. R. (Eds.). (1992). *The mammalian auditory pathway: Neuroanatomy.* New York: Springer.

Weedman, D. L., & Ryugo, D. K. (1996). Projections from auditory cortex to the cochlear nucleus in rats: Synapses on granule cell dendrites. *Journal of Comparative Neurology, 371,* 311–324.

Wiederhold, M. (1970). Variations in the effects of electric stimulation of the crossed olivocochlear bundle on cat single auditory-nerve fiber responses to tone bursts. *Journal of the Acoustical Society of America, 48,* 966–977.

Wiederhold, M. (1986). Physiology of the olivocochlear system. In R. A. Altschuler, D. W. Hoffman, & R. P. Bobbin (Eds.), *Neurobiology of hearing: The cochlea* (pp. 349–370). New York: Raven Press.

Weiss, T. F., & Rose, C. (1988). A comparison of synchronization filters in different auditory receptor organs. *Hearing Research, 33,* 175–180.

Winer, J. J. (1992). The functional architecture of the medial geniculate body and the primary auditory cortex. In D. B. Webster, A. N. Popper, & R. R. Fay (Eds.), *The mammalian auditory pathway: Neuroanatomy* (pp. 222–409). New York: Springer.

Winslow, R. L., & Sachs, M. B. (1987). Effect of electrical stimulation of the crossed olivocochlear bundle on auditory nerve response to tones in noise. *Journal of Neurophysiology, 57,* 1002–1021.

Winslow, R. L., & Sachs, M. B. (1988). Single-tone intensity discrimination based on auditory-nerve rate responses in backgrounds of quiet, noise, and with stimulation of the crossed olivocochlear bundle. *Hearing Research, 35,* 165–190.

Winter, I. M., & Palmer, A. R. (1991). Intensity-coding in low-frequency auditory-nerve fibers of the guinea pig. *Journal of the Acoustical Society of America, 90,* 1958–1967.

Wise, L. Z., & Irvine, D. R. F. (1983). Auditory response properties of neurons in deep layers of cat superior colliculus. *Journal of Neurophysiology, 49,* 674–685.

Wise, L Z., & Irvine, D. R. F. (1985). Topographic organization of interaural intensity difference sensitivity in deep layers of cat superior colliculus: Implications for auditory spatial representation. *Journal of Neurophysiology, 54,* 185–211.

Wong, J. C., Miller, R. L., Calhoun, B. M., Sachs, M. B., Young, E. D. (1998). Effects of high sound levels on responses to the vowel "eh" in cat auditory nerve. *Hearing Research, 123,* 61–77.

Woolsey, C. N. (1961). Organization of cortical auditory system. In W. A. Rosenblith (Ed.), *Sensory communication* (pp. 235–257). Cambridge: MIT Press.

Woolsey, C. N., & Walzl, E. M. (1942). Topical projection of nerve fibers from local regions of the cochlea to the cerebral cortex of the cat. *Bulletin of The Johns Hopkins Hospital, 71,* 315–344.

Wright, D., Hebrank, J. H., & Wilson, B. (1974). Pinna reflections as cues for localization. *Journal of the Acoustical Society of America, 56,* 957–962.

Wu, S. H., & Kelly, J. B. (1994). Physiological evidence for ipsilateral inhibition in the lateral superior olive: synaptic responses in mouse brain slice. *Hearing Research, 73,* 57–64.

Yan, J., & Suga, N., (1996). Corticofugal modulation of time-domain processing of biosonar information in bats. *Science, 273,* 1100–1103.

Yang, L., Monsivais, P., & Rubel, E. W. (1999). The superior olivary nucleus and its influence on nucleus laminaris: A source of inhibitory feedback for coincidence detection in the avian auditory brainstem. *Journal of Neuroscience, 19,* 2313–2325.

Yates, G. K. (1995). Cochlear structure and function. In B.C.J. Moore (Ed.), *Hearing* (pp. 41–74). San Diego: Academic Press.

Yates, G. K., Johnstone, B. M., Patuzzi, R. B., & Robertson, D. (1992). Mechanical preprocessing in the mammalian cochlea. *Trends in Neurosciences, 15,* 57–61.

Yin, T. C. T., & Chan, J. C. K. (1990). Interaural time sensitivity in medial superior olive of cat. *Journal of Neurophysiology, 64,* 465–488.

Yin, T. C. T., Chan, J. C. K., & Carney, L. H. (1987). Effects of interaural time delays of noise stimuli on low-frequency cells in the cat's inferior colliculus: III. Evidence for cross-correlation. *Journal of Neurophysiology, 58,* 562–583.

Young, E. D. (1984). Response characteristics of neurons of the cochlear nuclei. In C. Berlin (Ed.), *Hearing science* (pp. 423–460). San Diego: College-Hill Press.

Young, E. D. (1998). Cochlear nucleus. In G. Shepherd (Ed.), *The synaptic organization of the brain* (4th ed., pp. 121–157). New York: Oxford University Press.

Young, E. D., & Barta, P. E. (1986). Rate responses of auditory nerve fibers to tones in noise near masked threshold. *Journal of the Acoustical Society of America, 79,* 426–442.

Young, E. D., Robert, J.-M., & Shofner, W. P. (1988). Regularity and latency of units in ventral cochlear nucleus: Implications for unit classification and generation of response properties. *Journal of Neurophysiology, 60,* 1–20.

Young, E. D., Spirou, G. A., Rice, J. J., & Voigt, H. F. (1992). Neural organization and responses to complex stimuli in the dorsal cochlear nucleus. *Philosophical Transactions of the Royal Society, London B, 336,* 407–413.

Zhang, M., & Zwislocki, J. J. (1996). Intensity-dependent peak shift in cochlear transfer functions at the cellular level, its elimination by sound exposure, and its possible underlying mechanisms. *Hearing Research, 96,* 46–58.

Zhang, Y., Suga, N., & Yan, J. (1997). Corticofugal modulation of frequency processing in bat auditory system. *Nature, 387,* 900–903.

Zheng, J., Shen, W., He, D. Z., Long, K. B., Madison, L. D., & Dallos, P. (2000). Prestin is the motor protein of cochlear outer hair cells. *Nature, 405,* 149–155.

Zook, J. M., & Casseday, J. H. (1982). Cytoarchitecture of auditory system in lower brainstem of the mustache bat, *Pteronotus parnelli. Journal of Comparative Neurology, 207,* 1–13.

Zwislocki, J. J. (1986). Analysis of cochlear mechanics. *Hearing Research, 22,* 155–169.

CHAPTER 10

Auditory Perception and Cognition

STEPHEN MCADAMS AND CAROLYN DRAKE

The sound environment in which we live is extraordinarily rich. As we scurry about in our little animal lives, we perceive sound sources and the sequences of events they emit and must adapt our behavior accordingly. How do we extract and make use of the information available in this highly structured acoustic array?

Sounds arise in the environment from the mechanical excitation of bodies that are set into vibration. These bodies radiate some of their vibratory energy into the surrounding air (or water) through which this energy propagates, getting bounced off some objects and partially absorbed by different materials. The nature of the acoustic wave arising from a source depends on the mechanical properties both of that source and of the interaction with other objects that set it into vibration. Many of these excitatory actions are extended through time, and this allows a listener to pick up important information concerning both the source and the action through an analysis of the sequences of events produced. Further, most environments contain several vibrating structures, and the acoustic waves impending on the eardrums represent the sum of many sources, some near, others farther away.

To perceive what is happening in the environment and adjust its behavior appropriately to the sound sources present, a listening organism must be able to disentangle the acoustic information from the many sources and evaluate the properties of individual events or sequences of events arising from a given source. At a more cognitive level, it is also useful to process the temporal relations among events in more lengthy sequences to understand the nature of actions on objects that are extended in time and that may carry important cultural messages such as in speech and music for humans. Finally, in many cases, with so much going on, listening must be focused on a given source of sound. Furthermore, this focusing process must possess dynamic characteristics that are tuned to the temporal evolution of the source that is being tracked in order to understand its message.

Aspects of these complex areas are addressed in this chapter to give a nonexhaustive flavor for current work in auditory perception and cognition. We focus on auditory scene analysis, timbre and sound source perception, temporal pattern processing, and attentional processes in hearing and finish with a consideration of developmental issues concerning these areas. The reader may wish to consult several general texts for additional information and inspiration (Bregman, 1990; Handel, 1989; McAdams & Bigand, 1993; Warren, 1999, with an accompanying CD), as well as compact discs of audio demos (Bregman & Ahad, 1995; Deutsch, 1995; Houtsma, Rossing & Wagenaars, 1987).

AUDITORY SCENE ANALYSIS

It is useful for an organism to build a mental representation of the acoustic environment in terms of the behavior of sound sources (objects set into vibration by actions upon them) in order to be able to structure its behavior in relation to them. We can hear in the same room and at the same time the noise of someone typing on a keyboard, the sound of someone walking, and the speech of someone talking in the next room. From a phenomenological point of view, we hear all of these sounds as if they arrive independently at our ears without distortion or interference among them, unless, of course, one source is much more intense than the others, in which case it would mask them, making them inaudible or at least less audible.

The acoustic waves of all sources are combined linearly in the atmosphere, and the composite waveform is then analyzed as such by the peripheral auditory system (Figure 10.1; see Chap. 9, this volume). Sound events are not opaque like most visual objects are. The computational problem is thus to interpret the complex waveform as a combination of sound-producing events. This process is called *auditory scene analysis* (Bregman, 1990) by analogy with the analysis of a visual scene in terms of objects (see Chap. 5, this volume, for a comparison of how these two sensory systems have come to solve analogous problems). Contrary to vision, in which a contiguous array of stimulation of the sensory organ corresponds to an object (although this is not always the case, as with partially occluded or transparent objects), in hearing the stimulation is a distributed frequency array mapped onto the basilar membrane. For a complex sound arising from a given source, the auditory system must thus reunite the sound components coming from the same source that have previously been channeled into separate auditory nerve fibers on the basis of their frequency content. Further, it must separate the information coming from distinct sources that contain close frequencies that would stimulate the same auditory nerve fibers. This is the problem of *concurrent organization*. The problem of *sequential organization* concerns perceptually connecting (or binding) over time successive events emitted by the same source and segregating events

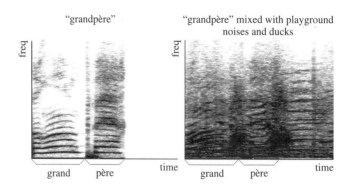

Figure 10.1   Spectrogram of (a) a target sound—the word *grandpère* ("grandfather" in French)—and (b) the target sound embedded in a noisy environment (a children's playground with voices and ducks). NOTE: A spectrogram represents time on the horizontal axis and frequency on the vertical axis. The level at a given frequency is coded by the darkness of the spectrographic trace. Note that in many places in the mixture panel, the frequency information of the target sound is strongly overlapped by that of the noisy environment. In particular, the horizontal lines representing harmonic frequency components of the target word become intermingled with those of other voices in the mixture.

coming from independent sources in order to follow the message of only one source at a time.

This section examines the mechanisms that are brought into play by the auditory system to analyze the acoustic events and the behavior over time of sound sources. The ultimate goal of such a system would be to segregate perceptually actions that occur simultaneously; to detect new actions in the environment; to follow actions on a given object over time; to compute the properties of sources to feed into categorization, recognition, identification, and comprehension processes; and to use knowledge of derived attributes to track and extract sources and messages. We consider in order the processes involved in auditory event formation (concurrent grouping), the distinction of new event arrival from change of an ongoing event, auditory stream formation (sequential grouping), the interaction of concurrent and sequential grouping factors, the problem posed by the transparency of auditory events, and, finally, the role of schema-based processes in auditory organization.

Auditory Event Formation (Concurrent Grouping)

The processes of concurrent organization result either in the *perceptual fusion* or *grouping* of components of the auditory sensory representation into a single auditory event or in their *perceptual segregation* into two or more distinct events that overlap in time. The nature of these components of the sensory representation depends on the dual coding scheme in the auditory periphery. On the one hand, different parts of the acoustic frequency spectrum are represented in separate anatomical locations at many levels of the auditory system, a representation that is called tonotopic (see Chap. 9, this volume). On the other hand, even within a small frequency range in

which all the acoustic information is carried by a small number of adjacent auditory nerve fibers, different periodicities in the stimulating waveform can be discerned on the basis of the temporal pattern of neural discharges that are time-locked to the stimulating waveform (see Chap. 9, this volume). The term *auditory event* refers to the unity and limited temporal extent that are experienced when, for example, a single sound source is set into vibration by a time-limited action on it. Some authors use the term *auditory objects,* but we prefer to distinguish objects (as vibrating physical sources) from perceptual events. A single source can produce a series of events.

A relatively small number of acoustic cues appear to signal either common behavior among acoustic components (usually arising from a single source) or incoherent behavior between components arising from distinct sources. The relative contribution of a given cue for scene analysis, however, depends on the perceptual task in which the listener is engaged: Some cues are more effective in signaling grouping for one attribute, such as identifying the pitch or vowel quality of a sound, than for another attribute, such as judging its position in space. Furthermore, some cues are more resistant than are others to environmental transformations of the acoustic waves originating from a vibrating object (reflections, reverberation, filtering by selective absorption, etc.).

Candidate cues for increasing segregation of concurrent sounds include inharmonicity, irregularity of spacing of frequency components, asynchrony of onset or offset of components, incoherence of change over time of level and frequency of components, and differences in spatial position.

Harmonicity

In the environment two unrelated sounds rarely have frequency components that line up such that each frequency is an integer multiple of the fundamental frequency (F0), which is called a harmonic series. It is even less likely that they will maintain this relation with changes in frequency over time. A mechanism that is sensitive to deviations from harmonicity and groups components having harmonic relations could be useful for grouping acoustic components across the spectrum that arise from a single source and for segregating those that arise from distinct sources.

Two main classes of stimuli have been used to study the role of harmonicity in concurrent grouping: harmonic complexes with a single component mistuned from its purely harmonic relation and complexes composed of two or more sets of harmonic components with a difference in fundamental frequency (Figures 10.2a–b).

Listeners report hearing out a single, mistuned harmonic component from the rest of the complex tone if its harmonic rank is low and the mistuning is around 2% of its nominal frequency (Moore, Peters, & Glasberg, 1985). If mistuning is sufficient, listeners can match the pitch of the segregated harmonic, but this ability deteriorates at component frequencies above approximately 2000 Hz, where temporal information in the neural discharge pattern is no longer reliably related to waveform periodicities (Hartmann, McAdams, & Smith, 1990). A mistuned harmonic can also affect the virtual pitch (see Chap. 11, this volume) of the whole complex, pulling it in the direction of mistuning. This pitch shift increases for mistunings up to 3% and then decreases beyond that, virtually disappearing beyond about 8% (Hartmann, 1988; Hartmann et al., 1990; Moore, Glasberg, & Peters, 1985). This relation between mistuning and pitch shift suggests a harmonic-template model with a tolerance function on the harmonic sieve (Duifhuis, Willems, & Sluyter, 1982) or a time-domain autocoincidence processor (de Cheveigné, 1993) with a temporal margin of error. Harmonic mistuning can also affect vowel perception by influencing whether the component frequency is integrated into the computation of the spectral envelope that determines the vowel identity (Darwin & Gardner, 1986). By progressively mistuning this harmonic, a change in vowel percept has been recorded up to about 8%

Figure 10.2 Stimuli used to test concurrent grouping cues.

NOTE: a) Harmonicity tested with the mistuned harmonic paradigm. A harmonic stimulus without the fundamental frequency still gives a pitch at that frequency (dashed line). A shift of at least 2% but no more than 8% in the frequency of the fourth harmonic causes the harmonic to be heard separately but still contributes to a shift in the pitch of the complex sound. b) Harmonicity tested with the concurrent vowel paradigm. In the left column two vowels (indicated by the spectral envelopes with formant peaks) have the same fundamental frequency (F0). The resulting spectrum is the sum of the two, and the new spectral envelope does not correspond to either of the vowels, making them difficult to identify separately. In the right column, the F0 of one of the vowels is shifted, and two separate groups of harmonics are represented in the periodicity information in the auditory nerve, making the vowels more easily distinguished. c) Spectral spacing. An even harmonic in an odd-harmonic base, or vice versa, is easier to hear out than are the harmonics of the base. d) Onset/offset asynchrony. When harmonics start synchronously, they are fused perceptually into a single perceptual event. An asynchrony of the onset of at least 30–50 ms makes the harmonic easier to hear out. An asynchrony of the offset has a relatively weak effect on hearing out the harmonic. e) Level comodulation (comodulation masking release). The amplitude envelopes of a sine tone (black) and a narrow band noise with a modulating envelope (white) are shown. The masking threshold of the sine tone in the noise is measured. When flanking noise bands with amplitude envelopes identical to that of the on-signal band are added, the masked threshold of the sine tone decreases by about 3 dB. f) Frequency comodulation. A set of harmonics that are coherently modulated in frequency (with a sinusoidal vibrato in this example) are heard as a single event. Making the modulation incoherent on one of the harmonics makes it easier to hear out because of the time-varying inharmonicity that is created.

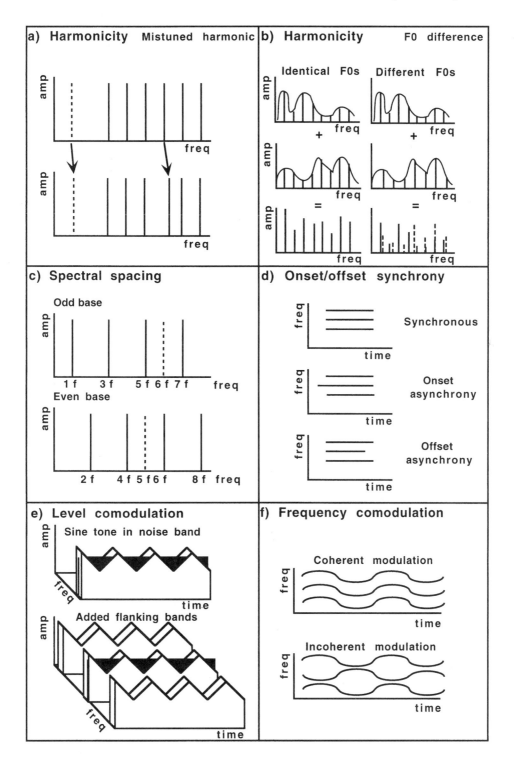

a) Harmonicity   Mistuned harmonic

b) Harmonicity   F0 difference

Identical F0s   Different F0s

c) Spectral spacing

Odd base

1 f   3 f   5 f 6 f 7 f   freq

Even base

2 f   4 f 5 f 6 f   8 f freq

d) Onset/offset synchrony

Synchronous

Onset asynchrony

Offset asynchrony

e) Level comodulation

Sine tone in noise band

Added flanking bands

f) Frequency comodulation

Coherent modulation

Incoherent modulation

mistuning, as for the pitch-shift effect. Note that above 2% mistuning, the component is heard as a separate event, but it continues to affect pitch and vowel perception up to a mistuning of about 8%.

A difference in fundamental frequency (ΔF0) of 2% across two sets of harmonics forming different synthetic speech formants[1] gives an impression of two sources with the same vowel identity (Cutting, 1976; Gardner, Gaskill, & Darwin, 1989), but much larger ΔF0s are necessary to affect the identity of consonant-vowel (CV) syllables. In four-formant CV syllables in which perceptual segregation of the second formant (F2) changes the identity from /ru/ to /li/, a 58% ΔF0 on F2 gave /li/ plus an additional buzz, whereas 4% gave an impression of two sources, both being /ru/ (Darwin, 1981). Fundamental frequency differences increase the intelligibility of a target speech stream mixed with a nonsense stream up to approximately 3%. Intelligibility remains relatively constant thereafter, but with a drop at the octave (Brokx & Nooteboom, 1982). At this 2:1 frequency ratio, the frequency components of the higher-F0 complex would coincide perfectly with the even-ranked components of the lower-F0 complex. In more controlled experiments in which pairs of synthesized vowels are mixed and must both be identified, performance increases up to a 3% ΔF0 (Assmann & Summerfield, 1990; Scheffers, 1983).

One question raised by these studies is how the harmonic structure of the source is exploited by a segregation mechanism. At the small differences in F0 that give significant identification improvement, it is clear that cochlear frequency selectivity would be in-sufficient. A mechanism might be used that operates on the temporal fine structure of the neural discharge pattern in the auditory nerve fiber array. Two possibilities have been examined by experimentation and modeling (de Cheveigné, 1993). One proposes that the extraction process uses the harmonicity of the *target* event. The other hypothesizes inversely that the harmonicity of the *background* is used to cancel it out. In line with the cancellation hypothesis, results from concurrent double-vowel experiments show that it is easier to identify periodic target vowels than inharmonic or noisy ones, but that the harmonicity of the target vowel itself has no effect (de Cheveigné, Kawahara, Tsuzaki, & Aikawa, 1997; de Cheveigné, McAdams, Laroche, & Rosenberg, 1995; de Cheveigné, McAdams, & Marin, 1997; Lea, 1992). The harmonic cancellation mechanism is extremely sensitive because improvement in vowel identification can be obtained with a ΔF0 as small as 0.4% (de Cheveigné, 1999).

Regularity of Spectral Spacing

The results from studies of harmonicity suggest a role for temporal coding rather than spectral coding in concurrent grouping. This view is complicated, however, by results concerning the regularity of spectral spacing, that is, the pattern of distribution of components along the frequency dimension. If a listener is presented with a base spectrum composed of only the odd harmonics plus one even harmonic, the even harmonic is more easily heard out than are its odd neighbors (Figure 10.2c). This is true even at higher harmonic numbers, where spectral resolution[2]

---

[1] Formants are regions in the frequency spectrum where the energy is higher than in adjacent regions. They are due to the resonance properties of the vocal tract and determine many aspects of consonant and vowel identity (see Chap. 12, this volume).

[2] The frequency organization along the basilar membrane in the cochlea (see Chap. 9, this volume) is roughly logarithmic, so higher harmonics are more closely spaced than are lower harmonics. At sufficiently high ranks, adjacent harmonics no longer stimulate separate populations of auditory nerve fibers and are thus "unresolved" in the tonotopic representation.

is reduced. Note that the even harmonic surrounded by odd harmonics would be less resolved on the basilar membrane than would either of its neighbors. Contrary to the ΔF0 cue, harmonic sieve and autocoincidence models cannot account for these results (Roberts & Bregman, 1991). Nor does the underlying mechanism involve a cross-channel comparison of the amplitude modulation envelope in the output of the auditory filter bank, because minimizing the modulation depth or perturbing the modulation pattern by adding noise does not markedly reduce the difference in hearing out even and odd harmonics (Roberts & Bailey, 1993). However, perturbing the regularity of the base spectrum by adding extraneous components or removing components reduces the perceptual "popout" of even harmonics (Roberts & Bailey, 1996), confirming the spectral pattern hypothesis.

Onset and Offset Asynchrony

Unrelated sounds seldom start or stop at exactly the same time. Therefore, the auditory system assumes that synchronous components are part of the same sound or were caused by the same environmental event. Furthermore, the auditory system is extremely sensitive to small asynchronies in analyzing the auditory scene. A single frequency component in a complex tone becomes audible on its own with an asynchrony as small as 35 ms (Rasch, 1978). Onset asynchronies are more effective than offset asynchronies are in creating segregation (Figure 10.2d; Dannenbring & Bregman, 1976; Zera & Green, 1993). When a component is made asynchronous, it also contributes less to the perceptual properties computed from the rest of the complex. For example, a 30-ms asynchrony can affect timbre judgments (Bregman & Pinker, 1978). Making a critical frequency component that affects the estimation of a vowel sound's spectral envelope asynchronous by 40 ms changes the vowel identity (Darwin, 1984). Further-

more, the asynchrony effect is abolished if the asynchronous portion of the component (i.e., the part that precedes the onset of the vowel complex) is grouped with another set of components that are synchronous with it alone and that have a common F0 that is different from that of the vowel. This result suggests that it is indeed a grouping effect, not the result of adaptation (Darwin & Sutherland, 1984).

The effect of a mistuned component on the pitch of the complex (discussed earlier) is increasingly reduced for asynchronies from 80 to 300 ms (Darwin & Ciocca, 1992). This latter effect is weakened if another component groups with a preceding portion of the asynchronous component (Ciocca & Darwin, 1993). Note that in these results the asynchronies necessary to affect pitch perception are much greater than are those that affect vowel perception (Hukin & Darwin, 1995a).

Coherence of Change in Level

From Gestalt principles such as common fate (see Chap. 5, this volume), one might expect that common direction of change in level would be a cue for grouping components together; inversely, independent change would signal that segregation was appropriate. The evidence that this factor is a grouping cue, however, is rather weak. In experiments by Hall and colleagues (e.g., Hall, Grose, & Mendoza, 1995), a phenomenon called comodulation masking release is created by placing a narrow-band noise masker centered on a target frequency component (sine tone) that is to be detected (Figure 10.2e). The masked threshold of the tone is measured in the presence of the noise. Then, noise bands with similar or different amplitude envelopes are placed in more distant frequency regions. The presence of similar envelopes (i.e., comodulation) makes it possible to detect the tone in the noise at a level of about 3 dB lower than in their absence. The masking seems to be released to some extent by the presence of co-modulation on the distant noise bands. Some authors have attributed this phenomenon to the grouping of the noise bands into a single auditory image that then allows the noise centered on the tone to be interpreted as part of a different source, thus making detection of the tone easier (Bregman, 1990, chap. 3). Others, however, consider either that cross-channel detection of the amplitude envelope simply gives a cue to the auditory system concerning when the masking noise should be in a level dip, or that the flanking maskers suppress the on-signal masker (Hall et al., 1995; McFadden & Wright, 1987).

Coherence of Change in Frequency

For sustained complex sounds that vary in frequency, there is a tendency for all frequencies to change synchronously and to maintain the frequency ratios. As such, one might imagine that frequency modulation coherence would be an important cue in source grouping (Figure 10.2f). The effects of frequency modulation incoherence may have two origins: within-channel cues and cross-channel cues. Within-channel cues would result from the interactions of unresolved components that changed frequency incoherently over time, creating variations in beating or roughness in particular auditory channels. They could signal the presence of more than one source. Such cues are detectable for both harmonic and inharmonic stimuli (McAdams & Marin, 1990) but are easier to detect for the former because of the reliability of within-channel cues for periodic sounds. Frequency modulation coherence is not, however, detectable across auditory channels (i.e., in distant frequency regions) above and beyond the mistuning from harmonicity that they create (Carlyon, 1991, 1992, 1994). Although frequency modulation increases vowel prominence when the $\Delta F0$ is already large, there is no difference be-

tween coherent and incoherent modulation across the harmonics of several vowels either on vowel prominence (McAdams, 1989) or on vowel identification (Summerfield & Culling, 1992). However, frequency modulation can help group together frequency components for computing pitch. In a mistuned harmonic stimulus, shifts in the perceived pitch of the harmonic complex continue to occur at greater mistunings when all components are modulated coherently than when they are unmodulated (Darwin, Ciocca, & Sandell, 1994).

Spatial Position

It was thought early on that different spatial positions should give rise to binaural cues that could be used to segregate temporally and spectrally overlapping sound events. Although work on speech comprehension in noisy environments (e.g., Cherry's 1953 "cocktail party effect") emphasized spatial cues to allow listeners to ignore irrelevant sources, the evidence in support of such cues for grouping is in fact quite weak. An interaural time difference (ITD) is clearly a powerful cue for direction (see Chap. 9, this volume), but it is remarkably ineffective as a cue for grouping simultaneous components that compose a particular source (Culling & Summerfield, 1995; Hukin & Darwin, 1995b).

The other principal grouping cues generally override spatial cues. For example, the detection of changes in ITD on sine components across two successive stimulus intervals is similar when they are presented in isolation or embedded within an inharmonic complex. However, detection performance is much worse when they are embedded within a harmonic complex; thus harmonicity overrides spatial incoherence (Buell & Hafter, 1991). Furthermore, mistuning a component can affect its lateralization (Hill & Darwin, 1996), suggesting that grouping takes place on the basis of harmonicity, and only *then* is the spatial position computed on the basis of the lateralization cues for the set of components that have been grouped together (Darwin & Ciocca, 1992).

Lateralization effects may be more substantial when the spatial position is attended to over an extended time, as would be the case in paying sustained attention to a given sound source in a complex environment (Darwin & Carlyon, 1995). Listeners can attend across time to one of two spoken sentences distinguished by small differences in ITD, but they do not use such continuity of ITD to determine which individual frequency components should form part of a sentence. These results suggest that ITD is computed on the peripheral representation of the frequency components in parallel to a grouping of components on the basis of harmonicity and synchrony. Subsequently, direction is computed on the grouped components, and the listener attends to the direction of the grouped object (Darwin & Hukin, 1999).

General Considerations Concerning Concurrent Grouping

Note that there are several possible cues for grouping and segregation, which raises the possibility that what the various cues signal in terms of source structures in the environment can diverge. For example, many kinds of sound sources are not harmonic, but the acoustic components of the events produced by them would still start and stop at the same time and probably have a relatively fixed spatial position that could be attended to. In many cases, however, redundancy of segregation and integration cues works against ambiguities in inferences concerning grouping on the basis of sensory information. Furthermore, the cues to scene analysis are not all-or-none. The stronger they are, the more they affect grouping, and the final perceptual result is the best compromise on the basis of both the

strength of the evidence available and the perceptual task in which the listener is engaged (Bregman, 1993). As many of the results cited earlier demonstrate, the grouping and segregation of information in the auditory sensory representation precedes and thus determines the perceptual properties of a complex sound source, such as its spatial position, its pitch, or its timbre. However, the perceived properties can in turn become cues that facilitate sustained attending to, or tracking of, sound sources over time.

New Event Detection versus Perception of a Changing Event

The auditory system appears to be equipped with a mechanism that triggers event-related computation when a sudden change in the acoustic array is detected. The computation performed can be a resampling of some property of the environment, such as the spatial position of the source, or a grouping process that results in the decomposition of an acoustic mixture (Bregman, 1991). This raises the questions of what constitutes a sudden change indicating the arrival of a new event and how it can be distinguished from a more gradual change that results from an evolution of an already present event.

An example of this process is binaural adaptation and the recovery from such adaptation when an acoustic discontinuity is detected. Hafter, Buell, & Richards (1988) presented a rapid (40/s) series of clicks binaurally with an interaural time difference that gave a specific lateralization of the click train toward the leading ear (Figure 10.3a). As one increases the number of clicks in the train, accuracy in discriminating the spatial position between two successive click trains increases, but the improvement is progressively less (according to a compressive power function) as the click train is extended in duration. The binaural system thus appears to become

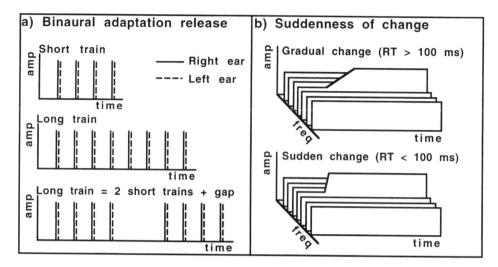

Figure 10.3 Stimuli used to test the resetting of auditory sampling of the environment upon new event detection.

NOTE: a) Binaural adapatation release. A train of clicks (interclick separation = 2.5 ms) is sent to the two ears with a small interaural time difference (ITD) that displaces the perceived lateralization of the sound toward the leading ear (the right ear in this example). The just noticeable ITD decreases as a function of the number of clicks in the train, but the relative contribution of later clicks is lesser than is that of the earlier clicks, indicating binaural adaptation. Release from adaptation is triggered by the detection of a new event, such as a discontinuity in the click train (e.g., a silent gap of 7.5 ms). b) Suddenness of change. The amplitude envelopes on harmonic components are shown. All harmonics are constant in level except one, which increases in level in the middle. A slow change in level (>100 ms) is heard as a change in the timbre of the event, whereas a sudden change (<100 ms) is heard as a new (pure-tone) event.

progressively quiet beyond stimulus onset for constant stimulation. However, if some kind of discontinuity is introduced in the click train (a longer or shorter gap between clicks, or a brief sound with a sudden onset in a remote spectral region, even of fairly low intensity), the spatial environment is suddenly resampled at the moment of the discontinuity. A complete recovery from the process of binaural adaptation appears to occur in the face of such discontinuities and indicates that the auditory system is sensitive to perturbations of regularity. Hafter and Buell (1985) proposed that at a fairly low level in the auditory system, multiple bands are monitored for changes in level that might accompany the start of a new signal or a variation in the old one. Sudden changes cause the system to resample the binaural in-

puts and to update its spatial map at the time of the restart, suggesting that knowledge about the direction of a source may rely more on memory than on the continual processing of ongoing information.

Similarly, an acoustic discontinuity can provoke the emergence of a new pitch in an otherwise continuous complex tone. A sudden interaural phase disparity or frequency disparity in one component of a complex tone can create successive-difference cues that make the component emerge (Kubovy, 1981; Kubovy, Cutting, & McGuire, 1974). In this case, the successive disparity triggers a recomputation of which pitches are present. Thus, various sudden changes trigger resampling. But how fast a change is "sudden"? If listeners must identify the direction of change in pitch for successive pure-tone events added in phase to a continuous harmonic complex (Figure 10.3b), performance is a monotone decreasing function of rise time; that is, the more sudden the change, the more the change is perceived as a new event with its own pitch, and the better is the performance. From these results Bregman, Ahad, Kim, and Melnerich (1994) proposed that "sudden" can be defined as basically less than 100 ms for onsets.

Auditory Stream Formation (Sequential Grouping)

The processes of sequential organization result in the perceptual integration of successive events into a single auditory stream or their perceptual segregation into two or more streams. Under everyday listening conditions, an auditory stream corresponds to a sequence of events emitted by a single sound source.

General Considerations Concerning Sequential Grouping

Several basic principles of auditory stream formation emerge from research on sequential grouping. These principles reflect regularities in the physical world that shaped the evolution of the auditory mechanisms that detect them.

1. *Source properties change slowly.* Sound sources generally emit sequences of events that are transformed in a progressive manner over time. Sudden changes in event properties are likely to signal the presence of several sources (Bregman, 1993).

2. *Events are allocated exclusively to streams.* A given event is assigned to one or another stream and cannot be perceived as belonging to both simultaneously (Bregman & Campbell, 1971), although there appear to be exceptions to this principal in interactions between sequential and concurrent grouping processes and in duplex perception (discussed later).

3. *Streaming is cumulative.* The auditory system appears by default to assume that a sequence of events arises from a single source until enough evidence to the contrary can be accumulated, at which point segregation occurs (Bregman, 1978b). Also, if a cyclical sequence is presented over a long period of time (several tens of seconds), segregation tends to increase (Anstis & Saida, 1985).

4. *Sequential grouping precedes stream attribute computation.* The perceptual properties of sequences depend on what events are grouped into streams, as was shown for concurrent grouping and event attributes. A corollary of this point is the fact that the perception of the order of events depends on their being assigned to the same stream: It is easier to judge temporal order on within-stream patterns than on across-stream patterns that are perceptually fragmented (Bregman & Campbell, 1971; van Noorden, 1975).

The cues that determine sequential auditory organization are closely related to the Gestalt principles of proximity and similarity (see Chap. 5, this volume). The notion of proximity in audition is limited here to the temporal distance between events, and similarity encompasses the acoustic similarity of successive events. Given the intrinsically temporal nature of acoustic events, grouping is considered in terms of continuity and rate of change in acoustic properties between successive events. In considering the acoustic factors that affect grouping in the following, keep in mind that not all acoustic differences are equally important in determining segregation (Hartmann & Johnson, 1991).

Frequency Separation and Temporal Proximity

A stimulus sequence composed of two alternating frequencies in the temporal pattern

ABA—ABA— (where "—" indicates a silence) is heard as a galloping rhythm if the tones are integrated into a single stream and as two isochronous sequences (A—A—A—A— and B———B———) if they are segregated. At slower tempos and smaller frequency separations, integration tends to occur, whereas at faster tempos and larger frequency separations, segregation tends to occur. Van Noorden (1975) measured the frequency separation at which the percept changes from integration to segregation or vice versa for various event rates. If listeners are instructed to try to hear the gallop rhythm or conversely to focus on one of the isochronous sequences, temporal coherence and fission boundaries are obtained, respectively (see Figure 10.4). These functions do not have the same form. The fission boundary is limited by the frequency resolution of the peripheral auditory system and is relatively unaffected by the event rate. The temporal coherence boundary reflects the limits of inevitable segregation and strongly depends on tempo. Between the two is an ambiguous region where the listener's perceptual intent plays a strong role.

Streaming is not an all-or-none phenomenon with clear boundaries between integration and segregation along a given sensory continuum, however. In experiments in which the probability of a response related to the degree of segregation was measured (Brochard, Drake, Botte, & McAdams, 1999), the probability varied continuously as a function of frequency separation. This does not imply that the percept is ambiguous. It is either one stream or two streams, but the probability of hearing one or the other varies for a given listener and across listeners.

It is not the absolute frequency difference that determines which tones are bound together in the same stream, but rather the relative differences among the frequencies. Bregman (1978a), for example, used a sequential tone pattern ABXY. If A and B are within a critical band (i.e., they stimulate overlapping sets of auditory nerve fibers) in a high frequency region, and if X and Y are within a critical band in a low frequency region, then A and B form one stream, and X and Y form another stream (see Figure 10.5). If X and Y are now moved to the same frequency region as A and B such that A and X are close and B and Y are close, without changing the frequency ratios between A and B nor between X and Y, then the relative frequency differences predominate and streams of A-X and B-Y are obtained.

The abruptness of transition from one frequency to the next also has an effect on stream segregation. In the studies just cited, one tone stops on one frequency, and the next tone begins at a different frequency. In many sound sources that produce sequences of events and vary the fundamental frequency, such as the voice, such changes may be more gradual. Bregman & Dannenbring (1973) showed that the inclusion of frequency ramps (going toward the next tone at the end and coming from the previous tone at the beginning) or even complete frequency glides between tones yielded greater integration of the sequence into a single stream.

The Cumulative Bias toward Greater Segregation

Anstis and Saida (1985) showed that there is a tendency for reports of a segregated percept to increase over time when listening to alternating-tone sequences. This stream biasing decays exponentially when the stimulus sequence is stopped and has a time constant of around 4 s on average (Beauvois & Meddis, 1997). Anstis and Saida proposed a mechanism involving the fatigue of frequency jump detectors to explain this phenomenon, but Rogers and Bregman (1993a) showed that an inductor sequence with a single tone could induce a bias toward streaming in the absence of jumps. The biasing mechanism requires

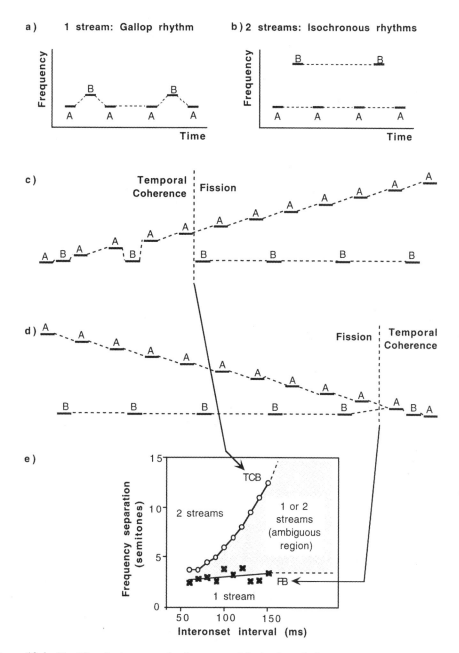

Figure 10.4 Van Noorden's temporal coherence and fission boundaries.

NOTE: A repeating "ABA—" pattern can give a percept of either a) a gallop rhythm or b) two isochronous sequences, depending on the presentation rate and AB frequency difference. c) To measure the temporal coherence boundary (TCB), the initial frequency difference is small and increases while the listener attempts to hold the gallop percept. d) To measure the fission boundary (FB), the initial difference is large and is decreased while the listener tries to focus on a single isochronous stream. In both cases, the frequency separation at which the percept changes is recorded. The whole procedure is repeated at different interonset intervals, giving the curves shown in (e).

SOURCE: Adapted from van Noorden (1975, Figure 2.7). Copyright © 1975 by Leon van Noorden. Adapted with permission.

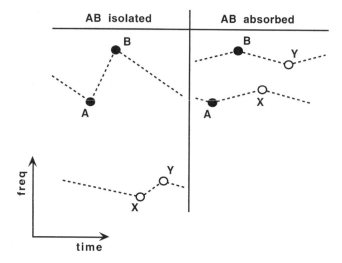

Figure 10.5　Two stimulus configurations of the type used by Bregman (1978) to investigate the effect of relative frequency difference on sequential grouping.
NOTE: Time is on the horizontal axis, and frequency is on the vertical axis. On the left, pure tones A and B are isolated from pure tones X and Y and are heard in a single stream together. Dashed lines indicate stream organization. On the right, A and B have the same frequency relation, but the insertion of X and Y between them causes their reorganization into separate streams because the A-X and B-Y differences are proportionally much smaller than are the A-B and X-Y differences.

the inductor stimulus to have the same spatial location and loudness as the test sequence (Rogers & Bregman, 1998). When discontinuities in these auditory attributes are present, the test sequence is more integrated—a sort of sequential counterpart to the resampling-on-demand mechanism discussed previously. Such a mechanism would have the advantage of preventing the auditory system from accumulating data across unrelated events.

Timbre-Related Differences

Sequences with alternating tones that have the same fundamental frequency (i.e., same virtual pitch) but that are composed of differently ranked harmonics derived from that fundamental (i.e., different timbres) tend to segregate (Figure 10.6a; van Noorden, 1975). Differences in spectral content can thus cause stream segregation (Hartmann & Johnson, 1991; Iverson, 1995; McAdams & Bregman, 1979). It is therefore not pitch per se that creates the streaming. Spectral differences can compete even with pitch-based patterns in determining the melodies that are heard (Wessel, 1979). Note that in music both pitch register and instrument changes produce discontinuities in spectral content.

Although other timbre-related differences can also induce segregation, not all perceptual attributes gathered under the term *timbre* (discussed later) do so. Listeners are unable to identify interleaved melodies any better when different amplitude envelopes are present on the tones of the two melodies than when they are absent, and differences in auditory roughness are only weakly useful for melody segregation, and only for some listeners (Hartmann & Johnson, 1991). However, dynamic (temporal) cues can contribute to stream segregation. Iverson (1995) played sequences that alternated between different musical instruments at the same pitch and asked listeners for ratings of the degree of segregation.

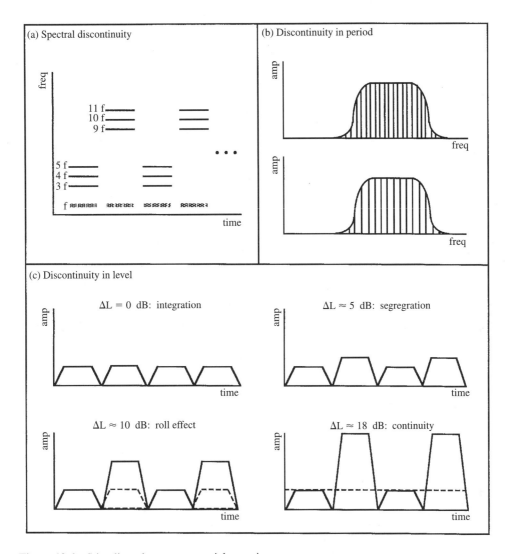

Figure 10.6 Stimuli used to test sequential grouping cues.

NOTE: a) Spectral discontinuity. An alternating sequence of tones with identical fundamental frequencies gives rise to a perception of constant pitch but differing timbres when the spectral content of the tones are different. This discontinuity in spectral content also creates a perceptual segregation into two streams. b) Discontinuity in period. A harmonic complex that is filtered in the high-frequency region gives rise to a uniform pattern of excitation on the basilar membrane, even if the period of the waveform (the fundamental frequency) is changed. The upper diagram has a lower F0 than has the lower diagram. There can be no cue of spectral discontinuity in a sequence of tones that alternates between these two sounds, yet segregation occurs on the basis of the difference in period, presumably carried by the temporal pattern of neural discharges in the auditory nerve. c) Discontinuity in level. A sequence of pure tones of constant frequency but alternating in level gives rise to several percepts depending on the relative levels. A single stream is heard if the levels are close. Two streams at half the tempo are heard if the levels differ by about 5 dB. A roll effect in which a louder half-tempo stream is accompanied by a softer full-tempo stream is obtained at certain rapid tempi when the levels differ by about 10 dB. Finally, at higher tempi and large differences in level, a louder pulsing stream is accompanied by a softer continuous tone.

Multidimensional scaling analyses of these ratings revealed a perceptual dimension related to the temporal envelope of the sound in addition to a more spectrum-based dimension. The temporal coherence boundary for alternating-tone or gallop sequences is situated at a smaller frequency separation if differences in temporal envelope are also present, suggesting that dynamic cues can combine with spectrum- or frequency-based cues (Singh & Bregman, 1997). Listeners can also use voice-timbre continuity rather than F0 continuity to disambiguate intersections in voices that cross in F0 contour (Culling & Darwin, 1993). When there is no timbre difference between crossing glides, bouncing contours are perceived (a pitch similarity effect), but when there is a difference, crossing contours are perceived (a timbre-similarity effect).

Differences in Period

Several studies have led to the conclusion that local differences in excitation patterns on the basilar membrane and fine-grained temporal information may also contribute interactively to stream segregation (Bregman, Liao & Levitan, 1990; Singh, 1987), particularly when the harmonics of the stimuli are resolved on the basilar membrane. Vliegen and Oxenham (1999) used an interleaved melody recognition task in which the tones of a target melody were interleaved with those of a distractor sequence. If segregation does not occur at least partially, recognition of the target is nearly impossible. In one condition, they applied a band-pass filter that let unresolved harmonics through (Figure 10.6b). Because the harmonics would not be resolved in the peripheral auditory system, there would be no cue based on the tonotopic representation that could be used to segregate the tones. However, segregation did occur, most likely on the basis of cues related to the periods of the waveforms carried in the temporal pat-

tern of neural discharges. In a study in which integration was required to succeed, a time shift was applied to the B tones in a gallop sequence (ABA—ABA—), and listeners were required to detect the time shift. This task is more easily performed when the A and B tones are integrated and the gallop rhythm is heard than when they are segregated and two isochronous sequences are heard (Figure 10.4; Vliegen, Moore, & Oxenham, 1999). It seems that whereas period-based cues in the absence of distinctive spectral cues can be used for segregation, as shown in the first study, they do not induce obligatory segregation when the listener tries to achieve integration to perform the task. Period-based cues are thus much weaker than spectral cues (Grimault, Micheyl, Carlyon, Arthaud, & Collet, 2000), suggesting that temporal information may be more useful in tasks in which selective attention can be used in addition to primitive scene-analysis processes.

Differences in Level

Level differences can also create segregation, although this effect is quite weak. Van Noorden (1977) found that alternating pure-tone sequences with constant frequency but level differences on the order of 5 dB segregated into loud and soft streams with identical tempi (Figure 10.6c). Hartmann and Johnson (1991) also found a weak effect of level differences on interleaved melody recognition performance. When van Noorden increased the level difference and the sequence rate was relatively fast (greater than 13 tones/s), other perceptual effects began to emerge. For differences of around 10 dB, a percept of a louder stream at one tempo accompanied by a softer stream at twice that tempo was obtained. For even greater differences (> 18 dB), a louder intermittent stream was accompanied by a continuous softer stream. In both cases, the more intense event would seem to be interpreted as being composed of two events of identical

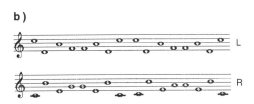

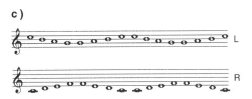

spectral content. These percepts are examples of what Bregman (1990, chap. 3) has termed the *old-plus-new heuristic* (discussed later).

Differences in Spatial Location

Dichotically presented alternating-tone sequences do not tend to integrate into a trill percept even for very small frequency separations (van Noorden, 1975). Similarly, listeners can easily identify interleaved melodies presented to separate ears (Hartmann & Johnson, 1991). Ear of presentation is not, however, a sufficient cue for segregation. Deutsch (1975) presented simultaneously ascending and descending musical scales such that the notes alternated between ears; that is, the frequencies sent to a given ear hopped around (Figure 10.7). Listeners reported hearing an up-down pattern in one ear and a down-up pattern in the other, demonstrating an organization based on frequency proximity despite the alternating ear of presentation. An interaural time difference is slightly less effective in creating segregation than is dichotic presentation (Hartmann & Johnson, 1991).

Figure 10.7   Melodic patterns of the kind used by Deutsch (1975).

NOTE: a) Crossing scales are played simultaneously over headphones. In each scale, the tones alternate between left (L) and right (R) earpieces. b) The patterns that would be heard if the listener focused on a given ear. c) The patterns reported by listeners.

Interactions between Concurrent and Sequential Grouping Processes

Concurrent and sequential organization processes are not independent. They can interact and even enter into competition, the final perceptual result depending on the relative organizational strength of each one. In the physical environment, there is a fairly good consensus among the different concurrent and sequential grouping cues. However, under laboratory conditions or as a result of compositional artifice in music, they can be made to conflict with one another. Bregman and Pinker (1978) developed a basic stimulus (Figure 10.8) for testing the situation in which a concurrent organization (fusion or segregation of B and C) and a sequential organization (integration or seg-

regation of A and B) were in competition for the same component (B). When the sequential organization is reinforced by the frequency proximity of A and B and the concurrent organization is weakened by the asynchrony of B and C, A and B form a single stream, and C is perceived with a pure timbre. If the concurrent organization is reinforced by synchrony while the sequential organization is weakened by separating A and B in frequency, A forms a stream by itself, and B fuses with C to form a second stream with a richer timbre.

The Transparency of Auditory Events

In line with the belongingness principle of the Gestalt psychologists, Bregman (1990,

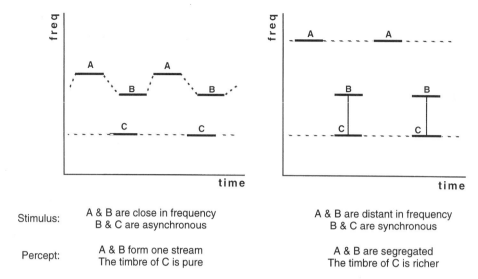

Stimulus: A & B are close in frequency   A & B are distant in frequency
            B & C are asynchronous   B & C are synchronous

Percept: A & B form one stream   A & B are segregated
            The timbre of C is pure   The timbre of C is richer

Figure 10.8   Schematic representative of some of the stimulus configurations used by Bregman and Pinker (1978) to study the competition between concurrent and sequential grouping processes.
NOTE: Pure tone A alternates with a complex tone composed of pure tones B and C. The relative frequency proximity of A and B and the asynchrony of B and C are varied. When A and B are close in frequency and B and C are sufficiently asynchronous (left diagram), an AB stream is formed, and C is perceived as having a pure timbre. When A and B are distant in frequency and B and C are synchronous (right diagram), A forms a stream by itself, and B and C fuse into a single event with a richer timbre.

chap. 7) has proposed the principle of exclusion allocation: A given bit of sensory information cannot belong to two separate perceptual entities simultaneously. In general, this principle seems to hold: Parts of a spectrum that do not start at the same time are exhaustively segregated into temporally overlapping events, and tones presented sequentially are exhaustively segregated into streams. There are, however, several examples of both speech and nonspeech sounds that appear to violate this principle.

Duplex Perception of Speech

If the formant transition specifying a stop consonant such as /b/ (see Chap. 12, this volume) is excised from a consonant-vowel syllable and is presented by itself, a brief chirp sound is heard. The remaining base part of the original sound without the formant transition gives a /da/ sound. If the base and transition

are remixed in the same ear, a /ba/ sound results. However, when the formant transition and base sounds are presented to opposite ears, listeners hear both a /ba/ sound in the ear with the base (integration of information from the two ears to form the syllable) and a simultaneous chirp in the other ear (Cutting, 1976; Rand, 1974). The formant transition thus contributes both to the chirp and to the /ba/—hence the term *duplex*. It is not likely that this phenomenon can be explained by presuming that speech processing is unconstrained by primitive scene analysis mechanisms (Darwin, 1991).

To account for this apparent paradox, Bregman (1990, chap. 7) proposes a two-component theory that distinguishes sensory evidence from perceptual descriptions. One component involves primitive scene analysis processes that assign links of variable strength among parts of the sensory evidence. The link strength depends both on the sensory evidence (e.g., the amount of asynchrony or mistuning for concurrent grouping, or the degree of temporal proximity and spectral dissimilarity for sequential grouping) and on competition among the cues. The links are evidence for belongingness but do not necessarily create disjunct sets of sensory information; that is, they do not provide an all-or-none partitioning. A second component then builds descriptions from the sensory evidence that *are* exhaustive partitionings for a given perceptual situation. Learned schemas can intervene in this process, making certain descriptions more likely than others, perhaps as a function of their frequency of occurrence in the environment. It is at this latter level that evidence can be interpreted as belonging to more than one event in the global description. But why should one allow for this possibility in auditory processing? The reason is that acoustic events do not occlude other events in the way that most (but not all) objects occlude the light reflected from other objects that are farther from the viewer. The acoustic signal arriving at the ears is the weighted sum of the waveforms radiating from different vibrating objects, where the weighting is a function of distance and of various transformations of the original waveform due to the properties of the environment (reflections, absorption, etc.). It is thus possible that the frequency content of one event coincides partially with that of another event. To analyze the properties of the events correctly, the auditory system must be able to take into account this property of sound, which, by analogy with vision, Bregman has termed *transparency.*

This theory presumes (a) that primitive scene analysis is performed on the sensory input prior to the operation of more complex pattern-recognition processes, (b) that the complex processes that build perceptual descriptions are packaged in schemas embodying various regularities in the sensory evidence, (c) that higher-level schemas can build from regularities detected in the descriptions built by lower-level schemas, (d) that the descriptions are constrained by criteria of consistency and noncontradiction, and (e) that when schemas (including speech schemas) make use of the information that they need from a mixture, they do not remove it from the array of information that other description-building processes can use (which may give rise to duplex-type phenomena). Although many aspects of this theory have yet to be tested empirically, some evidence is consistent with it, such as the fact that duplex perception of speech can be influenced by primitive scene-analysis processes. For example, sequential organization of the chirp component can remove it from concurrent grouping with the base stimulus, suggesting that duplex perception occurs in the presence of conflicting cues for the segregation and the integration of the isolated transition with the base (Ciocca & Bregman, 1989).

Auditory Continuity

A related problem concerns the partitioning on the basis of the surrounding context of sensory information present within overlapping sets of auditory channels. The *auditory continuity phenomenon,* also called auditory induction, is involved in perceptual restoration of missing or masked sounds in speech and music interrupted by a brief louder sound or by an intermittent sequence of brief, loud sound bursts (for reviews, see Bregman, 1990, chap. 3; Warren, 1999, chap. 6). If the waveform of a speech stream is edited such that chunks of it are removed and other chunks are left, the speech is extremely difficult to understand (Figure 10.9a). If the silent periods are replaced with noise that is loud enough to have masked the missing speech, were it present, and whose spectrum includes that of the original speech, listeners claim to hear continuous speech (Warren, Obusek, &

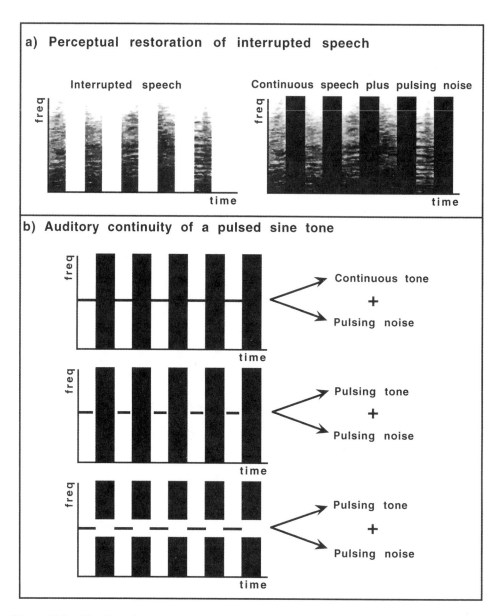

Figure 10.9   Stimuli used to test the auditory continuity phenomenon.
NOTE: a) Speech that is interrupted by silences is heard as such and is difficult to understand. If the silences are filled with a noise of bandwidth and level sufficient to have masked the absent speech signal, a pulsing noise is heard accompanied by an apparently continuous speech stream. b) Auditory continuity can be demonstrated also with a pulsed sine tone. When the silent gaps are filled with noise, a continuous tone is heard along with the pulsing noise. However, if small silent gaps of several milliseconds separate the tone and noise bursts, indicating to the auditory system that the tone actually ceased, then no continuity is obtained. Furthermore, the continuity effect does not occur if the noise does not have any energy in the frequency region of the tone.

Ackroff, 1972). Speech intelligibility can even improve if contextual information that facilitates identification of key words is present (Warren, Hainsworth, Brubaker, Bashford, & Healy, 1997).

Similar effects of continuity can be demonstrated with nonspeech stimuli, such as a sine tone interrupted by noise (Figure 10.9b) or by a higher-level sine-tone of similar frequency. An intermittent sequence superimposed on a continuous sound is heard, as if the more intense event were being partitioned into two entities, one that was the continuation of the lower-level sound preceding and following the higher-level event and another that was a sound burst. This effect works with pure tones, which indicates that it can be a completely within-channel operation. However, if any evidence exists that the lower-level sound stopped (such as short, silent gaps between the sounds), two series of intermittent sounds are heard. Furthermore, the spectrum of the interrupting sound must cover that of the interrupted sound for the phenomenon to occur; that is, the auditory system must have evidence that the interrupting sound could have masked the softer sound (Figure 10.9).

The partitioning mechanism has been conceived by Bregman (1990) in terms of an "old-plus-new" heuristic. The auditory system performs a subtraction operation on the high-level sound. A portion of the energy equivalent to that in the lower-level sound is assigned to the continuous stream, and the rest is left to form the intermittent stream. Indeed, the perceived levels of the continuous sound and intermittent sequence depend on the relative level change and are consistent with a mechanism that partitions the energy (Warren, Bashford, Healy, & Brubaker, 1994). However, the perceived levels are not consistent with a subtraction performed either in units of loudness (sones) or in terms of physical pressure or power (McAdams, Botte, & Drake, 1998). Furthermore, changes occur in the timbre of the high-level sounds in the presence of the low-level sounds compared to when these are absent (Warren et al., 1994). The relative durations of high- and low-level sounds are crucial to the phenomenon. The continuity effect is much stronger when the interrupting event is short compared to the uninterrupted portion. The perceived loudness is also a function of the relative levels of high and low portions, their relative durations, and the perceptual stream to which attention is being directed (Drake & McAdams, 1999). Once again, this continuity phenomenon demonstrates the existence of a heuristic for partitioning acoustic mixtures (if there is sufficient sensory evidence that a mixture indeed exists). It provides the listener with the ability to deal efficiently and veridically with the stimulus complexity resulting from the transparency of auditory events.

Schema-Based Organization

Much mention has been made of the possibility that auditory stream formation is affected by conscious, controlled processes, such as searching for a given source or event in the auditory scene. Bregman (1990) proposed a component that he termed *schema-based scene analysis* in which specific information is selected on the basis of attentional focus and previously acquired knowledge, resulting in the popout of previously activated events or the extraction of sought-after events. Along these lines, van Noorden's (1975) ambiguous region is an example in which what is heard depends in part on what one tries to hear. Further, in his interleaved melody recognition experiments, Dowling (1973a) observed that a verbal priming of an interleaved melody increased identification performance.

Other top-down effects in scene analysis include the role of pattern context (good continuation in Gestalt terms) and the use of previous knowledge to select target information from the scene. For example, a competition between good continuation and frequency proximity demonstrates that melodic pattern can affect the degree of streaming (Heise & Miller, 1951). Frequency proximity alone cannot explain these results.

Bey (1999; Bey & McAdams, in press) used an interleaved melody recognition paradigm to study the role of schema-based organization. In one interval an interleaved mixture of target melody and distractor sequence was presented, and in another interval an isolated comparison melody was presented. Previous presentation of the isolated melody gave consistently better performance than when the mixture sequence was presented before the comparison melody. Furthermore, if the comparison melody was transposed by 12, 13, or 14 semitones— requiring the listener to use a pitch-interval-based representation instead of an absolute-pitch representation to perform the task— performance was similar to when the isolated comparison melody was presented after the mixture. These results suggest that in this task an absolute-pitch representation constitutes the "knowledge" used to extract the melody. However, performance varied as a function of the frequency separation of the target melody and distractor sequence, so performance depended on both sensory-based organizational constraints and schema-based information selection.

TIMBRE PERCEPTION

Early work on timbre perception paved the way to the exploration of sound source perception. The word *timbre* gathers together a number of auditory attributes that until recently have been defined only by what they are not: Timbre is what distinguishes two sounds coming from the same position in space and having the same pitch, loudness,

and subjective duration. Thus, an oboe and a trumpet playing the same note, for example, would be distinguished by their timbres. This definition indeed leaves everything to be defined. The perceptual qualities grouped under this term are multiple and depend on several acoustic properties (for reviews, see Hajda, Kendall, Carterette, & Harshberger, 1997; McAdams, 1993; Risset & Wessel, 1999). In this section, we examine spectral profile analysis, the perception of auditory roughness, and the multidimensional approach to timbre perception.

Spectral Profile Analysis

The sounds that a listener encounters in the environment have quite diverse spectral properties. Those produced by resonating structures of vibrating objects have more energy near the natural frequencies of vibration of the object (string, plate, air cavity, etc.) than at more distant frequencies. In a frequency spectrum in which amplitude is plotted as a function of frequency, one would see peaks in some frequency regions and dips in others. The global form of this spectrum is called the spectral envelope. The extraction of the spectral envelope by the auditory system would thus be the basis for the evaluation of constant resonance structure despite varying fundamental frequency (Plomp & Steeneken, 1971; Slawson, 1968) and may possibly contribute to source recognition. This extraction is surely strongly involved in vowel perception, the quality of which is related to the position in the spectrum of resonance regions called *formants* (see Chap. 12, this volume). Spiegel and Green (1982) presented listeners with complex sounds in which the amplitudes were equal on all components except one. The level of this component was increased to create a bump in the spectral envelope. They showed that a listener is able to discriminate these spectral envelopes despite random variations in overall intensity, suggesting that it is truly the profiles that are being compared and not just an absolute change in intensity in a given auditory channel. This analysis is all the easier if the number of components in the spectrum is large and the range of the spectrum is wide (Green, Mason, & Kidd, 1984). Further, it is unaffected by the phase relations among the frequency components composing the sounds (Green & Mason, 1985). The mechanism that detects a change in spectral envelope most likely proceeds by estimating the level in each auditory channel and then by combining this information in an optimal way across channels (for a review, see Green, 1988).

Auditory Roughness

Auditory roughness is the sensory component of musical dissonance (see Chap. 11, this volume), but is present also in many environmental sounds (unhappy newborn babies are pretty good at progressively increasing the roughness component in their vocalizations, the more the desired attention is delayed). In the laboratory roughness can be produced with two pure tones separated in frequency by less than a critical band (the range of frequencies that influences the output of a single auditory nerve fiber tuned to a particular characteristic frequency). They interact within an auditory channel producing fluctuations in the amplitude envelope at a rate equal to the difference between their frequencies. When the fluctuation rate is less than about 20 Hz to 30 Hz, auditory beats are heard (cf. Plomp, 1976, chap. 3). As the rate increases, the perception becomes one of auditory roughness, peaking at around 70 Hz (depending on the center frequency) and then decreasing thereafter, becoming smooth again when the components are completely resolved into separate auditory channels (cf. Plomp, 1976, chap. 4). The temporal coding of such a

range of modulations has been demonstrated in primary auditory cortex in awake monkeys (Fishman, Reser, Arezzo, & Steinschneider, 2000). For two simultaneous complex harmonic sounds, deviations from simple ratios between fundamental frequencies create sensations of beats and roughness that correlate very strongly with judgments of musical dissonance (Kameoka & Kuriyagawa, 1969; Plomp & Levelt, 1965). Musical harmony thus has a clear sensory basis (Helmholtz, 1885; Plomp, 1976), although contextual factors such as auditory grouping (Pressnitzer, McAdams, Winsberg, & Fineberg, 2000) and acculturation (Carterette & Kendall, 1999) may intervene.

One sensory cue contributing to roughness perception is the depth of modulation in the signal envelope after auditory filtering (Aures, 1985; Daniel & Weber, 1997; Terhardt, 1974), which can vary greatly for sounds having the same power spectrum but differing phase relations among the components. The importance of such phase relations has been demonstrated in signals in which only one component out of three was changed in phase in order to leave the waveform envelope unmodified (Pressnitzer & McAdams, 1999b). Marked differences in roughness perception were found. The modulation envelope shape, after auditory filtering, thus contributes also to roughness, but as a factor secondary to modulation depth. In addition, the coherence of amplitude envelopes across auditory filters affects roughness: In-phase envelopes create greater roughness than do out-of-phase envelopes (Daniel & Weber, 1997; Pressnitzer & McAdams, 1999a).

The Multidimensional Approach to Timbre

One important goal in timbre research has been to determine the relevant perceptual dimensions of timbre (Plomp, 1970; Wessel,

1979). A systematic approach was made possible by the development of multidimensional scaling (MDS) analyses, which are used as exploratory data analysis techniques (McAdams, Winsberg, Donnadieu, De Soete & Krimphoff, 1995). These consist in presenting pairs from a set of sounds to listeners and asking them to rate the degree of similarity or dissimilarity between them. The (dis)similarity ratings are translated into distances by a computer algorithm that, according to a mathematical distance model, projects the set of sound objects into a multidimensional space. Similar objects are close to one another, and dissimilar ones are far apart in the space.

A structure in three dimensions representing the sounds of 16 musical instruments of the string and wind families was interpreted qualitatively by Grey (1977). The first dimension (called brightness; see Figure 10.10a) appeared to be related to the spectral envelope. The sounds having the most energy in harmonics of high rank are at one end of the dimension (oboe, O1), and those having their energy essentially confined to low-ranking harmonics are at the other end (French horn, FH). The second dimension (called spectral flux) was related to the degree of synchrony in the attacks of the harmonics as well as their degree of incoherent fluctuation in amplitude over the duration of the sound event. The flute (FL) had a great deal of spectral flux in Grey's set, whereas the clarinet's (C1) spectrum varied little over time. The position on the third dimension (called attack quality) varied with the quantity of inharmonic energy present at the beginning of the sound, which are often called the attack transients. Bowed strings (S1) can have a biting attack due to these transients, which is less the case for the brass instruments (e.g., trumpet, TP). To test the psychological reality of the brightness dimension, Grey and Gordon (1978) resynthesized pairs of sounds, exchanging their spec-

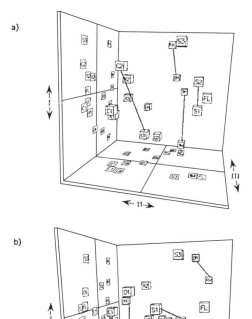

Figure 10.10 Three-dimensional timbre spaces found by a) Grey (1977) and b) Grey & Gordon (1978) from multidimensional scaling analyses of similarity judgments.

NOTE: Pairs of musical instrument sounds from the original Grey (1977) study were modified by exchanging their spectral envelopes in Grey & Gordon (1978) to test the hypothesis that dimension I was related to spectral envelope distribution. Note that the pairs switch orders along dimension I, with small modifications along other dimensions in some cases.

SOURCE: Adapted from Grey & Gordon (1978, Figures 2 and 3) with permission. Copyright © 1978 by the Acoustical Society of America.

tral envelopes (the patterns of bumps and dips in the frequency spectrum). This modification created a change in position along the brightness dimension, with a few shifts along other axes that can be fairly well predicted by the side-effects of the spectral envelope change on other acoustic parameters (Figure 10.10b).

This seminal work has been extended to (a) synthesized sounds representing orchestral instruments or hybrids among them, including more percussive sounds produced by plucking or striking strings or bars (Krumhansl, 1989; McAdams et al., 1995); (b) recorded sounds, including percussion instruments such as drums and gongs in addition to the standard sustained vibration instruments such as winds and bowed strings (Iverson & Krumhansl, 1993; Lakatos, 2000); and (c) car sounds (Susini, McAdams, & Winsberg, 1999). In some cases, new acoustical properties corresponding to the perceptual dimensions still need to be developed to explain these new timbre spaces. For example, attack quality is strongly correlated with the rise time in the amplitude envelope when impact-type sounds are included (Krimphoff, McAdams, & Winsberg, 1994). More advanced MDS procedures allow for individual items to be modeled not only in terms of dimensions shared with all the other items but also as possessing perceptual features that are unique and specific to them (Winsberg & Carroll, 1988). They also provide for the estimation of latent classes of listeners that accord differing weights to the perceptual dimensions (Winsberg & De Soete, 1993) and for the establishment of functional relations between the perceptual dimensions and the relevant acoustic parameters using MDS analyses constrained by stimulus properties (Winsberg & De Soete, 1997). All these advances in data analysis have been applied to musical timbre perception (Krumhansl, 1989; McAdams & Winsberg, 2000; McAdams et al., 1995).

Timbre Interval Perception

On the basis of such a multidimensional model of timbre perception, Ehresman and Wessel (1978) proposed a definition of a timbre interval, by analogy with a pitch interval in musical scales. According to their conception, a timbre interval is an oriented vector in the perceptual space. The equivalent to a transposition of a pitch interval (changing the absolute pitches while maintaining the pitch interval) would thus be a translation of the vector to a different part of the space, maintaining its length and orientation. Both musician and nonmusician listeners are sensitive to such abstract relations among timbres. However, when intervals are formed from complex musical instrument sounds, the specific features possessed by certain timbres often distort them (McAdams & Cunibile, 1992).

SOUND SOURCE PERCEPTION

Human listeners have a remarkable ability to understand quickly and efficiently the current state of the world around them based on the behavior of sound-producing objects, even when these sources are not within their field of vision (McAdams, 1993). We perceive the relative size and form of objects, properties of the materials that compose them, as well as the nature of the actions that had set them into vibration. On the basis of such perception and recognition processes, listening can contribute significantly to the appropriate behaviors that we need to adopt with respect to the environment. To begin to understand these processes more fully, researchers have studied the perception of object properties such as their geometry and material composition as well as the acoustic cues that allow recognition of sound sources. Although pitch can communicate information concerning certain source properties, timbre seems in many cases to be the primary vehicle for sound source and event recognition.

Perception of Source Shape

Listeners are able to distinguish sources on the basis of the geometry of air cavities and of solid objects. Changes in the positions of the two hands when clapping generate differences in the geometry of the air cavity between them that is excited by their impact and can be discriminated as such (Repp, 1987). Rectangular bars of a given material and constant length, but varying in width and thickness, have mechanical properties that give modes of vibration with frequencies that depend on these geometrical properties. When asked to match the order of two sounds produced by bars of different geometries to a visual representation of the cross-sectional geometry, listeners succeed as a function of the difference in ratio between width and thickness, for both metal and wood bars (Lakatos, McAdams, & Caussé, 1997). There are two potential sources of acoustic information in these bars: the ratio of the frequencies of transverse bending modes related to width and thickness and the frequencies of torsional modes that depend on the width-thickness ratio. Both kinds of information are more reliably present in isotropic metal bars than in anisotropic wood bars, and indeed listeners' judgments are more coherent and reliable in the former case.

The length of dowels and dimensions of plates can also be judged in relative fashion by listeners. Carello, Anderson, and Kunkler-Peck (1998) demonstrated that listeners can reproduce proportionally (but not absolutely) the length of (unseen) dowels that are dropped on a floor. They relate this ability to the inertial properties of the dowel, which may give rise to both timbral and rhythmic information (the "color" of the sound and the rapidity of its clattering), although the link between perception and acoustic cues was not established. Kunkler-Peck and Turvey (2000) presented the sounds of (unseen) rectangular and square plates to listeners and asked them to reproduce the vertical and horizontal dimensions for objects formed of metal, wood, and Plexiglas. Again listeners reproduced the proportional, but not absolute, dimensions. They further showed that listeners could identify the shape of plates across materials when asked to choose from among rectangles, triangles, and circles.

Perception of Source Material

There are several mechanical properties of materials that give rise to acoustic cues: density, elasticity, damping properties, and so on. With the advent of physical modeling techniques in which the vibratory processes extended in space and time are simulated with computers (Chaigne & Doutaut, 1997; Lambourg, Chaigne, & Matignon, 2001), fine-grained control of complex vibratory systems becomes available for perceptual experimentation, and a true psychomechanics becomes possible. Roussarie, McAdams, and Chaigne (1998) used a model for bars with constant cross-sectional geometry but variable material density and internal damping factors. MDS analyses on dissimilarity ratings revealed that listeners are sensitive to both mechanical properties, which are carried by pitch information and by a combination of amplitude envelope decay and spectral centroid, respectively, in the acoustic signal. Roussarie (1999) has further shown that listeners are sensitive to elasticity, viscoelastic damping, and thermoelastic damping in thin plates that are struck at constant force. He used a series of simulated plates that were hybrids between an aluminum plate and a glass plate. MDS analyses of dissimilarity ratings revealed monotonic relations between the perceptual and mechanical parameters. However, when listeners were required to identify the plate as either aluminum or glass, they used only the acoustic information related to damping factors, indicating an ability to select the most appropriate from among several sources of acoustic information, according to the perceptual task that must be performed.

Recognition and Identification of Sources and Actions

Studies of the identification of musical instruments have revealed the properties of the acoustic structure of a complex sound event to which listeners are sensitive (for a review, see McAdams, 1993). For example, if the attack transients at the beginning of a sound are removed, a listener's ability to identify instruments that have characteristic transients is reduced (Saldanha & Corso, 1964). Other studies have demonstrated the importance of spectral envelope and temporal patterns of change for identification of modified instrument tones (Strong & Clark, 1967a, 1967b).

A large class of sounds that has been relatively little studied until recently—ostensibly because of difficulties in analyzing and controlling them precisely under experimental conditions—consists of the complex acoustic events of our everyday environment. The breaking of glass, porcelain, or clay objects; the bouncing of wooden, plastic, or metal objects; the crushing of ice or snow underfoot; the scraping of objects against one another— all carry acoustic information both about the nature of the objects involved, about the way they are interacting, and even about changes in their geometric structure (a broken plate, becomes several smaller objects that vibrate independently).

Warren and Verbrugge (1984) asked listeners to classify a sound event as a breaking or bouncing glass object. The events were created by letting jars fall from different heights or from various acoustic manipulations of the recordings. Bouncing events were specified by simple sets of resonances with the same accelerating rhythmic pattern as the object came to rest. Breaking events were specified

by a broad-spectrum burst followed by a multiplicity of different resonating objects with uncorrelated rhythmic patterns. Thus, both the resonance cues (derived from a large unitary object or multiple smaller objects) and the rhythmic cues (unitary or multiple accelerating patterns) were possible sources of identification. To test these cues, the authors used synthetically reconstructed events in which the rhythmic patterns and spectral content (the various resonances present) were controlled. Most of the variance in identification performance was accounted for by the rhythmic behavior.

Cabe and Pittenger (2000) studied the listeners' sensitivities to the acoustic information in a given action situation: accurately filling a vessel. When water is poured into a cylindrical vessel and the rate of (silent) outflow and turbulent (splashy) inflow are controlled, listeners can identify whether the vessel is filling, draining, or remaining at a constant level. Their perception ostensibly depends on the fundamental resonance frequency of the unfilled portion of the vessel. Participants were asked to fill a vessel themselves while seeing, holding, and hearing the water pouring, or while only hearing the water pouring. They were fairly accurate at judging the moment at which the brim level was attained, although they tended to underestimate the brim level under auditory-only conditions. Consideration of the time course of available acoustic information suggests that prospective behavior (anticipating when the full-to-the-brim level will be reached) can be based on acoustic information related to changes in fundamental resonance frequency.

Work in the realm of auditory kinetics concerns the listeners' abilities to estimate the kinetic properties of mechanical events (mass, dropping height, energy). Guski (2000) studied the acoustic cues that specify such kinetic properties in events in which collisions between objects occur. He found that listeners' estimates of the striking force of a ball falling on a drumhead are linearly related to physical work (the energy exchange between the drum and the head at impact). They were less successful in judging the mass of the ball and could not reliably judge the dropping height. The acoustic cues that seem to contribute to these judgments include the peak level (a loudness-base cue) and the rhythm of the bouncing pattern of the ball on the drumhead. The former cue strongly affects judgments of force, which become unreliable if sound events are equalized in peak level. The rhythm cue depends on the energy of the ball and is thus affected by the height and the mass (hence, perhaps, the lower reliability of direct judgments of these parameters). The time interval between the first two bounces explains much of the variance in judgments of force and is strongly correlated with the amount of physical work. Considerations of the timbre-related spectral and temporal characteristics of individual bounces were not examined.

This nascent area of research provides evidence for human listeners' remarkable sensitivity to the forms and material compositions of the objects of their environment purely on the basis of the sounds they produce when set into vibration. The few results already available pave the way for theoretical developments concerning the nature of auditory source and event recognition, and may indeed reveal aspects of this process that are specific to the auditory modality.

TEMPORAL PATTERN PROCESSING IN HEARING

As described in the auditory scene analysis section, the acoustic mixture is perceptually organized into sound objects and streams. In this way, sound events that originate from a single source are perceptually grouped together and are not confused with events coming from other sources. Once auditory events and streams have been perceptually created, it is necessary to establish the relationship between successive events within a stream. We enter the realm of sequence perception, in which each event takes its existence from its relation with these surrounding events rather than from its own specific characteristics. An essential function of the perceptual system is thus to situate each event in time in relation to other events occurring within a particular time span. How do listeners follow the temporal unfolding of events in time? How do they select important information? How are they able to predict "what" and "when" something will occur in the future? The way in which the auditory system identifies the characteristics of each event (the "what") has been described in the section on sound source perception. We now discover the type of temporal information coding involved (the "when").

The Limits of Sequence Perception

Temporal processes occur over a wide range of rates (see Figure 10.11). In this section we focus on those that are relevant to sequence perception and temporal organization. Sound events are perceived as isolated if they are separated from surrounding events by about 1.5 s. This constitutes the upper limit of sequence perception and probably corresponds to the limits of echoic (sensory) memory (Fraisse, 1963). At the other extreme, if the onsets of successive tones are very close in time (less than about 100 ms), a single event is perceived, and the lower limit of sequence perception is surpassed. The zone of sequence perception falls between these two extremes (100–1500 ms interonset interval, or IOI). This range can be subdivided into three separate zones depending on sequence rate or tempo (ten Hoopen et al., 1994). It has been suggested that different

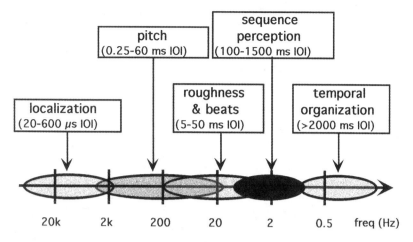

Figure 10.11 The temporal continuum.

NOTE: Event rate greatly influences the perceived nature of event sequences. At extremely fast rates, event attributes such as spatial position, pitch, and timbre are perceived, and at intermediate rates sequence attributes are perceived. Higher-level cognitive processes allow listeners to organize event structures over longer time spans. Event rate can be described in terms of the number of events per second (Hz) or the duration between the onset of successive events (interonset interval, or IOI).

processes are involved at different sequence rates: an intermediate zone (300–800 ms IOI) for which sequence processing is optimum and within which Weber's law applies; a fast zone (100–300 ms IOI) with a fixed time constant (Weber's law does not apply); and a slow zone (800–1500 ms IOI), also with a fixed time constant.

The Problem of Temporal Coding

Psychologists investigating temporal processing have to confront a tricky problem: the absence of an observable sensory organ for coding time (unlike the ear for hearing and the eye for vision). A detailed discussion of the possible existence of an internal clock or a psychological time base is beyond the scope of this chapter (see Block, 1990; Church, 1984; Killeen & Weisse, 1987). For our present concerns, it suffices to say that there is no single, identifiable part of the brain devoted to time perception. Numerous models have been proposed to explain temporal behavior, either by

the ticks of a clock (Creelman, 1962; Divenyi & Danner, 1977; Getty, 1975; Kristofferson, 1980; Luce, 1972; Sorkin, Boggs, & Brady, 1982; Treisman, 1963) or by concepts of information processing independent of a clock (Allan, 1992; Block, 1990; Michon, 1975; Ornstein, 1969). Not surprisingly, each model explains best the data for which it was developed. Thus, models without clocks best explain behavior that requires only temporal order processing, whereas models with clocks best explain behavior requiring relative or absolute duration coding.

For our present interests, it suffices to consider that our perceptual system provides an indication of the duration of events in relative terms (same, longer, or shorter) rather than absolute terms (the first tone lasts x beats, the second x beats; or the first tone occurred at 12:00:00, the second at 12:00:01). In the next sections we discover how information concerning these relative durations allows individuals to create elaborate and reliable temporal representations that are sufficient for adapting their behaviors to the environment. Of course, this representation is a simplification of the physically measurable temporal structure of events, but it does allow the listener to overcome processing constraints.

Coding Temporal Characteristics of Tones and Sequences

Single Tones

In the case of a single tone, the perceptual system probably retains an indication of the duration of the sound (*a* in Figure 10.12). However, the onset is usually more precisely coded than is the offset, due to the usually more abrupt nature of tone onsets (Schulze, 1989; P. G. Vos, Mates, & van Kruysbergen, 1995). It is less likely that there remains an absolute coding of the precise moment in time at which the tone occurred (*b* in Figure 10.12). Rather, there is probably an indication of the time of occurrence of the tone relative to other events. Listeners are able to indicate quite precisely whether two tones are perceived as occurring

simultaneously if their onsets occur within a relatively small time span (40 ms; Rasch, 1979). However, much larger differences in tone onsets are required to give a judgment about order, for instance, by indicating which tone occurs first (about 100 ms; Fitzgibbons & Gordon Salant, 1998).

Tone Sequences

If a tone is perceived as belonging to a sequence rather than being an isolated event, several types of temporal information must be coded. First, the temporal distance between successive events must be coded. A possible solution would be the coding of the duration of the interval between the offset of one tone and the onset of the following tone (*c* in Figure 10.12). However, numerous studies (Schulze, 1989; P. G. Vos et al., 1995) indicate that this parameter is not the most perceptually salient. Rather, the most dominant information concerns the duration between successive onsets (IOIs; *d* in Figure 10.12). For instance, the capacity to detect slight changes in tempo

Single tone

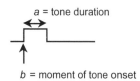

a = tone duration

b = moment of tone onset

Tone sequence

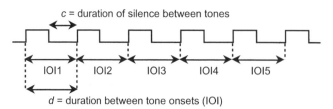

c = duration of silence between tones

IOI1   IOI2   IOI3   IOI4   IOI5

d = duration between tone onsets (IOI)

Figure 10.12   The physical parameters of isolated tones and tones within a sequence are not all of equal perceptual importance.
NOTE: The moment of tone onset (b) and the duration between successive tone onsets (d) appear to be the most perceptually salient.

between two sequences is unaffected by either tone duration (*a*) or off duration (*c*), but rather by the duration between the onsets of successive tones (*d*; J. Vos & Rasch, 1981; P. G. Vos et al., 1995; P. G. Vos, 1977). More precisely, it is not the physical onset of the tone, but rather the perceptual center (P-center) of the tone that determines the IOI, which in turn is influenced by tone duration, off duration, and the shape of the tone attack (P. G. Vos et al., 1995).

In the case of sequences of several events, it could be supposed that the temporal coding may involve the coding of the duration between the onset of each successive tone in the sequence. For instance, in the case of the sequence in Figure 10.12, this would involve the coding of IOI1, IOI2, IOI3, IOI4, and IOI5. This sort of coding is probably possible if the sequence does not contain more than five or six events, does not last longer than several seconds, and does not display a clearly-defined temporal structure (i.e., irregular sequences; Povel, 1981). However, this type of processing appears to be the exception rather than the rule.

Basic Temporal Organization Principles in Sequence Processing

Multiple-Look Model

Is the processing of a sequence of events the same as the sum of the processing of each individual event? The multiple-look model (Drake & Botte, 1993; Schulze, 1978; P. G. Vos, van Assen, & Franek, 1997) suggests that this is not the case. Listeners were presented with two isochronous sequences varying slightly in tempo (mean IOI). The sequences contained either a single interval (two tones) or a succession of intervals (2, 4, 6). Listeners were required to indicate which was the faster of the two sequences (tempo discrimination). The just noticeable difference

(JND) in relative tempo decreased as the number of intervals in the sequence increased. These findings suggest that the more observations the system has concerning the duration of intervals within the sequence (remember that they are all identical), the more precise is the memory code for that interval, and thus the more precise is the temporal coding. Therefore, the temporal coding of intervals contained within a sequence is more precise than is that of isolated intervals.

A second parameter enters into the equation: the degree of regularity of the sequence. If the sequence is regular (isochronous with all IOIs equal), the multiple-look process can work perfectly (no variability). However, if a high degree of irregularity is introduced into the sequence by varying the IOIs (increased standard deviation between IOI), relative tempo JNDs are considerably higher, indicating less efficient processing. It is therefore suggested that the multiple-look process incorporates an indication of both the mean and the variability of intervals within a sequence: The multiple-look process works more efficiently as the number of intervals increases and as the degree of variability decreases.

However, most environmental sequences (footsteps, music, speech) are not entirely regular but contain a low level of temporal irregularity. Does this interfere with a precise temporal coding? It appears not. Relative temporal JNDs are as low for quasi-regular sequences (with a low standard deviation) as they are for truly regular sequences (standard deviation = 0). These findings suggest the existence of a tolerance window by which the system treats sequences that vary within this window as if they were purely regular sequences.

Temporal Window

A third parameter influencing the multiple-look process concerns sequence rate or tempo: The faster the sequence, the greater the number of events over which an increase in sensitivity is observed. For relatively slow sequences (800–1500 ms IOI) JNDs decrease up to 2 or 3 intervals and then remain stable, whereas for fast sequences (200–400 ms IOI) adding additional intervals up to about 20 results in decreased JNDs. This finding suggests the existence of another factor involved in sequence processing: a temporal window.

The idea is that all events would be stored in a sensory memory buffer lasting several seconds (3 s according to Fraisse, 1982; 5 s according to Glucksberg & Cowen, 1970). It probably corresponds to echoic or working memory (see Crowder, 1993). During this time the exact physical characteristics remain in a raw state without undergoing any conscious cognitive processing (Michon, 1975, 1978). Higher-level processes have access to this information as long as it is available (until it decays), which allows the system to extract all relevant information (e.g., interval duration; Fraisse, 1956, 1963; Michon, 1975, 1978; Preusser, 1972). The existence of such an auditory buffer has been suggested by many psychologists under various names: psychological present (Fraisse, 1982), precategorical acoustic storage (Crowder & Morton, 1969), brief auditory store (Treisman & Rostran, 1972), nonverbal memory trace (Deutsch, 1975), and primary or immediate memory (Michon, 1975). One can imagine a temporal window gliding gradually through time, with new events arriving at one end and old events disappearing at the other due to decay. Thus only events occurring within a span of a few seconds would be accessible for processing at any one time, and only events occurring within this limited time window can be situated in relation to each other by the coding of relevant relational information.

Segmentation into Groups

One way to overcome processing limitations and to allow events to be processed together is to group the events into small perceptual units. These units result from a comparison process that compares incoming events with events that are already present in memory. If a new event is similar to those that are already present, it will be assimilated. If the new event differs too much (by its acoustical or temporal characteristics), the sequence will be segmented. This segmentation leads to the closure of one unit and the opening of the next. Elements grouped together will be processed together within a single perceptual unit, and thus can be situated in relation to each other.

An essential question concerns the factors that determine when one perceptual unit ends and the next one begins. A first indication was provided by Gestalt psychologists who described the physical characteristics of sounds that determine which events are perceived as belonging to a single unit (Koehler, 1929; Wertheimer, 1925). They considered that unit boundaries are determined by a relatively important perceptual change (pitch, loudness, articulation, timbre, duration) between successive events. For instance, two notes separated by a long temporal interval or by a large jump in pitch are perceived as belonging to separate groups. They described three principles: temporal proximity (events that occur relatively close in time), similarity (events that are relatively similar in timbre, pitch, loudness and duration), and continuity (events oriented in the same direction, i.e., progressive increase in pitch). Much research has confirmed the essential role of these principles in sequence segmentation (Bregman, 1990; Deutsch, 1999; Dowling & Harwood, 1986; Handel, 1989; Sloboda, 1985). They also appear to function with musical sequences (Clarke & Krumhansl, 1990; Deliège, 1987).

Temporal Regularity Extraction

Segmentation into basic perceptual units provides one means of overcoming memory limits and allows adjacent events to be processed together. However, this process poses the inconvenience of losing information concerning the continuity of the sequence over time between successive perceptual units. In order to maintain this continuity, a second basic process may occur in parallel: the extraction of temporal regularities in the sequence in the form of an underlying pulse. In this way the listener may extract certain temporal relationships between nonadjacent events. Thus, the process of segmentation breaks the sequence down into small processing units, whereas the process of regularity extraction pulls together temporally nonadjacent events.

Rather than coding the precise duration of each interval, our perceptual system compares each newly arriving interval with preceding ones. If the new interval is similar in duration to preceding intervals (within an acceptable temporal window, called the tolerance window), it will be categorized as "same"; if it is significantly longer or shorter than the preceding intervals (beyond the tolerance window), it will be categorized as "different." There may be an additional coding of "longer" or "shorter." Thus, two or three categories of durations (same/different, or same/longer/shorter) may be coded, but note that this is a relative, rather than an absolute, coding system.

One consequence of this type of processing is that if a sequence is irregular (each interval has a different duration) but all the interval durations remain within the tolerance window, then we will perceive this sequence as the succession of "same" intervals and therefore perceive a regular sequence. Such a tolerance in our perceptual system is quite understandable when we examine the temporal microstructure of performed music: Local lengthenings and shortenings of more than 10% are quite common and are not necessarily picked up by listeners as being irregularities per se (Drake, 1993a; Palmer, 1989; Repp, 1992).

Coding events in terms of temporal regularity is thus an economical processing principle that has other implications. If an incoming sequence can be coded in such a fashion, processing resources are reduced, thus making it easier to process such a sequence. Indeed, we can say that the perceptual system exploits this predisposition by actively seeking temporal regularities in all types of sequences. When listening to a piece of music, we are predisposed to finding a regular pulse, which is emphasized by our tapping our foot in time with the music (*tactus* in musical terms). Once this underlying pulse has been identified, it is used as an organizational framework with respect to which other events are situated.

The Hypothesis of a Personal Internal Tempo

The fact that we appear to be predisposed to processing temporal regularities and that temporal processing is optimum at an intermediate tempo has led Jones and colleagues (Jones, 1976; Jones & Boltz, 1989) to suggest that we select upcoming information in a cyclic fashion. Each individual would have a personal tempo, a rate at which incoming events would be sampled. For a given individual, events that occur at his or her personal tempo would be processed preferentially to events occurring at different rates.

Temporal Organization over Longer Time Spans

The temporal processes described so far occur within a relatively short time window of several seconds. When the sequence becomes more complicated (longer or having more events), the number of events that must be processed quickly goes beyond the limits of the buffer. However, it is clear that we are able to organize events over longer time spans; otherwise the perception of music and speech would be impossible. Consequently, simple concatenation models (Estes, 1972), which propose that the characteristics of each event are maintained in memory, are not able to account for the perception of long sequences because of problems of processing and memory overload. Imagine the number of intervals that would need to be stored and accessed when listening to a Beethoven sonata! We now explore how several coding strategies have been developed to overcome these limits and to allow the perception of longer and more complex sequences.

The organization of information into hierarchical structures has often been proposed as a means of overcoming processing and memory limits. This idea, originally formulated by Miller (1956), presupposes that the information processing system is limited by the quantity of information to be processed. By organizing the information into larger units, the limiting factor becomes the number of groups, not the number of events. Applying this principle to music perception, Deutsch and Feroe (1981) demonstrated that the units at each hierarchical level combine to create structural units at a higher hierarchical level. The presence of regularly occurring accents allows the listener to extract regularities at higher hierarchical levels, and thus attention can be guided in the future to points in time at which upcoming events are more likely to occur. This process facilitates learning and memorization (Deutsch, 1980; Dowling, 1973b; Essens & Povel, 1985; Halpern & Darwin, 1982). Sequences that are not structured in such a hierarchical fashion are harder to organize perceptually and require greater attentional resources. Events that occur at moments of heightened attention are better encoded and then remembered better than are events occurring at other moments in time (Dowling, 1973b). Learning and memorization are deteriorated, and listeners have difficulty in analyzing both temporal and nontemporal aspects of the sequence (Boltz, 1995). This type of hierarchical organization appears to function with music, of course, but with other types of natural sequences as well, such as speech, walking, and environmental sounds (Boltz, 1998; Boltz, Schulkind, & Kantra, 1991; Jones, 1976).

Two Types of Temporal Hierarchical Organizations

Two types of temporal hierarchical organizations have been proposed (see Figure 10.13; Drake, 1998; Jones, 1987; Lerdahl & Jackendoff, 1983) to work in parallel, each based on a basic process. One hierarchical organization is based on the combination of perceptual units (hierarchical segmentation organization). A second is created from the combination of underlying pulses (hierarchical metric organization). In both cases basic units combine to create increasingly larger perceptual units, encompassing increasingly larger time spans. Thus, a particular musical sequence may evoke several hierarchical levels at once. In theory, listeners may focus on each of these levels, switching attention from one to the other as desired.

Hierarchical segmentation organization involves the integration of small, basic groups into increasingly larger units that, in the end, incorporate whole musical phrases and the entire piece (levels A2, A3, and A4 in Figure 10.13). Similar segmentation processes probably function at each hierarchical level, except, of course, that the segmentation cues are more salient (larger temporal separation or larger pitch jump) at higher hierarchical levels (Clarke & Krumhansl, 1990; Deliège, 1993; Penel & Drake, 1998).

Hierarchical metric organization involves the perception of temporal regularities at

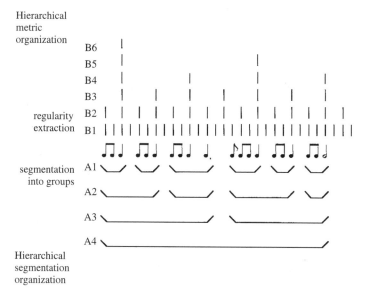

Figure 10.13 Grouping and metrical hierarchies in musical sequences.
NOTE: When listening to a tone sequence (here a musical rhythm), two basic processes function the same way in everyone: The sequence is perceptually segmented into small perceptual units (segmentation into groups, A), and a regular underlying pulse that retains a continuity between events is established (regularity extraction, B). Two types of hierarchical organization, each based on a basic process (hierarchical segmentation organization and hierarchical metric organization, respectively), allow the listener to organize events perceptually over longer time spans. The functioning of these organizational processes differs considerably across individuals.

multiple hierarchical levels. Regularly occurring events can be situated within a hierarchical structure by which multiples of the reference period (usually two, three, or four) are incorporated into larger units (level B3 in Figure 10.13), and these units can themselves be incorporated into increasingly larger units (levels B4, B5, and B6). Subdivisions (level B1) of the reference period are also possible. In Western tonal music, this type of organization corresponds to the metric structure involving the integration of regularly occurring beats, measures, and hyper-measures. Thus, events separated by time spans larger than the reference period can be processed together. Jones (1987) emphasized how these regularities allow the creation of expectations. The perception of regularly occurring accents (events that stand out perceptually from the

sequence background) facilitates the identification and implementation of higher hierarchical levels.

Many models of meter have been proposed (Desain, 1992; Lee, 1991; Longuet-Higgins & Lee, 1982; Longuet-Higgins & Lee, 1984; for a review of these models, see Essens, 1995), and these are perhaps the most popular aspect of temporal processing. Most of the models try to demonstrate that a computer is able to identify correctly the metric structure of a piece of music, thus demonstrating which factors may intervene (e.g., the position of long or accented events). These models are certainly interesting for both computer science and musicology, but their usefulness for psychologists is currently limited because of the rarity of appropriate comparison with human behavior. There are, however, two notable exceptions. In the first, Povel and Essens (1985) considered that an internal clock provides a regular beat around which rhythms are perceptually organized. They demonstrated that sequences that strongly induce a clock (sounds occurring at the same time as beats) are easier to reproduce than are sequences that do not induce a clock as strongly (sounds occurring between beats). In the second, Large and Jones (1999) proposed a neural net model designed to follow, in real time, the coding of an auditory sequence and to allow predictions about upcoming events. By the use of coupled oscillators and with the parameter values established by experimental data and theory, the model predictions are successfully confirmed by new experimental data.

ATTENTIONAL PROCESSES IN HEARING

Perceptual Organization Is an Active Process

We have described how listeners perceptually organize auditory scenes into objects, streams, and sources and how they follow changes over time. Listeners are active and through attentional processes are able to influence the resultant perceptual organization to a certain extent. What a listener tries to hear can affect the way a sound sequence is organized perceptually, indicating an interaction between top-down selection and perceptual integration or segregation (van Noorden, 1977). Indeed, the listener is "free" to focus attention on any individual auditory object or stream within an auditory stream, as was indicated in the section on auditory scene analysis (Alain, 2000; Giard, Fort, Mouchetant-Rostaing & Pernier, 2000). Luck and Vecera (Chap. 6, this volume) reviewed recent literature in visual attention. The reader is encouraged to compare the two sensory modalities in order to note similarities and differences between them.

Attentional Focus

In audition, attention is often considered as a spotlight aimed at a single auditory event (Näätänen, 1992; Scharf, 1998). Each perceived object within an auditory scene is potentially available for attentional focus. Listeners are unable to focus on more than one object at a time (Bigand, McAdams, & Forêt, 2000; Bregman, 1990). The process of focally attending to one particular object is known as *selective* or *focal attending*. Also, situations have been described in which listeners divide their attention between one or more objects, switching back and forth between them in a process know as *divided attention*. Selective or divided attention requires effort and becomes more difficult in more complex situations. For instance, focusing attention on a stream within a two-stream context is easier than focusing on the same stream within a three- or four-stream context (Brochard et al., 1999).

Attentional focus or selective attention results in enhanced processing of the selected object and limited processing of the remaining nonselected auditory scene. When attention is engaged, the representation of the object is more salient; semantic analysis is possible; cognitive decisions are faster; and the representation better resists decay. Conversely, when attention is directed elsewhere, stimuli are superficially processed; representations decay rapidly; and long-term storage is prevented. In short, selective attention enhances the representation of a target and inhibits the representation of distractors.

Such benefits have been demonstrated in the detection of pure tones (Scharf, 1998; Scharf, Quigley, Aoki, & Peachey, 1987). The detection of a pure tone in noise is facilitated if attention is drawn to that frequency by preceding it with a cue at that frequency. Facilitation progressively declines as the frequency difference between the cue and the target is increased. Scharf (1998) suggests that attention acts as a filter enhancing the detection of the target and attenuating the detection of a distractor (whose properties differ from those of the target). Contrary to Broadbent (1958), Scharf considers that these attentional filters are fitted with frequency-selective auditory filters. If a signal has a frequency tuned to the central frequency of the attentional filter, the representation of this signal is amplified. If the pitch of the signal falls outside the bandwidth of the attentional filter, the signal is attenuated and neglected. Similar effects are obtained with more complex stimuli (simultaneous presentation of complex sequences composed of subsequences varying in tempo and frequency). When attention is focused on one subsequence (by preceding the complex sequence by a single sequence cue), it is easy to detect a temporal irregularity located within it. However, when the temporal irregularity is located in a nonfocused subsequence (no preceding cue), the intensity level has to be increased by 15 dB to allow the same level of detection performance (Botte, Drake, Brochard, & McAdams, 1997).

Determinants of Attentional Focus

What determines which object will receive this privileged attentional focus? Two sets of factors have been described: stimulus-driven attentional capture and directed attentional focus.

Stimulus-Driven Attentional Capture

Certain characteristics of an auditory event or of an individual increase the probability than a particular stream or object will receive capture attention. First, physical characteristics of events may make one particular object more perceptually salient than others: For instance, loud events tend to capture attention more than relatively quiet events do (Cowan, 1988; Sokolov, 1963); in the case of music, relatively high-pitched events tend to capture attention more than low-pitched events do (Huron & Fantini, 1989). Second, sudden changes in the sound environment (the appearance or disappearance of a new object or stream) will tend to attract attention away from previously focused objects: The sudden appearance of a motor engine or the stopping of a clock's ticking usually lead to a change in attentional focus (Cowan, 1988; Sokolov, 1963). Furthermore, events with particular personal significance (your own name, or your own baby's crying) have enhanced perceptual salience and lead to a change in attentional focus for that particular object (Moray, 1959; Wood & Cowan, 1995).

Personal characteristics, such as a person's spontaneous internal tempo (or referent period), may lead to a preferential focusing on events occurring at one particular rate (Boltz, 1994; Jones, 1976). People with faster referent periods will tend to focus spontaneously on streams containing faster-occurring events. Similarly, the more skilled an individual is at organizing events over longer time spans (such as musicians compared with nonmusicians), the more likely it is that the individual will focus at a higher hierarchical level within a complex sequence such as music (Drake, Penel, & Bigand, 2000).

Directed Attentional Focus

Thus, in any given sound environment, attention will tend to be focused spontaneously on one particular object according to the factors just described. Listeners can actively control attention, but this ability is limited by characteristics of both the stimulus and the listener. In the case of a complex sound sequence composed of multiple subsequences, not all subsequences are equally easy to direct attention to. For instance, it is much easier to focus attention on subsequences with the highest or lowest pitch, rather than an intermediate pitch (Brochard et al., 1999). A corresponding finding has been observed in the perception of musical fugues in which it is easier to detect changes in the outer voices, in particular the voice with the highest pitch (Huron & Fantini, 1989). Similarly, it is easier to focus on one particular stream if it has been cued by tones resembling the target tones in some respect. The more physically similar a stream is to the object of spontaneous focus, the easier it is for a listener to direct attention to that particular object.

Individual characteristics also play an important role. The more a listener is familiar with a particular type of auditory structure, the easier it is for him or her to focus attention toward different dimensions of that structure. For instance, musicians can switch attention from one stream to another more easily than can nonmusicians, and musicians have access to more hierarchical levels than do nonmusicians (Drake et al., 2000; Jones & Yee, 1997).

Role of Attention in Auditory Organization

Much debate concerns whether stream formation is the result of attentional processes, precedes them, or is the result of some kind of interaction between the two.

More traditional approaches limit the role of attention to postorganizational levels (after object and stream formation). In the first cognitive model of attention proposed by Broadbent (1958), unattended information is prevented from reaching a central limited canal of conscious processing by a filter located after sensory storage and before the perceptual stage. Unattended information would therefore receive only extremely limited processing. Bregman (1990) holds stream formation to be a primarily primitive, preattentive process. Attention intervenes either as a partial selection of information organized within stream (a top-down influence on primitive organization) or as a focusing that brings into the foreground a particular stream from among several organized streams (the attended stream then benefits from further processing).

An alternative position (Jones, 1976; Jones & Boltz, 1989; Jones & Yee, 1993) considers that attention intervenes much earlier in processing, during the formation of streams themselves. The way in which an auditory scene is organized into streams depends on the listener's attentional focus: If an individual directs attention at some particular aspect of the auditory signal, this particular information will be a determinant in stream creation. Thus, Jones proposed that stream formation is the result of dynamic attentional processes with temporal attentional cycles. In this view, attention is viewed as a structuring and organizing process. It orchestrates information selection with a hierarchy of coupled oscillators. Therefore, fission is a breakdown of tracking caused by a noncorrelation between cyclic attentional processes and the periodicity of event occurrence. However, no effect of temporal predictability (Rogers & Bregman, 1993b) or of frequency predictability (van Noorden, 1977) on stream segregation has been found.

One way to disentangle this problem is to measure precisely when and where in the auditory pathway attention exerts its prime influence. Electrophysiological measures (Näätänen, 1992; Woods, Alho, & Algazi, 1994) consistently show that the earliest attentional modulation of the auditory signal appears 80 ms to 100 ms after stimulation, which is when the signal reaches the cortical level. Some authors have suggested that the efferent olivo-cochlear bundle that projects onto the outer hair cells (see Chap. 9, this volume) could be a device that allows attention to operate at a peripheral level (e.g., Giard, Collet, Bouchet & Pernier, 1993; Meric & Collet, 1994).

Using electrophysiological measures, unattended sounds seem to be organized perceptually. Sussman, Ritter, and Vaughan (1999) found electrophysiological evidence for a preattentive component in auditory stream formation using the mismatch negativity (MMN; Näätänen, 1995), an electroencephalographic (EEG) component based on an automatic, preattentive deviant detection system. MMN responses were found on deviant subsequences only when presented at a fast tempo that usually yields two auditory streams under behavioral measures. Within-stream patterns whose memory traces give rise to the MMN response appeared to have emerged prior to or at the level of the MMN system. Sussman, Ritter, and Vaughan (1998) observed, however, that if tempo and frequency separation were selected so that the stimulus sequence was in the ambiguous zone (van Noorden, 1977; see also Figure 10.4), the MMN was observed for the deviant sequence only in the attentive condition (attend to the high stream)—not in the inattentive condition with a distracting (reading) task. This physiological result confirms the behavioral finding that streaming can be affected by attentional focus in the ambiguous region. In a similar vein, Alain et al. (1994) found an interaction between the automatic perceptual analysis processes and volitional attentional processes in EEG measures.

In a paradigm derived from work on concurrent grouping (mistuned harmonic segregation), Alain, Arnott, and Picton (in press) found two major ERP components related to segregation: one related to automatic segregation processes that are unaffected by attentional focus but that varied with stimulus conditions related to segregation, and another that varied depending on whether listeners were actively attending to the sounds. These results suggest a model containing a certain level up to which perceptual organization is automatic and impermeable to attentional processes and above which the information produced by this stage can be further processed if attended to. This view is consistent with data showing that listeners have difficulty detecting a temporal deviation in one of several simultaneous streams if they are not cued to the target stream. It is also consistent with an apparent inhibition of nonfocused events as a kind of perceptual attenuation that has been estimated to be as much as 15 dB (Botte et al., 1997).

DEVELOPMENTAL ISSUES

Up to this point, we have examined the functioning of the human perceptual system in its final state: that of the adult. However, much can be learned about these systems by comparing this "final" state with "initial" or "transitional" states observed earlier in life. Differences may be related to (a) the functional characteristics and maturity of the auditory system (e.g., speed of information transmission, neuronal connectivity, and properties of the cochlea), (b) acculturation through passive exposure to regularities in the sound environment, and (c) specific learning, such as music tuition, in which musicians learn explicit organizational rules. The relative importance of these factors can be demonstrated by comparing the behavior of (a) infants (as young as possible to minimize all influences of learning), (b) children and adults varying in age (opportunities for acculturation increase with age), and (c) listeners with and without musical training (explicit learning—together with many other factors—increases with training). Of considerable interest is the question of the relative roles of passive exposure (and maturation) compared with explicit training in the development of these higher-level processes. Because it is impossible to find people without listening experience (except the recent emergence of profoundly deaf children fitted with hearing-aids and cochlear implants later in life), the usual experimental strategy has been to compare the performances of listeners who have received explicit training in a particular type of auditory environment (almost always music) with the performance of listeners who have not received such training. A newly emerging idea is to compare listeners from different cultures who have been exposed to different sound environments; commonalties in processing are considered to be fundamental, universal, or innate (Drake, in press; Krumhansl, Louhivuori, Toiviainen, Jaervinen, & Eerola, 1999; Krumhansl et al., 2000).

The dominant interactive hypothesis (Bregman, 1990; Deutsch, 1999; Dowling & Harwood, 1986; Drake et al., 2000; Handel, 1989; Jones, 1990; Sloboda, 1985) is that low-level perceptual processes (such as perceptual attribute discriminations, stream segregation, and grouping) are hardwired or innate, and thus more or less functional at birth. Slight improvements in functioning precision are predicted to occur during infancy, but no significant changes in functioning mode should be observed. However, higher-level cognitive processes (such as attentional flexibility and hierarchical organization) are less likely to be functional at birth. They will thus develop throughout life by way of passive exposure and explicit learning. These more "complex" processes do not appear from nowhere, but rather emerge from low-level processes as they extend in scope and combine into larger, more elaborate constructs.

Our knowledge about infants' and children's auditory perception and cognitive skills is currently extremely piecemeal (Baruch, 2001). Only a handful of auditory processes have been investigated. Moreover, of the stud-

ies that do exist, both the ages examined and the techniques used vary considerably. Researchers usually compare the performance of three sets of listeners: infants (aged 2 days to 10 months), children in midchildhood (aged 5–10 years), and adults (usually psychology students aged 18–25 years). Obviously, there is considerable room for change within each set of listeners (new-born infants and 1-year-olds do not have much in common!). There are also considerable periods in the developmental sequence that remain almost completely unexplored, probably because of experimental difficulties. For instance, we have very little idea of the perceptual abilities of toddlers and teenagers, but probably not for the same reasons. The tasks adopted are usually appropriate for each age group, but the degree of comparability between those used for different groups is debatable.

Despite these problems and limitations, general confirmation of the interactive developmental hypothesis is emerging, and it is possible to draw up a tentative picture of the auditory processes that are functional at birth, those that develop considerably during childhood through passive exposure, and those whose development is enhanced by specific training. We would like to emphasize, however, that this picture remains highly speculative.

Auditory Sensitivity and Precision

Most recent research indicates that infants' detection and discrimination thresholds are higher than those of adults, despite the presence of an anatomically mature peripheral auditory system at birth (e.g., Berg, 1993; Berg & Smith, 1983; Little, Thomas, & Letterman, 1999; Nozza & Wilson, 1984; Olsho, Koch, Carter, Halpin, & Spetner, 1988; Schneider, Trehub, & Bull, 1980; Sinnot, Pisoni, & Aslin, 1983; Teas, Klein, & Kramer, 1982;

Trehub, Schneider, & Endman, 1980; Werner, Folsom, & Mancl, 1993; Werner & Marean, 1991). Take, for example, the case of absolute thresholds. The magnitude of the observed difference between infants and adults has decreased significantly over recent years, mainly because of improvements in measurement techniques. However, even with the most sophisticated methods (observer-based psychoacoustic procedures), infants' thresholds remain 15 dB to 30 dB above those of adults. At six months the difference is 10 dB to 15 dB (Olsho et al., 1988). The difference continues to decrease with age (Schneider, Trehub, Morrongiello, & Thorpe, 1986), and by the age of 10 years, children's thresholds are comparable with those of adults (Trehub, Schneider, Morrongiello, & Thorpe, 1988).

It would be tempting to suggest that similar patterns of results have been found for the perception of various auditory attributes. In this field, however, the experimental data are so sparse and the developmental sequence so incomplete that such a conclusion would be premature. The best we can say is that most of the existing data are not incompatible with the proposed pattern (loudness: Jensen & Neff, 1993; Schneider & Trehub, 1985; Sinnot & Aslin, 1985; frequency selectivity: Olsho, 1985; Olsho et al., 1988; Sinnot & Aslin, 1985; Jensen & Neff, 1993; timbre: Trehub, Endman, & Thorpe, 1990; Clarkson, Martin, & Miciek, 1996; Allen & Wightman, 1995; and temporal acuity: Werner & Rubel, 1992).

Despite this poorer performance level in infants, the same functioning mode seems to underlie these low-level auditory processes. For instance, similar patterns of results in infants and adults indicate the existence in both groups of tuning curves and auditory filters (Abdala & Folsom, 1995), the double coding of pitch (pitch height and chroma; Demany & Armand, 1984, 1985), and the phenomenon of the missing fundamental and pitch extraction

from inharmonic tones (Clarkson & Clifton, 1995).

Primary Auditory Organization Processes

In a similar fashion, certain primary auditory organization processes appear to function early in life in the same way as they do in adults, although not necessarily as efficiently and not in more complex conditions.

Stream Segregation

As stream segregation is such an important process in auditory perception, it is surprising to note how few studies have investigated its development. Stream segregation has been demonstrated at ages 2 months to 4 months for frequency-based streaming (Demany, 1982) as well as in new-born infants, but only in easy streaming conditions (slow tempi and large pitch jumps) for timbre and spectral position-based streaming (McAdams & Bertoncini, 1997). Surprisingly, even less is known about how stream segregation develops during childhood. One exception is the study by Andrews and Dowling (1991), who demonstrated that even 5-year-olds are able to identify a familiar tune within a complex mixture based on pitch and timbre differences between tones. These abilities develop with age, although the differences may be due to changes in performance level rather than to changes in functioning mode. Elderly people do not show a deficit in this process compared with young adults (Trainor & Trehub, 1989).

Segmentation into Groups

Segmentation into groups has been demonstrated in 6- to 8-month-old infants (Trainor & Adams, 2000; Krumhansl & Jusczyk, 1990; Thorpe & Trehub, 1989) and in 5- to 7-year-old children (Bamberger, 1980; Drake, 1993a, 1993b; Drake, Dowling & Palmer, 1991;

Thorpe & Trehub, 1989). Similar segmentation principles are used by adult musicians and nonmusicians, although musicians are more systematic in their responses (Fitzgibbons, Pollatsek, & Thomas, 1974; Peretz & Morais, 1989).

Temporal Regularity Extraction

Temporal regularity extraction is functional at an early age: The capacity to detect a small change in tempo of an isochronous sequence is present in 2-month-old infants (Baruch & Drake, 1997). Children are able to synchronize with musical sequences by the age of 5 years (Dowling, 1984; Dowling & Harwood, 1986; Drake, 1997; Fraisse, Pichot, & Clairouin, 1969), and their incorrect reproductions of musical rhythms almost always respect the underlying pulse (Drake & Gérard, 1989). Both musicians and nonmusicians use underlying temporal regularities to organize complex sequences (Povel, 1985).

Tempo Discrimination

Tempo discrimination follows the same pattern over age: The same zone of optimal tempo is observed at 2 months as in adults, although there is a significant slowing and widening of this range during childhood (Baruch & Drake, 1997; Drake et al., 2000).

Simple Rhythmic Forms and Ratios

Like children and adults, infants demonstrate a processing preference for simple rhythmic and melodic forms and ratios (e.g., isochrony and 2:1 ratios; Trainor, 1997). Two-month-old infants discriminate and categorize simple rhythms (Demany, McKenzie, & Vurpillot, 1977; Morrongiello & Trehub, 1987), and young children discriminate and reproduce better rhythmic sequences involving 2:1 time ratios compared with more complex ratios (Dowling & Harwood, 1986; Drake, 1993b; Drake & Gérard, 1989).

Higher-Level Auditory Organization

In contrast to a noted general absence of changes with age and experience in the preceding sections, considerable differences are expected both in the precision and mode of functioning of more complex auditory processes. Because higher-level processes are conceived as being harder, researchers have simply not looked for (or published) their functioning in infants and children: It is never clear whether the absence of effect is due to the lack of process or to methodological limits. Very few studies investigate these processes in infants or children. However, some studies do demonstrate significant differences between different groups of adults (musicians and nonmusicians, different cultures, etc.). Whereas few studies have investigated higher-level processing in infants for simple and musical sequences, more is known about such processes for speech signals (see Chap. 12, this volume).

Hierarchical Segmentation Organization

This type of organization has been investigated with a segmentation paradigm that has been applied to children and adults but not to infants. Participants are asked to listen to a piece of music and then to indicate where they perceive a break in the music. In both children (Bertrand, 1999) and adults (Clarke & Krumhansl, 1990; Deliège, 1990; Pollard-Gott, 1983), the smallest breaks correspond to low-level grouping processes, described earlier, that are based on changes in the physical characteristics of events and temporal proximity. Larger groupings over longer time spans were observed only in adults. These segmentations correspond to greater changes in the same parameters. Such a hierarchy in segmentation was observed in both musicians and nonmusicians, although the principles used were more systematic in adult musicians. This type of organization has not been investigated in infants.

Hierarchical Metric Organization

The use of multiple regular levels has also not been investigated in infants. Whereas 4-year-old children do not demonstrate the use of this organizational principle, its use does increase with age. By the age of about 7 years, children use the reference period and one hierarchical level above or below this level (Drake, Jones & Baruch, 2000). However, the use of more hierarchical levels seems to be restricted to musicians (Bamberger, 1980; Drake, 1993b), and musicians tend to organize musical rhythms around higher hierarchical levels than do nonmusicians (Drake et al., 2000; Monahan, Kendall, & Carterette, 1987; Stoffer, 1985). The ability to use the metrical structure in music performance improves rapidly with musical tuition (Drake & Palmer, 2000; Palmer & Drake, 1997).

Melodic Contour

Infants aged 7 to 11 months can detect changes in melodic contours better than they can detect local changes in intervals, a pattern that is reflected in adult nonmusicians but not in adult musicians (Ferland & Mendelson, 1989; Trehub, Bull, & Thorpe, 1984; Trehub, Thorpe, & Morrongiello, 1987; for more details, see Chap. 11, this volume).

Focal Attending

Nothing is known about infants' ability to focus attention on particular events in the auditory environment. Four-year-old children spontaneously focus attention on the most physically salient event and have difficulty pulling attention away from this object and directing it toward others. Considerable improvements in this ability are observed up to the age of 10 years, and no additional improvement is observed for adult nonmusicans. How-

ever, adult musicians show a greatly enhanced ability to attend selectively to a particular aspect of an auditory scene, and this enhancement appears after only a couple of years of musical tuition (Drake et al., 2000).

Summary

The interactive developmental hypothesis presented here therefore provides a satisfactory starting point for future research. The existing data fit relatively well into this framework, but future work that more extensively investigates the principle findings concerning auditory perception and cognition in adults could conceivably invalidate such a position and lead to the creation of a completely different perspective.

CONCLUSIONS

One major theme running through this chapter has been that our auditory perceptual system does not function like a tape recorder, recording passively the sound information arriving in the ear. Rather, we actively strive to make sense out of the ever-changing array of sounds, putting together parts that belong together and separating out conflicting information. The result is the perception of auditory events and sequences. Furthermore, based on previous information and current desires, attentional processes help determine the exact contents of the perceived sound environment.

Such a dynamic approach to auditory perception and cognition has been developing gradually over the last 30 years, being greatly influenced by a handful of creative thinkers and experimentalists, to whom we hope we have done justice. In this chapter, the first in the *Stevens' Handbook* series devoted to auditory perception and cognition, we have tried to bring together evidence from a range of complementary fields in the hopes that the resulting juxtaposition of ideas will facilitate and enable future research to fill in the gaps.

REFERENCES

Abdala, C., & Folsom, R. C. (1995). The development of frequency resolution in human as revealed by the auditory brainstem response recorded with notched noise masking. *Journal of the Acoustical Society of America, 98*(2), 921–930.

Alain, C. A. (2000). Selectively attending to auditory objects. *Frontiers in Bioscience, 5,* 202–212.

Alain, C. A., Arnott, S. R., & Picton T. W. (2001). Bottom-up and top-down influences on auditory scene analysis: Evidence from event-related brain potentials. *Journal of Experimental Psychology: Human Perception and Performance, 27*(5), 1072–1089.

Alain, C. A., Woods, D. L., & Ogawa, K. H. (1994). Brain indices of automatic pattern processing. *NeuroReport, 6,* 140–144.

Allan, L. (1992). The internal clock revisited. In F. Macar, V. Pouthas, & W. J. Friedman (Eds.), *Time, action and cognition: Towards bridging the gap* (pp. 191–202). Dordrecht: Kluwer Academic.

Allen, P., & Wightman, F. (1995). Effects of signal and masker uncertainty on children's detection. *Journal of Speech and Hearing Research, 38*(2), 503–511.

Andrews, M. W., & Dowling, W. J. (1991). The development of perception of interleaved melodies and control of auditory attention. *Music Perception, 8*(4), 349–368.

Anstis, S., & Saida, S. (1985). Adaptation of auditory streaming to frequency-modulated tones. *Journal of Experimental Psychology: Human Perception and Performance, 11,* 257–271.

Assmann, P. F., & Summerfield, Q. (1990). Modeling the perception of concurrent vowels: Vowels with different fundamental frequencies. *Journal of the Acoustical Society of America, 88,* 680–697.

Aures, W. (1985). Ein Berechnungsverfahren der Rauhigkeit [A roughness calculation method]. *Acustica, 58,* 268–281.

Bamberger, J. (1980). Cognitive structuring in the apprehension and description of simple rhythms. *Archives of Psychology, 48,* 177–199.

Baruch, C. (2001). L'audition du bébé et du jeune enfant. *Année Psychologique, 101,* 91–124.

Baruch, C., & Drake, C. (1997). Tempo discrimination in infants. *Infant Behavior and Development, 20*(4), 573–577.

Beauvois, M. W., & Meddis, R. (1997). Time decay of auditory stream biasing. *Perception and Psychophysics, 59,* 81–86.

Berg, K. M. (1993). A comparison of thresholds for 1/3-octave filtered clicks and noise burst in infants and adults. *Perception and Psychophysics, 54*(3), 365–369.

Berg, K. M., & Smith, M. C. (1983). Behavioral thresholds for tones during infancy. *Journal of Experimental Child Psychology, 35,* 409–425.

Bertrand, D. (1999). *Groupement rythmique et représentation mentale de mélodies chez l'enfant.* Liège, Belgium: Université de Liège.

Bey, C. (1999). *Reconnaissance de mélodies intercalées et formation de flux auditifs: Analyse fonctionnelle et exploration neuropsychologique [Recognition of interleaved melodies and auditory stream formation: Functional analysis and neuropsychological exploration].* Unpublished doctoral dissertation, Ecole des Hautes Etudes en Sciences Sociales (EHESS), Paris.

Bey, C., & McAdams, S. (in press). Schema-based processing in auditory scene analysis. *Perception and Psychophysics.*

Bigand, E., McAdams, S., & Forêt, S. (2000). Divided attention in music. *International Journal of Psychology, 35,* 270–278.

Block, R. A. (1990). Models of psychological time. In R. A. Block (Ed.), *Cognitive models of psychological time* (pp. 1–35). Hillsdale, NJ: Erlbaum.

Boltz, M. G. (1994). Changes in internal tempo and effects on the learning and remembering of event durations. *Journal of Experimental Psychology: Learning, Memory, and Cognition, 20*(5), 1154–1171.

Boltz, M. G. (1995). Effects of event structure on retrospective duration judgments. *Perception & Psychophysics, 57,* 1080–1096.

Boltz, M. G. (1998). Task predictability and remembered duration. *Perception and Psychophysics, 60*(5), 768–784.

Boltz, M. G., Schulkind, M., & Kantra, S. (1991). Effects of background music on the remembering of filmed events. *Memory and Cognition, 19*(6), 593–606.

Botte, M. C., Drake, C., Brochard, R., & McAdams, S. (1997). Perceptual attenuation of nonfocused auditory stream. *Perception and Psychophysics, 59*(3), 419–425.

Bregman, A. S. (1978a). Auditory streaming: Competition among alternative organizations. *Perception and Psychophysics, 23,* 391–398.

Bregman, A. S. (1978b). Auditory streaming is cumulative. *Journal of Experimental Psychology: Human Perception and Performance, 4,* 380–387.

Bregman, A. S. (1990). *Auditory scene analysis: The perceptual organization of sound.* Cambridge: MIT Press.

Bregman, A. S. (1991). Using brief glimpses to decompose mixtures. In J. Sundberg, L. Nord, & R. Carleson (Eds.), *Music, language, speech and brain* (pp. 284–293). London: Macmillan.

Bregman, A. S. (1993). Auditory scene analysis: Hearing in complex environments. In S. McAdams & E. Bigand (Eds.), *Thinking in sound: The cognitive psychology of human audition* (pp. 10–36). Oxford: Oxford University Press.

Bregman, A. S., & Ahad, P. (1995). *Demonstrations of auditory scene analysis: The perceptual organization of sound.* Montréal, Québec, Canada: McGill University. Compact disc available at http://www.psych.mcgill.ca/labs/auditory/bregmancd.html.

Bregman, A. S., Ahad, P., Kim, J., & Melnerich, L. (1994). Resetting the pitch-analysis system: 1. Effects of rise times of tones in noise back-grounds or of harmonics in a complex tone. *Perception and Psychophysics, 56,* 155–162.

Bregman, A. S., & Campbell, J. (1971). Primary auditory stream segregation and perception of order in rapid sequences of tones. *Journal of Experimental Psychology, 89,* 244–249.

Bregman, A. S., & Dannenbring, G. L. (1973). The effect of continuity on auditory stream segregation. *Perception and Psychophysics, 13,* 308–312.

Bregman, A. S., Liao, C., & Levitan, R. (1990). Auditory grouping based on fundamental frequency and formant peak frequency. *Canadian Journal of Psychology, 44,* 400–413.

Bregman, A. S., & Pinker, S. (1978). Auditory streaming and the building of timbre. *Canadian Journal of Psychology, 32,* 19–31.

Broadbent, D. E. (1958). *Perception and communication.* London: Pergamon.

Brochard, R., Drake, C., Botte, M.-C., & McAdams, S. (1999). Perceptual organization of complex auditory sequences: Effect of number of simultaneous subsequences and frequency separation. *Journal of Experimental Psychology: Human Perception and Performance, 25,* 1742–1759.

Brokx, J. P. L., & Nooteboom, S. G. (1982). Intonation and the perceptual separation of simultaneous voices. *Journal of Phonetics, 10,* 23–36.

Buell, T. N., & Hafter, E. R. (1991). Combination of binaural information across frequency bands. *Journal of the Acoustical Society of America, 90,* 1894–1900.

Cabe, P. A., & Pittenger, J. B. (2000). Human sensitivity to acoustic information from vessel filling. *Journal of Experimental Psychology: Human Perception and Performance, 26,* 313–324.

Carello, C., Anderson, K. A., & Kunkler-Peck, A. J. (1998). Perception of object length by sound. *Psychological Science, 9,* 211–214.

Carlyon, R. P. (1991). Discriminating between coherent and incoherent frequency modulation of complex tones. *Journal of the Acoustical Society of America, 89,* 329–340.

Carlyon, R. P. (1992). The psychophysics of concurrent sound segregation. *Philosophical*

Transactions of the Royal Society, London B, 336, 347–355.

Carlyon, R. P. (1994). Detecting mistuning in the presence of synchronous and asynchronous interfering sounds. *Journal of the Acoustical Society of America, 95,* 2622–2630.

Carterette, E. C., & Kendall, R. A. (1999). Comparative music perception and cognition. In D. Deutsch (Ed.), *The psychology of music* (2nd ed., pp. 725–791). San Diego: Academic Press.

Chaigne, A., & Doutaut, V. (1997). Numerical simulations of xylophones: I. Time-domain modeling of the vibrating bars. *Journal of the Acoustical Society of America, 101,* 539–557.

Cherry, E. C. (1953). Some experiments on the recognition of speech, with one and two ears. *Journal of the Acoustical Society of America, 25,* 975–979.

Church, R. M. (1984). Properties of the internal clock. In J. Gibbon & L. Allan (Eds.), *Timing and time perception* (Vol. 423, pp. 566–582). New York: New York Academy of Sciences.

Ciocca, V., & Bregman, A. S. (1989). The effects of auditory streaming on duplex perception. *Perception and Psychophysics, 46,* 39–48.

Ciocca, V., & Darwin, C. J. (1993). Effects of onset asynchrony on pitch perception: Adaptation or grouping? *Journal of the Acoustical Society of America, 93,* 2870–2878.

Clarke, E. F., & Krumhansl, C. (1990). Perceiving musical time. *Music Perception, 7*(3), 213–252.

Clarkson, M. G., & Clifton, R. K. (1995). Infant's pitch perception: Inharmonic tonal complexes. *Journal of the Acoustical Society of America, 98*(3), 1372–1379.

Clarkson, M. G., Martin, R. L., & Miciek, S. G. (1996). Infants perception of pitch: Number of harmonics. *Infant Behavior and Development, 19,* 191–197.

Cowan, N. (1988). Evolving conceptions of memory storage, selective attention, and their mutual constraint within the human information-processing system. *Psychological Bulletin, 104,* 163–191.

Creelman, C. D. (1962). Human discrimination of auditory duration. *Journal of the Acoustical Society of America, 34,* 582–593.

Crowder, R. G. (1993). Auditory memory. In S. McAdams & E. Bigand (Eds.), *Thinking in sound: The cognitive psychology of human audition* (pp. 113–145). Oxford: Oxford University Press.

Crowder, R. G., & Morton, J. (1969). Precategorical acoustic storage (PAS). *Perception & Psychophysics, 5,* 365–373.

Culling, J. F., & Darwin, C. J. (1993). The role of timbre in the segregation of simultaneous voices with intersecting Fo contours. *Perception and Psychophysics, 34,* 303–309.

Culling, J. F., & Summerfield, Q. (1995). Perceptual separation of concurrent speech sounds: Absence of across-frequency grouping by common interaural delay. *Journal of the Acoustical Society of America, 98,* 758–797.

Cutting, J. E. (1976). Auditory and linguistic processes in speech perception: Inferences from six fusions in dichotic listening. *Psychological Review, 83,* 114–140.

Daniel, P., & Weber, R. (1997). Psychoacoustical roughness: Implementation of an optimized model. *Acustica, 83,* 113–123.

Dannenbring, G. L., & Bregman, A. S. (1976). Stream segregation and the illusion of overlap. *Journal of Experimental Psychology: Human Perception and Performance, 2,* 544–555.

Darwin, C. J. (1981). Perceptual grouping of speech components differing in fundamental frequency and onset time. *Quarterly Journal of Experimental Psychology, 33A,* 185–208.

Darwin, C. J. (1984). Perceiving vowels in the presence of another sound: Constraints on formant perception. *Journal of the Acoustical Society of America, 76,* 1636–1647.

Darwin, C. J. (1991). The relationship between speech perception and the perception of other sounds. In I. G. Mattingly & M. G. Studdert-Kennedy (Eds.), *Modularity and the motor theory of speech perception* (pp. 239–259). Hillsdale, NJ: Erlbaum.

Darwin, C. J., & Carlyon, R. P. (1995). Auditory grouping. In B. C. J. Moore (Ed.), *Hearing* (pp. 387–424). San Diego: Academic Press.

Darwin, C. J., & Ciocca, V. (1992). Grouping in pitch perception: Effects of onset asynchrony and ear of presentation of a mistuned component. *Journal of the Acoustical Society of America, 91,* 3381–3390.

Darwin, C. J., Ciocca, V., & Sandell, G. R. (1994). Effects of frequency and amplitude modulation on the pitch of a complex tone with a mistuned harmonic. *Journal of the Acoustical Society of America, 95,* 2631–2636.

Darwin, C. J., & Gardner, R. B. (1986). Mistuning a harmonic of a vowel: Grouping and phase effects on vowel quality. *Journal of the Acoustical Society of America, 79,* 838–845.

Darwin, C. J., & Hukin, R. W. (1999). Auditory objects of attention: The role of interaural time differences. *Journal of Experimental Psychology: Human Perception and Performance, 25,* 617–629.

Darwin, C. J., & Sutherland, N. S. (1984). Grouping frequency components of vowels: When is a harmonic not a harmonic? *Quarterly Journal of Experimental Psychology, 36A,* 193–208.

de Cheveigné, A. (1993). Separation of concurrent harmonic sounds: Fundamental frequency estimation and a time-domain cancellation model of auditory processing. *Journal of the Acoustical Society of America, 93,* 3271–3290.

de Cheveigné, A. (1999). Waveform interactions and the segregation of concurrent vowels. *Journal of the Acoustical Society of America, 106,* 2959–2972.

de Cheveigné, A., Kawahara, H., Tsuzaki, M., & Aikawa, K. (1997). Concurrent vowel identification: I. Effects of relative level and F0 difference. *Journal of the Acoustical Society of America, 101,* 2839–2847.

de Cheveigné, A., McAdams, S., Laroche, J., & Rosenberg, M. (1995). Identification of concurrent harmonic and inharmonic vowels: A test of the theory of harmonic cancellation and enhancement. *Journal of the Acoustical Society of America, 97,* 3736–3748.

de Cheveigné, A., McAdams, S., & Marin, C. M. H. (1997). Concurrent vowel identification: II. Effects of phase, harmonicity, and task. *Journal of the Acoustical Society of America, 101,* 2848–2856.

Deliège, I. (1987). Grouping conditions in listening to music: An approach to Lerdahl & Jackendoff's grouping preference rules. *Music Perception, 4,* 325–360.

Deliège, I. (1990). Mechanisms of cue extraction in musical grouping: A study of Sequenza VI for Viola Solo by L. Berio. *Psychology of Music, 18,* 18–45.

Deliège, I. (1993). Mechanisms of cue extraction in memory for musical time. *Contemporary Music Review, 9*(1&2), 191–205.

Demany, L. (1982). Auditory stream segregation in infancy. *Infant Behavior and Development, 5,* 261–276.

Demany, L., & Armand, F. (1984). The perceptual reality of tone chroma in early infancy. *Journal of the Acoustical Society of America, 1,* 57–66.

Demany, L., & Armand, F. (1985). A propos de la perception de la hauteur et du chroma des sons purs. *Bulletin d'Audiophonologie, 1–2,* 123–132.

Demany, L., McKenzie, B., & Vurpillot, E. (1977). Rhythm perception in early infancy. *Nature, 266,* 718–719.

Desain, P. (1992). A (de)composable theory of rhythm perception. *Music Perception, 9*(4), 439–454.

Deutsch, D. (1975). Two-channel listening to musical scales. *Journal of the Acoustical Society of America, 57,* 1156–1160.

Deutsch, D. (1980). The processing of structured and unstructured tonal sequences. *Perception & Psychophysics, 28,* 381–389.

Deutsch, D. (1995). *Musical illusions and paradoxes.* La Jolla, CA: Philomel Records. Compact disc available at http://www.philomel.com.

Deutsch, D. (Ed.). (1999). *The psychology of music* (2nd ed.). San Diego: Academic Press.

Deutsch, D., & Feroe, J. (1981). The internal representation of pitch sequences in tonal music. *Psychological Review, 88*(6), 503–522.

Divenyi, P. L., & Danner, W. F. (1977). Discrimination of time intervals marked by brief acoustic pulses of various intensities and spectra. *Perception & Psychophysics, 21*(2), 125–142.

Dowling, W. J. (1973a). The perception of interleaved melodies. *Cognitive Psychology, 5,* 322–327.

Dowling, W. J. (1973b). Rhythmic groups and subjective chunks in memory for melodies. *Perception & Psychophysics, 14,* 37–40.

Dowling, W. J. (1984). Development of musical schemata in children's spontaneous singing. In W. R. Crozier & A. J. Chapman (Eds.), *Cognitive processes in the perception of art* (pp. 145–163). Amsterdam: North-Holland.

Dowling, W. J., & Harwood, D. L. (1986). *Music cognition.* New York: Academic Press.

Drake, C. (1993a). Perceptual and performed accents in musical sequences. *Bulletin of the Psychonomic Society, 31*(2), 107–110.

Drake, C. (1993b). Reproduction of musical rhythms by children, adult musicians and adult nonmusicians. *Perception & Psychophysics, 53*(1), 25–33.

Drake, C. (1997). Motor and perceptually preferred synchronisation by children and adults: Binary and ternary ratios. *Polish Journal of Developmental Psychology, 3*(1), 41–59.

Drake, C. (1998). Psychological processes involved in the temporal organization of complex auditory sequences: universal and acquired processes. *Music Perception, 16*(1), 11–26.

Drake, C., & Bertrand, D. (2001). The quest for universals in temporal processing in music. *Annals of the New York Academy of Sciences, 930,* 17–27.

Drake, C., & Botte, M.-C. (1993). Tempo sensitivity in auditory sequences: Evidence for a multiple-look model. *Perception & Psychophysics, 54,* 277–286.

Drake, C., Dowling, W. J. & Palmer, C. (1991). Accent structures in the reproduction of simple tunes by children and adult pianists. *Music Perception, 8,* 315–334.

Drake, C., & Gérard, C. (1989). A psychological pulse train: How young children use this cognitive framework to structure simple rhythms. *Psychological Research, 51,* 16–22.

Drake, C., Jones, M. R., & Baruch, C. (2000). The development of rhythmic attending in auditory sequences: Attunement, referent period, focal attending. *Cognition, 77,* 251–288.

Drake, C., & McAdams, S. (1999). The continuity illusion: Role of temporal sequence structure. *Journal of the Acoustical Society of America, 106,* 3529–3538.

Drake, C., & Palmer, C. (1993). Accent structures in music performance. *Music Perception, 10*(3), 343–378.

Drake, C., & Palmer, C. (2000). Skill acquisition in music performance: Relations between planning and temporal control. *Cognition, 74*(1), 1–32.

Drake, C., Penel, A., & Bigand, E. (2000). Tapping in time with mechanically and expressively performed music. *Music Perception. 18,* 1–23.

Duifhuis, H., Willems, L. F., & Sluyter, R. J. (1982). Measurement of pitch in speech: An implementation of Goldsteins's theory of pitch perception. *Journal of the Acoustical Society of America, 83,* 687–695.

Ehresman, D., & Wessel, D. L. (1978). *Perception of timbral analogies,* IRCAM Report no. 13. Paris: IRCAM.

Essens, P. J. (1995). Structuring temporal sequences: Comparison of models and factors of complexity. *Perception & Psychophysics, 57*(4), 519–532.

Essens, P. J., & Povel, D. J. (1985). Metrical and nonmetrical representations of temporal patterns. *Perception & Psychophysics, 37*(1), 1–7.

Estes, W. K. (1972). An associative basis for coding and organization in memory. In A. W. Melton & E. Martin (Eds.), *Coding processes in human memory.* New York: Wiley.

Ferland, M. B., & Mendelson, M. J. (1989). Infant categorization of melodic contour. *Infant Behavior and Development, 12,* 341–355.

Fishman, Y. I., Reser, D. H., Arezzo, J. C., & Steinschneider, M. (2000). Complex tone processing in primary auditory cortex of the awake monkey: I. Neural ensemble correlates of roughness.

Journal of the Acoustical Society of America, 108, 235–246.

Fitzgibbons, P. J., & Gordon Salant, S. (1998). Auditory temporal order perception in younger and older adults. *Journal of Speech, Language, and Hearing Research, 41*(5), 1052–1060.

Fitzgibbons, P. J., Pollatsek, A., & Thomas, I. B. (1974). Detection of temporal gaps within and between perceptual tonal groups. *Perception & Psychophysics, 16,* 522–528.

Fraisse, P. (1956). *Les structures rythmiques.* Louvain, Belgium: Publications Universitaires de Louvain.

Fraisse, P. (1963). *The psychology of time.* New York: Harper & Row.

Fraisse, P. (1982). Rhythm and tempo. In D. Deutsch (Ed.), *The psychology of music* (pp. 149–180). New York: Academic Press.

Fraisse, P., Pichot, P., & Clairouin, G. (1969). Les aptitudes rythmiques: Etude comparée des oligophrènes et des enfants normaux. *Journal de Psychologie Normale et Pathologique, 42,* 309–330.

Gardner, R. B., Gaskill, S. A., & Darwin, C. J. (1989). Perceptual grouping of formants with static and dynamic differences in fundamental frequency. *Journal of the Acoustical Society of America, 85,* 1329–1337.

Getty, D. J. (1975). Discrimination of short temporal intervals: A comparison of two models. *Perception & Psychophysics, 18,* 1–8.

Giard, M.-H., Collet, L., Bouchet, P., & Pernier, J. (1993). Modulation of human cochlear activity during auditory selective attention. *Brain Research, 633,* 353–356.

Giard, M.-H., Fort, A., Mouchetant-Rostaing, Y., & Pernier, J. (2000). Neurophysiological mechanisms of auditory selective attention in humans. *Frontiers in Bioscience, 5,* 84–94.

Glucksberg, S., & Cowen, G. N. (1970). Memory for non-attended auditory material. *Cognitive Psychology, 1,* 149–156.

Green, D. M. (1988). Auditory profile analysis: Some experiments on spectral shape discrimination. In G. M. Edelman, W. E. Gall, & W. M. Cowan (Eds.), *Auditory function: Neurobiolog-*

ical bases of hearing (pp. 609–622). New York: Wiley.

Green, D. M., & Mason, C. R. (1985). Auditory profile analysis: Frequency, phase, and Weber's law. *Journal of the Acoustical Society of America, 77,* 1155–1161.

Green, D. M., Mason, C. R., & Kidd, G. (1984). Profile analysis: Critical bands and duration. *Journal of the Acoustical Society of America, 74,* 1163–1167.

Grey, J. M. (1977). Multidimensional perceptual scaling of musical timbres. *Journal of the Acoustical Society of America, 61,* 1270–1277.

Grey, J. M., & Gordon, J. W. (1978). Perceptual effects of spectral modifications on musical timbres. *Journal of the Acoustical Society of America, 63,* 1493–1500.

Grimault, N., Micheyl, C., Carlyon, R. P., Arthaud, P., & Collet, L. (2000). Influence of peripheral resolvability on the perceptual segregation of harmonic complex tones differing in fundamental frequency. *Journal of the Acoustical Society of America, 108,* 263–271.

Guski, R. (2000). Studies in auditive kinetics. In A. Schick, M. Meis, & C. Reckhardt (Eds.), *Contributions to psychological acoustics: Results of the 8th Oldenburg Symposium on Psychological Acoustics* (pp. 383–401). Oldenburg: Bis.

Hafter, E. R., & Buell, T. N. (1985). The importance of transients for maintaining the separation of signals in space. In M. Posner & O. Marin (Eds.), *Attention and performance XI* (pp. 337–354). Hillsdale, NJ: Erlbaum.

Hafter, E. R., Buell, T. N., & Richards, V. M. (1988). Onset-coding in lateralization: Its form, site, and function. In G. M. Edelman, W. E. Gall, & W. M. Cowan (Eds.), *Auditory function: Neurobiological bases of hearing* (pp. 647–676). New York: Wiley.

Hajda, J. M., Kendall, R. A., Carterette, E. C., & Harshberger, M. L. (1997). Methodological issues in timbre research. In I. Deliège & J. Sloboda (Eds.), *Perception and cognition of music* (pp. 253–306). Hove, England: Psychology Press.

Hall, J. W., Grose, J. H., & Mendoza, L. (1995). Across-channel processes in masking. In B. C. J.

Moore (Ed.), *Hearing* (pp. 243–266). San Diego: Academic Press.

Halpern, A. R., & Darwin, C. J. (1982). Duration discrimination in a series of rhythmic events. *Perception & Psychophysics, 31*(1), 86–89.

Handel, S. (1989). *Listening: An introduction to the perception of auditory events.* Cambridge, MA: MIT Press.

Hartmann, W. M. (1988). Pitch perception and the segregation and integration of auditory entities. In G. M. Edelman, W. E. Gall, & W. M. Cowan (Eds.), *Auditory function* (pp. 623–645). New York: Wiley.

Hartmann, W. M., & Johnson, D. (1991). Stream segregation and peripheral channeling. *Music Perception, 9,* 155–184.

Hartmann, W. M., McAdams, S., & Smith, B. K. (1990). Hearing a mistuned harmonic in an otherwise periodic complex tone. *Journal of the Acoustical Society of America, 88,* 1712–1724.

Heise, G. A., & Miller, G. A. (1951). An experimental study of auditory patterns. *American Journal of Psychology, 64,* 68–77.

Helmholtz, H. L. F. von. (1885). *On the sensations of tone as a physiological basis for the theory of music.* New York, from 1877 trans by A. J. Ellis of 4th German ed.: republ.1954, New York: Dover.

Hill, N. I., & Darwin, C. J. (1996). Lateralization of a perturbed harmonic: Effects of onset asynchrony and mistuning. *Journal of the Acoustical Society of America, 100,* 2352–2364.

Houtsma, A. J. M., Rossing, T. D., & Wagenaars, W. M. (1987). *Auditory demonstrations on compact disc.* Melville, NY: Acoustical Society of America. Compact disc available at http://asa.aip.org/discs.html.

Hukin, R. W., & Darwin, C. J. (1995a). Comparison of the effect of onset asynchrony on auditory grouping in pitch matching and vowel identification. *Perception and Psychophysics, 57,* 191–196.

Hukin, R. W., & Darwin, C. J. (1995b). Effects of contralateral presentation and of interaural time differences in segregating a harmonic from a vowel. *Journal of the Acoustical Society of America, 98,* 1380–1387.

Huron, D., & Fantini, D. (1989). The avoidance of inner-voice entries: Perceptual evidence and musical practice. *Music Perception, 7,* 43–48.

Iverson, P. (1995). Auditory stream segregation by musical timbre: Effects of static and dynamic acoustic attributes. *Journal of Experimental Psychology: Human Perception and Performance, 21,* 751–763.

Iverson, P., & Krumhansl, C. L. (1993). Isolating the dynamic attributes of musical timbre. *Journal of the Acoustical Society of America, 94,* 2595–2603.

Jensen, K. J., & Neff, D. L. (1993). Development of basic auditory discrimination in preschool children. *Psychological Science, 4,* 104–107.

Jones, M. R. (1976). Time, our last dimension: Toward a new theory of perception, attention, and memory. *Psychological Review, 83*(5), 323–355.

Jones, M. R. (1987). Dynamic pattern structure in music: Recent theory and research. *Perception & Psychophysics, 41*(6), 631–634.

Jones, M. R. (1990). Learning and development of expectancies: An interactionist approach. *Psychomusicology, 2*(9), 193–228.

Jones, M. R., & Boltz, M. (1989). Dynamic attending and responses to time. *Psychological Review, 96,* 459–491.

Jones, M. R., & Yee, W. (1993). Attending to auditory events: The role of temporal organization. In S. McAdams & E. Bigand (Eds.), *Thinking in sound: The cognitive psychology of human audition* (pp. 69–112). Oxford: Oxford University Press.

Jones, M. R., & Yee, W. (1997). Sensitivity to time change: the role of context and skill. *Journal of Experimental Psychology: Human Perception and Performance, 23,* 693–709.

Kameoka, A., & Kuriyagawa, M. (1969). Consonance theory: Part II. Consonance of complex tones and its calculation method. *Journal of the Acoustical Society of America, 45,* 1460–1469.

Killeen, P. R., & Weisse, N. A. (1987). Optimal timing and the Weber function. *Psychological Review, 94*(4), 445–468.

Koehler, W. (1929). *Gestalt psychology*. New York: Liveright.

Krimphoff, J., McAdams, S., & Winsberg, S. (1994). Caractérisation du timbre des sons complexes: II. Analyses acoustiques et quantification psychophysique [Characterization of the timbre of complex sounds: II. Acoustic analyses and psychophysical quantification]. *Journal de Physique, 4*(C5), 625–628.

Kristofferson, A. B. (1980). A quantal step function in duration discrimination. *Perception & Psychophysics, 27,* 300–306.

Krumhansl, C. L. (1989). Why is musical timbre so hard to understand? In S. Nielzén & O. Olsson (Eds.), *Structure and perception of electroacoustic sound and music* (pp. 43–53). Amsterdam: Excerpta Medica.

Krumhansl, C. L., & Jusczyk, P. W. (1990). Infants' perception of phrase structure in music. *Psychological Science, 1,* 70–73.

Krumhansl, C. L., Louhivuori, J., Toiviainen, P., Jaervinen, T., & Eerola, T. (1999). Melodic expectation in Finnish spiritual folk hymns: Convergence of statistical, behavioral, and computational approaches. *Music Perception, 17*(2), 151–195.

Krumhansl, C. L., Toivanen, P., Eerola, T., Toiviainen, P., Jaervinen, T., & Louhivuori, J. (2000). Cross-cultural music cognition: Cognitive methodology applied to North Sami yoiks. *Cognition, 76*(1), 13–58.

Kubovy, M. (1981). Concurrent-pitch segregation and the theory of indispensable attributes. In M. Kubovy & J. R. Pomerantz (Eds.), *Perceptual organization* (pp. 55–98). Hillsdale, NJ: Erlbaum.

Kubovy, M., Cutting, J. E., & McGuire, R. M. (1974). Hearing with the third ear: Dichotic perception of a melody without monaural familiarity cues. *Science, 186,* 272–274.

Kunkler-Peck, A. J., & Turvey, M. T. (2000). Hearing shape. *Journal of Experimental Psychology: Human Perception and Performance, 26,* 279–294.

Lakatos, S. (2000). A common perceptual space for harmonic and percussive timbres. *Perception and Psychophysics, 62,* 1426–1439.

Lakatos, S., McAdams, S., & Caussé, R. (1997). The representation of auditory source characteristics: Simple geometric form. *Perception & Psychophysics, 59,* 1180–1190.

Lambourg, C., Chaigne, A., & Matignon, D. (2001). Time-domain simulation of damped impacted plates: II. Numerical model and results. *Journal of the Acoustical Society of America, 109,* 1433–1447.

Large, E. W., Jones, M. R. (1999). The dynamics of attending: How people track time-varying events. *Psychological Review, 106*(1), 119–159.

Lea, A. (1992). *Auditory models of vowel perception.* Unpublished doctoral dissertation, University of Nottingham, Nottingham, England.

Lee, C. S. (1991). The perception of metrical structure: Experimental evidence and a model. In P. Howell, R. West, & I. Cross (Eds.), *Representing musical structure* (pp. 59–127). London: Academic Press.

Lerdahl, F., & Jackendoff, R. (1983). *A generative theory of tonal music.* Cambridge: MIT Press.

Little, V. M., Thomas, D. G., & Letterman, M. R. (1999). Single-trial analysis of developmental trends in infant auditory event-related potentials. *Developmental Neuropsychology, 16*(3), 455–478.

Longuet-Higgins, H. C., & Lee, C. S. (1982). The perception of musical rhythms. *Perception, 11,* 115–128.

Longuet-Higgins, H. C., & Lee, C. S. (1984). The rhythmic interpretation of monophonic music. *Music Perception, 1,* 424–440.

Luce, G. G. (1972). *Body time.* London: Temple Smith.

McAdams, S. (1989). Segregation of concurrent sounds: I. Effects of frequency modulation coherence. *Journal of the Acoustical Society of America, 86,* 2148–2159.

McAdams, S. (1993). Recognition of sound sources and events. In S. McAdams & E. Bigand (Eds.), *Thinking in sound: The cognitive psychology of human audition* (pp. 146–198). Oxford: Oxford University Press.

McAdams, S., & Bertoncini, J. (1997). Organization and discrimination of repeating sound sequences by newborn infants. *Journal of the Acoustical Society of America, 102,* 2945–2953.

McAdams, S., & Bigand, E. (Eds.). (1993). *Thinking in sound: The cognitive psychology of human audition.* Oxford: Oxford University Press.

McAdams, S., Botte, M.-C., & Drake, C. (1998). Auditory continuity and loudness computation. *Journal of the Acoustical Society of America, 103,* 1580–1591.

McAdams, S., & Bregman, A. S. (1979). Hearing musical streams. *Computer Music Journal, 3*(4), 26–43.

McAdams, S., & Cunibile, J. C. (1992). Perception of timbral analogies. *Philosophical Transactions of the Royal Society, London, Series B, 336,* 383–389.

McAdams, S., & Marin, C. M. H. (1990). *Auditory processing of frequency modulation coherence.* Paper presented at the Fechner Day '90, 6th Annual Meeting of the International Society for Psychophysics, Würzburg, Germany.

McAdams, S., & Winsberg, S. (2000). Psychophysical quantification of individual differences in timbre perception. In A. Schick, M. Meis, & C. Reckhardt (Eds.), *Contributions to psychological acoustics: Results of the 8th Oldenburg Symposium on Psychological Acoustics* (pp. 165–182). Oldenburg, Germany: Bis.

McAdams, S., Winsberg, S., Donnadieu, S., De Soete, G., & Krimphoff, J. (1995). Perceptual scaling of synthesized musical timbres: Common dimensions, specificities, and latent subject classes. *Psychological Research, 58,* 177–192.

McFadden, D., & Wright, B. A. (1987). Comodulation masking release in a forward-masking paradigm. *Journal of the Acoustical Society of America, 82,* 1615–1630.

Meric, C. & Collet, L. (1994). Attention and otoacoustic emissions: A review. *Neuroscience and Behavioral Review, 18,* 215–222.

Michon, J. A. (1975). Time experience and memory processes. In J. T. Fraser & N. Lawrence (Eds.), *The study of time* (pp. 2–22). Berlin: Springer.

Michon, J. A. (1978). The making of the present: A tutorial review. In J. Requin (Ed.), *Attention and performance VII* (pp. 89–111). Hillsdale, NJ: Erlbaum.

Miller, G. A. (1956). The magic number seven, plus or minus two: Some limits on our capacity for processing information. *Psychological Review, 63,* 81–97.

Monahan, C. B., Kendall, R. A., & Carterette, E. C. (1987). The effect of melodic and temporal contour on recognition memory for pitch change. *Perception & Psychophysics, 41*(6), 576–600.

Moore, B. C. J., Glasberg, B. R., & Peters, R. W. (1985). Relative dominance of individual partials in determining the pitch of complex tones. *Journal of the Acoustical Society of America, 77,* 1853–1860.

Moore, B. C. J., Peters, R. W., & Glasberg, B. R. (1985). Thresholds for the detection of inharmonicity in complex tones. *Journal of the Acoustical Society of America, 77,* 1861–1867.

Moray, N. (1959). Attention in dichotic listening: Affective cues and the influence of instructions. *Quarterly Journal of Experimental Psychology, 11,* 56–60.

Morrongiello, B. A., & Trehub, S. E. (1987). Age-related changes in auditory temporal perception. *Journal of Experimental Child Psychology, 44,* 413–426.

Näätänen, R. (1992). *Attention and brain function.* Hillsdale, NJ: Erlbaum.

Näätänen, R. (1995). The mismatch negativity: A powerful tool for cognitive neuroscience. *Ear & Hearing, 16,* 6–18.

Nozza, R. J., & Wilson, W. R. (1984). Masked and unmasked pure-tone thresholds of infants and adults: Development of auditory frequency selectivity and sensitivity. *Journal of Speech and Hearing Research, 27,* 613–622.

Olsho, L. W. (1985). Infant auditory perception: Tonal masking. *Infant Behavior and Development, 8,* 371–384.

Olsho, L. W., Koch, E. G., Carter, E. A., Halpin, C. F., & Spetner, N. B. (1988). Pure-tone sensitivity of human infants. *Journal of the Acoustical Society of America, 84*(4), 1316–1324.

Ornstein, R. E. (1969). *On the experience of time.* Harmondsworth, England: Penguin.

Palmer, C. (1989). Mapping musical thought to musical performance. *Journal of Experimental Psychology: Human Perception and Performance, 15,* 331–346.

Palmer, C., & Drake, C. (1997). Monitoring and planning capacities in the acquisition of music performance skills. *Canadian Journal of Experimental Psychology, 51*(4), 369–384.

Penel, A., & Drake, C. (1998). Sources of timing variations in music performance: A psychological segmentation model. *Psychological Research, 61,* 12–32.

Peretz, I., & Morais, J. (1989). Music and modularity. *Contemporary Music Review, 4,* 279–294.

Plomp, R. (1970). Timbre as a multidimensional attribute of complex tones. In R. Plomp & G. F. Smoorenburg (Eds.), *Frequency analysis and periodicity detection in hearing* (pp. 397–414). Leiden: Sijthoff.

Plomp, R. (1976). *Aspects of tone sensation: A psychophysical study.* London: Academic Press.

Plomp, R., & Levelt, W. J. M. (1965). Tonal consonance and critical bandwidth. *Journal of the Acoustical Society of America, 38,* 548–560.

Plomp, R., & Steeneken, J. M. (1971). Pitch versus timbre. *Proceedings of the 7th International Congress of Acoustics, Budapest, 3,* 377–380.

Pollard-Gott, L. (1983). Emergence of thematic concepts in repeated listening to music. *Cognitive Psychology, 15,* 66–94.

Povel, D. J. (1981). Internal representation of simple temporal patterns. *Journal of Experimental Psychology: Human Perception and Performance, 7,* 3–18.

Povel, D. J. (1985). Perception of temporal patterns. *Music Perception, 2*(4), 411–440.

Povel, D. J., & Essens, P. (1985). Perception of temporal patterns. *Music Perception, 2,* 411–440.

Pressnitzer, D., & McAdams, S. (1999a). An effect of the coherence between envelopes across frequency regions on the perception of roughness. In T. Dau, V. Hohmann, & B. Kollmeier (Eds.), *Psychophysics, physiology and models of hearing* (pp. 105–108). London: World Scientific.

Pressnitzer, D., & McAdams, S. (1999b). Two phase effects in roughness perception. *Journal of the Acoustical Society of America, 105,* 2773–2782.

Pressnitzer, D., McAdams, S., Winsberg, S., & Fineberg, J. (2000). Perception of musical tension for nontonal orchestral timbres and its relation to psychoacoustic roughness. *Perception and Psychophysics, 62,* 66–80.

Preusser, D. (1972). The effect of structure and rate on the recognition and description of auditory temporal patterns. *Perception & Psychophysics, 11*(3), 233–240.

Rand, T. C. (1974). Dichotic release from masking for speech. *Journal of the Acoustical Society of America, 55,* 678–680 (Letter to the editor).

Rasch, R. (1978). The perception of simultaneous notes as in polyphonic music. *Acustica, 40,* 21–33.

Rasch, R. A. (1979). Synchronization in performed ensemble music. *Acustica, 43*(2), 121–131.

Repp, B. H. (1987). The sound of two hands clapping: An exploratory study. *Journal of the Acoustical Society of America, 81,* 1100–1109.

Repp, B. H. (1992). Probing the cognitive representation of musical time: Structural constraints on the perception of timing perturbations. *Cognition, 44,* 241–281.

Risset, J. C., & Wessel, D. L. (1999). Exploration of timbre by analysis and synthesis. In D. Deutsch (Ed.), *The psychology of music* (2nd ed., pp. 113–168). San Diego: Academic Press.

Roberts, B., & Bailey, P. J. (1993). Spectral pattern and the perceptual fusion of harmonics: I. The role of temporal factors. *Journal of the Acoustical Society of America, 94,* 3153–3164.

Roberts, B., & Bailey, P. J. (1996). Regularity of spectral pattern and its effects on the perceptual fusion of harmonics. *Perception and Psychophysics, 58,* 289–299.

Roberts, B., & Bregman, A. S. (1991). Effects of the pattern of spectral spacing on the perceptual fusion of harmonics. *Journal of the Acoustical Society of America, 90,* 3050–3060.

Rogers, W. L., & Bregman, A. S. (1993a). An experimental evaluation of three theories of auditory stream segregation. *Perception and Psychophysics, 53,* 179–189.

Rogers, W. L., & Bregman, A. S. (1993b). An experimental study of three theories of auditory stream segregation. *Perception & Psychophysics, 53,* 179–189.

Rogers, W. L., & Bregman, A. S. (1998). Cumulation of the tendency to segregate auditory streams: Resetting by changes in location and loudness. *Perception and Psychophysics, 60,* 1216–1227.

Roussarie, V. (1999). *Analyse perceptive des structures vibrantes [Perceptual analysis of vibrating structures].* Unpublished doctoral dissertation, Université du Maine, Le Mans, France.

Roussarie, V., McAdams, S., & Chaigne, A. (1998). Perceptual analysis of vibrating bars synthesized with a physical model. *Proceedings of the 16th International Congress on Acoustics, Seattle,* 2227–2228.

Saldanha, E. L., & Corso, J. F. (1964). Timbre cues and the identification of musical instruments. *Journal of the Acoustical Society of America, 36,* 2021–2126.

Scharf, B. (1998). Auditory attention: The psychoacoustical approach. In H. Pashler (Ed.), *Attention* (pp. 75–117). Hove, England: Psychology Press.

Scharf, B., Quigley, S., Aoki, C., & Peachey, N. (1987). Focused auditory attention and frequency selectivity. *Perception and Psychophysics, 42*(3), 215–223.

Scheffers, M. T. M. (1983). *Sifting vowels: Auditory pitch analysis and sound integration.* Unpublished doctoral dissertation, University of Groningen, Groningen, Netherlands.

Schneider, B. A., & Trehub, S. E. (1985). Behavioral assessment of basic auditory abilities. In S. E. Trehub & B. A. Schneider (Eds.), *Auditory development in infancy* (pp. 104–114). New York: Plenum.

Schneider, B. A., Trehub, S. E., & Bull, D. (1980). High frequency sensitivity in infants. *Science, 207,* 1003–1004.

Schneider, B. A., Trehub, S. E., Morrongiello, B. A., & Thorpe, L. A. (1986). Auditory sensitivity in preschool children. *Journal of the Acoustical Society of America, 79*(2), 447–452.

Schulze, H. H. (1978). The detectability of local and global displacements in regular rhythmic patterns. *Psychological Research, 40*(2), 173–181.

Schulze, H. H. (1989). The perception of temporal deviations in isochronic patterns. *Perception & Psychophysics, 45,* 291–296.

Singh, P. G. (1987). Perceptual organization of complex-tone sequences: A tradeoff between pitch and timbre? *Journal of the Acoustical Society of America, 82,* 886–899.

Singh, P. G., & Bregman, A. S. (1997). The influence of different timbre attributes on the perceptual segregation of complex-tone sequences. *Journal of the Acoustical Society of America, 120,* 1943–1952.

Sinnot, J. M., & Aslin, R. N. (1985). Frequency and intensity discrimination in human infants and adults. *Journal of the Acoustical Society of America, 78,* 1986–1992.

Sinnot, J. M., Pisoni, D. B., & Aslin, R. M. (1983). A comparison of pure tone auditory thresholds in human infants and adults. *Infant Behavior and Development, 6,* 3–17.

Slawson, A. W. (1968). Vowel quality and musical timbre as functions of spectrum envelope and fundamental frequency. *Journal of the Acoustical Society of America, 43,* 97–101.

Sloboda, J. A. (1985). *The musical mind: The cognitive psychology of music.* Oxford: Oxford University Press.

Sokolov, E. N. (1963). Higher nervous functions: The orienting reflex. *Annual Review of Physiology, 25,* 545–580.

Sorkin, R. D., Boggs, G. J., & Brady, S. L. (1982). Discrimination of temporal jitter in patterned sequences of tones. *Journal of Experimental Psychology: Human Perception and Performance, 8,* 46–57.

Spiegel, M. F., & Green, D. M. (1982). Signal and masker uncertainty with noise maskers of varying duration, bandwidth, and center frequency. *Journal of the Acoustical Society of America, 71,* 1204–1211.

Stoffer, T. H. (1985). Representation of phrase structure in the perception of music. *Music Perception, 3,* 191–220.

Strong, W., & Clark, M. (1967a). Perturbations of synthetic orchestral wind-instrument tones. *Journal of the Acoustical Society of America, 41,* 277–285.

Strong, W., & Clark, M. (1967b). Synthesis of wind–instrument tones. *Journal of the Acoustical Society of America, 41,* 39–52.

Summerfield, Q., & Culling, J. F. (1992). Auditory segregation of competing voices: Absence of effects of FM or AM coherence. *Philosophical Transactions of the Royal Society, London, series B, 336,* 357–366.

Susini, P., McAdams, S., & Winsberg, S. (1999). A multidimensional technique for sound quality assessment. *Acustica/Acta Acustica, 85,* 650–656.

Sussman, E., Ritter, W., & Vaughan, J. H. G. (1998). Attention affects the organization of auditory input associated with the mismatch negativity system. *Brain Research, 789,* 130–138.

Sussman, E., Ritter, W., & Vaughan, J. H. G. (1999). An investigation of the auditory streaming effect using event-related brain potentials. *Psychophysiology, 36*(1), 22–34.

Teas, D. C., Klein, A. J., & Kramer, S. J. (1982). An analysis of auditory brainstem responses in infants. *Hearing Research, 7,* 19–54. *Attention* . New York: Academic

ten Hoopen, G., Boelaarts, L., Gruisen, A., Apon, I., Donders, K., Mul, N., & Akerboon, S. (1994). The detection of anisochrony in monaural and interaural sound sequences. *Perception & Psychophysics, 56*(1), 110–120.

Terhardt, E. (1974). On the perception of periodic sound fluctuations (roughness). *Acustica, 30,* 201–213.

Thorpe, L. A., & Trehub, S. E. (1989). Duration illusion and auditory grouping in infancy. *Developmental Psychology, 25,* 122–127.

Trainor, L. J. (1997). Effect of frequency ratio on infants' and adults' discrimination of simultaneous intervals. *Journal of Experimental Psychology: Human Perception and Performance, 23*(5), 1427–1438.

Trainor, L. J., & Adams, B. (2000). Infants' and adults' use of duration and intensity cues in the segmentation of tone patterns. *Perception and Psychophysics, 62*(2), 333–340.

Trainor, L. J., & Trehub, S. E. (1989). Aging and auditory temporal sequencing: Ordering the elements of repeating tone patterns. *Perception and Psychophysics, 45*(5), 417–426.

Trehub, S. E., Bull, D., & Thorpe, L. (1984). Infant's perception of melodies: The role of melodic contour. *Child Development, 55,* 821–830.

Trehub, S. E., Endman, M. W., & Thorpe, L. A. (1990). Infant's perception of timbre: Classification of complex tones by spectral structure. *Journal of Experimental Child Psychology, 49,* 300.

Trehub, S. E., Schneider, B. A., & Endman, M. (1980). Developmental changes in infant's sensitivity to octave-band noise. *Journal of Experimental Child Psychology, 29,* 283–293.

Trehub, S. E., Schneider, B. A., Morrongiello, B. A., & Thorpe, L. A. (1988). Auditory sensitivity in school-age children. *Journal of Experimental Child Psychology, 46*(2), 273–285.

Trehub, S. E., Thorpe, L., & Morrongiello, B. A. (1987). Organizational processes in infant's perception of auditory patterns. *Child Development, 58,* 741–749.

Treisman, M. (1963). Temporal discrimination and the indifference interval: Implications for a model of the "internal clock." *Psychological Monographs, 77*(13, Whole No. 576).

Treisman, M., & Rostran, A. B. (1972). Brief auditory storage: A modification of Sperling's paradigm applied to audition. *Acta Psychologica, 36,* 161–170.

van Noorden, L. P. A. S. (1975). *Temporal coherence in the perception of tone sequences.* Eindhoven, Netherlands: Eindhoven University of Technology.

van Noorden, L. P. A. S. (1977). Minimum differences of level and frequency for perceptual fission of tone sequences ABAB. *Journal of the Acoustical Society of America, 61,* 1041–1045.

Vliegen, J., Moore, B. C. J., & Oxenham, A. J. (1999). The role of spectral and periodicity cues in auditory stream segregation, measured using a temporal discrimination task. *Journal of the Acoustical Society of America, 106,* 938–945.

Vliegen, J., & Oxenham, A. J. (1999). Sequential stream segregation in the absence of spectral cues. *Journal of the Acoustical Society of America, 105,* 339–346.

Vos, J., & Rasch, R. (1981). The perceptual onset of musical tones. *Perception & Psychophysics, 29*(4), 323–335.

Vos, P. G. (1977). Temporal duration factors in the perception of auditory rhythmic patterns. *Scientific Aesthetics, 1,* 183–199.

Vos, P. G., Mates, J., & van Kruysbergen, N. W. (1995). The perceptual centre of a stimulus as the cue for synchronization to a metronome: Evidence from asynchronies. *Quarterly Journal of Experimental Psychology: Human Experimental Psychology, 48A*(4), 1024–1040.

Vos, P. G., van Assen, M., & Franek, M. (1997). Perceived tempo change is dependent on base tempo and direction of change: Evidence for a generalized version of Schulze's (1978) internal beat model. *Psychological Research, 59*(4), 240–247.

Warren, R. M. (1999). *Auditory perception: A new analysis and synthesis.* Cambridge: Cambridge University Press.

Warren, R. M., Bashford, J. A., Healy, E. W., & Brubaker, B. S. (1994). Auditory induction: Reciprocal changes in alternating sounds. *Perception and Psychophysics, 55,* 313–322.

Warren, R. M., Hainsworth, K. R., Brubaker, B. S., Bashford, J. A., & Healy, E. W. (1997). Spectral restoration of speech: Intelligibility is increased by inserting noise in spectral gaps. *Perception and Psychophysics, 59,* 275–283.

Warren, R. M., Obusek, C. J., & Ackroff, J. M. (1972). Auditory induction: Perceptual synthesis of absent sounds. *Science, 176,* 1149–1151.

Warren, W. H., & Verbrugge, R. R. (1984). Auditory perception of breaking and bouncing events: A case study in ecological acoustics. *Journal of Experimental Psychology: Human Perception and Performance, 10,* 704–712.

Werner, L. A., Folsom, R. C., & Mancl, L. R. (1993). The relationship between auditory brainstem response and behavioral thresholds in normal hearing infants and adults. *Hearing Research, 68,* 131–141.

Werner, L. A., & Marean, G. C. (1991). Method for estimating infant thresholds. *Journal of the Acoustical Society of America, 90,* 1867–1875.

Werner, L. A., & Rubel, E. W. (Eds.). (1992). *Developmental psychoacoustics.* Washington, D.C.: American Psychological Association.

Wertheimer, M. (1925). *Der Gestalttheorie.* Erlangen: Weltkreis-Verlag.

Wessel, D. L. (1979). Timbre space as a musical control structure. *Computer Music Journal, 3*(2), 45–52.

Winsberg, S., & Carroll, J. D. (1988). A quasi-nonmetric method for multidimensional scaling via an extended Euclidean model. *Psychometrika, 53,* 217–229.

Winsberg, S., & De Soete, G. (1993). A latent class approach to fitting the weighted euclidean model: CLASCAL. *Psychometrika, 58,* 315–330.

Winsberg, S., & De Soete, G. (1997). Multidimensional scaling with constrained dimensions: CONSCAL. *British Journal of Mathematical and Statistical Psychology, 50,* 55–72.

Wood, N. L., & Cowan, N. (1995). The cocktail party phenomenon revisited: How frequent are attention shifts to one's name in an irrelevant auditory channel? *Journal of Experimental Psychology: Learning, Memory and Cognition, 21,* 255–260.

Woods, D. L., Alho, K., & Algazi, A. (1994). Stages of auditory feature conjunction: An event-related brain potential study. *Journal of Experimental Psychology: Human Perception and Performance, 20,* 81–94.

Zera, J., & Green, D. M. (1993). Detecting temporal onset and offset asynchrony in multicomponent complexes. *Journal of the Acoustical Society of America, 93,* 1038–1052.

CHAPTER 11

Music Perception and Cognition

TIMOTHY C. JUSTUS AND JAMSHED J. BHARUCHA

INTRODUCTION

Music perception and cognition is the area of cognitive psychology devoted to determining the mental mechanisms underlying our appreciation of music, and in this chapter we review the major findings. We begin with the perception and cognition of pitch, which is the most thoroughly researched area in the field. We then consider perceptual organization in music in the dimension of time, followed by research in musical performance. Next, we review the literature concerning the cognitive neuroscience of music. Finally, we conclude with a discussion of musical universals and origins.

The size of the literature in this field prevents an exhaustive review in the course of a single chapter. The reader is referred to specific reviews in each section, including various chapters appearing in the edited volumes of Deutsch (1982, 1999b), McAdams and Bigand (1993), and Deliège and Sloboda (1997). Additional broad reviews include those by Dowling and Harwood (1986), Krumhansl (1991, 2000a), and Sloboda (1985). For psychologically informed discussions of issues in musical aesthetics, a topic

that will not be discussed here, works by Meyer (1956, 1967, 1973, 2000) and Raffman (1993) are recommended.

PITCH

The Constructive Nature of Pitch Perception

Pitch perception is an excellent example of the pattern-recognition mechanisms used by the auditory system to parse the simultaneous and successive sounds that make up the auditory scene into distinct objects and streams (Bregman, 1990; Chap. 10, this volume). When people listen to music or speech in a naturalistic setting, several instruments or voices may be sounded simultaneously. The brain's task is to parse the frequencies into sound sources. We will focus on the puzzle of virtual pitch and the missing fundamental, which demonstrates this constructive aspect of auditory perception.

Most periodically vibrating objects to which we attribute pitch, including the human vocal folds and the strings of musical instruments, vibrate at several sinusoidal component frequencies simultaneously (Figure 11.1). Typically, these frequencies or partials are approximately integer multiples (*harmonics*) of the fundamental frequency, and the complex is called a *harmonic spectrum*.

Thanks to Oded Ben-Tal, Carol Krumhansl, Susan Landau, Bruno Repp, Barbara Tillmann, Laurel Trainor, Sandra Trehub, and Steven Yantis for their helpful comments on this chapter.

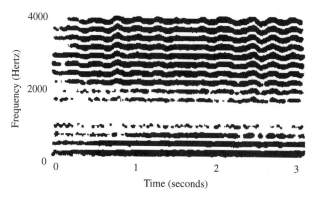

Figure 11.1 Harmonic structure in the human voice.

NOTE: When sustaining a single pitch, the human vocal folds vibrate at a fundamental frequency (e.g., 220 Hz) and at integer multiples of this frequency (440, 660, and so forth). The pitch of such harmonic spectra is matched to that of a sine wave tone at the fundamental frequency. In this case, the relative intensities of the higher-order harmonics have been modified by the shape of the vocal tract, which determines the vowel quality of the pitch (/i/).

Although each of these frequencies sounded alone would evoke a *spectral pitch,* when sounded simultaneously they perceptually fuse and collectively evoke a singular *periodicity pitch.* For harmonic spectra, the periodicity pitch can be matched to the spectral pitch of a pure tone sounded alone at the fundamental frequency (DeWitt & Crowder, 1987; Parncutt, 1989; Stumpf, 1898; Thurlow & Rawlings, 1959). This is not surprising because the fundamental is the most intense harmonic in most natural harmonic sources. However, one can remove the fundamental frequency from a harmonic spectrum and still hear it as the predominant *virtual pitch* (Terhardt, 1974), a phenomenon known as the *missing fundamental.* The perception of a virtual pitch when the fundamental frequency is missing has been the central puzzle motivating research in pitch perception since Helmholtz (1863/1954) and is the most important empirical constraint on any model of pitch.

Helmholtz attributed the missing fundamental to nonlinear distortion in peripheral hearing mechanisms. This was a plausible idea because difference frequencies can be introduced into a sound spectrum by nonlinear distortion, and the fundamental frequency is the difference between the frequencies of adjacent harmonics (see Green, 1976). However, the evidence indicates that it is an illusory percept resulting from the brain's attempt to reconstruct a coherent harmonic spectrum. In this respect, pitch perception is similar to the perception of illusory contours and other examples of constructive visual perception (Chap. 5, this volume). Three classes of evidence demonstrate that virtual pitch cannot be explained by nonlinear distortion alone. First, a virtual pitch cannot be masked by noise within the fundamental frequency's *critical band,* the range in which frequencies interact (see Chap. 10, this volume), but can only be masked by noise within the critical bands of the harmonics from which it is computed (Licklider, 1954). Second, virtual pitch can be induced centrally via dichotic presentation of subsets of harmonics (Houtsma & Goldstein, 1972). Finally, when the partials are not among the first 10 harmonics of the lowest frequency, the predominant virtual pitch corresponds neither to the fundamental nor to other distortion products (Hermann, 1912; de Boer, 1956; Schouten, Ritsma, & Cardozo, 1962).

This last piece of evidence has been the most challenging to explain. For example, a tone consisting of partials at 800, 1000, and 1200 Hz has a predominant periodicity pitch at 200 Hz. Here, 200 Hz is both the fundamental (the highest common divisor) and the difference frequency (a distortion product). However, a tone consisting of partials at 850, 1050 and 1250 Hz has neither a pitch at 50 Hz (the fundamental frequency) nor a pitch at 200 Hz (the difference frequency). Its pitch is somewhat ambiguous but is most closely matched to around 210 Hz. Wightman (1973a) attempted to explain this in terms of the temporal fine structure (i.e., the shape) of the time-domain waveform. He averaged the distances between salient peaks in the waveform resulting from adding the partials in cosine phase and found that the resulting period predicted the pitch. Unfortunately, the temporal fine structure of the waveform depends on the relative phases of the partials, whereas the pitch percept does not (Patterson, 1973; Green, 1976).

Most subsequent theories have postulated a pattern-recognition system that attempts to match the signal to a noisy or fuzzy harmonic template (e.g., Goldstein, 1973; Terhardt, 1972, 1974, 1979; Wightman, 1973b). The closest match of 850, 1050, and 1250 Hz is to a harmonic template with 210 Hz as the fundamental, whose fourth, fifth, and sixth harmonics are 840, 1050, and 1260 Hz. (Harmonics beyond the 10th play little role in pitch perception; hence, the pattern-matching process looks for the best match to low-order harmonics.) Some models have attempted to demonstrate how the to-be-matched harmonic template is learned through self-organizing neural net mechanisms (Cohen, Grossberg, & Wyse, 1995). Others have attempted to account for the brain's reconstruction of the har-

monic spectrum by using the probability distributions of temporal firing characteristics of phase-locked neurons.

Pitch Height and Pitch Class

Traditionally, pitch has been described as varying along a single dimension from low to high, called *pitch height*. Along this dimension, pitch is a logarithmic function of frequency. The Western equal-tempered tuning system divides each frequency doubling (*octave*) into twelve equally spaced steps (*semitones*) on a logarithmic scale, where one note is $2^{1/12}$ (about 1.06) times the frequency of the preceding note (Table 11.1, columns 1 and 3). Such a scale preserves the interval sizes under transformations and reflects the importance of relative rather than absolute pitch perception in music (Attneave & Olson, 1971).

However, this single dimension is not sufficient to describe our mental representation of pitch. Another dimension called *tone chroma* or *pitch class* underlies *octave equivalence*, the perceived similarity of tones an octave apart. Octave equivalence motivates the pitch naming system in Western music, such that tones an octave apart are named with the same letter (e.g., C, D, E) or syllable (e.g., do, re, mi). Shepard (1964) demonstrated this second dimension by generating tone complexes with octave-spaced frequencies whose amplitudes are largest in the middle frequency range and gradually diminish to the threshold of hearing in the high- and low-frequency ranges. Such tone complexes are known as Shepard tones and have a very salient pitch class but an ambiguous pitch height. The perceived direction of motion between two Shepard tones is based on the distance between the two pitch classes. When the distance in either direction between the two complexes is the same (the interval of a tritone; e.g., C to F#), the percept is ambiguous, although there are consistent individual differences in how these tone pairs are

Table 11.1   The 12 Pitch Classes and Intervals within a Single Octave.

Pitch	Interval with C	Frequency relationship with C (equal tempered)	Frequency ratio with C (approx.)	Diatonicity in C Major	Function in C Major	Chord in C Major
C	unison (octave)	262 Hz (524 Hz)	1:1 (2:1)	diatonic	tonic	C Major (I), CDE
C#, Db	minor second	$262 (2^{1/12}) = 278$ Hz	16:15	nondiatonic		
D	major second	$262 (2^{2/12}) = 294$ Hz	9:8	diatonic	supertonic	d minor (ii), DFA
D#, Eb	minor third	$262 (2^{3/12}) = 312$ Hz	6:5	nondiatonic		
E	major third	$262 (2^{4/12}) = 330$ Hz	5:4	diatonic	mediant	e minor (iii), EGB
F	perfect fourth	$262 (2^{5/12}) = 350$ Hz	4:3	diatonic	subdominant	F Major (IV), FAC
F#, Gb	tritone	$262 (2^{6/12}) = 371$ Hz	45:32	nondiatonic		
G	perfect fifth	$262 (2^{7/12}) = 393$ Hz	3:2	diatonic	dominant	G Major (V), GBD
G#, Ab	minor sixth	$262 (2^{8/12}) = 416$ Hz	8:5	nondiatonic		
A	major sixth	$262 (2^{9/12}) = 440$ Hz	5:3	diatonic	submediant	a minor (vi), ACE
A#, Bb	minor seventh	$262 (2^{10/12}) = 467$ Hz	16:9	nondiatonic		
B	major seventh	$262 (2^{11/12}) = 495$ Hz	15:8	diatonic	leading tone	b diminished (vii°), BDF

NOTE: The Western system divides the octave into 12 logarithmically spaced pitch classes, seven of which have specific functions as the diatonic notes in a particular key. Different combinations of two pitches give rise to 12 kinds of intervals, the consonance of which is correlated with how well the frequency ratio can be approximated by a simple integer ratio. Within a key, the seven diatonic chords are formed by combining three diatonic pitches in thirds. (The choice of C as the reference pitch for this table is arbitrary.)

perceived (Deutsch, 1986, 1987, 1991; Repp, 1994). This circular dimension of pitch class can be combined with the linear dimension of pitch height to create a helical representation of pitch (Figure 11.2). Additional geometric models of musical pitch include the *circle of fifths* (Figure 11.3) as a third dimension (see Shepard, 1982). However, even these additional dimensions do not fully capture the perceived relatedness between pitches in music, among other reasons because of the temporal-order asymmetries found between pitches in musical contexts (Krumhansl, 1979, 1990). This is a general concern for spatial representations of similarity given that geometric distances must be symmetric (Krumhansl, 1978; Tversky, 1977).

Pitch Categorization, Relative Pitch, and Absolute Pitch

Listeners are able to detect small differences in frequency, differences as small as 0.5% (Weir, Jesteadt, & Green, 1977). The pitch-class categories into which we divide the dimension of frequency are much larger; a semitone is a frequency difference of about 6%. Some musicians perceive these intervals categorically (Burns & Ward, 1978; Siegel & Siegel, 1977a, 1977b). This kind of categorical perception is characterized by clear category boundaries in a categorization task and an enhanced ability to discriminate stimuli near or across category boundaries, relative to stimuli in the center of a category (Studdert-Kennedy, Liberman, Harris, & Cooper, 1970). Pitch classes differ from stronger instances of categorical perception, as in speech, in that it is still possible to discriminate between different examples within the same category (see Chap. 12, this volume). For example, Levitin (1996, 1999) has pointed out that although musicians do assign nonfocal pitches (those near the boundary) to the nearest category, they will rate the focal pitch of the category as the best member or prototype and give lower ratings to pitches that are higher and lower than this reference pitch.

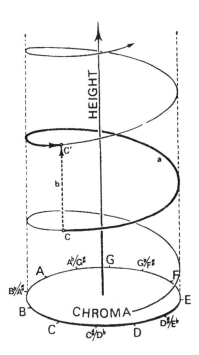

Figure 11.2   The pitch helix.
NOTE: The psychological representation of musical pitch has at least two dimensions, one logarithmically scaled linear dimension corresponding to pitch height and another circular dimension corresponding to pitch class or tone chroma.
SOURCE: From Shepard (1965). Copyright © 1965 by Stanford University Press. Reprinted by permission.

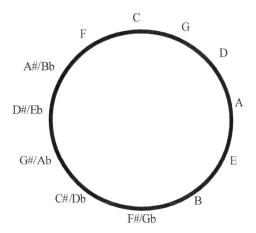

Figure 11.3   The circle of fifths.
NOTE: The circle of fifths represents the similarity between the 12 major keys, with any two adjacent keys on the circle differing in only one pitch. It also represents the sequential transition probabilities between major chords. For example, a C-Major chord is very likely to be followed by a G-Major or F-Major chord, and very unlikely to be followed by an F#-Major chord.

Although few listeners are able to assign names consistently to pitches, most people have the ability known as *relative pitch*. This allows them to recognize the relationship between two pitches and to learn to name one pitch if given the name of the other. Listeners with *absolute pitch* can identify the names of pitches in the absence of any reference pitch. Considering the helical model of pitch height and pitch class (Figure 11.2), it seems that the mental representation of the pitch class circle does not contain set labels for the listener with relative pitch but does for the listener with absolute pitch. Despite the popular misnomer of "perfect" pitch, absolute pitch is not an all-or-none phenomenon; many musicians display

absolute pitch only for the timbre of their primary instrument (see Miyazaki, 1989), and many musicians display absolute pitch only for particular pitches, such as the 440-Hz A to which orchestras tune (see Bachem, 1937). Furthermore, many musicians with relatively strong absolute pitch identify the white notes of the piano (C, D, E, and so on) better than they identify the black notes (C#, D#, and so on). Reasons for this latter phenomenon may be exposure to the white notes of the piano early in the course of childrens' musical instruction (Miyazaki, 1988), the prevalence of these pitches in music generally, or the differences in the names given to the black and white notes of the piano (Takeuchi & Hulse, 1991). The first notion is consistent with the critical period hypothesis for absolute pitch, namely, that children will acquire the ability if taught to name pitches at an early age (for a review, see Takeuchi & Hulse, 1993).

What is sometimes called latent absolute pitch ability has received additional attention. Levitin (1994) designed a study in which participants sang the opening line of a familiar popular song, using the album cover as a visual cue. Of these individuals, 12% sang in the key of the original song, and 44% percent came within two semitones of the original key. Levitin suggests that absolute pitch is actually two separate abilities: *pitch memory,* a common ability in which pitch information is stored veridically along with relational information, and *pitch labeling,* a less-common ability in which the listener has verbal labels to assign to pitch categories.

Consonance and Dissonance

Two pitches, whether played simultaneously or sequentially, are referred to as an *interval.* Consonance and dissonance refer to particular qualities of intervals. *Tonal consonance* or *sensory consonance* refers to the degree to which two tones sound smooth or fused, all else being equal. *Musical consonance* refers to a similar quality as determined by a specific musical context and the musical culture of the listener more generally (Krumhansl, 1991). The opposite qualities are tonal and musical dissonance, the degree of perceived roughness or distinctness. Intervals that can be expressed in terms of simple frequency ratios; for example, unison (1:1), the octave (2:1), perfect fifth (3:2), and perfect fourth (4:3) are regarded as the most consonant (Table 11.1, columns 1–4). Intermediate in consonance are the major third (5:4), minor third (6:5), major sixth (5:3), and minor sixth (8:5). The most dissonant intervals are the major second (9:8), minor second (16:15), major seventh (15:8), minor seventh (16:9), and the tritone (45:32).

Helmholtz (1863/1954) proposed that tonal consonance was related to the absence of interactions or beating between the harmonic spectra of two pitches, an idea that was supported in the model of Plomp and Levelt (1965). They calculated the dissonance of intervals formed by complex tones based on the premise that dissonance would result when any two members of the pair of harmonic spectra lay within a critical band. The model's measurements predicted that the most consonant intervals would be the ones that could be expressed with simple frequency ratios, which has been confirmed by psychological study (DeWitt & Crowder, 1987; Vos & van Vianen, 1984).

Scales and Tonal Hierarchies of Stability

As mentioned previously, our perception of pitch can be characterized by two primary dimensions: pitch height and pitch class. These two dimensions correspond roughly to the first and second of Dowling's (1978) four levels of abstraction for musical scales. The most abstract level is the *psychophysical scale,* which relates pitch in a logarithmic manner to frequency. The next level is the *tonal material,* the pitch categories into which the octave is divided (e.g., the 12 pitch-class categories of the Western system). For specific pieces of music, two additional levels are added. The third level in Dowling's scale scheme is the *tuning system,* a selection of five to seven categories from the tonal material to be used in a melody. In Western classical music, this corresponds to the selection of the seven notes of a major or minor scale, derived by a cycle of [2, 2, 1, 2, 2, 2, 1] semitones for the major (e.g., C D E F G A B C) and [2, 1, 2, 2, 1, 2, 2] semitones for the natural minor (e.g., A B C D E F G A). Such scales consisting of a series of five whole tones and two semitones are *diatonic,* and within a musical context the members of the scale are the *diatonic notes* (Table 11.1, column 5). Finally, the fourth level is *mode.* In this level a tonal hierarchy is established in which particular notes within the tuning system are given more importance or stability than are others (Table 11.1, column 6). These last two levels go hand-in-hand for Western listeners, as a particular hierarchy of stability is automatically associated with each tuning system. Musical works or sections thereof written primarily using one particular tuning system and mode are said to be in the *key* that shares its name with the first note of the scale. Although the psychophysical scale is universal, tonal material, tuning systems, and modes reflect both psychoacoustic constraints and cultural conventions. We return to this issue in the final section. For a very thorough exploration of scales both Western and non-Western, the reader is directed to the review by Burns (1999).

Within a tonal context such as the diatonic scale, the different pitches are not of equal importance but rather are differentiated in a hierarchy of stability, giving rise to the quality of *tonality* in Western music and in many genres of non-Western music. This stability is a subjective property that is a function of both the salience of the tone in the context and the extent to which it typically occurs in similar contexts. One method that has illustrated such hierarchies of stability is the probe-tone method devised by Krumhansl and colleagues (see Krumhansl, 1990). In the original study using this technique (Krumhansl & Shepard, 1979), an ascending or descending major scale was played (the tonal context) and then was followed by one of the twelve chromatic notes (the probe tone), and the participants were asked to rate how well the final tone completed the context. Listeners with musical training rated diatonic tones (the scale tones) more highly than they did nondiatonic tones (the nonscale tones). The ratings produced by the musicians also suggested that they were affected by their knowledge of how each particular tone functions within the tonality established by the scale. For a major tonal context (e.g., C Major), the tonic received the high-

est rating, followed by the dominant (G), mediant (E), subdominant (F), submediant (A), supertonic (D), leading tone (B), and then the nondiatonic tones (Figure 11.4, upper left; see also Table 11.1, columns 5–6). A similar pattern held for minor tonal contexts, with the primary exception that the mediant (E-flat in a c minor context) is second in rating to the tonic. This is consistent with the importance of the relative major tonality when in a minor context. Although the nonmusicians in this study based their judgments primarily on pitch height, other studies have suggested that nonmusicians also perceive tonal hierarchies (Cuddy & Badertscher, 1987; Hébert, Peretz, & Gagnon, 1995).

Krumhansl and Kessler (1982) used the set of probe-tone ratings for each key, collectively called a *key profile* (Figure 11.4, upper left), to create a set of measurements of key distance, allowing the 24 keys to be represented in a multidimensional space. The correlations between the different key profiles (Figure 11.4, lower left) were in agreement with what one would predict from music-theoretical concepts of key distance. The analysis algorithm solved the set of key-profile correlations in four dimensions. Although most four-dimensional solutions are difficult to visualize, undermining their utility, patterns in these particular data allowed for a different representation. Because two-dimensional plots of the first and second dimensions and of the third and fourth dimensions were roughly circular (Figure 11.4, upper right), the data could be represented as a three-dimensional torus, in which the angles of the two circular representations were translated into the two angular positions on the torus, one for each of its circular cross sections (Figure 11.4, lower right). In this representation, the major and minor keys can be visualized spiraling around the outer surface of the torus. The order of both the major and minor key spirals are that of the circle of fifths, and the relative positions of the two

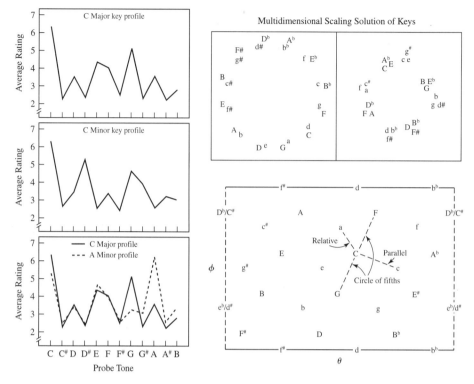

Figure 11.4   Tonal hierarchies and keys.

NOTE: A musical context establishes a hierarchy of stability for the 12 pitch classes, with characteristic hierarchies for major and minor keys. Diatonic notes are regarded as more stable than nondiatonic notes, with the tonic and dominant as the most stable (upper left). Correlations between the 24 key profiles (lower left) produce a multidimensional scaling solution in four dimensions (upper right), which can be represented as a flattened torus (lower right). See text for further discussion.

SOURCE: From Krumhansl & Kessler (1982). Copyright © 1982 by the American Psychological Association. Reprinted by permission.

spirals reflect the similarity between relative keys (sharing the same diatonic set, such as C Major and a minor) and parallel keys (sharing the same tonic, such as C Major and c minor).

Tonal hierarchies for major and minor keys have played a role in numerous other experiments. They are predictive of melodic expectation (Schmuckler, 1989), of judgments of phrase completeness (Palmer & Krumhansl, 1987a, 1987b), and of the response time needed to make judgments of key membership (Janata & Reisberg, 1988). They are also employed in the Krumhansl-Schmuckler key-

finding algorithm (described in Krumhansl, 1990, chap. 4), which calculates a 12-dimensional vector for a presented piece of music and correlates it with each of the 24 12-dimensional tonal hierarchies. The probe-tone method also has been used to study the tonal hierarchies of two non-Western systems, the North Indian system (Castellano, Bharucha, & Krumhansl, 1984) and the Balinese system (Kessler, Hansen, & Shepard, 1984).

Related to the probe-tone method is a similar technique in which a musical context is followed by two tones, which participants are asked to rate with respect to similarity or good continuation. Ratings are higher when the pair includes a stable pitch in the tonal hierarchy, and this effect is even stronger when the stable pitch is the second note in the pair (Krumhansl, 1990). This results in the observation that the ratings between one tone-pair ordering and its reverse are different, and these differences are greatest for pairs in which only one tone is stable in the preceding context. Multidimensional scaling was performed on these data as well, but rather than measuring the similarities (correlations) between the 24 key profiles, the similarities in this case were those between the 12 tones of a single key. The analysis found a three-dimensional solution in which the points representing the 12 pitches roughly lie on the surface of a cone, with the tonal center at the vertex. One factor clearly represented by this configuration is pitch class; the tones are located around the cone in order of their positions on the pitch-class circle. A second factor is the importance of the pitches in the tonal hierarchy; they are arranged such that tones with high positions in the hierarchy are located near the vertex, closer to the tonal center and to each other than are the remaining less-stable tones.

Chords and Harmonic Hierarchies of Stability

Harmony is a product not only of a tonal hierarchy of stability for pitches within a musical context but also of a harmonic hierarchy of stability for chords. A *chord* is simply the simultaneous (or sequential) sounding of three or more notes, and the Western system is built particularly on the triads within the major and minor keys. A *triad* is a chord consisting of three members of a scale, where each pair is spaced by the interval of a major or minor third. Thus there are four types of triads: major, minor, diminished, and augmented, depending on the particular combination of major and minor thirds used. In a major or minor key, the kind of triad built on each scale degree depends on the particular series of semitones and whole tones that make up the scale (Table 11.1, column 7). For example, in the key of C Major the seven triads are C Major (I), d minor (ii), e minor (iii), F Major (IV), G Major (V), a minor (vi), and b diminished (vii°). The tonic (I), dominant (V), and subdominant (IV) are considered to be the most stable chords in the key by music theorists, followed by ii, vi, iii, and vii°. (Note that the use of the word *harmonic* in the sense of musical harmony is distinct from the acoustic sense, as in *harmonic spectra*.)

This hierarchy of harmonic stability has been supported by psychological studies as well. One approach involves collecting ratings of how one chord follows from another. For example, Krumhansl, Bharucha, and Kessler (1982) used such judgments to perform multidimensional scaling and hierarchical clustering techniques. The psychological distances between chords reflected both key membership and stability within the key; chords belonging to different keys grouped together with the most stable chords in each key (I, V, and IV) forming an even smaller cluster. Such rating methods also suggest that the harmonic stability of each chord in a pair affects its perceived relationship to the other, and this depends on the stability of the second chord in particular (Bharucha & Krumhansl, 1983). Additionally, this chord space is plastic and changes when a particular tonal context is introduced; the distance between the members of a particular key decreases in the context of that key (Bharucha & Krumhansl, 1983; Krumhansl, Bharucha, & Castellano, 1982).

Convergent evidence is provided from studies of recognition memory in which two chord sequences are presented and participants must decide if they are the same or different, or, in the case in which all sequences differ, judge at which serial position the change occurred. In such studies, tonal sequences (reflecting a tonal hierarchy) are more easily encoded than are atonal sequences; nondiatonic tones in tonal sequences are often confused with more stable events; and stable chords are easily confused with each other (Bharucha & Krumhansl, 1983). Additionally, the probability of correctly detecting a change in a particular chord is systematically related to that chord's role in the presented tonal context (Krumhansl, Bharucha, & Castellano, 1982). Finally, nondiatonic chords in tonal sequences disrupt the memory for prior and subsequent chord events close in time (Krumhansl & Castellano, 1983).

There are some compelling similarities between the cognitive organization of chords and that of tones described in the previous section. For both tones and chords, a musical context establishes a hierarchy of stability in which some events are considered more important or stable than others. In both cases, the psychological space representing tones or chords is modified in a musical context in three principal ways (Bharucha & Krumhansl, 1983; Krumhansl, 1990). First, an important event in the hierarchy of stability is considered more similar to other instances of itself than is a less important event (*contextual identity*). Second, two important events in the hierarchy of stability are considered more similar to each other than are less important events (*contextual distance*). Third, the asymmetry in a pair of similarity judgments is largest when the first event is less important in the hierarchy and the second event is more important (*contextual asymmetry*). These results support the idea that stable tones and chords in tonal contexts serve as cognitive reference points (Rosch, 1975a) and are compelling examples of how musical organization can reflect domain-general principles of conceptual representation.

Harmonic Perception, Representation, and Expectation

Implicit knowledge of the relationships between the chords in Western music has also been shown in the chord-priming paradigm of Bharucha and colleagues (Bharucha & Stoeckig, 1986, 1987; Tekman & Bharucha, 1992, 1998). In each trial of this paradigm the participants are presented with two chords, a prime and a target, and are required to respond to some aspect of the target. The task is typically to identify whether the target chord is in tune or mistuned, although onset asynchrony (Tillmann & Bharucha, in press) and phoneme discrimination tasks (Bigand, Tillmann, Poulin, D'Adamo, & Madurell, 2001) have been used as well. The variable of interest, however, is the harmonic relationship between the two chords, which is related to the probability that these events will occur in sequence with each other in Western music. The results of the original study (Bharucha & Stoeckig, 1986) indicated that responses to tuned target chords that were in a close harmonic relationship with the prime were faster and more accurate than were responses to such chords distantly related to the prime. The data also revealed a response bias in that participants were more likely to judge a related target chord as more consonant; in an intonation task a close target is likely to be judged as tuned, whereas a distant target is likely to be judged as mistuned. Such priming is generated at a cognitive level, via activation spreading through a representation of tonal relationships, rather than by perceptual priming of specific frequencies (Bharucha & Stoeckig, 1987). Furthermore, priming occurs automatically even when more informative veridical information about the chord progression has been made explicitly available (Justus & Bharucha, 2001), suggesting that the mechanisms of priming are informationally encapsulated to some degree (see Fodor,

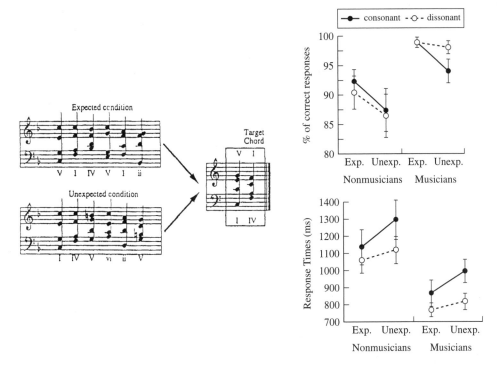

Figure 11.5 Chord priming by a global harmonic context.

NOTE: Musical contexts establish expectations for subsequent events, based on the musical schema of the listener. A target chord (F Major in the figure) is processed more efficiently at the end of a context that establishes it as the most stable event (the tonic chord) than a context that establishes it as a moderately stable event (the subdominant chord), even when the immediately preceding chord (C Major in the figure) is precisely the same. This is evidenced by both error rates and response times, and is true of both musician and nonmusician listeners.

SOURCE: From Bigand et al. (1999). Copyright © 1999 by the American Psychological Association. Reprinted by permission.

1983, 2000). Both musicians and nonmusicians demonstrate harmonic priming, and evidence from self-organizing networks suggests that this implicit tonal knowledge may be learned via passive exposure to the conventions of Western music (Bharucha, 1987; Tillmann, Bharucha, & Bigand, 2000).

Global harmonic context can influence the processing of musical events even when the local context is precisely the same. Bigand and Pineau (1997) created pairs of eight-chord sequences in which the final two chords were identical for each pair. The first six chords, however, established two different harmonic contexts, one in which the final chord was highly expected (a tonic following a dominant) and the other in which the final chord was less highly expected (a subdominant following a tonic). Target chords were more easily processed in the former case, indicating an effect of global harmonic context (Figure 11.5). Furthermore, different contexts can be established by harmonic structure that occurs several events in the past. Bigand, Mandurell, Tillmann, and Pineau (1999) found that target chords are processed more efficiently when they are more closely related to the overarching harmonic context (as determined by the harmony of a preceding phrase), even when all chords in the second phrase are identical. Tillmann and colleagues (Tillmann & Bigand, 2001; Tillmann, Bigand, & Pineau, 1998) have compared the mechanisms of harmonic priming and semantic priming. They note that although two distinct mechanisms have been proposed for language— one from spreading activation and another from structural integration—the former alone can account for reported harmonic priming results.

Melodic Perception, Representation, and Expectation

The composition of a melody generally reflects the tonal hierarchy of stability, frequently returning to a set of stable reference points. The tonal hierarchy affects the listener's melodic expectation; less stable tones within a tonal context are usually followed immediately by nearby, more stable tones. Bharucha (1984a, 1996) has referred to this convention and the expectation for it to occur as *melodic anchoring*. Conversely, different melodies will recruit a particular tonal hierarchy to varying degrees depending on its fit with the structure of the melody (Cuddy, 1991), requiring a degree of tonal bootstrapping on the part of the listener.

An additional constraint on melodies is that the individual notes of the melody must be *streamed* or perceptually grouped as part of the same event unfolding over time, and the rules that determine which events will and will not be grouped together as part of the same melody are explained in part by the Gestalt principles of perceptual organization (Bregman, 1990; Deutsch, 1999a; Chap. 10, this volume). For example, whether a series of tones is heard as a single melody or is perceptually streamed into two simultaneous melodies depends on the tempo, the tones' similarity in pitch height, and other factors, including timbral similarity. Composers often follow compositional heuristics when composing melodies, such as an avoidance of part crossing, to help the perceiver stream the voices (see Huron, 1991). This is of particular importance for counterpoint and other forms of polyphony, in which multiple voices singing or playing simultaneously must be streamed correctly by the listener if they are to be perceived as distinct events. Conversely, composers can exploit auditory streaming to create virtual polyphony, the illusion that multiple voices are present rather than one. For example, the solo string and woodwind repertoire of the Baroque period often contains fast passages of notes alternating between different registers, creating the impression that two instruments are playing rather than one.

Similar principles can also explain higher-order levels of melodic organization. Narmour (1990) has proposed a theory of melodic structure, the implication-realization model, which begins with elementary Gestalt principles such as similarity, proximity, and good continuation. The responses of listeners in continuity-rating and melody-completion tasks have provided empirical support for some of these principles (Cuddy & Lunney, 1995; Krumhansl, 1995; Thompson, Cuddy, & Plaus, 1997; see also Schellenberg, 1996, 1997). According to Narmour, these basic perceptual rules generate hierarchical levels of melodic structure and expectation when applied recursively to larger musical units.

Another body of research has examined the memory and mental representation of specific melodies. Studies of melody recognition when melodies are transposed to new keys suggest that melodic fragments are encoded with respect to scales, tonal hierarchies, and keys (Cuddy & Cohen, 1976; Cuddy, Cohen, & Mewhort, 1981; Cuddy, Cohen, & Miller, 1979; Cuddy & Lyons, 1981; Dewar, Cuddy, & Mewhort, 1977). Melodies are processed and encoded not only in terms of the musical scale in which they are written but also independently in terms of their *melodic contour,* the overall shape of the melody's ups and downs. When discriminating between atonal melodies, in which there are no tonal hierarchies, listeners rely mainly on the melodic contour (Dowling & Fujitani, 1971). Furthermore, within tonal contexts melodies and their tonal answers (transpositions that alter particular intervals by semitones to preserve the key) are just as easily confused as are exact transpositions (Dowling, 1978). One explanation of this result is that the contour, which is represented separately from the specific interval information, is processed relative to the framework provided by the scale.

TIME

Tempo

Among the temporal attributes of music are tempo, rhythmic pattern, grouping, and meter. The *tempo* describes the rate at which the basic pulses of the music occur. Several lines of evidence suggest a special perceptual status for temporal intervals ranging from approximately 200 ms to 1,800 ms, and in particular those ranging from approximately 400 ms to 800 ms. Both the *spontaneous tempo* and the *preferred tempo*—those at which humans prefer to produce and hear an isochronous pulse—are based on a temporal interval of about 600 ms (Fraisse, 1982). The range of about 200 to 1,800 ms also describes the range of accurate synchronization to a presented isochronous pulse, a task at which we become proficient early (Fraisse, Pichot, & Chairouin, 1949) and which we find easier than reacting *after* each isochronous stimulus (Fraisse, 1966).

Rhythmic Pattern

A *rhythmic pattern* is a short sequence of events, typically on the order of a few seconds, and is characterized by the periods between the successive onsets of the events. The interonset periods are typically simple integer multiples of each other; 85% to 95% of the notated durations in a typical musical piece are of two categories in a ratio of either 2:1 or 3:1 with each other (Fraisse, 1956, 1982). The limitation of durations to two main categories may result from a cognitive limitation; even musically trained subjects have difficulty distinguishing more than two or three duration categories in the range below 2 s (Murphy, 1966). Listeners distort near-integer ratios toward integers when repeating rhythms (Fraisse, 1982), and musicians have difficulty reproducing rhythms that cannot be represented as approximations of simple ratios (Fraisse, 1982; Sternberg, Knoll, & Zukofsky, 1982). Rhythms of simple ratios can be reproduced easily at different tempi, which is not true for more complex rhythms (Collier & Wright, 1995). However, the simplicity of the ratio cannot explain everything. Povel (1981) found that even if the ratios in a rhythmic pattern are integers, participants may not appreciate this relationship unless the structure of the pattern makes this evident. For example, a repeating sequence with intervals of 250-750-250-750 ms is more difficult than 250-250-250-750 ms, a pattern in which the 1:3 ratio between the elements of the pattern is emphasized by the pattern itself.

Grouping

A *group* is a unit that results from the segmentation of a piece of music, much as text can be segmented into sections, paragraphs, sentences, phrases, words, feet, and syllables. Rhythmic patterns are groups containing subordinate groups, and they can be combined to form superordinate groups such as musical phrases, sequences of phrases, sections, and movements. Lerdahl and Jackendoff (1983) proposed that the psychological representation of a piece of music includes a hierarchical organization of groups called the *grouping structure*. Evidence supporting grouping mechanisms was found by Sloboda and Gregory (1980), who demonstrated that clicks placed in a melody were systematically misremembered as occurring closer to the boundary of the phrase than they actually did, just as in language (Garrett, Bever, & Fodor, 1966). Furthermore, there are constraints on what can constitute a group. For example, a preference for listening to groups that end with a falling pitch contour and long final duration is present in infants as young as 4 months of age (Krumhansl & Jusczyk, 1990; Jusczyk & Krumhansl, 1993).

Grouping can occur perceptually even when there is no objective basis for it, a phenomenon called *subjective rhythmization*. Within the range of intervals of approximately 200 ms to 1,800 ms, an isochronous pattern will appear to be grouped in twos, threes, or fours (Bolton, 1894); when asked to synchronize with such a pattern, subjects illustrate their grouping by lengthening and accenting every other or every third event (MacDougall, 1903). Grouping is not independent of tempo; groups of larger numbers are more likely at fast tempi (Bolton, 1894; Fraisse, 1956; Hibi, 1983; Nagasaki, 1987a, 1987b; Peters, 1989). Rhythmic pattern also affects grouping; events separated by shorter intervals in a sequence will group into a unit that is the length of a longer interval (Povel, 1984). Finally, grouping is qualitatively different at different levels of the hierarchy. Levels of organization less than about 5 s form groups within the psychological present (Fraisse, 1982; see also Clarke, 1999).

For both grouping and meter, Lerdahl and Jackendoff's (1983) *A Generative Theory of Tonal Music (GTTM)* describes a set of well-formedness rules and preference rules for deciding which perceptual interpretation to assign to a particular musical passage. The well-formedness rules are absolute, whereas the preference rules are like the Gestalt principles in that they are ceteris paribus (all else being equal) rules. With the exception of work by Deliège (1987), the empirical worth of the grouping rules has not often been studied.

Meter

Meter is a hierarchical organization of beats. The first essential characteristic of meter is isochrony; the beats are equally spaced in time, creating a pulse at a particular tempo (Povel, 1984). A *beat* has no duration and is used to divide the music into equal *time spans*, just as in geometry a point divides a line into segments. The beat is thus not a feature of the raw musical stimulus, but something the listener must infer from it. For example, if a new event occurs almost every second, a beat is perceived every second, whether or not there is an event onset.

Povel (1984) proposed a model of meter in which the most economical *temporal grid* is chosen. In this model a temporal grid is a sequence of isochronous intervals with two parameters: duration (establishing a tempo) and phase. Each interval in a rhythmic pattern is a possible grid duration. The temporal grid is chosen based on the degree to which it fulfills three requirements: fixing the most elements in the rhythmic pattern, not fixing many empty points in time, and specifying the non-fixed elements within the grid. Rhythms can be metrical to varying degrees. The strength of the meter and the ease of reproducibility are related, which led Essens and Povel (1985) to suggest that highly metrical rhythms induce an internal clock that helps the listener encode the rhythm in terms of the meter. Metrical strength is also associated with an asymmetry in discrimination; it is easier to discriminate between two similar rhythmic patterns when the more strongly metrical one is presented first (Bharucha & Pryor, 1986).

The second characteristic of meter is a hierarchy of perceived stress, or a *metrical hierarchy,* such that events occurring on some beats are perceived to be stronger and longer than are those on the others, even if these events are not acoustically stressed. A metrical hierarchy arises when there is more than one level of metrical organization (Lerdahl & Jackendoff, 1983). The level of the hierarchy at which the isochronous pulse is the most salient is called the basic metrical level or *tactus,* and this level is often chosen such that the time span between tactus beats is between 200 ms and 1,800 ms, the tempo range that is processed most accurately. The two most common meters are duple (alternating stressed and unstressed beats, as in a march) and triple (stressed following by two unstressed, as in a waltz). In duple meter, the tactus has two beats per cycle, and the first superordinate level has one beat (the stressed beat or downbeat) per cycle. There may be subordinate metrical levels as well, arising from subdivisions of each beat into two or three. These different levels create a hierarchy of importance for the different beats in the measure; beats that are represented at higher hierarchical levels are regarded as stronger or more stable than the others.

Empirical support for the perception of metrical hierarchies comes from experiments in which participants judged the completeness of music ending on different beats of the meter (Palmer & Krumhansl, 1987a, 1987b) as well as from experiments in which participants rated the appropriateness of probe tones entering at different metrical positions or decided if the probe tones entered in the same metrical position as they had before (Palmer & Krumhansl, 1990). However, Handel (1998) showed that information about meter is not used consistently when participants discriminate between different rhythms when the figural (grouping) organization is the same. He

questioned whether the concept of meter is necessary and suggested that the apparent discrepancy between the importance of meter in rhythm production and perception may be resolved by noting that metrical rhythms are better reproduced because they are easier, and not because they are metrical.

Event Hierarchies and Reductions

In addition to the grouping and metrical hierarchies, Lerdahl and Jackendoff (1983) proposed two kinds of *reduction* in *GTTM.* Reductions for music were first proposed by musicologist Heinrich Schenker (1935), who was able to capture the elaboration of underlying structures in the musical surface. The concept of reduction in general implies that the events in music are heard in a hierarchy of relative importance. Such event hierarchies are not to be confused with the tonal hierarchies described in the preceding section, although the two interrelate in important ways (Bharucha, 1984b; Deutsch, 1984; Dowling, 1984). *Event hierarchies* refer to the temporal organization of a specific piece of music, where more important musical events are represented higher in the hierarchy, whereas *tonal hierarchies* refer to the organization of categories of pitch events, where some pitch classes are regarded as more stable in the context. A tonal hierarchy plays a role in the organization of an event hierarchy. The two reductions of *GTTM* are time-span reduction and prolongational reduction. The *time-span reduction* relates pitch to the temporal organization provided by meter and grouping; this reduction is concerned with relative stability within rhythmic units. The *prolongational reduction* relates harmonic structure to the information represented by the time-span reduction; this reduction is concerned with the sense of tension and relaxation in the music (see also Krumhansl, 1996). *GTTM* adopts a tree structure notation for these reductions, which represents how one event is subordinate to or an elaboration of the other. Branches on such trees must be nonoverlapping, adjacent, and recursive, just as are the grouping and rhythmic hierarchies.

There is a marked correspondence between the hierarchical representation of musical events in time as postulated in *GTTM* and the hierarchical representation of relative syllabic stress in phonology (Liberman & Prince, 1977; Selkirk, 1980). Additionally, music and speech have comparable phrase lengths, and in both cases phrases are typically characterized by a pitch contour that rises and then falls over the course of the phrase. Although comparisons have often been made between the structure of music and language (e.g., Bernstein, 1976), only in these phonological aspects is the analogy well supported. The evidence and theory suggesting syntactic or semantic parallels in music and language are less compelling.

The Relationship between Time and Pitch

A final issue in musical timing is the degree of interaction between the pitch-based and rhythmic components of music. Some accounts have emphasized an independent and additive relationship between the two in determining musical expectation (Bigand, 1997; Monahan & Carterette, 1985; Monahan, Kendall, & Carterette, 1987; Palmer & Krumhansl, 1987a, 1987b; Smith & Cuddy, 1989). Others have argued that there is a stronger dependence and interactive relationship between the two, as evidenced by judgments of melodic completion (Boltz, 1989a, 1989b), duration estimation (Boltz, 1989c, 1991b, 1993b; Jones & Boltz, 1989; Jones, Boltz, & Klein, 1993), recall (Boltz, 1991a; Boltz & Jones, 1986), and recognition (Bigand & Pineau, 1996; Boltz, 1993a; Jones, Summerell, & Marshburn, 1987; Jones & Ralston, 1991).

Boltz (1998) suggested that most musical sequences are highly coherent events, in that temporal structure and nontemporal structure are correlated and listeners encode these two dimensions together in memory. This is supported by the fact that participants can accurately give a duration judgment for a coherent musical sequence regardless of whether they attend to the duration or pitch alone or to the combination of both. For incoherent sequences, accurate duration estimates can be given only when that dimension is attended (Boltz, 1992, 1998).

Jones (1987; Jones & Boltz, 1989) has proposed a theory of dynamic attending in which different kinds of accent structures are attributed to both pitch and rhythmic organization in music. Accent coupling occurs in a melody when both melodic and temporal accents coincide. Such markers reorient attention, and manipulating them can cause differences in the detection and recognition of musical targets (Jones, Boltz, & Kidd, 1982; Jones, Kidd, & Wetzel, 1981).

MUSICAL PERFORMANCE AND ABILITY

Study of musical performance can yield insights into the mental representations used to interpret and plan the production of a piece and can provide additional clues to the kinds of information to which listeners attend when interpreting the performance. More generally, musical performance offers an opportunity to study complex motor behavior and the acquisition of cognitive skill. The reader is referred to additional reviews by Palmer (1997), Gabrielsson (1999), and Sloboda (1984, 1985, 1988).

Interpretation and Planning

The errors that musicians make are not random; mistakes often reflect the underlying representations of the music and the plan for executing the performance. We often think of pitch errors as being extremely salient, but Repp (1996b) has illustrated that the majority of errors made by trained pianists go undetected; errors vary along a continuum of perceptual salience. Conversely, trained pianists will automatically correct some errors in the score without realizing they are doing so, particularly when the error occurs in the middle of a phrase. This is a musical analogue of the proofreader's error (Sloboda, 1976).

Palmer and colleagues have used production errors in piano performance as an index of the kinds of representations that musicians use when planning; specifically, these errors reflect knowledge of diatonicity, melody, and harmony. The kind of musical knowledge emphasized in the errors will vary depending on the type of musical context, such as whether it is homophonic, having one primary melodic line, or polyphonic, having multiple melodic lines (Palmer & van de Sande, 1993). This approach also supports the idea that performers break a piece of music into segments that reflect the phrase structure of the piece for the purposes of planning (Palmer & van de Sande, 1995). The performer's representation of the local temporal organization of music has also been investigated by measuring errors in performance. Drake, Dowling, and Palmer (1991) found that pianists were more successful at reproducing melodies when different kinds of accent structures (metrical, melodic, and rhythmic) coincided and less successful when they conflicted. Furthermore, accent structures can affect the way in which the performer varies intensity, interonset timing, and articulation (Drake & Palmer, 1993).

Another cue to how performers process music is their eye movements when reading a score. Pianists' saccades reflect the relative harmonic or melodic content of the piece being played, with more vertical saccades for ho-mophonic music, in which information at each time point can be chunked into one harmonic event, and series of horizontal saccades for polyphonic music, in which multiple melodic lines are occurring simultaneously (Van Nuys & Weaver, 1943; Weaver, 1943). The number of notes that performers can produce after the removal of the music they are reading, referred to as the *eye-hand span,* is affected by the phrase structure in music. When the end of the phrase is just beyond the average length of an eye-hand span, the span is stretched up to a limit. Conversely, when the end of the phrase is before the average length of the span, the span is contracted (Sloboda, 1977; see Sloboda, 1984, for a review of music reading). Phrase lengths are constrained by capacity limits as well as structure, as evidenced by performance errors (Palmer & van de Sande, 1993).

Communication of Structure

A second major class of experiments in musical performance involves how musicians, through the nuances of the performance, communicate structure to the listener. The written notation of Western music represents pitch and duration much more explicitly than it does the structural and expressive principles, such as phrasing and tension-relaxation. However, the performer provides information about these unwritten aspects of the piece to the listener, often through systematic deviations from the notated music. In many cases the qualities that lead a listener to describe a performance as "musical" are changes in tempo, dynamics, and synchrony, done in a systematic way as to bring the structure of the piece across to the listener, as will be explained next. Investigations of this issue usually involve mastered performances by expert musicians, unlike the previous body of research, which requires errors (for a review, see Gabrielsson, 1999).

Performance expression can affect the listener's perception of rhythm, melody, and harmony. One piece of information that can be provided to the listener through deviations from the exact is the meter of the piece. For example, experienced musicians can tell the difference between two different recordings of the same piece played by performers who read the piece with the bar lines drawn in different phases (Sloboda, 1983). Performers also have a tendency to place the primary voice or melody slightly ahead of the other voices. This has been found both for ensembles (Rasch, 1988) and for individual pianists (Goebl, 2001; Palmer, 1989; Repp, 1996a). Different melodic intentions on the part of the performer result not only in different degrees of melodic lead, but also in different melodic interpretations on the part of the listener (Palmer, 1996). Additionally, performance expression may enhance the listener's perception of key modulation (Thompson & Cuddy, 1997).

Musicians cannot help but play nuances; even when asked to play mechanically, expressive timing differences remain (Drake & Palmer, 1993; Palmer, 1989; Penel & Drake, 1998; Repp, 1999a, 1999c). Listeners prefer and expect certain kinds of tempo deviation, particularly a slowing of tempo at the ends of musical phrases. In an analysis of performances of a Schumann piano work, Repp (1992b) found that systematic deviations from an exact tempo occurred during a recurring melodic gesture. Musicians but not nonmusicians prefer to hear this kind of temporal nuance when listening to synthesized musical performances (Repp, 1992a). Furthermore, evidence suggests that listeners expect to hear a slowing of tempo at the end of a musical phrase; a lengthening is more difficult for the listener to detect when it is placed at the end of a phrase relative to the middle (Repp, 1992c, 1998b, 1999b; see Figure 11.6). Converging evidence comes from

the study of expressive imitation; pianists can imitate phrases with expressive timing deviations well only if the deviations are related to the structure of the music (Clarke, 1993; Clarke & Baker-Short, 1987; but see Repp, 2000). There may be a connection between such temporal elements in music and kinematics, as suggested by Truslit (1938; see Repp, 1993). Just as biologically realistic variations in movement velocity are perceived as constant (see Viviani & Stucchi, 1992), music may appear to progress at a constant tempo when played with expressive timing deviations (Friberg & Sundberg, 1999; Penel, 2000; Repp, 1998a).

Musical Expertise and Skill Acquisition

There is also a growing body of research on the acquisition of skills involved in the performance of music, specifically piano performance. Children with more musical training plan their movements earlier, are quicker to detect and correct their errors, and are able to move past mistakes (Palmer & Drake, 1997). In addition, musical training as well as practice with a particular piece are associated with improvements in tempo, pitch accuracy, and relative timing of events (Drake & Palmer, 2000). Furthermore, the mental representations of motor events in musical performance may become more conceptual and less tied to motor representations for advanced musicians, as suggested by a transfer of learning study done by Palmer and Meyer (2000). Sloboda, Clarke, Parncutt, and Raekallio (1998) conducted a study of fingering accuracy in Czerny piano exercises and suggested that expert pianists have overlearned rule-governed response sequences that are triggered by familiar patterns in a score.

Differences also exist between musicians with different kinds of performance experience. Pianists whose primary emphasis is solo performance do worse than accompanists in

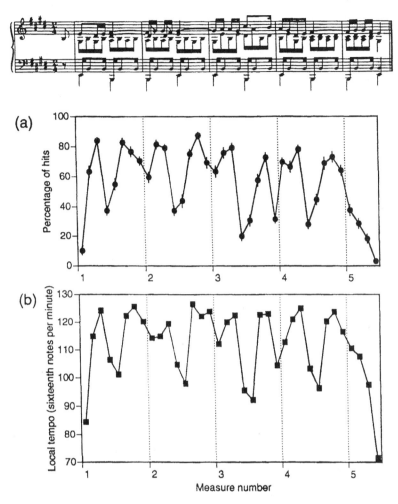

Figure 11.6   The representation of time in a musical context.
NOTE: Musical phrase structure warps the perception of time. A listener's ability to detect an experimental lengthening (a) in a mechanical performance of Chopin's Etude in E Major (Op. 10, No. 3) is correlated with the points in time where musicians typically provide such lengthening (b).
SOURCE: From Repp (1999b). Copyright © 1999 by the Psychonomic Society. Reprinted by permission.

sight-reading but show greater improvements with repeated practice (Lehmann & Ericsson, 1993). Proficient sight-readers also plan farther ahead; Sloboda (1977) found that when reading melodies, good instrumentalists had eye-hand spans of up to seven notes.

A related set of issues concern the environmental factors that are associated with (and perhaps causally related to) the development of musical skill. Not surprisingly, one major predictor of musical skill is the amount of formal practice undertaken (Ericsson, Krampe, & Tesch-Romer, 1993; Sloboda, Davidson, Howe, & Moore, 1996). Additionally, children who are successful in their private instrumental lessons tend to have parents who are highly involved in their children's early stages of learning and who also listen to (but not necessarily perform) music themselves (Davidson, Howe, Moore, & Sloboda, 1996).

One study of students' impressions of their music teachers revealed that effective initial teachers are perceived by their pupils as having positive personal characteristics (such as friendliness), but at later stages of learning, performance and professional skills are weighted more heavily (Davidson, Moore, Sloboda, & Howe, 1998). Other studies have addressed the effects of sibling role models and peer opinions on the progress of musical training in children (for a review, see Davidson, Howe, & Sloboda, 1997). Links between musical development and personality (Kemp, 1997) and gender (O'Neill, 1997) have also been suggested. Although notions of individual differences in musical development are often based on the concept of innate talent, not all music psychologists agree with this interpretation (see Sloboda, Davidson, & Howe, 1994; Howe, Davidson, & Sloboda, 1998, with commentaries)..

THE COGNITIVE NEUROSCIENCE OF MUSIC

Having reviewed the literature to this point from the perspective of cognitive psychology, we must now ask how the mental algorithms related to music cognition are implemented in the brain. Initially, such investigations focused on the perception of pitch. More recently, the kinds of processing explored in these studies have expanded to other levels of musical organization. Three general categories of approach have emerged: neuropsychological studies involving patients with damaged or resected brain regions of interest, neuroimaging studies concerned with patterns of metabolism and blood flow, and electroencephalography or the measurement of small electrical potentials on the surface of the head. Peretz (1993, 2001) has provided reviews of the first area, and Besson (1997) has provided a review of the third.

Neuropsychology

The animal literature provided one of the first clues regarding the processing of pitch in the brain. Research on cats lends support to the idea that the auditory cortex is required for a unified pitch percept, including the extraction of the missing fundamental, but not for simple frequency discriminations, which may be computed subcortically (but see Johnsrude, Penhune, & Zatorre, 2000). Heffner and Whitfield (1976) trained cats in a conditioned avoidance paradigm using complex tones as stimuli. First the cats were trained to avoid a shock by ceasing to lick a cup when a rising tone pair was played. Falling pairs were not associated with the shock and thus were ignored by the cats. After this training, pairs of harmonic complexes were presented such that when the component frequencies were rising in pitch, the implied fundamental frequency was falling, and vice versa. The cats continued their avoidance behavior as if they were processing the stimuli according to the implied fundamental frequency of the tone complexes. In a later study, Whitfield (1980) demonstrated that cats trained in such a manner who then received ablations of auditory cortex could be retrained to make responses to individual frequencies of complex tones (the spectral pitches), but not to the pitch implied by the group of frequencies as a whole (the virtual pitch).

Adapting this paradigm to humans, Zatorre (1988) found that an intact right primary auditory cortex, located in Heschl's gyrus, was needed to extract virtual pitch from harmonic complexes with missing fundamental frequencies. Patients who had undergone temporal lobe excisions that included the right Heschl's gyrus were impaired in pitch extraction, whereas patients with complementary lesions on the left side or more anterior regions in the temporal lobe were not impaired.

These results suggested that the right primary auditory cortex and perhaps more posterior secondary auditory cortices are necessary for pitch processing.

A preferred role for right temporal cortex as well as the right frontal cortex in the processing of pitch was also suggested by a study involving a short-term pitch retention task (Zatorre & Samson, 1991). Individuals with unilateral temporal and frontal excisions were asked to perform two pitch tasks. None of the patients were impaired on the control task, which was a comparison of two pitches over a delay. However, when the delay contained distracter pitches, all of the groups of right-hemisphere (and not left-hemisphere) patients were impaired relative to controls.

Pitch extraction therefore seems to rely more heavily on right- than on left-hemisphere mechanisms. The picture is more complex, however, for the perception and cognition of pitch sequences or melodies. Early studies suggested that the right auditory cortex plays a prominent role in melodic processing (e.g., Schulhoff & Goodglass, 1969; Shankweiler, 1966) and that the role of the left hemisphere was limited to the more verbal aspects of music such as the lyrics (e.g., Gardener, Silverman, Denes, Semenza, & Rosenstiel, 1977; for a review, see Zatorre, 1984). However, a frequently cited psychological study by Bever and Chiarello (1974) showed that musicians and nonmusicians have different hemispheric asymmetries, left and right respectively, as suggested by corresponding contralateral ear advantages for melodic perception. Peretz and Morais (1980) suggested that these differences are due to a global versus local processing difference for melodies in the right and left hemispheres, respectively. Nonmusicians also recruit the left hemisphere more significantly when they process in a more analytic manner, as evidenced by an increasing right-ear advantage.

This global-local distinction between the right and left hemispheres for melodic perception was also supported by Peretz (1990) in a neuropsychological study. Left-hemisphere damage was associated with a failure to use local information (intervals), and right-hemisphere damage was associated with a failure to use either global (contour) or local information, recalling the distinction between scale and contour proposed by Dowling (1978). This is consistent with at least two interpretations: one in which local processing occurs bilaterally or one in which it occurs in the left hemisphere but is dependent on prior global processing in the right. The former interpretation is supported by Liégeois-Chauvel, Peretz, Babaï, Laguitton, & Chauvel (1998), who in a study of 65 patients who underwent unilateral temporal cortectomy found a functional asymmetry in contour and interval processing. Their data support a role for bilateral posterior temporal gyrus in interval processing and a role for the right posterior temporal gyrus in contour processing.

The temporal dimension of music has been less systematically investigated than has the pitch dimension. In addition to the hemispheric asymmetry in melodic perception, Peretz (1990) found that damage to either hemisphere resulted in an impairment in rhythm perception but not in meter perception (see also Shapiro, Grossman, & Gardener, 1981), which supports the distinctness of these musical constructs as well as a possible primacy for metrical over rhythmic perception, as Lerdahl and Jackendoff's (1983) *GTTM* would suggest. Liégeois-Chauvel et al. (1998) also found that the anterior portion of the temporal lobe, bilaterally, was essential for determining meter. The double dissociation between pitch and rhythmic ability in these two studies suggests that these two components of music are anatomically separable to some degree (see Figure 11.7).

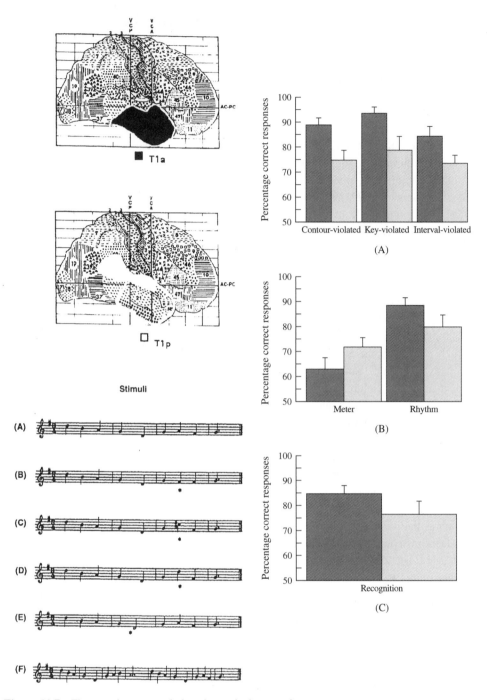

Figure 11.7 The superior temporal plane in musical processing.

NOTE: Discrimination and recognition of melodies and rhythmic patterns are impaired more following excision of the posterior part of the superior temporal plane (T1p, white bars) than more anterior regions of the temporal lobe (T1a, black bars). The pattern reverses for a metrical discrimination between duple meter (marches) and triple meter (waltzes). For the discrimination task, stimuli were presented in pairs (F) of the initial melody (A) and one of the following: (B) contour change, (C) key violation, (D) interval change with contour preserved, or (E) rhythmic change.

SOURCE: From Liégeois-Chauvel et al. (1998). Copyright © 1998 by Oxford University Press. Reprinted by permission.

Neuroimaging

To date, the neuroimaging studies in the field of music cognition have in many cases shared similar motivations with the neuropsychological studies, addressing the location and lateralization of pitch and melodic processing. An additional approach has been to identify the brain regions associated with high-level musical processing, including regions associated with musical short-term memory (Zatorre, Evans, & Meyer, 1994), musical imagery and music-related semantic retrieval (Halpern & Zatorre, 1999; Zatorre, Halpern, Perry, Meyer, & Evans, 1996), and absolute pitch processing (Zatorre, Perry, Beckett, Westbury, & Evans, 1998). We discuss the last area more fully as an example.

Imaging studies of absolute pitch implicate a stronger role for the left hemisphere than does much of the previously discussed neuropsychological work on pitch. An anatomical magnetic resonance imaging (MRI) study has demonstrated a leftward anatomical asymmetry in musicians with absolute pitch in the planum temporale, the surface of the superior temporal gyrus posterior to Heschl's gyrus (Schlaug, Jäncke, Huang, & Steinmetz, 1995; but see Westbury, Zatorre, & Evans, 1999). Left frontal regions may be involved as well. Using positron-emission tomography (PET), Zatorre et al. (1998) examined musicians with absolute pitch (AP) and relative pitch (RP) on a pitch-judgment task of relative pitch (major/minor third identification). In a passive listening condition both groups showed activation to bilateral superior temporal gyrus, right inferior frontal cortex, and right occipital cortex. The left posterior dorsolateral frontal (DLF) region was highly activated in the AP possessors but not at all in the musicians with only RP. In the active task, additional activation for the AP participants was observed in areas including the *right* DLF cortex, but the previous activity in right inferior frontal cortex disappeared, and for the RP participants

the previously inactive left posterior DLF region was recruited. The authors interpreted the automatic activation of left DLF cortex in the AP participants as the association between the pitches and their verbal labels. (The same area is activated in the active condition for both groups as the verbal label for the interval is being retrieved.) The authors also speculated that the lack of right inferior frontal activation during the active condition for AP listeners reflects the fact that they need not rely on auditory working memory to label the interval; they can use each note's verbal label to make that judgment.

Electroencephalography

Event-related potential (ERP) research has a strong advantage over brain imaging in temporal resolution, and the musical issues explored with this methodology—including pattern recognition, expectancy violation, and structural integration—reflect the exploitation of this advantage. Electrophysiological support for the harmonic hierarchy of stability was provided by Janata (1995), who showed that the P300 component was sensitive to the degree of harmonic expectancy. Comparing the processing of sentences and musical sequences that varied in syntactic congruity, Patel, Gibson, Ratner, Besson, and Holcomb (1998) found that the P600 components for language and music were indistinguishable and associated in both cases with increasing difficulty of syntactic integration. Patel (1998) suggested that although music and language have distinct syntax, the integrative mechanisms may overlap. This study found a music-specific component, the right antero-temporal negativity (RATN) in the range of 300 ms to 400 ms, which may be the right hemisphere analogue to another language ERP, the left anterior negativity (LAN). The ERP responses to *semantic* violations in language (e.g., the N400) seem to be distinct from those to pitch violations (Besson & Macar, 1987; Besson,

Faïta, Peretz, Bonnel, & Requin, 1998). The ERPs related to harmonic processing are also distinct from those related to the perception of sensory consonance (Regnault, Bigand, & Besson, 2001).

Several ERP studies have also investigated the differences in auditory and musical processing between musicians and nonmusicians. Tervaniemi, Ilvonen, Karma, Alho, and Näätänen (1997) found that the mismatch negativity (MMN), a measure of preattentive auditory cortex change detection, was greater in musical participants than in less musical participants when exposed to repetitive tone sequences containing infrequent order changes (but not pitch changes), even when the task was to ignore the sounds and read a self-selected book. Koelsch, Gunter, Friederici, and Schröger (2000) found that nonmusician participants displayed two characteristic ERPs when listening to chord sequences containing unexpected notes, furnished by Neapolitan chords in one experiment and tone clusters in another. The first was an early right-hemispheric anterior negativity (ERAN, also known as RATN), which the authors interpreted as the violation of culturally determined sound expectancy, and the second was a late bilateral-frontal negativity (P5) believed to reflect the integration of the unexpected chords into the previous context (see also Maess, Koelsch, Gunter, & Friederici, 2001). Although these kinds of effects are similar for musicians and nonmusicians, musical expertise and familiarity with a musical passage are associated with larger amplitudes and shorter latencies of the ERP response to pitch-based and rhythmic violations (Besson & Faïta, 1995).

The picture of how music is implemented in the brain has changed over the past 20 years. Rather than being viewed as a highly lateralized right-hemisphere counterpart of language, it is beginning to be regarded as a set of different cognitive abilities, many of which are located in both hemispheres but have subtle laterality differences depending on the particular computation at hand. The study of the biology of music has suggested both that the brain contains regions that may be developmentally specified for particular tasks (such as pitch computation within right posterior superior temporal cortex) and that the brain combines distinct mechanisms and domains (such as pitch and temporal organization) to create emergent forms of cognition. Additionally, music allows us to observe how enculturation can affect the development of the physical structure of the brain.

MUSICAL UNIVERSALS AND ORIGINS

In the final section we examine issues related to the origins of musical knowledge, both developmentally through the lifetime of the individual and historically through the existence of our species. A general reason why music is a good domain for the study of cognition is that it is mediated both by innate knowledge, which is universal across all humans and is part of our evolutionary history as a species, and by learned knowledge, which can vary across cultures and is a product of cultural evolution. Note that this is different from the issue of individual differences and talents (Sloboda et al., 1994; Howe et al., 1998). Rather than considering the genetic and environmental sources of variability between individuals, we address the evolutionary and cultural sources of the knowledge that is common to the members of a given community. We focus on knowledge of pitch relationships, reflecting the field's emphasis in this area.

Developmental Music Cognition

One important aspect of music cognition that seems to be universal and is present in infancy is the perceptual fusion of harmonic spectra into pitches. Infants as young as seven months can categorize harmonic complexes based on pitch, including those with a missing fundamental. Clarkson and Clifton (1985) first trained babies to respond with a head turn to a change in pitch, which could be accomplished by attending to the fundamental frequency or the spectral envelope of a harmonic complex. When the infants met a criterion on this task, they proceeded to a perceptual constancy trial in which they had to ignore changing frequency spectra that did not contain the implied fundamental frequency. The processing of pitch by 7-month-olds is very similar to that of adults in that pitch analysis is easier if the upper partials are greater in number (Clarkson, Martin, & Miciek, 1996), show a high degree of harmonicity (Clarkson & Clifton, 1995), and are not masked by noise (Montgomery & Clarkson, 1997). Infants do, however, require that harmonic spectra consist of low, more easily resolvable frequencies than adults do (Clarkson & Rogers, 1995). Studying even younger infants—4-month-olds—Bundy, Colombo, and Singer (1982) used a heart-rate habituation paradigm to demonstrate similar pitch processing earlier in development.

Further, infants as young as 3 months display octave equivalence (Demany & Armand, 1984), suggesting the universality of the two dimensions of pitch discussed in the first section: pitch height and pitch class. Startle responses are observed when melodies are presented a second time with some of the original tones shifted a seventh or ninth, but not an octave (as long as the melodic contour is not disrupted). Not only does the octave have preferred status in music, but so do the perfect fifth and other intervals with simple ratios (Schellenberg & Trehub, 1996a, 1996b; Trainor, 1997; Trainor & Heinmiller, 1998; Trainor & Trehub, 1993a, 1993b). Though universal, knowledge about pitch class and the

special nature of certain intervals may not require special innate representations but rather may be a result of the passive internalization of harmonic regularities in the auditory environment (Terhardt, 1974; Bharucha & Mencl, 1996). Still, such early effortless learning may reflect innate biases that favor the octave, perfect fifth, and other intervals with simple frequency ratios as natural prototypes (Rosch, 1975b) because they are relatively easy to learn and represent.

Melodic contour is also a salient musical property in infancy, and its importance in musical representation may also qualify as a universal. Using a head-turning paradigm, Trehub and colleagues have shown that while infants categorize transposed melodies (same intervals and contour) as the same melody and changed-interval melodies (with the same contour) as the same melody, they discriminate between changed-contour melodies (Trehub, Bull, & Thorpe, 1984; Trehub, Thorpe, & Morrongiello, 1985; Trehub, Thorpe, & Morrongiello, 1987; see also Ferland & Mendelson, 1989). This use of contour as a way to represent melodies remains in late childhood even though children improve in their ability to detect interval changes (Morrongiello, Trehub, Thorpe, & Capodilupo, 1985). Such studies have also demonstrated an asymmetry in discrimination not unlike that found by Bharucha and Pryor (1986) for rhythm; interval changes are easier for children to discriminate when the more consonant variant is presented first (Schellenberg & Trehub, 1996a).

Not all elements of music appear with such precocity, however. The importance of the seven diatonic tones within a tonal context is something that Western listeners apparently have to learn. Infants at 8 months of age discriminate when a melody is changed within the same key (diatonic change) as well as they do when it is changed outside of the key (nondiatonic change), whereas adults do much better at the latter and actually worse than infants on the former (Trainor & Trehub, 1992). This contrasts with the fact that infants of the same age can discriminate between melodies based on Western scales but not melodies based on nondiatonic scales or scales with intervals smaller than semitones (Trehub, Thorpe, & Trainor, 1990), as well as between melodies based on major triads and augmented triads (Cohen, Thorpe, & Trehub, 1987). The ability to represent melodies within Western diatonic contexts does appear by school age; 4- to 6-year-old children are better at detecting a change of tone within a diatonic context than within a nondiatonic context, but infants are not affected by this manipulation (Trehub, Cohen, Thorpe, & Morrongiello, 1986).

The importance of particular tones within the diatonic scale as cognitive reference points

may emerge even later during the school-age period. Krumhansl and Keil (1982) reported that although children at age 6 and 7 give preferential ratings to diatonic tones at the end of melodies, it is not until 8 or 9 that the notes of the tonic triad are given preferential ratings to the other diatonic tones (but see Cuddy & Badertscher, 1987; Speer & Meeks, 1985). Trainor and Trehub (1994) strengthened this result by showing that 5-year-olds can detect out-of-key melodic changes better than they can within-key melodic changes, and that 7-year-olds have the additional ability to detect out-of-harmony within-key melodic changes (Figure 11.8).

The developmental picture of music perception thus suggests that there may be universal, core musical principles such as pitch perception and a preference for the octave and perfect fifth, and other culture-specific

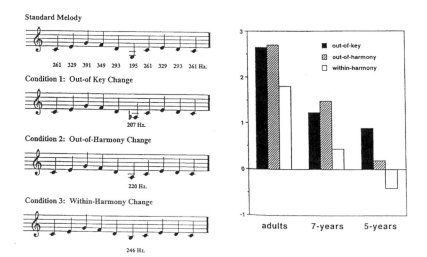

Figure 11.8   The development of tonal-harmonic knowledge in Western children.
NOTE: The ability to detect a changed note between a standard melody and three kinds of comparison melodies (left), as measured by d-prime scores (right), suggests that 5-year-olds can represent notes in a melody in terms of key-membership (diatonic or nondiatonic) but that the ability to represent them in terms of the implied harmony within the key does not emerge until age 7. In addition to these changes, adults can detect changes that do not alter the harmony. They remain better at detecting out-of-harmony than within-harmony changes, however, suggesting that the representation of a melody is based on the implied harmonic structure.
SOURCE: From Trainor and Trehub (1994). Copyright © 1994 by the Psychonomic Society. Reprinted by permission.

musical concepts that emerge only later in childhood such as specific scales and tonal hierarchies.

Cross-Cultural Music Cognition

Many of the features of music perception that appear early in development are found also in the universal features of music across cultures. Dowling and Harwood (1986) suggested that several features are common to virtually all of the world's musical systems. These include (a) the octave as a basic principle in pitch organization, (b) a logarithmic pitch scale, (c) discrete pitch levels, (d) five to seven unequally spaced pitches in a scale, (e) hierarchies of stability for pitch, and (f) melodic contour as an important organizational device.

These universals may stem from basic features of auditory cognition, and basic features of human cognition more generally. We have discussed how octave equivalence may be innate or learned very early as a consequence of universal environmental features. A logarithmic pitch scale follows easily from the constraint of octave equivalence; if each successive frequency doubling results in a pitch of the same category, then changes in pitch within each octave must be logarithmic as well. Discrete pitch levels with five to seven pitches in each octave may be an example of the short-term memory limitation for categories on a continuous dimension proposed by G. A. Miller (1956). The unequal levels of stability assigned to each of the notes of the scale have been suggested to be an example of Rosch's (1975a) cognitive reference points (Krumhansl, 1979), and the importance of melodic contour may stem from its similarity to prosodic patterns in speech (see Fernald, 1992).

The specifics of musical systems vary across cultures, and this kind of knowledge is often the kind that does not emerge until later childhood. One example concerns the specific sets of pitches chosen for the scales of a given culture. Western infants are equally good at detecting mistunings in their native major and minor scales and in Indonesian scales (e.g., the pélog scale of Java), whereas Western adults show a strong advantage for the scales of their own culture (Lynch, Eilers, Oller, & Urbano, 1990). Furthermore, estimations of interval sizes given by adults show an effect of the musical scale systems of the culture (Perlman & Krumhansl, 1996). The differences in perception of the native and nonnative scales are apparent by late childhood even in nonmusicians, although these differences are accelerated in children with formal musical training (Lynch & Eilers, 1991). Adult musicians and nonmusicians may show the opposite trend, suggesting that skills learned in musical training eventually can be applied to music of other cultures (Lynch, Eilers, Oller, Urbano, & Wilson, 1991).

The specific tonal hierarchies of stability also vary across cultures. Using the probe-tone technique with Western and Indian participants listening to North Indian *ragas,* Castellano et al. (1984) found that although the structure in the melodies themselves influenced the responses of both Western and Indian listeners, tacit knowledge of the underlying scales significantly influenced the responses of only the Indian listeners. This tacit knowledge was presumably from prior exposure to pieces of music based on the same scales. Similar effects of enculturation on music cognition were found in a comparison between Western and Balinese listeners for their respective musical systems (Kessler et al., 1984). Recently, studies using two distinct musical styles of Scandinavia have combined cross-cultural approaches with statistical and computational modeling (Krumhansl, 2000b; Krumhansl, Louhivuori, Toiviainen, Järvinen, & Eerola, 1999; Krumhansl, Toivanen, Eerola, Toiviainen, Järvinen, & Louhivuori, 2000).

Evolutionary Psychology of Music

A final topic in music cognition is how the relevant neural structure was shaped by natural selection throughout the evolution of our species (e.g., Wallin, Merker, & Brown, 2000). Many authors have examined the possible selection pressures for musical behaviors themselves as an explanation for how music evolved in our species (e.g., Brown, 2000; Dowling & Harwood, 1986; Huron, 1999; G. Miller, 2000). Generally, these arguments center on the premise that music provided a reproductive advantage for the individual in the context of the social group or via mechanisms of sexual selection, as originally suggested by Darwin (1871). These approaches reflect a more general trend in psychology to regard cognitive abilities as specific adaptive solutions to evolutionary problems (see Tooby & Cosmides, 1992).

This kind of approach to the evolutionary psychology of music has been criticized by Justus and Hutsler (2000, 2001), who have pointed out two critical issues that have been ignored in recent treatments of music evolution. The first is that much of what we regard as music is a product of cultural or memetic transmission (Blackmore, 2000; Dawkins, 1976; Mead, 1964), as cross-cultural differences suggest. It is not necessary to explain the adaptive utility of the culturally-transmitted features of music from an evolutionary perspective; the evolutionary selection pressure in this case was for more general learning, linguistic, and mimetic abilities, whereas the musical knowledge was culturally selected. Second, many of the innate capacities that humans apply to music perception and music making may not have evolved as musical processes per se, but rather are processing mechanisms and knowledge selected for their utility within other domains such as auditory perception, conceptual representation, language, timing, and emotion. The lat-

ter idea is similar to the concept of exaptation, which Gould and colleagues have used to describe morphological forms that arise not because of direct selection pressures, but rather are the inevitable result of selection pressures for other attributes (Gould & Lewontin, 1979; Gould & Vrba, 1982; for a general application to cognition, see Lewontin, 1990; for counterarguments in the domain of language, see Pinker & Bloom, 1990).

An examination of the developmental psychology of music, along with cross-cultural and evolutionary approaches, suggests that music is a reflection of both innate, universal cognitive mechanisms as well as cultural processes. Future integration of these three approaches may lead to answers to the most important questions of how and why our species came to be musical.

REFERENCES

Attneave, F., & Olson, R. K. (1971). Pitch as a medium: A new approach to psychophysical scaling. *American Journal of Psychology, 84,* 147–166.

Bachem, A. (1937). Various types of absolute pitch. *Journal of the Acoustical Society of America, 9,* 146–151.

Bernstein, L. (1976). *The unanswered question.* Cambridge: Harvard University Press.

Besson, M. (1997). Electrophysiological studies of music processing. In I. Deliège & J. Sloboda (Eds.), *Perception and cognition of music* (pp. 217–250). Hove, England: Psychology Press.

Besson, M., & Faïta, F. (1995). An event-related potential (ERP) study of musical expectancy: Comparison of musicians and non-musicians. *Journal of Experimental Psychology: Human Perception and Performance, 21,* 1278–1296.

Besson, M., Faïta, F., Peretz, I., Bonnel, A.-M., & Requin, J. (1998). Singing in the brain:

Independence of lyrics and tunes. *Psychological Science, 9,* 494–498.

Besson, M., & Macar, F. (1987). An event-related potential analysis of incongruity in music and other non-linguistic contexts. *Psychophysiology, 24,* 14–25.

Bever, T., & Chiarello, R. (1974). Cerebral dominance in musicians and nonmusicians. *Science, 185,* 537–539.

Bharucha, J. J. (1984a). Anchoring effects in music: The resolution of dissonance. *Cognitive Psychology, 16,* 485–518.

Bharucha, J. J. (1984b). Event hierarchies, tonal hierarchies, and assimilation: A reply to Deutsch and Dowling. *Journal of Experimental Psychology: General, 113,* 421–425.

Bharucha, J. J. (1987). Music cognition and perceptual facilitation: A connectionist framework. *Music Perception, 5,* 1–30.

Bharucha, J. J. (1996). Melodic anchoring. *Music Perception, 13,* 383–400.

Bharucha, J. J., & Krumhansl, C. L. (1983). The representation of harmonic structure in music: Hierarchies of stability as a function of context. *Cognition, 13,* 63–102.

Bharucha, J. J., & Mencl, W. E. (1996). Two issues in auditory cognition: Self-organization of octave categories and pitch-invariant pattern recognition. *Psychological Science, 7,* 142–149.

Bharucha, J. J., & Pryor, J. H. (1986). Disrupting the isochrony underlying rhythm: An asymmetry in discrimination. *Perception & Psychophysics, 40,* 137–141.

Bharucha, J. J., & Stoeckig, K. (1986). Response time and musical expectancy: Priming of chords. *Journal of Experimental Psychology: Human Perception and Performance, 12,* 403–410.

Bharucha, J. J., & Stoeckig, K. (1987). Priming of chords: Spreading activation or overlapping frequency spectra? *Perception & Psychophysics, 41,* 519–524.

Bigand, E. (1997). Perceiving musical stability: The effect of tonal structure, rhythm, and musical expertise. *Journal of Experimental Psychol-ogy: Human Perception and Performance, 23,* 808–822.

Bigand, E., Madurell, F., Tillmann, B., & Pineau, M. (1999). Effect of global structure and temporal organization on chord processing. *Journal of Experimental Psychology: Human Perception and Performance, 25,* 184–197.

Bigand, E., & Pineau, M. (1996). Context effects on melody recognition: A dynamic interpretation. *Current Psychology of Cognition, 15,* 121–134.

Bigand, E., & Pineau, M. (1997). Global context effects on musical expectancy. *Perception & Psychophysics, 59,* 1098–1107.

Bigand, E., Tillmann, B., Poulin, B., D'Adamo, D. A., & Madurell, F. (2001). The effect of harmonic context on phoneme monitoring in vocal music. *Cognition, 81,* B11–B20.

Blackmore, S. (2000). *The meme machine.* Oxford: Oxford University Press.

Bolton, T. L. (1894). Rhythm. *American Journal of Psychology, 6,* 145–238.

Boltz, M. G. (1989a). Perceiving the end: Effects of tonal relationships on melodic completion. *Journal of Experimental Psychology: Human Perception and Performance, 15,* 749–761.

Boltz, M. G. (1989b). Rhythm and "good endings": Effects of temporal structure on tonality judgments. *Perception & Psychophysics, 46,* 9–17.

Boltz, M. G. (1989c). Time judgments of musical endings: Effects of expectancies on the "filled interval effect." *Perception & Psychophysics, 46,* 409–418.

Boltz, M. G. (1991a). Some structural determinants of melody recall. *Memory & Cognition, 19,* 239–251.

Boltz, M. G. (1991b). Time estimation and attentional perspective. *Perception & Psychophysics, 49,* 422–433.

Boltz, M. G. (1992). The remembering of auditory event durations. *Journal of Experimental Psychology: Learning, Memory, and Cognition, 18,* 938–956.

Boltz, M. G. (1993a). The generation of temporal and melodic expectancies during musical listening. *Perception & Psychophysics, 53,* 585–600.

Boltz, M. G. (1993b). Time estimation and expectancies. *Memory & Cognition, 21,* 853–863.

Boltz, M. G. (1998). The processing of temporal and nontemporal information in the remembering of event durations and musical structure. *Journal of Experimental Psychology: Human Perception and Performance, 24,* 1087–1104.

Boltz, M. G., & Jones, M. R. (1986). Does rule recursion make melodies easier to reproduce? If not, what does? *Cognitive Psychology, 18,* 389–431.

Bregman, A. S. (1990). *Auditory scene analysis: The perceptual organization of sound.* Cambridge: MIT Press.

Brown, S. (2000). The "musilanguage" model of music evolution. In N. L. Wallin, B. Merker, & S. Brown (Eds.), *The origins of music* (pp. 271–300). Cambridge: MIT Press.

Bundy, R. S., Colombo, J., & Singer, J. (1982). Pitch perception in young infants. *Developmental Psychology, 18,* 10–14.

Burns, E. M. (1999). Intervals, scales, and tuning. In D. Deutsch (Ed.), *The psychology of music* (2nd ed., pp. 215–264). San Diego: Academic Press.

Burns, E. M., & Ward, W. D. (1978). Categorical perception—phenomenon or epiphenomenon: Evidence form experiments in the perception of melodic musical intervals. *Journal of the Acoustical Society of America, 63,* 456–468.

Castellano, M. A., Bharucha, J. J., & Krumhansl, C. L. (1984). Tonal hierarchies in the music of North India. *Journal of Experimental Psychology: General, 113,* 394–412.

Clarke, E. F. (1993). Imitating and evaluating real and transformed musical performances. *Music Perception, 10,* 317–343.

Clarke, E. F. (1999). Rhythm and timing in music. In D. Deutsch (Ed.), *The psychology of music* (2nd ed., pp. 473–500). San Diego: Academic Press.

Clarke, E. F., & Baker-Short, C. (1987). The imitation of perceived rubato: A preliminary study. *Psychology of Music, 15,* 58–75.

Clarkson, M. G., & Clifton, R. K. (1985). Infant pitch perception: Evidence for responding to pitch categories and the missing fundamental. *Journal of the Acoustical Society of America, 77,* 1521–1528.

Clarkson, M. G., & Clifton, R. K. (1995). Infants' pitch perception: Inharmonic tonal complexes. *Journal of the Acoustical Society of America, 98,* 1372–1379.

Clarkson, M. G., Martin, R. L., & Miciek, S. G. (1996). Infants' perception of pitch: Number of harmonics. *Infant Behavior and Development, 19,* 191–197.

Clarkson, M. G., & Rogers, E. C. (1995). Infants require low-frequency energy to hear the pitch of the missing fundamental. *Journal of the Acoustical Society of America, 98,* 148–154.

Cohen, M. A., Grossberg, S., & Wyse, L. L. (1995). A spectral network model of pitch perception. *Journal of the Acoustical Society of America, 98,* 862–879.

Cohen, A. J., Thorpe, L. A., & Trehub, S. E. (1987). Infants' perception of musical relations in short transposed tone sequences. *Canadian Journal of Psychology, 41,* 33–47.

Collier, G. L., & Wright, C. E. (1995). Temporal rescaling of simple and complex ratios in rhythmic tapping. *Journal of Experimental Psychology: Human Perception and Performance, 21,* 602–627.

Cuddy, L. L. (1991). Melodic patterns and tonal structure: Converging evidence. *Psychomusicology, 10,* 107–126.

Cuddy, L. L., & Badertscher, B. (1987). Recovery of the tonal hierarchy: Some comparisons across age and levels of musical experience. *Perception & Psychophysics, 41,* 609–620.

Cuddy, L. L., & Cohen, A. J. (1976). Recognition of transposed melodic sequences. *Quarterly Journal of Experimental Psychology, 28,* 255–270.

Cuddy, L. L., Cohen, A. J., & Mewhort, D. J. (1981). Perception of structures in short melodic sequences. *Journal of Experimental Psychology: Human Perception & Performance, 7,* 869–883.

Cuddy, L. L., Cohen, A. J., & Miller, J. (1979). Melody recognition: The experimental application of musical rules. *Canadian Journal of Psychology, 33,* 148–157.

Cuddy, L. L., & Lyons, H. I. (1981). Music pattern recognition: A comparison of listening to and studying tonal structure and tonal ambiguities. *Psychomusicology, 1,* 15–33.

Cuddy, L. L., & Lunney, C. A. (1995). Expectancies generated by melodic intervals: Perceptual judgments of melodic continuity. *Perception & Psychophysics, 57,* 451–462.

Darwin, C. (1871). *The descent of man.* London: Murray.

Davidson, J. W., Howe, M. J. A., Moore, D. G., & Sloboda, J. A. (1996). The role of parental influences in the development of musical ability. *British Journal of Developmental Psychology, 14,* 399–412.

Davidson, J. W., Howe, M. J. A., & Sloboda, J. A. (1997). Environmental factors in the development of musical performance skill. In D. J. Hargreaves & A. C. North (Eds.), *The social psychology of music* (pp. 188–206). Oxford: Oxford University Press.

Davidson, J. W., Moore, D. G., Sloboda, J. A., & Howe, M. J. A. (1998). Characteristics of music teachers and the process of young instrumentalists. *Journal of Research in Music Education, 46,* 141–161.

Dawkins, R. (1976). *The selfish gene.* Oxford: Oxford University Press.

de Boer, E. (1956). *On the residue in hearing.* Unpublished doctoral dissertation, University of Amsterdam.

Deliège, I. (1987). Grouping conditions in listening to music: An approach to Lerdahl & Jackendoff's grouping preference rules. *Music Perception, 4,* 325–360.

Deliège, I., & Sloboda, J. (Eds.). (1997). *Perception and cognition of music.* Hove, England: Psychology Press.

Demany, L., & Armand, F. (1984). The perceptual reality of tone chroma in early infancy. *Journal of the Acoustical Society of America, 76,* 57–66.

Deutsch, D. (Ed.). (1982). *The psychology of music.* New York: Academic Press.

Deutsch, D. (1984). Two issues concerning tonal hierarchies: Comment on Castellano, Bharucha, and Krumhansl. *Journal of Experimental Psychology: General, 113,* 413–416.

Deutsch, D. (1986). A musical paradox. *Music Perception, 3,* 275–280.

Deutsch, D. (1987). The tritone paradox: Effects of spectral variables. *Perception & Psychophysics, 41,* 563–575.

Deutsch, D. (1991). The tritone paradox: An influence of language on music perception. *Music Perception, 8,* 335–347.

Deutsch, D. (1999a). Grouping mechanisms in music. In D. Deutsch (Ed.), *The psychology of music* (2nd ed., pp. 299–348). San Diego: Academic Press.

Deutsch, D. (Ed.). (1999b). *The psychology of music* (2nd ed.). San Diego: Academic Press.

Dewar, K. M., Cuddy, L. L., & Mewhort, D. J. (1977). Recognition memory for single tones with and without context. *Journal of Experimental Psychology: Human Learning and Memory, 3,* 60–67.

DeWitt, L. A., & Crowder, R. G. (1987). Tonal fusion of consonant musical intervals. *Perception & Psychophysics, 41,* 73–84.

Dowling, W. J. (1978). Scale and contour: Two components of a theory of memory for melodies. *Psychological Review, 85,* 341–354.

Dowling, W. J. (1984). Assimilation and tonal structure: Comment on Castellano, Bharucha, and Krumhansl. *Journal of Experimental Psychology: General, 13,* 417–420.

Dowling, W. J., & Fujitani, D. S. (1971). Contour, interval, and pitch recognition in memory for melodies. *Journal of the Acoustical Society of America, 49,* 524–531.

Dowling, W. J., & Harwood, D. L. (1986). *Music cognition.* San Diego: Academic Press.

Drake, C., Dowling, W. J., & Palmer, C. (1991). Accent structures in the reproduction of simple tunes by children and adult pianists. *Music Perception, 8,* 315–334.

Drake, C., & Palmer, C. (1993). Accent structures in music performance. *Music Perception, 10,* 343–378.

Drake, C., & Palmer, C. (2000). Skill acquisition in music performance: Relations between planning and temporal control. *Cognition, 74,* 1–32.

Essens, P. J., & Povel, D.-J. (1985). Metrical and nonmetrical representations of temporal patterns. *Perception & Psychophysics, 37,* 1–7.

Ericsson, K. A., Krampe, R. T., & Tesch-Romer, C. (1993). The role of deliberate practice in the acquisition of expert performance. *Psychological Review, 100,* 363–406.

Ferland, M. B., & Mendelson, M. J. (1989). Infants' categorization of melodic contour. *Infant Behavior and Development, 12,* 341–355.

Fernald, A. (1992). Human maternal vocalizations to infants as biologically relevant signals: An evolutionary perspective. In J. H. Barkow, L. Cosmides, & J. Tooby (Eds.), *The adapted mind: Evolutionary psychology and the generation of culture* (pp. 391–428). Oxford: Oxford University Press.

Fodor, J. A. (1983). *The modularity of mind: An essay on faculty psychology.* Cambridge: MIT Press.

Fodor, J. A. (2000). *The mind doesn't work that way: The scope and limits of computational psychology.* Cambridge: MIT Press.

Fraisse, P. (1956). *Les structures rythmiques.* Lovain, Belgium: Editions Universitaires.

Fraisse, P. (1966). L'anticipation de stimulus rythmiques: Vitesse d'établissement et précision de la synchronisation. *L'Année Psychologique, 66,* 15–36.

Fraisse, P. (1982). Rhythm and tempo. In D. Deutsch (Ed.), *The psychology of music* (pp. 149–180). New York: Academic Press.

Fraisse, P., Pichot, P., & Chairouin, G. (1949). Les aptitudes rythmiques: Etude comparée des oligophrènes et des enfants normaux. *Journal de Psychologie Normale et Pathologique, 42,* 309–330.

Friberg, A., & Sundberg, J. (1999). Does music performance allude to locomotion? A model of final ritardandi derived from measurements of stopping runners. *Journal of the Acoustical Society of America, 105,* 1469–1484.

Gabrielsson, A. (1999). The performance of music. In D. Deutsch (Ed.), *The psychology of music* (2nd ed., pp. 501–602). San Diego: Academic Press.

Gardner, H., Silverman, J., Denes, G., Semenza, C., & Rosenstiel, A. K. (1977). Sensitivity to musical denotation and connotation in organic patients. *Cortex, 13,* 242–256.

Garrett, M., Bever, T., & Fodor, J. (1966). The active use of grammar in speech perception. *Perception & Psychophysics, 1,* 30–32.

Goebl, W. (2001). Melody lead in piano performance: Expressive device or artifact? *Journal of the Acoustical Society of America, 110,* 563–572.

Goldstein, J. L. (1973). An optimum processor theory for the central formation of the pitch of complex tones. *Journal of the Acoustical Society of America, 54,* 1496–1516.

Gould, S. J., & Lewontin, R. C. (1979). The spandrels of San Marco and the Panglossian paradigm: A critique of the adaptationist programme. *Proceedings of the Royal Society of London B, 205,* 581–598.

Gould, S. J., & Vrba, E. S. (1982). Exaptation: A missing term in the science of form. *Paleobiology, 8,* 4–15.

Green, D. M. (1976). *An introduction to hearing.* Hillsdale, NJ: Erlbaum.

Halpern, A. R., & Zatorre, R. J. (1999). When that tune runs through your head: A PET investigation of auditory imagery for familiar melodies. *Cerebral Cortex, 9,* 697–704.

Handel, S. (1998). The interplay between metric and figural rhythmic organization. *Journal of Experimental Psychology: Human Perception and Performance, 24,* 1546–1561.

Hébert, S., Peretz, I., & Gagnon, L. (1995). Perceiving the tonal ending of tune excerpts: The roles of pre-existing representation and musical expertise. *Canadian Journal of Experimental Psychology, 49,* 193–209.

Heffner, H., & Whitfield, I. C. (1976). Perception of the missing fundamental by cats. *Journal of the Acoustical Society of America, 59,* 915–919.

Helmholtz, H. von. (1954). *On the sensation of tone as a physiological basis for the theory of music.* New York: Dover. (Original work published 1863)

Hermann, L. (1912). Neue Versuche zur Frage der Unterbrechungstöne. *Pflüger's Archiv für die gesamte Physiologie des Menschen und der Tiere, 146,* 249–294.

Hibi, S. (1983). Rhythm perception in repetitive sound sequence. *Journal of the Acoustical Society of Japan, 4,* 83–95.

Houtsma, A. J. M., & Goldstein, J. L. (1972). The central origin of the pitch of complex tones: Evidence from musical interval recognition. *Journal of the Acoustical Society of America, 54,* 520–529.

Howe, M. J. A., Davidson, J. W., & Sloboda, J. A. (1998). Innate talents: Reality or myth? *Behavioral and Brain Sciences, 21,* 399–442.

Huron, D. (1991). The avoidance of part-crossing in polyphonic music: Perceptual evidence and musical practice. *Music Perception, 9,* 93–104.

Huron, D. (1999). An instinct for music: Is music an evolutionary adaptation? The 1999 Ernest Bloch Lectures, *Music and mind: Foundations of cognitive musicology.* Department of Music, University of California, Berkeley.

Janata, P. (1995). ERP measures assay the degree of expectancy violation of harmonic contexts in music. *Journal of Cognitive Neuroscience, 7,* 153–164.

Janata, P., & Reisberg, D. (1988). Response-time measures as a means of exploring tonal hierarchies. *Music Perception, 6,* 161–172.

Johnsrude, I. S., Penhune, V. B., & Zatorre, R. J. (2000). Functional specificity in the right human auditory cortex for perceiving pitch direction. *Brain, 23,* 155–163.

Jones, M. R. (1987). Dynamic pattern structure in music: Recent theory and research. *Perception & Psychophysics, 41,* 621–634.

Jones, M. R., & Boltz, M. G. (1989). Dynamic attending and responses to time. *Psychological Review, 96,* 459–491.

Jones, M. R., Boltz, M. G., & Kidd, G. (1982). Controlled attending as a function of melodic and temporal context. *Perception & Psychophysics, 32,* 211–218.

Jones, M. R., Boltz, M. G., & Klein, J. M. (1993). Expected endings and judged duration. *Memory & Cognition, 21,* 646–665.

Jones, M. R., Kidd, G., & Wetzel, R. (1981). Evidence for rhythmic attention. *Journal of Experimental Psychology: Human Perception and Performance, 7,* 1059–1072.

Jones, M. R., & Ralston, J. T. (1991). Some influence of accent structure on melody recognition. *Memory & Cognition, 19,* 8–20.

Jones, M. R., Summerell, L., & Marshburn, E. (1987). Recognizing melodies: A dynamic interpretation. *Quarterly Journal of Experimental Psychology, 39A,* 89–121.

Jusczyk, P. W., & Krumhansl, C. L. (1993). Pitch and rhythmic patterns affecting infants' sensitivity to musical phrase structure. *Journal of Experimental Psychology: Human Perception and Performance, 19,* 627–640.

Justus, T. C., & Bharucha, J. J. (2001). Modularity in musical processing: The automaticity of harmonic priming. *Journal of Experimental Psychology: Human Perception and Performance, 27,* 1000–1011.

Justus, T. C., & Hutsler, J. J. (2000). Origins of human musicality: Evolution, mind, and culture. In C. Woods, G. Luck, R. Brochard, F. Seddon, & J. A. Sloboda (Eds.), *Proceedings of the Sixth International Conference on Music Perception and Cognition* (pp. 1151–1160). Keele, England: European Society for the Cognitive Sciences of Music.

Justus, T. C., & Hutsler, J. J. (2001). *Fundamental issues in the evolutionary psychology of music: The contributions of culture and recruited cognitive domains.* Manuscript submitted for publication.

Kemp, A. E. (1997). Individual differences in musical behaviour. In D. J. Hargreaves & A. C. North (Eds.), *The social psychology of music* (pp. 25–45). Oxford: Oxford University Press.

Kessler, E. J., Hansen, C., & Shepard, R. N. (1984). Tonal schemata in the perception of music in Bali and the West. *Music Perception, 2,* 131–165.

Koelsch, S., Gunter, T., Friederici, A., & Schröger, E. (2000). Brain indices of music processing: "Nonmusicians" are musical. *Journal of Cognitive Neuroscience, 12,* 520–541.

Krumhansl, C. L. (1978). Concerning the applicability of geometric models to similarity data: The interrelationship between similarity and spatial density. *Psychological Review, 85,* 445–463.

Krumhansl, C. L. (1979). The psychological representation of musical pitch in a tonal context. *Cognitive Psychology, 11,* 346–374.

Krumhansl, C. L. (1990). *Cognitive foundations of musical pitch.* Oxford: Oxford University Press.

Krumhansl, C. L. (1991). Music psychology: Tonal structures in perception and memory. *Annual Review of Psychology, 42,* 277–303.

Krumhansl, C. L. (1995). Music psychology and music theory: Problems and prospects. *Music Theory Spectrum, 17,* 53–80.

Krumhansl, C. L. (1996). A perceptual analysis of Mozart's piano sonata K. 282: Segmentation, tension, and musical ideas. *Music Perception, 13,* 401–432.

Krumhansl, C. L. (2000a). Rhythm and pitch in music cognition. *Psychological Bulletin, 126,* 159–179.

Krumhansl, C. L. (2000b). Tonality induction: A statistical approach applied cross-culturally. *Music Perception, 17,* 461–479.

Krumhansl, C. L., Bharucha, J. J., & Castellano, M. A. (1982). Key distance effects on perceived harmonic structure in music. *Perception & Psychophysics, 32,* 96–108.

Krumhansl, C. L., Bharucha, J. J., & Kessler, E. J. (1982). Perceived harmonic structure of chords in three related musical keys. *Journal of Experimental Psychology: Human Perception and Performance, 8,* 24–36.

Krumhansl, C. L., & Castellano, M. A. (1983). Dynamic processes in music perception. *Memory & Cognition, 11,* 325–334.

Krumhansl, C. L., & Jusczyk, P. W. (1990). Infants perception of phrase structure in music. *Psychological Science, 1,* 1–4.

Krumhansl, C. L., & Keil, F. C. (1982). Acquisition of the hierarchy of tonal functions in music. *Memory & Cognition, 10,* 243–251.

Krumhansl, C. L., & Kessler, E. J. (1982). Tracing the dynamic changes in perceived tonal organization in a spatial representation of musical keys. *Psychological Review, 89,* 334–368.

Krumhansl, C. L., Louhivuori, J., Toiviainen, P., Järvinen, T., & Eerola, T. (1999). Melodic expectation in Finnish spiritual folk hymns: Convergence of statistical, behavioral, and computational approaches. *Music Perception, 17,* 151–195.

Krumhansl, C. L., & Shepard, R. N. (1979). Quantification of the hierarchy of tonal functions within a diatonic context. *Journal of Experimental Psychology: Human Perception and Performance, 5,* 579–594.

Krumhansl, C. L., Toivanen, P., Eerola, T., Toiviainen, P., Järvinen, T., & Louhivuori, J. (2000). Cross-cultural music cognition: Cognitive methodology applied to North Sami yoiks. *Cognition, 76,* 13–58.

Lehmann, A. C., & Ericsson, K. A. (1993). Sight-reading ability of expert pianists in the context of piano accompanying. *Psychomusicology, 12,* 182–195.

Lerdahl, F., & Jackendoff, R. (1983). *A generative theory of tonal music.* Cambridge: MIT Press.

Levitin, D. J. (1994). Absolute memory for musical pitch: Evidence from the production of learned melodies. *Perception & Psychophysics, 56,* 414–423.

Levitin, D. J. (1996). Do absolute pitch possessors have categorical perception? *International Journal of Psychology, 31,* 10.

Levitin, D. J. (1999). Absolute pitch: Self-reference and human memory. *International Journal of Computing Anticipatory Systems, 4,* 255–266.

Lewontin, R. C. (1990). The evolution of cognition. In D. N. Osherson & E. E. Smith (Eds.), *An invitation to cognitive science: Vol. 3: Thinking* (pp. 229–246). Cambridge: MIT Press.

Liberman, M., & Prince, A. (1977). On stress and linguistic rhythm. *Linguistic Inquiry, 8,* 249–336.

Licklider, J. C. R. (1954). Periodicity and place pitch. *Journal of the Acoustical Society of America, 26,* 945.

Liégeois-Chauvel, C., Peretz, I., Babaï, M., Laguitton, V., & Chauvel, P. (1998). Contribution of different cortical areas in the temporal lobes to music processing. *Brain, 121,* 1853–1867.

Lynch, M. P., & Eilers, R. E. (1991). Children's perception of native and nonnative musical scales. *Music Perception, 9,* 121–132.

Lynch, M. P., Eilers, R. E., Oller, K. D., & Urbano, R. C. (1990). Innateness, experience, and music perception. *Psychological Science, 1,* 272–276.

Lynch, M. P., Eilers, R. E., Oller, K. D., Urbano, R. C., & Wilson, R. (1991). Influences of acculturation and musical sophistication on perception of musical interval patterns. *Journal of Experimental Psychology: Human Perception and Performance, 17,* 967–975.

Maess, B., Koelsch, S., Gunter, T. C., & Friederici, A. D. (2001). Musical syntax is processed in Broca's area: An MEG study. *Nature Neuroscience, 4,* 540–545.

MacDougall, R. (1903). The structure of simple rhythmic forms. *Psychological Review, Monograph Supplements, 4,* 309–416.

McAdams, S., & Bigand, E. (Eds.). (1993). *Thinking in sound: The cognitive psychology of human audition.* Oxford: Oxford University Press.

Mead, M. (1964). *Continuities in cultural evolution.* New Haven, CT: Yale University Press.

Meyer, L. B. (1956). *Emotion and meaning in music.* Chicago: University of Chicago Press.

Meyer, L. B. (1967). *Music, the arts, and ideas: Patterns and predictions in twentieth-century culture.* Chicago: University of Chicago Press.

Meyer, L. B. (1973). *Explaining music: Essays and explorations.* Berkeley: University of California Press.

Meyer, L. B. (2000). *The spheres of music: A gathering of essays.* Chicago: University of Chicago Press.

Miller, G. (2000). Evolution of human music through sexual selection. In N. L. Wallin, B. Merker, & S. Brown (Eds.), *The origins of music* (pp. 329–360). Cambridge: MIT Press.

Miller, G. A. (1956). The magical number seven, plus or minus two: Some limits on our capacity for processing information. *Psychological Review, 63,* 81–97.

Miyazaki, K. (1988). Musical pitch identification by absolute pitch possessors. *Perception & Psychophysics, 44,* 501–512.

Miyazaki, K. (1989). Absolute pitch identification: Effects of timbre and pitch region. *Music Perception, 7,* 1–14.

Monahan, C. B., & Carterette, E. C. (1985). Pitch and duration as determinants of musical space. *Music Perception, 3,* 1–32.

Monahan, C. B., Kendall, R. A., & Carterette, E. C. (1987). The effect of melodic and temporal contour on recognition memory for pitch change. *Perception & Psychophysics, 41,* 576–600.

Montgomery, C. R., & Clarkson, M. G. (1997). Infants' pitch perception: Masking by low- and high-frequency noises. *Journal of the Acoustical Society of America, 102,* 3665–3672.

Morrongiello, B. A., Trehub, S. E., Thorpe, L. A., & Capodilupo, S. (1995). Children's perception of melodies: The role of contour, frequency, and rate of presentation. *Journal of Experimental Child Psychology, 40,* 279–292.

Murphy, L. E. (1966). Absolute judgments of duration. *Journal of Experimental Psychology, 71,* 260–263.

Nagasaki, H. (1987a). Correlations of stress and timing in periodic tapping. *Human Movement Science, 6,* 161–180.

Nagasaki, H. (1987b). Frequency dependence of rhythm in periodic tapping. *Human Movement Science, 6,* 247–256.

Narmour, E. (1990). *The analysis and cognition of basic melodic structures: The implication-realization model.* Chicago: University of Chicago Press.

O'Neill, S. A. (1997). Gender and music. In D. J. Hargreaves & A. C. North (Eds.), *The social psychology of music* (pp. 46–63). Oxford: Oxford University Press.

Palmer, C. (1989). Mapping musical thought to musical performance. *Journal of Experimental Psychology: Human Perception & Performance, 15,* 331–346.

Palmer, C. (1996). On the assignment of structure in music performance. *Music Perception, 14,* 23–56.

Palmer, C. (1997). Music performance. *Annual Review of Psychology, 48,* 115–138.

Palmer, C., & Drake, C. (1997). Monitoring and planning capacities in the acquisition of music performance skills. *Canadian Journal of Experimental Psychology, 51,* 369–384.

Palmer, C., & Krumhansl, C. L. (1987a). Independent temporal and pitch structures in perception of musical phrases. *Journal of Experimental Psychology: Human Perception and Performance, 13,* 116–126.

Palmer, C., & Krumhansl, C. L. (1987b). Pitch and temporal contributions to musical phrase perception: Effects of harmony, performance timing, and familiarity. *Perception & Psychophysics, 41,* 505–518.

Palmer, C., & Krumhansl, C. L. (1990). Mental representation for musical meter. *Journal of Experimental Psychology: Human Perception and Performance, 16,* 728–741.

Palmer, C., & Meyer, R. K. (2000). Conceptual and motor learning in music performance. *Psychological Science, 11,* 63–68.

Palmer, C., & van de Sande, C. (1993). Units of knowledge in music performance. *Journal of Experimental Psychology: Learning, Memory, & Cognition, 19,* 457–470.

Palmer, C., & van de Sande, C. (1995). Range of planning in music performance. *Journal of Experimental Psychology: Human Perception & Performance, 21,* 947–962.

Parncutt, R. (1989). *Harmony: A psychoacoustical approach.* New York: Springer.

Patel, A. D. (1998). Syntactic processing in language and music: Different cognitive operations, similar neural resources? *Music Perception, 16,* 27–42.

Patel, A. D., Gibson, E., Ratner, J., Besson, M., & Holcomb, P. J. (1998). Processing syntactic relations in language and music: An event-related potential study. *Journal of Cognitive Neuroscience, 10,* 713–717.

Patterson, R. D. (1973). The effects of relative phase and the number of components on residue pitch. *Journal of the Acoustical Society of America, 53,* 1565–1572.

Penel, A. (2000). *Variations temporelles dans l'interpretation musicale: Processus perceptifs et cognitifs.* Unpublished doctoral dissertation, University of Paris.

Penel, A., & Drake, C. (1998). Sources of timing variations in music performance: A psychological segmentation model. *Psychological Research, 61,* 12–32.

Peretz, I. (1990). Processing of local and global musical information by unilateral brain-damaged patients. *Brain, 113,* 1185–1205.

Peretz, I. (1993). Auditory agnosia: A functional analysis. In S. McAdams and E. Bigand (Eds.), *Thinking in sound: The cognitive psychology of human audition.* Oxford: Oxford University Press.

Peretz, I. (2001). Music perception and recognition. In B. Rapp (Ed.), *The handbook of cognitive neuropsychology: What deficits reveal about the human mind* (pp. 519–540). Philadelphia: Psychology Press.

Peretz, I., & Morais, J. (1980). Modes of processing melodies and ear asymmetry in non-musicians. *Neuropsychologia, 18,* 477–489.

Perlman, M., & Krumhansl, C. L. (1996). An experimental study of internal interval standards in Javanese and Western musicians. *Music Perception, 14,* 95–116.

Peters, M. (1989). The relationship between variability of intertap intervals and interval duration. *Psychological Research, 51,* 38–42.

Pinker, S., & Bloom, P. (1990). Natural language and natural selection. *Behavioral and Brain Sciences, 13,* 707–754.

Plomp, R., & Levelt, W. J. M. (1965). Tonal consonance and the critical bandwidth. *Journal of the Acoustical Society of America, 38,* 548–560.

Povel, D.-J. (1981). Internal representation of simple temporal patterns. *Journal of Experimental Psychology: Human Perception and Performance, 7,* 3–18.

Povel, D.-J. (1984). A theoretical framework for rhythm perception. *Psychological Research, 45,* 315–337.

Raffman, D. (1993). *Language, music, and mind.* Cambridge: MIT Press.

Rasch, R. A. (1988). Timing and synchronization in performed ensemble music. In J. A. Sloboda (Ed.), *Generative processes in music: The psychology of performance, improvisation, and composition* (pp. 70–90). Oxford: Oxford University Press.

Regnault, P., Bigand, E., & Besson, M. (2001). Different brain mechanisms mediate sensitivity to sensory consonance and harmonic context: Evidence from auditory event-related brain potentials. *Journal of Cognitive Neuroscience, 13,* 241–255.

Repp, B. H. (1992a). A constraint on the expressive timing of a melodic gesture: Evidence from performance and aesthetic judgment. *Music Perception, 10,* 221–241.

Repp, B. H. (1992b). Diversity and commonality in music performance: An analysis of timing microstructure in Schumann's "Träumerei." *Journal of the Acoustical Society of America, 92,* 2546–2568.

Repp, B. H. (1992c). Probing the cognitive representation of musical time: Structural constraints on the perception of timing perturbations. *Cognition, 44,* 241–281.

Repp, B. H. (1993). Music as motion: A synopsis of Alexander Truslit's (1938) *Gestaltung und Bewegung in der Musik. Psychology of Music, 21,* 48–73.

Repp, B. H. (1994). The tritone paradox and the pitch range of the speaking voice: A dubious connection. *Music Perception, 12,* 227–255.

Repp, B. H. (1996a). Patterns of note onset asynchronies in expressive piano performance. *Journal of the Acoustical Society of America, 100,* 3917–3932.

Repp, B. H. (1996b). The art of inaccuracy: Why pianists' errors are difficult to hear. *Music Perception, 14,* 161–184.

Repp, B. H. (1998a). The detectability of local deviations from a typical expressive timing pattern. *Music Perception, 15,* 265–290.

Repp, B. H. (1998b). Variations on a theme by Chopin: Relations between perception and production of timing in music. *Journal of Experimental Psychology: Human Perception and Performance, 24,* 791–811.

Repp, B. H. (1999a). Control of expressive and metronomic timing in pianists. *Journal of Motor Behavior, 31,* 145–164.

Repp, B. H. (1999b). Detecting deviations from metronomic timing in music: Effects of perceptual structure on the mental timekeeper. *Perception & Psychophysics, 61,* 529–548.

Repp, B. H. (1999c). Relationships between performance timing, perception of timing perturbations, and perceptual-motor synchronization in two Chopin preludes. *Australian Journal of Psychology, 51,* 188–203.

Repp, B. H. (2000). Pattern typicality and dimensional interactions in pianists' imitation of expressive timing and dynamics. *Music Perception, 18,* 173–211.

Rosch, E. (1975a). Cognitive reference points. *Cognitive Psychology, 7,* 532–547.

Rosch, E. (1975b). Universals and cultural specifics in human categorization. In R. Breslin, S. Bochner, & W. Lonner (Eds.), *Cross-cultural perspectives on learning* (pp. 117–206). New York: Halsted Press.

Schellenberg, E. G. (1996). Expectancy in melody: Tests of the implication-realization model. *Cognition, 58,* 75–125.

Schellenberg, E. G. (1997). Simplifying the implication-realization model of melodic expectancy. *Music Perception, 14,* 295–318.

Schellenberg, E. G., & Trehub, S. E. (1996a). Children's discrimination of melodic intervals. *Developmental Psychology, 32,* 1039–1050.

Schellenberg, E. G., & Trehub, S. E. (1996b). Natural musical intervals: Evidence from infant listeners. *Psychological Science, 7,* 272–277.

Schenker, H. (1935). *Der freie Satz.* Vienna: Universal Edition.

Schlaug, G., Jäncke, L., Huang, Y, & Steinmetz, H. (1995). In vivo evidence of structural brain asymmetry in musicians. *Science, 267,* 699–701.

Schmuckler, M. A. (1989). Expectation in music: Investigations of melodic and harmonic processes. *Music Perception, 7,* 109–150.

Schouten, J. F., Ritsma, R. J., & Cardozo, B. L. (1962). Pitch of the residue. *Journal of the Acoustical Society of America, 34,* 1418–1424.

Schulhoff, C., & Goodglass, H. (1969). Dichotic listening, side of brain injury and cerebral dominance. *Neuropsychologia, 7,* 149–160.

Selkirk, E. (1980). The role of prosodic categories in English word stress. *Linguistic Inquiry, 11,* 563–605.

Shankweiler, D. (1966). Effects of temporal-lobe damage on perception of dichotically presented melodies. *Journal of Comparative and Physiological Psychology, 62,* 115–119.

Shapiro, B. E., Grossman, M., & Gardner, H. (1981). Selective processing deficits in brain damage populations. *Neuropsychologia, 19,* 161–169.

Shepard, R. N. (1964). Circularity in judgments of relative pitch. *Journal of the Acoustical Society of America, 36,* 2346–2353.

Shepard, R. N. (1965). Approximation to uniform gradients of generalization by monotone transformations of scale. In D. I. Mostofsky (Ed.), *Stimulus generalization.* Stanford, CA: Stanford University Press.

Shepard, R. N. (1982). Geometrical approximations to the structure of musical pitch. *Psychological Review, 89,* 305–333.

Siegel, J. A., & Siegel, W. (1977a). Absolute identification of notes and intervals by musicians. *Perception & Psychophysics, 21,* 143–152.

Siegel, J. A., & Siegel, W. (1977b). Categorical perception of tonal intervals: Musicians can't tell *sharp* from *flat*. *Perception & Psychophysics, 21,* 399–407.

Sloboda, J. A. (1976). The effect of item position on the likelihood of identification by inference in prose reading and music reading. *Canadian Journal of Psychology, 30,* 228–237.

Sloboda, J. A. (1977). Phrase units as determinants of visual processing in music reading. *British Journal of Psychology, 68,* 117–124.

Sloboda, J. A. (1983). The communication of musical metre in piano performance. *Quarterly Journal of Experimental Psychology, 35,* 377–396.

Sloboda, J. A. (1984). Experimental studies of musical reading: A review. *Music Perception, 2,* 222–236.

Sloboda, J. A. (1985). *The musical mind: The cognitive psychology of music.* Oxford: Oxford University Press.

Sloboda, J. A. (Ed.). (1988). *Generative processes in music: The psychology of performance, improvisation, and composition.* Oxford: Oxford University Press.

Sloboda, J. A., Clarke, E. F., Parncutt, R., & Raekallio, M. (1998). Determinants of finger choice in piano sight-reading. *Journal of Experimental Psychology: Human Perception and Performance, 24,* 185–203.

Sloboda, J. A., Davidson, J. W., & Howe, M. J. A. (1994). Is everyone musical? *The Psychologist, 7,* 354–359.

Sloboda, J. A., Davidson, J. W., Howe, M. J. A., & Moore, D. G. (1996). The role of practice in the development of expert musical performance. *British Journal of Psychology, 87,* 354–359.

Sloboda, J. A., & Gregory, A. H. (1980). The psychological reality of musical segments. *Canadian Journal of Psychology, 34,* 274–280.

Smith, K. C., & Cuddy, L. L. (1989). Effects of metric and harmonic rhythm on the detection of pitch alterations in melodic sequences. *Journal of Experimental Psychology: Human Perception and Performance, 15,* 457–471.

Speer, J. R., & Meeks, P. U. (1985). School children's perception of pitch in music. *Psychomusicology, 5,* 49–56.

Sternberg, S., Knoll, R. L., & Zukofsky, P. (1982). Timing by skilled musicians. In D. Deutsch (Ed.), *The psychology of music* (pp. 181–239). New York: Academic Press.

Studdert-Kennedy, M., Liberman, A. M., Harris, K., & Cooper, F. S. (1970). The motor theory of speech perception: A reply to Lane's critical review. *Psychological Review, 77,* 234–249.

Stumpf, C. (1898). Konsonanz und Dissonanz. *Beiträge zur Akustik und Musikwissenschaft, 1,* 1–108.

Takeuchi, A. H., & Hulse, S. H. (1991). Absolute pitch judgments of black- and white-key pitches. *Music Perception, 9,* 27–46.

Takeuchi, A. H., & Hulse, S. H. (1993). Absolute pitch. *Psychological Bulletin, 113,* 345–361.

Tekman, H. G., & Bharucha, J. J. (1992). Time course of chord priming. *Perception & Psychophysics, 51,* 33–39.

Tekman, H. G., & Bharucha, J. J. (1998). Implicit knowledge versus psychoacoustic similarity in priming of chords. *Journal of Experimental Psychology: Human Perception and Performance, 24,* 252–260.

Terhardt, E. (1972). Zur Tonhöhenwahrnehmug von Klängen. *Acoustica, 26,* 173–199.

Terhardt, E. (1974). Pitch, consonance, and harmony. *Journal of the Acoustical Society of America, 55,* 1061–1069.

Terhardt, E. (1979). Calculating virtual pitch. *Hearing Research, 1,* 155–182.

Tervaniemi, M., Ilvonen, T., Karma, K., Alho, K., & Näätänen, R. (1997). The musical brain: Brain waves reveal the neurophysiological basis of musicality in human subjects. *Neuroscience Letters, 226,* 1–4.

Thompson, W. F., & Cuddy, L. L. (1997). Music performance and the perception of key. *Journal of Experimental Psychology: Human Perception and Performance, 23,* 116–135.

Thompson, W. F., Cuddy, L. L., & Plaus, C. (1997). Expectancies generated by melodic intervals: Evaluation of principles of melodic implication in a melody-completion task. *Perception & Psychophysics, 59,* 1069–1076.

Thurlow, W. R., & Rawlings, I. L. (1959). Discrimination of number of simultaneously sounding tones. *Journal of the Acoustical Society of America, 31,* 1332–1336.

Tillmann, B., & Bharucha, J. J. (in press). Effect of harmonic relatedness on the detection of temporal asynchronies. *Perception & Psychophysics.*

Tillmann, B., Bharucha, J. J., & Bigand, E. (2000). Implicit learning of tonality: A self-organizing approach. *Psychological Review, 107,* 885–913.

Tillmann, B., & Bigand, E. (2001). Global context effect in normal and scrambled musical sequences. *Journal of Experimental Psychology: Human Perception and Performance, 27,* 1185–1196.

Tillmann, B., Bigand, E., & Pineau, M. (1998). Effects of global and local contexts on harmonic expectancy. *Music Perception, 16,* 99–117.

Tooby, J., & Cosmides, L. (1992). The psychological foundations of culture. In J. H. Barkow, L. Cosmides, & J. Tooby (Eds.), *The adapted mind: Evolutionary psychology and the generation of culture* (pp. 19–136). Oxford: Oxford University Press.

Trainor, L. J. (1997). Effect of frequency ratio on infants' and adults' discrimination of simultaneous intervals. *Journal of Experimental Psychology: Human Perception and Performance, 23,* 1427–1438.

Trainor, L. J., & Heinmiller, B. M. (1998). The development of evaluative responses to music: Infants prefer to listen to consonance over dissonance. *Infant Behavior & Development, 21,* 77–88.

Trainor, L. J., & Trehub, S. E. (1992). A comparison of infants' and adults' sensitivity to Western musical structure. *Journal of Experimental Psychology: Human Perception and Performance, 18,* 394–402.

Trainor, L. J., & Trehub, S. E. (1993a). Musical context effects in infants and adults: Key distance. *Journal of Experimental Psychology: Human Perception and Performance, 19,* 615–626.

Trainor, L. J., & Trehub, S. E. (1993b). What mediates infants' and adults' superior processing of the major over the augmented triad? *Music Perception, 11,* 185–196.

Trainor, L. J., & Trehub, S. E. (1994). Key membership and implied harmony in Western tonal music: Developmental perspectives. *Perception & Psychophysics, 56,* 125–132.

Trehub, S. E., Bull, D., & Thorpe, L. A. (1984). Infants' perception of melodies: The role of melodic contour. *Child Development, 55,* 821–830.

Trehub, S. E., Cohen, A. J., Thorpe, L. A., & Morrongiello, B. A. (1986). Development of the perception of musical relations: Semitone and diatonic structure. *Journal of Experimental Psychology: Human Perception and Performance, 12,* 295–301.

Trehub, S. E., Thorpe, L. A., & Morrongiello, B. A. (1985). Infants' perception of melodies: Changes in a single tone. *Infant Behavior & Development, 8,* 213–223.

Trehub, S. E., Thorpe, L. A., & Morrongiello, B. A. (1987). Organizational processes in infants' perception of auditory patterns. *Child Development, 58,* 741–749.

Trehub, S. E., Thorpe, L. A., & Trainor, L. J. (1990). Infants' perception of *good* and *bad* melodies. *Psychomusicology, 9,* 5–15.

Truslit, A. (1938). *Gestaltung und Bewegung in der Musik.* Berlin: Vieweg.

Tversky, A. (1977). Features of similarity. *Psychological Review, 84,* 327–352.

Van Nuys, K., & Weaver, H. E. (1943). Memory span and visual pauses in reading rhythms and melodies. *Psychological Monographs, 55,* 33–50.

Viviani, P., & Stucchi, N. (1992). Biological movements look uniform: Evidence of motor-perceptual interactions. *Journal of Experimental Psychology: Human Perception and Performance, 18,* 603–623.

Vos, J., & van Vianen, B. G. (1984). Thresholds for discrimination between pure and tempered intervals: The relevance of nearly coinciding harmonics. *Journal of the Acoustical Society of America, 77,* 176–187.

Wallin, N. L., Merker, B., & Brown, S. (Eds.). (2000). *The origins of music.* Cambridge: MIT Press.

Weaver, H. E. (1943). A study of visual processes in reading differently constructed musical selections. *Psychological Monographs, 55,* 1–30.

Weir, C., Jesteadt, W., & Green, D. M. (1977). Frequency discrimination as a function of frequency and sensation level. *Journal of the Acoustical Society of America, 61,* 178–184.

Westbury, C. F., Zatorre, R. J., & Evans, A. C. (1999). Quantifying variability in the planum temporale: A probability map. *Cerebral Cortex, 9,* 392–405.

Whitfield, I. C. (1980). Auditory cortex and the pitch of complex tones. *Journal of the Acoustical Society of America, 67,* 644–647.

Wightman, F. L. (1973a). Pitch and stimulus fine structure. *Journal of the Acoustical Society of America, 54,* 397–406.

Wightman, F. L. (1973b). The pattern-transformation model of pitch. *Journal of the Acoustical Society of America, 54,* 407–416.

Zatorre, R. J. (1984). Musical perception and cerebral function: A critical review. *Music Perception, 2,* 196–221.

Zatorre, R. J. (1988). Pitch perception of complex tones and human temporal-lobe function. *Journal of the Acoustical Society of America, 82,* 566–572.

Zatorre, R. J., Evans, A. C., & Meyer, E. (1994). Neural mechanisms underlying melodic perception and memory for pitch. *Journal of Neuroscience, 14,* 1908–1919.

Zatorre, R. J., Halpern, A., Perry, D. W., Meyer, E., & Evans, A. C. (1996). Hearing in the mind's ear: A PET investigation of musical imagery and perception. *Journal of Cognitive Neuroscience, 8,* 29–46.

Zatorre, R. J., Perry, D. W., Beckett, C. A., Westbury, C. F., & Evans, A. C. (1998). Functional anatomy of musical processing in listeners with absolute pitch and relative pitch. *Proceedings of the National Academy of Sciences of the United States of America, 95,* 3172–3177.

Zatorre, R. J., & Samson, S. (1991). Role of the right temporal neocortex in retention of pitch in auditory short-term memory. *Brain, 114,* 2403–2417.

CHAPTER 12

Speech Perception

PETER W. JUSCZYK AND PAUL A. LUCE

By the time we are adults, speech perception seems to be an effortless process. Unless we find ourselves communicating in a very noisy environment or listening to someone with an extremely strong nonnative accent, we seem to perceive the words of utterances produced by different talkers with no apparent difficulties. Moreover, perceiving speech from a variety of different talkers seems to be something that young children are able to accomplish with little, if any, direct instruction. Why, then, has it been so difficult to build mechanical devices or computer interfaces that can respond directly to human vocal commands? In this chapter we explore the nature of speech perception by adults and infants. We examine the ways in which researchers have attempted to explain how speech perception occurs, beginning with early research that focused on attempts to identify acoustic correlates of the building blocks of words (i.e., phonemes) and moving to more recent efforts to understand how listeners segment and recognize words from fluent speech. Moreover, because developmental research can provide insights into the nature of the capacities and mechanisms that underlie speech perception, we review major findings on the origins and development of speech perception capacities during infancy.

EARLY RESEARCH ON SPEECH PERCEPTION

Research on the perception of speech began in earnest during the 1950s. The major focus of research was on how listeners could recover the correct phonetic segments from the speech signal. There were three issues at the heart of most early studies; these were invariance, constancy, and perceptual units. All of these matters are crucial for understanding how the acoustic signal is transformed into phonetic segments. We consider each in turn.

Invariance

Each element in the periodic table has a unique atomic number corresponding to the number of protons in its nucleus. Hence, if we know how many protons are present, we know the identity of the element. If speech worked in the same way, then each phonetic segment would be specified by a unique set of acoustic properties. Unfortunately, the situation is considerably more complex, as Delattre, Liberman, and Cooper (1955) discovered when they sought acoustic invariants for consonants such as [d]. When they examined the acoustic realizations for [d] produced with different following vowels (e.g., [di], [da], [du]), they found no obvious common acoustic properties that specified [d] across these contexts. Instead, the acoustic characteristics of [d] were strongly influenced by the following vowel. This phenomenon, by which consonant and vowel segments are produced simultaneously rather than sequentially, is referred to as *coarticulation*. An example of how coarticulation affects the acoustic characteristics of the consonants [b] and [d] is shown in the spectrograms presented in Figure 12.1.

Although a single set of acoustic features that identifies a particular phonetic segment in all contexts might not exist, a weaker version of the acoustic invariance might still hold. There might be equivalence classes of acoustic features that identify a particular phonetic segment in different contexts (e.g., one set of features before [a], another set before [u], etc.) However, other evidence refutes even this weaker hypothesis. Liberman, Delattre, and Cooper (1952) found that an identical burst of acoustic noise, when placed in front of the vowels [a], [i], and [u], resulted in the perception of the syllables [pi], [ka], [pu]. In other words, the same noise was perceived as a [p] in some contexts, but as a [k] in other contexts. These findings undermined any simple notion of identifying phonetic segments based on invariant acoustic properties.

In response to these findings, many investigators explored alternative acoustic descriptions of speech in hopes of achieving a description that would reveal invariant properties of phonetic segments (Blumstein & Stevens, 1978; Kewley-Port, 1983; Sawusch, 1992; Searle, Jacobson, & Rayment, 1979; Stevens, 1998; Sussman, McCaffrey, & Matthews, 1991). Others embraced the view that phonetic segments are not specified by acoustic invariants and sought other explanations of phonetic perception (Fowler, 1986; Fowler & Rosenblum, 1991; Liberman, Cooper, Harris, & MacNeilage, 1963; Liberman & Mattingly, 1985; Liberman & Whalen, 2000).

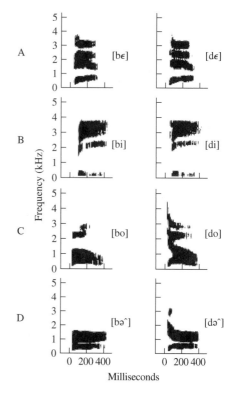

Figure 12.1 Spectrograms of consonant-vowel syllables consisting of [b] and [d] produced in the context of four different vowels.
NOTE: (A) [bɛ] and [dɛ], as in "bet" and "debt"; (B) [bi] and [di], as in "bead" and "deed"; (C) [bo] and [do], as in "boat" and "dote"; and (D) [bɚ] and [dɚ], as in "birth" and "dearth." The dark bands in each graph correspond to the formants. For example, four formants are visible in the two spectrograms in A; these correspond, from bottom to top, to the first, second, third, and fourth formants. The darkness of the bands reflects the intensity of acoustic energy concentrated at particular spectral frequencies for a given moment in time. Note that for [d] the initial portion of the second and third formants (i.e., the formant transitions) sometimes fall and sometimes rise in frequency depending on the vowel that follows it. Also note that the spacing of the different formants varies with the vowel contexts. In the case of [e], the second and third formants are so close in their spectral frequencies that they are hard to distinguish in the spectrograms.

Constancy

There are additional sources of variability in speech sounds with which the human perceptual system must also cope. When different talkers produce the same speech segment, the acoustic characteristics of their productions will differ. Women's voices tend to be higher pitched than men's voices, and a wide range of acoustic variability occurs even within a particular sex.

Individual differences in talkers' voices are a natural consequence of the sizes and shapes of their vocal tracts. The length and mass of the vocal folds, as well as the overall length of the vocal tract, affect the typical fundamental frequency (or pitch) of one's voice. Other factors (e.g., the flexibility of the tongue, the state of one's vocal folds, etc.) affect the acoustic characteristics of the speech also. As a result, the production of a particular word by one talker might actually be more similar acoustically to the production of a different word by another talker than it is to the second talker's production of the same word (Ladefoged & Broadbent, 1957). Peterson and Barney (1952) examined productions of different English vowels by 76 talkers. They found that tokens of a particular vowel produced by some talkers actually overlapped with the productions of a different vowel produced by other talkers.

There is also considerable variability in productions of the same target by a single talker. Changing one's speaking register from adult-directed speech to child-directed speech changes not only pitch but other acoustic properties of speech as well (Fernald et al., 1989; Kuhl et al., 1997). In addition, variations in speaking rate lead to concomitant changes in the acoustic signal. Phonetic distinctions linked to the rate of temporal change of certain acoustic features (such as [b] vs. [w]) are likely to be affected by changes in speaking rate (Liberman, Delattre, Gerstman, & Cooper, 1956; J. L. Miller & Liberman,

1979). Thus, listeners cannot use the absolute duration of some acoustic feature as a cue to a phonetic distinction. Other types of speech contrasts are also affected by changes in speaking rate. For example, Summerfield (1975) found that differences in the voicing characteristics of voiced (e.g., [d]) and voiceless (e.g., [t]) stops tend to decrease as speaking rate speeds up. Moreover, the nature of the acoustic changes that ensue is not always predictable a priori (Port, 1976). Not surprisingly, then, how listeners cope with the intra- and intertalker variability in speech garnered the attention of many researchers.

Perceptual Units

Many early studies assumed that the elementary unit of perception was the minimal-sized unit that could distinguish two different word forms, namely, the phoneme or phonetic segment. Phonemes contrast minimally with each other according to certain features (Jakobson, Fant, & Halle, 1952). Thus, [b] contrasts with [p] on a voicing feature, with [m] on an oral/nasal manner of articulation feature, with [d] on a place of articulation feature, and so on. According to Jakobson et al., "The distinctive features are the ultimate distinctive entities of language since no one of them can be broken down into smaller linguistic units" (p. 3). However, distinctive features combine into one concurrent bundle, corresponding to the phonetic segment. It was only natural that researchers assumed that direct acoustic correlates of such units would exist. The development of the pattern playback synthesizer enabled researchers to determine how elements in the acoustic signal affected speech perception (F. S. Cooper, Delattre, Liberman, Borst, & Gerstman, 1952; F. S. Cooper, Liberman, & Borst, 1951). The patterns used to generate speech sounds with this synthesizer were based on spectrographic analyses of speech. The time × frequency × intensity analysis provided in a spectrogram reveals that acoustic energy is concentrated in bands in the acoustic spectrum. These bands, called *formants,* correspond to the natural resonant frequencies of the vocal tract during the production of a given speech sound. When researchers began to seek the acoustic features corresponding to phonetic segments, it was soon discovered that there was no way to divide the formants of a consonant-vowel (CV) syllable, such as /di/ into pieces corresponding to each of the individual segments (Liberman, Cooper, Shankweiler, & Studdert-Kennedy, 1967). No portion of the formant patterns corresponds to the /d/ alone. Rather, listeners hear either a /di/ or a nonspeech sound. Based on these observations, Liberman and his colleagues concluded that even the beginning portions of the acoustic signal carry information about the consonant and the vowel simultaneously.

Much research has been directed at identifying the elementary unit of perception. Savin and Bever (1970) found that listeners were faster at detecting syllable targets than at detecting phoneme targets. They concluded that syllables are the basic units of speech perception and that phonemes are derived secondarily from these (see also Massaro, 1972). Nevertheless, under different circumstances, faster monitoring times have been reported for phonemes (Cutler, Norris, & Williams, 1987; Healy & Cutting, 1976; Mills, 1980; Swinney & Prather, 1980) or for units larger than syllables (McNeill & Lindig, 1973). However, the methods used in many of these studies have been criticized (Mehler, Segui, & Frauenfelder, 1981). It is fair to say that no strong consensus emerged regarding the basic perceptual unit. Indeed, there were proponents for a range of different sized units, including demi-syllables (Fujimura, 1976), context-sensitive allophones (Wickelgren, 1969), syllables (Cole & Scott, 1974; Mehler, Dommergues, Frauenfelder, & Segui, 1981;

Studdert-Kennedy, 1974), and even context-sensitive spectra (Klatt, 1979).

A BOTTOM-UP VIEW OF SPEECH PERCEPTION

Because phonemes are the elementary sound units used in constructing the words of a language, a general assumption was that perceiving words first requires the recovery of the sequence of phonemes that makes up the word. Although the range of topics considered in this section is by no means exhaustive of those investigated in earlier studies, they attracted a lion's share of researchers' attention. The four topics discussed here all pertain to the goal of understanding how phonemes are extracted from the speech signal.

Categorical Perception

When researchers at Haskins Laboratories began to manipulate information in the acoustic signal to determine its importance for the perception of phonemes such as the stop consonants /b/, /d/, and /g/, they discovered an interesting phenomenon about the way that physical differences in the speech signal relate to perceived changes in the phonemes. Using a speech synthesizer to create these sounds, Liberman, Harris, Hoffman, and Griffith (1957) noted that these sounds differed primarily in spectral information (i.e. the onset frequency and extent of the second formant transition). By varying this information in small steps to produce additional stimuli, they created an acoustic continuum for stop consonant sounds differing in place of articulation, ranging from [b] to [d] to [g]. However, when listeners were asked to label the individual sounds from the continuum, they did not report intermediate sounds as gradually shading from one phoneme to another. Rather, listeners consistently tended to report them as acceptable instances of [b], [d], or [g]. The changeover from one phonemic category to another was abrupt, as manifested by steep slopes in the identification curves plotted from listener's labeling of the stimuli along the continuum. Moreover, when asked to discriminate pairs of stimuli from the continuum, listeners' success in discriminating these stimulus pairs was predicted by the phonemic labels that they assigned to each stimulus. As Liberman et al. noted, "a listener can better discriminate between sounds that lie on the opposite sides of a phoneme boundary than he can between sounds that fall within the same phoneme category" (p. 358). This finding was surprising because for most acoustic stimuli listeners typically discriminate many more distinctions between stimuli than they can provide distinct labels for. Pollack (1952) found that average listeners could discriminate about 1,200 pitch differences between 100 Hz and 8000 Hz but that they could consistently use only about seven labels within this pitch range. By comparison, Liberman et al.'s subjects' abilities to discriminate acoustic differences for stop consonants was roughly equivalent to their identification of stimuli as instances of the phoneme categories /b/, /d/, or /g/.

Categorical perception was found to occur also along other dimensions of phonetic contrast, such as voicing (Liberman, Harris, Kinney, & Lane, 1961; Lisker & Abramson, 1970) and manner of articulation (Miyawaki et al., 1975). Three consistent facts from the studies are taken as hallmarks of categorical perception (Studdert-Kennedy, Liberman, Harris, & Cooper, 1970). First, adults' labeling of stimuli from such continua indicated abrupt, steep slopes between adjacent phonemic categories (ranging from 80–100% identification of an instance as a member of a particular phoneme category to only 0–20% identification of the next step along the continuum as an instance of that same phoneme

category). Second, discrimination of stimuli from within the same phonemic category tended to be poor, whereas discrimination of equal-sized acoustic differences between stimuli from different phonemic categories was good. Third, peaks in the discriminability of stimulus pairs along a continuum corresponded to the category boundaries obtained in labeling the stimuli.

Categorical perception is characteristic of how listeners respond to many consonantal contrasts. By comparison, perception of vowel contrasts is said to be continuous. Fry, Abramson, Eimas, and Liberman (1962) explored a continuum that ranged from /I/ to /ɛ/ to /æ/ and found that discrimination among items from within the same vowel category was quite good. Thus, rather than categorical, the perception of vowel contrasts is similar to the discrimination of stimulus differences along nonspeech continua (Pollack, 1952, 1953).

Initial indications were that categorical perception was unique to how certain speech contrasts are processed. When similar kinds of acoustic differences were used to construct nonspeech analogs of speech contrasts, listeners' perception of the nonspeech contrasts was continuous, even though their perception of the same changes in speech contexts was categorical (Liberman, Harris, Eimas, Lisker, & Bastian, 1961). The belief that categorical perception was unique to speech became a core element of arguments for the existence of a special mode of perception for speech processing (Liberman, 1970; Liberman et al., 1967).

Speech versus Nonspeech Processing

Researchers have undertaken many investigations to establish whether speech and nonspeech sounds are processed in the same manner. The earliest investigations centered on categorical perception. Direct comparisons of speech and nonspeech processing initially indicated that categorical perception was restricted to speech (Liberman, Harris, Kinney, et al., 1961; Mattingly, Liberman, Syrdal, & Halwes, 1971; Miyawaki et al., 1975). However, studies of the perception of nonspeech stimuli with multiple components that varied in relation to each other (much like speech sounds) told a different story. The relationships manipulated in these later studies (e.g., varying the timing of one component with respect to another) were often analogous to phonetic dimensions such as voicing, and this analogy prompted claims that a set of general auditory mechanisms underlies the discrimination of the speech contrasts (J. D. Miller, Weir, Pastore, Kelly, & Dooling, 1976; Pisoni, 1977). Moreover, categorical perception was found also for stimulus continua with no ready analogs in speech, such as musical chords (Blechner, 1977; Locke & Kellar, 1973; Zatorre & Halpern, 1979) and the flicker-fusion threshold of visual stimuli (Pastore et al., 1977). Such findings undermined the view that categorical perception is unique to speech processing. (For more extensive discussion of these issues, see Harnad, 1987.)

Proponents of a specialized mode of speech processing have offered other grounds for believing that speech and nonspeech sounds are processed differently. Marked differences exist in the rate at which speech and nonspeech sounds can be processed. Liberman et al. (1967) reported that human listeners can process speech at rates of 25 to 30 phonetic segments per second. Other reports indicate that adults are capable of processing 400 words per minute, though with some difficulty (Orr, Friedman, & Williams, 1965). By comparison, rates of 30 nonspeech sounds per second seem to be beyond the temporal resolving capacity of the human ear (G. A. Miller & Taylor, 1948). In fact, human listeners are unable to assign the correct ordering to a sequence of different nonspeech

sounds occurring at a rate of four sounds per second (R. M. Warren, 1974; R. M. Warren, Obusek, Farmer, & Warren, 1969). Evidently, the overlap in phonetic segments caused by coarticulation enables listeners to process speech information at higher transmission rates.

Further grounds for specialized speech processing mechanisms concern certain types of context-effects that occur in speech processing. As earlier, changes in speaking rates affect how certain acoustic elements are perceived in the signal. J. L. Miller and Liberman (1979) demonstrated that perception of the acoustic information for a stop/glide distinction (i.e., [b] vs. [w]) varies with speaking rates. They generated a continuum from [ba] to [wa] by gradually changing the duration of formant transitions present between the onset of these sounds and the vowel. Changes in speaking rates were created by varying the overall duration of the syllables. Shorter syllables occur in faster speaking rates; longer syllables occur in slower speaking rates. The point along the continuum at which the perceived syllable shifted from [ba] to [wa] varied systematically with speaking rate. J. L. Miller and Liberman attributed such effects to specialized perceptual mechanisms that compensate for speaking rate differences. This view was challenged by Pisoni, Carrell, and Gans (1983), who found similar effects for the perception of nonspeech tone analogs to the J. L. Miller and Liberman stimuli. Pisoni et al. argued that a general auditory processing mechanism could account for both the speech and nonspeech findings.

Another finding implicating possible differences in speech and nonspeech processing comes from studies of duplex perception. In these studies subjects hear a particular portion of a speech syllable in one ear, such as an isolated third formant transition, and the rest of the syllable in the other ear (Liberman, Isenberg, & Rakerd, 1981). Listeners hear both a complete syllable and a chirp or tone corresponding to the isolated third formant transition. Liberman et al. argued that these signals are perceived simultaneously as speech and nonspeech, suggesting two different processors for these signals. Subsequent studies showed that various stimulus or procedural manipulations independently affect the speech and nonspeech percepts (Bentin & Mann, 1990; Nygaard, 1993; Nygaard & Eimas, 1990). However, researchers have challenged interpretations of the findings on duplex perception on a number of grounds (Fowler, 1990; Fowler & Rosenblum, 1990; Hall & Pastore, 1992; Nusbaum, Schwab, & Sawusch, 1983; Pastore, Schmeckler, Rosenblum, & Szczesiul, 1983). For instance, Pastore et al. (1983) demonstrated that duplex perception can be obtained also for musical chords when one note is played in one ear and the other two notes are played to the opposite ear. Clearly, more research is required to understand the full implications of duplex perception for speech processing mechanisms.

Perhaps the strongest evidence for different modes of speech and nonspeech perception comes from investigations using sine wave speech. Sine wave speech stimuli are produced by replacing the formants of syllables with frequency-modulated sine waves that follow the center frequency of the formants (Bailey, Summerfield, & Dorman, 1977; Best, Morrongiello, & Robson, 1981; Remez, Rubin, Pisoni, & Carrell, 1981). Listeners process such signals in distinctive ways depending on whether they are told that they are hearing poor-quality synthetic speech or a series of beeps or tones (Remez et al., 1981). The argument here is that the specialized speech processor is engaged when subjects are expecting to hear speech, and a general auditory processor is used when subjects are told that they will be hearing beeps or tones. Because the acoustic information is identical in both cases, the differences in process-

ing must be attributable to subjects' engagement of specialized speech processing mechanisms in the former situation, but not in the latter.

To conclude, despite many efforts to determine whether there is a special mode of perception for processing speech, there is still considerable debate about this issue.

Selective Adaptation

During the 1970s many researchers speculated that feature detectors might explain how phonemes are extracted from the acoustic signal during speech processing (Abbs & Sussman, 1971; Liberman, 1970; Stevens, 1972). This view received a significant boost from findings reported by Eimas and his colleagues (Eimas, Cooper, & Corbit, 1973; Eimas & Corbit, 1973). Phonetic feature accounts pointed to binary oppositions between similar speech sounds. For instance, [b] and [p] share all phonetic features except for voicing, where they have contrasting values ([b] is voiced and [p] is voiceless). Researchers in other domains have argued that underlying sensory mechanisms are often organized as opponent processes in which prolonged stimulation of one member of an opponent process pair temporarily depresses its sensitivity while leaving the other member of the pair unaffected (Hurvich & Jameson, 1969). This changes the point at which stimulation of the two pair members cancel each other out. Eimas and Corbit (1973) hypothesized that this might hold for speech sounds with opposite values on a phonetic feature dimension, such as voicing. Using a voicing continuum ranging from [ba] to [pa], they first identified the phonetic category boundary for each of their subjects. Next, each subject was repeatedly exposed to a stimulus from one of the two endpoints of the continuum; then they were tested for the location of their phonetic category boundaries. Subjects exposed to [ba] adaptors were more likely to label stimuli from the region of the original category boundary as *pa,* whereas those exposed to the [pa] adaptor were much more likely to label the same stimuli as *ba.* Eimas and Corbit interpreted these results as evidence for the existence of feature detectors.

Subsequent studies reported selective adaptation effects for other types of phonetic feature contrasts, such as place of articulation (W. E. Cooper & Blumstein, 1974). In addition, selective adaptation effects were found to be greater for adaptors that were prototypical instances of a phonemic category than for less typical instances of the category (J. L. Miller, Connine, Schermer & Kluender, 1983; Samuel, 1982).

However, subsequent research showed that the phonetic feature detector model was implausible. First, findings indicated that selective adaptation effects did not transfer across syllable position or vowel context (Ades, 1974; W. E. Cooper, 1975; Sawusch, 1977). Such findings ruled out the possibility that the same feature detector could detect a particular phonetic property across all contexts, suggesting instead separate detectors for each context. Second, other findings suggested that detectors responded to acoustic, rather than phonetic, properties. Tartter and Eimas (1975) found that adaptation with nonspeech chirp stimuli was sufficient to produce significant shifts of phonemic category boundaries. Also, Sawusch and Jusczyk (1981) found that when listeners were exposed to an adaptor [spa] that was acoustically more similar to one end of a continuum [ba] yet phonetically similar to the other end of the continuum [pa], adaptation effects followed the acoustic properties of the stimuli. Such findings seemed to suggest that any feature detectors underlying speech processing were tuned to acoustic rather than to phonetic properties. However, Remez (1980) called into question the notion that feature detectors were involved in speech processing. He created a stimulus series with [ba] as one endpoint of a continuum and a nonspeech buzz as the other endpoint. Adaptation with either endpoint resulted in a significant shift in the category boundary on this continuum. The fact that selective adaptation effects occur on such an artificial continuum with no known correspondence to any phonetic dimension casts serious doubt on claims that selective adaptation effects reflect the action of detectors mediating acoustic-phonetic correspondences.

Normalization

We have already noted some problems that occur as a result of intra- and intertalker differences in the production of speech. Given these, it is not surprising that the ways in which listeners compensate for such variability became an important focus of research. Ladefoged and Broadbent (1957) manipulated the perceived dimensions of a talker's vocal tract by raising or lowering the first and second formants of a synthesized version of the sentence "Please say what this word is." This sentence was followed by utterances of four target words: *bit, bet, but,* and *bat.* Although the acoustic characteristics of the carrier sentence varied across the test trials, the acoustic properties of the target words remained unchanged. Listeners' judgments of the target words varied with their perceptions of the talker's voice. Ladefoged and Broadbent concluded that the carrier phrase allowed listeners to calibrate the vowel space of the perceived talker on a particular trial, leading them to adjust their interpretations of the target words accordingly. Subsequent investigations supported the view that listeners estimate the typical vowel space of a given talker from a small speech sample (Gerstman, 1968; Shankweiler, Strange, & Verbrugge, 1977). However, other studies indicated that providing listeners with examples of a talker's vowels did not significantly improve their identification of words with similar vowels (Shankweiler et al., 1977; Verbrugge, Strange, Shankweiler, & Edman, 1976).

An alternative view of normalization assumes that invariant acoustic features specify the identity of particular phonemes (Blumstein & Stevens, 1980; Fant, 1960; Stevens, 1960; Stevens & Blumstein, 1978). By this view, listeners focus on invariant features and ignore the articulatory characteristics of different individuals. In other words, listeners essentially strip away the information relating to a particular talker's voice and use the invariant acoustic cues to phonetic segments to recognize particular words (Nearey, 1989; Syrdal & Gopal, 1986). Properties of the signal such as pitch are deemed to guide the interpretation of formant frequencies produced by different talkers (Suomi, 1984). Sussman (1986) has proposed that innately specified neuronal cell assemblies may encode both absolute and relative formant frequencies. Connections between these cell assemblies and higher-order assemblies could eliminate information related to vocal tract size and thus allow the derivation of invariant properties required for normalization.

The alternative view, just considered, assumes that listeners rely on a frequency-based recalibration of the signal. Others have argued that listeners achieve normalization not by extracting out static acoustic invariants, but by recovering the underlying articulatory dynamics from the speech signal (Verbrugge & Rakerd, 1986). The latter claim is based on research with silent-centered syllables. These are consonant-vowel-consonant (CVC) syllables in which the middle 60% of the signal is removed, leaving only the beginning and ending formant transitions with a silent period inbetween. Listeners correctly identify the vowels from such patterns even when a range of

tokens from different males and females is used. Verbrugge and Rakerd concluded that "vowels can be characterized by higher-order variables (patterns of articulatory and spectral *change*) that are independent of a specific talker's vocal tract dimensions" (p. 56).

Although these accounts of normalization differ in the mechanisms proposed to serve this function, they agree that listeners cope with talker variability by stripping away such information from the acoustic signal. In other words, talker-specific information is discarded to achieve successful perception of the linguistic message. However, talker variability does have an impact on the perception of speech sounds, in terms of both the accuracy (Creelman, 1957) and the speed (Mullennix, Pisoni, & Martin, 1989; Summerfield, 1975; Summerfield & Haggard, 1973) of word recognition. This has led some investigators to question whether the successful recovery and recognition of words from fluent speech involves stripping talker-specific characteristics from the acoustic signal (Goldinger, 1996; Houston & Jusczyk, 2000; Jusczyk, 1993; Pisoni, 1992). The latter view is discussed in more detail in relation to issues considered in the next section.

SPOKEN WORD RECOGNITION: MODELS AND ISSUES

Early work in the field of speech perception was dominated by research on the discrimination and categorization of phonetic segments. In the 1970s a new research emphasis began to emerge that focused on the processes and representations responsible for the perception of spoken *words*. This focus grew from the recognition that a comprehensive theory of spoken language comprehension must account for more than the perception of individual consonants, vowels, and syllables.

Models

The history of research on spoken word recognition is largely a history of word recognition models. To its credit, the field has been extensively driven by the development, testing, and refinement of its theories. Thus, to understand the nature and substance of the issues that occupy the field today, one must have some appreciation for the models that have inspired current empirical research. We briefly review four current models of spoken word recognition: Cohort, TRACE, Shortlist, and the Neighborhood Activation Model.

Cohort

Cohort theory (Marslen-Wilson & Tyler, 1980; Marslen-Wilson & Welsh, 1978) proposes that input in the form of a spoken word activates a set of similar items in memory, referred to as the word-initial *cohort*. The cohort consists of all spoken words known to the listener that begin with the initial segment or segments of the input word. For example, the word *elephant* may activate in memory the cohort members *echo, enemy, elder, elevator,* and so on. Once activated, the cohort is winnowed based on both bottom-up (acoustic-phonetic) and top-down (syntactic and semantic) information until a single candidate remains, at which time recognition is achieved. In early versions of the theory, activation is a function of an exact match between acoustic-phonetic information at the beginnings of words and representations in memory. According to the theory, acoustic-phonetic information is solely responsible for establishing the cohort, and the recognition system tracks the input so closely that minimally discrepant featural information is sufficient to remove an inconsistent candidate from play (P. Warren & Marslen-Wilson, 1987, 1988). In addition, both early and more recent versions of the theory propose a specific and restricted competition process: Words in the cohort are

not assumed to affect the activation levels of one another; the effect of a competitor on its target arises through its mere presence in the cohort as a candidate for recognition. For example, recognition of the input word *elephant* must wait until the word diverges—or becomes unique—from its competitor, *elevator* (see, however, Marslen-Wilson, Tyler, Waksler, & Older, 1994).

Cohort theory has been very successful in focusing attention on the temporal dynamics of spoken word recognition. In particular, the theory provides an elegant account of the earliness of word recognition, stating that spoken words, in the absence of overlapping cohort competitors, may be identified well before their offsets. The theory also proposes an explicit mechanism for the effects of context on word recognition: Top-down information may speed recognition by eliminating competitors from the cohort. The early theory's strong emphasis on exact match between input and representation, its rejection of sublexical levels of representation (discussed later), and its lack of computational specificity are among its notable shortcomings. Many of these concerns have been addressed by a more recent, computationally explicit version of the theory (Gaskell & Marslen-Wilson, 1997, 1999) that adopts a distributed representational format for modeling the mapping of form onto meaning. Nevertheless, the newer theory still preserves the notion of lexical competition without lateral inhibition and eschews intermediate sublexical representations between feature and word.

TRACE

The TRACE model of spoken word recognition (McClelland & Elman, 1986) is an interactive-activation (or local-connectionist) model of spoken word recognition. The TRACE model consists of three levels of primitive processing units corresponding to features, phonemes, and words. These processing units have excitatory connections between levels and inhibitory connections within levels. These connections serve to raise and lower activation levels of the nodes depending on the stimulus input and on the activity of the overall system.

The hallmark of TRACE is its interactivity. By passing activation between levels, the model serves to confirm and accentuate evidence in the input corresponding to a given feature, phoneme, and word. For example, evidence consistent with voicing (as in the consonants /b/, /d/, or /g/) will cause the voiced feature at the lowest level of the model to become active, which in turn will pass its activation to all voiced phonemes at the next level of units, which will in turn activate words containing those phonemes. Moreover, through lateral inhibition among units within a level, winning hypotheses may easily come to dominate other competing units that are also momentarily consistent with the input. Thus, evidence for the word *cat* at the lexical level will cause *cat*'s unit to send inhibitory information to similar, competing lexical units (e.g., for *pat*), helping to ensure that the best candidate word will win.

TRACE has been enormously influential, owing primarily to its computational specificity and to the broad range of phenomena for which it attempts to account (Norris, 1994). Simulations of the model are readily available, making direct tests of the model's behavior relatively easy to conduct. However, TRACE incorporates a decidedly questionable architecture: Its systems of nodes and connections are duplicated over successive time slices of the input—a rather inelegant (and psychologically implausible) means of dealing with the temporal dynamics of spoken word recognition.

Shortlist

Like TRACE, Norris' (1994) Shortlist model is a connectionist model of spoken word recognition. In the first stage of the model, a shortlist of word candidates is derived that consists of lexical items that match the bottom-up speech input. In the second stage of processing, the shortlist of lexical items enters into a network of word units, much like the lexical level of TRACE. Lexical units at this second level of processing compete with one another (via lateral inhibitory links) for recognition.

The Shortlist model is attractive for two primary reasons: First, the model attempts to provide an explicit account of segmentation of words from fluent speech via mechanisms of lexical competition. Among the first computationally explicit models, Shortlist was purposefully designed to simulate effects of subsequent context on spoken word recognition, thereby attempting to account for the process by which individual words are pulled out of the speech stream. Second, Shortlist improves on the highly unrealistic architecture of TRACE, in which single words are represented by a plethora of identical nodes across time.

Recently, the Shortlist model has attracted considerable attention as the prime example of an autonomous model of recognition. Unlike TRACE, Shortlist does not allow for top-down lexical influences on its phoneme units; flow of information between phoneme and word is unidirectional and bottom-up. Thus, the Shortlist model embodies the notion—which has received some empirical support (Burton, Baum, & Blumstein, 1989; Cutler, Norris, et al., 1987; McQueen, 1991)—that the processing of phonemes in the input is unaffected by (or autonomous of) top-down, lexical influences. This central tenet of the Shortlist model (and its companion model, Merge) has engendered a lively debate in the literature between the autonomist and interactionist positions (see Norris, McQueen, & Cutler, 2000, and the accompanying responses). As yet, no unequivocal support has emerged for either side. However, Shortlist remains a particularly attractive alternative to the TRACE model, primarily because of its more plausible architecture and its superiority in accounting for lexical segmentation in fluent speech.

Neighborhood Activation Model and PARSYN

Over the past few years, Luce and colleagues have devoted considerable effort to modeling the processes of activation and competition. According to their Neighborhood Activation Model (NAM; Luce & Pisoni, 1998; Luce, Pisoni, & Goldinger, 1990), stimulus input directly activates a set (or neighborhood) of similar-sounding acoustic-phonetic patterns in memory. The activation levels of the acoustic-phonetic patterns are a function of their degree of match with the input. In turn, these patterns activate a set of word decision units tuned to the patterns. The word decision units compute probabilities for each pattern based on (a) the frequency of the word to which the pattern corresponds, (b) the activation level of the pattern (which depends on the pattern's match to the input), and (c) the activation levels and frequencies of all other words activated in the system. The word decision unit that computes the highest probability wins, and its word is recognized. In short, word decision units compute probability values based on the word's acoustic-phonetic similarity to the input, the word's frequency, and the activation levels and frequencies of all other words activated in memory.

NAM predicts that multiple activation has its consequences: Spoken words with many similar-sounding neighbors should be processed more slowly and less accurately than are words with few neighbors. That is, NAM predicts effects of *neighborhood density* arising from competition among multiply activated representations of words in memory. These predictions have been confirmed in many studies: Words in high-density similarity neighborhoods are indeed processed

less quickly and less accurately than are words in low-density neighborhoods (Cluff & Luce, 1990; Goldinger, Luce, & Pisoni, 1989; Goldinger, Luce, Pisoni, & Marcario, 1992; Luce & Pisoni, 1998; Vitevitch & Luce, 1998, 1999).

Recently, Luce, Goldinger, Auer, and Vitevitch (2000) instantiated NAM in a more explicit processing model called PARSYN. PARSYN has three levels of units: (a) an input allophone level, (b) a pattern allophone level, and (c) a word level. Connections between units within a level are mutually inhibitory with one exception: Links among allophone units at the pattern level are facilitative across temporal positions. Connections between levels are facilitative also with one exception: The word level sends inhibitory information back to the pattern level, essentially quelling activation in the system once a single word has gained a marked advantage over its competitors.

PARSYN is designed to simulate the effects of both *neighborhood activation* and *probabilistic phonotactics* on the processing of spoken words. Effects of neighborhood density arise primarily from lateral inhibition at the lexical level. Effects of probabilistic phonotactics arise from interconnections and activation levels of units at the pattern level. Moreover, PARSYN was developed to overcome two significant shortcomings of NAM. First, PARSYN is an attempt to account better for the temporal dynamics of recognition, including the ebb and flow of neighborhood activation and phonotactic constraints. In addition, PARSYN incorporates a sublexical level of representation missing in the original NAM. We discuss the issue of sublexical representations in more detail later.

Issues

We now turn to a discussion of several core issues that occupy much attention in current research and theory on spoken word recognition, all of which are related directly or indirectly to the original issues addressed by the cohort model. These are (a) the nature of lexical activation and competition, (b) the nature of sublexical and lexical representations and their interactions, (c) segmentation of spoken words from fluent speech, and (d) representational specificity of spoken words.

Activation and Competition in Spoken Word Recognition

Current models of spoken word recognition typically share the assumption that the perception of spoken words involves two fundamental processes: activation and competition (see Luce & Pisoni, 1998; Marslen-Wilson, 1989; McClelland & Elman, 1986; Norris, 1994). Although there is some consensus that the input activates a set of candidates in memory that are subsequently discriminated among, the details of the activation and competition processes are still in dispute.

Activation.   In their characterization of the activation process, models of spoken word recognition fall into roughly two categories. *Radical activation models* (e.g., TRACE, Shortlist, PARSYN) propose that form-based representations that are consistent with stimulus input may be activated at any point in the speech stream. For example, spoken input corresponding to *cat* may activate *pat* based on the overlapping vowel and final consonant, even though the two words differ initially. Of course, most radical activation models afford priority to *cat* in recognition, primarily because of the relative temporal positions of the mismatch and overlap. Nevertheless, radical activation models propose that any consistency between input and representation may result in some degree of activation. *Constrained activation models* hold that form-based representations respond only to specific portions of the input, such as word beginnings (Marslen-Wilson, 1987, 1989) or strong syllables (Cutler, 1989; Cutler

& Norris, 1988). A primary example is the Cohort model, which gives word-initial information priority in activating the set of representations (i.e., the cohort) that compete for recognition. A fundamental assumption of Cohort is the *minimal discrepancy hypothesis;* namely, minimally inconsistent or discrepant information in speech input suffices to exclude representations from the recognition process (P. Warren & Marslen-Wilson, 1987, 1988). Thus, word-initial featural information indicating a /k/, as in *cat,* inhibits activation of all representations not beginning with /k/ (e.g., *pat;* see Marslen-Wilson, Moss, & Van Halen, 1996). This same hypothesis also incorporates the notion of the *divergence* or *uniqueness point.* According to the Cohort model, a word is recognized at the precise moment when it diverges from all other candidates in the lexicon (the divergence or uniqueness point). As a spoken word is processed in time, competitors are eliminated from the cohort by discrepant bottom-up information until only one candidate remains (Marslen-Wilson, 1989). Crucially, information after the uniqueness point is predicted to have no demonstrable effect on lexical activation, even if this information is consistent with the competitor.

Evidence in favor of the minimal discrepancy hypothesis comes from a series of gating experiments examining the role of coarticulatory information in listeners' abilities to guess the identities of words based on their fragments (P. Warren & Marslen-Wilson, 1987, 1988). Listeners were remarkably sensitive to fine acoustic-phonetic detail and did not wait until the ends of segments to identify a word correctly. The implications of this work are clear: Minimally discrepant information in speech controls perceptual choice, ruling out alternatives (i.e., competitors) at the earliest possible point in time.

However, research on form-based (or sound-based) priming has not supported the minimal discrepancy hypothesis. For example, Connine, Blasko, and Titone (1993) found facilitative priming effects between rhyming nonword primes and real-word targets, suggesting that overlapping word-initial information is not crucial for activation of competitors. Marslen-Wilson et al. (1996; see also Marslen-Wilson & Zwitserlood, 1989) also obtained rhyme-priming effects in an intramodal, auditory prime–auditory target task, although they found no evidence of rhyme priming in a cross-modal task using auditory primes and visual targets (see Connine, Titone, Deelman, & Blasko, 1997, for a discussion of this last finding).

Luce et al. (2000) used primes and targets that were phonetically similar but shared no position-specific segments (e.g., *shun-gong*). Processing times were significantly slower for targets following phonetically related primes than to targets following unrelated primes. This result is consistent with the radical activation account, given that none of the prime-target pairs shared word-initial segments. Further support for radical activation models was obtained by Allopena, Magnuson, and Tanenhaus (1998). Using a paradigm that tracked eye movements as subjects followed spoken instructions to manipulate objects on a computer screen, Allopena et al. found that rhyming competitors are activated early in recognition. When asked to click on a picture of a *beaker,* subjects' fixation probabilities indicated that they also considered a picture of a *speaker* to be a likely candidate. Remarkably, fixation probabilities to the competitor started increasing prior to offset of the spoken word, suggesting that eye movements closely tracked competitor activation. Thus, shared word-initial information is not necessary to activate competitors (the spoken word *beaker* resulted in increased probabilities to fixate on the picture of the *speaker*).

All told, evidence from both intramodal phonetic priming and eye movement studies casts doubt on the minimal discrepancy hypothesis. Moreover, results from research on the activation of embedded words in longer carrier words (e.g., *lock* in *hemlock;* Luce & Cluff, 1998; Luce & Lyons, 1999; Shillcock, 1990; Vroomen & de Gelder, 1997) and from a number of other sources (Andruski, Blumstein, & Burton, 1994; Charles-Luce, Luce, & Cluff, 1990; Cluff & Luce, 1990; Goodman & Huttenlocher, 1988; see also Mattys, 1997) also call the hypothesis into question, thus supporting the general claims of radical activation models.

Although consistent with a radical activation account of spoken word recognition, the data point more toward a modification, rather than an outright rejection, of the Cohort model's original claims regarding the nature of the activated competitor environment. A marked left-to-right bias exists in the processing of spoken words, supporting the spirit, if not the precise detail, of the Cohort model (see Luce, 2001). Under optimal listening conditions, word onsets appear to determine strongly the activation of competitors in memory, and unfolding acoustic-phonetic information over time guides the activation process. However, that activation of form-based representations is not exclusively limited to onsets.

Competition. In activation-competition models the hallmark of the lexical recognition process is competition among multiple representations of words activated in memory. As a result, the role of competition has been a primary focus of research and theory on spoken word recognition in the last few years (e.g., Cluff & Luce, 1990; Goldinger, Luce, & Pisoni, 1989; Marslen-Wilson, 1989; McQueen, Norris, & Cutler, 1994; Norris, McQueen, & Cutler, 1995; Vitevitch & Luce, 1998, 1999).

Evidence for competition among form-based lexical representations activated in memory has come from a variety of experimental paradigms. For example, Luce and colleagues (Cluff & Luce, 1990; Luce & Pisoni, 1998) have shown that *similarity neighborhood density* and *frequency,* both indexes of lexical competition, have demonstrable effects on processing time and accuracy in speeded single-word shadowing, auditory lexical decision, and perceptual identification. Recall that a similarity neighborhood is defined as a collection of words that are similar to a given target word. For example, the target word *cat* has neighbors *pat, kit, catty, cad, scat,* and so on (for details, see Luce & Pisoni, 1998; Luce et al., 2000).

Neighborhoods may vary on both the density and frequency of the words that comprise them. Some words (e.g., *cat*) have many high frequency neighbors, whereas others (e.g., *try*) have fewer, less frequent neighbors. As previously noted, Luce and colleagues have shown that words residing in densely populated similarity neighborhoods, in which lexical competition is predicted to be strong, are processed less quickly and less accurately than are words residing in sparsely populated neighborhoods. Moreover, in similarity neighborhoods composed of high-frequency words, competition is more severe than in neighborhoods of low-frequency words, resulting in slower and less accurate processing (see also Goldinger et al., 1989; Goldinger et al., 1992; Luce et al., 2000.)

Although there is now considerable evidence for competitive effects in spoken word recognition, debate continues over the precise mechanisms underlying lexical competition. As noted earlier, lateral inhibition among lexical representations is a fundamental feature of the competitive process in models of recognition such as TRACE, Shortlist, and PARSYN. The Cohort model, on the other hand, eschews the notion of lateral inhibition in favor of a competitive process that is modulated primarily by top-down (context-driven) and bottom-up (stimulus driven) facilitation

and inhibition (Marslen-Wilson, 1987, 1990; see, however, Marslen-Wilson et al., 1996). More recently, Gaskell and Marslen-Wilson (1997, 1999) have proposed that speech input consistent with many lexical representations (or neighbors) results in more diffusely activated distributed representations, producing effects of lexical competition in the absence of lateral inhibition. In short, although most agree that lexical items activated in memory somehow compete, there is little consensus regarding the exact mechanisms of this lexical interaction.

The Nature of Lexical and Sublexical Representations

Research on lexical competition has focused primarily on interactions among representations of *words*. However, an equally crucial topic concerns the nature of sublexical (or segmental) representations. Some have argued against the existence of any sort of sublexical representation intervening in the mapping between feature and word (Marslen-Wilson & Warren, 1994). Indeed, a lively debate has arisen among the proponents of sublexical representations concerning the nature of the interaction—or lack thereof—between segmental and lexical representations. We first consider the argument against sublexical representations and then discuss recent research examining the consequences of sublexical patterning (or probabilistic phonotactics) for lexical processing. The available evidence suggests a role for sublexical representations, although the debate over the interaction of lexical and sublexical units is still very much alive (see Norris et al., 2000; Pitt & Samuel, 1995).

Against Sublexical Representations. Mainstream speech perception researchers have long assumed that the speech waveform is recoded into successively more abstract representations, proceeding from acoustic to phonetic feature, from phonetic feature to segment, from segment to syllable, and, ultimately, to lexical representation (Pisoni & Luce, 1987). This central dogma was challenged by Marslen-Wilson and Warren (1994; see also Klatt, 1979, for a similar view), who argued for a direct mapping of feature to word, with no intervening representations. Drawing inspiration from Streeter and Nigro (1979) and Whalen (1984, 1991), Marslen-Wilson and Warren generated a set of cross-spliced words and nonwords in which coarticulatory information signaling phonetic segments mismatched. For example, the initial consonant and vowel of the word *jog* was spliced onto the final consonant from the word *job,* creating a subcategorical mismatch between the coarticulatory information in the vowel of the spliced stimulus and the final consonant. That is, information in the vowel of the spliced stimulus was consistent with the final consonant /g/, *not* the spliced consonant /b/. Similar nonword stimuli were constructed with mismatching coarticulatory information between the vowel and final consonant (e.g., the consonant and vowel of *smod* was cross-spliced with the final consonant of *smob*).

The results from experiments examining subcategorical mismatch in spliced word and nonword stimuli suggested that mismatching coarticulatory information had consequences only for stimuli that activated lexical representations (i.e., words cross-spliced with other words and words cross-spliced with nonwords). Nonwords cross-spliced with other nonwords (e.g., *smob*) failed to show effects of subcategorical mismatch. According to Marslen-Wilson and Warren, mismatching coarticulatory information can be detected only when representations at the lexical level are activated. Thus, the failure to observe subcategorical mismatch for nonwords is presumably a direct consequence of the absence of sublexical representations that can detect the mismatching information in the nonwords that are cross-spliced with other nonwords.

Later research revealed that conclusions regarding the demise of the segmental representation were premature. Two problems arose, one empirical and one theoretical. First, McQueen, Norris, and Cutler (1999) demonstrated that the asymmetry between cross-spliced words and nonwords varied as a function of task demands, a demonstration that calls into question the empirical basis of Marslen-Wilson and Warren's original conclusions. Equally as damning, it has been shown that models with a phonemic level of representation could simulate Marslen-Wilson and Warren's original data pattern, thus removing the theoretical underpinnings for their claims that sublexical representations are not operative in spoken word recognition.

Evidence for Two Levels of Processing: Probabilistic Phonotactics. At present, there is little compelling evidence against intermediate representations in spoken word recognition. Indeed, recent research on probabilistic phonotactics strongly suggests that sublexical representations have demonstrable effects on processing of both words and nonwords (Pitt & Samuel, 1995).

Probabilistic phonotactics refers to the relative frequencies of segments and sequences of segments in syllables and words. Using estimates of positional probabilities based on a computerized lexicon, Treiman, Kessler, Knewasser, Tincoff, and Bowman (1996) found that participants' performance on rating and blending tasks was sensitive to probabilistic differences among phonetic sequences. Participants in the rating task judged high-probability patterns to be more "English-like" than low-probability patterns (see also Vitevitch, Luce, Charles-Luce, & Kemmerer, 1997). When subjects were asked to combine two sound patterns into a single item in the blending task, high-probability sequences tended to remain intact more often than did low-probability sequences.

Vitevitch et al. (1997) examined the effects of probabilistic phonotactic information on *processing times* for spoken stimuli. They used disyllabic nonwords composed of phonetic sequences that were legal in English but varied in their segmental and sequential probabilities. Using a speeded single-word shadowing task, Vitevitch et al. found that disyllabic nonwords composed of common segments and sequences of segments were repeated faster than were nonwords composed of less common segments and sequences.

Taken together, these studies demonstrate that information regarding the legality and probability of phonotactic patterns has demonstrable influences on the representation and processing of spoken stimuli (see also Massaro & Cohen, 1983). A potential anomaly has arisen, however: The effects of phonotactics that have been demonstrated thus far seem to contradict the predictions of—and evidence for—the class of models that emphasizes the roles of activation and competition in spoken word recognition. Recall that according to NAM, spoken words that sound like many other words (i.e., words in dense similarity neighborhoods) should be recognized more slowly and less accurately than are words with few similar-sounding words (i.e., words in sparse similarity neighborhoods). A contradiction is revealed by the observation that high-probability segments and sequences of segments are found in words occurring in high-density neighborhoods, whereas low-probability segments and sequences of segments are found in words occurring in low-density neighborhoods. Thus, NAM predicts that high-probability phonotactic stimuli should be processed *more slowly* than low probability phonotactic stimuli, in contrast to the findings of Vitevitch et al. (1997).

To explore these seemingly contradictory results, Vitevitch and Luce (1998; see also Vitevitch & Luce, 1999) presented participants in a speeded auditory shadowing task with monosyllabic words and nonwords that varied on similarity neighborhood density and phonotactic probability. They generated two sets of words and nonwords: (1) high phonotactic probability/high neighborhood density stimuli and (2) low phonotactic probability/low neighborhood density stimuli. Vitevitch and Luce replicated the pattern of results obtained in the Vitevitch et al. (1997) study for nonwords: High probability/density nonwords were repeated more quickly than were low probability/density nonwords. However, the words followed the pattern of results predicted by NAM. That is, high probability/density words were repeated more slowly than were low probability/density words.

Vitevitch and Luce (1998, 1999) suggested that two levels of representation and processing—one lexical and one sublexical—are responsible for differential effects of phonotactics and neighborhoods (see also Cutler & Norris, 1979; Foss & Blank, 1980; McClelland & Elman, 1986; Norris, 1994; Radeau, Morais, & Segui, 1995). In particular, Vitevitch and Luce suggested that facilitative effects of probabilistic phonotactics reflect differences among activation levels of *sublexical* units, whereas effects of similarity neighborhoods arise from competition among *lexical* representations. Models of spoken word recognition such as TRACE, Shortlist, and NAM propose that lexical representations compete with and/or inhibit one another (see Cluff & Luce, 1990; Goldinger, Luce, & Pisoni, 1989; Marslen-Wilson, 1989; McQueen, Norris, & Cutler, 1994; Norris, McQueen, & Cutler, 1995). Thus, words occurring in dense similarity neighborhoods succumb to more intense competition among similar sounding words activated in memory, resulting in slower processing. Apparently, effects of lexical competition overshadow any benefit these high-density words accrue from having high probability phonotactic patterns. Because nonwords do not make direct contact with a single lexical unit and thus do not immediately initiate large-scale lexical competition, effects of segmental and sequential probabilities emerge for these stimuli. That is, in the absence of strong lexical competition effects associated with word stimuli, higher activation levels of sublexical units (i.e., those with higher phonotactic probabilities) afford advantage to high-probability nonwords (see Luce & Large, in press).

Research on phonotactics and neighborhood activation thus supports the hypothesis of two levels of representation and process in spoken word recognition. Thus, recognition models such as TRACE, Shortlist, and PARSYN, which incorporate *both* lexical and sublexical levels of representation and processing, may more accurately account for effects of spoken word recognition as a function of neighborhood activation and probabilistic phonotactics than can models such as NAM and Cohort.

Segmentation of Spoken Words from Fluent Speech

To this point, we have focused on research devoted primarily to understanding the perception of isolated spoken words. However, since the 1970s (and even earlier; e.g., G. A. Miller, Heise, & Lichten, 1951), much research has examined the perception of words in larger units. Indeed, Marslen-Wilson's seminal work on cohort theory addressed the role of sentential context on recognition (see also Cole & Jakimik, 1980). Recent work continuing along this path has focused in particular on the fundamental issue of how spoken words are segmented from fluent speech.

The listener's phenomenal experience of continuous speech is one of a succession of discretely produced words. However, the search for reliable acoustic information marking the beginnings and endings of words has met with little success (Nakatani & Dukes, 1977; Lehiste, 1972). Given that the signal fails to mark consistently the boundaries of words in spoken discourse, a crucial question in research on spoken word recognition concerns the means by which the perceptual system segments the continuous stream of speech. Four traditional solutions to the problem of segmentation have been proposed: phonetic, prosodic, lexical, and phonotactic.

According to the *phonetic solution,* the speech signal may provide cues to the position-specificity of phonemes (which are sometimes referred to as *context-sensitive allophones;* Church, 1987), thus providing the listener with information regarding beginnings and endings of words. For example, syllable-initial and syllable-final stops are phonetically and acoustically distinct, distinguished in part by degree of aspiration (e.g., Davidson-Nielson, 1974; Dutton, 1992). In particular, aspirated /t/ is always syllable-initial (see Church, 1987). Previous research has demonstrated that some phonetic cues may be used in segmentation. Among the possible cues to word boundaries that have been shown to facilitate segmentation are allophonic variation of /l/ and /r/ (Nakatani & Dukes, 1977, 1979), aspiration of word-initial stops, and duration of word-initial segments (Christie, 1977). This collection of cues, among others (see Dutton, 1992), may assist the listener in identifying consonants as pre- or postvocalic, thus indicating whether a given consonant occurs at the beginning or end of a syllable or word. To date, however, the lack of success at identifying all but a restricted set of possible phonetic cues to word boundaries suggests that the phonetic solution may be severely limited.

According to the *prosodic solution* to the segmentation problem, listeners parse the speech stream by exploiting rhythmic characteristics of their language (Cutler, 1996; Cutler & Norris, 1988; Cutler & Butterfield, 1992; Vroomen, van Zon, & de Gelder, 1996). The most notable hypothesis representing the prosodic solution to the segmentation problem is embodied in Cutler and Norris's (1988) *metrical segmentation strategy* (MSS). MSS asserts that lexical access is attempted based on each strong syllable. Cutler and Norris argued that because most strong syllables in English are word-initial (see Cutler & Carter, 1987), a strategy of attempting lexical access at each strong syllable would meet with frequent success.

Many models of spoken word recognition espouse the *lexical solution,* whereby segmentation is a byproduct of the recognition process. Cole and Jakimik (1980) proposed that words in fluent connected speech are recognized one at a time in sequential order. The word-by-word assumption obviates the need for any explicit segmentation process because the recognition of a word makes evident both the end of the just-recognized word and the beginning of the next word. Likewise, the Cohort model (Marslen-Wilson, 1992; Marslen-Wilson & Welsh, 1978; Marslen-Wilson & Zwitserlood, 1989) characterizes word recognition as a strictly sequential process in which segmentation is accomplished incidentally as each word in the speech stream is recognized. Although both models have intuitive appeal and appear to match our experience of recognizing one spoken word after another, the phenomenon of lexical embeddedness is problematic for approaches that assume that segmentation is a byproduct of recognition (see also Tabossi, Burani, & Scott, 1995). In particular, it is unclear how a word-by-word approach would deal with the presence of a short word embedded in a longer lexical item (e.g., *cat* in *catatonic*; see McQueen & Cutler, 1992; McQueen, Cutler, Briscoe, & Norris, 1995; Luce, 1986; Luce & Lyons,

1999; see also Bard, Shillcock, & Altmann, 1988; Grosjean, 1985).

Other models of spoken word recognition espousing the lexical solution to segmentation emphasize the role of *competition* among lexical candidates (e.g., Norris, McQueen, & Cutler, 1995; Vroomen & de Gelder, 1995). For example, in Shortlist, segmentation occurs via a competitive process in which the unit most closely matching the *entire* input receives the most activation.

Recently, research on spoken language has focused on a fourth potential solution to the segmentation problem: probabilistic phonotactics (see Massaro & Cohen, 1983). If listeners are sensitive to variations in the frequencies of segments and their sequences, probabilistic phonotactics may provide useful information for segmentation. Norris, McQueen, Cutler, and Butterfield (1997) demonstrated that listeners take into account phonotactic information when attempting to detect real words embedded in nonsense words (accomplishing this, of course, requires the identification of the boundaries of the target words). Norris et al. demonstrated that participants were able to detect words embedded in nonsense words faster and more accurately when the additional segments of the nonsense words formed phonotactically legal syllables (or possible words) than when the additional segments did not constitute well-formed syllables in English. That is, subjects were faster and more accurate at detecting "apple" in "vuffapple," where "vuff" is itself a phonotactically legal syllable, than "apple" in "fapple," in which the additional segment "f" does not constitute a legal syllable. These results suggest that listeners are able to make use of phonotactic information on-line in parsing fluent speech.

McQueen (1998) used word spotting to investigate the role of phonotactics as a cue to syllable boundaries in Dutch. He hypothesized that two-segment sequences (or biphones) that do not occur *within* syllables signal syllable boundaries. McQueen embedded real Dutch words at the beginnings or ends of disyllabic nonsense words. The boundaries between the two syllables consisted of biphones that do or do not occur within syllables in Dutch. Presumably, biphones that do not occur within syllables should make detection of words embedded in nonwords easier by marking a syllable boundary. McQueen found that participants were faster and more accurate at recognizing words whose boundaries were aligned with phonotactically specified syllable boundaries than at recognizing those that were misaligned, demonstrating that participants are able to use phonotactic information about biphones to identify boundaries of syllables (and thus of possible words).

Gaygen and Luce (2001) also investigated the potential role of probabilistic phonotactics in the segmentation of words from continuous speech. They hypothesized that if listeners encounter a sequence of segments that do not typically occur within words (i.e., a low-probability sequence), they may hypothesize the presence of a word boundary, thus facilitating segmentation. To test this hypothesis, Gaygen and Luce embedded CVC words in a sequence of CVC stimuli, forming triads of CVC items in which the middle CVC could be a word. For example, the participant's task might be to detect the word *rack* in the sequence *moid rack doog*. The last consonant of the first nonword and the first consonant of the target word could be high or low in probability. (In the example, the *dr* in *moid rack* is high in probability.) If phonotactics aids segmentation, low-probability sequences of segments should make target detection easier. Their results demonstrated that low phonotactic probabilities at the beginnings of the target words did indeed speed detection, providing further support for the hypothesis that phonotactics aids segmentation.

Although the available evidence supports some role for probabilistic phonotactics in the segmentation of spoken words, it has become increasingly clear that segmentation is best viewed as a constraint-satisfaction problem in which the perceiver employs various solutions—phonetic, prosodic, lexical, and phonotactic—to determine the beginnings and endings of words in fluent speech.

Representational Specificity

Theories of spoken word recognition have traditionally assumed, either implicitly (e.g., McClelland & Elman, 1986; Luce & Pisoni, 1998; Norris, 1994) or explicitly (e.g., Jackson & Morton, 1984), that lexical items are represented in memory by abstract phonological codes that preserve only information that is relevant for lexical discrimination. In many current models of word recognition, stimulus variation—arising from factors such as differences in speaking rates and the identities of the talkers—is treated as irrelevant information that is discarded early in the encoding process. For example, feature-based accounts of speech perception (see Klatt, 1989; Pisoni & Luce, 1987; Marslen-Wilson & Warren, 1994) have proposed that speech sounds and words are processed using the elemental features of linguistic description (e.g., [vocalic], [consonantal], [sonorant]). However, spoken words may differ on many physical dimensions that are not captured by these features. The normalization process is responsible for winnowing the information in the speech signal and extracting only the featural information that is relevant for identification. This process thereby serves a substantial data reduction function that may ultimately result in considerable economy of process and representation.

Despite the arguments that have been made for abstract lexical representations in memory, recent research (see Goldinger, 1996, 1998, for reviews) has suggested that putatively irrelevant surface details of words (e.g., information specific to a given talker) are preserved in some form in memory. These findings regarding specificity effects have led to the proposal (e.g., Goldinger, 1996, 1998) that lexical items are represented in memory by exemplar-based representations that preserve, rather than discard, much of the physical detail of the stimulus.

Research has demonstrated that variation in the surface details of spoken stimuli (usually measured by changes in the identity of the talker, hereafter referred to broadly as changes in voice) has implications for both identification and memory. Typically, subjects have more difficulty in identifying (Mullennix, Pisoni, & Martin, 1989), recognizing (Church & Schacter, 1994; Goldinger, 1996; Palmeri, Goldinger, & Pisoni, 1993; Schacter & Church, 1992; Sheffert, 1995, 1999a, 1999b), and recalling (Goldinger, Pisoni, & Logan, 1991; Martin, Mullennix, Pisoni, & Summers, 1989) lists of stimuli composed of words spoken by multiple talkers compared to lists composed of stimuli spoken by a single talker (see Palmeri, Goldinger, & Pisoni, 1993, for one interesting exception). One explanation for these effects is that normalization processes reduce resources available for encoding, rehearsal, or both.

The effects of changes in the surface details of stimuli between study and test in recognition memory experiments have been of particular interest in the literature (Church & Schacter, 1994; Schacter & Church, 1992). For example, Goldinger (1996) presented words in explicit (recognition) and implicit (perceptual identification in noise) tasks with varying delays between study and test. He found significant effects of voice in both recognition and identification, demonstrating that voice effects are not, in fact, restricted to implicit tasks. However, Goldinger found that effects of voice were reduced more by delay between study and test in the explicit task than in the implicit task. In another experiment, Goldinger manipulated voice and levels of processing in the study-test implicit-explicit format. His results demonstrated that effects of voice varied with level of processing, such that strongest effects of stimulus specificity were observed in the shallower processing conditions, especially for recognition memory.

Although somewhat varied, the overall results of studies examining the effects of voice on identification and memory are consistent with exemplar-based models of memory. According to these models, a new representation of a stimulus item is stored in memory each time it is encountered, and it is hypothesized that these representations preserve surface information about the stimulus. In this respect, exemplar-based models of speech perception bear a resemblance to viewpoint-dependent models of object-recognition described in by Tarr and Vuong (Chap. 7, this volume). In both domains, perceivers are held to store multiple representations of a particular distal stimulus: a visual object in one case and a word (or lexical item) in the other.

One advantage of exemplar-based models is that they have the potential for solving the long-standing problem of perceptual normalization in speech perception by dispelling the notion that the ultimate goal of the perceptual process is to map acoustic-phonetic information onto *abstract* form-based representations of words in memory. In exemplar-based models, the representational currency of the perceptual encoding process is more or less true to the details of the stimulus itself. In an application of this general theoretical approach to spoken word recognition, Goldinger (1996, 1998) has proposed an exemplar-based lexicon in which the individual memory traces themselves may encode both abstract and surface information (see also Luce & Lyons, 1998; Luce, Charles-Luce, &

McLennan, 1999) and in which the degree of stimulus specificity depends crucially on attentional factors during encoding.

THE DEVELOPMENT OF SPEECH PERCEPTION CAPACITIES: EARLY STUDIES

Motivated by the view that perceivers first recover the minimum sized units of organization and use these to build up representations of higher levels of linguistic organization, early studies focused on infants' abilities to perceive phonetic differences. What kinds of phonetic distinctions can infants perceive, and what mechanisms underlie their abilities? Are the mechanisms specific to speech perception, or are they used more generally in auditory processing? What are infants' capacities for coping with variability in the speech signal? In addition to these issues, which are familiar from adult studies, research with infants has provided the opportunity to explore how experience with a particular language affects the development of speech perception capacities.

Infants' Discriminative Capacities

When Eimas and his colleagues began investigating infant speech perception capacities, two questions motivated their study (Eimas, Siqueland, Jusczyk, & Vigorito, 1971). First, can infants discriminate a minimal phonetic contrast between two consonants? Second, if so, do they show categorical perception for this contrast? Eimas et al. used the high-amplitude-sucking procedure to test 1- and 4-month-olds on contrasts involving [ba] and [pa]. The different stimuli varied in voice onset time (VOT), which refers to the moment at which the vocal cords begin to vibrate relative to the release of closure in the vocal tract. If vocal chord vibration begins within

25 ms of the release of the lips, the resulting sound is heard as [b], whereas [p] is perceived if it is delayed by more than 25 ms (Abramson & Lisker, 1967). Eimas et al. presented infants with syllables that differed by 20 ms in VOT. For one group (between category), infants were familiarized with a syllable from one phonemic category (e.g., [ba]) and then were presented with one from the other phonemic category (e.g., [pa]). For another group (within category), both the familiarization syllable and the subsequent test syllable came from the same phonemic category (i.e., either two different [ba] stimuli or two different [pa] stimuli). Finally, a third group (control) continued to hear the original familiarization syllable for the entire test session. Relative to the control group, only infants in the between-category group significantly increased their sucking rates to the new syllable. Thus, infants could detect VOT differences, but, like adults, their discrimination of these differences is categorical.

Many subsequent studies explored infants' abilities to discriminate different types of phonetic contrasts. Infants were also found to discriminate consonant differences involving place of articulation (Eimas, 1974; Levitt, Jusczyk, Murray, & Carden, 1988; Moffitt, 1971; Morse, 1972) and manner of articulation (Eimas, 1975; Eimas & Miller, 1980b; Hillenbrand, Minifie, & Edwards, 1979). Not only do infants discriminate contrasts between initial segments of syllables, but they also detect contrasts at the ends of syllables (Jusczyk, 1977) and in the middle of multisyllabic utterances (Jusczyk, Copan, & Thompson, 1978; Jusczyk & Thompson, 1978; Karzon, 1985; Williams, 1977). Moreover, infants also discriminate vowel contrasts (Kuhl & Miller, 1982; Swoboda, Kass, Morse, & Leavitt, 1978; Swoboda, Morse, & Leavitt, 1976; Trehub, 1973). Like that of adults, infants' discrimination of vowel contrasts is continuous in that they can discriminate different tokens from the same vowel category (Swoboda et al., 1976).

Two different sorts of investigations suggested that prior experience is not a significant factor in infants' abilities to discriminate phonetic contrasts during the first few months of life. First, several investigations used speech sound contrasts not found in the language spoken in the infant's environment (Lasky, Syrdal-Lasky, & Klein, 1975; Streeter, 1976; Trehub, 1976). Even when infants had no prior experience with a particular phonetic contrast, they were able to discriminate it. Streeter (1976) found that Kikuyu-learning 1- to 4-month-olds distinguished a [ba]-[pa] contrast despite its absence in Kikuyu. A second kind of indication that infants' discrimination abilities do not depend on a long period of prior exposure to a language came from studies with newborns. Bertoncini, Bijeljac-Babic, Blumstein, and Mehler (1987) showed that infants only a few days old discriminate phonetic contrasts. Given adults' difficulties in discriminating contrasts outside of their native language (Miyawaki et al., 1975; Trehub, 1976), infants' abilities are quite remarkable.

Mechanisms Underlying Infants' Discriminative Capacities

When Eimas et al. (1971) conducted their study, categorical perception was still believed to be specific to speech processing. Consequently, their findings were taken as an indication that infants are innately endowed with specialized speech processing abilities. Eimas (1974, 1975) provided further support for this view when he found differences in infants' discrimination of the same information in speech and nonspeech contexts. However, other studies with infants demonstrated categorical discrimination of certain nonspeech contrasts (Jusczyk, Pisoni, Walley, & Murray, 1980). Strong parallels in how infants processed temporal order differences in non-

speech sounds and how they processed VOT differences in speech sounds suggested that a common auditory processing mechanism might enable discrimination of both kinds of contrasts (see also Jusczyk, Rosner, Reed, & Kennedy, 1989).

Proponents of specialized processing mechanisms also pointed to findings that even 2-month-olds demonstrate an ability to compensate for speaking rate differences in their perception of phonetic contrasts (Eimas & Miller, 1980a; J. L. Miller & Eimas, 1983). For example, infants' discrimination of acoustic cues to the stop/glide contrast between [b] and [w] varies with speaking rate changes; this led Eimas and Miller (1980a,b) to claim that infants possess specialized processing mechanisms to compensate for speaking rate changes. However, Jusczyk, Pisoni, Fernald, Reed, and Myers (1983) found that infants displayed the same pattern in responding to certain nonspeech sounds, suggesting that a general auditory processing mechanism underlies infants' discrimination performance with the speech and nonspeech stimuli.

More recently, Eimas and Miller (1992) demonstrated that 3- to 4-month-olds give evidence of a duplex perception effect when processing speech sounds. They presented an isolated third formant transition critical to distinguishing [da] from [ga] to one ear and the rest of the syllable to the opposite ear. Infants discriminated the patterns corresponding to [da] and [ga] not only in this situation but also when the third formant transition was greatly attenuated in its intensity. In contrast, when the attenuated third formant transitions were presented in isolation, infants' discrimination of these differences was significantly poorer. Because researchers have not yet undertaken comparable studies using nonspeech analogs of the speech stimuli used in duplex perception studies with infants, whether this phenomenon is specific to infants' processing of speech sounds remains to be seen.

How Infants Handle Variability in Speech

The available evidence suggests that even at a young age, infants appear to cope with the variability that exists in different talkers' productions of the same syllables. Kuhl and Miller (1982; Kuhl, 1976) used different tokens of the vowels [a] and [i] to explore 1- to 4-month-olds' abilities to perceive vowel contrasts. The different tokens varied in whether they were produced with a rising or falling pitch. During one phase of the experiment, infants were exposed first to the different tokens of one of the vowels and then to the different tokens of the other vowel. Despite the fact that the pitch characteristics of the tokens varied throughout the experiment, the infants still discriminated the vowel tokens. Kuhl and Miller concluded that even 1-month-olds had the means to generalize different tokens of the same vowel in order to perceive the phonetic contrast.

Subsequently, Kuhl (1979, 1983) showed that 6-month-olds handle variability in productions of the same syllable by different talkers. Infants were initially taught to respond to a vowel contrast between [a] and [i] that was produced by a single talker. Then, Kuhl (1979) gradually introduced tokens of the vowels produced by other talkers into the set to which infants were responding. The final set included tokens from three different talkers, including both males and females. Infants continued to respond to the vowel contrast, which led Kuhl to claim that infants have some capacity for perceptual normalization. Kuhl (1983) extended these findings to the more subtle vowel contrasts between [a] and [O]. Similarly, Jusczyk, Pisoni, and Mullennix (1992) found that even 2-month-olds have some capacity to cope with talker variability in perceiving phonetic contrasts. Nevertheless, the variability did have some impact on infants' encoding and subsequent recall of the sounds. In particular, 2-month-olds gave no evidence of discriminating tokens from multiple talkers

if a brief 2-min delay intervened between familiarization and testing. By comparison, infants given the same delay period but familiarized with tokens produced by a single talker discriminated the stimuli. These findings show that compensating for talker variability does tax infants' abilities to encode and remember speech.

In addition to coping with talker variability, infants display some capacity to handle variability caused by changes in speaking rate (Eimas & Miller, 1980a; J. L. Miller & Eimas, 1983).

Influences of Native Language on Underlying Perceptual Capacities

As noted earlier, infants under the age of 6-months seem to discriminate phonetic contrasts that are not present in their native language. Eventually, however, experience with a language does affect perceptual capacities. When do changes occur in the discrimination of nonnative language speech contrasts?

Werker and Tees (1984) found that sensitivity to nonnative speech contrasts begins to decline between 6 and 12 months. They tested English-learning 6- to 8-month-olds' perception of three phonetic contrasts: an English [ba]-[da] distinction, a Hindi [ta]-[Ta] distinction, and a Nthlakapmx [k'i]- [q'i] distinction. Although neither the Hindi nor the Nthlakapmx contrast occurs in English, the infants discriminated all of the contrasts. However, when 8- to 10-month-olds were tested, only some of them discriminated the two nonnative contrasts, although all of them discriminated the English contrast. By 10 to 12 months, the infants discriminated only the English contrast. Experiments conducted with Hindi-learning and Nthlakapmx-learning 10- to 12-month-olds showed that these infants had no difficulty discriminating the contrast from their respective native languages. Hence, the English-learners' decline in discriminating the Hindi and Nthlakapmx contrasts seems to stem from their lack of experience with these contrasts in the linguistic input. Subsequent research by Werker and Lalonde (1988) using a different Hindi contrast further confirmed the time course of English-learners' decline in sensitivity to such contrasts.

However, this decline in sensitivity does not extend universally to all nonnative contrasts. Best, McRoberts, and Sithole (1988) found no evidence of a similar decline in English-learners' abilities to perceive a contrast between two Zulu click sounds. Similarly, English-learning 10- to 12-month-olds continue to discriminate a place of articulation distinction for different ejective sounds in Ethiopian, although at this age they show a significant decline in discriminating a lateral fricative voicing distinction in Zulu (Best, Lafleur, & McRoberts, 1995). Also, Japanese-learning 6- to 8-month-olds discriminate the English [ra]-[la] contrast, but Japanese 10- to 12-month-olds do not (Tsushima et al., 1994). Clearly, although lack of direct experience with a particular contrast is a factor in the decline of sensitivity to nonnative contrasts, it is not the sole factor. The most favored explanation for why sensitivity declines for only some nonnative contrasts has to do with how these relate to contrasts in the native language (Best, 1995; Eimas, 1991; Flege, 1995; Werker, 1991). The perceptual assimilation model (Best, 1995) holds that nonnative contrasts that map onto two different native language phonemic categories or to no nonnative language categories are less likely to undergo a decline than are those that map onto a single phonemic category.

HOW PERCEPTUAL CAPACITIES ARE USED IN ACQUIRING LANGUAGE

In recent years there has been shift in emphasis in infant research toward viewing speech perception capacities in the context of acquiring a communication system. This view has had an important impact on the issues addressed in studies of infants' speech processing abilities. One major focus is on processes that are required for building a lexicon, such as the ability to segment words from fluent speech and to store sufficient information about their sound patterns to distinguish them from those of other words. Another important issue concerns how infants extract larger units of organization, which govern the relations that hold among the words in an utterance.

Segmenting Words

Even in speech directed to them, few utterances that infants hear consist of isolated words. In analyzing input directed to an infant between 6 and 9 months, van de Weijer (1998) found that excluding greetings, vocatives, and fillers, only about 9% of the speech consisted of one-word utterances. Thus, to learn the words of their native language, infants must be able to segment words from fluent speech. The most effective word segmentation cues are ones tailored to the sound structure of a particular language. Therefore, one might anticipate that an infant would need to learn about the sound organization of his or her native language before making much progress in segmenting words.

Infants learn much about the sound structure of their native language between 6 and 9 months. At 6 months, English learners are as likely to listen to lists of words from a foreign language, Dutch, as to words of native their language (Jusczyk, Friederici, Wessels, Svenkerud, & Jusczyk, 1993b). By 9 months, English learners listen significantly longer to English word lists, and Dutch learners listen significantly longer to Dutch lists. Because the prosodic characteristics of English and Dutch words are very similar (Reitveld & Koopmans-van Beinum, 1987; Schreuder &

Baayen, 1994), infants seem to have learned about the segmental characteristics of their language, such as what sounds and sequences of sounds (*phonotactic* patterns) are permissible in words. Indeed, when such information was removed from the words through low-pass filtering, infants no longer showed a preference for native language words. Furthermore, by 9 months, infants also have some knowledge of which phonotactic patterns occur frequently, as opposed to infrequently, within words (Jusczyk, Luce, & Charles-Luce, 1994). Similar gains are evident in knowledge of the prosodic characteristics of native language words. For example, the predominant stress pattern of English words has an initial strong syllable (i.e., one that carries prosodic stress) followed by one or more weak (or unstressed) syllables (Cutler & Carter, 1987). At 6 months, English learners are as likely to listen to lists of disyllabic words without the predominant stress pattern as they are to listen to words with it. However, by 9 months, English learners listen significantly longer to disyllabic words with the predominant strong/weak pattern than to words with a weak/strong pattern (Jusczyk, Cutler, & Redanz, 1993).

The knowledge that infants aged 6 to 9 months gain about native language sound structure provides information that could be exploited to segment words from fluent speech. Phonotactic cues (Brent & Cartwright, 1996; Cairns, Shillcock, Chater, & Levy, 1997) and prosodic stress cues (Cutler, 1990, 1994; Cutler & Norris, 1988) are considered to be useful in segmenting English words. It is striking, then, that infants first segment words around 7.5 months of age. Jusczyk and Aslin (1995) found that 7.5-month-olds, but not 6-month-olds, segmented monosyllabic words, such as *cup, dog, feet,* and *bike,* from fluent speech. In one experiment infants were familiarized with a pair of words (e.g., *cup* and *dog*) that were repeatedly spoken as isolated words. Then the infants heard four different six-sentence passages, two of which contained one of the familiarization words and two of which did not. Infants listened significantly longer to the passages with the familiarization words, suggesting that they recognized these words in fluent speech. In a second experiment, infants did equally well when they were familiarized with the passages first and then tested on the isolated words.

Subsequent research has been directed at how infants segment words from fluent speech. Jusczyk, Houston, and Newsome (1999) suggested that English learners begin segmenting words by relying on prosodic stress cues, linking word onsets to the occurrence of strong syllables. Using the same methods as Jusczyk and Aslin (1995) used, they found that (a) English-learning 7.5-month-olds segment words with strong/weak patterns (e.g. *doctor*), but not weak/strong words (e.g., *surprise*); (b) 7.5-month-olds missegment weak/strong words at the beginnings of strong syllables (e.g., they segment *prize* rather than *surprise*); and (c) it is not until 10.5 months that they segment weak/strong words. One prediction that follows from the claim that English learners begin segmenting words by relying on prosodic stress cues is that they should also show some ability to segment words in an unfamiliar language that has the same predominant word stress pattern. In fact, English-learning 9-month-olds have been shown to segment strong/weak words (e.g., *pendel*) from Dutch utterances (Houston, Jusczyk, Kuipers, Coolen, & Cutler, 2000).

Although prosodic stress cues might help infants to begin to segment words in a language, such as English or Dutch, they are not sufficient, as 7.5-month-olds' difficulties with weak/strong words illustrates. To progress, infants must draw on other sources of information in the input. As noted earlier, infants aged 6 to 9 months learn about the frequency with which certain phonotactic patterns appear in words. Indeed, some have argued that the ability to track recurring patterns in the input may suffice for segmenting words (Aslin, Saffran, & Newport, 1998; Saffran, Aslin, & Newport, 1996; Saffran, Newport, & Aslin, 1996). Saffran, Aslin, et al. (1996) presented 8-month-olds with a 2.5-min stream of continuous speech containing no other information to word boundaries but the statistical likelihood that one syllable follows another (i.e., transitional probabilities). When later tested on sequences from the familiarization stream, infants responded differentially to sequences corresponding to words, as opposed to part-words, suggesting they had segmented the words.

Other investigations have focused on how patterns that infants have already detected in the input could assist them in word segmentation. For example, 9-month-olds respond differently to phonotactic patterns that are more likely to occur within words than between words (i.e., as the last phonetic segment in one word and the first segment in the next word; Friederici & Wessels, 1993; Mattys, Jusczyk, Luce, & Morgan, 1999). Such findings suggest that infants have learned about the distribution of such sequences relative to word boundaries. Indeed, English-learning 9-month-olds were found to segment words only from contexts in which phonotactic cues suggest a likely word boundary (Mattys & Jusczyk, 2001). Thus, by 9 months, English learners can use phonotactic cues to segment words. However, they seem to require more time to develop their ability to use another possible word segmentation cue. It has been suggested that listeners may use information about the distribution of different phonetic variants (i.e., allophones) of a particular phoneme to segment words (Bolinger & Gerstman, 1957; Church, 1987; Hockett, 1955; Lehiste, 1960). Allophones are often restricted in the positions in which they can

appear within a word. Consider allophones of the English phoneme /t/. The aspirated allophone [tʰ] occurs at the beginnings of English words, whereas the unaspirated allophone [t] occurs at the ends of English words. Knowledge of which allophones occur in particular contexts could help to identify the possible locations of word boundaries. Although 2-month-olds can discriminate allophones relevant to word boundaries (Hohne & Jusczyk, 1994), English learners do not use this information until 10.5 months in segmenting words (Jusczyk, Hohne, & Bauman, 1999).

Many questions remain about how infants discover these kinds of cues and how they integrate them in segmenting words from fluent speech. Jusczyk, Hohne, et al. (1999) suggested that the tendency for English learners to use prosodic stress cues is rooted initially in the fact that the items that they are likely to hear frequently as isolated words (e.g., names and diminutives) are typically strong/weak patterns. Moreover, breaking the input into smaller chunks based on the occurrence of strong syllables provides a way of relating phonotactic sequences and allophones to potential word boundaries, thus facilitating the discovery of these types of word segmentation cues. Presumably, infants learning languages without predominant stress patterns begin with one potential word segmentation cue and learn to uncover other available cues in the signal.

Although not much is known about how or when infants integrate different word segmentation cues, when prosodic stress cues conflict either with statistical cues (Johnson & Jusczyk, in press) or with phonotactic cues (Mattys et al., 1999), infants aged 9 months or younger favor prosodic stress cues. However, the fact that 10.5-month-olds segment weak/strong words indicates that by this age other types of cues can outweigh prosodic stress cues. In addition, by 12 months, infants' segmentation seems to be governed by whether a particular parse yields items that could be possible words in a language (Johnson, Jusczyk, Cutler, & Norris, 2000). Furthermore, given the critical role that competition among lexical items plays in adults' recognition of words during on-line speech processing, then one might expect lexical competition to become a significant factor in infants' recognition of words as the lexicon develops. Indeed, Hollich, Jusczyk, and Luce (2000) have reported lexical competition effects in a word-learning task with 17-month-olds. Specifically, infants learned a new word from a sparse neighborhood more readily than they learned a new word from a dense neighborhood.

The word segmentation findings discussed thus far have involved the segmentation of words beginning with consonants. When words begin with initial vowels (whose onsets tend to be less prominently marked in the speech stream than do those of consonants), English-learners do not segment these until between 13 and 16 months (Mattys & Jusczyk, in press; Nazzi, Jusczyk, & Bhagirath, 1999).

Developing Lexical Representations

Once word segmentation begins, infants are positioned to store possible words and build a lexicon linking sound patterns to specific meanings. Infants store the sound patterns of frequently occurring words even when they lack a specific meaning to attach to them. Jusczyk and Hohne (1997) noted that 8-month-olds who were familiarized with three stories that were told once a day for 10 days during a two week period retained information about the sound patterns of frequently occurring words in the stories when tested two weeks later. Infants exposed to the stories listened significantly longer to lists of words from the stories than to lists of matched foil words, whereas infants who had not heard the stories displayed no preference for either list. These findings suggest that infants not only segment frequently occurring words but also encode them into memory.

How much do infants store about the sound patterns of words? One suggestion is that initially, infants must only encode sufficient detail about a word to distinguish it from other items in the lexicon (Charles-Luce & Luce, 1990, 1995; Jusczyk, 1993; Walley, 1988, 1993). In studies with French infants, Hallé and Boysson-Bardies (1994) found that 11-month-olds listen significantly longer to words that are likely to be familiar to them than to unfamiliar words. Subsequently, however, Hallé and Boysson-Bardies (1996) found that French 11-month-olds showed a similar preference when the initial consonants of the familiar words were changed to another consonant. The latter findings suggest that infants' representations of the sound patterns of the familiar words might not be fully detailed with respect to phonetic properties. In another investigation, Stager and Werker (1997) reported that despite 14-month-olds' abilities to discriminate two syllables [bI] and [dI] differing by a single phonetic feature, they could not succeed at a word-learning task that required them to attach these two syllables to distinctive objects. Thus, even though infants can detect fine distinctions among speech sounds, they might not encode the same detail in their representations of the sound patterns of words.

Nevertheless, a growing body of evidence suggests that infants' representations are detailed from the outset. Jusczyk and Aslin (1995) found that infants familiarized with an item such as *tup* did not listen significantly longer to a passage in which the word *cup* appeared repeatedly. This finding seems to indicate that representations of such words are very detailed. Other studies suggest that infants' representations of the sound patterns of words are so detailed as to include talker-specific information (Houston, Jusczyk, & Tager, 1998; Houston & Jusczyk, 2000).

Similarly, studies requiring infants to respond to the appropriate meaning of a particular sound pattern also suggest that they include considerable phonetic detail in their representations. Swingley, Pinto, and Fernald (1999) recorded the latency of 24-month-olds' looking responses to a visual target upon hearing its name. By systematically varying the distracter item paired with the target, they found that infants responded more slowly when the distracter shared an initial consonant with the target item (e.g., *dog* and *doll*) than when it did not (e.g., *doll* and *ball*). This finding suggests that infants' representations include detail about the initial consonants. To determine whether such phonetic detail might be stored by infants only when they know two different words that begin in the same way, Swingley and Aslin (2000) compared 18- to 23-month-olds' responses to correct pronunciations of a target versus mispronunciations that differed by a single phonetic feature (e.g., *baby* versus *vaby*). Infants' looking time latencies to the correct object were significantly delayed for mispronunciations of the targets versus correct pronunciations, suggesting that their representations of the target words must have already contained sufficient detail to distinguish them from these close mispronunciations.

Learning about Larger Units of Linguistic Organization

Recovering the underlying meaning of an utterance depends crucially on identifying the relationships that exist among its words. Beginning with arbitrary groupings of words would guarantee failure in discovering the grammatical organization of utterances in the native language. Thus, it is critical that language learners detect major constituents and their relations in the utterances. To do this,

they must divide the signal into the appropriately sized units.

The boundaries of units such as clauses are acoustically marked in both adult-directed (Lehiste, 1973; Nakatani & Dukes, 1977; Price, Ostendorf, Shattuck-Hufnagel, & Fong, 1991) and child-directed (Bernstein Ratner, 1986; Fisher & Tokura, 1996b) speech. Typically, pitch declines, final syllables lengthen, and pauses are likely to occur at clause boundaries. Infants are sensitive to the occurrence of these cues in the input. Hirsh-Pasek et al. (1987) found that English-learning 7- and 10-month-olds preferred passages in which pauses were inserted at clause boundaries, as opposed to in the middles of clauses (see also Morgan, 1994). Furthermore, clausal units seem to be used in infants' encoding and retrieval of speech information. Six-month-olds can better detect clausal units embedded in continuous speech than they can detect comparable nonclausal units (Nazzi, Kemler Nelson, Jusczyk, & Jusczyk, 2000). Even 2-month-olds remember speech information better when it is packaged in clausal units, as opposed to comparable, but nonclausal, word sequences (Mandel, Jusczyk, & Kemler Nelson, 1994; Mandel, Kemler Nelson, & Jusczyk, 1996).

The situation for units of organization smaller than clauses, such as phrases, is more mixed. Languages differ considerably in how they organize phrases within clauses. Languages that rely heavily on word order to convey syntactic information are likely to group words from the same phrase together. However, languages that allow for freer word orders might have elements from the same phrase in different portions of an utterance. Still, for a language such as English, phrasal units are often marked by acoustic cues (Price et al., 1991; Scott, 1982; Scott & Cutler, 1984). When such information is available in child-directed speech, English-learning 9-month-olds not only detect it (Jusczyk,

Hirsh-Pasek, Kemler Nelson, Kennedy, Woodward, & Piwoz, 1992) but also use it in encoding and remembering information (Soderstrom, Jusczyk, & Kemler Nelson, 2000). Nevertheless, even for languages such as English, syntactic phrases are not consistently marked in the input that the child receives (Fisher & Tokura, 1996a). Because the markers present in the speech signal tend to relate to prosodic phrases, they do not always pick out the same types of syntactic phrases. Indeed, English-learning 9-month-olds display listening preferences that accord with prosodic, rather than with syntactic, organization (Gerken, Jusczyk, & Mandel, 1994). Still, dividing utterances into units corresponding to prosodic phrases may help infants learn to identify syntactic phrases by facilitating the discovery of syntactic units such as grammatical morphemes (Jusczyk, 1999). In English, certain morphemes, such as function words, typically occur only at particular locations inside phrasal units. For instance, "the" marks the beginning of a noun phrase and is extremely unlikely to occur as the last word of a phrasal unit. Hence, grouping the input into prosodic phrases and noting regularities in how certain morphemes are distributed within such phrases may help delineate their syntactic roles.

CONCLUSIONS

Early research on speech perception by adults was largely concerned with the nature of the acoustic information that underlies the perception of phonetic segments. Efforts to isolate invariant acoustic cues led to the use of experimental paradigms in which listeners were asked to identify and discriminate isolated speech sounds. Similarly, when researchers began to explore infants' speech perception capacities, they, too, began by investigating infants' responses to phonetic differences in isolated syllables. In both instances, these early studies provided interesting information about the nature and limitations of our perceptual capacities to discriminate and categorize speech sounds. At the same time, this focus on minimal distinctions among speech sounds also influenced the way that researchers thought about the manner in which both on-line speech processing in adult listeners and the development of speech perception capacities takes place—namely, starting with the smallest units and moving to larger units of organization. However, once researchers began to focus on how adult listeners (and more recently infant listeners) process fluent speech, it became clear that the sequence of processes in on-line speech perception, and for that matter in development, need not require the extraction of the smallest possible units on the way to recognizing larger units such as words and phrases. In fact, one of the biggest challenges of future speech research with both infants and adults is to determine how the various pieces fit together during on-line processing. Given that fluent speech consists of a rapidly changing stream of sounds, is the most efficient scheme for recognizing words one that requires the extraction and combination of phonetic segments, or might word recognition occur with a less-than-complete specification of phonetic segments? Similarly, in acquiring the sound structure of their native language, must infants begin by recovering phonetic segments from utterances, or might the discovery of these minimal units of sound organization derive from infants' apprehension of larger units of organization? Finally, one question that preoccupied the earliest researchers in this field remains: Why do listeners perceive the continuous acoustic stream as a discrete sequence of phonetic segments?

REFERENCES

Abbs, J. H., & Sussman, H. M. (1971). Neurophysiological feature detectors and speech perception: A discussion of theoretical implications. *Journal of Speech and Hearing Research, 14,* 23–36.

Abramson, A. S., & Lisker, L. (1967). *Discriminability along the voice continuum: Cross language tests.* Paper presented at the Proceedings of the Sixth International Congress of Phonetic Sciences, Prague, Czechoslavakia.

Ades, A. E. (1974). How phonetic is selective adaptation? Experiments on syllable and vowel environment. *Perception & Psychophysics, 16,* 61–67.

Allopena, P. D., Magnuson, J. S., & Tanenhaus, M. K. (1998). Tracking the time course of spoken word recognition using eye movements: Evidence for continuous mapping models. *Journal of Memory and Language, 38,* 419–439.

Andruski, J. E., Blumstein, S. E., & Burton, M. (1994). The effect of subphonetic differences on lexical access. *Cognition, 52,* 163–187.

Aslin, R. N., Saffran, J. R., & Newport, E. L. (1998). Computation of probability statistics by 8-month-old infants. *Psychological Science, 9,* 321–324.

Bailey, P. J., Summerfield, A. Q., & Dorman, M. F. (1977). *On the identification of sine-wave analogs of certain speech sounds* [Status Report on Speech Research SR 51–52]. New Haven, CT: Haskins Laboratories.

Bard, E. G., Shillcock, R. C., & Altmann, G. T. M. (1988). The recognition of words after their acoustic offsets in spontaneous speech: Effect of subsequent context. *Perception & Psychophysics, 44,* 395–408.

Bentin, S., & Mann, V. A. (1990). Masking and stimulus intensity effects on duplex perception: A confirmation of the dissociation between speech and nonspeech modes. *Journal of the Acoustical Society of America, 88,* 64–74.

Bernstein Ratner, N. (1986). Durational cues which mark clause boundaries in mother-child speech. *Phonetics, 14,* 303–309.

Bertoncini, J., Bijeljac-Babic, R., Blumstein, S. E., & Mehler, J. (1987). Discrimination in neonates of very short CV's. *Journal of the Acoustical Society of America, 82,* 31–37.

Best, C. T. (1995). Learning to perceive the sound patterns of English. In C. Rovee-Collier & L. P. Lipsitt (Eds.), *Advances in infancy research* (Vol. 9, pp. 217–304). Norwood, NJ: Ablex.

Best, C. T., Lafleur, R., & McRoberts, G. W. (1995). Divergent developmental patterns for infants' perception of two non-native contrasts. *Infant Behavior and Development, 18,* 339–350.

Best, C. T., McRoberts, G. W., & Sithole, N. M. (1988). Examination of the perceptual reorganization for nonnative speech contrasts: Zulu click discrimination by English-speaking adults and infants. *Journal of Experimental Psychology: Human Perception and Performance, 14,* 345–360.

Best, C. T., Morrongiello, B., & Robson, R. (1981). Perceptual equivalence of acoustic cues in speech and nonspeech perception. *Perception & Psychophysics, 29,* 191–211.

Blechner, M. J. (1977). *Musical skill and the categorical perception of harmonic mode.* Unpublished doctoral dissertation, Yale University, New Haven, CT.

Blumstein, S. E., & Stevens, K. N. (1978). Acoustic invariance for place of articulation in stops and nasals across syllabic context. *Journal of the Acoustical Society of America, 62,* S26.

Blumstein, S. E., & Stevens, K. N. (1980). Perceptual invariance and onset spectra for stop consonants in different vowel environments. *Journal of the Acoustical Society of America, 67,* 648–662.

Bolinger, D. L., & Gerstman, L. J. (1957). Disjuncture as a cue to constraints. *Word, 13,* 246–255.

Brent, M. R., & Cartwright, T. A. (1996). Distributional regularity and phonotactic constraints are useful for segmentation. *Cognition, 61,* 93–125.

Burton, M. W., Baum, S. R., & Blumstein, S. E. (1989). Lexical effects on the phonetic categorization of speech: The role of acoustic structure. *Journal of Experimental Psychology: Human Perception and Performance, 15,* 567–575.

Cairns, P., Shillcock, R., Chater, N., & Levy, J. (1997). Bootstrapping word boundaries: A bottom-up corpus-based approach to speech segmentation. *Cognitive Psychology, 33,* 111–153.

Charles-Luce, J., & Luce, P. A. (1990). Similarity neighborhoods of words in young children's lexicons. *Journal of Child Language, 17,* 205–215.

Charles-Luce, J., & Luce, P. A. (1995). An examination of similarity neighborhoods in young children's receptive vocabularies. *Journal of Child Language, 22,* 727–735.

Charles-Luce, J., Luce, P. A., & Cluff, M. (1990). Retroactive influence of syllable neighborhoods. In G. T. Altmann (Ed.), *Cognitive models of speech processing* (pp. 173–184). Cambridge, MA: MIT Press.

Christie, W. (1977). Some multiple cues for juncture in English. *General Linguistics, 17,* 212–222.

Church, B. A., & Schacter, D. L. (1994). Perceptual specificity of auditory priming: Implicit memory for voice intonation and fundamental frequency. *Journal of Experimental Psychology: Learning, Memory, and Cognition, 20,* 521–533.

Church, K. (1987). Phonological parsing and lexical retrieval. *Cognition, 25,* 53–69.

Cluff, M. S., & Luce, P. A. (1990). Similarity neighborhoods of spoken bisyllabic words. *Journal of Experimental Psychology: Human Perception and Performance, 16,* 551–563.

Cole, R. A., & Jakimik, J. (1980). A model of speech perception. In R. A. Cole (Ed.), *Perception and production of fluent speech* (pp. 133–163). Hillsdale, NJ: Erlbaum.

Cole, R. A., & Scott, B. (1974). Toward a theory of speech perception. *Psychological Review, 81,* 348–374.

Connine, C. M., Blasko, D. G., & Titone, D. (1993). Do the beginnings of words have a special status in auditory word recognition? *Journal of Memory and Language, 32,* 193–210.

Connine, C. M., Titone, D., Deelman, T., & Blasko, D. (1997). Similarity mapping in spoken word recognition. *Journal of Memory and Language, 37,* 463–480.

Cooper, F. S., Delattre, P. C., Liberman, A. M., Borst, J. M., & Gerstman, L. J. (1952). Some experiments on the perception of synthetic speech sounds. *Journal of the Acoustical Society of America, 24,* 597–606.

Cooper, F. S., Liberman, A. M., & Borst, J. M. (1951). The interconversion of audible and visible patterns as a basis for research in the perception of speech. *Proceedings of the National Academy of Sciences, 37,* 318–325.

Cooper, W. E. (1975). Selective adaptation to speech. In F. Restle, R. M. Shiffrin, N. J. Castellan, H. Lindman, & D. B. Pisoni (Eds.), *Cognitive theory: Vol. 1* (pp. 23–54). Hillsdale, NJ: Erlbaum.

Cooper, W. E., & Blumstein, S. E. (1974). A "labial" feature analyzer in speech perception. *Perception & Psychophysics, 15,* 591–600.

Creelman, C. D. (1957). Case of the unknown talker. *Journal of the Acoustical Society of America, 29,* 655.

Cutler, A. (1989). Auditory lexical access: Where do we start? In W. D. Marslen-Wilson (Ed.), *Lexical Representation and Process* (pp. 342–356). Cambridge: MIT Press.

Cutler, A. (1990). Exploiting prosodic probabilities in speech segmentation. In G. T. M. Altmann (Ed.), *Cognitive models of speech processing: Psycholinguistic and computational perspectives* (pp. 105–121). Cambridge: MIT Press.

Cutler, A. (1994). Segmentation problems, rhythmic solutions. *Lingua, 92,* 81–104.

Cutler, A. (1996). Prosody and the word boundary problem. In J. L. Morgan & K. Demuth (Eds.), *Signal to Syntax* (pp. 87–99). Mahwah, NJ: Lawrence Erlbaum Associates.

Cutler, A., & Butterfield, S. (1992). Rhythmic cues to speech segmentation: Evidence from juncture misperception. *Journal of Memory & Language, 31,* 218–236.

Cutler, A., & Carter, D. M. (1987). The predominance of strong initial syllables in the English vocabulary. *Computer Speech and Language, 2,* 133–142.

Cutler, A. & Norris, D. (1979). Monitoring sentence comprehension. In W. E. Cooper & E. C. T. Walker (Eds.) *Sentence Processing: Psycholinguistic Studies Presented to Merrill Garrett.* Hillsdale: Erlbaum.

Cutler, A., & Norris, D. G. (1988). The role of strong syllables in segmentation for lexical access. *Journal of Experimental Psychology: Human Perception and Performance, 14,* 113–121.

Cutler, A., Norris, D. G., & Williams, J. N. (1987). A note on the role of phonological expectation in speech segmentation. *Journal of Memory and Language, 26,* 480–487.

Davidson-Nielson, N. (1974). Syllabification in English words with medial sp, st, sk. *Journal of Phonetics, 2,* 15–45.

Delattre, P. C., Liberman, A. M., & Cooper, F. S. (1955). Acoustic loci and transitional cues for consonants. *Journal of the Acoustical Society of America, 27,* 769–773.

Dutton, D. (1992). Allophonic variation and segmentation in spoken word recognition. Doctoral Dissertation State University of New York at Buffalo.

Eimas, P. D. (1974). Auditory and linguistic processing of cues for place of articulation by infants. *Perception & Psychophysics, 16,* 513–521.

Eimas, P. D. (1975). Auditory and phonetic coding of the cues for speech: Discrimination of the [r–l] distinction by young infants. *Perception & Psychophysics, 18,* 341–347.

Eimas, P. D. (1991). Comment: Some effects of language acquisition on speech perception. In I. G. Mattingly & M. Studdert-Kennedy (Eds.), *Modularity and the motor theory of speech perception* (pp. 111–116). Hillsdale, NJ: Erlbaum.

Eimas, P. D., Cooper, W. E., & Corbit, J. D. (1973). Some properties of linguistic feature detectors. *Perception & Psychophysics, 13,* 247–252.

Eimas, P. D., & Corbit, J. D. (1973). Selective adaptation of linguistic feature detectors. *Cognitive Psychology, 4,* 99–109.

Eimas, P. D., & Miller, J. L. (1980a). Contextual effects in infant speech perception. *Science, 209,* 1140–1141.

Eimas, P. D., & Miller, J. L. (1980b). Discrimination of the information for manner of articulation. *Infant Behavior & Development, 3,* 367–375.

Eimas, P. D., & Miller, J. L. (1992). Organization in the perception of speech by young infants. *Psychological Science, 3,* 340–345.

Eimas, P. D., Siqueland, E. R., Jusczyk, P. W., & Vigorito, J. (1971). Speech perception in infants. *Science, 171,* 303–306.

Fant, C. G. M. (1960). *Acoustic theory of speech production.* The Hague, Netherlands: Mouton.

Fernald, A., Taeschner, T., Dunn, J., Papousek, M., Boysson-Bardies, B. D., & Fukui, I. (1989). A cross-language study of prosodic modifications in mothers' and fathers' speech to preverbal infants. *Journal of Child Language, 16,* 477–501.

Fisher, C., & Tokura, H. (1996a). Prosody in speech to infants: Direct and indirect acoustic cues to syntactic structure. In J. L. Morgan & K. Demuth (Eds.), *Signal to syntax* (pp. 343–364). Mahwah, NJ: Erlbaum.

Fisher, C. L., & Tokura, H. (1996b). Acoustic cues to grammatical structure in infant-directed speech: Cross-linguistic evidence. *Child Development, 67,* 3192–3218.

Flege, J. E. (1995). Second language speech learning: Theory, findings, and problems. In W. Strange (Ed.), *Speech perception and linguistic experience: Theoretical and methodological issues* (pp. 229–273). Timonium, MD: York Press.

Foss, D. J., & Blank, M. A. (1980). Identifying the speech codes. *Cognitive Psychology, 12,* 1–31.

Fowler, C. A. (1986). An event approach to the study of speech perception from a direct-realist perspective. *Journal of Phonetics, 14,* 3–28.

Fowler, C. A. (1990). Sound-producing sources as objects of perception: Rate normalization and nonspeech perception. *Journal of the Acoustical Society of America, 88,* 1236–1249.

Fowler, C. A., & Rosenblum, L. D. (1990). Duplex perception: A comparison of monosyllables and slamming of doors. *Journal of Experimental Psychology: Human Perception and Performance, 16,* 742–754.

Fowler, C. A., & Rosenblum, L. D. (1991). Perception of the phonetic gesture. In I. G. Mattingly & M. Studdert-Kennedy (Eds.), *Modularity and the motor theory* (pp. 33–59). Hillsdale, NJ: Erlbaum.

Friederici, A. D., & Wessels, J. M. I. (1993). Phonotactic knowledge and its use in infant speech perception. *Perception & Psychophysics, 54,* 287–295.

Fry, D. B., Abramson, A. S., Eimas, P. D., & Liberman, A. M. (1962). The identification and discrimination of synthetic vowels. *Language and Speech, 5,* 171–189.

Fujimura, O. (1976). Syllables as concatenated demisyllables and affixes. *Journal of Acoustical Society of America, 59,* S55.

Gaskell, M. G., & Marslen-Wilson, W. D. (1997). Integrating form and meaning: A distributed model of speech perception. *Language and Cognitive Processes, 12,* 613–656.

Gaskell, M. G., & Marslen-Wilson, W. D. (1999). Ambiguity, competition, and blending in spoken word recognition. *Cognitive Science, 23,* 439–462.

Gaygen, D., & Luce, P. A. (2001). *Troughs and bursts: Probabilistic phonotactics and lexical activation in the segmentation of spoken words in fluent speech.* Manuscript submitted for publication.

Gerken, L. A., Jusczyk, P. W., & Mandel, D. R. (1994). When prosody fails to cue syntactic structure: Nine-month-olds' sensitivity to phonological vs syntactic phrases. *Cognition, 51,* 237–265.

Gerstman, L. (1968). Classification of self-normalized vowels. *EEE Transactions on Audio and Electroacoustics* (ACC-16), 78–80.

Goldinger, S. D. (1996). Words and voices: Episodic traces in spoken word identification and recognition memory. *Journal of Experimental Psychology: Learning, Memory, and Cognition, 22,* 1166–1183.

Goldinger, S. D. (1998). Echoes of echoes? An episodic theory of lexical access. *Psychological Review. Vol. 105,* 251–279.

Goldinger, S. D., Luce, P. A., & Pisoni, D. B. (1989). Priming lexical neighbors of spoken words: Effects of competition and inhibition. *Journal of Memory and Language, 28,* 501–518.

Goldinger, S. D., Luce, P. A., Pisoni, D. B., & Marcario, J. K. (1992). Form-based priming in spoken word recognition: The roles of competitive activation and response biases. *Journal of Experimental Psychology: Learning, Memory, and Cognition, 18,* 1210–1237.

Goldinger, S. D., Pisoni, D. B., & Logan, J. S. (1991). On the nature of talker variability effects on recall of spoken word lists. *Journal of Experimental Psychology: Learning, Memory, and Cognition, 17,* 152–162.

Goodman, J. C., & Huttenlocher, J. (1988). Do we know how people identify spoken words? *Journal of Memory and Language, 27,* 684–689.

Grosjean, F. (1985). The recognition of words after their acoustic offset: Evidence and Implications. *Perception & Psychophysics, 38,* 299–310.

Hall, M. D., & Pastore, R. E. (1992). Musical duplex perception: Perception of figurally good chords with subliminally distinguishing tones. *Journal of Experimental Psychology: Human Perception and Performance, 18,* 752–762.

Hallé, P. A., & de Boysson-Bardies, B. D. (1994). Emergence of an early receptive lexicon: Infants' recognition of words. *Infant Behavior and Development, 17,* 119–129.

Hallé, P., & de Boysson-Bardies, B. D. (1996). The format of representation of recognized words in infants' early receptive lexicon. *Infant Behavior & Development, 19,* 463–481.

Harnad, S. (Ed.). (1987). *Categorical perception: The groundwork of cognition.* Cambridge: Cambridge University Press.

Healy, A. F., & Cutting, J. E. (1976). Units of speech perception: Phoneme and syllable. *Journal of Verbal Learning and Verbal Behavior, 15,* 73–83.

Hillenbrand, J. M., Minifie, F. D., & Edwards, T. J. (1979). Tempo of spectrum change as a cue in speech sound discrimination by infants. *Journal of Speech and Hearing Research, 22,* 147–165.

Hirsh-Pasek, K., Kemler Nelson, D. G., Jusczyk, P. W., Wright Cassidy, K., Druss, B., & Kennedy,

L. (1987). Clauses are perceptual units for young infants. *Cognition, 26,* 269–286.

Hockett, C. F. (1955). *A manual of phonology: Vol. 21.* Baltimore: Waverly Press.

Hohne, E. A., & Jusczyk, P. W. (1994). Two-month-old infants' sensitivity to allophonic differences. *Perception & Psychophysics, 56,* 613–623.

Hollich, G., Jusczyk, P. W., & Luce, P. A. (2000). Infant sensitivity to lexical neighborhoods during word learning. *Journal of the Acoustical Society of America, 108,* 2481.

Houston, D. M., & Jusczyk, P. W. (2000). The role of talker-specific information in word segmentation by infants. *Journal of Experimental Psychology: Human Perception and Performance, 26,* 1570–1582.

Houston, D. M., Jusczyk, P. W., Kuipers, C., Coolen, R., & Cutler, A. (2000). Cross-language word segmentation by 9-month-olds. *Psychonomic Bulletin & Review, 7,* 504–509.

Houston, D. M., Jusczyk, P. W., & Tager, J. (1998). Talker-specificity and the persistence of infants' word representations. In A. Greenhill, M. Hughes, H. Littlefield, & H. Walsh (Eds.), *Proceedings of the 22nd Annual Boston University Conference on Language Development: Vol. 1* (pp. 385–396). Somerville, MA: Cascadilla Press.

Hurvich, L. M., & Jameson, D. (1969). Human color perception. *American Scientist, 57,* 143–166.

Jackson, A., & Morton, J. (1984). Facilitation of auditory recognition. *Memory and Cognition, 12,* 568–574.

Jakobson, R., Fant, C. G. M., & Halle, M. (1952). *Preliminaries to speech analysis.* Cambridge: MIT Press.

Johnson, E. K., & Jusczyk, P. W. (in press). Word segmentation by 8-month-olds: When speech cues count more than statistics. *Journal of Memory and Language.*

Johnson, E. K., Jusczyk, P. W., Cutler, A., & Norris, D. (2000). 12-month-olds show evidence of a possible word constraint. *Journal of the Acoustical Society of America, 108,* 2481.

Jusczyk, P. W. (1977). Perception of syllable-final stops by two-month-old infants. *Perception and Psychophysics, 21,* 450–454.

Jusczyk, P. W. (1993). From general to language specific capacities: The WRAPSA Model of how speech perception develops. *Journal of Phonetics, 21,* 3–28.

Jusczyk, P. W. (1999). Narrowing the distance to language: One step at a time. *Journal of Communication Disorders, 32,* 207–222.

Jusczyk, P. W., & Aslin, R. N. (1995). Infants' detection of sound patterns of words in fluent speech. *Cognitive Psychology, 29,* 1–23.

Jusczyk, P. W., Copan, H., & Thompson, E. (1978). Perception by two-month-olds of glide contrasts in multisyllabic utterances. *Perception & Psychophysics, 24,* 515–520.

Jusczyk, P. W., Cutler, A., & Redanz, N. (1993). Preference for the predominant stress patterns of English words. *Child Development, 64,* 675–687.

Jusczyk, P. W., Friederici, A. D., Wessels, J., Svenkerud, V. Y., & Jusczyk, A. M. (1993). Infants' sensitivity to the sound patterns of native language words. *Journal of Memory and Language, 32,* 402–420.

Jusczyk, P. W., Hirsh-Pasek, K., Kemler Nelson, D. G., Kennedy, L., Woodward, A., & Piwoz, J. (1992). Perception of acoustic correlates of major phrasal units by young infants. *Cognitive Psychology, 24,* 252–293.

Jusczyk, P. W., & Hohne, E. A. (1997). Infants' memory for spoken words. *Science, 277,* 1984–1986.

Jusczyk, P. W., Hohne, E. A., & Bauman, A. (1999). Infants' sensitivity to allophonic cues for word segmentation. *Perception & Psychophysics, 61,* 1465–1476.

Jusczyk, P. W., Houston, D., & Newsome, M. (1999). The beginnings of word segmentation in English-learning infants. *Cognitive Psychology, 39,* 159–207.

Jusczyk, P. W., Luce, P. A., & Charles-Luce, J. (1994). Infants' sensitivity to phonotactic patterns in the native language. *Journal of Memory and Language, 33,* 630–645.

Jusczyk, P. W., Pisoni, D. B., Fernald, A., Reed, M., & Myers, M. (1983). *Durational context effects in the processing of nonspeech sounds by infants.*

Paper presented at the Meeting of the Society for Research in Child Development, Detroit, MI.

Jusczyk, P. W., Pisoni, D. B., & Mullennix, J. (1992). Some consequences of stimulus variability on speech processing by 2-month-old infants. *Cognition, 43,* 253–291.

Jusczyk, P. W., Pisoni, D. B., Walley, A. C., & Murray, J. (1980). Discrimination of the relative onset of two-component tones by infants. *Journal of the Acoustical Society of America, 67,* 262–270.

Jusczyk, P. W., Rosner, B. S., Reed, M., & Kennedy, L. J. (1989). Could temporal order differences underlie 2-month-olds' discrimination of English voicing contrasts? *Journal of the Acoustical Society of America, 85,* 1741–1749.

Jusczyk, P. W., & Thompson, E. J. (1978). Perception of a phonetic contrast in multisyllabic utterances by two-month-old infants. *Perception & Psychophysics, 23,* 105–109.

Karzon, R. G. (1985). Discrimination of a polysyllabic sequence by one- to four-month-old infants. *Journal of Experimental Child Psychology, 39,* 326–342.

Kewley-Port, D. (1983). *Time-varying features as correlates of place of articulation in stop consonants* [Research on Speech Perception: Technical Report 3]. Bloomington: Indiana University.

Klatt, D. H. (1979). Speech perception: A model of acoustic-phonetic analysis and lexical access. *Journal of Phonetics, 7,* 279–312.

Klatt, D. H. (1989). Review of selected models of speech perception. In W. Marslen-Wilson (Ed.), *Lexical representation and process* (pp. 169–226). Cambridge, MA: Bradford.

Kuhl, P. K. (1976). Speech perception in early infancy: the acquisition of speech sound categories. In S. K. Hirsh, D. H. Eldridge, I. J. Hirsh, & S. R. Silverman (Eds.), *Hearing and Davis: Essays honoring Hallowell Davis* (pp. 265–280). St. Louis, MO: Washington University Press.

Kuhl, P. K. (1979). Speech perception in early infancy: Perceptual constancy for spectrally dissimilar vowel categories. *Journal of the Acoustical Society of America, 66,* 1668–1679.

Kuhl, P. K. (1983). Perception of auditory equivalence classes for speech in early infancy. *Infant Behavior and Development, 6,* 263–285.

Kuhl, P. K., Andruski, J. E., Chistovich, L. A., Kozhevnikova, E. V., Ryskina, V. L., Stolyarova, E. I., Sundberg, U., & Lacerda, F. (1997). Cross-language analysis of phonetic units addressed to infants. *Science, 277,* 684–686.

Kuhl, P. K., & Miller, J. D. (1982). Discrimination of auditory target dimensions in the presence or absence of variation in a second dimension by infants. *Perception & Psychophysics, 31,* 279–292.

Ladefoged, P., & Broadbent, D. E. (1957). Information conveyed by vowels. *Journal of the Acoustical Society of America, 29,* 98–104.

Lasky, R. E., Syrdal-Lasky, A., & Klein, R. E. (1975). VOT discrimination by four to six and a half month old infants from Spanish environments. *Journal of Experimental Child Psychology, 20,* 215–225.

Lehiste, I. (1960). *An acoustic-phonetic study of internal open juncture.* New York: Karger.

Lehiste, I. (1972). The timing of utterances and linguistic boundaries. *Journal of the Acoustical Society of America, 51,* 2018–2024.

Lehiste, I. (1973). Phonetic disambiguation of syntactic ambiguity. *Glossa, 7,* 107–122.

Levitt, A., Jusczyk, P. W., Murray, J., & Carden, G. (1988). The perception of place of articulation contrasts in voiced and voiceless fricatives by two-month-old infants. *Journal of Experimental Psychology: Human Perception and Performance, 14,* 361–368.

Liberman, A. M. (1970). Some characteristics of perception in the speech mode. In D. A. Hamburg (Ed.), *Perceptions and its disorders: Proceedings of the Association for Research in Nervous and Mental Diseases.* Baltimore, MD: Williams & Wilkins.

Liberman, A. M., Cooper, F. S., Harris, K. S., & MacNeilage, P. F. (1963). *A motor theory of speech perception.* Paper presented at the Proceedings of the Speech Communication Seminar, Royal Institute of Technology, Speech Transmission Laboratory, Stockholm, Sweden.

Liberman, A. M., Cooper, F. S., Shankweiler, D. P., & Studdert-Kennedy, M. G. (1967). Perception of the speech code. *Psychological Review, 74,* 431–461.

Liberman, A. M., DeLattre, P. D., & Cooper, F. S. (1952). The role of selected stimulus variables in the perception of unvoiced stop consonants. *American Journal of Psychology, 65,* 497–516.

Liberman, A. M., Delattre, P. C., Gerstman, L. J., & Cooper, F. S. (1956). Tempo of frequency change as a cue for distinguishing classes of speech sounds. *Journal of Experimental Psychology, 52,* 127–137.

Liberman, A. M., Harris, K. S., Eimas, P. D., Lisker, L., & Bastian, J. (1961). An effect of learning on speech perception: The discrimination of durations of silence with and without phonetic significance. *Language and Speech, 54,* 175–195.

Liberman, A. M., Harris, K. S., Hoffman, H. S., & Griffith, B. C. (1957). The discrimination of speech sounds within and across phoneme boundaries. *Journal of Experimental Psychology, 54,* 358–368.

Liberman, A. M., Harris, K. S., Kinney, J. A., & Lane, H. L. (1961). The discrimination of relative-onset time of the components of certain speech and non-speech patterns. *Journal of Experimental Psychology, 61,* 379–388.

Liberman, A. M., Isenberg, D., & Rakerd, B. (1981). Duplex perception of cues for stop consonants: Evidence for a phonetic mode. *Perception & Psychophysics, 30,* 133–143.

Liberman, A. M., & Mattingly, I. G. (1985). The motor theory of speech perception revised. *Cognition, 21,* 1–36.

Liberman, A. M., & Whalen, D. H. (2000). On the relation of speech to language. *Trends in Cognitive Science, 4,* 187–196.

Lieberman, P., Crelin, E. S., & Klatt, D. H. (1972). Phonetic ability and related anatomy of the newborn and adult human, Neanderthal man, and the chimpanzee. *American Anthropologist, 74,* 287–307.

Lisker, L., & Abramson, A. S. (1970). The voicing dimension: Some experiments in comparative phonetics. In B. Hala, M. Romportl, & P. Janota (Eds.), *Proceedings of the Sixth International Congress of Phonetic Sciences* (pp. 563–567). Prague, Czechoslavakia: Academia.

Locke, S., & Kellar, L. (1973). Categorical perception in a non-linguistic mode. *Cortex, 9,* 353–367.

Luce, P. A. (1986). A computational analysis of uniqueness points in auditory word recognition. *Perception & Psychophysics, 39,* 155–158.

Luce, P. A. (2001). *The minimal discrepancy hypothesis in spoken word recognition.* Manuscript submitted for publication.

Luce, P. A., Charles-Luce, J., & Mclennan, C. (1999). Representational specificity of lexical form in the production and perception of spoken words. *Proceedings of the 1999 International Congress of Phonetic Sciences,* 1889–1892.

Luce, P. A., & Cluff, M. S. (1998). Delayed commitment in spoken word recognition: Evidence from cross-modal priming. *Perception & Psychophysics, 60,* 484–490.

Luce, P. A., Goldinger, S. D., Auer, E. T., & Vitevitch, M. S. (2000). Phonetic priming, neighborhood activation, and PARSYN. *Perception & Psychophysics, 62,* 615–625.

Luce, P. A., & Large, N. (in press). Phonotactics, neighborhood density, and entropy in spoken word recognition. *Language and Cognitive Processes.*

Luce, P. A., & Lyons, E. A. (1998). Specificity of memory representations for spoken words. *Memory and Cognition, 26,* 708–715.

Luce, P. A., & Lyons, E. A. (1999). Processing lexically embedded spoken words. *Journal of Experimental Psychology: Human Perception and Performance, 25,* 174–183.

Luce, P. A., & Pisoni, D. B. (1998). Recognizing spoken words: The neighborhood activation model. *Ear and Hearing, 19,* 1–36.

Luce, P. A., Pisoni, D. B., & Goldinger, S. D. (1990). Similarity neighborhoods of spoken words. In G. Altmann (Ed.), *Cognitive models of speech perception: Psycholinguistic and computational perspectives.* Cambridge: MIT Press, (pp. 122–147).

Mandel, D. R., Jusczyk, P. W., & Kemler Nelson, D. G. (1994). Does sentential prosody help infants to organize and remember speech information? *Cognition, 53,* 155–180.

Mandel, D. R., Kemler Nelson, D. G., & Jusczyk, P. W. (1996). Infants remember the order of words in a spoken sentence. *Cognitive Development, 11,* 181–196.

Marslen-Wilson, W. D. (1987). Parallel processing in spoken word recognition. *Cognition, 25,* 71–102.

Marslen-Wilson, W. D. (1989). Access and integration: Projecting sound onto meaning. In W. D. Marslen-Wilson (Ed.), *Lexical access and representation* (pp. 3–24). Cambridge: Bradford.

Marslen-Wilson, W. D. (1990). Activation, competition, and frequency in lexical access. In G. T. M. Altmann (Ed.), *Cognitive models of speech processing* (pp. 148–172). Cambridge, MA: MIT Press.

Marslen-Wilson, W. D. (1992). Access and integration: Projecting sound onto meaning. In W. Marslen-Wilson (Ed.), *Lexical Representation and Process* (pp. 3–24). Cambridge, MA. MIT Press.

Marslen-Wilson, W. D., Moss, H. E., & van Halen, S. (1996). Perceptual distance and competition in lexical access. *Journal of Experimental Psychology: Human Perception and Performance, 22,* 1376–1392

Marslen-Wilson, W. D., & Tyler, L. K. (1980). The temporal structure of spoken language understanding. *Cognition, 8,* 1–71.

Marslen-Wilson, W. D., Tyler, L. K., Waksler, R., & Older, L. (1994). Morphology and meaning in the English mental lexicon. *Psychological Review, 101,* 3–33.

Marslen-Wilson, W. D., & Warren, P. (1994). Levels of perceptual representation and process in lexical access: Words, phonemes, and features. *Psychological Review, 101,* 653–675.

Marslen-Wilson, W. D., & Welsh, A. (1978). Processing interactions and lexical access during word recognition in continuous speech. *Cognitive Psychology, 10,* 29–63.

Marslen-Wilson, W. D., & Zwitserlood, P. (1989). Accessing spoken words: The importance of word onsets. *Journal of Experimental Psychology: Human Perception and Performance, 15,* 576–585.

Martin, C. S., Mullennix, J. W., Pisoni, D. B., & Summers, W. (1989). Effects of talker variability on recall of spoken word lists. *Journal of Experimental Psychology: Learning, Memory, and Cognition, 15,* 676–684.

Massaro, D. W. (1972). Preperceptual images, processing time, and perceptual units in auditory perception. *Psychological Review, 79,* 124–145.

Massaro, D. W., & Cohen, M. M. (1983). Phonological context in speech perception. *Perception & Psychophysics, 34,* 338–348.

Mattingly, I. G., Liberman, A. M., Syrdal, A. K., & Halwes, T. (1971). Discrimination in speech and non-speech modes. *Cognitive Psychology, 2,* 131–157.

Mattys, S. L. (1997). The use of time during lexical processing and segmentation: A review. *Psychonomic Bulletin & Review, 4,* 310–329.

Mattys, S. L., & Jusczyk, P. W. (2001). Phonotactic cues for segmentation of fluent speech by infants. *Cognition, 78,* 91–121.

Mattys, S. L., & Jusczyk, P. W. (in press). Do infants segment words or recurring contiguous patterns? *Journal of Experimental Psychology: Human Perception and Performance.*

Mattys, S. L., Jusczyk, P. W., Luce, P. A., & Morgan, J. L. (1999). Word segmentation in infants: How phonotactics and prosody combine. *Cognitive Psychology, 38,* 465–494.

McClelland, J. L., & Elman, J. L. (1986). The TRACE model of speech perception. *Cognitive Psychology, 18,* 1–86.

McNeill, D., & Lindig, K. (1973). The perceptual reality of the phoneme, syllables, words, and sentences. *Journal of Verbal Learning and Verbal Behavior, 12,* 419–430.

McQueen, J. M. (1991). The influence of the lexicon on phonetic categorization: Stimulus quality and word-final ambiguity. *Journal of Experimental Psychology: Human Perception and Performance, 17,* 433–443.

McQueen, J. M. (1998). Segmentation of continuous speech using phonotactics. *Journal of Memory and Language, 39,* 21–46.

McQueen, J. M., & Cutler, A. (1992). Words within words: Lexical statistics and lexical access. *Proceedings of the Second International Conference on Spoken Language Processing,* Banff, Canada, 221–224.

McQueen, J. M., Cutler, A., Briscoe, T., & Norris, D. (1995). Models of continuous speech recognition and the contents of the vocabulary. *Language & Cognitive Processes, 10,* 309–331.

McQueen, J. M., Norris, D. G., & Cutler, A. (1994). Competition in spoken word recognition: Spotting words in other words. *Journal of Experimental Psychology: Learning, Memory, & Cognition, 20,* 621–638.

McQueen, J. M., Norris, D. G., & Cutler, A. (1999). Lexical influence in phonetic decision making: Evidence from subcategorical mismatches. *Journal of Experimental Psychology: Human Perception and Performance, 25,* 1363–1389.

Mehler, J., Dommergues, J. Y., Frauenfelder, U., & Segui, J. (1981). The syllable's role in speech segmentation. *Journal of Verbal Learning & Verbal Behavior, 20,* 298–305.

Mehler, J., Segui, J., & Frauenfelder, U. (1981). The role of syllable in language acquisition and perception. In T. F. Myers, J. Laver, & J. Anderson (Eds.), *The cognitive representation of speech.* Amsterdam: North-Holland.

Miller, G. A., Heise, G. A., & Lichten, W. (1951). The intelligibility of speech as a function of the context of the test materials. *Journal of Experimental Psychology, 41,* 329–335.

Miller, G. A., & Taylor, W. G. (1948). The perception of repeated bursts of noise. *Journal of the Acoustical Society of America, 20,* 171–182.

Miller, J. D., Weir, C. C., Pastore, L., Kelly, W. J., & Dooling, R. J. (1976). Discrimination and labeling of noise-buzz sequences with varying noise-lead times: An example of categorical perception. *Journal of the Acoustical Society of America, 60,* 410–417.

Miller, J. L., Connine, C. M., Schermer, T., & Kluender, K. R. (1983). A possible auditory basis for internal structure of phonetic categories. *Journal of the Acoustical Society of America, 73,* 2124–2133.

Miller, J. L., & Eimas, P. D. (1983). Studies on the categorization of speech by infants. *Cognition, 13,* 135–165.

Miller, J. L., & Liberman, A. M. (1979). Some effects of later-occurring information on the perception of stop consonant and semivowel. *Perception & Psychophysics, 25,* 457–465.

Mills, C. B. (1980). Effects of context on reaction time to phonemes. *Journal of Verbal Learning and Verbal Behavior, 19,* 75–83.

Miyawaki, K., Strange, W., Verbrugge, R., Liberman, A. M., Jenkins, J. J., & Fujimura, O. (1975). An effect of linguistic experience: The discrimination of /r/ and /l/ by native speakers of Japanese and English. *Perception & Psychophysics, 18,* 331–340.

Moffitt, A. R. (1971). Consonant cue perception by twenty- to twenty-four-week old infants. *Child Development, 42,* 717–731.

Morgan, J. L. (1994). Converging measures of speech segmentation in prelingual infants. *Infant Behavior & Development, 17,* 387–400.

Morse, P. A. (1972). The discrimination of speech and nonspeech stimuli in early infancy. *Journal of Experimental Child Psychology, 13,* 477–492.

Mullennix, J. W., Pisoni, D. B., & Martin, C. S. (1989). Some effects of talker variability on spoken word recognition. *Journal of the Acoustical Society of America, 85,* 365–378.

Nakatani, L., & Dukes, K. (1977). Locus of segmental cues for word juncture. *Journal of the Acoustical Society of America, 62,* 714–719.

Nakatani, L. H., & Dukes, K. D. (1979). Phonetic parsing cues for word perception. Murray Hill, NJ: ATT Bell Laboratories Technical Memorandum (TM-79-1228-4).

Nazzi, T., Jusczyk, P. W., & Bhagirath, K. (1999, April). *Infants' segmentation of verbs from fluent speech.* Paper presented at the Biennial Meeting of the Society for Research in Child Development, Albuquerque, NM.

Nazzi, T., Kemler Nelson, D. G., Jusczyk, P. W., & Jusczyk, A. M. (2000). Six-month-olds' detection of clauses embedded in continuous speech: Effects of prosodic well-formedness. *Infancy, 1,* 123–147.

Nearey, T. M. (1989). Static, dynamic, and relational properties in vowel perception. *Journal of the Acoustical Society of America, 85,* 2088–2113.

Norris, D. (1994). Shortlist: A connectionist model of continuous speech recognition. *Cognition, 52,* 189–234.

Norris, D., McQueen, J. M., & Cutler, A. (1995). Competition and segmentation in spoken-word recognition. *Journal of Experimental Psychology: Learning, Memory and Cognition, 21,* 1209–1228.

Norris, D., McQueen, J. M., & Cutler, A. (2000). Merging information in speech recognition: Feedback is never necessary. *Brain and Behavioral Sciences, 23,* 299–325.

Norris, D., McQueen, J. M., Cutler, A., & Butterfield, S. (1997). The possible-word constraint in the segmentation of continuous speech. *Cognitive Psychology, 34,* 191–243.

Nusbaum, H. C., Schwab, E. C., & Sawusch, J. R. (1983). The role of the "chirp" identification in duplex perception. *Perception & Psychophysics, 33,* 323–332.

Nygaard, L. C. (1993). Phonetic coherence in duplex perception: Effects of acoustic differences and lexical status. *Journal of Experimental Psychology: Human Perception and Performance, 19,* 268–286.

Nygaard, L. C., & Eimas, P. D. (1990). A new version of duplex perception: Evidence for phonetic and nonphonetic fusion. *Journal of the Acoustical Society of America, 88,* 75–86.

Orr, D. B., Friedman, H. L., & Williams, J. C. C. (1965). Trainability of listening comprehension of speech discourse. *Journal of Educational Psychology, 56,* 148–156.

Palmeri, T. J., Goldinger, S. D., & Pisoni, D. B. (1993). Episodic encoding of voice attributes and recognition memory for spoken words. *Journal of Experimental Psychology: Learning, Memory, and Cognition, 19,* 309–328.

Pastore, R. E., Ahroon, W. A., Buffuto, K. A., Friedman, C. J., Puleo, J. S., & Fink, E. A.

(1977). Common factor model of categorical perception. *Journal of Experimental Psychology: Human Perception and Performance, 4,* 686–696.

Pastore, R. E., Schmeckler, M. A., Rosenblum, L., & Szczesiul, R. (1983). Duplex perception with musical stimuli. *Perception & Psychophysics, 33,* 469–473.

Peterson, G. E., & Barney, H. L. (1952). Control methods used in a study of the vowels. *Journal of the Acoustical Society of America, 24,* 175–184.

Pisoni, D. B. (1977). Identification and discrimination of the relative onset of two component tones: Implications for voicing perception in stops. *Journal of the Acoustical Society of America, 61,* 1352–1361.

Pisoni, D. B. (1992). Some comments on talker normalization. In Y. Tohkura, E. Vatikiotis-Bateson, & Y. Sagisaka (Eds.), *Speech perception, production, and linguistic structure* (pp. 143–151). Tokyo: IOS Press.

Pisoni, D. B., Carrell, T. D., & Gans, S. J. (1983). Perception of the duration of rapid spectrum changes: Evidence for context effects with speech and nonspeech signals. *Perception & Psychophysics, 34,* 314–322.

Pisoni, D. B., & Luce, P. A. (1987). Acoustic-phonetic representations in word recognition. *Cognition, 25,* 21–52.

Pitt, M. A., & Samuel, A. G. (1995). Lexical and sublexical feedback in auditory word recognition. *Cognitive Psychology, 29,* 149–188.

Pollack, I. (1952). The information in elementary auditory displays. *Journal of the Acoustical Society of America, 24,* 745–749.

Pollack, I. (1953). The information in elementary auditory displays: II. *Journal of the Acoustical Society of America, 25,* 765–769.

Port, R. F. (1976). The influence of speaking tempo on the duration of stressed vowel and medial stop in English trochee words. Unpublished doctoral dissertation, University of Connecticut.

Price, P. J., Ostendorf, M., Shattuck-Hufnagel, S., & Fong, C. (1991). The use of prosody in syntactic disambiguation. *Journal of the Acoustical Society of America, 90,* 2956–2970.

Radeau, M., Morais, J., & Segui, J. (1995). Phonological priming between monosyallbic spoken words. *Journal of Experimental Psychology: Learning, Memory, and Cognition, 15,* 378–387.

Reitveld, A. C. M., & Koopmans-van Beinum, F. J. (1987). Vowel reduction and stress. *Speech Communication, 6,* 217–229.

Remez, R. E. (1980). Susceptability of a stop consonant to adaptation on a speech-nonspeech continuum: Further evidence against feature detectors in speech perception. *Perception & Psychophysics, 27,* 17–23.

Remez, R. E., Rubin, P. E., Pisoni, D. B., & Carrell, T. D. (1981). Speech perception without traditional cues. *Science, 212,* 947–950.

Saffran, J. R., Aslin, R. N., & Newport, E. L. (1996). Statistical learning by 8-month-old infants. *Science, 274,* 1926–1928.

Saffran, J. R., Newport, E. L., & Aslin, R. N. (1996). Word segmentation: The role of distributional cues. *Journal of Memory and Language, 35,* 606–621.

Samuel, A. G. (1982). Phonetic prototypes. *Perception & Psychophysics, 31,* 307–314.

Samuel, A. G. (in press). Some empirical tests of Merge's architecture. *Language and Cognitive Processes.*

Savin, H. B., & Bever, T. G. (1970). The nonperceptual reality of the phoneme. *Journal of Verbal Learning and Verbal Behavior, 9,* 295–302.

Sawusch, J. R. (1977). Processing of place information in stop consonants. *Perception & Psychophysics, 22,* 417–426.

Sawusch, J. R. (1992). Auditory metrics for speech perception. In M. E. H. Schouten (Ed.), *The processing of speech: From the auditory periphery to word recognition* (pp. 315–321). Berlin: de Gruyter.

Sawusch, J. R., & Jusczyk, P. W. (1981). Adaptation and contrast in the perception of voicing. *Journal of Experimental Psychology: Human Perception and Performance, 7,* 408–421.

Schacter, D. L., & Church, B. A. (1992). Auditory priming: Implicit and explicit memory for words and voice. *Journal of Experimental Psychology: Learning, Memory and Cognition, 18,* 915–930.

Schreuder, R., & Baayen, R. H. (1994). Prefix stripping re-revisited. *Journal of Memory and Language, 33,* 357–375.

Scott, D. R. (1982). Duration as a cue to the perception of a phrase boundary. *Journal of the Acoustical Society of America, 71,* 996–1007.

Scott, D. R., & Cutler, A. (1984). Segmental phonology and the perception of syntactic structure. *Journal of Verbal Learning and Verbal Behavior, 23,* 450–466.

Searle, C. L., Jacobson, J. Z., & Rayment, S. G. (1979). Phoneme recognition based on human audition. *Journal of the Acoustical Society of America, 65,* 799–809.

Shankweiler, D. P., Strange, W., & Verbrugge, R. R. (1977). Speech and the problem of perceptual constancy. In R. Shaw & J. Bransford (Eds.), *Perceiving, acting, and knowing: Toward an ecological psychology* (pp. 315–345). Hillsdale, NJ: Erlbaum.

Sheffert, S. M. (1995). *Implicit and explicit memory for words and voices.* Unpublished doctoral dissertation, University of Connecticut.

Sheffert, S. M. (1999a). Contributions of surface and conceptual information on spoken word and voice recognition. *Perception & Psychophysics.*

Sheffert, S. M. (1999b). Format-specificity effects on auditory word priming. *Memory & Cognition.*

Shillcock, R. (1990). Lexical hypotheses in continuous speech. In G. T. Altmann (Ed.), *Cognitive models of speech processing* (pp. 24–49). Cambridge: MIT.

Soderstrom, M., Jusczyk, P. W., & Kemler Nelson, D. G. (2000). Evidence for the use of phrasal packaging by English-learning 9-month-olds. In S. C. Howell, S. A. Fish, & T. Keith-Lucas (Eds.), *Proceedings of the 24th Annual Boston University Conference on Language Development: Vol. 2* (pp. 708–718). Somerville, MA: Cascadilla Press.

Stager, C. L., & Werker, J. F. (1997). Infants listen for more phonetic detail in speech perception than in word-learning tasks. *Nature, 388,* 381–382.

Stevens, K. N. (1960). Toward a model for speech recognition. *Journal of the Acoustical Society of America, 32,* 47–55.

Stevens, K. N. (1972). The quantal nature of speech. In J. E. E. David & P. B. Denes (Eds.), *Human communication: A unified view*. New York: McGraw-Hill, (pp. 51–56).

Stevens, K. N. (1998). *Acoustic phonetics*. Cambridge: MIT Press.

Stevens, K. N., & Blumstein, S. E. (1978). Invariant cues for place of articulation in stop consonants. *Journal of the Acoustical Society of America, 64*, 1358–1368.

Streeter, L. A. (1976). Language perception of 2-month old infants shows effects of both innate mechanisms and experience. *Nature, 259*, 39–41.

Streeter, L. A., & Nigro, G. N. (1979). The role of medial consonant transitions in word perception. *Journal of the Acoustical Society of America, 65*, 1533–1541.

Studdert-Kennedy, M. G. (1974). The perception of speech. In T. A. Sebeok (Ed.), *Current trends in linguistics: Vol. 12*. The Hague, Netherlands: Mouton.

Studdert-Kennedy, M. G., Liberman, A. M., Harris, K. S., & Cooper, F. S. (1970). Motor theory of speech perception: A reply to Lane's critical review. *Psychological Review, 77*, 234–249.

Summerfield, Q. (1975). *Acoustic and phonetic components of the influence of voice changes and identification times for CVC syllables*. Belfast, Ireland: Queen's University of Belfast (unpublished ms.).

Summerfield, Q., & Haggard, M. P. (1973). *Vocal tract normalisation as demonstrated by reaction times* [Report of Speech Research in Progress 2]. Belfast, Ireland: Queen's University of Belfast.

Suomi, K. (1984). On talker and phoneme identification conveyed by vowels: A whole spectrum approach to the normalization problem. *Speech Communication, 3*, 199–209.

Sussman, H. M. (1986). A neuronal model of vowel normalization and representation. *Brain and Language, 28*, 12–23.

Sussman, H. M., McCaffrey, H. A., & Matthews, S. A. (1991). An investigation of locus equations as a source of relational invariance for stop place

categorization. *Journal of the Acoustical Society of America, 90*, 1309–1325.

Swingley, D., & Aslin, R. N. (2000). Spoken word recognition and lexical representation in young children. *Cognition, 76*, 147–166.

Swingley, D., Pinto, J., & Fernald, A. (1999). Continuous processing in word recognition at 24-months. *Cognition, 71*, 73–108.

Swinney, D. A., & Prather, P. (1980). Phonemic identification in a phoneme monitoring experiment: The variable role of uncertainty about vowel contexts. *Perception & Psychophysics, 27*, 104–110.

Swoboda, P., Kass, J., Morse, P. A., & Leavitt, L. A. (1978). Memory factors in infant vowel discrimination of normal and at-risk infants. *Child Development, 49*, 332–339.

Swoboda, P., Morse, P. A., & Leavitt, L. A. (1976). Continuous vowel discrimination in normal and at-risk infants. *Child Development, 47*, 459–465.

Syrdal, A. K., & Gopal, H. S. (1986). A perceptual model of vowel recognition based on the auditory representation of American English vowels. *Journal of the Acoustical Society of America, 79*, 1086–1100.

Tabossi, P., Burani, C., & Scott, D. (1995). Word identification in fluent speech. *Journal of Memory and Language, 34*, 440–467.

Tartter, V. C., & Eimas, P. D. (1975). The role of auditory and phonetic feature detectors in the perception of speech. *Perception & Psychophysics, 18*, 293–298.

Trehub, S. E. (1973). Infants' sensitivity to vowel and tonal contrasts. *Developmental Psychology, 9*, 91–96.

Trehub, S. E. (1976). The discrimination of foreign speech contrasts by infants and adults. *Child Development, 47*, 466–472.

Treiman, R., Kessler, B., Knewasser, S., Tincoff, R., & Bowman, M. (1996). English speakers' sensitivity to phonotactic patterns. Paper for volume on Fifth Conference on Laboratory Phonology.

Tsushima, T., Takizawa, O., Sasaki, M., Siraki, S., Nishi, K., Kohno, M., Menyuk, P., & Best, C. (1994). *Discrimination of English /r-l/ and /w-y/*

by Japanese infants at 6–12 months: Language specific developmental changes in speech perception abilities. Paper presented at the International Conference on Spoken Language Processing, Yokohama, Japan.

van de Weijer, J. (1998). *Language input for word discovery*. Unpublished doctoral dissertation, University of Nijmegen, Nijmegen, Netherlands.

Verbrugge, R. R., & Rakerd, B. (1986). Evidence of talker-independent information for vowels. *Language and Speech, 29,* 39–57.

Verbrugge, R. R., Strange, W., Shankweiler, D. P., & Edman, T. R. (1976). What information enables a listener to map a talker's vowel space? *Journal of the Acoustical Society of America, 60,* 198–212.

Vitevitch, M. S., & Luce, P. A. (1998). When words compete: Levels of processing in spoken word perception. *Psychological Science, 9,* 325–329.

Vitevitch, M. S., & Luce, P. A. (1999). Probabilistic phonotactics and neighborhood activation in spoken word recognition. *Journal of Memory and Language, 40,* 374–408.

Vitevitch, M. S., Luce, P. A., Charles-Luce, J., & Kemmerer, D. (1996). Phonotactic and metrical influences on the perception of spoken and nonsense words. *Language and Speech, 40,* 47–62.

Vitevitch, M. S., Luce, P. A., Charles-Luce, J., & Kemmerer, D. (1997). Phonotactics and syllable stress: Implications for the processing of spoken nonsense words. *Language and Speech, 40,* 47–62.

Vroomen, J., & de Gelder, B. (1995). Metrical segmentation and lexical inhibition in spoken word recognition. *Journal of Experimental Psychology: Human Perception and Performance, 21,* 98–108.

Vroomen, J., & de Gelder, B. (1997). Activation of embedded words in spoken word recognition. *Journal of Experimental Psychology: Human Perception and Performance, 23,* 710–720.

Vroomen, J., van Zon, M., & de Gelder, B. (1996). Cues to speech segmentation: Evidence from juncture misperceptions and word spotting. *Memory & Cognition, 24,* 744–755.

Walley, A. C. (1988). Spoken word recognition by young children and adults. *Cognitive Development, 3,* 137–165.

Walley, A. C. (1993). The role of vocabulary development in children's spoken word recognition and segmentation ability. *Developmental Review, 13,* 286–350.

Warren, P., & Marslen-Wilson, W. (1987). Continuous uptake of acoustic cues in spoken word recognition. *Perception & Psychophysics, 41,* 262–275.

Warren, P., & Marslen-Wilson, W. (1988). Cues to lexical choice: Discriminating place and voice. *Perception & Psychophysics, 31,* 21–30.

Warren, R. M. (1974). Auditory temporal discrimination by trained listeners. *Cognitive Psychology, 6,* 237–256.

Warren, R. M., Obusek, C. J., Farmer, R. M., & Warren, R. P. (1969). Auditory sequence: Confusion of patterns other than speech or music. *Science, 164,* 586–587.

Werker, J. F. (1991). The ontogeny of speech perception. In I. G. Mattingly & M. Studdert-Kennedy (Eds.), *Modularity and the motor theory of speech perception* (pp. 91–109). Hillsdale, NJ: Erlbaum.

Werker, J. F., & Lalonde, C. E. (1988). Cross-language speech perception: Initial capabilities and developmental change. *Developmental Psychology, 24,* 672–683.

Werker, J. F., & Tees, R. C. (1984). Cross-language speech perception: Evidence for perceptual reorganization during the first year of life. *Infant Behavior and Development, 7,* 49–63.

Whalen, D. H. (1984). Subcategorical phonetic mismatches slow phonetic judgments. *Perception & Psychophysics, 35,* 49–64.

Whalen, D. H. (1991) subcategorical phonetic mismatches and lexical access. *Perception & Psychophysics, 50,* 351–360.

Wickelgren, W. A. (1969). Context-sensitive coding in speech recognition, articulation, and development. In K. N. Leibovic (Ed.), *Information processing in the nervous system.* Berlin: Springer.

Williams, L. (1977). *The effects of phonetic environment and stress placement on infant discrimination of place of stop consonant artic-ulation.* Paper presented at the Second Annual Boston University Conference on Language Development, Boston.

Zatorre, R. J., & Halpern, A. R. (1979). Identification, discrimination, and selective adaptation of simultaneous musical intervals. *Perception & Psychophysics, 26,* 384–395.

CHAPTER 13

Neural Basis of Haptic Perception

KENNETH JOHNSON

The richness of sensation from the human hand is based on the variety of receptor types and related afferent fiber types sending information to the brain. The glabrous (hairless) skin and deeper tissues are innervated by 13 types of sensory afferents, comprising two groups of pain afferents (Raja, Meyer, Ringkamp, & Campbell, 1999), an itch afferent (Andrew & Craig, 2001; Schmelz, Schmidt, Bickel, Handwerker, & Torebjörk, 1997), two thermoreceptive types (one selectively responsive to cooling and one to warming; Darian-Smith, 1984), four proprioceptive types, which signal information about muscle length, muscle force, and joint angle (Clark & Horch, 1986), and four mechanoreceptive afferent types responsive to skin deformation. Haptic perception depends primarily on these four mechanoreceptive types and they are the main focus of this chapter. Proprioceptors are included in the discussion of joint angle perception.

The mechanoreceptive afferents consist of two types that innervate the epidermis densely (slowly adapting type 1, or SA1, afferents that end in Merkel cells and rapidly adapting, or RA, afferents that end in Meissner corpuscles) and two that are sparser and end in the deeper tissues (Pacinian, or PC, afferents that end in Pacinian corpuscles and slowly adapting type 2, or SA2, afferents that are thought to end in Ruffini complexes). The mechanore-

ceptors in the glabrous skin of the hand are illustrated in Figure 13.1. The innervation of the hairy skin of the back of the hand is less well studied, but it is different from that of the glabrous skin and of other hairy skin (Edin & Abbs, 1991; Vallbo, Olausson, Wessberg, & Kakuda, 1995). It contains afferent types that are similar to the four cutaneous mechanoreceptive afferents of the glabrous skin plus a small number of mechanoreceptive afferents that end in hair follicles.

Evidence from more than three decades of combined psychophysical and neurophysiological research, which began with Mountcastle's studies of the neural mechanisms of vibratory sensation (Mountcastle, LaMotte, & Carli, 1972; Talbot, Darian-Smith, Kornhuber, & Mountcastle, 1968), supports the idea that each afferent type serves a distinctly different sensory function and that, taken together, these functions explain tactual perceptual function. Furthermore, it is evident that the receptors of each of the afferent types are specialized to extract the information that is most relevant for their respective perceptual functions (Johnson, 2001). Much of the evidence for this division of function between the afferent systems is recent and is, therefore, the focus of this chapter. The central mechanisms of haptic perception have been reviewed recently (Burton & Sinclair, 1996; Hsiao & Vega Bermudez, 2001; Johnson & Yoshioka, 2001).

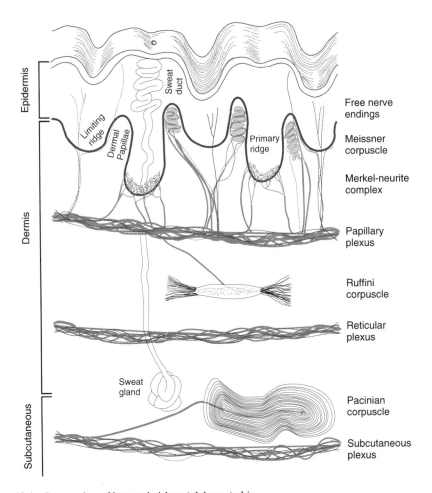

Figure 13.1 Innervation of human hairless (glabrous) skin.

NOTE: The skin of the palm and flexor surfaces of the fingers comprises two layers, the epidermis and dermis. The thickness of the epidermis is fairly constant over the glabrous surface of the hand; the distance from the skin surface to the dermal papillae is typically 0.6 mm whereas the distance to the tips of the primary ridges, which contain the sweat ducts, is typically 1.0 mm. The dermis is 2 to 3 mm thick and contains connective tissue (predominantly collagen and elastin fibers), blood vessels, sweat glands, and nerve plexuses. Three plexuses supply sensory endings to the epidermis and dermis. They also supply autonomic innervation to the sweat glands and blood vessels which is not shown. The large-caliber myelinated axons that supply morphologically distinct cutaneous mechanoreceptors are illustrated in green. The small myelinated and unmyelinated axons that supply free nerve endings (which are thermoreceptors, nociceptors, and itch receptors) are illustrated in red. The Meissner's corpuscles are located in the tips of the dermal papillae, which are as close to the surface of the skin within the dermis as is possible. The drawing illustrates the fact that Meissner's corpuscles are innervated by 2 to 6 large myelinated axons as well as small fibers, which are C fibers, whose function is not known (Johansson, Fantini & Hu, 1999; Paré, Elde, Mazurkiewicz, Smith, & Rice, 2001). A single Meissner axon can also innervate many Meissner's corpuscles (see text). The Merkel afferent terminals are located next to Merkel cells, which are specialized epidermal cells in the tips of the primary epidermal ridges. A single Merkel afferent axon innervates many (possibly hundreds) of Merkel cells on several primary ridges. Ruffini corpuscles (whose existence is questioned but are illustrated here because that is the accepted practice) are thought to be encapsulated strands of connective tissue and nerve endings. The Pacinian corpuscles are located in the deeper parts of the dermis and in the subcutaneous tissues. A single Pacinian axon innervates a single Pacinian corpuscle and, likewise, a single Pacinian corpuscle is innervated by a single afferent axon.

SOURCE: Adapted by Michel Paré from a drawing by R. W. Crosby (Mountcastle, 1974, page 299).

SA1, SA2, RA, and PC systems are referred to throughout the chapter (Johnson & Hsiao, 1992). Reference to the SA1 system, for example, means the SA1 receptors (the Merkel-neurite complex), the SA1 afferent nerve fiber population, and all the central neural pathways that convey the SA1 signal to memory and perception. This usage does not imply that there is no convergence between the systems in the central nervous system or that systems do not overlap. They may or may not do so. However, the available evidence supports the idea that the information from each of the afferent systems is segregated and processed separately at least through the early stages of cortical processing.

Combined psychophysical and neurophysiological studies have played a more prominent role in the study of somatosensation than in any other system because of the large number of afferent systems and because the receptors of all but the nociceptive and pruritic systems are so sensitive. Most manual activities engage most of the afferent systems, which makes it difficult to assign a particular function to a single afferent system without very careful hypothesis testing and elimination. The history of this endeavor is full of surprises, and nothing can be taken for granted. The first, very interesting surprise arises from the extreme sensitivity of Pacinian receptors to vibration. Adrian and Umrath (1929), in one of the first neurophysiological studies of sensory receptors, indented exposed Pacinian corpuscles with a probe mounted on the laboratory bench and observed a sustained discharge whose rate increased monotonically with increasing indentation. Because of this observation, the Pacinian corpuscle was thought to be a pressure receptor for two decades or more (and is still identified as such in some textbooks). Its complete insensitivity to sustained deformation and its extreme sensitivity to vibration were discovered later (Gray & Malcolm,

1950; Sato, 1961), but the reason for the sustained response to indentation was not discovered until Hunt (1961) showed (with an accelerometer mounted on the dissecting table) that a sensitive PC receptor responds to ambient vibrations transmitted through a building. Adrian and Umrath were evidently coupling ambient vibrations to their Pacinian corpuscle more effectively as they drove their probe more deeply into the corpuscle.

A second example, examined later, involves the neural basis of joint angle perception. The joint capsules are richly innervated with receptors, and nothing would seem more obvious than that joint angle perception is based on information provided by joint afferents; however, the evidence is to the contrary. An early (but not a critical) indication that joint afferents play no role or at best only a minor role came from the observation that joint replacements that involve removal of the joint capsule and its innervation produced little or no deficit in joint angle perception (Cross & McCloskey, 1973; Grigg, Finerman, & Riley, 1973; Moberg, 1972). Subsequent psychophysical and neurophysiological studies (discussed later) showed that joint afferents play no discernible role in the perception of flexion and extension at simple joints such as the knee and the elbow; at those simpler joints, joint angle perception depends on information provided by muscle spindle afferents. In the hand, where no single afferent provides unambiguous information about joint angle and hand conformation, the joint afferents appear to play a tertiary role, although that is disputed by some (as discussed later).

A third example, also examined later, involves the neural basis of tactile form perception (e.g., the ability to read Braille with the fingertips). Before form perception was studied in combined psychophysical and neurophysiological experiments, all the evidence pointed to the RA system. The RA system has several properties to recommend it. First, it innervates the skin more densely than does any other system (e.g., 50% more densely than the SA1 system), and innervation density is the primary correlate of spatial acuity over the surface of the body. Second, the RA receptor, the Meissner corpuscle, lies closer to the surface of the epidermis than does any other mechanoreceptor; it would, therefore, seem to be best suited to sense the fine spatial features of a surface. Third, form perception is enhanced by finger movement over a surface, and motion is required to activate the RA system. The effect of motion on form perception can be appreciated by placing a finger stationary on a surface with some structure, sensing the surface features, and then by moving the finger back and forth over the same surface. When the finger is stationary, the surface features are perceived only dimly; when the finger is in motion, the surface features are perceived clearly. One of David Katz's many pithy observations is that "movement [is] as indispensable for touch as light is for color sensations" (Katz, 1925/1970). A reasonable but erroneous interpretation is that the SA1 and RA systems are like the scotopic and photopic systems in vision: When the finger is stationary (like dim light) and only the SA1 system is active, resolution is poor. When the finger is moving (bright light), the RA system is active, and we perceive surface structure acutely. In fact, the SA1 system—not the RA system—is responsible for form perception. The scotopic-photopic analogy is apt but in reverse, as will be evident when the SA1 and RA systems are examined more closely: The RA system, like the scotopic system, is more sensitive, has substantially poorer spatial resolution, and has a limited dynamic range. The SA1 system, like the photopic system, is less sensitive, but it has substantially finer spatial resolution at the fingertips (the somatosensory fovea) and a much greater dynamic range. The effect of motion on form perception derives from the SA1 mechanoreceptors' much greater sensitivity to dynamic than to static stimuli.

The properties and functions of each of the afferent systems are summarized in Table 13.1. All the mechanoreceptive afferents are large, myelinated nerve fibers (6–12 μm diameter) with conduction velocities in the Aβ range (35–70 m/s); SA1 afferents are distinguished by a narrower range of axon diameters and conduction velocities (see Table 13.1). Two of the four afferent types, the RA and PC afferents, respond only to dynamic skin deformation. The other two, the slowly adapting SA1 and SA2 afferents, respond to sustained skin deformation with a sustained discharge, but they (SA1 afferents particularly) are much more sensitive to movement than to static deformation. The SA1 and RA afferents innervate the skin densely. Because the SA1 afferents innervate the skin densely and resolve spatial detail so well (about 0.5 mm at the fingertips), they convey high-resolution neural images of cutaneous stimuli to the brain. RA afferents have poorer spatial resolution but greater sensitivity than do the SA1s, and consequently they convey a dense image of skin motion. In contrast, the SA2 and PC afferents innervate the hand more sparsely, have larger receptive fields, and resolve spatial detail poorly. SA2 afferents are less sensitive to skin indentation than are SA1 afferents but they are more sensitive to skin stretch and therefore convey an image of skin stretch. Individual PC afferents are extremely sensitive to high-frequency vibration; the most sensitive among them respond to skin deformation of 10 nm or less at 200 Hz. As a result, the PC population conveys a precise temporal representation of vibrations acting on the hand. The neural response properties of these four cutaneous afferent types have been studied extensively in both human and nonhuman primates, and excepting SA2 afferents (discussed later), there are no interspecies differences.

Table 13.1   Afferent Systems and Their Properties.

Afferent type	SA1	RA	PC	SA2
Receptor	Merkel	Meissner	Pacinian	Ruffini
Location	Tip of epidermal sweat ridges	Dermal papillae (close to skin surface)	Dermis and deeper tissues	Dermis
Axon diameter	7–11 μm	6–12 μm	6–12 μm	6–12 μm
Conduction velocity	40–65 m/s	35–70 m/s	35–70 m/s	35–70 m/s
Sensory function	Form and texture perception	Motion detection, grip control	Perception of distant events through transmitted vibrations, tool use	Tangential force, hand shape, motion direction
Effective stimulus	Edges, points, corners, curvature	Skin motion	Vibration	Skin stretch
Response to sustained indentation	Sustained with slow adaptation	None	None	Sustained with slow adaptation
Frequency range	0–100 Hz	1–300 Hz	5–1000 Hz	0–? Hz
Peak sensitivity	5 Hz	50 Hz	200 Hz	0.5 Hz
Threshold for rapid indentation or vibration (best)	8 μm	2 μm	0.01 μm	40 μm
Threshold (mean)	30 μm	6 μm	0.08 μm	300 μm
Receptive field area (measured with rapid 0.5 mm indentation)	9 mm^2	22 mm^2	Entire finger or hand	60 mm^2
Innervation density (finger pad)	100/cm^2	150/cm^2	20/cm^2	10/cm^2
Spatial acuity	0.5 mm	3 mm	10+ mm	7+ mm

When single afferent axons are stimulated electrically in humans (Ochoa & Torebjörk, 1983; Vallbo, Olsson, Westberg, & Clark, 1984), the result is consistent with the functions inferred from combined psychophysical and neurophysiological experiments: Stimulation of an SA1 afferent produces a sensation of steady pressure located at the neuron's receptive field; stimulation of an RA afferent produces a sensation of tapping or flutter, also localized to the neuron's receptive field; stimulation of a PC afferent produces a sensation of vibration localized at the center of the PC's receptive field. Stimulation of SA2 afferents produces either sensation over a large skin area whose quality varies from afferent to afferent (Vallbo et al., 1984) or no sensation at all (Ochoa & Torebjörk, 1983).

PERCEPTUAL FUNCTION OF EACH AFFERENT SYSTEM

Neurophysiological, psychophysical, and combined psychophysical and neurophysiological studies discussed in this chapter support the idea that each of the afferent systems serves a distinctly different perceptual function. Moreover, the receptors in each of those systems appear to be specialized to extract the information that is most relevant to the system's perceptual role (Johnson, 2001).

The data reviewed in this chapter support the following hypotheses:

- The SA1 system is responsible for form and texture perception. SA1 afferents innervate the skin densely, and they resolve spatial features of .5 mm or less. The SA1 receptor, the Merkel-neurite complex, is selectively sensitive to a specific component of tissue strain (closely related to strain energy density), which confers sensitivity to edges, corners, points, and curvature.

- The RA system is responsible for the perception of events that produce low-frequency, low-amplitude skin motion. That includes the detection of microscopic surface features and low-frequency vibration. Its most important function may be the provision of feedback signals for grip control. The sensitive RA receptors are suspended within (Meissner) corpuscles that act as filters to shield the receptors from the low-frequency (<2 Hz), high-amplitude skin deformations that accompany typical manual tasks.

- The PC system is responsible for the perception of events transmitted to the hand as high-frequency vibrations through objects, probes, and tools held in the hand. The PC receptor, which is sensitive to nanometer-level skin motion, is protected from the confounding effects of high-amplitude, low-frequency stresses and strains that accompany manual tasks by steep mechanical filtering (provided by the multilayered, fluid-filled Pacinian corpuscle that surrounds the nerve ending).

- The SA2 system provides information used for the perception of hand conformation and for the perception of forces acting parallel to the skin surface. The SA2 receptors are especially sensitive to the deep tissue strain produced by skin stretch and changes in hand and finger shape. They are protected from the confounding effects of stimuli within their receptive fields by relative insensitivity to local skin deformation.

To illustrate these functions, consider the hypothesized role of each system as you take a key from a pocket and unlock a door. While you reach for the pocket, you shape your hand appropriately (SA2, muscle spindle, and possibly joint receptor systems) and slide it into the pocket. As you do so, you feel the texture of the pocket material and you isolate the key from the surrounding coins (both SA1 functions). Then you grasp the key with a force just sufficient to lift it from the pocket without slip (RA system), position it appropriately for insertion into the lock (SA1 system), and move it toward the lock. When the key touches the lock (signaled by the PC system), your grip force increases to avoid slip as you insert the key (RA afferents). On insertion you feel the key sliding into the lock, you feel the lock's mechanisms in operation, and you get a sense of the quality and precision of the locking mechanism (PC system). The evidence linking each system to its respective role is examined in the rest of the chapter.

SA1 SYSTEM

The SA1 receptors are Merkel-neurite complexes involving specialized (Merkel) epidermal cells that enfold the unmyelinated ends of SA1 axons (Iggo & Andres, 1982). Although there are synapse-like junctions between the Merkel cells and the axon terminals, action potentials appear to arise as the result of the deformation of mechanosensitive ion channels in the bare nerve endings (Diamond, Mills, & Mearow, 1988; Ogawa, 1996). As individual SA1 afferent axons approach the epidermis, they branch over an area of about 5 mm^2 and terminate in the basal layer of the epidermis at the tips of the epidermal sweat ridges (see Figure 13.1)

(Miller, Ralston, & Kasahara, 1960). This area is estimated from the minimal SA1 receptive field area (shown later in Figure 13.8). Throughout the receptive field, the SA1 discharge rate is approximately a linear function of indentation amplitude (Blake, Johnson, & Hsiao, 1997; Mountcastle, Talbot, & Kornhuber, 1966; Vega-Bermudez & Johnson, 1999a; but see Knibestöl & Vallbo, 1980). However, SA1 afferents are much more sensitive to the temporal and spatial structure of a stimulus than to indentation per se. Scanning a finger across a Braille dot, for example, evokes SA1 impulse rates that are 10 times greater than those that result from placing the finger on the dot without horizontal movement (Johnson & Lamb, 1981), and placing a finger on an edge can evoke SA1 impulse rates 20 times greater than those evoked by placing it on a smooth surface (Phillips & Johnson, 1981a).

Numerous studies link the SA1 system to form and texture perception. The distinction between form and texture perception adopted here is that form perception is the perception of the geometric structure of a surface or object, whereas texture perception corresponds to the subjective feel of a surface or object. Form perception depends on the geometry of the object's surface features; texture perception depends on the features' distributed, statistical properties. Form perception has many dimensions; texture perception has only two or possibly three dimensions (discussed later). Form perception can be studied with objective methods (i.e., the subject's responses can be scored for accuracy); texture perception cannot. A sheet of Braille text provides a good example of this distinction. After scanning a Braille passage, an observer can be asked to report the content of the passage or how rough it felt. The subject's character or word recognition can be scored for accuracy; the report of roughness cannot. The subject could have been asked a question about the spacing or density of the Braille dots, but the answer, in our view, would have been the result of form perception, not texture perception. Many combined psychophysical and neurophysiological studies have shown that the SA1 system accounts for both form and texture perception and that none of the other systems can do so. Form and texture perception are discussed separately.

Form Perception

Form perception is constant over a wide range of stimulus conditions. The ability to discriminate object or surface features and the capacity for pattern recognition at the fingertip are the same whether the object is contacted actively or is applied to the passive hand; they are affected only marginally by whether the object is stationary or moving relative to the skin; they are unaffected by scanning speed up to 40 mm/s and then decline slowly at higher scanning speeds; they are unaffected by contact force, at least over the range from 0.2–1 N; and they are affected only marginally by the height (relief) of spatial features over a wide range of heights (Johnson & Phillips, 1981; Loomis, 1981, 1985; Phillips, Johnson, & Browne, 1983; Vega-Bermudez, Johnson, & Hsiao, 1991).

The evidence that the SA1 system is responsible for form perception is based on its exclusive ability to account for spatial acuity at the fingertip and for the perception and discrimination of curvature. Figure 13.2 shows the human ability to discriminate three different kinds of stimuli with the distal pad of the index finger. The element width that results in performance midway between chance and perfect discrimination, between 0.9 mm and 1.0 mm, is close to the theoretical limit set by the density of SA1 and RA primary afferents at the fingertip (discussed later). Acuity declines progressively from the index to the fifth finger (Vega-Bermudez &

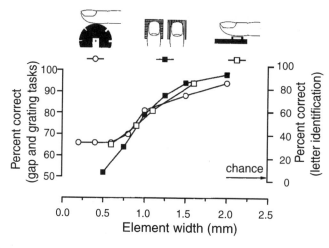

Figure 13.2 Gap detection, grating orientation discrimination, and letter recognition performance.
NOTE: The abscissa displays the basic element width for each task: gap size for the gap detection task, groove width (which equaled bar width) for the grating orientation discrimination task, and average bar and gap width within letters (one fifth the letter height) for the letter recognition task. Threshold is defined as the element size producing performance midway between chance and perfect performance (75% correct for gap detection and grating orientation discrimination, 52% for letter recognition).
SOURCE: Adapted from Johnson & Phillips (1981).

Johnson, 2001); it declines progressively at more proximal finger and hand locations (Craig & Lyle, 2001); and it declines progressively with age (Sathian, Zangaladze, Green, Vitek, & DeLong, 1997; J. C. Stevens & Choo, 1996; Wohlert, 1996). Whether these effects are due to changes in innervation density is not known. Spatial acuity at the lip and tongue (0.51 mm and 0.58 mm respectively; Van Boven & Johnson, 1994a) is significantly better than at the fingertip (Essick, Chen, & Kelly, 1999; Sathian & Zangaladze, 1996; Van Boven & Johnson, 1994a). An important point for the discussion that follows is that tactile spatial acuity is the same in humans and monkeys (Hsiao, O'Shaughnessy, & Johnson, 1993).

The capacity for spatial discrimination and pattern recognition illustrated in Figure 13.2 implies that at least one of the afferent systems must transmit a neural image of the stimulus with 1 mm resolution or better. That requires an innervation density of at least one affer-

ent per square millimeter, and it requires that the individual afferents be able to resolve the spatial details that humans resolve in discrimination experiments. Neither the PC nor the SA2 system comes close either on the basis of innervation density (Johansson & Vallbo, 1979b). Figure 13.3 shows the responses of typical human cutaneous afferents to Braille symbols scanned over their receptive fields. It is evident in Figure 13.3 that neither the PC nor the SA2 afferents convey any useful information about the form of the Braille patterns, whereas RA, and particularly SA1, afferents do. Precise estimates of SA1 and RA innervation densities are difficult. Because there are, as yet, no molecular markers for the axons of the different afferent types, estimates of innervation density are indirect; current estimates are based on the ratios of the different afferent types in random neurophysiological samples and counts of the total numbers of axons with diameters in the Aβ range (6–12 μm). Estimates of the SA1 and RA

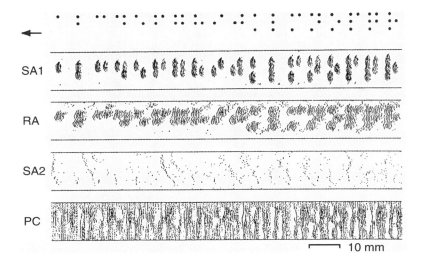

Figure 13.3   Responses of single human SA1, RA, SA2, and PC afferents to the Braille symbols A through R.

NOTE: The Braille symbols were scanned repeatedly from right to left over the afferent fibers' receptive fields (in effect, the receptive fields scanned from left to right) at 60 mm/s. Each tick mark represents the occurrence of an action potential. After each scan, the Braille pattern was shifted 0.2 mm at right angles to the scanning direction. Each receptive field was on a distal finger pad.

SOURCE: Adapted from Phillips, Johansson, & Johnson (1990).

densities at the fingertip are, respectively, 70 and 141 afferents/cm^2 in humans (Johansson & Vallbo, 1979b) and 134 and 178 afferents/cm^2 in monkeys (Darian-Smith & Kenins, 1980), but the differences between humans and monkeys are not statistically significant for reasons given by Johansson and Vallbo (1976). A reasonable estimate based on the two studies is 100 SA1 and 150 RA afferents/cm^2. These innervation densities correspond to mean spacings between SA1 and RA receptive field centers of 1.0 mm and 0.82 mm. Therefore, SA1 and RA systems are both potentially able to account for form perception.

Direct evidence that only the SA1 afferents account for the spatial resolution illustrated in Figure 13.2 comes from neurophysiological experiments in which SA1 and RA afferents were studied with the same periodic gratings as were used in the psychophysical experiments (Phillips and Johnson, 1981a).

Figure 13.4 illustrates SA1, RA, and PC responses to a grating identical to those used in the psychophysical experiments except that all groove widths are contained in the single grating. The RA illustrated here was the most sensitive to spatial detail of all the RAs tested. Note the SA1 afferent's response to edges and isolated features as compared with its responses to indentation by a flat surface. Note also that the human performance illustrated in Figure 13.2 begins to rise above chance at element sizes around 0.5 mm, which means that the system responsible for this behavior must begin to resolve spatial detail at 0.5 mm or below. As can be seen in Figure 13.4, SA1 responses to aperiodic grating convey information about spatial structure when the groove and ridge widths are 0.5 mm wide (leftmost bars and grooves); when the grooves and ridges are 1 mm wide, SA1s provide a robust neural image of the stimulus. In contrast, the RA illustrated in Figure 13.4 fails to signal

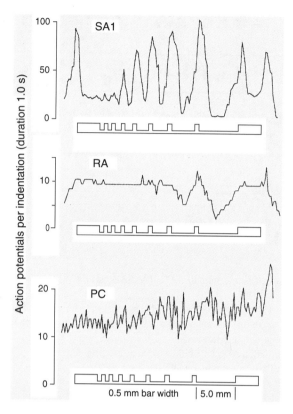

Figure 13.4 SA1, RA, and PC responses to an aperiodic grating pressed into the skin.
NOTE: The grating is shown in cross section beneath each response profile. The end bars are 3.0 mm
wide; the internal bars are 0.5 mm wide. The grooves are deeper than illustrated (2.0 mm deep) and are
0.5, 0.5, 0.75, 1.0, 1.5, 2.0, 3.0, and 5.0 mm wide. The grating indented the skin by 1 mm for 1 s and
then was raised and moved laterally 0.2 mm for the next indentation. The ordinate represents the number
of action potentials evoked during the 1-s period. RA and PC afferents responded during the indentation
phase only, which accounts for their smaller impulse counts. The abscissa for each plot represents the
position of the receptive field center relative to the grating; for example, the left peak in the SA1 response
profile (95 imp/s) occurred when the center of the SA1 receptive field was directly beneath the left edge
of the grating. The RA illustrated here was the most sensitive to spatial detail of all RAs studied. Most
RA responses dipped only during the 5-mm gap, and some barely registered the presence of the 5-mm
gap even though they responded vigorously at all grating positions. Testing progressed from right to left.
The progressive decline in PC responses results from adaptation to the repeated indentations.
SOURCE: Adapted from Phillips & Johnson (1981a).

the presence of a groove until it is at least
3 mm wide; most RAs require groove widths
that are greater than 3 mm. Kops and Gardner
(1996) have obtained nearly identical results
(discussed later).

A. W. Goodwin, Wheat, and their colleagues have taken an approach to the neural mechanisms of form perception that does
not rely on acuity; instead, they have investigated the neural mechanisms of curvature perception (A. W. Goodwin, Browning,
& Wheat, 1995; A. W. Goodwin, John, &
Marceglia, 1991; A. W. Goodwin & Wheat,
1992a, 1992b). When the skin is indented with
a curved surface, one of the cues to curvature
is the increase of contact area with increasing

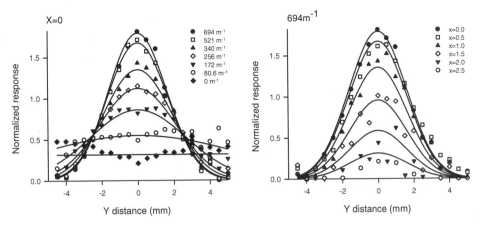

Figure 13.5   SA1 population response to indentation with spheres of varying curvature.
NOTE: The left plot shows the mean responses of SA1 afferents as a function of proximal-distal distance from the center of indentation. Data are shown for seven curved surfaces with radii ranging from 1.44 mm (curvature $= 694 \, m^{-1}$) to a flat surface (curvature $= 0 \, m^{-1}$). The right plot shows population response profiles in proximal-distal slices at varying distances from the center of indentation.
SOURCE: From Goodwin, Browning, & Wheat (1995). Reprinted with permission.

indentation; in fact, however, curvature is discriminated virtually as well (with a Weber fraction of 10–20%) when contact area is held constant as when it is not. Other experiments by A. W. Goodwin and his colleagues show that estimates of curvature are unaffected by changes in contact force and, conversely, that estimates of force are unaffected by changes in curvature. This latter finding is particularly surprising considering that SA1 firing rates are strongly affected by curvature (A. W. Goodwin et al., 1995; Srinivasan & LaMotte, 1987). These psychophysical observations suggest that the spatial profile of neural activity in one or more of the afferent populations is used for the perception of curvature and that a different signal (e.g., total discharge rate) is used for the perception of force. In fact, only the SA1 population response can account for the human ability to discriminate the curvature and orientation of a curved stimulus applied to the skin (Dodson, Goodwin, Browning, & Gehring, 1998; A. W. Goodwin et al., 1995). The SA1 population response provides a veridical neural image of curved

stimuli over a wide range of shapes and application forces (see Figure 13.5). RAs respond poorly to such stimuli and provide no signal that might account for the ability to discriminate curvature (A. W. Goodwin et al., 1995; Khalsa, Friedman, Srinivasan, & LaMotte, 1998; LaMotte, Friedman, Lu, Khalsa, & Srinivasan, 1998). Other studies with a reading device for the blind (discussed later) demonstrate the capacity for form perception provided by the RA system and show that it is substantially less acute than the performance illustrated in Figure 13.2. Thus, the evidence is that the SA1 system is the only system that can account for form perception and, furthermore, that it is specialized for the representation of stimulus form because of its sensitivity to edges, local features, and curvature.

SA1 Afferents Are Specialized for Representing Local Spatial Features

The response properties that most prominently distinguish the SA1 receptor as being specialized for representing local spatial

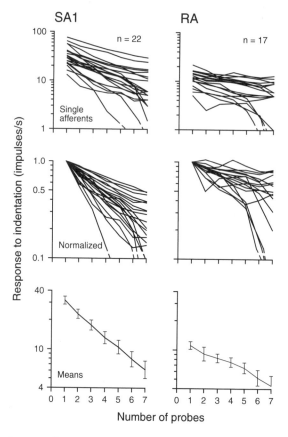

Figure 13.6 Surround suppression.

NOTE: The skin was indented 100 μm by one or more probes. One probe, the central probe, always indented the center of the receptive field; additional probes indented the skin at the vertices of a hexagon, each vertex being 1 mm from the center. The ordinates of the top two graphs represent the mean impulse rate (impulses per second, or ips) during the 200-ms indentation period. The response to two probes represents the mean impulse rate over all six possible placements of the second probe. The response to three probes represents the mean response over all 15 possible placements of the second and third probe, and so on. The top two graphs represent the responses of 22 SA1 and 17 RA afferents to varying numbers of probes. The middle two graphs are normalized to emphasize the differences in surround suppression between afferents. The bottom two graphs are the geometric means of the responses displayed in the top graphs. The SA1 and RA responses to seven probes are 20% and 50% of the responses to a single probe. Note that the intense surround suppression displayed here occurred even though the indentation depth was only one-tenth the probe spacing. The surround suppression was independent of indentation depth. SOURCE: Adapted from Vega-Bermudez & Johnson (1999b).

features are its spatial resolution (Figures 13.3 and 13.4) and its sensitivity to edges, points, and curvature (illustrated in Figures 13.4 to 13.7). This results from sensitivity to a specific component of the subcutaneous stress-strain field that is produced by skin surface deformation. Any cutaneous stimulus produces a complex pattern of stresses and strains (pressures and distortions) in the skin and in the subcutaneous tissues. Some components of stress and strain are particularly strong under points, edges, and regions

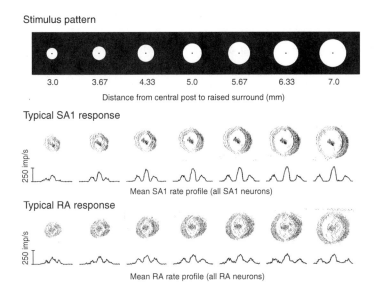

Stimulus pattern

3.0 3.67 4.33 5.0 5.67 6.33 7.0

Distance from central post to raised surround (mm)

Typical SA1 response

250 imp/s

Mean SA1 rate profile (all SA1 neurons)

Typical RA response

250 imp/s

Mean RA rate profile (all RA neurons)

Figure 13.7 Surround suppression produced by surface features.
NOTE: The stimulus is a smooth plastic surface (black) with holes (white) that are 0.6 mm deep. Within each hole is a square post, 0.4 mm wide by 0.6 mm tall (i.e., flush with the surrounding surface). The distance from the post to the surrounding surface varies from 3.0 mm to 7.0 mm. The methods are the same as in Figure 13.3. The trace beneath each raster represents the mean impulse rate in a swath 2 mm wide containing the peak response to the central post. The number of impulses evoked by the central post begins to decline when the edges of the hole come to within 6 mm of the post. When the surround closes to 3 mm, the SA1 response is reduced to 50% of its unsuppressed value; the RA response is reduced to 75% of its unsuppressed value. The overall result of this surround suppression is that neither the SA1 nor the RA afferents respond to the flat surface even though the pressure is substantial (the average pressure used by humans while scanning a surface), but they both respond intensely to the essential features of the surface, including the falling edge of each hole (the left edge). The RA illustrated here responds more robustly to the falling edge than does the SA1 illustrated here, but that is not typical; total impulse counts at the falling edges of raised and depressed objects average 53% and 54% of the counts at the rising edges for SA1 and RA afferents, respectively. Impulse rates at rising and falling edges are proportional to the cosine of the angle between the edge and the scanning direction.
SOURCE: Adapted from Blake, Johnson, & Hsiao (1997).

of curvature, whereas others are more sensitive to skin indentation per se. Still other components are particularly sensitive to skin stretch. Because different receptor types can be selectively sensitive to different components of stress and strain, different afferent types can be selectively sensitive to different aspects of skin deformation. For example, the SA2's insensitivity to curvature and local features and its sensitivity to skin stretch suggests that it is sensitive to horizontal tensile strain or a similar strain component. The SA1 sensitivity to curvature, local features, and edges comes from selective sensitivity to strain energy density (energy required to produce local deformation) at the Merkel-neurite complex (Phillips & Johnson, 1981b; Srinivasan & Dandekar, 1996).

This selective sensitivity to strain energy density confers a response property called surround suppression (Figures 13.6 and 13.7), which is exactly like that conferred by surround inhibition in the central somato sensory and visual pathways. In surround inhibition, stimuli in the center of the receptive field excite the neuron whereas stimuli in the surrounding region inhibit the response to the central stimulus. Neurons with this property are very sensitive to curvature and may be (depending on the balance between excitation and inhibition) completely insensitive to a uniform stimulus field. Surround suppression in the responses of tactile peripheral afferents confers similar response properties, but it is based entirely on mechanoreceptor sensitivity to strain energy density (or a closely related component of strain), not on synaptic mechanisms. Consequently, SA1 afferents respond strongly to points, edges, and curvature, as illustrated in Figures 13.4 to 13.7, and these responses are suppressed by the presence of stimuli in the surrounding skin. Also, because of this surround suppression SA1 afferents are minimally responsive to uniform skin indentation (e.g., Figures 13.4 and 13.7). Therefore, local spatial features such as edges, points, and curves are represented strongly in the neural image conveyed by the peripheral SA1 population response. RA afferents exhibit some surround suppression but the effect is weaker (e.g., Figure 13.6).

Other response properties that make the SA1 afferents particularly suited to the representation of spatial information are the following:

1. SA1 responses to stimulus elements on a surface are independent of contact pressure (Johnson & Lamb, 1981; Vega-Bermudez & Johnson, 1999b).

2. SA1 receptive fields grow minimally (relative to RA receptive fields) with increasing indentation depth (Vega-Bermudez & Johnson, 1999a). At the height of a Braille dot, 500 μm, RA receptive field areas are two-and-a-half times greater than are SA1 receptive field areas (Figure 13.8), which accounts for the differences in the SA1 and

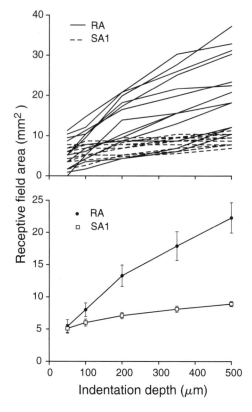

Figure 13.8 SA1 and RA receptive field area versus indentation depth.
NOTE: Each receptive field was sampled on a 1-mm triangular grid and receptive field area was calculated from the number of stimulus sites producing greater than 10% of the number of action potentials evoked at the point of maximum sensitivity. Each line in the top graph represents the relationship between receptive field area and indentation depth for a single afferent (RA, solid; SA1, dashed). The bottom graph displays the means (RA, filled circles; SA1, open squares).
SOURCE: Adapted from Vega-Bermudez & Johnson (1999a).

RA responses to Braille characters illustrated in Figure 13.3.

3. The spatial resolution of single SA1 afferents is affected minimally by changes in scanning velocity at velocities up to at least 80 mm/s (DiCarlo & Johnson, 1999; Johnson, Phillips, Hsiao, & Bankman, 1991).

4. Dispersion in the neural image of a spatial stimulus due to variation in conduction velocity is significantly less for SA1 than for RA afferents (Darian-Smith & Kenins, 1980; Knibestöl, 1975; Talbot et al., 1968). Consequently, there is less blurring due to conduction delay dispersion as a finger is scanned across a complex surface (Johnson & Lamb, 1981).

5. SA1 afferents represent the relative heights of object or surface features effectively. SA1 impulse rates increase linearly with increasing indentation depth for depths up to at least 1.5 mm (Mountcastle et al., 1966), whereas RA impulse rates rise rapidly for indentation depths up to 100 μm and then saturate by about 300-μm indentation (Blake, Johnson, & Hsiao, 1997; Blake, Hsiao, & Johnson, 1997; Vega-Bermudez & Johnson, 1999a).

6. SA1 responses to repeated skin indentation are practically invariant; the variability is about one impulse per trial regardless of the number of action potentials evoked (Vega-Bermudez & Johnson, 1999a). The result is a virtually noise-free neural image of the stimulus contacting the skin.

7. SA1 afferents respond with a sustained discharge to sustained skin deformation.

8. SA1 afferents are at least 10 times more sensitive to dynamic than to static stimuli (Johnson & Lamb, 1981).

The psychophysical correlate of (1) and (2) is that tactile pattern recognition is independent of contact force and indentation depth (Loomis, 1985); similarly, curvature perception is affected minimally by indentation depth (A. W. Goodwin et al., 1991). The psychophysical correlate of (3) and (4) is competent tactile spatial pattern recognition at scanning velocities of up to at least 80 mm/s (Vega-Bermudez et al., 1991). A correlate of (5) is the ability to judge indentation and object form independently (A. W. Goodwin & Wheat, 1992b). A correlate of (6) is a high-quality, invariant percept of an object contacting the skin. A perceptual correlate of (7) is that we perceive the form of an object or a surface even when it is stationary on the skin, and we do so almost as well (acuity threshold increases by only 25%) as when the object is moving (Phillips et al., 1983). The perceptual correlate of (8) is the increased intensity and clarity of the tactile image when we move our fingers over a surface. We can distinguish the fine detail of an object or surface almost as well when the finger is stationary as when it is moving, but it requires concentration. The difference between static and dynamic touch is similar to the difference between dim and bright light in vision.

SA1 Response Properties Account for Pattern Recognition Behavior

Human performance in a letter recognition task and the SA1 neural responses that underlie it are shown in Figure 13.9. The principal object of the experiment illustrated in Figure 13.9 was to compare pattern recognition behavior when letters are scanned actively and when the same letters are scanned across a passive finger (Vega-Bermudez et al., 1991). There was no detectable difference between the two conditions; even the detailed patterns of identifications and errors illustrated in Figure 13.9 were identical between active and passive touch. Accuracies in letter recognition ranged from 15% (N) to 98% (I), and more than 50% of the confusions were confined to 7% of all possible confusion pairs (22 out of 325 possible confusion pairs), which are enclosed in boxes in Figure 13.9. The confusions in all but five of those 22 pairs are highly asymmetric ($p < 0.001$). The frequency of occurrence of letters in English bears no relationship to the rates of correct responses, false positives, or total responses. Further, excluding I, J, and L, which had high hit rates and

Pooled (%)

Response

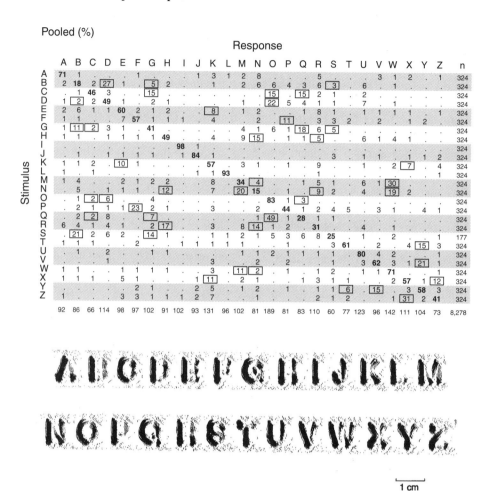

Stimulus	A	B	C	D	E	F	G	H	I	J	K	L	M	N	O	P	Q	R	S	T	U	V	W	X	Y	Z	n
A	71	1	.	.	.	1	.	.	.	1	3	1	2	8	.	.	.	5	.	.	.	3	1	2	.	1	324
B	2	18	2	[27]	1	.	[5]	2	.	.	1	.	2	6	.	6	4	3	6	[3]	.	6	.	1	.	.	324
C	.	1	46	3	.	.	[15]	.	.	.	.	.	.	.	[15]	.	[15]	2	1	.	2	.	.	.	.	.	324
D	1	[2]	2	49	1	.	2	1	.	.	.	.	1	.	[22]	5	4	1	1	.	7	.	1	.	.	.	324
E	2	6	1	1	60	2	1	2	.	.	[8]	.	1	2	.	.	1	8	1	.	1	1	1	.	1	1	324
F	1	1	.	.	7	57	1	1	1	.	.	4	.	.	2	.	[11]	.	3	3	2	.	2	.	1	2	324
G	1	[11]	[2]	3	1	.	41	.	.	.	.	4	1	6	1	[18]	6	[5]	.	.	.	.	.	.	.	.	324
H	1	1	.	1	1	1	1	49	.	.	.	4	.	9	[15]	.	1	1	[5]	.	6	1	4	1	.	.	324
I	.	1	.	.	1	1	1	.	98	1	.	.	.	.	.	.	.	.	.	.	.	.	.	.	.	.	324
J	.	1	.	1	1	1	1	.	1	84	1	.	.	.	.	.	.	3	.	1	1	.	.	1	1	2	324
K	1	1	2	.	[10]	1	.	.	.	.	57	.	3	1	.	1	.	9	.	.	1	.	2	[7]	.	4	324
L	1	.	1	.	.	.	.	.	1	1	93	.	.	.	.	.	.	1	.	.	.	.	.	.	.	1	324
M	1	4	.	.	2	1	2	2	.	.	8	.	34	[4]	.	.	1	5	1	.	6	1	[30]	.	.		324
N	.	5	.	.	1	1	1	.	[12]	.	.	.	7	.	[20]	15	.	1	.	[9]	2	.	4	.	[19]	2	324
O	.	1	[2]	[6]	.	.	4	.	.	.	.	.	.	.	83	1	[3]	.	.	.	.	.	.	.	.		324
P	.	2	1	1	1	[23]	2	1	.	.	3	.	.	2	.	44	1	2	4	5	.	3	1	.	4	1	324
Q	.	2	[2]	8	.	.	[7]	.	.	.	.	.	.	1	[49]	1	28	1	1	.	.	.	.	.	.		324
R	6	4	1	4	1	.	2	[17]	.	.	3	.	8	[14]	1	2	.	31	.	.	4	.	1	.	.	.	324
S	.	[21]	2	6	2	.	[14]	1	.	.	1	1	2	1	5	3	6	8	25	.	1	.	2	.	.	1	177
T	1	1	1	.	.	2	.	.	1	1	1	1	1	.	.	.	1	.	.	3	61	.	2	.	4	[15]	3	324
U	.	.	1	.	2	.	.	1	1	.	.	.	1	2	1	1	1	1	.	80	4	2	.	.		324
V	.	.	1	.	.	.	.	.	.	.	.	.	3	.	.	2	.	.	1	.	3	62	3	1	[21]	1	324
W	1	1	.	.	1	1	1	1	.	.	3	.	[11]	2	.	1	.	1	2	.	1	1	71	.	.	1	324
X	1	1	1	.	5	1	.	.	.	1	[11]	.	2	1	.	.	1	3	1	1	.	2	57	1	[12]	324
Y	.	.	.	.	2	1	.	.	2	5	.	1	2	.	.	1	.	1	1	[6]	.	[15]	.	3	58	3	324
Z	1	.	.	.	3	3	1	1	1	2	7	.	.	1	.	.	.	2	1	2	.	1	[31]	2	41	324
	92	86	66	114	98	97	102	91	102	93	131	96	102	81	189	81	83	110	60	77	123	96	142	111	104	73	8,278

1 cm

Figure 13.9   Confusion matrix of responses obtained from humans in a letter recognition task (top) and responses of a typical monkey SA1 afferent to the same letter stimuli (A through Z).

NOTE: The confusion matrix is derived from the pooled results of 64 subjects who performed either the active or passive letter identification task. The letters were raised 0.5 mm above the background and were 6 mm high. Matrix entries represent the frequencies of all possible responses to each letter (e.g., the letter A was called N on 8% of presentations). The numbers in the bottom row represent column sums. The numbers in the right-most column represent the number of presentations of each letter. Boxes around entries represent letter pairs whose mean confusion rates exceed 8%. For example, the mean confusion rate for B and G is 8% because G is called B on 11% of trials and B is called G on 5% of trails. The neural image (bottom) was derived from action potentials recorded from a single SA1 afferent fiber in a monkey. The stimuli consisted of the same embossed letters as in the letter recognition task scanned repeatedly from right to left across the receptive field of the neuron (equivalent to finger motion from left to right). Each black tick in the raster represents the occurrence of an action potential (see the note to Figure 13.3 for details).

SOURCE: Adapted from Vega-Bermudez, Johnson, & Hsiao (1991).

low false-positive rates, there was no relationship between hit and false positive rates. This suggests that the response patterns are not the result of cognitive biases.

The response of a typical SA1 afferent to repeated scans of the same raised letters as in the letter recognition experiment is shown at the bottom of Figure 13.9. Because all SA1 responses to these scanned letters are similar, it can be inferred that the raster plot at the bottom of Figure 13.9 approximates the neural images on which the pattern recognition behavior was based (Johnson & Lamb, 1981). The patterns of confusion seem to be explained largely by the responses shown at the bottom of Figure 13.9. For example, B is identified as B on only 18% of trials; instead, it is identified as D 50% more often than it is identified as B. Conversely, D is virtually never called B (Figure 13.9, top). The reason for this confusion can be explained by the SA1 surround suppression mechanism discussed earlier, which suppresses the response to the central horizontal bar of the B. The neural representation of the B resembles a D more than it does a B (see the raster plots at the bottom of Figure 13.9), and that accounts for the strong bias toward the letter D. For another example, C is often called G or Q, but G and Q are almost never called C. An explanation is that the subject learns quickly that internal and trailing features are often represented weakly or not at all; therefore, when the subject is presented with the letter C, lack of the features expected of a G or a Q in the neural representation is not a strong reason not to respond G or Q. Conversely, the strong representation of the distinctive features of the G and Q make confusion with a C unlikely. However, G and Q are confused frequently as expected from their neural representations. The performance illustrated in Figure 13.9 is for 64 naive subjects in their first testing session. Performance improved steadily on repeated testing (Vega-Bermudez et al., 1991).

One possible reason for the improvement is that subjects learn the idiosyncrasies of the neural representations (e.g., as soon as a subject recognizes the distinctive feature of the G in the neural representation, he or she is less likely to mistake a C for a G).

Importance of Spatial Acuity Measurements

Because the sensory mechanisms serving the lip, tongue, and fingertips are specialized for spatial information processing, it makes sense that a measure of spatial acuity would be a particularly sensitive indicator of function in these regions. Signs of this specialization are dense mechanoreceptive innervation (Darian-Smith, 1973; Darian-Smith & Kenins, 1980; Halata & Munger, 1983; Johansson & Vallbo, 1979b) and large somatosensory cortical representations (Kaas, Nelson, Sur, & Merzenich, 1981). This logic was pursued in a study of 24 subjects who underwent a surgical procedure to lengthen or shorten the mandible (bilateral split osteotomies), which crushes the nerve innervating the lip and chin (Van Boven & Johnson, 1994b). All subjects reported complete anesthesia after surgery. Although all subjects reported at least partial recovery of sensory function over the following year, only three recovered fully by their own assessment. The subjects were studied with 11 psychophysical tests that tested all sensory modalities before surgery, two weeks after surgery, and then at 1, 3, 6, and 12 months after surgery. The aim was to determine the diagnostic and predictive power of the tests. Recovery rates varied between subjects, but the order of recovery among the 11 psychophysical tests did not. Performance in the grating orientation discrimination task corresponded most closely with the subjects' own assessment of recovery, and it was the only test in which recovery to preinjury performance (in three subjects) was delayed until the subjects reported full recovery (Figure 13.10). The plot of subjects'

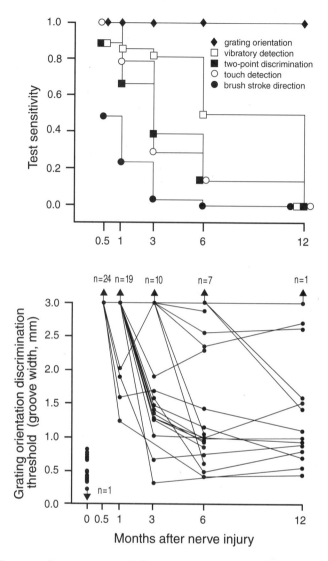

Figure 13.10   Five tests of sensory recovery after severe nerve injury.

NOTE: Twenty-four subjects were tested before and at intervals after surgery that severely damaged the nerve innervating the lip and chin. Test sensitivity is defined as the fraction of subjects with sensory impairment (by their own report) whose performance on the specific test was impaired (i.e., significantly poorer than their own preinjury performance). Brush-stroke directional discrimination dropped to zero sensitivity at six months, for example, because it detected no abnormalities even though 21 of 24 subjects described their tactile sensation as abnormal. The grating orientation test remained at 1.0 throughout because performance in that test was impaired in all subjects until they reported themselves symptom free (only 3 of 24 subjects in the first year). The bottom graph shows the grating orientation discrimination thresholds. The points at 0 months represent preinjury thresholds. The arrows at the top of the graph represent the number of subjects with thresholds greater than 3.0 mm, which was the coarsest grating in the battery.

SOURCE: Adapted from Van Boven & Johnson (1994a).

performance in the grating orientation test illustrated in the bottom panel of Figure 13.10 correlates closely with the subjects' own assessment of recovery.

A hypothesis that accounts for all the psychophysical findings is that the differences in recovery rates between tasks (Figure 13.10) were accounted for by their relative dependencies on innervation density. Brush-stroke directional discrimination recovered most rapidly among the 11 tests: Half the subjects could discriminate brush-stroke direction two weeks after surgery even though their lips were numb and they could not discriminate the orientations of gratings with 3.0 mm grooves and bars (preinjury thresholds averaged 0.51 mm). Brush-stroke direction can, in theory at least, be discriminated with two functioning afferents. Performance in tests such as touch detection with no known dependence on innervation density recovered at an intermediate rate. Warming detection and grating orientation discrimination recovered most slowly, and both are linked to innervation density. Warming detection exhibits spatial summation (Hardy & Oppel, 1937), which means that it depends on the number of responsive afferents. According to the innervation density hypothesis, the delayed recovery in warming detection is a result of the time required for reinnervation to populate the skin with enough warm afferents for normal detection performance. Accurate discrimination of grating orientation depends on perceiving the presence and orientation of the grooves and bars in the neural image of the stimulus. If spatial acuity is limited by innervation density in the lip in the same way as in the finger pad, then full recovery would not be possible without full reinnervation.

Next to brush-stroke direction, the two-point discrimination test was the least sensitive indicator of the subjects' sensory deficits. Before surgery, all subjects could discriminate two points (1 mm diameter) separated by

$500\ \mu$m from a single point with greater than 75% correct accuracy. At six months, all but three subjects returned to preinjury performance in the two-point discrimination test even though seven subjects could not yet discriminate the orientation of a grating with 3 mm grooves and bars (see Figure 13.10). The likely reason for subjects' ability to discriminate one from two points even though their spatial acuity was severely limited can be seen in Figure 13.6; the peak discharge rate evoked by a single point is about 40% greater than the peak discharge rate when two points indent the skin. A strong intensive cue distinguishes one from two points. An objective test of two-point discrimination at the fingertip has shown that subjects can discriminate two apposed, 0.5-mm diameter points from a single point with 85% accuracy (Johnson & Phillips, 1981). Subjects report that they can distinguish a single point from two apposed points because a single point feels sharper and more intense.

The traditional two-point limen test is a subjective test in which two points at varying separation are presented and the subject is asked, "Do you feel one or two points?" The variability within subjects, between subjects, and between studies is extreme (Van Boven & Johnson, 1994b). The problem is that two points create a continuum of sensations as they are spread apart (described as "point," "circle," "oval," "dumbbell," and "two points"; Gates, 1915) that finally results in the perception of two clearly separated regions of pressure. Where the subject draws the line between "one" and "two" is arbitrary. The objective and subjective forms of the two-point limen test were discussed recently by Craig and Johnson (2000). The history of this test, which played such a prominent role in the early history of experimental psychology, has been reviewed by Johnson, Van Boven, and Hsiao (1994).

The importance of spatial acuity as an index of sensory function raises the question,

"What is a good test of spatial acuity?" The problem is to measure the ability to sense the spatial structure of the stimulus without introducing nonspatial cues (mostly differences in perceived intensity). Gap detection, grating orientation discrimination, and letter recognition all yield the same threshold value at the fingertip, but gap detection is severely flawed. Gaps introduce edges, and SA1 afferents are very sensitive to edges (Figure 13.4); a surface with and without a gap will therefore evoke different discharge rates. SA1 responses to the edges of the gaps almost certainly account for the significantly greater than chance performance for gaps as small as 0.2 mm in the study illustrated in Figure 13.2. In that study of gap detection, genuine spatial acuity seems to have become dominant at a gap size of 0.8 mm, which resulted in an accurate estimate of spatial acuity at the fingertip. If the spatial acuity is poorer because of age, disease, or testing at a site of reduced acuity (Sathian et al., 1997; J. C. Stevens & Choo, 1996; Wohlert, 1996), however, the concern is that the intensive cues in gap detection will dominate and yield artificially low estimates. Gibson and Craig (2000) have tested this idea by measuring the ability to discriminate gratings from smooth surfaces at the fingertip, the pad of the proximal phalanx of the index finger, and the pad at the base of the thumb. Gratings with groove widths less than 1 mm were reliably discriminated from smooth surfaces at all three sites even though the grating orientation discrimination thresholds at the three sites were 1.24 mm, 4.35 mm, and 5.73 mm, respectively.

The grating orientation discrimination task was designed to eliminate spurious cues by making the total contact area and edge content identical in all presentation conditions. A possible problem is that the relationship between the grating orientation and the skin-ridge orientation may affect the afferent discharge rates and thereby introduce an intensive cue on which discrimination might be based (Phillips & Johnson, 1981a; Wheat & Goodwin, 2000). If this is true, subjects should be able to discriminate a grating from a uniform surface better at some orientations than at others, but Craig (1999) has shown that this is not so. Craig and Kisner (1998) have provided an extensive analysis of the spatial factors affecting grating orientation discrimination.

Two-alternative forced-choice designs are inherently vulnerable to spurious cues. A different approach is to make the number of alternatives so large that a simple, unidimensional cue (e.g., differences in perceived intensity) cannot account for more than a small fraction of the correct responses; for example, when subjects identify raised letters, there can be little doubt that performance is based on appreciation of the spatial structure of the neural images evoked by the letters. Consistency between measures based on grating orientation discrimination and letter recognition is evidence that both measure spatial acuity effectively (Vega-Bermudez & Johnson, 2001). Threshold measures from both grating orientation discrimination and letter recognition at the finger pad are repeatable between studies (Johnson & Phillips, 1981; Loomis, 1985; Sathian & Zangaladze, 1996; Vega-Bermudez et al., 1991; see also subsequent references), between subjects (Van Boven & Johnson, 1994b), and in longitudinal testing within subjects (Van Boven & Johnson, 1994a; Vega-Bermudez et al., 1991). Essick et al. (1999) report similar results in a study of letter recognition at the tongue. Grating orientation discrimination has the advantage of having been used widely in normative and clinical studies (Craig, 1999; Johnson & Phillips, 1981; Sathian & Zangaladze, 1996; Van Boven, Hamilton, Kauffman, Keenan, & Pascual-Leone, 2000; Van Boven & Johnson, 1994a, 1994b; Wohlert, 1996).

Texture Perception

Our knowledge of texture perception and its neural mechanisms has changed markedly in the last decade. A major step is the demonstration that texture perception involves two strong dimensions, roughness and softness, and a weaker third dimension that is related to friction. Multidimensional scaling studies have shown that texture perception includes soft-hard and smooth-rough as independent perceptual dimensions; surface hardness and roughness can occur in almost any combination, and they account for most or all of texture perception (Hollins, Bensmaïa, Karlof, & Young, 2000; Hollins, Faldowski, Rao, & Young, 1993). A third dimension (sticky-slippery) improves the multidimensional scaling fit in some subjects. Thus, it appears that texture perception has two strong dimensions and, possibly, a third weaker dimension. An important question is whether texture perception is the product of inbuilt neural mechanisms (e.g., color vision) or whether it is just a description of complex sensory experience (in the same way that a sea can be described as smooth or rough). In fact, there is strong evidence, described later, that the smooth-rough dimension is based on inbuilt neural mechanisms. Whether this is so for the other texture dimensions is not yet clear.

It is important to distinguish between the objective and subjective components of texture perception in the same way that it is important to distinguish between frequency and pitch or between intensity and loudness in audition. In this chapter the terms *coarseness* (e.g., spacing between surface features) and *compliance* (e.g., millimeters of deformation per gram force) are used to characterize the physical properties of an object or surface, whereas the terms *roughness* (or smoothness) and *softness* (or hardness) are used only as descriptors of subjective experience. If a subject judges one surface to be coarser or more compliant than another, it is an objective description of the physical properties of the stimulus, which can be scored for accuracy. Studies of this objective capacity show that the Weber fractions for coarseness and compliance judgments are 2% to 5% and 7% to 8%, respectively (Lamb, 1983; Morley, Goodwin, & Darian-Smith, 1983; Tan, Durlach, Beauregard, & Srinivasan, 1995). However, if subjects say that one surface is rougher or softer than another, they are neither right nor wrong; they are merely describing subjective experiences. When texture elements are small, subjective reports of roughness magnitude are an inverted U-shaped function of element spacing, which peaks when the element spacing is about 3 mm (Connor, Hsiao, Phillips, & Johnson, 1990). Therefore, an increase in element spacing that is clearly discernable as an increase in coarseness (i.e., an increase greater than 2–5%) can produce either an increase or a decrease in roughness depending on the initial element spacing relative to the peak of the inverted U-shaped function. The following discussion concerns the neural mechanisms of the subjective sense of roughness and softness.

Roughness Perception

Roughness perception has been studied extensively (Blake, Johnson, et al., 1997; Hollins, Bensmaïa, Karlof, & Young, 2000; Lederman, 1974; Lederman 1983; Meenes & Zigler, 1923; Meftah, Belingard, & Chapman, 2000; Sathian, Goodwin, John, & Darian-Smith, 1989; S. S. Stevens & Harris, 1962). There is no simple summary of these studies: They demonstrate that roughness perception is unidimensional (the test of unidimensionality consists of the ability to assign numbers on a unidimensional continuum and to make greater-than and less-than judgments); that it depends on element height, diameter, shape, compliance, and density; and that (although the effect of each is generally consistent with one's expectation from subjective experience) the relationship is complex and nonlinear. Important early observations were that scanning velocity, contact force, and friction between the finger and a surface have minor or no effects on judgments of roughness magnitude (Lederman, 1974; Taylor & Lederman, 1975). Although the physical determinants of roughness perception are complex, the evidence is that the neural mechanisms are simple.

A series of combined psychophysical and neurophysiological studies have examined the neural coding mechanisms underlying roughness perception by using exactly the same stimulus surfaces in roughness magnitude estimation experiments and in neurophysiological experiments (Blake, Johnson, et al., 1997; Connor et al., 1990; Connor & Johnson, 1992; Yoshioka, Gibb, Dorsch, Hsiao, & Johnson, 2001). The experimental design followed the method of multiple working hypotheses and sequential elimination of hypotheses by falsification (Platt, 1964; Popper, 1959). The multiple working hypotheses laid out in the first study of the series (Connor et al., 1990) were of the type "Perceived roughness is based on the neural measure X in afferent population Y." The neural measures, X, were measures of mean impulse rate, measures of impulse rate fluctuation within single afferents (temporal variation), and measures of variation in firing rate between afferents (spatial variation). The afferent populations, Y, were the SA1, RA, PC, and SA2 populations. Thus, there were more than a dozen initial working hypotheses (each of the three neural coding hypothesis types combined with each of the four afferent fiber types). The test of each neural coding hypothesis was consistency, which was tested by plotting the mean roughness judgment against the putative neural measure for each surface in the study. A hypothesis was rejected only when there was no consistent (one-to-one) relationship between the two (i.e., when two or more surfaces evoked nearly identical putative neural coding mea-

sures but very different roughness judgments). Altogether, 62 surfaces that varied in surface geometry were used: Element spacings varied from 100 μm to 6.2 mm; element heights varied from 280 μm to 2.0 mm; and element widths varied from 0 mm (a sharp element) to 2.5 mm. The single neural coding hypothesis that survived was that perceived roughness depends on the mean absolute difference in firing rates between SA1 afferents with receptive field centers separated by 2 mm to 3 mm (hereafter called spatial variation). The correlation between this coding measure and subjects' roughness magnitude judgments was 0.97 or greater in every study. Every other putative neural code failed the consistency test in one or more studies.

The consistency test is shown in Figure 13.11 for nine hypothetical neural coding measures derived from a study with 18 raised-dot surfaces that varied in dot diameter and spacing (Connor et al., 1990). The surfaces, which ranged from almost glassy smooth to very rough, were scanned repeatedly across the receptive fields of monkey SA1, RA, and PC afferents to obtain a statistically accurate description of the population responses to these surfaces. It is evident in Figure 13.11 that roughness is not based on mean impulse rate in any of these three afferent systems; smooth and rough surfaces evoked the same impulse rates. Perceived roughness could not have depended on mean impulse rate. Spatial and temporal neural coding mechanisms based on PC responses failed for a similar reason. Because PCs are so sensitive and because they respond so vigorously to smooth and rough surfaces alike, there was little gradation in their spatial or temporal responses and therefore no basis for roughness perception. This rejection of all neural codes based on PC responses is consistent with a study by Lederman, Loomis, and Williams (1982), which showed that strong vibratory adaptation (which depressed the responses of PC

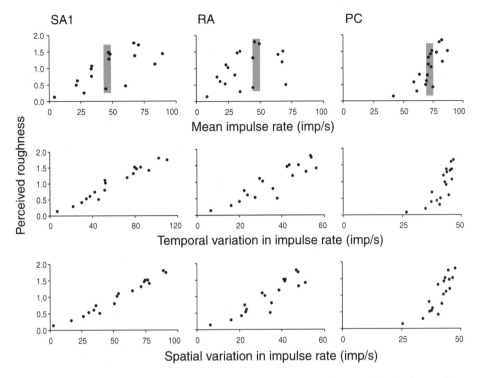

Figure 13.11   Consistency plots of subjective roughness versus putative neural codes for roughness.
NOTE: The stimulus patterns were 18 raised-dot patterns (Connor, Hsiao, Phillips, & Johnson, 1990) comprising dot arrays with six dot spacings and three dot diameters; the dots were 350 μm high. The surfaces varied widely in roughness. The smoothest surface was judged to be almost perfectly smooth; the roughest surface was judged to be about as rough as 36-grit sandpaper. The ordinate of each graph represents the mean subjective roughness judgment for each of the 18 surfaces. The abscissa represents one of the neural response measures tested in this study. Mean impulse rate was just the mean impulse rates of all afferents of a single type averaged across all stimulus sweeps. Temporal variation in firing rate was measured as the mean absolute difference in firing rates between periods separated by 100 ms. Spatial variation in firing rates was measured as the mean absolute difference in firing rates between afferents with receptive field centers separated by 2–3 mm. The gray bars highlight the fact that some of the smoothest and some of the roughest surfaces evoke essentially the same mean firing rates. Therefore, there is no consistent relationship between roughness judgments and mean firing rate; roughness perception cannot be based on mean firing rate.
SOURCE: Adapted from Connor, Hsiao, Phillips, & Johnson (1990).

afferents and reduced the subjective magnitudes of high frequency stimuli) had no effect on perceived roughness. The tightest relationship in the study by Connor et al. was between spatial variation in SA1 impulse rates and roughness judgments (0.98 correlation coefficient). The relationship was linear as well as consistent even though nothing in the analysis predisposed the relationship to linearity (discussed later); the putative neural measures were computed without reference to the psychophysical outcome. A measure of temporal variation in SA1 firing rates was only slightly less well correlated. Comparable measures of RA impulse rates were more poorly correlated, but they cannot be said to have failed the consistency test in any clear and unambiguous way in this study.

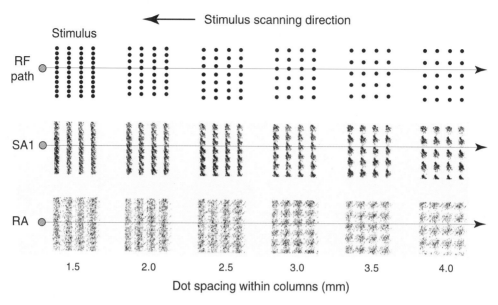

Figure 13.12   Typical SA1 and RA responses to six dot patterns used by Connor & Johnson (1992).
NOTE: Filled circles in the top row represent raised dots, 0.5 mm diameter and 0.5 mm high. The horizontal spacing between dot centers was 4 mm in all six patterns; the vertical spacing ranged from 1.5 mm to 4.0 mm. The middle and bottom rows illustrate the neural responses of typical SA1 and RA afferents. The method of display is the same as that in Figure 13.3. The large gray circle at the left of each row and the line extending to the right represent the neuron's receptive field and one of many paths through the dots. The line shows that when a finger scans across one of the sparser patterns from left to right, a particular afferent might be silent, partially activated, or maximally activated depending on the position of its receptive field. As vertical separation increases, fewer afferents are activated strongly. Consequently, any neural response measure derived from the responses of single afferents and averaged across the population (mean impulse rate, any measure of spike timing, etc.) will decline relative to the pattern with 1.5 mm vertical spacing in which none of the trajectories is silent. That is the logic; analysis of the neural responses showed it to be true. If roughness perception depends on a neural response measure of this kind, the pattern with 4.0 mm spacing will be judged to be smoother than the surface with 1.5 mm spacing. In fact, it is much rougher.
SOURCE: Adapted from Connor & Johnson (1992).

Human afferents have been studied with a subset of the raised-dot surfaces used by Connor et al. (1990; Phillips, Johansson, & Johnson, 1992). The result was that human and monkey SA1, RA, and PC responses were indistinguishable (some sense of the similarity can be seen by comparing Figures 13.3 and 13.12). SA2 responses (see Figure 13.3), in contrast, were like nothing seen in monkey neurophysiological studies. Measures of mean impulse rate and temporal and spatial variation in SA2 impulse rates all failed the consistency test because the SA2s were uniformly unresponsive to all the stimulus patterns (Phillips et al., 1992; Phillips & Matthews, 1993).

The second study by Connor and Johnson (1992) was aimed at distinguishing between temporal and spatial coding mechanisms. The class of all possible neural coding mechanisms can be subdivided into those based on summed measures of firing within single neurons (within-neuron codes) and those based on differences in firing between neurons (between-neuron codes). Examples of within-neuron codes are mean or summed firing rates over populations of active neurons and summed measures of temporal firing in single neurons. The surfaces illustrated in Figure 13.12 were designed so that a graded decline in element density in the direction orthogonal to the scanning direction would cause a graded decline in the number of active neurons. The logic was that all measures based on within-neuron codes would have to decline as the number of active neurons declined. By the same logic, measures based on between-neuron codes would grow as the population activity becomes less uniform. Logic of this kind requires direct neurophysiological verification; within- and between-neuron coding measures based on neurophysiological data like that presented in Figure 13.12 showed the logic to be correct. In these experiments, roughness judgments cannot be consistent with both within- and between-neuron codes because one (within-fiber codes) declines whereas the other (between-fiber codes) rises as the patterns become more sparse. In fact, the surfaces displayed on the right of Figure 13.12 (the sparser patterns) were judged to be much rougher than were the surfaces displayed at the left. Within-neuron codes were anticorrelated with the roughness judgments whereas between-fiber codes were positively correlated with the roughness judgments. All temporal codes and all mean-rate codes (i.e., all within-neuron codes) therefore failed the consistency test. The correlation between spatial variation in SA1 firing rates and roughness judgments for all surfaces in the study was 0.98; the analogous measure of RA firing rates was less closely correlated but did not fail the consistency test unambiguously. The power of this study is that it rejected all within-neuron measures; there are many possible temporal codes, and being certain that all had been tested would be difficult if they were addressed one by one.

The third study in this series (Blake, Johnson, et al., 1997) was aimed at distinguishing between neural codes based on SA1 and RA responses. Previous studies by Blake, Hsiao, et al. (1997) had shown that RA impulse rates are quite insensitive to the heights of scanned, raised elements with heights above 0.3 mm. Psychophysical studies with textured patterns with element heights ranging from 0.3 mm to 0.6 mm showed that roughness judgments rise linearly with element height. Because RA responses are insensitive to changes in element height above 300 μm, there was no consistent relationship between roughness judgments and any measure of the RA responses evoked by these surfaces. Spatial variation in SA1 discharge rate, in contrast, was correlated strongly (0.97) with the roughness judgments. Thus, only a single putative neural mechanism survived the first three studies, and it was almost perfectly correlated with subjects' roughness judgments in every study.

The hypothesis that spatial variation in SA1 firing rates accounts for roughness perception faces a severe challenge in accounting for the perceived roughness of textured surfaces with element densities greater than the SA1 innervation density (100 per cm^2). Many fine surfaces with element densities greater than 100 per cm^2 (e.g., fine sandpapers) are rough. How can a mechanism based on differences in firing rates between afferents with receptive field centers separated by about 2 mm account for the perceived roughness of surfaces with features separated by tenths of millimeters? The only previous study that examined the responses of SA1 afferents to finely textured surfaces suggested that SA1 afferents do not resolve spatial detail well in the submillimeter range (Darian-Smith, Davidson, & Johnson, 1980). An alternative possibility is that the PC system might take over responsibility for roughness perception for finely textured surfaces. Katz

(1925/1970) showed long ago that we can discriminate surface texture by dragging a probe over the surface and that this ability depends on vibrations transmitted through the probe (see also Klatzky & Lederman, 1999). PC afferents (discussed later) are exquisitely sensitive to minute vibrations whether transmitted through a probe held in the hand or induced by direct contact with a finely textured surface (Brisben, Hsiao, & Johnson, 1999; Srinivasan, Whitehouse, & LaMotte, 1990). These observations have prompted a duplex theory of roughness perception in which a spatial mechanism accounts for the perceived roughness of coarser surfaces and a vibratory mechanism, presumably mediated by PC afferents, accounts for the perceived roughness of finer surfaces (Hollins & Risner, 2000). Hollins, Fox, and Bishop (2000) provided evidence for this hypothesis by showing that intense, high-frequency vibration can make a relatively smooth surface feel less smooth.

A fourth combined psychophysical and neurophysiological study employing 20 gratings with spatial periods ranging from 0.1 mm to 2.0 mm has addressed these issues (Yoshioka et al., 2001). As in previous studies, there was no consistent relationship between PC responses and roughness judgments because the PCs were activated so strongly and uniformly by finely and coarsely textured surfaces alike. SA1 afferents responded to the finely textured surfaces in a graded manner, and the mean absolute difference in SA1 firing rates between afferents was correlated strongly (0.97) with subjective roughness estimates. The neural basis for Hollins' observations (Hollins, Fox, & Bishop, 2000) is unclear; the intense, high-frequency vibration could have affected the discharge of SA1 and RA afferents as well as PC afferents, or it could have affected some central interaction between the PC and SA1 systems.

The outcome of a long series of studies is that spatial variation in the SA1 discharge rate accounts for roughness perception nearly perfectly (see Figure 13.13). The correlation between psychophysical roughness magnitude estimates and spatial variation in the SA1 discharge was greater than 0.97 in every study. Every other neural coding hypothesis has been rejected not because it fitted the data less well than did the SA1 spatial variation hypothesis but because it was completely inconsistent with the psychophysical data. The consistency test has resulted in the rejection of all neural codes based on PC responses (Connor et al., 1990; Lederman et al., 1982; Yoshioka et al., 2001), all codes based on RA responses (Blake et al., 1997; Johnson & Hsiao, 1994; Lederman et al., 1982), all codes based on SA2 responses (Phillips et al., 1992; Phillips & Matthews, 1993), all codes based on mean impulse rate (Connor et al., 1990; Connor & Johnson, 1992), and all temporal codes (Connor & Johnson, 1992).

The mean absolute difference in firing rates between SA1 afferents with receptive field centers separated by 2 mm to 3 mm may seem abstract, but it corresponds, in fact, to a simple neurophysiological mechanism (Connor et al., 1990; Connor & Johnson, 1992). Every neuron within the central nervous system whose receptive field includes regions of inhibition and excitation (which is, as far as is known, virtually all neurons in somatosensory cortex) computes a measure of the spatial variation in skin deformation. More accurately, its discharge rate is proportional to the difference in discharge rates between afferents arising from the excitatory and inhibitory subregions of the receptive field. The principal importance of the mechanism is that it confers selectivity for particular stimulus features and their orientations. However, the summed discharge rate of a population of such neurons can form the basis for roughness perception. In fact, neurons with exactly the properties hypothesized to account for roughness perception have been demonstrated in somatosensory

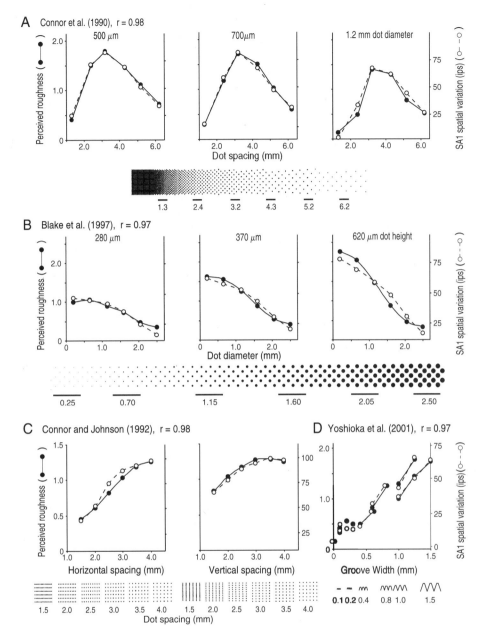

Figure 13.13   Roughness magnitude and spatial variation in SA1 firing rate from four studies.

NOTE: The left ordinate and filled circles in each graph represent mean roughness judgments for individual surfaces. The right ordinate and open circles represent spatial variation in SA1 impulse rates evoked by the same surfaces. The top row illustrates data from a study employing raised-dot patterns in which dot spacing and dot diameter were varied independently (Connor, Hsiao, Phillips, & Johnson, 1990). The middle row shows data from a study in which dot diameter and dot height were varied widely (Blake, Hsiao, & Johnson, 1997). The two left graphs on the bottom row show data from a study in which the horizontal dot spacing (i.e., dot spacing in the scanning direction) and vertical dot spacing (i.e., dot spacing orthogonal to the scanning direction; see Figure 13.12) were varied independently (Connor & Johnson, 1992). The right graph shows data from a study employing scanned grating in which the grating period ranged from 0.1 to 2.0 mm (Yoshioka, Gibb, Dorsch, Hsiao, & Johnson, 2001). The correlation between roughness judgments and this putative neural code was 0.97 or greater in all studies.

SOURCE: Adapted from Yoshioka, Gibb, Dorsch, Hsiao, & Johnson (2001).

cortex (DiCarlo & Johnson, 2000). Such a mechanism has several things to recommend it. Like roughness perception, it is unidimensional and is affected only secondarily by factors such as scanning velocity and contact force (DiCarlo & Johnson, 1999). The combined psychophysical studies described earlier and the existence of neurons with the hypothesized properties suggest that roughness perception is based on such a mechanism.

Linearity as the Basic Law of Psychophysics

These studies of the neural mechanisms underlying subjective experience bear on the search for the metrics that govern our internal representations of the external world. The original formulation, which persisted for nearly a hundred years, was Fechner's (1860/1966), who used Weber's law to infer that physical and subjective intensity are related by a logarithmic function. S. S. Stevens (1957) showed, however, that when subjects are asked to report their sense of subjective intensity with direct numerical report or by selecting an equivalent physical intensity in another modality, the result is a power law relationship. Based on these observations, S. S. Stevens advocated the power law as the basic law of subjective intensity (1961a). Almost immediately, MacKay (1963) showed that we cannot distinguish the two laws without peering into the underlying mechanisms because magnitude estimation and cross-modality matching yield a power law even if the relationship between physical and subjective intensity is logarithmic.

A third proposal entered the picture in 1963 (Mountcastle, Poggio, & Werner, 1963): Subjective intensity is a linear function of the neural response measure on which it is based. The basis of that idea was the occurrence of power law relationships between physical intensities and evoked neural responses with exponents matching the psychophysical exponents. S. S. Stevens did not explicitly adopt this idea of linearity, but he observed that "the exponents are what they are because of the nature of the sensory transducers" (Stevens, 1961b, p. 28) and he repeatedly surveyed and highlighted correspondences between primary sensory neural responses and the power law (1970, 1975). This implies his acceptance of the idea of linearity. If the power law is established by primary neural response mechanisms, then subjective intensity is linearly related to those neural responses. A weakness of those comparisons is that none of the neural responses whose exponents were being compared with psychophysical exponents had been established as the basis of subjective intensity.

The roughness coding studies described earlier do establish a link between subjective intensity and its neural basis, and they are direct. They involve no a priori assumptions about the relationship between physical stimuli and subjective experience or about the relationship between neural activity and subjective experience—except for causality (which is the principle underlying the consistency test). Nothing in the analysis methods predisposed the relationship to linearity; consistency plots of the type illustrated in Figure 13.11 reveal consistent relationships whatever their form might be. In fact, a linear relationship between perceived roughness and spatial variation in SA1 firing rates emerged in every study, as illustrated in Figure 13.13. These studies show that roughness perception is proportional to the neural code on which it is based. If this is so for roughness perception, why should it be otherwise for other intensive continua? A possibility is that this linearity applies more broadly to the metrical structure of perception (Johnson, Hsiao, & Blake, 1996; Johnson, Hsaio, & Yoshioka, 2001).

Softness Perception

The essential nature of the second major texture dimension, soft-hard, can be appreciated by pressing first the keys of a typewriter or computer keyboard and then other, softer objects. Perceived softness does not depend on the relationship between force and object displacement (i.e., compliance); the fact that the space bar gives way easily does not make it soft. A soft object conforms to the finger or hand as it is manipulated, but conformation is not sufficient; the keyboard keys that are molded to conform to the skin of a fingertip feel as hard as flat keys do. The essence of softness is progressive conformation to the contours of the fingers and hand in proportion to contact force. The degree of softness is signaled by the rate of growth of contact area with contact force and by the uniformity of pressure across the contact area. Conversely, the essence of hardness is invariance of object form with changes in contact force. Resistance to deformation signals the hardness of an object or surface.

Like smoothness or roughness, softness or hardness is subjective. Except for a study by Harper and Stevens (1964), most psychophysical studies have focused on the objective ability to discriminate compliance. Harper and Stevens showed that subjective softness judgments were related to the compliance of their test objects by a power function with exponent 0.8 and that hardness and softness judgments were reciprocally related. The most extensive study of the objective ability to discriminate compliance is by Srinivasan and LaMotte (1995), who used cutaneous anesthesia and various modes of stimulus contact to show that cutaneous information alone is sufficient to discriminate the compliance of objects with deformable surfaces. Subjects discriminate softness when an object is applied to the passive, immobile finger as accurately as when they actively palpate the object, and this passive ability is unaffected by randomizing the velocity and force of application.

No combined psychophysical and neurophysiological experiments systematically address the neural mechanisms of hardness perception, but the likely mechanism can be inferred from what is known about the response properties of each of the afferent types. Just as in roughness perception, the a priori possibilities are intensive temporal or spatial codes in one or more of the cutaneous afferent populations. Intensive codes are unlikely because random changes in velocity and force, which do not affect discrimination performance, have strong effects on afferent impulse rates (Srinivasan & LaMotte, 1996). Purely temporal codes seem unlikely in this context. Because perceived softness (or hardness) is based on perceived changes in object form with changing contact force, the system responsible for the perception of object form (i.e., the SA1 system) would seem to be implicated. Thus, it is likely that the SA1 system is responsible for both principal dimensions of texture (roughness and hardness) as well as for the perception of form.

RA SYSTEM

Individual RA afferent nerve fibers end as unmyelinated, disk-like bladders within Meissner's corpuscles (Figure 13.1), which occur in dermal pockets between the sweatduct and adhesive ridges (Guinard, Usson, Guillermet, & Saxod, 2000; Miller et al., 1960; Munger & Ide, 1988). The disk-like expansions of the terminal axons increase the membrane area available to transduce mechanical stimuli. Meissner's corpuscles are as close to the surface of the epidermis as is possible within the dermis (Quilliam, 1978). This and the disk-like expansions may account in part for the greater sensitivity of RA afferents to minute skin deformation relative to SA1 afferents, whose receptors are on the tips of the deepest epidermal ridges. The number of corpuscles innervated by each RA axon in the finger pad can be estimated from the innervation density (150/cm^2; see also the earlier discussion), the number of RA axons entering each corpuscle (1–9 RA axons; Cauna, 1956), and the Meissner corpuscle density (40/mm^2 in a young adult, declining to about 15/mm^2 in an elderly person; Bolton, Winkelmann, & Dyck, 1964). If each corpuscle receives two RA axons on average (Cauna, 1956), then each RA afferent innervates 20 to 50 corpuscles depending on a person's age. This innervation number may help to preserve functional innervation density despite the loss of receptors with age. The breadth of the terminal arbor, about 5 mm^2, can be inferred from the minimal RA receptive field area (Figure 13.8).

RA afferents can be distinguished in neurophysiological recordings from the slowly adapting SA1 and SA2 afferents by their lack of response to sustained skin deformation. They are distinguished from the PC afferents by their much smaller receptive fields and by being most sensitive to vibratory stimuli in the range from 40 Hz to 60 Hz. RA thresholds in this frequency range vary from 2 to 20 μm peak-to-peak vibratory amplitude (Mountcastle et al., 1972). PCs are most sensitive in the range from 150 Hz to 300 Hz; they are orders of magnitude more sensitive; and because of their sensitivity, their receptive field areas are orders of magnitude larger.

RA afferents have been linked to sensory function in several studies. What links all the functions attributed to RAs is the detection of minute motion on the surface of the skin. The detection of slip and of sudden changes in load force that require reflexive changes in grip force may be the most important of these. The beneficial effect of the larger RA receptive field areas compared with SA1 receptive field areas (Figure 13.8) is that an isolated event at the skin surface (e.g., localized slip that portends widespread slip) is signaled by many RA afferents.

The detection, discrimination, and scaling of low-frequency cutaneous vibration was the first function attributed to RA afferents; the percept associated with the activation of RAs was flutter (i.e., a feeling of rapid skin movement; Mountcastle, 1975). Combined psychophysical and neurophysiological studies showed that only the RA thresholds could account for the detection of vibration at low frequencies and that only PC thresholds could account for detection thresholds at high frequencies (Mountcastle et al., 1972), which provided proof of Verrillo's (1963) duplex theory of vibratory detection. The combined studies concluded that vibratory frequency discrimination depends on the periodicity of the evoked afferent response (Mountcastle, 1975) and that the ability to scale vibratory intensity depends on the integrated impulse rate in the RA population response (Johnson, 1974).

Grip Control

When the skin of the fingers is anesthetic, we lose manual dexterity. This is partly because of the loss of form perception (e.g., consider your own tactile sensations while buttoning and unbuttoning a button) but it is also because of the loss of sensory information required for grip control. Unexpected slip between the skin and an object held in the hand and sudden, unexpected changes in load force both require rapid, reflexive adjustments of grip force. RA afferents appear to provide the information required for such reflexive adjustments (Johansson & Westling, 1984, 1987; Macefield, Hager-Ross, & Johansson, 1996; Srinivasan et al., 1990).

When we lift an object with the fingers, we increase our grip and lift forces in parallel; when the object lifts off, we stop increasing grip force. The key to success lies in increasing the grip force in relation to the lift force so that the slip threshold (the least lateral force between the skin and the object that produces slip) is always greater than the lift force. Once the object is lifted, the slip threshold (which is proportional to and controlled by grip force) must be kept above the object's weight and above any other forces that might pull the object out of the hand. An interesting complication is that the coefficient of surface friction (which determines the relationship between grip force and slip threshold; slip threshold = grip force × coefficient of friction) varies by a factor of three or four between objects. If the surface of an object is slippery (coefficient of friction is low) and grip force is increased too slowly relative to lift force, the object slips out of grasp. Johansson and Westling (1987) showed that we sense the coefficient of friction and begin to adjust our grip force appropriately within the first 0.1 s of contact with an object. Once lifted, minute slips of which we are unaware (but which are detected by an accelerometer within the object that is held) cause reflexive adjustments to grip force. Sudden changes in load force have the same effect (Macefield et al., 1996). If we were unable to detect slip, the only way to hold objects securely would be to grip all objects as though they were slippery, and that is just what we do when our fingers are anesthetized (Johansson & Westling, 1984).

How do we sense the coefficient of friction without apparent macroscopic slip? Which afferents signal slip and changes in load force? The answer to both questions lies in the response of RA afferents. Only RA afferents respond consistently and with sufficiently short latency to account for the reflexive changes that accompany sudden changes in load force (Macefield et al., 1996). SA1, RA, and PC afferents all respond to minute slips, so the RA role is inferred by elimination. PC afferents are eliminated by experimental manipulations believed to affect only SA1 and RA receptors: Topical anesthesia eliminates reflexive responses to slip, and, conversely, weak electrical stimulation at the cutaneous interface elicits reflexive increases in grip force as though the object had slipped (Johansson & Westling, 1984, 1987). Topical anesthesia and weak electrical stimulation are presumed to affect the SA1 and RA receptors which lie at the dermal-epidermal margin (Figure 13.1) but not the Pacinian receptors, which are mostly distant from the skin surface. The argument that RAs are slip detectors is based partly on experiments by Srinivasan et al. (1990), who showed that small surface features are required for slip detection and that RA afferent responses account for the limits of slip detection. The only conceivable basis for sensing the coefficient of friction within the first 100 ms of contact is that slippery surfaces allow more slippage as the skin conforms to the surface and that this is detected by one of the afferent systems. SA1, RA, and PC afferents respond vigorously during the contact phase, but Johansson and Westling (1987) could detect a consistent relationship between these responses and the coefficient of friction only in some RA afferents. This observation, combined with the fact that RAs are slip detectors, that RAs respond most vigorously during the period when coefficient of friction is being sensed, and that only RAs reliably signal sudden changes in load force, suggests that RAs provide the sensory information on which grip control is based.

Other RA Functions

RA afferents are about four times more sensitive to cutaneous deformation than are the SA1 afferents; therefore, they are responsible for the perception of surface features under some conditions. For example, LaMotte and Whitehouse (1986) have shown that because of its greater sensitivity, the RA system is responsible for the human ability to detect small (2 μm tall) surface features. The most sensitive SA1 afferents required feature heights of 8 μm or more. A four-to-one difference in sensitivity between RA and SA1 afferents shows up repeatedly in different studies. RA afferents are four times more sensitive to rapid indentation than are SA1 afferents; median thresholds in a study by Johansson and Vallbo (1979a) were 14 μm and 56 μm, respectively. RA and SA1 responses to vibratory stimuli are similar in most respects; the major difference, besides a difference in best frequencies, is that RAs are about four times more sensitive (Freeman & Johnson, 1982). The lower RA response thresholds are paralleled by lower saturation thresholds relative to SA1 afferents (as discussed earlier; Blake, Johnson, & Hsiao, 1997; Vega-Bermudez & Johnson, 1999a), which suggests that RA and SA1 afferents play complementary roles. As mentioned earlier, the RA and SA1 systems are in some respects like the scotopic and photopic systems in vision. The RA system, like the scotopic system, has greater sensitivity but poorer spatial resolution and limited dynamic range. The SA1 system, like the photopic system, is less sensitive but has higher spatial resolution and operates over a wider dynamic range.

Optacon Studies

The Optacon (optical to tactile converter) is a reading device for the blind that converts spatial images on a page into patterns of vibration on 144 pins applied to a finger pad (Bliss, 1969). A wide range of studies with the Optacon have characterized pattern recognition ability (e.g., Kops & Gardner, 1996); pattern masking, temporal integration, and response competition (e.g., Craig, 2000); effects of aging (Muijser, 1990); stimulus integration and competition between fingers and between hands (e.g., Evans, Craig, & Rinker, 1992); and the effects of attention (e.g., Craig & Evans, 1995). Because of the large number of psychophysical studies conducted with the Optacon (Craig & Rollman, 1999), it was important to learn that the Optacon activates RA and PC but not SA1 afferents (Gardner &

Palmer, 1989) and that PCs provide little, if any, useful information about the spatial pattern of stimulation delivered by the Optacon (Palmer & Gardner, 1990). Therefore, psychophysical studies with the Optacon aimed at spatial information processing (i.e., almost all Optacon studies) are practically pure studies of RA function, but the fact that PCs are activated strongly must be kept in mind.

The capacity for form perception based on RA input alone is provided by Optacon studies of grating orientation discrimination and letter recognition. Kops and Gardner (1996) have shown that the orientation of a grating presented to a finger pad with the Optacon can be discriminated only when the pattern grooves exceed 5 mm; this is about five times the threshold when SA1 afferents are activated (Figure 13.2). The Optacon grating orientation threshold is consistent with the RA inability to resolve gaps less than 3 mm to 5 mm wide, as illustrated in Figure 13.4. When letter recognition (the intended use of the Optacon) is tested, the threshold letter heights in trained subjects are 15 mm or more— that is, at least three times greater than when naive subjects contact raised letters directly (reviewed in Johnson & Hsiao, 1992).

Motion Perception

The neural mechanisms of motion perception—an important aspect of tactile perception—are not well understood. Most natural stimuli that move across the skin produce asymmetric skin stretch as well as progressive, temporal activation of all receptor types (see Figure 13.3), and these provide a wide range of cues to motion (Essick, 1998; Olausson, Wessberg, & Kakuda, 2000). Pattern motion is a robust aspect of the sensory experience evoked by the Optacon, which demonstrates that the RA system is sufficient for motion perception. The stimulus factors that affect motion perception with the Optacon have been studied extensively (Gardner &

Sklar, 1994). A particularly interesting result of studies with the Optacon is that finger position affects the integration of motion information from two fingers (Rinker & Craig, 1994). If the RA system is responsible for motion processing, then it should integrate information from the skin in a way that is consistent with the motion of the object rather than motion across the skin. The relationship between cutaneous motion and object motion is complex. For example, when the right hand is laid flat on a surface, right-to-left surface motion beneath the hand produces (anatomically defined) medial-to-lateral motion across the fingers and the thumb (i.e., from the fifth finger toward the thumb). When an object is grasped between thumb and forefinger, the same object motion relative to the fingers produces motion across the thumb pad in the opposite direction (i.e., lateral-to-medial motion), but we are unaware of the change in the motion pattern. If the cutaneous motion were unchanged, it would signal an object rotating between the thumb and forefinger. The system that integrates motion on the skin obviously accounts for finger position. Rinker and Craig (1994) used two Optacon displays to show that this is how motion information is integrated by the RA system. When the hand is flat, medial-to-lateral motion on the thumb biases the perception of motion on the index finger toward medial-to-lateral motion; when the thumb and index finger assume the position of a precision grip, the bias reverses. This implies that somewhere within the RA system, neuronal responses to moving stimuli are affected by the shape and position of the hand.

PC SYSTEM

Pacinian corpuscles, which occur in the dermis and deeper tissues, are large onion-like receptors comprising corpuscles within corpuscles separated from one another by fluid spaces; each fluid space shields the next corpuscle from the large, low-frequency deformations that accompany most manual tasks (Hubbard, 1958; Loewenstein & Skalak, 1966). This filter cascade protects the receptor within it from all but high-frequency vibrations. The most sensitive Pacinian corpuscles respond with action potentials to vibratory amplitudes as small as 3 nm applied directly to the corpuscle (Bolanowski & Zwislocki, 1984) and 10 nm applied to the skin (Brisben et al., 1999). Because the receptor is so sensitive, receptive field boundaries are difficult to define. The most sensitive PCs have receptive fields that may include an entire hand or even an entire arm; an insensitive PC may have a receptive field restricted to a single finger pad. Each corpuscle receives a single axon, and each PC axon terminates in a single corpuscle. The history, structure, and electrophysiological properties of this interesting receptor are reviewed by Bell, Bolanowski, and Holmes (1994). There are about 2,500 Pacinian corpuscles in the human hand, and they are about twice as numerous in the fingers as in the palm (about 350 per finger and 800 in the palm; reviewed by Brisben et al., 1999).

Transmitted Vibrations

Early psychophysical and neurophysiological studies showed that only the PC system can account for the human ability to detect high-frequency vibratory stimuli (Lindblom & Lund, 1966; Mountcastle et al., 1972; Verrillo, 1963). The detection and perception of distant events by vibrations transmitted through tools, probes, and objects held in the hand may be the most important function served by the PC system. When we are skilled in the use of a tool or a probe, we perceive distant events almost as if our fingers were present at the working surfaces of the tool or probe. A possibility that has not been examined is that a substantial part of skill acquisition with a tool or probe consists of learning to associate the transmitted vibrations with events at the working surface of the tool or probe. Katz (1925/1970) provided an early demonstration of this by showing that we can discriminate the roughness of a surface with a probe as well as we can with direct finger contact and that this capacity is lost when vibrations in the probe are damped. A recent study has shown that when subjects grasp a probe, transmitted vibrations with amplitudes less than 10 μm at the hand can be detected (the mean is 30 μm; Figure 13.14).

The hypothesis that the PC system is responsible for the perception of vibrations transmitted through an object held in the hand supposes not just that Pacinian receptors detect the transmitted vibration but that the PC population transmits a neural image of the vibratory signal that is sufficient to account for this perceptual capacity. Work on the human ability to detect and discriminate complex vibratory stimuli (Formby, Morgan, Forrest, & Raney, 1992; Lamore, Muijser, & Keemink, 1986; Weisenberger, 1986) has shown that we are sensitive to the temporal structure of high-frequency stimuli that only activate PC afferents; for example, humans can discriminate the frequency with which a 250-Hz carrier stimulus is modulated for modulation frequencies as high as 60 Hz, and we can detect the presence of this modulation through the cutaneous sense as well as we can through audition (Formby et al., 1992).

The PC system acts as an extremely steep high-pass filter. Between 20 Hz and 150 Hz, the human threshold for detecting transmitted vibration falls from 5.6 μm to 0.03 μm, which amounts to a drop of 52 dB per decade (Figure 13.14). This is close to the filtering characteristic of a mechanism that is sensitive to the third temporal derivative of tissue displacement (60 dB per decade; dashed line in Figure 13.14, which is called jerk because

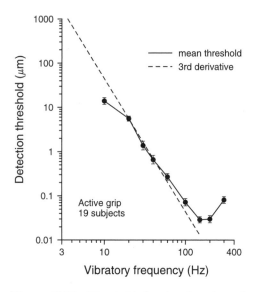

Figure 13.14   Threshold for the detection of transmitted vibration when subjects grasp a 32 mm diameter cylindrical rod.

NOTE: Vibrations were produced by a linear motor mounted at one end of the rod. Vibratory amplitudes were measured with a three-dimensional accelerometer mounted on the rod. The ordinate represents the mean threshold amplitude measured as half the vibratory peak-to-peak excursion. Filled circles and solid lines represent the psychophysical thresholds. The dashed line has the slope of a detector sensitive to the third derivative of stimulus motion (i.e., 60 dB/decade).

SOURCE: Adapted from Brisben, Hsiao, & Johnson (1999).

it corresponds to the rate of change of acceleration). Our hands are used constantly in manual tasks that subject the hand to large dynamic forces, but we remain sensitive to minute vibrations in the object being grasped even though we grip it with great force. If it were not for this filtering, the Pacinian receptors would be overwhelmed by these forces. Peak-to-peak motion of 1 cm at 2 Hz will not activate the PC system if the dashed line in Figure 13.14 is an accurate representation of its threshold.

SA2 SYSTEM

SA2 afferents are distinguished from SA1 afferents by four properties: (a) Their receptive field areas are about five times larger, and their borders are not so clearly demarcated (Johansson & Vallbo, 1980); (b) they are about six times less sensitive to skin indentation (Johansson & Vallbo, 1979a; Johansson, Vallbo, & Westling, 1980); (c) they are two to four times more sensitive to skin stretch (Edin, 1992); and (d) their interspike intervals are more uniform (Chambers, Andres, von Duering, & Iggo, 1972; Edin, 1992). The differences in sensitivity and receptive field size between SA1 and SA2 afferents can be seen in the responses to Braille dots illustrated in Figure 13.3, which are, in effect, receptive field plots.

Both SA1 and SA2 afferents respond to forces that are orthogonal and parallel to the skin surface, but between them the SA1 afferents are biased toward responsiveness to orthogonal forces and SA2 afferents to parallel forces (Macefield et al., 1996). SA2 responses to raised dot patterns, to Braille patterns (Figure 13.3), and to curved surfaces suggest that they play no role in form perception. Based on SA2 responses to curved surfaces, A. W. Goodwin, Macefield, and Bisley (1997, p. 2887) concluded that "SA2 responses are unlikely to signal information to the brain about the local shape of an object."

Because of their sensitivity to skin stretch, the most obvious role for SA2 afferents is to signal the magnitude and direction of forces acting parallel to the skin surface. This may serve two related perceptual functions. The first is to signal the direction of an object moving across the skin; when an object moves across the skin, it often produces skin stretch in its wake that provides a strong cue to the object motion and direction. Olausson et al. (2000) showed that the SA2 afferents sense

this pattern of skin stretch and provide a more effective signal of motion direction than do the SA1 afferents. The second possible function is to signal the direction and magnitude of the force transmitted to the hand by an object held in the hand (Macefield et al., 1996); for example, when we pull an object with a rope we perceive its resistance to movement (or, if it is active, how hard it pulls back) by the force tangential to the skin surface. The SA2 afferents are ideally suited to transduce the skin stretch that is correlated with this tangential force. Combined psychophysical and neurophysiological experiments and hypothesis testing are required to determine whether they play this role. A very interesting possibility, discussed later, is that SA2 afferents send a neural image of skin stretch that plays a significant—or possibly even the dominant—role in our perception of hand conformation.

A puzzle is that SA2 afferents occur frequently in the glabrous skin of humans (Hulliger, Nordh, Thelin, & Vallbo, 1979; Johansson & Vallbo, 1979b) but I am aware of no report of SA2 afferents in monkey glabrous skin. The difference cannot be explained by differences in classification criteria between studies because several investigators have conducted neurophysiological recording experiments in both species. A. W. Goodwin and his colleagues studied neural responses to curved surfaces in both monkeys and humans and found that the responses of SA1 afferents are virtually identical in the two species (e.g., compare Figure 4 in A. W. Goodwin et al., 1995, with Figure 3 in A. W. Goodwin et al., 1997), but nothing like the human SA2 responses to curved surfaces (Figure 4 in A. W. Goodwin et al., 1997) has been observed in the monkey. Similarly, Johnson and his colleagues studied neural responses to scanned raised dots in both monkeys (Blake, Hsiao, & Johnson, 1997; Connor et al., 1990; Johnson & Lamb, 1981) and humans (Phillips, Johansson, & Johnson, 1990, 1992) and found that SA1 responses are virtually identical in the two species (compare SA1 responses in Figures 13.3 and 13.12), but nothing like the human SA2 responses to raised dots illustrated in Figure 13.3 has been observed in studies of monkey afferents. A caution in concluding that SA2 afferents are absent in monkey glabrous skin is that neurophysiological studies in monkeys have focused heavily on afferents innervating the distal finger pads.

Perception of Hand Conformation

Before considering the sensory mechanisms underlying the perception of hand conformation, it is useful to close one's eyes and introspect while adopting different hand shapes (and being careful to avoid contact between the fingers). The result is a powerful, accurate image of the shape of the hand; moving the thumb and the tip of one of the fingers to within a millimeter or two of one another without visual feedback illustrates the accuracy of this image. There are three possible sources of this capacity—joint afferents, muscle length afferents, and cutaneous afferents—and each has its proponents.

The evidence is strong that muscle spindle (length transducer) afferents provide the essential information on which, for example, elbow and knee joint angle perception is based (Clark, Horch, Bach, & Larson, 1979; G. M. Goodwin, McCloskey, & Matthews, 1972; Matthews, 1988). After anesthetizing the joint capsule and the skin around the knee, joint angle sense is normal. A simple and elegant demonstration of the role of muscle spindles in the perception of joint angle comes from vibrating the biceps or triceps of the arm, which activates muscle spindle afferents strongly (G. M. Goodwin et al., 1972). When the biceps are vibrated, blindfolded subjects behave as though the elbow is extended 30° or more beyond its actual location; vibrating the triceps has the opposite effect. These experi-

ments make muscle spindles prime candidates as the basis for the perception of hand conformation, but the evidence indicates that this function is shared with joint and cutaneous afferents in the hand.

The mechanisms underlying the perception of joint angle in the hand may be different because the accurate perception of hand conformation and finger position is so important and because the hand is so complex. Three layers of complexity make computing hand conformation based on information that is signaled by muscle spindles difficult: (a) 20 joint angles are required to specify hand conformation, and the coordinate transforms required to go from a specific set of angles to a specific hand conformation are complex; (b) the relationship between muscle length and even a single joint angle is not simple (Biggs, Horch, & Clark, 1999); and (c) muscle spindle discharge is affected by efferent motor activity as well as muscle length (Matthews, 1988). Hulliger, Nordh, & Vallbo (1982) have shown that spindle responses signal passive finger joint position accurately but that during active finger movements the efferent control of spindle activity cancels the discharge produced by changes in joint angle. If muscle spindles play a role in the perception of finger position, they do so with compensation for the efferent effects that accompany motor acts (Matthews, 1988). Regardless of these theoretical concerns, the psychophysical evidence is that muscle spindles do play a role. For example, when the flexor and extensor muscles are disengaged from the distal phalanx of the middle finger (by flexing the middle finger fully while extending the other four fingers), the ability to detect and discriminate distal joint motion is reduced (Gandevia, Hall, McCloskey, & Potter, 1983). If the joint is moved (passively) very slowly, however, disengaging the muscles has no detrimental effect (i.e., the perception of static finger position is unaffected by removing the muscle length cues; Taylor & McCloskey, 1990).

Muscles that flex and extend the fingers are located in the forearm; consequently, their tendons are often exposed during surgery at the wrist. It would seem that if spindle afferents from these muscles contribute to the perception of finger position, then pulling these tendons and applying vibration that excites the muscle spindles should result in a clear percept of finger motion (as in the biceps and triceps), but the results are equivocal (Gelfan & Carter, 1967; Matthews & Simmonds, 1974; McCloskey, Cross, Honner, & Potter, 1983; Moberg, 1972, 1983). The conclusions from such studies are split evenly between those who find a strong role for muscle length receptors in the perception of finger position and those who do not. The positive findings definitely verify a role for spindle afferents. The negative findings bear on the strength of this signal relative to those from joint and cutaneous afferents.

Joint receptors would seem to be ideally positioned to signal joint angle, but the evidence is that they are least important in joint angle perception. Neurophysiological recordings from median, ulnar, and radial nerves in humans show that joint afferents (afferents terminating in joint receptors) are rare (Hulliger et al., 1979) and that they signal joint angle either at the extremes of extension and flexion or in the midrange (in which case the signal is affected strongly by motor activity; Edin, 1990). Burke, Gandevia, and Macefield (1988, page 357) concluded that joint receptor response properties are "inappropriate for a major role in kinesthesia." Injection of a local anesthetic into the capsule of the proximal interphalangeal joint has been reported to have a substantial (Ferrell, Gandevia, & McCloskey, 1987) or a minor (Clark, Grigg, & Chapin, 1989) effect on the discrimination of finger joint angle. The fact that replacing a finger joint with a silastic implant has a

minimal effect on joint angle acuity (Cross & McCloskey, 1973) joins the other observations to suggest that joint afferents play a minor role.

All cutaneous receptor types are active while the hand is in motion, and they provide a rich potential basis for the perception of hand conformation. Three hundred cutaneous afferents have been studied during active and passive hand movements (Burke et al., 1988; Edin & Abbs, 1991; Hulliger et al., 1979). The results of Hulliger et al. (1979) are typical: 57% of RA, 66% of SA1, 94% of SA2, and 100% of PC afferents were active during hand movements; when motion stopped, RA and PC afferents fell silent, but 17% of SA1 and 81% of SA2 afferents remained active. Edin (1992) has shown that cutaneous afferents on the back of the hand and especially SA2 afferents provide a robust signal of joint angle. He showed that ordinary hand movements produce skin strain of 10% to 15% over a large part of the back of the hand and that both SA1 and SA2 afferents respond in a near-linear manner to this strain but that the SA2s are more sensitive. The most sensitive SA1 and SA2 afferents respond with about 1.5 imp/s and 5 imp/s per percent change in skin stretch, respectively. The relationship between joint angle and skin stretch varies with skin location, but Edin estimates SA1 and SA2 sensitivities of about 0.25 imp/s and 0.5 imp/s per degree of change in metacarpophalangeal joint angle; the comparable sensitivities for type Ia and II muscle spindles in the appropriate muscles are 0.25 imp/s and 0.35 imp/s (Edin & Vallbo, 1990). Cutaneous afferents from the glabrous skin undoubtedly respond to hand conformation in a similar way. Human subjects can detect movement of about 0.5° or less at almost all joints of the body (Clark & Horch, 1986), and they can track the angle of one finger joint with the homologous joint of the other hand to within about 1° (Rymer & D'Almeida, 1980). This implies that we resolve the afferent discharge of the relevant afferents with an accuracy of better than 0.5 imp/s per afferent.

Edin (1992) made a compelling argument that the perception of mouth conformation (independent of jaw movement) must be based entirely on information from cutaneous afferents because there are apparently no muscle spindles in facial muscles. Therefore, there is a precedent for the role of cutaneous afferents in the perception of hand conformation. (An introspective comparison of lip movements with the jaw closed and hand movements provides a convincing demonstration of the potential role of cutaneous afferents.) Later experiments (Collins & Prochazka, 1996; Collins, Refshauge, & Gandevia, 2000; Edin & Johansson, 1995) showed that experimentally induced skin stretch near a joint does produce the illusion of joint movement. Collins et al. (2000) showed that both muscle and skin afferents contribute to the perception of finger position and that, in addition, cutaneous input serves to localize the percept to the appropriate finger. The evidence cited previously suggests that SA2 afferents underlie the role assigned to cutaneous afferents, but SA1 afferents cannot be ruled out.

Thus there is compelling evidence that muscle length afferents, cutaneous afferents, and possibly joint afferents all contribute to the perception of finger position and hand conformation. Many studies of the neural mechanisms of finger position have demonstrated that spindle, joint, and skin afferents each play a role under some or all circumstances and that each has its potential weaknesses. An argument cited earlier against a role for spindle afferents in the perception of hand conformation is the confounding effect of efferent drive during active movements (Hulliger et al., 1982; but see Matthews, 1988). A similar argument against joint afferents is the confounding effect of motor activity on their responses during active movements (Edin, 1990). A comparable argument against cutaneous afferents is the confounding effect of the mechanical deformation and vibration to which the hand is subject in many manual tasks. It may be that reliance on multiple systems protects this perceptual capacity from the vulnerabilities of each. The perception of hand conformation may be like balance—a function so critical that it is served by multiple sensory systems (Fitzpatrick and McCloskey, 1994; Lackner et al., 1999).

CONCLUSION

The available evidence suggests a sharp division of function between the four cutaneous afferent systems that innervate the human hand. The SA1 system provides a high-quality neural image of the spatial structure of objects and surfaces that contact the skin, and this is the basis of form and texture perception. The RA system provides a neural image of motion signals from the whole hand. From this, the brain extracts information that is critical for grip control as well as information about the motion of objects that contact the skin. The PC system provides a neural image of vibrations transmitted to the hand from objects contacting the hand or, more frequently, from objects grasped in the hand. This provides the basis for the perception of distant events, possibly in a manner analogous to some of the perceptual mechanisms of audition. The SA2 system provides a neural image of skin stretch over the whole hand. The evidence is less secure, but the most likely hypothesis is that the brain extracts information about hand conformation from the dorsal SA2 image (and the ventral image when the hand is empty). When the hand is occupied, the ventral SA2 image may signal forces acting on objects held in the hand.

REFERENCES

Adrian, E. D., & Umrath, K. (1929). The impulse discharge from the Pacinian corpuscle. *Journal of Physiology, 68,* 139–154.

Andrew, D., & Craig, A. D. (2001). Spinothalamic lamina I neurons selectively sensitive to histamine: A central neural pathway for itch. *Nature Neuroscience, 4,* 72–77.

Bell, J., Bolanowski, S. J., & Holmes, M. H. (1994). The structure and function of Pacinian corpuscles: A review. *Progress in Neurobiology, 42,* 79–128.

Biggs, J., Horch, K., & Clark, F. J. (1999). Extrinsic muscles of the hand signal fingertip location more precisely than they signal the angles of individual finger joints. *Experimental Brain Research, 125,* 221–230.

Blake, D. T., Hsiao, S. S., & Johnson, K. O. (1997). Neural coding mechanisms in tactile pattern recognition: The relative contributions of slowly and rapidly adapting mechanoreceptors to perceived roughness. *Journal of Neuroscience, 17,* 7480–7489.

Blake, D. T., Johnson, K. O., & Hsiao, S. S. (1997). Monkey cutaneous SAI and RA responses to raised and depressed scanned patterns: Effects of width, height, orientation, and a raised surround. *Journal of Neurophysiology, 78,* 2503–2517.

Bliss, J. C. (1969). A relatively high-resolution reading aid for the blind. *IEEE Transactions on Man-Machine Systems, 10,* 1–9.

Bolanowski, S. J., & Zwislocki, J. J. (1984). Intensity and frequency characteristics of Pacinian corpuscles: I. Action potentials. *Journal of Neurophysiology, 51,* 793–811.

Bolton, C. F., Winkelmann, R. K., & Dyck, P. J. (1964). A quantitative study of Meissner's corpuscles in man. *Transactions of the American Neurological Association, 89,* 190–192.

Brisben, A. J., Hsiao, S. S., & Johnson, K. O. (1999). Detection of vibration transmitted through an object grasped in the hand. *Journal of Neurophysiology, 81,* 1548–1558.

Burke, D., Gandevia, S. C., & Macefield, G. (1988). Responses to passive movement of receptors in joint, skin and muscle of the human hand. *Journal of Physiology, 402,* 347–361.

Burton H., & Sinclair, R. J. (1996). Somatosensory cortex and tactile perceptions. In L. Kruger (Ed.), *Pain and touch* (pp. 105–177). San Diego: Academic Press.

Cauna, N. (1956). Nerve supply and nerve endings in Meissner's corpuscles. *American Journal of Anatomy, 99,* 315–350.

Chambers, M. R., Andres, K. H., von Duering, M., & Iggo, A. (1972). The structure and function of the slowly adapting type II mechanoreceptor in hairy skin. *Quarterly Journal of Experimental Physiology, 57,* 417–445.

Clark, F. J., Grigg, P., & Chapin, J. W. (1989). The contribution of articular receptors to proprioception with the fingers in humans. *Journal of Neurophysiology, 61,* 186–193.

Clark, F. J., & Horch, K. W. (1986). Kinesthesia. In K. R. Boff, L. Kaufman, & J. P. Thomas (Eds.), *Handbook of perception and human performance: Vol. 1. Sensory processes and perception* (pp. 1–62). New York: Wiley.

Clark, F. J., Horch, K. W., Bach, S. M., & Larson, G. F. (1979). Contributions of cutaneous and joint receptors to static knee-position sense in man. *Journal of Neurophysiology, 42,* 877–888.

Collins, D. F., & Prochazka, A. (1996). Movement illusions evoked by ensemble cutaneous input from the dorsum of the human hand. *Journal of Physiology, 496,* 857–871.

Collins, D. F., Refshauge, K. M., & Gandevia, S. C. (2000). Sensory integration in the perception of movements at the human metacarpophalangeal joint. *Journal of Physiology, 529,* 505–515.

Connor, C. E., Hsiao, S. S., Phillips, J. R., & Johnson, K. O. (1990). Tactile roughness: Neural codes that account for psychophysical magnitude estimates. *Journal of Neuroscience, 10,* 3823–3836.

Connor, C. E., & Johnson, K. O. (1992). Neural coding of tactile texture: Comparisons of spatial and temporal mechanisms for roughness perception. *Journal of Neuroscience, 12,* 3414–3426.

Craig, J. C. (1999). Grating orientation as a measure of tactile spatial acuity. *Somatosensory and Motor Research, 16,* 197–206.

Craig, J. C. (2000). Processing of sequential tactile patterns: Effects of a neutral stimulus. *Perception and Psychophysics, 62,* 596–606.

Craig, J. C., & Evans, P. M. (1995). Tactile selective attention and temporal masking. *Perception and Psychophysics, 57,* 511–518.

Craig, J. C., & Johnson, K. O. (2000). The two-point threshold: Not a measure of tactile spatial resolution. *Current Directions in Psychological Science, 9,* 29–32.

Craig, J. C., & Kisner, J. M. (1998). Factors affecting tactile spatial acuity. *Somatosensory and Motor Research, 15,* 29–45.

Craig, J. C., & Lyle, K. B. (2001). A comparison of tactile spatial sensitivity on the palm and fingerpad. *Perception and Psychophysics, 63,* 337–347.

Craig, J. C., & Rollman, G. B. (1999). Somesthesis. *Annual Review of Psychology, 50,* 305–331.

Cross, M. J., & McCloskey, D. I. (1973). Position sense following surgical removal of joints in man. *Brain Research, 55,* 443–445.

Darian-Smith, I. (1973). The trigeminal system. In A. Iggo (Ed.), *Handbook of sensory physiology: Vol. 2. The somatosensory system* (pp. 271–314). Berlin: Springer.

Darian-Smith, I. (1984). Thermal sensibility. In I. Darian-Smith, V. B. Mountcastle, & J. M. Brookhart (Eds.), *Handbook of physiology: Vol. 3. Sensory processes* (pp. 879–914). Bethesda, MD: American Physiological Society.

Darian-Smith, I., Davidson, I., & Johnson, K. O. (1980). Peripheral neural representation of spatial dimensions of a textured surface moving across the monkey's finger pad. *Journal of Physiology, 309,* 135–146.

Darian-Smith, I., & Kenins, P. (1980). Innervation density of mechanoreceptive fibers supplying glabrous skin of the monkey's index finger. *Journal of Physiology, 309,* 147–155.

Diamond, J., Mills, L. R., & Mearow, K. M. (1988). Evidence that the Merkel cell is not the transducer in the mechanosensory Merkel cell-neurite complex. *Progress in Brain Research, 74,* 51–56.

DiCarlo, J. J., & Johnson, K. O. (1999). Velocity invariance of receptive field structure in somatosensory cortical area 3b of the alert monkey. *Journal of Neuroscience, 19,* 401–419.

DiCarlo, J. J., & Johnson, K. O. (2000). Spatial and temporal structure of receptive fields in primate somatosensory area 3b: Effects of stimulus scanning direction and orientation. *Journal of Neuroscience, 20,* 495–510.

Dodson, M. J., Goodwin, A. W., Browning, A. S., & Gehring, H. M. (1998). Peripheral neural mechanisms determining the orientation of cylinders grasped by the digits. *Journal of Neuroscience, 18,* 521–530.

Edin, B. B. (1990). Finger joint movement sensitivity of non-cutaneous mechanoreceptor afferents in the human radial nerve. *Experimental Brain Research, 82,* 417–422.

Edin, B. B. (1992). Quantitative analysis of static strain sensitivity in human mechanoreceptors from hairy skin. *Journal of Neurophysiology, 67,* 1105–1113.

Edin, B. B., & Abbs, J. H. (1991). Finger movement responses of cutaneous mechanoreceptors in the dorsal skin of the human hand. *Journal of Neurophysiology, 65,* 657–670.

Edin, B. B., & Johansson, N. (1995). Skin strain patterns provide kinaesthetic information to the human central nervous system. *Journal of Physiology, 487,* 243–251.

Edin, B. B., & Vallbo, Å. B. (1990). Dynamic response of human muscle spindle afferents to stretch. *Journal of Neurophysiology, 63,* 1297–1306.

Essick, G. K. (1998). Factors affecting direction discrimination of moving tactile stimuli. In J. W. Morley (Ed.), *Neural aspects of tactile sensation* (pp. 1–54). Amsterdam: Elsevier.

Essick, G. K., Chen, C. C., & Kelly, D. G. (1999). A letter-recognition task to assess lingual tactile acuity. *Journal of Oral and Maxillofacial Surgery, 57,* 1324–1330.

Evans, P. M., Craig, J. C., & Rinker, M. A. (1992). Perceptual processing of adjacent and nonadjacent tactile nontargets. *Perception and Psychophysics, 52,* 571–581.

Fechner, G. T. (1966). *Elements of psychophysics* (H. E. Adler, Trans.). New York: Holt, Rinehart and Winston. (Original work published 1860)

Ferrell, W. R., Gandevia, S. C., & McCloskey, D. I. (1987). The role of joint receptors in human kinaesthesia when intramuscular receptors cannot contribute. *Journal of Physiology, 386,* 63–71.

Fitzpatrick, R., & McCloskey, D. I. (1994). Proprioceptive, visual and vestibular thresholds for the perception of sway during standing in humans. *Journal of Physiology, 478,* 173–186.

Formby, C., Morgan, L. N., Forrest, T. G., & Raney, J. J. (1992). The role of frequency selectivity in measures of auditory and vibrotactile temporal resolution. *Journal of the Acoustical Society of America, 91,* 293–305.

Freeman, A. W., & Johnson, K. O. (1982). A model accounting for effects of vibratory amplitude on responses of cutaneous mechanoreceptors in macaque monkey. *Journal of Physiology, 323,* 43–64.

Gandevia, S. C., Hall, L. A., McCloskey, D. I., & Potter, E. K. (1983). Proprioceptive sensation at the terminal joint of the middle finger. *Journal of Physiology, 335,* 507–517.

Gardner, E. P., & Palmer, C. I. (1989). Simulation of motion on the skin: I. Receptive fields and temporal frequency coding by cutaneous mechanoreceptors of Optacon pulses delivered to the hand. *Journal of Neurophysiology, 62,* 1410–1436.

Gardner, E. P., & Sklar, B. F. (1994). Discrimination of the direction of motion on the human hand: A psychophysical study of stimulation parameters. *Journal of Neurophysiology, 71,* 2414–2429.

Gates, E. J. (1915). The determination of the limens of single and dual impression by the method of constant stimuli. *American Journal of Psychology, 26,* 152–157.

Gelfan, S., & Carter, S. (1967). Muscle sense in man. *Experimental Neurology, 18,* 469–473.

Gibson, G. O., & Craig, J. C. (2000). Measures of tactile sensitivity with and without a latex glove. *Psychonomic Society.*

Goodwin, A. W., Browning, A. S., & Wheat, H. E. (1995). Representation of curved surfaces in responses of mechanoreceptive afferent fibers innervating the monkey's fingerpad. *Journal of Neuroscience, 15,* 798–810.

Goodwin, A. W., John, K. T., & Marceglia, A. H. (1991). Tactile discrimination of curvature by humans using only cutaneous information from the fingerpads. *Experimental Brain Research, 86,* 663–672.

Goodwin, A. W., Macefield, V. G., & Bisley, J. W. (1997). Encoding of object curvature by tactile afferents from human fingers. *Journal of Neurophysiology, 78,* 2881–2888.

Goodwin, G. M., McCloskey, D. I., & Matthews, P. B. C. (1972). The contribution of muscle afferents to kinaesthesia shown by vibration induced illusions of movement and by the effects of paralysing joint afferents. *Brain, 95,* 705–748.

Goodwin, A. W., & Wheat, H. E. (1992a). Human tactile discrimination of curvature when contact area with the skin remains constant. *Experimental Brain Research, 88,* 447–450.

Goodwin, A. W., & Wheat, H. E. (1992b). Magnitude estimation of force when objects with different shapes are applied passively to the fingerpad. *Somatosensory and Motor Research, 9,* 339–344.

Gray, J. A. B., & Malcolm, J. L. (1950). The initiation of nerve impulses by mesenteric Pacinian corpuscles. *Proceedings of the Royal Society of London, Series B: Biological Sciences, 137,* 96–114.

Grigg, P., Finerman, G. A., & Riley, L. H. (1973). Joint-position sense after total hip replacement. *Journal of Bone and Joint Surgery: American Volume, 55,* 1016–1025.

Guinard, D., Usson, Y., Guillermet, C., & Saxod, R. (2000). PS-100 and NF 70-200 double immunolabeling for human digital skin Meissner corpuscle 3D imaging. *Journal of Histochemistry and Cytochemistry, 48,* 295–302.

Halata, Z., & Munger, B. L. (1983). The sensory innervation of primate facial skin: II. Vermilion border and mucosa of lip. *Brain Research, 286,* 81–107.

Hardy, J. D., & Oppel, T. W. (1937). Studies in temperature sensation: III. The sensitivity of the body to heat and the spatial summation of the end organ responses. *Journal of Clinical Investigation, 16,* 533–540.

Harper, R., & Stevens, S. S. (1964). Subjective hardness of compliant materials. *Quarterly Journal of Experimental Psychology, 16,* 204–215.

Hollins, M., Bensmaïa, S., Karlof, K., & Young, F. (2000). Individual differences in perceptual space for tactile textures: Evidence from multidimensional scaling. *Perception and Psychophysics, 62,* 1534–1544.

Hollins, M., Faldowski, R., Rao, S., & Young, F. (1993). Perceptual dimensions of tactile surface texture: A multidimensional-scaling analysis. *Perception and Psychophysics, 54,* 697–705.

Hollins, M., Fox, A., & Bishop, C. (2000). Imposed vibration influences perceived tactile smoothness. *Perception, 29,* 1455–1465.

Hollins, M., & Risner, S. R. (2000). Evidence for the duplex theory of tactile texture perception. *Perception and Psychophysics, 62,* 695–705.

Hsiao, S. S., O'Shaughnessy, D. M., & Johnson, K. O. (1993). Effects of selective attention of spatial form processing in monkey primary and secondary somatosensory cortex. *Journal of Neurophysiology, 70,* 444–447.

Hsiao, S. S., & Vega-Bermudez, F. (2001). Attention in the somatosensory system. In R. J. Nelson (Ed.), *The somatosensory system: Deciphering the brain's own body image* (pp. 197–217). Boca Raton: CRC Press.

Hubbard, S. J. (1958). A study of rapid mechanical events in a mechanoreceptor. *Journal of Physiology, 141,* 198–218.

Hulliger, M., Nordh, E., Thelin, A. E., & Vallbo, Å. B. (1979). The responses of afferent fibres from the glabrous skin of the hand during voluntary finger movements in man. *Journal of Physiology, 291,* 233–249.

Hulliger, M., Nordh, E., & Vallbo, Å. B. (1982). The absence of position response in spindle afferent units from human finger muscles during accurate position holding. *Journal of Physiology, 322,* 167–179.

Hunt, C. C. (1961). On the nature of vibration receptors in the hind limb of the cat. *Journal of Physiology, 155,* 175–186.

Iggo, A., & Andres, K. H. (1982). Morphology of cutaneous receptors. *Annual Review of Neuroscience, 5,* 1–31.

Johansson, O., Fantini, F., & Hu, H. (1999). Neuronal structural proteins, transmitters, transmitter enzymes and neuropeptides in human Meissner's corpuscles: A reappraisal using immunohistochemistry. *Archives of Dermatological Research 291,* 419–424.

Johansson, R. S., & Vallbo, Å. B. (1976). Skin mechanoreceptors in the human hand: An inference of some population properties. In Y. Zotterman (Ed.), *Sensory functions of the skin in primates* (pp. 171–184). Oxford: Pergamon Press.

Johansson, R. S., & Vallbo, Å. B. (1979a). Detection of tactile stimuli: Thresholds of afferent units related to psychophysical thresholds in the human hand. *Journal of Physiology, 297,* 405–422.

Johansson, R. S., & Vallbo, Å. B. (1979b). Tactile sensibility in the human hand: Relative and absolute densities of four types of mechanoreceptive units in glabrous skin. *Journal of Physiology, 286,* 283–300.

Johansson, R. S., & Vallbo, Å. B. (1980). Spatial properties of the population of mechanoreceptive units in the glabrous skin of the human hand. *Brain Research, 184,* 353–366.

Johansson, R. S., Vallbo, Å. B., & Westling, G. (1980). Thresholds of mechanosensitive afferents in the human hand as measured with von Frey hairs. *Brain Research, 184,* 343–351.

Johansson, R. S., & Westling, G. (1984). Roles of glabrous skin receptors and sensorimotor memory in automatic control of precision grip when lifting rougher or more slippery objects. *Experimental Brain Research, 56,* 550–564.

Johansson, R. S., & Westling, G. (1987). Signals in tactile afferents from the fingers eliciting adaptive motor responses during precision grip. *Experimental Brain Research, 66,* 141–154.

Johnson, K. O. (1974). Reconstruction of population response to a vibratory stimulus in quickly adapting mechanoreceptive afferent fiber population innervating glabrous skin of the monkey. *Journal of Neurophysiology, 37,* 48–72.

Johnson, K. O. (2001). The roles and functions of cutaneous mechanoreceptors. *Current Opinion in Neurobiology, 11,* 455–461.

Johnson, K. O., & Hsiao, S. S. (1992). Neural mechanisms of tactual form and texture perception. *Annual Review of Neuroscience, 15,* 227–250.

Johnson, K. O., & Hsiao, S. S. (1994). Evaluation of the relative roles of slowly and rapidly adapting afferent fibers in roughness perception. *Canadian Journal of Physiology and Pharmacology, 72,* 488–497.

Johnson, K. O., Hsiao, S. S., & Blake, D. T. (1996). Linearity as the basic law of psychophysics: Evidence from studies of the neural mechanisms of roughness magnitude estimation. In O. Franzén, R. S. Johansson, & L. Terenius (Eds.), *Somesthesis and the neurobiology of the somatosensory cortex* (pp. 213–228). Basel: Birkhäuser.

Johnson, K. O., Hsiao, S. S., & Yoshioka, T. (2001). Neural coding and the basic law of psychophysics, *The Neuroscientist,* In press.

Johnson, K. O., & Lamb, G. D. (1981). Neural mechanisms of spatial tactile discrimination: Neural patterns evoked by Braille-like dot patterns in the monkey. *Journal of Physiology, 310,* 117–144.

Johnson, K. O., & Phillips, J. R. (1981). Tactile spatial resolution: I. Two-point discrimination, gap detection, grating resolution, and letter recognition. *Journal of Neurophysiology, 46,* 1177–1191.

Johnson, K. O., Phillips, J. R., Hsiao, S. S., & Bankman, I. N. (1991). Tactile pattern recognition. In O. Franzén & J. Westman (Eds.), *Information processing in the somatosensory system* (pp. 305–318). London: Macmillan.

Johnson, K. O., Van Boven, R. W., & Hsiao, S. S. (1994). The perception of two points is not the spatial resolution threshold. In J. Boivie, P. Hansson, & U. Lindblom (Eds.), *Touch, temperature, and pain in health and disease: Mechanisms and assessments* (3rd ed., pp. 389–404). Seattle, WA: IASP Press.

Johnson, K. O., & Yoshioka, T. (2001). Neural mechanisms of tactile form and texture perception. In R. J. Nelson (Ed.), *The somatosensory system: Deciphering the brain's own body image* (pp. 73–101). Boca Raton: CRC Press.

Kaas, J. H., Nelson, R. J., Sur, M., & Merzenich, M. M. (1981). Organization of somatosensory cortex in primates. In F. O. Schmitt, F. G. Worden, & S. G. Dennis (Eds.), *The organization of the cerebral cortex* (pp. 237–261). Cambridge: MIT Press.

Katz, D. (1970). *The world of touch* (L. E. Krueger, Trans.). Hillsdale, NJ: Erlbaum. (Original work published 1925)

Khalsa, P. S., Friedman, R. M., Srinivasan, M. A., & LaMotte, R. H. (1998). Encoding of shape and orientation of objects indented into the monkey fingerpad by populations of slowly and rapidly adapting mechanoreceptors. *Journal of Neurophysiology, 79,* 3238–3251.

Klatzky, R. L., & Lederman, S. J. (1999). Tactile roughness perception with a rigid link interposed between skin and surface. *Perception and Psychophysics, 61,* 591–607.

Knibestöl, M. (1975). Stimulus-response functions of slowly adapting mechanoreceptors in the human glabrous skin area. *Journal of Physiology (London), 245,* 63–80.

Knibestöl, M., & Vallbo, Å. B. (1980). Intensity of sensation related to activity of slowly adapting mechanoreceptive units in the human hand. *Journal of Physiology, 300,* 251–267.

Kops, C. E., & Gardner, E. P. (1996). Discrimination of simulated texture patterns on the human hand. *Journal of Neurophysiology, 76,* 1145–1165.

Lackner, J. R., DiZio, P., Jeka, J., Horak, F., Krebs, D., & Rabin, E. (1999). Precision contact of the fingertip reduces postural sway of individuals with bilateral vestibular loss. *Experimental Brain Research, 126,* 459–466.

Lamb, G. D. (1983). Tactile discrimination of textured surfaces: Psychophysical performance measurements in humans. *Journal of Physiology, 338,* 551–565.

Lamore, P. J. J., Muijser, H., & Keemink, C. J. (1986). Envelope detection of amplitude-modulated high-frequency sinusoidal signals by skin mechanoreceptors. *Journal of the Acoustical Society of America, 79,* 1082–1085.

LaMotte, R. H., Friedman, R. M., Lu, C., Khalsa, P. S., & Srinivasan, M. A. (1998). Raised object on a planar surface stroked across the fingerpad: Responses of cutaneous mechanoreceptors to shape and orientation. *Journal of Neurophysiology, 80,* 2446–2466.

LaMotte, R. H., & Whitehouse, J. M. (1986). Tactile detection of a dot on a smooth surface: Peripheral neural events. *Journal of Neurophysiology, 56,* 1109–1128.

Lederman, S. J. (1974). Tactile roughness of grooved surfaces: The touching process and the effects of macro- and microsurface structure. *Perception and Psychophysics, 16,* 385–395.

Lederman S. J. (1983) Tactual roughness perception: Spatial and temporal determinants. *Canadian Journal of Psychology, 37,* 498–511.

Lederman, S. J., Loomis, J. M., & Williams, D. A. (1982). The role of vibration in the tactual perception of roughness. *Perception and Psychophysics, 32,* 109–116.

Lindblom, U., & Lund, L. (1966). The discharge from vibration-sensitive receptors in the monkey foot. *Experimental Neurology, 15,* 401–417.

Loewenstein, W. R., & Skalak, R. (1966). Mechanical transmission in a Pacinian corpuscle: An analysis and a theory. *Journal of Physiology, 182,* 346–378.

Loomis, J. M. (1981). On the tangibility of letters and Braille. *Perception and Psychophysics, 29,* 37–46.

Loomis, J. M. (1985). Tactile recognition of raised characters: A parametric study. *Bulletin of the Psychonomic Society, 23,* 18–20.

Macefield, V. G., Hager-Ross, C., & Johansson, R. S. (1996). Control of grip force during restraint of an object held between finger and thumb: Responses of cutaneous afferents from the digits. *Experimental Brain Research, 108,* 155–171.

MacKay, D. M. (1963). Psychophysics of perceived intensity: A theoretical basis for Fechner's and Stevens' laws. *Science, 139,* 1213–1216.

Matthews, P. B. C. (1988). Proprioceptors and their contribution to somatosensory mapping: Complex messages require complex processing. *Canadian Journal of Physiology and Pharmacology, 66,* 430–438.

Matthews, P. B. C., & Simmonds, A. (1974). Sensations of finger movement elicited by pulling upon flexor tendons in man. *Journal of Physiology, 239,* 27P–28P.

McCloskey, D. I., Cross, M. J., Honner, R., & Potter, E. K. (1983). Sensory effects of pulling or vibrating exposed tendons in man. *Brain, 106,* 21–37.

Meenes, M., & Zigler, M. J. (1923). An experimental study of the perceptions of roughness and smoothness. *American Journal of Psychology, 34,* 542–549.

Meftah, E. M., Belingard, L., & Chapman, C. E. (2000). Relative effects of the spatial and temporal characteristics of scanned surfaces on human perception of tactile roughness using passive touch. *Experimental Brain Research, 132,* 351–361.

Miller, M. R., Ralston H. J., & Kasahara M. (1960). The pattern of cutaneous innervation of the human hand, foot and breast. In W. Montagna (Ed.), *Advances in biology of skin* (pp. 1–47). Oxford: Pergamon.

Moberg, E. (1972). Fingers were made before forks. *Hand, 4,* 201–206.

Moberg, E. (1983). The role of cutaneous afferents in position sense, kinaesthesia, and motor function of the hand. *Brain, 106,* 1–19.

Morley, J. W., Goodwin, A. W., & Darian-Smith, I. (1983). Tactile discrimination of gratings. *Experimental Brain Research, 49,* 291–299.

Mountcastle, V. B. (1974). *Medical Physiology.* St. Louis: Mosby.

Mountcastle, V. B. (1975). The view from within: Pathways to the study of perception. *Johns Hopkins Medical Journal, 136,* 109–131.

Mountcastle, V. B., LaMotte, R. H., & Carli, G. (1972). Detection thresholds for stimuli in humans and monkeys: Comparison with threshold events in mechanoreceptive afferent nerve fibers innervating the monkey hand. *Journal of Neurophysiology, 35,* 122–136.

Mountcastle, V. B., Poggio, G. F., & Werner, G. (1963). The relation of thalamic cell response to peripheral stimuli varied over an intensive continuum. *Journal of Neurophysiology, 26,* 807–834.

Mountcastle, V. B., Talbot, W. H., & Kornhuber, H. H. (1966). The neural transformation of mechanical stimuli delivered to the monkey's hand. In A. V. de Reuck & J. Knight (Eds.), *Touch, heat, pain and itch* (pp. 325–351). London: Churchill.

Muijser, H. (1990). The influence of spatial contrast on the frequency-dependent nature of vibration sensitivity. *Perception and Psychophysics, 48,* 431–435.

Munger, B. L., & Ide, C. (1988). The structure and function of cutaneous sensory receptors. *Archives of Histology and Cytology, 51,* 1–34.

Ochoa, J. L., & Torebjörk, H. E. (1983). Sensations evoked by intraneural microstimulation of single mechanoreceptor units innervating the human hand. *Journal of Physiology, 342,* 633–654.

Ogawa, H. (1996). The Merkel cell as a possible mechanoreceptor cell. *Progress in Neurobiology, 49,* 317–334.

Olausson, H., Wessberg, J., & Kakuda, N. (2000). Tactile directional sensibility: Peripheral neural mechanisms in man. *Brain Research, 866,* 178–187.

Palmer, C. I., & Gardner, E. P. (1990). Simulation of motion on the skin: IV. Responses of Pacinian corpuscle afferents innervating the primate hand to stripe patterns on the Optacon. *Journal of Neurophysiology, 64,* 236–247.

Paré, M., Elde, R., Mazurkiewicz, J. E., Smith, A. M., & Rice, F. L. (2001). The Meissner corpuscle revised: A multi-afferented mechanoreceptor with nociceptor immunochemical properties. *Journal of Neuroscience, 21,* 7236–7246.

Phillips, J. R., Johansson, R. S., & Johnson, K. O. (1990). Representation of Braille characters in human nerve fibers. *Experimental Brain Research, 81,* 589–592.

Phillips, J. R., Johansson, R. S., & Johnson, K. O. (1992). Responses of human mechanoreceptive afferents to embossed dot arrays scanned across fingerpad skin. *Journal of Neuroscience, 12,* 827–839.

Phillips, J. R., & Johnson, K. O. (1981a). Tactile spatial resolution: II. Neural representation of bars, edges, and gratings in monkey primary afferents. *Journal of Neurophysiology, 46,* 1192–1203.

Phillips, J. R., & Johnson, K. O. (1981b). Tactile spatial resolution: III. A continuum mechanics model of skin predicting mechanoreceptor responses to bars, edges, and gratings. *Journal of Neurophysiology, 46,* 1204–1225.

Phillips, J. R., Johnson, K. O., & Browne, H. M. (1983). A comparison of visual and two modes of tactual letter resolution. *Perception and Psychophysics, 34,* 243–249.

Phillips, J. R., & Matthews, P. B. C. (1993). Texture perception and afferent coding distorted by cooling the human ulnar nerve. *Journal of Neuroscience, 13,* 2332–2341.

Platt, J. R. (1964). Strong inference. *Science, 146,* 347–353.

Popper, K. (1959). *The logic of scientific discovery.* New York: Basic Books.

Quilliam, T. A. (1978). The structure of finger print skin. In G. Gordon (Ed.), *Active touch* (pp. 1–18). Oxford: Pergamon Press.

Raja, S. N., Meyer, R. A., Ringkamp, M., & Campbell, J. N. (1999). Peripheral neural mechanisms of nociception. In P. D. Wall & R. Melzack (Eds.), *Textbook of pain* (pp. 11–58). Edinburgh: Churchill Livingstone.

Rinker, M. A., & Craig, J. C. (1994). The effect of spatial orientation on the perception of moving tactile stimuli. *Perception and Psychophysics, 56,* 356–362.

Rymer, W. Z., & D'Almeida, A. (1980). Joint position sense: The effects of muscle contraction. *Brain, 103,* 1–22.

Sathian, K., Goodwin, A. W., John, K. T., & Darian-Smith, I. (1989). Perceived roughness of a grating: Correlation with responses of mechanoreceptive afferents innervating the monkey's fingerpad. *Journal of Neuroscience, 9,* 1273–1279.

Sathian, K., & Zangaladze, A. (1996). Tactile spatial acuity at the human fingertip and lip: Bilateral symmetry and interdigit variability. *Neurology, 46,* 1464–1466.

Sathian, K., Zangaladze, A., Green, J., Vitek, J. L., & DeLong, M. R. (1997). Tactile spatial acuity and roughness discrimination: Impairments due to aging and Parkinson's disease. *Neurology, 49,* 168–177.

Sato, M. (1961). Response of Pacinian corpuscles to sinusoidal vibration. *Journal of Physiology, 159,* 391–409.

Schmelz, M., Schmidt, R., Bickel, A., Handwerker, H. O., & Torebjörk, H. E. (1997). Specific C-receptors for itch in human skin. *Journal of Neuroscience, 17,* 8003–8008.

Srinivasan, M. A., & Dandekar, K. (1996). An investigation of the mechanics of tactile sense using two-dimensional models of the primate fingertip. *Journal of Biomechanical Engineering, 118,* 48–55.

Srinivasan, M. A., & LaMotte, R. H. (1987). Tactile discrimination of shape: Responses of slowly and rapidly adapting mechanoreceptive afferents to a step indented into the monkey fingerpad. *Journal of Neuroscience, 7,* 1682–1697.

Srinivasan, M. A., & LaMotte, R. H. (1995). Tactual discrimination of softness. *Journal of Neurophysiology, 73,* 88–101.

Srinivasan, M. A., & LaMotte, R. H. (1996). Tactual discrimination of softness: Abilities and mechanisms. In O. Franzén, R. S. Johansson, & L. Terenius (Eds.), *Somesthesis and the neurobiology of the somatosensory cortex* (pp. 123–135). Basel: Birkhäuser.

Srinivasan, M. A., Whitehouse, J. M., & LaMotte, R. H. (1990). Tactile detection of slip: Surface microgeometry and peripheral neural codes. *Journal of Neurophysiology, 63,* 1323–1332.

Stevens, J. C., & Choo, K. K. (1996). Spatial acuity of the body surface over the life span. *Somatosensory and Motor Research, 13,* 153–166.

Stevens, S. S. (1957). On the psychophysical law. *Psychological Review, 64,* 153–181.

Stevens, S. S. (1961a). To honor Fechner and repeal his law. *Science, 133,* 80–86.

Stevens, S. S. (1961b). The psychophysics of sensory function. In W. A. Rosenblith (Ed.), *Sensory Communication* (pp. 1–34). Cambridge: MIT Press.

Stevens, S. S. (1970). Neural events and the psychophysical law. *Science, 170,* 1043–1050.

Stevens, S. S. (1975). *Psychophysics: Introduction to its perceptual, neural and social aspects.* New York: Wiley.

Stevens, S. S., & Harris, J. R. (1962). The scaling of subjective roughness and smoothness. *Journal of Experimental Psychology, 64,* 489–494.

Talbot, W. H., Darian-Smith, I., Kornhuber, H. H., & Mountcastle, V. B. (1968). The sense of flutter-vibration: Comparison of the human capacity with response patterns of mechanoreceptive afferents from the monkey hand. *Journal of Neurophysiology, 31,* 301–334.

Tan, H. Z., Durlach, N. I., Beauregard, G. L., & Srinivasan, M. A. (1995). Manual discrimination of compliance using active pinch grasp: The roles of force and work cues. *Perception and Psychophysics, 57,* 495–510.

Taylor, J. L., & McCloskey, D. I. (1990). Ability to detect angular displacements of the fingers made at an imperceptibly slow speed. *Brain, 113,* 157–166.

Taylor, M. M., & Lederman, S. J. (1975). Tactile roughness of grooved surfaces: A model and the effect of friction. *Perception and Psychophysics, 17,* 23–36.

Vallbo, Å. B., Olausson, H., Wessberg, J., & Kakuda, N. (1995). Receptive field characteristics of tactile units with myelinated afferents in hairy skin of human subjects. *Journal of Physiology, 483,* 783–795.

Vallbo, Å. B., Olsson, K. A., Westberg, K. G., & Clark, F. J. (1984). Microstimulation of single tactile afferents from the human hand: Sensory attributes related to unit type and properties of receptive fields. *Brain, 107,* 727–749.

Van Boven, R. W., Hamilton, R. H., Kauffman, T., Keenan, J. P., & Pascual-Leone, A. (2000). Tactile spatial resolution in blind Braille readers. *Neurology, 54,* 2230–2236.

Van Boven, R. W., & Johnson, K. O. (1994a). The limit of tactile spatial resolution in humans: Grating orientation discrimination at the lip, tongue and finger. *Neurology, 44,* 2361–2366.

Van Boven, R. W., & Johnson, K. O. (1994b). A psychophysical study of the mechanisms of sensory recovery following nerve injury in humans. *Brain, 117,* 149–167.

Vega-Bermudez, F., & Johnson, K. O. (1999a). SA1 and RA receptive fields, response variability, and population responses mapped with a probe array. *Journal of Neurophysiology, 81,* 2701–2710.

Vega-Bermudez, F., & Johnson, K. O. (1999b). Surround suppression in the responses of primate SA1 and RA mechanoreceptive afferents mapped with a probe array. *Journal of Neurophysiology, 81,* 2711–2719.

Vega-Bermudez, F., & Johnson, K. O. (2001). Differences in spatial acuity between digits. *Neurology, 56,* 1389–1391.

Vega-Bermudez, F., Johnson, K. O., & Hsiao, S. S. (1991). Human tactile pattern recognition: Active versus passive touch, velocity effects, and patterns of confusion. *Journal of Neurophysiology, 65,* 531–546.

Verrillo, R. T. (1963). Effect of contactor area on the vibrotactile threshold. *Journal of the Acoustical Society of America, 35,* 1962–1966.

Weisenberger, J. M. (1986). Sensitivity to amplitude-modulated vibrotactile signals. *Journal of the Acoustical Society of America, 80,* 1707–1715.

Wheat, H. E., & Goodwin, A. W. (2000). Tactile discrimination of gaps by slowly adapting afferents: Effects of population parameters and anisotropy in the fingerpad. *Journal of Neurophysiology, 84,* 1430–1444.

Wohlert, A. B. (1996). Tactile perception of spatial stimuli on the lip surface by young and older adults. *Journal of Speech and Hearing Research, 39,* 1191–1198.

Yoshioka, T., Gibb, B., Dorsch, A. K., Hsiao, S. S., & Johnson, K. O. (2001). Neural coding mechanisms underlying perceived roughness of finely textured surfaces. *Journal of Neuroscience, 21,* 6905–6916.

CHAPTER 14

Touch and Haptics

MARK HOLLINS

This chapter is the second of three dealing with somesthesis. The previous chapter described the anatomy and physiology of the cutaneous senses. The present chapter is devoted to the perceptual phenomena and psychophysical abilities that these physiological mechanisms make possible (although the way in which they do so is in many cases unclear). The last of the three chapters deals with temperature and pain, which are almost separate modalities from *touch* in the narrow sense (i.e., the acquisition and processing of nonnoxious mechanical information).

The present chapter is for the most part organized around the two domains—space and time—within which sensory information is arrayed. Although every tactile stimulus has both spatial and temporal aspects, an attempt has been made to treat them separately in the first half of the chapter. Some of the ways in which spatial and temporal factors interact are then discussed. The chapter concludes with a consideration of *haptic touch,* in which exploratory movement (e.g., of the hand) is used strategically to influence the ways in which the skin will be stimulated by environmental objects.

Preparation of this chapter was supported by NIH Program Project grant DE07509.

SPATIAL FACTORS IN TOUCH

A Puzzling Result

We start our discussion of spatial factors in touch with some puzzling results of an experiment by the perceptual theorist James J. Gibson (1962). He had subjects lay their hand on a table, and into their upturned palm he firmly pressed a cookie cutter, lowering it with a system of levers so that unsteadiness on the part of the experimenter would not influence the results. There were six of these stimulus objects, about 2.5 cm across, with simple shapes such as a triangle, a teardrop, and a star. Subjects had been shown all six stimuli in advance and were asked merely to identify the one presented on each of a series of trials. Given the remarkable ability people have to detect, discriminate, and identify objects by touch in everyday life, it might be expected that Gibson's subjects would have had no trouble identifying these large and familiar patterns. In fact, however, they responded correctly on only 29% of trials, barely better than a chance level (17%). In the first part of this chapter we consider some possible reasons that this seemingly easy task is actually so difficult.

Point Localization

One possibility is that our perception of exactly where on the skin we are touched is not very accurate. If subjects' perception of where the different parts of the cookie cutter were located were in error—particularly if the direction and size of these errors differed haphazardly from one region of the palm to another—then it would clearly be impossible to appreciate the overall shape of the stimulus. It is reasonable to ask, then, just how accurate localization ability is.

This question fascinated one of the earliest and most creative of sensory researchers, Ernst Heinrich Weber (1795–1878), and he invented a simple method of addressing it (Weber, 1852/1965). With powdered carbon he blackened the slightly rounded tip of a knitting needle and touched it to the skin of a blindfolded subject. After the stimulus was removed, the subject tried to touch the same spot with a short probe. The subject was allowed to move the probe about on the skin until he or she was confident that it was superimposed on the spot originally touched. However, subjects typically were imperfect in their responses, and Weber was able to determine the magnitude of their errors by measuring the distance from the probe to the black mark left behind by the original stimulus.

One of Weber's major findings was that accuracy depends very much on the part of the body that is stimulated. On the lips and fingertips, for example, errors were typically on the order of a millimeter, whereas on the thigh they ranged up to 16 mm. On the palm—where Gibson's cookie cutters were presented—Weber found localization errors on the order of 4 mm.

Using a variety of methods, researchers in the century and a half since Weber's report have carried out further studies of point localization ability. For example, the subject may be asked to touch the probe to the skin without moving it about (Cole, 1929) or to indicate the spot touched by marking it on a drawing (Culver, 1970). In a recently introduced method used to measure point localization on the forearm, subjects looked at the arm after the stimulus had been removed and aimed a narrow beam of light at the spot that they believed had been stimulated; red goggles allowed subjects to see the arm and the beam of light but not the array of red-ink dots on the skin that enabled the experimenter to specify the locations of the stimulus and the response (Green & Flammer, 1989). Despite the fact that these methods measure somewhat different things (e.g., some explicitly involve visual perception while others do not), they give results that are roughly consistent with one another, as well as with Weber's original findings. His discovery that the accuracy of point localization increases as one examines more and more distal sites on a limb has proven especially robust (Weinstein, 1968); Weber may in fact have underestimated the steepness of this change, for Loomis (1979) has reported that point localization on the finger pad is better than was previously supposed—on the order of .2 mm. Loomis's use of a thin, precisely positioned stimulus and a forced-choice procedure enabled him to show how accurate localization can be under optimal conditions.

But how do these findings bear on our original question of whether errors of localization can explain the relative inaccuracy with which patterns impressed on the skin are perceived? If the different portions of one of Gibson's cookie cutters were misperceived by several millimeters, would this distort the resulting percept enough to make subjects confuse, for example, a star with a triangle? Perhaps, if the perceived locations of different parts of a pattern were displaced in different directions. The fact is, however, that errors of localization are not entirely haphazard. In Culver's (1970) study, for example, stimuli delivered to various locations on the palm were consistently perceived as closer to the thumb than they actually were. If a patterned stimulus behaved as a series of such points, the effect of consistent errors would be to shift the perceived pattern across the skin, rather than to distort it. While the inaccuracy of point localization may therefore make some contribution to the difficulty of tactile pattern perception, it does not appear to be a major factor. We must look elsewhere for the near-chance performance of Gibson's (1962) subjects.

Two-Point Threshold

The fact that pattern perception cannot be understood in terms of point localization alone implies that the elements of the pattern are not processed in isolation. We must consider the rules that govern the perception of stimuli made up of more than one point to determine ways in which they interact. For example, it might be the case that when two adjacent points are stimulated, they merge perceptually into a single perceived point, so that they cannot be told apart; this would cause any information about the spatial arrangement of the points to be lost. The question here is one of *tactile acuity:* How close together can two tactile stimuli be before they blend together to produce a sensation with no internal structure?

There are several ways to measure acuity, one of which was devised by Weber (1834/1996) himself. It is called the two-point threshold. In this method, two points, such as the slightly blunted points of a compass, are touched simultaneously to neighboring spots on the skin, and the subject is asked whether the resulting sensation is of one point or two. When the stimuli are far apart, they are perceived as clearly separate, but when close together they are perceived as one. The two-point threshold is the intermediate distance at which the two points can just be discerned. Although two-point threshold is typically two to four times greater than the error of localization at the same site, these two measures of spatial precision vary in much the same way

from one part of the body to another: The best performance is achieved on the lips and fingertips, the worst on the torso and proximal regions of the limbs (Weinstein, 1968).

In fact, spatial acuity in a given cutaneous region appears to be roughly indicative of the degree to which that region participates in exploring the environment. To put this somewhat vague concept on a more rigorous and quantitative footing, Vierordt (1870), a contemporary of Weber's, carried out a detailed analysis of the way tactile acuity changes along the arm, from shoulder to fingertip. He discovered that acuity (expressed as the reciprocal of two-point threshold) shows a steady increase from shoulder to elbow; beyond the elbow it continues to rise, but at a faster rate than before; and further abrupt increases in the rate of change occur at succeeding joints. Why does acuity rise faster and faster on succeeding segments of the limb? Vierordt's answer was that acuity at each spot on the arm reflects its mobility—its potential to be moved into a variety of positions. Thus, a spot on the upper arm can be moved about on the surface of an imaginary sphere whose center is at the shoulder and whose radius is the distance of that spot from the shoulder. Points on the forearm can occupy a much greater range of positions, because for each possible position of the upper arm, the flexion of the elbow can vary. The implication of Vierordt's *law of mobility* is that acuity is most important for those parts of the body that move about exploring the environment.

Despite the importance of this and other discoveries (e.g., Stevens, 1982, 1989, 1992) made using the two-point threshold, this method of measuring acuity has some shortcomings. The most important of these is that when the two points are separated by a distance of less than the two-point threshold, so that they are not perceived as distinct, they nevertheless feel subtly different from a single point (e.g. dumbbell-shaped, or unitary but elongated). A variety of these intermediate sensations began to be noticed soon after Weber invented the method, and the way in which they successively supplant one another was documented by Gates (1915). At least on the fingertip and other sensitive regions, signal-detection procedures cannot be used to measure two-point threshold because the subject can always tell the difference between one point and two, even when the two points are contiguous; at small separations such judgments probably depend more on intensity cues, such as how much force is delivered or how much skin is stimulated, than on the spatial distribution of the stimulus (Johnson & Phillips, 1981; Johnson, Van Boven, & Hsiao, 1994).

Spatial Summation

Relevant to the possibility that intensity cues influence performance on seemingly spatial tasks is work by Greenspan and colleagues on a phenomenon called *spatial summation*. This term refers to a pooling or combining of the sensory effects of stimulus elements delivered at different spots. Greenspan and McGillis (1991) demonstrated this phenomenon by delivering pressure through a contactor that varied in size. More directly comparable to the tasks we have been considering, however, is the report of Greenspan, Thomadaki, and McGillis (1997), who stimulated the skin on the back of a finger, midway between base and tip, with a pair of small contactors, simultaneously applied 5 mm apart. This separation is somewhat below the two-point threshold for this body site, as shown by the fact that subjects reported the perceptual experience of only a single site's being stimulated (although we may wonder whether the stimulus was perceived as elongated!). This dual stimulus was applied repeatedly, with gradually increasing force, until the subject reported a sensation of pressure. The result of inter-

est was that the total force required (about 14 g; i.e., 7 g per contactor) was only slightly greater than that needed in control measurements using only a single contactor (12 g). Thus, the forces delivered through two contactors combined almost as effectively as they would have if applied through a single contactor. Because of spatial summation, which varies in a somewhat unpredictable way with experimental conditions, it is difficult to eliminate categorically intensity cues when determining two-point threshold. This makes the latter a problematic index of tactile acuity.

Vierck and Jones (1969) studied a different measure of spatial performance: the ability to discriminate the size of disks (or the length of lines: Jones & Vierck, 1973) pressed against the skin. Size difference thresholds were found to be almost an order of magnitude lower than two-point thresholds on the same body site, a difference that the investigators attributed to the greater biological significance of size judgments as compared to judgments of separation. Size discrimination is clearly a remarkable spatial ability, but it may depend on subjects' perceiving the amount, rather than the geometrical distribution, of stimulated skin. It is therefore not an unambiguous measure of spatial acuity, which would require a stimulus set in which factors such as the amount of skin stimulated were held constant.

Resolution Acuity

For this purpose Johnson and Phillips (1981) used gratings (i.e., patterns consisting of a series of ridges separated by grooves). Within each of their gratings the grooves and ridges were of equal width, but some gratings were finer than others. A motor pressed the stimuli into the skin of the finger pad for 2.5 s. The subject's task was to distinguish on each trial the orientation of the grating, that is, whether it was presented with the ridges parallel or perpendicular to the axis of the finger. Performance was at a chance level when narrow (0.5 mm) grooves were used but improved steadily as groove width increased, reaching a threshold level (75% correct) at a groove width of about 0.9 mm—roughly a third of the two-point threshold at the same site (Weinstein, 1968). This resolution limit is similar to the spacing of SA I mechanoreceptors in the finger pad, a correspondence suggesting that receptor spacing is the limiting factor in true spatial acuity (Johnson & Phillips, 1981; Chap. 13, this volume). Johnson and Phillips found that a receptor-spacing analysis also did a reasonable job of accounting for levels of performance on other spatial tasks, such as letter recognition (see Figure 14.1).

What are the implications of tactile acuity for Gibson's (1962) experiment in shape perception? Resolution acuity is only about one-sixth as keen on the palm as it is on the fingertip (Craig & Lyle, 2001), a level so poor

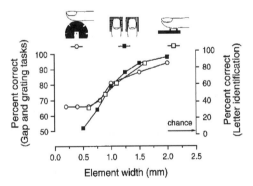

Figure 14.1   The ability to detect gaps, determine the orientation of gratings, and identify letters is plotted as a function of the size of the stimuli.
NOTE: The three tasks are illustrated at the top. The abscissa is scaled in terms of the size of the fundamental elements of each stimulus: gap width, bar or groove width for the gratings, and (by hypothesis) one-fifth of letter height.
SOURCE: From Johnson, Van Boven, & Hsiao (1994). Reprinted by permission of the International Association for the Study of Pain.

as to interfere substantially with discernment of Gibson's patterns. Thus, acuity probably played a major role in accounting for the near-chance level of performance that his subjects exhibited. As we will see, however, other factors may also have been involved.

A mathematically more elaborate approach to the question of whether resolution is the limiting factor in pattern perception has been undertaken by Loomis (1981, 1982, 1990). Borrowing a technique that has been widely employed in the study of visual perception (De Valois & De Valois, 1990), Loomis has studied the spatial frequency composition of patterns, and the ability of the somatosensory system to detect the presence of these spatial frequencies. The spatial frequency of a repeating pattern is the number of cycles (cycle = ridge + groove) that fit within a unit length. Thus, a grating in which ridges .5 mm wide are separated by grooves of the same width has a spatial frequency of 1 cycle/mm. Although tactile gratings are usually rectangular in profile (e.g., Johnson & Phillips, 1981; Lederman & Taylor, 1972), spatial frequency analysis becomes much more powerful when cast in terms of sinusoidal, rather than rectangular, variations, because any pattern can be mathematically analyzed into a set of sinusoidal components. An embossed letter of the alphabet, for example, consists of a large number of such components, differing from one another in orientation, spatial frequency, amplitude, and phase. Generally speaking, the low spatial-frequency components contribute to the overall shape of a stimulus, whereas the high spatial-frequency components make up its details. Loomis has proposed that inaccuracies of pattern perception can be attributed mainly to an inability to perceive spatial frequencies above a cutoff value, which can be determined on the basis of resolution measurements.

If printed letters equal in size to the embossed ones are viewed at arm's length, or even from as far away as 5 m, they are much more easily recognized than are their tangible counterparts (Loomis, 1990). Both Johnson and Phillips (1981) and Loomis (1990) attribute this difference between modalities primarily to the fact that the retinal mosaic of visual receptors is more fine-grained, relative to the letters imaged on it, than is the fingertip's mosaic of tactile receptors relative to the tangible letters. To test this explanation, Loomis (1981, 1982, 1990) blurred visual stimuli to eliminate the highest spatial frequencies, presumably making the representations of letters at the receptoral level equally "sharp" in the two modalities. Consistent with the prediction, this blurring impaired letter recognition performance to about the same level as that obtained in the tactile task, and the confusion matrices for vision and touch (showing the distribution of specific errors made by the subjects, as in mistaking a C for a G) showed many similarities (Loomis, 1982). These results support the view that the somatosensory system's limited spatial resolution is one of the main reasons we have difficulty identifying detailed patterns presented to the sense of touch.

However, Loomis's work also turned up an additional difference between vision and touch. In each sense performance gradually improved as larger and larger letters were presented, and in vision this increase occurred at just the rate predicted by Loomis's model. For touch, however, the improvement was more gradual: For small letters, where resolution is undoubtedly a major factor, the model did a good job of predicting the subjects' relatively poor performance, but for larger letters, where resolution should be less important, actual performance fell far short of that predicted by the model. Loomis (1990, p. 117) concluded that "there seems to be some factor limiting tactile performance in addition to the spatial low-pass filtering of the cutaneous transfer from skin to cortex."

One such factor may be that when multiple points on the skin that are separated by much more than the two-point threshold are stimulated, their perceived locations can differ from what they would be if presented individually. This was demonstrated by Green (1982), who touched subjects at two places on the forearm simultaneously. The stimuli, plastic disks 4 mm in diameter, were pressed against the skin for 2 s. After the stimuli were removed, the subject was permitted to view the forearm and was asked to make two chalk marks on it at the sites where he or she thought the stimuli had been applied. Surprisingly, the subject's errors were much greater than is normally the case in a point localization task, and they showed a consistent pattern: The stimuli were perceived as closer to each other than they actually had been. The effect was a large one: When the stimuli were actually 10 cm apart, subjects generally made chalk marks separated by only 6 cm. Green's findings suggest that the subjective representations of multiple stimuli are somehow drawn together, as if attracted to one another. We will see later that similar phenomena occur in a variety of stimulus situations; the general term *funneling* (von Békésy, 1958) is often applied to this family of perceptual distortions.

Significantly for our discussion, Green (1982) also found that the degree of underestimation of the distance between points varied with their actual separation, and with the orientation of their alignment: Judgment was more accurate for points separated transversely on the forearm than for those separated longitudinally. These findings imply that a two-dimensional shape—if thought of as a large number of points arranged in a pattern—could be distorted in shape as well as in size by the phenomenon he described. Such distortions may have made a contribution to the difficulty that Gibson's (1962) subjects had in identifying the patterns pressed into the skin of their palms.

One feature of almost all the studies considered so far is that the stimuli remained motionless after being brought into firm contact with the skin. This method of stimulus presentation produces a reasonably clear initial sensation, but almost immediately the sensory experience begins to fade and blur, a process called *adaptation*. It is easy to see that adaptation may have played a role in impairing the performance of Gibson's (1962) subjects because his apparatus abruptly lowered the cookie cutter onto the palm and then held it motionless. If subjects were unable to perceive it clearly at the outset, they would be even less likely to do so later. In other words, subjects had only one brief chance to detect the pattern. Gibson himself recognized the importance of this factor, and he sought to reduce adaptation by having the experimenter apply the cookie cutter by hand, causing some moment-to-moment variation in the pressure applied by different parts of the stimulus pattern. The result was a clear improvement in performance, from 29% to 49%. Although subjects still had great difficulty in identifying the patterns, the difference between conditions shows how greatly touch is enhanced by stimulus changes that occur over time. We pursue this theme in the next section of the chapter by turning to a detailed examination of temporal factors in touch.

TEMPORAL FACTORS IN TOUCH

The process of adaptation is a complex one that depends on several factors. One is that the skin accommodates itself to forces that are imposed on it. This mechanical adjustment can be demonstrated by firmly pressing a stimulus (such as the flat end of a rod) against the skin for several seconds and then quickly removing it. The depression left behind in the skin indicates that localized shifting and deformation of cutaneous and subcutaneous tissue has occurred. It was once believed (Nafe & Wagoner, 1941) that feelings of pressure continue only as long as these movements do, and that adaptation represents stimulus failure; however, this finding was obtained with a weight that continued to sink into the skin for up to 30 s. Later research using controlled, quickly achieved displacements showed that the sensation can outlast the movement by seconds (Horch, Clark, & Burgess, 1975). Adaptation thus depends on a combination of mechanical and neural factors.

Continuous movement of a stimulus slows (although it does not entirely prevent) its subjective fading. The most widely used method of producing continuous movement in the laboratory is to vibrate the stimulus probe along a line perpendicular to the skin surface. The amplitude and frequency of vibration can be varied independently of one another as well as of the overall duration of stimulation; this independence of stimulus dimensions has made vibration a powerful tool for analyzing tactile mechanisms. An additional advantage of vibration as a stimulus is that the technology for producing and measuring it, and the mathematics needed to describe it, are well developed (Griffin, 1990).

Is Vibrotaction a Submodality?

One of the earliest questions to be asked about vibration was whether *vibrotaction* is a separate submodality. Early evidence favoring this possibility was put forward by Treitel (1897), a physician who tested responsiveness to vibration by placing the base of a tuning fork in contact with the skin. His testing of patients with neurological problems revealed that in some cases responsiveness to vibration was impaired, while other aspects of touch, such as localization of a cotton swab touched to the skin, remained normal. Other cases showed the reverse pattern. Although later clinical work has shown that selective impairment or sparing of vibrotaction depends on many factors, Treitel's hypothesis of selective damage to particular afferent channels remains a plausible explanation in some cases (Boivie, 1994).

Not content with clinical evidence alone, Treitel (1897) added to the case for a vibrotactile submodality by making measurements on neurologically normal individuals. He found that both vibrotaction and spatial aspects of touch varied with the location on the body at which the tests were performed. Importantly, however, the two were not strongly correlated. For example, he found that two-point threshold is (as we have seen) several times lower on the fingertips than on the palm, whereas vibratory sensibility is nearly equal at these two sites. Even more remarkable, the vibration of a 220-Hz tuning fork is not felt at all on the tongue, although by other measures the sense of touch here is as keen as on the fingertip. The implication of these dissociations is that vibrotaction is independent of steady touch—that it is a separate submodality.

The idea of a separate "vibratory sense" later gained wider acceptance through the work of David Katz (1925/1989). Katz reiterated earlier arguments and added several new ones. Some of these, such as the claim that vibratory sensations feel more "alive" than those produced by pressure, are descriptive only and have little or no evidentiary value. However, Katz made more provocative observations as well. For example, he pointed out that vibrotaction has a remarkable ability to convey information about events that occur at some distance from the skin, such as the movement of the wheels of one's car along the street—unlike pressure sensitivity, which confines itself mainly to the properties of objects that we are actually touching.

However, Katz's claim (1930, p. 90) that vibrotaction is "a completely independent sense which has a correspondingly specific nervous apparatus" went well beyond his data and was not without its critics. Geldard (1940), among others, maintained that vibrotaction is simply the response of the pressure sense to rapid, repeated changes in pressure. The argument would probably have continued indefinitely had our understanding of the matter not been dramatically advanced by physiological discoveries (see Chap. 13, this volume), especially the finding that electrical stimulation of some cutaneous afferents gives rise to a sensation of repetitive tapping (RAs) or vibration (PCs), while stimulation of other afferents (SAs) produces only a sensation of pressure (Ochoa & Torebjörk, 1983; Vallbo, Olsson, Westberg, & Clark, 1984). Although all mechanoreceptive afferents will apparently respond to vibration of sufficient intensity, only a subset give rise, by their activity, to the feeling of vibration. Though hardly "a completely independent sense," then, vibrotaction does appear to reflect the operation of a somewhat specialized component of the sense of touch.

Vibrotactile Channels

Yet even vibrotaction is not a unitary submodality, for its behavior depends on the frequency of the vibratory stimulus. Verrillo (1963, 1965) measured the detection threshold of vibration (i.e., the smallest amplitude at which the vibration could be felt). Stimuli were delivered through a vibrating disk—the tip of a cylindrical contactor—pressed against the skin. A stationary ring, concentric with the contactor and separated from it by 1 mm all around, was pressed against the skin to reduce the spread of vibrations across the surface. Verrillo (1963) discovered that at high frequencies, threshold decreased as the stimulated area (the size of the contactor) increased: In other words, spatial summation occurred. At low frequencies, however, there was no spatial

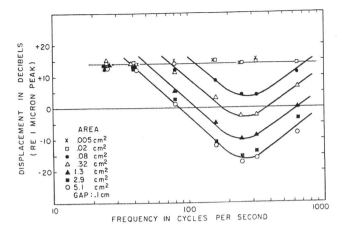

Figure 14.2   Threshold amplitude is plotted as a function of the frequency of vibration.
NOTE: The parameter is the area of the contactor through which stimulation is delivered. Larger contactors permit spatial summation to occur, enabling the U-shaped Pacinian channel to become increasingly prominent.
SOURCE: From Verrillo (1963). Used with permission of the Acoustical Society of America.

summation. Thus, the rules for detecting vibration are different at high and low frequencies (see Figure 14.2). Later work showed that *temporal summation*—that is, neural integration over time (Gescheider, Berryhill, Verrillo, & Bolanowski, 1999)—likewise occurs only at high frequencies (Gescheider, 1976; Verrillo, 1965).

Except when very small contactors and short bursts of vibration are used, threshold amplitude changes systematically as a function of frequency. Threshold is nearly the same at all frequencies from 10 Hz to about 60 Hz, but above 60 Hz it falls abruptly as frequency increases, reaching a minimum in the neighborhood of 250 Hz. At still higher frequencies, threshold rises again, so that the function above 60 Hz is U-shaped (see Figure 14.2).

Based primarily on these three lines of evidence—spatial summation, temporal summation, and frequency dependence—Verrillo (1968) proposed that different populations of cutaneous mechanoreceptors, along with their central connections, determine vibrotac-

tile thresholds at low and high frequencies, respectively. At a given frequency, one receptor population or the other is more sensitive, and it is that one that mediates threshold detection at that frequency. By comparing his psychophysical measurements with physiological data obtained by other researchers, notably Sato (1961), Verrillo (1966) realized that the dominant vibratory receptors at high frequencies are Pacinian corpuscles. He could not identify with certainty the low-frequency receptors, and so he labeled them the "non-Pacinian" mechanism. Subsequent work (described later) by Verrillo and others has confirmed and extended these ideas.

Mountcastle and his colleagues shed further light on the receptoral basis of vibrotaction with studies combining human psychophysical results with recordings from primary afferents in monkeys (Mountcastle, Talbot, Darian-Smith, & Kornhuber, 1967; Talbot, Darian-Smith, Kornhuber, & Mountcastle, 1968). They confirmed the identification of the high-frequency mechanism with Pacinian corpuscles and also provided persuasive evidence that the low-frequency receptors are Meissner corpuscles. These researchers also realized the significance of a qualitative difference between the sensations elicited by low- and high-frequency vibrations. At low frequencies one has the impression of very rapid tapping: Although the taps occur too rapidly to be counted, the subject feels that they *could* be counted, if only they could be slowed down. At high frequencies of vibration, in contrast, one is no longer aware of individual movements of the probe. Mountcastle and his colleagues called the low-frequency sensation *flutter* and the high-frequency sensation *vibration*. Microneurography has confirmed their belief that flutter involves activity of the Meissner channel, whereas vibration (in their sense of the term) reflects Pacinian activity. Although their terminological distinction is a valid one, we will for the sake of simplicity avoid the term *flutter* and use *vibration* in its broadest sense (i.e., to refer to repetitive mechanical stimuli of any frequency and to the sensations of intermittency to which they give rise).

Vibrotactile Adaptation

As noted earlier, we adapt to a continuing vibratory stimulus, although the process is much slower than the perceptual fading of a steady pressure stimulus. Hahn (1966) measured the effect of an adapting stimulus by presenting it continuously for an extended period of time, then turning it off and quickly measuring detection threshold by using a weaker vibration of the same frequency. The time course of adaptation was determined by using adapting stimuli of different durations, ranging from 10 s to 25 min, and measuring threshold after each was turned off. Exposure to the adapting stimulus caused threshold to rise, rapidly at first, and then more slowly; the process required at least 15 min to run to completion. Following offset of the adapting stimu-

lus, threshold returned gradually to its original level. Other measurements showed that a brief (1 s) suprathreshold stimulus of fixed amplitude grew subjectively weaker as adaptation proceeded, but rebounded during the recovery period.

Hahn next found (1968) that adaptation was frequency-selective: A low-frequency (10 Hz) adapting stimulus raised the threshold for a test stimulus at the same frequency but had little effect on high-frequency (200 Hz) threshold; similarly, 200-Hz adaptation desensitized the finger only to high-frequency stimuli. These results support the idea that two or more receptor populations are involved in vibrotaction. The frequency selectivity of vibrotactile adaptation was explored further by Verrillo and Gescheider (1977) and Gescheider, Frisina, and Verrillo (1979). By determining the relative ability of adapting stimuli of a given frequency to raise threshold at various test frequencies, they were able to show that threshold is raised in proportion to the adapting stimulus's ability to stimulate (and thereby to desensitize) the channel that is determining threshold. The adapting stimulus's ability to activate other channels is irrelevant. In other words, threshold is set within each channel individually, depending on its recent history of activation. This *channel independence* is consistent with physiological work showing that signals from different classes of mechanoreceptive afferents are kept largely segregated until after they reach the cerebral cortex (Mountcastle, Talbot, Sakata, & Hyvärinen, 1969), by which point adaptation has already adjusted their "gain" (O'Mara, Rowe, & Tarvin, 1988).

Vibrotactile Masking

A psychophysical paradigm that, like adaptation, makes test stimuli harder to detect, is *masking*. Masking is typically produced by a brief, intense stimulus that is presented just before, during, or after a test stimulus and obscures it; the subject feels the masking stimulus but is not sure whether a faint test stimulus occurred as well. Masking is thus different from adaptation, in which a temporally extended stimulus gradually desensitizes the system, making it harder to feel a test stimulus even after the adapting stimulus has been turned off. Despite the differences in procedure, and presumably in mechanism, masking and adaptation paradigms can be used to explore many of the same issues. For example, like adaptation, masking obeys rules of channel independence (Gescheider, Verrillo, & Van Doren, 1982; Hamer, Verrillo, & Zwislocki, 1983).

In fact, masking has been used to demonstrate that more than two channels— apparently four in all—can participate in the detection of vibratory stimuli (Bolanowski, Geschieder, Verrillo, & Checkosky, 1988; Gescheider, Sklar, Van Doren, & Verrillo, 1985). These researchers label the easily identifiable Pacinian system the *P channel* and call other channels *NP* (for non-Pacinian). By close comparison of psychophysical data with electrophysiological measurements made by themselves and others, Bolanowski et al. (1988) reached the following conclusions: NP I is the low-frequency channel studied originally by Verrillo and identified by Mountcastle et al. (1967) with Meissner afferents; NP II probably reflects the activity of SA II afferents, although the case for this is not absolutely compelling; and NP III is associated with SA I afferents.

Although all four of these channels are able to detect vibratory stimuli, the last two probably do not make important contributions to the "vibration sense" as this term is traditionally understood. First, these two channels require extreme conditions of vibratory stimulation: either very low frequency (NP III) or very high amplitude (NP II). This means that they do not participate in the response to

many vibrations in everyday life. Second, intraneural microstimulation indicates that activity in SA I afferents is perceived as steady (or only gradually changing) pressure (Ochoa & Torebjörk, 1983), and there is circumstantial evidence that SA II afferents, which are sensitive to skin stretch, contribute primarily to sensations of bodily movement. The vibration sense therefore appears to be mediated almost entirely by the RA and Pacinian systems. Because there is no doubt that these afferent classes are the peripheral components of the NP I and P channels, respectively, this chapter will for simplicity use the former terms in referring both to afferents and to psychophysical channels.

Regardless of the terminology employed, the dissection of channels permitted by masking demonstrates the usefulness of this experimental paradigm. However, masking is interesting in itself, apart from its ability to separate channels. For example, a 700-msec masking stimulus's ability to raise the threshold of a very brief test stimulus is greatest when the test is presented just as the masker begins or ends (Gescheider, Bolanowski, & Verrillo, 1989). This result suggests that both the onset and offset of a stimulus are treated as salient events by the sense of touch.

Intensity Discrimination

When test and masker are presented to the same spot on the skin at the same time, the test stimulus can be considered an increment superimposed on a pedestal (the masker), and the subject's task is one of intensity discrimination. Pedestals of different durations can be used, however, and performance depends on the length of the pedestal: Difference thresholds are lower with a long pedestal than with a short one (Gescheider, Bolanowski, Verrillo, Arpajian, & Ryan, 1990). There are probably several reasons for this improvement. One is that the parts of the pedestal that mask most effectively (i.e., its beginning and end) are separated in time from the test stimulus when a long pedestal is used. Another factor may be that additional processes are engaged by long exposure to a pedestal. The situation in which pedestal and increment are both short involves masking in relatively pure form; but when the pedestal begins seconds before the increment, the subject may begin adapting to it, reducing its effectiveness as a masker.

Goble and Hollins (1993) directly tested the effect of adaptation on intensity discrimination by using an adapting stimulus that ended a full second before the test stimuli were presented—too long for the former to mask the latter. By manipulating the intensity of the adapting stimulus, they could vary the subject's state of adaptation independently of other factors. Intensity difference threshold was measured by forced-choice tracking in which subjects judged which of two brief test stimuli was more intense. They found that when the adapting stimulus was equal in amplitude to the weaker of these two stimuli, the difference threshold was lower than when no adapting stimulus was presented. Apparently, adaptation reduces the perceived intensity of test stimuli equal to it in amplitude but has little or no effect on increments above this level. Perceptually diminishing the pedestal makes the increment more readily detectable. This is a highly desirable arrangement from a functional point of view, because continuous perception of an ongoing vibration is of less value to the organism than is detection of a sudden change in stimulation; it is thus not surprising that adaptation enhances discrimination in other sensory systems as well (e.g., Greenlee & Heitger, 1988; McBurney, Kasschau, & Bogart, 1967).

Whatever the factors that determine vibrotactile increment threshold in a particular situation, one of the most important—and expected—results is that the higher the stan-

dard stimulus (i.e., the pedestal), the greater must the increment be if it is to be detected. If the necessary increment (ΔI) increased in direct proportion to the standard (I), this result would constitute an example of Weber's law (see Chap. 3, Vol. 4 of this series). In fact, ΔI is usually found to be not quite proportional to I: The fraction $\Delta I/I$ decreases slightly, but consistently, as the intensity of the standard increases. This gradual increase in the relative keenness of vibrotactile intensity discrimination at higher levels of stimulation is sometimes called the *near miss to Weber's law* (Gescheider et al., 1990), after a similar and perhaps related phenomenon that occurs in audition (McGill & Goldberg, 1968). Although it varies somewhat as a function of standard amplitude and other stimulus parameters, the Weber fraction for vibration intensity is generally found to lie between 0.1 and 0.3 (Craig, 1974; Gescheider et al., 1990; Goble & Hollins, 1993; LaMotte & Mountcastle, 1975).

Difference thresholds tell us how discriminable a set of stimuli are, but do not provide us with information about their subjective intensities, such as whether one vibration feels 10% or 20% stronger than another. If we wish to learn about the scaling of perceived intensity (i.e., how it grows as a function of stimulus amplitude), we must obtain measurements that directly address this question. One way of doing this is with magnitude estimation, a technique (described more fully in Chap. 3, Vol. 4 of this series) in which the subject assigns numbers to stimuli indicating their perceived intensity. For vibration, this produces a two-branched function (see Figure 14.3) in which perceived intensity grows rapidly at low stimulus amplitudes, and then, often after a distinct break, grows more slowly at high amplitudes (Gescheider, 1976; Verrillo, 1982; Verrillo, Fraioli, & Smith, 1969). Similar functions are obtained all across the frequency spectrum, ruling out the

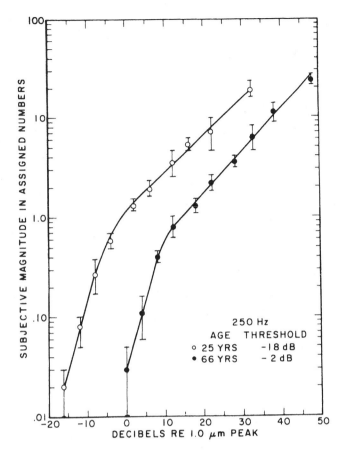

Figure 14.3 The perceived intensity of 250-Hz vibration is plotted as a function of stimulus amplitude, for both younger (open symbols) and older (filled symbols) participants.

NOTE: In each case the function has two branches, the significance of which is unknown. The horizontal separation between the data for the two groups of subjects makes the additional point that sensitivity to high-frequency vibration declines with age.

SOURCE: From Verrillo (1982). Reprinted by permission of Psychonomic Society, Inc.

possibility that one of the branches is due to the RA channel and the other to the Pacinian channel. The significance of the two branches remains unknown. Perhaps it represents the dependence of perceived intensity on two factors—such as the number of responding afferents and the rate at which they are firing—that change in their relative importance as amplitude increases.

To determine how signals from the RA and Pacinian channels are integrated into an overall impression, Hollins and Roy (1996) had subjects estimate the perceived intensity of a large number of vibratory stimuli of different frequencies and amplitudes. The stimuli were 1 s in duration and were delivered to the index finger pad. Using the results from the lowest and highest frequencies, Hollins and Roy modeled the loudness functions of the RA and Pacinian channels, respectively. Then they compared the results obtained at intermediate frequencies with the predictions of different combination rules. Although perceived intensity was generally greater when vibrations activated both channels than when they activated only one, estimates fell below predictions based on simple addition of signals from the two channels. These results suggest a moderate level of antagonism or mutual inhibition between the channels, as distinct from the channel independence that is typically obtained in the context of threshold measurements (as described earlier). This interaction is fortunate from the point of view of perceptual constancy because it enables stimuli of different frequencies but the same sensation level (i.e., the same number of decibels above detection threshold) to be more nearly equal in subjective intensity than they otherwise would be.

Frequency Discrimination

Vibrations can be discriminated on the basis of their frequency as well as on the basis of amplitude. When stimuli of different frequencies are to be compared, however, to what relative values should the experimenter set their amplitudes? One possibility would be to make the stimuli equal in amplitude. If this approach were adopted, however, subjects could base their judgments partly on differences in perceived intensity among the stimuli. Most researchers in this area strive to eliminate such cues by equating the subjective intensities of the stimuli through matching procedures: The goal is to force subjects to rely on some subjective cue other than intensity.

This additional cue is often referred to as vibratory pitch—a metaphor for the auditory dimension of the same name. At least since the days of Katz, sensory researchers have noted a deep similarity between the sensory experience produced by a tactile vibration and that produced by a sound. Naive subjects will sometimes report that they actually hear a tactile vibration, even when steps (earphones and loud masking nose) have been taken to rule out this possibility. This synesthesia-like

confusion presumably reflects the fact that both types of sensory stimuli involve temporal oscillations, and indicates that some of the information-processing mechanisms in the two modalities are analogous. Whatever the significance of this similarity between hearing and touch, it has given rise to the use of the terms *loudness* (i.e., subjective intensity) and *pitch* to refer to those subjective dimensions of vibrotaction that are primarily dependent on amplitude and frequency, respectively.

Goff (1967) was not the first person to measure vibrotactile frequency discrimination (Dunlap, 1911; Knudsen, 1928), but she was the first to control precisely for loudness differences (by adjusting all stimuli to equal the loudness of a 100-Hz standard). Vibratory stimuli were applied to the index finger pad, and the method of limits was used to measure frequency difference thresholds (Δf) for each of a series of standards ranging from 25 Hz to 200 Hz. Goff found that Δf increased as the frequency of the standard increased; in fact, the former increases were proportionally greater than the latter, so that the Weber fraction tended upward as higher portions of the frequency spectrum were examined. The pattern of results across frequencies was the same at two loudness levels (using standards of 20 and 35 dB SL), although Weber fractions were somewhat lower overall at the higher level, ranging from 0.2 at 25 Hz to 0.4 at 200 Hz.

The results of Mountcastle and his colleagues (Mountcastle, Talbot, Sakata, & Hyvärinen, 1969; Mountcastle, Steinmetz, & Romo, 1990) differ somewhat from those of Goff in that the former found the Weber fraction to remain relatively invariant across frequencies. Whereas Mountcastle's and Goff's results were roughly comparable at low frequencies, Mountcastle's difference thresholds at 200 Hz were only a fraction of those that Goff obtained. Perhaps in Goff's study the skin did not perfectly follow the movements of the vibrator at high frequencies, because the steady force they exerted on one another was very slight (8 g).

Physiological recordings by Mountcastle et al. (1969, 1990) show that the activity of RA afferents, and of the cortical neurons that receive their signals, is entrained with sufficient temporal precision to explain frequency discrimination at low frequencies. It is not clear how the equally good psychophysical performance of Mountcastle's subjects at high frequencies is to be explained, however, given the looser temporal structure of the responses of cortical neurons to frequencies in the Pacinian range. An answer to this and other unresolved questions in the area of frequency discrimination will require additional research.

Another possible contributor to vibrotactile pitch perception is the relative activity levels in the RA and Pacinian systems that a stimulus evokes. Morley and Rowe (1990) confirmed von Békésy's (1957a) observation that the pitch of a vibratory stimulus of a given frequency may change as its amplitude increases, and they went on to show that the amount and even the direction of this shift varies from one person to another (as well as from one frequency to another). They concluded that these intersubject differences precluded any simple explanation of pitch in terms of across-channel activity ratios. Roy and Hollins (1998) found, however, that such a model could account for magnitude estimates of pitch if the loudness functions of the individual subjects were taken into account. According to their model, pitch depends on the ratio of Pacinian loudness signals to the sum of loudness signals in the Pacinian, RA, and SA I channels combined. While it may account for overall impressions of pitch, however, this ratio mechanism is probably not precise enough to play an important role in frequency discrimination.

COMBINING SPATIAL AND TEMPORAL INFORMATION

The atmosphere exerts on the skin a pressure that is both uniform and (virtually) unchanging; therefore, we do not feel it. All effective tactile stimuli involve changes in both space and time. In the preceding sections we focused on stimuli that involve mainly one or the other type of change, but even in these situations the separation is not complete: A spatial pattern must be brought into contact with the skin before it can be held motionless against it, and vibration is delivered through a contactor that stimulates only a small region of skin. In everyday life, however, tactile stimuli that engage our attention tend to be complex events that robustly convey both spatial and temporal information. The principles of spatial and temporal processing described in preceding sections provide only a partial understanding of the way we perceive these complex stimulus events, apparently because some of these events activate specialized information-processing mechanisms within the somatosensory system. This part of the chapter is divided into sections dealing with a number of spatiotemporal phenomena, arranged in increasing order of the extent to which they are "emergent"—that is, the extent to which they depend on information-processing mechanisms that cannot be understood in terms of space or time alone.

Texture Perception

The movement of a textured surface across the skin is a spatiotemporal event because the skin is spatially deformed (i.e., locally stretched and indented) in a way that changes systematically over time. Katz (1925/1989) made extensive observations on the perception of such surfaces, but his stimuli were not well specified, and he was able to reach only qualitative conclusions. Lederman (1974, 1983;

Lederman & Taylor, 1972) brought a new level of rigor to work in this area, using as stimuli a series of precisely machined metal gratings; subjects used magnitude estimation to report the perceived roughness of these surfaces. Lederman found that the spatial parameters of the gratings (especially groove width) exerted a major influence on subjects' perceptions, and that the major temporal variable, speed of movement of the finger across the grating, had little effect. By developing a mathematical model that incorporated known skin parameters, Taylor and Lederman (1975) were able to show that a spatial index of stimulation—the instantaneous volumetric displacement of the skin from its resting position—did a good job of accounting for the roughness of all but the finest surfaces (where irregularities in the gratings made prediction uncertain). Further evidence against temporal coding was provided by Lederman, Loomis, & Williams (1982), who found that adapting vibrotactile channels did not affect the roughness of the surfaces.

A further comparison of the relative ability of hypothetical spatial and temporal coding mechanisms to account for roughness was offered by Connor and Johnson (1992). Their stimuli were two-dimensional arrays (rows and columns) of bumps embossed on plastic surfaces. In examining a surface, subjects moved their fingertip from side to side across it (i.e., along the rows and across the columns). As the separation of adjacent columns was increased, allowing skin to sink lower into the intervening gaps, the surfaces were perceived as increasingly rough. This is an unsurprising result, given that both spatial variation (deviation of the skin from its resting configuration at any given moment) and temporal variation (vertical changes in the position of any one spot on the skin with the passage of time) were increasing. By varying the separation of adjacent rows, however, Connor and Johnson were able to compare the effects of

these two variables: Increased row separation increases spatial variation but decreases overall temporal variation (because points on the skin that lie between rows will not move up and down). In fact, subjects judged the surfaces to grow rougher as the spacing between rows increased, demonstrating the preeminence of spatial factors. Connor and Johnson also examined the neural basis of spatial encoding; they found SA I afferents, rather than those mediating vibrotaction, to be responsible (see Chap. 13, this volume).

Katz (1925/1989), however, had hypothesized that very fine surfaces—with features smaller than those of Lederman's gratings or Connor's dot patterns—are temporally coded. As the finger moves across them, he maintained, microscopic vibrations are set up in the skin, and these serve as cues to the nature of the surface. Katz had noted that much can be learned about a surface when one touches it indirectly, for example, through a stylus or thimble that transmits vibrations but prevents spatial coding (Klatzky & Lederman, 1999). Several lines of evidence now indicate that Katz's *duplex theory* of tactile texture perception (spatial coding of coarse surfaces and vibrotactile coding of fine surfaces) is correct (Hollins, Bensmaïa, & Roy, in press). First, holding a surface motionless against the skin virtually eliminates the perception of fine textures—those with features smaller than about 100 microns—but leaves the distinctiveness of coarser surfaces relatively unimpaired (see Figure 14.4; Hollins & Risner, 2000). Second, vibrotactile adaptation reduces the perceived roughness of fine surfaces while leaving the roughness of coarse surfaces (as Lederman et al., 1982, found) relatively unaffected (Bolanowski, 1998; Hollins, Bensmaïa, & Risner, 1998). Third, adaptation can also interfere with the ability to discriminate fine surfaces from one another (Hollins, Bensmaïa, & Washburn,

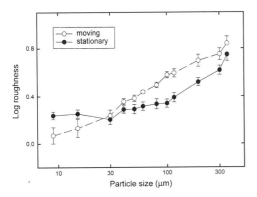

Figure 14.4 The perceived roughness of sandpaper increases as an orderly power function of particle size when the paper is drawn across the fingertip (open symbols).
NOTE: When vibration is eliminated by holding the papers motionless against the skin, the finer surfaces all feel the same. Data are the mean magnitude estimates of eight observers.
SOURCE: From Hollins and Risner (2000). Reprinted by permission of Psychonomic Society, Inc.

in press). And fourth, surreptitiously vibrating a textured surface causes subjects to judge it as rougher (Hollins, Fox, & Bishop, 2001), presumably because rough surfaces normally produce more cutaneous vibration than smooth ones do.

Moreover, recent work indicates that temporal processing can contribute to the perception of even relatively coarse textures. Cascio and Sathian (2001) asked participants to give magnitude estimates of the roughness of a series of tactile gratings that all had the same groove width (1 mm), but that varied in ridge width and in the speed with which they moved across the skin. By holding groove width (which powerfully engages spatial processing) constant, the investigators sought to isolate the more subtle effects of other variables. Roughness was found to increase moderately with increasing speed, and to decrease (as first reported by Lederman and Taylor, 1972) with increasing ridge width. Importantly, these two effects were equivalent when

plotted as a function of the temporal frequency of stimulation, suggesting its importance as an underlying variable. Indeed, when Cascio and Sathian presented pairs of gratings differing in ridge width and speed but having the same temporal frequency, subjects were virtually unable to distinguish them. Additional evidence that temporal cues play a role in the discrimination of coarse gratings has been reported by Gamzu and Ahissar (2001).

Even rats have two ways to encode the roughness of surfaces. Carvell and Simons (1995) trained rats to use their whiskers to examine surfaces: They obtained a reward when they correctly indicated which of two grooved surfaces was coarser. By testing the rats with most whiskers removed, the investigators found that at least two whiskers were needed to discriminate among coarse surfaces. The necessity of simultaneously touching two spots on the surface indicates spatial coding. With only a single whisker remaining, however, the rats were able to discriminate among very fine surfaces, necessarily on the basis of temporal coding.

Although they can be isolated in the laboratory, spatial and temporal coding mechanisms normally work together to enable the perception of the roughness (and perhaps other qualities) of surfaces. At least to a first approximation, it seems possible to understand roughness perception by carefully applying the principles of spatial and temporal processing, described in previous sections. This cannot be said of all tactile phenomena, however. We turn next to a family of perceptual distortions whose understanding requires, at the very least, an extrapolation of the rules of sensory processing considered up to this point.

Perceptual Attraction

We saw earlier (Green, 1982) that when two rods are pressed against the skin simultaneously, and separated by a distance considerably greater than the two-point threshold, they are consistently perceived as being closer to each other than they actually are. This illusion of proximity apparently grows more marked when the stimulus array is only briefly presented: von Békésy (1955) reported that when the base of a wire frame (resembling the bottom of a coat hanger) is pressed slowly into the skin, subjects perceive it more or less accurately, but when it is tapped briskly against the skin, the resulting perception is compressed. He found that a similar perceptual fusion into a somewhat diffuse, centrally located event occurs when two brief taps are simultaneously presented at widely separated locations on the forearm, or when a number of vibrators arranged in a row are simultaneously activated (von Békésy, 1957a, 1957b). Von Békésy (1958) used the term *funneling* to describe this type of perceptual event; the idea is that as signals from the ends of an array are processed, they shift toward a middle location. He believed that inhibition among sensory cells is primarily responsible.

An important part of von Békésy's notion of funneling is that the centrally located percept is stronger than it would be if only a single stimulus were presented. Sometimes when two or more stimuli are delivered simultaneously, however, one of them (especially if it is of lower intensity) may be rendered undetectable, without causing any obvious enhancement of the other(s); this is considered a form of masking. Masking diminishes as the test and masking stimuli are moved farther apart on the body surface (Sherrick, 1964). When the target and masker are close together, masking is thought to involve interference between their neural representations, whereas masking between widely separated stimuli probably depends primarily on attentional factors.

So far we have considered only situations in which two or more stimuli are presented at the same time. Equally remarkable perceptual phenomena have been found to occur, however, when a stimulus at one location is presented slightly before a stimulus at another location. For example, Helson (1930; Helson & King, 1931) employed an array of three contactors lined up on the forearm. Each in turn was briefly activated so that a spatially and temporally ordered series of three taps was presented. When the intervals between the taps were equal, subjects reported that they seemed equally separated in space; when the interval between (say) the first and second taps was made shorter than that between the second and third taps, however, the distance between the first and second contactors seemed shorter as well. An orderly mathematical relationship between time and perceived distance was obtained. Helson called this systematic perceptual distortion the *tau effect*.

Some insight into the nature of this effect was provided by Geldard (1982; Geldard & Sherrick, 1972), who used a slightly different paradigm: delivering two taps through one contactor and then a third tap through another contactor. The first tap served to alert the subject to prepare for a trial, as well as to establish a benchmark with which the perceived locations of later taps could be compared. After a relatively long interval (about 1 s), the second and then the third tap were presented in close (15–250 ms) succession. Geldard's subjects reported that the middle tap seemed to be occurring at a spot intermediate between the locations of the two contactors. Interestingly, it was this tap alone that was perceptually displaced, as if drawn toward the final one; the latter was subjectively unaffected, as was the initial tap, which was so well separated in time from later events that it did not interact with them.

An elaborated version of the illusion was created when the middle tap was replaced by a series of taps, closely spaced in time and all delivered through the same contactor. In this situation, each of these taps appears to be at a different place: Later members of the series are mislocalized closer and closer to the "attractant" (terminal contactor). Thus, a tap that precedes the final one by a tenth of a second will likely appear to be midway between the contactors, whereas a tap preceding the final one by only 20 ms will appear to be virtually superimposed on it. Because the overall experience is of a stimulus jumping from place to place, Geldard called the phenomenon *saltation*.

Although Geldard used somewhat shorter time intervals than did Helson, their observations are so compatible that it is likely that saltation and tau reflect the same process. Little is known about the underlying physiology, but some of Geldard's psychophysical results offer clues about it. First, saltation can occur only over a limited distance: A tap on the shoulder will not be drawn toward a later one delivered to the foot. Second, these spatial limits on saltation are smaller in high-acuity regions of the body (e.g., the finger) than in low-acuity regions (e.g., the back), suggesting that the underlying events occur at a level where the representation of inputs from different regions of skin reflects the innervation density of those regions. Third, saltation does not occur across the body midline. Saltation is thus not mediated by interactions occurring in the skin, such as mechanical waves that travel from place to place; but it is equally unlikely to reflect events occurring at such a high level of processing that the representation of space is an isotropic and homogenous one. Phenomena resembling cutaneous saltation have been described for the visual and auditory modalities (Geldard, 1976, 1982).

Movement Perception

Another tactile space-time illusion is apparent movement, which, like saltation, has parallels in vision and audition (Lakatos & Shepard, 1997; Sherrick, 1968b; Chap. 4, this volume).

Tactile apparent movement between two spots on the skin is most easily obtained when each spot is stimulated with a burst of tapping or vibration, rather than with the small number of taps typically used to elicit saltation (Kirman, 1974). The effectiveness of a rapid series of pressure stimuli suggests that apparent movement may be nothing more than a series of small saltations, with a densely packed array of "phantoms" (mislocalized stimuli), each occurring somewhat later than its predecessor and therefore seeming incrementally closer to the second vibrator. The smoothness of apparent movement contrasts with the discreteness of saltation, in which the experience is one of distinct stimuli materializing in different places; however, the difference in step size in the two situations may account for this qualitative difference. A more telling distinction is that although saltation does not cross the body midline (Geldard, 1982), apparent movement readily does so; in fact, under carefully arranged conditions a stimulus can be perceived as moving through the air from one hand to the other (Sherrick, 1968a). If the two illusions are distinct, however, they belong to the same family, sharing the feature that the percept of an early stimulus is drawn toward a later one.

Movement of an object along the skin is, of course, an important event, and it is not surprising that specialized mechanisms should be in place to respond to it—or, in the case of apparent movement, to "infer" its occurrence on the basis of fragmentary evidence. Almost as important as detecting the occurrence of movement, however, is identifying its direction: A raindrop trickling down the neck can be safely ignored, but an insect crawling upward cannot. It is not always easy to make such directional judgments, however. Dreyer, Hollins, and Whitsel (1978) used forced-choice procedures to determine if subjects could tell whether a brush was sweeping up or down the forearm. Subjects' judgments grew more accurate as the length of the brush's path increased, so the researchers were able to use the path length that was just sufficient to support 75%-correct responding as a (reciprocal) indicator of the ability to discriminate direction. This ability turned out to be keenest for intermediate velocities, in the neighborhood of 3 cm/s to 25 cm/s. Essick, Bredehoeft, McLaughlin, and Szaniszlo (1991) subsequently showed that optimal velocity varies somewhat from one region of skin to another, generally being lowest in regions where spatial acuity is high.

Performance falls off for different reasons at the two ends of the velocity continuum. At high speeds the sensation is of the brush slapping a small region of skin; in view of the perceptual distortions described in the last section, it is not surprising that this shortening of the path is accomplished mostly by a shift in the felt position of stimulus onset rather than of stimulus offset (Whitsel et al., 1986). At low velocities, however, the perceived path of the brush, though long, is meandering (Hall & Donaldson, 1885; Langford, Hall, & Monty, 1973). The fact that direction discrimination is most accurate at those moderate velocities for which path length is undistorted (Whitsel et al., 1986) illustrates the extent to which a moving stimulus evokes a complex percept whose multiple aspects are subtly interrelated.

Pattern Masking

In the last section we considered situations in which the individual stimuli—a tap, a burst of vibration delivered through a small round contactor, a brush moving in a straight line— carry little spatial information. It is possible, however, to present spatially patterned stimuli in order to determine how they interact with others occurring at different locations or at different times. The most widely used method of presenting such patterns is with a densely packed array of thin, vibrating rods or pins. The Optacon, a reading aid for the visually impaired (Bliss, Katcher, Rogers, & Shepard, 1970), incorporates such an array, which has served as a model for experimental versions. Typically, the volar surface of the subject's distal finger pad rests on the gently curving 6 × 24-pin array, and patterns are presented by activation of predetermined subsets of the pins.

The subject is usually asked not simply to detect the occurrence of a pattern, but to identify it by choosing from a set of alternatives. Performance (percent correct) on a large number of these baseline trials can then be compared with performance on other trials in which an additional stimulus, a masker, is presented either to the same region of the array just before or after the target, or to a different location. *Pattern masking* refers to masking that interferes with the subject's ability to identify a pattern, even if its occurrence is still noted. In one such study, Craig (1982) presented target stimuli and maskers to the same area of the finger pad. The 26-ms target was in the shape of a letter of the alphabet, which the subject attempted to identify by typing a response at a keyboard. Craig used two types of masking stimuli. In one, all the pins in the array were activated; the other type were nonsense patterns made up of elements (lines, curves) resembling the features of letters. Although the patterned maskers contained fewer vibrating pins than the uniform masker and therefore were, in some sense, weaker, they were much more effective in interfering with the subject's ability to identify the targets. This difference is probably the result of several factors. First, a patterned masker may combine perceptually with the target, forming a composite whose components are hard to distinguish (Evans & Craig, 1986; Mahar & Mackenzie, 1993); second, individual pattern maskers may resemble some members of the target set, and to the extent that they are perceived will therefore tend to elicit responses that are likely to be incorrect (Craig, 2000); and third, the masker may distort the target by causing small shifts in the positions of its components (Craig, 1989), although so far the evidence for this is inconclusive.

Masking does not require that target and masker be exactly synchronous: Some impairment of performance occurs even if the masking stimulus slightly precedes (forward masking) or follows (backward masking) the target. When subjects have only to report the occurrence of a tap or vibration, masking appears to be most effective when the stimuli are delivered at the same time (Sherrick, 1964), or at least received by the brain simultaneously (Gilson, 1969). In the case of pattern masking, however, Weisenberger and Craig (1982) were able to demonstrate, by presenting a test pattern and a masker to adjacent regions of the finger pad, that backward masking with a stimulus onset asynchrony of 50 ms or so is actually more effective than simultaneous masking—a result analogous to the visual phenomenon called *metacontrast*. Apparently, the complex processing required for target identification is most vulnerable to disruption once it is fully underway. A measurable amount of backward pattern masking occurs even with a stimulus onset asynchrony of 100 ms, for both stationary and scanned presentation of the test pattern (Craig, 1980), a fact that probably helps to explain why Braille is seldom read at a rate of more than one character per 150 ms (Craig, 2000).

The spatiotemporal interactions studied in this section appear to be shortcomings or failures of the sense of touch because they involve stimuli that are mislocalized, or rendered unrecognizable or undetectable. We should be cautious, however, in drawing conclusions about their effects on everyday perception. They demonstrate limits on the tactile ability to accurately perceive isolated stimuli or, at most, simple patterns; in most real-world situations, however, we are typically confronted with larger and more complex objects—a garment, a sandwich, a gerbil—that come into shifting contact with various parts of the body. As Kirman (1973) eloquently maintained, the ability to detect the information in these complex patterns of stimulation may actually be enhanced by some of the spatiotemporal interactions that hinder performance under impoverished stimulus conditions. Masking, for example, may serve to highlight edges or other major features of an object by deemphasizing small irregularities; and apparent movement may reveal to the observer the real movement of an object that comes into intermittent contact with the skin.

Up to this point we have considered only situations in which stimuli are applied to the skin of a passive observer. Patterns of stimulation become even more complicated when the observer is actively exploring objects in the environment, because parts of the body are then shifting with respect to one another, as well as with respect to external objects. Perception under conditions of active stimulus examination is called *haptics,* and it is to this subject that we now turn.

HAPTICS

When the electricity goes out, we grope in a drawer or toolbox for a flashlight; we can judge the size of an unseen fish by the pull it exerts on the line; and we feel the slipperiness of icy patches on the sidewalk and adjust our gait accordingly. These are all examples of haptics—a remarkably efficient and accurate form of perception. Klatzky, Lederman, & Metzger (1985) documented a key haptic ability by asking subjects to examine by touch a series of everyday objects, such as a baseball glove, a paintbrush, and a tea bag, and to name them as quickly as possible. They were free to use both hands and to lift the objects off the

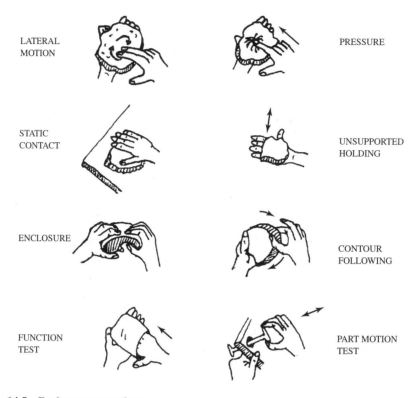

LATERAL MOTION

PRESSURE

STATIC CONTACT

UNSUPPORTED HOLDING

ENCLOSURE

CONTOUR FOLLOWING

FUNCTION TEST

PART MOTION TEST

Figure 14.5   Exploratory procedures.
SOURCE: From Lederman and Klatzky (1987). Reprinted by permission of Academic Press.

table. With vision and hearing blocked, and no lists to choose from, subjects nevertheless took only a couple of seconds to name each object after first touching it. There were few errors.

Subjects' expert performance during haptic exploration is in marked contrast to their flawed performance during many apparently simpler tactile tasks, such as estimating the distance between two stimulated spots on the skin. What accounts for this difference in performance?

Exploratory Procedures

One of the most important factors is that during haptic activity we are able to interact in different ways with an object. We can lift it, tap it, rub it, and so on. Lederman and Klatzky (1987) called these different motor activities *exploratory procedures* (EPs; see Figure 14.5), and showed that they are related to the type of information that a perceiver seeks about an object. Lederman and Klatzky asked blindfolded subjects to examine, on each trial, a series of four objects (a "standard" followed by three comparison objects), and to say which of the comparison objects was most like the standard with regard to a particular property or dimension. The stimuli were small objects especially made for the study, such as miniature pillows covered with various fabrics and stuffed with beads or fiber, and irregularly shaped pieces of wood, Styrofoam, and other materials. The authors videotaped the subjects while they were examining the objects, and later examined the tapes to determine how much time they devoted to the use of various EPs, such as lateral motion, pressure, enclosure, and unsupported holding.

Lederman and Klatzky (1987) found that the subjects used different exploratory procedures, depending on the stimulus property they had been asked to judge. For example, when asked to compare the surface textures of the objects, subjects spent much more time executing lateral motion than any other EP. When asked to judge the hardness of the same objects, however, pressing on the object became the main EP employed. Is the use of particular EPs for extracting particular types of information merely a culturally determined habit? Or does it help to make haptics more efficient? A second experiment by Lederman and Klatzky settled this question in favor of the latter conclusion. Subjects were asked to compare objects on particular dimensions, as before, but were now permitted to use only a particular EP on a given trial: They were carefully trained to perform each EP in a standardized way on command. Accuracy of performance was the primary measure. The authors found that, in general, performance on a particular dimension was best when subjects were instructed to use the EP that had been spontaneously used for that dimension in the first experiment. For example, pressure enabled the best performance when subjects judged the hardness of objects; lateral movement did so when they judged texture; and unsupported holding did so when they judged weight. Some information about a property was generally obtained even with nonoptimal EPs, although this was not always the case: Lateral movement, for example, did not significantly enable subjects to judge the weight of stimuli.

The overall picture, then, is that persons systematically use particular methods of exploration depending on what they are trying to learn about an object. But the issue is not one of tactics only, but of strategy. Lederman and Klatzky (1990) found that when asked to identify an object, subjects typically adopt a multistage approach, first using what might be called a general purpose exploratory procedure (such as gently enclosing the object in the hand) that gives a modest amount of information about a range of properties, and then following up with more specialized EPs that target properties found in the initial stage to be potentially informative.

The systematic, goal-driven behavior of subjects as they actively examine an object certainly helps to explain the accuracy and efficiency of haptic exploration. But why are particular EPs so effective for specific dimensions in the first place? The answer appears to be that a particular type of interaction with the object causes the tissues of the hand to be stimulated by the object in a way that will reveal a particular property. Lateral movement of the finger across a surface reveals texture information in part because it sets up vibrations in the skin—a rich source of information about surface texture. But are there other reasons for the effectiveness of haptic perception, reasons that cannot be reduced to the efficiency of cutaneous stimulation?

J. J. Gibson (1962), who developed the cookie-cutter experiment with which we began this chapter, certainly thought so. He believed that active exploration was inherently more effective in learning about objects than was any passive stimulation, no matter how carefully arranged by the experimenter. In fact, his experiment showed that subjects' poor performance in identifying the shapes of cookie cutters pressed into the palm contrasted markedly with excellent performance when they were allowed to palpate the stimuli with their fingertips. This comparison was not a fair one, however, both because acuity is better on the fingertips than on the palm and because movement of stimuli across the skin occurred in the active condition only. Gibson himself sought to address the latter issue by including an additional passive condition in which the stimulus was twisted back and forth while being held against the palm; this produced an intermediate level of performance.

Later researchers continued to refine Gibson's experimental design in order to compare active and passive touch under conditions that were more nearly equivalent with respect to stimulation of the skin. Schwartz, Perey, and Azulay (1975) presented all stimuli to a single index finger, eliminating body site as a confound. They found that performance when the subject traced the form with the fingertip was equivalent to that obtained when the subject remained motionless and the experimenter slowly turned the object so that its contour moved sequentially across the skin. Cronin (1977) presented all stimuli to the palm rather than the fingertip; she, too, found that participants were equally accurate whether the object moved across the skin or the skin moved across the object. Heller and Myers (1983) likewise presented all stimuli to the palm, but the way in which the stimuli moved on the skin during passive stimulation was different from Cronin's method: She, like Gibson, applied the whole shape to the palm at once and twisted it, whereas Heller and Myers touched only part of the shape to the palm at a time, in a way that resembled "a spinning saucer as it comes to rest" (p. 228). Perhaps because of this procedural difference, Heller and Myers found performance in this passive condition to be inferior to that achieved with active examination of the stimuli.

Unfortunately, no firm conclusion about the claimed superiority of active touch in form perception can be based on these early studies because they did not precisely equate the spatiotemporal pattern of skin stimulation in the active and passive conditions. Vega-Bermudez, Johnson, and Hsiao (1991) made progress toward resolving the issue, however, by using not only the same body site (finger) but also the same pattern of stimulation in ac-

tive and passive conditions: Either the finger moved rightward across the embossed letters, or the letters moved leftward under the stationary finger pad. Performance was virtually identical under these two conditions, and even the confusion matrices were closely comparable.

In summary, it appears that when the pattern and amount of cutaneous stimulation can be equated across active and passive conditions, the ability to recognize two-dimensional forms is thereby also equated (the same equivalence applies in the case of texture judgments: Heller, 1989; Lamb, 1983; Lederman, 1981). But we cannot say with certainty how this conclusion would fare in the case of three-dimensional objects like those used by Klatzky et al. (1985) because active exploration of them is a complex affair that brings into play special cognitive operations (Klatzky & Lederman, 1993) and strongly engages subjects' attention.

Attention

Differences in the level or distribution of attention between active conditions (where attention is consistently engaged) and passive conditions (where it may wander) may in fact help to explain the active versus passive differences in performance that have sometimes been reported. When attention itself is brought under experimental control, however, it appears to follow the same rules whether the hand or the object moves. Many current studies of attention employ some version of an experimental paradigm developed by Posner, Snyder, and Davidson (1980), which capitalizes on the fact that attention is usually spatial in nature (i.e., focused on a particular location). In Posner's experiments, subjects know in advance that a visual target stimulus will be presented in one of two or more locations; a fraction of a second before it is presented, a *cue* stimulus occurs, revealing that the target is likely to be presented in one particular location. Posner et al. (1980) found that subjects respond more quickly to a stimulus if they know where to expect it; not surprisingly, a misleading cue slows performance relative to baseline (the reader should consult Chap. 6, this volume, for a more complete discussion of this experimental approach and the theoretical issues it raises).

Using this paradigm, Butter, Buchtel, and Santucci (1989) subsequently demonstrated that tactile attention can also be directed to a cued location. An ingenious study by Lakatos and Shepard (1997) showed that these locations are represented perceptually not just as regions of the body, but as places in the three-dimensional space that the body occupies. On a verbal command, their subjects focused attention on a particular part of the body, such as "left calf" or "right wrist"; after 2 s, a second announcement directed their attention elsewhere. Simultaneous with the second command, puffs of air were delivered to several locations, and the subject indicated whether a puff had been delivered to the second locus of attention. The experiment rests on the assumption that attention must arrive at the second location before this decision can be made; latency of response is therefore taken as a measure of how long it takes to shift tactile attention between locations. The surprising result was that attention appears to move through a mental representation of three-dimensional space, rather than a representation of the body surface alone: For example, it took longer for attention to be shifted from the right wrist to the left arm than from the right wrist to the left wrist (the latter distance being shorter, since the subject's arms were extended forward). A follow-up experiment supported the existence of a space-based representation by demonstrating that changes in the positions of the arms and legs modified response latencies in the expected direction.

We cannot, however, anticipate every tactile stimulus, or even shift our attention to it while it is still present. How is perception affected when the stimulus falls outside of the attended region? We know that the response to a stimulus is slowed under these conditions (Butter et al., 1989), but is perception itself otherwise affected? This question has been addressed by Sathian and Burton (1991), who had subjects pull four fingers (the index and middle fingers of both hands) across separate gratings simultaneously (see Figure 14.6). At least three of the gratings were identical; the fourth was sometimes the same as well, but half the time it had embedded within it a short region of grating that was coarser or finer than the rest. A trial consisted of the subject traversing the gratings, resting a moment, and then doing so again. He or she then had to indicate whether the grating with the embedded region had been encountered during the first or the second traverse. The experimenter brought attention into play by tapping one finger of the subject just before each traverse. During the target-present traverse, the tap could be delivered either to the finger receiving the target (in which case the tap constituted a valid cue), or to some other finger (in which case it was an invalid cue). Presumably, attention is drawn to the tapped finger, and the question is whether this focusing of attention helps in detecting the embedded region. In fact, valid cuing did not increase accuracy in the task just described, indicating that spatially focused attention is not needed for detecting suddenly occurring regions that differ in texture from their surroundings.

However, when the subject's task was to distinguish gratings with embedded rough areas from others with embedded smooth regions (the condition illustrated in Figure 14.6), attention (valid cuing) was helpful. The same was true when subjects struggled to distinguish uniform gratings differing in roughness or to detect a target defined by its *lack* of

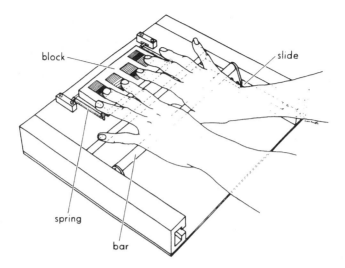

Figure 14.6 The apparatus used by Sathian and Burton (1991) in a series of experiments on selective attention.

NOTE: As participants pull the sliding bar toward them with their thumbs, the index and middle fingers of both hands are drawn across tactile gratings. In the specific experiment shown, the target grating contains an embedded region of increased roughness (i.e., more widely spaced ridges), whereas the distractor gratings contain embedded regions of decreased roughness.

SOURCE: From Sathian and Burton (1991). Reprinted by permission of Psychonomic Society, Inc.

an embedded region. The results resemble those obtained in studies of visual attention (Treisman & Gormican, 1988). Apparently, perception in the absence of focused attention is relatively crude: Salient events or features are noted, but their properties are only dimly appreciated. Similar findings have been obtained with vibrotactile stimuli (Whang, Burton, & Shulman, 1991).

Attention in the tactile modality probably does more than highlight some stimuli at the expense of others, however. Research on the visual system indicates that sometimes attention also plays a role in perceptually unifying an object's many properties (Treisman & Gelade, 1980). Such perceptual binding would make an especially valuable contribution to haptic perception and would perhaps help to explain the remarkable ability of subjects to grasp and identify quickly a wide range of everyday objects (Klatzky et al., 1985).

Kinesthetic Contributions

An additional and extremely important factor in haptic perception is kinesthesis—a detailed awareness of the body's own movements (the interested reader should consult Chap. 8, this volume, for a discussion of the contribution kinesthesis makes to motor control). A variety of receptors within the body's musculoskeletal system contribute to kinesthesis. The role of joint receptors has long been recognized, but in the past three decades it has been shown that receptors in muscles also make an important contribution. These receptors normally become active when a muscle is stretched and trigger a compensatory reflex contraction. But they also influence our perception of where the parts of our body are positioned in space: Exciting muscle receptors by applying vibration to the biceps, for example, makes the arm feel more extended than it is (Goodwin, McCloskey, & Matthews,

1972); increasing their level of activation further can create the unpleasant sensation that the forearm is bending backward at the elbow (Craske, 1977). Normally, however, signals from joints and muscles work together to provide a unified and accurate sense of how the parts of the body are positioned relative to one another (Gandevia & McCloskey, 1976). More recently, it has been shown that even some *cutaneous* receptors have a kinesthetic function. Gently pulling sideways on the skin overlying the knuckles, for example by means of threads that are glued to the skin, can create the illusion that the fingers are flexing or extending (Collins & Prochazka, 1996; Edin & Johansson, 1995). Such stimulation presumably mimics the skin stretching that occurs normally when the fingers actually do move. The receptors in this case are believed to be mechanoreceptors of the SA II variety, whose end organs (Ruffini cylinders) bear a superficial but perhaps not coincidental resemblance to some stretch receptors in muscle. It has also been hypothesized (Merton, 1964) that a centrally generated record of motor commands contributes to kinesthetic spatial awareness in much the same way that a sense of the effort expended in lifting an object contributes to its perceived heaviness (Flanagan & Bandomir, 2000; Flanagan, Wing, Allison, & Spencely, 1995; Gandevia & McCloskey, 1977). However, this is now considered unlikely (McCloskey & Torda, 1975).

Kinesthetic signals can convey information not just about the disposition of parts of the body, but also about the geometry of objects that we interact with. If, while walking along a dark road at night, you stumble over a stick and kick it out of your path, the brief encounter gives you some sense of the stick's dimensions, even though your foot has come into contact with only a small section of it. More controlled and extended wielding of an object (such as swinging a hammer) gives you an even clearer impression of its length,

orientation, and other properties. This ability to learn about objects by wielding them has been the subject of considerable research (recently summarized by Turvey, 1996). In general, these investigations show that our perception of the dimensions of such objects is mediated by the sensing of specific mechanical quantities that manifest themselves when we swing, lift, or otherwise manipulate the object.

For example, Solomon and Turvey (1988) showed that rotational inertia plays a key role in sensing the length of a wielded rod. Their subjects reached behind a screen and grasped a rod by one end, swinging it to and fro. Regardless of the plane in which the rod was swung, or how rapidly it was moved, subjects had a reasonably accurate perception of its length (demonstrated by moving a visible surface until it seemed to be at the same distance from the observer as the far end of the rod). To determine what aspect of the stimulus situation was mediating subjects' performance, Solomon and Turvey added a weight to the rod—a metal block that could be attached to it at any of several positions. Regardless of its location, the block increased the weight of the rod by the same amount, but its contribution to rotational inertia varied with position because inertia takes into account both the weight of the block and (the square of) its distance from the end by which the rod is held. The crucial result was that the perceived length of the rod was a power function of the overall moment of inertia. The applicability of Stevens' law to this situation implies that rotational inertia acts as a bona fide stimulus variable. More complex mechanical quantities appear to play a mediating role in more subtle judgments, such as the direction of a bend in the rod (Turvey, 1996).

An additional question is how kinesthetic signals combine with tactile ones to produce an overall appreciation of the size, shape and location of touched—but not necessarily wielded—objects in our environment. That there is a unified central representation of space is suggested by a number of recent findings, including the results of Lakatos and Shepard's (1997) attentional study, described earlier, and the discovery that the distracting effect of a stimulus to one hand on the ability to make tactile judgments using the other depends on the separation between the hands (Spence, personal communication, July 2, 2000). The fact that distortions of haptic space (Armstrong & Marks, 1999; Hollins & Goble, 1988) closely resemble those that occur when it is the stimulus, rather than the hand, that moves (Langford et al., 1973; Whitsel et al., 1986) are also consistent with the idea that there is a single, if not entirely veridical, spatial representation of the body and its immediate environment.

This merging of tactile and kinesthetic signals is not, however, a seamless one, as Aristotle's illusion shows: When two fingers are crossed, an object, such as a pencil placed between them, feels to some observers like two separate objects (Benedetti, 1985). If kinesthetic information about the positions of the fingers were accurately combined with tactile signals caused by the pencil, there would be no illusion. Perhaps in this situation the internal spatial representation into which tactile signals are integrated is a compromise between the normal positions of the fingers and their current, somewhat anomalous positions.

A more quantitative way of examining the combination rules for tactile and kinesthetic signals was devised by Pont et al. (1999). They asked subjects to examine curved surfaces (arching plastic strips) by touching each one with three fingers simultaneously. Subjects were to choose from an array of such surfaces—each examined with fingers spread apart—the one that best matched the curvature of a standard examined with the fingers close together. The results showed that match-

ing was disturbed by changes in finger separation: A given surface felt more curved when the fingers were splayed (so that the outer fingers contacted more steeply sloping regions) than when they were close together. This result suggests that, as in the case of Aristotle's illusion, subjects are only partially compensating for changes in finger separation.

CONCLUSION

In summary, we have seen that touch is a complex affair. This most essential of the senses is less specialized for extracting spatial information from the environment than is vision, and less specialized for temporal information than is audition. Yet it does a creditable job in both domains, resolving spatial details with submillimeter accuracy and detecting vibration over a nine-octave range of frequencies. Spatial and temporal processing often intersect, enhancing abilities such as texture discrimination but also causing substantial perceptual distortions such as the tau effect. Adding to the complexity—and power—of touch is that it operates in close cooperation with motor systems. Although active and passive touch are equally accurate when they involve the same cutaneous stimulation, only active touch is able to influence what patterns of stimulation the skin will receive and to draw fully on kinesthetic as well as tactile signals. The haptic ability to examine and identify an unseen object is a sensory and cognitive achievement that we are only beginning to understand.

REFERENCES

Armstrong, L., & Marks, L. E. (1999). Haptic perception of linear extent. *Perception & Psychophysics, 61*, 1211–1226.

Benedetti, F. (1985). Processing of tactile spatial information with crossed fingers. *Journal of*

Experimental Psychology: Human Perception and Performance, 11, 517–525.

Bliss, J. C., Katcher, M. H., Rogers, C. H., & Shepard, R. P. (1970). Optical-to-tactile image conversion for the blind. *IEEE Transactions on Man-Machine Systems, MMS-11,* 58–65.

Boivie, J. (1994). Sensory abnormalities in patients with central nervous system lesions as shown by quantitative sensory tests. In J. Boivie, P. Hansson, & U. Lindblom (Eds.), *Progress in pain research and management: Vol. 3. Touch, temperature, and pain in health and disease: Mechanisms and assessments* (pp. 179–191). Seattle: IASP Press.

Bolanowski, S. J. (1998). Tactile channels and their interactions. In S. Grondin & Y. Lacouture (Eds.), *Fechner Day 98: Proceedings of the Fourteenth Annual Meeting of the International Society for Psychophysics* (pp. 103–108). Quebec, Canada: International Society for Psychophysics.

Bolanowski, S. J., Jr., Gescheider, G. A., Verrillo, R. T., & Checkosky, C. M. (1988). Four channels mediate the mechanical aspects of touch. *Journal of the Acoustical Society of America, 84,* 1680–1694.

Butter, C. M., Buchtel, H. A., & Santucci, R. (1989). Spatial attentional shifts: Further evidence for the role of polysensory mechanisms using visual and tactile stimuli. *Neuropsychologia, 27,* 1231–1240.

Carvell, G. E., & Simons, D. J. (1995). Task- and subject-related differences in sensorimotor behavior during active touch. *Somatosensory and Motor Research, 12,* 1–9.

Cascio, C. J., & Sathian, K. (2001). Temporal cues contribute to tactile perception of roughness. *Journal of Neuroscience, 21,* 5289–5296.

Cole, L. E. (1929). The localization of tactual space: A study of average and constant errors under different types of localization. *Genetic Psychology Monographs, 5*(5), 339–447.

Collins, D. F., & Prochazka, A. (1996). Movement illusions evoked by ensemble cutaneous input from the dorsum of the human hand. *Journal of Physiology, 496,* 857–871.

Connor, C. E., & Johnson, K. O. (1992). Neural coding of tactile texture: Comparison of spatial and temporal mechanisms for roughness perception. *Journal of Neuroscience, 12,* 3414–3426.

Craig, J. C. (1974). Vibrotactile difference thresholds for intensity and the effect of a masking noise. *Perception & Psychophysics, 15,* 123–127.

Craig, J. C. (1980). Modes of vibrotactile pattern generation. *Journal of Experimental Psychology: Human Perception and Performance, 6,* 151–166.

Craig, J. C. (1982). Vibrotactile masking: A comparison of energy and pattern maskers. *Perception & Psychophysics, 31,* 523–529.

Craig, J. C. (1989). Interference in localizing tactile stimuli. *Perception & Psychophysics, 45,* 343–355.

Craig, J. C. (2000). Processing of sequential tactile patterns: Effects of a neutral stimulus. *Perception & Psychophysics, 62,* 596–606.

Craig, J. C., & Lyle, K. B. (2001). A comparison of tactile spatial sensitivity on the palm and fingerpad. *Perception & Psychophysics, 63,* 337–347.

Craske, B. (1977). Perception of impossible limb positions induced by tendon vibration. *Science, 196,* 71–73.

Cronin, V. (1977). Active and passive touch at four age levels. *Developmental Psychology, 13,* 253–256.

Culver, C. M. (1970). Errors in tactile localization. *American Journal of Psychology, 83,* 420–427.

De Valois, R. L., & De Valois, K. K. (1990). *Spatial vision.* New York: Oxford University Press.

Dreyer, D. A., Hollins, M., & Whitsel, B. L. (1978). Factors influencing cutaneous directional sensitivity. *Sensory Processes, 2,* 71–79.

Dunlap, K. (1911). Palmesthetic difference sensibility for rate. *American Journal of Physiology, 29,* 108–114.

Edin, B. B., & Johansson, N. (1995). Skin strain patterns provide kinaesthetic information to the human central nervous system. *Journal of Physiology, 487,* 243–251.

Essick, G. K., Bredehoeft, K. R., McLaughlin, D. F., & Szaniszlo, J. A. (1991). Directional sensitivity along the upper limb in humans. *Somatosensory and Motor Research, 8,* 13–22.

Evans, P. M., & Craig, J. C. (1986). Temporal integration and vibrotactile backward masking. *Journal of Experimental Psychology: Human Perception & Performance, 12,* 160–168.

Flanagan, J. R., & Bandomir, C. A. (2000). Coming to grips with weight perception: Effects of grasp configuration on perceived heaviness. *Perception & Psychophysics, 62,* 1204–1219.

Flanagan, J. R., Wing, A. M., Allison, S., & Spencely, A. (1995). Effects of surface texture on weight perception when lifting objects with a precision grip. *Perception & Psychophysics, 57,* 282–290.

Gamzu, E., & Ahissar, E. (2001). Importance of temporal cues for tactile spatial-frequency discrimination. *Journal of Neuroscience, 21,* 7416–7427.

Gandevia, S. C., & McCloskey, D. I. (1976). Joint sense, muscle sense, and their combination as position sense, measured at the distal interphalageal joint of the middle finger. *Journal of Physiology, 260,* 387–407.

Gandevia, S. C., & McCloskey, D. I. (1977). Sensations of heaviness. *Brain, 100,* 345–354.

Gates, E. J. (1915). The determination of the limens of single and dual impression by the method of constant stimuli. *American Journal of Psychology, 26,* 152–157.

Geldard, F. A. (1940). The perception of mechanical vibration: I. History of a controversy. *Journal of General Psychology, 22,* 243–269.

Geldard, F. A. (1976). The saltatory effect in vision. *Sensory Processes, 1,* 77–86.

Geldard, F. A. (1982). Saltation in somesthesis. *Psychological Bulletin, 92,* 136–175.

Geldard, F. A., & Sherrick, C. E. (1972). The cutaneous "rabbit": A perceptual illusion. *Science, 178,* 178–179.

Gescheider, G. A. (1976). Evidence in support of the duplex theory of mechanoreception. *Sensory Processes, 1,* 68–76.

Gescheider, G. A., Berryhill, M. E., Verrillo, R. T., & Bolanowski, S. J. (1999). Vibrotactile temporal summation: Probability summation or neural integration? *Somatosensory and Motor Research, 16,* 229–242.

Gescheider, G. A., Bolanowski, S. J., Jr., & Verrillo, R. T. (1989). Vibrotactile masking: Effects of stimulus onset asynchrony and stimulus frequency. *Journal of the Acoustical Society of America, 85,* 2059–2064.

Gescheider, G. A., Bolanowski, S. J., Jr., Verrillo, R. T., Arpajian, D. J., & Ryan, T. F. (1990). Vibrotactile intensity discrimination measured by three methods. *Journal of the Acoustical Society of America, 87,* 330–338.

Gescheider, G. A., Frisina, R. D., & Verrillo, R. T. (1979). Selective adaptation of vibrotactile thresholds. *Sensory Processes, 3,* 37–48.

Gescheider, G. A., Sklar, B. F., Van Doren, C. L., & Verrillo, R. T. (1985). Vibrotactile forward masking: Psychophysical evidence for a triplex theory of cutaneous mechanoreception. *Journal of the Acoustical Society of America, 78,* 534–543.

Gescheider, G. A., Verrillo, R. T., & Van Doren, C. L. (1982). Prediction of vibrotactile masking functions. *Journal of the Acoustical Society of America, 72,* 1421–1426.

Gibson, J. J. (1962). Observations on active touch. *Psychological Review, 69,* 477–491.

Gilson, R. D. (1969). Vibrotactile masking: Some spatial and temporal aspects. *Perception & Psychophysics, 5,* 176–180.

Goble, A. K., & Hollins, M. (1993). Vibrotactile adaptation enhances amplitude discrimination. *Journal of the Acoustical Society of America, 93,* 418–424.

Goff, G. D. (1967). Differential discrimination of frequency of cutaneous mechanical vibration. *Journal of Experimental Psychology, 74,* 294–299.

Goodwin, G. M., McCloskey, D. I., & Matthews, P. B. C. (1972). The contribution of muscle afferents to kinaesthesia shown by vibration induced illusions of movement and by the effects of paralysing joint afferents. *Brain, 95,* 705–748.

Green, B. G. (1982). The perception of distance and location for dual tactile pressures. *Perception & Psychophysics, 31,* 315–323.

Green, B. G., & Flammer, L. J. (1989). Localization of chemical stimulation: Capsaicin on hairy skin. *Somatosensory and Motor Research, 6,* 553–566.

Greenlee, M. W., & Heitger, F. (1988). The functional role of contrast adaptation. *Vision Research, 28,* 791–797.

Greenspan, J. D., & McGillis, S. L. B. (1991). Stimulus features relevant to the perception of sharpness and mechanically evoked cutaneous pain. *Somatosensory and Motor Research, 8,* 137–147.

Greenspan, J. D., Thomadaki, M., & McGillis, S. L. B. (1997). Spatial summation of perceived pressure, sharpness and mechanically evoked cutaneous pain. *Somatosensory and Motor Reseach, 14,* 107–112.

Griffin, M. J. (1990). *Handbook of human vibration.* New York: Harcourt Brace Jovanovich.

Hahn, J. F. (1966). Vibrotactile adaptation and recovery measured by two methods. *Journal of Experimental Psychology, 71,* 655–658.

Hahn, J. F. (1968). Low-frequency vibrotactile adaptation. *Journal of Experimental Psychology, 78,* 655–659.

Hall, G. S., & Donaldson, H. H. (1885). Motor sensations on the skin. *Mind, 10,* 557–572.

Hamer, R. D., Verrillo, R. T., & Zwislocki, J. J. (1983). Vibrotactile masking of Pacinian and non-Pacinian channels. *Journal of the Acoustical Society of America, 73,* 1293–1303.

Heller, M. A. (1989). Texture perception in sighted and blind observers. *Perception & Psychophysics, 45,* 49–54.

Heller, M. A., & Myers, D. S. (1983). Active and passive tactual recognition of form. *Journal of General Psychology, 108,* 225–229.

Helson, H. (1930). The Tau effect: An example of psychological relativity. *Science, 71,* 536–537.

Helson, H., & King, S. M. (1931). The tau effect: An example of psychological relativity. *Journal of Experimental Psychology, 14,* 202–217.

Hollins, M., Bensmaïa, S., & Risner, R. (1998). The duplex theory of tactile texture perception. In S. Grondin & Y. Lacouture (Eds.), *Fechner Day 98: Proceedings of the Fourteenth Annual Meeting of the International Society for Psychophysics* (pp. 115–120). Quebec, Canada: International Society for Psychophysics.

Hollins, M., Bensmaïa, S. J., & Roy, E. A. (in press). Vibrotaction and texture perception. In

O. Franzén, R. Johansson, & L. Terenius (Eds.), *Brain mechanisms of tactile perception.* Basel, Switzerland: Birkhäuser.

Hollins, M., Bensmaïa, S. J., & Washburn, S. (in press). Vibrotactile adaptation impairs discrimination of fine, but not coarse, textures. *Somatosensory and Motor Research.*

Hollins, M., Fox, A., & Bishop, C. (2001). Imposed vibration influences perceived tactile smoothness. *Perception, 30,* 1455–1465.

Hollins, M., & Goble, A. K. (1988). Perception of the length of voluntary movements. *Somatosensory Research, 5,* 335–348.

Hollins, M., & Risner, S. R. (2000). Evidence for the duplex theory of tactile texture perception. *Perception & Psychophysics, 62,* 695–705.

Hollins, M., & Roy, E. A. (1996). Perceived intensity of vibrotactile stimuli: The role of mechanoreceptive channels. *Somatosensory and Motor Research, 13,* 273–286.

Horch, K. W., Clark, F. J., & Burgess, P. R. (1975). Awareness of knee joint angle under static conditions. *Journal of Neurophysiology, 38,* 1436–1447.

Johnson, K. O., & Phillips, J. R. (1981). Tactile spatial resolution: I. Two-point discrimination, gap detection, grating resolution, and letter recognition. *Journal of Neurophysiology, 46,* 1177–1191.

Johnson, K. O., Van Boven, R. W., & Hsiao, S. S. (1994). The perception of two points is not the spatial resolution threshold. In J. Boivie, P. Hansson, & U. Lindblom (Eds.), *Progress in pain research and management: Vol. 3. Touch, temperature, and pain in health and disease: Mechanisms and assessments* (pp. 389–404). Seattle: IASP Press.

Jones, M. B., & Vierck, C. J., Jr. (1973). Length discrimination on the skin. *American Journal of Psychology, 86,* 49–60.

Katz, D. (1930). The vibratory sense [University of Maine Studies, 2nd Series, No. 14. *The vibratory sense and other lectures*]. *The Maine Bulletin, 32*(10), 90–104.

Katz, D. (1989). *The world of touch* (L. E. Krueger, Ed. and Trans.). Hillsdale, NJ: Erlbaum. (Original work published 1925)

Kirman, J. H. (1973). Tactile communication of speech: A review and an analysis. *Psychological Bulletin, 80,* 54–74.

Kirman, J. H. (1974). Tactile apparent movement: The effects of interstimulus onset interval and stimulus duration. *Perception & Psychophysics, 15,* 1–6.

Klatzky, R. L., & Lederman, S. J. (1993). Toward a computational model of constraint-driven exploration and haptic object identification. *Perception, 22,* 597–621.

Klatzky, R. L., & Lederman, S. J. (1999). Tactile roughness perception with a rigid link interposed between skin and surface. *Perception & Psychophysics, 61,* 591–607.

Klatzky, R. L., Lederman, S. J., & Metzger, V. A. (1985). Identifying objects by touch: An "expert system." *Perception & Psychophysics, 37,* 299–302.

Knudsen, V. O. (1928). "Hearing" with the sense of touch. *Journal of General Psychology, 1,* 320–352.

Lakatos, S., & Shepard, R. N. (1997). Time-distance relations in shifting attention between locations on one's body. *Perception & Psychophysics, 59,* 557–566.

Lamb, G. D. (1983). Tactile discrimination of textured surfaces: Psychophysical performance measurements in humans. *Journal of Physiology, 338,* 551–565.

LaMotte, R. H., & Mountcastle, V. B. (1975). Capacities of humans and monkeys to discriminate between vibratory stimuli of different frequency and amplitude: A correlation between neural events and psychophysical measurements. *Journal of Neurophysiology, 38,* 539–559.

Langford, N., Hall, R. J., & Monty, R. A. (1973). Cutaneous perception of a track produced by a moving point across the skin. *Journal of Experimental Psychology, 97,* 59–63.

Lederman, S. J. (1974). Tactile roughness of grooved surfaces: The touching process and effects of macro- and microsurface structure. *Perception & Psychophysics, 16,* 385–395.

Lederman, S. J. (1981). The perception of surface roughness by active and passive touch. *Bulletin of the Psychonomic Society, 18,* 253–255.

Lederman, S. J. (1983). Tactual roughness perception: Spatial and temporal determinants. *Canadian Journal of Psychology, 37,* 498–511.

Lederman, S. J., & Klatzky, R. L. (1987). Hand movements: A window into haptic object recognition. *Cognitive Psychology, 19,* 342–368.

Lederman, S. J., & Klatzky, R. L. (1990). Haptic object classification: Knowledge-driven exploration. *Cognitive Psychology, 22,* 421–459.

Lederman, S. J., Loomis, J. M., & Williams, D. A. (1982). The role of vibration in the tactual perception of roughness. *Perception & Psychophysics, 32,* 109–116.

Lederman, S. J., & Taylor, M. M. (1972). Fingertip force, surface geometry, and the perception of roughness by active touch. *Perception & Psychophysics, 12,* 401–408.

Loomis, J. M. (1979). An investigation of tactile hyperacuity. *Sensory Processes, 3,* 289–302.

Loomis, J. M. (1981). On the tangibility of letters and braille. *Perception & Psychophysics, 29,* 37–46.

Loomis, J. M. (1982). Analysis of tactile and visual confusion matrices. *Perception & Psychophysics, 31,* 41–52.

Loomis, J. M. (1990). A model of character recognition and legibility. *Journal of Experimental Psychology: Human Perception and Performance, 16,* 106–120.

Mahar, D. P., & Mackenzie, B. D. (1993). Masking, information integration, and tactile pattern perception: A comparison of the isolation and integration hypotheses. *Perception, 22,* 483–496.

McBurney, D. H., Kasschau, R. A., & Bogart, I. M. (1967). The effect of adaptation on taste jnds. *Perception & Psychophysics, 2,* 175–178.

McCloskey, D. I., & Torda, T. A. G. (1975). Corollary motor discharges and kinaesthesia. *Brain Research, 100,* 467–470.

McGill, W. J., & Goldberg, J. P. (1968). A study of the near-miss involving Weber's law and pure-tone intensity discrimination. *Perception & Psychophysics, 4,* 105–109.

Merton, P. A. (1964). Human position sense and sense of effort. *Symposia of the Society for Experimental Biology, 18,* 387–400.

Morley, J. W., & Rowe, M. J. (1990). Perceived pitch of vibrotactile stimuli: Effects of vibration amplitude, and implications for vibration frequency coding. *Journal of Physiology, 431,* 403–416.

Mountcastle, V. B., Steinmetz, M. A., & Romo, R. (1990). Frequency discrimination in the sense of flutter: Psychophysical measurements correlated with postcentral events in behaving monkeys. *Journal of Neuroscience, 10,* 3032–3044.

Mountcastle, V. B., Talbot, W. H., Darian-Smith, I., & Kornhuber, H. H. (1967). Neural basis of the sense of flutter-vibration. *Science, 155,* 597–600.

Mountcastle, V. B., Talbot, W. H., Sakata, H., & Hyvärinen, J. (1969). Cortical neuronal mechanisms in flutter-vibration studied in unanesthetized monkeys: Neuronal periodicity and frequency discrimination. *Journal of Neurophysiology, 32,* 452–484.

Nafe, J. P., & Wagoner, K. S. (1941). The nature of sensory adaptation. *Journal of General Psychology, 25,* 295–321.

Ochoa, J., & Torebjörk, E. (1983). Sensations evoked by intraneural microstimulation of single mechanoreceptor units innervating the human hand. *Journal of Physiology, 342,* 633–654.

O'Mara, S., Rowe, M. J., & Tarvin, R. P. C. (1988). Neural mechanisms in vibrotactile adaptation. *Journal of Neurophysiology, 59,* 607–622.

Pont, S. C., Kappers, A. M. L., & Koenderink, J. J. (1999). Similar mechanisms underlie curvature comparison by static and dynamic touch. *Perception & Psychophysics, 61,* 874–894.

Posner, M. I., Snyder, C. R. R., & Davidson, B. J. (1980). Attention and the detection of signals. *Journal of Experimental Psychology: General, 109,* 160–174.

Roy, E. A., & Hollins, M. (1998). A ratio code for vibrotactile pitch. *Somatosensory and Motor Research, 15,* 134–145.

Sathian, K., & Burton, H. (1991). The role of spatially selective attention in the tactile perception of texture. *Perception & Psychophysics, 50,* 237–248.

Sato, M. (1961). Response of Pacinian corpuscles to sinusoidal vibration. *Journal of Physiology, 159,* 391–409.

Schwartz, A. S., Perey, A. L., & Azulay, A. (1975). Further analysis of active and passive touch in pattern discrimination. *Bulletin of the Psychonomic Society, 6,* 7–9.

Sherrick, C. E., Jr. (1964). Effects of double simultaneous stimulation of the skin. *American Journal of Psychology, 77,* 42–53.

Sherrick, C. E. (1968a). Bilateral apparent haptic movement. *Perception & Psychophysics, 4,* 159–160.

Sherrick, C. E. (1968b). Studies of apparent tactual movement. In D. R. Kenshalo (Ed.), *The skin senses* (pp. 331–344). Springfield, IL: Thomas.

Solomon, H. Y., & Turvey, M. T. (1988). Haptically perceiving the distances reachable with handheld objects. *Journal of Experimental Psychology: Human Perception and Performance, 14,* 404–427.

Stevens, J. C. (1982). Temperature can sharpen tactile acuity. *Perception & Psychophysics, 31,* 577–580.

Stevens, J. C. (1989). Temperature and the two-point threshold. *Somatosensory and Motor Research, 6,* 275–284.

Stevens, J. C. (1992). Aging and spatial acuity of touch. *Journal of Gerontology (Psychological Sciences), 47,* 35–40.

Talbot, W. H., Darian-Smith, I., Kornhuber, H. H., & Mountcastle, V. B. (1968). The sense of flutter-vibration: Comparison of the human capacity with response patterns of mechanoreceptive afferents from the monkey hand. *Journal of Neurophysiology, 31,* 301–334.

Taylor, M. M., & Lederman, S. J. (1975). Tactile roughness of grooved surfaces: A model and the effect of friction. *Perception & Psychophysics, 17,* 23–26.

Treisman, A. M., & Gelade, G. (1980). A feature-integration theory of attention. *Cognitive Psychology, 12,* 97–136.

Treisman, A. M., & Gormican, S. (1988). Feature analysis in early vision: Evidence from search asymmetries. *Psychological Review, 95,* 15–48.

Treitel. (1897). Ueber das Vibrationsgefühl der Haut. *Archiv für Psychiatrie und Nervenkrankheiten, 29,* 633–640.

Turvey, M. T. (1996). Dynamic touch. *American Psychologist, 51,* 1134–1152.

Vallbo, Å. B., & Johansson, R. S. (1978). The tactile sensory innervation of the glabrous skin of the human hand. In G. Gordon (Ed.), *Active touch: The mechanism of recognition of objects by manipulation: A multi-disciplinary approach* (pp. 29–54). Oxford, UK: Pergamon Press.

Vallbo, Å. B., Olsson, K. Å., Westberg, K.-G., & Clark, F. J. (1984). Microstimulation of single tactile afferents from the human hand. *Brain, 107,* 727–749.

Vega-Bermudez, F., Johnson, K. O., & Hsiao, S. S. (1991). Human tactile pattern recognition: Active versus passive touch, velocity effects, and patterns of confusion. *Journal of Neurophysiology, 65,* 531–546.

Verrillo, R. T. (1963). Effect of contactor area on the vibrotactile threshold. *Journal of the Acoustical Society of America, 35,* 1962–1966.

Verrillo, R. T. (1965). Temporal summation in vibrotactile sensitivity. *Journal of the Acoustical Society of America, 37,* 843–846.

Verrillo, R. T. (1966). Vibrotactile sensitivity and the frequency response of the Pacinian corpuscle. *Psychonomic Science, 4,* 135–136.

Verrillo, R. T. (1968). A duplex mechanism of mechanoreception. In D. R. Kenshalo (Ed.), *The skin senses* (pp. 139–156). Springfield, IL: Thomas.

Verrillo, R. T. (1982). Effects of aging on the suprathreshold responses to vibration. *Perception & Psychophysics, 32,* 61–68.

Verrillo, R. T., Fraioli, A. J., & Smith, R. L. (1969). Sensory magnitude of vibrotactile stimuli. *Perception & Psychophysics, 6,* 366–372.

Verrillo, R. T., & Gescheider, G. A. (1977). Effect of prior stimulation on vibrotactile thresholds. *Sensory Processes, 1,* 292–300.

Vierck, C. J., Jr., & Jones, M. B. (1969). Size discrimination on the skin. *Science, 163,* 488–489.

Vierordt, K. (1870). Die Abhängigkeit der Ausbildung des Raumsinnes der Haut von der Beweglichkeit der Körpertheile. *Zeitschrift für Biologie, 6,* 53–72.

von Békésy, G. (1955). Human skin perception of traveling waves similar to those on the cochlea. *Journal of the Acoustical Society of America, 27,* 830–841.

von Békésy, G. (1957a). Neural volleys and the similarity between some sensations produced by tones and by skin vibrations. *Journal of the Acoustical Society of America, 29,* 1059–1069.

von Békésy, G. (1957b). Sensations on the skin similar to directional hearing, beats, and harmonics of the ear. *Journal of the Acoustical Society of America, 29,* 489–501.

von Békésy, G. (1958). Funneling in the nervous system. *Journal of the Acoustical Society of America, 30,* 399–412.

Weber, E. H. (1965). [Excerpt from] Ueber den Raumsinn und die Empfindungskreise in der Haut und im Auge [D. Cantor, Trans.]. In R. J. Herrnstein & E. G. Boring (Eds.), *A source book in the history of psychology* (pp. 140–148). Cambridge, MA: Harvard University Press. (Original work published 1852)

Weber, E. H. (1996). *De subtilitate tactus* ["*De tactu*"; H. E. Ross, Trans.]. In H. E. Ross & D. J. Murray (Eds.), *E. H. Weber on the tactile senses* (2nd ed.) (pp. 21–136). Hove, England: Erlbaum. (Original work published 1834)

Weinstein, S. (1968). Intensive and extensive aspects of tactile sensitivity as a function of body part, sex, and laterality. In D. R. Kenshalo (Ed.), *The skin senses* (pp. 195–222). Springfield, IL: Thomas.

Weisenberger, J. M., & Craig, J. C. (1982). A tactile metacontrast effect. *Perception & Psychophysics, 31,* 530–536.

Whang, K. C., Burton, H., & Shulman, G. L. (1991). Selective attention in vibrotactile tasks: Detecting the presence and absence of amplitude change. *Perception & Psychophysics, 50,* 157–165.

Whitsel, B. L., Franzén, O., Dreyer, D. A., Hollins, M., Young, M., Essick, G. K., & Wong, C. (1986). Dependence of subjective traverse length on velocity of moving tactile stimuli. *Somatosensory Research, 3,* 185–196.

CHAPTER 15

Temperature and Pain Perception

RICHARD H. GRACELY, MICHAEL J. FARRELL, AND MASILO A. B. GRANT

INTRODUCTION

A common homeostatic thread runs through temperature and pain sensation. Thermal and noxious information from the skin and viscera drive reflex and conscious behaviors that are critical for survival. The tolerance of the internal human environment for changes in temperature is extremely limited, and temperature sensation is a pivotal component of homeothermic processes. Acute pain is a compelling impetus for action, and it is ignored at an organism's peril. Pain and temperature sensation also have similar anatomical elements and share many psychophysical attributes. Consequently, it is very appropriate that the perceptions of pain and temperature are discussed in a single forum. This chapter examines first temperature sensation and then pain sensation to provide details of the common and unique features of these experiences.

TEMPERATURE SENSATION

The internal human environment operates optimally within a tight temperature range that is modulated by metabolic, sudomotor (efferent control of sweat glands), vascular, and behavioral responses. Two major sources of temperature information must be monitored to maintain thermal homeostasis: the temperature of

the internal environment and the temperature of the interface between the body and the external environment. The sensation of temperature at the interface between the body and the external environment is an experience served by separate mechanisms depending on the direction of the temperature change. The sensation of coolness and warmth differ in overall sensitivity, and in the relative effects of the extent, temporal profile, and site of stimulation. As described in the next section, the perception of temperature also includes a hedonic dimension of pleasantness or unpleasantness that is determined by inputs from both the skin interface and the body core.

The Temperature Sensation Pathway

Current understanding of the systems mediating temperature sensation is based on anatomical, electrophysiological, behavioral, psychophysical and functional brain imaging evidence. Separate systems monitor cutaneous and internal temperature. Information from the skin and viscera are integrated at a supraspinal level to produce a multidimensional sensory experience.

Electrophysiological recordings from peripheral nerves have revealed two populations of fibers that respond to thermal stimulation of the skin. Both warm and cold fibers respond in similar fashion to respective changes in temperature. Warm fibers have sluggish responses to temperature changes in the range of 29 °C to 40 °C (Darian-Smith et al., 1979). The frequency of discharge of warm fibers increases with increases in stimulus temperature and is directly related to the rate of temperature change (Hallin, Torebjork, & Wiesenfeld, 1982; Hensel & Iggo, 1971; Konietzny & Hensel, 1977). Responses of warm fibers abate as stimulating temperatures approach the noxious range. Cooling also inhibits warm fiber activity (Darian-Smith et al., 1979; Hensel & Iggo, 1971; LaMotte & Campbell, 1978). Likewise, cold fibers demonstrate increasing rates of discharge with falling temperatures (Adriaensen, Gybels, Handwerker, & Van Hees, 1983; Darian-Smith, Johnson, & Dykes, 1973; Hensel & Iggo, 1971; Leem, Willis, & Cheung, 1993; Lynn & Carpenter, 1982). Warming inhibits cold fiber activity. The functional distinction of cool and warm fibers appears to be genuinely dichotomous; there are very few reports of fibers that respond to both increases and decreases of temperature in the innocuous range.

Cold-sensitive cutaneous free nerve endings of Aδ primary afferents terminate in lamina 1 of the dorsal horn of the spinal cord (Christensen & Perl, 1970; Darian-Smith et al., 1973; Johnson, Darian-Smith, & LaMotte, 1973). Warm-sensitive afferents are unmyelinated C fibers. The terminations of warm fibers are inadequately described but, like cold fibers, are probably distributed in lamina 1 of the dorsal horn (Christensen & Perl, 1970; Kumazawa & Perl, 1978). Both cold and warm fibers have spot-like receptive fields (Darian-Smith et al., 1973, 1979; Hallin et al., 1982; Hensel & Iggo, 1971; Konietzny & Hensel, 1977). Warm fibers are much more sparsely distributed than are cold fibers (Adriaensen et al., 1983; Darian-Smith et al., 1973; Davies, Goldsmith, Hellon, & Mitchell, 1983; Lynn & Carpenter, 1982). Second-order neurons responsive to cold and warm stimu-

lation of the skin ascend in the spinothalamic tract (Dostrovsky & Craig, 1996; Kumazawa & Perl, 1978). Thermal stimulation of the skin leads to activation of the ventral-posterior nuclei of the thalamus, cerebellum, somatosensory cortex and insula (Becerra et al., 1999; Berman, Kim, Talati, & Hirsch, 1998; Casey, Minoshima, Morrow, & Koeppe, 1996; Davis, Kwan, Crawley, & Mikulis, 1998; Davis et al., 1999; J. Lee, Dougherty, Antezana, & Lenz, 1999; Lenz et al., 1993). Activation of the insula cortex demonstrates a strong relationship to the magnitude of sensations associated with cooling of the skin (A. D. Craig, Chen, Bandy, & Reiman, 2000).

Temperature-sensitive structures are not confined to the skin. A completely different system subserves internal temperature sensation. Cells in the preoptic anterior hypothalamus (POAH), thalamus, and spinal cord respond to cooling and warming in vitro and in vivo (Boulant, 1998; Hori, Minato, & Kobayashi, 1999; Kobayashi & Takahashi, 1993; Pehl, Simon, & Schmid, 1997; Travis, Bockholt, Zardo-Smith, & Johnson, 1995). Animal studies that manipulate the temperature of these central nervous system structures have implicated their role in shaping both behaviors and autonomic responses that modify internal body temperature (Corbit, 1973; Corbit & Ernits, 1974). Electrophysiological studies of temperature-sensitive central nervous system (CNS) structures have reported more pronounced cell activity after comparable degrees of warming versus cooling (Cabanac & Dib, 1983; Dib & Cabanac, 1984; Klir & Heath, 1994). The pathways through which POAH-mediated effects are realized (suggested) but may be bilateral and modulated by the nucleus raphe magnus caudally (Berner, Grahn, & Heller, 1999; Kanosue, Yanase-Fujiwara, & Hosono, 1994; Kanosue, Zhang, Yanase-Fujiwara, & Hosono, 1994) and via thalamic and prefrontal projections within the cerebrum (Morimoto, Murakami,

& Sakata, 1988; Sakata, Morimoto, & Murakami, 1989; Shibata, Hori, Kiyohara, & Nakashima, 1988).

Temperature Psychophysics

Temperature Detection and Discrimination Thresholds

The discrimination threshold is the smallest change in a stimulus that can be detected. The detection threshold is the case of discrimination in which the smallest amount of stimulus is perceived as compared to its absence. However, thresholds are a measure of sensory acuity, not a quantification of stimulus attributes, and there are circumstances in which no sensation of warm or cold is experienced at the skin under ambient conditions. The absence of any experience of warm or cool is termed *thermal neutrality* and is dependent on adaptation within a restricted temperature range. A thermal stimulus applied within the range of thermal neutrality is perceived initially as a sensation consistent with the valance of the stimulus (Kenshalo, 1970). Over a period of seconds to minutes adaptation occurs, and no sensation of warm or cool is associated with the persisting stimulus. Stimuli that increase or decrease skin temperature beyond the range of thermal neutrality continue to evoke corresponding sensations for as long as the stimulus is applied. Effecting a change of skin temperature outside the range of thermal neutrality does not invariably result in a sensory experience that is consistent with the valence of the stimulus. Progressive increases in temperature of cold skin are reported as a decrease in coolness, then as the onset of thermal neutrality, and finally as the onset, or detection threshold, of warmth. The converse progression of experiences occurs during cooling of warm skin (see Figure 15.1).

Thermal neutrality provides an absence of sensation against which detection thresh-olds can be measured. The bounds of thermal neutrality in Figure 15.1 are represented as 31 °C to 36 °C. More recent studies examining detection thresholds for warm and cold stimuli have adopted a tighter range of baseline temperatures (31.5–35 °C) consistent with current views of thermal neutrality at normal core temperatures (Bartlett, Stewart, Tamblyn, & Abrahamowicz, 1998; Chen, Rainville, & Bushnell, 1996; Claus, Hilz, & Neundorfer, 1990; Gray, Stevens, & Marks, 1982; Hilz, Stemper, Axelrod, Kolodny, & Neundorfer, 1999). The magnitude of detection thresholds reported by studies conforming with a more stringent range of thermal neutrality are invariably smaller for cooling than for warming despite large regional differences across the surface of the skin. Thresholds for temperature increases and decreases can differ by an order of magnitude between areas such as the face and the relatively insensitive feet (Greenspan, Taylor, & McGillis, 1993; J. C. Stevens & Choo, 1998; J. C. Stevens, Marks, & Simonson, 1974). The detection of warm stimuli is remarkably variable within regions. Careful mapping of the thermal sensitivity of the forearm has revealed substantial areas, in excess of 5 cm^2, that lack any appreciation of heat stimuli in the innocuous range (B. G. Green & Cruz, 1998). Detection thresholds in excess of 44 °C have been recorded in these insensitive areas; these values correspond with the activation threshold of some C nociceptors. Warmth-insensitive fields do not differ in cold sensitivity, nor are there substantial within-region differences in cold detection thresholds.

Suprathreshold Stimuli and Temperature Sensation

Suprathreshold ratings behave in a power-function relationship with cutaneous cool and warm stimuli (Marks & Stevens, 1972; Refinetti, 1989; J. C. Stevens et al., 1974). The exponents and intercepts of the equations

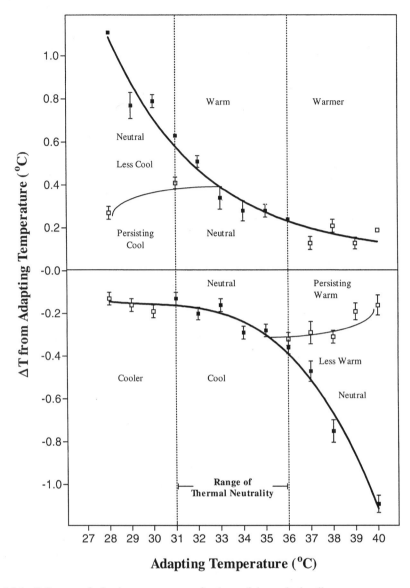

Figure 15.1 Influence of adapting temperature of ratings of thermal stimuli.

NOTE: The stimuli used to evoke the sensations represented in this graph were applied to the forearm with a Peltier thermode. The thermode remained at an adapting temperature for 40 min before brief stimuli (10 s) were administered. Adapting temperatures between 31 °C and 36 °C were considered within the range of thermal neutrality. Closed squares represent values for warm and cool detection thresholds. Under conditions of thermal neutrality, detection of warm or cool represents the onset of a sensation in the absence of any preceding sense of temperature. Closed squares outside the range of thermal neutrality represent the temperature change required to evoke a sensation of opposite polarity to the adapting sensation. The open squares correspond to the magnitudes for discrimination of stimuli evoking sensations of similar quality to the sensation associated with the adapting temperature. At low adapting temperatures, further decreases in temperature are perceived as an increase in coolness (first three open squaress on the left of the graph below 0 °C ΔT). At low adaptation temperatures, initial increases in temperature are perceived as reduction in coolness (first two open squares on left of graph between 0.2 °C and 0.4 °C ΔT). Further increases in temperature result in thermal neutrality before the threshold for detection of warm is exceeded. The converse sequence of sensations results from any fall in temperature from a high adaptation temperature.

SOURCE: Modified from Kenshalo (1971).

describing the relationship between thermal stimuli and ratings vary as a function of polarity and stimulus paradigm. Generally, the sense of cold is more closely bound to stimulus intensity, although both warm and cold sensations demonstrate remarkable variation depending on the spatial and temporal characteristics of stimuli.

Spatial Summation of Warm and Cold Stimuli. Intensity ratings of cold and warm stimuli are dependent to a large degree on the spatial extent of stimuli. Near the threshold for cold and warm, stimulus intensity can be traded for area of stimulation to produce comparable ratings of sensation (Marks & Stevens, 1973; J. C. Stevens & Marks, 1971, 1979). Spatial summation operates almost uniformly across the range of sensory intensity for cold. The exponent of the cold stimulus-response relationship remains constant for different areas of stimulation, averaging 1.07, whereas the intercept increases systematically as the spatial extents of stimuli increase (J. C. Stevens & Marks, 1979). The spatial summation of warmth is most pronounced near threshold and abates as the intensity of sensation increases. As the area of stimulation increases, the exponent of the warm stimulus-response relationship diminishes, ranging from 0.67 at an area of 200 cm^2 to 2.00 at 4.7 cm^2 on the back (J. C. Stevens et al., 1974). Increasing the area of warm stimulation near threshold has a dramatic effect. Radiation of extensive areas of the trunk has resulted in detection thresholds of 0.004 °C for warm stimulation (Hardy & Oppel, 1937). Summation of warmth occurs during stimulation of discontinuous areas and has been reported for stimuli applied to left and right hands (Hardy & Oppel, 1937).

Spatial Discrimination of Warm and Cold Stimuli. The accuracy of thermal stimulus location differs according to valence

in a pattern that reflects the relative effects of spatial summation for warmth and coolness. Localization of warm stimuli is remarkable for its inaccuracy at intensities near threshold. In a pointed illustration of poor warm stimulus location, Cain (1973) cited instances of radiant heat on the trunk that were localized to the ventral or dorsal surface opposite to that of the stimulus. With increasing stimulus intensity, in an inverse relationship to spatial summation, localization of warmth becomes more accurate (Taus, Stevens, & Marks, 1975). Both cold and warm stimuli are localized with greater accuracy across, rather than within, dermatomes (D. K. Lee, McGillis, & Greenspan, 1996). Irrespective of configuration, cold stimuli are invariably localized more reliably than are warm stimuli.

Referral is a feature of temperature sensation. Manipulation of skin temperature at one site on the forearm will provoke sensations under a second stimulator that is held at a neutral temperature. The magnitude of this effect is more pronounced for warming of the skin, although both warming and cooling lead to perceptions of commensurate, albeit smaller, changes in temperature at sites as far as 16 cm proximal to stimulation at the wrist (B. G. Green, 1978). The referral of thermal sensation occurs between fingers and can lead to dominance of one modality when conflicting cooling and warming stimuli are presented to alternate fingers (B. G. Green, 1977). Spatially alternating warm and cool stimulators produces sensations of heat or heat pain in a phenomenon dubbed the *thermal grill effect* (A. D. Craig & Bushnell, 1994). Heat and heat pain are occasionally experienced paradoxically during cooling of the skin (Greenspan et al., 1993; Hamalainen, Vartiainen, Karvanan, & Jarvilento, 1982). Reaction-time measures suggest that paradoxical heat sensations are conveyed by small-diameter C fibers, presumably warm-sensitive, that are disinhibited by a mechanism mediated by the cold sensory system (Susser, Sprecher, & Yarnitsky, 1999).

Temporal Patterns of Response to Warm and Cold Stimuli. The temporal characteristics of thermal stimuli influence the appreciation of warmth and coolness. The detection of changes in skin temperature diminishes as the duration of stimuli fall below 1 s. Psychophysical paradigms that incorporate reaction time tend to produce greater estimates of warm thresholds because of the substantial delays between stimulus and response that are a consequence of the conduction velocity of C fibers (Dyck et al., 1993; Hilz et al., 1999; Pertovaara & Kojo, 1985; Yarnitsky & Ochoa, 1991; Yarnitsky & Sprecher, 1994). Cold detection thresholds are not influenced by stimulus rise rates as much as are warm detection thresholds.

Temperature sensation is subject to adaptation. Sequential ratings of a constant thermal stimulus lessen over periods that differ according to valence, region, and the difference between initial ratings and thermal neutrality. Adaptation is most pronounced for stimuli within the range of thermal neutrality (Kenshalo & Scott, 1966). Adaptation to more extreme temperatures does occur, but not to an extent sufficient to abolish the sense of either warmth or coolness associated with a persistent stimulus.

The Hedonic Dimension of Temperature Sensation

Increases and decreases in skin temperature evoke sensations that can be described in terms of magnitude, locus, and polarity. The perception of temperature also includes a hedonic dimension that arises from the integration of afferent input from the skin and viscera. Sensations of warmth and coolness are associated with feelings of pleasantness and unpleasantness (Cabanac, 1992). The valence of these feelings is dependent on the current homeostatic need. As core temperature increases, cooling of the skin becomes more pleasant, and warming of the skin becomes more unpleasant, whereas a fall in core temperature is associated with converse appraisals of the affective quality of cooling and warming (Attia & Engel, 1981; Cabanac, 1969; Marks & Gonzalez, 1974; Mower, 1976). Under conditions of a neutral core temperature, thermal stimulation of the skin is perceived as either neutral or unpleasant depending on the magnitude of the stimulus (see Figure 15.2). Thus, the hedonic dimension of temperature acts as an index of homeothermic integrity. This is in contrast to ratings of the intensity of skin warmth or coolness that remain stable as core temperature fluctuates (Mower, 1976). Input from internal temperature–sensitive structures to feelings of pleasantness and unpleasantness is the sole contribution of visceral afferents to the sensation of temperature.

Feelings of pleasure or discomfort associated with temperature sensation provide the impetus for behaviors that are compatible with the restoration of homeostasis. Many behaviors including choice of clothing, adjusting the temperature of a shower, fanning the face, moving vigorously, or reducing activity are motivated by the hedonic of temperature sensation (Jeong & Tokura, 1993; Kim & Tokura, 1994; Ohnaka, Tochihara, & Watanabe, 1994; Shoemaker & Refinetti, 1996). When provided with the opportunity, animals will directly heat or cool their hypothalamus under conditions of hypothermia or hyperthermia, respectively (Corbit, 1973; Corbit & Ernits, 1974). Behaviors that maximize thermal pleasure and attenuate thermal unpleasantness are generally rewarded with the achievement of neutrality.

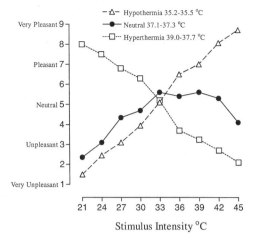

Figure 15.2 Ratings of thermal unpleasantness during varying core temperatures.
NOTE: Icons in this graph represent mean ratings of thermal pleasantness at different stimulus temperatures. The three groups of ratings were collected under conditions of hypothermia, neutral core temperature, and hyperthermia. Subjects immersed their right hands in an adapting bath in excess of 10 min until they experienced the absence of either warm or cool sensations. The stimuli consisted of immersion in a second bath for 3 s before the hand was returned to the adapting bath. Stimuli were rated for intensity and unpleasantness. Core temperature had no effect on intensity ratings (for results, see Mower, 1976). Unpleasantness ratings were strongly related to core temperature. During hypothermia cool stimuli were unpleasant, and warm stimuli were pleasant. The converse relationship was apparent for hyperthermia. At a neutral core temperature, extreme stimuli of either valence were rated as unpleasant, and mid-range stimuli were described as neutral.
SOURCE: Modified from Mower (1976).

Conclusion

Fluctuations in the temperature of the external environment are monitored by the somesthetic temperature sense with differential acuity depending on the valence of temperature change. The sense of cool is more acute and behaves more predictably across variable stimulus conditions than does the sense of warm. The sense of a fall or rise in skin temperature is occasionally subject to distortions but is not systematically affected by core temperature. The compatibility of skin temperature with the maintenance of thermal homeostasis shapes the hedonic dimension of temperature sensation. Feelings of pleasantness and unpleasantness associated with the sense of temperature are a powerful impetus for behaviors that restore and maintain thermal homeostasis.

PAIN

There is much about pain that is shared with other sensory experiences. Indeed, a defining quality of pain, unpleasantness, is an important attribute of other sensations, including thirst, hunger, and temperature. It is the plasticity of responses that makes pain unique. Plasticity is not confined to pain; many sensations exhibit a range of responses to similar stimuli under variable temporal and spatial conditions. What is remarkable about pain is the extent to which the stimulus-response function can vary across time and space. Under some conditions pain is absent following major injury, whereas in other circumstances brushing the skin with cotton thread can provoke excruciating pain. Perceptual localization can bear little, if any, relationship to the site of stimuli, and the mere expectation of pain can provoke commensurate sensory experiences. The current definition of pain acknowledges that stimulus and response are associative at best and incorporates the possibility of sensation in the absence of stimulation: "An unpleasant sensory and emotional experience associated with actual or potential tissue damage, or described in terms of such damage" (Merskey & Bogduk, 1994, p. 210).

The complex neural architecture of the pain system permits significant modulation at each synapse in the afferent nervous system. Peripheral efferent actions, local modulating circuits, descending excitatory and inhibitory pathways, and extensive supraspinal networks characterize the anatomy and physiology of the pain system. Estimates of pain magnitude may be reliably reported during stable physiological and environmental conditions. However, many extraneous factors induce plasticity of pain responses. The passage of time is possibly the most important factor in the association between stimuli and pain.

The Pain Pathway

Tissue damage or impending damage activates *nociceptors*. Nociceptors do not demonstrate morphological specialization but consist exclusively of free nerve endings. The receptive fields of nociceptors are more variable than are warm and cold receptors, ranging from spot-like fields to complex areas exceeding 300 mm^2 (Olausson, 1998; Schmidt, Schmelz, Ringhamp, Handwerker, & Torebjork, 1997; Treede, Meyer, & Campbell, 1990). Fibers with free nerve endings that respond to noxious stimuli are small-diameter myelinated Aδ and unmyelinated C-fiber primary afferents (Hallin & Torebjork, 1973).

Nociceptive afferents can be classified functionally according to responses to different stimulus modalities. The majority of nociceptive C-afferents are activated by intense mechanical and heat stimuli (CMH fibers; Raja, Meyer, Ringkamp, & Campbell, 1999). Many of this phenotypic subgroup respond also to cold and chemical stimuli, prompting the label "polymodal." Nociceptive C-afferents with preferential responses to single stimulus modalities have been identified (Schmidt et al., 1995). Extensive search techniques have also revealed C as well as some Aδ afferents that are not activated by noxious stimuli under physiological conditions (Meyer, Davis, Cohen, Treede, & Campbell, 1991). These mechanically insen-sitive afferents play a role in nociception following tissue damage. The population of Aδ nociceptive afferents consists of two major functional groups. The majority of myelinated nociceptive fibers are classified as high-threshold mechanoreceptors (Treede, Meyer, Raha, & Campbell, 1992). These fibers can be activated also by very intense thermal stimuli (53 °C) and become thermally sensitive following injury, and they have been dubbed A-fiber mechano-heat nociceptors (AMHs; Burgess & Perl, 1967; Fitzgerald & Lynn, 1977; Perl, 1968; Treede, Meyer, & Campbell, 1998). A second subgroup of AMH fibers (type 2) are rapidly activated by thermal stimuli (Bromm & Treede, 1987). Both type 1 and type 2 AMH fibers are activated by intense cold stimuli (<0 °C; Simone & Kajander, 1997).

The cell bodies of nociceptive afferents are in the dorsal root ganglia. Proximal axons of nociceptive afferents synapse onto second-order projection neurons in characteristic layers of the substantia gelatinosa of the spinal cord and homologous structures in the trigeminal system in the brain stem. Spinal cord neurons receiving nociceptive input exhibit two distinct functional profiles (Price & Dubner, 1977). Under physiological conditions, nociceptive-specific (NS) cells are activated exclusively by Aδ and C nociceptive afferents. Wide dynamic range (WDR) dorsal horn neurons receive input from a variety of afferent fibers, including nociceptive fibers, and consequently have much lower thresholds for activation. Both NS and WDR neurons are subject to considerable modulation from local and descending circuits (Doubell, Mannion, & Woolf, 1999).

In common with temperature sensation, nociceptive information projects to supraspinal structures via the contralateral spinothalamic tract (Willis, 1989). However, projections from WDR and NS neurons are not confined to the spinothalamic pathway.

Nociceptive information also ascends in the spinoreticular, spinohypothalamic and spinopontoamygdaloid pathways (Guilbaud, Bernard, & Besson, 1994). Supraspinal processing of pain occurs in a widely distributed network. Different components of this network may be associated with individual components of the pain experience. Many of investigations of the neuroanatomical correlates of nociception focus on the distinction between the sensory/discriminative and motivational/affective domains of the pain experience. Pain discrimination encompasses localization, magnitude estimation, and qualitative appraisal. The motivational/affective component of pain includes the primary hedonic quality of the experience as well as arousal and secondary affective responses. Secondary pain affect refers to emotional responses associated with persistent pain that stem from appraisal of the meaning and implications of the experience. The planning and execution of motor responses is an important consequence of pain that falls outside the sensory/discriminative, motivational/affective schema.

The evidence to date indicates that the sensory/discriminative component of pain is subserved by the "lateral" pain system (for reviews, see Treede, Apkarian, Bromm, Greenspan, & Lenz, 2000; Treede, Kenshalo, Gracely, & Jones, 1999). Spinothalamic projections terminate among lateral thalamic nuclei, including the ventral posterior lateral nucleus, ventral posterior medial nucleus, ventral posterior inferior nucleus, and the posterior part of the ventromedial nucleus (VMpo). Neurons within the lateral thalamus relay nociceptive input to the somatosensory cortices (SI, SII). The insula receives projections from VMpo and corticocortical connections with SI and SII through the posterior parietal complex. However, as noted below, the laterally located insula may also participate in the processing of affec-

tive/motivational dimension of pain experience. Lesions incorporating the lateral thalamus or the somatosensory cortices lead to impairments of pain identification and localization (Bassetti, Bogousslavsky, & Regali, 1993; Greenspan, Joy, McGillis, Checkosky, & Bolanowski, 1997; Greenspan, Lee, & Lenz, 1999). Functional brain imaging has revealed relationships between pain intensity and activity in the elements of the lateral pain system that further support the role of these structures in pain discrimination (Coghill, Sang, Maisog, & Iadarola, 1999).

Medial cortical and subcortical structures have been implicated in the processing of the hedonic dimension of pain (see Price, 2000, for a review). Medial thalamic nuclei, including the centrolateral nucleus, ventrocaudal part of the medial dorsal nucleus, and the parafascicular nucleus, receive input from the spinothalamic tract that is subsequently relayed to the anterior cingulate cortex, notably Brodmann area 24. The insula also receives projections from medial thalamic nuclei. Excluding the spinothalamic tract, ascending pathways project directly to the reticular activating system, hypothalamus, and amygdala. The prefrontal cortex receives input from the amygdala and has reciprocal connections with the anterior cingulate. The contemporaneous autonomic activation, arousal, and fear associated with the onset of pain is most probably a function of the direct connections between the dorsal horn and reticular and limbic terminations of the spinoreticular, spinohypothalamic, and spinopontoamygdaloid pathways. Clinical treatments suggest that the anterior cingulate plays a critical role in this system. The preservation of pain sensation and abolition of affective distress associated with noxious stimuli has been observed subsequent to frontal lobotomy; this effect is attributed to transection of the cingulum (Foltz & White, 1962). Indeed, surgical cingulotomy continues to be advocated as a treatment for intractable pain (Pillay & Hassenbusch, 1992). Functional brain images generated under experimental conditions of similar pain intensity and disparate pain unpleasantness—achieved either with hypnotic suggestion or thermal stimuli of different duration—have provided further support for the anterior cingulate as a critical component of the network responsible for pain unpleasantness (Rainville, Duncan, Price, Carrier, & Bushnell, 1997; Tolle et al., 1999). The anterior insula also appears to be important for the experience of pain unpleasantness. Lesions of the insula produce marked reductions in withdraw responses and emotional responses to painful stimuli despite the absence of primary sensory deficits (Berthier, Starkstein, & Leiguarda, 1988).

The neuroanatomical correlates of motor responses associated with pain are frequently identified in the context of functional brain imaging studies involving noxious stimuli (Coghill et al., 1999). Supraspinal activations attributed to painful stimulation include the supplementary motor cortex, lenticular nuclei, and cerebellum. The contribution of supraspinal components of the motor system to the experience of pain has not been subject to empirical study to date.

The pain system is not confined to ascending pathways. Activity from supraspinal sites descends to influence processing at the spinal connection between primary afferents and the ascending projection system, forming a feedback loop between the brain and spinal processing systems (Dubner & Ren, 1999).

Under conditions of tissue injury, propagation of potentials along nociceptive primary afferents in a proximal to distal direction (antidromic activity) results in the release of vasoactive substances from nociceptor terminals that contribute to inflammation (Rossi & Johansson, 1998). Dorsal horn circuitry modulates antidromic nociceptor activity and neurogenic inflammation (Willis, 1999). This peripheral efferent pathway of the pain system constitutes the final link in an integrated network that is capable of intrinsic modulation and manipulation of the extrinsic factors (e.g., inflammatory mediators) that precipitate and maintain nociceptive activity.

Pain Experience

Duration significantly influences the experience and expression of pain. A natural history of pain incorporating immediate, secondary, and tertiary phases, articulated by Descartes (1664) over 300 years ago, has continuing relevance for the phenomenology of pain. Pain provoked by potentially injurious stimulation is a warning signal indicating that tissue damage is imminent or in progress. This signal quickly elicits feelings of aversion and both conscious and reflex behaviors of withdrawal and escape from harm. Actions associated with the immediate phase of pain reduce the risk of tissue damage and the persistence of pain. If these injury-avoidance actions fail, the organism experiences a secondary stage characterized by agitation and the search for relief. In the event that relief is not forthcoming, tertiary pain is a period during which recovery is facilitated by protection and immobilization of the injured area.

Subtle semantic issues differentiate Descartes's model and contemporary descriptions of pain duration used in empirical studies and the clinic. Brief (milliseconds to seconds) noxious stimuli are referred to as phasic, and stimuli that persist for seconds to minutes are referred to as tonic. In most instances noxious phasic and tonic stimuli do not produce tissue damage. These stimuli are analogous to the immediate stage of pain. Experimental models of prolonged pain in animals are usually injurious, resolving within minutes to hours (acute pain) or persisting for days to weeks (chronic pain). Strategies such as administration of algesic substances (chemicals that cause pain and inflammation) and of excessive levels of exercise using heavy weights have been used to produce durable pain in humans (Breus, O'Connor, & Ragan, 2000; LaMotte, Shain, Simone, & Tsai, 1991). The temporal distinction between acute and chronic pain in experimental models differs from the clinical situation in humans, in which acute pain is a function of normal healing time (weeks) and pain continuing after the resolution of injury is considered chronic (months; Bonica, 1977). Experimental phasic and tonic pains are also occasionally described as acute.

The duration of noxious stimuli influences the nature of experimental paradigms that explore pain sensation. Phasic and tonic stimuli are readily assessed by psychophysical studies of human pain perception under physiological conditions. The phenomenology of persistent pain is commonly assessed with models of tissue inflammation. Sensory testing with phasic and tonic stimuli is used to characterize stimulus-response changes associated with tissue inflammation. The consequences of noxious stimulation can be evaluated by self-report in humans and by behavioral and physiological measures in humans and animals.

Human Report: Pain Psychophysics

Most modalities capable of evoking pain sensation produce a nonpainful sensation at low stimulus intensities. Unlike sensory detection thresholds that involve a decision about the presence or absence of a sensation, pain thresholds involve a decision about the quality of the evoked sensation. Establishing the very presence of pain depends on the human ability to describe conscious experience. All other measures in animal and man infer this presence. Proponents of behavioral or physiological measures argue with some validity that verbal report is simply another behavior with similar problems of interpretation

(Craig & Prkachin, 1983). However, the case for primacy of self-report is compelling. Pain is defined by subjective experience, and nonverbal measures are validated, when possible, by correlating them to verbal report. The importance of subjective report is not just a topic of academic debate; it is also based on medical ethics. Pain is a significant clinical problem—a major reason for seeking medical care. Health care providers making decisions about analgesic doses might prefer the objectivity of a notional pain meter versus a patient's subjective appraisal. Readers need only place themselves within the perspective of the patient to appreciate that pain is a personal experience. Consider the scenario of awaking during the night in a hospital with severe pain, and one's requests for analgesics are denied because an attached medical device indicates an absence of pain! Verbal report of self-experience must be considered the yardstick by which all other measures of pain are compared (Gracely, 1990).

Though primary, verbal reports are also pliable. A change in reported pain can represent an actual change in pain sensation, a change in labeling behavior, or a combination of these effects. The evaluation of pain and the influence of labeling behavior, or response bias, has been controversial, focusing considerable attention on the problems of pain assessment. Part of the controversy has centered on the use of psychophysical methods—such as sensory decision theory (SDT)—that independently assesses sensory sensitivity and response bias (Chapman, 1977; Clark & Yang, 1983). The current consensus is that SDT is a powerful tool but that the parameters cannot be automatically interpreted in terms of pain sensitivity and pain response criterion (Coppola & Gracely, 1983; Rollman, 1977). These issues are most appropriately addressed by experimental designs that either control the factors that are assumed to influence the response criterion or deliberately manipulate these factors to assess the influence of extraneous effects.

The clinical relevance of pain leads to an additional difference between pain and other sensory modalities. Sensory psychophysics is usually concerned with the relative difference between stimuli. The common variable of interest in ratio scaling is the slope of the psychophysical function, the rate at which sensation grows as stimulus intensity is increased. The intercept or absolute height of the psychophysical function is evaluated in some models, but the result is either ignored or purposefully rendered meaningless (S. S. Stevens, 1975). In contrast, the absolute magnitude of a pain sensation is usually the most important variable in a human study. An experiment evaluating the effect of an analgesic may reduce this absolute magnitude with little change in the slope or in the relative differences between stimuli-evoked sensations.

The Pain Threshold

The pain threshold is assessed by standard psychophysical methods. In some cases the methods must be modified to avoid excessive pain stimulation. For example, the classic *method of limits* is usually modified to present only ascending series (Gracely & Naliboff, 1996). Choice of a method is a compromise between increasing precision and minimizing discomfort. Simple methods are often adequate for the detection of dramatic changes found in the clinic. When greater precision is needed, methods are chosen that minimize bias and discomfort. Several titration methods achieve this objective through the use of interactive algorithms that base the intensity of a stimulus on the subject's previous behavior (Gracely, Lota, Walter, & Dubner, 1988). These methods have the advantage of presenting stimuli near pain threshold, avoiding excessively painful stimulation and efficiently calculating a threshold with the minimum number of trials.

The measurement of pain threshold is brief and easily performed and inflicts minimal discomfort. However, the information gained from the pain threshold is limited to sensitivity at the bottom of the pain range and may not predict suprathreshold sensitivity. In addition, determination of the pain threshold may be more vulnerable to psychological factors and other sources of response bias (Gracely & Naliboff, 1996).

Suprathreshold Pain Psychophysics

As emphasized in the beginning of this section, focusing on the slope of the stimulus-response function does not address the applied need of measuring absolute pain intensity. However, variations of ratio scaling have been used to approach this difficult goal. Tursky (1976) used S. S. Stevens's scaling methods to quantify category labels, such as mild, moderate, and intense, to assess pain intensity. In a simple application of this method, subjects described the pain intensity produced by experimental stimuli by choosing specific descriptors. The previously determined numbers were substituted for each descriptor and were analyzed. Figure 15.3 shows that this strategy can result in psychophysical functions to painful electrical stimuli that are very similar to those produced by matching the intensity of the pain sensations to a metric response, such as the duration of a button press or the force of a handgrip squeeze. Verbal category scales have also been analyzed by other methods ranging from simple assumptions of equal category intervals to methods that determine scale values based on the ability to discriminate between stimuli (Gracely, 1979; LaMotte & Campbell, 1978; McArthur, Cohen, & Schandler, 1989).

The methods employed by Tursky (1976) and others are based on the concept that choices of meaningful words tend to anchor judgments to an absolute standard. An alternative ratio-scaling method does not use

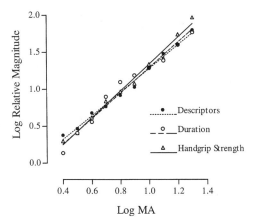

Figure 15.3 Psychophysical functions derived from verbal descriptor scaling and from cross-modality matching to pain evoked by electro-cutaneous stimulation.

NOTE: Log relative magnitude of the intensity of the pain sensations is plotted against log electrical current in milliamperes. For each response, 24 subjects rated the sensations produced by up to 10 stimulus values presented 10 times each in a random sequence. The verbal descriptor function (filled circles, slope 1.6) was derived from choices of 13 words or phrases describing sensory intensity (e.g., weak, moderate, very intense) printed on a single page in a random configuration that did not imply the relative weighting of the respective words. Previously ratio-scaled values for each choice were used for the analysis. Cross-modality matches included duration of a button press (open circles, slope 1.7) and the force of a handgrip squeeze (open triangles, slope 1.8). The theoretical equivalence of these measures is supported by the similar functions shown in the figure.

SOURCE: Modified from Gracely, McGrath, & Dubner (1978).

verbal labels but matches subjective pain intensity directly to the intensity of a separate, nonpainful sensory modality. The method of magnitude matching (J. C. Stevens & Marks, 1980) has demonstrated utility for the absolute measurement of painful heat stimuli using visual brightness as the comparative standard (Duncan, Feine, Bushnell, & Boyer, 1988).

One of the most widely used pain-scaling methods anchors responses to a finite space

symbolizing the full range of possible pain experience. The visual analog scale (VAS) is usually presented as a 10-cm horizontal line labeled at the ends by descriptive phrases such as "no pain" and "worst pain imaginable." Subjects indicate pain magnitude by marking the line. The absence of verbal cues along the continuum of responses removes any prompt for memory in experiments using repeated measures. Measuring pain with line length can be an advantage when literacy is an issue, and it can also be conducive for international studies. VAS scales demonstrate ratio-scaling properties and are sensitive to analgesic agents (Price, McGrath, Rafii, & Buckingham, 1983; Price, Von der Gruen, Miller, Rafii, & Price, 1985). The VAS may be subject to rating biases that are known to influence scales with a limited response space (S. S. Stevens, 1975). Questions also arise regarding the capacity of the VAS to discriminate between different dimensions of pain (Gracely & Naliboff, 1996). However, the influence of the bounded space can be reduced by the use of longer scales (i.e., 15 cm), and rating biases and errors of discrimination can be minimized by the use of careful instructions (Price et al., 1983).

Ratio scaling usually requires that the same stimulus set be delivered to each subject in a group. Fixed stimuli can be problematic among groups with divergent pain sensitivity or in experiments in which sensitivity changes within subjects, such as analgesic studies. The most intense stimuli in a fixed set can potentially cause unacceptable levels of pain in the most sensitive subjects. This problem can be overcome by administering stimuli at equal intervals in subjective space (Gracely, Dubner, & McGrath, 1979). Some methods automatically find subjectively equal stimulus intensities. Adaptive methods use computer technology to continuously adjust stimulus intensity to maintain responses at predefined subjective levels. If a pain threshold is defined as the interval between two subjective responses (no pain, very faint pain), adaptive levels can also find intervals between suprathreshold subjective levels such as mild and moderate or strong and intense. In practice, these methods determine stimulus intensities that correspond to specific threshold- and suprathreshold-level responses in the same session (Gracely et al., 1988). These methods address the problem of differences in individual stimulus ranges, avoiding the administration of a stimulus that is excessively painful for a particular subject. These methods also minimize extraneous cues that an analgesic has been administered. During analgesia these procedures increase the stimulus intensity to maintain the same level of response, minimizing obvious signs of reduced range of sensation and response that occur with conventional methods. Two types of adaptive procedures have been applied to suprathreshold pain assessment. One method determines probabilities of the entire response history (Duncan, Miron, & Parker, 1992). Another adapts Cornsweet's (1962) staircase method to suprathreshold assessment. There is evidence that the probability method produces more stable results whereas the staircase method assesses the time course of analgesic interventions. However, each method can be made to approach the other by changing parameters (Gracely & Naliboff, 1996).

Stimulus Parameters and Pain Responses

Psychophysical procedures have established that pain responses to noxious modalities behave in a predictable manner under normal physiological conditions. Pain thresholds and suprathreshold ratings can be reliably measured within individuals on different occasions for a given modality using a consistent paradigm (Anton, Euchner, & Handwerker, 1992; Janal, Clark, & Carroll, 1991; Nussbaum & Downes, 1998). However, sensitivity to one modality does not usually correlate with sensitivity to other stimulus modalities, either at threshold or at suprathreshold levels (Janal, Glusman, Kuhl, & Clark, 1994). Consequently, pain sensitivity cannot be considered a trait because it does not operate uniformly in an individual across modalities.

In common with temperature sensation, pain responses are affected by the spatial extent of noxious stimuli, although the impact of stimulus parameters varies across modalities. Noxious heat summates spatially to a uniform degree along the stimulus-response function analogous to the behavior of cold sensation (Defrin & Urca, 1996; Nielsen & Arendt-Nielsen, 1997). Mechanical pain summates spatially to only a modest degree at threshold, whereas increasing the area of chemical stimulation of the skin by as much as 15 times does not produce a significant change in pain intensity (Green, 1990; Greenspan, Thomadaki, & McGillis, 1997).

The response to a single noxious stimulus can demonstrate an idiosyncratic temporal profile. Pain following the application of a brief noxious stimulus to an extremity can be experienced as two discrete sensations. A sufficiently noxious stimulus provokes a pricking, well-localized "first pain" that is followed by a diffuse, burning "second pain" (Lewis & Pochin, 1938). The phenomena of first and second pain are the consequence of the different conduction velocities of Aδ and C fibers. Stubbing or burning a toe evokes Aδ-mediated activity that travels up the leg at velocities of about 20 m/s, while the C-fiber-mediated activity travels at only about 1 m/s. Due to the long length of the primary afferents, the Aδ-mediated activity arrives at the spinal cord near a full second before the C-fiber-mediated activity, and the experience of first and second pain are separated by this relatively long time interval. In contrast, the experience of first and second pain occurs almost simultaneously after painful stimulation of the face due to the short primary afferent length.

Pain responses are influenced by the temporal attributes of stimuli. Temporal summation of noxious stimuli is usually assessed with sequential stimuli of fixed duration. The alternative strategy, increasing the duration of a single stimulus across trials, is feasible for some stimulus modalities but can increase the risk of tissue damage. Temporal summation of painful stimuli bears a relationship to frequency that highlights the plasticity of the pain pathway. Electrical or thermal stimuli—of sufficient intensity to activate C fiber nociceptors—delivered at 0.3 Hz to 3 Hz provoke increasingly intense sensations of pain (Price, Hu, Dubner, & Gracely, 1977). Temporal summation tends to plateau after four or five stimuli, peaking at almost twice the intensity of sensation evoked by the initial stimulus (Magerl, Wilk, & Treede, 1998). The quality of pain also changes as the intensity increases; it tends to become exclusively burning second pain. Frequency-dependent temporal summation of pain is presumably due to spinal cord mechanisms. Electrophysiological recordings from primary afferents in humans have established stable or attenuated responses during the course of repeated stimuli (Olausson, 1998; Slugg, Meyer, & Campbell, 2000; Treede et al., 1998). Recordings from cells in the dorsal horn of animals have revealed progressive increases in discharge subsequent to regular nociceptive C-fiber input (Mendell & Wall, 1965). The electrophysiological behavior of spinal cord neurons in animals, referred to as *windup,* is the presumed mechanism of frequency dependent temporal summation of pain in humans.

The reliability of responses to noxious stimuli under consistent testing procedures is testimony to the capacity of individuals to employ an internal subjective standard for the description of pain. However, this standard is subject to considerable modification by environmental and cognitive factors. Attention to, or away, from a painful stimulus influ-ences ratings of sensory intensity (Arntz & de Jong, 1993; Arntz, Dreessen, & DeJong, 1994). The description of an experimental stimulus can also affect responses (Eccleston, 1995). Instruction effects are possibly mediated through their influence on mood state (Crombez, Baeyens, & Eelen, 1994). Levels of fear or anxiety correlate with pain ratings, and manipulation of mood state has been employed with psychophysical paradigms to investigate the affective domain of pain (Rhudy & Meagher, 2000). Psychophysical ratings are also subject to social conditioning. A study of the influence of gender on experimenter-subject interactions found that men rated stimuli as less painful in the presence of a female experimenter (Levine & De Simone, 1991).

The Hedonics of Pain

Pain motivation can be evaluated by the same methods used to assess thermal motivation, though with an important difference. Unlike the thermal senses, which can be either pleasant or unpleasant, pain for most individuals is only unpleasant. Pain intensity and unpleasantness are intertwined and increase together. Discriminating pain intensity from pain unpleasantness is more difficult than is separating pleasantness and unpleasantness from the intensity of innocuous thermal stimuli.

Intensity and unpleasantness have been used interchangeably to describe the experience of pain. The need to define and distinguish these dimensions was emphasized by early laboratory studies of analgesia. For many years, experimenters could not demonstrate any effect of morphine on radiant heat pain thresholds in healthy volunteers. In the classic paper titled "Pain, one mystery solved," Beecher (1966) finally demonstrated morphine analgesia to painful electrical stimulation. Beecher proposed an explanation, in two parts, for the sensitivity of his methods: (a) Electrically evoked pain sensations are

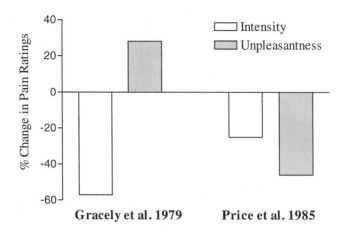

Figure 15.4 Experimental demonstrations of opioid analgesia.
NOTE: This figure shows the analgesic effects reported from two studies of opioid medications. Each bar represents the percentage change in pain rating from pre- to postopioid administration. The histograms on the left show the effects of 1.1 μg/kg fentanyl on verbal descriptor scales of the sensory intensity and unpleasantness of pain evoked by electrical tooth-pulp stimulation. The histograms on the right show the effects of 0.08 mg/kg morphine on visual analog scales of the sensory intensity and unpleasantness of painful heat stimuli. Intensity ratings were reduced significantly in both studies, whereas unpleasantness ratings showed opposite effects.
SOURCE: Modified from Gracely, Dubner, & McGrath (1979) and Price, Von der Gruen, Miller, Rafii, & Price (1985).

accompanied by a significant level of emotional "reaction component," and (b) morphine selectively reduces the reaction component of pain sensation. Previous failures to demonstrate morphine analgesia were attributed to the insufficient reaction component produced by the heat-pain threshold and other methods.

Beecher's studies of morphine analgesia profoundly influenced prevailing thought about narcotic action. Clinical textbooks indicated that opioid analgesia represented a selective reduction of pain unpleasantness, echoed in the clinical phrase, "patients frequently report that the pain is still present but that they feel more comfortable" (Jaffe & Martin, 1975, p. 248). However, subsequent animal evidence suggested that opioid analgesia includes a significant attenuation of the sensory-discriminative aspects of pain sensation (see Mayer & Price, 1976), and this action was supported by human experiments.

Figure 15.4 shows examples of two human studies that used different drugs, stimuli, and measurement methods. Both show that in comparison to placebo, opioid analgesics significantly reduce ratings of the intensity of the evoked pain sensations (Gracely et al., 1979; Price et al., 1985). These results suggest a revision of Beecher's explanation. Opiate analgesia is due in part to a reduction in pain sensation, and Beecher may have failed to show this effect because he measured the pain threshold to radiant heat rather than using more robust methods that administer stimulation throughout the subjective pain range.

Although Beecher's concept of narcotic action has been revised, his emphasis on dual pain dimensions remains an important concept in pain evaluation. Figure 15.4 illustrates conditions under which pain intensity and unpleasantness vary independently. Placebo reduced the unpleasantness of electrical tooth-pulp pain but had no effect on the unpleasantness of heat-pain sensation (Price et al., 1985). In comparison to placebo, the combination of fentanyl and ambulation actually increased pain unpleasantness at the same time that sensory intensity was reduced (Gracely et al., 1979). These results emphasize the importance of separating these two pain dimensions, which are mediated by different neural systems and are likely influenced differentially by analgesic treatments. The different effects of unpleasantness in these studies were likely due to the presence of nausea in the study by Gracely et al. (1979), an effect consistent with clinical observations that administration of opiates may often produce dysphoria in controls and euphoria in patients (Jaffe & Martin, 1975). These results are examples that pain unpleasantness is determined by multiple innate and external factors, some of which are poorly understood.

In practice, ratings of sensory intensity and unpleasantness are often highly correlated, leading to recommendations that these elements be combined into a single overall dimension of pain magnitude (Turk, Rudy, & Salovey, 1985). However, a simple model accommodates both this correlation and the independence of unpleasantness. The unpleasantness system can be modeled as a variable-gain amplifier with sensory intensity as input. The output of the amplifier will obviously be correlated with the input. However, the variable of interest is the gain of the amplifier, not its output. Unpleasantness gain can be computed as the relative ratio or difference between unpleasantness and intensity ratings. A number of studies have used this strategy to demonstrate effects of interventions on unpleasantness gains and of static differences in gain over specific pain syndromes (Gracely et al., 1979; Price, Barrell, & Gracely, 1980; Price & Harkins, 1992; Price, Harkins, & Baker, 1987). Hypnotic analgesia can differentially affect pain intensity and unpleasantness, and studies of functional brain

imaging suggest that instruction to reduce either pain dimension leads to activation of different cerebral regions (Rainville et al., 1997; Rainville, Carrier, Hofbauer, Bushnell, & Duncan, 1999). Pain unpleasantness is an important variable that cannot be ignored in studies of pain mechanisms and pain control.

Pain Hedonics and Pain Emotion

Pain's capacity to provoke an affective response is not confined to the primary feeling state of unpleasantness. Pain also contains a secondary, affective component that involves cognitive appraisal and emotional qualities. This stage encompasses anxiety, fear, and despair. At present, there is no consistent nomenclature, and many terms are used interchangeably to describe primary and secondary components (Gracely, 1992; Price, 2000). The secondary affective component of pain can be evident under experimental conditions during phasic and tonic stimulation. However, secondary affect is most pronounced when pain persists. Altered mood states—notably depression—frequently occur in association with chronic pain (Magni, Marchetti, Moreschi, Merskey, & Luchini, 1993). Redressing maladaptive appraisals of pain and the adoption of cognitive coping strategies are important treatment strategies in cases in which persistent pain has adverse emotional and functional impact (Jensen, Turner, Romano, & Karoly, 1991; Keefe, Dunsmore, & Burnett, 1992).

Persistent Pain and Hyperalgesia

The call to action of acute pain is not always successful. Withdrawal mechanisms are not adequate to avoid all injuries, and they do not protect against the onset of disease. The major burden of pain—and the most keenly investigated aspect of this sensory experience—is in the realm of disease and injury. Ongoing nociceptor activity associated with injury and inflammation has a potent influence on the stimulus-response characteristics of pain sensation. Responses to noxious stimuli at the site of an injury are amplified considerably, and previously innocuous stimuli provoke pain. This up-regulation of pain responses can also be observed at areas surrounding the injury that have not been damaged. Ongoing pain and increased sensitivity after injury initially serve a biological function by facilitating behaviors that are likely to promote tissue repair. Pain at this acute stage serves to protect the injured area by providing a stable environment for maximizing healing. In this stage, pain does not provoke movement; movement provokes pain. However, up-regulation of the pain system can persist after tissue healing and constitutes a major health problem.

The pioneering studies of Lewis and Hardy (Hardy, Wolff, & Goodell, 1950; Lewis, 1936), using a wide range of experimental and clinical models, have inspired a new generation of research incorporating models that minimize the risk of tissue damage. Intradermal injections or topical applications of algesic substances provoke intense local burning pain and erythema (reddening of the skin, or flare) without long-term effects on tissue integrity (Helme & McKernan, 1985; Simone, Baumann, & LaMotte, 1989). Capsaicin is possibly the most widely used agent in models of prolonged pain. The active ingredient of chili peppers, capsaicin is a neurotoxin that acts selectively on nociceptive C-afferents to provoke ongoing discharge and antidromic release of peptides (Jancso, Kiraly, & Jancso-Gabor, 1977; Lembeck & Holzer, 1979).

Ongoing noxious stimulation associated with injection of capsaicin leads to sensory and vascular changes that are characterized according to their proximity to the injection site (see Figure 15.5; LaMotte et al., 1991). The bleb of tissue at the site of infil-tration is analgesic due immediately to possible receptor fatigue following massive release of available neurotransmitters and subsequently to degeneration of nociceptor fibers (Simone, Nolano, Johnson, Wendelschafer-Crabb, & Kennedy, 1998). An irregularly shaped reddening of the skin extending well beyond the bleb is tangible evidence of neurogenic inflammation, a process involving release of vasoactive substances, including substance P and calcitonin gene-related peptide (P. G. Green, Basbaum, & Levine, 1992; Khalil & Helme, 1989), from the terminals of cutaneous nociceptors. Responses to extrinsic stimuli applied around the injected region undergo dramatic changes that persist well after the spontaneous pain has resolved, and mirror results found after clinical injury. Responses to thermal and mechanical stimulation of the skin in proximity to the injection site are notable for a pronounced fall in pain thresholds and increased ratings of suprathreshold stimuli. This primary area is usually slightly smaller than the area of flare. A secondary, larger area surrounding the primary region and extending well beyond the limits of the flare becomes sensitized to mechanical stimulation. The secondary area does not demonstrate any change of responses to thermal stimuli. Mechanical sensitivity in the primary and secondary areas has two distinct functional subtypes. All of the sensitized skin has lowered thresholds and increased suprathreshold ratings to punctate stimuli, a modality that is in the usual domain of noxious stimuli. This effect abates gradually from the infiltration site to the margin of the secondary area, where a sharp distinction marks the return of normal sensitivity (Huang, Ali, Travison, Campbell, & Meyer, 2000). Within the confines of the secondary area is a smaller region that is sensitized to normally innocuous brushing of the skin. A puff of air producing hair follicle movement can be sufficient to elicit this form of mechanical sensi-

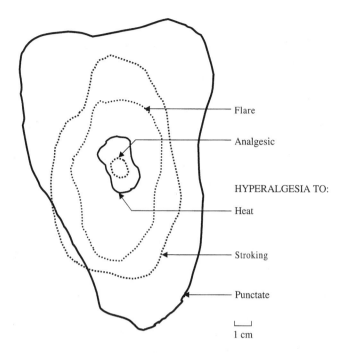

Figure 15.5   Topography of stimulus-response changes following injection of intradermal capsaicin.
NOTE: The lines in this figure represent the perimeters of areas of altered sensitivity after an intradermal injection of capsaicin. The raised bleb at the site of infiltration remains analgesic for long periods (median 22 hr). The area of flare does not correspond with any of the sensory changes. However, thermographic measures usually reveal vascular changes that extend beyond the limits of the visible reddening of the skin. Sensitivity to stroking (allodynia) occupies a smaller area but is not confined by the perimeter of punctate hyperalgesia. A variety of peripheral and central changes explains the different areas of sensitivity (see text for details).
SOURCE: Modified from LaMotte, Shain, Simone, & Tsai (1991).

tivity. Brushing sensitivity tends to be an all-or-nothing response, bearing little relationship to the intensity of stimulation. The phenomenon of increased sensitivity to noxious stimuli is referred to as hyperalgesia, specifically primary hyperalgesia near the injection site (or area of clinical injury) and secondary hyperalgesia outside of the injected (or injured) area. Brush-evoked mechanical sensitivity is called allodynia. The defining quality of allodynia is that pain responses are evoked by stimuli at intensities that do not evoke pain under normal physiological conditions.

Empirical studies have revealed an extensive range of mechanisms that contribute to changes in pain stimulus-response functions in animal and human models of hyperalgesia. Microneurography and psychophysics have evaluated the time course of peripheral changes during the development of hyperalgesia in humans. Ongoing activity in C fibers has been implicated as a major contributor to the burning pain associated with intradermal injections of capsaicin (Culp, Ochoa, Cline, & Dotson, 1989; Koltzenburg, Lundberg, & Torebjork, 1992; Torebjork, Lundberg, & LaMotte, 1992). Under conditions of tissue injury, mechanically insensitive afferents develop spontaneous activity and become sensitized to mechanical and thermal stimuli (Schmidt et al., 1995). These usually "silent nociceptors" may be particularly important for spontaneous pain and mechanical sensitivity in the primary area after tissue damage (Meyer et al., 1991; Schmelz, Schmid, Handwerker, & Torebjork, 2000). Recordings from $A\delta$ and C nociceptive fibers with receptive fields in the area of primary hyperalgesia reveal response changes that parallel increased pain responses to thermal stimuli (Torebjork, LaMotte, & Robinson, 1984). Both C and $A\delta$ nociceptors undergo expansion of receptive fields to mechanical stimulation in proximity to the site of injury, contributing to sensitization through spatial summation (Thalhammer & LaMotte, 1982). The sensitization of nociceptive fibers in the area of primary hyperalgesia is not sufficient to produce activation by brushing of the skin. Microneurographic recordings from nociceptive fibers with receptive fields in the region of secondary hyperalgesia have revealed an absence of any stimulus-response changes following the onset of hyperalgesia (Handwerker & Reeh, 1991; LaMotte, Lundberg, & Torebjork, 1992). Allodynia, and also hyperalgesia to pinprick, in the area of secondary hyperalgesia cannot be explained by peripheral sensitization.

Punctate hyperalgesia in the secondary area is conveyed by nociceptive fibers but is mediated by central sensitization at the level of the spinal cord. Recent evidence implicates type 1 A fiber mechano heat nociceptors as the peripheral afferents responsible for punctate hyperalgesia (Ziegler, Magerl, Meyer, & Treede, 1999).

The peripheral components contributing to allodynia fall outside the usual neuroanatomy of nociception. Microneurography and analgesic blocks have excluded peripheral nociceptors as the neural substrates of allodynia (Koltzenburg et al., 1992; LaMotte et al., 1991; Torebjork et al., 1992). The nature of stimuli evoking allodynia and the reversal of brush-evoked pain by $A\beta$ blockade via ischemia or pressure suggest that low-threshold, rapidly adapting mechanoreceptors are integral to the experience of brush-evoked pain (Gracely, Lynch, & Bennett, 1992). Sensitivity to brushing is presumably due to sensitization of WDR neurons via a heterosynaptic mechanism (Cervero & Laird, 1996). Input to the spinal cord that is usually associated with light touch is misconstrued as pain under conditions of hyperalgesia.

Mechanisms contributing to up-regulation of the pain system are not confined to changes in peripheral nociceptors and dorsal horn neurons. Electrophysiological recordings of supraspinal structures in animal models of inflammatory pain and recent reports of functional brain imaging in humans have identified altered cerebral responses following the development of hyperalgesia (Baron, Baron, Disbrow, & Roberts, 1999; Guilbaud, Benoist, Neil, Kayser, & Gautron, 1987; Iadarola et al., 1998; Vin-Christian, Benoist, Gautron, Levante, & Guilbaud, 1992). Although some of these responses faithfully reflect an increase in ascending input, the quality of changes suggests that additional supraspinal modulation of nociceptive signals are associated with tissue inflammation.

In summary, injury, whether induced by experimental methods, accidental trauma, or disease, dramatically changes the functional attributes of the pain pathway. Peripheral nociceptors become increasingly sensitive to stimuli and release substances that contribute to inflammation. Spinal cord neurons involved in nociception demonstrate amplified responses to noxious input after injury, also responding to low levels of tactile input as if it were arising from nociceptive afferents. Supraspinal structures exhibit patterns of response under conditions of tissue damage that suggest further up-regulation of the pain pathway. Augmented pain responses evoked by injury that persist beyond the time of normal healing are a major cause of suffering. The multiple mechanisms contributing to post injury pain and sensitization are obvious research targets for the development of new analgesic treatments.

Pain Modulation

The Gate Control Theory

In 1965 Wall and Melzack published the gate control theory (Melzack & Wall, 1965), postulating that the pain system does not provide a faithful indication of injurious stimulation. This landmark theory proposed that circuits within the substantia gelatinosa, extending the length of the spinal cord, modulate activity at the synaptic connection between nociceptors and the spinal projection system. According to this model, input from nonnociceptive afferents could "close the gate," inhibiting pain transmission. This mechanism explains the common experience that rubbing an injured area can reduce pain. The theory also postulated that pathways descending from the brain could control this gate. This important mechanism provided a means of reducing the interference of attention-grabbing pain in flight or fight situations. At these times survival is enhanced by temporarily ignoring pain-signaled tissue injury.

Endogenous Opioids and Stimulation-Produced Analgesia

The introduction of the gate control theory was followed by two important, interrelated discoveries. Stimulation of the periaqueductal gray (PAG) area in the midbrain was found to suppress reaction to painful stimuli, although responses to other environmental stimuli remain unaffected (Reynolds, 1969). A few years later, Hughes et al. (1975) isolated the first endogenous opioid-like compound that was found to bind at PAG sites, activating descending pathways that inhibited spinal nociception. Ablating these descending tracts attenuated the analgesia produced by electrical stimulation or opioid infusion of the PAG (Basbaum, Clanton, & Fields, 1976). This finding, combined with the observation that stimulation-produced analgesia was reversed by the narcotic antagonist naloxone (Akil, Mayer, & Liebeskind, 1976) and evidence of cross-tolerance between stimulation-produced analgesia and opioid-administration (Mayer & Hayes, 1975), led to the conclusion that electrical stimulation of PAG recruited a descending inhibitory system that is activated under physiological conditions by internal release of endorphins or external administration of opioids.

Ensuing studies have revealed the complexity of this system. At least three types of opioid receptors—mu (μ), delta (δ) and kappa (κ)—are distributed throughout the central nervous system, including the spinal cord, midbrain, amygdala, medulla, pons, thalamus, and cortex (Kanjhan, 1995). Different opioids have different affinities for these receptors (see Yaksh, 1997, for a review). For example, morphine has affinity for the mu and kappa receptors, whereas nalbuphine has affinity for kappa receptors but blocks activity associated with the mu receptor. Naloxone is an example of an antagonist that binds and blocks activity in both mu and kappa receptors. Endogenous opioid peptides include the group of enkephalins, endorphins, dynorphins, and endomorphins (Fields & Basbaum, 1999).

Intrinsic systems also mediate analgesia independently of the opioid systems. These include the activation of a widespread system of diffuse noxious inhibitory controls (DNIC), systems that evoke localized analgesia (Villanueva & Le Bars, 1995) and cortical attentional mechanisms.

Activation of Endogenous Analgesic Systems

How are these various endogenous analgesic systems activated? The natural conditions of flight or fight are logical candidates, simulated in the laboratory by exposure to numerous experimental stressors. Experimental stress activates neural, endocrine, and behavioral networks that result in cardiovascular arousal and reduced pain sensitivity (McCubbin, 1993). The type of analgesia activated by stress seems to be dependent on the type of stressor used (Lewis, Cannon, & Liebeskind, 1980). In rats, low-severity, intermittent foot shock causes opioid analgesia, whereas high-severity, continuous foot shock produces nonopioid-mediated analgesia. Other stress modalities such as heat withdrawal and swim stress similarly produce both opioid and nonopioid analgesia (Kavaliers, 1987; Mogil, Sternberg, Balian, Liebeskind, & Sadowski, 1996).

Human experiments have shown that laboratory stressors, such as electric foot shock, reduce ratings of painful stimulation (Willer, Dehen, & Cambier, 1981). Anecdotal evidence of analgesia during combat or sports competitions suggests that these situations provide a human analog of natural flight or fight situations in animals. Physical exertion and competitive sports are associated with laboratory analgesia (Koltyn, 2000). The cognitive set of competition may be sufficient to evoke analgesia even in the absence of exertion (Sternberg, Bokat, Alboyadjian, & Gracely, 2001).

Cognitive Factors in Pain Modulation

In addition to human studies of naturalistic stress analgesia, there is substantial interest in the influence of psychological factors such as anxiety, expectation, information, and distraction, and in analgesic states produced by interventions such as acupuncture, hypnosis, and placebo. Studies of these mechanisms provide information about pain mechanisms and the degree to which extraneous, often subtle, factors can influence pain reports. These factors can be a nuisance variable in applied analgesia studies or can constitute valid treatments in their own right. Placebo analgesia provides an excellent example of this group of cognitive interventions because the manipulation and its consequence has been documented in specific experiments and in numerous applied studies of analgesic agents.

The Placebo Effect

Placebo analgesia is a striking example of pain modulation. Belief that one has received a powerful analgesic produces profound relief in some subjects and about half the efficacy of the active drug in group studies (Evans, 1985). The magnitudes of placebo effects are dependent on the context of the delivery; placebo morphine is more powerful than is placebo aspirin. Studies have shown that the color, shape, and number of placebo pills influence effect size (Buckalew & Coffield, 1982). The impact of extraneous factors depends on the patient's expectancy and can be influenced by the clinician's expectancies (Gracely, Dubner, Deeter, & Wolskee, 1985). The placebo effect is not limited to the administration of placebos. The factors that enhance the placebo response may be maximized during active treatments, providing an adjunctive benefit to the therapeutic action of the treatment. This benefit can be substantial; a recent review concluded that the placebo effect in the pharmacological treatment of depression is twice as great as that due to the pharmacological action of the medication (Kirsch & Sapirstein, 1999).

There is a large body of anecdote and literature on the placebo effect that must be interpreted with caution. In many cases the evidence for the efficacy of placebos is not obtained from studies designed to assess this efficacy, and other social, psychological, physiological, and statistical factors may masquerade as a potent placebo effect (Ernst & Resch, 1995; Kienle & Kiene, 1997). Studies designed to assess the mechanisms of placebo analgesia are of considerable interest to academics and clinicians treating patients with intractable pain. Soon after the demonstration of endogenous opioids, a study of placebo analgesia following extraction of third molar teeth found evidence consistent with a mechanism in which administration of a placebo caused the release of endogenous opioids (Levine, Gordon, & Fields, 1978). A subsequent study using a similar design replicated this result (Gracely, Dubner, Wolskee, & Deeter, 1983). However, an additional control group in the latter study showed that the placebo effect occurred when the endorphin receptors were blocked, and this study also suggested that endorphins increased pain regardless of whether placebos were administered. Thus, the placebo effect can occur independently of opioid processes, although these processes may be involved in specific cases of analgesia. Endogenous opioids have been implicated in experimental studies with pain evoked by tourniquet ischemia (Benedetti, 1996; Grevert & Goldstein, 1977), although other studies have implicated cognitive factors of expectation and demonstrated different placebo effects within a single dermatome, an effect that is not likely due to endogenous opioids (Price et al., 1999). The placebo effect is not confined to pain and must be mediated by many effector mechanisms. It seems likely that endogenous opioids play a variable role in placebo analgesia. Given the ubiquitous nature of placebo, the search for common factors that trigger placebo effects is of considerable importance. Expectations of the patient and clinician appear to play an important role (Evans, 1985; Gracely, 2000).

CONCLUSION

Experimental psychology has contributed substantially to contemporary views of temperature and pain sensation. Psychophysics has quantified the accuracy of the body's thermometer and early warning system under stable conditions and during perturbations that challenge homeostasis. The sense of temperature change and the appreciation of noxious stimuli are not remarkable for their accuracy or for the subtle nuances of sensory experience that characterize other senses. Under some conditions, thermal stimuli may fail to evoke a response or elicit a paradoxical sensation. Responses to noxious stimuli can vary considerably depending on psychological context, tissue integrity, and stimulus duration. However, the functional implications of sensations arising from temperature change and noxious stimuli are associated with motivational drive rather than perceptual precision. The hedonic quality of pain and temperature sensation shapes behaviors that maintain integrity of the organism.

REFERENCES

Adriaensen, H., Gybels, J., Handwerker, H. O., & Van Hees, J. (1983). Response properties of thin myelinated (A-delta) fibers in human skin nerves. *Journal of Neurophysiology, 49,* 111–122.

Akil, H., Mayer, D. J., & Liebeskind, J. C. (1976). Antagonism of stimulation-produced analgesia by naloxone, a narcotic antagonist. *Science, 191,* 961–962.

Anton, F., Euchner, I., & Handwerker, H. O. (1992). Psychophysical examination of pain induced by defined CO_2 pulses applied to the nasal mucosa. *Pain, 49,* 53–60.

Arntz, A., & de Jong, P. (1993). Anxiety, attention and pain. *Journal of Psychosomatic Research, 37,* 423–431.

Arntz, A., Dreessen, L., & De Jong, P. (1994). The influence of anxiety on pain: Attentional and attributional mediators. *Pain, 56,* 307–314.

Attia, M., & Engel, P. (1981). Thermal alliesthesial response in man is independent of skin location stimulated. *Physiology and Behavior, 27,* 439–444.

Baron, R., Baron, Y., Disbrow, E., & Roberts, T. P. (1999). Brain processing of capsaicin-induced secondary hyperalgesia: A functional MRI study. *Journal of Neurology, 53,* 548–557.

Bartlett, G., Stewart, J. D., Tamblyn, R., & Abrahamowicz, M. (1998). Normal distributions of thermal and vibration sensory thresholds. *Muscle and Nerve, 21,* 367–374.

Basbaum, A. I., Clanton, C. H., & Fields, H. L. (1976). Opiate and stimulus-produced analgesia: Functional anatomy of a medullospinal pathway. *Proceedings of the National Academy of Sciences of the United States of America, 73,* 4685–4688.

Bassetti, C., Bogousslavsky, J., & Regali, F. (1993). Sensory sydromes in parietal stroke. *Journal of Neurology, 43,* 1942–1949.

Becerra, L. R., Breiter, H. C., Stojanovic, M., Fishman, S., Edwards, A., Comite, A. R., Gonzalez, R. G., & Borsook, D. (1999). Human brain activation under controlled thermal stimulation and habituation to noxious heat: An fMRI study. *Magnetic Resonance in Medicine, 41,* 1044–1057.

Beecher, H. K. (1966). Pain: One mystery solved. *Science, 151,* 840–841.

Benedetti, F. (1996). The opposite effects of the opiate antagonist naloxone and the cholecystokinin antagonist proglumide on placebo analgesia. *Pain, 64,* 535–543.

Berman, H. H., Kim, K. H., Talati, A., & Hirsch, J. (1998). Representation of nociceptive stimuli in primary sensory cortex. *Neuroreport, 9,* 4179–4187.

Berner, N. J., Grahn, D. A., & Heller, H. C. (1999). 8-OH-DPAT-sensitive neurons in the nucleus raphe magnus modulate thermoregulatory output in rats. *Brain Research, 831,* 155–164.

Berthier, M., Starkstein, S., & Leiguarda, R. (1988). Asymbolia for pain: A sensory-limbic disconnection syndrome. *Annals of Neurology, 24,* 41–49.

Bonica, J. J. (1977). Neurophysiologic and pathologic aspects of acute and chronic pain. *Archives of Surgery, 112,* 750–761.

Boulant, J. A. (1998). Hypothalamic neurons: Mechanisms of sensitivity to temperature. *Annals of the New York Academy of Sciences, 856,* 108–115.

Breus, M. J., O'Connor, P. J., & Ragan, S. T. (2000). Muscle pain induced by novel eccentric exercise does not disturb the sleep of normal young men. *Journal of Pain, 1,* 67–76.

Bromm, B., & Treede, R. D. (1987). Human cerebral potentials evoked by CO_2 laser stimuli causing pain. *Experimental Brain Research, 67,* 153–162.

Buckalew, L. W., & Coffield, K. E. (1982). An investigation of drug expectancy as a function of capsule color and size and preparation form. *Journal of Clinical Psychopharmacology, 2,* 245–248.

Burgess, P. R., & Perl, E. R. (1967). Myelinated afferent fibres responding specifically to noxious stimulation of the skin. *Journal of Physiology, 190,* 541–562.

Cabanac, M. (1969). Plaisir ou deplaisir de la sensation thermique et homeothermie. *Physiology and Behavior, 4,* 359–364.

Cabanac, M. (1992). Pleasure: The common currency. *Journal of Theoretical Biology, 155,* 173–200.

Cabanac, M., & Dib, B. (1983). Behavioural responses to hypothalamic cooling and heating in the rat. *Brain Research, 264,* 79–87.

Cain, W. S. (1973). Spatial discrimination of cutaneous warmth. *American Journal of Psychology, 86,* 169–181

Casey, K. L., Minoshima, S., Morrow, T. J., & Koeppe, R. A. (1996). Comparison of human cerebral activation pattern during cutaneous warmth, heat pain, and deep cold pain. *Journal of Neurophysiology, 76,* 571–581.

Cervero, F., & Laird, J. M. (1996). Mechanisms of touch-evoked pain (allodynia): A new model. *Pain, 68,* 13–23.

Chapman, C. R. (1977). Sensory decision theory methods in pain research: A reply to Rollman. *Pain, 3,* 295–305.

Chen, C. C., Rainville, P., & Bushnell, M. C. (1996). Noxious and innocuous cold discrimination in humans: Evidence for separate afferent channels. *Pain, 68,* 33–43.

Christensen, B. N., & Perl, E. R. (1970). Spinal neurons specifically excited by noxious or thermal stimuli: Marginal zone of the dorsal horn. *Journal of Neurophysiology, 33,* 293–307.

Clark, W. C., & Yang, J. C. (1983). Applications of sensory decision theory to problems in laboratory and clinical pain. In R. Melzack (Ed.), *Pain Measurement and Assessment.* New York: Raven Press (pp. 15–25).

Claus, D., Hilz, M. J., & Neundorfer, B. (1990). Thermal discrimination thresholds: A comparison of different methods. *Acta Neurologica Scandinavica, 81,* 533–540.

Coghill, R. C., Sang, C. N., Maisog, J. M., & Iadarola, M. J. (1999). Pain intensity processing within the human brain: A bilateral, distributed mechanism. *Journal of Neurophysiology, 82,* 1934–1943.

Coppola, R., & Gracely, R. H. (1983). Where is the noise in SDT pain assessment? *Pain, 17,* 257–266.

Corbit, J. D. (1973). Voluntary control of hypothalamic temperature. *Journal of Comparative and Physiological Psychology, 83,* 394–411.

Corbit, J. D., & Ernits, T. (1974). Specific preference for hypothalamic cooling. *Journal of Comparative and Physiological Psychology, 86,* 24–27.

Cornsweet, T. N. (1962). The staircase-method in psychophysics. *Journal of Psychology, 75,* 485–491.

Craig, A. D., & Bushnell, M. C. (1994). The thermal grill illusion: Unmasking the burn of cold pain. *Science, 265,* 252–255.

Craig, A. D., Chen, K., Bandy, D., & Reiman, E. M. (2000). Thermosensory activation of insular cortex. *Nature Neuroscience, 3,* 184–190.

Craig, K. D., & Prkachin, K. M. (1983). Nonverbal measures of pain. In R. Melzack (Ed.), *Pain Measurement and Assessment* (pp. 173–179). New York: Raven Press.

Crombez, G., Baeyens, F., & Eelen, P. (1994). Sensory and temporal information about impending pain: The influence of predictability on pain. *Behaviour Research and Therapy, 32,* 611–622.

Culp, W. J., Ochoa, J., Cline, M., & Dotson, R. (1989). Heat and mechanical hyperalgesia induced by capsaicin: Cross modality threshold modulation in human C nociceptors. *Brain, 112,* 1317–1331.

Darian-Smith, I., Johnson, K. O., & Dykes, R. (1973). "Cold" fiber population innervating palmar and digital skin of the monkey: Responses to cooling pulses. *Journal of Neurophysiology, 36,* 325–346.

Darian-Smith, I., Johnson, K. O., LaMotte, C., Shigenaga, Y., Kenins, P., & Champness, P. (1979). Warm fibers innervating palmar and digital skin of the monkey: Responses to thermal stimuli. *Journal of Neurophysiology, 42,* 1297–1315.

Davies, S. N., Goldsmith, G. E., Hellon, R. F., & Mitchell, D. (1983). Facial sensitivity to rates of temperature change: Neurophysiological and psychophysical evidence from cats and humans. *Journal of Physiology, 344,* 161–175.

Davis, K. D., Kwan, C. L., Crawley, A. P., & Mikulis, D. J. (1998). Functional MRI study of thalamic and cortical activations evoked by cutaneous heat, cold, and tactile stimuli. *Journal of Neurophysiology, 80,* 1533–1546.

Davis, K. D., Lozano, R. M., Manduch, M., Tasker, R. R., Kiss, Z. H., & Dostrovsky, J. O. (1999). Thalamic relay site for cold perception in humans. *Journal of Neurophysiology, 81,* 1970–1973.

Defrin, R., & Urca, G. (1996). Spatial summation of heat pain: A reassessment. *Pain, 66,* 23–29.

Descartes, R. (1664). *L'homme.* Paris: Angot.

Dib, B., & Cabanac, M. (1984). Skin or hypothalamus cooling: A behavioral choice by rats. *Brain Research, 302,* 1–7.

Dostrovsky, J. O., & Craig, A. D. (1996). Cooling-specific spinothalamic neurons in the monkey. *Journal of Neurophysiology, 76,* 3656–3665.

Doubell, T. P., Mannion, R. J., & Woolf, C. J. (1999). The dorsal horn: State-dependent sensory processing plasticity and the generation of pain. In P. D. Wall & R. Melzack (Eds.), *Textbook of pain* (pp. 165–182). Edinburgh, England: Livingstone.

Dubner, R., & Ren, K. (1999). Endogenous mechanisms of sensory modulation. *Pain* (Suppl. 6), 45–53.

Duncan, G. H., Feine, J. S., Bushnell, M. C., & Boyer, M. (1988). Use of magnitude matching for measuring group differences in pain perception. In R. Dubner, G. F. Gebhart, & M. R. Bond (Eds.), *Proceedings of the 5th World Congress on Pain, 3* (383–390). Seattle: Elsevier.

Duncan, G. H., Miron, D., & Parker, S. R. (1992). Yet another adaptive scheme for tracking thresholds. *Annual Meeting of the International Society for Psychophysics, 8,* 1–5.

Dyck, P. J., Zimmerman, I., Gillen, D. A., Johnson, D., Karnes, J. L., & O'Brien, P. C. (1993). Cool, warm, and heat-pain detection thresholds: Testing methods and inferences about anatomic distribution of receptors. *Neurology, 43,* 1500–1508.

Eccleston, C. (1995). The attentional control of pain: Methodological and theoretical concerns. *Pain, 63,* 3–10.

Ernst, E., & Resch, K. L. (1995). Concept of true and perceived placebo effects. *BMJ, 311,* 551–553.

Evans, F. J. (1985). Expectancy, therapeutic instructions, and the placebo response. In B. Tursky & G. E. Schwartz (Eds.), *Placebo: Theory, research and mechanisms* (pp. 215–228). New York: Guilford Press.

Fields, H. L., & Basbaum, A. I. (1999). Central nervous system mechanisms of pain modulation. In P. D. Wall & R. Melzack (Eds.), *Textbook of pain* (pp. 309–329). Edinburgh, England: Livingstone.

Fitzgerald, M., & Lynn, B. (1977). The sensitization of high threshold mechanoreceptors with myelinated axons by repeated heating. *Journal of Physiology, 265,* 549–63.

Foltz, E. L., & White, L. E. J. (1962). Pain relief by frontal cingulotomy. *Journal of Neurosurgery, 19,* 89–100.

Gracely, R. H. (1979). Psychophysical assessment of human pain. In J. J. Bonica (Ed.), *Advances in Pain Research and Therapy: Vol. 3* (pp. 805–824). New York: Raven Press.

Gracely, R. H. (1990). Pain psychophysics. In C. R. Chapman & J. D. Loeser (Eds.), *The measurement of pain* (pp. 211–229). New York: Raven Press.

Gracely, R. H. (1992). Affective dimensions of pain: How many and how measured? *APS Journal, 1,* 243–247.

Gracely, R. H. (2000). Charisma and the art of healing: Can nonspecific factors be enough? In M. Devor, M. C. Rowbotham, & Z. Wiensenfeld-Hallin (Eds.), *Proceedings of the 9th World Congress on Pain, 16,* 1045–1067.

Gracely, R. H., Dubner, R., Deeter, W. R., & Wolskee, P. J. (1985). Clinicians' expectations influence placebo analgesia. *Lancet, 1,* 43.

Gracely, R. H., Dubner, R., & McGrath, P. A. (1979). Narcotic analgesia: Fentanyl reduces the intensity but not the unpleasantness of painful tooth pulp sensations. *Science, 203,* 1261–1263.

Gracely, R. H., Dubner, R., Wolskee, P. J., & Deeter, W. R. (1983). Placebo and naloxone can alter post-surgical pain by separate mechanisms. *Nature, 306,* 264–265.

Gracely, R. H., Lota, L., Walter, D. J., & Dubner, R. (1988). A multiple random staircase method of psychophysical pain assessment. *Pain, 32,* 55–63.

Gracely, R. H., Lynch, S. A., & Bennett, G. J. (1992). Painful neuropathy: Altered central processing maintained dynamically by peripheral input. *Pain, 51,* 175–194.

Gracely, R. H., McGrath, F., & Dubner, R. (1978). Ratio scales of sensory and affective verbal pain descriptors. *Pain, 5,* 5–18.

Gracely, R. H., & Naliboff, B. D. (1996). Measurement of pain sensation. In L. Kruger (Ed.), *Pain and touch* (pp. 243–313). San Diego: Academic Press.

Gray, L., Stevens, J. C., & Marks, L. E. (1982). Thermal stimulus thresholds: Sources of variability. *Physiology and Behavior, 29,* 355–360.

Green, B. G. (1977). Localization and thermal sensation: An illusion and synthetic heat. *Perception and Psychophysics, 22,* 331–337.

Green, B. G. (1978). Referred thermal sensations: Warmth versus cold. *Sensory Processes, 2,* 220–230.

Green, B. G. (1990). Spatial summation of chemical irritation and itch produced by topical application of capsaicin. *Perception and Psychophysics, 48,* 12–18.

Green, B. G., & Cruz, A. (1998). "Warmth-insensitive fields": Evidence of sparse and irregular innervation of human skin by the warmth sense. *Somatosensory and Motor Research, 15,* 269–275.

Green, P. G., Basbaum, A. I., & Levine, J. D. (1992). Sensory neuropeptide interactions in the production of plasma extravasation in the rat. *Neuroscience, 50,* 745–749.

Greenspan, J. D., Joy, S. E., McGillis, S. L. B., Checkosky, C. M., & Bolanowski, S. J. (1997). A longitudinal study of somethetic perceptual disorders in an individual with a unilateral thalamic infarct. *Pain, 72,* 13–25.

Greenspan, J. D., Lee, R. R., & Lenz, F. A. (1999). Pain sensitivity alterations as a function of lesion location in the parasylvian cortex. *Pain, 81,* 273–282.

Greenspan, J. D., Taylor, D. J., & McGillis, S. L. (1993). Body site variation of cool perception thresholds, with observations on paradoxical heat. *Somatosensory and Motor Research, 10,* 467–474.

Greenspan, J. D., Thomadaki, M., & McGillis, S. L. (1997). Spatial summation of perceived pressure, sharpness and mechanically evoked cutaneous pain. *Somatosensory and Motor Research, 14,* 107–112.

Grevert, P., & Goldstein, A. (1977). Effects of naloxone on experimentally induced ischemic pain and on mood in human subjects. *Proceedings of the National Academy of Sciences of the United States of America, 74,* 1291–1294.

Guilbaud, G., Benoist, J. M., Neil, A., Kayser, V., & Gautron, M. (1987). Neuronal response thresholds to and encoding of thermal stimuli during carrageenin-hyperalgesic-inflammation in the ventro-basal thalamus of the rat. *Experimental Brain Research, 66,* 421–431.

Guilbaud, G., Bernard, J. F., & Besson, J. M. (1994). Brain areas involved in nociception and pain. In P. D. Wall & R. Melzack (Eds.), *Textbook of pain* (pp. 113–128). Edinburgh, England: Livingstone.

Hallin, R. G., & Torebjork, H. E. (1973). Electrically induced A and C fiber responses in intact human skin nerves. *Experimental Brain Research, 16,* 309–320.

Hallin, R. G., Torebjork, H. E., & Wiesenfeld, Z. (1982). Nociceptors and warm receptors innervated by C fibres in human skin. *Journal of Neurology, Neurosurgery and Psychiatry, 45,* 313–319.

Hamalainen, H., Vartiainen, M., Karvanen, L., & Jarvilehto, T. (1982). Paradoxical heat sensations during moderate cooling of the skin. *Brain Research, 251,* 77–81.

Handwerker, H. O., & Reeh, P. W. (1991). Pain and inflammation. In M. R. Bond, J. E. Charlton, & C. J. Woolf (Eds.), *Proceedings of the Sixth World Congress on Pain* (pp. 59–70). Amsterdam: Elsevier.

Hardy, J. D., & Oppel, T. W. (1937). Studies in temperature sensation: III. The sensitivity of the body to heat and spatial summation of the end-organ responses. *Journal of Clinical Investigation, 16,* 533–540.

Hardy, J. D., Wolff, H. C., & Goodell, H. (1950). Experimental evidence on the nature of cutaneous hyperalgesia. *Journal of Clinical Investigation, 29,* 115–140.

Helme, R. D., & McKernan, S. (1985). Neurogenic flare responses following topical application of capsaicin in humans. *Annals of Neurology, 18,* 505–509.

Hensel, H., & Iggo, A. (1971). Analysis of cutaneous warm and cold fibres in primates. *Pflügers*

Archive European Journal of Physiology, 329, 1–8.

Hilz, M. J., Stemper, B., Axelrod, F. B., Kolodny, E. H., & Neundorfer, B. (1999). Quantitative thermal perception testing in adults. *Journal of Clinical Neurophysiology, 16,* 462–471.

Hori, A., Minato, K., & Kobayashi, S. (1999). Warming-activated channels of warm-sensitive neurons in rat hypothalamic slices. *Neuroscience Letters, 275,* 93–96.

Huang, J. H., Ali, Z., Travison, T. G., Campbell, J. N., & Meyer, R. A. (2000). Spatial mapping of the zone of secondary hyperalgesia reveals a gradual decline of pain with distance but sharp borders. *Pain, 86,* 33–42.

Hughes, J., Smith, T. W., Kosterlitz, H. W., Fothergill, L. A., Morgan, B. A., & Morris, H. R. (1975). Identification of two related pentapeptides from the brain with potent opiate agonist activity. *Nature, 258,* 577–580.

Iadarola, M. J., Berman, K. F., Zeffiro, T. A., Byas-Smith, M. G., Gracely, R. H., Max, M. B., & Bennett, G. J. (1998). Neural activation during acute capsaicin-evoked pain and allodynia assessed with PET. *Brain, 121,* 931–947.

Jaffe, J. H., & Martin, W. R. (1975). Narcotic analgesics and antagonists. In L. S. Goodman & A. Gilman (Eds.), *The pharmacological basis of therapeutics* (pp. 245–283). New York: Macmillan.

Janal, M. N., Clark, W. C., & Carroll, J. D. (1991). Multidimensional scaling of painful and innocuous electrocutaneous stimuli: Reliability and individual differences. *Perceptual Psychophysics, 50,* 108–116.

Janal, M. N., Glusman, M., Kuhl, J. P., & Clark, W. C. (1994). On the absence of correlation between responses to noxious heat, cold, electrical and ischemic stimulation. *Pain, 58,* 403–411.

Jancso, G., Kiraly, E., & Jancso-Gabor, A. (1977). Pharmacologically induced selective degeneration of chemosensitive primary sensory neurones. *Nature, 270,* 741–743.

Jensen, M. P., Turner, J. A., Romano, J. M., & Karoly, P. (1991). Coping with chronic pain: A critical review of the literature. *Pain, 47,* 249–283.

Jeong, W. S., & Tokura, H. (1993). Different thermal conditions of the extremities affect thermoregulation in clothed man. *Eur J Appl Physiol, 67,* 481–485.

Johnson, K. O., Darian-Smith, I., & LaMotte, C. (1973). Peripheral neural determinants of temperature discrimination in man: A correlative study of responses to cooling skin. *Journal of Neurophysiology, 36,* 347–370.

Kanjhan, R. (1995). Opioids and pain. *Clinical an Experimental Pharmacology and Physiology, 22,* 397–403.

Kanosue, K., Yanase-Fujiwara, M., & Hosono, T. (1994). Hypothalamic network for thermoregulatory vasomotor control. *American Journal of Physiology, 267,* R283–R288.

Kanosue, K., Zhang, Y. H., Yanase-Fujiwara, M., & Hosono, T. (1994). Hypothalamic network for thermoregulatory shivering. *American Journal of Physiology, 267,* R275–R282.

Kavaliers, M. (1987). Evidence for opioid and non-opioid forms of stress-induced analgesia in the snail, Cepaea nemoralis. *Brain Research, 410,* 111–115.

Keefe, F. J., Dunsmore, J., & Burnett, R. (1992). Behavioral and cognitive-behavioral approaches to chronic pain: Recent advances and future directions. *Journal of Consulting and Clinical Psychology, 60,* 528–536.

Kenshalo, D. R. (1970). Psychophysical studies of temperature sensitivity. In W. D. Neff (Ed.), *Contributions to sensory physiology.* New York: Academic Press (pp. 19–74).

Kenshalo, D. R. (1971). The cutaneous senses. In J. W. Kling & L. A. Riggs (Eds.), *Woodworth & Schlosberg's experimental psychology* (pp. 117–168). New York: Holt, Rinehart and Winston.

Kenshalo, D. R., & Scott, H. H. J. (1966). Temporal course of thermal adaptation. *Science, 151,* 1095–1096.

Khalil, Z., & Helme, R. D. (1989). Sequence of events in substance P-mediated plasma extravasation in rat skin. *Brain Research, 500,* 256–262.

Kienle, G. S., & Kiene, H. (1997). The powerful placebo effect: Fact or fiction? *Journal of Clinical Epidemiology, 50,* 1311–1318.

Kim, H. E., & Tokura, H. (1994). Effects of time of day on dressing behavior under the influence of ambient temperature fall from 30 degrees C to 15 degrees C. *Physiology and Behavior, 55,* 645–650.

Kirsch, I., & Sapirstein, G. (1999). Listening to Prozac but hearing placebo: A meta-analysis of antidepressant medication. In I. Kirsch (Ed.), *How expectancies shape behavior* (pp. 303–320). Washington, DC: American Psychological Association.

Klir, J. J., & Heath, J. E. (1994). Thermoregulatory responses to thermal stimulation of the preoptic anterior hypothalamus in the red fox (Vulpes vulpes). *Comparative Biochemistry and Physiology Part A: Physiology, 109,* 557–566.

Kobayashi, S., & Takahashi, T. (1993). Whole-cell properties of temperature-sensitive neurons in rat hypothalamic slices. *Proceedings of the Royal Society of London. Series B, Biological Sciences, 251,* 89–94.

Koltyn, K. F. (2000). Analgesia following exercise: A review. *Sports Medicine, 29,* 85–98.

Koltzenburg, M., Lundberg, L. E., & Torebjork, H. E. (1992). Dynamic and static components of mechanical hyperalgesia in human hairy skin. *Pain, 51,* 207–219.

Konietzny, F., & Hensel, H. (1977). The dynamic response of warm units in human skin nerves. *Pflügers Archive—European Journal of Physiology, 370,* 111–114.

Kumazawa, T., & Perl, E. R. (1978). Excitation of marginal and substantia gelatinosa neurons in the primate spinal cord: Indications of their place in dorsal horn functional organization. *Journal of Comparative Neurology, 177,* 417–434.

LaMotte, R. H., & Campbell, J. N. (1978). Comparison of responses of warm and nociceptive C-fiber afferents in monkey with human judgments of thermal pain. *Journal of Neurophysiology, 41,* 509–528.

LaMotte, R. H., Lundberg, L. E., & Torebjork, H. E. (1992). Pain, hyperalgesia and activity in nociceptive C units in humans after intradermal injection of capsaicin. *Journal of Physiology, 448,* 749–764.

LaMotte, R. H., Shain, C. N., Simone, D. A., & Tsai, E. F. (1991). Neurogenic hyperalgesia: Psychophysical studies of underlying mechanisms. *Journal of Neurophysiology, 66,* 190–211.

Lee, D. K., McGillis, S. L., & Greenspan, J. D. (1996). Somatotopic localization of thermal stimuli: I. A comparison of within- versus across-dermatomal separation of innocuous thermal stimuli. *Somatosensory and Motor Research, 13,* 67–71.

Lee, J., Dougherty, P. M., Antezana, D., & Lenz, F. A. (1999). Responses of neurons in the region of human thalamic principal somatic sensory nucleus to mechanical and thermal stimuli graded into the painful range. *Journal of Comparative Neurology, 410,* 541–555.

Leem, J. W., Willis, W. D., & Chung, J. M. (1993). Cutaneous sensory receptors in the rat foot. *Journal of Neurophysiology, 69,* 1684–1699.

Lembeck, F., & Holzer, P. (1979). Substance P as neurogenic mediator of antidromic vasodilation and neurogenic plasma extravasation. *Naunyn—Schiederberg's Archives of Pharmacology, 310,* 175–183.

Lenz, F. A., Seike, M., Richardson, R. T., Lin, Y. C., Baker, F. H., Khoja, I., Jaeger, C. J., & Gracely, R. H. (1993). Thermal and pain sensations evoked by microstimulation in the area of human ventrocaudal nucleus. *Journal of Neurophysiology, 70,* 200–212.

Levine, F. M., & De Simone, L. L. (1991). The effects of experimenter gender on pain report in male and female subjects. *Pain, 44,* 69–72.

Levine, J. D., Gordon, N. C., & Fields, H. L. (1978). The mechanism of placebo analgesia. *Lancet, 2,* 654–657.

Lewis, J. W., Cannon, J. T., & Liebeskind, J. C. (1980). Opioid and nonopioid mechanisms of stress analgesia. *Science, 208,* 623–625.

Lewis, T. (1936). Experiments relating to cutaneous hyperalgesia and its spread through somatic nerves. *Clinical Science, 2,* 373–421.

Lewis, T., & Pochin, E. E. (1938). The double response of the human skin to a single stimulus, *Clinical Science, 3,* 67–76.

Lynn, B., & Carpenter, S. E. (1982). Primary afferent units from the hairy skin of the rat hind limb. *Brain Research, 238,* 29–43.

Magerl, W., Wilk, S. H., & Treede, R. D. (1998). Secondary hyperalgesia and perceptual wind-up following intradermal injection of capsaicin in humans. *Pain, 74,* 257–268.

Magni, G., Marchetti, M., Moreschi, C., Merskey, H., & Luchini, S. R. (1993). Chronic musculoskeletal pain and depressive symptoms in the National Health and Nutrition Examination: I. Epidemiologic follow-up study. *Pain, 53,* 163–168.

Marks, L. E., & Gonzalez, R. R. (1974). Skin temperature modifies the pleasantness of thermal stimuli. *Nature, 247,* 473–475.

Marks, L. E., & Stevens, J. C. (1972). Perceived cold and skin temperature as functions of stimulation level and duration. *American Journal of Psychology, 85,* 407–419.

Marks, L. E., & Stevens, J. C. (1973). Spatial summation of warmth: Influence of duration and configuration of the stimulus. *American Journal of Psychology, 86,* 251–267.

Mayer, D. J., & Hayes, R. L. (1975). Stimulation-produced analgesia: Development of tolerance and cross-tolerance to morphine. *Science, 188,* 941–943.

Mayer, D. J., & Price, D. D. (1976). Central nervous system mechanisms of analgesia. *Pain, 2,* 379–404.

McArthur, D. L., Cohen, M. J., & Schandler, S. L. (1989). A philosophy for measurement of pain. In C. R. Chapman & J. D. Loeser (Eds.), *Issues in pain measurement.* New York: Raven Press.

McCubbin, J. A. (1993). Stress and endogenous opioids: Behavioral and circulatory interactions. *Biological Psychology, 35,* 91–122.

Melzack, R., & Wall, P. D. (1965). Pain mechanisms: A new theory. *Science, 150,* 971–979.

Mendell, L. M., & Wall, P. D. (1965). Responses of dorsal cord cells to peripheral cutaneous unmyelinated fibres. *Nature, 206,* 97–99.

Merskey, H., & Bogduk, N. (1994). *Classification of chronic pain: Description of chronic pain syndromes and definition of pain terms.* Seattle, WA: IASP Press.

Meyer, R. A., Davis, K. D., Cohen, R. H., Treede, R. D., & Campbell, J. N. (1991). Mechanically insensitive afferents (MIAs) in cutaneous nerves of monkey. *Brain Research, 561,* 252–261.

Mogil, J. S., Sternberg, W. F., Balian, H., Liebeskind, J. C., & Sadowski, B. (1996). Opioid and nonopioid swim stress-induced analgesia: A parametric analysis in mice. *Physiology and Behavior, 59,* 123–132.

Morimoto, A., Murakami, N., & Sakata, Y. (1988). Changes in hypothalamic temperature modulate the neuronal response of the ventral thalamus to skin warming in rats. *Journal of Physiology, 398,* 97–108.

Mower, G. D. (1976). Perceived intensity of peripheral thermal stimuli is independent of internal body temperature. *Journal of Comparative Physiology and Psychology, 90,* 1152–1155.

Nielsen, J., & Arendt-Nielsen, L. (1997). Spatial summation of heat induced pain within and between dermatomes. *Somatosensory and Motor Research, 14,* 119–125.

Nussbaum, E. L., & Downes, L. (1998). Reliability of clinical pressure-pain algometric measurements obtained on consecutive days. *Physical Therapy, 78,* 160–169.

Ohnaka, T., Tochihara, Y., & Watanabe, Y. (1994). The effects of variation in body temperature on the preferred water temperature and flow rate during showering. *Ergonomics, 37,* 541–546.

Olausson, B. (1998). Recordings of polymodal single c-fiber nociceptive afferents following mechanical and argon-laser heat stimulation of human skin. *Experimental Brain Research, 122,* 44–54.

Pehl, U., Simon, E., & Schmid, H. A. (1997). Properties of spinal neuronal thermosensitivity in vivo and in vitro. *Annals of the New York Academy of Sciences, 813,* 139–145.

Perl, E. R. (1968). Myelinated afferent fibres innervating the primate skin and their response to noxious stimuli. *Journal of Physiology, 197,* 593–615.

Pertovaara, A., & Kojo, I. (1985). Influence of the rate of temperature change on thermal thresholds in man. *Experimental Neurology, 87,* 439–445.

Pillay, P. K., & Hassenbusch, S. J. (1992). Bilateral MRI-guided stereotactic cingulotomy for intractable pain. *Stereotactic and Functional Neurosurgery, 59,* 33–38.

Price, D. D. (2000). Psychological and neural mechanisms of the affective dimension of pain. *Science, 288,* 1769–1772.

Price, D. D., Barrell, J. J., & Gracely, R. H. (1980). A psychophysical analysis of experimental factors that selectively influence the affective dimension of pain. *Pain, 8,* 137–149.

Price, D. D., & Dubner, R. (1977). Neurons that subserve the sensory-discriminative aspects of pain. *Pain, 3,* 307–338.

Price, D. D., & Harkins, S. W. (1992). The affective-motivational dimension of pain: A two stage model. *APS Journal, 1,* 229–239.

Price, D. D., Harkins, S. W., & Baker, C. (1987). Sensory-affective relationships among different types of clinical and experimental pain. *Pain, 28,* 297–307.

Price, D. D., Hu, J. W., Dubner, R., & Gracely, R. H. (1977). Peripheral suppression of first pain and central summation of second pain evoked by noxious heat pulses. *Pain, 3,* 57–68.

Price, D. D., McGrath, P. A., Rafii, A., & Buckingham, B. (1983). The validation of visual analogue scales as ratio scale measures for chronic and experimental pain. *Pain, 17,* 45–56.

Price, D. D., Milling, L. S., Kirsch, I., Duff, A., Montgomery, G. H., & Nicholls, S. S. (1999). An analysis of factors that contribute to the magnitude of placebo analgesia in an experimental paradigm. *Pain, 83,* 147–156.

Price, D. D., Von der Gruen, A., Miller, J., Rafii, A., & Price, C. (1985). A psychophysical analysis of morphine analgesia. *Pain, 22,* 261–269.

Rainville, P., Carrier, B., Hofbauer, R. K., Bushnell, M. C., & Duncan, G. H. (1999). Dissociation of sensory and affective dimensions of pain using hypnotic modulation. *Pain, 82,* 159–171.

Rainville, P., Duncan, G. H., Price, D. D., Carrier, B., & Bushnell, M. C. (1997). Pain affect encoded in human anterior cingulate but not somatosensory cortex. *Science, 277,* 968–971.

Raja, S. N., Meyer, R. A., Ringkamp, M., & Campbell, J. N. (1999). Peripheral neural mechanisms of nociception. In P. D. Wall & R. Melzack (Eds.), *Textbook of pain* (pp. 11–58). Edinburgh, England: Livingstone.

Refinetti, R. (1989). Magnitude estimation of warmth: Intra- and intersubject variability. *Perception and Psychophysics, 46,* 81–84.

Reynolds, D. V. (1969). Surgery in the rat during electrical analgesia induced by focal brain stimulation. *Science, 164,* 444–445.

Rhudy, J. L., & Meagher, M. W. (2000). Fear and anxiety: Divergent effects on human pain thresholds. *Pain, 84,* 65–75.

Rollman, G. B. (1977). Signal detection theory measurement of pain: A review and critique. *Pain, 3,* 187–211.

Rossi, R., & Johansson, O. (1998). Cutaneous innervation and the role of neuronal peptides in cutaneous inflammation: A minireview. *Eur J Dermatol, 8,* 299–306.

Sakata, Y., Morimoto, A., & Murakami, N. (1989). Responses of thalamic neurons in rats to skin cooling and hypothalamic temperature. *American Journal of Physiology, 256,* R1293–R1298.

Schmelz, M., Schmid, R., Handwerker, H. O., & Torebjork, H. E. (2000). Encoding of burning pain from capsaicin-treated human skin in two categories of unmyelinated nerve fibres. *Brain, 123,* 560–571.

Schmidt, R., Schmelz, M., Forster, C., Ringkamp, M., Torebjork, E., & Handwerker, H. (1995). Novel classes of responsive and unresponsive C nociceptors in human skin. *Journal of Neuroscience, 15,* 333–341.

Schmidt, R., Schmelz, M., Ringkamp, M., Handwerker, H. O., & Torebjork, H. E. (1997). Innervation territories of mechanically activated C nociceptor units in human skin. *Journal of Neurophysiology, 78,* 2641–2648.

Shibata, M., Hori, T., Kiyohara, T., & Nakashima, T. (1988). Convergence of skin and hypothalamic temperature signals on the sulcal prefrontal cortex in the rat. *Brain Research, 443,* 37–46.

Shoemaker, J. A., & Refinetti, R. (1996). Day-night difference in the preferred ambient temperature of human subjects. *Physiology and Behavior, 59,* 1001–1003.

Simone, D. A., Baumann, T. K., & LaMotte, R. H. (1989). Dose-dependent pain and mechanical hyperalgesia in humans after intradermal injection of capsaicin. *Pain, 38,* 99–107.

Simone, D. A., & Kajander, K. C. (1997). Responses of cutaneous A-fiber nociceptors to noxious cold. *Journal of Neurophysiology, 77,* 2049–2060.

Simone, D. A., Nolano, M., Johnson, T., Wendelschafer-Crabb, G., & Kennedy, W. R. (1998). Intradermal injection of capsaicin in humans produces degeneration and subsequent reinnervation of epidermal nerve fibers: corelation with sensory function. *Journal of Neuroscience, 18,* 8947–8959.

Slugg, R. M., Meyer, R. A., & Campbell, J. N. (2000). Response of cutaneous A- and C-fiber nociceptors in the monkey to controlled-force stimuli. *Journal of Neurophysiology, 83,* 2179–2191.

Sternberg, W. F., Bokat, C., Alboyadjian, A., & Gracely, R. H. (2001). Sex-dependent components of the analgesia produced by athletic competition. *The Journal of Pain, 2,* 65–74.

Stevens, J. C., & Choo, K. K. (1998). Temperature sensitivity of the body surface over the life span. *Somatosensory and Motor Research, 15,* 13–28.

Stevens, J. C., & Marks, L. E. (1971). Spatial summation and the dynamics of warmth sensation. *Perception and Psychophysics, 9,* 391–398.

Stevens, J. C., & Marks, L. E. (1979). Spatial summation of cold. *Physiology and Behavior, 22,* 541–547.

Stevens, J. C., & Marks, L. E. (1980). Cross-modality matching functions generated by magnitude estimation. *Perception and Psychophysics, 27,* 379–389.

Stevens, J. C., Marks, L. E., & Simonson, D. C. (1974). Regional sensitivity and spatial summa-

tion in the warmth sense. *Physiology and Behavior, 13,* 825–836.

Stevens, S. S. (1975). *Psychophysics: Introduction to its perceptual, neural and social prospects.* New York: Wiley.

Susser, E., Sprecher, E., & Yarnitsky, D. (1999). Paradoxical heat sensation in healthy subjects: Peripherally conducted by A delta or C fibres? *Brain, 122,* 239–246.

Taus, R. H., Stevens, J. C., & Marks, L. E. (1975). Spatial localization of warmth. *Perception and Psychophysics, 17,* 194–196.

Thalhammer, J. G., & LaMotte, R. H. (1982). Spatial properties of nociceptor sensitization following heat injury of the skin. *Brain Research, 231,* 257–265.

Tolle, T. R., Kaufmann, T., Siessmeier, T., Lautenbacher, S., Berthele, A., Munz, F., Zieglgansberger, W., Willoch, F., Schwaiger, M., Conrad, B., & Bartenstein, P. (1999). Region-specific encoding of sensory and affective components of pain in the human brain: A positron emission tomography correlation analysis. *Annals of Neurology, 45,* 40–47.

Torebjork, H. E., LaMotte, R. H., & Robinson, C. J. (1984). Peripheral neural correlates of magnitude of cutaneous pain and hyperalgesia: Simultaneous recordings in humans of sensory judgments of pain and evoked responses in nociceptors with C-fibers. *Journal of Neurophysiology, 51,* 325–339.

Torebjork, H. E., Lundberg, L. E., & LaMotte, R. H. (1992). Central changes in processing of mechanoreceptive input in capsaicin-induced secondary hyperalgesia in humans. *Journal of Physiology, 448,* 765–780.

Travis, K. A., Bockholt, H. J., Zardetto-Smith, A. M., & Johnson, A. K. (1995). In vitro thermosensitivity of the midline thalamus. *Brain Research, 686,* 17–22.

Treede, R. D., Apkarian, A. V., Bromm, B., Greenspan, J. D., & Lenz, F. A. (2000). Cortical representation of pain: Functional characterization of nociceptive areas near the lateral sulcus. *Pain, 87,* 113–119.

Treede, R. D., Kenshalo, D. R., Gracely, R. H., & Jones, A. K. (1999). The cortical representation of pain. *Pain, 79,* 105–111.

Treede, R. D., Meyer, R. A., & Campbell, J. N. (1990). Comparison of heat and mechanical receptive fields of cutaneous C-fiber nociceptors in monkey. *Journal of Neurophysiology, 64,* 1502–1513.

Treede, R. D., Meyer, R. A., & Campbell, J. N. (1998). Myelinated mechanically insensitive afferents from monkey hairy skin: Heat-response properties. *Journal of Neurophysiology, 80,* 1082–1093.

Treede, R. D., Meyer, R. A., Raja, S. N., & Campbell, J. N. (1992). Peripheral and central mechanisms of cutaneous hyperalgesia. *Progress in Neurobiology, 38,* 397–421.

Turk, D. C., Rudy, T. E., & Salovey, P. (1985). The McGill Pain Questionnaire reconsidered: Confirming the factor structure and examining appropriate uses. *Pain, 21,* 385–397.

Tursky, B. (1976). The development of a pain perception profile: A psychological approach. In M. Weisenberg & B. Tursky (Eds.), *Pain: New perspectives in therapy and research* (pp. 171–194). New York: Plenum Press.

Villanueva, L., & Le Bars, D. (1995). The activation of bulbo-spinal controls by peripheral nociceptive inputs: Diffuse noxious inhibitory controls. *Biological Research, 28,* 113–125.

Vin-Christian, K., Benoist, J. M., Gautron, M., Levante, A., & Guilbaud, G. (1992). Further evidence for the involvement of SmI cortical neurons in nociception: Modifications of their responsiveness over the early stage of a carrageenin-induced inflammation in the rat. *Somatosensory and Motor Research, 9,* 245–261.

Willer, J. C., Dehen, H., & Cambier, J. (1981). Stress-induced analgesia in humans: Endogenous opioids and naloxone-reversible depression of pain reflexes. *Science, 212,* 689–691.

Willis, W. D. (1989). The origin and destination of pathways involved in pain transmission. In P. D. Wall & R. Melzack (Eds.), *Textbook of pain* (pp. 112–127). Edinburgh, England: Livingstone.

Willis, W. D., Jr. (1999). Dorsal root potentials and dorsal root reflexes: A double-edged sword. *Experimental Brain Research, 124,* 395–421.

Yaksh, T. L. (1997). Pharmacology and mechanisms of opioid analgesic activity. *Acta Anesthesiologica Scandinavica, 41,* 94–111.

Yarnitsky, D., & Ochoa, J. L. (1991). Warm and cold specific somatosensory systems: Psychophysical thresholds, reaction times and peripheral conduction velocities. *Brain, 114,* 1819–1826.

Yarnitsky, D., & Sprecher, E. (1994). Thermal testing: Normative data and repeatability for various test algorithms. *Journal of the Neurological Sciences, 125,* 39–45.

Ziegler, E. A., Magerl, W., Meyer, R. A., & Treede, R. D. (1999). Secondary hyperalgesia to punctate mechanical stimuli: Central sensitization to A-fibre nociceptor input. *Brain, 122,* 2245–2257.

CHAPTER 16

Taste

BRUCE P. HALPERN

INTRODUCTION

This chapter is an overview of our current understanding of the taste system (or *gustation*), especially the human taste system. Taste in humans and in other mammals is an oral chemoreceptive—and also thermoreceptive and mechanoreceptive—sensory and perceptual system (Cruz & Green, 2000; Halpern, 1999; Oakley, 1985). The human taste system normally responds during drinking, biting, licking, chewing, and swallowing. Some of the central nervous system gustatory areas (see O'Doherty, Rolls, Francis, Bowtell, & McGlone, 2001; Rolls, 1997) are presumably also involved in relevant recall, perception, and cognition, in the presence or absence of oral tastants. To start this overview of taste, this chapter first introduces two contending theoretical and empirical approaches to gustation and then examines regional taste responsiveness of the human mouth. Next, gustatory anatomy, gustatory physiology, and human taste psychophysics are presented. In these latter sections, the brief outlines of gustatory organization presented in this introduction are amplified; relevant data are considered; and additional issues are addressed.

Knowledge of vertebrate taste structures and functions increased substantially during the second half of the 20th century. This improved understanding included information on the genetics and molecular biology of taste receptor cells, the anatomy and function of peripheral and central nervous system (CNS) gustatory structures, and behaviorally derived categorizations and descriptions of tastants and their interactions. Only a limited portion of this vast literature can be referenced in the present chapter. More comprehensive and detailed presentations—including noteworthy information on clinical and developmental aspects of human gustation, methods for studying human taste judgments, and taste in nonhuman organisms—are available in other works (e.g., Beauchamp & Bartoshuk, 1997; Doty, 1995; Finger, Silver, & Restrepo, 2000; Getchell, Doty, Bartoshuk, & Snow,

I thank Linda M. Bartoshuk, Graham A. Bell, France Bellisle, Gordon C. Birch, Paul A. S. Breslin, John Caprio, Frank A. Catalanotto, Robert J. Contreras, Annick Faurion, Patricia M. Di Lorenzo, John A. DeSimone, Marion E. Frank, Robert A. Frank, John I. Glendinning, Barry G. Green, Göran Hellekant, Howard C. Howland, Frank C. Keil, Sue C. Kinnamon, Linda M. Kennedy, Kenzo Kurihara, David G. Laing, Harry T. Lawless, Darryl James Mayeaux, Herbert L. Meiselman, Julie A. Mennella, Ulric Neisser, Ann C. Noble, Michael O'Mahony, Michael J. Owren, Cathy A. Pelletier, Joel Porte, John Prescott, Edmund T. Rolls, Stephen D. Roper, Thomas R. Scott, Burton Slotnick, Alan Spector, Michael J. Spivey, Daniel N. Tapper, Michael G. Tordoff, James. M. Weiffenbach, and Takashi Yamamoto for assistance with the preparation of this chapter, and Jeannine F. Delwiche, Robert P. Erickson, and Steven Yantis for very helpful feedback on earlier drafts.

1991; Lawless & Heymann, 1997; Murphy, 1998).

Notwithstanding the increased understanding of taste achieved during the 20th century, some gustatory issues that existed at the time of the previous edition of this handbook (Bartoshuk, 1988) continue to be debated, and some misunderstandings that were clarified nonetheless are still repeated. A principal discord in gustatory science concerns the organizational and informational characteristics of mammalian taste systems, and a persistent confusion involves the likelihood and properties of taste reports evoked when tastants are applied to various areas of the human tongue.

Organizational and Informational Characteristics of Mammalian Taste Systems

Two disparate answers are offered for the organizational and informational characteristics of mammalian taste systems. One, identified as the basic tastes model (see Delwiche, 1996; Halpern, 1997, 1999; Lawless, 2000) has four core postulates.

First, very few distinguishable taste categories exist. Each of these categories is considered a *basic taste*. The basic tastes are generally specified to be bitter, salty, sour, and sweet. A fifth basic taste, variously designated glutamate-taste, savory, or, by some, umami, is sometimes added. In this framework, human oral perceptions that do not correspond to one or more of these basic taste categories are considered to be nongustatory (i.e., dependent upon other sensory systems, especially olfaction or chemesthesis [or the common chemical sense]. See Bryant & Silver, 2000).

Second, each member of this small set of taste perceptions is quite distinct and separate from the others. It is asserted that the basic tastes can always be recognized in mixtures of tastants unless the concentrations are such that some basic tastes are suppressed by effects of other tastants in the mixture. This ability to resolve the components of a mixed sensory input is sometimes referred to as characterizing an *analytic* sensory or perceptual system. Concordant with the postulates of a small set of noninteracting members, human taste, per se, is believed to have little cognitive involvement.

Third, physiological responses of the gustatory system are characterized by distinct and separate mechanisms that correspond to the very limited set of taste perceptions. These nonoverlapping mechanisms are considered to begin at the taste receptor cells and continue in direct fashion throughout the sensory system. The (four or five) separate taste mechanisms are often regarded as so independent that each can be designated a neural *labeled line*. A particular gustatory labeled line (e.g., the sweet mechanism) is thought to be activated by rather specific receptor processes in certain taste receptor cells. Activity in a particular gustatory labeled line would denote the degree to which that basic taste was present.

Fourth, different identifiable tastants, which can be specified at the level of single pure chemicals, activate one or another of the separate gustatory mechanisms. Each of these pure chemicals is called a *basic taste stimulus*. It is asserted that a particular basic taste stimulus will arouse, at least primarily, only one fundamental taste mechanism and that it will initiate biologically relevant activity in only one basic taste labeled line. If descriptions of the taste of a pure chemical contain several basic tastes, or if a tastant activates multiple gustatory mechanisms, the most intense response is taken as meaningful, and the others are described as *side tastes* and considered to lack perceptual or sensory importance. The thus-identified basic taste stimulus for a gustatory category, mechanism, or labeled line component cell is described as the *best stimulus*.

In turn, the activated taste receptor cell or gustatory neuron is called an *X-best structure,* where X may be either the chemical name of the basic taste stimulus—for example, sodium chloride (NaCl)—or the basic taste category label, in this instance salt or salty.

The majority of taste researchers accept, in part or in whole, the basic tastes model (see Frank, 2000; Lundy & Contreras, 1999; McCaughey & Scott, 1998; Sato, Ogawa, & Yamashita, 1994; Scott & Giza, 2000; Smith & Vogt, 1997).

The contrasting answer for the organizational and informational characteristics of mammalian taste systems is known as the *across-fiber-pattern* or *population* model (see Halpern, 1997, 1999). The population model rejects each of the postulates and corollaries of the basic tastes model. Instead, the across-fiber-pattern model posits, first, that there are a sizeable number of taste categories, certainly more than four or five. None of these many taste categories are viewed as the fundamental elements from which all other taste perception or cognitions are constructed, and therefore the concept of basic tastes is rejected. The model proposes that one pure-chemical tastant may evoke several of these gustatory categories, and that a mixture of tastants may elicit a gustatory experience that is a new *synthesis* and is not analyzable into the components of the mixture. For this framework, the physiological instantiations are initiated at the taste receptor cell level of the gustatory system by partially overlapping oral responses to tastants (as well as some oral thermal and mechanical events). The pattern of responses across ensembles of taste receptor cells, and across subsequent arrays of peripheral and CNS gustatory neurons, is considered to specify taste categories dynamically. It is believed that the activity or responsiveness of any one individual gustatory receptor cell or neuron, in isolation, is not biologically meaningful. Thus, the concept of an exclusive best stimulus is considered inapplicable, and all responses to tastants by taste receptor cells or neurons are potentially information-carrying when the full cluster of neural elements is considered. On the other hand, it is expected that chemically diverse tastants (e.g., sweeteners) may elicit taste perceptions with shared characteristics, reflecting responses with common patterns but perhaps with different elements.

The across-fiber-pattern model, in its full or strong form, is accepted by only a minority of taste researchers (e.g., Erickson, 2000, 2001; Faurion, 1987). However, hybrid models, which consider individual taste receptor cells and the primary afferent neurons that are activated by them to be insufficiently selective to denote all tastants reliably, and therefore propose population gustatory processing rather than labeled lines in the CNS, have gained acceptance (Gilbertson, Damak, & Margolskee, 2000; Smith, St. John, & Boughter, 2000).

These opposing models for the organizational and informational characteristics of vertebrate taste systems lead to different research strategies and foci. Interest in the across-fiber-pattern model encourages measurements of the judged complexity of tastants, suggests that limits on the descriptions or variety of tastants may be inadvisable, and recommends that responses to oral tastants by arrays of gustatory neurons, assembled into a synthesized population or, better, studied simultaneously, are the most appropriate data for understanding CNS taste physiology.

In contrast, adherence to the basic tastes model suggests that attention to transduction processes in taste receptor cells in relation to basic taste stimuli should receive major emphasis, together with human judgments of tastants, which are limited to basic taste categories, and responses of individual gustatory neurons to the same stimuli.

Taste Reports Evoked When Tastants Are Applied to Various Areas of the Human Mouth

Taste descriptions such as sweet, sour, salty, and bitter, as well as other descriptions, can be evoked from all taste-bud-bearing areas of the human tongue when suitable concentrations of appropriate tastants are applied to these regions. This was unequivocally demonstrated by Collings in 1974. Thus, diagrams suggesting that one or another of these taste description can be evoked only from particular areas of the human tongue are incorrect. Bartoshuk (1988) has traced the history of this misunderstanding.

However, stimulation of the several lingual (i.e., tongue) and palatal taste receptor regions with the same tastants does reveal differences in sensitivity (detection or recognition thresholds) and in the rate of change in judged intensity (Lawless, 2000). On the tongue, recognition thresholds for urea, sucrose, NaCl, and quinine hydrochloride (in these studies, the only accepted recognition responses are, respectively, bitter, sweet, salty, and bitter) are all lowest at the front of the tongue, although average differences in these recognition thresholds from one taste-bud-bearing lingual region to another are less than a factor of three. Palatal recognition thresholds for urea and quinine hydrochloride (QHCl) are lower than at any tongue locus; for NaCl and citric acid (with sour the "correct" recognition response for citric acid), the thresholds are higher. At the front of the tongue, rates of change (slope) of judged intensity with tastant concentration are equivalent for the five tastants used. Some differences in intensity slopes do occur between tongue taste bud regions, but again, none reach a factor of three.

It may be that the regional taste sensitivity and intensity differences that occur with gustatory stimulation within the human mouth (e.g., Collings, 1974; Doty, Bagla, Morgenson, & Mirza, 2001; Sandick & Cardello, 1981) are essentially laboratory phenomena, small enough to allow the several taste bud loci to be considered equivalent and redundant under normal circumstances. Conversely, the regional differences in oral taste function may be viewed as sufficiently diverse and sizeable to imply that gustatory responses to normal foods or beverages are patterns that depend in part on these differences. Later in this chapter these variations will be related to expectations from the basic tastes model.

GUSTATORY ANATOMY

Peripheral Anatomy: Taste Buds and Papillae

Taste buds, the human gustatory receptor organs, occur in predictable locations in the mouth (the oral cavity) as well as in the oropharynx and throat (Figure 16.1A). Individual mammalian taste buds are 20 μm to 40 μm in diameter and 40 μm to 50 μm long, and they contain 40 to 100 cells (Figure 16.1C; Herness & Gilbertson, 1999; Stewart, DeSimone, & Hill, 1997). The dimensions of human taste buds seem to be at the upper end of the mammalian size range (Arvidson & Friberg, 1980).

In human adults oral loci of taste buds are the tongue (i.e., lingual taste buds) and the soft palate (Figure 16.1A); extraoral loci are the epiglottis and larynx (for general information on locations and characteristics of human taste buds, see Halpern, 1977; Miller, 1989, 1994; Miller & Bartoshuk, 1991; Mistretta, 1984, 1986, 1991; Oakley, 1986; Pritchard, 1991). Only taste buds in the oral cavity, which are believed to play the principal role in taste-dependent human behavior, are discussed in detail here.

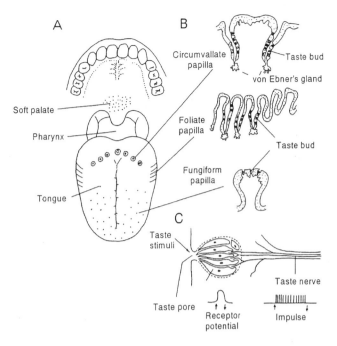

Figure 16.1   Schematic drawings of locations of the taste buds in the mouth (A); transverse sections of circumvallate, foliate, and fungiform papillae (B); and a taste bud and taste nerve fibers with electrical events (C).
SOURCE: From Yamamoto, Nagai, Shimura, & Yasoshima (1998). Copyright © 1998. Reprinted with permission.

Lingual Papillae

On the adult human tongue, taste buds are restricted to distinctive epithelial structures called papillae, which are organized entities that both protrude above the dorsal tongue surface and extend below the surface. There are four classes of human lingual papillae, but only three may contain taste buds: fungiform, foliate, and circumvallate papillae (ordered from the front to the back of the tongue). The fourth class of lingual papillae, filiform papillae, never has taste buds.

Estimates of the overall number of human lingual taste buds in the fungiform, foliate, and circumvallate papillae vary widely, and individual differences are large. Approximately 3,000 to perhaps as many as 12,000 taste buds are on the human tongue. A middle value, 5,000 taste buds, will be taken

as a typical total for the human tongue. Human taste buds each contain about 40 to 60 receptor cells, yielding about 300,000 taste receptor cells for the human tongue, with the possibility of as many as 720,000. Even the conservative estimate of 300,000 lingual taste bud receptor cells exceeds by a factor of approximately 10 the total number of human afferent auditory receptor cells, the inner hair cells of our two cochleas (Geisler, 1998; Gulick, Gescheider, & Frisina, 1989; Pickles, 1988).

The very large number of taste receptor cells distributed across the adult human tongue, comprising a lingual gustatory receptor array that substantially exceeds the total number of afferent auditory receptor cells, is interesting. One might propose that if location of stimulation on this taste sensory surface is preserved in the CNS and is coupled with regional differences in responses to tastants, a spatial, and perhaps even temporal, pattern of CNS responses could result. These possibilities will be discussed in later sections. Briefly, nonhuman neurophysiological data and, as noted in the introduction, human psychophysical observations demonstrate that there are regional differences in responses to tastants, and anatomical location *is* preserved in the CNS. These data have functional consequences, in that humans can localize tastants on the tongue (Shikata, McMahon, & Breslin, 2000), as well as selectively remove from the mouth objects with specified gustatory characteristics (Delwiche, Lera, & Breslin, 2000).

Fungiform Papillae

The taste-bud-bearing papillae of the anterior region of the human tongue are called *fungiform papillae* (Figures 16.1A and 16.1B). About 750 of these mushroom-shaped (hence fungiform) papillae occur on the anterolateral dorsum of the tongue, but the middle of the tongue, excluding the tip, lacks fungiform papillae. The grossly visible portion of these papillae extends outward from the surface of the human tongue and bares 0 to 27 taste buds; the probability of taste buds is correlated with the diameter of the papilla. Human fungiform papillae average three to four taste buds, although the mean number of fungiform papillae with taste buds is highest at the tip of the human tongue. About half of the fungiform papillae exhibit no taste bud pores (openings from taste buds to the mouth) (Figure 16.1C), implying that approximately 50% of fungiform papillae have no taste buds (Arvidson, 1976, 1979; Arvidson & Friberg, 1980; Kullaa-Mikkonen & Sorvari, 1985; Kuznicki & Cardello, 1986; Zuniga et al., 1993). Studies in humans, summarized in the section on taste psychophysics, indicate that an absence of a taste bud means no responses to tastants.

The density (quantity per unit measure) of taste buds in the fungiform papillae re-gion of the human tongue shows an almost 200-fold individual difference at the tip of the tongue, ranging from 3.0 taste buds/cm^2 to 512 taste buds/cm^2, with a mean of about 115 taste buds/cm^2. In contrast, the mean density further posterior in the fungiform papillae region is approximately 23 taste buds/cm^2, with a range from 0 taste buds/cm^2 to 86 taste buds/cm^2. Across all individuals' tongues, the rank-order correlation between tip and midregion fungiform papillae taste bud densities was 0.82, suggesting that a particular fungiform papillae taste bud density may characterize each individual. In agreement with the observed high fungiform papillae taste bud density at the front of the human tongue, it was noted in the introduction that human lingual gustatory thresholds for urea, sucrose, NaCl, and QHCl are lowest at the front of the tongue.

Development of fungiform papillae in humans and other species has been described in detail by Mistretta (1991, 1998). Mature papillae are found before birth in humans. Papillary structures on the anterolateral tongue that approximate the distribution of adult fungiform papillae are present by the 10th to 13th fetal week, and at this time some have pore-like openings. Studies on human fetuses find full-size lingual taste buds, in papillae and with openings through the epithelium (i.e., pores) to the oral cavity, by the 15th week of gestation (a little more than one third of full term). By the 20th week, which is 50% of a typical full term, taste buds are comparable to those at term (Bradley & Stern, 1967; Hersch & Ganchrow, 1980). These anatomical data suggest that the human gustatory system functions in utero and that it thus might provide some gustatory input at birth. Studies on premature infants and full-term neonates confirm this supposition (Beauchamp & Moran, 1986; Crook & Lipsitt, 1976; Desor, Maller, & Andrews, 1975; Lipsitt, 1977; Mennella & Beauchamp, 1997; Nowliss & Kessen, 1976).

Foliate Papillae

Another category of lingual gustatory papillae, the *foliate papillae,* occur as folds or ridges and grooves on the two lateral margins of the human tongue, approximately half the distance between the tip and the root of the tongue (Figures 16.1A and 16.1B). Limited data indicate approximately 120 to 140 taste buds in each of the human foliate papillae, for a total of perhaps 1,000 foliate papillae taste buds on each side of the tongue, all in grooves below the surface of the tongue. About one third of all human taste buds occur in the foliate papillae (Bradley, Stedman, & Mistretta, 1985).

Circumvallate Papillae

On the posterior region of the human tongue, a third class of taste-bud-bearing papillae occurs: the *circumvallate papillae* (Figures 16.1A and 16.1B). A V-shaped array of circumvallate papillae can be observed, with the vertex at the back of the mouth. Each of these 8 to 12 papillae has a central region that extends above the tongue surface but generally has no taste buds in adult humans. This central mound is surrounded by a deep moat-like depression containing large numbers of taste buds in its walls. Approximately 200 to 700 taste buds are found in each human circumvallate papilla. Consequently, about 2,400 to 8,000 taste buds occur in the human circumvallate papillae. Almost one half of all human taste buds occur in the circumvallate papillae (Kuznicki & Cardello, 1986; Oakley, 1986).

Soft Palate

The taste buds in the human soft palate are generally described as not being associated with papillae (Figure 16.1A and 16.1B; Miller & Bartoshuk, 1991). However, Henkin, Graziadei, and Bradley (1969, page 795) noted "that adult palates may contain a large number of papillae . . . mainly near the junc-

tion of the hard and soft palates. Histologic examination of one of these papillae shows that it is not anatomically significantly different from a lingual fungiform papillae and that it contains taste buds whose appearance and location are more like those from a fungiform than from a circumvallate papilla."

Fine Structure of Taste Buds

Taste buds are complex receptor organs. Mature human taste buds contain a variety of taste receptor cells, immature receptor cells, peripheral portions of sensory (afferent) neurons, and basal cells (Figure 16.1C; J. C. Kinnamon, 1987). Several different types of taste bud receptor cells are described in some vertebrates, but there appears to be only one type in humans (Arvidson, Cottler-Fox, and Friberg, 1981; Reutter & Witt, 1993). Close to their mucosal end, near the oral cavity, the mature taste receptor cells of a human taste bud cluster together, forming intercellular connections (Arvidson, Cottler-Fox, & Friberg, 1981) that are termed *tight junctions* (DeSimone & Heck, 1993; Simon & Wang, 1993). These tight junctions limit penetration of large molecules into the spaces between the receptor cells but may readily permit movement of ions between receptor cells (Stewart et al., 1997). Both these aspects of taste buds' tight junctions are important. Penetration through this diffusion barrier into the spaces between the cells, called the paracellular space (Glendinning, Chaudhari, & Kinnamon, 2000), may easily occur for small ions such as H^+, Na^+ and K^+ (DeSimone & Heck, 1993; Simon & Wang, 1993). These positively charged ions (cations) exist in significant concentrations in many foods, especially after manipulation and hydration within the mouth. As will be discussed in the section on transduction, the presence of increased cation concentrations in the paracellular space can modulate receptor cell responses to tastants, could directly interact with membrane sites on basolateral (sides and bottom) portions of taste bud receptor cells (Stewart et al., 1997), and may be a significant aspect of human gustatory transduction.

Above the tight junctions, human taste bud receptor cells form microvilli, extensions of their cell membrane that provide considerable surface area. Tastants of any molecular size or complexity may reach the microvilli because they are located in a space that opens either directly (fungiform papillae and palatal taste buds) or indirectly (foliate and circumvallate papillae taste buds) to the oral cavity. The space in which the receptor cells' microvilli are located is designated the pore chamber or pore pit. The opening between this chamber and the oral cavity is the taste bud pore (Figure 16.1C), which is about 15 μm in diameter. Human taste bud microvilli are restricted to the pore chamber and do not extend through the pore (Arvidson, 1976; Arvidson, Cottler-Fox, & Friberg, 1981; J. C. Kinnamon, 1987; Kullaa-Mikkonen & Sorvari, 1985; Reutter & Witt, 1993).

Taste Bud Receptor Cells Are Not Permanent

The individual receptor cells of vertebrate taste buds are not permanent structures (Beidler & Smith, 1991; Finger & Simon, 2000; J. C. Kinnamon, 1987; Mistretta, 1986; Oakley, 1986). This has been directly determined by a measurement technique that requires an intravascular injection of radioactive substances that are incorporated into cells that differentiate from precursor cells in the taste bud while the radioactive pulse is present (the DNA precursor, tritiated thymidine), or of a substance that prevents such differentiation. In those mammals that have been studied, basal cells of taste buds continuously differentiate into immature receptor cells. The newly born receptor cells migrate through the taste bud, and some, or possibly all, eventually form tight junctions with other receptor cells near the mucosal end of the taste bud, producing

microvilli above the tight junctions and associations with neuron terminals or other receptor cells below the tight junctions. In laboratory rats the average time period between differentiation into a receptor cell and disappearance from the taste bud is 7 to 10 days. In other words, 50% of the taste bud cells live about 10 days. However, others have a much longer residence in the taste bud. About 25% remain for 20 days, and at least 10% remain for more than 30 days. Researchers do not know the functional implications of a majority of transient taste bud receptor cells combined with a small population of relatively long-lived cells or the characteristics of taste bud receptor cell replacement in humans.

Neural Innervation of Taste Buds: Three Cranial Nerves

Mammalian taste buds typically receive gustatory afferent innervation from branches of three cranial nerves: the 7th (facial), 9th (glossopharyngeal), or 10th (vagus; Smith & Davis, 2000; Smith & Vogt, 1997). These several afferent nerves serve distinct taste receptor populations, located on regions of the oral cavity that have separate embryological origins (Halpern, 1977). This arrangement is quite different from the auditory, olfactory, vestibular, or visual systems, for which single cranial nerves provide all afferent input to the central nervous system. However, taste has substantial similarities with the complex and heterogeneous somesthetic system. For example, as in somesthesis (Chap. 13, this volume), the multiple gustatory afferent nerves serve receptor organs located in anatomically different cutaneous regions, show unique response profiles, and have distinguishable CNS termination zones.

The oral cavity, including the immediate vicinity of taste buds, receives extensive innervation from the fifth cranial nerve (the trigeminal nerve; Bryant & Silver, 2000; Green & Lawless, 1991; Silver & Finger,

1991; Zotterman, 1967). Interactions between taste receptor cells and the trigeminal nerve have sometimes been suggested. However, as discussed in the section on taste psychophysics, application of tastants to a papilla innervated only by the trigeminal nerve does not elicit human taste responses (Arvidson & Friberg, 1980).

The Chorda Tympani Nerve Branch of the Facial Nerve (Cranial 7). Taste buds of fungiform papillae, and of the most anterior portion of the foliate papillae, are innervated by the chorda tympani branch of the facial nerve (Halpern, 1977; Oakley, 1986). The name of this nerve branch derives from its route through the middle ear, where it is located behind the tympanic membrane (Zotterman, 1967). Gustatory neural recordings from the human chorda tympani nerve are discussed in the section on gustatory physiology.

Human taste alterations or losses may occur with damage to the chorda tympani during therapeutic middle ear surgery or dental surgery and may be produced by disease or trauma that involve the middle ear (Boucher, Fahrang, Azérad, & Faurion, 2000; Costanzo & Zasler, 1991; Doty, Bartoshuk, & Snow, 1991; Pritchard, 1991; Schuknecht, 1974; Zuniga, Chen, & Miller, 1994). For example, dental extraction of third molars may cause human taste deficits, especially reductions in taste intensity, because the chorda tympani approaches and enters the tongue joined with the lingual branch of the trigeminal nerve, which travels near the third molars (Shafer, Frank, Gent, & Fischer, 1999).

The same anatomical joining of the chorda tympani and lingual nerves permits controlled study of these nerves in humans. Procedures that anesthetize the lingual branch of the trigeminal nerve after its admixture with the chorda tympani, such as some employed to control discomfort in dentistry, will reversibly anesthetize the chorda tympani and lingual nerve axons on one side (Catalanotto, Bartoshuk, Östrom, Gent, & Fast, 1993). After unilateral blocks, whole-mouth judged intensity for the highest concentrations of NaCl and QHCl *increases* significantly, as does judged intensity for several concentrations of citric acid and sucrose. However, with a bilateral chorda tympani/lingual block, intensity for most concentrations of NaCl, as well as for the highest concentrations of citric acid and sucrose, *decreases*. The increases in intensity with unilateral blocks suggest that a reduction of inhibition at CNS loci of taste input via nonchorda tympani routes more than compensates for the loss of chorda tympani input. Gustatory responses in rat CNS have suggested that inhibitory effects may be significant in taste (Di Lorenzo, 2000) and that release from taste-induced inhibition may occur when only the chorda tympani is blocked by instilling topical anesthetic into the external ear canal (Halpern & Nelson, 1965).

In order to examine the effect in humans of reversibly blocking only the chorda tympani nerve, anesthetic is injected into the wall of the external ear canal. This produces *increased* taste intensity at contralateral circumvallate papillae, but total loss of taste intensity near the tip of the tongue ipsilateral to the injection, and ipsilateral decreases in intensity at the foliate and circumvallate papillae, as well as at the palate and during a swallow (Yanagisawa, Bartoshuk, Catalanotto, Karrer, & Dveton, 1998). That ipsilateral taste intensity decreases for many oral taste bud regions after the ipsilateral chorda tympani block suggests that in the human CNS, gustatory input from the chorda tympani may produce extensive response enhancement.

The Greater Superficial Petrosal Nerve Branch of the Facial Nerve (Cranial 7). Human taste buds of the soft palate are thought to be innervated by the greater superficial petrosal branch of the facial nerve (Pritchard, 1991), which reaches the soft palate as part of the lesser palatine nerve. No human neurophysiological data are available for this nerve, but complete third molar extractions produce long-lived reductions in taste intensity upon palatal stimulation (Shafer et al., 1999).

Other Cranial Gustatory Nerves.   The taste buds of most of the foliate papillae, and of all circumvallate papillae, are innervated by the lingual branch of the glossopharyngeal nerve, while the vagus nerve (cranial 10) is thought to innervate most or all extraoral taste buds (Kuznicki & Cardello, 1986; Oakley, 1986).

CNS Anatomy

"Higher Primates" versus Other Vertebrates

Much of the gustatory CNS anatomy (midbrain, diencephalon, and cerebral cortex) of the "higher primate" rhesus and cynomolgus monkeys—and, apparently, humans—differs substantially from that of other mammals. These broad anatomical differences represent direct connections from gustatory nuclei in the hindbrain to thalamus, and then to multiple cerebral cortical areas (Figure 16.2) (Beckstead, Morse, & Norgren, 1980; Pritchard, 1991; Rolls, 1995, 1997; Rolls, Critchley, Browning, & Hernadi, 1998; Scott & Plata-Salamán, 1999). It is not known how early in the primate radiation these differences begin.

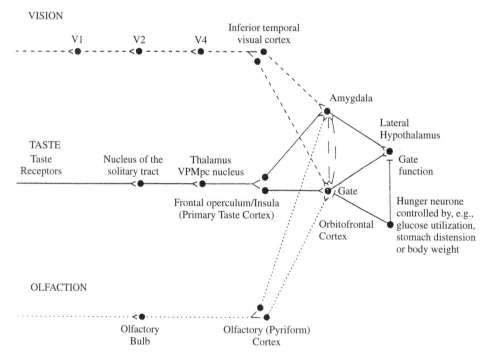

Figure 16.2   Schematic diagram of the taste pathways in primates (center) showing how they converge with olfactory and visual pathways.

NOTE: The gate function shown refers to the finding that the responses of taste neurons in the orbitofrontal cortex are modulated by hunger. VPMpc is the ventralposteromedial thalamic nucleus; V1, V2, and V4 are visual cortical areas.

SOURCE: From Rolls (1995). Copyright © 1995. Reprinted with permission.

More specifically, the primate peripheral gustatory nerves terminate ipsilaterally in a hindbrain nucleus, the nucleus of the solitary tract (Figure 16.2). A major difference from other mammals appears at this point. Gustatory output from the higher primate nucleus of the solitary tract goes directly to a forebrain region, the ventral-posterior medial nucleus of the dorsal thalamus. From the dorsal thalamus, connections exist to a primary gustatory cortical area (probably the rostral part of the frontal operculum and adjoining insula), and thence to secondary gustatory cortex (caudolateral orbitofrontal cortex) and tertiary gustatory cortex (perhaps a medial area of the orbitofrontal cortex). Only after taste input has reached the primate cerebral cortex are there connections to structures such as the amygdala and the hypothalamus. In addition, the primate secondary gustatory cortex receives connections from other cortical areas, such as the rhinal sulcus and ventral rostral insular cortex.

Human CNS Gustatory Anatomy

It is assumed that the overall gustatory anatomy of humans at the levels of the hindbrain (nucleus of the solitary tract) and dorsal thalamus (ventral-posterior medial nucleus) is somewhat similar to that of other primates, though no doubt with important differences. Traumatic lesions associated with apparent loss of taste perception (ageusia) identify a human cerebral cortical gustatory region at the anterior end of the Sylvian fissure (Bronstein, 1940a, 1940b). The noninvasive technique of functional magnetic resonance imaging (fMRI; see Chap. 5, Vol. 4 of this series) confirms the existence of human cortical gustatory responsiveness in the Sylvian fissure area. With whole-tongue gustatory stimulation the operculum represents about one third of all human fMRI activations; the insula represents 27%. Activation is bilateral in the operculum and the superior insula, but it

is mainly unilateral in the inferior insula and is concentrated in the hemisphere considered dominant on the basis of handedness (Faurion et al., 1999; Van de Moortele et al., 1997). The inferior insula may represent a second cortical gustatory area.

O'Doherty et al. (2001) has also observed consistent fMRI activation of human orbitofrontal cortex, as well as the frontal operculum, insula, and dorsal anterior cingulate, evoked by oral stimulation with 1 molar (M) glucose and 100 millimolar (mM) NaCl. For the orbitofrontal cortex, the areas activated by the two tastants are separated by an average of 39 mm. The orbitofrontal cortex responses may be related to hedonic evaluations, and the separation between areas activated by glucose and NaCl might be related to pleasantness and unpleasantness of tastants. A report that activation of orbitofrontal cortex is produced by presenting vanilla to the anterior nares, and that differential activation was elicited by more pleasant stroking of the hand, supports the hedonic involvement of orbitofrontal cortex (Figure 16.2; Francis et al., 1999). A different imaging technology, positron-emission tomography (PET; see Chap. 5, Vol. 4 of this series), also indicates that oral gustatory stimulation with a variety of tastants activates areas in the insula, frontal and parietal operculum, and orbitofrontal cortex (Small et al., 1999). For the insula and operculum, at least, 73% of the activation is in the right hemisphere.

Overall, the general outline of human cortical gustatory areas seems similar to that of nonhuman higher primates. For humans, cerebral cortical taste regions include the Sylvian fissure area, the insula and operculum, and the orbitofrontal cortex. The latter region appears to be a secondary taste area that includes a convergence of chemosensory and nonchemosensory afferent inputs and a possible separation of positive and negative hedonic loci.

GUSTATORY PHYSIOLOGY

Transduction

Sweetener Transduction

Multiple-step reception and amplification sequences are reported for sweeteners (Brand, 1997; Gilbertson et al., 2000; Stewart et al., 1997). These sequences involve (a) interaction of the sweetener with a selectively sensitive protein receptor molecule that is located partially outside and partially inside the apical membrane of taste bud receptor cells (a transmembrane protein; Dulac, 2000), leading to (b) structural alterations in a specific protein on the inside of the apical membrane (a G-protein; Herness & Gilbertson, 1999) situated close to and functionally coupled with the receptor molecule, which then causes (c) changes in the activation levels of enzymes within the taste bud, and eventually, because of biological amplification produced by acceleration of reaction rates by the enzymes, (d) increased probability of opening of ion channels in the basolateral membrane of the taste bud receptor cell. The latter is thought to lead to alteration of charge movement across the taste bud membrane, perhaps causing additional changes in ion channels and eventually modulation of transmitter release across synapses. The change in transmitter release would modulate the activity of the primary afferent gustatory neurons innervating the receptor cells.

One sequence of extracellular and intracellular signals of this sort is submitted for sugars that act as sweeteners; a slightly different one is proposed for some other sweeteners (Brand, 1997; Gilbertson et al., 2000; Striem, Pace, Zehavi, Naim, & Lancet, 1989). In all cases, the nature of the apical membrane receptor molecule thought to be necessary in the first step is crucial. Candidate taste bud apical membrane receptor molecules for sweeteners are now available (Chandrashekar et al., 2000; Dulac, 2000; Gilbertson et al., 2000; Glendinning et al., 2000; Hoon et al., 1999). These data represent major contributions that molecular biology has made to gustatory science, although both the number of such receptor molecules and their relevance to human taste remain to be determined.

However, a general model of the essential physicochemical characteristics of receptor molecules for all sweeteners, or of all sweeteners themselves, remains elusive (Glendinning et al., 2000; Khan, 1979; Lee, 1979; Schiffman, Hopfinger, & Mazur, 1986). Most recent approaches are elaborations of the Shallenberger and Acree proton donor–proton acceptor model (Eggers, Acree, & Shallenberger, 2000; Shallenberger, 1977; Shallenberger & Acree, 1967, 1969, 1971). The initial version of this model proposes that to be a sweetener, a tastant must have a covalently bound proton site that provides hydrogen bonding and is separated from an electronegative site by 300 picometers. This concept is symbolized by AH-B. It is thought that a compatible AH-B site on the gustatory receptor molecule would interact with the sweetener's site. Analysis of amino acid sweeteners indicates that the two interaction loci of the original AH-B model are insufficient (Kier, 1972). Thus, researchers have proposed a third binding site, located about 350 picometers from the "A" binding site of the AH-B model and about 530 picometers from the "B" binding site. Nonetheless, even with this third variable (γ), the AH-B γ model of sweeteners is limited to post hoc rationalizations of how molecules identified by psychophysical procedures as "sweet" resemble each other (Schiffman et al., 1986).

More complex elaborations of the AH-B γ concept also exist. One is the multipoint attachment (MPA) theory, which proposes "eight fundamental recognition sites" of a hypothetical human sweetness receptor and "15 potential interaction points of sweeteners with the human sweetness receptor" (Nofre, Tinti, & Glaser, 1996, page 753). The taste bud receptor in MPA theory is thought to be "a seven-pass transmembrane receptor coupled to a G protein," basically similar to those of the multiple-step (second messenger) transduction models discussed earlier. A possible limitation of MPA theory is the concern that as the number of variables of any model increases, fit with physical reality is likely to improve, but the conceptual power and generality of the model may be diminished.

A quite separate and complementary approach to all the AH-B-related models characterizes sweeteners based on the volumes of the sweetener molecules, on their interactions with water, and on how the sweetener-water complex may affect a hypothetical receptor for hydrated sweeteners (Birch, 1997a, 1997b; Birch, Parke, Siertsemak, & Westwell, 1997; Parke & Birch, 1999).

Acid-Tastant Transduction

Inorganic and hydrocarbon-based acids are effective stimuli for many vertebrate taste receptor cells. This may not be surprising because organic acids are common in plant tissues. Many researchers have proposed that in mammals a paracellular pathway in which hydrogen ions (H^+) diffuse past the tight junctions between taste bud receptor cells and either modulate intracellular charge states or interact with membrane receptor sites on the basolateral portions of the receptor cells is a major mechanism for gustatory responses to acids (DeSimone & Heck, 1993; Glendinning et al., 2000; Herness & Gilbertson, 1999; Simon & Wang, 1993; Stewart et al., 1997). Potentially relevant channels or pumps that interact with H^+ exist on the basolateral membrane of some mammals. Another factor is the discontinuity between the pH of acids and nonhuman gustatory neural responses to partially dissociated weak acids (Beidler, 1971, 1978; Ogiso, Shimizu, Watanabe, & Tonosaki,

2000; Pfaffmann, 1959). Thus, some of the apical ion channels, such as those through which Na^+ can pass, or other mechanisms that have been identified in some mammals (Kinnamon, 1996) and other vertebrates, are likely to have a role in human responses to acid tastants.

Salt-Stimulus Transduction

Gustatory responses to NaCl are widespread if not ubiquitous across animals. However, the human taste receptor cell mechanism(s) that transduce the presence of NaCl into biological activity differ from those in many mammals. Biophysical, biochemical, neurophysiological, and behavioral data indicate that in some mammals a class of sodium channels located in the apical portion of taste buds is necessary for normal responses to NaCl (Boughter & Gilbertson, 1999; Gilbertson et al., 2000; Glendinning et al., 2000; Halpern, 1998; Herness & Gilbertson, 1999). Because these sodium channels can be blocked by the synthetic chemical amiloride, they are designated amiloride-sensitive sodium channels. However, this taste transduction mechanism for NaCl is absent in certain strains of mammals, shows no selectivity for sodium salts and other tastants in some mammals, and is not associated with gustatory neural responses to NaCl recorded from the glossopharyngeal nerve of mammals. Consequently, amiloride-sensitive sodium channels cannot be the only means by which mammalian gustatory systems transduce NaCl. For humans, treatment of the tongue with amiloride does not alter the frequency with which NaCl is called salty, the initial intensity of the saltiness, or changes in the intensity of saltiness over time (Halpern, 1998; Halpern & Darlington, 1998). These data indicate that for humans amiloride-sensitive sodium channels are not the transduction mechanism by which salt stimuli initiate perceptions of saltiness (Kinnamon, 1996).

How, then, might the human taste system transduce NaCl? Apical sodium channels or transporters that are amiloride-insensitive may be relevant (S. C. Kinnamon, 1996). In addition, a paracellular pathway (DeSimone & Heck, 1993; Simon & Wang, 1993; Stewart et al., 1997) that permits small cations such as Na^+ to diffuse through the tight junctions between taste bud receptor cells and thereby to reach the basolateral region of receptor cells may play a role in humans' describing NaCl and other sodium salts as "salty" (Delwiche, Halpern, & DeSimone, 1999; Herness & Gilbertson, 1999). Support for the importance of a paracellular pathway in human taste responses to sodium salts is provided by measurement of simple taste reaction time (RT) to sodium chloride, sodium acetate, sodium glutamate, sodium ascorbate, and sodium gluconate. As the molecular weight of these molecules increases, simple taste RT also increases (Spearman's $\rho = 0.933$). More specifically, a mathematical model predicts that simple taste RT for sodium salts increases in a linear fashion with molecular volume of the salt. The underlying reasoning is that because larger salts have less permeability, more time is required for the salts to reach the basolateral locus of action. For the formal model, because the cation is always Na^+, it can be ignored, and molecular volume is approximated by the square root of the anionic weights. This model fits the relationship between sodium salt size and simple taste RT with $r = 0.94$, $p = 0.01$ (Delwiche et al., 1999), suggesting that for NaCl and other sodium salts, a paracellular pathway between human taste bud receptor cells that allows access to the basolateral region of the cells is both functional and significant.

Bitter-Stimulus Transduction

The great chemical diversity of substances that humans are likely to describe as bitter suggests that more than one gustatory transduction mechanism and amplification sequence is likely to be involved (Bartoshuk, 1988; Stewart et al., 1997). Nonetheless, a general model for bitter compounds and for a bitterness receptor has been developed (Kubo, 1994; Shallenberger & Acree, 1971). This model is based on the structural chemistry of diterpenes and glycosides, and it has a conceptual similarity to the AH-B models of sweeteners and sweetener receptors. For bitter stimuli the model postulates both a bitter unit (consisting of a DH and an A group, separated by 150 picometers) and a hydrophobic portion of the molecule. The DH and A components are thought to hydrogen bond with a membrane receptor site, whereas the hydrophobic portion of the molecule aligns with the lipid phase of the cell membrane. It is unclear how this model relates to inorganic bitter stimuli.

Other models for transduction of bitter stimuli derive from biophysical, biochemical, and neurophysiological approaches using many different nonhuman vertebrate tissues and organs (e.g., K. Kurihara, Katsuragi, Matsuoka, Kashiwayanagi, & Kumazawa, 1994). In most, but not all (T. Sato, Okada, & Miyamoto, 1994) cases, multiple transduction mechanisms for bitter-stimuli are described with each mechanism pertinent only to certain molecules or ions, and perhaps present only in particular vertebrates (Brand, 1997; Dulac, 2000; Gilbertson et al., 2000; Glendinning et al., 2000; Herness & Gilbertson, 1999; Kinnamon, 2000). Putative membrane-bound bitter-stimulus receptor molecules, including some derived from human tissues, have now been identified (Adler et al., 2000; Chandrashekar et al., 2000; Dulac, 2000; Hoon et al., 1999), as well as associated G-proteins and several different second messengers. Which of these various transduction pathways actually functions in human judgments of bitterness, if any, has not been determined.

Glutamate-Tastant Transduction

In nonprimate mammals and in catfish, millimolar concentrations of glutamate and some of its salts—for example, monosodium glutamate (MSG)—appear to interact selectively with taste bud membrane-bound receptor sites that control the probability that apical membrane ion channels will be open (Brand, 1997; Herness & Gilbertson, 1999; Glendinning et al., 2000; Kinnamon, 1996). This mechanism is facilitated when guanosine 5′-monophosphate (GMP) or inosine 5′-monophosphate (IMP) is presented together with glutamates, an observation that is compatible with human judgments of combinations of glutamates and ribonucleotides such as GMP and IMP (Halpern, 2000). The extent to which the glutamate transduction mechanisms of laboratory rodents and catfish occurs in humans is unknown.

Fatty Acid-Tastant Transduction

Fat and fatty acids are often necessary and desirable components of human food systems (McGee, 1984; McWilliams, 1985). The current belief is that the oral sensory stimulation derived from fats includes modification of the physical structure of foods, and perhaps also involves the fact that fats serve as a medium in which lipid-soluble tastants can approach taste receptor cells, but excludes fats themselves as tastants. Nonetheless, present data suggest that fat break down products may be tastants. Biophysical measurements across the cell membranes of isolated rat circumvallate papilla taste bud receptor cells (whole-cell patch clamping) find that the permeability to K^+ ions is reduced by approximately 80% to 90% when particular fatty acids, at $10\,\mu M$, are present outside the cell. In the absence of patch clamping, the effect would be to depolarize the cell, thus increasing transmitter release. The effective fatty acids are all *cis*-polyunsaturated, such as *cis*-arachidonic, *cis*-linoleic, and *cis*-linolenic acids. Trans-fatty acids, such as *trans, trans*-linoleic acid, are ineffective, as are lauric acid and oleic acid. Effects are fully reversible and repeatable, but slow. A second possible taste bud mechanism for responses to fatty acids is suggested by histological studies on rat circumvallate papilla taste bud tissues using a selective stain for a fatty acid transport system. In the taste buds, the immunohistochemical staining shows that a fatty acid transporter is present, most heavily in the apical regions of the receptor cells. This transporter might be involved in moving fatty acids into taste bud receptor cells (Gilbertson, 1998; Gilbertson et al., 2000; Herness & Gilbertson, 1999). It is unknown if the suggested fatty acid transduction mechanisms, detected by biophysical and histochemical observations on rat circumvallate papillae, actually represent fatty acid gustatory response pathways in rats or humans.

Gustatory Neural Responses

Taste Bud Receptor Cell Responses

No human or nonhuman primate data on responses of single taste bud receptor cells to tastants are available, but recordings made with penetrating microelectrodes from individual mammalian fungiform papillae taste bud receptor cells in rats and hamsters do exist (Beidler, 1961; Kimura & Beidler, 1961). No two cells give identical receptor potentials (Figure 16.1C), but all cells respond to tastants from two or more categories. Later studies of taste bud receptor cells using patch clamping (see Purves et al., 2001), a technique that is less traumatic for the cell and can measure very small movements of charge, confirm the observation that individual mammalian taste bud receptor cells respond to a number of different tastants (Gilbertson, Boughter, Zhang, and Smith, 2001; Herness, 2000).

As with fungiform papillae taste buds, responses have been recorded from individual foliate papillae taste bud receptor cells. Instead of direct measures of change in transmembrane voltage or current, as was done with fungiform papillae cells, a technique is used that images intracellular calcium (Ca^{2+}; see Berridge, Lipp, & Bootman, 2000; Higdon & Gruenstein, 2001) to detect increases of Ca^{2+} concentration in foliate papillae receptor cells within tissue slices. Of those foliate papillae taste bud receptor cells that are responsive, most (67%) show changes in internal Ca^{2+} to only one of the five bitter stimuli tested (cycloheximide, denatonium, sucrose octaacetate, phenylthiocarbamide, and QHCl), although 26% respond to two; 7% respond to three of the five (Caicedo & Roper, 2001). One interpretation of these data is that for bitter stimuli, at least, most individual taste bud receptor cells are not broadly tuned, but instead respond to only one category of bitter stimuli. However, these observations may be limited to foliate papillae. Furthermore, even though in humans the foliate papilla QHCl recognition threshold is comparable to that for the anterolateral tongue region or a circumvallate papilla (see the section on taste psychophysics), because most of the receptor cells (82%) fail to show Ca^{2+} increase responses to any of the five bitter-stimuli, the meaning for human gustation of the apparently narrow tuning of rat foliate papilla taste bud receptor cells is unclear.

Individual Primary Afferent Gustatory Neurons

No data exist on neurophysiological responses of human individual afferent neurons innervating taste bud receptor cells. On the other hand, analogous results to the nonhuman single taste bud receptor cell observations just discussed are available from individual primary afferent neurons innervating nonhuman taste bud receptor cells (Figure 16.1C). These data indicate broad tuning of afferent gustatory neurons, that is, responses to a range of tastants, often representative of several different gustatory categories. However, larger neural responses are usually recorded to a subset of those tastants that are used, and these tastants often belong to only one or two categories of tastants, such as sweeteners or salt stimuli (Beidler & Tonosaki, 1985; Frank, 2000; McCaughey & Scott, 1998; Smith, St. John, & Boughter, 2000). As suggested in the introduction, there are divergent interpretations of the typically relatively broad but usually differential responsiveness to tastants of taste bud receptor cells and gustatory primary afferent neurons.

Single-unit peripheral gustatory neural responses have been recorded from several different nonhuman primates (Danilova, Hellekant, Roberts, Tinti, & Nofre, 1998; Hellekant, Danilova, & Ninomiya, 1997; Hellekant, Danilova, Roberts, & Ninomiya, 1997; Hellekant, Ninomiya, & Danilova, 1997, 1998; Ogawa, Yamashita, Noma, & Sato, 1972; Sato et al., 1994). These studies generally sum action potentials over 5 s or more and use as a response criterion a frequency during a tastant presentation that exceeds by at least two standard deviations the variability during equally long periods of solvent presentation. Under these processing and response criterion conditions, for 48 chimpanzee chorda tympani single units, it is reported that the best stimuli for each peripheral gustatory afferent neuron can be characterized as either sweeteners, QHCl plus other tastants, or NaCl plus other tastants (Hellekant, Ninomiya, et al., 1997). Responses of the sweetener-best units are described as occurring only to these best stimuli, as the basic tastes model would expect, although NaCl also elicits responses. More multifaceted stimulus profiles occur for the other chimpanzee gustatory unit classes, with the "QHCl-best plus" units also responding to HCl and an organic acid, as well as to amiloride, lithium chloride (LiCl), potassium chloride (KCl), and xylitol. Finally the "NaCl plus" units are divided into three subsets, depending on whether only NaCl, LiCl, MSG, and xylitol are effective stimuli, whether only NaCl, LiCl, and KCl are, or whether NaCl, KCl, MSG, and GMP are, with the latter two molecules being the most effective stimuli for this third "NaCl plus" subset.

If one adopts the basic tastes model's argument that only the largest gustatory neural responses are meaningful, even the rather broad patterns of response just described could provide supporting evidence. One immediate problem is determining which responses, though statistically reliable, are too small to matter. Suppose that a criterion is adopted that responses (in this case, the number of action potentials averaged over 5,000 ms) must be at least 25% of the largest response to have a sensory meaning. With this criterion, the sweetener-best units also respond to NaCl; the QHCl-best units respond meaningfully to various metallic chloride salts as well as to acids and the sweetener xylitol; one NaCl-best subset also responds to LiCl, MSG, and xylitol, whereas the other subset responds to NaCl, KCl, and LiCl; and the MSG-best units (i.e., one of the "NaCl plus" subsets) respond to GMP, NaCl, LiCl, KCl, and sodium saccharin. Of course, the selectivity of these units can be manipulated down or up by lowering or raising the criterion for a sufficiently large response. Decreasing or increasing the tastant concentrations can also have this effect. In both cases the operation is rather arbitrary.

A further complication is the data analysis method. Calculating the average number of action potentials over 5,000 ms (5 s) assumes that brief clusters of responses within this time period either do not occur or have no sensory meaning. However, RTs for human taste quality identification are about 1,000 ms (Halpern,

1991; Kelling & Halpern, 1988), one fifth of the time over which the chimpanzee neural responses are averaged. A 1,000-ms taste identification RT indicates that humans generate sufficient taste responses, transmit them to the CNS, decide what is being tasted, and do something about it, all in less than one second. Consequently, analysis in fractions-of-a-second periods of the nonhuman primate gustatory neural responses is needed. Suppose this were done for fifth-of-a-second intervals (i.e., averaging action potentials every 200 ms instead of every 5,000 ms). Suppose, further, that during one and only one of the 200 ms-intervals, a tastant reliably evokes about 25 action potentials. This would be quite respectable on a time scale in which action potentials are counted over 200-ms, but it would be very small when averaged over 5,000 ms. The action potential numbers over 200 ms are hypothetical, but data supplied by Hellekant, Ninomiya, et al. (1997) illustrate brief action potential bursts during stimulation with tastants, and list many "ineffective" tastants that produce only 25 action potentials over 5,000 ms.

Time intervals of 200 ms may seem unreasonably short for gustatory neural action potential averaging because human taste quality identification RTs are about 1,000 ms. However, a taste stimulus *duration* of only 50 ms is long enough to permit human descriptions of tastants. In addition, simple taste RTs, in which subjects report only the presence of a tastant, are about 400 ms to 700 ms, with the briefest being less than 300 ms (Halpern, 1991).

Human Peripheral Gustatory Neural Responses

In humans, only multiunit peripheral nerve gustatory response data are available (Diamant, 1968; Diamant, Funakoshi, Ström, & Zotterman, 1963; Diamant, Oakley, Ström, Wells, & Zotterman, 1965; Diamant &

Zotterman, 1959; Oakley, 1985, 1986; Zotterman, 1967). Gustatory afferent responses are recorded from the cut human chorda tympani nerve during therapeutic middle ear surgery in which patients are maintained under general anesthesia. The time of stimulus solution arrival at the tongue is not precisely known, but responses all rise from baseline to maximum in less than 1 s, reaching two thirds of maximum in about 200 ms. Responses fall much more slowly, taking about 15 s to decrease to about one third of maximum, and over 1 min to decline to baseline. Sometimes, magnitude estimates of taste intensity are obtained a few days before chorda tympani nerve recording. Both power functions and linear equations fit the neural data and the intensity judgments. For any one patient, there is good correspondence between the neural and psychophysical data, but less between patients (Halpern, 1991). In general, the speed of human gustatory neural responses is commensurate with taste RTs, and for any one individual, neural and psychophysical response magnitudes have similar rankings.

Human CNS Gustatory Neural Responses

No human single-unit or multiple-unit CNS gustatory cortex neural response data are available. However, another neural response measure from human cortical gustatory areas, called gustatory evoked magnetic fields (GEM), is available (Kobayakawa et al., 1999; Saito, Kobayakawa, Ayabe-Kanamura, Gotow, & Ogawa, 2000). The general method is known as magnetoencephalography (MEG). MEG measurements may access the activity of groups of cerebral cortical cells with less distortion and more spatial resolution than do electroencephalographic (EEG) methods: "Magnetoencephalography involves the measurement of neuromagnetic signals outside the head. Just like an electric current passing through a wire generates a magnetic field,

so does an ionic current within the brain. An advantage of magnetoencephalography over electroencephalography is that neuromagnetic signals penetrate the skull and scalp without any significant distortion. As a result, the spatial resolution of MEG can be higher than that of EEG." (Huiskamp, 2001). Dynamic MEG responses elicited by gustatory stimuli have been designated GEM; they reflect some aspects of the activity of a population of cortical cells that is localized in space and time. It is thought that postsynaptic potentials are the major source of GEM.

Human gustatory cortical activity believed to represent the primary gustatory cortical area is localized by MEG to the region of transition between the opercular cortex and the insula (Kobayakawa et al., 1999). Average activation times are 155 ± 45 ms for 1 M NaCl and 267 ± 92 ms for 3 mM saccharin. These cortical GEM latencies are 300 ms to 500 ms shorter than median simple taste RTs to similar solutions (Kelling & Halpern, 1987). No activation was detected in orbitofrontal cortex, but this may be due to the orientation of the magnetic field detection coils in their superconducting quantum interference device (SQUID).

TASTE PSYCHOPHYSICS

Taste Buds and Papillae

Single Fungiform Papillae

Histological examination of human fungiform papillae after psychophysical testing reveals that almost 60% of these papillae contain no taste buds. Stimulation of these nontaste-bud fungiform papillae with relatively high concentration tastants never evokes taste responses. In contrast, in almost every instance (96%) stimulation of the papillae that have taste buds does elicit taste responses (Arvidson & Friberg, 1980). These twin observations indicate that although trigeminal nerve terminals are probably present in all fungiform papillae (Bryant & Silver, 2000; Mistretta, 1991; Zahm & Munger, 1985), these chemesthetic afferent nerve endings are not, in the absence of taste buds, sufficient to permit human taste responses to NaCl, sucrose, citric acid, or QHCl solutions. It may be that the access through the superficial layer of the papillary epithelium that is provided by the pore of a mature human taste bud is necessary for these tastant solutions to initiate perceptually recognized responses by way of trigeminal afferents. In similar fashion, tastants applied to oral areas without taste buds cannot be localized (Shikata et al., 2000).

Many additional psychophysical data on responses to gustatory stimulation of individual human fungiform papillae are available (Bealer & Smith, 1975; Cardello, 1978; Halpern, 1987; Harper, Jay, & Erickson, 1966; Kuznicki & Cardello, 1986; Kuznicki & McCutcheon, 1979; Sandick & Cardello, 1981). The general outcomes are that a range of descriptions of taste quality can be elicited from stimulation of an individual fungiform papilla, even when that papilla is subsequently shown to have only a single taste bud; that fungiform papillae without taste buds are unresponsive to gustatory stimuli; and that thresholds are higher, often by a factor of 10 or more, than those for which multiple-papillae areas are stimulated. These three psychophysical observations provide important constraints for interpretations of functional anatomy. They show that a human fungiform papilla must have at least one taste bud if stimulation by tastants is to occur, that a single fungiform papilla taste bud is sufficient for responsiveness to many tastants, and that sensory output of taste buds of separate fungiform papillae is combined (apparently in the CNS) such that overall system sensitivity is very substantially enhanced, thus demonstrating appreciable spatial summation in human taste (see Delwiche, Buletic, and Breslin, 2001a). A strong implication is that human gustatory perception is not dependent on taste-bud-bearing fungiform papillae that respond to only one or two categories of tastants. It is possible that the receptor cells that comprise each taste bud in a human papilla, individually or in groups, respond to only one or two categories of tastants (e.g., Beidler & Tonosaki, 1985). However, as already summarized under gustatory neural responses in the gustatory physiology section, in non-human mammals individual taste bud receptor cells respond to a range of tastants.

Number of Fungiform Papillae Stimulated and Taste Judgments

During tasting outside the laboratory, it is quite unlikely that only a single fungiform papilla at the front of the tongue will be stimulated, or even that localized natural tastant concentrations will be different from one of these fungiform papillae to its immediate neighbors. Consequently, gustatory sensitivity related to total number of papillae stimulated or to cumulative area of the fungiform papillae region involved, comparable to stimulus-area relationships observed in the somesthetic system (Chap. 13, this volume), seems likely and is in fact observed. For example, mean detection threshold for NaCl decreases as the number of fungiform papillae included increases (Doty et al., 2001). The largest number of fungiform papillae per unit area of the tongue (i.e., density) is greatest at the front of the tongue (also known as the anterodorsal tip region). As noted in the introduction, thresholds for a number of tastants are lowest at the front of the tongue. However, fungiform papillae density does not predict taste judgments for all measures or tastants. Thus, threshold for citric acid, but not citric acid sourness, varies with density of fungiform papillae. Correlation between estimated fungiform papillae taste bud density and citric acid threshold is modest although significant ($r = -0.42$; Zuniga et al., 1993). Also, change in judged sweetness of sucrose does not differ between oral taste-bud populations (Collings, 1974). For two other tastants, QHCl and 6-n-propyl-2-thiouracil (PROP), each subject's judgments of bitterness intensity, measured with a labeled magnitude scale (see Green et al., 1996), does increase with the number of fungiform papillae receiving the tastant solution (Delwiche, Buletic, & Breslin, 2001b). Nonetheless, between subjects, difference in the number of papillae or in papilla density does not relate to subjects' PROP sensitivity, and is not a good predictor of judged bitterness.

In general, it appears that factors besides the density of fungiform papillae taste buds are important in determining taste thresholds and that specification of taste bud or papilla density, or of the dorsal anterolateral tongue area on which tastants are applied, is not sufficient to predict judgments of gustatory intensity. Of the various psychophysical measures, thresholds may be most closely related to the number of fungiform papillae reached and, presumably, to the number of taste buds stimulated (the presence of taste bud pores was often not verified). Many physiological and structural differences between individuals might underlay the observed failure of fungiform papillae counts or density to account fully for the psychophysical data. These differences could include characteristics and degrees of expression of transduction mechanisms, properties of interactions among taste bud receptor cells, the nature of afferent innervation of taste buds by gustatory nerves, and CNS processing.

Single Foliate Papillae

Highly controlled presentation of tastants to foliate papillae is difficult because the stimuli must penetrate into folds extending below the tongue surface before reaching the pores of the many (120 to 140) taste buds that line each fold. Foliate papilla-evoked gustatory thresholds and intensity judgments differ in a tastant-dependent manner from other oral taste bud populations (Collings, 1974). For example, citric acid recognition thresholds for single foliate papilla are lower than at all other lingual or oral (palate) locations, but NaCl and urea thresholds are higher. In contrast to urea, QHCl thresholds are similar to other regions with taste buds. With intensity judgments, the slope for citric acid is steeper than at other loci, and urea and QHCl differ from each other.

Single Circumvallate Papillae

Psychophysical studies of single circumvallate papilla recognition thresholds, taste intensity slopes, and taste descriptions show both responses to many tastants and some differences from the more anterior, fungiform and foliate papillae regions, as well as from the palatal taste bud area. Recognition thresholds for stimulation of a circumvallate or a foliate papilla with urea or QHCl are similar, but judged intensity of QHCl increases more rapidly for a circumvallate papilla than elsewhere in the mouth. Citric acid applied to a circumvallate papilla is generally described as sour, but intensity is low, and threshold is high. In contrast, sucrose evokes responses with sensitivity and intensity that are comparable to those of most other oral locations except the tip of the tongue and exceeds the tip region in the likelihood that a concentrated sucrose solution will be described as sweet (Collings, 1974; Sandick & Cardello, 1981).

Single Papilla Functional Differences and Models of Gustatory Organization

Stimulation of a single foliate papilla is likely to involve about 30 times as many taste buds as would a single fungiform papilla; stimulation of a circumvallate papilla likely involves

50 to 200 times as many taste buds. If numbers of taste buds were the sole factor, circumvallate papillae would be expected to have lower thresholds than foliate or fungiform papillae and steeper intensity slopes, with the fungiform papillae achieving a distant third in every measure. In contrast, fungiform papillae thresholds for a number of tastants are lower than elsewhere on the tongue, and they become lower still when a small number of these papillae are stimulated in unison. Furthermore, threshold for a particular basic-taste tastant is higher at one locus than at other loci but lower with other tastants, and intensity functions increase for some tastants but decrease for others from one taste bud region to another. To explain these data, substantial variations in gustatory receptor cell or CNS processing of the same tastants are necessary. This seems contrary to the expectations of the basic tastes model. In this context the differences between effects of urea and QHCl are of particular interest, because both are considered bitter stimuli. These psychophysical data demonstrate that multiple transduction mechanisms for tastants of a single category exist in humans, as they do in other vertebrates.

Tastants and Taste Response Categories

The basic tastes model of gustatory function indicates that tastants should elicit only one meaningful gustatory category and that the best stimuli for a particular category—be it sweet or sour, bitter, salty, or glutamate-taste—should be indiscriminable, with concentration as the only necessary variable (see the introduction). These basic tastes postulates have been tested for several tastants. Results are discussed in the context of each tastant class and taste description category.

Sweeteners and Sweetness

A wide variety of plant-based and human-created substances are sweeteners (Bakal,

1997; Beidler, 1978; Birch, 1997a; Glendinning et al., 2000; Guesry & Secrétin, 1991; Hough, 1989; Lee, 1979; Schiffman et al., 1986; Yoshida & Saito, 1969). Human sweetness recognition thresholds for these sweeteners extend over a seven-log unit range, from nanomolar concentration for the protein thaumatin through about $20\,\mu M$ for sodium saccharin to about 3 mM for sucrose. Detection thresholds for sweeteners can be 1 to 3 log units lower (Breslin, 2000; Lawless, 2000; Pfaffmann, 1959; Stevens, Cruz, Hoffman, & Patterson, 1995). There is a great diversity of noncarbohydrate sweeteners in addition to the well-known sugars, for example, several chloride salts, including NaCl at or below concentrations of 20 mM and calcium chloride ($CaCl_2$) through 10 mM (ca. 25% sweet reports, Tordoff, 1996), and plant-derived glycosides (Birch, 1997a; Lee, 1979) such as stevioside, which is effective at a 1 mM concentration (Schiffman, Lockhead, & Maes, 1983) elicit reports of sweetness.

All sweeteners could evoke essentially the same perceptual experience, as the basic tastes model predicts (Schifferstein, 1996), or sweetness could be as heterogeneous a cognitive category as sweeteners are chemically, permitting observers to distinguish and differentiate various sweeteners more or less readily. One approach to the possible unitary nature of human responses to sweeteners is to ask whether pairs of sweeteners, at concentrations that are described as sweet, can be made indiscriminable to individual judges solely by adjusting the concentration of one of the tastants. This absence of discriminability occurs for the sugars fructose, glucose, maltose, and sucrose (Breslin, 2000; Breslin, Beauchamp, & Pugh, 1996; Breslin, Kemp, & Beauchamp, 1994). This is an important observation because it suggests that for these carbohydrate sweeteners, at least, a unitary perception provides a complete description and could be based on one gustatory mechanism. In support of this concept is the observation that the modal description of two chemically quite different sweeteners, sucrose and sodium saccharin, presented in various ways to the anterior region of the tongue, is always the word "sweet" (Halpern, 1987; Kelling & Halpern, 1988).

In further agreement with the concept of sweetness as an independent and self-contained taste category are reports that several plant-derived substances (taste modifiers) selectively block judged sweetness of tastants and have little or no effects on responses to other tastants (e.g., Bartoshuk, 1977; Breslin, 2000; Kennedy & Halpern, 1980; Kurihara et al., 1988; Meiselman & Halpern, 1970; Meiselman, Halpern, & Dateo, 1976; Riskey, Desor, & Vellucci, 1982; V. V. Smith & Halpern, 1983). Deducing a single sweetness mechanism from these data may nonetheless be inappropriate because an analysis of the underlying biophysics and biochemistry suggests that these taste modifiers penetrate into taste receptor cells, acting at one or more of the amplification steps (Kennedy, Bourassa, & Rogers, 1993).

Despite the already cited observations that the taste of several sugars can differ only in intensity and that chemically disparate sweeteners may have the same taste, human judgments of sweeteners do not always conform to a unitary concept of sweetness. For example, when low sugar concentrations are studied, sweetness recognition thresholds for sucrose and fructose are similar but are different from and independent of a third sugar, glucose. In addition, individuals' thresholds for glucose decrease over time, whereas those for fructose remain constant (Eylam & Kennedy, 1998; Kennedy, Eylam, Poskanzer, & Saikku, 1997). When a more diverse set of sweeteners is used, including sugars, proteins, saccharin, and D-leucine, recognition thresholds for one sweetener have little correlation with the thresholds for other sweeteners;

the largest correlation is $r = 0.37$ (Faurion, Saito, & MacLeod, 1980). Attempts to determine the possible number of sweetness categories by matching suprathreshold intensities of 12 sweeteners to a range of sucrose concentrations find four factors, represented by (a) chloroform, (b) D-leucine, (c) thaumatin and stevioside, and (d) sugars plus the other sweeteners. Finally, pair-wise intensity comparisons of 40 tastants, during which nontaste input via retronasal olfaction is minimized by a constant air flow into the anterior nares, also results in a four-fold grouping of sweeteners (Faurion, 1992).

In general, it appears unlikely that all sweeteners produce the same taste experience or utilize a single gustatory mechanism, but a small number of sweetener-activated mechanisms, perhaps only three or four, may suffice. Both the psychophysical data and the physiological results reviewed under the section on gustatory physiology support multiple sweetness mechanisms. Human judgments of the full range of sweeteners indicate that sweetness is a complex cognition rather than a unitary perception whose only dimension is intensity. Notwithstanding the observation that the sweetness of a limited set of sugars can be matched simply by adjusting concentration, a broader view of sweeteners fails to confirm this prediction of the basic tastes model.

Acid Tastants and Sourness

If strong acids (i.e., acids that are highly dissociated in solution, where dissociation means that they are separated into ions) are, with reference to human taste, little more than sources of hydrogen ions (H^+), then at concentrations at which taste quality descriptions are given to these solutions, it should be possible to find concentrations of a strong acid that judges cannot discriminate from a solution of another strong acid. This is the case for hydrochloric (HCl), nitric (HNO_3), and sulfuric (H_2SO_4) acids tasted at equal pH values, all at concentrations between 5 mM and 10 mM (Breslin & Beauchamp, 1994). In this experiment, aqueous concentrations of HCl that produce a pH of either 2.5 or 3.1 are taken as a standard, and the discriminability from the HCl solution of various concentrations of HNO_3 and H_2SO_4 is examined. When the HNO_3 or H_2SO_4 matches the pH of the HCl, subjects can not discriminate between them (Paul A. S. Breslin, personal communication, October, 2000). It appears that for these relatively low concentrations of strong acids—thresholds for these acids are approximately 1 mM, that is, pH 3 in pure water (Pfaffmann, 1959; Breslin, 2000)—a single gustatory perception or cognitive category is elicited, even though the three strong acids dissociate into quite different anions in addition to the common H^+ cation.

The perceptual or cognitive characteristics of the single gustatory category for strong acids are not specified by a lack of discriminability within the category. It might be assumed that the word "sour" would be a complete description of the taste of acids, but this is not the case. When subjects are required to divide total taste intensity among sweet, sour, salty, bitter, and other taste quality descriptions, and solutions are presented using sip-and-spit whole-mouth stimulation, HCl and H_2SO_4 are approximately 16% bitter and approximately 13% salty, as well as approximately 65% sour (Settle, Meehan, Williams, Doty, & Sisley, 1986). If tastant solutions are flowed over a small area of the anterodorsal tongue tip region, HCl at 3.2 mM or 10 mM, very similar to the Breslin and Beauchamp (1994) indiscriminability concentration range, is never predominantly "sour." Salty descriptions are always present for HCl under these circumstances, but if a complex characterization of HCl is permitted, including acid, sour, salty-sour, and sour-sweet, this set of descriptions often represents the majority of all reports (Kelling & Halpern,

1988). The latter observations suggest that HCl, though adding only hydrogen and chloride ions (H^+ and Cl^-) to the water solvent, and sometimes considered the archetypal sour stimulus, produces a complex human taste cognition. Similar results occur for the organic acid tastant, citric acid. In this case there are large individual differences in descriptions, as well as frequent use of multiple adjectives (O'Mahony, Hobson, Garvey, Davies, & Brit, 1976).

Furthermore, if acids activate only one gustatory mechanism and produce a unitary perception, descriptions of acids should be the same for different taste bud regions, with concentration as the only significant factor. This is not observed. Citric acid at 125 mM, applied to groups of 4 to 10 fungiform papillae on the anterior portion of the tongue, is described almost equally as salty, bitter, and sour, with salty predominating (Sandick & Cardello, 1981). However, when the same solution is applied to a single circumvallate papilla, most of the taste intensity is assigned to sour, with a low proportion of bitter and an even lower proportion of salty.

An additional complexity is a discontinuity between the pH of acids and human judgments of the intensity of partially dissociated weak acids (Ganzevles & Kroeze, 1987; Gibson & Hartman, 1919; Norris, Noble, & Pangborn, 1984; Pfaffmann, 1959). When pH of organic acids is made equal and careful buffering is employed, human ratings of sourness intensity remain unequal, indicating that differences due to anions must be the determining factor.

Overall, human judgments of sourness are not a simple function of H^+, and tastes of acids, including HCl, include descriptions such as salty and bitter in addition to sour. Because application of the same acid tastants to different taste bud regions elicits different descriptions, the gustatory mechanisms activated at these loci must also differ.

Salt Stimuli and Saltiness

NaCl is the archetypical salt-taste stimulus for humans (Gillette, 1985; Lynch, 1987; O'Donnell, 1998). When NaCl solutions are flowed over a small area of the anterodorsal tongue tip region, descriptions of 500 mM NaCl are at least 90% salty when subjects do free-choice profiling. At a lower concentration, 250 mM NaCl is 95% salty (Halpern & Darlington, 1998; Kelling & Halpern, 1988). With sip-and-spit presentations of 100 mM NaCl, the description selected is 100% salty when nine descriptors (bitter, metallic, none, other, salty, soapy, sulfurous, sour, sweet) are available (Hettinger, Frank, & Myers, 1996). However, in contrast, delivery of a range of NaCl concentrations to a single circumvallate papilla often produces descriptions of sour or bitter (Sandick & Cardello, 1981). It appears that NaCl's status as the best stimulus for saltiness is primarily dependent on input from the anterodorsal tongue, fungiform papilla region.

The connection between NaCl and saltiness is further complicated by the frequent observations that the taste of NaCl solutions varies with concentration. For example, at concentrations less that 10 times detection threshold, descriptions of sweet are common for sip-and-spit or anterodorsal tongue presentations of NaCl, but at higher concentrations, reports of sweet disappear, and those of salty became more frequent. However, even at concentrations of 30 mM to 100 mM, NaCl—though predominately salty—is also bitter (Halpern & Darlington, 1998; Hettinger, Frank, & Myers, 1996; Kelling & Halpern, 1988; Pfaffmann, 1959; Pfaffmann, Bartoshuk, & McBurney, 1971).

Bitter Stimuli and Bitterness

The substances that humans are likely to categorize as bitter are as diverse chemically as are the sweeteners. Bitter stimuli include inorganic salts such as KCl, $CaCl_2$, magnesium chloride ($MgCl_2$) and magnesium sulfate ($MgSO_4$), and a host of organic compounds: methylated xanthines (e.g., caffeine), alcohols, alkaloids (including quinolines, nicotine, and strychnine), chloropyrazinecarboxamides (e.g., amiloride), many amino acids, catechins, denatonium benzoate, flavanols, phenols, isomerized humulones (from hops), PROP, steroid glucosides, the acetylated sugar sucrose octa-acetate (SOA), and urea (Belitz & Wieser, 1985; Guinard, Hong, Zoumas-Morse, Budwig, & Russell, 1994; Halpern, 1994; Herness & Gilbertson, 1999; Kato, Rhue, & Nishimura, 1989; Ney, 1979; Usuki & Kaneda, 1980). Most of these compounds are of plant origin; many are components of human foods or beverages (Mattes, 1994; Noble, 1994).

A basic question for bitterness is whether all bitter stimuli elicit a single gustatory category. The basic tastes model predicts such a unitary bitterness category. The across-fiber-pattern model is less clear but suggests that multiple categories for bitter stimuli are not surprising and that no one best stimulus for bitterness exists. Some psychophysical measures do indicate that bitterness is not unitary. For example, complete cross-adaptation occurs between some bitter stimuli, but only partial cross-adaptation occurs between others (McBurney, 1978), and detection thresholds for these stimuli have a 2,000-fold range (Breslin, 2000; Lawless, 2000; Pfaffmann, 1959; Pfaffmann et al., 1971). In addition, when a number of chemically diverse bitter stimuli are judged for total and bitterness intensity with both the labeled magnitude scale and ranking for bitterness, at least three clusters of bitter-stimuli are found: (a) epicatechin, L-phenylalanine, L-tryptophan, and urea; (b) PROP; (c) caffeine, denatonium benzoate, quinine, $MgSO_4$, SOA, and tetralone (a mixture of iso-alpha-acids), with an indication that $MgSO_4$, rather than being grouped with some of the other bitter stimuli, might represent a fourth cluster (Delwiche et al., 2001a). Overall, it appears that bitterness is a complex gustatory cognitive category, rather than a unitary taste perception. The human psychophysical data that indicate this outcome are reinforced by the chemical diversity of bitter stimuli and the putative multiple transduction mechanisms for these tastants.

Two bitter stimuli, phenylthiocarbamide and PROP, are of special interest. This is the case because threshold for these bitter stimuli is a heritable trait and is reported to correlate with the density of lingual taste buds and their pores (although not by Delwiche et al., 2001b), as well as with intensity judgments for PROP. Individuals with relatively high PROP thresholds (e.g., greater than $200\,\mu M$) are designated nontasters; those with PROP thresholds below $100\,\mu M$ are designated either medium tasters or supertasters. All nonageusic individuals are apparently able to discriminate between PROP and solvent and to make magnitude estimates of suprathreshold PROP. Supertasters are distinguished from medium tasters by their steeper magnitude estimate function for PROP (Bartoshuk, 1988, 2000; Bartoshuk, Duffy, & Miller, 1994; Lawless, 1996; Miller & Bartoshuk, 1991; Prutkin et al., 2000; Sposato, 2000).

If sensitivity to PROP, as well as classification as nontaster, taster, or supertaster, are indexes of general gustatory ability or are predictive of food choice, measures of taste responses to PROP would be important guides to human taste function and would be useful in understanding food-related behaviors. However, connections between taste judgments of PROP, judgments of other tastants, and preferences for foods remain unsettled. Contradictory results exist for predictions of gustatory sensitivity to acetic acid,

caffeine, quinine salts, sucrose, or KCl, and correlations between PROP sensitivity and food choice are inconsistent (Delwiche et al., 2001a; Drewnowski, Henderson, & Shore, 1997; Drewnowski, Henderson, Shore, & Barratt-Fornell, 1998; Drewnowski, Kristal, & Cohen, 2001; Ly & Drewnowski, 2001; Marks, Borg, & Westerlund, 1992; Sato, Okada, Miyamoto, & Fujiyama, 1997; Sposato, 2000; Tepper & Nurse, 1998). It is possible that the manner in which psychophysical procedures are applied is a crucial factor in the divergent results for correlations between PROP and other tastants, with intensity judgments perhaps distorted unless psychophysical measurement instruments have appropriate upper criteria (Bartoshuk, 2000; Prutkin et al., 2000). Regardless, when bitter stimuli are both rated and ranked, some subjects give low intensity ratings to all bitter stimuli, but rank bitter stimuli as do other subjects, with PROP not correlated with other bitter stimuli (Delwiche et al., 2001a).

Glutamate Tastants, MSG, and Umami

Many amino acids and their derivatives are tastants. Glutamic acid is of particular interest both because it is widely distributed in nature and because a salt, MSG, is often added in the preparation of foods (Lawless, 1996; Yamaguchi & Ninomiya, 1998). The taste of MSG, the sodium salt of L-glutamic acid, is most simply characterized as glutamate taste (Ikeda, 1912). However, MSG together with certain ribonucleotides, particularly IMP and GMP, is often described as an umami tastant (Kuninaka, 1981; Lawless, 1996, 2000; Maga, 1987; Yamaguchi, 1987). Use of the term *umami* to characterize human gustatory judgments of MSG, with or without IMP or GMP, is linguistically moot because in Japanese the word often connotes a cognitive category (Yamaguchi & Ninomiya, 1998) of taste, or perhaps flavor, with definitions that include deliciousness, flavor, relish, gusto, and zest (Inoue, 1983). In effect, the Japanese word *umami* can denote a really good taste of something—a taste or flavor that is an especially appropriate exemplar of the flavor of that something (Backhouse, 1978).

One direct test of the appropriateness of the term *umami* for the taste of MSG is to ask native speakers of Japanese to describe an MSG solution. For 1 M MSG applied to single fungiform papillae at the tip of the tongue, reports are predominately bitter or salty (in Japanese), but never umami. Comparable descriptions are provided by native speakers of English, suggesting that whether or not umami is part of ones's lexicon, spontaneous taste description of MSG use other terms (Halpern, 1987). With a more complex judgment task and a lower concentration (214 mM), MSG is first soapy, then bitter (Zwillinger & Halpern, 1991). These descriptions are compatible with reports that the taste of MSG itself is unpleasant (Faurion, 1987; Yamaguchi, 1991). However, none of these data indicate whether MSG elicits a singular basic taste and should therefore be placed in the pantheon of the basic tastes model, or whether it produces one of an almost infinite number of human gustatory experiences, as the across-fiber-pattern model suggests (O'Mahony & Ishii, 1987; Yamaguchi, 1987, 1998).

Descriptions of MSG as bitter, salty, soapy, and unpleasant would not seem to recommend it as an ingredient to improve the flavor of foods. Nonetheless, at low concentrations and in the appropriate food systems, the pleasantness and acceptability of the food is increased by the addition of MSG, often accompanied by even lower concentrations of IMP or GMP. Alternatively, soy sauce, tomato, certain cheeses, or mushrooms are used, supplying glutamic acid or ribonucleotides while meeting criteria of naturalness (Halpern, 2000; Yamaguchi, 1998).

Age and Tasting

Sensory systems often change their characteristics in older individuals. However, age does not consistently alter all judgments of tastants.

Sweeteners

For sucrose, the sweetener most used in aging studies, significant increases of detection thresholds as a function of age occur in some reports (Moore, Nielsen, & Mistretta, 1982; Richter & Campbell, 1940; Stevens et al., 1995), but not in others (Cowart, 1989; Stevens, 1996; Weiffenbach, Baum, & Burghauser, 1982). Observed elevations are not very large, averaging less than four-fold, and they are sometimes revealed only by repeated testing. Suprathreshold judgments of the sweetness of sucrose solutions are little affected by age (Cowart, 1989; Gilmore & Murphy, 1989; Murphy & Gilmore, 1989, 1990; Weiffenbach, Tylenda, & Baum, 1990), in agreement with the proposal that aging effects on judgments of sucrose are not very noteworthy. Because sweeteners appear to differ in the gustatory mechanisms that they activate and because judgments of one sweetener often poorly predict those to others, the modest effects of aging on taste responses to sucrose may not generalize to other sweeteners.

Acid Tastants

Most, if not all, age-related studies of gustation that include an acid tastant use citric acid, thus precluding any general conclusions regarding acid tastants and age. Detection thresholds for citric acid do not vary with age in one study (Weiffenbach et al., 1982), but they do in another (Stevens, 1996). Judged sourness intensity of citric acid significantly decreases with age (Murphy & Gilmore, 1989).

Salt Stimuli

As with other tastants, effects of age on gustatory judgments of NaCl depend on the measure. With sip-and-spit presentations, NaCl detection threshold increases, but judged saltiness intensity does not change (Cowart, 1989; Murphy & Gilmore, 1989, 1990; Weiffenbach et al., 1990).

General Age Effects

A significant decrease with age occurs in a taste identification task in which responses are scored as correct when a solution of sucrose is identified as sweet, QSO_4 as bitter, NaCl as salty, and citric acid as sour (Cowart, 1989). However, the specific measure and the health status of the aged individuals may be major factors. A longitudinal investigation over 10-year time spans found no alteration in judgments of taste intensity among healthy older people (Weiffenbach, 1994). Overall, it remains unclear whether all aspects of human taste judgments tend to become worse with age and, at a broader level, whether advancing age, per se, or events and conditions that are more likely to exist in older individuals, underlie those changes that do occur.

SUMMARY

Mammalian taste systems are much more complex than might have been envisioned at the middle of the 20th century. The gustatory receptor cells themselves are transient structures that contain a wide variety of transduction mechanisms. Some details of these transduction mechanisms are now known, and candidate receptor molecules for initial interactions with tastants have been identified. Often, the degree to which these observations can be generalized to humans is unresolved. It is known that the CNS gustatory anatomy of humans and other higher primates is fundamentally different from that of most mammals, further limiting facile generalizations. Imaging techniques such as fMRI and PET, as well as recording approaches such as MEG, are revealing the complex CNS functional anatomy and processing of the human taste system. A fundamental theoretical issue—the organizational and informational characteristics of the human taste system—remains debatable: Both the basic tastes model and the across-fiber-pattern model have received empirical support. It seems likely that a middle ground, rather than either extreme theoretical position, best characterizes the complexity of the human gustatory system.

REFERENCES

Adler, E., Hoon, M. A., Mueller, K. L., Chandrashekar, J., Ryba, N. J., & Zuker, C. S. (2000). A novel family of mammalian taste receptors. *Cell, 100,* 693–702.

Arvidson, K. (1976). Scanning electron microscopy of fungiform papillae on the tongue of man and monkey. *Acta Otolaryngol, 81,* 496–502.

Arvidson, K. (1979). Location and variation in number of taste buds in human fungiform papillae. *Scandinavian Journal of Dental Research, 87,* 435–442.

Arvidson, K., Cottler-Fox, M., & Friberg, U. (1981). Fine structure of taste buds in human fungiform papilla. *Scandinavian Journal of Dental Research, 89,* 297–306.

Arvidson, K., & Friberg, U. (1980). Human taste: Response and taste bud number in fungiform papillae. *Science, 209,* 807–808.

Backhouse, A. E. (1978). *Japanese taste terms.* Unpublished doctoral dissertation, University of Edinburgh, Edinburgh, Scotland.

Bakal, A. (1997, March). A satisfyingly sweet overview. *Prepared Food,* 47–50.

Bartoshuk, L. M. (1977). Modification of taste quality. In G. G. Birch, J. G. Brennan, & K. J.

Parker (Eds.), *Sensory properties of foods* (pp. 5–26). London: Applied Science.

Bartoshuk, L. M. (1988). Taste. In R. C. Atkinson, R. J. Herrenstein, G. Lindzey, & R. D. Luce (Eds.), *Stevens' handbook of experimental psychology* (2nd ed., pp. 461–499). New York: Wiley.

Bartoshuk, L. M. (2000). Comparing sensory experiences across individuals: Recent psychophysical advances illuminate genetic variation in taste. *Chemical Senses, 25,* 447–460.

Bartoshuk, L. M., Duffy, V. B., & Miller, I. J. (1994). PTC/PROP tasting: Anatomy, psychophysics, and sex effects. *Physiology and Behavior, 56,* 1165–1171.

Bealer, S. L., & Smith, D. V. (1975). Multiple sensitivity to chemical stimuli in single human taste papillae. *Physiology and Behavior, 14,* 795–799.

Beauchamp, G. K., & Bartoshuk, L. M. (Eds.). (1997). *Tasting and smelling: Handbook of perception and cognition* (2nd ed.). San Diego: Academic Press.

Beauchamp, G. K., & Moran, M. (1986). Taste in young children. In H. L. Meiselman & R. S. Rivlin (Eds.), *Clinical measurement of taste and smell* (pp. 305–315). New York: Macmillan.

Beckstead, R. M., Morse, J. R., & Norgren, R. (1980). The nucleus of the solitary tract in the monkey: Projections to the thalamus and brain stem nuclei. *The Journal of Comparative Neurology, 190,* 259–282.

Beidler, L. M. (1961). Biophysical approaches to taste. *American Scientist, 49,* 421–431.

Beidler, L. M. (Ed.). (1971). *Handbook of sensory physiology: Volume 4. Chemical senses. Section 2. Taste.* Berlin: Springer-Verlag.

Beidler, L. M. (1978). Biophysics and chemistry of taste. In E. C. Carterette & M. P. Friedman (Eds.), *Handbook of perception: Volume 6A. Tasting and smelling* (pp. 3–18). New York: Academic Press.

Beidler, L. M., & Smith, J. C. (1991). Effects of radiation therapy and drugs on cell turnover and taste. In T. V. Getchell, R. L. Doty, L. M. Bartoshuk, & J. B. Snow Jr. (Eds.), *Smell and taste in health and disease* (pp. 753–763). New York: Raven Press.

Beidler, L. M., & Tonosaki, K. (1985). Multiple sweet receptor sites and taste theory. In D. W. Pfaff (Ed.), *Taste, olfaction, and the central nervous system* (pp. 47–64). New York: Rockefeller University Press.

Belitz, H.-D., & Wieser, H. (1985). Bitter compounds: Occurrence and structure-activity relationships. *Food Reviews International, 1,* 271–354.

Berridge, M. J., Lipp, P., & Bootman, M. D. (2000). The versatility and universality of Ca^{2+} signaling. *Nature Reviews of Molecular and Cellular Biology, 1,* 11–21.

Birch, G. G. (1997a, February). Sweeteners: A question of taste. *Chemistry and Industry,* 90–94.

Birch, G. G. (1997b). Sweet sensation. *Biologist, 44,* 451–453.

Birch, G. G., Parke, S., Siertsemak, R., & Westwell, J. M. (1997). Importance of molar volumes and related parameters in sweet taste chemoreception. *Pure and Applied Chemistry, 69,* 685–692.

Boucher, Y., Fahrang, F., Azérad, J., & Faurion, A. (2000). Effect of dental deafferentation on gustatory sensitivity. *ISOT 2000 and ECRO 2000 Abstracts,* Brighton UK, 155.

Boughter, J. D., Jr., & Gilbertson, T. A. (1999). From channels to behavior: An integrative model of NaCl taste. *Neuron, 22,* 213–215.

Bradley, R. M., Stedman, H. M., & Mistretta, C. M. (1985). Age does not affect number of taste buds and papillae in adult rhesus monkeys. *The Anatomical Record, 212,* 246–249.

Bradley, R. M., & Stern, I. B. (1967). The development of the human taste bud during the foetal period. *Journal of Anatomy, 101,* 743–752.

Brand, J. G. (1997). Biophysics of taste. In G. K. Beauchamp & L. M. Bartoshuk (Eds.), *Tasting and smelling: Handbook of perception and cognition* (2nd ed., pp. 1–24). San Diego: Academic Press.

Breslin, P. A. S. (2000). Human gustation. In T. F. Finger, W. L. Silver, & D. Restrepo (Eds.), *The neurobiology of taste and smell* (2nd ed., pp. 423–461). New York: Wiley-Liss.

Breslin, P. A. S., & Beauchamp, G. K. (1994). Strong acids are indiscriminable at equal pH. *Chemical Senses, 19,* 447.

Breslin, P. A. S., Beauchamp, G. K., & Pugh, E. N. (1996). Monogeusia for fructose, glucose, sucrose, and maltose. *Perception and Psychophysics, 58,* 327–341.

Breslin, P. A. S., Kemp, S., & Beauchamp, G. K. (1994). Single sweetness signal. *Nature, 369,* 447–448.

Bronstein, W. S. (1940a). Cortical representation of taste in man and monkey. I. Functional and anatomical relations of taste, olfaction, and somatic sensibility. *Yale Journal of Biology and Medicine, 12,* 719–736. Cited in Rolls, E. T. (1995), Central anatomy and neurophysiology. In R. L. Doty (Ed.), *Handbook of olfaction and gustation* (pp. 549–573). New York: Marcel Dekker.

Bronstein, W. S. (1940b). Cortical representation of taste in man and monkey. II. The localization of the cortical taste area in man, a method of measuring impairment of taste in man. *Yale Journal of Biology and Medicine, 13,* 133–156. Cited in Rolls, E. T. (1995), Central anatomy and neurophysiology. In R. L. Doty (Ed.), *Handbook of olfaction and gustation* (pp. 549–573). New York: Marcel Dekker.

Bryant, B., & Silver, W. L. (2000). Chemesthesis: The common chemical sense. In T. F. Finger, W. L. Silver, & D. Restrepo (Eds.), *The neurobiology of taste and smell* (2nd ed., pp. 73–100). New York: Wiley-Liss.

Caicedo, A., & Roper, S. D. (2001). Taste receptor cells that discriminate between bitter stimuli. *Science, 291,* 1557–1560.

Cardello, A. V. (1978). Chemical stimulation of single human fungiform taste papillae: Sensitivity profiles and locus of stimulation. *Sensory Processes, 2,* 173–190.

Catalanotto, F. A., Bartoshuk, L. M., Östrom, K. M., Gent, J. F., & Fast, K. (1993). Effects of anesthesia of the facial nerve on taste. *Chemical Senses, 18,* 461–470.

Chandrashekar, J., Mueller, K. L., Hoon, M. A., Adler, E., Feng, L., Guo, W., Zuker, C. S., & Ryba, N. J. (2000). T2Rs function as bitter taste receptors. *Cell, 100,* 703–711.

Collings, V. B. (1974). Human taste responses as a function of locus of stimulation on the tongue and soft palate. *Perception and Psychophysics, 16,* 169–174.

Costanzo, R. M., & Zasler, N. D. (1991). Head trauma. In T. V. Getchell, R. L. Doty, L. M. Bartoshuk, & J. B. Snow Jr. (Eds.), *Smell and taste in health and disease* (pp. 711–730). New York: Raven Press.

Cowart, B. J. (1989). Relationships between taste and smell across the adult life span. *Annals of the New York Academy of Sciences, 561,* 39–55.

Crook, C. K., & Lipsitt, L. P. (1976). Neonatal nutritive sucking: Effects of taste stimulation upon sucking rhythm and heart rate. *Child Development, 47,* 518–522.

Cruz, A., & Green, B. G. (2000). Thermal stimulation of taste. *Nature, 403,* 889–892.

Danilova, V., Hellekant, G., Roberts, T., Tinti, J. M., & Nofre, C. (1998). Behavioral and single chorda tympani taste fiber responses in the common marmoset, *Callithrix jacchus jacchus.* In C. Murphy (Ed.), *Olfaction and taste XII: An international symposium* (Vol. 855, pp. 160–164). New York: Annals of the New York Academy of Sciences.

Delwiche, J. F. (1996). Are there "basic" tastes? *Trends in Food Science and Technology, 7,* 411–415.

Delwiche, J. F., Buletic, Z., & Breslin, P. A. S. (2001a). Covariation in individuals' sensitivities to bitter compounds: Evidence supporting multiple receptor/transduction mechanisms. *Perception and Psychophysics, 63,* 761–776.

Delwiche, J. F., Buletic, Z., & Breslin, P. A. S. (2001b). Relationship of papillae number to bitter intensity of quinine and PROP within and between individuals. *Physiology and Behavior, 74,* 1–9.

Delwiche, J. F., Halpern, B. P., & DeSimone, J. A. (1999). Anion size of sodium salts and simple taste reaction times. *Physiology and Behavior, 66,* 27–32.

Delwiche, J. F., Lera, M. F., & Breslin, P. A. S. (2000). Selective removal of a target stimulus localized by taste in humans. *Chemical Senses, 25,* 181–187.

DeSimone, J. A., & Heck, G. L. (1993). Cell biology of the lingual epithelium. In S. A. Simon & S. D. Roper (Eds.), *Mechanisms of taste transduction* (pp. 201–223). Boca Raton, FL: CRC Press.

Desor, J. A., Maller, O., & Andrews, K. (1975). Ingestive responses of human newborns to salty, sour, and bitter stimuli. *Journal of Comparative and Physiological Psychology, 89,* 966–970.

Diamant, H. (1968). Comparison between neural and psychophysical recordings of taste stimulations. *Acta Oto-laryngologica, 65,* 51–54.

Diamant, H., Funakoshi, M., Ström, L., & Zotterman, Y. (1963). Electrophysiological studies on human taste nerves. In Y. Zotterman (Ed.), *Olfaction and taste* (pp. 193–203). Oxford, England: Pergamon Press.

Diamant, H., Oakley, B., Ström, L., Wells, C., & Zotterman, Y. (1965). A comparison of neural and psychophysical responses to taste stimuli in man. *Acta Physiologica Scandinavica, 64,* 67–74.

Diamant, H., & Zotterman, Y. (1959). Has water a specific taste? *Nature, 183,* 191–192.

Di Lorenzo, P. (2000). The neural code for taste in the brainstem: Response profiles. *Physiology and Behavior, 69,* 87–96.

Doty, R. L. (Ed.). (1995). *Handbook of olfaction and gustation.* New York: Dekker.

Doty, R. L., Bagla, R., Morgenson, M., & Mirza, N. (2001). NaCl thresholds: Relationship to anterior tongue locus, area of stimulation, and number of fungiform papillae. *Physiology and Behavior, 72,* 373–378.

Doty, R. L., Bartoshuk, L. M., & Snow, J. B. (1991). Causes of olfactory and gustatory disorders. In T. V. Getchell, R. L. Doty, L. M. Bartoshuk, & J. B. Snow Jr. (Eds.), *Smell and taste in health and disease* (pp. 449–462). New York: Raven Press.

Drewnowski, A., Henderson, S. A., & Shore, A. B. (1997). Genetic sensitivity to 6-n-propylthiouracil (PROP) and hedonic responses to bitter and sweet tastes. *Chemical Senses, 22,* 27–37.

Drewnowski, A., Henderson, S. A., Shore, A. B., & Barratt-Fornell, A. (1998). Sensory responses to 6-n-propylthiouracil (PROP) or sucrose solutions and food preferences in young women. In C. Murphy (Ed.), *Olfaction and taste XII: An international symposium* (Vol. 855, pp. 797–801). New York: Annals of the New York Academy of Sciences.

Drewnowski, A., Kristal, A., & Cohen, J. (2001). Genetic taste responses to 6-*n*-propylthiouracil among adults: A screening tool for epidemiological studies. *Chemical Senses, 26,* 483–489.

Dulac, C. (2000). The physiology of taste, vintage 2000. *Cell, 100,* 607–610.

Eggers, S. C., Acree, T. E., & Shallenberger, R. S. (2000). Sweetness chemoreception theory and sweetness transduction. *Food Chemistry, 68,* 45–49.

Erickson, R. P. (2000). The evolution of neural coding ideas in the chemical senses. *Physiology and Behavior, 69,* 3–13.

Erickson, R. P. (2001). The evolution and implications of population and modular neural coding ideas. In M. Nicolelis (Ed.), *Progress in brain research: Vol. 130. Advances in neural population coding* (pp. 9–29). Amsterdam: Elsevier.

Eylam, S., & Kennedy, L. M. (1998). Identification and characteristics of human fructose or glucose taste variants with hypogeusia for one monosaccharide but not for another. In C. Murphy (Ed.), *Olfaction and taste XII: An international symposium* (Vol. 855, pp. 170–174). New York: Annals of the New York Academy of Sciences.

Faurion, A. (1987). MSG as one of the sensitivities within a continuous taste space: Electrophysiological and psychophysical studies. In Y. Kawamura & M. R. Kare (Eds.), *Umami: A basic taste* (pp. 387–408). New York: Dekker.

Faurion, A. (1992). The physiology of sweet taste and molecular receptors. In M. Mathlouthi, J. A. Kanters, & G. G. Birch (Eds.), *Sweet-taste chemoreception* (pp. 291–315). New York: Elsevier.

Faurion, A., Cerf, B., Van de Moortele, P.-F., Lobel, E., MacLeod, P., & Le Bihan, D. (1999). Human taste cortical areas studied with functional magnetic resonance imaging: Evidence of functional lateralization related to handness. *Neuroscience Letters, 277,* 189–192.

Faurion, A., Saito, S., & MacLeod, P. (1980). Sweet taste involves several distinct receptor mechanisms. *Chemical Senses, 5,* 107–121.

Finger, T. F., Silver, W. L., & Restrepo, D. (Eds.). (2000). *The neurobiology of taste and smell* (2nd ed.). New York: Wiley-Liss.

Finger, T. F., & Simon, S. A. (2000). Cell biology of taste epithelium. In T. F. Finger, W. L. Silver, & D. Restrepo (Eds.), *The neurobiology of taste and smell* (2nd ed., 287–314). New York: Wiley-Liss.

Francis, S., Rolls, E. T., Bowtell, R., McGlone, F., O'Doherty, J. O., Browning, A., Clare, S., & Smith, E. (1999). The representation of pleasant touch in the brain and its relationships with taste and olfactory areas. *NeuroReport, 10,* 453–459.

Frank, M. E. (2000). Neuron types, receptors, behavior, and taste quality. *Physiology and Behavior, 69,* 53–62.

Ganzevles, P. G., & Kroeze, J. H. (1987). Effects of adaptation and cross-adaptation to common ions on sourness intensity. *Physiology and Behavior, 40,* 641–646.

Geisler, C. D. (1998). *From sound to synapse.* New York: Oxford University Press.

Getchell, T. V., Doty, R. L, Bartoshuk, L. M., & Snow, J. B., Jr. (Eds.) (1991). *Smell and taste in health and disease.* New York: Raven Press.

Gibson, L., & Hartman, T. (1919). The comparative sapidity of hydrochloric, sulphuric and acetic acids: I. *American Journal of Psychology, 30,* 311–313.

Gilbertson, T. A. (1998). Gustatory mechanisms for the detection of fat. *Current Opinion in Neurobiology, 8,* 447–452.

Gilbertson, T. A., Boughter, J. D., Jr., Zhang, H., & Smith, D. V. (2001). Distribution of gustatory sensitivities in rat taste cells: Whole-cell responses to apical chemical stimulation. *The Journal of Neuroscience, 21,* 4931–4941.

Gilbertson, T. A., Damak, S., & Margolskee, R. F. (2000). The molecular physiology of taste transduction. *Current Opinion in Neurobiology, 10,* 519–527.

Gillette, M. (1985). Flavor effects of sodium chloride. *Food Technology, 39,* 47–52, 56.

Gilmore, M. M., & Murphy, C. (1989). Aging is associated with increased Weber ratios for caffeine, but not for sucrose. *Perception and Psychophysics, 46,* 555–559.

Glendinning, J. I., Chaudhari, N., & Kinnamon, S. C. (2000). Transduction and molecular biology. In T. F. Finger, W. L. Silver, & D. Restrepo (Eds.), *The neurobiology of taste and smell* (2nd ed., pp. 315–351). New York: Wiley.

Green, B. G., Dalton, P., Cowart, B., Shaffer, G., Rankin, K., & Higgins, J. (1996). Evaluating the "Labeled Magnitude Scale" for measuring sensations of taste and smell. *Chemical Senses, 21,* 323–334.

Green, B. G., & Lawless, H. T. (1991). The psychophysics of somatosensory chemoreception in the nose and mouth. In T. V. Getchell, R. L. Doty, L. M. Bartoshuk, & J. B. Snow Jr. (Eds.), *Smell and taste in health and disease* (pp. 235–253). New York: Raven Press.

Guesry, P. R., & Secrétin, M.-C. (1991). Sugars and nonnutritive sweeteners. In M. Gracey, N. Kretchmer, & E. Rossi (Eds.), *Sugars in nutrition* (pp. 33–53). New York: Raven Press.

Guinard, J.-X., Hong, D. Y., Zoumas-Morse, C., Budwig, C., & Russell, G. F. (1994). Chemoreception and perception of the bitterness of isohumulones. *Physiology and Behavior, 56,* 1257–1263.

Gulick, W. L., Gescheider, G. A., & Frisina, R. D. (1989). *Hearing.* New York: Oxford University Press.

Halpern, B. P. (1977). Functional anatomy of the tongue and mouth of mammals. In J. A. W. M. Weijnen & J. Mendelson (Eds.), *Drinking behavior: Oral stimulation, reinforcement and preference* (pp. 1–92). New York: Plenum Press.

Halpern, B. P. (1987). Human judgments of MSG taste: Quality and reaction times. In Y. Kawamura & M. R. Kare (Eds.), *Umami: A basic taste* (pp. 325–354). New York: Dekker.

Halpern, B. P. (1991). More than meets the tongue: Temporal characteristics of taste intensity and quality. In H. T. Lawless & B. P. Klein (Eds.),

Sensory science theory and applications in foods (pp. 37–105). New York: Dekker.

Halpern, B. P. (1994). Overview: Kirin international symposium on bitter taste. *Physiology and Behavior, 56,* 1265–1266.

Halpern, B. P. (1997). Psychophysics of taste. In G. K. Beauchamp & L. M. Bartoshuk (Eds.), *Tasting and smelling: Handbook of perception and cognition* (2nd ed., pp. 77–123). San Diego: Academic Press.

Halpern, B. P. (1998). Amiloride and vertebrate gustatory responses to NaCl. *Neuroscience and Biobehavioral Reviews, 23,* 5–47.

Halpern, B. P. (1999). Taste. In R. A. Wilson & F. Keil (Eds.), *The MIT encyclopedia of the cognitive sciences* (pp. 826–828). Cambridge: Bradford Books.

Halpern, B. P. (2000). Glutamate and the flavor of foods. *Journal of Nutrition, 130,* 910S–914S.

Halpern, B. P., & Darlington, R. B. (1998). Effects of amiloride on gustatory quality descriptions and temporal patterns produced by NaCl. *Chemical Senses, 23,* 501–511.

Halpern, B. P., & Nelson, L. M. (1965). Bulbar gustatory responses to anterior and to posterior tongue stimulation in the rat. *American Journal of Physiology, 209,* 105–110.

Harper, H. W., Jay, J. R., & Erickson, R. P. (1966). Chemically evoked sensation from single human taste papillae. *Physiology and Behavior, 1,* 319–325.

Hellekant, G., Danilova, V., & Ninomiya, Y. (1997). Primate sense of taste: Behavioral and single chorda tympani and glossopharyngeal nerve fiber recordings in the rhesus monkey, *Macaca mulatta. Journal of Neurophysiology, 77,* 978–993.

Hellekant, G., Danilova, V., Roberts, T., & Ninomiya, Y. (1997). The taste of ethanol in a primate model: I. Chorda tympani nerve responses in *Macaca mulatta. Alcohol, 14,* 473–484.

Hellekant, G., Ninomiya, Y., & Danilova, V. (1997). Taste in chimpanzees: II. Single chorda tympani fibers. *Physiology and Behavior, 61,* 829–841.

Hellekant, G., Ninomiya, Y., & Danilova, V. (1998). Taste in chimpanzees III. Labeled-line coding in sweet taste. *Physiology and Behavior, 65,* 191–200.

Henkin, R. I., Graziadei, P. P. G., & Bradley, D. F. (1969). The molecular basis of taste and its disorders. *Annals of Internal Medicine, 71,* 791–821.

Herness, S. (2000). Coding in taste receptors: The early years of intracellular recording. *Physiology and Behavior, 69,* 21–27.

Herness, M. S., & Gilbertson, T. A. (1999). Cellular mechanisms of taste transduction. *Annual Review of Physiology, 61,* 873–890.

Hersch, M., & Ganchrow, D. (1980). Scanning electron microscopy of developing papillae on the tongue of human embryos and fetuses. *Chemical Senses, 5,* 331–341.

Hettinger, T. P., Frank, M. E., & Myers, W. E. (1996). Are the tastes of polycose and monosodium glutamate unique? *Chemical Senses, 21,* 341–347.

Higdon, M., & Gruenstein, E. (2001, August 25). Imaging vs. photometry . . . Which Do I Choose? Available at http://www.intracellular.com/app05.html.

Hoon, M. A., Adler, E., Lindemeier, J., Battey, J. F., Ryba, N. J., & Zuker, C. S. (1999). Putative mammalian taste receptors: A class of taste-specific GPCRs with distinct topographic selectivity. *Cell, 96,* 541–551.

Hough, L. (1989). Sucrose, sweetness and sucralose. *International Sugar Journal, 91,* 23–32.

Huiskamp, G. (2001, August 25). Physics of medical imaging 2001. EEG and MEG techniques. Available at http://www.mbfys.kun.nl/~geertjan/.

Ikeda, K. (1912). On the taste of the salt of glutamic acid. *Eighth International Congress of Applied Chemistry, 38*(8c), 147.

Inoue, J. (1983). *Inoue's smaller Japanese-English dictionary*. Tokyo: Tuttle.

Kato, H., Rhue, M. R., & Nishimura, T. (1989). Role of free amino acids and peptides in food taste. In R. Teranishi, R. G. Butler, & F. Shahidi (Eds.), *Flavor chemistry: Trends and developments* [ACS Symposium 388] (pp. 158–174). Washington, DC: American Chemical Society.

Kelling, S. T., & Halpern, B. P. (1987). Taste judgments and gustatory stimulus duration: Simple taste reaction times. *Chemical Senses, 12,* 543–562.

Kelling, S. T., & Halpern, B. P. (1988). Taste judgments and gustatory stimulus duration: Taste quality, taste intensity, and reaction time. *Chemical Senses, 13,* 559–586.

Kennedy, L. M., Bourassa, D. M., & Rogers, M. (1993). The cellular and molecular neurobiology of sweet taste: Studies with taste-altering compounds. In M. Mathlouthi, J. A. Kanters, & G. G. Birch (Eds.), *Sweet-taste chemoreception* (pp. 317–351). New York: Elsevier.

Kennedy, L. M., Eylam, S., Poskanzer, J. E., & Saikku, A.-R. (1997). Genetic analyses of sweet taste transduction. *Food Chemistry, 60,* 311–321.

Kennedy, L. M., & Halpern, B. P. (1980). Extraction, purification, and characterization of a sweetness-modifying component from Ziziphus jujuba. *Chemical Senses, 5,* 123–147.

Khan, R. (1979). Molecular basis of sweetness. *Journal of the Chemical Society of Pakistan, 1,* 33–35.

Kier, L. B. (1972). A molecular theory of sweet taste. *Journal of Pharmaceutical Sciences, 61,* 1394–1397.

Kimura, K., & Beidler, L. M. (1961). Microelectrode study of taste receptors of rat and hamster. *Journal of Cellular and Comparative Physiology, 58,* 131–140.

Kinnamon, J. C. (1987). Organization and innervation of taste buds. In T. F. Finger & W. L. Silver (Eds.), *Neurobiology of taste and smell* (277–297). New York: Wiley.

Kinnamon, S. C. (1996). Taste transduction: Linkage between molecular mechanisms and psychophysics. *Food Quality and Preference, 7,* 153–159.

Kinnamon, S. C. (2000). A plethora of taste receptors. *Neuron, 25,* 507–510.

Kobayakawa, T., Ogawa, H., Kaneda, H., Ayabe-Kanamura, S., Endo, H., & Saito, S. (1999).

Spatio-temporal analysis of cortical activity evoked by gustatory stimulation in humans. *Chemical Senses, 24,* 201–209.

Kubo, I. (1994). Structural basis for bitterness based on rabdosia diterpenes. *Physiology and Behavior, 56,* 1203–1207.

Kullaa-Mikkonen, A., & Sorvari, T. E. (1985). A scanning electron microscope study of the dorsal surface of the human tongue. *Acta Anatomica, 123,* 114–130.

Kuninaka, A. (1981). Taste and flavor enhancers. In R. Teranishi, R. A. Flath, & H. Sugisawa (Eds.), *Flavor research: Recent Advances* (pp. 305–353). Basel: Dekker.

Kurihara, K., Katsuragi, Y., Matsuoka, I., Kashiwayanagi, M., & Kumazawa, T. (1994). Receptor mechanisms of bitter substances. *Physiology and Behavior, 56,* 1125–1132.

Kurihara, Y., Ookubo, K., Takashi, H., Kodama, H., Akiyama, Y., Yagi, A., & Halpern, B. (1988). Studies on the taste modifiers: I. Purification and structure determination of sweetness inhibiting substances in leaves of *Ziziphus jujuba. Tetrahedron, 44,* 61–66.

Kuznicki, J. T., & Cardello, A. V. (1986). Psychophysics of single taste papillae. In H. L. Meiselman & R. S. Rivlin (Eds.), *Clinical measurement of taste and smell* (pp. 200–225). New York: Macmillan.

Kuznicki, J. T., & McCutcheon, N. B (1979). Cross-enhancement of the sour taste on single human taste papillae. *Journal of Experimental Psychology: General, 108,* 68–89.

Lawless, H. T. (1996). Flavor. In M. P. Friedman & E. C. Carterette (Eds.), *Cognitive ecology* (pp. 325–380). San Diego: Academic Press.

Lawless, H. T. (2000). Taste. In E. B. Goldstein (Ed.), *Blackwell handbook of perception* (pp. 601–635). Malden, MA: Blackwell.

Lawless, H. T., & Heymann, H. (1997). *Sensory evaluation of food: Principles and practices.* New York: Chapman & Hall.

Lee, C. K. (1979). Carbohydrate sweeteners: Structural requirements for taste. *World Review of Nutrition and Dietetics, 33,* 142–197.

Lipsitt, L. P. (1977). Taste in human neonates: Its effects on sucking and heart rate. In J. M. Weiffenbach (Ed.), *Taste and development: The genesis of sweet preference* [DHEW Publication No. (NIH) 77-1068] (pp. 125–145). Bethesda, MD: Public Health Service, National Institutes of Health.

Lundy, R. F., Jr., & Contreras, R. J. (1999). Gustatory neuron types in rat geniculate ganglion. *The Journal of Neurophysiology, 82,* 2970–2988.

Ly, A., & Drewnowski, A. (2001). PROP (6-n-Propylthiouracil) tasting and sensory responses to caffeine, sucrose, neohesperidine dihydrochalcone and chocolate. *Chemical Senses, 26,* 41–47.

Lynch, N. M. (1987). In search of the salty taste. *Food Technology, 41,* 82–83 and 85–86.

Maga, J. A. (1987). Organoleptic properties of umami substances. In Y. Kawamura & M. R. Kare (Eds.), *Umami: A basic taste* (pp. 41–73). New York: Dekker.

Marks, L. E., Borg, G., & Westerlund, J. (1992). Differences in taste perception assessed by magnitude matching and by category-ratio scaling. *Chemical Senses, 17,* 493–506.

Mattes, R. D. (1994). Influences on acceptance of bitter foods and beverages. *Physiology and Behavior, 56,* 1229–1236.

McBurney, D. H. (1978). Psychological dimensions and perceptual analyses of taste. In E. C. Carterette & M. P. Friedman (Eds.), *Handbook of perception: Vol. 6A. Tasting and smelling* (pp. 125–155). New York: Academic Press.

McCaughey, S. A., & Scott, T. R. (1998). The taste of sodium. *Neuroscience and Biobehavioral Reviews, 22,* 663–676.

McGee, H. (1984). *On food and cooking.* New York: Scribner's.

McWilliams, M. (1985). *Food fundamentals* (4th ed.). New York: Macmillan.

Meiselman, H. L., & Halpern, B. P. (1970). Effects of *Gymnema sylvestre* on complex taste elicited by amino acids and sucrose. *Physiology and Behavior, 5,* 1379–1384.

Meiselman, H. L., Halpern, B. P., & Dateo, G. P. (1976). Reduction of sweetness judgments by extracts from the leaves of *Ziziphus jujuba. Physiology and Behavior, 17,* 313–317.

Mennella, J. A., & Beauchamp, G. K. (1997). The ontogeny of human flavor perception. In G. K. Beauchamp & L. M. Bartoshuk (Eds.), *Tasting and smelling: Handbook of perception and cognition* (2nd ed., pp. 199–221). San Diego: Academic Press.

Miller, I. J. (1989). Variation in human taste bud density as a function of age. In C. Murphy, W. S. Cain, & D. M. Hegsted (Eds.), *Nutrition and the chemical senses in aging: Recent advances and current research needs* (Vol. 561, pp. 307–319). New York: Annals of the New York Academy of Sciences.

Miller, I. J. (1994). Structural and functional features of human fungiform papillae. In K. Kurihara, N. Suzuki, & H. Ogawa (Eds.), *Olfaction and Taste XI* (p. 26). Tokyo: Springer-Verlag.

Miller, I. J., & Bartoshuk, L. M. (1991). Taste perception, taste bud distribution, and spatial relationships. In T. V. Getchell, R. L. Doty, L. M. Bartoshuk, & J. B. Snow Jr. (Eds.), *Smell and taste in health and disease* (pp. 205–233). New York: Raven Press.

Mistretta, C. M. (1984). Aging effects on anatomy and neurophysiology of taste and smell. *Gerodontology, 3,* 131–136.

Mistretta, C. M. (1986). Taste anatomy and neurophysiology in early development and old age. In H. L. Meiselman & R. S. Rivlin (Eds.), *Clinical measurement of taste and smell* (pp. 283–304). New York: Macmillan.

Mistretta, C. M. (1991). Developmental neurobiology of the taste system. In T. V. Getchell, R. L. Doty, L. M. Bartoshuk, & J. B. Snow Jr. (Eds.), *Smell and taste in health and disease* (pp. 35–64). New York: Raven Press.

Mistretta, C. M. (1998). The role of innervation in induction and differentiation of taste organs: Introduction and background. In C. Murphy (Ed.), *Olfaction and taste XII: An international symposium* (Vol. 855, pp. 1–13). New York: Annals of the New York Academy of Sciences.

Moore, L. M., Nielsen, C. R., & Mistretta, C. M. (1982). Sucrose taste thresholds: Age-related differences. *Journal of Gerontology, 37,* 64–69.

Murphy, C. (Ed.) (1998). *Olfaction and taste XII: An international symposium* (Vol. 855). New York: Annals of the New York Academy of Sciences.

Murphy, C., & Gilmore, M. M. (1989). Quality-specific effects of aging on the human taste system. *Perception and Psychophysics, 45,* 121–128.

Murphy, C., & Gilmore, M. M. (1990). Effects of aging on sensory functioning: Implications for dietary selection. In R. L. McBride & H. J. H. MacFie (Eds.), *Psychological basis of sensory evaluation* (pp. 19–39). London: Elsevier.

Ney, K. H. (1979). Bitterness of lipids. *Fette, Seifen, Anstrichmittel, 81,* 467–469.

Noble, A. C. (1994). Bitterness in wine. *Physiology and Behavior, 56,* 1251–1255.

Nofre, C., Tinti, J. M., & Glaser, D. (1996). Evolution of the sweetness receptor in primates: II. Gustatory responses of nonhuman primates to nine compounds known to be sweet in man. *Chemical Senses, 21,* 747–762.

Norris, M. B., Noble, A. C., & Pangborn, R. M. (1984). Human saliva and taste responses to acids varying in anions, titratable acidity, and pH. *Physiology and Behavior, 32,* 237–244.

Nowliss, G. H., & Kessen, W. (1976). Human newborns differentiate differing concentrations of sucrose and glucose. *Science, 191,* 865–866.

Oakley, B. (1985). Taste response of the human *chorda tympani* nerve. *Chemical Senses, 10,* 469–481.

Oakley, B. (1986). Basic taste physiology: Human perspectives. In H. L. Meiselman & R. S. Rivlin (Eds.), *Clinical measurement of taste and smell* (pp. 5–18). New York: Macmillan.

O'Doherty, J., Rolls, E. T., Francis, S., Bowtell, R., & McGlone, F. (2001). The representation of pleasant and aversive taste in human brain. *The Journal of Neurophysiology, 85,* 1313–1321.

O'Donnell, C. D. (1998, March). A short salt synopsis. *Prepared Foods,* 51–54.

Ogawa, H., Yamashita, S., Noma, A., & Sato, M. (1972). Taste responses in the macaque monkey chorda tympani. *Physiology and Behavior, 9,* 325–331.

Ogiso, K., Shimizu, Y., Watanabe, K., & Tonosaki, K. (2000). Possible involvement of undissociated acid molecules in the acid response of the rat. *The Journal of Neurophysiology, 83,* 2776–2779.

O'Mahony, M., Hobson, A., Garvey, J., Davies, M., & Brit, C. (1976). How many tastes are there for low concentration "sweet" and "sour" stimuli? Threshold implications. *Perception, 5,* 147–154.

O'Mahony, M., & Ishii, R. (1987). The umami taste concept: Implications for the dogma of four basic types. In Y. Kawamura & M. R. Kare (Eds.), *Umami: A basic taste* (pp. 75–93). New York: Dekker.

Parke, S. A., & Birch, G. G. (1999). Solution properties and sweetness response of selected bulk and intense sweeteners. *Journal of Agricultural and Food Chemistry, 47,* 1378–1384.

Pfaffmann, C. (1959). The sense of taste. In J. Field (Ed.), *Handbook of physiology: Vol. 1. Section 1, Neurophysiology* (pp. 507–533). Washington, DC: American Physiological Society.

Pfaffmann, C., Bartoshuk, L. M., & McBurney, D. H. (1971). Taste psychophysics. In L. M. Beidler (Ed.), *Handbook of sensory physiology: Vol. 4. Chemical senses, Section 2, Taste* (pp. 75–101). Berlin: Springer.

Pickles, J. O. (1988). *An introduction to the physiology of hearing* (2nd ed.). San Diego: Academic Press.

Pritchard, T. C. (1991). The primate gustatory system. In T. V. Getchell, R. L. Doty, L. M. Bartoshuk, & J. B. Snow Jr. (Eds.), *Smell and taste in health and disease* (pp. 109–125). New York: Raven Press.

Prutkin, J., Duffy, V. B., Etter, L., Fast, K., Gardner, E., Lucchina, L. A., Snyder, D. J., Tie, K., Weiffenbach, J., & Bartoshuk, L. M. (2000). Genetic variation and inferences about perceived taste intensity in mice and men. *Physiology and Behavior, 69,* 161–173.

Purves, D., Augustine, G. J., Fitzpatrick, D., Katz, L. C., LaMantia, A.-S., McNamara, J. O., & Williams, S. M. (Eds.) (2001). *Neuroscience,* (2nd ed.). Sunderland, MA: Sinauer Associates.

Reutter, K., & Witt, M. (1993). Morphology of vertebrate taste organs and their nerve supply. In S. A. Simon & S. D. Roper (Eds.), *Mechanisms of taste transduction* (pp. 29–82). Boca Raton, FL: CRC Press.

Richter, C. P., & Campbell, K. H. (1940). Sucrose taste thresholds of rats and humans. *American Journal of Physiology, 128,* 291–297.

Riskey, D. R., Desor, J. A., & Vellucci, D. (1982). Effects of gymnemic acid concentration and time since exposure on intensity of simple tastes: A test of the biphasic model for the action of gymnemic acid. *Chemical Senses, 7,* 143–152.

Rolls, E. T. (1995). Central taste anatomy and neurophysiology. In R. L. Doty (Ed.), *Handbook of olfaction and gustation* (pp. 549–573). New York: Dekker.

Rolls, E. T. (1997). Taste and olfactory processing in the brain and its relation to the control of eating. *Critical Reviews in Neurobiology, 11,* 263–287.

Rolls, E. T., Critchley, H. D., Browning, A., & Hernadi, I. (1998). The neurophysiology of taste and olfaction in primates, and umami flavor. In C. Murphy (Ed.), *Olfaction and taste XII: An international symposium* (Vol. 855, pp. 426–437). New York: Annals of the New York Academy of Sciences.

Saito, S., Kobayakawa, T., Ayabe-Kanamura, S., Gotow, N., & Ogawa, H. (2000). Magnetoencephalographic imaging of gustatory brain areas. *ISOT 2000 and ECRO 2000 Abstracts,* Brighton UK, 100–101.

Sandick, B., & Cardello, A. V. (1981). Taste profiles from single circumvallate papillae: Comparison with fungiform profiles. *Chemical Senses, 6,* 197–214.

Sato, M., Ogawa, H., & Yamashita, S. (1994). Gustatory responsiveness of chorda tympani fibers in the cynomolgus monkey. *Chemical Senses, 19,* 381–400.

Sato, T. Okada, Y., & Miyamoto, T. (1994). Receptor potential of the frog taste cell in response to bitter stimuli. *Physiology and Behavior, 56,* 1133–1139.

Sato, T. Okada, Y., Miyamoto, T., & Fujiyama, R. (1997). Distribution of non-tasters for phenylthiocarbamide and high sensitivity to quinine hydrochloride of the non-tasters in Japanese. *Chemical Senses, 22,* 547–551.

Schifferstein, H. N. J. (1996). Cognitive factors affecting taste intensity judgments. *Food Quality and Preference, 7,* 167–175.

Schiffman, S. S., Hopfinger, A. J., & Mazur, R. H. (1986). The search for receptors that mediate sweetness. In P. M. Conn (Ed.), *The receptors: Vol. 4* (pp. 315–377). New York: Academic Press.

Schiffman, S. S., Lockhead, E., & Maes, F. W. (1983). Amiloride reduces the taste intensity of Na^+ and Li^+ salts and sweeteners. *Proceeding of the National Academy of Sciences, USA, 80,* 6136–6140.

Schuknecht, H. F. (1974). *Pathology of the ear.* Cambridge: Harvard University Press.

Scott, T. R., & Giza, B. K. (2000). Issues of gustatory neural coding: Where they stand today. *Physiology and Behavior, 69,* 65–76.

Scott, T. R., & Plata-Salamán, C. R. (1999). Taste in the monkey cortex. *Physiology and Behavior, 67,* 489–511.

Settle, R. G., Meehan, K., Williams, G. R., Doty, R. L., & Sisley, A. C. (1986). Chemosensory properties of sour tastants. *Physiology and Behavior, 36,* 619–623.

Shafer, D. M., Frank, M. E., Gent, J. F., & Fischer, M. E. (1999). Gustatory function after third molar extraction. *Oral Surgery, Oral Medicine, Oral Pathology, Oral Radiology and Endodontics, 87,* 419–428.

Shallenberger, R. S. (1977). Chemical clues to the perception of sweetness. In G. G. Birch, J. G. Brennan, & K. J. Parker (Eds.), *Sensory properties of foods* (pp. 91–100). London: Applied Science.

Shallenberger, R. S., & Acree, T. E. (1967). Molecular theory of sweet taste. *Nature, 216,* 480–482.

Shallenberger, R. S., & Acree, T. E. (1969). Molecular structure and sweet taste. *Journal of Agricultural and Food Chemistry, 17,* 701–703.

Shallenberger, R. S., & Acree, T. E. (1971). Chemical structure of compounds and their sweet and bitter taste. In L. M. Beidler (Ed.), *Handbook of sensory physiology: Vol. 4. Chemical senses Section 2, Taste* (pp. 221–277). Berlin: Springer.

Shikata, H., McMahon, D.B.T., & Breslin, P. A. S. (2000). Psychophysics of taste lateralization on anterior tongue. *Perception and Psychophysics, 62,* 684–694.

Silver, W. L., & Finger, T. F. (1991). The trigeminal system. In T. V. Getchell, R. L. Doty, L. M. Bartoshuk, & J. B. Snow Jr. (Eds.), *Smell and taste in health and disease* (pp. 97–108). New York: Raven Press.

Simon, S. A., & Wang, Y. (1993). Chemical responses of lingual nerves and lingual epithelia. In S. A. Simon & S. D. Roper (Eds.), *Mechanisms of taste transduction* (pp. 225–252). Boca Raton, FL: CRC Press.

Small, D. M., Zald, D. H., Jones-Gotman, M., Zatorre, R. J., Pardo, J. V., Frey, S., & Petrides, M. (1999). Human cortical gustatory areas: A review of functional neuroimaging data. *NeuroReports, 10,* 7–14.

Smith, D. V., & Davis, B. J. (2000). Neural representations of taste. In T. F. Finger, W. L. Silver, & D. Restrepo (Eds.), *The neurobiology of taste and smell* (2nd ed., pp. 353–394). New York: Wiley-Liss.

Smith, D. V., St. John, S. J., & Boughter, J. D., Jr. (2000). Neuronal cell types and taste quality coding. *Physiology and Behavior, 69,* 77–85.

Smith, D. V., & Vogt, M. B. (1997). The neural code and integrative processes of taste. In G. K. Beauchamp & L. M. Bartoshuk (Eds.), *Tasting and smelling: Handbook of perception and cognition* (2nd ed., pp. 25–76). San Diego: Academic Press.

Smith, V. V., & Halpern, B. P. (1983). Selective suppression of judged sweetness by ziziphins. *Physiology and Behavior, 30,* 867–874.

Sposato, D. J. (2000). Individual differences in bitter taste perception of saccharin and acesulfame-k. Unpublished master's thesis, Cornell University, Ithaca, NY.

Stevens, J. C. (1996). Detection of tastes in mixtures with other tastes: Issues of masking and aging. *Chemical Senses, 21,* 211–221.

Stevens, J. C., Cruz, L. A., Hoffman, J. M., & Patterson, M. Q. (1995). Taste sensitivity and

aging: High incidence of decline revealed by repeated threshold measures. *Chemical Senses, 20,* 451–459.

Stewart, R. E., DeSimone, J. A., & Hill, D. L. (1997). New perspectives in gustatory physiology: Transduction, development, and plasticity. *American Journal of Physiology (Cell Physiology 41), 272,* C1–C26.

Striem, B. J., Pace, U., Zehavi, U., Naim, M., & Lancet, D. (1989). Sweet tastants stimulate adenylate cyclate coupled to GTP-binding protein in rat tongue membranes. *Biochemical Journal, 260,* 121–126.

Tepper, B. J., & Nurse, R. J. (1998). PROP taster status is related to fat perception and preference. In C. Murphy (Ed.), *Olfaction and taste XII: An international symposium* (Vol. 855, pp. 802–804). New York: Annals of the New York Academy of Sciences.

Tordoff, M. G. (1996). Some basic psychophysics of calcium salt solutions. *Chemical Senses, 21,* 417–424.

Usuki, R., & Kaneda, T. (1980). Bitter taste of oxidized fatty acids. *Agricultural and Biological Chemistry, 44,* 2477–2481.

Van de Moortele, P.-F., Cerf, B., Lobel, E., Paradis, A.-L., Faurion, A., & Le Bihan, D. (1997). Latencies in fMRI time-series: Effects of slice acquisition order and perception. *NMR in Biomedicine, 10,* 230–236.

Weiffenbach, J. M. (1994). Human sensory function for taste is robust across the adult lifespan. In K. Kurihara, N. Suzuki, & H. Ogawa (Eds.), *Olfaction and taste: Vol. 11.* (pp. 551–553). Tokyo: Springer.

Weiffenbach, J. M., Baum, B. J., & Burghauser, R. (1982). Taste thresholds: Quality specific variations with human aging. *Journal of Gerontology, 37,* 372–377.

Weiffenbach, J. M., Tylenda, C. A., & Baum, B. J. (1990). Oral sensory changes in aging. *Journal of Gerontology: Medical Sciences, 45,* M121–M125.

Witty, M. (1999, May). Proteins pack muscle to modify taste. *Prepared Foods,* 69–71.

Yamaguchi, S. (1987). Fundamental properties of umami in human taste sensation. In

Y. Kawamura & M. R. Kare (Eds.), *Umami: A basic taste* (pp. 41–73). New York: Dekker.

Yamaguchi, S. (1991). Basic properties of umami and effects in humans. *Physiology and Behavior, 49,* 833–841.

Yamaguchi, S. (1998). Basic properties of umami and its effects on food flavor. *Food Reviews International, 14,* 139–176.

Yamaguchi, S., & Ninomiya, K. (1998). What is umami? *Food Reviews International, 14,* 123–138.

Yamamoto, T., Nagai, T., Shimura, T., & Yasoshima, Y. (1998). Roles of chemical mediators in the taste system. *Japanese Journal of Pharmacology, 76,* 325–348.

Yanagisawa, K., Bartoshuk, L. M., Catalanotto, F. A., Karrer, T. A., & Dveton, J. F. (1998). Anesthesia of the chorda tympani nerve and taste phantoms. *Physiology and Behavior, 63,* 329–335.

Yoshida, M., & Saito, S. (1969). Multidimensional scaling of the taste of amino acids. *Japanese Psychological Research, 11,* 149–166.

Zahm, D. S., & Munger, B. L. (1985). The innervation of the primate fungiform papilla: Development, distribution and changes following selective ablation. *Brain Research Reviews, 9,* 147–186.

Zotterman, Y. (1967). The neural mechanism of taste. In Y. Zotterman (Ed.), *Sensory mechanisms: Progress in brain research, 23* (pp. 139–154). Amsterdam: Elsevier.

Zuniga, J. R., Chen, N., & Miller, I. J. J. (1994). Effects of chorda-lingual nerve injury and repair on human taste. *Chemical Senses, 19,* 657–665.

Zuniga, J. R., Davis, S. H., Englehardt, R. A., Miller, I. J. J., Schiffman, S. S., & Phillips, C. (1993). Taste performance on the anterior human tongue varies with fungiform taste bud density. *Chemical Senses, 18,* 449–460.

Zwillinger, S. A., & Halpern, B. P. (1991). Time-quality tracking of monosodium glutamate, sodium saccharin, and a citric acid-saccharin mixture. *Physiology and Behavior, 49,* 855–862.

CHAPTER 17

Olfaction

PAMELA DALTON

INTRODUCTION

Olfaction is the most ancient of the distal senses (hearing and vision being the other two). Its precursors can be found in the most primitive single-celled organisms, which reflects the need for every organism to sense its chemical environment. In vertebrates the primary function of the olfactory system is to detect and process volatile chemicals in air. Because animals are themselves the source for volatile chemicals, olfaction for many vertebrates, including lower mammals, is a critical determinant of such behavioral processes as kin recognition, reproductive behavior, and spatial organization. In humans, olfaction provides essential information for guiding ingestive behavior, for orienting in the environment, and for making risk assessments of situations; it also adds greatly to affective appreciation of our surroundings. In addition, olfaction appears to play a role in social relationships, from mother-infant bonding to sexual attraction to group synchrony.

Olfaction is also, in many respects, the least well understood of the distal senses. Our limited understanding of olfaction is partly a reflection of the dominance of vision and au-

dition as sources of distal information for humans. In addition, though, the olfactory system involves a complicated sensory interface that does not correspond to simple or familiar physical models. The difficulty of building an artificial nose, for example, attests to our lack of devices to detect and identify chemical information. However, within the past decade developments in molecular biology have led to substantial advances in our knowledge of olfaction, and molecular approaches to investigating transduction and coding of olfactory sensory signals have greatly illuminated basic mechanisms underlying olfaction. There is reason to hope that an understanding of these molecular and cellular components of olfactory processing will finally lead to an understanding of how odor quality is determined. However, molecular approaches, though sophisticated, fail to provide a functional perspective on sensory processing. Consequently, psychophysical and behavioral studies of olfactory processing remain essential to a comprehensive view of olfaction.

Prior reviews of olfaction depended heavily on the use of nonhuman animal models as tools to study olfaction. The rapid development of techniques and approaches to study directly the structure and function of human olfactory systems makes it possible to rely less on extrapolations from studies of lower

I wish to thank Drs. Bill Whitlow, Monique Smeets, Nancy Rawson and Tyler Lorig for helpful discussions and comments on earlier versions of this chapter.

primates and other animal models than in the past. Thus, this necessarily selective review focuses primarily on studies of human olfaction, with references made to studies in other species as confirmation or contradiction or where no human data presently exists.

This review begins by describing the anatomical basis for olfaction, from sensory surface to central nervous system (CNS) processing. This structural description is followed by an examination of the basics of sensory processing, a description of standard methods for studying olfaction, and an overview of basic results from psychophysical analyses. The psychophysics of olfaction is followed by a review of olfaction in higher-level cognition, and the review concludes by briefly describing clinical pathologies of olfaction.

ANATOMY AND PHYSIOLOGY

Four features distinguish the olfactory system from other regions of the CNS. First, the olfactory receptor cell body is in direct contact with the external environment, whereas other CNS sensory neurons are more centrally located and hence protected. Second, olfactory neurons have a single unbranched axon that projects directly to the brain without a synapse on intermediate neurons. Third, unlike most other vertebrate CNS neurons, olfactory neurons are replaced continuously throughout the normal life span, which is probably related to the potential for damage and dysfunction produced by their direct exposure to volatiles and irritants in the environment. Fourth, the chemical molecules that are the basis for olfaction remain physically present after initiating the sensory transduction process. Although some of these features provide unique advantages, particularly in terms of investigational access to the CNS, others pose special challenges for understanding the chemical, biological, and psychological processes involved in olfactory perception.

Morphology of the Nasal Cavity

The nasal cavity can be divided into three parts: the nasal vestibule, the respiratory region, and the olfactory region. The septum, consisting of a bony plate and a cartilaginous wall, divides the nasal cavity into two symmetrical halves. On average, in humans the total surface area of both nasal cavities is approximately 150 cm^2, and the total volume is about 15 ml. The anterior portion of the nasal cavity opens in the nostril, whereas the posterior part opens into the rhinopharynx. Volatile chemicals can be inhaled into the nasal cavity orthonasally through the nostril (or nares) or can enter retronasally from the mouth or during swallowing (thus enabling the significant contribution of olfactory perception to food flavor). These odor plumes are broken up by convolutions in the tissue that are called turbinates (see Figure 17.1). Actual exposure to odorants depends on patterns of airflow through a geometrically complex structure, and only recently have models been developed that allow quantitative analysis of flow patterns. Early attempts to determine flow patterns tried lining the noses of human subjects with litmus paper and having the subjects inhale ammonia fumes (Paulsen, 1882), but this technique proved unreliable (!). It was replaced by the development of physical models of the nasal cavity. Although early models were typically cast directly from the noses of human cadavers, modern anatomical casts have been developed from three-dimensional information provided by CT scans.

Given the anatomical complexity, it is perhaps not surprising that little is known about the normal range of variation in human nasal cavity dimensions or how those variations affect airflow patterns. It seems likely, however, that anatomical deformities, such as a deviated

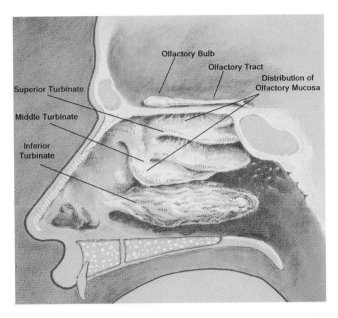

Figure 17.1 Anatomy of the nasal passages, showing the turbinates, the location of the olfactory epithlium, and orthonasal and retronasal odorant flow.

septum or nasal polyps, and variations due to race or pathology contribute to variations in how odorants are presented to the receptor surface. Studies using acoustic rhinometry have reported systematic differences between African American, Caucasian, and Indian noses, for example. However, the functional relevance of these morphological differences, if any, has not been elucidated (Gurr, Diver, Morgan, MacGregor, & Lund, 1995).

The human nasal passages contain two different types of secretory mucosae: respiratory and olfactory. The primary functions of the respiratory epithelium are to humidify, filter, and warm the incoming air during inspiration. Respiratory epithelium covers much of the upper two thirds of the nasal passages, except for those locations containing olfactory epithelium. The primary function of the olfactory epithelium is to detect odorants in the inspired air. The olfactory epithelium is located on both sides of the upper portion of the nasal cavity and the olfactory cleft and in humans occupies a total area of about 3 cm^2 to 5 cm^2, as compared with 20 cm^2 to 200 cm^2 in dogs. For many years the olfactory epithelium was commonly depicted as being limited to the region within the olfactory cleft, a misconception that appears to have evolved from an early paper that stated that the olfactory neuroepithelium was restricted to the nasal septum and superior turbinate (von Brunn, 2000). However, this statement actually contradicted published figures in the same paper showing extension of the olfactory epithelium onto the middle turbinate and septum (Lanza & Clerico, 1995). Recent anatomical (Feron, Perry, McGrath, & Mackay-Sim, 1998) and functional (Restrepo, Okada, Teeter, Lowry, & Cowart, 1993) studies have confirmed the existence of olfactory epithelium in these regions through biopsies.

Sensory Innervation of the Nasal Cavity

Chemosensory Systems

The nasal cavity in vertebrates contains receptors of as many as five different chemosensory

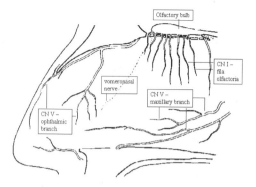

Figure 17.2 Sensory innervation of the nasal cavity in humans, showing the olfactory, trigeminal, vomeronasal, and nervus terminalis.
SOURCE: From Lang (1989).

systems (see Figure 17.2), but at present only two of these systems (olfactory and trigeminal) are known to play a role in human chemosensation.

The olfactory epithelium contains cells of three types: olfactory receptor neurons (ORNs), their precursors (basal cells), and sustentacular cells (serving glia-like supportive functions). The ORNs are located beneath a watery mucus layer in this epithelium; on one end of each receptor, projections of the hair-like olfactory cilia extend down into the watery layer covering the membrane. The receptor sites for odorant molecules are on the cilia, and as such, the cilia are the structures involved in the initial stages of olfactory signal transduction (Lowe & Gold, 1991). Odor information is transmitted via the bundles of axons that form the olfactory nerve (cranial nerve I), which extend from the olfactory receptor cells in the olfactory epithelium through the cribriform plate and synapse, unbranched, within the olfactory bulb, a small structure in the base of the forebrain where receptor input is integrated.

In addition to the olfactory receptors, the nasal cavity is innervated by unmyelinated, free nerve endings of the maxillary and ethmoid branches of the trigeminal nerve, which

are capable of detecting chemically and mechanically stimulated sensations of pungency, irritation, warmth, and coolness. Formerly referred to as the common chemical sense, the cutaneous mucosal sensation elicited by chemical stimulation is now known as *chemesthesis* (Green, Mason, & Kare, 1990). The appeal of this term is that it does not imply that chemical sensitivity is a separate sensory modality but rather includes chemical sensitivity as a general property of the cutaneous senses, along with thermal and mechanical sensitivity. The primary function of chemesthesis in the nose is presumed to involve detection and avoidance of caustic or reactive chemicals in airway mucosal tissue and the lungs (Green et al., 1990). Nevertheless, it should be recognized that the appreciation of spicy foods, carbonated beverages, and cooling vapors (i.e., menthol) relies largely on the sensations of chemesthesis. In combination with olfactory sensations, intranasal chemesthetic sensations also contribute significantly to the overall perceptual intensity and quality for many volatile chemicals. Olfactory-chemesthetic interactions may take the form of additive, synergistic, or suppressive combinations and are described elsewhere in this review.

A third chemosensory system found in the nasal passage of some amphibians, most reptiles, and many mammals, including New World primates, is the vomeronasal organ (VNO), or organ of Jacobsen. In mammals, the VNO is cigar-shaped and is located rostral of the olfactory region, near the base of the nasal cavity. The VNO may respond to some of the same odorous stimuli as does the olfactory system, but it can also detect stimuli that are higher in molecular weight than can be detected by olfactory sensory neurons. Through direct contact with liquids such as urine and other secretions, the VNOs of many animals can even respond to nonvolatile compounds.

Extensive studies of the VNO's structure and function, conducted in rodents, lagomorphs, and ungulates, have conclusively demonstrated the importance of this organ for detecting chemical signals used in social interactions and reproduction (Wysocki & Meredith, 1987). However, whether humans (or Old World primates) possess a functioning VNO has been the focus of much recent debate (Monti-Bloch, Jennings-White, & Berliner, 1998) and is still not decided.

In animals that possess a functioning VNO, the medial wall of the lumen contains bipolar sensory neurons and supporting cells. The axons of these cells penetrate the basement membrane of the sensory epithelium, exit the VNO, cross the nasal septum and the cribriform plate, and enter the brain to synapse in the accessory olfactory bulb, which is embedded within the main olfactory bulb (Wysocki, 1979). Although some studies have claimed to find evidence of cells of bipolar appearance in fetal and adult human VNO, there is no evidence showing intact neural connections with the brain. Of course, the lack of a functional VNO in humans does not preclude the possibility of chemical communication via pheromones, as many species, including one mammal (pig; Dorries, Adkins-Regan, & Halpern, 1997) exhibit responses to pheromones without the presence or use of a VNO.

A fourth sensory system in the nose of most, if not all, non-human vertebrates is the nervus terminalis (TN, or cranial nerve 0). The TN has a peripheral distribution on the nasal septum, courses along the ventromedial surface of the olfactory bulbs, and connects with the forebrain by means of several nerve bundles that project to the medial and lateral septal nuclei, olfactory tubercle, and preoptic areas. During mammalian embryogenesis, the olfactory, vomeronasal, and terminalis systems originate from a common placode. Once differentiated, however, the TN is the only nerve that projects directly from the nose to particular regions in the forebrain that have been shown to be involved in the reception and coordination of stimuli that evoke behavioral and hormonal changes relevant to reproduction (Demski & Schwanzel-Fukuda, 1987). The functions of the TN are not well identified, but there are indications that it may respond to sensory but not chemosensory stimuli, that it controls blood vessels and glands in the nose, and that it has peptide-containing fibers that may control reproductive development and behavior (Demski, 1993).

The fifth sensory system in the nasal cavity is the septal organ of Masera (SO), a small patch of olfactory epithelium located near the base of the nasal septum and separated from the main olfactory epithelium by a section of respiratory epithelium that progressively lose olfactory features over the course of embryonic development (Giannetti, Pellier, Oestreicher, & Astic, 1995). Electro-olfactogram (EOG) recordings from the rat septal olfactory organ have established this structure as a functioning component of the mammalian intranasal chemosensory system, with broad-range chemosensitivity and responsiveness to some odorants at lower concentrations than those required to elicit responses in the main olfactory neuroepithelium (Marshall & Maruniak, 1986). From this evidence it appears that the SO could have an orienting or alerting function and provide information relevant to the assessment of many odor stimuli.

Olfactory Receptor Neurons

ORNs are specialized primary bipolar neurons with direct axonal connections to the CNS, and they are located in the basal two thirds of the epithelium. The mature cell body is $5\,\mu$m to $8\,\mu$m in diameter. ORNs have been shown to differentiate from basal cells at the base of the epithelium, and at any given point in time, the epithelium consists of transitional forms between the basal cells and the mature receptor neurons (Graziadei & Monti Graziadei, 1979).

ORNs are relatively unique among neurons for two reasons: First, they are the only neurons in the nervous system that are directly exposed to the external environment; second, they have a limited life span (approximately one month) but continue to regenerate from basal cells throughout adult life. From these observations it has been inferred that the high metabolic cost to sustain this continued receptor turnover is advantageous only if damage to the receptors occurs as an intrinsic byproduct of exposure to chemical molecules or other conditions from the external environment (Halpern, 1982).

Like other CNS neurons, ORNs develop unbranched, unmyelinated axon processes that penetrate the skull into the cranial cavity and terminate in the olfactory bulb. The dendrite of the olfactory receptor neuron ends in cilia, where the initial steps in odor transduction take place (Lowe & Gold, 1991). It is here that an odorant molecule interacts with a receptor protein located within the cilia (see Figure 17.3).

The multigene family of olfactory receptor proteins may contain as many as 1,000 different members in rats (Buck & Axel, 1991), 500 to 750 members in humans, and 100 members in zebra fish and catfish. Although it is frequently claimed that a single olfactory neuron expresses only one of the olfactory receptor genes, the evidence to support this is limited (Malnic, Hirono, Sato, & Buck, 1999); furthermore, despite the fact that coexpression of multiple olfactory receptors has never been reported, this issue deserves much more study.

Signal Transduction in ORNs

Signal transduction in vertebrate ORNs commences in the olfactory cilia when odorant molecules bind to specific receptors. This in-

teraction stimulates a cascade of biochemical events that ultimately produce an action potential that is transmitted along the axon of the olfactory neuron to the olfactory bulb (for a review, see Schild & Restrepo, 1998).

The development of methods that allow comparisons between the responses of freshly biopsied human and rodent ORNs to selected odorant mixtures has led to considerable progress in understanding the function and selectivity of these neurons (Rawson et al., 1997). For example, in contrast with olfactory neurons from other species, human ORNs can respond to odorants with either increases or decreases in calcium, raising the possibility that coding of odor quality may rely on different mechanisms in humans and other species. The ability of the primary human ORNs to generate excitatory or inhibitory responses provides a potential mechanism for enhancing the discrimination ability of the peripheral olfactory system (Schild & Restrepo, 1998).

Central Neuroanatomy

The central olfactory system receives information about odor molecules from the ORNs. Because a single odor, such as the smell of a rose, may be composed of a combination of hundreds of different odor molecules, the central olfactory system is charged with integrating signals from a large variety of odorant receptors. The first relay station for the integration of this information is the main olfactory bulb (MOB). The MOB contains seven layers: (a) olfactory nerve layer, (b) glomerular layer, (c) external plexiform layer, (d) mitral cell layer, (e) internal plexiform layer, (f) granule cell layer (cells containing GABA, which inhibits mitral and tufted cells), and (g) the ependymal zone (where the progenitors of many bulb cells are found). The main signal-processing layer is the second glomerular layer. Because the sep-

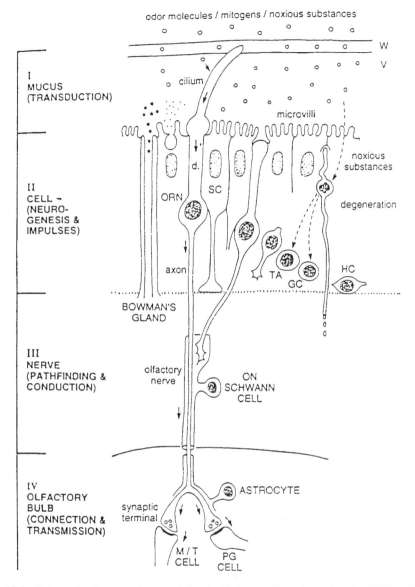

Figure 17.3   Schematic diagram of the peripheral olfactory pathway, showing the ORN at different stages of development and its relations with different extracellular environments.

NOTE: (I) Olfactory cilia are contained in the mucus layer, consisting of water (w) and viscous (v) sublayers and secreted by the Bowman's glands the supporting cells (SC), respectively. (II) The olfactory neuron bodies and dendrites (d) are contained in the epithelium, where they integrate the receptor potentials and generate impulse responses. Neurogenesis by stem cells replaced degenerating ORNs. GC: globose cell; HC: horizontal cell; TA: transiently amplifying. (III) Olfactory axons span the epithelium, olfactory nerves, and bulb. In the nerve, the axons are in bundles surrounded by the processes of special (ON) Schwann cells. (IV) ORN axon terminals make synapses onto the dendrites of M/T and periglomerular (PG) cells in the olfactory glomeruli.

SOURCE: From Shepherd (1994).

tum divides the right from the left nasal cavity, bilateral integration of odor information from the two nostrils occurs only in the brain, via the medial olfactory tract. This anatomical feature has been exploited to examine such perceptual issues as the locus of olfactory adaptation (Cain, 1977a) or the odor quality of mixtures (Sobel, Khan, Saltman, Sullivan, & Gabrieli, 1999).

The MOB in mammals contains several thousands of signal-processing cells known as glomeruli (approximately 2000/bulb in rabbits and mice and 3000/bulb in rats). Just as the percentage of the nasal cavity that is comprised of olfactory epithelium is larger in animals that rely heavily on olfaction (rats, dogs) than in humans, so too is the relative size of the olfactory bulb. The transfer of information through the bulb involves a single synapse from ORN terminals to one of the two kinds (mitral or tufted cells) of principal or output neurons. Each glomerulus contains a single primary dendrite from a mitral cell (the main output neurons of the olfactory bulb) and the axon terminals from many ORNs. After receiving the synaptic contact from the ORNs within the glomerulus, each mitral cell sends a single axon out of the bulb toward more central olfactory structures. In mice, for example, each glomerulus receives axonal inputs from several thousand ORNs and may be innervated by the dendrites of as many as 20 mitral cells, whose axons then send the information to the primary olfactory cortex. A second class of output neurons, the tufted cells, are morphologically similar to the mitral cells but have their soma located in the glomerular layer (Nickell & Shipley, 1995). Some tufted cells project their axons to higher cortical structures, whereas some remain within the olfactory bulb and function as local circuit neurons. The glomeruli serve as the first point of convergence of peripheral information: The axonal inputs that a single glomerulus receives originate from ORNs expressing only one type of odorant receptor.

The olfactory bulb is not only necessary for the integration and relay of peripheral odor information to higher cortical areas, but it is also critical for maintaining the integrity of the peripheral sensory epithelium. Surgical removal of the bulb in vertebrates results in retrograde degeneration of mature olfactory neurons. However, the epithelium appears capable of at least partial anatomical and biochemical recovery. For example, studies in hamsters have shown that this degeneration is followed by a wave of basal cell differentiation that reconstitutes the epithelium to approximately 60% of its former thickness (Costanzo & Graziadei, 1983). These newly developed olfactory axons will grow and penetrate the forebrain, forming ectopic glomeruli that synapse with local neurons (Graziadei & Monti Graziadei, 1979). This remarkable regenerative capacity of the epithelium occurs even in the absence of the target tissue, the olfactory bulb.

Collectively, the regions that are directly innervated by the outputs of the MOB have been referred to as primary olfactory cortex. Figure 17.4 summarizes the major efferent pathways of the main olfactory system. The primary olfactory cortex includes the piriform, periamygdaloid, transition, and the lateral entorhinal cortices. The functionality of these regions for olfactory perception has been established through the use of neuroimaging techniques, such as functional magnetic resonance imaging (fMRI), magnetic source imaging (MSI), and positron-emission tomography (PET), in which activation in these regions can be temporally and spatially correlated with various levels or types of odor processing (Kobal & Kettenman, 2000; Yousem et al., 1999; Zald & Pardo, 2000).

The olfactory system also connects secondarily with other brain regions presumably for

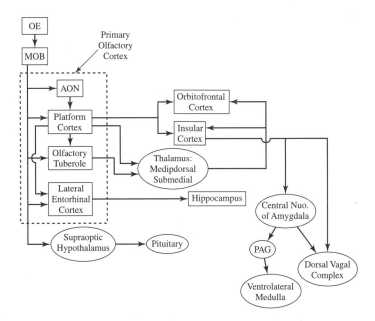

Figure 17.4   The major efferent pathways of the central olfactory system.
NOTE: Regions within thick dashed lines are within the primary olfactory cortex. Cortical regions are indicated within rectangles, and subcortical regions are indicated within ovals. AON: anterior olfactory nucleus; MOB: main olfactory bulb; OE: olfactory epithelium; PAG: periaqueductal gray.
SOURCE: From McLean & Shipley (1995).

integrating olfactory information with other sensory systems and higher cortical functions. For example, the MOB directs input to the entorhinal cortex (deOlmos, Hardy, & Heimer, 1978), as does the primary olfactory cortex, and projections from these structures connect with the hippocampus (Schwerdtfeger, Buhl, & Germroth, 1990), a structure that is important in memory function. Such a connection may enable the formation and associative strength of olfactory memories. Olfactory information may also integrate with taste, somatosensory, and visceral information. Recent data suggest that both MOB and piriform cortex connections to the insular cortex may be involved in integration of olfaction and visceral responses, observed in such behaviors as the orienting response to novel odor stimuli or the poorly understood response of nausea to unpleasant, but not toxic, odors. Another region that may be involved in higher-level in-

tegration of multimodal sensory information is the orbitofrontal cortex, which in primates has been shown to have neurons responsive to taste, smell, and somatosensory input—sensory systems that jointly contribute to flavor perception (Francis et al., 1999; Rolls, 1997).

Accessory Olfactory System

In macrosmatic mammals (animals that rely on smell for survival), the olfactory system consists of two subdivisions: the main and accessory olfactory systems. Although parallel, these two systems function separately in the integration of specific odor types. ORNs in the olfactory epithelium respond primarily to volatile chemicals and transmit this information to the main olfactory bulb, whereas ORNs located in the vomeronasal organ, which respond to many nonvolatile compounds, project exclusively to the accessory olfactory bulb, located at the dorsocaudal limit of the MOB. Although the connections between the MOB and the accessory olfactory bulb (AOB) and more central olfactory structures are parallel, they do not overlap.

SPECIAL PROBLEMS IN OLFACTION: THE STIMULUS AND ENVIRONMENT

A major challenge to conducting research in olfaction is related to measurement of stimulus concentration and delivery. For example, estimating the effective odorant concentration necessary to elicit perception is a formidable task because the odorant molecules that provide the physical basis for signaling the system must be transported into the body, dispersed in a geometrically complex structure (the nasal cavity), and transported through multiple types of substrate, including air, mucus, and blood *prior to* reaching the receptor environs. However, recent advances in anatomically accurate three-dimensional models of the nasal cavities, as well as the development of finite element models of transport and uptake across this mesh (Keyhani, Scherer, & Mozell, 1997), have facilitated the calculation of odorant deposition across the olfactory region as a function of air-flow rate, mass air concentration, and physicochemical properties of the odorants.

The initial events in olfactory perception occur in the 5- to 30-μm-thick (Menco, 1980) mucus layer that lines the olfactory epithelium and provides a constant aqueous environment around the receptors that serves to protect the cilia of olfactory neurons. This mucus is a viscoelastic gel, composed of a web of glycoprotein molecules and water containing dissolved proteins, enzymes, and electrolytes with a serous watery layer below the gel. Olfactory mucus merges into respiratory mucus without a clear-cut distinction, although the two types of epithelium are readily dis-

tinguishable. Olfactory and respiratory mucus are produced by different glands and therefore differ in composition; however, a continuous layer of mucus bathes the entire nasal epithelium, and some mixing occurs.

In addition to protecting the receptors, olfactory mucus plays a critical role in facilitating access and clearance of odorant molecules to and from receptor sites (M. L. Getchell & Mellert, 1991; T. V. Getchell, Margolis, & Getchell, 1984; Hornung & Mozell, 1977b; Moulton, 1976). Several physical factors regulate the access and diffusion times of an odorant in olfactory mucus, including the viscosity of the mucus and the length of the diffusion path (i.e., the depth of the mucus; M. L. Getchell & Mellert, 1991). In addition, a number of enzymes that are capable of metabolizing odorants have been localized in olfactory mucosa. The metabolic activity of these enzymes can serve as a mechanism for odorant removal, can transform odor quality or generate new odorants (particularly for enzymes that metabolize steroids and pheromones), and can change the solubility of odorants and their rate of diffusion through mucus to receptor sites on olfactory neurons. Mucus also contains secretory proteins, the first of which to be identified was odorant-binding protein (OBP). OBPs have been suggested to serve a transport function, binding hydrophobic odorant molecules to effect transport to the olfactory mucosa or to faciliate their removal from the receptor vicinity after they have been desorbed from receptor sites on the neurons (M. L. Getchell & Mellert, 1991).

Odorant Accumulation and Clearance

The delivery of odorant molecules to the receptor environment occurs cyclically during normal respiration. A complexity in olfaction that is not present in vision and audition is the potential for accumulation of the physical signal. That is, inhaled molecules can accumulate in the mucus surrounding the olfactory receptors and potentially damage tissue as well as delay recovery of receptor response and interfere with temporal coding of chemical signals. Because signal termination is critical, both for the recovery of sensitivity following stimulation and for temporally binding the signal from different receptors responding to the same odor, it is not surprising that several different mechanisms act in concert to clear odorant molecules from the receptor environment. Hornung and Mozell (Hornung & Mozell, 1977b; Hornung & Mozell, 1980) investigated the fate of tritiated butanol and octane in the nasal passages of bullfrogs and demonstrated that the odorants were removed from the olfactory mucosa in three ways: by mucociliary transport to the internal nares and buccal cavity, by uptake into the circulatory system, and by desorption back into the air compartment. In the vertebrate nose a continuous flow of mucus, ranging up to 23 mm/min, ensures an efficient washing of the olfactory epithelium and a steady elimination of odorants to the pharynx, from where they are swallowed (Pelosi, 1996). Odorant molecules can also be transported away from the olfactory region by absorption and uptake into the circulatory system via capillaries in the nasal bed. In addition to these biophysical events, studies by Pelosi and colleagues (Pelosi, 1996) have shown that enzymes present in the mucus itself are capable of degrading odorant molecules or altering their conformation or structure. This enzymatic activity can serve a protective function to neutralize toxic molecules as well as clear odorants from areas of maximum chemosensitivity in order to effect signal termination.

Alterations in these biophysical mechanisms may contribute to impairments in olfactory function. For example, certain pathophysiologic and rhinitic conditions that lead to changes in mucus rheology are associated with decreased olfactory sensitivity (e.g., chronic sinusitis, among others; Min, Yun, Song, Cho, & Lee, 1995; Passali, Bellussi, & Lauriello, 1995), whereas senescence is associated with changes in the nasal mucosa (Joki & Saano, 1997), reduced regional blood flow, and decreases in olfactory acuity and recovery of sensitivity following stimulation (Stevens & Cain, 1987; Stevens, Cain, Schiet, & Oatley, 1989).

INFORMATION CODING IN THE OLFACTORY SYSTEM

Perhaps the most remarkable property of the mammalian olfactory system is its ability to encode and thus discriminate thousands of odorant stimuli. Novel compounds, mixtures, and even randomly synthesized chemicals are frequently perceived as distinct, discriminable, and meaningful. To a first approximation, the olfactory system seems optimally designed to accommodate the unpredictability and dynamic nature of the olfactory world.

This exceptional ability appears to result from a sequence of information-processing events that occur in series within several distinct anatomical structures: the olfactory epithelium in the nasal cavity (where olfactory receptor neurons are activated by odorants), the olfactory bulb (where signals from the ORNs are received) and the olfactory cortex (where information from the olfactory bulb is then relayed to various other brain regions). The identification and cloning of genes that encode olfactory receptors have provided new tools for investigating these questions, resulting in enormous strides in the last decade in investigations of the molecular basis of quality coding in the olfactory system. At present, however, these investigations have not yielded a basis for classification of odorants on perceptual dimensions.

Theories of Odor Quality

Odor quality is one of the most significant features of the experience of an odor. Unlike the gustatory system, which comprises multiple primary taste qualities (sweet, sour, salty, bitter, and umami, the savory taste associated with glutamate; see Chap. 16, this volume) that can be independently characterized at the neurophysiological level, the olfactory system has, thus far, failed to yield a classification system that would satisfactorily account for the diverse range of quality sensations it is capable of discriminating.

Attempts to classify odors into discrete qualitative categories have occurred throughout ancient and modern history (for a review, see Cain, 1988). From the broad scheme of Linnaeus's (1756) seven-category perceptual classification system to Henning's more modern attempts to explain odor qualities in terms of combinations of odor dimensions (Boring, 1928), most classification systems have been based on heuristics and have failed on empirical grounds. A significant step in constructing theoretical frameworks for odor quality was taken by Amoore (1962), who unlike his predecessors sought to explain odor qualities on the basis of a set of seven primary odor dimensions (ethereal, camphoraceous, musky, floral, minty, pungent, and putrid) and relate those dimensions to physicochemical properties of odors having those qualities. Although the resulting stereochemical theory of olfaction (Amoore, 1962) is one of the most widely described theories of olfactory function, the concept of odor primaries (or at least these odor primaries) has not found empirical support. Admittedly, specific heuristic classification schemes have been of great practical utility for describing and organizing the dimensions of olfactory stimuli in professions that rely on sensory evaluations, such as perfumery or wine tasting. Of greater interest to the research community, however, have been techniques that use multidimensional scaling, in which odorants are rated on various dimensions for similarity or dissimilarity and the emergence of one or more factors (such as intensity, hedonics, etc.) permits the profiling and ordering of multiple odorants in an n-dimensional space (Dravnieks, 1982).

It is noteworthy, however, that repeated failures to identify a meaningful set of primary odor qualities with underlying neurophysiological organization has not quelled all attempts to relate some aspect of physicochemical features for a given odorant molecule with its perceived quality. Over the past 100 years a diverse range of theories have been examined in the hopes of devising some reasonably encompassing system to relate odor quality to properties of the stimulus molecules. Factors such as molecular size and shape, the positions or profile of their functional groups, their vibrational energy (Wright, 1977), solubility (Hornung & Mozell, 1977a), and activity coefficients (Keyhani et al., 1997) have been implicated as correlates of olfactory quality and discriminability. Unfortunately, the large number of potential physicochemical parameters and the presence of significant intercorrelations between many of them has limited the ability of any theory to predict odor quality from knowledge of the odorant's molecular features. Although rapid progress in studies of the molecular basis for olfactory codes has produced optimism that a metric to classify and predict odor quality from some emergent dimension of the odorant structure is within reach, such a dimension has yet to be identified.

Peripheral versus Central Coding

The mammalian olfactory system can obviously discriminate between thousands of different odorants, yet the precise locus of the sensory coding that leads to this impressive discrimination has only recently been addressed. Does specificity arise at the level of the peripheral receptors? If so, this would require a large number of receptors with high affinity and specificity for odor ligands. Alternatively, specificity could occur more centrally, by processing of the peripheral input from only a few receptors with overlapping specificities.

From the early work of Gesteland and colleagues, many electrophysiological studies have established that different olfactory sensory neurons respond to different odorants or sets of odorants (Firestein, Picco, & Menini, 1993; Gesteland, Lettvin, & Pitts, 1965; T. V. Getchell, 1974; Sicard, 1985). More recently, Buck and Axel's (1991) identification of the gene family that codes for odorant receptors has led to the use of molecular tools for investigating the cellular responses to odorants. With this approach, the relevant parameters of the neurobiological basis for olfactory coding have been tentatively established. For example, the apparent specificity of receptor expression coupled with the estimated size of the

gene family encoding receptor proteins has prompted suppositions that the mammalian ability to discriminate thousands of different odorant molecules may be, in part, due to the ligand specificities of olfactory receptors expressing different genes. Such a supposition also presumes that some degree of quality coding occurs at this first stage of olfactory perception. Evidence against a one-to-one scheme for quality coding at the level of the receptor comes from studies showing that a single olfactory receptor can recognize multiple odorants and that one odorant is recognized by multiple odorant receptors (Malnic et al., 1999). If, however, receptors expressing the same protein respond in such a broadly selective fashion to multiple odorants, where in the system do the final steps of odor quality coding occur?

As illustrated by the schematic in Figure 17.5, a first, rough level of qualitative organization appears to derive from the zonal expression of olfactory neurons that expresses

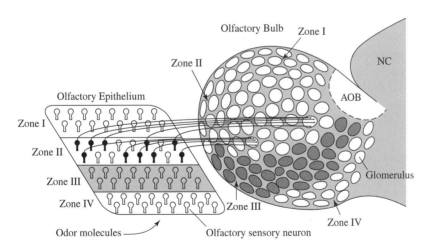

Figure 17.5   Schematic diagram illustrating the axonal connectivity pattern between the nose and the MOB.
NOTE: The OE in mice is divided into four zones (I–IV) that are defined by the expression of odorant receptors. Olfactory receptor neurons in a given zone of the epithelium project to glomeruli located in a corresponding zone of the MOB. Axons of sensory neurons expressing the same odorant receptor converge to only a few defined glomeruli. NC: neocortex; AOB: accessory olfactory bulb.
SOURCE: From Mori, Nagao, & Yoshihara (1999).

a given olfactory receptor. Neurons expressing a particular olfactory receptor are confined to one of four zones in the epithelium, where they are randomly interspersed with neurons expressing other olfactory receptors (Breer & Strotmann, 1997; Ressler, Sullivan, & Buck, 1994). The possibility of a spatially organized map of olfactory information has been suggested by data collected over the past five decades. Since the early studies of Adrian (1950), considerable physiological evidence has accumulated to suggest that the odorant activation in the olfactory epithelium occurs in a highly distributed fashion and that different odorants produce different spatial patterns of neural activation on the mucosal sheet (Kauer & Moulton, 1974; Kent & Mozell, 1992; Mackay-Sim & Kesteven, 1994; Thommesen & Doving, 1977; Youngentob & Kent, 1995). A recent study by Malnic and colleagues (Malnic et al., 1999), which used a combination of calcium imaging and single-cell reverse transcriptase-PCR to identify odorant receptors for aliphatic odorants with related structures but different odor qualities, provides an illustrative example of how these spatial codes could be translated into meaningful sensory codes for quality.

Figure 17.6 shows the recognition profiles of 14 olfactory neurons and their receptors to 19 different odorants that were tested in this study. This figure illustrates several important points about the mechanisms that are generally acknowledged to underlie odor discrimination. First, a single olfactory receptor could recognize multiple odorants (average = four) and the odorants recognized by a single olfactory receptor appeared to be related by the length of their carbon chain and, to a lesser degree, by their functional groups. That is, all but one of the olfactory receptors tested recognized only odorants with consecutive carbon chain lengths. And none of the olfactory receptors recognized odorants belonging to all four classes of odorants (carboxylic acids, aliphatic alcohols, bromocarboxylic acids, and dicarboxylic acid). Second, they observed that a single odorant could be recognized by multiple receptors, with 11 out of 17 odorants recognized by two or more olfactory receptors (and probably additional ones that were not obtained and tested). The third (and arguably the most important) finding is that different odorants were recognized by different combinations of olfactory receptors. That is, each odorant that elicited a response in more than one neuron was recognized by a different combination of neurons. This direct physiological evidence that the receptor code for a single odorant is combinatorial, with activation in each olfactory receptor serving as one of the overlapping yet nonidentical components, suggests that if odorants with related structures can be recognized by overlapping subsets of olfactory receptors, they can share components of an overall distinct receptor code.

A subsequent level of organization is imposed through the connections from the receptors to glomeruli in the olfactory bulb: Axons of neurons expressing the same olfactory receptor converge at fixed sites in the bulb (Figure 17.5; Ressler et al., 1994; Vassar, Ngai, & Axel, 1993). Using in situ hybridization techniques, the patterns of expression of olfactory receptor genes have been examined in several different species from catfish to humans: Of the estimated 6 million to 12 million ORNs in the human, those expressing the same receptor protein all converge precisely to the same two glomeruli in the olfactory bulb. Using genetic approaches to study the organization of the primary olfactory projection, Mombaerts et al. (Mombaerts et al., 1996) have confirmed that the projection of the olfactory epithelium onto the glomeruli of the olfactory bulb converges the axons of sensory neurons that express the same primary olfactory receptor (POR) onto two glomeruli

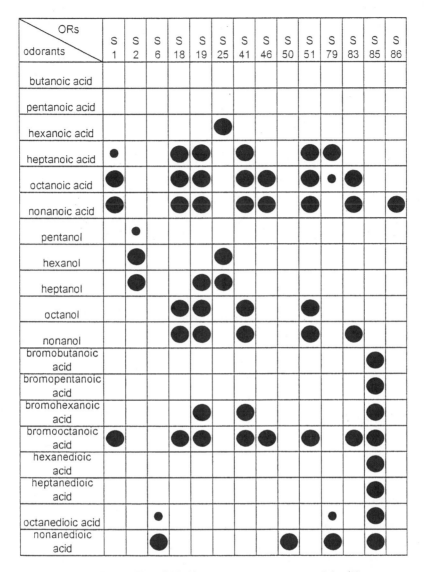

Figure 17.6   The recognition profiles of 14 olfactory receptor neurons and the olfactory receptors they expressed.
NOTE: Test odorants are shown on the left, and the ORs identified in the responsive neurons are shown on top. Filled circles indicate responses to 100 μm odorants, with smaller circles indicating a relatively weak response (less than half the change in fluorescence intensity elicted by KCl).
SOURCE: From Malnic, Hirono, Sato, & Buck (1999).

per bulb—one each on the medial and lateral surfaces.

Thus, both molecular and genetic studies have substantiated the findings from many prior anatomical and physiological studies that suggested that the glomeruli served as functional units for the integration of olfactory information. From this perspective, the patterning of the primary olfactory projection has the effect of transforming odorant stimuli (i.e., chemical information) into a code across neural space, such that the constellation of glomeruli activated by a single chemical will differ from that constellation activated by another. Hence, it seems increasingly plausible that central structures in the olfactory system will be charged with interpreting a combinatorial code distributed across glomerular space in order to generate the odor percept associated with chemical stimuli.

A combinatorial coding mechanism can account for a significant amount of psychophysical data on cross-adaptation, whereby exposure to one odorant diminishes the response to another. By this scheme, odorants that exhibited significant cross-adaptation (i.e., mutually suppressed odor intensity) would tend to be those that shared more of the components of their combinatorial code, whereas odorants that cross-adapted to a lesser degree would be those that had less overlap in their olfactory-receptor codes. The ability of multiple odors to stimulate a subset of the same receptors is consistent also with the psychophysical observation that exposure to any odorant appears to suppress the response to any subsequent odorants to a slight but observable degree (Köster, 1971).

Biological Basis of Artificial Olfaction

Numerous commercial applications (e.g., in the food, beverage, fragrance, chemical, and medical diagnostic industry) exist for instrumentation capable of broadband chemical detection and quantification. Traditional on-line chemical sensing has used an approach in which a single sensor is created for each analyte or ligand to be detected. However, an increased understanding of the neurobiological principles underlying mammalian olfactory discrimination ability has led to the development of advanced instrumentation that simulates the functions of the mammalian olfactory system (see Figure 17.7). Combining semiselective sensor arrays with higher-order pattern recognition capability (e.g., the same

distributed specificity phenomenon that appears to be the basis for odor quality discrimination in mammals), artificial noses are capable of on-line detection, discrimination, and quantification of multiple analytes in complex mixtures. Although they presently lack the range and sensitivity of the human nose, they are proving to be useful as complements to psychophysical assessment because they can avoid some of the common difficulties inherent in human sensory assessment, including (a) subjectivity and context-dependence of human response, (b) variability between individuals, (c) adaptation and fatigue, (d) susceptibility to infections that can impair olfactory ability, (e) sensitivity changes with age, and (f) health risks from exposure to certain toxic odors (Dickinson, White, Kauer, & Walt, 1998). It is likely that with advances in both sensory technology and computational power, their use will become more widespread.

OLFACTORY PSYCHOPHYSICS

Methodological Issues

Animal studies have always played a central role in understanding olfaction, and they will continue to be essential for elucidating basic molecular, cellular, and physiological mechanisms of olfactory processing. However, understanding the varieties of human olfactory experience, which depend on experiential and cognitive factors as well as genetic ones, can only be achieved through carefully controlled human experimental research. Fortunately, the analytic reach of such research continues to expand because of increases in the sophistication of available technology (e.g., fMRI) and in experimental methodology. Table 17.1 presents a summary of methods to measure the response of the olfactory system in humans at different levels of analysis, spanning the range from single-unit recordings of

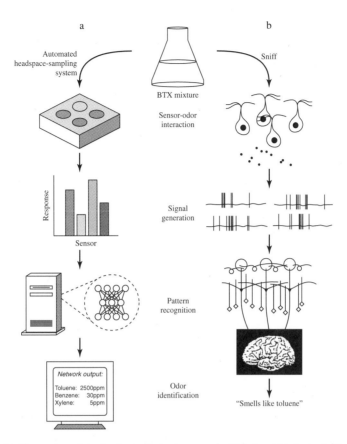

Figure 17.7   An illustration of the basic analogies between artificial and biological olfaction.
NOTE: (a) Headspace volatiles from a benzene-toluene-xylene (BTX) mixture are collected by an au-
tosampler and delivered to an array of cross-reactive transducers. Each sensor responds to the mixture
of odorants in a unique way, giving rise to characteristic patterns that are then fed into a computer-based
pattern-recognition algorithm for identification and, ideally, quantification. (b) Inhaled volatiles above a
solution are presented to a distributed array of broadly specific receptor proteins present in the cilia of
the olfactory receptor neurons. Odorant-receptor binding generates a series of action-potential patterns
that are relayed to the various layers of the olfactory bulb, and these are passed on to the higher-level
brain regions for identification of the input odors.
SOURCE: From Dickinson, White, Kauer, & Walt (1998).

peripheral olfactory receptors to the integrated
psychophysical response yielding a detection,
recognition, or perceived intensity judgment.

Stimulus Control

It should come as no surprise that the difficulty of preparing, measuring, and delivering
an olfactory stimulus has had more than a minimal impact on the research progress of the
field. The challenges of stimulus control in

olfaction, a modality in which almost no devices for stimulus control/delivery are com-
mercially available, can dim the enthusiasm
of the most ardent investigator. In a broad
sense, there are three methods for generating
odors and delivering them to the nasal cavity, namely, static olfactometry, dynamic olfactometry, and chamber exposure.

The first and least technically complex
method is static olfactometry. This method

Table 17.1   Methods for Studying Chemosensory Response

Methods	Description	Species
Psychophysical Methods		
Detection Thresholds	Minimum amount of stimulus concentration necessary to discriminate odor from blank (absolute) or discriminate two stimuli from one another (differential)	r, h
Direct Scaling	Judged intensity of odor stimulus using one of a variety of scaling methods, e.g, magnitude estimation, category scales, visual-analog scales or hybrids (category-ratio) scales.	h
Cross-Modality Scaling	Rated intensity of odor stimulus by adjusting a stimulus in another modality (e.g., tone, light, pressure) iso-intense.	h
Odor Identification	Name generation or n-alternative forced-choice identification of a range of common odorants	h
Electrophysiological Methods		
Electro-Olfactogram	Summated generator potentials of olfactory neurons recorded from the intact olfactory epithelium	r, h, a
Cortical EEG	Activity of dendritic potentials from the cerebral cortex in response to odorant presentation, recorded by placing external electrodes on various locations on the scalp	h
Event-Related Potentials	Positive and negative electric potentials from the cerebral cortex that are time-locked to the presentation of a stimulus	h
Single-Unit, Multi-Unit Recording	Intracellular and Extracellular measures of cell potential in response to electrical or odorant stimulation	r, h, a, i
Imaging Methods		
Position-Emission Tomography (PET)	Localization of brain activity by measurements of regional cerebral blood flow (via a radioactive tracer molecule) that indicate areas of the brain (showing metabolic changes associated with synaptic activity associated with odorant exposure.	r, h
functional Magnetic Resonance Imaging (fMRI)	Spatially- and temporally-resolved localization of transient increases in oxygenated haemoglobin in the red blood cells signifying cortical activity that can be correlated with presentation of an olfactory stimulus	h
CA^{2+} Imaging	Changes in intra-cellular calcium following odorant application, observed by loading biopsied ORNs with fura-2 or other calcium sensitive dye that fluoresces under light	r, h, a

r = rodent, h = human, a = amphibian, i = insect.

typically uses containers to hold and deliver odors; most often, the containers are odorless and either glass bottles or plastic, squeeze-type bottles, each with a dilution of the odorant in an odorless solvent. A typical set of stimuli contains a series of multiple bottles, each holding a decreasing concentration of the odorant in a fixed dilution scheme (e.g., binary, tertiary, log).

It is important to recognize that the actual stimulus of interest—the amount of odorant that is available to the subject's nose—is the concentration of the odorant in vapor phase (i.e., the headspace), not the amount of odorant in the solution. Vapor phase concentration varies proportionately with the concentration of odorant in solution according to a factor known as the *partition coefficient*. This coefficient may differ dramatically among different odorants, among the same odorant diluted with different solvents, and sometimes among concentrations of the same odorant-solvent pair (Cain, Cometto-Muñiz, & de Wijk, 1992). Unfortunately, the majority of olfactory studies has reported the concentration of the odorant in solution, not the concentration in vapor phase. Direct measurement of the vapor-phase concentration of the odorant in the headspace using gas chromatography provides a reliable method of (a) ascertaining the actual vapor-phase stimulus available in the headspace of each bottle and (b) ensuring the stability of that stimulus over time and with usage. This, of course, entails access to a gas chromatograph and training in its use.

The importance of the partition coefficient for determining headspace concentration means that the choice of solvent for odorant dilutions is also critical. Distilled, deionized water is a readily accessible solvent, but some odorants are not stable in it, and many odorants are not water-soluble. Alternatives that have been used (depending on the solubility of the odorant and solvent) are filtered mineral oil, propylene glycol, polyethylene glycol, and glycerol. However, the choice of solvent can significantly alter the partition coefficient of the odorant between the liquid and vapor phases, thus rendering meaningless any comparisons of detection thresholds obtained for an odorant in different solvents, without measures of the headspace concentration.

In order to ensure that the concentration sniffed from the headspace above the liquid solution is not diluted with surrounding room air, it is preferable to use a system that allows a spout or nose piece to be inserted directly inside one or both nostrils (Figure 17.8). During respiration, the average tidal volume (the amount of air that enters and leaves the lungs in one respiratory cycle) of normal young men is 0.50 L (Lambertsen, 1974). Studies by Laing (1983) have revealed that the average human sniff lasts 0.4 s, has a volume of 200 cm^3, and reaches a flow rate of 30 L/min. Thus, the size of the container should pro-

Figure 17.8 Threshold assessment using static olfactometry, in which the subject attempts to detect the odorant by sniffing the odorized air in the headspace of each bottle.
NOTE: Teflon nosepieces provide a snug fit in the nostrils, thereby preventing dilution of the odorant concentration.

vide an adequate volume of headspace to enable a normal sniff that remains undiluted until well past the olfactory region. Following stimulus delivery, the depleted headspace over the odorant solution must re-equilibrate in order to regain concentration. Depending on the activity coefficient of the odorant, re-equilibration of the headspace can require up to 30 min. However, in a series of empirical tests, Dravnieks (1975) found that gentle swirling of the odorant in a circular pattern reduces this re-equilibration time to less than 1 min.

In many situations, especially where rapid or field assessment of olfactory sensitivity is the goal, static olfactometry (particularly when coupled with GC analysis of the headspace concentration) provides a more than adequate level of stimulus control. From a practical perspective, it is also a relatively simple, convenient, and portable method of determining olfactory sensitivity in a noninvasive fashion. However, when there is a need for a high degree of control over the concentration or temporal onset of the odorant, dynamic olfactometry may be the more appropriate choice. Dynamic olfactometry involves delivering a continuous, well-regulated gas flow that contains odorized air mixed in varying proportions with a carrier gas (typically odorless air or nitrogen). Modern olfactometers permit the experimenter to vary the odorant concentration while simultaneously holding constant the other critical variables of volume flow rate, temperature, odorant purity, and relative humidity (Prah, Sears, & Walker, 1995). During active smelling (e.g., sniffing, inhaling), the volume of odorized air available for each trial should exceed the subject's maximum inhalation volume. To avoid stimulus artifacts from trigeminal stimulation during passive smelling, the odorant stream should not be blasted into the nose discretely, but should instead be inserted into a continuously flowing airstream that is held at a constant flow volume, temperature, and humidity. However, a short (e.g., 25 ms to 66% of asymptote) rise time of the odorant pulse is critical for odorant delivery in studies that record odorant-evoked potentials (Prah et al., 1995). Modern air-dilution olfactometers therefore employ electronic mass flow controllers for precision in flow control and digital computer control of stimulus delivery for versatility and precision to the timing and duration of the stimulus presentation.

Dissociating a subject's breathing and odorant stimulation during passive stimulation has allowed investigators to specify and control the time course of stimulation (an important feature for measuring electro-cortical responses to odorants), but it has been criticized for altering the natural manner in which people ordinarily deliver odorant stimuli (i.e., through sniffing or inhaling). This concern was given empirical support by Laing's (1985) demonstration that optimum odor sensitivity is obtained when subjects are allowed to employ their own idiosyncratic sniffing patterns, by Lorig et al.'s results that cortical odorant-evoked activity differs during active versus passive odorant delivery (Lorig, Matia, Peszka, & Bryant, 1996), and by Sobel et al.'s findings that humans adjust their sniff durations to compensate for increases and decreases in nasal patency (Sobel, Khan, Hartley, Sullivan, & Gabrieli, 2000). All of these findings suggest that somatosensory stimulation induced by airflow through the nostrils may serve as input to the olfactory cortex and be necessary for computation of an accurate olfactory percept (Sobel et al., 1998, 1999).

Static and dynamic olfactometric techniques both have enormous utility for measuring sensitivity and perceived intensity of odorous stimuli over brief durations. However, investigations that examine temporal factors more relevant to naturalistic exposures or in which the intent is to expose multiple sites of chemosensory mucosa (eyes, nose, throat) require larger volumes of stimuli or whole-body exposure capability, such as is available in environmental chambers. Environmental chambers provide perhaps the most naturalistic and ecologically valid exposure scenarios for evaluating odor and irritant perception under controlled conditions, and many studies of perceived indoor air quality and simulated occupational exposure have been conducted using such facilities. They can provide a more than adequate volume of odorized air, and in the case of evaluations of odor/irritant interactions, they allow the gaseous material to contact all relevant mucosal surfaces (ocular, nasal, throat) that would be stimulated in a natural environment. Because environmental conditions can interact both with odorant concentration in the chamber and with the characteristics of the nasal passages of the subject, careful control and monitoring of temperature, humidity, and airflow are standard features of most environmental chambers. In addition, such chambers must have a system of generating an odorized air stream and a way of mixing it adequately with the room air in order to create a uniform concentration without disturbing air currents. To ensure that the chemical concentration in the chamber is both uniform over time and at the target concentration, the investigator should use both an on-line method (e.g., a total hydrocarbon analyzer) and an off-line method (e.g., collecting air into Tedlar bags and analyzing via gas chromatography) for measuring actual odorant concentration during exposures. Although exposures in environmental chambers are perhaps the most complex and expensive to conduct, they have an unmatched potential for clarifying the basis of olfactory perception in many situations.

Individual Variation

Olfactory thresholds and responses to odorants in general exhibit considerable interindividual variation, the sources of which have gone largely unexplored. For thresholds, this variability often exceeds several orders of magnitude, rendering most standard compilations for threshold values of little practical utility. Although differences in threshold methodology (ascending, descending, staircase), stimulus preparation (e.g., choice of solvent), and delivery method (static vs. dynamic) undoubtedly contribute to the observed variation, these factors cannot explain the considerable range of sensitivity that is often observed within a single study. After accounting for (or preferably eliminating) vari-

ation due to poor stimulus control, true individual differences often still exist. Several factors may be involved in this variation, and their existence should be recognized and allowed to guide the choice of subject selection for any particular study.

The first factor to be addressed is the variation that is caused by differences in subjects' prior experiences. Such experiences fall into two categories: experience with the specific psychophysical test procedure and experience (or exposure to) the specific chemical odorant. In the case of the former factor, it is easy to imagine the significant differences in threshold that would obtain for a single threshold measurement of an individual who was completely naive to a psychophysical procedure and an individual who has participated in many previous threshold tests. Consistent with this intuition, numerous investigators have found increases in sensitivity with repeated testing. Cain and Gent (1991) found that subjects became progressively more sensitive with practice, and the reliability of their olfactory thresholds increased with repeated tests over the course of four days. Rabin and Cain (1986) found that thresholds declined over three sessions and that this practice generalized from one odorant to another. In a similar study, de Wijk (1989) tested subjects over many sessions and reported threshold stability after approximately 30 hours of practice.

Another important source of variation stems from an individual's experience with a specific odorant. Interestingly, depending on the frequency and periodicity of exposure, such experience can either increase or decrease sensitivity. A specific decrease in olfactory sensitivity is most easily observed in studies of individuals who are regularly or occupationally exposed to a volatile chemical. For example, textile workers with daily exposure to acetone exhibited acetone thresholds that were eight times higher than those of control subjects who were not regularly exposed to acetone, whereas their butanol thresholds (a chemical to which neither group had regular exposure) did not differ (Wysocki, Dalton, Brody, & Lawley, 1997).

Aging effects on olfactory thresholds (as well as suprathreshold intensity) can also be quite profound, although decrements in sensitivity may distribute themselves in a heterogenous fashion across a variety of odorants (Wysocki & Gilbert, 1989). Irrespective of the stimulus employed, it is not uncommon to find that elderly adults exhibit thresholds that are two to ten times higher than those of young adults (Cain & Stevens, 1989; Stevens & Cain, 1987). In studies that do not wish to test effects of aging explicitly, limiting the upper bound of the subject recruitment to 55 years old is a reasonably conservative strategy to eliminate possible confounds due to aging (Doty, 1991).

Although significant effects of gender can be found on several measures of olfactory processing such as memory for odors, odor identification, and hedonic ratings (Cain, 1982; Doty, Applebaum, Zusho, & Settle, 1985; Gilbert, Knasko, & Sabini, 1997), systematic gender influences on olfactory sensitivity have been elusive: As many studies have found heightened sensitivity for females as have not (Doty, Gregor, & Settle, 1986; Koelega, 1970; Koelega & Köster, 1974; Punter, 1983; Venstrom & Amoore, 1968). Moreover, in contrast to the anecdotal experience that females appear more sensitive to real-world odors, most laboratory effects of gender differences have been small. However, recent evidence showing that females, but not males, in their reproductive years can dramatically increase sensitivity to an odor following repeated test exposures provides a satisfying confirmation of real-world observations and suggests an activational role of sex hormones on olfactory processes in humans (Dalton, Doolittle, & Breslin, in press).

Olfactory Sensitivity: Absolute Thresholds

In olfaction, as in other sensory modalities, the amount of stimulation required to activate a sensory system is presumed to reflect in some direct fashion the sensitivity of the system. From a psychophysical tradition, one of the most widely used methods to assess olfactory sensitivity is to establish the lowest concentration of a stimulus that a subject can detect, or the absolute threshold.

Psychophysical techniques based on the measurement of an absolute threshold were operationally developed by Fechner in 1860 (Herrnstein & Boring, 1965) predicated on the idea that conscious perception of a stimulus required exceeding a critical level or threshold of mental event. Following considerable refinement of these early techniques, it is now recognized that at very low levels of stimulation, subjects rarely perceive any qualitative information about the odorant stimulus but are instead able only to indicate (often with low confidence) the presence of an odorant when compared with an odorless blank (*detection threshold*). The lowest concentration at which an odor quality becomes perceptible, thus allowing recognition of the odorant stimulus, is termed the *recognition threshold*. Recognition occurs at a concentration as much as three times higher than the detection threshold.

A common way of obtaining accurate and reliable thresholds that also eliminates the influence of a subject's bias (either liberal or conservative) to report the presence or absence of a stimulus is to use a forced-choice technique. Rather than just presenting the odor stimulus and asking the subjects whether an odor is perceived or not (yes/no technique), the forced-choice method requires subjects to indicate on a given trial which of two stimuli (an odor and a blank) has a stronger smell. This has the advantages of (a) reminding the subject on every trial the characteristics of the odorless blank (which, it should be noted, may always elicit some slight odor sensation) and (b) allowing the subject to use short-term memory for the characteristics of the odor stimulus.

Apart from variation caused by individual differences in sensitivity, the estimation of an average olfactory threshold for a substance will depend greatly on the specific methodology used to obtain it. Just as a forced-choice stimulus presentation will result in greater sensitivity than a yes/no technique, odor thresholds will vary according to whether the odorant concentrations are presented in ascending, descending, or random order. Ascending presentations tend to produce low threshold estimates; descending presentations tend to produce higher threshold estimates (perhaps due to adaptation from suprathreshold stimulation); and randomized presentations fall somewhere in between. Adaptation from successive presentations of the same stimulus or randomized stimuli clearly plays a significant, if underappreciated, role and mandates the employment of interstimulus intervals of sufficient duration (minimum 30 s) for recovery.

Individual and methodological variations aside, the use of psychophysical threshold techniques has shown that an odorant's ability to elicit a detectable olfactory sensation varies from odorant to odorant across many orders of magnitude (see Table 17.2). For example, tertiary-butyl mercaptan (the odorant that is added to odorless natural gas to allow its detection) can be detected in concentrations less than one part per billion in air, whereas much higher concentrations are required for detection of many other everyday odors, such as acetone (nail polish remover) or isopropyl (rubbing) alcohol.

The basis for this impressive variation in potency across different odorants has been explored by studying the relation between

Table 17.2   Human Odor Detection Thresholds of Selected Compounds

Compound	Odor Threshold in Air (ppm)
Methanol	141
Acetone	15
Isopropyl Alcohol	10
Formaldehyde	.87
Chlorine	.50
Camphor	.05
Menthol	.04
Hydrogen Sulfide	.017
t-butyl mercaptan	.00033
Vanillin	.000035

Taken from Devos et al. (1990) Standardized Human Olfactory Thresholds.

psychophysical potency and physicochemical factors. By using thresholds for members of specific aliphatic series obtained by Laffort (e.g., alcohols, acids, alkanes) and plotting those thresholds as a function of carbon chain length, Cain (1988) depicted a progressive increase in sensitivity with carbon chain length (Figure 17.9). The consistency of this progression for other aliphatic series, including esters, ketones, hydrocarbons, and acids suggested a relation between potency at threshold and

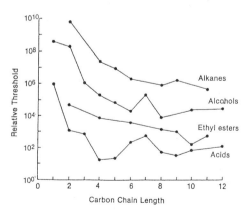

Figure 17.9   The association between carbon chain length for four aliphatic series and odor potency.
SOURCE: Data taken from Laffort, Patte, & Etcheto (1974), from a figure by Cain (1988).

odorant solubility, and solubility has indeed been incorporated as a parameter in a number of models that have shown moderate success in the prediction of olfactory thresholds in humans (Davies & Taylor, 1959; Keyhani et al., 1997; Laffort, 1977).

Suprathreshold Odor Judgments

Traditional psychophysics has focused on the measurement of sensitivity at threshold. However, the past 30 years have seen an increased interest in measuring the response of the olfactory system to suprathreshold stimuli (e.g., Marks, 1974). Although many factors can have similar effects on peri-threshold and suprathreshold odor responses, measurement techniques for the two types of responses will vary significantly. Most notably, at suprathreshold levels the detectability of the odor stimulus is assumed, and other attributes of the stimulus are the focus of interest.

Often, preparing stimuli for suprathreshold assessments is less complex than is preparing stimuli for measuring responses at threshold. However, the actual odor stimulus is still the vapor-phase concentration in the headspace of the stimulus vessel or bottle. Thus, the choice of appropriate solvent, careful measurement and mixing of the solutions, and an independent (e.g., gas chromatograph) assessment of the vapor-phase concentration are all warranted in suprathreshold measurement as well. Nevertheless, perhaps because suprathreshold assessments require less preparation and test administration time and because the stimuli are less altered by time, use, or contamination, this type of evaluation is widely used in basic and applied sensory research.

In general, the measurement of sensitivity or response to suprathreshold olfactory stimuli can be classified into three types. The first type involves the direct scaling of stimulus attributes, such as intensity or pleasantness; the second type involves determin-ing a difference threshold between two stimuli (e.g., the minimum increase in stimulus concentration that allows discrimination between two concentrations); and the third type involves assessments such as stimulus identity or memorability. Human performance on other types of suprathreshold judgments, such as odor identification or memorability, is discussed in the sections on clinical evaluations of olfactory ability and memory for odors, respectively. Accordingly, only issues involved in intensity discrimination and suprathreshold measurement and factors influencing judgments of suprathreshold intensity are reviewed here.

Among humans at least, responses to odors can be described in terms of a number of perceptual attributes, such as intensity, pleasantness, and various qualities. The measurement of perceived intensity, however, is perhaps the attribute of an olfactory stimulus that is most frequently obtained, and numerous psychophysical techniques exist for such purposes, including category scales, line scales (or visual analog scales), and ratio scales (see Chap. 3, Vol. 4 of this series). Category scales have the advantage of being easy to comprehend and use, but they often employ a limited set of response alternatives and limit the subject's ability to make finer discriminations along the stimulus continuum, especially because most olfactory studies have used scales containing seven or fewer categories. Line (or visual analog) scales may be less susceptible to number preferences or memory effects and can also allow assignment of responses to an infinite number of categories. Ratio scales (e.g., magnitude estimation/production) require subjects to assign numbers relative to the magnitude of sensations elicited by numerous stimuli. More recently, hybrid scaling techniques, such as category-ratio scales (e.g., the Labeled Magnitude Scale; Green et al., 1996), have served as alternatives to magnitude estimation in the scaling of olfactory stimuli, as they yield ratio data but allow subjects to use natural language descriptors, rather than numbers, to scale sensation.

Data obtained from the use of ratio scaling techniques such as magnitude estimation or magnitude production have shown that the exponent of the psychophysical function for most odorants falls well below 1, implying a compression of sensation magnitude over stimulus magnitude. However, there can be considerable variation in the slope of the psychophysical function for different odorants, as

revealed by individual exponents that range from 0.10 to 0.71. At least some of the variation can be explained by the fact that higher concentrations of many odorants will elicit not only odor but also sensory irritation, the contribution of which will lead to a steeper psychophysical function. Data from a study evaluating two scaling methods for olfactory stimuli (Green et al., 1996) illustrate the difference nicely. In this study, the psychophysical function for intensity of phenylethyl alcohol (Figure 17.10), which in

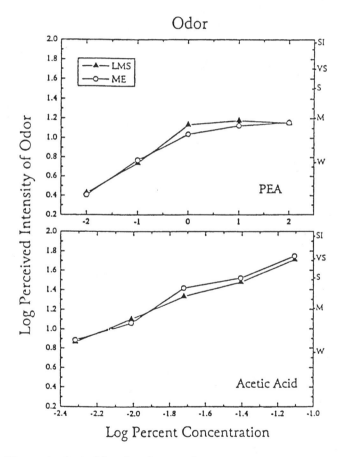

Figure 17.10 The psychophysical functions for two odorants.
NOTE: Psychophysical functions were obtained using magnitude estimation (ME) and the labeled magnitude scale (LMS): acetic acid, which stimulates both the olfactory and trigeminal system, and phenyl ethyl alcohol, which in vapor phase only stimulates olfactory sensation Labels on the right axis refer to the semantic descriptors used by the LMS: W = weak, M = moderate, S = strong, VS = very strong, SI = strongest imaginable.
SOURCE: From Green et al. (1996).

vapor phase appears to stimulate only olfactory sensations, is quite shallow, with a slope of approximately 0.3 across the lower concentrations and a slope of zero (implying an inability to resolve differences in concentration) across the higher ones. In contrast, intensity data for acetic acid, which is a trigeminal as well as an olfactory stimulant at the higher concentrations, were well described by a single power function with a slope of approximately 0.7.

Although resolving differences in odorant concentration would appear to be an important function of the olfactory system in real-world situations, there has been a paucity of research investigating this question. In general, the few modern studies of olfactory intensity discrimination have found that the Weber fractions (i.e., the size of the increment in odorant concentration required to produce a just noticeable difference, or JND, divided by the concentration) for different odorants fall within the range of 0.15 to 0.35 (Cain, 1977b; Slotnick & Ptak, 1977; Stone & Bosley, 1965), suggesting that although olfactory discrimination potential may not exhibit the sensitivity of that found in vision or audition, people are able to resolve small differences at least for some odorants.

Mixture Perception

Although most experimental research is conducted on the perception and response to single chemical odorants, in the real world the vast majority of odors that we perceive are composed of complex mixtures of many different odorants. Even when we perceive the odor of a single chemical, we often assess this against a background composed of many hundreds of sub- and peri-threshold chemical compounds. Thus, understanding both the ways in which we perceive mixtures and our capacity to discriminate the constituents of complex mixtures are central to a complete accounting of olfactory processes. Whereas human olfactory ability seems optimally equipped to discriminate the many hundreds of different odors that we encounter regularly, general observations seem to suggest that we can discriminate very few constituents of mixtures and that most mixtures are perceived as a unitary whole that is difficult to decompose into constituent parts, at least to the untrained nose.

Beginning with the simplest level of mixture analysis—binary mixtures—Cain and Drexler (1974) described a set of outcomes that could result when mixtures were smelled. They proposed that relative to the unmixed components, the perceived strength of a mixture could show complete additivity, hyper-additivity, or one of three types of hypoadditivity (partial when the mixture smells more intense than the stronger component smelled alone; compromise when the mixture smells more intense than one component smelled alone but less than the other; or compensation when the mixture smells weaker than both the stronger and weaker component; Cain & Drexler, 1974; Laing, Panhuber, Willcox, & Pittman, 1984). In addition to outcomes involving the total intensity of the mixture, Laing and colleagues (Laing et al., 1984) described mixture effects that can be observed on the perception of individual components in which reciprocity between odorants in a binary mixture is rarely encountered. For example, in a mixture of limonene (citrus) and propionic acid (vinegar), limonene strongly suppresses the perceived intensity of the propionic acid, whereas the acid has little effect on the perception of limonene (Bell, Laing, & Panhuber, 1987). In contrast, in an equi-intense mixture of limonene and carvone (spearmint), the carvone suppressed the odor of limonene without exhibiting any reduction in its own smell (Laing, 1988).

Humans have shown a remarkably limited capacity to identify or discriminate the components of mixtures. In a series of experiments, Laing and his colleagues (Laing & Glemarec, 1992; Laing & Francis, 1989) asked trained and untrained subjects and experienced flavorists and perfumers to identify the constituents of mixtures containing from one to five common odorants. Although trained subjects performed more accurately than did untrained subjects and although perfumers and flavorists performed substantially better than did untrained subjects, the average subject was limited to identifying no more than three components in a five-component mixture. This result, together with the finding that multicomponent mixtures are frequently not judged as more complex than single odorants or binary mixtures (Moskowitz & Barbe, 1977), supports the notion that mixtures are perceived in holistic fashion, and this reflects the strongly synthetic nature of olfactory processing.

Both peripheral and central mechanisms can be involved in the perception of mixtures. Laing (1991) suggested several peripheral mechanisms that could account for mixture suppression, including (a) competition for receptor sites, (b) allosteric effects whereby occupation of a site by one odorant adjacent to the binding site of another odorant affects binding of the latter odor, and (c) intracellular effects whereby odorant-stimulated release of certain substances (e.g., calcium) could inhibit the transduction process for another odorant that might compete for the same receptor sites on an olfactory neuron. Bell et al. (1987) investigated metabolic activity in glomeruli of the olfactory bulb in rats for two kinds of binary odor mixtures: one in which humans perceived only one odorant and one in which they perceived both odorants. In the former mixture, metabolic activity of the glomeruli specific to the suppressed odor was greatly reduced, whereas in the latter mixture the researchers observed metabolic activity characteristic of both components. They

concluded that mixture suppression was primarily peripheral in origin; that is, one odorant's ability to suppress another in the mixture was likely to be determined by chemical properties that in turn determined competition for receptor sites in the olfactory epithelium. Suppression need not be confined to the periphery, however, especially given the potential for modification of the input in the olfactory bulb via lateral inhibition (Shepherd, 1974) and the presumed convergence from the olfactory bulb to the primary olfactory cortex (Staubli, Fraser, Faraday, & Lynch, 1987).

One psychophysical approach to investigating the peripheral versus central suppression involved comparing the degree of suppression observed when two odorants were delivered simultaneously but separately to each nostril (dichorhinic stimulation) or simultaneously as a mixture to both nostrils (birhinal stimulation). The lack of peripheral convergence of olfactory information argued for any observed interactions under dichorhinic conditions to be of central origin. Using these techniques, some investigations found similarities in suppression (Cain, 1977a), whereas others found strong suppression during birhinal but not during dichorhinic stimulation (Laing & Willcox, 1987). However, even under conditions of birhinal stimulation, there is evidence that each nostril may transmit very different information to the cortex. Building on the earlier findings of Mozell, Kent, and Murphy (1991), who showed that the deposition patterns of odorants with different solubilities varied as a function of flow rate, Sobel et al. (1999) familiarized subjects with each component of a binary mixture and then presented that mixture dichorhinically and asked subjects to rate the similarity of the mixture to each component. Because of the effects of the normal nasal cycle, patency and flow rate differed between the nostrils of most subjects by more than 20%. As predicted by Mozell et al.'s model, the perception from the least patent nostril was rated as similar to the low solubility component, whereas the perception from the more patent nostril was judged as similar to the component of higher solubility (Sobel et al., 1999).

Multimodal Interactions

Olfactory information is often processed in combination with stimuli from other sensory systems. Two interactions are of particular importance for understanding human chemosensory processing: the interaction of taste and olfaction, to produce flavor perception, and the interaction of chemesthesis and olfaction. The perception of flavor is probably the quintessential example of multimodal interactions: Activation in two peripherally distinct neural systems, olfaction and gustation, gives rise to a unified oral sensation (see Chap. 16, this volume). When suprathreshold mixture solutions of taste and odorant stimuli have been taken in the mouth and judged for overall perceived intensity, almost perfect additivity of sensation is observed: The intensity of the mixtures of ethyl butyrate (odorant) and sodium saccharin (taste; Murphy, Cain, & Bartoshuk, 1977) and sucrose and NaCl (taste) and citral and anethol (odorant; Gillan, 1983) were judged only slightly less than the sum of the perceived intensities of the unmixed components. Multimodal mixtures showed less suppression than did within-modality mixtures (Gillan, 1983). When asked to apportion the overall intensity judgment between the modalities of smell and taste, however, subjects often show considerable taste-smell confusion and resolve most flavor sensations by ascribing them to taste. For example, the rated taste intensity of a mixture containing saccharin (taste) and ethyl butyrate (odorant) decreased by 80% when the nostrils were closed and the contribution of retronasal olfactory stimulation was eliminated (Murphy et al., 1977).

Although quality congruency of the odor and taste solution had no effect on stimulus additivity at suprathreshold concentrations of taste-odor mixtures (Murphy & Cain, 1980), this did not hold true for integration at subthreshold levels. Dalton and colleagues (Dalton, Doolittle, Nagata, & Breslin, 2000) used psychophysical methods to demonstrate cross-modal summation of subthreshold concentrations of gustatory and olfactory stimuli. In a series of experiments, they showed that the threshold for benzaldehyde was significantly decreased by the presence of a subthreshold concentration of saccharin in the mouth (Figure 17.11), but not by the presence of water or monosodium glutamate (MSG, which was selected because benzaldehyde-MSG was an incongruous flavor to the test population). This outcome implicated a central locus of convergence for gustatory and olfactory information and raised the possibility that the enhancement in neural response to an odor-taste combination may reflect associations based on prior experience (Rolls, 1997).

Despite the strong contribution of retronasal olfactory cues to the overall perception of flavor, flavor sensation is almost always localized to the oral cavity, not the nose (Murphy & Cain, 1980). This illusion may be mediated through the oral somatosensory stimulation that almost always accompanies actual taste stimulation but does not necessarily accompany odor unless the olfactory stimulus has both olfactory and chemesthetic properties.

Intranasal chemesthesis is always experienced in combination with odor perception, except in rare circumstances, for example, following stimulation with carbon dioxide or among individuals who are anosmic (i.e., lacking a functional sense of smell). Early observations suggested that trigeminal stimulation had an inhibitory influence over the perception of odor (Cain & Murphy, 1980).

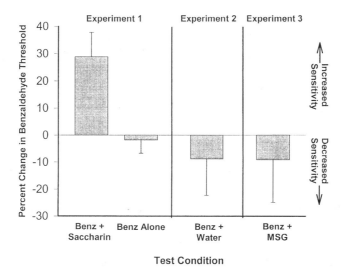

Figure 17.11 Subthreshold integration of smell and taste.
NOTE: Median percent changes from baseline odor threshold for benzaldehyde when subjects simultaneously held a subthreshold saccharin solution (Experiment 1), deionized water (Experiment 2), or subthreshold monosodium glutamate solution (Experiment 3) in their mouths while sniffing. Only the threshold obtained when saccharin was in the mouth differed significantly from zero.
SOURCE: From Dalton, Doolittle, Nagata, & Breslin (2000).

A formal investigation of the interaction between these two modalities suggested that at suprathreshold concentrations strong mutual inhibition between odor and chemesthesis occurs (Cain & Murphy, 1980).

Chemesthesis and olfaction may interact at subthreshold chemesthetic levels as well. Because sensory irritation of the upper airways is a widely cited health effect in indoor air and occupational environments (U.S. Department of Health and Human Services, 1994) and because almost any odorant at a sufficiently high concentration evokes not only odor but also chemesthetic sensations, investigators have used various techniques to determine the concentration at which an odorant elicits chemesthetic sensations. Direct scaling of irritant sensation in individuals with intact olfactory and trigeminal systems has led to extreme variability in results, as these separate modalities tend to be experienced as a unified percept in the nose; hence, responses to

odor intensity may be confused with chemesthetic sensations. One approach to evaluating odor and chemesthesis separately has been to measure nasal detection thresholds to odorants in subjects with a normal sense of smell and compare them with those obtained from anosmic individuals (Cometto-Muñiz & Cain, 1990, 1991). The concentration at which a normosmic can detect a chemical is assumed to correspond to the odor threshold, whereas the concentration at which an anosmic can detect is assumed to correspond to the nasal irritation threshold. However, evidence from electrophysiological and anatomical studies suggests that chemesthetic perception may be diminished among individuals who lack a functional sense of smell (Finger & Bottger, 1993; Roscher et al., 1996). Thus, the recent development of a psychophysical method to measure separately thresholds for odor and chemesthesis in subjects with a functional sense of smell has led to rapid progress in this area (Cometto-Muñiz & Cain, 1998; Wysocki et al., 1997). This technique, called nasal lateralization, relies on the fact that irritants, but not pure olfactory stimuli, can be localized to the nasal mucosa. Thus, presenting a chemical vapor to one nostril and clean air to the other nostril will permit a smell, but not a localizable sensation, as long as the concentration does not exceed the threshold for trigeminal nerve activation. Once the concentration of the vapor exceeds the irritant threshold, the vapor stimulus will be able to be reliably localized to the stimulated nostril. Data using this technique have been used to measure both odor and irritation thresholds in individuals with a normal sense of smell.

FUNCTIONAL CHANGES ACROSS TIME

Neural Plasticity: Neurogenesis across the Life Span and Recovery from Injury

The olfactory system is a highly plastic region of the nervous system. Continuous remodeling of neuronal circuits in the olfactory bulb takes place throughout life as a result of constant turnover of primary sensory olfactory neurons in the periphery. The olfactory epithelium of adult animals retains the capacity for neurogenesis, and the olfactory receptor neurons are capable of replacement throughout the animal's life span (Graziadei & Monti Graziadei, 1977). They can also reconstitute wholly or in part after direct damage (i.e., chemical lesions or nerve injury) or retrograde neuronal degeneration. During recovery, replacement neurons differentiate from basal cells, and their axons grow and reestablish connections with the olfactory bulb.

Degenerative changes in the olfactory epithelium are a common correlate of aging. These changes include a reduction in the thickness of the epithelium because of recep-

tor neuron loss, intermingling of respiratory cells with olfactory neurons and supporting cells, and extensive patchy replacement of olfactory by respiratory epithelium. Olfactory loss is frequently associated with a number of age-related conditions, including the early stages of neuro-degenerative diseases, medication use, or injuries (Mesholam, Moberg, Mahr, & Doty, 1998; Murphy, 1999).

The pathophysiology underlying senescence- and disease-related losses in olfactory acuity is still unknown, but a number of mechanisms have been proposed, including decreased capacity for neurogenesis/regeneration with age, cumulative damage from environmental pollutants and diseases (such as upper respiratory infections or nasal-sinus disease), genetically programmed cell aging, or a combination of all of these (Farbman, 1990). When Rawson and colleagues (Rawson, Gomez, Cowart, & Restrepo, 1998) examined olfactory tissue biopsy specimens from older (64–85 years) and younger (20–45 years) individuals, however, they found as many ORNs in the biopsies of older subjects as they did in biopsies of younger individuals. Moreover, ORNs from older individuals were much more responsive to stimulation by multiple odorants than were ORNs from younger individuals, suggesting that age-related decrements in olfactory acuity may reflect a decreased specificity in the receptor response, rather than simply decreased receptor density or responsivity.

Admittedly, the olfactory system is remarkably resistant to the functional effects of some types of peripheral damage. For example, experimentally induced chemical lesions that destroy roughly 95% to 98% of the olfactory epithelium do not produce significant alterations in odor sensitivity, as measured by detection ability in rats (Youngentob, Schwob, Sheehe, & Youngentob, 1997). This robustness has been interpreted to reflect both the capacity of the normal epithelium to sustain environmental insults and the importance of maintaining olfactory function for the organism.

Surgical techniques, such as olfactory nerve transection, in which all nerve fibers that project to the olfactory bulb are severed, have been more likely to produce a total loss of olfactory function (e.g., Yee & Costanzo, 1998), similar to what is observed following traumatic head injury in humans. Following nerve transection in rats and mice, the axons reconnect with glomeruli in the bulb, but even after recovery the odor receptor map is significantly altered (Costanzo, 2000). What are the functional consequences of changes in the mapping of the receptor neurons? Patients who have sustained impaired olfactory function as a consequence of traumatic head injury (and from whom it is possible to obtain information about pre- and postinjury odor quality) have reported that many formerly familiar odorants produce detectable, but unique and unidentifiable, odor sensations. As is true in animal transection studies, feedback and training can facilitate discrimination of these "new" odors, but in most cases the odorant never reacquires its preinjury qualities, suggesting that the patterns of neural innervation in the olfactory bulb are critical to the perception of odor quality.

Life Span Effects: Aging

Aging has an effect on most sensory processes, and olfaction provides no exception. Although aging has been discussed as a determining factor in the regenerative capacity of the neuroepithelium, aging has substantial effects on olfactory function that can lead to significant impairments in quality of life and may render the elderly susceptible to certain environmental hazards. Age-related deficits in olfaction have been found for threshold and suprathreshold sensitivity as well as odor identification performance. The

ability to detect or recognize peri-threshold concentrations of odorants may constitute the earliest demonstration of age-related losses. Relative to a young cohort, significantly elevated detection and recognition thresholds have been observed for a broad range of odorant compounds, although some studies have suggested that age-related declines are not uniform across all substances tested (Figure 17.12; Wysocki et al., 1989).

Even in the absence of observable disease or injury, the normal process of aging leads to significant and quantifiable decreases in olfactory ability, which can be observed both on threshold and suprathreshold performance. Psychophysical studies have shown that many, if not most, individuals experience measurable age-related losses in olfactory sensitivity, beginning as early as the sixth decade. Such losses can ultimately be profound: Doty (1991) estimated that by the ninth decade more than 75% of individuals were clinically *hyposmic,* experiencing major difficulties in perceiving and identifying odorants. However, both psychophysical and anatomical studies suggest that such decrements may reflect more the contributions of physiological rather than chronological age, with poor health, medications, and environmental exposures being major contributors to a decline in olfactory function (Loo, Youngentob, Kent, & Schwob, 1996; Schiffman, 1997).

Exposure Effects: Adaptation, Cross-Adaptation and Sensitization

Sensory adaptation is a common property of all sensory systems and is thought to be an important functional mechanism for preventing saturation in the nervous system and maintaining the organism's sensitivity to new information. In the olfactory system, adaptation has been operationally defined as the decrease in sensitivity or response to an odorant after exposure to that odorant. Numerous studies have

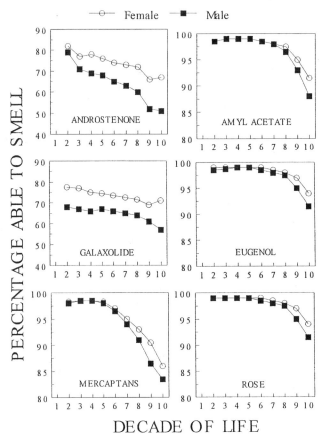

Figure 17.12 The percentage of respondents to the National Geographic Smell Survey who were able to smell the six test odorants, as a function of gender and age.
SOURCE: After Gilbert & Wysocki (1987).

examined short-term adaptation and recovery to a wide variety of odorants. These studies show that although the decline in perceived intensity follows a characteristic exponential decay function, the rate and degree of adaptation and the temporal kinetics of recovery are both concentration- and duration-dependent (e.g., Berglund, 1974; Cain, 1974). At the extreme, where studies have used prolonged exposure durations, the level of adaptation can rise to the level of the adapting stimulus and yield the impression that the odor has completely disappeared. Although relatively few in number, studies of the parametric features of adaptation in both vertebrate and inverte-

brate animal models appear to replicate the findings in psychophysical studies of adult humans (Colbert & Bargmann, 1995; Wuttke & Tompkins, 1999).

A defining feature of olfactory adaptation is that the exposure-induced decrease in sensitivity or perceived intensity is specific to the adapting odorant. In his seminal study on olfactory adaptation, Köster (1971) proposed a number of general rules that characterized the parameters of adaptation and cross-adaptation to olfactory stimuli. Cross-adaptation, defined as a decrease in sensitivity (or perceived intensity) to one odor after exposure to a different odor, has been

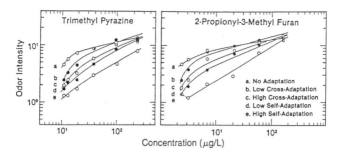

Figure 17.13 Families of psychophysical functions for the odor intensity of two structurally different but perceptually similar odorants, trimethyl pyrazine (TMP) and 2-propionyl-3-methyl furan (PMF) under various conditions of self-adaptation and of cross-adaptation of one substance by another.
NOTE: Although both odorants exhibit mutual cross-adaptation, the degree of self-adaptation is always greater than the degree of cross-adaptation.
SOURCE: From Cain & Polak (1992).

interpreted as a measure of the degree to which odors share common sensory channels (e.g., Cain & Polak, 1992). Although adaptation to one odor may generalize to a small subset of other chemicals that share structural or perceptual features with the adapting odorant (see Figure 17.13; Cain & Polak, 1992; Pierce, Wysocki, Aronov, Webb, & Boden, 1996), the degree of cross-adaptation is almost always less than the degree of adaptation resulting from the same stimulus, providing that the stimuli are equated for intensity and duration (Köster, 1971). No adapting substance has been found to enhance the sensitivity to another substance. In addition, most cross-adaptational relationships are nonreciprocal. Although this difference can be minimized by equating the two stimuli for perceived intensity, one substance influences the sensitivity to another substance to a larger degree than the second one influences the sensitivity to the first.

Measures of Adaptation

Olfactory adaptation can manifest itself in an elevation of the detection threshold, in a reduction in perceived intensity, or in slowed reaction times to detect or identify the odor. In addition, adaptation to one or more odors may alter other measures of olfactory performance: It is well established that adaptation to one odorant may cross-adapt (reduce the response to) another odorant (Cain, 1970; Pierce et al., 1996), and there is evidence that in an adapted olfactory system there are shifts in perception of odor qualities, particularly of mixtures (Köster & de Wijk, 1991; Lawless, 1987). Thus, understanding the sources of variation in the degree and rate of adaptation is critical to assessing the detectability or quality of an odor over time under environmentally realistic conditions.

The effects of adaptation can be measured using psychophysical methods to assess changes in olfactory threshold and perceived intensity, electrophysiological methods to monitor activity in receptor cells and secondary neurons, and neuroimaging methods to evaluate activity in central cortical structures that process olfactory and related information. Using psychophysical techniques, changes in threshold to the exposure odorant can be sensitive indexes of an adapted olfactory system; however, measuring thresholds is time-consuming, and sensitivity cannot be measured during the process of adaptation. Unlike threshold measurements, the perceived intensity of an odor can be monitored during adaptation by direct scaling methods (magnitude estimation, category scaling, visual analog scales) or by cross-modality matching procedures (finger span, auditory matching), thus providing a dynamic measure of the adapted olfactory system.

There is considerable merit in investigating adaptation phenomena using multiple methods, for it is generally believed that olfactory adaptation occurs at multiple levels in the olfactory system (e.g., Cometto-Muñiz & Cain, 1995): Transient or persistent decreases in odor intensity and sensitivity can be accompanied by changes in both peripheral and central responses to olfactory input (Hummel, Knecht, & Kobal, 1996). In studies examining peripheral mechanisms, investigators have shown that both aggregate (EOG) and single cell electrophysiological responses from olfactory neurons in animals (e.g., rat) are attenuated following repeated stimulation by an odorant (Ottoson, 1956). However, attempts to compare the magnitude of the decline in receptor response with the decline in response or the reported intensity of odor have led investigators to conclude that receptor adaptation alone cannot account for the psychophysical loss (T. V. Getchell & Shepherd, 1978; Hummel et al., 1996). Thus, researchers continue to look for other loci of the adaptive process.

The temporal kinetics of the recovery from adaptation may differ when viewed at the neural versus the perceptual level. For example, the duration of adaptation at the periphery that is considered long-lasting is on the order of minutes (Zufall & Leinders-Zufall, 1997), yet both anecdotal and experimental examples of perceptual adaptation appear much more durable, and decreased sensitivity often persists for hours beyond the original exposures (Colbert & Bargmann, 1995; Gagnon, Mergler, & Lapare, 1994). There is evidence that repetitive exposure can induce a form of adaptation of even longer durations. When

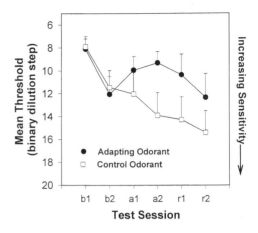

Figure 17.14 Olfactory adaptation following long-term exposure to an odorant.
NOTE: Average olfactory detection thresholds for two odorants, either citralva (lemon) or isobornyl acetate (balsam): The adapting odorant was kept in the subject's home for 2 weeks, and the control odorant was experienced only during threshold testing in the laboratory. Sensitivity to these two odorants was tested weekly on six sessions: two prior to exposure (baseline), two during home-exposure (adaptation), and two after removal of the odorant from the home (recovery).
SOURCE: From Dalton & Wysocki (1996).

individuals were exposed to odors in their homes for 6 hours per day for 2 weeks, adaptation was evident for hours after leaving the home environment to be tested in the laboratory, and recovery to baseline olfactory sensitivity for the adapting odorant did not occur for more than 2 weeks following the last exposures (see Figure 17.14; Dalton & Wysocki, 1996). The neural basis, if any, for such persistence remains in question.

Variation in the dynamic responses to odor exposure can also be attributed to subject factors, such as age, exposure history, and cognitive/emotional factors. For example, in one of the few studies that directly examined variation in adaptation kinetics, Stevens et al. (1989) found that the degree of recovery from adaptation appeared to decrease with age (see Figure 17.15). Because assessments of

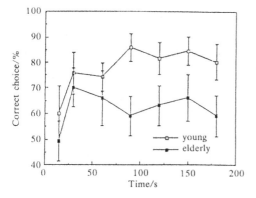

Figure 17.15 Decreased recovery from adaptation as a function of age, as shown by the average olfactory recovery curves following adaptation to butanol for 10 older and 10 younger subjects.
SOURCE: From Stevens, Cain, Schiet, & Oatley (1989).

olfactory acuity status rely on repetitive exposures to test stimuli, the potential for decreased recovery following even brief odor stimulation could account for some of the apparent elevations in threshold and diminished sensitivity to suprathreshold stimuli that are observed among the elderly. Sustained occupational exposure to an odorant (acetone) over weeks, months, or years can lead to a reduction in sensitivity and response to its odor and irritation (Dalton, Wysocki, Brody, & Lawley, 1997; Wysocki et al., 1997). There are at least three possible causes underlying this persistent adaptation. First, peripheral changes such as down-regulation of receptors could account for the elevated thresholds and reduced responses. Second, the circulatory system can provide a vehicle for transporting odorants that have been absorbed from the nasal cavity and lungs and dissolved into fat stores in the body. Odorants can be measured in the blood after short exposure durations, and such blood-borne odorants have been shown to elicit responses in olfactory receptors (Maruniak, Silver, & Moulton, 1983). Desorbed odorants may be carried to the receptor environment during expiration by dif-

fusion from the blood stream in the lungs (Maruniak, Mason, & Kostelc, 1983; Van Dishoeck & Versteeg, 1957) or may stimulate receptors by diffusing out of the blood stream into the nasal capillary bed (Maruniak et al., 1983) and cause continuous adaptation of the olfactory receptors as they are exhaled. A third possibility is that higher levels of cognitive/emotional processing are involved in modulating the adaptation process. Repetitive occupational exposure may modify beliefs about the risk from exposure to an odorant; in studies where expectations or beliefs about chemical safety were manipulated prior to exposure, characteristic patterns of adaptation occurred only for subjects who were led to believe that the exposure odorant was a benign natural odorant (Dalton, 1996).

Induced Sensitivity

Exposure to a static background level of odor induces adaptation, yet this situation is not fully representative of our everyday experience in chemical environments, in which our olfactory systems regularly receive punctate stimulation by a diverse range of odorants. The resulting complexity and unpredictability of the chemical world that an organism may encounter can pose a considerable burden on an olfactory system that may therefore need to develop sensitivity to thousands of discriminable odorants. One solution to this problem is to alter the sensory capabilities of the olfactory system according to the surrounding chemical environment in order to enhance sensitivity to odorants that are of particular relevance. Thus, in contrast to the adaptation that results from exposures at chronic, unvarying levels, intermittent or punctate exposures to odorants frequently lead to impressive increases in sensitivity to those specific odors. An example of such alterations comes from perfumers, flavor chemists, and chefs, who often report dramatic increases in the

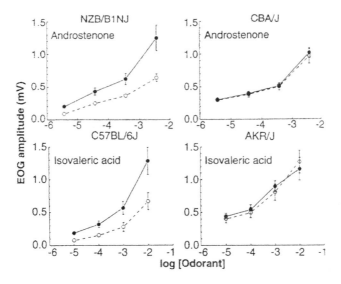

Figure 17.16 Peak amplitudes of the EOG as a function of the log odorant concentration for the indicated strains of mice.
NOTE: Solid circles: androstenone or isovaleric-exposed; open circles: control. No changes in EOG amplitude were observed for the control odorant, isoamyl acetate.
SOURCE: Adapted from Wang, Wysocki, & Gold (1993).

detectability of volatiles to which they are regularly exposed in the course of their occupational activities.

Whether this apparent increase in sensitivity is due to a change in sensory or attentional processes remains unresolved on the basis of such anecdotes. However, experimental studies have demonstrated impressive increases in sensitivity from regular exposure to certain odorants. Wysocki, Dorries, and Beauchamp (1989) investigated the inducibility of sensitivity to androstenone, a volatile steroid that nearly half the adult human population cannot smell. With regular daily exposure to androstenone, sensitivity was induced in 10 of 20 subjects who were initially unable to smell it. To explore the locus of this effect (whether peripheral or central in origin), Wang, Wysocki, and Gold (1993) measured the peripheral response of aggregated olfactory receptors (EOG) to androstenone and isovaleric acid before and after 2- or 4-week periods of daily exposure in two strains

of mice that were initially low in sensitivity to either of those compounds. Although repeated exposure to these odorants led to an odorant-specific induction of peripheral sensitivity, this occurred only in inbred strains that were initially insensitive to the exposure odorant (see Figure 17.16). Finding evidence of stimulus-induced plasticity in a sensory receptor neuron for two unrelated odorants raises the possibility that olfactory induction is a general phenomenon that allows the olfactory system to develop maximal sensitivity to the proximal environment. For example, the ability of young females to sensitize to odors may confer specific advantages for reproductive behaviors such as mother-infant bonding, selection of nutritive food sources, and avoidance of toxicants (Dalton, Doolittle, & Breslin, in press).

There is evidence that induction of specific sensitivities can occur in the developing olfactory system as well. For newborn, weanling, and even adult rabbits, prenatal exposure to specific maternal diets leads to both enhanced peripheral sensitivity (EOG response) and an increased preference to the odors of those diets; moreover, this can occur even in the absence of postnatal experience with those odors (Hudson & Distel, 1998).

OLFACTORY COGNITION

From the perspective of cognitive psychology, the process of odor perception is a classic information-processing task in which the response to an odor can be influenced both by properties of the stimulus (concentration, quality) and by information that the stimulus activates in long-term memory. Many odors emanate from sources that are unlocalizable and diffuse, and they are difficult to identify when experienced outside of their typical contexts (Davis, 1981; de Wijk & Cain, 1994b). Consequently, the response to an odor stimulus has the potential to be greatly influenced by top-down (conceptually-driven) factors in the complex environment surrounding the exposure, which can include the social context as well as the perceiver's expectations or cognitive capacities.

In fact, a variety of top-down processes has been shown to influence judgments about the detectability, intensity, and hedonic characterization of an odor. For example, enhancing bottles containing odorized solutions as well as those containing odorless solvents with irrelevant color cues increased the likelihood of people's reporting the presence of an odor in either stimulus type (Engen, 1972). This manipulation also increased perceived odor intensity (Zellner & Kautz, 1990). Informing subjects that an aerosol delivery of water was either a pleasant or unpleasant odorous substance produced reports of odor experience that were consistent with the hedonic characterization (Knasko, Gilbert, & Sabini, 1990). Studies like these suggest that higher-level

cognition may play a large role in determining our everyday odor experiences because of the degree to which factors such as context or expectations were able to bias reported odor perceptions.

Odor Memory

Perhaps more than stimuli in other modalities, odors are believed to evoke vivid and complex memories readily. Moreover, the formation of odor memories has important functional significance in humans, particularly at early stages of development. Beginning shortly after birth, human infants appear able to form complex associations to olfactory stimuli, independent of semantic memory formation (Porter & Winberg, 2000; Sullivan et al., 1991), that may play an important role in the subsequent development of preferences and infant-mother bonds.

Until recently, however, investigations of memory for odors and odor-evoked memories were relatively few, and those that did exist were poorly integrated with the broad research field of memory and cognition for other modalities. Methods to investigate different aspects of memory function that have been developed for verbal and visual memory studies are now being applied to the study of olfactory memory. Although much of the evidence from recent studies supports the perspective that odor memory is not a separate memory system that is characterized by different parameters than memory for other forms of information, the lack of a systematic body of research in this area should forestall premature conclusions.

Measures of Memory: Familiarity and Identification

Odor recognition remains the most common and direct measure of odor memory (Schab & Crowder, 1995) because the response options for subjects who are asked to recall odors are limited to generating the name or other verbal label that has been given to the odor. Nevertheless, one cannot rule out the possibility that odors are dually encoded as are pictures (Snodgrass, Wasser, Finkelstein, & Goldberg, 1974) or that recognition memory for odors is based at least in part on the recognition of covertly generated and associated visual or verbal representations of olfactory information.

Early studies of short-term odor memory concluded that odor recognition was characterized by imperfect odor encoding, little subsequent forgetting, and no effects of odor familiarity or identifiability. However, subsequent evidence for significant forgetting of odors at retention intervals of 1 min to 2 min prompted Schab and Crowder (1995) to suggest that the flat forgetting function at shorter intervals may be due to a longer encoding process for odors that effectively shortens the nominal retention interval. Long-term odor memory experiments yielded results and conclusions that were very similar to many of the early short-term recognition studies. For example, Rabin and Cain (1984) showed that recognition memory accuracy is positively correlated with stimulus familiarity and identifiability, but that forgetting is rather minimal even over durations of up to one week. In general, the most striking consistency is the relatively flat forgetting curve obtained with odors, suggesting that once established, odor memories are relatively resistant to subsequent interference. This may be due to two features of the encoding process that limit the amount of interference: (a) Odors are likely to be encoded as relatively structureless stimuli without feature redundancy, and (b) experimental odors may be encoded differently than nonexperimental odors experienced in everyday contexts (Schab, 1991). As is true for odor identification, aging appears to decrease recognition memory performance for odors. Murphy and her colleagues (Murphy, Cain,

Gilmore, & Skinner, 1991) compared recognition across various retention intervals for symbols, faces, and odors among young and elderly individuals. Memory for odors among the elderly decayed dramatically across a 6-month retention interval relative to their memory for graphic stimuli (see Figure 17.17). Although odor and graphic memory among the younger subjects showed some forgetting, performance even at 6 months was always above chance. Notably, memory performance for odors at all retention intervals was characterized by an extremely high false alarm rate (0.35–0.50).

Additional studies have established the importance of semantic encoding on odor memory performance by demonstrating that elaboration at encoding (verbal or semantic) can enhance odor recognition (Lyman & McDaniel, 1986, 1990). When tested after a 7-day retention interval, subjects who had generated verbal definitions or related personal episodes to odors recognized significantly more odors than those who had generated visual images or encoded the odors without an orienting task (Lyman & McDaniel, 1990).

In contrast to recognition memory performance, the ability to identify odors by name remains a difficult task throughout the life span, especially when the task involves free recall rather than recognition of a limited set of odor names (see Herz & Engen, 1996, for a review). In general, people find it more difficult to provide names for odors, even relatively familiar ones, than for pictures (Murphy et al., 1991). The basis for this relatively poor performance in free odor identification has been attributed to an inherent weak link between odors and language (Engen, 1987) or a byproduct of the way in which we learn odors (e.g., we typically learn that certain objects possess smells rather than that certain smells can be described with verbal labels). However, it has also been suggested that poor identification performance

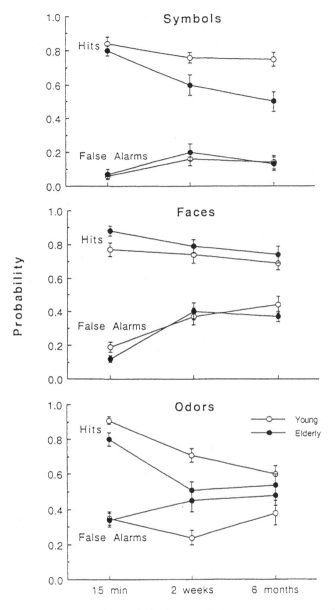

Figure 17.17   Recognition memory for symbols, faces, and odors among younger and older people at three retention intervals.
SOURCE: From Murphy, Cain, Gilmore, & Skinner (1991).

could as well be limited by deficiencies in discrimination and resolution of odors (Cain, de Wijk, Lulejian, Schiet and See, 1998). In side-by-side comparisons of odors, where the demands on memory are limited, discrimination errors with common odors are still made (Eskenazi, Cain, & Friend, 1986; Rabin, 1988). Although identification ability improves dramatically when subjects are given a small set of odor labels to select from, it should be noted that presentation of a verbal label can prompt a percept that is consistent with the presented name, even when the actual odor stimulus is a different, but perceptually similar, odor (de Wijk & Cain, 1994a). This underscores the extent to which odor perception is both a top-down (conceptually-driven) and a bottom-up (stimulus-driven) process.

Features of Odor Memory and Comparison with Other Sensory Systems

Memory for odors has traditionally been compared with memory for visual and verbal information on several dimensions of performance, such as the shape of the retention function and sensitivity to interference effects (see Richardson & Zucco, 1989, for a review). Although the shape of the forgetting curve for odors is comparable to the curve for other types of memory, odor memory does appear less sensitive to the effects of retroactive interference (although strong proactive interference effects are found; Lawless & Engen, 1977). This finding has generally been attributed to the presumed unitary representation of odors in memory.

In making comparisons involving visual/ verbal and olfactory memory, it is prudent to acknowledge that although memory processes subserving these different modalities may appear to differ, the observed differences in memory performance may result from fundamental differences in the stimulus materials themselves. For example, recent findings showing that stimulus familiarity increases odor recognition performance are in conflict with the results of verbal/visual recognition memory studies in which unfamiliar (i.e., distinctive) stimuli are recognized better but recalled worse than familiar/common ones. However, as Schab and Crowder (1995) noted, the quality of stimulus encoding differs significantly between these three types of stimuli: Word- and picture-frequency effects occur for stimuli that are easily and meaningfully encoded but not for stimuli that are truly unfamiliar (e.g., nonwords). For odors, which are

less easily encoded and may be more similar to nonwords than words, the benefits of distinctiveness may be outweighed by the benefits of familiarity (Schab & Crowder, 1995).

Odor Hedonics

Preference and Hedonic Response

Perhaps more than other sensory stimuli, the perception of an odor will often prompt a rapid hedonic response (Schiffman, 1974). Studies that have explored the nature and quality of olfactory representations through multidimensional scaling have consistently found that two factors underlie people's responses to odors: intensity and pleasantness (hedonic tone). However, the search for an emergent dimension by which some odors are judged pleasant and others unpleasant has not been fruitful. The simplest hypothesis, that objects producing bad odors are likely to be dangerous or toxic and that those producing good odors are likely to be beneficial (or at least nontoxic), is not readily supported or refuted by existing data. For example, methyl salicylate (oil of wintergreen) is highly toxic if ingested in adequate quantities, yet it is used as a flavoring at low concentrations and is generally considered to have a pleasant, healthy smell (Dalton, 1996). Similarly, some odors that elicit strongly negative hedonic responses (e.g., the smell of vomit) would hardly be judged as toxic or life-threatening.

However, odors need not be judged as noxious for them to be perceived as threatening or aversive. In a series of studies examining the interaction between health cognitions and odor perception, subjects were exposed to odors under one of three characterizations about the consequences of exposure (harmful, healthful, and neutral). Those individuals given a harmful bias reported significantly more health symptoms following exposure and more intense odor and irritation during exposure than did those given a neutral or healthful bias (Dalton, 1996, 1999; Dalton et al., 1997). The overall pattern of results from these and other studies (e.g., Shusterman, 1992) suggests that many of the health-related effects of exposure to odorants are mediated not by a direct effect of chemical exposure but by cognitive variables that influence hedonics, such as mental models of the relationship between environmental odors and health.

Development of Hedonic Responses

One approach to understanding the hedonic dimension of responses to odors is to examine the extent to which the origins of hedonic preferences to olfactory stimuli are innate or learned. This is not a simple question, and investigators wishing to tackle this problem have needed to address numerous methodological issues, including choices about which odors to use and which affective reactions to measure. For example, odor stimuli should be iso-intense and should not elicit trigeminal sensation (the avoidance of which is mediated by the pain system and is therefore innate). The measurement of hedonic responses in preverbal children has required the use of inferential techniques to evaluate odor responses. Two basic approaches have been used: (a) measuring movements toward or away from an odor, under the assumption that such responses indicate preference and aversion, respectively, and (b) recording facial expressions as stereotypic indicators of internal states signifying approach and avoidance (Steiner, 1974, 1976; but see Gilbert, Fridlund, & Sabini, 1987). Both types of responses to odors have been evident shortly after birth (Engen, Lipsitt, & Kaye, 1963; Reiser, Yonas, & Wikner, 1976; Sarnat, 1978; Self, Horowits, & Paden, 1972). Some odors having biological relevance to infants, such as maternal odors, have been found to mediate approach behavior. For example, 2- to 3-day-old infants orient more to a breast pad that was previously worn by their lactating mother than to one worn by an unfamiliar lactating female (Russell, 1976; Schaal, 1986). However, this finding may not indicate that maternal odors inspire positive affective reactions, but may serve merely to indicate that preference is based on acquired attraction or familiarity, especially given the possibility that prenatal exposure to maternal odors occurs and influences postnatal response (Hepper, 1995).

Although earlier studies of children younger than five indicated that they were more tolerant of odors than adults and often responded positively to some odors (e.g., sweat and feces) that adults and older children found offensive, these studies also suffered from methodological difficulties. For example, forced-choice methodologies embedded in the context of a game circumvent the tendency of young children to answer positively phrased questions in the affirmative (Schmidt & Beauchamp, 1988). Using these techniques, studies of olfactory preferences and aversions in children have shown that children do exhibit a pattern of preferences and aversion to a range of odors that is fairly similar to that shown by adults (see Figure 17.18; Schmidt & Beauchamp, 1988; Strickland, Jessee, & Filsinger, 1988), although the question of whether children exhibit greater tolerance to malodors than do adults has not been explored adequately.

Obviously, the lack of evidence for innate hedonic reactions to odors applies primarily to humans. For many nonhuman animals (vertebrate and invertebrate), there are clear examples of innate chemical tropisms mediated by pheromone compounds that serve to initiate and maintain specific behaviors (i.e., food search or reproduction; Cheal & Sprott, 1971).

Evidence from cross-cultural studies indicates that a substantial degree of the hedonic response to odors may be related to

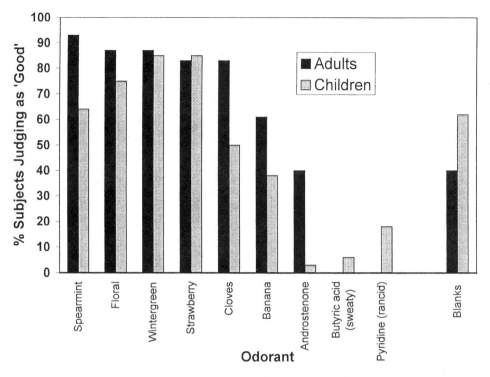

Figure 17.18   Hedonic ratings of "good" for a range of odorants by adults and 5-year-old children.
SOURCE: From Schmidt & Beauchamp (1988).

culture-specific experiences that can evoke different patterns of cognitive and emotional responses (Rozin, 1973). Results from the 1986 National Geographic Smell Survey (Gilbert & Wysocki, 1987) showed that a significantly larger number of Asians from Malaysia, Singapore, and Thailand said that they would eat something that smelled like mercaptan (an odor that smells like rotten eggs) than did non-Asian respondents from those same countries, a behavior that may be based on specific dietary experiences. This type of culture-specific learning may occur quite early in development: Recent evidence indicates that flavor volatiles from the maternal diet and odors from other activities during pregnancy (i.e., smoking, alcohol consumption) can modify postnatal flavor preferences (Mennella & Beauchamp, 1991, 1998; Mennella, Jagnow, & Beauchamp, 2001) even

in the absence of specific postnatal experience. Thus, we cannot assume that an odor preference represents a hard-wired, rather than a learned, event just because it is present at birth. In general, the preponderance of data on responses to odors in infants and young children suggests that, as yet, we cannot differentiate the origins of preference on this basis.

Olfaction and Emotion

The notion that olfactory processes are closely linked to emotional experience has become dogma in both popular and scientific literature. Some of the basis for this linkage stems from assumptions about the functionality of the neuroanatomical projections from the olfactory system to substrates that subserve nonverbal aspects of emotion and memory. Prior to Papez's (1937) discoveries that linked certain cortical and subcortical structures to emotion, the area now called the limbic system was known as the rhinencephalon, or smell brain. Unlike other sensory systems, the first cortical relay for olfaction is not the thalamus but rather the primary olfactory cortex, which then links with the amygdala-hippocampal complex of the limbic system (Eichenbaum, 1996). Moreover, the olfactory bulbs have projections to the amygdala that are more direct than are those of other sensory inputs (Aggelton & Mishkin, 1986).

It has been suggested that the unique neural interconnections between the olfactory and limbic systems may account for the Proust phenomenon, in which memories evoked by odors seem more accurate and emotionally tinged than do those evoked by other sensory stimuli (Herz & Cupchik, 1995). Although there is no evidence to support the contention that odor-evoked memories are more accurate, several studies have suggested that such memories have greater emotional potency, as measured by the number of emotional descriptors used during recall (e.g., Herz, 1998). However, verification of emotional arousal on autonomic or other physiologic measures during the recall of such memories is lacking. Moreover, as Ehrlichman and Bastone (1992) observed, mere neuroanatomical proximity between structures subserving olfactory and emotional processing does not prove that they are closely linked in behavior and experience. The amygdala serves as a sensory gateway to the emotions for all manner of sensory stimuli (Aggelton & Mishkin, 1986).

A number of studies have attempted to measure the effects of normatively rated pleasant or unpleasant odors on self-reported mood with equivocal results. In general, the magnitude of negative reactions to malodors seems to outweigh greatly the positive reactions to pleasant odors. In natural environments, perceptions of malodors have been shown to decrease positive mood states (Deane &

Sanders, 1978; Schiffman, Miller, Suggs, & Graham, 1995; Taylor et al., 1997) and increase symptom reporting. However, although many laboratory studies have shown that subjects predict that exposure to unpleasant odors will negatively affect mood or task performance, there is less evidence of the effectiveness of either pleasant or unpleasant odors to modulate mood or performance (Gilbert et al., 1997; Knasko, 1992; Knasko, 1993; Rotton, 1983; Rotton, Barry, Frey, & Soler, 1978). It is possible that the perceived control over the odor, the duration of the exposure, and the context in which exposure occurs (laboratory vs. home environment) are critical to observing an effect on mood states and behavior.

Evidence from neuroimaging studies has shown that the limbic system (amygdala) is involved in the processing of olfactory stimuli that are judged to be aversive. Zald and Pardo (1997) exposed healthy subjects to aversive olfactory stimuli while measuring regional cerebral blood flow (rCBF) with PET. Exposure to a highly aversive odorant (hydrogen sulfide) produced strong rCBF increases in both amygdala and in the left orbitofrontal cortex, whereas exposure to less aversive odorants produced rCBF increases in the orbitofrontal cortex but not in the amygdala (see Figure 17.19). Activity within the left amygdala was significantly associated with subjective ratings of perceived aversiveness. While this demonstrates a link between activity in the limbic system and the subjective perception of a malodor, such effects are not restricted to the processing of olfactory stimuli: In a subsequent study, aversively rated gustatory stimuli (saline solutions) also produced rCBF increases in the amygdala and orbitofrontal cortex (Zald, Lee, Fluegel, & Pardo, 1998).

Although both anecdotal and experimental evidence suggests that the perception of an odor may evoke pleasure or displeasure, influence mood, or in some individuals,

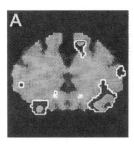 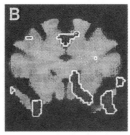 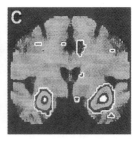

Figure 17.19   PET scan of cerebral activation during aversive olfactory stimulation.
NOTE: Changes in rCBF (relative to the no-odor control) are rendered in white-outlined regions (amygdala and orbitofrontal cortex). The two largest responses occurred bilaterally within the amygdala (Panel C). Activation within the left hemisphere included the amygdala, as well as areas lateral to the amygdala extending to the inferior insula. A weaker bilateral band of activity extended from anterior to posterior along the ventral surface of the frontal lobe to the junction of the frontal and temporal lobes (Panels A and B). This area is consistent with the localization of primary olfactory cortex (POC) as defined by histological studies and overlaps with the location of human POC visualized previously by PET (15, 31). SOURCE: From Zald & Pardo (1997).

stimulate long-forgotten emotional memories, it is still too early to conclude that such effects are unique to olfactory experience. The possibility exists that olfactory stimuli function more as secondary facilitators of emotional reactions in combination with other stimuli. For example, the magnitude of the acoustic startle reflex has been attenuated during exposure to pleasant odors and exacerbated during exposure to unpleasant ones (Ehrlichman, Brown, Zhu, & Warrenburg, 1995; Kaviani, Wilson, Checkley, Kumari, & Gray, 1998).

Perhaps through their significance as indicators of the acceptability of air quality or food, the perception of malodors seems to be intricately linked with the perception of health and disease. Ancient beliefs may prevail here: Prior to the discovery of germ theory, unpleasant odors were deemed to be carriers of disease, and good odors were thought to be potentially curative (Levine & McBurney, 1986). In modern times, unidentified odors have been documented as eliciting more than 50% of the reported outbreaks of psychogenic illness (Colligan & Murphy, 1982), and they play a large role in the perception of sick build-

ing syndrome and concerns about indoor and outdoor air quality.

The motivational potency of pleasant odors is less obvious. Undoubtedly, the most powerfully positive odors for human behavior are those related to food, and the degree of such influences will presumably vary with satiety (Cabanac, 1979). As noted by Engen (1982), however, except perhaps in cases of starvation, the motivational ability of pleasant odors to attract will almost always be less powerful than the tendency of unpleasant odors to elicit avoidance. Taken together with the evidence from PET studies, the behavioral reactions to unpleasant odors appear to show linkage of some types of olfactory processes and affective states.

CLINICAL PROBLEMS OF OLFACTION

Within the past decade, clinical problems of olfaction have been the recipient of renewed interest from both the medical and research profession. From a clinical perspective, olfactory dysfunction can have a substantial impact on quality of life, lead to nutritional problems, and increase susceptibility to the hazards of fire, exposure to chemical toxins, and ingestion of spoiled food (Cowart, Young, Feldman, & Lowry, 1997). From a research perspective, increased understanding of the etiologies of and prognoses for clinical disorders of olfaction might shed light on both normal olfactory function and the vulnerabilities of this system.

Types of Olfactory Dysfunction

It is important to distinguish between two major types of olfactory impairment: disorders of conduction, in which odorous molecules are prevented from reaching the olfactory epithelium, and disorders of perception, in which there is dysfunction in the transmission or reception of the electrical signal. In the former, an anatomic obstruction—frequently due to swelling or congestion, as observed in nasal-sinus disease—prevents the inspired air and odorous molecules from reaching the olfactory epithelium. In the latter, a decreased density of olfactory neurons or the disruption of axonal connections between neurons and the olfactory bulb or primary olfactory cortex prevents the olfactory signal from being transmitted to those cortical areas that are necessary for perception. For example, the olfactory losses in Alzheimer's disease are in part a consequence of the histopathological changes (e.g., neurotic plaques, neurofibrillary tangles, and degeneration) that occur in olfactory pathways, including the olfactory epithelium (Ohm & Braak, 1987; Reyes et al., 1987; Talamo et al., 1989).

Applied Olfaction: Psychophysical Measures of Clinical Olfactory Function

Three classifications of olfactory losses have been described: anosmia (the absence of smell), hyposmia (diminished sensitivity of smell), and dysosmia (distortion of normal smell). Two subcategories of dysosmia include phantosmia (perception of an unpleasant smell when none is present) and parosmia (the perception of a distorted odor in response to a particular stimulus). Although dysosmia is more difficult to quantify in a psychophysical test, anosmia and hyposmia can be quantified by measuring responses to odors at both threshold and suprathreshold concentrations. Most of the chemosensory clinical research centers have established criteria for olfactory dysfunction that rely on the measurement of odor detection thresholds for one or more chemicals (e.g., butanol, pyridine, phenyl ethyl alcohol) and performance on a multiple-item odor identification task (Cain, 1989; Cowart et al., 1997; Doty, Shaman, & Dann, 1984). These measures employ a forced-choice format with a limited number of response alternatives and are therefore less prone to subjective biases and variability than are scaling measures or questionnaires.

Using a battery of tests can greatly assist in identifying the nature of the olfactory problem. For example, hyposmia can be distinguished from anosmia and quantified by measuring sensitivity at threshold. In contrast, odor identification serves as a global assessment tool that provides information on the ability to perceive olfactory stimuli, discriminate qualities, and associate the proper verbal label with an odor. A careful selection of response alternatives can provide insight into the nature of the errors made by subjects. For example, inclusion of a near-miss alternative can serve to confirm a diagnosis of hyposmia (diminished olfactory ability) versus anosmia (loss of olfactory ability), whereas normal threshold sensitivity coupled with poor identification performance and complaints about odor distortions can verify the presence of dysosmia (Cowart et al., 1997).

Etiologies of and Prognosis for Olfactory Dysfunction

The majority of cases of smell dysfunction appear to arise from three primary causes: (a) nasal-sinus disease (NSD; approximately 30%), which may lead to generalized inflammatory processes that can change the composition of the mucus in the olfactory epithelium or, alternatively, through edema, can change the patterns of airflow and odorant deposition (Cowart et al., 1997); (b) prior upper-respiratory tract infection (URI; 14–26%; Cowart et al., 1997; Mott & Leopold, 1991) that may result in viral damage to peripheral olfactory receptors (Jafek et al., 1990); and (c) head trauma (10–19%), which is generally due to tearing or severing of the olfactory neuron axons where they pass through the cribriform plate. Less common causes include congenital deficiencies (i.e., Kallman's disease), neurodegenerative diseases (i.e., Parkinson's or Alzheimer's disease), and exposure to environmental toxicants.

Although anosmia or hyposmia from NSD frequently responds to anti-inflammatory drugs such as corticosteroid therapy (Cain, Gent, Goodspeed, & Leonard, 1988), and some post-viral and head-trauma anosmias spontaneously recover, no effective treatment for other smell disorders presently exists. Research into factors that may play a role in neural regeneration in the olfactory epithelium (e.g., Vitamin A) is currently seen as one promising avenue to pursue (Yee & Rawson, 2000).

FUTURE DIRECTIONS FOR OLFACTORY RESEARCH

This chapter has attempted to review the state of our knowledge about olfaction, especially human olfaction, at a time when our knowledge is rapidly expanding on several fronts.

A landmark finding of the past decade—the identification of the gene family that codes for olfactory receptors—has provided new tools for investigating the molecular basis for olfactory perception and has led to new insights about the organization of olfaction. At the same time, increasingly sophisticated psychophysical and behavioral studies of olfactory processing have shown the importance of a multilevel approach for understanding the role of olfaction in human experience.

Four directions for future research stand out clearly at the moment. One direction is to continue to use the identification of specific olfactory receptors through techniques of molecular biology to guide the development of a principled basis for a theory of olfactory qualities. Coupled with computational modeling of how olfactory signals are processed, this approach seems very promising. A second direction is to use the powerful computational and imaging tools of modern biology to understand how chemical signals are actually presented to the sensory surface as well as how they are taken up and expelled. A third direction is to take advantage of the continuing refinement of imaging techniques to explore olfactory processing in terms of the activation of brain pathways in normal healthy adults. Finally, and perhaps most importantly, improving our understanding of how psychological processes determine the impact of olfactory experience on human behavior has both practical and theoretical implications that may allow olfaction to assume a more prominent place in discussions of the human senses.

REFERENCES

Adrian, E. D. (1950). Sensory discrimination with some recent evidence from the olfactory organ. *British Medical Bulletin, 6,* 330–333.

Aggelton, J. P., & Mishkin, M. (1986). The amygdala: Sensory gateway to the emotions. In

R. Plutchik & H. Kellerman (Eds.), *Emotion: Theory, research, and experience* (pp. 281–299). Orlando, FL: Academic.

Amoore, J. E. (1962). The stereochemical theory of olfaction: I. Identification of the seven primary odours. *Proceedings of the Scientific Section: Toilet Goods Association, 37,* 1–12.

Bell, G. A., Laing, D. G., & Panhuber, H. (1987). Odor mixture suppression: Evidence for a peripheral mechanism in human and rat. *Brain Research, 426,* 8–18.

Berglund, U. (1974). Dynamic properties of the olfactory system. *Annals of the New York Academy of Sciences, 237,* 17–27.

Boring, E. G. (1928). A new system for the classification of odors. *American Journal of Psychology, 40,* 345–349.

Breer, H., & Strotmann, J. (1997). Olfactory receptor gene expression. *Cell and Developmental Biology, 8,* 189–195.

Buck, L., & Axel, R. (1991). A novel multigene family may encode odorant receptors: A molecular basis for odor recognition. *Cell, 65,* 175–187.

Cabanac, M. (1979). Sensory pleasure. *Quarterly Review of Biology, 54,* 1–29.

Cain, W. S. (1970). Odor intensity after self-adaptation and cross-adaptation. *Perception & Psychophysics, 7,* 271–275.

Cain, W. S. (1974). Perception of odor intensity and the time-course of olfactory adaptation. *ASHRAE Transactions, 80,* 53–75.

Cain, W. S. (1977a). Bilateral interaction in olfaction. *Nature, 268,* 50–52.

Cain, W. S. (1977b). Differential sensitivity for smell: "Noise" at the nose. *Science, 195,* 796–798.

Cain, W. S. (1982). Odor identification by males and females: Predictions versus performance. *Chemical Senses, 7,* 129–142.

Cain, W. S. (1988). Olfaction. In *Stevens' handbook of experimental psychology* (pp. 409–459). New York: Wiley.

Cain, W. S. (1989). Testing olfaction in a clinical setting. *Ear, Nose, and Throat Journal, 68,* 316–328.

Cain, W. S., Cometto-Muñiz, J. E., & de Wijk, R. A. (1992). Techniques in the quantitative study of human olfaction. In M. J. Serby & K. L. Chobor (Eds.), *Science of olfaction* (pp. 279–308). New York: Springer.

Cain, W. S., de Wijk, R., Lulejian, C., Schiet, F., & See, L. C. (1998). Odor identification: Perceptual and semantic dimensions. *Chemical Senses, 23,* 309–326.

Cain, W. S., & Drexler, M. (1974). Scope and evaluation of odor counteraction and masking. *Annals of the New York Academy of Sciences, 237,* 427–439.

Cain, W. S., & Gent, J. F. (1991). Olfactory sensitivity: Reliability, generality, and association with aging. *Journal of Experimental Psychology: Human Perception and Performance, 17,* 382–391.

Cain, W. S., Gent, J. F., Goodspeed, R. B., & Leonard, G. (1988). Evaluation of olfactory dysfunction in the Connecticut Chemosensory Clinical Research Center. *Laryngoscope, 98,* 83–88.

Cain, W. S., & Murphy, C. L. (1980). Interaction between chemoreceptive modalities of odour and irritation. *Nature, 284,* 255–257.

Cain, W. S., & Polak, E. H. (1992). Olfactory adaptation as an aspect of odor similarity. *Chemical Senses, 17,* 481–491.

Cain, W. S., & Stevens, J. C. (1989). Uniformity of olfactory loss in aging. *Annals of the New York Academy of Sciences, 561,* 29–38.

Cheal, M. L., & Sprott, R. L. (1971). Social olfaction: A review of the role of olfaction in a variety of animal behaviors. *Psychological Reports, 29,* 195–243.

Colbert, H. A., & Bargmann, C. I. (1995). Odorant-specific adaptation pathways generate olfactory plasticity in C elegans. *Neuron, 14,* 803–812.

Colligan, M. J., & Murphy, L. (1982). A review of mass psychogenic illness in work settings. In M. Colligan, J. Pennebaker, & L. Murphy (Eds.), *Mass psychogenic illness: A social psychological analysis* (pp. 33–52). Hillsdale, NJ: Erlbaum.

Cometto-Muñiz, J. E., & Cain, W. S. (1990). Thresholds for odor and nasal pungency. *Physiology & Behavior, 48,* 719–725.

Cometto-Muñiz, J. E., & Cain, W. S. (1991). Nasal pungency, odor, and eye irritation thresholds for homologous acetates. *Pharmacology, Biochemistry and Behavior, 39,* 983–989.

Cometto-Muñiz, J. E., & Cain, W. S. (1995). Olfactory Adaptation. In R. L. Doty (Ed.), *Handbook of olfaction and gustation.* New York: Dekker. (pp. 257–281).

Cometto-Muñiz, J. E., & Cain, W. S. (1998). Trigeminal and olfactory sensitivity: Comparison of modalities and methods of measurement. *International Archives of Occupational and Environmental Health, 71,* 105–110.

Costanzo, R. (2000). Rewiring the olfactory bulb: Changes in odor maps following recovery from nerve transection. *Chemical Senses, 25,* 199–205.

Costanzo, R. M., & Graziadei, P. P. C. (1983). A quantitative analysis of changes in the olfactory epithelium following bulbectomy in hamster. *Journal of Comparative Neurology, 215,* 370–381.

Cowart, B. J., Young, I. M., Feldman, R. S., & Lowry, L. D. (1997). Clinical disorders of smell and taste. In G. K. Beauchamp & L. M. Bartoshuk (Eds.), *Handbook of perception and cognition: Vol. 8. Tasting and smelling* (pp. 175–198). New York: Academic Press.

Dalton, P. (1996). Odor perception and beliefs about risk. *Chemical Senses, 21,* 447–458.

Dalton, P. (1999). Cognitive influences on health symptoms from acute chemical exposure. *Health Psychology, 18,* 579–590.

Dalton, P., Doolittle, N., & Breslin, P. A. S. (in press). Gender-specific induction of enhanced sensitivity to odors. *Nature Neuroscience.*

Dalton, P., Doolittle, N., Nagata, H., & Breslin, P. A. S. (2000). The merging of the senses: Integration of subthreshold taste and smell. *Nature Neuroscience, 3,* 431–432.

Dalton, P., & Wysocki, C. J. (1996). The nature and duration of adaptation following long-term exposure to odors. *Perception & Psychophysics, 58,* 781–792.

Dalton, P., Wysocki, C. J., Brody, M. J., & Lawley, H. J. (1997). Perceived odor, irritation and health symptoms following short-term exposure to acetone. *American Journal of Industrial Medicine, 31,* 558–569.

Davies, J. T., & Taylor, F. H. (1959). The role of adsorption and molecular morphology in olfaction: The calculation of olfactory thresholds. *Biological Bulletin, 117,* 222–228.

Davis, R. G. (1981). The role of nonolfactory context cues in odor identification. *Perception & Psychophysics, 30,* 83–89.

Deane, M., & Sanders, G. (1978). Annoyance and health reactions to odor from refineries and other industries in Carson, California. *Environmental Research, 15,* 119–132.

Demski, L. S. (1993). Terminal nerve complex. *Acta Anatomica (Basel), 148,* 81–95.

Demski, L. S., & Schwanzel-Fukuda, M. (1987). *The terminal nerve (nervus terminalis): Structure, function and evolution* (Vol. 519). New York: The New York Academy of Sciences.

deOlmos, J., Hardy, H., & Heimer, L. (1978). The afferent connections of the main and the accessory olfactory bulb formations in the rat: An experimental HRP-study. *Journal of Comparative Neurology, 181,* 213–244.

Devos, M., Patte, F., Rouault, J., Laffort, P., & Van Gemert, L. J. (1990). *Standardized human olfactory thresholds* (Vol. 1). New York: Oxford University Press.

de Wijk, R. A. (1989). *Temporal factors in human olfactory perception.* Unpublished doctoral dissertation, University of Utrecht, Netherlands.

de Wijk, R. A., & Cain, W. S. (1994a). Odor identification by name and by edibility: Life-span development and safety. *Human Factors, 36,* 182–187.

de Wijk, R. A., & Cain, W. S. (1994b). Odor quality: Discrimination versus free and cued identification. *Perception and Psychophysics, 56,* 12–18.

Dickinson, T. A., White, J., Kauer, J. S., & Walt, D. R. (1998). Current trends in "artificial nose" technology. *Trends in Biotechnology, 16,* 250–258.

Dorries, K. M., Adkins-Regan, E., & Halpern, B. P. (1997). Sensitivity and behavioral responses to the pheromone androstenone are not mediated by the vomeronasal organ in domestic pigs. *Brain, Behavior and Evolution, 49,* 53–62.

Doty, R. L. (1991). Olfactory capacities in aging and Alzheimer's disease. *Annals of the New York Academy of Sciences, 640,* 20–27.

Doty, R. L., Applebaum, S., Zusho, H., & Settle, R. G. (1985). Sex differences in odor identification ability: A cross-cultural analysis. *Neuropsychologia, 23,* 667–672.

Doty, R. L., Gregor, T. P., & Settle, R. G. (1986). Influence of intertrial interval and sniff-bottle volume on phenyl ethyl alcohol odor detection thresholds. *Chemical Senses, 11,* 259–264.

Doty, R. L., Shaman, P., & Dann, M. (1984). Development of the University of Pennsylvania smell identification test: A standardized microencapsulated test of olfactory function. *Physiology & Behavior, 32,* 489–502.

Dravnieks, A. (1975). Instrumental aspects of olfactometry. In D. G. Moulton, A. Turk, & J. W. Johnston Jr. (Eds.), *Methods in olfactory research* (pp. 1–61). London: Academic Press.

Dravnieks, A. (1982). Odor quality: Semantically generated multidimensional profiles are stable. *Science, 218,* 799–801.

Ehrlichman, H., & Bastone, L. (1992). Olfaction and emotion. In M. J. Serby & K. L. Chobor (Eds.), *Science of olfaction* (pp. 410–438). New York: Springer.

Ehrlichman, H., Brown, S., Zhu, J., & Warrenburg, S. (1995). Startle reflex modulation during exposure to pleasant and unpleasant odors. *Psychophysiology, 32,* 150–154.

Eichenbaum, H. (1996). Olfactory perception and memory. In R. Llinas & P. Churchland (Eds.), *The mind-brain continuum* (pp. 173–202). Cambridge: MIT Press.

Engen, T. (1972). The effect of expectation on judgments of odor. *Acta Psychologica, 36,* 450–458.

Engen, T. (1982). *The perception of odors.* New York: Academic.

Engen, T. (1987). Remembering odors and their names. *American Scientist, 75,* 497.

Engen, T., Lipsitt, L. P., & Kaye, H. (1963). Olfactory responses and adaptation in the human neonate. *Journal of Comparative and Physiological Psychology, 56,* 73–77.

Eskenazi, B., Cain, W. S., & Friend, K. (1986). Exploration of olfactory aptitude. *Bulletin of the Psychonomic Society, 24,* 203–206.

Farbman, A. (1990). Olfactory neurogenesis: Genetic or environmental controls? *Trends in Neurosciences, 13,* 382–385.

Feron, F., Perry, C., McGrath, J. J., & Mackay-Sim, A. (1998). New techniques for biopsy and culture of human olfactory epithelial neurons. *Archives of Otolaryngology, Head and Neck Surgery, 124,* 861–866.

Finger, T. E., & Bottger, B. (1993). Peripheral peptidergic fibers of the trigeminal nerve in the olfactory bulb of the rat. *Journal of Comparative Neurology, 334,* 117–124.

Firestein, S., Picco, C., & Menini, A. (1993). The relation between stimulus and response in olfactory receptor cells of the tiger salamander. *Journal of Physiology, 468,* 1–10.

Francis, S., Rolls, E. T., Bowtell, R., McGlone, F., O'Doherty, J., Browning, A., Clare, S., & Smith, E. (1999). The representation of pleasant touch in the brain and its relationship with taste and olfactory areas. *Neuroreport, 10,* 453–459.

Gagnon, P., Mergler, D., & Lapare, S. (1994). Olfactory adaptation, threshold shift and recovery at low levels of exposure to methyl isobutyl ketone (MIBK). *Neurotoxicology, 15,* 637–642.

Gesteland, R., Lettvin, J., & Pitts, W. (1965). Chemical transmission in the nose of the frog. *Journal of Physiology, 181,* 525–559.

Getchell, M. L., & Mellert, T. K. (1991). Olfactory mucus secretion. In T. V. Getchell, R. L. Doty, L. M. Bartoshuk, & J. B. Snow Jr. (Eds.), *Smell and taste in health and disease* (pp. 83–95). New York: Raven Press.

Getchell, T. V. (1974). Unitary responses in frog olfactory epithelium to sterically related molecules at low concentrations. *Journal of General Physiology, 64,* 241–261.

Getchell, T. V., Margolis, T. V., & Getchell, M. L. (1984). Perireceptor and receptor events in vertebrate olfaction. *Progress in Neurobiology, 23,* 317–345.

Getchell, T. V., & Shepherd, G. M. (1978). Responses of olfactory receptor cells to step pulses of odour at different concentrations in the salamander. *Journal of Physiology, 282,* 521–540.

Giannetti, N., Pellier, V., Oestreicher, A. B., & Astic, L. (1995). Immunocytochemical study of the differentiation process of the septal organ of Masera in developing rats. *Brain Research: Developmental Brain Research, 16,* 287–293.

Gilbert, A. N., Fridlund, A. J., & Sabini, J. (1987). Hedonic and social determinants of facial displays to odors. *Chemical Senses, 12,* 355–363.

Gilbert, A. N., Knasko, S. C., & Sabini, J. (1997). Sex differences in task performance associated with attention to ambient odor. *Archives of Environmental Health, 52,* 195–199.

Gilbert, A. N., & Wysocki, C. J. (1987). The smell survey. *National Geographic. Sept., 122,* 514–525.

Gillan, D. J. (1983). Taste-taste, odor-odor, and taste-odor mixtures: Greater suppression within than between modalities. *Perception and Psychophysics, 33,* 183–185.

Graziadei, P. P. C., & Monti Graziadei, G. A. (1977). Continuous nerve cell renewal in the olfactory system. In M. Jacobson (Ed.), *Handbook of sensory physiology* (pp. 55–83). Berlin: Springer.

Graziadei, P. P. C., & Monti Graziadei, G. A. (1979). Neurogenesis and neuron regeneration in the olfactory system of mammals: I. Morphological aspects of differentiation and structural organization of the olfactory sensory neurons. *Journal of Neurocytology, 8,* 1–18.

Green, B. G., Dalton, P., Cowart, B. J., Shaffer, G., Rankin, K. R., & Higgins, J. (1996). Evaluating the "Labeled Magnitude Scale" for measuring sensations of taste and smell. *Chemical Senses, 21,* 323–334.

Green, B. G., Mason, J. R., & Kare, M. R. (Eds.). (1990). *Chemical senses: Vol. 2. Irritation.* New York: Dekker.

Gurr, P., Diver, J., Morgan, N., MacGregor, F., & Lund, V. (1995). Acoustic rhinometry of the indian and anglo-saxon nose. *Rhinology, 34,* 156–159.

Halpern, B. P. (1982). Environmental factors affecting chemoreceptors: An overview. *Environmental Health Perspectives, 44,* 101–105.

Hepper, P. (1995). Human fetal "olfactory" learning. *International Journal of Perinatal Psychology, 2,* 147–151.

Herrnstein, R. J., & Boring, E. G. (1965). *A source book in the history of psychology.* Cambridge: Harvard University Press.

Herz, R. S. (1998). Are odors the best cues to memory? A cross-modal comparison of associative memory stimuli. *Annals of the New York Academy of Sciences, 855,* 674.

Herz, R. S., & Cupchik, G. C. (1995). The emotional distinctiveness of odor-evoked memories. *Chemical Senses, 20,* 517–528.

Herz, R. S., & Engen, T. (1996). Odor memory: Review and analysis. *Psychonomic Bulletin and Review, 3,* 300–313.

Hornung, D. E., & Mozell, M. M. (1977a). Factors influencing the differential sorption of odorant molecules across the olfactory mucosa. *Journal of General Physiology, 69,* 343–361.

Hornung, D. E., & Mozell, M. M. (1977b). Odorant removal from the frog olfactory mucosa. *Brain Research, 128,* 158–163.

Hornung, D. E., & Mozell, M. M. (1980). Tritiated odorants to monitor retention in the olfactory and vomernasal organs. *Brain Research, 181,* 488–492.

Hudson, R., & Distel, H. (1998). Induced peripheral sensitivity in the developing vertebrate olfactory system. *Annals of the New York Academy of Sciences, 855,* 109–115.

Hummel, T., Knecht, M., & Kobal, G. (1996). Peripherally obtained electrophysiological responses to olfactory stimulation in man: Electro-olfactograms exhibit a smaller degree of desensitization compared with subjective intensity estimates. *Brain Research, 717,* 160–164.

Jafek, B. W., Hartman, D., Eller, P. M., Johnson, E. W., Strahan, R. C., & Moran, D. T. (1990). Postviral olfactory dysfunction. *American Journal of Rhinology, 4,* 91–100.

Joki, S., & Saano, V. (1997). Influence of aging on ciliary beat frequency and on ciliary response to leukotriene D4 in guinea-pig tracheal epithelium. *Clinical and Experimental Pharmacology and Physiology, 24,* 166–169.

Kauer, J. S., & Moulton, D. G. (1974). Responses of olfactory bulb neurones to odor stimulation of small nasal areas in the salamander. *Journal of Physiology, 243,* 717–737.

Kaviani, H., Wilson, G. D., Checkley, S. A., Kumari, V., & Gray, J. A. (1998). Modulation of the human acoustic startle reflex by pleasant and unpleasant odors. *Journal of Psychophysiology, 12,* 353–361.

Kent, P., & Mozell, M. M. (1992). The recording of odorant-induced mucosal activity patterns with a voltage-sensitive dye. *Journal of Neurophysiology, 68,* 1804–1819.

Keyhani, K., Scherer, P. W., & Mozell, M. M. (1997). A numerical model of nasal odorant transport for the analysis of human olfaction. *Journal of Theoretical Biology, 186,* 279–301.

Knasko, S. C. (1992). Ambient odor's effect on creativity, mood, and perceived health. *Chemical Senses, 17,* 27–35.

Knasko, S. C. (1993). Performance, mood, and health during exposure to intermittent odors. *Archives of Environmental Health, 48,* 305–308.

Knasko, S. C., Gilbert, A. N., & Sabini, J. (1990). Emotional state, physical well-being and performance in the presence of feigned ambient odor. *Journal of Applied Social Psychology, 20,* 1345–1357.

Kobal, G., & Kettenman, B. (2000). Olfactory functional imaging and physiology. *International Journal of Psychophysiology, 36,* 157–163.

Koelega, H. S. (1970). Extraversion, sex, arousal and olfactory sensitivity. *Acta Psychologica, 34,* 51–66.

Koelega, H. S., & Köster, E. P. (1974). Some experiments on sex differences in odor perception. *Annals of the New York Academy of Sciences, 237,* 234–246.

Köster, E. P. (1971). *Adaptation and cross-adaptation in olfaction.* Doctoral Dissertation. Utrecht University, Utrecht (unpublished).

Köster, E. P., & de Wijk, R. A. (1991). Olfactory adaptation. In D. G. Laing, R. L. Doty, & W. Breipohl (Eds.), *The human sense of smell* (pp. 199–215). New York: Springer.

Laffort, P. (1977). Some aspects of molecular recognition by chemoreceptors. In J. LeMagnen & P. MacLeod (Eds.), *Olfaction and taste: Vol. 6* (pp. 17–25). London: Information Retrieval.

Laffort, P., Patte, F., & Etcheto, M. (1974). Olfactory coding on the basis of physico-chemical properties. *Annals of the New York Academy of Sciences, 237,* 193–208.

Laing, D. G. (1988). Relationship between the differential adsorption of odorants by the olfactory mucus and their perception in mixtures. *Chemical Senses, 13,* 463–471.

Laing, D. G., & Willcox, M. (1987). An investigation of the mechanisms of odor suppression using physical and dichorhinic mixtures. *Behavioural Brain Research, 26,* 79–87.

Laing, D. G. (1983). Natural sniffing gives optimum odour perception for humans. *Perception, 12,* 99–117.

Laing, D. G. (1985). Optimum perception of odor intensity by humans. *Physiology & Behavior, 34,* 569–574.

Laing, D. G. (1991). Characteristics of the human sense of smell when processing odor mixtures. In D. G. Laing, R. L. Doty, & W. Breipohl (Eds.), *The human sense of smell* (pp. 241–259). New York: Springer.

Laing, D. G., & Francis, G. W. (1989). The capacity of humans to identify odors in mixtures. *Physiology & Behavior, 46,* 809–814.

Laing, D. G., & Glemarec, A. (1992). Selective attention and the perceptual analysis of odor mixtures. *Physiology & Behavior, 52,* 1047–1053.

Laing, D. G., Panhuber, H., Willcox, M. E., & Pittman, E. A. (1984). Quality and intensity of binary odor mixtures. *Physiology & Behavior, 33,* 309–319.

Lambertsen, C. J. (1974). Physical and mechanical aspects of respiration. In V. B. Mountcastle (Ed.), *Medical physiology* (pp. 1361–137). St. Louis, MO: Mosby.

Lang, J. (1989). *Clinical anatomy of the nose, nasal cavity and paranasal sinuses.* New York: Thieme Medical Publishers, Inc.

Lanza, D. C., & Clerico, D. M. (1995). Anatomy of the human nasal passages. In R. L. Doty (Ed.),

Handbook of olfaction (pp. 53–73). New York: Dekker.

Lawless, H. T. (1987). An olfactory analogy to release from mixture suppression in taste. *Bulletin of the Psychonomic Society, 25,* 266–268.

Lawless, H. T., & Engen, T. (1977). Associations to odors: Interference, memories, and verbal labeling. *Journal of Experimental Psychology, 3,* 52–59.

Levine, J. M., & McBurney, D. H. (1986). The role of olfaction in social perception and behavior. In C. P. Herman, M. P. Zanna, & E. T. Higgins (Eds.), *The Ontario Symposium: Vol. 3. Physical appearance, stigma, and social behavior* (pp. 179–217). Hillsdale, NJ: Erlbaum.

Linnaeus, C. (1756). *Systema naturae.* Ninth edition. Leiden: Theodor Haak (Lugdunum Batavorum).

Loo, A. T., Youngentob, S. L., Kent, P. F., & Schwob, J. E. (1996). The aging olfactory epithelium: Neurogenesis, response to damage, and odorant-induced activity. *Developmental Neuroscience, 14,* 881–900.

Lorig, T. S., Matia, D. C., Peszka, J., & Bryant, D. N. (1996). The effects of active and passive stimulation on chemosensory event-related potentials. *International Journal of Psychophysiology, 23,* 199–205.

Lowe, G., & Gold, G. H. (1991). The spatial distributions of odorant sensitivity and odorant-induced currents in salamander olfactory receptor cells. *Journal of Physiology, 442,* 147–168.

Lyman, B. J., & McDaniel, M. A. (1986). Effects of encoding strategy on long-term memory of odours. *The Quarterly Journal of Experimental Psychology, 38A,* 753–765.

Lyman, B. J., & McDaniel, M. A. (1990). Memory for odors and odor names: Modalities of elaboration and imagery. *Journal of Experimental Psychology: Learning, Memory, and Cognition, 16,* 656–664.

Mackay-Sim, A., & Kesteven, S. (1994). Topographic patterns of responsiveness to odorants in the rat olfactory epithelium. *Journal of Neurophysiology, 71,* 150–160.

Malnic, B., Hirono, J., Sato, T., & Buck, L. B. (1999). Combinatorial receptor codes for odors. *Cell, 96,* 713–723.

Marks, L. E. (1974). *Sensory processes: The new psychophysics* (Vol. 1). New York: Academic Press.

Marshall, D. A., & Maruniak, J. A. (1986). Masera's organ responds to odorants. *Brain Research, 26,* 329–332.

Maruniak, J. A., Mason, J. R., & Kostelc, J. G. (1983). Conditioned aversions to an intravascular odorant. *Physiology & Behavior, 30,* 617–620.

Maruniak, J. A., Silver, W. L., & Moulton, D. G. (1983). Olfactory receptors respond to blood-borne odorants. *Brain Research, 265,* 312–316.

McLean, J. H., & Shipley, M. T. (1995). Neuroanatomical substrates of olfaction. In M. J. Serby & K. L. Chobor (Eds.), *Science of Olfaction* (pp. 126–171). New York: Springer-Verlag.

Menco, B. P. M. (1980). Qualitative and quantitative freeze-fracture studies on olfactory and nasal respiratory structures of frog, ox, rat and dog: I. A general survey. *Cell Tissue Research, 207,* 183–209.

Mennella, J. A., & Beauchamp, G. K. (1991). The transfer of alcohol to human milk: Effects on flavor and the infant's behavior. *New England Journal of Medicine, 325,* 981–985.

Mennella, J. A., & Beauchamp, G. K. (1998). The infant's response to scented toys: Effects of exposure. *Chemical Senses, 23,* 11–17.

Mennella, J. A., Jagnow, C. P., & Beauchamp, G. K. (2001). Pre- and post-natal flavor learning by human infants. *Pediatrics, 107,* e88. (electronic format).

Mesholam, R. I., Moberg, P. J., Mahr, R. N., & Doty, R. L. (1998). Olfaction in neurodegenerative disease: A meta-analysis of olfactory functioning in Alzheimer's and Parkinson's diseases. *Archives of Neurology, 55,* 84–90.

Min, Y., Yun, Y., Song, B. H., Cho, Y. S., & Lee, K. S. (1995). Recovery of nasal physiology after functional endoscopic sinus surgery: Olfaction and mucociliary transport. *ORL: Journal of Otorhino-laryngology and Its Related Specialties, 57,* 264–268.

Mombaerts, P., Wang, F., Dulac, C., Chao, S. K., Nemes, A., Mendelsohn, M., Edmondson, J., & Axel, R. (1996). Visualizing an olfactory sensory map. *Cell, 87,* 675–686.

Monti-Bloch, L., Jennings-White, C., & Berliner, D. (1998). The human vomeronasal system: A review. *Annals of the New York Academy of Sciences, 855,* 373–389.

Mori, K., Nagao, H., & Yoshihara, Y. (1999). The olfactory bulb: Coding and processing of odor molecule information. *Science, 286,* 711–715.

Moskowitz, H. R., & Barbe, C. D. (1977). Profiling of odor components and their mixtures. *Sensory Processes, 1,* 212–226.

Mott, A. E., & Leopold, D. A. (1991). Disorders in taste and smell. *Medical Clinics of North America, 75,* 1321–1353.

Moulton, D. G. (1976). Spatial patterning of response to odors in the peripheral olfactory system. *Physiological Reviews, 56,* 578–593.

Mozell, M. M., Kent, P. F., & Murphy, S. J. (1991). The effect of flow rate upon the magnitude of the olfactory response differs for different odorants. *Chemical Senses, 16,* 631–649.

Murphy, C. L. (1999). Loss of olfactory function in dementing disease. *Physiology & Behavior, 66,* 177–182.

Murphy, C. L., & Cain, W. S. (1980). Taste and olfaction: Independence versus interaction. *Physiology & Behavior, 24,* 601–605.

Murphy, C. L., Cain, W. S., & Bartoshuk, L. M. (1977). Mutual action of taste and olfaction. *Sensory Processes, 1,* 204–211.

Murphy, C. L., Cain, W. S., Gilmore, M. M., & Skinner, R. B. (1991). Sensory and semantic factors in recognition memory for odors and graphic stimuli: Elderly versus young persons. *American Journal of Psychology, 104,* 161–192.

Nickell, W. T., & Shipley, M. T. (1995). Neurophysiology of the olfactory bulb. In M. J. Serby & K. L. Chobor (Eds.), *The science of olfaction* (pp. 172–212). New York: Springer-Verlag.

Ohm, T. G., & Braak, H. (1987). Olfactory bulb changes in Alzheimer's disease. *Acta Neuropathologica, 73,* 365–369.

Ottoson, D. (1956). Analysis of the electrical activity of the olfactory epithelium. *Acta Physiologica Scandinavica Supplementum, 355,* 1–83.

Papez, J. W. (1937). A proposed mechanism of emotion. *Archives of Neurology and Psychiatry, 38,* 725–743.

Passali, D., Bellussi, L., & Lauriello, M. (1995). The rheological characteristics of nasal mucus in patients with rhinitis. *European Archives of Oto-rhino-laryngology, 252,* 348–352.

Paulsen, E. (1882). Experimentalle Untersuchungen uber die Stronmungen der Luft in der Nasenhohle. *Sitzung.K.Akad.Wissensch., 85,* 348.

Pelosi, P. (1996). Perireceptor events in olfaction. *Journal of Neurobiology, 30,* 3–19.

Pierce J. D., Jr., Wysocki, C. J., Aronov, E. V., Webb, J. B., & Boden, R. M. (1996). The role of perceptual and structural similarity in cross-adaptation. *Chemical Senses, 21,* 223–237.

Porter, R. H., & Winberg, J. (2000). Unique salience of maternal breast odors for newborn infants. *Neuroscience and Biobehavioral Reviews, 23,* 439–449.

Prah, J. D., Sears, S. B., & Walker, J. C. (1995). Modern approaches to air dilution olfactometry. In R. L. Doty (Ed.), *Handbook of olfaction and gustation* (pp. 227–255). New York: Dekker.

Punter, P. H. (1983). Measurement of human olfactory thresholds for several groups of structurally related compounds. *Chemical Senses, 7,* 215–235.

Rabin, M. D. (1988). Experience facilitates olfactory quality discrimination. *Perception and Psychophysics, 44,* 532–540.

Rabin, M. D., & Cain, W. S. (1984). Odor recognition: Familiarity, identifiability, and encoding consistency. *Journal of Experimental Psychology: Learning, Memory, and Cognition, 10,* 316–325.

Rabin, M. D., & Cain, W. S. (1986). Determinants of measured olfactory sensitivity. *Perception & Psychophysics, 39,* 281–286.

Rawson, N. E., Gomez, G., Cowart, B. J., & Restrepo, D. (1998). The use of olfactory receptor neurons (ORNs) from biopsies to study changes in aging and neurodegenerative diseases. In C. L. Murphy (Ed.), *Olfaction and taste: Vol. 12: An International Symposium* (pp. 701–707). New York: New York Academy of Sciences.

Rawson, N. E., Gomez, G., Cowart, B. J., Brand, J. G., Lowry, L. D., Pribitkin, E. A., & Restrepo, D. (1997). Selectivity and response characteristics of human olfactory neurons. *Journal of Neurophysiology, 77,* 1606–1613.

Reiser, J., Yonas, A., & Wikner, K. (1976). Radial localization of odors by human newborns. *Child Development, 47,* 856–859.

Ressler, K. J., Sullivan, S. L., & Buck, L. (1994). A molecular dissection of spatial patterning in the olfactory system. *Current Opinion in Neurobiology, 4,* 588–596.

Restrepo, D., Okada, Y., Teeter, J. H., Lowry, L. D., & Cowart, B. (1993). Human olfactory neurons respond to odor stimuli with an increase in cytoplasmic Ca++. *Biophysical Journal, 64,* 1961–1966.

Reyes, P. F., Golden, G. T., Fagel, P. L., Fariello, L., Katz, L., & Carner, E. (1987). The prepiriform cortex in dementia of the Alzheimer type. *Archives of Neurology, 44,* 644–645.

Richardson, J. T., & Zucco, G. M. (1989). Cognition and olfaction: A review. *Psychological Bulletin, 105,* 352–360.

Rolls, E. T. (1997). Taste and olfactory processing in the brain and its relation to the control of eating. *Critical Reviews in Neurobiology, 11,* 263–287.

Roscher, S., Mohammadian, P., Schneider, A., Wendler, J., Hummel, T., & Kobal, G. (1996). Olfactory input facilitates trigeminal chemosensitivity. *ECRO Abstracts, 21,* 24.

Rotton, J. (1983). Affective and cognitive consequences of malodorous pollution. *Basic and Applied Social Psychology, 4,* 171–191.

Rotton, J., Barry, T., Frey, J., & Soler, E. (1978). Air pollution and interpersonal attraction. *Journal of Applied Social Psychology, 8,* 57–71.

Rozin, E. (1973). *The flavor-principle cookbook.* New York: Hawthorn Books.

Russell, M. J. (1976). Human olfactory communication. *Nature, 260,* 520–522.

Sarnat, H. B. (1978). Olfactory reflexes in the newborn infant. *Journal of Pediatrics, 92,* 624–626.

Schaal, B. (1986). Presumed olfactory exchanges between mother and neonate in humans. In J. LeCamus & J. Conier (Eds.), *Ethology and psychology* (pp. 101–110). Toulouse, France: Privat-IEC.

Schab, F. R. (1991). Odor memory: Taking stock. *Psychological Bulletin, 109,* 242–251.

Schab, F. R., & Crowder, R. G. (1995). Odor recognition memory. In F. R. Schab & R. G. Crowder (Eds.), *Memory for odors* (pp. 9–20). Mahwah, NJ: Erlbaum.

Schiffman, S. S. (1974). Physicochemical correlates of odor quality. *Science, 185,* 112–117.

Schiffman, S. S. (1997). Taste and smell losses in normal aging and disease. *JAMA, 278,* 1357–1362.

Schiffman, S. S., Miller, E. A. S., Suggs, M. S., & Graham, B. G. (1995). The effect of environmental odors emanating from commercial swine operations on the mood of nearby residents. *Brain Research Bulletin, 37,* 369–375.

Schild, D., & Restrepo, D. (1998). Transduction mechanisms in vertebrate olfactory receptor cells. *Physiological Reviews, 78,* 429–466.

Schmidt, H. J., & Beauchamp, G. K. (1988). Adult-like preferences and aversions in three-year old children. *Child Development, 59,* 1138–1143.

Schwerdtfeger, W. K., Buhl, E. H., & Germroth, P. (1990). Disynaptic olfactory input to the hiccocampus mediated by stellate cells in the entorhinal cortex. *Journal of Comparative Neurology, 292,* 163–177.

Self, P. A. F., Horowits, F. D., & Paden, L. Y. (1972). Olfaction in newborn infants. *Developmental Psychology, 7,* 349–363.

Shepherd, G. M. (1974). *The synaptic organization of the brain.* New York: Oxford University Press.

Shepherd, G. M. (1994). Discrimination of molecular signals by the olfactory receptor neuron. *Neuron, 13,* 771–790.

Shusterman, D. (1992). Critical review: The health significance of environmental odor pollution. *Archives of Environmental Health, 47,* 85.

Sicard, G. (1985). Olfactory discrimination of structurally related molecules: Receptor cell responses to camphoraceous odorants. *Brain Research, 326,* 203–212.

Slotnick, B. M., & Ptak, J. E. (1977). Olfactory intensity difference thresholds in rats and humans. *Physiology & Behavior, 19,* 795–802.

Snodgrass, J. G., Wasser, B., Finkelstein, M., & Goldberg, L. B. (1974). On the fate of visual and verbal memory codes for pictures and words: Evidence for a dual coding mechanism in recognition memory. *Journal of Verbal Learning & Verbal Behavior, 13,* 27–37.

Sobel, N., Khan, R. M., Hartley, C. A., Sullivan, E. V., & Gabrieli, J. D. (2000). Sniffing longer rather than stronger to maintain olfactory detection threshold. *Chemical Senses, 25,* 1–8.

Sobel, N., Khan, R., Saltman, A., Sullivan, E. V., & Gabrieli, J. D. (1999). The world smells differently to each nostril. *Nature, 402,* 282–286.

Sobel, N., Prabhakaran, V., Desmond, J. E., Glover, G. H., Goodes, R. L., Sullivan, E. V., & Gabrieli, J. D. (1998). Sniffing and smelling: Separate subsystems in the human olfactory cortex. *Nature, 392,* 282–286.

Staubli, U., Fraser, D., Faraday, R., & Lynch, G. (1987). Olfaction and the "data" memory system in rats. *Behavior Neuroscience, 101,* 757–765.

Steiner, J. E. (1974). Discussion paper: Innate discrimative facial expressions to taste and smell stimulation. *Annals of the New York Academy of Sciences, 237,* 229–233.

Steiner, J. E. (1976). Further observations on sensory motor coordinations induced by gustatory and olfactory stimuli. *Israeli Journal of Medical Science, 12,* 1231.

Stevens, J. C., & Cain, W. S. (1987). Old-age deficits in the sense of smell as gauged by thresholds, magnitude matching, and odor identification. *Psychology and Aging, 2,* 36–42.

Stevens, J. C., Cain, W. S., Schiet, F. T., & Oatley, M. W. (1989). Olfactory adaptation and recovery in old age. *Perception, 18,* 265–276.

Stone, H., & Bosley, J. J. (1965). Olfactory discrimination and Weber's Law. *Perceptual and Motor Skills, 20,* 657–665.

Strickland, M., Jessee, P. O., & Filsinger, E. E. (1988). A procedure for obtaining young children's reports of olfactory stimuli. *Perception & Psychophysics, 44,* 379–382.

Sullivan, R. M., Taborsky-Barba, S., Mendoza, R., Itano, A., Leon, M., Cotman, C. W., Payne, T. F., & Lott, I. (1991). Olfactory classical conditioning in neonates. *Pediatrics, 87,* 511–518.

Talamo, B. R., Rudel, J. S. R., Kosik, K. S., Lee, V. M., Neff, S., Adelman, L., & Kauer, J. S. (1989). Pathological changes in olfactory neurons in patients with Alzheimer's disease. *Nature, 337,* 736–739.

Taylor, S. M., Sider, D., Hampson, C., Taylor, S. J., Wilson, K., Walter, S. D., & Eyles, J. D. (1997). Community health effects of a petroleum refinery. *Ecosystem Health, 3,* 27–43.

Thommesen, G., & Doving, K. B. (1977). Spatial distribution of the EOG in the rat: A variation with odor quality. *Acta Physiologica Scandinavica, 99,* 270–280.

U. S. Department of Health and Human Services. (1994). *NIOSH pocket guide to chemical hazards.* No. 94-116. Washington, DC: U.S. Government Printing Office.

Van Dishoeck, H. A. E., & Versteeg, N. (1957). On the problem of haematogenic olfaction. *Acta Oto-Laryngologica, 47,* 396–401.

Vassar, R., Ngai, J., & Axel, R. (1993). Spatial segregation of odorant receptor expression in the mammalian olfactory epithelium. *Cell, 74,* 309–318.

Venstrom, D., & Amoore, J. E. (1968). Olfactory threshold in relation to age, sex or smoking. *Journal of Food Science, 33,* 264–265.

von Brunn, A. (2000). Beitrage zur mikroskopischen Anatomie der menschlichen Nasenhohle. *Arch.Mikr.Anat., 39,* 632–651.

Wang, H. W., Wysocki, C. J., & Gold, G. H. (1993). Induction of olfactory receptor sensitivity in mice. *Science, 260,* 998–1000.

Wright, R. H. (1977). Odor and molecular vibration: Neural coding of olfactory information. *Journal of Theoretical Biology, 64,* 473–502.

Wuttke, M. S., & Tompkins, L. (1999). Olfactory Adaptation is TRP-independent in Drosophila Larvae. *Journal of Neurogenetics, 14,* 41–62.

Wysocki, C. J. (1979). Neurobehavioral evidence for the involvement of the vomeronasal system in mammalian reproduction. *Neuroscience and Biobehavioral Reviews, 3,* 301–341.

Wysocki, C. J., Dalton, P., Brody, M. J., & Lawley, H. J. (1997). Acetone odor and irritation thresholds obtained from acetone-exposed factory workers and from control (occupationally non-exposed) subjects. *American Industrial Hygiene Association Journal, 58,* 704–712.

Wysocki, C. J., Dorries, K. M., & Beauchamp, G. K. (1989). Ability to perceive androstenone can be acquired by ostensibly anosmic people. *Proceedings of the National Academy of Sciences of the United States of America, 86,* 7976–7978.

Wysocki, C. J., & Gilbert, A. N. (1989). National Geographic smell survey: Effects of age are heterogenous. In C. L. Murphy, W. S. Cain, & D. M. Hegsted (Eds.), *Nutrition and the chemical senses in aging: Recent advances and current research needs* (pp. 12–28). New York: New York Academy of Sciences.

Wysocki, C. J., & Meredith, J. (1987). The vomeronasal system. In T. Finger & W. Silver (Eds.), *Neurobiology of taste and smell* (pp. 125–150). New York: Wiley.

Yee, K. K., & Costanzo, R. M. (1998). Changes in odor quality discrimination following recovery from olfactory nerve transection. *Chemical Senses, 23,* 513–519.

Yee, K. K., & Rawson, N. E. (2000). Retinoic acid enhances the rate of olfactory recovery after olfactory nerve transection. *Developmental Brain Research, 124,* 129–132.

Youngentob, S. L., & Kent, P. F. (1995). Enhancement of odorant-induced mucosal activity patterns in rats trained on an odorant identification task. *Brain Research, 670,* 82–88.

Youngentob, S. L., Schwob, J. E., Sheehe, P. E., & Youngentob, L. M. (1997). Odorant threshold following methyl bromide-induced lesions of the olfactory epithelium. *Physiology and Behavior, 62,* 1241–1252.

Yousem, D. M., Maldjian, J. A., Siddiqi, F., Hummel, T., Alsop, D. C., Geckle, R. J., Bilker, W. B., & Doty, R. L. (1999). Gender effects on odor-stimulated functional magnetic resonance imaging. *Brain Research, 818,* 480–487.

Zald, D. H., Lee, J. T., Fluegel, K. W., & Pardo, J. V. (1998). Aversive gustatory stimulation activates limbic circuits in humans. *Brain, 121,* 1143–1154.

Zald, D. H., & Pardo, J. V. (1997). Emotion, olfaction and the human amygdala: Amygdala activation during aversive olfactory stimulation. *Proceedings of the National Academy of Sciences USA, 94,* 4119–4124.

Zald, D. H., & Pardo, J. V. (2000). Functional neuroimaging of the olfactory system in humans. *International Journal of Psychophysiology, 36,* 165–181.

Zellner, D. A., & Kautz, M. A. (1990). Color affects perceived odor intensity. *Journal of Experimental Psychology: Human Perception and Performance, 16,* 391–397.

Zufall, F., & Leinders-Zufall, T. (1997). Identification of long-lasting form of odor adaptation that depends on the carbon monoxide/cGMP second-messenger system. *Journal of Neuroscience, 8,* 2703–2712.

Author Index

Subject Index